Nineteenth-Century Literature Criticism

Topics Volume

Guide to Gale Literary Criticism Series

When you need to review criticism of literary works, these are the Gale series to use:

If the author's death date is: **You should turn to:**

After Dec. 31, 1959
(or author is still living)

CONTEMPORARY LITERARY CRITICISM

for example: Jorge Luis Borges, Anthony Burgess,
William Faulkner, Mary Gordon,
Ernest Hemingway, Iris Murdoch

1900 through 1959

TWENTIETH-CENTURY LITERARY CRITICISM

for example: Willa Cather, F. Scott Fitzgerald,
Henry James, Mark Twain, Virginia Woolf

1800 through 1899

NINETEENTH-CENTURY LITERATURE CRITICISM

for example: Fyodor Dostoevsky, Nathaniel Hawthorne,
George Sand, William Wordsworth

1400 through 1799

LITERATURE CRITICISM FROM 1400 TO 1800
(excluding Shakespeare)

for example: Anne Bradstreet, Daniel Defoe,
Alexander Pope, François Rabelais,
Jonathan Swift, Phillis Wheatley

SHAKESPEAREAN CRITICISM

Shakespeare's plays and poetry

Antiquity through 1399

CLASSICAL AND MEDIEVAL LITERATURE CRITICISM

for example: Dante, Homer, Plato, Sophocles, Vergil,
the Beowulf Poet

Gale also publishes related criticism series:

CHILDREN'S LITERATURE REVIEW

This series covers authors of all eras who have written for
the preschool through high school audience.

SHORT STORY CRITICISM

This series covers the major short fiction writers of all nationalities
and periods of literary history.

ISSN 0732-1864

Volume 28

Nineteenth-Century Literature Criticism

Topics Volume

Excerpts from Criticism of Various
Topics in Nineteenth-Century Literature,
including Literary and Critical Movements,
Prominent Themes and Genres, Anniversary
Celebrations, and Surveys of National Literatures

Laurie Sherman

Editor

Michael W. Jones
Marie Lazzari
Thomas Ligotti
Michelle L. McClellan
Joann Prosyniuk

Associate Editors

 Gale Research Inc. · *DETROIT · NEW YORK · LONDON*

STAFF

Laurie Sherman, *Editor*

Michael W. Jones, Marie Lazzari, Thomas Ligotti,
Michelle L. McClellan, Joann Prosyniuk, *Associate Editors*

Susan Windisch Brown, Ian A. Goodhall, Tina N. Grant,
Alan Hedblad, Grace N. Jeromski, David Kmenta,
Ronald S. Nixon, Mark Swartz, Debra A. Wells, *Assistant Editors*

Jeanne A. Gough, *Permissions & Production Manager*
Linda M. Pugliese, *Production Supervisor*
Suzanne Powers, Maureen A. Puhl, Jennifer Van Sickle, *Editorial Associates*
Donna Craft, Lorna Mabunda, James Wittenbach, *Editorial Assistants*

Victoria B. Cariappa, *Research Manager*
H. Nelson Fields, Judy Gale, Maureen Richards, *Editorial Associates*
Paula Cutcher, Robin Lupa, Jill M. Ohorodnik, *Editorial Assistants*

Sandra C. Davis, *Permissions Supervisor (Text)*
Josephine M. Keene, Denise M. Singleton, Kimberly F. Smilay, *Permissions Associates*
Maria L. Franklin, Michele Lonoconus, Camille P. Robinson, Shalice Shah,
Rebecca A. Stanko, *Permissions Assistants*

Patricia A. Seefelt, *Permissions Supervisor (Pictures)*
Margaret A. Chamberlain, *Permissions Associate*
Pamela A. Hayes, Lillian Quickley, *Permissions Assistants*

Mary Beth Trimper, *Production Manager*
Shanna G. Philpott, *External Production Assistant*

Arthur Chartow, *Art Director*
C. J. Jonik, *Keyliner*

Laura Bryant, *Production Supervisor*
Louise Gagné, *Internal Production Associate*
Yolanda Y. Latham, *Internal Production Assistant*

Contents

Preface   vii

Authors to Be Featured in Forthcoming Volumes   xi

Acknowledgments   xiii

The American Frontier in Literature

English Decadent Literature of the 1890s

English Romantic Poetry

Preface

The study of literature embraces many disciplines, including history, sociology, psychology, and philosophy. To thoroughly comprehend a literary work, it is often necessary to understand the history and culture of the author's nation, the literary movements the author belonged to or disdained, the political passions and social concerns of the author's era, and the themes common to the literature of the author's nation. Thus, to gain a fuller perspective on an author, a student often needs to examine many social, historical, and literary factors.

Many schools reflect the necessity for such a broad view of literature by including historical and thematic surveys in their curricula. In these courses, themes that recur throughout many works of literature are examined, the literary tempers of various historical eras are assessed, and literary and critical movements are defined. Increasingly, comparative literature courses and thematic surveys of foreign literature are being offered by colleges and universities, introducing students to the most significant literature of many nations. In order to provide important information on the variety of subjects encountered by the general reader or student of literature, *Nineteenth-Century Literature Criticism (NCLC)* has extended its scope by creating the *NCLC* Topics volumes. Once a year, *NCLC* devotes an entire volume to criticism of literary topics that cannot be addressed by our regular format.

Scope of the Series

NCLC is designed to serve as an introduction to the authors of the nineteenth century and to the most significant interpretations of these authors' works. Since a vast amount of relevant critical material confronts the student, *NCLC* presents significant passages from the most important published criticism to aid students in the location and selection of critical commentary.

Standard volumes of *NCLC* comprise surveys of the careers of ten to fifteen authors who represent a variety of nationalities and genres. The authors selected include the most important writers of the era, as well as lesser-known figures whose significant contributions to literary history are important to the study of nineteenth-century literature. Each author entry represents a historical overview of the critical response to the author's work: early criticism is presented to indicate initial reactions, later selections represent any rise or decline in the author's reputation, and current analyses provide students with a modern perspective. Every attempt is made to identify and include excerpts from seminal essays on each author's work.

Topics Volumes

The *NCLC* Topics volumes enhance the usefulness of the series by examining literary topics that cannot be covered under the author approach used in the rest of the series. Such topics include literary and critical movements, significant genres, important themes and subjects in nineteenth-century literature, literary reaction to political and historical events, prominent literary anniversaries, and discussions of foreign literatures often overlooked by English-speaking readers. *NCLC* 28, for example, examines the following five topics: American Frontier Literature, the wide-ranging body of fiction and nonfiction works inspired by westward expansion in nineteenth-century America; English Decadent Literature, a highly stylized literary movement that celebrated the sensual qualities in art; the English Romantic Poets, whose emphasis on nature, moral purity, and spirituality produced a "golden age" of poetry; the Gothic Novel, a genre characterized by romance and mystery that influenced the development of modern horror and science fiction; and Russian Nihilism, a political and literary movement advocating individual freedom from political, social, and cultural mandates.

The subjects of topic entries are chosen for their usefulness and timeliness; the length of each entry is determined by the importance of the topic and the amount of criticism available in English. Topics considered are restricted as much as possible to the period 1800 to 1899, and only literary movements and subjects that had their greatest influence during this period are discussed. In some cases this means that we will include discussion of authors who are covered in *Twentieth-Century Literary Criticism (TCLC)* or in *Literature Criticism from 1400 to 1800 (LC 1400-1800),* but no criticism from these series has been duplicated.

Organization of the Book

Each topic entry consists of the following elements:

- The *introduction* briefly defines the subject of the entry and provides social and historical information important to an understanding of the criticism.

- The list of *representative works* identifies writings by authors associated with the subject. Arranged chronologically by date of first book publication, the list also indicates the genre of each work. In those instances when the first publication was in a language other than English, the title and date of the first English-language edition are given in brackets. Unless otherwise indicated, dramas are dated by first performance, rather than first publication.

- The *criticism* is arranged thematically. Entries commonly begin with general surveys of the subject or essays providing historical or background information, followed by essays that develop particular aspects of the topic. For example, the entry devoted to the Gothic novel begins by outlining the development, major works, and most prominent characteristics of the genre. This is followed by a selection focusing on Gothic themes and techniques as well as discussions of significant developments of the genre in the United States and in Scotland. Examinations of the influence and legacy of the Gothic novel conclude the critical portion of the entry. Each section has a separate title heading and is identified with a page number in the table of contents for easy access.

  The critic's name is given at the beginning of each piece of criticism; when an unsigned essay is later attributed to a critic, the critic's name appears in brackets at the beginning of the excerpt and in the bibliographic citation. Anonymous essays are headed by the title of the journal in which they appeared. Publication information (such as publisher names and book prices) and parenthetical numerical references (such as footnotes or page and line references to specific editions of works) have been deleted at the editors' discretion to provide smoother reading of the text.

- Critical excerpts are prefaced by *annotations* providing the reader with information about both the critic and the criticism that follows. Included are the critic's reputation, individual approach to literary criticism, and particular expertise in the subject under discussion. Also noted are the relative importance of a work of criticism, the scope of the excerpt, and the growth of critical controversy or changes in critical trends regarding the subject. In some cases, these notes include cross references to related criticism in the entry.

- A complete *bibliographic citation* designed to facilitate the location of the original essay or book follows each piece of criticism.

- *Illustrations* throughout the entry include portraits of the authors under discussion, important manuscript pages, letters, magazine covers, book illustrations, and reproductions of artwork associated with the topic.

- The bibliography of *further reading* appearing at the end of each subject entry lists additional secondary sources on the topic, in some cases including essays for which the editors could not obtain reprint rights. Where appropriate, the bibliography also lists significant English-language anthologies of primary sources discussed in the entry.

The acknowledgments section lists the copyright holders who have granted permission to print material in this volume of *NCLC*. It does not, however, list every book or periodical consulted for the volume.

Cumulative Indexes

Each volume of *NCLC* includes a cumulative index listing all the authors who have appeared in *Contemporary Literary Criticism, Twentieth-Century Literary Criticism, Nineteenth-Century Literature Criticism, Literature Criticism from 1400 to 1800, Classical and Medieval Literature Criticism,* and *Short Story Criticism.* Topic entries devoted to a single author will be listed in this index. Also included are cross-references to the Gale series *Authors & Artists for Young Adults, Children's Literature Review, Authors in the News, Contemporary Authors, Contemporary Authors Autobiography Series, Dictionary of Literary Biography, Concise Dictionary of American Literary Biography, Something about the Author, Something about the Author Autobiography Series,* and *Yesterday's Authors of Books for Children.* This index, which lists birth and death dates when available, will be particularly valuable for those authors who are identified with a certain period but whose death dates cause them to be placed in another, or for those authors whose careers span two periods. For example, Fyodor Dostoevsky is found in *NCLC,* yet Leo Tolstoy, another major nineteenth-century Russian novelist, is found in *TCLC* because he died after 1899.

Each new volume in Gale's Literary Criticism Series includes a cumulative topic index, which lists all literary topics treated in *NCLC, TCLC, LC 1400-1800* and the *CLC Yearbook.*

Each *NCLC* Topics volume also includes a cumulative nationality index listing all authors who have appeared in regular *NCLC* volumes. Authors are listed by nationality, followed by the volume numbers in which they appeared.

Titles discussed in the topic entries are not included in the *NCLC* cumulative title index.

A Note to the Reader

When writing papers, students who quote directly from any volume in Gale's Literary Criticism Series may use the following general forms to footnote reprinted criticism. The first example pertains to material drawn from periodicals, the second to material reprinted from books.

[1]T. S. Eliot, "John Donne," *The Nation and the Athenaeum,* 33 (9 June 1923), 321-32; excerpted and reprinted in *Literature Criticism from 1400 to 1800,* Vol. 10, ed. James E. Person, Jr. (Detroit: Gale Research, 1989), pp. 28-9.

[1]Clara G. Stillman, *Samuel Butler: A Mid-Victorian Modern* (Viking Press, 1932); excerpted and reprinted in *Twentieth-Century Literary Criticism,* Vol. 33, ed. Paula Kepos (Detroit: Gale Research, 1989), pp. 43-5.

Suggestions Are Welcome

In response to suggestions, several features have been added to *NCLC* since the series began, including annotations to excerpted criticism, an index listing authors in all Gale literary criticism series, entries devoted to a single work by a major author, more extensive illustrations, and an index listing all the literary works discussed in the series.

Readers who wish to suggest authors to appear in future volumes, or who have other comments and suggestions for expanding the coverage and enhancing the usefulness of the series, are cordially invited to write the editors.

Authors to Be Featured in Forthcoming Volumes

Matthew Arnold (English poet and critic)—The author of such major poems as "The Scholar Gypsy" and "Dover Beach," Arnold was also one of the most influential thinkers of the Victorian era. His writings on culture, religion, and literature have been particularly esteemed. This entry will include essays written for the 1988 centenary of Arnold's death.

Charles Baudelaire (French poet)—Baudelaire is considered one of the greatest poets in world literature. His influential collection *Les fleurs du mal* (*The Flowers of Evil*), which has earned him recognition as the first modern poet, candidly reflects his obsession with moral, physical, and psychological corruption.

Charles Darwin (English naturalist and scientific writer)—While not the originator of the theory of evolution, Darwin gave it extensive support in his *On the Origin of Species by Natural Selection.* In addition to the disturbing effect this work had on religious convictions and institutions, something which Darwin did not intend, it also inspired an optimistic belief in the historical progress and improvement of human life.

Toru Dutt (Indian poet and translator)—Dutt was one of India's first prominent women writers. She is best known for her English translations of French poetry and her original English poems adapted from Hindu epics.

William Hazlitt (English critic and essayist)—Hazlitt was one of the most important and influential commentators during the Romantic age in England. In his literary criticism and miscellaneous prose he combined discerning judgment with strongly stated personal opinion, producing essays noted for their discursive style, evocative descriptions, and urbane wit.

Felicia Hemans (English poet)—Hemans was one of the most popular poets of the early nineteenth century. Focusing on religious, patriotic, and domestic subjects, her verse was memorized and declaimed by several generations of English and American school children.

Francis Jeffrey (Scottish journalist, critic, and essayist)—An influential literary critic, Jeffrey was also a founder and editor (1803-1829) of the prestigious Edinburgh Review. A liberal Whig, Jeffrey often allowed his political beliefs to color his critical opinions, and his commentary is judged the most characteristic example of "impressionistic" critical thought during the first half of the nineteenth century. Today, he is best remembered for his brutal attacks on the early Romantic poets, exemplified by the first sentence of a review of William Wordsworth's *Excursion:* "This will never do."

Charles-Marie-René Leconte de Lisle (French poet)—Leconte de Lisle was the leader of the Parnassians, a school of French poets that rejected the tenets of Romanticism in favor of emotional restraint, clarity of expression, and attention to artistic form. Inspired by the civilizations of ancient Greece, Scandinavia, and India, as well as by his love of nature, Leconte de Lisle's poetry has been described as impassive and pessimistic yet sensitive and acutely attuned to beauty.

Herman Melville (American novelist, novella and short story writer, and poet)—A major figure in American literature, Melville is recognized for his exploration of complex metaphysical and moral themes in his novels and short fiction. *NCLC* will devote an entry to his novella *Billy Budd,* a symbolic inquiry into the nature of good and evil, innocence and guilt.

John Henry Newman (English theologian and writer)—An influential theologian, Newman was a key figure in the Oxford movement, whose adherents advocated the independence of the Church of England from the state and sought to establish a doctrinal basis for Anglicanism in the Church's evolution from Catholicism. Newman's subsequent conversion to Roman Catholicism inspired his best-known work, *Apologia pro vita sua,* an eloquent spiritual autobiography tracing the development of his beliefs.

Alfred Tennyson (English poet and dramatist)—Often regarded as the poet whose work is most representative of the tastes and values of the Victorian era, Tennyson remains one of the most popular authors in the history of literature. The prosodic skills demonstrated in such memorable poems as "The Charge o the Light Brigade" and *In Memoriam* have especiall contributed to his high standing among critics ar readers.

Acknowledgments

The editors wish to thank the copyright holders of the excerpted criticism included in this volume, the permissions managers of many book and magazine publishing companies for assisting us in securing reprint rights, and Anthony Bogucki for assistance with copyright research. We are also grateful to the staffs of the Detroit Public Library, the Library of Congress, the University of Detroit Library, the Wayne State University Purdy/Kresge Library Complex, and University of Michigan Libraries for making their resources available to us. Following is a list of copyright holders who have granted us permission to reprint material in this volume of *NCLC*. Every effort has been made to trace copyright, but if omissions have been made, please let us know.

COPYRIGHTED EXCERPTS IN *NCLC*, VOLUME 28, WERE REPRINTED FROM THE FOLLOWING PERIODICALS:

American Literature, v. 19, March, 1947. Copyright 1947, renewed 1974 Duke University Press, Durham, NC. Reprinted with permission of the publisher.—*American Quarterly,* v. XVIII, Winter, 1966 for "The Success Theme in Great Plains Realism" by Lewis O. Saum; v. 37, Winter, 1985 for "The American Eve: Miscegenation and a Feminist Frontier Fiction" by Leland S. Person. Copyright 1966, 1985, American Studies Association. Both reprinted by permission of the publisher and the respective authors.—*The Aylesford Review,* v. VIII, Autumn, 1966 for "Aubrey Beardsley and 'The Savoy' " by Robert M. Booth.—*Boston University Journal,* v. XXV, 1977. Copyright © 1977 by the trustees of the Boston University. Reprinted by permission of the author.—*The Journal of Aesthetics and Art Criticism,* v. XVII, September, 1958; v. XX, Spring, 1962. Copyright © 1958, 1962 by The American Society for Aesthetics. Reprinted by permission of the publisher.—*Mosaic: A Journal for the Interdisciplinary Study of Literature,* v. XIV, Summer, 1981. © *Mosaic* 1981. Acknowledgment of previous publication is herewith made.—*PMLA,* v. 84, March, 1969; v. 86, October, 1971. Copyright © 1969, 1971, by the Modern Language Association of America. Both reprinted by permission of the Modern Language Association of America.—*Russian Literature,* v. XI, May 15, 1982 for "Nihilism, Aesthetics, and 'The Idiot' " by Charles A. Moser. © 1982, by Elsevier Science Publishers B.V. (North-Holland). All rights reserved. Reprinted by permission of the publisher and the author.—*Slavic and East-European Journal,* n.s. Vol. 21, Winter, 1977. © 1977 by AATSEEL of the U.S., Inc. Reprinted by permission of the publisher.—*Studies in the Novel,* v. VI, Summer, 1974. Copyright 1974 by North Texas State University. Reprinted by permission of the publisher.—*Studies in Romanticism,* v. IV, Autumn, 1964. Copyright 1964 by the Trustees of Boston University. Reprinted by permission of the publisher.—*Theoria,* Pietermaritzburg, v. XLVIII, May, 1977. Reprinted by permission of the publisher.—*West Virginia University Bulletin: Philological Studies,* v. 3, September, 1939. Reprinted by permission of the publisher.—*The Western Historical Quarterly,* v. XIII, January, 1982 for "Making Use of the Frontier and the American West" by Vernon Carstensen. Copyright 1982 by The Western Historical Quarterly. Reprinted by permission of the publisher and the author.—*The Yearbook of English Studies,* v. 1, 1971. © Modern Humanities Research Association 1971. All rights reserved. Reprinted by permission of the Editor and the Modern Research Humanities Association.

COPYRIGHTED EXCERPTS IN *NCLC*, VOLUME 28, WERE REPRINTED FROM THE FOLLOWING BOOKS:

Abrams, M. H. From "English Romanticism: The Spirit of the Age," in *Romanticism Reconsidered: Selected Papers from the English Institute.* Edited by Northrop Frye. Columbia University Press, 1963. Copyright © 1963 Columbia University Press. Used by permission of the publisher.—Armitage, Susan H. From "Women's Literature and the American Frontier: A New Perspective on the Frontier Myth," in *Women, Women Writers, and the West.* Edited by L. L. Lee and Merrill Lewis. The Whitston Publishing Company, 1979. Copyright 1979 L. L. Lee and Merrill Lewis. Reprinted by permission of the editors.—Barnett, Louise K. From *The Ignoble Savage: American Literary Racism, 1790-1890.* Greenwood Press, 1975. Copyright © 1975 by Louise K. Barnett. All rights reserved. Reprinted by permission of Greenwood Publishing Group, Inc., Westport, CT.—Beaty, Frederick L. From *Light from Heaven: Love in British Romantic Literature.* Northern Illinois University Press, 1971. Copyright © 1971 by Northern Illinois University Press. All rights reserved. Reprinted with permission of Northern Illinois University Press, DeKalb, IL.—Bergonzi, Bernard. From *The Turn of a Century: Essays on Victorian and Modern English Literature.* Barnes & Noble, 1973. © Bernard Bergonzi, 1973. All rights reserved. Reprinted by permission of Barnes & Noble Books, a division of Littlefield, Adams & Co., Inc. In Canada by permission of Peters, Fraser & Dunlop Group Ltd.—Bloom, Harold. From *Romanticism and Consciousness: Essays in Criticism,* Norton, 1970. Reprinted by permission of W. W. Norton & Company, Inc.—Bowra, C. M. From *The Romantic Imagination.* Cambridge, Mass.: Harvard University Press, 1949. Copyright 1949 by the President and Fellows of Harvard College. Renewed © 1977 by the Literary Estate of Cecil Maurice Bowra. Excerpted by permission of Harvard University Press.—Buckley, Jerome Hamilton. From *The Victorian Temper: A Study in Literary Culture.* Cambridge, Mass.: Harvard University Press, 1951. Copyright 1951 by the President and Fellows of Harvard College. Renewed 1979 by Jerome Hamilton Buckley. Excerpted by permission of the publishers and the

The American Frontier in Literature

INTRODUCTION

The phrase "American frontier" is most often associated with the settling of the western part of the continent during the nineteenth century, and much of what is commonly classified as frontier literature is concerned with this episode in American history. Comprising novels, short stories, dramas, and poetry, as well as travel essays by explorers and surveyors, and diaries and letters of pioneers and settlers, frontier literature evidences several prominent themes, characters, and dramatic situations. For example, many early writers depicted the New World as an Edenic promised land where hardworking, God-fearing individuals could build a civilization free from the corruption of European society. The struggles of this new civilization to conquer the physical hardships of pioneering and to wrest control of the land from the indigenous peoples provided many of the characters and events depicted in frontier literature. To most writers, the ultimate success of colonization was never in doubt, and nineteenth-century writing about the frontier generally reflects the doctrine of Manifest Destiny, the belief that the settlement of the continent by Americans of European descent and the subjugation of the native population were both right and inevitable. The promises of Manifest Destiny were fulfilled in a remarkably short time; by the end of the century the frontier had been conquered even as fictional portrayals of the frontier experience reached new heights of popularity and literary quality. Increasingly recognized by critics as a major contribution to the development of a national literature in the United States, the literature and mythology of the frontier has also had a profound impact on the American national consciousness, shaping in particular the American ideals of egalitarianism, independence, and democracy.

REPRESENTATIVE WORKS

Austin, Mary
  The Land of Little Rain (nature essays) 1903
Biddle, Nicholas, and Allen, Paul, eds.
  History of the [Lewis and Clark] Expedition (journals) 1814
Bird, Robert Montgomery
  Nick of the Woods; or, The Jibbenainosay (novel) 1837
Bleecker, Ann Eliza
  The History of Maria Kittle (novel) 1793
Brown, Charles Brockden
  Wieland; or, The Transformation (novel) 1798
  Edgar Huntly; or, Memoirs of a Sleep-Walker (novel) 1799
  Ormond; or, The Secret Witness (novel) 1799
  Clara Howard (novel) 1801; also published as *Philip Stanley; or, The Enthusiasm of Love,* 1807
Bryant, Daniel
  The Adventures of Daniel Boone (biography) 1813

Cary, Alice
  Clovernook; or, Recollections of Our Neighborhood in the West (novel) 1852
Cather, Willa
  O Pioneers! (novel) 1913
  My Ántonia (novel) 1918
Cheney, Harriet V.
  A Peep at the Pilgrims (novel) 1824
Child, Lydia Maria
  Hobomok; A Tale of Early Times (novel) 1824
Cooper, James Fenimore
  The Pioneers; or, The Sources of the Susquehanna (novel) 1823
  The Last of the Mohicans (novel) 1826
  The Prairie (novel) 1827
  The Wept of Wish-ton-Wish (novel) 1829
  The Pathfinder; or, The Inland Sea (novel) 1840
  The Deerslayer; or, The First War Path (novel) 1841
  Wyandotté; or, The Hutted Knoll (novel) 1843
  The Chainbearer; or, The Littlepage Manuscripts (novel) 1845
  Satanstoe; or, The Littlepage Manuscripts (novel) 1845
  The Redskins; or, Indian and Injin: Being the Conclusion of the Littlepage Manuscripts (novel) 1846
Crèvecoeur, J. Hector St. John de
  Letters from an American Farmer (nonfiction) 1782
Custer, George A.
  My Life on the Plains (autobiography) 1874
Farnham, Eliza W.
  California, In-Doors and Out; or, How We Farm, Mine, and Live Generally in the Golden State (essay) 1856
Filson, John
  The Discovery, Settlement, and Present State of Kentucke [includes appendix "The Adventures of Col. Daniel Boon"] (history and biography) 1784
  Life and Adventures of Colonel Daniel Boon, the First White Settler of the State of Kentucky (biography) 1824
Flint, Timothy
  Francis Berrian; or, The Mexican Patriot (novel) 1826
  George Mason, The Young Backwoodsman (novel) 1829
  The Shoshonee Valley (novel) 1830
  Biographical Memoir of Daniel Boone, the First Settler of Kentucky, Interspersed with Incidents in the Early Annals of the Country (biography) 1833
Fuller, Margaret
  Summer on the Lakes, in 1843 (travel essay) 1844
Garland, Hamlin
  Main-Travelled Roads: Six Mississippi Valley Stories (short stories) 1891
  Prairie Songs: Being Chants Rhymed and Unrhymed of the Level Lands of the Great West (poetry) 1893
  Boy Life on the Prairie (novel) 1899
  Other Main-Travelled Roads (short stories) 1910
  A Son of the Middle Border (autobiography) 1917

1

A Daughter of the Middle Border   (autobiography) 1921

The Book of the American Indian   (biography and short stories)   1923

Trail-Makers of the Middle Border   (autobiography) 1926

Back-Trailers from the Middle Border   (autobiography) 1928

Harte, Bret
The Luck of Roaring Camp, and Other Sketches   (short stories)   1869

Stories of the Sierras, and Other Sketches   (short stories) 1872

California Stories   (short stories)   1884

On the Frontier   (short stories)   1884

Holley, Mary Austin
Texas, Observations, Historical, Geographical, and Descriptive, In a Series of Letters, Written during a Visit to Austin's Colony, with a View to a Permanent Settlement in That Country, in the Autumn of 1831   (letters)   1833

Hopkins, Sarah Winnemucca
Life among the Piutes   (autobiography)   1883

Howard, H. R.
The Life and Adventures of John A. Murrell, the Great Western Land Pirate   (novel)   1847

Irving, Washington
A Tour on the Prairies   (travel essay)   1835

King, Clarence
Mountaineering in the Sierra Nevada   (sketches)   1872

Kirkland, Caroline M.
A New Home—Who'll Follow? Or, Glimpses of Western Life   (novel)   1839

Forest Life. 2 vols.   (novel)   1842

Kirkland, Joseph
Zury: The Meanest Man in Spring County   (novel) 1887

London, Jack
The Son of the Wolf   (novel)   1900

The Call of the Wild   (novel)   1903

Muir, John
The Mountains of California   (nature essays)   1894

Our National Parks   (essays)   1901

My First Summer in the Sierra   (essays)   1911

The Yosemite   (essays)   1912

Parkman, Francis
The California and Oregon Trail   (essay)   1849

Paulding, James K.
The Backwoodsman   (poem)   1818

Pike, Zebulon M.
An Account of Expeditions to the Sources of the Mississippi and through the Western Parts   (travel essay)   1810

Ridge, John Rollin
The Life and Adventures of Joaquin Murieta, the Celebrated California Bandit   (novel)   1854

Rölvaag, Ole
I de dage—: Fortælling om Norske nykommere i Amerika   (novel)   1924

I de dage—: Riket grundlaegges   (novel)   1925
    [These works were translated and published as
        Giants in the Earth: A Saga of the Prairie, 1927]

Peder Seier   (novel)   1928
    [*Peder Victorious: A Tale of the Pioneer Twenty
        Years Later,* 1929]

Rowlandson, Mary White
The Sovereignty and Goodness of God; better known as *The Narrative of Mrs. Mary Rowlandson*   (captivity narrative)   1682

Rowson, Susannah
Reuben and Rachel   (novel)   1798

Seaver, James Everett
Narrative of the Life of Mrs. Mary Jemison   (biography) 1824

Sedgwick, Catharine Maria
Hope Leslie; or, Early Times in the Massachusetts. 2 vols.   (novel)   1827

Simms, William Gilmore
The Yemassee   (novel)   1835

The Wigwam and the Cabin   (novel)   1845

The Cassique of Kiawah   (novel)   1859

Soule, Caroline A.
The Pet of the Settlement: A Story of Prairie-Land   (novel)   1860

Twain, Mark
The Celebrated Jumping Frog of Calaveras County, and Other Sketches   (sketches)   1867

Roughing It   (novel)   1872

The Adventures of Tom Sawyer   (novel)   1876

Life on the Mississippi   (autobiographical novel)   1883

The Adventures of Huckleberry Finn   (novel)   1884

Wister, Owen
The Virginian: A Horseman of the Plains   (novel)   1902

DEFINITIONS OF FRONTIER LITERATURE

EDWIN FUSSELL

[*An American educator and critic, Fussell is the author of numerous works on American literature. In the following excerpt, he discusses the significance of the West and the frontier as concepts in the development of American literature.*]

For an understanding of early American literature, the word West, with all its derivatives and variants, is the all but inevitable key. Yet no word commonly associated with the American identity and destiny has been, and continues to be, more frequently misused and sentimentalized. As Caroline Kirkland asked well over a century ago about "the 'West' ": "How much does that expression mean to include? I never have been able to discover its limits." (The superficial retort would be that an expression which includes everything means nothing.) Mrs. Kirkland's near contemporary George Catlin still more pointedly observed: "Few people even know the true definition of the term 'West;' and where is its location?— phantom-like it flies before us as we travel." And in a review of Charles Fenno Hoffman, *A Winter in the West. By a New-Yorker* (1835), an unknown analyst puzzled the matter out at considerable length:

> "The West," however, is a vague designation of any place in North America. Although there be a distinct meaning in the phrase, well understood by the person using it, yet paradoxical as this is, it points to no locality. Twenty years ago the Alleghany range might, by most people, be considered in these new countries. Ten years ago, the Mississippi was

the *ne plus ultra* for five-sixths of Americans. The imaginary line which limited the bounds of the West, has thus been continually changing, till at length it has found a natural correspondence in the "woods where rolls the Oregon," and on the shore laved by the Pacific. Still the phrase has a local meaning. The mind of a citizen of Philadelphia referring to the West, does not now reach beyond the Mississippi. When an inhabitant of Ohio speaks of the West, he means beyond that river; and when one of Missouri talks of this still receding land, he fixes himself, as he geographically is, in the centre of the Union, and locates the West far beyond his Pawnee or Comanche neighbors, along the distant peaks that give rise to the Oregon and Missouri.

Especially in early nineteenth-century American thought and expression, the term West is not only all-inclusive but it perpetually vacillates between what might be called an absolute meaning (location) and what might be called a relative meaning (direction), the first of which is entirely arbitrary while the second is dependent upon the time, the location, and the linguistic habits of the speaker. The word must be interpreted anew for each new use, according to its presumed function in the context, and this function is not always easy to determine, for American speakers normally intend both the absolute and relative senses of the word, however vaguely, together with some sort of doctrinal connection between them, usually implicit. The American West is almost by definition indefinite and indefinable, or at least changing, pluralistic, and ambiguous in signification.

To envisage America's ambiguous civilization in the light of the West is also to become involved with both our difference from, and our continuity with, the Eastern Hemisphere. As Walt Whitman continually reminds us, the germs of American civilization were long harbored in Europe, or even farther East, and therefore American civilization is not a simple malady, although modern Europeans often act as if it were. However much they have been associated with the United States by Europeans and Americans alike, the concepts of the West and the frontier, and nearly every one of their component or sustaining elements, are un-American in origin. In "Walking," Thoreau correctly surmised that "the island of Atlantis, and the islands and gardens of the Hesperides, a sort of terrestrial paradise, appear to have been the Great West of the ancients, enveloped in mystery and poetry." (And vice versa, of course.) Thoreau might also have mentioned the poets and philosophers of Renaissance Europe, who likewise looked beyond the Atlantic for their Utopias, cities in the sun, and brave new worlds. Unlike the ancients, they not only looked but saw. And those who came to America not only saw but were seen, not only by those who remained at home but by themselves. American civilization and, within it, American literature, result from the confrontation and reciprocal interaction of Old World predispositions and New World actualities.

Oddly enough, the myth of the West was further reinforced by Christian tradition. Christ Himself (according to St. Matthew) predicted that the Son of Man would spring from the East and flash across to the West. And who can really estimate how much of the continuing emotional charge and nuisance value of such conventional counters as Old World and New World was once derived from analogies with Old and New Testaments, old and new dispensations, prophecy and redemption, order and liberty, Eden lost and (to be) regained? Our bibliolatrous forefathers were well aware of

these remotely gratifying sanctions, and if their enlightened children were not, they were fortified to comparable political ends by universal history (from the European point of view), with its delightful teachings about the inevitably progressive and Westward course of empires. In 1807, one of John Adams' friends preserved a tradition that the following lines were "drilled into a Rock on the shore of Monument Bay in our old Colony of Plymouth, and were supposed to have been written and engraved there by some of the first emigrants":

> The Eastern nations sink, their glory ends
> And Empire rises where the sun descends.

"However this may be," said Adams of the unlikely tale, "I have heard these verses for more than sixty years. . . . There is nothing . . . more ancient in my Memory than the observation that Arts, Sciences and Empire had travelled Westward: and in Conversation it was always added, since I was a Child that their next Leap would be over the Atlantick into America." Adams' reassuring memory was perhaps overstocked with such verses, for the second line of this couplet appears to have been slightly misquoted from "The Rising Glory of America," a Princeton graduation poem by Philip Freneau and Hugh Henry Brackenridge, and of no more venerable date than 1771.

Interpenetration of the Western myth with the actual events comprising the expansion of the United States from a strip of Atlantic colonies to a continental nation, produced not only American civilization but the complex phenomenon known to historians (though not very clearly understood) as the Westward Movement. For the period between the Revolution and the Civil War, these two phenomena—American civilization and the Westward Movement—are to all intents and purposes interchangeable. The Westward Movement is also the inclusive term within which the more limited term the West must always be approached, as the West, so defined, is the inclusive term containing the still more restricted term the frontier. Regrettably, these terms do not become clearer as they shrink in comprehensiveness—neither do they become clearer as time goes on—but on the contrary intensify their inherent ambiguities. From the outset, the American concept of the frontier reveals a shifting character and a striking ambivalence; and these are found in all the major American writers through Whitman, and, in a tentative and somewhat inchoate form, in the works of J. Hector St. John de Crèvecœur, writing on the verge of American political independence, and of Charles Brockden Brown, writing soon after.

In Crèvecœur's *Letters from an American Farmer* (1782), a naïve narrator named James conducts us from idyl ("On the Situation, Feelings, and Pleasures of an American Farmer"), to definition ("What Is an American"), and then through a tour of the colonies to disintegration and disaster ("Distresses of a Frontier Man"). "If they be not elegant," says the local minister of these letters, "they will smell of the woods, and be a little wild," for they come "from the edge of the great wilderness, three hundred miles from the sea." Crèvecœur's frontier farmer catches pigeons which he fancies "breed toward the plains of Ohio, and those about Lake Michigan," and like Franklin and Jefferson imagines that "many ages will not see the shores of our great lakes replenished with inland nations, nor the unknown bounds of North America entirely peopled. Who can tell how far it extends?" Within the verge of this conception, but on the hither edge of a conception

"Emigrants to the West," an illustration by William de la Montagne Cary for A Popular History of the United States *by William Cullen Bryant and Sydney Howard Gay.*

which is about to controvert and supplant it, he offers the famous definitions of Americanism:

> What then is the American, this new man? . . . *He* is an American, who leaving behind him all his ancient prejudices and manners, receives new ones from the new mode of life he has embraced, the new government he obeys, and the new rank he holds. . . . Americans are the western pilgrims, who are carrying along with them that great mass of arts, sciences, vigour, and industry which began long since in the east; they will finish the great circle.

But this conventional conception of the frontier as cutting edge for happy American progress runs into difficulty when the narrator thinks of actual pioneers. Sharply dissociating himself from their barbarism, he moves to new ground and a new metaphor, the frontier as neutral territory, or middle condition (in middle-class eighteenth-century English parlance). James has subtly changed his place of residence from the edge of the wilderness to "the middle settlements," the "intermediate space" between ocean and woods, where "a sort of resurrection" transcends constitutive opposition, and the idyl of agrarianism naturally occurs. In Crèvecœur's triple-tiered civilization, those who live near the ocean are "bold and enterprising" but dull—except Nantucketers who "go to whaling . . . as a landman undertakes to clear a piece of swamp"—while those who live in the woods are horridly fascinating, and are described at length in connection with the Westward Movement. The pioneers are "the most hideous parts of our society. They are a kind of forlorn hope, preceding by ten or twelve years the most respectable army of veter-

ans which come after them. . . . Such is our progress, such is the march of the Europeans toward the interior parts of this continent. In all societies there are off-casts; this impure part serves as our precursors or pioneers." Entirely forgetting what the *Letters* were supposed to smell like, Crèvecœur now tells us of woods which corrupt. "Thus our bad people are those who are half cultivators and half hunters; and the worst of them are those who have degenerated altogether into the hunting state. As old ploughmen and new men of the woods, as Europeans and new made Indians, they contract the vices of both."

At the end, as colonial civilization collapses in Revolution, and Loyalist Crèvecœur's intermediate space is devastated by incursions of Loyalist Indians, the fictive farmer is once more driven to reconceive his frontier. " You know the position of our settlement. . . . To the west it is inclosed by a chain of mountains, reaching to—; to the east, the country is as yet but thinly inhabited." The distressed frontiersman imagines himself farther West than he actually is and decides to "revert into a state approaching nearer to that of nature," even to the extent of turning half hunter. "You may therefore, by means of anticipation," he warns his correspondent, "behold me under the Wigwham." In the course of a typically French critique of the failing English empire, the new man undergoes a still further metamorphosis. Gladly will James learn from the Noble Savages—previously described as "a race doomed to recede and disappear before the superior genius of the Europeans"—and gladly teach them civilized ways, or "chearfully go even to the Mississippi" in quest of peace. Going native is the same as pioneering, and the only imaginable direction is West.

Post-Revolutionary American writing never more clearly reveals the New World's traumas than when attempting to march toward the interior; perhaps in part because until the 1820's, the only imaginable direction for American literature proved impossible to travel. In a prefatory note to *Edgar Huntly; or, Memoirs of a Sleep-Walker* (1799), Charles Brockden Brown spoke of the need to investigate "sources of amusement to the fancy and instruction to the heart, that are peculiar to ourselves," with special emphasis upon "the incidents of Indian hostility, and the perils of the Western wilderness." As advertised, *Edgar Huntly* contains the famous portrait of Old Deb, a malingering Delaware woman whose tribe has removed after "encroachments." Unfortunately, the border warfare she instigates is operatic to the point of parody, the vaunted wilderness where it occurs is only a nearby suburban desert, and the connection between wilderness warfare and the somnambulistic nightmares otherwise informing the novel is obscure. Yet indirectly and much more significantly Brown shows European emigrants and American natives penetrating the unknown future and unwittingly going savage. "Was I still in the vicinity of my parental habitation, or was I thousands of miles distant?" He was perhaps the first American writer to suspect that the West might more profitably be defined as a condition of the soul than as a physiographical region. In *Ormond; or, The Secret Witness* (1799), the protagonist has mysteriously been outside "the precincts of civilized existence," and among other places "beyond the Mississippi," or "in the heart of desert America"; his ardent sister has fought in the patriot armies "on the frontiers." Their tales enlarge our heroine's little Atlantic seaboard world to include "men, in their two forms, of savage and refined," for, on the threshold of development, America is neither, or both. The adolescent hero of *Clara Howard; or, The Enthusiasm of Love* (1801) hysterically pictures himself adventuring by canoe to the Pacific Ocean. By this time Brown's ambition had clearly outrun American history and American geographical knowledge.

An earlier novel is still more illuminating. In *Wieland; or, The Transformation. An American Tale* (1798), a European seeking conversion of the Indians emigrates to the New World, and as far inland as "the shores of the Ohio." In the next generation, fanatical piety turns to religious mania in the son, who murders wife and children, and takes his own life, as if he were an Indian in such an atrocity-novel as Mrs. Ann Eliza Bleecker's *History of Maria Kittle* (1797). Evidently the chaos created by young Wieland is in Brown's parable to be thought of as resulting from a reciprocity of forces at the meeting point between savagery and civilization. "It was worthy of savages trained to murder, and exulting in agonies. . . . Surely, said I, it is a dream." (There are many similar passages.) Consequently, Clara Wieland and her uncle decline further participation in the American dream and flee to Europe. " 'I confess I came over with an intention to reside among you,' " the uncle observes, " ' but these disasters have changed my views.' " *Wieland* is an indispensable chapter in the story of Europe mythically projecting the New World and then reacting to the actual creation; ironically, it was published in the year of the Alien and Sedition Acts, and allegedly deals with events "between the conclusion of the French and the beginning of the revolutionary war."

In the supplementary "Memoirs of Carwin, the Biloquist,"

Brown's "villain" is pointedly identified as a native American—from "a western district of Pennsylvania"—who has been corrupted by prolonged residence in Europe. After helping produce the Wielands' cultural regression, Carwin entertains the idea of burying himself in the wilderness—in order to write!—but finally settles for the tranquilizing pursuit of rural competence, presumably in Crèvecœur's intermediate space. Had Brown been able to fuse these polar actions within a single unified vision, he might have earned in our literary history approximately the position occupied by Cooper, for the narrative which *Wieland* so inefficiently embodies bears many an anticipatory resemblance to the Leatherstocking Tales. But 1798 was simply too early; not even Thomas Jefferson had a sufficiently clear idea what the continent was like, or what American development might portend. Clara Wieland's self-description is inevitably the description of her creator, his contemporaries, and their yet undefined nation: "My ideas are vivid, but my language is faint; now know I what it is to entertain incommunicable sentiments. . . . What but ambiguities, abruptnesses, and dark transitions, can be expected from the historian who is, at the same time, the sufferer of these disasters?"

The West was won by American literature in the next generation, and it was not an easy victory. As journalistic publicists were always saying: "The American mind will be brought to maturity along the chain of the great lakes, the banks of the Mississippi, the Missouri, and their tributaries in the far northwest. There, on the rolling plains, will be formed a republic of letters which, not governed like that on our seaboard, by the great literary powers of Europe, shall be free, indeed." But even a promotional tract had to concede that in the actual West "the very atmosphere of society is averse to mental culture, and all refinement is so systematically as well as practically decried, as to have fallen into absolute discredit." The apparent paradox is easily explained: a kind of nihilistic and anarchic cultural regression was the immediate local effect of the continually advancing frontier line, and, by the very nature of the process, it was superficial and temporary. Americanization was a delayed reaction in the rear, and a vastly different affair. It probably began in the minds of writers desperately trying to make some kind of provisional sense of their rapidly evolving civilization. From variously brilliant responses to the challenge of the new West, which in at least the geographical sense was plainly to become the greater part of a new America, they developed a genuinely American literature. As Margaret Fuller said in a volume of Western travels: "I trust by reverent faith to woo the mighty meaning of the scene, perhaps to foresee the law by which a new order, a new poetry, is to be evoked from this chaos." The new order of literature evoked from the chaos is a matter of record, and we have no choice but to assume that it tells us the fundamental truth about the Westward Movement. (If it does not, we shall never know it.) Neither have we cause for complaint, for the truth told by American literature is considerably more fascinating, if somewhat less comforting, than the tales of the forest found in our history books.

Of course, it is equally true that without the real and imagined experiences of actual pioneering to serve as informing principle and guiding light, nineteenth-century American literature as we know it would never have come into being. Insofar as it resulted from a series of aesthetic transformations, through which intrinsically meaningless pioneer experiences were elevated to the status of ideas and forms, American literature may in its origins fairly be called an effect of the frontier; re-entering society, it became a continuing cause (a far more important cause than the actual frontier) toward the creation of the American character, nationalism, democracy, or whatever other values (a few of them more elevating than these) are actually found in the literature. Given the American situation, it was perhaps to have been expected that some people would resent the intrusions of a higher truth into literature, that they would attack the truth from the cover of anti-intellectual "realism," and that the attacks would come from the most anti-intellectual of the American sections. Almost from the beginning, second-rate writers like Daniel Drake, residing in what they were pleased to consider the real West, fulminated against Cooper, for example, arguing that "in delineating the West, no power of genius can supply the want of opportunities for personal observation on our natural and social aspects. No western man can read those works with interest." The simple truth is that the American West was neither more nor less interesting than any other place, except in mythology or in the swollen egos of Westerners, until by interpretation the great American writers—all of whom happened to be Eastern—made it seem so. This they did by conceiving its physical aspects (forests, rivers, lakes, clearings, settlements, prairies, plains, deserts) and its social aspects (isolation, simplicity, improvisation, criticism, chaos, restlessness, paradox, irony) as expressive emblems for the invention and development of a new national civilization, and not as things in themselves.

Most Americans preferred an easier progress, and rather mindlessly found it in insignificant puns about different orders of movement. "The expansive future is our arena, and for our history. We are entering on its untrodden space. . . . We are the nation of human progress, and who will, what can, set limits to our onward march? . . . The far-reaching, the boundless future will be the era of American greatness. In its magnificent domain of space and time, the nation of many nations is destined to manifest to mankind the excellence of divine principles." Those exhilarating analogous progressions from East to West and from present to future were surcharged with teleological nationalism cartographically advancing from right to left, Old World to New, reality to beatitude. Yet paradoxically the American West—as chaos, matrix, or embryo—was also "earlier," and therefore the past. By moving his point of observation Eastward, the nationalistic writer commanded a double vision, and conveniently close to home. Under the guise of the past he foretold the future, as under the pretense of describing the Revolutionary colonies he secretly visited the West. Of "The Spy. A Tale of the Revolution," whose setting was Maryland, and which was included in *Tales of the Border,* James Hall explained:

> Although the title which we have chosen for this volume, would seem to confine us, in the selection of our scenes, to an imaginary line which forms the boundary of our settled population, yet, in fact, the limit which it imposes refers rather to time than place, for ours is a moving frontier, which is continually upon the advance. What is now the *border,* has but recently assumed that character, and if we trace back the history of our country to its earliest period, in search of the stirring scenes attendant upon a state of war, we shall find ourselves rapidly travelling towards the shores of the Atlantic. There has been a point in the history of every state in the Union, when a portion of its territory was a wilderness. . . . It is this circumstance which ren-

ders the whole of our broad empire so rich in materials for the novelist.

The same time-space equations ambiguously supported American appropriation of Condorcet's social-stages-of-history theory, as posthumously propounded in *Outlines of an Historical View of the Progress of the Human Mind* (1795). That optimistic program for egalitarian democracy supplied a philosophic rationale for expansion of civilization in the New World—if necessary through obliteration of "those savage nations still occupying there immense tracts of country"—and, best of all, it placed the Anglo-Americans, with the French, in the vanguard of progress. Unfortunately, the topography and climate of America practically prescribed certain physiographical concentrations of economic activity: commerce on the East Coast, cattle-raising far to the West of the nation's granaries. Condorcet considered the pastoral condition inevitably more primitive than agriculture, and agriculture more primitive than commerce. In this view, Westward progress meant cultural regress. It is not surprising, then, that at the heart of the American language, radically divergent conceptions of the national destiny were impounded in conflicting notions of "back" ("backwoodsman") and "front" (frontiersman"), which reflected the antithetical regressive and progressive readings of the Westward Movement and, ultimately, the conflicting European-community vs. isolationist interpretations of American history. The frontier was the meeting point between these readings. From their interpenetration on the neutral ground of national becoming, early nineteenth-century writers zealously looked for a new culture, genetically European but better, and certainly no a pallid compromise between our old home and a disheartening environment. After all, "front" implied not only "back," but also a duality of direction, a "fronting both ways," or even an oppositional situation surreptitiously sexual and procreative; as Margaret Fuller incomparably announced: "Male and female represent the two sides of the great radical dualism." Naturally the hopes and fears of the American writer were drawn to this provocative and realistic symbol of the cultural antagonisms which beset him. Somewhere out West, as analogously on the frontier within his own soul, a struggle was being enacted between the failing forms of the paternal civilizations and the threat of absolute formlessness. Through a sort of secular miracle, new forms and values might yet emerge from the deathlock, expressive of the new time and place, and indeed constituting them. And at this point, the anticipated miracle miraculously occurred—not literally on the frontier or magically in the forest, but in the minds and on the tongues of men.

Frederick Jackson Turner [in his *The Frontier in American History,* 1920] carefully called attention to the way that "in American thought and speech the term 'frontier' has come to mean the edge of settlement, rather than, as in Europe, the political boundary," and he also insisted that "the American frontier is sharply distinguished from the European frontier—a fortified boundary line running through dense populations." It is not easy to understand how these two significations could have been kept apart in the early days, and of course they were not. Always in relationship with each other, the European and Western meanings of the word together formed a trope, and should properly be called "the frontier metaphor." Consequently, what the American frontier means is its genesis: a new situation, vaguely sensed, and requiring designation, was denoted by an old word with an adaptable meaning. The mingling of meanings helps explain why the American frontier was sometimes a line and sometimes a space, as it also helps explain why it was a militantly nationalistic concept unrelated to any other nation. Either way, the frontier was a figure of speech, gradually but never entirely sloughing European implications as it assumed new functions in a new context, and thus incidentally a splendid illustration of the Americanizing process Turner used it to describe. The frontier was the imaginary line between American civilization and nature, or the uncreated future, and everything that came to depend upon that line was ironically reversible.

Not merely in this primary sense was the frontier metaphor the leading formal principle of early American literature. A further threshold was crossed when American writers learned to double their basic metaphor, especially the frontier-as-space, by involving it with social, psychological, philosophical, or other situations analogously reconciling opposites through interpenetration and transcendence. Doubling was easiest in the case of phrases like "neutral ground" and "debatable land," which originated in the actual conditions of early American history, and were formally and intentionally the same as Crèvecœur's "intermediate space." Gradually they came to signify the Western frontier and proliferated into a whole series of similar terms. Then by a simple extension of meaning comparable to the extension through which the old word frontier was first applied to conditions in the new West, Cooper could say that in frontier communities gentle and common folk "meet, as it might be, on a sort of neutral ground," and Orestes Brownson could discuss the fluid relations between prose and poetry in terms of the Western border: "No man can define the exact boundary line between them; and it is only when at a considerable distance from the line, that we can tell whether we are in the territory of the one or of the other. On each side of the line, there is and always must be a disputed territory."

As Bronson Alcott revealingly wrote of Emerson's early works, and the criticisms of them: "These I deem first fruits of a new literature. . . . Nature and the Soul are conjoined. The images are American. The portrait is set in a frame of western oak." On the philosophical side, the Western frontier became more and more entangled with Transcendental dialectic imported from Germany by way of British oversimplifications and spatially displayed on the expansive fields of American geographical and spiritual progress. Dialectic was the all-but-universal mode of reconciling opposites, and opposites were rife. In addition to the intrinsic and almost unavoidable opposites (life-death, known-unknown, good-evil), early nineteenth-century thinkers were infatuated with such pairs as civilization-nature (especially popular in the United States), mind-matter, reason-understanding, reason-imagination, imagination-fancy, organism-mechanism, self-society, subject-object, poet-nature, fiction-fact, poetry-prose, heart-head, synthesis-analysis—real or imaginary dichotomies spotting the gray debris of Cartesian confusion and Kantian clarification. For Romantic thought, these pairs rested on a special feeling for duality-in-unity, or the reverse, most vigorously articulated by Teufelsdröckh-Carlyle, whose American vogue in the 1830's amounted to a craze; Thoreau and Whitman judged him essentially Western, as, in a way, he was. "Consider them [two Goethe characters] as the two disjointed Halves of the singular Dualistic Being of ours," he would go on and on, while the Americans gaped, "a Being, I must say, the most utterly Dualistic; fashioned, from the very heart of it, out of Positive and Negative . . . everywhere

out of *two* mortally opposed things, which yet must be united in vital love, if there is to be any *Life;*—a Being, I repeat, Dualistic beyond expressing." Around 1840 Thoreau reported that a sagacious lecturer—it would have been Emerson or Alcott—was effectively making his point by holding up "one finger to express individuality, and two for dualism."

This central intellectual structure of the age was quite literally a meta-physics. As Emerson retrospectively noted: "The magnet was thrown into Europe, and all philosophy has taken a direction from it." Perhaps the first, and certainly the most influential philosopher who was thought to have taken direction was Kant. His *Versuch, den Begriff der negativen Grössen in die Weltweisheit einzuführen* (1763) contained a tantalizing distinction between "real" and "logical" opposition, and was widely misinterpreted as arguing that universal laws might be derived from electromagnetic polarity. In *Biographia Literaria* (1817), Coleridge propped his theory of imagination with a preliminary discussion of Kant's treatise, whence he transcendentally extracted from the "effective pioneer" a "master-thought," the "inter-penetration of the counteracting powers [any powers], partaking of both." It was an easy step to the famous definition of "the poet, described in *ideal* perfection," and especially his unifying esemplastic power revealing itself "in the balance or reconciliation of opposite or discordant qualities." In *The Friend* (1818), Coleridge elicited from "the phænomena of electricity the operation of a law which reigns through all nature, the law of POLARITY, or the manifestation of one power by opposite forces." And his retrospect was the same as Emerson's: the "new light" of the day was "the discovery of electricity," and "the new path, thus brilliantly opened, became the common road to all departments of knowledge."

Unfortunately, the new light illuminated an ancient roadblock. "A believer in Unity, a seer of Unity," Emerson typically confessed, "I yet behold two." Dualism haunted this representative American mind. "All the universe over, there is but one thing, this old Two-Face . . . of which any proposition may be affirmed or denied." He summed up his problem in a *Journal* entry ambivalently headed "*The Two Statements, or Bipolarity.*" Emerson was finally unable to share some people's enthusiastic interpretations of Kant as the author of discontinuity: "If, as Hedge thinks . . . the world is not a dualism [!], is not a bipolar unity, but is *two*, is Me and It, then is there the alien, the unknown, and all we have believed and chanted out of our deep instinctive hope is a pretty dream." The national literature being at stake, Emerson rejected the "Infernal Twoness" in favor of the "Supernal Oneness" (Poe's terms), namely a polar, paradoxical, ironic, ambiguous monism which remains to this day the signature of American thought and expression. Unity was the spirit of the age, or as Emerson said in a variety of contexts: " 'T is indifferent whether you say, all is matter, or, all is spirit; and 't is plain there is a tendency in the times to an identity-philosophy," a magnificent instance of American fascination with form at the expense of content.

For reasons comprehending American history from the Declaration of Independence through the Civil War, the passion for unity was more frenetic in the United States than elsewhere. In 1836, Brownson instructed his compatriots in *New Views of Christianity, Society, and the Church,* where Our Lord was Americanized along the mythical-dialectic border. "We are to reconcile spirit and matter," he declared. "Nothing else remains for us to do. Stand still we cannot. . . .

Progress is our law and our first step is Union." Theological in application but philosophical and political in origin, Brownson's argument was shaped by a constitutive opposition comprising the whole experience of mankind: "Spiritualism" (Catholicism, "the Eastern World") vs. "Materialism" (Protestantism, "the Western World"). Having supplied His own dilemma, God triumphantly produced the ecumenical American answer: "This antithesis generates perpetual and universal war. It is necessary then to remove it and harmonize, or unite the two terms. Now, if we conceive Jesus as standing between spirit and matter, the representative of both—God-Man—the point where both meet and lose their antithesis . . . we shall have his secret thought and the true idea of Christianity." By perfect analogy and reciprocal causation, the standpoint between spirit and matter was precisely the point where civilization and nature met and American life was perpetually reborn. On the frontier, Christ turned into Leatherstocking, Crèvecœur's new man suffered still another forest-change (Turner's phrase), and the Second Coming was subsumed in the Westward Movement. Under auspices so benign, even the minor writer could chant his deep instinctive hopes. Daniel Boone, according to William Gilmore Simms, "was not merely a hunter. He was on a mission. The spiritual sense was strong in him. He felt the union between his inner and the nature of the visible world, and yearned for their intimate communion."

In "The Young American" (1844), Emerson wrote: "Luckily for us, now that steam has narrowed the Atlantic to a strait, the nervous, rocky West is intruding a new and continental element into the national mind, and we shall yet have an American genius." And then, somehow, Emerson's gaze wandered, and when he looked again, his visionary powers were gone. "It is to be remembered that the flowering time is the end," he said in an 1853 lecture: "we ought to be thankful that no hero or poet hastens to be born." After a trip to St. Louis in the same year he wrote Carlyle: "Room for us all, since it has not ended, nor given sign of ending, in bard or hero." In fact, the flowering time was almost over, and the heroic poets hastening to their literal or figurative graves. Just before his death Cooper wrote in a new introduction to *The Prairie:* "Since the original publication of this book [1827] . . . the boundaries of the republic have been carried to the Pacific." Already the end was in sight, for those who had eyes to see. "In 1820, Missouri was the 'far West,' and Independence the boundary of civilization. Now, in 1854, there is no 'far West.' It has been crowded overboard into the Pacific Ocean. . . . Pioneer life and pioneer progress must soon pass away for ever, to be remembered only in story."

But the West Coast never was a frontier in the primary metaphorical sense of neutral territory between advancing civilization and nature lying beyond; and when California was admitted to the Union in 1850, with Oregon following in 1859, all the other straggling frontiers to the East were by the same action effectually blocked off. No longer was the West a field of boundless opportunity, but a mopping-up operation. During the 1850's and 1860's the figurative frontier and the teleological West were drained of expressive value, and disappeared from literary currency. The West exerted serious imaginative impact in the United States only so long as it remained a living idea, which was only so long as it survived in real potentiality; the winning of the actual West brought the Westward Movement of American writing to a natural and inevitable end a few years after the closing of the frontier.

Thus, by the time Mark Twain arrived on the scene, the frontier and the West were gone, though their memory left minor, vestigial traces on almost everything he wrote. He exploded the final trace in *A Connecticut Yankee in King Arthur's Court,* where the Wild West show comes to a rude end with the Boss blowing up his own "civilization-factories" on a "kind of neutral ground." This symbolic explosion of the frontier metaphor may perhaps be taken for Mark Twain's signing off as the Buffalo Bill of American literature, a role evidently foisted upon him by the long-held expectation of a Great American Writer emanating from the Great West, and more or less willingly played at in such early books as *Roughing It* (1872) and *The Gilded Age* (1873). After the Civil War, practically no Americans either knew or cared what they meant by the West, though apparently Mark Twain suspected, for the main point of his role as literary Westerner increasingly came to be its ludicrously anachronistic irrelevance—hence such standing jokes as the Arkansas legislature, territorial governments, the backwoods, the Choctaw language, Sherman chasing Indians, or, for that matter, Buffalo Bill—or its sentimental value as an image of youth. Inevitably his deepest desires found expression through a small boy's dwindling dream, nourished by a mythical river running through land settled on both banks and concluding: "And so there ain't nothing more to write about, and I am rotten glad of it. . . . But I reckon I got to light out for the Territory ["for howling adventures amongst the Injuns"] ahead of the rest, because Aunt Sally she's going to adopt me and sivilize me, and I can't stand it. I been there before." And there he would stay, the "Territory" of 1885 not being worth lighting out for, as can be verified in any historical atlas; and as appears in the opening of *Tom Sawyer Abroad* (1894), Huck Finn on second thought decided not to try for it. The geographical axis of *The Adventures of Huckleberry Finn* ("SCENE: THE MISSISSIPPI VALLEY. TIME: FORTY TO FIFTY YEARS AGO.") is conspicuously North-South, and the only realistic direction of escape revealingly lies to the East, the same line of escape taken by the author. Neither was Mark Twain born "on the frontier," as so often alleged, for the frontier, however defined, was in 1835 far West of Florida, Missouri, if, indeed, it was anywhere at all, except as an object of thought or figure of speech. (pp. 3-25)

Edwin Fussell, in his Frontier: American Literature and the American West, *Princeton University Press, 1965, 450 p.*

JAY B. HUBBELL

[*An American critic and educator, Hubbell was considered an authority on American literature, particularly that of the southern United States. He served as editor of* American Literature *from 1928 to 1954, and maintained that American writing deserved the same serious scholarship as had previously been reserved for British literature. In the following excerpt, Hubbell reflects on the ways in which the frontier has influenced American literature.*]

The frontier, as I see it, has made two distinct and important contributions to our literature: it has given our writers a vast field of new materials, and it has given them a new point of view, which we may call American.

Our early nineteenth-century authors fell heir to a new and varied natural background, which appealed strongly to the Romantic imagination. Here they found the primeval forest, practically gone from Europe, and the great plains, not to be paralleled in Europe outside of Russia; they found rivers which made the Thames and the Tweed seem like pigmies, and mountains loftier than the Alps. Here was a new country, practically as large as the whole of Europe and rivaling Europe in its natural wonders and in its variety of climate and topography. To the imagination of Romantic poets, America was almost Utopia come true; it was Nature (with a capital) comparatively uncorrupted by the defiling hand of man.

The American scene, too, was filled with new and striking character types. There was that romantic and mysterious child of Nature, the Indian, who enjoyed a vogue in the literatures of Europe before America had a literature. There was a whole tribe of frontier and semifrontier types: the half-breed, the trader, the hunter, the trapper, the bush-ranger (*coureur de bois*), the scout, the missionary, the frontier soldier, the cowboy, the sheepherder, the miner, the ranger, the gambler, the Pike, the "bad man," the "greaser," the squatter, the Mormon, the circuit rider, the lumberjack, the Hoosier, the poor white, the Southern mountaineer, who lives in a curiously retarded frontier region; and we may perhaps include the varied types found in the Western oil fields of today. To these we must add the frontier women, less numerous but not less interesting than the men. All these frontier types were racy, individual, and quite distinct from European types. And their variety was greatly increased by the presence on the border of contrasting racial strains: Indian, English, Scotch-Irish, German, Scandinavian, French, and Spanish.

It was in many respects a sordid and futile life which the pioneers led, but it abounded in adventure, change, and freedom; and it was close to nature. On the border, truth was often stranger than the wildest of fiction. It is no wonder that our novelists have found in frontier life a wealth of incidents or that a few writers like Frank Norris have seen in the westward movement the last great epic event in our history.

One must not forget that the conquest of a great continent has not found expression adequate to its magnitude or importance. Cooper's Leather-Stocking Tales have a certain epic quality, but for too many of our writers the frontier has been a legend rather than a reality. Most of the novels that deal with the frontier were written by men who had no first-hand experience of pioneer life. Consequently our frontier fiction is, as a rule, no "document" for the social historian; it represents a literary convention. Most of our major writers, living in metropolitan centers, had little opportunity to know frontier life; and the pioneers themselves were seldom writers, or even readers, of books. Socially, the frontier represents a primitive stage, an unliterary stage. Many other stages—not necessarily many years—had to follow before the descendants of the pioneers had any vital interest in describing the frontier and before the West had reached the economic and cultural level at which literature begins to be produced. Indeed, some parts of the West cannot be said even yet to have reached that level. It is not surprising, then, that many aspects of frontier life vanished before being accurately described; and now that the frontier is gone never to return, much of that life will probably never be adequately recorded. Few, except an occasional Hamlin Garland, care what the reality was. The popular novel, the cheap magazine, and the motion picture theater have commercialized the legend of the frontier; Zane Grey flourishes and Andy Adams is practically forgotten.

The study of the frontier as literary subject matter is much less difficult than the accurate appraisal of the frontier influence in other directions. For here we deal with an influence which is indirect, protean, incessantly changing, interplaying with other factors almost equally elusive. The frontier influence in *The Last of the Mohicans* and "The Outcasts of Poker Flat" is easy to see, but what of the indirect frontier influence in Emerson's "The American Scholar" and Whitman's "Song of the Open Road"? Here we need to walk warily and to remember that this particular field has not yet been systematically studied. I merely suggest tentatively certain conclusions which I believe further investigation will warrant, and I do this primarily to suggest what lines our study should follow.

The frontier had an influence upon many of our writers who never saw it. The appeal of this vast Western hinterland to the imagination of those who lived upon the Atlantic seaboard is difficult to estimate, but it undoubtedly existed. If Henry James could explain the difference between Turgenev and the typical French novelist by saying that the back door of the Russian's imagination was always open upon the endless Russian steppes, surely the existence of the American frontier helps to explain some of the differences between Emerson and Whitman and their British contemporaries, Carlyle and Tennyson. Hawthorne told Howells that he "would like to see some part of the country on which the . . . shadow of Europe had not fallen"; and even the domestic Longfellow longed to share Frémont's exhilarating experiences in the Far West, although he sighed, "Ah, the discomforts!"

If our literature is a reflection of the national character, it should be strongly colored by our experience with the frontier. For it was chiefly the frontier influence which, as Norman Foerster has said, "transformed the European type into such men as Jefferson, Jackson, Lincoln, and Theodore Roosevelt, or, among the writers, Emerson, Whitman, and Mark Twain." [Frederick J.] Turner believed that the frontier supplied the key to the American character. "To the frontier," said he, "the American intellect owes its striking characteristics. That coarseness and strength combined with acuteness and inquisitiveness; that practical, inventive turn of mind, quick to find expedients; that masterful grasp of material things, lacking in the artistic but powerful to effect great ends; that restless, nervous energy; that dominant individualism, working for good and for evil, and withal that buoyancy and exuberance which comes with freedom—these are traits of the frontier, or traits called out elsewhere because of the existence of the frontier."

To what extent are these frontier traits to be seen in our literature? Mr. Turner himself, in a letter to the writer, said, "I thoroughly agree that what is distinctive in American, in contrast to general English literature, comes out of our experience with the frontier, broadly considered." It is natural, I think, to conclude that there is, in the writings of such men as Whitman, Mark Twain, and William James, something distinctively American which comes indirectly from the frontier; but it is no easy matter to put one's finger upon it and say, here it is. A good case can be made out for much of our political writing, which is closer to our life than most of what is known as belles-lettres. Indeed, Bliss Perry finds that the dominant note in American literature is the civic note, which surely owes much to frontier democracy. Henry Seidel Canby has argued, too, that the "nature book," perhaps the only new literary type which America has given the world, grew out of our fathers' experience with the frontier and our own longing for the vanished frontier environment.

Much of what we are accustomed to call American literature, however, has no discernible connection with the frontier; the work of Edgar Allan Poe is a conspicuous example. Much of our literature is un-American, imitative of Europe. Too often, as John Macy has pointed out, it is distinguished by just those qualities which the American intellect is supposed to lack: it is dainty, polished, fanciful, sentimental, feminine, and "literary." The contemporary revolt against our cis-Atlantic Victorians, however, would indicate that many of our older writers were out of harmony with what now seems to be the genuine American tradition.

American literature has become a national literature—if we may now call it national—largely through what Van Wyck Brooks, in a letter to the writer, called "the sublimation of the frontier spirit." American literature has become increasingly American. It may be well here to try to indicate the part which the frontier has played in the nationalization of our literature.

The American Revolution, the historians tell us, was in large measure due to the political and economic influence of the frontier. In the new environment had grown up a people to whom the English were comparative strangers. Under the stress of the common struggle, first against France and later against England, a new national consciousness had developed in the thirteen colonies, which finally declared themselves a new nation. The frontier conception of democracy, modified of course by European political theory and experience, was written into the Declaration of Independence. Eventually it brought about something akin to a social and economic revolution in American life.

With the achievement of political independence and with the natural reaction against all things English, it was inevitable that there should arise a demand for a national literature which would express the new national culture. It was felt that a nation whose political and social life was based on democratic principles should have a literature quite unlike that of undemocratic Britain. A good deal of ignorance of literary history and a certain lack of logic are seen in the reasoning of the advocates of a national literature; and the literature which they prophesied was not born full-grown like Minerva from the brain of Jove. Nevertheless from the early nineteenth century down to the present there has been a succession of declarations of cultural and intellectual independence from England. These include Emerson's "The American Scholar," Whitman's Preface to *Leaves of Grass,* Mark Twain's *Innocents Abroad,* and Van Wyck Brooks's *America's Coming of Age.* The new national literature, however, did not come in response to the immediate demand. It was the Romantic movement, and not the outmoded neoclassical literary tradition, which gave American writers the technical methods of putting the national life into literature. Ultimately, however, as Carl Van Doren has pointed out, the Revolution became one of the "three matters of American romance," the other two being the settlement and the frontier.

Perhaps the influence of Jacksonian democracy had something to do with Whitman's attempt to create a native American literature. Whitman of course was not a frontiersman, but there is a certain analogy between what he and the Jacksonian democrats tried to accomplish. Emerson was too much the scholar and the gentleman to attempt all that Whitman tried to do, but he saw hope even in the Jacksonians for the future of American literature. Lamenting the cultural dependence of America upon England, he wrote in his *Journals*

in 1834: "I suppose the evil may be cured by this rank rabble party, the Jacksonism of the country, heedless of English and all literature—a stone cut out of the ground without hands;—they may root out the hollow dilettantism of our cultivation in the coarsest way, and the newborn may begin again to frame their own world with greater advantage."

The Civil War gave a great impetus to national tendencies in all fields and did much to complete the work left incomplete by the Revolution. It brought about "the birth of a nation," and in literature it led to what Fred Lewis Pattee has called "the second discovery of America." By abolishing slavery and settling the question of secession, the war made the nation a political unit that it had never been before. Americans gradually ceased to say, "The United States *are,*" and began to say, "The United States *is.*" Political and military leadership passed from New England and the South to the more thoroughly American Middle West, which, in Lowell's phrase, gave us "the first American," Abraham Lincoln. The Civil War stimulated the progress of the economic or industrial revolution, which, more than any other influence besides the frontier, has made the whole country an economic and cultural unit. In ante-bellum days American literature was little more than an aggregation of sectional literatures; after the war it became national in a sense of the word not applicable before that time.

In the Americanization of our literature the West, especially the Middle West, played a leading part. The writings of New Englanders and New Yorkers did not satisfy the West. Edward Eggleston, jealous of the literary domination of New England, wrote *The Hoosier Schoolmaster* to show that Indiana furnished as rich materials for the novelist as Massachusetts. Bret Harte and other young men, so he tells us, were trying to create a California literature. A more important spokesman for the West was Mark Twain. What Ibsen and Tolstoy were to nineteenth-century Europe, that or something like it Mark Twain was to the United States: a new region had found a spokesman, and what he had to say did not resemble the work of Hawthorne and Longfellow. A new spirit also began to move the reconstructed and reviving South; and the more cosmopolitan spirit of the Middle Atlantic states blended with the influence of the South and the West to create something approximating a national point of view in our literature.

Meanwhile the best work of nearly all the great New Englanders had been done. The Romantic impulse had become conventional, and the influence of European realism was becoming apparent. Upon Howells, a Westerner by birth, had descended the editorial mantle of the *Atlantic Monthly.* But Howells was thoroughly de-Westernized, and New England assimilated him without great difficulty. It was to his friend Mark Twain that New England objected as representing the Western barbarians of literature. At the Whittier birthday dinner of the *Atlantic* in 1877, the custodians of the Brahmin tradition condemned in no uncertain manner the vulgarity of the literary West. Howells tells us that of the Boston-Cambridge group only Francis James Child and Charles Eliot Norton made anything of the man whom Howells regarded as "the Lincoln of our literature"; even Lowell did not warm to him. The current of events, however, was too strong for the Brahmins. Howells himself went to New York, thereby admitting that the literary scepter had passed from Boston. New York is now our publishing center, our literary capital, if we have one; but the productive center of American literature is perhaps nearer Chicago. Certainly the Middle West aspires to cultural as well as industrial leadership, and it is significant that the favorite background of contemporary fiction is the Middle West.

One must not, as I have said, push the frontier influence too far. Our literary history is the result of the interplay of complex and changing influences, political, economic, social, cultural, educational—sectional, national, foreign. Properly to understand and appraise the influence of the frontier, one must thoroughly understand other influences and their interrelations.

The frontier influence is not the only influence making for nationalism in American literature. At least two other historical factors have had a part in it. In the first place, many of the immigrants who came to this country from the very beginning did not represent the English type in race, in religious beliefs, or in social status. They were, to a large extent, nonconformists; nor were these by any means confined to New England, as we too often suppose. The nonconformists played a large part in the development of the American bourgeoisie, with its well-known attitude toward art and literature. Immigration, moreover, was itself a selective process. The more restless and the more aggressive came, whereas the conservative, as a rule, remained in Europe. The character of our immigrants accounts in part for the peculiar American blend of radicalism and conservatism which strikes our foreign critics as odd. Many of the immigrants, however, even in Colonial times, were not English or even British. Mr. Mencken and Professor Schlesinger has argued that the fine arts in America have been developed largely by men of mixed blood. At any rate, the typical American would not be a typical Englishman even had there been no influence from the frontier.

Another influence making for nationalism is the economic or industrial revolution. In the course of a century American life has become predominantly urban; and it is based very largely upon machinery. As a result, American life is to a great degree uniform throughout the country. The same tendency toward standardization is found in our books, our magazines, and our schools. Even those who rebel against the tyrannous uniformity of American life and thought seem to rebel *en masse,* as it were, and merely substitute the conventions of the *American Mercury* for those of the *Saturday Evening Post*— as if one could by any such change of front become individual and original.

In our eagerness to point out the national tendencies in our literature, one should not overlook the sectional. Most of those engaged in research in American literature have been prejudiced against the sectional approach by the poor quality of existing sectional studies. Even the political historians have neglected sectional tendencies, except as they concern the slavery issue, so much that Turner has felt it necessary in a recent article to urge a new study of sectionalism in American history. The frontier influence, in the main a national one, has at times made for sectionalism. In Colonial times it was the frontier which created the first sectionalism of West against East. In recent years we have seen the semifrontier West, sometimes allied with the South, arrayed against the industrial belt of North and East.

To understand the literary influence of the frontier, one must study it in connection with the influences which came from Europe. Influences from abroad have increased rather than diminished, for the revolution in methods of transportation and communication has brought Europe closer to New York than Boston and Philadelphia were a century ago. European literary fashions have to a large extent determined the manner in which our writers have portrayed the pioneers.

Before bringing this essay to a conclusion, it seems necessary to insist that, if our literary historians are to continue to use the term *frontier,* it must be carefully defined. To a layman, it would seem that even the historians sometimes use the term loosely. "In the census reports," says Turner, "it is treated as the margin of that settlement which has a density of two or more to the square mile. The term is an elastic one, and for our purposes does not need sharp definition. We shall consider the whole frontier belt, including the Indian country and the outer margin of the 'settled area' of the census reports." In justice to Turner, it should be stated that he was, in his own words, attempting only "to call attention to the frontier as a fertile field for investigation, and to suggest some of the problems which arise in connection with it." Professor Paxson notes that "The American frontier was a line, a region, or a process, according to the context in which the word is used," but even he attempts no exact definition of the term.

Careful historians like Paxson and Turner doubtless have a fairly definite meaning in mind even though they do not take the trouble of defining the word. Many persons without the scholar's feeling for accuracy use the term very loosely. The word has acquired certain connotations which do not properly belong to it. It has a poetic flavor; it suggests something native, something fine and romantic which other countries conspicuously lack. But to one who has read Hamsun's *Growth of the Soil,* the opening pages of Butler's *Erewhon,* or the *Oxford Book of Australasian Verse,* it is permissible to doubt whether the American frontier is quite unique. We are in danger of forgetting the sordid side of the American frontier. Among Westerners in particular the term has much the same glamour that the *Old South* has in Virginia or the *Pilgrim Fathers* in New England. There is a halo about the forehead of the pioneer. Such provincial pride, amounting sometimes to ancestor worship, inevitably interferes with the historian's seeing things as they are. After all, are the economic and geographic influences implied in the term *frontier* essentially different from those to be found in sparsely settled regions the world over?

Our literary historians have used the word *frontier* more loosely than the historians; the term has become increasingly vague and ambiguous. Like the *Celtic spirit,* the *Greek influence, Romanticism, Classicism,* and *Realism,* the term *frontier* may be made to mean whatever the user wishes it to mean. The frontier should not be identified with all the national influences in our literature; it should not be identified with the geographic environment. The frontier passes; the natural background remains, often unchanged. The Adirondacks and the Marshes of Glynn once belonged to the frontier, but not today.

In literature there are two fairly definite uses of the word which seem legitimate. We may properly refer to the frontier as a literary background. There is no ambiguity here except when we include semifrontier regions, as we often do. We may also use the word when we refer to the beginnings of literary activity on the frontier, as in Professor Rusk's *The Literature of the Middle Western Frontier.*

A third common use of the term, however, calls for closer

definition. We have too often identified the frontier with *all* the national influences in our literary history. The sources of the national spirit are, as I have tried to indicate, more numerous; and the whole problem is quite complex. If we do not use the term more carefully, we shall soon find it as thoroughly discredited as Taine's famous formula: race, environment, and epoch. I do not think we can dispense with the term, but I do expect that we shall use it more accurately. If we do not, the results of our investigation may be no more creditable to American scholarship than are the works of certain of our predecessors whom we need not name here. (pp. 274-84)

> *Jay B. Hubbell, "The Frontier in American Literature," in his* South and Southwest: Literary Essays and Reminiscences, *Duke University Press, 1965, pp. 269-84.*

DEVELOPMENT OF FRONTIER LITERATURE

VERNON CARSTENSEN

[Carstensen is an American educator who has served as president of the Western Historical Society. In the following excerpt, he comments on the development of American frontier literature to the end of the nineteenth century.]

For two centuries or longer the immense and varied experience of occupying this continent, all embraced within the terms frontier and American West, has served the different purposes of American writers, scholars, artists, entertainers, politicians, and business men. Ray Billington's delightful book, *Land of Savagery, Land of Promise,* tells us of the many uses Europeans have made of the American westering experience.

The terms *frontier* and *American West* are, of course, pleasantly imprecise. They are sometimes interchangeable, sometimes they only overlap, and sometimes they strike out on their own, depending on who uses them, for what purpose, and when. The frontier as an area of new land settlement moved from Jamestown and Plymouth to the Pacific, but the *West,* as a term applied to areas of new settlement, came into use to describe the region beyond the Appalachians. Thereafter, as one dictionary maker has it, the American West, "at any particular time," embraced "that part of the United States west of the earlier settled region." In some minds, particularly those nurtured in the eastern part of the country, the region of the Great Plains and beyond seems to be permanent frontier country. (p. 5)

The business of occupying this continent was one of the great adventures of modern times, but it was over much sooner than many expected. When Thomas Jefferson took the oath as president in 1801, he congratulated his countrymen on their good fortune. They were shielded from the turmoil of Europe and they possessed "a chosen country, with room enough for our descendants to the thousandth and thousandth generation." When he spoke, the boundaries of the Republic extended only to the Mississippi. He underestimated the pull of the new lands, a pull no doubt enormously strengthened by the new secular religion he had helped to shape—a religion that included notions of liberty and equality, representative government, and belief in progress. He may also have overestimated the chilling effect on immigrants that might have been expected from the warning of learned men of France that the New World was a land where plants, animals, and men degenerated. Immigrants apparently did not believe the warnings if they read them. By mid-century the Republic had expanded to the Pacific, and before the end of the century the frontier had all but disappeared.

The world had never seen anything like the hasty, tumultuous, often chaotic conquest of this vast, incredibly rich continent. Settlers came in constantly increasing numbers. They came singly, they came in families, sometimes as members of communities to claim and use the farmlands, the forests, the grasslands, the mineral lands, the water power sites, the townsites or anything else of real or imagined value. By the early 1840s the first caravans of land seekers were crossing the plains and mountains to make farms in the Willamette Valley in Oregon, and by the end of that decade gold drew multitudes to California. The Indians could delay encroachment, but they could not stop the march. Wherever these settlers entered the wild lands to make their farms and plantations, to build their villages and towns, they faced dangers, hardships, privation, and almost endless manual labor. They were mostly strangers to each other, but they were reasonably quick to establish and maintain order, aided lightly by the federal government. Their politicians, preachers, and editors never tired of reminding them that they were laying the foundations for a new civilization.

English and European appetite for information about the New World was insatiable, as the makers of books quickly discovered. The famous and the unknown came to look and to write about what they saw on the eastern seaboard and in regions of new settlement. Fredericka Bremer from Sweden invited her countrymen to colonize Wisconsin and Minnesota and turn that region into a new Scandinavia, and they tried. George Ruxton discovered the mountain men for the grateful and enthusiastic readers of *Blackwood's Magazine.* There were scores and scores of others who came and who wrote.

Americans, too, made books about what was going on. Timothy Dwight, once president of Yale, visited the frontier of New York and New England in the 1790s and characterized the pioneers he saw as men who could not live in a regular society. "They are too idle, too talkative, too passionate, too prodigal and too shiftless to acquire either property or character." He rejoiced that the vast western wilderness was sufficiently alluring to "draw them away from the land of their nativity," where they would only cause trouble if they had stayed. In striking contrast, those who wrote the numerous settlers' guidebooks and the gazetteers viewed the pioneers as a stalwart, self-reliant people, carriers of civilization, worthy of the great opportunities the new lands offered.

James Fenimore Cooper was the first American novelist to exploit the frontier with dramatic success. In 1823 he published *The Pioneers,* the first of the Leatherstocking Tales. English publishers promptly pirated the work, and it was also translated into the major European languages. In Russia there were thirty-two editions by 1927. Cooper's success encouraged other writers to make use of the frontier. Washington Irving toured the prairies in the 1830s and published an account of his experiences. He later wrote about Astoria and Captain Bonneville. A decade later Francis Parkman spent a summer on the Oregon Trail. His account of his adventures,

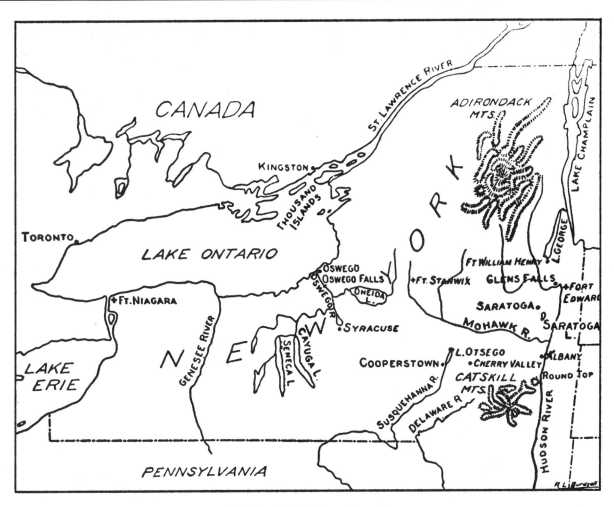

The sites of the Leatherstocking tales.

published in 1849, enjoyed enduring popularity. The mining camps of California became a source of delight in literary circles in Boston and London when Bret Harte published *The Luck of Roaring Camp and Other Sketches.* Thereafter, there came a flood of good books, both fiction and nonfiction, that used frontier material. Some writers wrote about what they had seen; others based their work on careful research.

In the last half of the nineteenth century Erastus Beadle, printer and publisher, and his various associates found a new market to be served by the dime novel. In 1860 Beadle published *Malaeska: The Indian Wife of a White Hunter,* and it sold briskly, even though it was a reprint of a book first published twenty years before. This was followed by *Seth Jones, or the Captive of the Frontier.* Success led him to hire a number of writers to produce western thrillers that dealt with almost all aspects of the real or imagined excitement and dangers of life on the frontier. There were wild tales about Indians, trappers, traders, mountain men, explorers, backwoodsmen, rafters, gold hunters, and soldiers. By the 1880s cowboys and cattle thieves began to take their place among other frontier types in the popular novels and the pulp magazines of the early twentieth century.

Meanwhile, as Billington has told us in rich detail, scores of European writers turned out an endless stream of frontier

thrillers. Karl May became, and still remains, a household name in Germany, and Mayne Reid in England saw his books appear as dime novels in America, while at the same time they found a vast and enduring following in Russia. Indeed, Anton Chekhov has a short story about two Russian schoolboys who, under the spell of Mayne Reid, plan to walk across Siberia on their way to the California frontier where they will fight tigers and savages, find gold and ivory, and drink gin.

There were many others during the nineteenth century who sought and found ways of making use of the frontier. There were artists and photographers whose pictures found a ready sale, exhibitors who collected artifacts and animals for show in the East and in Europe, and entertainers, like Buffalo Bill Cody, who appeared in "The Scouts of the Prairie" in 1872. The show, written by Ned Buntline, drew large audiences in Chicago, New York, and Boston.

There were also collectors of records of the westering experience. For example, Lyman C. Draper, while still in his twenties and with no sure means of support, committed himself to gathering records and recollections of pioneer life in the border settlements after the Revolution. In 1854 he became secretary of the Wisconsin State Historical Society. His extensive collections laid the foundation for the great historical library of the society. Hubert H. Bancroft was a somewhat different user of the frontier. A San Francisco printer and bookseller, Bancroft began collecting California records and books in the late 1850s and then undertook to assemble the documents and other records needed to produce his history of the Pacific Coast states—which, you may recall, includes Texas. He organized a staff to write the accounts he published under his own name. By the end of the 1880s he had published a thirty-nine volume set, and according to John W. Caughey, he had made a profit of nearly a half-million dollars. Ultimately, he sold his great collection to the University of California in Berkeley.

Professional, that is to say, academic, historians were reasonably quick to make use of the frontier as a subject for instruction and investigation. History in general found little room in the American college curriculum until the late nineteenth century. When the [American Historical Association] was formed in 1884, only nine of the forty-one persons who attended the first meeting were professors of history. But a brighter day was coming, as colleges and universities multiplied, enrollments increased and the professional training of historians took shape.

In 1888 James Bryce published his great book, *The American Commonwealth.* "Western America," he wrote, "is one of the most interesting subjects the modern world has seen. There has been nothing in the past resembling its growth, and probably there will be nothing in the future. . . . The West is the most American part of America; that is to say, the part where those features which most distinguish America come out in the strongest relief." Five years later Frederick Jackson Turner read his famous paper ["The Significance of the Frontier in American History"]. All of us recognize these words. "Up to our own day American history has been in a large degree the history of the colonization of the Great West." Turner offered a hypothesis more attractive than anything then available. The place of the frontier experience in the growth of the nation provided one of the dominating themes of American historical studies for the next half century.

The nineteenth century produced many frontier types that promised to assume a permanent heroic character to serve literary and other purposes. Daniel Boone and Davy Crockett led a parade that included warriors, both Indian and white, pathfinders, mountain men, missionaries, prospectors, and even a few outlaws and politicians. During the last decades of the century the cowboy emerged in the dime novels, but initially he was something of a roughneck. A few articles on cowboys appeared in literary journals such as *Harper's Magazine* and *Century.* And then, in 1902, the cowboy finally won full literary respectability in [Owen Wister's] *The Virginian.* . . . (pp. 6-9)

Wister's view of the cowboy and the West would have startled Timothy Dwight. Listen to his description of cowboys in a Medicine Bow saloon.

> City saloons rose into my vision and I instantly preferred this Rocky Mountain place. More death it undoubtedly saw, but less of vice, than did its New York equivalents. And death is a thing much cleaner than vice. Moreover, it was by no means vice that was written upon these wild manly faces. . . . Daring, laughter, endurance—these were what I saw on the countenances of the cowboys. And this very first day of my knowledge of them marks a date with me. For something about them, and the idea of them, smote my heart, and I have never for-

gotten it, nor ever shall, as long as I live. In their flesh our natural passions ran tumultuous; but often in their spirit sat hidden a true nobility, and often beneath its unexpected shining their figures took a heroic stature.

Wister brought together the vital and durable ingredients of the American morality play: a western landscape, the cowboy hero, wrong-doers who would have to be destroyed violently to assure the establishment of law and order in the new land.

[Theodore] Roosevelt wrote Wister that he was delighted with the book. Henry James approved, with some reservations. The book was enthusiastically received. The reviewer in the *Atlantic Monthly* came very close to saying that this was a thinking man's western. The book went through fifteen reprints during the first year, and it would retain its popularity over the years as a book, a play, a number of movies, and serials on radio and TV.

Wister's success called forth a mighty flood of western, mostly cowboy books that found an apparently insatiable market while carrying readers farther and farther away from the West that really was. (pp. 10-11)

> *Vernon Carstensen, "Making Use of the Frontier and the American West," in* The Western Historical Quarterly, *Vol. XIII, No. 1, January, 1982, pp. 5-16.*

JAMES K. FOLSOM

[*Folsom is an American educator who has written extensively on western American literature. In the following excerpt, he examines aspects of American culture that helped shape the development of the Western novel.*]

The semi-arid regions of the North American continent which lie within the boundaries of the United States and are conventionally referred to as the American West posed a cultural challenge to the westering Anglo-European settlers of which the magnitude has only fairly recently been realized. Only since Walter Prescott Webb's epoch-making study *The Great Plains* (1931) have systematic attempts been made to understand the enormous cultural adaptations made inevitable by the staggering environmental differences between the trans-Mississippi West and the well-watered area east of the Father of Waters. These differences are most obviously seen in terms of the striking contrasts among the inhabitants of both regions: the Horse Indians, though ethnically related to their eastern cousins, are culturally totally divorced from them; differences between the agricultural Pueblo Indians and their eastern agricultural counterparts are more striking than are similarities; the eastern farmer has been metamorphosed into the western rancher; and his prosaic farmhand into the romantic cowboy, "the hired man on horseback," in Eugene Manlove Rhodes's evocative phrase.

Yet these obvious differences, striking and important as they admittedly are, have caused many observers to rush into the tempting but unsound conclusion that the trans-Mississippi American West—especially in its literary reflections—has absolutely nothing to do with that eastern America which preceded, and in a sense produced it. In fact, many of the same factors which drove Americans across the wide Missouri had brought them across the Big Water some centuries before. Horace Greeley's famous remark "Go West, young man, go West" is, from this perspective, only an echo of Bishop Berkeley's almost equally well-known line, "Westward the course of empire takes its way," of a century earlier: and though present residents of California may unthinkingly assume the line was written with their university in mind, in actuality it was written much earlier, in honor of another infant western college—Yale.

In one sense, of course, fascination with the strange and novel is a perennial human trait. The equally reliable tales of humans abducted by gods and spacemen (in some modern versions the two are equated) have probably fascinated *Homo sapiens* since he first learned that a fire was just as desirable a place to socialize as it was to roast his dinner; but at least in the European imagination these traditional tales had, over the centuries, developed a kind of presumed historicity more or less unique to western society. Prester John had given way to Marco Polo, and the stories "of the cannibals that each other eat, / The Anthropophagi, and men whose heads / Do grow beneath their shoulders," though they may have beguiled Desdemona did not fool Othello for one minute. The reason behind this is not far to seek. One need remember only that that same Renaissance which produced one of the greatest cultural awakenings the West was ever to know produced a scientific revolution as well, of which a disciplined curiosity was its intellectual expression and an age of exploration its technological offshoot. Richard Hakluyt's *Voyages* (1589-1600) had proved so popular that they had been continued by Samuel Purchas (d. 1626) in several further volumes as *Purchas his Pilgrimes* and imitated by a host of others. The prestigious British Royal Society had been founded in 1660 with the encouragement of navigation and discovery as one of its primary aims, and with the New World as one of its primary targets.

Yet the New World explored by the English was substantially different from the other lands discovered by them, if only because it was not the seat of an older and more sophisticated civilization, but quite the reverse: it was, to their eyes at least, a virgin land on which their destiny might be writ afresh without the hindrances of the past. What chronicle to write on this tabula rasa was the problem, then as now, facing the literary recorder.

In this regard it is important to remark that, although the early colonists might well know what they were fleeing from, there was little agreement concerning what in fact they were fleeing toward. The most articulate view, at least at first, stemmed from the notions of eighteenth-century primitivism, for which Jean Jacques Rousseau was the most widely quoted, though by no means unique, spokesman. Rousseau's famous remark that man is born free, and yet is everywhere in chains had an obvious political implication: remove man from his chains and he would again be free. Once free, the nobility of his nature would emerge and then, again to quote Bishop Berkeley, "there shall be sung another golden age."

Perhaps the clearest American spokesman for this view was a transplanted Frenchman, one J. Hector St. John de Crèvecoeur, whose *Letters from an American Farmer* (1782) painted an optimistic picture of what man might make of himself in this New World, freed from the artificial restraints imposed on him by a landed gentry, a whimsical aristocracy, and an established church. Although the *Letters* are not primarily fiction (except perhaps in the sense that Huckleberry Finn uses the term when he claims that Mark Twain told, in *Tom Sawyer,* the truth mostly, except for a few "stretchers"), they do contain fictional elements, most notably in the third

letter, significantly titled "What Is an American?" This letter contains the story of one Andrew the Hebridean, an imaginary immigrant whose person is the archetype of the American colonizer and whose history is the archetype of the American success story. Thus early in American writing the longing for a new start and the rewards it will bring—two themes of primary importance to subsequent western writing—have become inextricably entwined in American myth.

Yet this optimistic view of the flowering of human destiny in the Garden of the Lord, a new Eden untainted by artificially imposed restraints, though persuasive, by no means carried the day. It rang peculiarly hollow in the ears of the American Puritans, many of whom had selected the infant colonies as a desirable position from which to view the Battle of Armageddon which they presumed to be imminent. In 1741, only forty years prior to Crèvecoeur's *Letters,* Jonathan Edwards in his famous sermon "Sinners in the Hands of an Angry God" had darkly warned that "probably the bigger part of adult persons that ever will be saved, will be brought in now in a little time," a clear prophecy that the end was near. Nor did one have to be of Edwards's millennial persuasion to discover the logical flaw in Rousseau's views: for if man was born free, but is everywhere in chains, who made the chains?

The lines of the debate were clearly drawn and passionately argued throughout the eighteenth and nineteenth centuries. The prime metaphor in the controversy was "nature," and the debate, which often discussed external nature, equally often concerned itself with two contrary views of human nature. Was man basically a noble creature whose innate goodness was entrapped within a cage of artificial and whimsical social restraints? Or was he, as William Bradford had warned in *Of Plymouth Plantation* (1630), a being whose nature was hopelessly corrupt, and to whom liberty was merely a euphemism for license?

The obvious focus for this debate was the native inhabitant of the New World, the Indian. Was this classic "man in a state of nature" a "noble savage," as good primitivist theory would have it, or was he, as actual contact in the field suggested, merely a savage whose nobility was presumed rather than demonstrated? Mary Rowlandson's extremely successful *Narrative* (1682) of her earlier captivity among the Indians during King Philip's War (1675-76) had established a durable literary genre still popular today, the so-called "captivity narrative" which details the harrowing experiences of white captives among fiendish Native Americans. Timothy Flint, whose first novel *Francis Berrian, or The Mexican Patriot* (1826) can make a good claim to being the first Western ever written, later penned *The Shoshonee Valley: A Romance* (1830) specifically to refute "the wild and pernicious sophism of Rousseau, that the savage is happier, than the social state," a philosophical position firmly adhered to by the novel's protagonist William Weldon, who discovers the magnitude of his logical error when he and his family are murdered by the supposedly peaceful Shoshoni. By 1830 Flint is working within a well-established tradition, pioneered most successfully by Charles Brockden Brown in *Edgar Huntly; or Memoirs of a Sleep-Walker* (1799), in which the Indians are ruthless and implacable enemies.

Somewhat unfairly, James Fenimore Cooper was viewed by his nineteenth-century compatriots as the primary American literary spokesman for Rousseau's position, and it is not surprising then that many attacks on Rousseau focus on Cooper. Perhaps the best example is Robert Montgomery Bird's excellent novel, now unfortunately generally ignored, *Nick of the Woods or the Jibbenainosay: A Tale of Kentucky* (1837), which is written, he tells us, to set the record straight, for Cooper "had thrown a poetical illusion over the Indian character" by depicting him as "a new style of the beau-ideal." Not so: "in his natural barbaric state" the Indian "is a barbarian," and that's that.

This contrary tradition was from its inception representative of a western rather than an eastern point of view, serving an avowedly political purpose in justifying harsh policies toward the Indian opponents of American westward expansion. The point is interesting in another way as clearly exemplifying a further legacy to modern western American writing—the profound western regional distrust of what Vardis Fisher was much later to call "the Eastern establishment." Even when East and West were both east of the Mississippi, the westerner's sense of himself as markedly different from his eastern compatriots had emerged and was clearly reflected in his writing.

A serious literary argument pitting easterner against westerner erupted very early in American letters. This debate, which is with us yet today, expressed itself primarily in terms of an apparently straightforward question: who, it was asked, was better able to express the facts of western life, the easterner working from book knowledge or the westerner who knew the western experience at first hand? The western position, simplistically stated, was that the eastern writer simply got his facts wrong, and since he knew nothing of the bases of western life could not possibly be expected to say anything sensible about it. As early as 1827, in a review of James Fenimore Cooper's recently published *The Prairie,* Timothy Flint clearly articulates what is to become a perennial western American literary complaint. *The Prairie,* it will be remembered, represents Cooper's one extended literary foray into the Great Plains, an area which Flint knew well, and about which he had written *Francis Berrian* only one year previously. Flint, as an avowed proponent of that progress he feels inevitable when the Great Plains are opened to the benefits of civilization, has little use for the more tragic view of history proposed by Cooper, and the basic thrust of his argument is that Cooper's profound reservations about the course of "progress" are not well taken. Philosophically, the point is certainly arguable, yet Flint's line of attack is curious. Basically, he dismisses Cooper's argument because Cooper has gotten his facts wrong. "Of all natural scenery," Flint sniffs, "one would think, a prairie the most easy to imagine, without having seen it," but apparently even this simple task is beyond Cooper's abilities. "We shall read him with pleasure only," Flint concludes, "when he selects scenery and subjects, with which he is familiarly conversant." The analogical reasoning behind this line of argument is, though tempting, implicitly misleading; for Flint has adduced, as the sole criterion for literary merit, simple and absolute fidelity to literal fact.

Flint's argument is certainly valid to a degree, and Mark Twain, also writing from a western perspective, is later (1895) to expand it in "Fenimore Cooper's Literary Offenses," justifiably one of his most famous essays. Twain mercilessly exposes what Flint had also noted in another place (1828), that in Cooper's writing "probability is violated at every step." Twain's account of how, in *The Deerslayer,* five of six Indians miss an easy jump into a passing boat must strike a sympathetic chord in any readers who have felt their enjoyment of

much western story nullified by the sheer preposterousness of the action. The litany is familiar, and needs no more than brief mention: incredible feats of marksmanship and woodcraft, impossible coincidences, and the like which fill much western fiction can be traced back, in some cases specifically, to eastern misapprehensions about the West in general and to the legacy of Cooper in particular.

At the same time, the case is not so open and shut as Flint and Twain make it appear. The difficulty goes to the heart of the whole concept of western literary "realism," and indeed to a more wide-ranging discussion of the nature of realism in American fiction generally. The question finally comes down to an ambiguity in the American literary experience existing from its origins. Is reality primarily definable in external terms, or is it instead the expression of some kind of internal state? In his 1851 preface to *The House of the Seven Gables,* Nathaniel Hawthorne was to see the dilemma clearly. He, following a nineteenth-century critical commonplace, divided imaginative literature into two types, exemplified by what he called the "Novel" and the "Romance." The novel, he said, aims at "a very minute fidelity . . . to the probable and ordinary course of man's experience." The romance, contrariwise, although it too must present "the truth of the human heart," may "present that truth under circumstances . . . of the writer's own choosing or creation." To the nineteenth-century novelist, one great literary problem becomes that of how to present these two contrary aspects of "the truth of the human heart" within one story, to find a vehicle which combines the reality of factual detail with that other reality represented by the romance. The magnitude of the problem may be seen in Hawthorne's handling of *The Scarlet Letter* (1850), which he prefaces with a long essay, "The Custom House," ostensibly explaining how the manuscript of the romance came into his possession, but actually an attempt to provide a novelistic balance to his romantic story, thus arriving at a fictional truth combining both novelistic and romantic aspects of fiction. Whatever his actual beliefs, Hawthorne liked to adopt the literary stance that the separation of novelistic and romantic elements in his own fiction was not completely fortunate. Each perspective was valid, he would argue, but each by itself incomplete.

To the student of western literature, Melville's *Moby-Dick* (1851), often mentioned as a kind of frontier novel of the sea, is perhaps more interesting. Melville attempts the same union of these two different aspects of the "truth of the human heart" by combining the romantic story of the monomaniac Captain Ahab's pursuit of the Great White Whale with the novelistic cetology chapters which fill much of the novel. Of particular significance for western story is the fact that in *Moby-Dick* the cetological (novelistic) chapters become less evident as the story progresses, while the (romantic) story of the hunt becomes more important. In one sense, then, *Moby-Dick* represents a penetration through the external world of everyday reality into a realm equally real in another, mythical sense, yet not primarily factual. The Great White Whale may finally be understood only in terms of the contradictory meanings we project upon him.

Something of this penetration through the comfortable surface world we know into a more sinister internal world we only sense is at the "heart of darkness" in many western novels which can superficially be dismissed as blood-and-thunder or pure escape. Mary Rowlandson's *Narrative* of her Indian captivity, mentioned earlier, depends upon precisely this effect of penetration through the comfortable surface to an understanding of that malevolence which lies concealed beneath it. She has, literally and metaphorically, gone West to grow up with the country, and her newly won maturity is achieved only at the price of her loss of innocence. The reality she has discovered in the West is a reality of terror, one which she would just as soon forget. Offhandedly she tells us, after her safe return to her family, "I can remember the time, when I used to sleep quietly without workings in my thoughts, whole nights together, but now it is other ways with me." Her dream of westering has turned into a nightmare.

Penetration through experience, then, rather than travel over it is the perspective romantic western fiction offers which novelistic fiction cannot. It is useless to condemn Cooper's *The Last of the Mohicans* on the grounds that it is unrealistic, in the sense of being shaky in its factual bases. The point can readily be conceded without denigrating Cooper's genius, for his purpose in that novel is not primarily to take us on a journey across country; rather the journey takes us finally to an apocalyptic vision of inner space, a vision true to our internal perceptions of reality in which identities merge and things become their opposites rather than to the external world where Mingoes, Delawares, French, and English are easily labeled.

In the last analysis, the most important legacy of earlier American writing to western fiction is one of ambiguity. The great debate which had gone on ever since the first English explorers penetrated into the Great Plains—the debate over whether this new land was the Garden of the Lord or, contrariwise, the Great American Desert—is one to which presumably there is a factual answer. In fact, as Henry Nash Smith pointed out in *Virgin Land* (1950), the answer depends as much on the predispositions one brings to the problem as it does on the alleged facts. Whether what we see is a reflection of the world outside or a projection instead of our inner wishes and, on occasion, hidden fears is a philosophical problem at least as old as the Republic. From its forebears western writing inherits a method of exploring this problem in terms of discussion of a series of profound and unsettling paradoxes. What is the West itself—the Garden of the Lord or the Great American Desert? Who inhabits the West—noble savages or merely savages? Most important of all, what—realistically considered—are the chances for a new start when you bring your old self with you? (pp. 141-47)

James K. Folsom, "Precursors of the Western Novel," in A Literary History of the American West, *sponsored by The Western Literature Association, Texas Christian University Press, 1987, pp. 141-51.*

NONFICTION WRITING ABOUT THE FRONTIER

THOMAS J. LYON

[*Lyon is an American educator who has served as the editor of* Western American Literature. *In the following excerpt, he surveys descriptions of the American West written in the nineteenth and early twentieth centuries by explorers, government surveyors, and naturalists.*]

The Function of the nature essayist, as Henry Beston pointed out [in his "Foreword" to Herbert Faulkner West's *The Nature Writers*], is like that of the poet. Both attempt to reforge a fundamental continuity between inner and outer, so that for the reader the world is alive again, seen precisely for what it is, and the mind is alive to it. To have known the beauty of the world, seen with unclouded eyes the sheer wonder of a clear river or a mesa or a cottonwood tree, is to be in some sense and for that time, psychologically whole. The deepest attraction of the nature essay, probably, is this basic rightness of gestalt. Good nature writing is a recapturing of the child's world, the world before fragmentation, the world as poets and artists can see it. The best nature writing has this, and has also the reliability of science, for a true completeness must, logically, include the objective aspect of mind as well.

In the West, the nature essay also reflects the European and eastern newcomers' drive to be at home in a new land: first to explore it, to list its ingredients and learn its history, then to settle in it, finally to cherish and defend it. For several decades beginning with Lewis and Clark, western nature writing was done by travelers, and by necessity took the form of brief sketches within journal-like narratives. Perhaps its chief quality or charm, at this stage, is the wonder of newness as the writer, far from what he regarded as civilization, burst upon the vast freedom of the prairies or was awed by the abundance of animal life or the wild strangeness of distant, snow-draped mountains floating above the heat waves of summer. By definition, an explorer is not at home, and it is not surprising that the writing of most early observers lacks some of the closeness and thoroughness which distinguishes the best of the genre, and which seems to come from a true immersion in an environment. Nevertheless, even in the early years, there are occasional passages which show that the writer was deeply moved by the wilderness—Meriwether Lewis looking down from a hilltop on the confluence of the Yellowstone and the Missouri, or Prince Maximilian silently descending the Missouri at night, almost thirty years later, listening to the elk and the wolves on shore, and the buffalo thrashing their way across the river. These are some of the great moments of newness.

By the latter decades of the nineteenth century, the first freshness was gone. At this point, with the work of a few important writers, chief among them John Muir and Mary Austin, the western nature essay took a turn onto a more profound level. Muir and Austin, and others, spent the requisite time to become dwellers, as opposed to travelers, and the deep perception of place they developed was significant not only for the nature essay, but perhaps also for the general maturation of western regional literature. With them, the post-frontier era begins. They came to believe that the frontier challenge was not of physical movement to a new place, but of the enlargement of understanding. "The secret of learning the mesa life," Austin wrote, "is to sit still, and to sit still, and to keep on sitting still." (pp. 221-22)

The classics of nature writing, beginning with the first great work of the modern era, Gilbert White's *The Natural History of Selborne* (1789), and including such later books as Henry David Thoreau's *Walden* (1854), John Muir's *The Mountains of California* (1894), Mary Austin's *The Land of Little Rain* (1903), Henry Beston's *The Outermost House* (1928), Joseph Wood Krutch's *The Voice of the Desert* (1954), and Edward Abbey's *Desert Solitaire* (1968), are works of a settled, home-knowing and home-loving consciousness. Place, after all, is a logical center and starting point: from a home ground one may venture thoughts on the human condition—as all of the major nature writers do—in terms of a solidly naturalistic perspective (the cycle of the four seasons being the most common reference and pattern for the writing), and from a practical involvement with the earth. The best nature writers are connected in this way; they have, as it were, a bit of the home place under their fingernails.

In the early decades of nature writing about the West, we do not often find the familiarized expression of the placed. On the other hand, we would be remiss to ignore the genuine excitement of space and wildness the West offered, "once upon a time." Among the details of travel and food-getting leaps up the occasional great moment:

> [Lewis]   Thursday April 25th, 1805
> . . . our rout lay along the foot of the river hills. when we had proceeded about four miles, I ascended the hills from whence I had a most pleasing view of the country, particularly of the wide and fertile vallies formed by the missouri and the yellowstone rivers, which occasionally unmasked by the wood on their borders disclose their meanderings for many miles in their passage through these delightfull tracts of country. I could not discover the junction of the rivers immediately, they being concealed by the wood; however, sensible that it could not be distant I determined to encamp on the bank of the Yellow stone river which made it's appearance about 2 miles South of me. the whol face of the country was covered with herds of Buffaloe, Elk & Antelopes; deer are also abundant, but keep themselves more concealed in the woodland. the buffaloe Elk and Antelope are so gentle that we pass near them while feeding, without appearing to excite any alarm among them; and when we attract their attention, they frequently approach us more nearly to discover what we are. . . .

This is a journal entry by a man traveling with a purpose, with several purposes in fact, and it was not meant as literature; but there is no mistaking the Adamic undercurrent, the consciousness of Meriwether Lewis that he was indeed in a singular, privileged vanguard.

The records of the travels of Thomas Nuttall, who made three explorations into the West in 1811, 1819, and 1834, suggest a more deliberate approach to the essay form and to literature. In Nuttall's writings about the West, which appear in scattered paragraphs in his later ornithological and botanical works and most conspicuously in *A Journal of Travels into the Arkansa Territory, During the Year 1819,* there is a more informed documentation of natural history than was possible for Lewis, and in addition more reflection in the classic manner of the personal essay. Nuttall reveals his love of nature, and a scheme of values in which geology and wild flora and fauna seem of considerably greater interest than detail of travel and camp, and he also essays general comments on the relationship of civilization and wilderness, somewhat after the manner of Crèvecoeur, so that what emerges from his journals and his more formal writings is something close to a literary persona.

Nuttall, who was born in England in 1786 and died there in 1859, was one of the most thorough of the early generalists in American natural history. His *Genera of North American Plants* (1818) and *A Manual of the Ornithology of the United States and Canada* (1832) were authoritative for their time, and were in heavy use throughout the nineteenth century—

the birdbook ("Nuttall," as it was familiarly known) into the twentieth. Despite Washington Irving's characterization of him as absent-minded ("he went groping and stumbling along among the wilderness of sweets, forgetful of everything but his immediate pursuit," Irving said of Nuttall's accompaniment of the Astorians in 1811), it is clear that Nuttall was, in another sense, absolutely present. His success as a collector and taxonomist suggests the point, and his writings go far to prove it. Unfortunately, we have no record of his trip partway with the Astorians, and his 1834 journal has also been lost, but we do have an account of his middle, southwestern excursion. In 1819, Nuttall traveled up the Arkansas River into what is now Oklahoma, and after passing through seemingly endless climax forest along the lower portions of the river, came finally into higher and more open country. We see him here at the prime moment for the eastern traveler. He immediately fell to studying the prairie vegetation, in which he delighted wholeheartedly.

> The surface of these woodless expanses was gently undulated, and thickly covered with grass knee high, even to the summits of the hills. . . . The flowers, which beautify them at this season of nature's vigour, communicated all the appearance of a magnificent garden, fantastically decked with innumerable flowers of the most splendid hues.

In common with nearly all travelers to the frontier, up to the present, the naturalist commented on the state of civilization of the few settlers in the area, as if the very dominance and beauty of the wild called forth cultural generalizations. It was a new world, fresh, and human activity stood freshly revealed. The settlers did not impress Nuttall favorably.

> It is to be regretted that the widely scattered state of the population in this territory, is but too favorable to the spread of ignorance and barbarism. . . . the rising generation are growing up in mental darkness, like the French hunters who have preceded them, and who have almost forgot that they appertain to the civilized world.

The European model was Nuttall's apparent standard, for he referred to wilderness as "a dead solemnity, where the human voice is never heard to echo, where not even ruins of the humblest kind recall [sic] its history to mind, or prove the past dominion of man."

But the wilderness was where the new plants and birds were, and it was to wilderness that Nuttall returned again and again. In 1834 he resigned his position at Harvard to travel once more to the West, this time with Nathaniel Wyeth, the Cambridge merchant who designed to enter the fur trade, and with a young Philadelphia ornithologist, John Kirk Townsend. The party went all the way to the Pacific, and Nuttall continued by ship to Hawaii, always and indefatigably in search of new plants. The West was Nuttall's Eden, where he could roam free and give names to almost everything before him; he left it and America with a deep sense of loss, recorded in his "Preface" to Michaux's *North American Sylva* in 1841: " . . . and I must now bid a long adieu to the 'New World,' its sylvan scenes, its mountains, wilds, and plains; and henceforth, in the evening of my career, I return, almost an exile, to the land of my nativity."

In his supplements to the *Sylva,* a work first published in 1810–1813 and considerably enlarged by Nuttall for a new edition in 1841, the naturalist occasionally departs from botanical description to engage in short narratives about his own experiences with western trees. His aesthetic joy is evident and unabashed, leading his science writing into the realm of the literary essay:

> As we sailed along the smooth bosom of these extensive streams [the "deep Wahlamet" and the "wide Oregon"], for many miles we never lost sight of the long-leaved Willow, which seemed to dispute the domain of the sweeping flood, fringing the banks of the streams and concealing the marshes entirely from view; at every instant, when touched by the breeze, displaying the contrasted surface of their leaves, above of a deep and lucid green, beneath the bluish-white of silver: the whole scene, reflected by the water and in constant motion, presented a silent picture of exquisite beauty.

John Kirk Townsend, Nuttall's companion on the 1834 journey, left a record which has been called "the most readable and exciting account ever written of the continental crossing." First published in 1839, the *Narrative of a Journey Across the Rocky Mountains, to the Columbia River, and a Visit to the Sandwich Islands, Chili, &c.* is certainly readable—in part because Townsend, a member of a prominent Philadelphia family, wrote an urbane, faintly amused, often more than faintly scornful, prose which interests the reader as much in the writer's character as in the scenes portrayed. Townsend is an early specimen of the tourist. His account contains short descriptions of camas bulbs and chokecherries, among the somewhat scanty natural history references, but this traveler's attention seems to have been mainly on topography-in-general and on the details and stories of camp life. He is an example of the writer on the move. However, there was an occasion when Townsend took a leisurely look around himself—he was ill, and was offended by the brawling of the trappers at a rendezvous, and so stayed apart—and the result is a pleasant Rocky Mountain pastoral scene:

> *30th.*—Our camp here is the most lovely one in every respect, and as several days have elapsed since we came, and I am convalescent, I can roam about the country a little and enjoy it. The pasture is rich and very abundant, and it does our hearts good to witness the satisfaction and comfort of our poor jaded horses. Our tents are pitched in a pretty little valley or indentation in the plain, surrounded on all sides by low bluffs of yellow clay. Near us flows the clear deep water of the Sidkadee [Green River], and beyond, on every side, is a wide and level prairie, interrupted only by some gigantic peaks of mountains and conical butes [sic] in the distance.

One early naturalist whose writing seems to reflect a more spirited engagement with the wilderness was Alexander Philip Maximilian, Prince of Wied-Neuwied, a small principality on the Rhine. Maximilian not only "wintered-over" in the wilderness, a distinctive accomplishment according to the measurement of frontier veterans, but he also paid attention to the sounds and smells of the wild and to the complex life of Indian encampments, so that his account, *Travels in the Interior of North America,* 1832-1834, is one of the richest and most precise of early travel documents. During his young manhood in the Prussian army (he fought in the Napoleonic Wars, rose to the rank of major, and was decorated with the Iron Cross), Maximilian had become intensely interested in natural history, and had pursued his studies in the Amazon jungles for three years (1815-1817) after leaving the military. He collected and named flora and fauna, and made the first

detailed studies of native tribes in the Amazon Basin. Later, after identifying and arranging his South American collections and after corresponding with Thomas Say, the American entomologist who had accompanied the Long expedition to the front range of the Rockies in 1819-1820, "Prince Max" determined to extend his nature studies to North America. In April, 1833, he set out by steamboat from St. Louis, bound for the upper Missouri, eager to see the primitive part of America. His narrative, in common with others of this early period, is largely concerned with travel, but Maximilian seemed to have a more relaxed approach than most—perhaps because he traveled with a manservant—and there are numerous occasions when he simply sat still and watched.

> I often passed my time in the lofty and shady forest which extended beyond the willow thickets on the banks, at the border of the open prairie. Sitting on an old trunk, in the cool shade, I could observe at leisure the surrounding scene. I saw the turkey buzzards, that hovered above the hills, contending against the high wind, while a couple of falcons frequently made a stoop at them, doubtless to defend their nest. A couple of ravens likewise flew about them. The red-eyed finch, the beautiful *Sylvia aestiva,* the *Sylvia striata,* and the wren, flew around me, the latter singing very prettily.

When, in the fall of 1833, he made the turn at Fort Union and started back down the Missouri, Maximilian was deeply impressed by the abundance of wildlife:

> Buffaloes and elks had crossed the river before us, and we heard the noise they made in the water at a considerable distance. The island was covered with lofty trees, and in many places, with tall plants, especially artemisia, but had many grassy and open spots, and we found on it five buffaloes, and several troops of elks and Virginian deer. A white wolf looked at us from the opposite bank, and the great cranes flew slowly and heavily before us.

Appended to his travel narrative, the German prince included some two hundred fifty pages of detailed observations on the Indian life he had seen and to some degree taken part in, covering food, clothing, games, rituals, language (including sign language), stories, and social relations; the contrast with Townsend, who at one point simply said of an Indian village, "I scarcely know how to commence a description of the *tout en semble* of the camp, or to frame a sentence which will give an adequate idea of the extreme filth, and most horrific nastiness of the whole vicinity," is instructive. Where Townsend was put off, Maximilian sat down comfortably in a Sioux tipi, hesitated not to accept the proffered dish of freshly cooked dog, and pronounced it "excellent."

Among the writings of mountain men, Osborne Russell's *Journal of a Trapper,* which he readied for publication in 1848, is a remarkable document. Its descriptions of place are innocently heartfelt, and the appended essays on animals and Indian tribes of the Rocky Mountains are enlivened by a quaint, untutored, workmanlike approach. Though Russell was modest about his own writing, and felt that he was trespassing on poets' territory when he attempted to describe the mountain wilderness, it is clear that he himself had the poetic spirit. In his second summer in the West (1835), he wandered into the Lamar River valley in what is now Yellowstone National Park, and formed an immediate attachment to that beautiful area, calling it "Secluded Valley." "I almost wished I could spend the remainder of my days in a place like this," he wrote. He returned to the Lamar several times during his years as a trapper, often attempting to describe the peculiar hold the landscape had upon him. Not a tourist but a working trapper, and often in danger, Russell nevertheless was keenly sensitive to the fact that in wilderness lay a special power.

> There is something in the wild romantic scenery of this valley which I cannot nor will I, attempt to describe but the impressions made upon my mind while gazing from a high eminence on the surrounding landscape one evening as the sun was gently gliding behind the western mountain and casting its gigantic shadows across the vale were such as time can never efface from my memory. . . .

This trapper went out of his way to engage the wilderness at its most potent. In the depth of winter, 1841, having stayed on in the mountains after the last rendezvous had been held and the beaver business had declined, Russell rode out from the Indian camp he had been staying in, just east of the Great Salt Lake.

> The 3d day of Feby. I took a trip up the mountain to hunt Sheep I ascended a spur with my horse sometimes riding and then walking until near the top where I found a level bench where the wind had blown the snow off. . . .
>
> the air was calm serene and cold and the stars shone with an uncommon brightness after sleeping till about Midnight I arose and renewed my fire My horse was continually walking backwards and forwards to keep from freezing I was upwards of 6,000 ft above the level of the lake, below me was a dark abyss silent as the night of Death I set and smoked my pipe for about an hour and then laid down and slept until near daylight—My Chief object in Sleeping at this place was to take a view of the lake when the Sun arose in the morning.

Shortly after the mountain man's day had faded began the era of the government surveyor. Well provisioned and equipped for the most part, working as officials on a mission, the surveyors of the middle and later decades of the nineteenth century corrected and completed the mapping of the West, made it known to all through their reports, and served thus to edge the "country in the mind" out of the unknown and mythic, toward the account books. However, the writing of some of these men—John Charles Frémont, Howard Stansbury, William Henry Brewer, Clarence King, and especially Clarence E. Dutton—is nowhere near as dry as their assigned work might suggest. Their reports are informed with excellent geological understanding and often ecological insight. The immensity of the West, and the great views from high points necessary for mapping, and the sheer exhilaration of contact with wilderness, all worked to bring their documents alive. Some of the writing is very good indeed.

Frémont (1813-1890), who in 1842 mapped the Oregon Trail through South Pass in minute detail and whose later expeditions likewise took on historical and political importance, had an enjoyment of mountain wilderness, at least in its summer season, which considerably brightens his journal report. The Wind River range, which he first visited in August of 1842, seemed to speak to him in terms quite other than the march-tempo tunes of manifest destiny, future railroads, and future mines which he heard nearly everywhere else in the ten or fifteen thousand miles of western travel covered by his expeditions. Here in the mountains he came closest to writing simply of nature as nature. It is as if the Wind Rivers stunned him into a purely aesthetic response.

> It is not by the splendor of far-off views, which have lent such a glory to the Alps, that these impress the mind; but by a gigantic disorder of enormous masses, and a savage sublimity of naked rock, in wonderful contrast with innumerable green spots of rich floral beauty, shut up in their stern recesses.

Later, describing a climb to the summit of the range, he commented that "a stillness the most profound and a terrible solitude forced themselves constantly on the mind as the great features of the place." There was no conceivable use for these gigantic mountains, no obvious material reason for people to be there. Captain Frémont went on, of course, to California and a gold rush fortune, a senatorship, even the Republican nomination for President; yet his reports, and his unfinished *Memoirs of My Life* (1887) often reflect a kind of wistfulness in their descriptions of place, as if Frémont did in fact, at least half-consciously, surmise what he was leaving behind.

Howard Stansbury (1806-1863), who as a Captain in the Topographical Engineers made a hardship-plagued survey of the Great Salt Lake and its surrounding desert in 1849, wrote a straightforward account of the area which presents its ruggedness clearly. But Stansbury too, perhaps to a greater degree than Frémont, was awake to wild beauty. In *Exploration and Survey of the Valley of the Great Salt Lake of Utah* (1852), describing a desert where he and his men had to carry water for their mules (rationing them to two pints per day), and where their own survival was very much in question, he calls the area "a landscape full of wild and peculiar beauty." In the course of setting up triangulation points, the party came upon the pelican colonies of Gunnison Island in the Great Salt Lake, and Stansbury's description of the scene reveals a lively aesthetic awareness:

> The whole neck and the shores of both of the little bays were occupied by immense flocks of pelicans and gulls, disturbed now for the first time, probably, by the intrusion of man. They literally darkened the air as they rose upon the wing, and, hovering over our heads, caused the surrounding rocks to re-echo with their discordant screams. The ground was thickly strewn with their nests, of which there must have been some thousands. Numerous young, unfledged pelicans, were found in the nests on the ground, and hundreds half-grown, huddled together in groups near the water, while the old ones retired to a long line of sand-beach on the southern side of the bay, where they stood drawn up, like Prussian soldiers, in ranks three or four deep, for hours together, apparently without motion.

Stansbury's appreciation for the desert—typically the least hospitable of environments, a kind of test for the nature lover—comes through his account despite his comments on its difficulty. What called forth his best writing—even extending him to metaphor at times—was the experience of absolute space and starkness in the reaches of the Great Basin, where life forms were sharply outlined and precious.

In 1860, the State Legislature of California sponsored what it hoped would be "an accurate and complete Geological Survey of the State." Taking part in this significant undertaking were two men whose writings have lasted into our time, William Henry Brewer (1828-1910) and Clarence King (1842-1901). Both were graduates of the Sheffield Scientific School of Yale University, capable wilderness travelers in the West, and competent, not to say graceful, writers, with King decidedly the more literary of the two. Brewer, who had grown up on a farm in upstate New York, maintained a commonsensical outlook and a practical realism in the many letters he sent home from the California survey, letters gathered into a continuous account a century later; King, in his best-known and most consciously artistic work, *Mountaineering in the Sierra Nevada* (1872), used some of the survey experiences as a starting point only, to create a classic series of sketches and adventures. In him, we see the first literary man in the history of the western nature essay.

Brewer's charm as a writer is that of the ordinary man given heavy responsibilities and difficulties, who meets these and has time and mind left over for appreciating beauty. He climbed mountains for the view as much as for survey work, and seemed to delight in recording what lay below. From a hill at the southern end of San Francisco Bay, he wrote, "The valley looked like a map, and the head of the bay, with its swamps intersected and cut up with winding streams and bayous crossing and winding in every direction, made by far the prettiest arabesque picture of the kind I have ever seen." On one memorably clear day, from the summit of Mount Diablo, Brewer was able to see, he said, forty thousand square miles, from the Pacific to the Sierra Nevada. "What a grand sight!" he exclaimed, in typically unembellished enthusiasm. As the Survey progressed, Brewer became fit and hardy, and relished the outdoor life. He wrote several times that he liked camp life best, and never, whatever the weather, caught a cold in the wilderness. But Brewer, although it has been said that his writings "must . . . be considered the founding statement of California mountaineering," does not transmute wilderness fitness into philosophy. His contribution to the western nature essay is more in the line of topographical realism and precision.

Clarence King was a writer—at the very least we can say he was a would-be writer—a fact immediately apparent as one turns from other surveyors' reports to the opening of *Mountaineering in the Sierra Nevada*: "The western margin of this continent is built of a succession of mountain chains folded in broad corrugations, like waves of stone upon whose seaward base beat the mild small breakers of the Pacific." With an amazingly comprehensive grasp of geological history as expressed in present landforms, King laid out for his readers a view of the West—in *Mountaineering* and later in *Systematic Geology* (1878), his major contribution to the Fortieth Parallel Survey—which would not be surpassed until the photographs from space in the 1960s. King was also an excellent storyteller, whose account in *Mountaineering* departed from the daily journal record to create incident and character in almost novelistic fashion. No one before King, in the western travel essay, had this sort of range. If he had brought his gifts to maturity, King might have been a major western writer. Even so, his contribution is important. The distinctive finish he added to survey notes may be seen by comparing an account of his with one of Brewer's, of the same view in the Kings River Canyon district of the Sierra Nevada. Brewer says, in his serviceable way,

> The rocks are granite, very light-colored, the soil light-gray granite sand. Here and there are granite knobs or domes, their sides covered with loose angular bowlders, among which grow bushes, or here and there a tree. Sometimes there are great slopes of granite, almost destitute of soil, with only an oc-

casional bush or tree that gets a rooting in some crevice. Behind all this rise the sharp peaks of the crest, bare and desolate, streaked with snow; and, since the storms, often great banks of clouds curl around their summits.

King attempts to express the scene as an involving, rhythmic pattern:

> I believe no one can study from an elevated lookout the length and depth of one of these great Sierra cañons without asking himself some profound geological questions. Your eyes range along one or the other wall. The average descent is immensely steep. Here and there side ravines break down the rim in deep lateral gorges. Again, the wall advances in sharp, salient precipices, rising two or three thousand feet, sheer and naked, with all the air of a recent fracture. At times the two walls approach each other, standing in perpendicular gateways. Toward the summits the cañon grows, perhaps, a little broader, and more and more prominent lateral ravines open into it, until at last it receives the snow drainage of the summit, which descends through broad, rounded amphitheatres, separated from each other by sharp, castellated snow-clad ridges.

The difference is small, perhaps, in point of imagery or diction, but the sense of organization is telling.

If King, writing with both geological insight and artistic care for leading the eye, helped to bring the West into sharper focus, he did not venture into a philosophy of nature or wilderness in any overt way, not even as far as the sober Brewer had. There are hints in King—speaking of the forest belt of the Sierra, he said, "Lifted above the bustling industry of the plains and the melodramatic mining theatre of the foot-hills, it has a grand, silent life of its own, refreshing to contemplate even from a hundred miles away"—but only hints. King's career led him elsewhere.

Perhaps the finest of the surveyors, as a writer, was Clarence Dutton (1841-1912), whose work has even been said to belong "properly with that of Thoreau, Burroughs, Muir. . ." As a captain in the U. S. Army, Dutton spent parts of the years 1875 through 1881 studying the geology of the "Four Corners" region of the Southwest, and described his findings in four major works: *Report on the Geology of the High Plateaus of Utah* (1880), *The Physical Geology of the Grand Cañon* (1882), *Tertiary History of the Grand Cañon District* (1882), a book which has recently been reprinted and which is perhaps the climax to "surveyor's prose," and finally, *Mount Taylor and the Zuni Plateau* (1885). Dutton had the large grasp of King, as regards landforms and the immensities of geologic time, and a remarkably lucid style, complemented in *Tertiary History* by the equally remarkable artwork of William H. Holmes. The plateau and canyon country stands forth, as it were, in the depth-revealing light of late afternoon in Dutton's works, and although he did not become a dweller, and thus perhaps did not penetrate so deeply into the place-mind as Thoreau, say, or Muir, he is nevertheless a consummate tour guide. He is a master of the authoritative overview which yet has a poetic tone, for example in introducing a mountain range in south-central Utah: "The Tushar is also a composite structure, its northern half being a wild bristling cordillera of grand dimensions and altitudes, crowned with snowy peaks, while the southern half is conspicuously tabular."

In *Tertiary History,* Dutton raises an epistemological and aesthetic point which, in the works of subsequent writers about western wilderness, has become an important theme: that which is totally wild cannot be easily assimilated into the prepared categories of civilized perception. In fact, it will be distorted by them. A new apprehension is called for, and this seems not to be a simple acquisition but something which must be slowly lived into. Speaking of the Grand Canyon's inner gorge, Dutton wrote,

> Forms so new to the culture of civilized races and so strongly contrasted with those which have been the ideals of thirty generations of white men cannot indeed be appreciated after the study of a single hour or day.

In accordance with this thought, Dutton's mode of presentation was an attempt at complete realism—escaping, or trying to escape, those received conventions of thirty generations.

> There is no need, as we look upon them [the Vermilion Cliffs], of fancy to heighten the picture, nor of metaphor to present it. The simple truth is quite enough. I never before had a realizing sense of a cliff 1,800 to 2,000 feet high. I think I have a definite and abiding one at present.

Dutton did not always abide by these strictures, but the stated respect for terrain-as-it-is reveals a certain emotional dedication; only a perfect purity on the part of the observer, a non-embellishing expression, could do justice to the unique landscape. It is clear that Dutton felt such a mission, though he found it impossible to fulfill. He avoided any explicit comments in the area of the dialectic which has, from the beginnings of American literature, been suggested by the opposition of civilization and wilderness—there was, after all, perhaps little place for this in a government report. But his statements in favor of directness and accuracy show that he was aroused by the incomparable wilderness of the canyon country, and inspired to a kind of purgation of motive and expression. The main thing was to see clearly.

Dutton's degree of success can be suggested only by samples of a certain length. We need to be with this observer for several hours at least, to appreciate his patience and attentiveness. Perhaps an afternoon and evening watching the Vermilion Cliffs will serve as an example. In the bright light, depth and proportion are flattened.

> But as the sun declines there comes a revival. The half-tones at length appear, bringing into relief the component masses; the amphitheaters recede into suggestive distances; the salients silently advance toward us; the distorted lines range themselves into true perspective; the deformed curves come back to their proper sweep; the angles grow clean and sharp; and the whole cliff arouses from lethargy and erects itself in grandeur and power as if conscious of its own majesty. Back also come the colors, and as the sun is about to sink they glow with an intense orange vermilion that seems to be an intrinsic luster emanating from the rocks themselves.

With Clarence Dutton, the western nature essay may be said to have reached the upper limit of the pictorial. The West was being described to visual near-perfection. While it is true that a certain tactile sensitivity must be among the powers of a landscape-describer, it seems clear that Dutton, King, Brewer, Stansbury, and Frémont, along with the other writers discussed to this point (with the partial exceptions of Osborne Russell and Prince Maximilian), limited their descriptions to

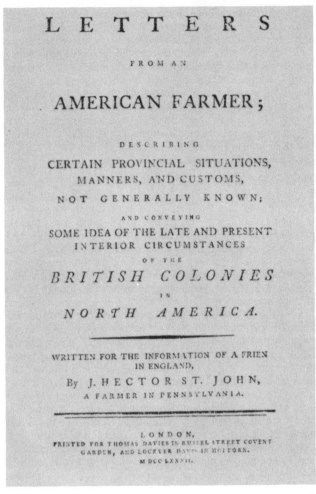

Title page of Letters from an American Farmer.

the visual realm. This limitation suggests a certain distance, a lack of grit, sound, and smell; and this in turn may explain why the early writers make almost no profound psychological or philosophical comments about wilderness—that is, about their experience in it and what this experience might mean for a civilized inheritor of the European and Judaeo-Christian tradition. There are only intimations. It is as if the wild had not been deeply enough entered, or assimilated; the observer remained apart, bringing back ever more detailed and precise reports, until finally almost everything knowable had been accounted for in the picture, but still the complete engagement had not been made.

In the writings of John Muir (1838-1914), the body comes alive to the wilderness, and with this important, almost baptismal step (to use one of Muir's metaphors), the western nature essay reaches toward maturity and significance. The intellectual response to nature is not neglected—in fact, Muir's first published nature essays were scientific in nature and grew out of a geological controversy—but it is placed within a context of physical and emotional immersion into the wild. Muir's great contribution to western writing was to bring the holistic or participant experience alive, but at the same time not to relegate the intellect and science to vagueness. Muir's writing, at its best, vivifies science.

John Muir's emergence as a mature thinker—better said, his emergence into a radical, perhaps historically important consciousness—began in the summer of 1869, his "first summer in the Sierra." Thirty-one years old, a man without a career except, as he said, to walk God's wilderness, Muir had been offered a more or less supernumerary job as a sheepherder-supervisor. The band of two thousand sheep trailed from the hot foothills up into the forests and finally to the edge of the little-known alpine zone, and as the summer developed, Muir rapidly opened out into an ecstatic, wakeful relationship with the wild mountains, a feeling of deep continuity which would be the basis of his understanding of geological processes, his compassion for all life forms, and his subsequent explanation and defense of all that was wild. His eventual command of a first-rate prose style, which in its flexibility and emphasis upon the activity of nature could evoke some of the excitement of a wilderness experience, was also rooted in the awakening of 1869. That summer was the key, and Muir was aware that something dramatic was happening to him. On July 7, he wrote in his journal,

> Never while anything is left of me shall this first camp be forgotten. It has fairly grown into me, not merely as memory pictures, but as part and parcel of mind and body alike. The deep hopper-like hollow, with its majestic trees through which all the wonderful nights the stars poured their beauty. The flowery wildness of the high steep slope toward Brown's Flat, and its bloom-fragrance descending at the close of the still days. . . . The great sungold noons, the alabaster cloud-mountains, the landscape beaming with consciousness like the face of a god.

Two weeks later, the emergence continued.

> No pain here, no dull empty hours, no fear of the past, no fear of the future. These blessed mountains are so compactly filled with God's beauty, no petty personal hope or experience has room to be. Drinking this champagne water is pure pleasure, so is breathing the living air, and every movement of the limbs is pleasure, while the whole body seems to feel beauty when exposed to it as it feels a campfire or sunshine, entering not by the eyes alone, but equally through all one's flesh like radiant heat, making a passionate ecstatic pleasure-glow not explainable.

The traditionally limited and separate point of consciousness of Western civilization is here being transcended. A larger, apparently limitless identity is emerging—two years later, Muir wrote, "the solid contents of a human soul is the whole world"—which became the root of his life and thought. From this new viewpoint, Muir was able to see or intuit natural facts and relationships that other, perhaps better trained, observers had not noticed. For example, he proved that glaciers had played an important role in the formation of Yosemite Valley, a fact that both Clarence King and Josiah Whitney of the California Survey had missed. The important point for Muir's own development, however, was that his intellect was enabled and enlivened by his inner feeling for relationship and process, his sharing with the mountains, as it were, one body. He literally felt the mountains, lying on boulders in order to sense their grain and possible cleavage lines, sleeping out tentless where night happened to overtake him, climbing numerous peaks, wading streams, and going almost foodless, so that what he called his "loving study" could proceed with maximum, filterless perception. Muir's studies and experiences in the Sierra suggest a revolutionary transformation or reversion of consciousness, into a state of mind which accords with the physical interweavings and mutualisms of ecology.

The writing which proceeded from this vision is characteristically vivid, imagistically. But it suggests a life within the pictures by paying attention, above all, to movement and to interconnection. There are few static scenes in Muir's books: always the wind is making the flower stalks nod or bending the trees in great arcs, and the streams are catching at the down-hanging grass stems along the bank; when the sun rose over the Grand Canyon, Muir saw it "stinging" the uppermost cliffs. Even in his later, comparatively not so active works, such as *The Yosemite* (1912), the sense of movement is basic, as in his description of the giant sequoia:

> The immensely strong, stately shafts are free of limbs for one hundred and fifty feet or so. The large limbs reach out with equal boldness in every direction, showing no weather side, and no other tree has foliage so densely massed, so finely molded in outline and so perfectly subordinated to an ideal type. A particularly knotty, angular, ungovernable-looking branch, from five to seven feet in diameter and perhaps a thousand years old, may occasionally be seen pushing out from the trunk as if determined to break across the bounds of the regular curve, but like all the others it dissolves in bosses of branchlets and sprays as soon as the general outline is approached.

With prose that modelled activity and the interpenetration of subject and object, Muir was able to arouse a caring response on the part of his readers. In *The Mountains of California* (1894), *Our National Parks* (1901), *My First Summer in the Sierra* (1911), and in the posthumously published *Travels in Alaska* (1917) and *Steep Trails* (1918), the attempt was to express a physical-spiritual joyfulness, an engaged awareness which could inspire ecological sensitivity. Importantly, Muir's initial effect was contemporaneous with the closing of the frontier, and perhaps indicated the acceptability of a new style of thought. His fundamental recognition was that the world is a living system, not an endless flat plane consisting of resources which may be used up, serially, by an always-advancing people. Nor was the world, for Muir, an object of any sort, not even the "pretty" sort. His is thus the first post-frontier mind in western literature. He had the science of the great surveyors, but he went the necessary step further to make himself completely at home in the mountains, and to become capable of ecological vision.

> We are governed more than we know, and most when we are wildest. Plants, animals, and stars are all kept in place, bridled along appointed ways, *with* one another, and *through the midst* of one another. . . .

Mary Austin (1868-1934) had a similar attitude toward nature, though perhaps more forthrightly mystical and less scientific than Muir's. She realized the importance of the territory he had opened up, and paid him tribute in her first book, *The Land of Little Rain* (1903); by the end of her career, she had made a significant extension of the Muir line, as it might be called, by prophesying that the consciousness of the unity of mind and nature would become not just a literary theme but the ground of an entirely new culture. This would happen, according to Austin, in the American West. She also paid a good deal of attention to Native Americans and their philosophies, an area in which Muir had small interest, and she absolutely relished the details of folk life on the land, finding in native and folk adaptations instances of ecological wisdom. Her essays on natural history, found in *The Land of Little Rain, The Flock* (1906), *California, the Land of the Sun* (1914), and *The Land of Journeys' Ending* (1924), are distinguished by a leisurely, spacious, and at the same time almost microscopic attention. There is no hurry in Mary Austin's books. Time and the seasons will come around again; the flocks will be moved a few miles a day, toward the lowlands in fall, toward the mountains in spring; the dust devils way out on the alkali flats will whirl again when the winds are right. The chief thing is to be alert, unhurried, ready, because vision and the "Deep-self," her term for the ultimate consciousness that one's self and the environment are not two, may awaken at any time.

The primary experience had first come to Mary Austin at the age of six, near her family home in Illinois. Fifteen years later, while riding in the hills near her brother's homestead in California, she was reconfirmed in the fundamental, mystical center which was to inspire all of her writings. As her third-person autobiography, *Earth Horizon* (1932), has it,

> It was a dry April, but not entirely barren; mirages multiplied on every hand, white borage came out and blue nemophilia; where the run-off of the infrequent rains collected in hollows, blue lupine sprang up as though pieces of the sky had fallen. On a morning Mary was walking down one of these, leading her horse, and suddenly she was aware of poppies coming up singly through the tawny, crystal-sanded soil, thin, piercing orange-colored flames. And then the warm pervasive sweetness of ultimate reality, the reality first encountered so long ago under the walnut tree. Never to go away again; never to be completely out of call. . . .

Her resolute holding to this center, and to a degree her promotion of it in her role as a literary figure later in life, served to isolate Austin somewhat and perhaps helped make her life more difficult. But her chosen path also allowed her to concentrate and to see. Her neighbors in Independence, California, after the publication of *The Land of Little Rain,* could not understand how she drew so much out of the apparent barrenness of an ordinary, vacant field next to her house. But Austin, who unlike most of her townsmen was not looking for gold or planning to move water, had time to look meditatively and to see the riches in "My Neighbor's Field." She sat out on the mesas in the same way, at the edge of the wilderness desert, until the dry and seemingly hostile landscape became for her a land of abundance. The ecological givens of place were not irritations to her but matter for the opening of vision. She spent hours of outdoor stillness to get the one right word for the dry foothills, and got it, to her satisfaction: "puckery." Her great contribution to the western essay is just such a distillation and purity of image.

To Austin, however, especially in later years, this vision was not solely imagistic but also had historical, analytic, and prophetic aspects. When invited to a conference of prominent southwesterners in 1927, on the subject of the proposed Boulder Dam, she alone was outspoken against it. Man should be learning and adapting to natural conditions, not rushing to change them. Austin's case against dams would move no "realists," probably, but she believed that time and the gradual influence of the land and its native people upon the incoming races, the water movers, would prove her right. The Southwest, she thought, the environment itself, operating "subtly

below all other types of adjustive experience," will work to produce a new, land-harmonious culture. It will be, she said, "the *next* great and fructifying world culture." This future, for Mary Austin, begins in any moment of true seeing. To an alert mind, any natural object will do; one could be walking casually through a stand of junipers, surely an ordinary environment, and quite suddenly touch the core of things.

> Not one of all the ways by which a tree strikes freshly on your observation,—with a greener flush, with stiffened needles, or slight alterations of the axis of the growing shoots, accounts for this flash of mutual awareness. You walk a stranger in a vegetating world; then with an inward click the shutter of some profounder level of consciousness uncloses and admits you to sentience of the mounting sap.

Aesthetic communion is also the heart of the work of John Charles Van Dyke (1856-1932), a New Jersey librarian and professor of art history at Rutgers College, whose experience in the West began in Minnesota in 1868 and encompassed long stays in Montana, Arizona, and California. Again, as with Muir and Austin, the opening of perception to a specific environment led eventually to an ecological vision and a critique of civilization. In *Nature for Its Own Sake* (1898), *The Desert* (1904), *The Mountain* (1916), *The Grand Canyon of the Colorado* (1920), and *The Open Spaces* (1922), which represent Van Dyke's western writings, he covers nearly all of the subjects of the western nature essay, and in his firm, Muirian, anti-anthropocentric position, strikes the western essay's major tone perfectly. Though he did not overtly promote or even assert a mystical consciousness, as did Mary Austin, there is evidence of Van Dyke's having transcended the limited, egoistic view. Speaking of the Grand Canyon, he said, "And we, if we would understand the Canyon, must largely eliminate the human element of it. It is insignificant." The ideal point of view, apparently, is Mind, not ego.

> The utilitarians look at it [the Colorado River] and perhaps wonder how they can harness it, make it turn wheels, generate electricity, or irrigate the earth. It now serves no "purpose" and is quite "useless"—useless to man, who still cherishes the idea that the world was made exclusively for him.

The origin of the larger vision is unmediated aesthetic experience—simply being aware of light, rain clouds, color in fog banks, the lightness and drift of clouds, the roll of the divides and swales—to list a few of the topic headings in *Nature for Its Own Sake.* Van Dyke teaches awareness by narrative example, for instance in the opening chapter of *The Mountain,* an autobiographical account of riding across the high plains of Montana toward the Rockies, by noticing the air becoming thinner and the light brighter. More often, he gives minutely detailed lectures in which the usually-passed-over beauties of nature are set up for notice. The attention to detail is extraordinary, almost dissective, and yet the sense of the whole is kept alive, as a kind of diapason, by the fact that all of the scenes and details are, after all, being known by one careful, meditative consciousness. The feeling of interested participation is great, and is one of the positive beauties of Van Dyke's writing.

Van Dyke also directly attacked what he considered to be false approaches to nature, for example "fancy" and the "pathetic fallacy." Like Clarence Dutton, he thought a stripped, illusionless and traditionless perception, unfiltered by any predisposition to dualistic judgments, was the only means by which the wild could be apprehended.

> . . . Nature neither rejoices in the life nor sorrows in the death. She is neither good nor evil; she is only a great law of change that passeth understanding.
>
> The fault is not in the subject [desert wildlife]. It is not vulgar or ugly. The trouble is that we perhaps have not the proper angle of vision. If we understood all, we should admire all.
>
> If we could but rid ourselves of the false ideas, which, taken *en masse,* are called education, we should know that there is nothing ugly under the sun, save that which comes from human distortion.

The ideal of a direct and perfected awareness is a major theme in the western nature essay, still very much alive. It was clearly John Van Dyke's guiding thought, and it led him more and more to wilderness, as an environment conducive to such perception. "The great spaces of the wilderness have a quality of beauty about them that no panorama of civilized lands can equal or even suggest," he wrote in *The Mountain.* This beauty was for Van Dyke not an object but a personal, mind-awakening renewal. "He [the] climber of a wilderness mountain] is back to a primitive faith from which he never should have wandered." In his autobiography, *The Open Spaces,* he describes sleeping out in the arid, spacious West, and summarizes his thought: "What a strange feeling, sleeping under the wide sky, that you belong only to the universe. You are back to your habitat, to your original environment, to your native heritage." Anything less than this was, for Van Dyke, civilized and partial, and vision-obstructing.

Muir, Austin, and Van Dyke represent the flowering of the post-frontier vision. But it should not be supposed that the closing of the frontier automatically or widely conferred such an outlook. Many writers simply exploited the West as a tourist's curiosity—some continue to do so. Some appeared to approach the level of sensitivity of the three authors cited, but then seemed to fall short. George Wharton James (1858-1923), for example, who praised the curative powers of the southwestern deserts in his best book, *The Wonders of the Colorado Desert* (1906), and gave tours of the West in such works as *California, Romantic and Beautiful* (1914) and *Utah, Land of Blossoming Valleys* (1922), was apparently greatly attracted to the wildness of mountain and desert which Muir and Austin had found so meaningful. Indeed, James found a personal regeneration in the desert after losing, in a scandal, his former career as a minister. But he wrote quickly and excitedly, as a promoter or converter rather than one who had rested deeply in the self-nature continuum. He described himself as having been " 'on the jump' for many years," indicating perhaps the nature of his relationship with any one particular place. Even so, there are passages in his works, for example the last several pages of *The Wonders of the Colorado Desert,* which intimate a great deal.

> The desert is nothing if it is not sincere. It is sincere to brutality. Open, bare, exposed it lies, and yet it is not dead. It is alive with a fiery aliveness that takes you into its heart and compels you to be as it is, open, frank, sincere.

The lure of the desert, according to James, is that it can deepen one who will cross the line into wildness and revoke all former claims. "There is no knowing of self in the whirl of the cities," he asserts. But the boosterism in James suggests a certain incompleteness. For him, the underground aquifers in the desert were, simply, "inexhaustible," and should be tapped. Where John Van Dyke had argued that "the deserts should never be reclaimed. They are the breathing-space of the West and should be preserved forever," James rather trippingly stated, in summarizing vast water projects in Utah, "Thus the good work of irrigation goes on." Having it both ways—the desert is good, and reclaiming the desert is good—James shows a positive attitude. But it is legitimate to ask if he was thinking through the matter of aridity completely.

Authors from California and the southwestern deserts dominate the western nature essay from the close of the frontier onward into our time. Among the few good writers dealing with the interior, mountain West was Enos Mills (1870-1922), a philosophical follower of John Muir and a Colorado mountaineer of very extensive experience in the wild. Mill's debt to Muir is clearly great—he dedicated his first major book to Muir, quoted him at length when the scene under discussion apparently seemed to require an extra dimension in the writing (see Mills's *Your National Parks* [1917], for example), and even used several Muirisms in something very like their original form—but he also had a great fund of personal experience, particularly with animals, which enabled him to make a unique contribution to western literature. In *Wild Life on the Rockies* (1909), *The Spell of the Rockies* (1911), and *Wild Animal Homesteads* (1923), the sense of being involved with myriad life forms—beaver, mountain lions, wolves, coyotes, skunks, grizzlies, and a host of birds—is particularly strong. From 1886 on, Mills spent a great deal of time in lone mountain rambles, having as a base camp a small cabin near Longs Peak, and he came to know the Rockies with a lover's intimacy. He was a true dweller. Where Henry Thoreau had referred to himself humorously as an inspector of snowstorms, Mills actually had a government job in precisely that line, walking the continental divide to measure snow depth. "I lived intensely through ten strong days and nights, and gave to my life new and rare experiences," he said of one inspection trip. "I went beyond the trails and visited the silent places alone."

The demands of winter travel in the wilderness helped to develop in Mills a remarkable hardiness and insouciance, which in his accounts often reaches toward the philosophical dimension. His writing also shows a profound understanding of territory, in the animal-behavior sense: the absolute interdependence of animal and habitat. Walking quietly, alone, and sitting still in concealment for long periods, he observed intensely, and upon occasion attempted to take part in, the often dramatic scenes unfolding around him. He also entered the animals' home life, and in a sense did make it his own by writing with emotion for his home ground and his wild neighbors. This connection, like his hardiness, suggests much, philosophically. But Mills, a self-educated man, was reticent about deep interpretations, seeming to pass them off in almost formulaic sentences. ("Silence sounds rhythmic to all, and attunes all minds to the strange message, the rhapsody of the universe," he said once, for example, speaking of the quiet of the high country.) Chiefly, he seemed content to let his adventures speak for themselves. His narratives showed the wilderness as a friendly place, by and large, where night and winter held no genuine terrors. In comparison to his contemporaries Muir, Austin, and Van Dyke, Mills may seem less intellectual, perhaps, less in command of the cultural references of Western civilization; but his fearless absorption into the wild gives his writing original life and a vivid sense of place. He was at home in the mountains.

Mills was also, like all twentieth-century nature writers, disturbed by the swift passing of large-scale wilderness. Like John Muir (indeed, perhaps partly because of a youthful meeting with Muir), he entered the political arena on the side of the shrinking wild, using his writing to awaken readers to the awesomeness of their moment in history. In an explosive change occupying only a few decades, man had become capable of transforming the planet, and of losing sight of the most fundamental connections. In *Your National Parks*, Mills wrote,

> Once, like a web of joy, trails overspread all the wild gardens of the earth. The long trail is gone, and most others are cut to pieces and ruined. The few broken remnants are but little used.

(pp. 222-42)

Thomas J. Lyon, "The Nature Essay in the West," in A Literary History of the American West, *sponsored by The Western Literature Association, Texas Christian University Press, 1987, pp. 221-65.*

LLOYD HUSTVEDT

[*Hustvedt is an American educator who specializes in Scandinavian studies. In the following excerpt, he examines diaries and letters of Norwegian immigrants who settled in the prairie Midwest during the mid nineteenth century.*]

In seventeenth-century England a letter from New England was "venerated as Sacred Script, or as writing of some Holy Prophet, t'was carried many miles where diverse came to hear it" [Samuel Eliot Morison, *Builders of the Bay Colony*]. This was no less true for letters sent to Norway by Norwegian immigrants from the Middle West two centuries later. Through these letters a new discovery of America took place, forming an image for both writer and reader which in the main was positive in tone. What the earlier explorers had said about America hardly meant much to the average Norwegian. But when they began to read in their own homes firsthand information from friends and relatives what America was really like, "America Fever" often followed. These letters were read with more than curiosity: there was self-interest and questions were raised with a purpose. They faced a major decision: a choice between the Old and the New World. As we know, many chose the latter. Hence many of the "America Letters" go beyond the information they yield and the image they create; they were an active and vital agent in the migration movement itself.

In many Norwegian households terms like Illinois, Wisconsin, Iowa, Minnesota and the Dakotas, together with settlement names like Muskego, Koshkonung, and Winneshiek County became as familiar as the names of their own neighboring provinces. On the other hand difficult Indian place names were offset with familiar postmarks like Sogn, Norway, Vang, Trondheim and Christiania. In time, Norwegian rural emigrants were apt to meet more friends and relatives in America than if they sought work in Oslo or Bergen.

While it is more than risky to make firm generalizations about immigrant letters and diaries, one can point to some dominant attitudes. Despite the many experiences that could be cited to prove the contrary, America was the land of opportunity and promise. One finds an unfailing faith in the freedom of the new land, and that most writers were sincerely pious and deeply religious. All in all, idealistic hope prevailed over realistic disappointments.

Despite the permeating optimism, this literature makes clear that upon arrival in America all was not success and sunshine. They began at the bottom of the ladder, most were poor and ignorant of the English language, and there were an alarming number of deaths during the Atlantic crossing. Diseases like malaria, cholera, typhoid, pneumonia and measles took a heavy toll after arrival. When some seventy persons died one winter in the Muskego settlement, Soren Bache advanced the theory that newly broken soil exuded noxious fumes, but optimistically concluded that these fumes fortunately dissipated with time [*Chronicle of Old Muskego: The Diary of Soren Bache, 1839-1847*]. They faced hard work and, we can only conclude, at a pace they had not known before. There were for many periods of loneliness and isolation. They could find themselves cheated by sharp-dealing Yankees and at times by their own countrymen. But the majority did survive and worked their way to "better days."

Among the early letter writers and an American enthusiast was Gjert G. Hovland. He settled first near Buffalo, New York, in 1831 and then moved to Illinois in 1835, being among the first Norwegian settlers there. "Nothing has made me more happy and contented," he wrote, "than the fact that we left Norway and journeyed to this new country. We have gained more since our arrival here than I did during all the time I lived in Norway." Hovland goes on to tell how he sold his fifty-acre farm in New York for five dollars an acre and that he bought 160 acres of better land in Illinois for $1.25 an acre. He gave details on taxes, wages, prices, quality of soil and the availability of wood and water. He felt that there were good laws in this country and emphasized that there was complete religious freedom. He also aimed a barb at Norwegian officialdom: There were no "useless expenditures for support of persons . . . who are no benefit but rather a harm to the country." He stated that "prosperity and contentment are to be seen almost everywhere one goes." He added, however, "everyone must work for a living here, whether he is of low or high estate." He recommended emigration, save for those who were unsuited for work. Hovland's letters were published in local newspapers and otherwise recopied perhaps in the hundreds and circulated throughout Norway [Theodore C. Blegen, ed. *Land of Their Choice: The Immigrants Write Home*].

A different view is presented by Sjur J. Haaeim. Hovland's letters had inspired him to emigrate. When he arrived in Illinois, he found only the crudest huts as homes; the children were half naked and their parents were in rags. He had been among those who had moved on to Missouri where he found conditions still worse. After losing his land there, he moved back to Illinois. Neither did he think highly of his fellow immigrants: "Some left Norway because of hatred for the clergy and other officials, others because of their hatred for their neighbors, still others because of vices. When all these came together in one neighborhood, one can imagine what kind of life they lead in these American forests." There was not, he continued, a church within 100 miles, and he declared that "we are living in the worst conceivable state of heathendom in the whole world." He also appealed for financial assistance so that he and his family might return to Norway. His letter, sent to a Bergen bishop who strongly opposed emigration, was published in a Bergen newspaper.

The greatest influence on the early migration came through Ole Rynning, a son of a minister, well educated and idealistic. At the age of twenty-eight, he led an immigrant party into the ill-fated Beaver Creek settlement south of Chicago in 1837. The land which looked good in the late summer stood under water in the spring. An epidemic invaded the community, many died, and survivors fled. Before Rynning himself died in the fall of 1838, he wrote an extended letter to the Norwegian people under the title, *True Account of America for the Information and Help of Peasant and Commoner.* Since there were so many conflicting reports, he hoped to set the records straight. A friend said about Rynning: "A great and good idea formed the central point of his thinking," namely, "to provide the poor, oppressed Norwegian workman a happier home on this side of the sea. . . . Nothing could shake his belief that America would become a place of refuge for the masses" (cited in Svein Nelsson's *Billed Magazine,* 1:84, 95).

His message contains thirteen brief chapters which answer specific questions. It moves from general information about America to discussions on the Norwegian settlements that were forming. He provided detailed advice on preparations for emigrations, the best routes to the West, medicines, supplies, tools and equipment one should bring and emphasized the need for a reliable guide and interpreter. Regarding slavery he anticipated the Civil War: "There will in all likelihood come a separation between the states or else bloody civil disputes." The book, published first in 1838, saw a second edition in 1839 and was reprinted in Sweden, and became popularly known as the "America Book." Persons who could hardly read learned to do so as they struggled through the pages word for word.

Not all immigrant letters entered the public sphere or took any particular stand as to the merits of migration. Such a collection would be the letters of Gro Svendsen who settled near Estherville, Iowa, in 1862. In simple language she recorded her experiences that for her spelled America. Two novels have been based on these letters, but they seem less rewarding than the letters themselves. Gro was born in Hallingdal, Norway, of rural aristocracy, much loved and perhaps shielded by her parents. There was no need for her to emigrate, but she had learned to love Ole Svendsen who planned to do so. Her parents would not let her go. "How I want to go with you," she wrote, "and yet I am not sure I shall be strong enough to leave my parents forever. I love them; I am their child; they will have to deal with me as they wish." She advised Ole to speak with her parents, and he must have spoken well; for they sailed for the New World in April, 1862. She was twenty-one years old, and Ole turned twenty-two during the crossing [*Frontier Mother: The Letters of Gro Svendsen*].

Regarding her last glimpse of Norway she wrote: "It's far in the distance like a blue mist—nothing more. I am heavy hearted." Regarding a storm, she recorded: "The dark winds beat against us in sullen fury." When a bird was killed by the captain's dog, she was heartbroken: "Poor little creature that sought haven with us, only to be ruthlessly torn to pieces." But when this same dog whelped, she was delighted with the five puppies. When an infant was buried at sea, she explained that "the ship's carpenter made a little coffin and filled it half full of sand." When it was lowered into the sea "It was strangely quiet and solemn. The waves hurried to cover the little coffin."

Everything along the way seemingly excited her interest and observation. She borrowed books from the captain and studied the ship's maps. The church spires in Quebec shone "like silver in the morning sun." When she saw some women loaded down with trinkets, she became critical: "No moderation, no taste, vulgar." A child was born to her mother-in-law on board ship. She cared for it and held it when the captain performed baptism. Later this child was buried in St. Ansgar's Cemetery. Her simple words were, "He was ill the few days he lived on earth . . . from the third of June to the tenth of July. Then he fell asleep."

She told of her dreams. Many were happy dreams, but they could also be sad and foreboding. She knew that she had caused her parents "unspeakable sorrow" and pleaded that they not be sad on her account. Although dark moods of loneliness overcame her, she never expressed regret over leaving. "My husband fully understands what sacrifices I made when I left everything most precious to me to go with him into the unknown; . . . with him alone can I share my joys and sorrows." But solemn confessions like this can be followed abruptly with progress reports: "I also want you to know that we bought a cow for which we paid fifteen dollars, and she now has a little calf."

Through her letters we can follow the development of their farm. There was gradual acquisition of livestock; first came oxen, then horses. There were crop failures due mostly to locusts and encounters with thunderstorms, blizzards, prairie fires and snakes. "Life here," she wrote, "is very different from our mountain valley. One must readjust oneself to learn all over again. Even to the preparation of food. . . . We are told that women of America have leisure time, but I haven't yet met any woman who thought so."

Gro waited seven months before she told her parents that her husband had been drafted into the Union Army. He left the day their second child was baptized: "What I endured that day," she wrote, "I could never tell you. . . . I stood like a frightened bird with my young alone, bewildered and forsaken." Despite her premonitions that she would not see him again, he returned safely.

After three years she confessed that "Our house is very small and humble, but it is a shelter from the cold winter. I shall say no more about it. However, next spring . . . we hope to build a large comfortable house." Normally the first years of pioneering were the most difficult. This may not have been true for the Svendsens. In the eleventh year, 1873, after the grasshoppers had ravaged, she stated, "Times have been hard this fall, much harder than any since we came to this land. The future is uncertain. No one knows what tomorrow will bring."

She had a never-ending interest in education. She wrote much about books and reading. With her first child on her arm she attended English school and later found herself teaching school three days a week at twelve dollars a month. She watched carefully the growth of her children. The oldest learned to manage oxen. The second had the sharpest mind of all her children, while Albert puzzled her. He asked "strange and disturbing questions" on such subjects as creation. When her daughter Sigri died in 1876, dreary resignation to fate followed, but her interests revived when a new Sigri was born.

The process of Americanization can be detected. Her early criticism of American clothing and schools abated. She took a lively interest in local politics and was proud that her husband had been an American soldier. She argued for more American names for her later children like Albert, Steffen and Louise. The American tendency must have gone quite far when they named their pony Horace Greeley.

She was deeply religious and interested in the church but not in its controversies on theological questions. She praised their first minister, Halvard Hande, because he was concerned more with human needs than with theological debate, but he left to become editor of a newspaper. In the midst of thoughts about her duties as parent and mother she gave birth to her tenth child in 1878. She died at the age of thirty-seven, and her remarkable letters came to an end.

In the case of Gro Svendsen we are not dealing with fame or distinction. She was hardly unusual in terms of education or experience. But, without these letters little would be left today save for a name on a tombstone in Esterville, Iowa. She had, to be sure, more gift than most to express her thoughts and experiences, but nevertheless thoughts and experiences that have been shared by countless immigrant women.

What happened later? Ole Svendsen sold his Iowa farm and moved to North Dakota. The tenth child died in 1881; Steffen and Bergit died of diphtheria in the fall of that year. Svend, the oldest, died in 1882, nineteen years old. Her husband went on to build a prosperous farm (the kind Gro had dreamed about), and lived to seventy-eight years old.

Diaries, if hidden away in desk drawers, made no impact on the migration movement itself and remain largely sources of interest for later readers. Because it covers the early period of Norwegian settlement, the diary kept by Soren Bache from 1839 to 1847 merits our attention. Bache's father was a man of means, and three of his brothers were educated in England. Soren, the fourth son, motivated by reading Rynning's "America Book," left Norway in 1839, well supplied with the money for travel and land purchases. One Johannes Johansen, a former office worker, came along as a companion. This may have been his father's doing as it was rumored that Soren was an impractical dreamer.

They arrived in New York on September 4 and reached Chicago eighteen days later. Enroute he was much saddened to learn of the death of Ole Rynning, whom he had obviously hoped to visit. They devoted that fall to exploring land in Illinois, visited the Norwegian settlements and found mixed circumstances. They also pressed north to Jefferson Prairie and Koskonung in Wisconsin, both regions being embryo Norwegian settlements. They returned to the Fox River settlement in Illinois, where they spent a tedious winter.

Not until the middle of June, 1840, could they resume exploration. They concluded that being close to Lake Michigan would be an advantage and that health conditions were better in Wisconsin. By September, one year after arrival, Bache and Johansen had acquired considerable land in Muskego, some twenty miles southwest of Milwaukee. From the beginning ethnic issues entered the picture: "The Irishman sold his land to Johansen today for the price he originally paid for it. Since we had already bought the land next to him he could not expect to get a single one of his countrymen as a neighbor. This was undoubtedly the reason he sold out" [*Chronicle of Old Muskego*].

They first built a sod hut, but later excavated into a mound to ground level and erected a two-story building (24 x 18 feet), a building which would serve as a community center for the Muskego settlers for a number of years. The mound proved to be an Indian grave. Bache attended English school during the winter. He unfortunately dismisses the entire year of 1841 by saying, "Nothing remarkable happened during this long period." He had helped with such improvements as were necessary to put land under cultivation. He moved to Milwaukee during the winter of 1841-1842 to attend school. The following spring he returned to Norway for a visit and returned a year later. With him came the first trained clergyman to serve the Norwegian immigrants, Clause Lauritz Clausen.

A number of entries point to the strife and splintering that would take place in Norwegian-American Church life. After Clausen's ordination Bache writes: "A large number of settlers gathered in our house to enroll as members of the Lutheran Church." But adds, "I did not join because I wish to see what would develop out of the innovations Clausen had introduced in the service." When the second theologian J. W. C. Dietrichsen, arrived a year later, he registered skepticism. He had met him on his way to work: "A strapping young man. His tall powerful build and rosy cheeks reminded me of some young giant from the Norwegian mountains. He had come to maintain among (the immigrants) the Lutheran faith. . . . Time will tell how successful he will be."

Bache's family had financed the major costs of building a church in Muskego, claimed to be the first among the Norwegian settlers. Bache was not pleased with the dedication ceremonies. Both Clausen and Dietrichsen spoke: "Their sermons were largely a condemnation of those who had not joined the church and a cry of woe over those who had withdrawn from it." Dietrichsen, he continued, "aimed at inspiring remorse and anguish in the hearts of the people for having left Norway. . . . It must be said that the sermon as a whole was mixed with too much nonsense. . . . Thus ended the events of this day which will be long remembered because of Clausen's and Dietrichsen's bravado and sorry behavior. If their thoughts and deeds are recorded in history they will be a poor example for the coming generation to follow."

Bache was a restless spirit. Being financially independent he could make frequent excursions into the other Norwegian settlements in Wisconsin. Not all of his entries discussed serious matters: "When bedtime came a pallet was spread for me on the upstairs floor. After I had retired the nobleman's hound came and wanted to be my bedfellow. As I would not agree to this, he evened the score by doing unmentionable things in the corner."

Without being a blind booster, Bache supported emigration and spoke disparagingly about those who could not find happiness here. Despite his position he returned himself to Norway in 1847, never to return to America or the community he helped build. He had participated in acquiring the first trained clergyman, through him his family had helped to build a church, and he had aided in establishing the first Norwegian newspaper, *Nordlyset*, in 1847.

Elisabeth Koren's charming diary covers the years 1853 to 1855, and shifts the scene to Iowa. Parts of this state had been opened up to Norwegian settlers by none other than the earlier-mentioned Reverend Clausen. There was need for a minister, and Ulrik Vilhelm Koren, twenty-seven years old, responded. About one month before leaving for the United States in September, 1853, he married Elisabeth Hysing, twenty-one years old, and the daughter of a distinguished headmaster of a high school. She came out of an intellectual environment and was accustomed to gracious living in a manor house. During the crossing she read Schiller, Dickens and Washington Irving. Through her diary we can learn in detail what it is like to travel cabin class. The journey, attended by incessant storms, took two months. She was aware of what was going on among the less fortunate: "There is much sickness in steerage. Eleven are already dead. One man lost his wife and two or three children, one poor woman and six children" [*The Diary of Elisabeth Koren: 1853-1855*].

Their sojourn in New York must have differed greatly from most immigrants'. They ate well, lived in comfortable hotels, associated with distinguished Scandinavians, saw exhibits and attended a play, *Uncle Tom's Cabin,* which she found to be "frightfully distorted." They traveled in reasonable comfort as far as Milton, Wisconsin, but there all luxury ended. The trek from Wisconsin to Washington Prairie near Decorah, Iowa, in December in open vehicles was an arduous one. No preparations had been made for a parsonage when they arrived. On Christmas Eve they moved in with Erik Egge, his wife and two small children. Their one-room cabin measured fourteen by sixteen feet. Elizabeth could only write: "What a contrast between this evening and a year ago." They lived under similar conditions for ten months. During this time the new minister traveled extensively, leaving his young wife alone with her host family: "Everything looks as usual here this evening. Erik fills the room with his awful tobacco; Helene (Erik's wife) yawning over her stockings, blows her nose and sighs a bit. Per (the child) at last talked himself to sleep, having experienced many kinds of misfortune throughout the day—he overturned a mug of beer on the floor, and fell down in the mud outside the door; he was picked up out of this, and amid many an angry exclamation, was wiped off with dirty straw which serves in place of a door mat, and then chased into the house with a whack."

There was much that jolted her delicate sensibilities. Pigs, calves, sheep and chickens could invade their cabin if the door was left open. In many households she found unkempt and unsanitary conditions and unwashed children smeared with molasses. Other things pained her: "I hear such cries and shouts at Katterud's. They are breaking sod. It is shameful the way they whip the poor oxen." In the main she entered her new life with good humor and courage. She often longed for intellectual conversation, but all the same became fond of her neighbors, and learned, in fact, to know and appreciate the rural segment of Norwegian society which had earlier been closed to her. She marvelled over how handsome many of the pioneer men of rural origin were. When her host, however, took off his shoes and socks and rubbed his feet with turpentine while she was eating, she felt that frontier rustic habits had gone too far.

Because her husband read her diary regularly, she may have withheld much. At times she confesses her loneliness: "I do not understand why all at once I can become so sad, or depressed, or whatever I should call it. It starts with a longing for Vilhelm, then everything about me seems so empty; I become rather faint and have to take a little walk and look around. That helps sometimes, especially if I happen to see something beautiful, as today when I saw a new kind of bluebird. . . . And then when I can, I avoid thinking of Vilhelm or of anyone at home or in Norway." But with time, this lady "to the manor born" became involved in matters like

salting down pork and filling ticks with freshly threshed straw for their new home.

This diary which makes a book of more than three-hundred pages covers only fifteen months. The last entry is for December 3, 1854. Their first child, Henriette, was born nine days later. The diary hardly deals with any emotional crisis; rather it reveals the intelligence, fortitude and clear vision of the author, and how she made the transition from high station in her homeland to the primitive conditions of an unfinished society in the new.

Hans Tollefsrud's unpublished diary deals with secondary migration. He left his wife and family in Wisconsin on New Year's Eve in 1851 for the gold fields of California; he came home late summer of 1856. He went by ship to Panama, crossed the isthmus and picked up another ship on the Pacific side for San Francisco. He entered a rough and tumble world. They stopped in Kingston, Jamaica, on the way for coal and water. There were 500 soldiers on board. "They also went into town," he wrote, "got drunk and started to fight with the blacks. This was no time to go on land, but rather try to find the best place on ship in order not to get hurt. . . . There were many wounded and also dead on both sides. It was the worst fight I had ever seen and I do not need to say how scared I was." When crossing parts of Panama on foot, he noted, "We all have pistols in one hand and a knife in the other." He was curious about everything and spent much time in Panama City waiting for his ship. With much Lutheran naivete he explored the Catholic churches. He listened to sermons "but could not understand a word." "The priest," he noted, "was dressed in black and had a golden band which reached all the way to his heels. Often he would kneel at the altar, and each time the sexton took hold of the band and held it up. If the reason was to prevent it from touching the floor or to give the congregation an opportunity to look at his behind, I do not know." He puzzled over the containers made of marble which contained water and the finger-dipping and subsequent crossing of oneself. After viewing their funeral customs he turned to rare judgment: "Any dog has better sense than these raw Spaniards. I have to call them that." Regarding communion he noted that the priest "took some big swallows each time. I believe he was drinking to wash away their sins."

He discussed the voyage to San Francisco, but noted only briefly that the captain committed suicide on the way. He began to look for gold on March 11, 1852, but found nothing the first day. As things turn out he alternates between working for others and gold digging. He rejoiced over letters he received from home, written for his wife by the Reverend C. L. Clausen, who seemed to be everywhere. There were long periods of isolation, and loneliness set in especially when the weather did not permit work. On January 1, 1853, one year after his departure, he reflected and took inventory. The date was also his birthday. "I feel I have reason to be sad. And then I think of how I have used this past year. Badly, if I had to be judged. . . . How I desire to be home and have fun and fool around with my family—if only for a half-day."

Without any trace of self-pity he can tell of hardship, endurance, frustration and disappointment. At times his style resembles that of the Icelandic sagas: "This morning I found a dead man. He had been ravaged by wild animals. He probably had been caught in a storm and froze to death." He reported on a fire in Maupville: "Fifteen whorehouses burnt down plus more, and the murderer from Rabbit Creek escaped from jail with two million six hundred thousand dollars." Or we might consider this account: "Johns shot Rick, so he fell dead on the floor. Rick first went to Johns to egg him on. He had his loaded revolver with him. After he tried to punch Johns a couple times and failed, he reached inside his coat, but Johns had his pistol handier and shot first. He hit Rick in the chest and he didn't say another word." At times the dramatic and the mundane stand side by side: "The murderer was hanged today. The crowd stood between three and four thousand. Syrom returned from Marysville with mules and oxen." When a Norwegian by the name of Ole Olson tried to cheat him on a note for $400, he took legal measures which led to arrest. When they met at the office of the Justice of Peace, Tollefsrud stated: "I felt a complete sense of shame for my countryman, which I knew that he too sensed. Olson did not say much. After a few minutes Ole Nielson wanted to reconcile us. I said I was willing but that the matter was now in the hands of the law."

On August 16, 1856, he bid farewell to his friends, and he could write that it "did not take place without tears." He may not have left rich, but he left with a certain class. When he boarded the stagecoach he was well dressed and carried a cane as behooves a man of some worth. But underneath his coat was a pistol for protection against possible robbers. He arrived home in Wisconsin one month later.

The purpose of this delivery has been to give you some glimpses into the variety of experiences and responses that enter the field of immigrant history. None of these sources alone tells the full story, but collectively they add a human dimension that might be lost in the synthesis of historical scholarship. Diaries, journals and letters are the human fires that smolder underneath the footnotes. (pp. 38-51)

Lloyd Hustvedt, "Immigrant Letters and Diaries," in The Prairie Frontier, *Sandra Looney, Arthur R. Huseboe, Geoffrey Hunt, eds., The Nordland Heritage Foundation, 1984, pp. 38-51.*

FRONTIER FICTION

WALLACE STEGNER

[Stegner is an American novelist, short story writer, educator, and critic who has written extensively on life in the American West and the nature of the American Dream. In the following excerpt, he discusses how the experience of the frontier has shaped the fiction of the American West.]

The Western, horse opera, has . . . been studied in considerable detail, though it must be admitted that critics rarely approach it from the near, or literary side. They mount it from the right, like Indians, and ride it hard as myth, as folklore, as a part of the history of ideas, or as a demonstration of Freudian or Jungian psychology. I don't recall ever seeing a Western discussed for its original social or psychological insights, for the complexity or depth of its characters, for its poetic evocativeness, for its narrative techniques, or for its prose style. It wouldn't pay to do it, for a Western is not a unique performance but a representative one. Its characters are not individuals but archetypes or stereotypes, and its themes are less interesting for their freshness or their truth

to history than for their demonstration of a set of mythic patterns.

I do not intend to get caught in the argument about whether the Western is, or can be, literature on the highest level. I only want to establish its relation to another kind of western story-telling which is not mythic but literary. This literature is western with a small *w,* and only the fact that it all takes place west of the 100th meridian permits us to put it under one rubric, or to put this class of writing beside the Western. Variety is, at least superficially, one of its marked characteristics. As a westerner, I would love to believe that there is some spirit, attitude, faith, experience, tone, something, that binds all small-*w* western stories together as manifestations of a coherent regional culture. And yet I confess I have doubts: in order to get an *unum* out of our *pluribus,* do all of us define "West" and "western" too narrowly, forgetting what does not fill our bill?

It is not exactly classified information that there are many Wests. Neither is it unknown that they have certain things in common—aridity above all else, and the special clarity of light, the colors, the flora and fauna, and the human adjustments that have resulted from aridity. Most of the Wests have been touched by the magic figure of the horseman, and so almost any of them may be a legitimate home for horse opera. And all the Wests are late, large, and new. Those are the basic resemblances. Otherwise, there are almost as many divergent as convergent lines.

Is it legitimate to speak of western literature, except in reference to the Western? Can one find a relation between a story by Willa Cather and one by Steinbeck, Mary Austin, or Walter Van Tilburg Clark? One is fairly sure about such a novel as *Horseman, Pass By,* by Larry McMurtry, because it is an affectionate requiem to the old-time Texas cattleman, whatever they did to it when they made it into the movie *Hud.* But what of McMurtry's latest, *The Last Picture Show,* a sort of small-town *Studs Lonigan?* It is laid in west Texas; is it a "western" novel? Is Bernard Malamud's *A New Life* a western novel? Its setting is Oregon State College in Corvallis. Is Nathanael West's *The Day of the Locust* a western novel? It takes place in Los Angeles. Are Eugene Burdick's *The Ninth Wave* and George Stewart's *Storm* western novels? Both are laid in the San Francisco Bay Area, which was held to be the West when Bret Harte wrote about it.

Literature is one of the things that emerge as by-products when you throw people of an advanced civilization into an unrecorded, history-less, art-less new country. Western writing is only the last stage of what occurred on every American frontier. West Virginia was once as west as west Texas; the literary development of the two should have been approximately the same. According to the organic theory that dominated our cultural self-examination from the Connecticut Wits through Emerson and Whitman to Hamlin Garland and the local colorists, each new part of the continent should have a seedtime of a generation or two, and then reap a harvest. Once it had set its roots, it should develop some variety of that "rocky, continental quality" that Emerson thought he felt in the Mississippi Valley, and start speaking out in its own native voice.

The process took place in New England, it took place in the middle Atlantic states, it occurred like realized prophecy in the Midwest, where literary nativism spread in a series of waves from Indiana to the Dakotas. It began to happen in

Gold Rush California and in the cowboy Southwest: it put out belated shoots in the Pacific Northwest and in Mormon country. But I think it cannot be said to have happened plainly all over the West.

Despite large individual differences, midwestern writers from Eggleston to Dreiser and Lewis have tended to be earthy, plain, and realistic. Southern fiction from Poe to Faulkner has had strong infusions of the gothic, the grotesque, the highly colored, the "tall," and it has had its consistent and repetitive themes: color, the lost cause, the persistence of the family fabric and tradition. But when one asks if there are comparable likenesses among western writers, one hedges. Well, probably not. And then again, perhaps yes. Or perhaps only maybe.

I believe that a number of things happened to inhibit, interrupt, and in places block the organic cultural growth the West had a right, from the experience of the rest of America, to expect. One inhibiting factor was simply the West's variety. Climate, physiographic features, resources, characteristic occupations, ethnic mixtures were so various that they began to produce a Plains tradition, a desert tradition, a lumberwoods tradition, a Californian or Mormon or Mexican border tradition, and it is at least open to question whether these have enough in common to be recognizable components of a western tradition.

Moreover, the "fiction factories" that first took hold of the most colorful western themes and characters swiftly petrified them into the large, simple formulas of myth. First the Beadles with their dime novels, then the Wild West Shows, then Street and Smith and the pulp magazines, then the movies, and now television, have found those formulas to be all but foolproof, as good now as they were a hundred years ago. As a result, they do not change; they are only reassembled from interchangeable parts. They remain predictable, serene, and timeless, fantasies of self-reliance and aggression, sexually symbolic or curiously asexual, depending on which critic you read, apparently good for another century and perhaps forever.

This one area of western writing has been so calcified that it escapes the organic imperative: it is not necessary to be homegrown in order to write it. (pp. 187-90)

Variety, dispersion, and constant immigration on the one hand and mythic petrifaction on the other had the effect of producing either stories with little family resemblance, or stories with altogether too much. And history intervened to break up many forming regional patterns. Those patterns develop best in rural isolation; but time and change have often been so syncopated in the West that there has been no time for a native character to form and find its voice.

Settlement in the West was not only late, it was irregular. The mining West, and to a degree the timber, the grazing, and the homestead Wests, were raided, not settled; and sometimes raided for one resource after another, by different breeds of raiders. Despite their colorful history, there has hardly been a *continuous* community life in an Aspen or a Telluride; and when oilfields are superimposed on cattle country in Texas, or subdivisions superimposed on orchards in California, something disruptive has happened in the life of both people and towns. Folklore, more often than not an improvisation on an occupational theme—logging, riverboating, railroading, cowboying—is *only* an improvisation, and though it may be curiously lasting, it lasts as the Western lasts: it is cut loose

like a balloon from the actual and continuing lives of men and women.

Few western places can show, even during their short life, the uninterrupted life of a Maine fishing village or a county seat in Indiana or Iowa or a southern town clustered around the courthouse square. Western people have been notably migrant, and much of the West has happened during the age of swift communication, since the invention of the telegraph. Moreover, urbanization, which is as culturally shattering an experience as the frontier itself, has often followed so hot upon settlement that the only constant in western life has been change. Regional patterns that would have developed in isolation were effaced or blurred, half-formed. The living past, having little apparent relevance to the present, became a dead past, sometimes a pool of nostalgia. To the natural letdown of the second and third generation cheated of the hardships and dangers that kept their parents busy has been added the strangeness and unfriendliness and dissatisfaction of ways that have more in common with New York, London, Paris, Vienna, or Prague than with the brief and strenuous annals of the West.

What I have been saying is of course true to some degree of almost the whole of America, but it is particularly true west of the Missouri. Fearing the loss of what little tradition we have, we cling to it hard; we are hooked on history. If the Western continues to exist in a timeless West, carefully landscaped, around Sedona, Arizona and Kanab, Utah—country suitable for "cutting them off at the pass"—western literature

John Filson

of the small-*w* kind is generally scrupulous in sticking to real places and real experience. But it is a literature almost without a Present.

Western writers of fiction have shown a disinclination, perhaps an emotional inability, to write about the contemporary; and when they occasionally do, we are not inclined to think of their books as western. Not one critic in five hundred would designate *Storm* or *A Shooting Star* "western" novels, but *The Oxbow Incident* would make it because it includes cowboys, and *The City of Trembling Leaves* might make it because, though contemporary and urban (Reno) it exploits the scenery of the Sierra and the Nevada desert, and makes a thematic point of its western-ness.

I shall have more to say about the amputated Present in western writing. For the moment, I only want to emphasize that we do save the term "western"—small-*w*—for fiction of a certain kind, a kind not so petrified as the Western, but related to it. It is almost by definition historical and rural, or at least limited to the life characteristic of the periods of raid and settlement, the beginnings of a new civilization. Its actions do cluster around certain large and recurrent themes; its characters, however individually conceived, do illustrate certain tribal qualities and virtues, and so may be said to emphasize a type. Limited as I have limited it—which I think is the way most of us limit it—western literature does have elements of a large, loose cohesiveness.

Themes recur: nostalgia, for instance, the elegiac tone. Henry Nash Smith, Folsom, and other critics have pointed out the debt that much western writing owes to Fenimore Cooper, and in nothing is the debt more apparent than in this lament for the noble and lost, the last of a race or a breed or a kind. Chingachgook, the last of the Mohicans, has a thousand descendants. Some, like Noel Loomis's "Grandfather out of the Past," are as authentically native as Chingachgook himself. But the "last survivor" figures are various. The old prospector in Walter Van Tilburg Clark's "The Wind and the Snow of Winter," the cowhands and hispaños in Eugene Manlove Rhodes' "Paśo por Aquí," badman Scratchy Wilson in Stephen Crane's "The Bride Comes to Yellow Sky," Captain Forrester in Willa Cather's *A Lost Lady,* the wilderness in Guthrie's *The Big Sky,* the sea of grass in Conrad Richter's novel of the same name, all are touched with the tone of nostalgic regret. It is a tone that may seem odd in a new country, and yet it may express something quintessentially American: our sadness at what our civilization does to the natural, free, and beautiful, to the noble, the self-reliant, the brave. Many of the virtues of the typical western hero are virtues seen as defeated, gone by, no longer honored.

The regret, in fact, seems almost as compulsive as our need to "break" the wilderness and plant our civilization. Like many other American attitudes, it seems accentuated in the West, perhaps because the West *was* the last home of frontier freedom and largeness, perhaps because as horsemen's country it always had more glamor than clodhopper country, perhaps because in spite of its virile tradition the West itself is fragile—it does not heal readily, the ugliness we create stays visible, bare, and glaring. In a way it is a more honest region than most.

Whenever western fiction does approach the contemporary, the theme of ugliness and vulgarity is likely to show. Willa Cather, in love with the frontier's spaciousness and health, revolted from the villages and towns it had bred: compare *O*

Pioneers! with *A Lost Lady* or *One of Ours.* Mari Sandoz, another Nebraskan who always struck me as wishing she had been born a Sioux, did her native state bleakly in *Capitol City,* a very different Nebraska from the Niobrara frontier of *Old Jules.* Bernard DeVoto, putting his hometown of Ogden into *The Crooked Mile* and other novels, could find nothing good to say of it, though that same country, when it was prowled by Utes and mountain men, heated his imagination to incandescence. And those are not isolated instances. The typical western writer loves the past, despises the present, of his native region.

In a way, the dichotomy between the past and present is a product of two forces frequently encountered in both western fiction and the Western: the freedom-loving, roving man and the civilizing woman. Given the circumstances of western settlement and the legitimate inclinations of the sexes, it was natural that the West should find this theme strong in its history, and make it into something pervasive in its literature. The bride comes to Yellow Sky and the old male freedom slouches off, defeated, with its bootheels punching funnel-shaped holes in the sand. The schoolmarm comes to Wyoming, and after a suitable interval of male skylarking and lynching, the Virginian wears a collar. An eastern young lady in New Mexico is the person to whom the hispaño speaks of the desert rock on which old passersby have scribbled their elegiac greeting and farewell, "Pasó por Aquí." It is inescapable. Long before I had heard this theme stated, and before I knew enough western literature to state it myself, I had put it into Bo and Elsa Mason in *The Big Rock Candy Mountain.* Almost every writer who has dealt with family stresses on the frontier has found it in his hands, because he probably grew up with it in his own family. Male freedom and aspiration versus female domesticity, wilderness versus civilization, violence and danger versus the safe and tamed. It is in *The Big Sky,* in *Giants in the Earth,* in Vardis Fisher's *Toilers of the Hills,* in a cartridge-belt full of indistinguishable Westerns. Done in almost diagrammatic mythic terms or done as realistic fiction, it is as inextricable from western writing as the theme of color is inextricable from the literature of the South.

Allied to it—all these major themes nest and interlock—is the conflict between law as stated in the books and enforced by sheriffs and right as defined by private judgment and enforced by gun, fist, or rope. In practice, the dispute is often but not invariably between fallible book law and the higher moral law. Like the conflict between man-wilderness and woman-civilization, the law theme has an impeccably historical basis, though it is more prominent in stories of mining camps or cowtowns than in those that chronicle the homesteader or sodhouse frontier. The sodhouse frontier was more likely to get its drama out of the location of the county seat or a dispute between landholders—conflicts essentially *within* the structure of established law—than out of lynching bees or walkdowns. Often the woman theme is intertwined with the law theme, as in that source-book *The Virginian,* in Guthrie's *These Thousand Hills,* in Richter's *Sea of Grass,* in the movie *High Noon.* Sometimes the mythic and lawless patterns are turned upside down, as in *The Oxbow Incident,* where private judgment turns out wrong and innocents are hanged, or in Oakley Hall's *Warlock,* which attempts some corrections in the traditional drawing of gunmen and marshals.

The correctives are needed, for one result of condoning handmade personal justice is to encourage vigilantism; and it is true, as DeVoto pointed out in that essay on Wister, that the Johnson County War looks far more innocent in *The Virginian* than it does to the eye of history. If one assumes that fantasy has no social consequences, then one can take all Westerns and some western literature as harmless ways of discharging the aggressive ego. If one assumes otherwise, then most Westerns and some western books are unconsciously immoral, and perhaps dangerous, in the terms of the civilization that has replaced the frontier.

Immoral or upright, dangerous or merely self-reliant, the protagonist of either kind of western story has heroic virtues, horseback virtues—and that goes whether he is the Virginian or Per Hansa with his feet in a Dakota furrow. Often the structure of a story is created by the testing of the hero, sometimes in one of those walkdown situations between rival gunfighters, sometimes in moral crises where book law has presumably broken down and personal justice must be administered, sometimes in the simple risks and endurances that tell a boy he is a man or reassure a man that he is still one.

Of this last kind are two stories that I like as well as any ever written about the West: H. L. Davis' "Open Winter" and Paul Horgan's "To the Mountains." I have done much the same sort of thing in my story "Genesis," included in *Wolf Willow,* and have discovered something in the process of writing it. Very often this testing of the hero has the quality of an ordeal, and in consequence these stories are generally longer than short stories, shorter than novels: the ordeal must go on a good while to be a true ordeal, but it cannot go on too long or it becomes excruciating. One of the classical examples is the section called "The Crawl," in Frederick Manfred's story of old Hugh Glass, called *Lord Grizzly.* In special and modified terms, Walter Clark's "Hook" is another of those testings of the indomitable spirit, and H. L. Davis' "Homestead Orchard" shows us another boy becoming a man.

The virtues required to survive all these testings are the "manly" virtues of tenacity, courage, the ability to bear pain and hardship, an assured self-trust, generosity, a certain magnanimity of spirit. They do not differ much from the virtues that collectively make up Hemingway's "grace under pressure"; and as Malcolm Cowley has pointed out, Hemingway's virtues are essentially Indian virtues. Western writing is full of them; myth or literature, it is heroic to a degree, and even when fine and honest writers take a hard look at the myths, as Clark does in *The Oxbow Incident* or Milton Lott does in *The Last Hunt,* or A. B. Guthrie does in *The Big Sky,* they do not ever question the validity of heroism.

And that is one of the biggest reasons why to some modern critics the literature we call western seems remote, unreal, uncontemporary, anachronistic, belated. For heroism does not survive into modern literature, or seems not to, and writing which deals with the heroic and the rural seems to have little to say to people whose lives are fully urban and whose minds have grown skeptical or scornful of heroes. At least since Chekhov and Dostoevsky, the main streams of European and American literature have dealt increasingly with victims, not heroes. Look for victims among western stories and you may find them occasionally, as in Crane's "Blue Hotel." "Blue Hotel," beautiful and right as it is, is more "modern" than "western."

The difference in attitude was dramatized by Leslie Fiedler in an essay in which he told of getting off the train at Missou-

la, Montana, an easterner fresh from the *Partisan Review* offices, and seeing a large, grave, booted, tall-hatted man pass by. The man's face was serene, weathered, and to Fiedler vacant, bemused by an unquestioning faith in what to Fiedler were romantic and untenable fictions. Fiedler records his impression in one line: " 'Healthy!' I thought in contempt."

I want to suggest neither that this "Montana face" was indeed noble and that Fiedler was a diseased New York intellectual, nor that Fiedler was right and the Montana face was the product of a pathetic illusion. I want only to underscore the point I made earlier about the absence of a present in western literature and in the whole tradition we call western. It remains rooted in the historic, the rural, the heroic; it does not take account of time and change. That means that it has no future either, except to come closer and closer to the stereotypes of the mythic, unless it can expand its vision of itself and include things like a Leslie Fiedler lecturing to classes of undergraduates at the University of Montana.

Nostalgia, however tempting, is not enough. Disgust for the shoddy present is not enough. And forgetting the past entirely is a dehumanizing error. One of the lacks, through all the newly swarming regions of the West, is that millions of westerners, old and new, have no sense of a personal and *possessed* past, no sense of any continuity between the real western past which has been mythicized almost out of recognizability and a real western present that seems as cut-off and pointless as a ride on a merry-go-round that can't be stopped. The heroism of a forming civilization has become a thing to smile at, the civilization a thing to be savagely repudiated. The strenuousness of a hundred western years can be dissolved in strobe lights to the pounding of folk rock that has plenty to do with rock but little to do with folk. You can make the Haight-Ashbury scene in San Francisco, or be a teenage disturber of the peace on the Sunset Strip, you can work in an office in Denver or Dallas, and hear only the strident present, and be persuaded that the past does not exist, that Ford was right when he said history is bunk. But if you are any part of an artist, and a lot of people are some part of one, if you have any desire to understand, and thus to help steer, a civilization that seems to have got away from us, then I think you don't choose between the past and the present; you try to find the connections, you try to make the one serve the other.

No western writer that I know has managed to do it, unless it be Wright Morris in his sequence of novels about Nebraska, and they have a tendency to be hard on both past *and* present. Nobody has quite made a western Yoknapatawpha County or discovered a historical continuity comparable to that which Faulkner traced from Ikkemotubbe the Chickasaw to Montgomery Ward Snopes. Maybe it isn't possible, but I wish someone would try. I might even try myself.

God knows what happens in a future menaced by our incontinent fertility as a species and our incontinent willingness to accept a merely "bearable" world with none of the old western space and elbow room and self-reliance in it. God knows what happens to the heroic virtues when organization and programming have rendered them no longer viable. Maybe we will all sit and watch Westerns on TV, testing ourselves only in fantasy and by standards we no longer think applicable to our real lives. Maybe we will all revolt away from everything we mean and into some "other culture." But I hope we will find ways of recognizing at least parts of ourselves in the literature and history the past has left us, and I hope we will find ways of bringing some of the historic self-reliance and some of the heroic virtues back into our world, which in its way is more dangerous than Comanche country ever was.

I share the nostalgia that I have attributed to most writers of the West. I share their frequent distaste for the uglified and over-engineered and small-spirited civilization that threatens to turn us into one gigantic anthill. But I do not think we can forget the one or turn away from the other. In the old days, in blizzardy weather, we used to tie a string of lariats from house to barn so as to make it from shelter to responsibility and back again. With personal, family, and cultural chores to do, I think we had better rig up such a line between past and present. If we do, the term "western literature" will be enlarged beyond its ordinary limitations, and its accomplishments not so easily overlooked. (pp. 191-201)

Wallace Stegner, "History, Myth, and the Western Writer," in his The Sound of Mountain Water, *Doubleday & Company, Inc., 1969, pp. 186-201.*

LEWIS O. SAUM

[*In the following excerpt, Saum examines the success theme in fictional accounts of life on the Great Plains.*]

In an early short story titled "On the Divide," Willa Cather wrote of pioneer Nebraska that "it causes no great sensation there when a Dane is found swinging to his own windmill tower, and most of the Poles after they have become too careless and discouraged to shave themselves keep their razors to cut their throats with." This grimly facetious aside calls to mind an often remarked mood in a sizable body of literature. Ole Rölvaag, Willa Cather, Hamlin Garland and others sought realistically to portray the pioneer farmer's struggles with the Great Plains. Often, as Cather did in the above remark, they conveyed an image unhappy to behold. Psychopathic loneliness, soul-crushing melancholy, stultification of tender sensibilities, physical brutalization of men and spiritual destruction of women appear as stock themes. Thus, in a characteristic appraisal, Walter Prescott Webb in his study of Great Plains culture spoke of the farm literature as one "of *people,* of poverty, of unremitting toil, small reward, and ceaseless effort, the basis of stark realism."

But these authors did not portray futility. However, grotesque pioneer life may appear in such Cather stories as "On the Divide" and "A Wagner Matinée," her depictions involve generally "affirmative conclusions." The characters of this literary genre do not stand in awe-struck helplessness before the malign powers of the plains. On the contrary, they experience very real triumphs, and it may well be that, from the perspective of material accomplishment, they emerge more nearly successful than defeated. On the level of the immediate and particular, for example, they frequently show a striking ability to improvise. Though often considered a novel of despair, Ole Rölvaag's *Giants in the Earth,* a story of Norwegian settlers in eastern Dakota, presents a prolonged study in the human capacity for extemporization. The psychological deterioration of the wife and the ultimate tragedy of her husband have blurred the fact that the latter prevails in almost every particular that he turns his hand to. As Rölvaag's biographers have noted, his Per Hansa embodies the Norwegian Askeladd motif. He represents the child of fortune. In him "the fairy-tale influence is manifest and palpable."

At the end of their first growing season on the plains, Per Hansa and his fellows drive wagons the ninety miles back to Worthington for winter supplies. Here, against an economic backdrop, hardship and inadequacy might well obtrude. However, the chronicle of this trip, for all its rustic simplicity, fails utterly to convey an impression of deprivation. Encountering a fellow-Norwegian couple whose lot is less enviable, Per Hansa showers upon them the fruit of his own apparent good fortune. The two men strike a bargain to provide an evening meal—a pail of Per Hansa's vegetables and a bit of milk from the couple's cow. But the agreement means little to the hero of this story. He gives them each a pailful, and, when the husband broaches the subject of potatoes on credit, Per Hansa leaves him eight pailfuls and a promise: " 'I'll bring you a whole load. . . . I'll take the money when I get it.' " Indeed, he becomes almost overbearing in his munificence. As a parting gesture he lays out a fish, a pailful of carrots and his finest melon, and, while driving off, he shouts back good-naturedly: " 'Don't kill yourselves eating now!' " He appears here as a sojourner from a smiling land; "he couldn't remember when life had been so much fun!" In Worthington things go equally well. A widow and her children become the objects of Per Hansa's generosity. He deals effectively with the lumberman, getting "all the lime he needed, more lumber than he expected, and even some nails thrown into the bargain." In the general store he senses his financial impotence but uneasiness gives way to his usual exuberance. Even the trader seems infected by it. Though evidently driving a sound bargain, he stands the Norwegians to two rounds from his own stock while filling their liquor bottles. As Per Hansa himself had reflected while eating rooster with the widow and her boys, "it all seemed exactly like a fairy tale."

Near the end of a chapter titled "Facing the Great Desolation," Rölvaag shows Per Hansa engaged in late fall tasks following his supply trip to Worthington. While at the Minnesota town, he purchased with an air of mystery an inexplicably large amount of twine and rope. Having returned, indeed even while the wagons make their way westward, he prepares to bring off his coup. Per Hansa has been eyeing the Sioux River and now he constructs nets with which to fish it. Moreover, as he informed Beret, but not his excited boys, he would take ducks from the nearby marsh with the net as well. Thus, on waking one morning Beret finds her fully-clothed husband stretched beside her, and to her irritation, what appears to be a pile of clothes heaped in the middle of the floor. Impeccable housekeeper that she is, Beret seizes upon the eyesore but finds that it is not hastily discarded apparel—"it was a new net, sheeted and fully rigged, as a new net ought to be!" And this singularly impressive work is no empty exercise. Soon the Sioux River yields its bounty to the nets and the mastery of Per Hansa. "Heaps" of safely frozen fish now lie outside the prairie dwelling. The ducks of the marsh have no more success in evading the wily Norwegian and his net: "Per Hansa had figured out every detail in his mind; if the ducks got the best of him on one tack, he would fool them on another; into the net somehow they must go!" Thus early winter finds Per Hansa and his boys distributing gifts of ducks throughout the neighborhood, and with what had seemed a peculiarly large salt purchase from Worthington, filling every available container with salt fish, evidently with an eye for economic betterment.

Triumphs come easily to Per Hansa, and not all are won by the net. In the same fall and winter when fish and game fall so readily to his prey, he dazzles his neighbors with the interior aspect of his sod-house. The widow in Worthington had apprised him of the use of lime for white-washing dirt walls, and part of his deal with the lumberman had been for that article. Now when his fellows come, Per Hansa basks in the warmth of his "little triumph"—"Why . . . why . . . what in the world was this? . . . My stars, how fine it looked!" For Beret, the newly done walls are a mixed blessing. The maddeningly unbroken whiteness of the winter plains has now forced itself into the sanctuary of her home; it blinds her and she hangs her head to give tired eyes the relief of the brown-black dirt floor. Still, she realizes that "Per Hansa could accomplish the most marvellous things. . . ." Her husband both recognizes and savors his victories. "It seemed to him that he never liked his neighbors so well" as when they stood awe-stricken before the gleaming whiteness of his walls. Indeed, he strays into simple conceit and an exchange between him and the stolid Hans Olsa shows him unwittingly hurling defiance at the forces which ultimately would destroy him:

> "You have made it pretty fine inside, Per Hansa; but He Who is now whitening the outside of your walls does fully as well. . . . You shouldn't be vain in your own strength, you know!"

> "Oh, nonsense, Hans Olsa!" laughed Per Hansa. "What are you prating about? . . . Here, take along a couple more ducks for Sörrina!" . . .

Fish nets and white-washed walls evidence man's prevailing in precise and particular endeavors. To be sure, these microcosmic victories occasionally act as little more than dramatic contrasts for ultimate and complete failure of some sort. But to a degree that seems generally to have gone unrecognized, they represent details in a general pattern wherein the characters of the plains literature subdue their environment. In these stories, man, not nature, emerges triumphant.

As Carl Van Doren once noted, Herbert Quick's *Vandemark's Folly* contains unsatisfying, "romantic conventions," and so, perhaps, it occupies a position on the peripheries of this class of fiction. The Iowa prairies give in readily; trees spring up with little attention; Vandemark, the pioneer, drains Hell Slew and goes on to comfortable prosperity. Though inserted partly in irony and partly in allusion to unforeseen trials yet ahead, Vandemark's reflections at the outset of the chapter "The Plow Weds the Sod" reveal the facility of the process:

> This morning it had been wilderness; now it was a field. . . . Surely this was a new world! Surely, this was a world in which a man with the will to do might make something of himself. No waiting for the long processes by which the forests were reclaimed; but a new world with new processes, new neighbors, new ideas, new opportunities, new victories easily gained.

It was easier on the Iowa prairies—"new victories easily gained"—but the upshot was the same in Cather's Nebraska, Fisher's Idaho, Rölvaag's Dakota and even Garland's middle border.

Between parts one and two of *O Pioneers!*, Willa Cather makes an abrupt transition from the realm of man's struggle with nature to the realm of human inter-relations. The titles, "The Wild Land" and "Neighboring Fields," reflect the change. At the end of part one, Alexandra Bergson feels "the future stirring." Though lacking their sister's prophetic foresight, Lou and Oscar have at least become resigned to life on the Nebraska Divide, no longer seeking excuses to flee. Berg-

son affairs now encompass overt land speculation—" 'let's try to do like the shrewd ones,' " Alexandra urges Lou. Pioneers have tamed the wild land and can now turn to each other. As part two opens, John Bergson, father of Alexandra, Lou and Oscar, has been dead sixteen years:

> . . . he would not know the country under which he has been asleep. The shaggy coat of the prairies . . . has vanished forever. From the Norwegian graveyard one looks out over a vast checker-board, marked off in squares of wheat and corn. . . . Telephone wires hum along the white roads. . . . From the graveyard gate one can count a dozen gaily painted farm-houses. . . .

> The Divide is now thickly populated. The rich soil yields heavy harvests; the dry, bracing climate and the smoothness of the land make labor easy for men and beasts.

It was, of course, no child's play working this transformation. But Willa Cather spends little time describing the obstacles. She gives John Bergson, lying on his deathbed, a brief interval in which to reflect upon his failure to harness the land. And after his death, a succession of bad years pushes the settlers to the wall. But this latter calamity of drouth and failure seems unconvincing. It is anticlimactic—"the last struggle of a wild soil against the encroaching plowshare." Artistically, it seems a contrivance, the better to exhibit Alexandra's strength. Practically, it provides the milieu in which she can copy the tactics of Charley Fuller in town and turn to the aggrandizement of the Bergson holdings.

A reviewer of Vardis Fisher's *Toilers of the Hills* described the life of Dock and Ope Hunter as "a long agony relieved only by a kind of litany of pain." However adequate this may seem at first glance, it fails to note another way in which their agony was relieved—by ultimate, complete success in subduing the Idaho hills. To be sure, Ope has sunk into pitiable and unresisting apathy. But Dock and those around him have mastered the techniques of dry farming; they have overcome the disastrous combination of wheat roots only six inches long and soil moisture which begins a full foot beneath the surface. Though no longer caring, Ope muses over her husband's conquest:

> [she] knew what great emotions, of glory . . . and of sadness, were shaking him deeply in this year of triumph. He was a little afraid, she knew, to believe that he had won, that the other men had won or were winning; he was afraid that he would wake from a dream and find before him, not fields of gold, but grain burnt to the ground and acres of weeds, and hawks crying out of the sky . . . she went back down the years, remembering the first of starvation and loneliness, and the others that came after, one and another, and another, each with its trial and loss, each adding little by little to Dock's victory . . .

Viewing it in retrospect, Ope recognizes that she has been more hindrance than help to her husband. The victory over Antelope belongs to Dock; but victory it is nonetheless.

With apparently appropriate grimness, Ole Rölvaag titled the final, tragic chapter of *Giants in the Earth* "The Great Plain Drinks the Blood of Christian Men and Is Satisfied." The first page of the chapter generalizes about the hazards of the wilderness—Indians, madness, heat, storms, prairie fires, drunkenness, "toil and travail, famine and disease." However, immediately thereafter, still in a general vein, Rölvaag does a *volte-face.* He is not, he indicates, chronicling disaster, but quite the opposite:

> And it was as if nothing affected the people in those days. They threw themselves into the Impossible, and accomplished the Unbelievable. If anyone succumbed in the race—and that often happened—another would come and take his place. Youth was in the race; the unknown, the untried, the unheard-of was in the air; people caught it, were intoxicated by it, threw themselves away, and laughed at the cost. Of course it was possible—everything was possible out here. There was no such thing as the Impossible any more. The human race has not known such faith and such self-confidence since history began. . . .

His was a tale of magnificent accomplishment, not futility. That final chapter reveals the Dakota prairie drinking the blood of two particular men, Hans Olsa and Per Hansa. Hans Olsa represents stolidity; he is a powerful and righteous man, slow in thought and action. He provides the illumination of contrast for the volatile, inspired and even whimsical genius of his comrade, the hero Per Hansa. The affairs of these two individuals as they end their travails bear out fully the sanguine generalization with which Rölvaag prefaced the chapter.

Hans Olsa has prospered. He now owns 480 acres. He has fenced his third quarter-section and uses it exclusively for pasturing a "large herd." This last manifestation of plenty brings him down. During the blizzards of 1881 he goes there to look after his cattle, becomes overheated in repairing a shed, and consequently takes to his deathbed with pneumonia. From the mystic and half-crazed perspective of Beret, Hans Olsa has done *too* well. Thus, she berates her husband, Per Hansa, for the preoccupation with worldly success which he shares with the dying man:

> "You know what our life has been: land and houses, and then more land, and cattle! That has been his whole concern—that's been his very life. Now he is beginning to think about not having laid up treasures in heaven. . . ."

Called to the bedside of this man who has laid up treasures here instead of in the hereafter, Per Hansa accepts the dying charge, not of a man fleeing a world of poverty and frustration, but of one reluctantly leaving a manifestly going concern. Per Hansa must take care of "a couple of little debts" which he owed in Sioux Falls. Then Hans Olsa instructs him as to the stipulations of payment on the various debts owed him—stipulations which turn out to be gratifyingly generous. His wife, Sorïne, should stay on the farm, "for this was the country of the future—of that he was certain." Per Hansa must advise her and see that she hires "an honest and capable manager." If Little-Hans shows any scholarly aptitude, he should go to St. Olaf College. "Or if the Lord had destined him for the ministry—But that was probably expecting too much. . . ."

Per Hansa's is paramountly a success story. Grasshoppers, storms, hardships—the ingenious mastery of this redoubtable Norwegian has prevailed over all. In the fall before the winter of tragedy, he works himself and his sons unstintingly, and hires a number of men besides. "He needed all the help he could get; for there was the new house to be built, the crops to be harvested, the fall plowing that must be done . . ." He

took satisfaction from the unprecedented snows of that fateful winter; they assured a bumper crop next season. In the next fall, he told the boys, they would build a new barn. They would avoid the mistakes of "that fool Torkel Tallaksen," whose structures were unsurpassed in attracting attention. "But they were going to have a real show barn, just the same—red with white cornices, because he always thought those colors looked the best. . . ." Their building would incorporate some of the features and devices utilized by "the big farmers in the East" about whom he had been reading in the *Skandinaven.* Per Hansa enriched whatever he touched.

Even more dramatically than in the case of Hans Olsa, success becomes Per Hansa's undoing. To be sure, other things victimize him, perhaps even the fates; but he is nominated as sacrifice to the dark forces existing within his wife's bothered mind largely because of a record free of failure. Driven to morbid despondence by the psychopathic religiosity of an obsessed Beret (who urges upon him the necessity of a minister rather than a doctor), the dying Hans Olsa prevails upon his bosom friend to set off into the storms to fetch one able to point the way to eternal peace. Per Hansa recognizes the dangers and even the hopelessness of such a venture—"God pity him who had to travel the prairie these days!" But Hans Olsa cries out to his long-time comrade, " 'Oh, Per Hansa! . . . There never was a man like you . . . !' " And by means of insidious egging and a final insult, Beret ultimately compels her husband to try. However, she does so not just at the urgings of her own, angry God. She does so partly in light of Per Hansa's exclusively triumphant record: " '. . . we all have a feeling that nothing is ever impossible for you—and I thought that perhaps you might find a way out of this, too!' " The central figure of this powerful novel has not experienced too many setbacks; he has experienced too few. As Allan Nevins put it in a review, "he is too gallant of soul, too sure of his powers, too high-spirited to turn back while it is yet time."

Because he was involved in working a major change of direction in American writing, Hamlin Garland exceeds in literary significance most of the authors who depicted the life of the plains farmer. Moreover, he often receives credit for having given the classically grim account of that existence. In the autobiographical *A Son of the Middle Border,* Garland described a return trip to the West after six years' absence. What he saw caused him anguish, and he asked himself the often-quoted question: " 'Why have these stern facts never been put into our literature . . . ?' " It was, of course, a rhetorical question calling for remedy more than for answer. It set the tone for his most important work, the collection of short stories titled *Main-Travelled Roads.* In light of this source of inspiration, Lars Åhnebrink's assessment of these stories seems judicious—they were meant "mainly to present a protest against the romantic portrayal of the Middle West." However, there is a tendency to overemphasize the sternness with which Garland conveyed the facts of *Main-Travelled Roads.* In *The American Mind* Henry Steele Commager, for example, referred to the life represented in that work as one "where every house had its message of sordid struggle and half-hidden despair, and all the good days were in the past . . ." *Main-Travelled Roads,* according to John T. Flanagan, told the "bitter truth of the hopeless struggles" waged by coulee dweller and plains pioneer. Indeed, Flanagan felt that Garland erred in being too single in his purpose of revealing the grim, thus overlooking the lighter contrasts. Even more extremely, Lucy Lockwood Hazard wrote [in her *The*

Frontier in American Literature] that these stories "are all variations of the same theme: the ugliness, the monotony, the bestiality, the hopelessness of life on the farm." "An analysis of one," she assured her readers, "will give the spirit of all."

But does it? Certainly the main-traveled road of the West "is long and wearyful, and has a dull little town at one end and a home of toil at the other." However, only two of the stories in the work as originally published convey despair and hopelessness in any thorough, descriptive and convincing fashion. In "Up the Coulé" Howard McLane returns to the Wisconsin farm of his childhood after a long absence which has brought him prosperity in the arts. His evident well-being stands in embarrassing contrast to the condition of his farm-locked brother, Grant, and of his mother. The farm has crushed the old woman and has defeated and embittered the brother. And Howard can not change the gloomy picture. When he offers to stake his brother to a better life, Grant turns him down: " 'You can't help me now. It's too late!' " "Under the Lion's Paw," which Hazard considers typical of the entire book, presents an indictment of unearned increment. Driven out of Kansas by grasshoppers, Tim Haskins rents a run-down farm from land speculator Jim Butler for three years with the option of buying or re-renting at the end of that term. Haskins works "like a fiend," and Jim Butler, returning at the end of the three years, notes with satisfaction the improvements that his renter has made. Consequently, he doubles the rent and the buying price. If Haskins will not meet the terms, he can get out. This blow to the helpless renter should not cause one to overlook the fact that it was *man*, not prairie farm nature, which confounded Tim Haskins. He had mastered the *land* and made it fairly bloom.

But Garland's main-traveled road provides ample contrasts to scenes of distress. Follow it far enough, he directed his readers in an opening epigram, and "it may lead past a bend in the river where the water laughs eternally over its shallows." In the six stories originally contained in this collection, as the author himself remarked many years later, these latter, sanguine aspects appear far more commonly than is often supposed.

First of all, Garland evidently had no monomania for depicting the mud and the dung of the cowlot. Indeed, in these stories the farm seems as much a unifying *locus* as it does a unifying *theme*. In at least two of the selections the farm background of the characters strikes one as being almost coincidental. "The Return of a Private" is pre-eminently what the title indicates. The opening story, "A Branch-Road," deals with youthful love and its ultimate triumph, and apparently depends little, if at all, upon the Iowa farm setting. One commentator, noting the purposeful arrangement of these stories, wrote that *Main-Travelled Roads* begins with a tale of "young" love, and, in "Mrs. Ripley's Trip," closes with "the ashes of an old one."

More importantly for the consideration at hand, the characters of this work have the ability to accomplish things. Their lives do not consist of unrelieved futility. In "A Branch-Road" the lovers, Will Hannan and Agnes Dingman, have a misunderstanding and in a prideful huff Will leaves for the far West. Seven years later he returns to Rock River and is horrified and guilt-stricken at the transformation in Agnes, who is now married to a handsome but essentially brutal and boorish man. What had once been a beautiful and vigorous woman is now hardly more than a skeleton. However, Agnes has not fallen victim to prairie farm penury. Her father-in-

law has been in the position to foreclose mortgages on helpless widows. Her husband has a taste for "fast nags" and the wherewithal to indulge it. She has simply fallen in with a family whose spirit is informed by "a petty utility." Will and Agnes had erred grievously; but, as he tells her, they could still right the situation. He has money, and she and her baby must leave with him. Feeling the obligation to lift the blight from her life, Will holds out, in good faith and with ability to perform, an immediate European vacation, a fine home in Houston, his salary, cattle, books, a piano, the theater and concerts. When everyone else is away, the three simply leave—"and the world lay before them."

The first part of the disjointed story titled "Among the Corn Rows" depicts Rob Rodemaker's affairs on his Dakota prairie homestead and conveys general comments on the situation there. Through his spokesman, a rather artificially injected editor Seagraves, Garland passes basically optimistic judgments. For example, Rob symbolizes "the nameless longing of expanding personality." His kind would destroy hate, prejudice and class distinctions. Practically, Rob is a man of capabilities:

> He had dug his own well, built his own shanty, washed and mended his own clothing. He could do anything and do it well. He had a fine field of wheat, and was finishing the ploughing of his entire quarter-section.

He has " 'good reasons' " for liking the new country:

> "The soil is rich, the climate good so far, an' if I have a couple o' decent crops you'll see a neat upright goin' up here, with a porch and a baywinder."

Then Rob boards the train for Waupac County, Wisconsin to find something the plains can not provide—a wife. Among the corn rows, he finds Julia Peterson—overworked, too young yet to be broken by it, and, like Agnes Dingman, forced to slave, not out of necessity, but to meet the demands of a harsh man. Her miserly Norse father could hire help, but Julia, a strong girl, does the work for nothing. Rob courts her during one afternoon in the corn rows, and they leave that night for Dakota. Evidently, ease does not await them. But a young man who can spare a dollar to still the tongue of a too-observant little brother must have some future.

And "Mrs. Ripley's Trip," the final story of the book as originally published, ends on a note of at least qualified triumph. Mrs. Ripley, an old farm woman, has been away from "Yaark State" twenty-three years and now suddenly she announces to an astounded husband that she is returning for a visit. The old pair do little more than eke out a living, and so, a worried Ethan Ripley views it as a near impossibility. But, "troubles always slid off his back like punkins off a haystack," and he tells a tearfully moved wife:

> "Wal, the upshot is, I sent t' town for some things I calc'late you'd need. An' here's a ticket to Georgetown, and ten dollars."

In fact, Mrs. Ripley, by herself, had put away enough money coin by coin, to finance the excursion. Of course, the old lady's sojourn was no colossal stroke; but for humble people in a simple setting it had trenchant import. The vacation over,

> she took up her burden again, never more thinking to lay it down . . . (but) her trip was a fact now;

no chance could rob her of it. She had looked forward twenty-three years toward it, and now she could look back at it accomplished.

Much of the same ambivalence regarding success pervades *Jason Edwards,* the story of an "average man" who meets defeat in the Boston labor market and then succumbs to the lure of the land speculators' West, where trout-filled brooks run by every homestead. The Dakota prairie treats him little better than the stifling and squalid city. Brought down by drouth, Edwards encounters the final calamity in the form of a hailstorm. It ruins him both financially and physically. But salient features of the novel have a quite different ring. First of all, Jason Edwards plays a peculiarly subordinate role in the book and his misfortunes are more nearly disclosed than described. Walter Reeves holds the book together. This simple young man with capacity and determination rises to the heights in Boston editorial circles and comes to love Jason's daughter Alice, a girl whose future as a singer seems assured. Affluence and happiness await her if she marries Reeves, but a feeling of personal obligation compels her to go with her luckless family. Years later Reeves and the hailstorm arrive almost simultaneously at the Edwards farm. In the wake of the storm Reeves persuades Alice to marry him and persuades her family to occupy an extra house he owns in the East. Reeves, it appears, could have spared them all of their hardship. In succoring them now, he was acting as "sort of a special providence," but he had been willing and able to play "lieutenant of God" all along. Only Jason's pride and his daughter's willfulness had stood in the way.

In his preface which so clearly anticipated Frederick Jackson Turner's effort of a few months later, Garland made it clear that it was not the frontier itself which brought ruin to its prospective inhabitants. Indeed,

> the West has been the escape-valve of social discontent in the great cities of America. Whenever the conditions of his native place pressed too hard upon him, the artisan or the farmer has turned his face toward the prairies and forests of the West. The emigrant not only bettered his own fortunes, on the whole, but he bettered the conditions of his fellows who remained, by reducing the competition for employment.

The frontier had held out a true promise, which had been translated into a mythic and hopeful dream. "But to-day this dream—this most characteristic American emotion—is almost gone. Free land is gone. . . . What will be the outcome?"

One can find reasons both abundant and apparent for the prevalence of the success theme in this literature. Some of them have ready application only to particular individuals. In the case of Hamlin Garland, for example, there is good cause for supposing that the literary flavor characterizing the writing of W. D. Howells and others of the 1880s and 1890s had a stronger influence than analyses of *Main-Travelled Roads* often indicate. Garland took some philosophical implications from the same men who inspired Emile Zola, but, as Lars Åhnebrink has pointed out [in his *Crumbling Idols: Twelve Essays on Art Dealing Chiefly with Literature, Painting, and the Drama by Hamlin Garland*], the Frenchman's subject matter proved too grimly brutal. He bemoaned the "satyriasic French novelists" who could "scent a suggestive situation with the nostrils of a vulture" and sought instead a presentation of "healthy and vigorous men and women."

Pursuit of the same theme has led another scholar to argue that Garland tailored his early "realistic" work more nearly to fit editorial predilections than to convey artistic or reformist convictions. In a surprising number of cases, B. O. Flower's radical *Arena* received Garland pieces *after* they had been submitted to such journals as the *Century* and *Harper's Weekly.* For Garland, he wrote, "reform and realism were never in themselves primary literary or intellectual pursuits. They were accessory for a time to his campaign for intellectual and literary success." He compromised readily. When he felt the pressure of Middle West antagonism he turned, according to Lars Åhnebrink, "with relief and joy to the Rocky Mountain area and its heroic and romantic types."

Both Garland and Quick were products of the farming frontier and both experienced enough disgruntlement with conditions there to espouse the doctrines of Henry George. However, neither felt strongly enough to take direct exception to the existing state of things. Thus, as Lewis Atherton has shown, Garland, evidencing "the needless conflict of wealth versus humanism," could debase himself in the presence of Henry Ford, a man truly successful by time-honored American standards. And Quick, though he spoke in his autobiography of his "wild radicalism," made an essentially positive assessment of the life he knew. Writing in the 1920s, he noted the prevalence of "the view-point of contempt, of which we have successful literary products in recent years." But, he added, there was another approach—"that of the searcher for whatever good he can find." He left no doubt as to his position:

> . . . my revolt was based on my high estimate of the good in our present system, and the yearning to take away the barriers that bar the growth of our inherent beneficent tendencies. Our other friends seem to be prone to shut their eyes to the good, and impliedly to demand the destruction of a thing which is sound in the main. . . . My attitude has always been one of admiration for what the human race has done for itself and confidence in what it might accomplish. . . . There is so much that is good in any community if one only gives it its true value.

An outlook so positive would be highly unlikely to inspire vengefully realistic literary creations.

Even the immigrant Rölvaag, in whom the ambivalence between optimism and pessimism is patent, at times unashamedly espoused America's positive bent for progressive accomplishment. In an interview he once recalled his impressions of America after returning from a visit to Norway. Aboard a New York streetcar he sat enthralled as the motorman manifested his Americanness. Though the track was blocked by horses, the driver set his car in motion shoving the animals forward for two blocks:

> And all the while I sat there in the car thrilled to the core of my being. . . . This was America— hurry and rush, clang, clang, over the top—if you can't do it one way, try another! Such a thing as that would never have happened in a European street . . . [nor] been done by a European motorman. And I liked it, I liked it.

With precisely that spirit, he imbued Per Hansa.

In a study of Willa Cather's search for values William Randall III portrayed *O Pioneers!* and *My Ántonia* as embodiments of one of the dominant cultural concepts of nineteenth-century America, a concept that readily embraced total mastery of the land. She gave artistic localization, he wrote, to what Henry Nash Smith described in American thinking as the garden of the world—the scene of abundant and innocent agrarian simplicity. Cather's Nebraska is "paradisiac in the extreme." Her farmers of the Divide appear like Adam and Eve with one difference: they have to fabricate their Eden. The garden of the Middle West is disciplined nature, not wild nature. As John Ward put it, "a corn field surrounded by a split rail fence" provided the backdrop for the ideal American scene. In *O Pioneers!* Alexandra Bergson's efforts eventuate almost hurriedly in "triumph." The outcome of the endeavors of "The Wild Land" is, according to Randall, "more successful than that of any other activity recorded in a Willa Cather novel." Though the garden established is more nearly the theme of *My Ántonia*, it is readily recognizable at the outset of part two of *O Pioneers!:*

> When you go out of the house into the flower garden, there you feel again the order and fine arrangement manifest all over the great farm; in the fencing and hedging, in the windbreaks and sheds, in the symmetrical pasture ponds. . . . There is even a white row of beehives in the orchard, under the walnut trees.

Nebraska quickly becomes "neatly classical squares, triangles, and rectangles of fertile soil." Indeed, tragedy and defeat enter the Divide country only *after* the physical garden has been realized. Thus, Marie Shabata and Emil Bergson have their last, fatal meeting under a white mulberry tree in the orchard, through the hedgerows of which Frank Shabata shoots and kills them.

In more general terms the writers of Great Plains realism evidently used human achievements as contrivances for dramatic impact. By according their characters accomplishments, they could all the more effectively in turn impart an aura of disaster. This contrapuntal device took on two readily observable, though often intermingled, dimensions—one chronological, one sexual. As an illustration of the former, Tim Haskins in "Under the Lion's Paw" experiences heartwarming progress which only heightens the reader's outrage when the farmer's good fortune is obliterated by a Jim Butler bent upon unearned increment. Here, success dramatizes subsequent failure. In *Giants in the Earth,* Per Hansa's situation illustrates both dimensions. On the one hand, his complete mastery and self-confidence heighten the tragedy of his own ultimate destruction, and, on the other, they provide a background against which his wife's despairing religiosity and psychological disintegration stand out in brilliant illumination.

In a reference to the writings of Garland and Cather, Vernon L. Parrington remarked that, however convincing, they stopped short of penetrating to "the hidden core of futility." Literary naturalism, what Lars Åhnebrink has called a portrayal of *"life as it is in accordance with the philosophic theory of determinism,"* provided the means of illuminating that final facet. By and large, the writers of prairie-plains realism refused its use, and by so doing left their characters happily free to work their own destinies.

In *Toilers of the Hills* Vardis Fisher has Ope reflect upon man's struggle with Idaho nature in a way which is almost tritely naturalistic. The efforts of the dry farm pioneers seemed to her "like the drama of ants trying to build their kingdom in a plowed field." They were "tiny things lost here and there among their efforts, scarring the grey breast of the

earth and sending up clouds of dust." They seemed "no less absurd than hopeless." Yet, for all its grimness, the book does not partake of pessimistic determinism. The above metaphor represented only the plaintive forebodings of the wife, the deterioration of whom Fisher so studiously chronicles. The husband's outlook is informed by a quite different notion, one which ultimately brings him triumph. When Herbert Quick's Jacob Vandemark realizes his growing desire for the girl he has befriended and when he senses a threat to her well being, he readies himself for violence. "It is," Vandemark muses, "the way of all male animals. . . . " However, this vague note of naturalistic atavism passes quickly, never to be resurrected. Willa Cather, of course, came to epitomize unyielding and traditional opposition to the deterministic hallmark of naturalism.

In *The Beginnings of Naturalism in American Fiction* Lars Åhnebrink analyzed the writings of Hamlin Garland along with those of Stephen Crane and Frank Norris. And most assuredly, grimly deterministic conventions appear in his depictions of the middle border. In "Up the Coulé" Grant McLane notes bitterly that a man like himself is "just like a fly in a pan of molasses." Jason Edwards' daughter Alice recognizes life as a "relentless, horrible struggle." The frontiersman Bailey of *The Moccasin Ranch* while watching a human tragedy taking place sees it as "infinitesimal."

> He came also to feel that the force which moved these animaliculae was akin to the ungovernable sweep of the wind and snow—all inexplicable, elemental, unmoral.

However, in spite of such patent illustrations, Åhnebrink considers Garland's pessimism and determinism to have been "fairly superficial" and to have originated primarily from social indignation. The son of the middle border was keenly aware of corruption and oppression, but he believed in the efficacy of reform. Thus, directly before his deterministic reflection Bailey negates its force by concluding that the unhappy affair involving husband, wife and lover "was born of conventions largely." And in *Jason Edwards,* Garland's closest approximation of naturalism, men and their institutions, not blind forces, confound the "average man." Why must we live on the pitiless prairie?, Alice asks. Because, she answers, "men push us out." Even the crucial hailstorm itself fails clearly to manifest malignly uncontrollable powers. When a heckler challenges the village radical to blame it on the administration or taxation, he retorts in a confidently Georgeian vein:

> "I'll bet I can. If we hadn't give away s' much land to the railroad an' let landsharks gobble it up, an' if we'd taxed 'em as we ought to, we wouldn't be crowded away out here where it can't rain without blowing hard enough to tear the ears off a cast-iron bull-dog."

However grim and miserable her plight, Lucretia Burns of *Prairie Folks* "might have sung like a bird if men had been as kind to her as Nature." In the same story when Lily the schoolteacher asks her beau, Radbourn, what is the way out for people like Sim Burns and his wife, the young man—here speaking for Garland—has ready answers. First, he suggests the preaching of "noble discontent" in place of the "soporific" message of orthodox religion. Then, he launches upon a point by point outline of the Henry George system. A shrug of the shoulders would have been a more appropriate reflection of pessimistic determinism. For Garland, "the universe was friendly if only man would make it so." His harshest writings seemed to indicate that little more was needed than the institution of the single tax.

Both Vernon L. Parrington and Henry Steele Commager have noted the philosophical inadequacy of Cather and Garland, and have noted admiringly that it was avoided by Ole Rölvaag in *Giants in the Earth*—it portrays "futility," "the end is futility." By the 1920s when Rölvaag wrote this novel, the deterministic element had grown more subtle and had been internalized. The forces impinging upon men's lives were more nearly psychological or physiological than sociological or economic as they had been for earlier naturalists. The futility was "moral," wrote Commager, because in the physical and material realm Per Hansa could achieve handsomely. Though the "Norns of his fathers" and the "hidden weakness of fearful souls" ultimately destroyed him, the singular Norwegian was, according to Parrington, "the strong, the capable one who never failed, who was cunning enough to outwit fate itself. . . ." Whatever dark determinisms were at play, there is no doubting Per Hansa's mastery of the Dakota plains.

Finally and most evidently, these writers combined accomplishment and success with harshness and tragedy because in an authentic portrayal the former were as important as the latter. In the concluding paragraph of *Let the Hurricane Roar*, Rose Wilder Lane has the prairie mother musing as she studies her dugout-born child.

> Somehow, without quite thinking it, she felt that a light from the future was shining in the baby's face. The big white house was waiting for him, and the acres of wheat fields, the fast driving teams and swift buggies. If he remembered at all this life in the dugout, he would think of it only as a brief prelude to more spacious times.

The almost saccharine hopefulness calls to mind Edmund Wilson's dissatisfaction with far grimmer pieces of western literature for their unconvincing sunniness. Still, such depictions do more than glaringly misrepresent. If, as Wilson Clough suggests, "self-pitying outcries" seem comparatively absent from the literature of the western locale, it has something to do with the fact that "the west, historically, has always implied the chance to move on, to refuse the final despair of economic or social defeat. . . ." Thus, the celebrational tone has at least partial congruity in literary treatments.

But fellow men often proved less tractable than the land; and the unhappy aspects of Great Plains literature frequently enter *after* the pioneer has worked his will upon the natural setting. Thus, one of William Randall's judgments of *O Pioneers!* has general appropriateness.

> In a larger sense, it can be regarded as a kind of allegory on Western man and his entire history. It shows him—as he has historically been—as much more successful in dealing with his physical environment than with his fellow man: Alexandra's saga follows a success-failure pattern as she moves away from relatively simple problems and toward the more complex.

In *The Moccasin Ranch*, Hamlin Garland telescoped the theme of unhappy completion into ten months of Dakota homesteading. The chapter titles—"March," "May," "June," "August," "November" and "December"—accentuate the process of maturation. In "March" and "May" the virgin land has a "mystical and glorious" effect upon the settlers; they revel in the "wonder and beauty of the new world." They set about their tasks in a "holiday mood," and simplicity and hard work forestall the entry of "envy and hatred and suspicion." But the elation passes and the mood of the land grows "gray and sad" as problematical human interrelations develop. In "December" a pioneer woman, wife of a weak and ineffectual man, abandons her home to flee with the lover by whom she is pregnant. The inability of Garland's spokesman in the story to ascribe guilt and innocence, right and wrong, conveys the loss of idyllic simplicity. Complexity had routed certainty. Even into Hamlin Garland's well ordered moral world, doubt and ambivalence had crept. At the outset, God was there, just behind the "western clouds"; but now the land was "accursed."

The sombre tone of the most distinguished literary portrayals of the Great Plains farm in the *post*-pioneer setting provide an inferential substantiation of the "success-failure" pattern. In his novel of the Saskatchewan prairies, *Our Daily Bread*, Frederick Philip Grove spares his readers nearly all of the details of how John Elliot achieved affluence. Elliot had been a dreamer, "but his dreams had a way of coming true." He now has pure-bred stock, the best equipment that money can buy, and a barn that would grace an agricultural college. But his "one great dream of family life" means more to him. That dream, so immensely difficult of attainment, provides the subject matter of Grove's gloomy novel. Social and economic complements to the domestic ruin of *Our Daily Bread* appear in Lois Phillips Hudson's *The Bones of Plenty*, a tale of North Dakota farm life in the 1930s, and in Sophus K. Winther's Grimsen family trilogy. The latter, though it opens in the nonfrontier setting of eastern Nebraska in 1898, exhibits some of the "success" which, in this literature, antedates the "failure." A modicum of "hope and challenge" obtains at the opening of *Take All to Nebraska*. However, it hurriedly gives way to the dominant overtones of frustration and tragedy.

The transformation of assurance and accomplishment into despair and futility appears most plainly in the writing of Rölvaag. He wove that pattern into *Giants in the Earth*, indeed into the entire trilogy. In essential isolation with only the land to subdue, Per Hansa scores victory after victory. In contrast, the opening section of *Peder Victorious* ("The Song of Life's Dismay") shows his boyish son pondering the meaning of an angry schism within the now established Lutheran community and the suicide of a young girl compelled to make open church confession of an alleged pregnancy and stillbirth. Near the end of the third volume, *Their Fathers' God*, Peder learns one of the great truths of the trilogy—" 'that Success and Happiness can't be hitched together. . . .' " In the closing scenes of that work Peder's Catholic wife wilfully torments her own child, and a wrathful Peder smashes her vessel of holy water and grinds her rosary and crucifix beneath his heel. But in earlier days there had been giants in the earth. And it was not mordant playfulness nor irony that had led Per Hansa to name his prairie-born son, Peder Victorious. (pp. 579-98)

Lewis O. Saum, "The Success Theme in Great Plains Realism," in American Quarterly, *Vol. XVIII, No. 4, Winter, 1966, pp. 579-98.*

Title page for The Frontier Series.

DARYL JONES

[*In the following excerpt, Jones discusses the dime novel Western.*]

> The thirst for works of the imagination is as strong and universal at the present time as at any former period; and we trust that of the floods which annually pour in upon the reading world, there are some fountains at which the soul may drink and feel itself refreshed and invigorated.

> —*The Western Monthly Magazine, 1833*

Perhaps it was in part the note of confidence sounded in this opening statement of Isaac Appleton Jewett's "Themes for Western Fiction" that won him, in December 1833, the first annual prize for the best essay to appear in the pages of *The Western Monthly Magazine.* Addressed to the writers of America, Jewett's essay made an impassioned plea for a new and distinctly national literature which would draw its subject matter from the rich artistic resources offered by the wilderness West. Citing the wealth of material available to writers in the landscape, characters, and incidents of the frontier, Jewett predicted that it would be from those works of the imagination which distilled the emotional impact of the West that the soul would someday drink and feel refreshed.

Though eloquently phrased, Jewett's call for a national literature nurtured on the frontier experience was not so much a new and original proposal as it was the reflection of a trend well advanced in American letters. Already, at least two epic poems, Daniel Bryan's *The Mountain Muse* (1813) and James Kirk Paulding's *The Backwoodsman* (1818), had heralded the opening of the West; *The Pioneers* (1823), *The Last of the Mohicans* (1826), and *The Prairie* (1827) had won Cooper a prominent place in American literature; and numerous short stories, novels, and pioneer biographies had emerged from the pens of Gilbert Imlay, Hugh Henry Brackenridge, Charles Brockden Brown, James McHenry, N. M. Hentz, William Joseph Snelling, Timothy Flint, Matthew St. Clair Clarke, and James Hall. The late thirties, forties, and fifties spawned an even greater body of literature that utilized frontier settings and incidents. Skilled writers like Cooper, Paulding, and Hall continued to produce Western fiction, and soon they found themselves joined by a coterie of talented newcomers, most notably Robert Montgomery Bird, whose *Nick of the Woods* (1837) won instant acclaim, and William Gilmore Simms, who dramatized life on the Southern Border both in *The Yemassee* (1835) and in the series of works known collectively as the *Border Romances* (1834-1840).

During this same period a number of less talented writers— James Strange French, Nathaniel B. Tucker, Charles W. Webber, Charles Fenno Hoffman, Emerson Bennett, A. W. Arrington, John Esten Cooke, and Mayne Reid—ground out Western fiction that proved immensely popular. Emerson Bennett's *The Prairie Flower* (1849) and *Leni-Leoti* (1849) sold one hundred thousand copies each, and Bennett's rivals were nearly as successful. Yet with the possible exception of an occasional work by Mayne Reid, these popular novels were poorly written, highly melodramatic, and embarrassingly derivative. John Myers, the hero of Cooke's *Leatherstocking and Silk* (1854), for instance, is an unintentionally amusing replica of Natty Bumppo who, in even the most extreme circumstances, seems incapable of saying anything more profound than "Anan?" By the late 1850s such novels were the rule rather than the exception. Indeed, to such an extent had Western fiction degenerated by 1858 that in June of that year William T. Coggeshall, then the Ohio State Librarian, told the Beta Theta Pi fraternity of Ohio University that "Tomahawks and wigwams, sharp-shooting and hard fights, log cabins, rough speech, dare-devil boldness, bear-hunting and corn-husking, prairie flowers, bandits, lynch-law and no-law-at-all miscellaneously mixed into 25 cents novels . . . represent the popular idea of Western Literature."

One result of this sudden deterioration in the quality of literature concerning the West has been that interpreters of the early Western have concentrated their efforts almost exclusively on works produced before 1860—particularly those by Cooper, Simms, and Bird. For the same reason, interpreters who credit Wister's *The Virginian* with resurrecting the Western from the murky realm of sub-literature have dealt exclusively with works penned after 1902—those by Andy Adams, Eugene Manlove Rhodes, William McLeod Raine, Emerson Hough, Zane Grey, Frederick Faust, and a host of more recent writers in the six-gun and sagebrush school. Consequently, with regard to the Western, the period between 1860 and 1900 might justly be termed "the forgotten era." Critics of the Western have, of course, concerned themselves with selected works by such writers as Mark Twain, Bret Harte, Hamlin Garland, and Stephen Crane—even though it remains a moot point as to whether or not the works in question are in fact "Westerns." Yet these same critics largely ignore the development during this period of that variety of story which, indisputably, is a Western.

At least two factors account for this critical neglect. On the one hand, almost all Westerns written between 1860 and 1902 appeared as dime novels or story papers printed on cheap pulp paper—a notoriously ephemeral medium. Thus, only a relatively small number of dime novels survive today, and the majority of these are inaccessible to scholars; they are either in the hands of private collectors, or they are crumbling, uncatalogued and unmicrofilmed, in the rare book vaults of a few major libraries. On the other hand, critics have, with some justification, neglected dime novel Westerns because of the genre's undeniable mediocrity. Nevertheless, it was the dime novelist—working in the comparative anonymity of a large publishing house, meeting rigid deadlines, and looking to sales as the sole measure of his artistry—who gradually, over a period of more than fifty years, fashioned many of the Western's most characteristic elements.

As a medium for the dissemination of popular fiction, the dime novel was not a strikingly original development but rather the culmination of a trend in publishing that began in the 1830s. Although the population of the United States was at that time approaching twenty million people, most of whom were literate, the majority of readers were denied access to popular literature by the high cost of hardbound books, and the limited number of libraries. All of this changed with the introduction of the steam rotary press—which lowered printing costs—and the subsequent development of new techniques in marketing and mass distribution. As early as 1839, inspired innovators in the field of publishing began tapping the potential of the mass audience; Wilson & Company of Boston initiated the publication of the weekly story paper with *Brother Jonathan,* a compilation of several short stories and chapters from serial novels, printed on cheap paper, organized in newspaper format, and issued at minimal cost to both publisher and reader. The experiment was an instant success. Other firms, spurred by the example of *Brother Jonathan,* printed their own versions, and succeeding years saw the rise of such popular story papers as *The Flag of Our Union, The New York Ledger, The New York Weekly,* and *The Youth's Companion.*

Although popular fiction in the form of fifteen- and twenty-cent serial novelettes appeared throughout the forties and fifties—series like Ballou's *The Weekly Novelette* or *Gleason's Literary Companion*—the dime novel *per se* did not appear until Erastus and Irwin Beadle, heartened by their initial success with a pamphlet entitled *The Dime Song Book,* conceived the idea of printing entire novels complete under one cover, to be sold for a dime. Engaging the services of a business associate named Robert Adams, and moving from Buffalo to New York City in 1858, they formed the publishing firm which later came to be known as the House of Beadle and Adams. In June 1860 they released the first dime novel: *Malaeska: The Indian Wife of the White Hunter.* Written by an established domestic novelist, Mrs. Ann S. Stephens, this tale of white hunters and noble savages sold 65,000 copies within a few months—a reception that virtually assured the success of the Beadle venture.

The popularity enjoyed by Beadle and Adams' "yellow-back novels" soon attracted other firms into the field. Over the years, the House of Beadle and Adams encountered its stiffest competition from five rivals. In 1863, one of the Beadle print-

ers, George Munro, set out on his own and promptly launched a lucrative series called Munro's Ten Cent Novels. In 1867, Robert DeWitt expanded his small publishing house and released the first of 1,118 dime novels that he was to publish in the next ten years. And in 1870, Norman Munro, George's brother, entered the field. Still, the greatest success fell to two relative latecomers, Frank Tousey and Street & Smith. Together with a host of smaller competitors, these firms—based in New York City and aiming their stories at a predominantly eastern audience—dominated the market until the early decades of the twentieth century, when the combined effects of rising second-class postal rates and the burgeoning film industry precipitated the decline of the dime novel.

Though classified under the rubric "dime novel," pulp thrillers released by these firms actually varied widely in format. Some, like *The New York Weekly,* were simply story papers; save for their sensational, black and white woodcut illustrations, they resembled an ordinary newspaper. Others, particularly those that flourished from 1860 to 1888, were issued semi-monthly as seven by five inch pamphlets averaging one hundred pages and priced at a dime. After 1888, publishers enlarged the format to twelve by eight inches in an effort to accommodate larger illustrations on the front cover; dime novels of this period ran from sixteen to thirty-two pages in length, and sold for only a nickel. In the 1890s these so-called "nickel weeklies" began to appear with color illustrations, and shortly thereafter some stories assumed the format of the modern paperback novel. Publishers were not, however, reluctant to release a story in more than one format, or even to reprint the same story several times under different titles. If a tale serialized in a weekly story paper received a favorable reception, publishers promptly re-released it as the latest number of an ongoing series of novels "complete under one cover."

Although formats varied, the stories were nearly all alike. Generally, they were 30,000 to 50,000 words of stirring action, inflated description, and—since authors were paid to fill a predetermined format—padded prose. They dealt with pirates, detectives, highwaymen, bootblacks, and soldiers. They concerned adventure, history, love, war, romance, life in the city and life on the sea. Popular as they were, however, all of these types of stories were outstripped in popularity by the Western. After classifying stories published by Beadle and Adams alone, Philip Durham concluded that "approximately three-fourths of the dime novels deal with the various forms, problems, and attitudes of life on the frontier, and that more than half are concerned with life in the trans-Mississippi West."

It is difficult, in retrospect, to comprehend the full extent of the popularity that the dime novel enjoyed, but it must have been phenomenal. During banner years, various firms were publishing concurrently as many as 101 different series, and some series ran to more than a thousand titles. Novels with an initial printing of 60,000 to 70,000 copies often went through ten or twelve editions in a single year. For instance, one of the earliest Westerns published by Beadle and Adams, Edward S. Ellis' *Seth Jones; or, The Captives of the Frontier,* sold out of its first printing of 60,000 copies almost immediately; translated into half a dozen languages, it eventually sold more than 600,000 copies. Sales figures similar to these were not uncommon. William Everett, writing in the prestigious *North American Review* in 1864, explained that he had been astonished to learn that by April 1, 1864 "an aggregate of five millions of Beadle's Dime Books had been put in circulation." Such sales, "almost unprecedented in the annals of booksellers," led Everett to conclude that Beadle's yellow-back novels had "undoubtedly obtained greater popularity than any other series of works of fiction published in America." In a similar comment addressed fifteen years later to readers of the *Atlantic Monthly,* W. H. Bishop contended that dime novel and story paper literature presented "an enormous field of mental activity, the greatest literary movement, in bulk, of the age, and [one] worthy of a very serious consideration for itself. Disdained as it may be by the highly cultivated for its character, the phenomenon of its existence cannot be overlooked."

And yet, for the most part, the dime novel phenomenon has been overlooked, especially as it concerns the evolution of the Western. Although Merle Curti made some initial forays into the subject in 1937, it was not until the publication in 1950 of Henry Nash Smith's *Virgin Land: The American West as Symbol and Myth* that scholars began to realize the significance of the dime novel as a cultural document. In recent studies of selected Western heroes, Kent Ladd Steckmesser, Don Russell, and William Settle have attempted to determine the role played by the dime novel in the legend-making process. Still, few attempts have been made to assess the influence of the dime novel upon the development of the Western itself. Unquestionably, the influence was profound. But what was the nature of that influence? Specifically, what influenced the development in the dime novel of those characteristic elements that have since become standard fare in the popular Western?

Certainly, the answer lies somewhere in the interplay of cultural and aesthetic dynamics. In the last four decades of the nineteenth century the United States became an industrialized nation. Between 1860 and 1870 alone, the total number of manufacturing establishments rose by eighty percent, and the value of manufactured products by one hundred percent. In railroads, mining, lumber, meat packing, iron and steel, and oil, whole industries grew up overnight, contributing not only to the national wealth but also to the independent fortunes of a new breed of capitalists—railroad builders like Vanderbilt, Stanford, and Harriman, lumber kings like Weyerhauser, meat packers like Armour and Swift, steel barons like Carnegie and Hewitt, oil men like John D. Rockefeller. Exercising aggressive business practices, and favored by lenient governmental control, these captains of industry engineered the growth of mighty trusts and monopolies that changed forever the nature of American life. Absorbing or eliminating competition, trusts developed in nearly every domain of American industry-in silver, nickel, and zinc, in rubber, leather, and glass, in sugar, salt, and crackers, in cigars, whiskey, and candy, in oil, gas, and electricity. By the turn of the century, the International Harvester Company manufactured nearly all of the nation's farm implements, Standard Oil had a practical monopoly on refining, and United States Steel made two-thirds of the country's steel products. A survey taken in 1904 showed that 319 industrial trusts had swallowed up about 5300 previously independent businesses, and that 127 utilities (including railroads) had absorbed some 2400 smaller enterprises.

For the average American, industrialization and economic growth ushered in a new and uncertain way of life. His food, his clothes, his household furnishings, his tools, the transpor-

tation he employed, were made or controlled by trusts. Mechanization threatened to eliminate his job. Affected, too, was the business life of his community. Local shops and industries went out of business, unable to compete with distant corporations. Factories closed, mortgages were assumed by Eastern banks or insurance companies, and more and more of his neighbors gave up their shops and small businesses to go to work for giant corporations whose policies exposed the wage earner to the vicissitudes of vast economic forces. Neighborhoods, too, changed as immigrants arrived in great numbers. Even the nature of the home and family changed as women and children left the home and entered the working world. Between 1870 and 1900 the proportion of women in industry rose from one eighth to one fifth, and the number of child workers between the ages of ten and fifteen rose to one and three-quarter millions. The result of this new and uncertain way of life was that the optimism with which Americans had greeted the first stirrings of the economic revolution in the early part of the century gradually eroded in the years following the Civil War. Optimism continued to be the ostensible mood of the age, but as the deleterious effects of economic growth upon the social, legal, and moral landscape of society became increasingly evident, the average American began to entertain grave doubts about the future.

Around him he saw all of the problems that accompany rapid economic change. Mechanization and the influx of immigrant labor depressed wages while prices spiraled. Severe financial panics disrupted the economy in 1873 and again in 1893. The conflict between capital and labor, long suppressed, at last erupted into the large-scale industrial violence of the great railroad strike of 1877. Strikes occurred thereafter with increasing frequency; from 1881 to 1905 the nation experienced thirty-seven thousand strikes, including the tragic Haymarket riot of 1886, the Pullman strike of 1894, and the Cripple Creek War in the Colorado coal fields. The decline in the quality of life was particularly evident in the crowded cities, where housing conditions were poor, where the crime rate was high, and where prostitution was becoming a serious problem among unemployed working girls. Yet the average American felt that there was little he could do to alter the ominous course of progress. Industrialization, urbanization, class polarization, and control of society by big business and the international agricultural market were gargantuan forces which seemingly led to the abridgment of personal freedoms and the decline of traditional morality. But though totally subject to these forces, powerless to effect any real change in his life, the common man could yet find needed diversion in popular fiction. Here, at least, there existed a world where the grim realities of everyday life did not intrude.

Observers of the time were quick to locate the allure of cheap fiction. Reverend Jonathan B. Harrison, after investigating social conditions among mill-hands in a New England factory town in 1880, was convinced that "the only effect of this kind of reading is that it serves 'to pass away the time,' by supplying a kind of entertainment, a stimulus or opiate for the mind, and that these people resort to it and feel a necessity for it in much the same way that others feel they must have whiskey or opium" [*Certain Dangerous Tendencies in American Life, and Other Papers*]. Mrs. Jennie C. Croly, a humanitarian noted for her efforts to help New York working girls, shared a more penetrating insight in testimony before the Senate Committee on Education and Labor in 1883. Working girls read pulp fiction, she explained, because "they want something very different from what they have in their daily lives. . . . They are crazy for something that is outside of themselves, and which will make them forget the hard facts of their daily lives."

Dime novelists, too, were sensitive to the needs of their audience. Eugene T. Sawyer, author of several Nick Carter detective novels and countless stories in Street & Smith's Log Cabin Library and *New York Weekly,* recognized that the primary appeal of sensational pulp fiction lay in its power to transport readers beyond the confines of their commonplace lives. "To a man whose life is measured by yards of ribbon and pounds of cheese, or bounded by the four dingy walls of a counting house," Sawyer explained, "a dime novel is a revelation and a delight. Most of my readers are mere 'supers' on the stage of life. . . . Nothing romantic ever happens to them. For all these, hungry for something to take them out of themselves, the dime novel provides a thrill per page" [Gelett Burgess, "The Confessions of a Dime Novelist," *Dime Novel Roundup,* No. 105 (May 15, 1941)].

Though dime novelists aimed their stories at a predominantly working-class audience, the appeal of the genre in fact pervaded the entire culture. Dime novels provided a source of entertainment and diversion for any individual of any social class who sought relief from the anxieties of the age. Again, somewhat defensively perhaps, Sawyer explained: "It is not, however, only the 'submerged tenth' who reads cheap stories. I have been into bookshops and seen bankers and capitalists gravely paying their nickels for the same tales their own elevator boys read. . . . Such yarns are about as good a remedy for brain fag as you could find. They're easy to read and require little effort of the mind. You can read "The Pirate of the Caribees' when your nerves forbid ethical discussions." Similarly, an author formerly employed by Beadle and Adams argued in retrospect that "It is a mistake to assume that the 'Beadle' appeal was merely to newsboys and bootblacks or the half-baked intelligences of the community. Take the 'Nick Carter' stories for example, and they were to be found in the hands of men of large business interests and public affairs who did not hesitate to acknowledge that they sought mental relaxation in following the marvelous detective's hairbreadth adventures" ["Dime Novel Days," *Dime Novel Roundup,* No. 112, (January 15, 1942)]. Clearly, the intrinsic entertainment value of dime novels—arising from their patterned experience of excitement, suspense, and release—provided a variety of mental relaxation that cut across class distinctions and stimulated broad audience appeal.

Yet a study of the evolution of the Western formula in the dime novel suggests that other, less obvious factors contributed to the popularity of pulp stories, and that these factors influenced the nature of the stories themselves. From its initial appearance in 1860 to its demise late in the second decade of the twentieth century, the dime novel Western responded to the anxieties and aspirations of the age—a function clearly reflected in the standardized setting, stereotyped characters, and conventionalized plots which developed in the stories. (pp. 1-15)

No single factor, of course, adequately accounts for the phenomenal popularity that the dime novel Western enjoyed in its time. Undoubtedly, much of its success resulted from its intrinsic entertainment value as an autonomous artistic construct—its unity of setting, character, and action, and its ordered vision of reality. So, too, its popularity no doubt resulted in part from its reliance upon an archetypal structure that

reflects and embodies the most fundamental and universal concerns of mankind. Yet both of these factors characterize all popular art forms. Neither distinguishes the Western from any other popular formula, nor does either satisfactorily account for the enduring popularity of the Western *per se.* It seems, rather, that the Western's unique character and its ensuing popularity result largely from factors which are expressly cultural.

The Western evolved as an expression of nineteenth century America's prevailing attitude toward history, progress, and the national destiny. In the early part of the century, apocalyptic visions and physiocratic theories had nurtured a poetic conception of the national destiny based on the conquest of the wilderness and the future foundation of a pastoral utopia in the West. As popularly conceived, this utopia would combine the respective advantages of civilization and wilderness while transcending the disadvantages of each; it would be a land of plenty, of human bliss, of freedom and equality. For this reason Americans revered progress, seeing in the historical process a trend toward the perfection of society and the realization of an ideal world. Yet as the century progressed the utopian vision became increasingly difficult to sustain. Gargantuan economic and social forces associated with the industrial revolution steadily polarized society, corrupted political and social institutions, and precipitated moral decline. Giant corporations swallowed up small businesses, monopolized industry, manipulated Government policy. The public became dependent on trusts like Armour, International Harvester, Weyerhauser, Standard Oil, and United States Steel for its jobs, food, clothing, housing, and transportation. Disputes between capital and labor led to bloody confrontations and paralyzing strikes. Mechanization and the influx of immigrant labor depressed wages, created unemployment, and forced many men and women into crime and vice. Americans in larger and larger numbers soon came to the realization that progress and perfection were not necessarily related. Indeed, as Cooper had predicted long before, the trend of history seemed ominous; instead of improving, the quality of life was perceptibly deteriorating. America's glorious future, once a virtual certainty, was becoming a matter for grave doubt. In the face of growing disillusionment and anxiety, the mass of Americans sought reassurance that the ideal world was still a golden possibility. And in the setting, characters, and plots of the dime novel Western they found this reassurance.

That we are still reluctant today to abandon our vision of an ideal world, a moment's glance at a newsstand, a theater marquee, or a television program guide will instantly confirm. The medium has changed, but the popular Western lives on. To be sure, the message is neither so simple nor so reassuring as it once was. With the advance of the twentieth century have come cultural and worldwide dilemmas which have brought about significant alterations in the familiar formula: external conflicts are more commonly internalized; characters are more frequently morally ambivalent; plot situations are more complex and their resolutions more often equivocal. No longer a simple nobleman like Daniel Boone or Buffalo Bill, the Western hero of today is difficult to understand and classify. Often he is the dedicated professional of television's *Have Gun, Will Travel,* but he may also be the psychopathic killer of Sergio Leone's *For a Fistful of Dollars* or the living anachronism of *Butch Cassidy and the Sundance Kid.* He may even be the drunken buffoon of *Cat Ballou.* But though the formula has changed, vestiges of the standardized setting, stereotyped characters, and conventionalized plots that evolved in the dime novel are yet recognizable. In the saloons of Matt Dillon's Dodge City walk the shades of the bumbling sidekicks and tainted women who once stood beside Deadwood Dick in the boom towns of South Dakota. In television's *Grizzly Adams,* the buckskin-clad descendants of Daniel Boone still stare into the big sky, though with a more critical and worldly eye than did the patriarch of the wilds. So, too, western knights-errant rove the same rolling plains that Buffalo Bill roamed decades ago, though these days their guns are most often for hire. Altered, inverted, even parodied, the popular Western formula nonetheless survives. And it will continue to survive as long as it extends to humanity some glimmer of hope that a golden age still lies ahead. (pp. 165-68)

> *Daryl Jones, in his* The Dime Novel Western, *Bowling Green State University Popular Press, 1978, 186 p.*

FRONTIER PROTAGONISTS

RICHARD SLOTKIN

[*Slotkin is an American educator, critic, and fiction writer whose works reflect his interest in American history and in the development of an American mythology. In the following excerpt, he provides a detailed analysis of John Filson's "The Adventures of Col. Daniel Boon" (1784), asserting the importance of Filson's characterization in the development of the mythological frontier hero. For additional commentary by Slotkin, see excerpt below.*]

In 1784 John Filson, a schoolmaster turned surveyor and land speculator, returned from two years in Kentucky. In Wilmington, the metropolis of his home state of Delaware, he published *The Discovery, Settlement and Present State of Kentucke,* an elaborate real-estate promotion brochure designed to sell farm lands in the Dark and Bloody Ground to easterners and Europeans. Sales resistance was likely to be high. The Revolution had just ended, and the bloody Indian wars which had decimated the Kentucky settlements were still sputtering out in petty raids and secret murders. Thus Filson faced the classic problem of writers about the frontier since Underhill's time: how to portray the promise of the frontier without destroying his own credibility by glossing over the obviously perilous realities of the pioneer's situation.

Filson attempted to persuade his audience by composing, as an appendix to that book, a literary dramatization of a hero's immersion in the elemental violence of the wilderness and his consequent emergence as the founder of a nascent imperial republic. In "The Adventures of Col. Daniel Boon" Filson created a character who was to become the archetypal hero of the American frontier, copied by imitators and plagiarists and appearing innumerable times under other names and in other guises—in literature, the popular arts, and folklore—as the man who made the wilderness safe for democracy. The Boone narrative, in fact, constituted the first nationally viable statement of a myth of the frontier.

A myth is a narrative which concentrates in a single, dramatized experience the whole history of a people in their land. The myth-hero embodies or defends the values of his culture

in a struggle against the forces which threaten to destroy the people and lay waste the land. Myth grows out of the timeless desire of men to know and be reconciled to their true relationship to the gods or elemental powers that set in motion the forces of history and rule the world of nature. In the case of the American colonies, whose people were not native to the soil, this desire took the form of a yearning to prove that they truly belonged to their place, that their bringing of Christian civilization to the wilderness represented the fulfillment of their own destiny as children of Jehovah (rather than a perversion of that destiny) and of the land's destiny as the creation of God. (This yearning, common to all the colonies, was most clearly and intensely articulated by the Puritans.)

Filson's narrative, then, to qualify as myth, would have to draw together all the significant strands of thought and belief about the frontier that had been developed in the historical experience of the colonies, concentrate those experiences in the tale of a single hero, and present that hero's career in such a way that his audience could believe in and identify with him. Moreover, the tale would have to be constructed in such a way that it could grow along with the culture whose values it espoused, changing and adjusting to match changes in the evolution of that culture. Otherwise the tale would lose that essential quality of seeming to be drawn from the original sources of cultural experience. Ultimately, Filson's tale would have to dramatize convincingly the interdependence of Boone's destiny, the historical mission of the American people, and the destiny appointed for the wilderness by natural law and divine Providence. The evidence suggests that the Boone legend first put before the public by Filson did, in fact, fulfill these requirements. (pp. 268-69)

"The Adventures of Col. Daniel Boon" is the key to the immortality of Filson's vision of the West and of the fame of his hero, Daniel Boone. This chapter of *Kentucke* proved far more popular than the rest of the book. It was lifted out of its context and reprinted as a separate pamphlet, in anthologies of Indian war narratives and captivity narratives, and in popular literary periodicals in both Europe and the United States. It became the vehicle by which Filson's version of the frontier myth was transmitted to the literary giants of the American Renaissance and to the European Romantics. The narrative crystallizes everything that Filson had to say about the West, echoing his vision of its utopian future and paralleling the narrative movement into the wilderness that *Kentucke* as a whole follows. The Boone narrative does not state Filson's ideas explicitly (this is left for the "Conclusion"); the ideas are implicit within the drama of its events. This structuring of the book permitted Filson to concentrate on the depiction of Boone's character and allowed later writers to change the context in which the narrative was set, in accordance with changing interpretations of the frontier. For this reason, and because Boone himself was the sort of figure who continued to generate popular legends, the Boone narrative finally proved pregnant of more meanings than its author could have intended.

The Boone narrative, though ostensibly Boone's own narration of his adventures, is actually Filson's careful reworking of Boone's statements and of the legends that Filson had heard about Boone from his fellow frontiersmen. The narrative is a literary myth, artfully contrived to appeal to men concerned with literature; it is not folk legend. Filson selects incidents for portrayal and breaks into the strict chronology of events in order to establish in his reader's mind a sense of the rhythm of Boone's experience and to emphasize certain key images and symbols that define the meaning of Boone's experience. Boone's "Adventures" consist of a series of initiations, a series of progressive immersions that take him deeper into the wilderness. These initiations awaken Boone's sense of his own identity, provide him with a natural moral philosophy, and give him progressively deeper insights into the nature of the wilderness. Each immersion is followed by a return to civilization, where Boone can apply his growing wisdom to the ordering of his community, and by a momentary interlude of meditation and contemplation, in which Boone can review his experience, interpret it, and formulate the wisdom gained from it. As a result of these rhythmic cycles of immersion and emergence, he grows to become the commanding genius of his people, their hero-chief, and the man fit to realize Kentucky's destiny.

Filson casts Boone's adventures as a personal narrative, developed by the Puritans as a literary form of witness to an experience of God's grace. "The Adventures of Col. Daniel Boon" combines the conventions of form and substance of three types of personal narratives—the conversion narrative of the type written by Jonathan Edwards in his "Personal Narrative"; the narrative of personal triumph in battle, as written by Mason and Church; and the captivity narrative, the account of ordeals suffered at the hands of the wilderness's human children, the Indians. But Filson revolutionizes the Puritan forms by substituting nature or the wilderness for Jehovah as his symbol of deity. The impression conveyed by the Puritan personal narrative is that of a tightly closed, systematic, intimate universe, bound together by explicitly articulated, organic bonds between God and man—a universe manageable in size but containing all important things. The wilderness is the realm of chaos, impinging on the ordered cosmos but somehow outside the world protected by God. Filson, however, substitutes all of the wilderness landscape, its ambiguous and even hellish elements as well as its pure and paradisiacal qualities (its wigwams as well as its settlements), for the Word of God in the symbolic universe of Boone's personal narrative. He thus expands the boundaries of that universe to include the wild continent as an integral and vital part of the divine plan for the regeneration of man. At the same time, by retaining the individual experience as the central focus and source of perspective in his narrative, he preserves the sense of organic unity and order that the Puritan form possessed.

The Boone narrative begins with an account of and an apology for the hero's motivation for leaving his family and moving to Kentucky. The account is carefully calculated to overcome the objections made by opponents of emigration from Increase Mather to Buffon. If a man is civilized, why would he leave society for the savage solitude of the forest? And if he is not civilized, how can he be set up as a hero for civilized men to emulate? Boone's justification is largely pragmatic: the final results of his act are good, whatever his motives. He creates a new society through his emigration, and he does not destroy the existing society by leaving it. He returns in the end to his family. Thus the trinity of values on which Anglo-American society is based—social progress, piety, and the family—is invoked at the outset as the basic standard for judging Boone's actions. But Filson reinforces this defense by having Boone present himself as a man nurtured in the values of the eighteenth century, so that he can further justify his emigration by appealing to the "divinities" of natural reli-

gion—natural law, human reason (and the desire for knowledge), and divine Providence:

> CURIOSITY is natural to the soul of man, and interesting objects have a powerful influence on our affections. Let these influencing powers actuate, by the permission or disposal of Providence, from selfish or social views, yet in time the mysterious will of heaven is unfolded, and we behold our own conduct, from whatever motives excited, operating to answer the important designs of heaven. Thus we behold Kentucke, lately an howling wilderness, . . . rising from obscurity to shine with splendor, equal to any other of the stars of the American hemisphere.

This passage provides a major insight into the pattern of experience that is rhythmically repeated throughout the Boone narrative and the whole of *Kentucke*. Boone enters the wilderness in a state of innocence and naïveté, unsure of his own motivations and of the ultimate outcome of his adventures, but trusting in the strength of his own character and the goodness of nature to create ultimate good out of present confusion. This trusting immersion in the wilderness ultimately results in the attainment of self-knowledge and an understanding of the design of God—a state of awareness which Boone attains when he is able to stand above his experience, view it from outside, and exercise his reason upon it in order to reduce it to its essential order.

This pattern of experience is followed in the first crucial section of the narrative, in which Boone is initiated into a knowledge of the wilderness of Kentucky. With four friends, he enters Kentucky in 1769, after a fatiguing journey and "uncomfortable weather as a prelibation of our future suffering." The naïve hero is exposed to a series of experiences that give him direct knowledge of both the terror and the beauty of Kentucky. His arrival is a pastoral idyll, in which the wilderness appears to be the bucolic retreat of a divine country squire. Even the buffalo are compared to domesticated cattle. Behind the picture of peace there is a bare suggestion that the violence of man may disrupt the natural harmony: "The buffaloes were more frequent than I have seen cattle in the settlements, browsing on the leaves of the cane, or croping [*sic*] the herbage on those extensive plains, fearless, because ignorant, of the violence of man." But Boone himself is as ignorant of the threat as are the buffalo.

Boone's description of the wilderness has a peculiarly neoclassic flavor about it, with nature appearing as an artful landscape designer and master gardener, the creator of the well-wrought forest. At another level nature is Boone's hostess, welcoming him into a formal garden planted with an eye toward elegance of form and color, with animals provided apparently for the amusement of the guests:

> We . . . passed through a great forest, on [*sic*] which stood myriads of trees, some gay with blossoms, others rich with fruits. Nature was here a series of wonders and a fund of delight. Here she displayed her ingenuity and industry in a variety of fruits and flowers, beautifully coloured, elegantly shaped, and charmingly flavoured; and we were diverted with innumerable animals presenting themselves perpetually to our view.

In the eyes of Filson's Boone, the beauty of wild nature lies in the extent to which it imitates cultivated nature and implies that civilization is itself the crown of natural evolution.

Into this idyllic and civil landscape the violence of man intrudes, catching the innocents unaware. Boone and one companion are captured, their other friends driven off, their camp and furs plundered. The two men manage to escape their captors and return to camp, where they find Boone's brother Squire arrived before them. This coincidence provides Boone with an opportunity for one of those philosophical asides in which he finds the essential meaning of his experience and derives from that meaning a practical wisdom. In this case he discovers that friendship and human society are balm for the hurts inflicted by human enmity and evil: "[Our] meeting so fortunately in the wilderness made us reciprocally sensible of the utmost satisfaction. So much does friendship triumph over misfortune . . . and substitute . . . happiness in [its] room." Soon his companion is killed by Indians, and Boone and Squire are left alone in the wilderness. Yet he can still maintain his cheerfulness and confidence, indulge in civilized conversation, and articulate a stoic philosophy of asceticism and self-control:

> Thus situated, many hundred of miles from our families in the howling wilderness, I believe few would have enjoyed the happiness we experienced. I often observed to my brother. You see now how little nature requires to be satisfied. Felicity . . . is rather found in our own breasts than in the enjoyment of external things . . . it requires but a little philosophy to make a man happy. . . . This consists in a full resignation to the Will of Providence, and a resigned soul finds pleasure in a path strewed with briars and thorns.

Boone's initiation into knowledge of the wilderness cannot be accomplished, however, while even one civilized amenity remains to him. He must be stripped to the barest essentials for survival, in order to meet nature directly and without encumbrances. Thus, when their supplies run low, Squire returns to the settlement, leaving Boone with no trace of civilized life except his rifle—"without bread, salt or sugar, without company of my fellow creatures or even a horse or dog." The dark elements in the wilderness have all but subdued the light. Death has nearly triumphed over life, loneliness has succeeded companionship, and melancholy passions have all but toppled the controlling power of "philosophy and fortitude." But at this point the narrative takes a sudden turn, and Boone's melancholy is converted into a vision of the beauty and order of nature, which strengthens his spirit and gives him the determination to settle permanently in Kentucky.

Boone's melancholy takes the form of a morbid introspection, a dwelling on the insecurity of his position and his separation from his wife and family. This melancholy nearly destroys him and is overcome only when the beauty of the natural landscape forces him to turn his eyes outward. In the Puritan narrative of life in the wilderness, salvation depended on the opposite process. The Puritan needed the sense of insecurity to make vivid his dependence on God, and he pursued a course of rigorous introspection precisely in order to develop that sense of personal weakness. Where the protagonist of the Puritan captivity, yearning for God's felt presence, hearkened to a voice from the church or from his Bible, Filson's hero hears the voice of God calling him deeper into the wilderness. Filson's God makes himself apparent through the landscape, and the Word of God becomes apparent to the reader as the landscape alters Boone's attitude gradually from gloom to light and peace. Boone ascends from the wilderness to a commanding height, from which he can view the wilderness at a distance and (figuratively) take in the whole vista of Kentucky. The scene serves to comfort him, as biblical texts comforted the Puritan:

> One day I undertook a tour through the country, and the diversity and beauties of nature . . . expelled every gloomy and vexatious thought. Just at the close of day the gentle gales retired and left the place to the disposal of a profound calm. Not a breeze shook the most tremulous leaf. I had gained the summit of a commanding ridge, and, looking round with astonishing delight, beheld the ample plains, the beauteous tracts below. On the other hand, I surveyed the famous river Ohio that rolled in silent dignity, marking the western boundary of Kentucke with inconceivable grandeur. At a vast distance I beheld the mountains lift their venerable brows, and penetrate the clouds. All things were still. I kindled a fire near a fountain of sweet water, and feasted on the loin of a buck, which a few hours before I had killed. The sullen shades of night soon overspread the whole hemisphere, and the earth seemed to gasp for the hovering moisture. . . . I laid me down to sleep, and I awoke not until the sun had chased away the night.

This scene is the crisis of the book, for from this first initiation into the knowledge of nature Boone derives the "philosophy and fortitude" and the vision of future paradise in Kentucky which enable him to emerge from the later ordeals he must face. The scene is crucial to the successful operation of the narrative as a myth, since it is here that the human hero achieves communion with the gods of nature.

Filson's method of conveying this special relationship between man and God through the mediation of nature differs substantially, however, from that used by his cultural ancestors, and this change signifies an important shift in Americans' conceptions of their place in the wilderness. Filson's symbolism is implicit in his landscape and is communicated to the reader only in terms of Boone's changed perception of the objects around him. Both Edwards in his *Personal Narrative* and Jefferson in his descriptions in *Notes on Virginia* isolated the elements of divinity or of natural law which are present in the landscape and described them explicitly to the reader. To Jefferson such scenes were the basis for theories of natural evolution and geologic change. Edwards prepared for his vision of God in nature by reading his Bible, and he gained his first insights from a text ("I am the Rose of Sharon and the Lily of the Valleys"), rather than from a direct view of nature. It was only after he had read his Bible that the appearance of nature altered for him and there seemed to be "a calm, sweet cast, or appearance of divine glory, in almost every thing." The God in Edwards's landscape is a transcendent being, whose nature makes itself apparent in the landscape but whose essence is not the landscape. And where Filson's Boone does not mention "God" once in this description (as if to imply that nature is God enough), Edwards noted each of the several specific aspects which make up God's nature, his "excellency, his wisdom, his purity and love," and his biblical role as "the Redeemer."

Boone's (or Filson's) vision is closer to the Indian vision of nature (as expressed, for example, in the conversion of the Sioux priest Black Elk), in which the seeker or hunter achieves a sense of kinship with all nature and nature's creatures and, through this natural kinship, a kinship with the gods. However, there remains a vital difference between Boone's and Black Elk's visions. In Filson's account, nature is not as concretely seen as in Black Elk's. Conventions of landscape portrayal intervene, to give Filson's descriptions a slightly abstract quality; and where he does go into detail, in the sections on Kentucky flora and fauna, the tone is scientific and impersonal. Boone appreciates the wisdom and moral intention of the God of nature through his intimacy with the landscape; for Black Elk, the intimacy is so intense that the gods become his grandfathers, the beasts his brothers and sisters and gods by turns, and he himself both god, man, and beast. Later writers, such as Timothy Flint and Fenimore Cooper, who developed the implications of Filson's narrative to their ultimate point, came closer to expressing in convincing and evocative terms the character of this hunter's vision of man's and God's places in the cosmos. Filson's vision is still bound to the conventions of description favored by the landscape artists and writers of the early Romantic period. God's nature becomes apparent through man's perceptions of symbolic relationships within the real world, rather than through direct supernatural revelation or mystical insight. These patterns of symbolic relationship in the natural world are then interpreted with a high degree of artifice, of intellectual plan, as in Jefferson's "Natural Bridge" and "Potomac Gap."

The spiritual impact of Boone's experience (as Filson sees it) is to make him the perfect stoic—patient as an Indian, indifferent to danger, fearless, and content to live as the wilderness demands, by hunting and hiding in solitude. Moreover, Filson enables him to articulate his philosophy in a series of maxims and observations on social order and personal self-reliance. He does not, like a painter, leave the meaning implicit in his symbolic experience. Rather, he draws applications from his experience as a Puritan would, deriving practical standards of behavior and judgment. Thus he generalizes from his own stoic calm: "How unhappy such a situation for a man tormented by fear, which is vain if no danger comes, and if it does, only augments the pain. It was my happiness to be destitute of this afflicting passion, with which I had the greatest reason to be affected." Nothing in nature can hold fear for him now: even the "prowling wolves" and their "perpetual howlings" merely "diverted my nocturnal hours." But human institutions could never create in him this sense of inner peace and self-possession. Boone rejects both the comforts of civilization and the commercial values which characterize established urban societies like that of England: "I was surrounded with plenty in the midst of want. I was happy in the midst of dangers and inconveniences. In such diversity it was impossible that I should be disposed to melancholy. No populous city, with all the varieties of commerce and stately structures, could afford so much pleasure to my mind, as the beauties of nature I found here."

Before Filson's Boone moves deeper into the wilderness, his "second paradise," he returns to the East to tell his family and friends his vision of the West and to convince them to organize a settlement in Kentucky. This return marks the end of Boone's first initiation into the wilderness and starts him on another series of initiations, which will make him a political and military leader capable of organizing and defending a civilized community in the wilderness. His first attempt ends in failure, when Indian attacks and the difficulty of the season force his emigrant caravan to turn back to the settlements on Clench River. Boone's meditation on this failure calls up a vision of the mountain pass in which disaster has overtaken the party. As in the earlier landscape, this description is a blend of symbols which define the divine truth im-

plicit in the scene. But where the earlier description saw nature as a pastoral realm of order and promise, the description of the pass is more akin to sublime than to pastoral painting. Disproportionately huge rocks, shattered by wind and water—images of ruin and destruction and human weakness—embody a vision of the dark power of nature. The vision calls up in Boone a sense of the mortality of all natural things, the geologic cycles by which mountains rise and fall and the convulsions in which the civilizations of men are destroyed: "The aspect of these cliffs is so wild and horrid it is impossible to behold them without terror. The spectator is apt to imagine that nature had formerly suffered some violent convulsion; and that these are the dismembered remains of the dreadful shock; the ruins not of Persepolis or Palmyra, but a world!"

The theme of this section of the narrative is the antithesis of the first. Nature is now seen as uncontrolled and callous of human sentiments and concerns. The institutions of man, though subject like Persepolis and Palmyra to natural decay, offer the only hope of succor and moral order. The wild disorder of the natural scene is contrasted with a little fable of the social contract. Boone, having been aided by his countrymen at Clench River, sets aside his own plans and instead serves his people as an officer in Lord Dunmore's War of 1774. As a consequence of this service, Boone becomes a partner of Henderson's Transylvania Company and takes a party west to survey the Wilderness Road and establish the settlement of Boonesborough on the Kentucky River. In the rest of this section of the narrative, Boone experiences a series of similar initiations into the various societal arrangements and value systems then contending for mastery in the West.

The narrative continues to suggest that sentiment is the bond which seals the social contract. Filson has Boone mention pointedly that his wife and daughter were the first white women to settle in Kentucky, as if this is the sign of civilization. Sentimental concern for women and children, as Filson points out in his discussion of Indian "Manners," is the quality which distinguishes the white from the Indian society. Thus it is inevitable that one of the tests in Boone's initiation into the responsibilities of civilized leadership should involve the rescue of three young girls (including his own daughter) from the ungentle hands of Indian raiders. This incident was to be developed in elaborate detail by many later writers of the Romantic period—Cooper in *The Last of the Mohicans* and other of the Leatherstocking tales, Imlay in *The Emigrants,* and Brown in *Edgar Huntly*—but Filson treats it rather briefly. He was not, after all, writing a novel; it was enough for his purposes to suggest that the Indians had no sentimental regard for the female and that Boone did. An audience raised on captivity narratives could fill in the blank spaces from memory.

The differences in social values between the frontiersmen, the Indians, and the commercial civilization of Britain and the eastern states are clarified for Boone in the course of his capture by the Shawnee, his march with them to the British Fort Detroit, and his adoption into the tribe. Like the hero-victim of the captivity narrative, Boone is tempted to turn apostate and become a Shawnee or British subject. His captivity forces Boone into acquaintance with the serpent in his garden of Kentucky. If he adopts the standards of the British or the Indians, Boone will incur a second fall of man; he will prove himself a new Adam with the identical weaknesses of the old. The Indians represent a fallen race, a people who have failed to realize the arcadian possibilities of the land and their own human capacity for civilized behavior. The white scalp-buyers and renegades like Simon Girty, against whom Boone was later to fight, also succumb to the evil temptation of the wilderness and realize their potential for evil and inhuman rapacity, rather than sentiment and humanity. Boone resists the temptation to become an Indian or a scalp-hunter because he brings to his ordeal the mind and heart of an eighteenth-century gentleman-philosophe (albeit in rudimentary form).

For the Puritan, resistance to temptation depended upon the degree to which man subordinated his will, intellect, and emotions to the revealed Word of God. In the conversion experience and the captivity narrative, this sentiment of subordination is evoked by an unanticipated and overwhelming providential event, which mere reason proves incapable of predicting or fully explaining. Heart, mind, and spirit are regenerated or created anew, and the premises of reasoning as well as the motives of willful action are so altered by their purification as to be unintelligible to the unregenerate. The mind and heart of Filson's Boone, on the other hand, are sequentially rather than apocalyptically educated. His reasoning mind accumulates and analyzes a continually accreting store of experience, both immediate or personal and traditional or historical. Where the Puritan is saved from sin by the infusion of sudden grace in an uninformed (or misinformed) spirit, Boone is saved by the power of his mind and the growing store of experience on which his reason operates. In Filson's work, this contrast between Boone's rationalism and the Puritan insistence on a mystical immediacy of revelation as ways of approaching knowledge of God appears as a contrast between Boone's rational and the Indian's mythopoeic and superstitious apprehension of nature.

After his capture, Boone is carried by the Indians to Fort Detroit, where Governor Hamilton treats him "with great humanity" and offers the Indians "one hundred pounds sterling" to release Boone. A group of English gentlemen, disturbed by Boone's situation, offer him a purse of money for his "wants." In these brief incidents Filson sketches a caricature of English social values. Hamilton and his fellow gentlemen are courteous and generous to the captive, but at the same time they are engaged in buying scalps and captives from the Indians. Their values are largely commercial, and their valuation of Boone is purely monetary. The Indians, on the other hand, have none of this British hypocrisy. They refuse the price offered for Boone, despite the fact that it represents a king's ransom. Similarly, Boone refuses the offer of a purse because to accept it would be inconsistent with the honor of an independent man ("I refused, with many thanks for their kindness; adding, that I never expected it would be in my power to recompense their generosity"). While the Indians do not offer Boone money for his comforts, they recognize his worth as a man and a hunter and adopt him into the tribe as an equal. Where the British are hypocritical in their courtesy, the Shawnee are affectionate and loyal within their family bonds. They accept their adopted brother as virtually a blood member of the tribe:

> I . . . was adopted, according to their custom, into a family where I became a son, and had a great share in the affection of my new parents, brothers, sisters, and friends. I was exceedingly familiar and friendly with them, always appearing cheerful and satisfied as possible, and they put great confidence in me.

Yet Boone remains superior to the Indians: he masters their technique of living, without surrendering his consciousness of "white" social values or his personal philosophy of self-reliance and self-restraint. Thus he plays cleverly on the childish vanity of his adopted brothers and stays clear of their jealousy of his skill with a rifle:

> I often went a hunting with them, and frequently gained their applause for my activity at our shooting matches. I was careful not to exceed many of them in shooting; for no people are more envious than they in this sport. I could observe, in their countenances and gestures, the greatest expressions of joy when they exceeded me; and when the reverse happened, of envy.

Boone can become as intimate as an Indian with the conditions of wilderness life, engage in long solitary hunts, and even allow his soul to be harrowed by the terrors of the wilderness landscape without succumbing to the Indian's debilitating religious terror. His prowess and his dispassionate, calculated personal diplomacy quickly make him one of the most prominent and respected braves in the tribe:

> The Shawanese King took great notice of me, and treated me with profound respect, and entire friendship, often entrusting me to hunt at liberty. I frequently returned with the spoils of the woods, and as often presented some of what I had taken to him, expressive of duty to my sovereign. My food and lodging was, in common, with them, not so good indeed as I could desire, but necessity made every thing acceptable.

If Boone is allowed the liberty of hunting by himself, why does he not immediately seek his freedom? The question was to perplex many later writers, who assumed that Boone stayed because he found the Indian life very much to his liking. Filson does not explain the considerations which in fact determine Boone on staying with the Indians for a long period of time, but most likely they are pragmatic. Boone is fairly deep in Indian country and would run very grave risks in escaping by himself because of the winter season and the scarcity of game. Later he becomes aware that an assault on Boonesborough is being planned, and he waits to spy out the Indians' plans as they mature. In addition, he needs time to lull the Indians' suspicion of him. Filson's reasons for omitting Boone's motives for staying were based on literary considerations: to detail Boone's calculations would have vitiated Boone's initiation into knowledge of the Indian way. In order for Boone to know the Indians' life, he has to be truly immersed in it, accept (however temporarily) all of its assumptions and manners, and set aside the moral and political predilections of his own people. During the course of his life with the Indians, the values that belong to Boone as a white frontiersman gradually assert themselves, and this is a sign that his acceptance of the Indians has been simply another step in the larger initiation into his knowledge of himself and his own people's essential values. In the world Filson creates for Boone, knowledge and values proceed always from experience. Only when experience is completed does Filson's hero formulate its philosophic meaning.

The first sign of Boone's awakening sense of his true nature is his observation that the Shawnee lands have great potential for farming: "I hunted some [for the Indians], and found the land, for a great extent about this river, to exceed the soil of Kentucke, if possible, and remarkably well watered." He sees the land as a husbandman, not simply as a hunter, a perception which sets him off from the Indians. His sentimental feeling for his family's situation, another sign of his difference from the Indians, revives when he notes the gathering of an army of warriors, armed and painted "in a fearful manner" for an attack on Kentucky. Boone's reaction to these perceptions is swift: he makes his escape, despite the season, and returns to Boonesborough after a foodless march—a sort of purification ordeal-by-hunger.

On his return Boone first leads the settlers in their successful resistance to a prolonged siege by four hundred Indians and eleven French Canadian officers. Then he makes a circuit to Carolina and back to retrieve his wife and family, who had returned to their home thinking Boone was dead. The events of this section reveal Boone's ability to apply the knowledge of Indian psychology, the wilderness environment, and the principles of political organization which he has gained in his several initiations. Boone's skills include his leadership of a reconnaissance raid deep into Indian territory around the flank of the approaching army, the clever diplomacy by which he delays the Indians' attack, and his grasp of military measures to thwart their attempts to undermine the palisade. (Despite the fact that the French were about to enter the Revolution on the colonial side, the Indian-Canadian army flew French colors next to British as they marched against Boonesborough, a fact which Filson's Boone notes without comment. Apparently the French of Canada regarded the British as temporary allies in their continuing struggle against the Anglo-Americans of the thirteen colonies.)

Boone's triumph over the Indians is only temporary, and after his return from Carolina he and his colony face the darkest period of their history. In this last adventure in the narrative Boone receives his final test, his final initiation into self-knowledge and the wisdom and power of leadership. The prowess which he has gained in his initiations into the knowledge of nature and the techniques of Indian war is not enough to make him leader of a civilized community. Simon Girty and Alexander McKee, the two "abandoned [white] men"

who lead the next Indian assault on Kentucky, have as much prowess as Boone; but the civilized leader must possess those sentiments and sympathies which are at the basis of social cohesion, and these qualities the renegades have abandoned. In his last ordeal, as Boone experiences the depths of defeat and personal misery, his powers of rational control are all but overthrown by the tragedies which overtake his family and his nation. The land itself, as if in sympathy with the state of Boone's soul, goes through a period of barren fruitlessness and famine. It renews its vigor only when Boone renews his powers of self-control and his hopeful vision of the future.

The dark chapter begins with a disastrous hunting expedition. Boone and his brother, hunting food for the settlers, whose grain and corn crops have been ruined by Indian raids, are attacked by Indians. The brother is killed, and Boone himself is hunted through the woods by the Indians and their hunting dogs. The paragraph which recounts this misadventure ends with the observation that "winter soon came on, and was very severe." Thus Filson directly associates Boone's personal tragedy with the state of the land. The severity of the winter and the Indians' attacks force the settlers to abandon their reliance on the products of husbandry—corn and wheat—and turn to hunting buffalo for their sustenance like the Indians. But the Kentuckians have a philosophy which enables them to resign themselves to hardship: "Being a hardy race of people, and accustomed to difficulties and necessities, they were wonderfully supported through all their sufferings, until the ensuing Fall, when we received abundance from the fertile soil." The Puritans were wont to claim that they were "wonderfully supported" in their sufferings; but where the Puritans' support came from the transcendent Jehovah, the Kentuckians' support derives from their belief in their own hardihood and in the coming renewal of the land's fertility. The Kentuckians thus adopt the philosophy which their culture hero Daniel Boone discovered in his first initiation into the wilderness.

With the coming of spring all the powers of darkness seem

Hamlin Garland in South Dakota.

to gather for a last effort at destroying Kentucky. In 1782 the Indians and their British masters were to make a last effort to throw back the frontier and render invalid all American claims to the West. While Boone (in Filson's account) is apparently unaware of the threat to the nation at large, he knows that the year will see Kentucky saved or destroyed. To prevent the settlers from planting the corn that could carry them through another dark winter, the Indians send numerous raiding parties ahead of their main army and inflict a series of defeats on the settlers. Under McKee and Girty all the tribes of the Ohio country gather against Kentucky, as in Puritan times French officers mustered all hell and Canada against New England. Their rage and bloodthirstiness are excited to fever pitch by the monstrous sadism of the renegades, men who had abandoned both those human sympathies and sentiments which mark the civilized man and the tribal loyalties which ennoble the Indian.

McKee and Girty are Boone's antitypes, men who have experienced the same initiation into the wilderness that Boone underwent but who were degraded by the experience. They embody all the negative, evil possibilities inherent in the emigration to the wilderness. At the climactic Battle of Blue Licks, Boone and the renegades meet head on, and the result is a tragic setback for Boone and his countrymen. Filson's account of the battle is brief and incomplete; he neglects to explain how so canny a frontiersman as Boone comes to fall into Girty's trap at Blue Licks, although such an explanation would certainly have enhanced his hero's reputation for prowess. Filson is not interested here in showing us more of Boone's skill. Instead, the Battle of Blue Licks gives him an opportunity to show Boone under the stress of strong passions and at last victorious over them. This is Boone's decisive struggle between the newly awakened sentiments of grief and his philosophy of rational self-control and attention to duty.

According to Filson's account, the Kentuckians under Boone and two other militia colonels, Todd and Trigg, pursue Girty's army on its retreat from an unsuccessful siege of Bryant's Station and assault a small party, on the other side of Licking River, which they take to be a rear guard. But this small rear guard is bait for a trap, which Girty springs when the Kentuckians cross over. (In historical fact, Boone and his fellow colonels were not deceived by the ruse. They had decided against attacking; but when Major McGary went berserk with battle-madness and precipitated the assault, Boone and the others could only join in and make the best of a desperate situation.) The Indians fire from their hiding places in brushy ravines on the riverside hills, and "an exceeding fierce battle immediately began, for about fifteen minutes, when we, being overpowered by numbers, were obliged to retreat." Among the dead are Colonels Todd and Trigg and Boone's second son, killed at his father's side at the height of the assault. Sixty-seven other Kentuckians are killed and seven captured; four of the latter are tortured to death "in a most barbarous manner, by the young warriors, to train them up to cruelty."

The horrid details of the assault and the retreat do not emerge till Boone returns to the field some days after the battle, with Logan's relief force, to bury the dead. Then the terror and grief of his recollections shake him, and the "dreadful scene" before him is made still more poignant by the fact that his son lies among the mutilated dead:

> [We] returned to bury the dead, and found their bo-

dies strewed everywhere, cut and mangled in a dreadful manner. This mournful scene exhibited a horror almost unparalleled: Some torn by wild beasts; those in the river eaten by fishes; all in such putrified condition, that no one could be distinguished from another.

Yet from this scene of desolation new hope is born. As in Rogers's *Ponteach,* the hero's powers of reason triumph over grief by subordinating his emotions to the moderate level necessary for an efficient discharge of his duties. He accompanies Clark's punitive expedition against the Shawnee towns and, as he sees again the land that he found so fertile even in his captivity, he experiences a revival of his hopes for its agricultural development. His ordeal and Kentucky's are over. Both have emerged wiser in the ways of the wilderness, better able to organize and control their own affairs, and emotionally awakened to the bonds of sympathy and sentiment that hold civilization together.

Boone signifies his emergence in a concluding review of his adventures, in which he interprets the meaning of his part and projects a vision of the future. It is in this "Conclusion" that his ultimate character as a hero emerges. The section vaguely resembles one of those "improvements" that Cotton Mather attached to Hannah Dustin's captivity narrative, but its substance is not abstractly philosophical or theological. Filson has Boone recount his vision in a series of images and incidents drawn from the drama of his experiences. The symbols which give meaning to this vision derive their primary significance from the narrative alone, not from some biblical or other source outside the narrative. This self-contained quality and the fact that Boone's philosophic principles are voiced primarily as perceptions and experiences (rather than as abstract lessons or messages) make the Boone narrative the nearest approach in the eighteenth century to a truly novelistic treatment of the myth of the frontier.

Boone begins his concluding statement with a text, drawn from the words of an Indian chief rather than from the Bible: "To conclude, I can now say that I have verified the saying of an old Indian who signed Col. Henderson's deed. Taking me by the hand, at the delivery thereof, Brother, says he, we have given you a fine land, but I will believe you will have much trouble settling it." Witnessing to the truth of this prophecy, Boone laments his losses and troubles, the hardships he has suffered at the hand of nature and the Indians. But the lament, like each of Boone's initiations, ends with a vision of the good that arises from the cruelties and hardships of the wilderness:

> My footsteps have often been marked with blood, and therefore I can truly subscribe to [Kentucky's] original name [Dark and Bloody Ground]. Two darling sons, and a brother have, I lost by savage hands, which have also taken from me many horses and abundance of cattle. Many dark and sleepless nights have I been companion for owls, separated from the chearful society of men, scorched by the Summer's sun, and pinched by the Winter's cold, and instrument ordained to settle the wilderness. But now the scene is changed: Peace crowns the sylvan shade.

Boone's lament bears a close resemblance to Mary Rowlandson's concluding plaint, dwelling on the sleepless nights, the loneliness, and the discomfort experienced in the wilderness sojourn. But where the Puritan Mrs. Rowlandson believed that her captivity represented God's intention to chastise her and make more taxing the settlement of the wilderness, Boone claims that he is "an instrument ordained by God to settle the wilderness." Even in suffering, Boone is essentially the hero, the man of power.

The Boone narrative establishes its meaning through a rhythmic repetition of a single pattern of experience, reinforced by an imagistic connection between the state of Boone's mind and the state of the real landscape. This pattern of experience constitutes the essence of Filson's "myth." It begins with a total immersion of Boone in an experience of the wilderness, continues with his tasting both the promise and the terror of the Indian's world, and culminates in his achievement of a deeper perception of the nature of the wilderness and of his own soul and his assertion of rational control over his environment. The reader is led to assume that the result of this assertion of control will be to realize, through agrarian cultivation, nature's inherent power to sustain civilization. But in the narrative itself this result is seen only through Boone's perceptions of the land. It is the imagistic logic of literature that leads the reader unconsciously to draw a causal connection between Boone's perception of Kentucky's promise and the realization of a western arcadia. If Boone sees Kentucky as paradise, one feels, then it really is (or may really become) a paradise.

What is extraordinary about Filson's handling of this literary logic is that he portrays Boone's arcadian vision of the West as emerging from a thorough grounding in the evils and hardships of the wilderness, implying that these very evils are productive of the highest good for Boone's character and consequently for the character of the Kentucky settlements. The passage in which he describes his "footsteps" as "marked with blood" is followed by a vision of peace:

> What thanks, what ardent and ceaseless thanks, are due to that all-superintending providence which has turned cruel war into peace, brought order out of confusion, made the fierce savages placid, and turned away their hostile weapons from our country! May the same Almighty Goodness banish the accursed monster war, . . . rapine, and insatiable ambition. Let peace, descending from her native heaven, bid her olives spring amid the joyful nations; and plenty, in league with commerce, scatter blessings from her copious hands.

To Filson this vision represents Boone's realization of his true character and his true vision of the West. As a hero of the Enlightenment, enamored of peace and order, Boone views the promise of the West as dependent on its ability to produce an agrarian arcadia, cultivated to a symmetrical and orderly beauty, offsetting the sublime and terrible picture of what convulsions man and nature are capable of producing. Beyond the liberty to delight in this promise in "peace and safety . . . with my once fellow-sufferers," to enjoy the gratitude of his countrymen for his services, and to contemplate the prospect of Kentucky's becoming "one of the most opulent and powerful states of North America," Boone requires nothing further of nature. With this statement his narrative concludes. (pp. 278-94)

Richard Slotkin, "Narrative into Myth: The Emergence of a Hero (1784)," in his Regeneration through Violence: The Mythology of the American Frontier, 1600-1860, *Wesleyan University Press, 1973, pp. 268-312.*

HENRY NASH SMITH

[*Smith is an American educator who has written extensively on the works of American novelists, particularly the works of Mark Twain. In the following excerpt, he compares contradictory interpretations of Daniel Boone's significance as a frontier hero in various accounts of his life. For additional commentary by Smith, see excerpt below.*]

During the summer of 1842, following his sophomore year at Harvard, Francis Parkman made a trip through northern New York and New England. After spending several days admiring the scenery along the shores of Lake George, he noted in his journal: "There would be no finer place of gentlemen's seats than this, but now, for the most part, it is occupied by a race of boors about as uncouth, mean, and stupid as the hogs they seem chiefly to delight in." The tone is even blunter than that of Timothy Dwight's famous description of backwoodsmen in this area a generation earlier, but it embodies a comparable aristocratic disdain. Observers from Eastern cities made similar comments about uncultivated farmers along every American frontier. The class bias underlying the judgment was one of the dominant forces shaping nineteenth-century attitudes toward the West.

When Parkman got away from farms and hogs, out into the forest, his tone changed completely. He wrote, for example, that a woodsman named James Abbot, although coarse and self-willed, was "a remarkably intelligent fellow; has astonishing information for one of his condition; is resolute and independent as the wind." The young Brahmin's delight in men of the wilderness comes out even more forcibly in the journal of his Far Western trip four years later. *The Oregon Trail* presents the guide Henry Chatillon, a French-Canadian squaw man, as a hero of romance—handsome, brave, true, skilled in the ways of the plains and mountains, and even possessed of "a natural refinement and delicacy of mind, such as is rare even in women."

Parkman's antithetical attitudes toward backwoods farmers and the hunters and trappers of the wilderness illustrate the fact that for Americans of that period there were two quite distinct Wests: the commonplace domesticated area within the agricultural frontier, and the Wild West beyond it. The agricultural West was tedious; its inhabitants belonged to a despised social class. The Wild West was by contrast an exhilarating region of adventure and comradeship in the open air. Its heroes bore none of the marks of degraded status. They were in reality not members of society at all, but noble anarchs owning no master, free denizens of a limitless wilderness.

Parkman's love of the Wild West implied a paradoxical rejection of organized society. He himself was the product of a complex social order formed by two centuries of history, and his way of life was made possible by the fortune which his grandfather had built up as one of the great merchants of Boston. But a young gentleman of leisure could afford better than anyone else to indulge himself in the slightly decadent cult of wildness and savagery which the early nineteenth century took over from Byron. Historians call the mood "primitivism." Parkman had a severe case. In later life he said that from his early youth "His thoughts were always in the forest, whose features possessed his waking and sleeping dreams, filling him with vague cravings impossible to satisfy." And in a preface to *The Oregon Trail* written more than twenty years after the first publication of the book he bewailed the advance of humdrum civilization over the wide empty plains of Colorado since the stirring days of 1846.

Such a mood of refined hostility to progress affected a surprising number of Parkman's contemporaries. Nevertheless, it could hardly strike very deep in a society committed to an expansive manifest destiny. A romantic love of the vanishing Wild West could be no more than a self-indulgent affectation beside the triumphant official cult of progress, which meant the conquest of the wilderness by farms and towns and cities. If there was a delicious melancholy for sophisticated and literary people in regretting the destruction of the primitive freedom of an untouched continent, the westward movement seemed to less imaginative observers a glorious victory of civilization over savagery and barbarism. For such people—and they were the vast majority—the Western hunter and guide was praiseworthy not because of his intrinsic wildness or half-savage glamor, but because he blazed trails that hard-working farmers could follow.

One of the most striking evidences of the currency of these two conflicting attitudes toward the westward movement is the popular image of Daniel Boone. The official view was set forth in a greatly admired piece of allegorical sculpture by Horatio Greenough in the National Capitol, which depicted the contest between civilization and barbarism as a fierce hand-to-hand struggle between Boone and an Indian warrior. George C. Bingham's painting "The Emigration of Daniel Boone" (1851) showed the celebrated Kentuckian leading a party of settlers with their wives and children and livestock out into a dreamily beautiful wilderness which they obviously meant to bring under the plow.

These empire-building functions were amply documented by the facts of history. Boone had supervised the Treaty of Sycamore Shoals which extinguished the Indian claim to much of Kentucky, he had blazed the Wilderness Trail through the forest, and after leading the first settlers to Boonesborough in 1775, he had stoutly defended this outpost of civilization against the Indians during the troubled period of the Revolution. His functions as founder of the commonwealth of Kentucky had been celebrated as early as 1784 by John Filson, first architect of the Boone legend, in *The Discovery, Settlement and Present State of Kentucke.* Filson represents Boone as delighting in the thought that Kentucky will soon be one of the most opulent and powerful states on the continent, and finding in the love and gratitude of his countrymen a sufficient reward for all his toil and sufferings. The grandiose epic entitled *The Adventures of Daniel Boone,* published in 1813 by Daniel Bryan, nephew of the hero, is even more emphatic concerning his devotion to social progress. Complete with Miltonic councils in Heaven and Hell, the epic relates how Boone was chosen by the angelic Spirit of Enterprise to bring Civilization to the trans-Allegheny wilderness. When he is informed of his divine election for this task, Boone's kindling fancy beholds Refinement's golden file smoothing the heathen encrustations from the savage mind, while Commerce, Wealth, and all the brilliant Arts spread over the land. He informs his wife in a Homeric leave-taking that the sovereign law of Heaven requires him to tread the adventurous stage of grand emprise, scattering knowledge through the heathen wilds, and mending the state of Universal Man. Faithful to his mission even in captivity among the Indians, he lectures the chief Montour on the history of the human race, concluding with reflections on

How Philanthropy

And social Love, in sweet profusion pour
Along Refinement's pleasure-blooming Vales,
Their streams of richest, life-ennobling joy.

By the side of Boone the empire builder and philanthropist, the anonymous popular mind had meanwhile created an entirely different hero, a fugitive from civilization who could not endure the encroachment of settlements upon his beloved wilderness. A dispatch from Fort Osage in the Indian territory, reprinted in *Niles' Register* in 1816, described an interview with Boone and added: "This singular man could not live in Kentucky when it became settled. . . . he might have accumulated riches as readily as any man in Kentucky, but he *prefers the woods,* where you see him in the dress of the roughest, poorest hunter."

Boone's flight westward before the advance of the agricultural frontier—actually dictated by a series of failures in his efforts to get and hold land—became a theme of newspaper jokes. The impulse that produced Western tall tales transformed him into the type of all frontiersmen who required unlimited elbow room. "As civilization advanced," wrote a reporter in the New York *American* in 1823, "so he, from time to time, retreated"—from Kentucky to Tennessee, from Tennessee to Missouri. But Missouri itself was filling up: Boone was said to have complained, "I had not been two years at the licks before a d—d Yankee came, and settled down *within an hundred miles of me!!*" He would soon be driven on out to the Rocky Mountains and would be crowded there in eight or ten years. Edwin James, chronicler of the Stephen H. Long expedition, visiting Fort Osage in 1819, heard that Boone felt it was time to move again when he could no longer fell a tree for fuel so that its top would lie within a few yards of the door of his cabin. This remark set James, a native of Vermont, to thinking about the irrational behavior of frontiersmen. He had observed that most inhabitants of new states and territories had "a manifest propensity, particularly in the males, to remove westward, for which it is not easy to account." There was an apparently irresistible charm for the true Westerner in a mode of life "wherein the artificial wants and the uneasy restraints inseparable from a crowded population are not known, wherein we feel ourselves dependent immediately and solely on the bounty of nature, and the strength of our own arm. . . ." The Long party came upon a man more than sixty years old living near the farthest settlement up the Missouri who questioned them minutely about the still unoccupied Platte Valley. "We discovered," noted James with astonishment, "that he had the most serious intention of removing with his family to that river."

Seizing upon hints of Boone's flight before the advance of civilization, Byron paused in his description of the siege of Ismail in the eighth canto of *Don Juan* to insert an extended tribute to him. Although Byron's Boone shrank from men of his own nation when they built up unto his darling trees, he was happy, innocent, and benevolent; simple, not savage; and even in old age still a child of nature, whose virtues shamed the corruptions of civilization. Americans quoted these stanzas eagerly.

Which was the real Boone—the standard-bearer of civilization and refinement, or the child of nature who fled into the wilderness before the advance of settlement? An anonymous kinsman of Boone wrestled with the problem in a biographical sketch published a few years after the famous hunter's death in 1820. It would be natural to suppose, he wrote, that the Colonel took great pleasure in the magnificent growth of the commonwealth he had founded in the wilderness. But such was not the case. Passionately fond of hunting, "like the unrefined Savage," Boone saw only that incoming settlers frightened away all the game and spoiled the sport. He would "certainly prefer a state of nature to a state of Civilization, if he were obliged to be confined to one or the other."

Timothy Flint's biography, perhaps the most widely read book about a Western character published during the first half of the nineteenth century, embodies the prevalent confusion of attitudes. Flint says that Boone delighted in the thought that "the rich and boundless valleys of the great west—the garden of the earth—and the paradise of hunters, had been won from the dominion of the savage tribes, and opened as an asylum for the oppressed, the enterprising, and the free of every land." The explorer of Kentucky

> had caught some glimmerings of the future, and saw with the prophetic eye of a patriot, that this great valley must soon become the abode of millions of freemen; and his heart swelled with joy, and warmed with a transport which was natural to a mind so unsophisticated and disinterested as his.

Yet we learn only a few pages later that he was driven out of Kentucky by "the restless spirit of immigration, and of civil and physical improvement." Even in Missouri, "the tide of emigration once more swept by the dwelling of Daniel Boone, driving off the game and monopolizing the rich hunting grounds." In despair,

> he saw that it was in vain to contend with fate; that go where he would, American enterprize seemed doomed to follow him, and to thwart all his schemes of backwoods retirement. He found himself once more surrounded by the rapid march of improvement, and he accommodated himself, as well as he might, to a state of things which he could not prevent.

On yet other occasions Flint credits Boone with a sophisticated cult of pastoral simplicity greatly resembling his own, which he had imitated from Chateaubriand. When the frontiersman seeks to induce settlers to go with him into the new land, he is represented as promising them that the original pioneers, in their old age, will be surrounded by

> consideration, and care, and tenderness from children, whose breasts were not steeled by ambition, nor hardened by avarice; in whom the beautiful influences of the indulgence of none but natural desires and pure affections would not be deadened by the selfishness, vanity, and fear of ridicule, that are the harvest of what is called *civilized and cultivated life.*

The debate over Boone's character and motives lasted into the next decade. The noted Western Baptist minister and gazetteer, John M. Peck, prepared a life of Boone for Jared Sparks's Library of American Biography in 1847 which repeatedly attacked the current conception of the hero as a fugitive from civilization. Peck says that Boone left North Carolina for the Kentucky wilderness because of the effeminacy and profligacy of wealthy slaveowners who scorned the industrious husbandman working his own fields. But by the time the biographer interviewed the aged hero in Missouri in 1818, Boone had become aware of an imposing historical mission. Although he had not consciously aimed to lay the foundations of a state or nation, he believed that he had been "a creature of Providence, ordained by Heaven as a pioneer in the

wilderness, to advance the civilization and the extension of his country."

James H. Perkins of Cincinnati, writing in 1846 in the *North American Review,* was equally interested in the problem of Boone's motives, but inclined to a more modest interpretation. Boone, he said, was a white Indian. Although he and his companions were not at all like the boasting, swearing, drinking, gouging Mike Finks of the later West, they were led into the wilderness not by the hope of gain, nor by a desire to escape the evils of older communities, nor yet by dreams of founding a new commonwealth, but simply by "a love of nature, of perfect freedom, and of the adventurous life in the woods." Boone "would have pined and died as a nabob in the midst of civilization. He wanted a frontier, and the perils and pleasures of a frontier life, not wealth; and he was happier in his log-cabin, with a loin of venison and his ramrod for a spit, than he would have been amid the greatest profusion of modern luxuries."

If one detects a patronizing note in this account, it goes along with a greater respect for the simple, hearty virtues that are left to the frontiersman. Such a view seems to have become general in the 1840's. William H. Emory of the Army of the West which invaded New Mexico in 1846 invoked the figure of the Kentuckian to convey his impression of an American settler in the Mora Valley northeast of Santa Fé: "He is a perfect specimen of a generous open-hearted adventurer, and in appearance what, I have pictured to myself, Daniel Boone, of Kentucky, must have been in his day."

Yet the issue long remained unsettled. As a character in fiction Boone could still be made the spokesman of a stilted primitivism. Glenn, the young Eastern hero of John B. Jones's shoddy *Wild Western Scenes,* published in 1849, is traveling in the vicinity of Boone's last home in Missouri, and there encounters the venerable pioneer. The highly implausible conversation between the two men indicates to what unhistorical uses the symbol of Boone could be put. The Westerner asks Glenn whether he has become disgusted with the society of men. Glenn, who happens to be just such a rhetorical misanthrope as the question implies, welcomes the opportunity to set forth his views:

> I had heard [he declares] that you were happy in the solitude of the mountain-shaded valley, or on the interminable prairies that great the horizon in the distance, where neither the derision of the proud, the malice of the envious, nor the deceptions of pretended love and friendship, could disturb your peaceful meditation; and from amid the wreck of certain hopes, which I once thought no circumstances could destroy [it is a matter of disappointment in love], I rose with a determined vow to seek such a wilderness, where I would pass a certain number of my days engaging in the pursuits that might be most congenial to my disposition. Already I imagine I experience the happy effects of my resolution. Here the whispers of vituperating foes cannot injure, nor the smiles of those fondly cherished, deceive.

Boone clasps the young coxcomb's hand in enthusiastic agreement. If Daniel Bryan's epic represents the limit of possible absurdity in making Boone the harbinger of civilization and refinement, this may stand as the opposite limit of absurdity in making him a cultural primitivist. The image of the Wild Western hero could serve either purpose. (pp. 51-8)

Henry Nash Smith, "Daniel Boone: Empire Builder or Philosopher of Primitivism?" in his Virgin Land: The American West as Symbol and Myth, *Cambridge, Mass.: Harvard University Press, 1950, pp. 51-8.*

RICHARD SLOTKIN

[*In the following excerpt, Slotkin examines variations of the frontier hero in the fiction of the "Southwest school" written during the 1830s and 1840s. For additional commentary by Slotkin, see excerpt above.*]

The [American West] . . . experienced in an acute form the ambivalent association of democratic idealism and unprincipled materialism that characterized the society as a whole [during the period of industrialization]. This combination was especially dismaying to those who identified themselves as spokesmen for traditional values—self-restraint, deference, conservative business ethics, religious "otherworldliness." And it was this circumstance that lay behind the emergence of the "Southwest school" of writers as an important and popular literary tendency in 1835-50.

Usually "Southwestern" stories were concerned with life in the backwash of the frontier, Crèvecoeur's borderland between the realm of the Indian and hunter, and that of the settled and established farming community. Southwestern writers exploited their region and its characters for local color, affecting to stand between the rough characters of the backwash region and their genteel readership in Cincinnati, Philadelphia, or New York. There was a certain amount of realism, an emphasis on the gritty quality of life, crudity of manners, violence, crime, and poverty; a certain amount of sensationalism in the depiction of violence, linked to a folkloric tendency to hyperbole that converted aggression to humor; and a certain amount of condescension to the "types" represented in the stories. The writers of the Southwestern school were mostly Whigs and conservatives, representatives of the professional class, not infrequently politicians. If their stories were intended to popularize and mythologize their region, they were also meant as satires on the primitive side of their section's life-style—satires that pointed, indirectly, toward more respectable values and behavior.

Although the writers themselves were mostly residents of the region and began publishing in local papers, their primary outlets were the nationally oriented urban journals of the Metropolitan North. Magazines like *Police Gazette* and *Spirit of the Times* catered to an urban and lower-class audience, and the preoccupations of that audience shaped their choice of material. Tales of urban criminality tended to make ironic juxtapositions of rich and poor. The law is seen to punish the poor man who becomes an outlaw by robbing the wealthy; but it does not rebuke the wealthy who, by their selfishness, create the conditions of poverty that drive men to crime. One of the conventional plots—which George Lippard treated on an epic scale in *Monks of Monk Hall* (1844)—was that of the poor girl driven to crime or prostitution by an indifferent society and a wealthy seducer. George Wilkes, the pro-labor editor of both *Police Gazette* and *Spirit of the Times,* made a media heroine of sorts out of Helen Jewett—a prostitute murdered by a wealthy man, who was acquitted after a sensational trial.

The context in which the Southwestern stories appeared was therefore entirely Metropolitan; and the juxtaposition of urban and Frontier stories suggested a significant relationship between the two worlds. To some extent the journals preserve the original premise that the Frontier is an alternative to and an escape from the rigors of the Metropolis. These suggestions harmonize with the editorial stance of the papers, which favored the whole range of policies associated with the Frontier Myth—Manifest Destiny, Homestead legislation, and subsidized railroads. But the association of Southwestern with Metropolitan crime stories implies another kind of connection—an identity between the corruptions of Metropolitan society and those of a Frontier approaching closure.

In the Southwest of fiction, the Frontier has passed, and the predatory impulse turned inward produces a society in which economic competition reaches a limit of violent unrestraint that tests the tolerance of social bonding itself. The typical Southwestern heroes are lower-class "confidence men," slick in a horse swap; or men of prodigious capacities for violence. Augustus Baldwin Longstreet's *Georgia Scenes* (1835) offers a typical pantheon of Southwestern types, including two cracker-barrel entrepreneurs who passionately prevaricate, exaggerate, distort, and defraud each other in order to emerge victorious in "The Horse Swap." Pride as well as cash value is at stake: the Frontiersman must overcome his opponent at any cost, competition is a value in itself. In "The Fight," this violence becomes explicitly verbal and physical, and the unrestrained character of a frontier brawl is set before the reader, complete with gouging, kicking, biting off body parts, and foul language. Among themselves, as in their warfare with the Indian, the Frontiersmen have learned to give and take no quarter; every war is a war of extermination, and every exchange a potential *casus belli.*

The Southwest contains its left-over Leatherstockings as well, and these speak directly of the nature of the change that has overtaken the border. Some old hunters and Indian fighters adjust or even run for Congress like Davy Crockett and Simon Suggs. Others, like the legendary keelboatman Mike Fink, bring to quarrels with fellow whites the same code of violence and revenge that shaped their behavior toward Indians—with the result that they are killed off by the hand of justice or the outcome of blood feud.

Viewed from the perspective of a post-Frontier social order, the Indian fighter of the past becomes a far more ambiguous and threatening figure than Cooper's Leatherstocking. The difference is registered in the critique and revision of Cooper by the western writer James Hall and the southern novelist Robert M. Bird. For Cooper, the Frontier hero had been a mediator between two races representing opposite poles of a spectrum of natural "gifts" or moral propensities. Since Indian and white participate in a common universe of natural and moral law, the Indian's different moral vision has a kind of legitimacy; and through the interpretation of the Leatherstocking figure, Indian morals can even offer a useful critique of civilized values and behavior. To be sure, Cooper's Indians perish and his whites inherit the land; but the mediation of Leatherstocking suggests that this process involves—below the violence—a passing on of legitimate authority from the elder race to the younger. But for Hall and Bird there is no question of Indian legitimacy or moral authority. They criticize Cooper as a sentimentalist for evoking sympathy for Indian values and representing their response to civilization as a moral critique. For Hall and Bird the Indian response is simply the rage of the wild beast against the cage: visceral, unreasoning, an expression of a nature innately incapable of civilization.

By attributing innate depravity to the Indian, Hall and Bird discredit the Frontier hero's role as interpreter and critic of society. Both writers vest the principle of social authority unambiguously in civilized, military-aristocratic characters. Their Frontiersmen are rendered as unstable, dangerous, even schizophrenic by their existence in the void between antitheses of Red and White. The title character of Bird's *Nick of the Woods* (1837) is the most melodramatic version of this sort of hero. Nathan Slaughter had been a fanatical Quaker, who sought license for his hyperintense religiosity in the isolation of the forest. When his family is massacred by Indians his Christian fanaticism becomes inverted, and he becomes a demonic avenger called by the Indians "Jibbenainosay" and by the whites "Nick of the Woods." The offsetting impulses of gentility and violence (white gifts and Indian nurture) that made Natty Bumppo so capable an interpreter between Indians and whites cannot be balanced in Nathan's world or soul: they split his personality in two. So the principles of savagery and civilization, freedom and order, Frontiersman and citizen are revealed as antithetical.

Hall's portrayal of the type is less sensational in style, and pretends to historical accuracy. But his classic sketch of the "Indian Hater" (1835) points to the same conclusions about the antisocial consequences that follow from a too-devoted enjoyment of the life of the Frontier hero. His brief account of the life of Colonel John Moredock was a well-known and frequently reprinted piece of Frontier history and legend; and after its satirical apotheosis as a parody in Melville's *The Confidence-Man* (1857) it became the work most frequently associated with Hall's name. Hall depicts the Indian hater as a spiritual type common in the Frontier era: a man of solitary and self-willed character who suffers some misfortune at Indian hands—the massacre of family and loved ones—and becomes thereafter a professional Indian killer. The Indian hater's mission is to exterminate red men as a matter of principle, and he will make any sacrifice of health or interest necessary to fulfill this mission. Flint's Boone is represented as an "artist" in his worthy passion of hunting; Hall extends some of this quality to the Indian hater. Yet so closely linked with the animal and the Indian have they become that both the professional hunter and the professional Indian fighter come close to perishing when the things they love to kill have at last been exterminated.

According to Hall, the origin of Indian hating lies in the fact that the people living on the crest of Frontier expansion constitute "a peculiar race," which generation after generation has persisted in keeping ahead of the tide of emigration, "who shunned the restraints, while they despised the luxuries of social life." This race represents a primitive survival of an earlier epoch of our national history, for "America was settled in an age when certain rights, called those of *discovery* and *conquest*, were universally acknowledged; and when the possession of a country was readily conceded to the strongest." Although better notions have entered social life with "the spread of knowledge, and the dissemination of religious truth," such improvements have not touched the consciousness of a pioneer race which persistently flees contact with the more advanced society that follows them. Hall goes so far as to assert that the chief motive of this race is not to kill the Indian or conquer the woods, but simply to escape from civilization: as Melville said, not so much sailing for any haven

ahead, as fleeing from all havens astern. Conflict with the Indian rises from his desire to "monopolize" the land, where the pioneer asserts that the hunting grounds must be "free to all."

Hall goes on to give the history of a representative of this pioneer race, Colonel John Moredock, a man of superhuman prowess, whose family was massacred by Indians; and who became, as a result, a passionate hunter and slayer of Indians, who "never in his life failed to embrace an opportunity to kill a savage." Despite this proclivity, he was accounted a good husband and provider, a useful citizen who was considered as a candidate for governor, but declined the honor. In Melville's retelling of the tale, this decline is a sacrifice Moredock makes to his darling passion; but Hall insists on his good qualities as a citizen. The implication in Melville's version is that Moredock's desire for revenge remains a passion, even after the frontier situation which gave birth to it and in a manner justified it has passed; at this point Hall avoids the question or allows it to drop, and ends on a note emphasizing the colonel's eventual socialization. The principle, in both cases, is the same, however: the colonel cannot make one with society unless he lets the obsession for private revenge go and ceases to be "the Indian hater."

Yet the character of Indian fighter or hunter may be, as Hall suggests, as ingrained as a racial trait or a personal identity. Thomas Bangs Thorpe, in his famous short story "The Big Bear of Arkansas," plays with this idea and develops some of its implications. The narrator of the story is the typical "genteel" observer of Southwestern fiction, here journeying down the Mississippi on a steamboat. Into the smoking room bursts Jim Doggett, an "alligator-horse" type of frontiersman, speaking in dialect and calling himself "The Big Bear of Arkansaw." Doggett at first comes on like a Frontier booster as he hyperbolically sings the praises of his home countryside in Arkansas, "the creation State, the finishing-up country—a State where the *sile* runs down to the center of the 'arth, and government gives you a title to every inch of it." However, in his proper character, Jim Doggett is a hunter, a bear hunter—in fact, *the* bear hunter of all the world. As he says of his dog, "I never could tell whether he was made expressly to hunt bear, or whether bear was made expressly for him to hunt."

Jim Doggett's dilemma is that his skill has virtually denuded the country of bears, and those that remain are so demoralized by his skill that they scarcely resist him anymore. The hunter's profession is gone, his competitive prowess no longer evoked by an antagonistic and abundant nature. Life becomes dull and monotonous, until nature responds to Doggett's silent wish and sends him a bear of bears, the "Big Bear of Arkansaw" from which he will take his nickname. The Big Bear is colossal in size, a match for Doggett and his hound in cunning, who also has quasi-magical powers and who, on one occasion, walks right through a fusillade unscathed. Doggett feels that it is not he who hunts bear, but the bear who hunts him. Frustrated and humiliated, he determines to kill the bear, die, or "go to Texas"; and as if in response, the Big Bear comes walking "through his fence," and virtually offers himself to the gun.

The outcome of the hunt is, however, spiritually troubling to Doggett, who is forced to conclude that it was not his skill that gained him the victory, but some mystical choice on the bear's part—that he was "a Creation bear," unhuntable, and died "when his time come." If we are to take Doggett at his word, the killing of the last bear represents the final extinction of the active principle of wildness in the wilderness—an extinction for which man is the instrument, but Nature herself the ordainer. Doggett is left with the name of the thing he killed and of the place whose spirit the animal was—he *is* "The Big Bear of Arkansaw"—but Doggett is also an anachronism, and the last view of him is indeed pathetic: a garrulous, tipsy, backwoodsman booster who vanishes from the steamboat in the night, going back to bear-less Arkansas.

Johnson Jones Hooper's *Some Adventures of Captain Simon Suggs* (1845) presents the quintessential post-Frontier Southwesterner as a rogue and confidence man. In Hooper, the political and social dimensions of the Southwestern version of "the hunter" emerge quite clearly. Captain Suggs is a satire on Andrew Jackson, his border constituency, and his picked successor, Martin Van Buren. Suggs converts the ideology of democracy-in-mobility into a maxim: "It is good to be shifty in a new country." And he makes the most of the ambiguity inherent in the word "shifty," through a career of fraud and chicanery.

> The shifty Captain Suggs is a miracle of shrewdness. He possesses, in an eminent degree, the tact which enables a man to detect the *soft spots* in his fellow, and to assimilate himself to whatever company he may fall in with. Besides, he has a quick, ready wit, which has extracted him from many an unpleasant predicament, and which makes him whenever he chooses to be so—and that is always—very companionable. In short, nature . . . sent him into the world a sort of he-Pallas, ready to cope with his kind, from infancy, in all the arts by which men *"get along"* in the world; if she made him, in respect of his moral conformation, a beast of prey, she did not refine the cruelty by denying him the fangs and the claws.

This miracle of predation chooses his victims from within the society, beginning with the cheating and befooling of both his hard-shell Baptist preacher-father and their Negro slave. Neither patriarch nor servant, authority nor subordinate, is safe from exploitation by the shifty Suggs, as he makes his way in the world. His typical victims, however, are not embodiments of traditional authority—noble planters or worthy barristers. Rather, they are representatives of the nouveaux riches, the would-be gentlemen of the Frontier, whose pretensions to gentility and status constitute their chief vanity, and the weak spots that Suggs exploits. Thus Suggs overcomes and takes advantage of a Frontier militia muster, where various "worthies" contest his right to the captaincy; of a camp meeting, where a Frontier ranter finds Simon stealing his thunder and his collection; of a puffed-up citizen named General Witherspoon, who is, it transpires, a hog drover by profession.

In Suggs, Hooper finds a voice to satirize Jacksonian man on two levels: through the captain's easy distortion of his victims' pretensions, his showing up of their vanities; and through the captain's own amoral and unrestrained predation. In a true Frontier situation, Sugg's type might have figured as the military aristocrats' sly and ingenious hunter-scout; behind the Frontier, given license to compete for economic and political power, he is something like a menace.

The satiric mode and the presence of resources that are still relatively abundant soften the impact of Suggs's criminality in Hooper's stories. But other Southwestern stories took a darker view, focusing on the careers of the infamous badmen and outlaws who infested the river and forests in the early nineteenth century. James Hall's *The Harpe's Head* is in this vein, and there were any number of paperback potboilers that rendered the careers of Southwestern bandits in the most sensationalistic terms. The Harpes, within this paradigm, represented a survival of two psychopathic primitives into the post-Frontier era. In an earlier time, they would have been renegades like Simon Girty and exhibited their sadism inciting Indians to torture their captives; now they are rapists, robbers and murderers, river pirates and road agents who must be hunted down like wild beasts—yet who can, and do, pass for civilized men in backwoods farming communities.

More troublesome than the throwback Harpes were outlaws of the type of Samuel Rogers and John Murrell—men who carried the striving for success too far, and who turned ferries or taverns or toll stations into bases for the robbery and murder of travelers. Of these, the most notable character was John Murrell, a man who began as a frontier highwayman, but who adjusted his criminal enterprise to suit the new conditions of a post-Frontier society—and so threatened that society profoundly. Murrell's story was told by H. R. Howard in two paperback versions, and also in the *National Police Gazette*. The first of these concentrates on Murrell himself, and was part of a series of books on famous western criminals written by Howard. The second focuses not on Murrell, but on the man who brought Murrell to justice, Virgil A. Stewart.

The Life and Adventures of John A. Murrell, the Great Western Land Pirate (1847) represents the great outlaw as part of that outcast "social refuse" that inhabits Frontier districts and wild tracts. Howard asserts also that the story of Murrell's fall constitutes a significant part of that story of the wilderness's "redemption into civilization" which begins with the Indian wars. However, he sees in Murrell no mere Frontier brigand, but a man of prepossessing intellectual and even moral endowment (phrenologically cast) who converted the motives and energy of the western brigand into "a science . . . confederating all the various elements of the region into a single combination." Murrell is to Frontier outlawry what [John Jacob] Astor is to Frontier fur trapping. And like Astor he has "risen" from poverty. That Murrell's parents were poor should not in itself be a motive for a life of crime: but in Murrell's household the mother—who ought to have been the embodiment of all the sacred values—was "course [*sic*] and immodest," taught Murrell to steal, and gave him his "barbarous and vicious nature." Pursuing a career of theft, chicanery, and murder, Murrell eventually arrives in Alabama, where a combination of circumstances give him his great idea. Taking advantage of local panic engendered by rumors of a "servile insurrection," Murrell devises a scheme for a lucrative racket involving seducing slaves to run away from their masters to "freedom" with him. Once in Murrell's confederates' hands, the slave can either be resold, returned for reward, or—if necessity requires it—murdered, gutted, weighted with stones, and dropped in a swamp. Similarly, free northern blacks could be kidnapped and smuggled south. The operation of such a large-scale racket requires a certain amount of conspiracy between Murrell and "respectable" society—law enforcement officers, judges, and of course a class of purchasing planters who would "ask no questions."

Out of the associations created by the runaway-slave racket, Murrell builds a network of political influence and protection which, in Howard's account, amounts to a secret society, a

Mafia capable finally of achieving political control of whole districts—and perhaps more. Thus while Murrell follows a course of crime in the Suggsian manner—masquerading as a preacher, a merchant, and so on; a confidence man as much as an armed robber, perhaps more so—he secretly plans his "Mystic Clan" to avenge himself at the expense of a world that had impoverished, scorned, and imprisoned him. The aim of the Mystic Clan is to incite a servile insurrection among blacks in the southwest and Deep South by urging the "malevolent serf[s]" to assert an "equality of hate." In the disorder and terror of the uprising, Murrell's Clan may rise to power, manipulating the ignorant blacks; or if the rebellion looks as if it will fail, they can use it as a cover to loot the plantations, with the cooperation of their black dupes.

Power in the Clan is concentrated in the "Grand Council," with chapters in every community throughout the region. The Council itself meets secretly in a swamp hideout, protected by primitive jungle. Their strategy with the blacks will be to select the most "vicious and daring" of them, then "commence poisoning their minds by telling them how monstrously they are mistreated; that they are entitled to their freedom as much as their masters, and that all of the wealth of the country is the proceeds of black people's labor . . . then sting them with their own degraded condition, by comparing it with the pomp and ease" of their masters. Murrell's agents are told to represent themselves as emissaries from the Free States, and instruct the blacks to "butcher every white man in the slaveholding states." Initiation into this bloody mission requires a bloodcurdling oath sworn on a skeleton, which magically "spoke," and other ceremonies of a Grand Guignol character. Although the plot is appalling, Howard cannot withhold the comparison of his antihero to "Alexander or . . . Napoleon." When Murrell's impulse is thwarted, the rage of the criminal underclass builds. Now Murrell, an Indian-hater/avenger type who has perversely chosen the upper classes of his own race for an object, determines that the basis of the organization will not be profit but "unrelenting massacre. . . . The negroes . . . were promised revenge for past wrongs, possession of the delicate-skinned daughters and wives of their former masters. . . . Day by day the dark sedition widened."

The downfall of Murrell is recounted in detail in Howard's second book, which features the career of the man hunter Virgil Stewart. Stewart is a diligent small entrepreneur and land speculator who sells merchandise to Indians and settlers and operates a small farm. Asked by a friend to help recover a stolen slave, Stewart comes upon Murrell, and recognizes him; but dissembles, and becomes friendly with the murderous conspirator, learning from him the gory details of Murrell's business. Murrell takes his "friend" to the swamp hideout, for induction into the Mystic Clan. The hideout is described as "the Garden of Eden," a wilderness paradise like the Dark and Bloody Ground of Kentucky—mingling wilderness beauty and fecundity with fearsome shapes of terror and racial war. Stewart, alias "Hues," gains the trust of the conspirators by means of a speech in which he cites the law of the jungle, by which the strongest rule, as justification for their actions: "We consider every thing under the control of our power as our right." Like the "pioneer race" in Hall's account of Moredock, the right of conquest is the only law they recognize. With tongue in cheek, Hues/Stewart compares them to Roman patriots, striking for Liberty.

His situation is not unlike that of the Indian captive—or bet-

ter, of Daniel Boone among the Indians, feigning acceptance of the ritual of adoption, but yearning for his home and planning escape. Seizing an opportunity, Stewart returns to his community and exposes the plot. Vigilante organizations form (Murrell's Mafia may control the official structure), and the region is swept by a wave of what an unfriendly eye might term witch-hunting. Murrell, himself caught and jailed, turns state's evidence. Suspected black and white conspirators are hunted down, lynched or legally executed, or otherwise punished. Yet so powerful is the conspiracy that, years later, Stewart still fears their desire for vengeance will dog him to death.

The fear roused by Murrell's conspiracy was genuine, and well reported in the regional and national press. What Howard and other dime novelists made of Murrell was a national myth, embodiment of destructive forces within a society cut off from expansion at the borders, aggression against passive nature and alien Indians. The story invokes the class/race tensions inherent in the existence of slavery and ties them to poor-white dissatisfactions through the character of Murrell. These in turn are magnified by association with radical abolitionism, "a poisonous swarm" from the "great northern hive of fanatics and incendiaries."

The specter that Murrell's career awakes is the specter of a slave uprising, a war of races that will at the same time be a war of classes, motivated by the resentment of rich and poor. Wars with red savages speak of expansion and progress; those with black savages and white "renegades" speak of social self-destruction. In the backwash of the Frontier, the confrontation with class differences and conflicts is inescapable; the idea of the *permanence* and necessity of class subordination is inescapable. Yet the Frontier ideology, the Frontier impulse, requires that systems of subordination and limitation be overturned and exploded.

But the same Frontier values that generate the peculiar form of "dangerous class" represented by a Murrell offer an antidote to that danger in the figure of the vigilante, a prototype of the private citizen detective. Virgil Stewart is an early version of the type: a common man who is drawn almost inadvertently into the path of adventure; who gains intimacy with the dangerous class through a form of disguised captivity; but who ultimately turns the dangerous class's talents for renegadery, conspiracy, and extralegal violence against itself. His adventure parallels that of the Indian fighter, with the difference that for Daniel Boone or Leatherstocking the dangerous class is an unambiguously identified racial "other." Although racial "darkness" taints Murrell and his Clan, it does not entirely define them. Like the Indian fighter, the vigilante is usually represented as a necessary figure in a relatively primitive state of society. James Hall delineates the character of the vigilante in the same volume in which he sets forth the character of the Indian hater, and he represents the exponent of "Linch's law" as the representative man of a transitional stage from the world of the Indian hater and pioneer to that of the completed settlement. Like the Indian hater, the vigilante fulfills a social and civilizing mission by exercising a privilege of violence that goes beyond legal or conventional prohibitions. He thus shares some of the "dangerous" character of the criminals he pursues—just as the Indian hater shares the traits of the savage.

This privilege can safely be exercised only within the primitive framework; and if the vigilante pursues his enterprise after the establishment of civilized law, he becomes as antisocial a figure as the Indian hater who persists in secret murder after the time of race war has passed. Hall deals with this dangerous potential anecdotally by informing us that the vigilante abnegates his privilege in deference to the arrival of legitimate and effective law enforcement. The vigilante is more easily assimilated into the political structure of a completed settlement than the Indian hater, for all of his adventure has been within the boundaries of society and defensive of social bonds.

The dubious element in the vigilante figure is not, however, so easily dispelled. We see the persistence of the "dangerous class" identification in Cooper's portrayal of the Bush clan in *The Prairie.* The ending of Virgil Stewart's adventure also represents the vigilante as permanently altered by his adventure, and thus isolated from full participation in his society. Stewart's relation to the society he has rescued is as problematic as that of the returned captive Mary Rowlandson to hers: Stewart is driven into incognito by fear of Murrell's surviving confederates, who have infiltrated legitimate government; and even those whom he has saved doubt the incredible tale he has to tell, and mistrust him for having so readily played the "Clansman," leaving him in a position of moral isolation.

The problem of the dangerous classes behind the frontier, and the vigilante solution to that problem, persisted in both social fact and literary mythology. . . . The vigilante is the prototype of a kind of Frontier hero that would emerge after the Civil War as a substitute for the Indian-fighter/scout type represented by Leatherstocking. His personal characteristics and the special form of his adventure would be fully developed in a new genre, set in the cities rather than the wilderness—the detective story. (pp. 127-36)

> Richard Slotkin, *"The Backwash of a Closing Frontier: Industrialization and the Hiatus of Expansion, 1820-1845,"* in his The Fatal Environment: The Myth of the Frontier in the Age of Industrialization, 1800-1890, *Atheneum, 1985, pp. 109-37.*

HENRY NASH SMITH

[*In the following excerpt, Smith discusses conflicting attitudes toward the figure of the yeoman farmer in fiction of the agricultural West. For additional commentary by Smith, see excerpt above.*]

Although it was endlessly exciting for nineteenth-century Americans to contemplate the pioneer army moving westward at the command of destiny, and the Sons of Leatherstocking performing their improbable exploits in the wilderness, these themes had only an indirect bearing upon the major trends of economic and social development in American society. The forces which were to control the future did not originate in the picturesque Wild West beyond the agricultural frontier, but in the domesticated West that lay behind it.

With each surge of westward movement a new community came into being. These communities devoted themselves not to marching onward but to cultivating the earth. They plowed the virgin land and put in crops, and the great Interior Valley was transformed into a garden: for the imagination, the Garden of the World. The image of this vast and constantly growing agricultural society in the interior of the continent became one of the dominant symbols of nineteenth-century American society—a collective representation, a po-

George Sterling, Mary Austin, Jack London, and Jimmy Hopper.

etic idea (as Tocqueville noted in the early 1830's) that defined the promise of American life. The master symbol of the garden embraced a cluster of metaphors expressing fecundity, growth, increase, and blissful labor in the earth, all centering about the heroic figure of the idealized frontier farmer armed with that supreme agrarian weapon, the sacred plow. Although the idea of the garden of the world was relatively static, resembling an allegorical composition . . . , its role in expressing the assumptions and aspirations of a whole society and the hint of narrative content supplied by the central figure of the Western farmer give it much of the character of a myth. (pp. 123-24)

The yeoman ideal that was . . . to dominate the social thinking of the Northwest had emerged as a fusion of eighteenth-century agrarian theory with the observation of American experience beyond the Alleghenies. But the process had been slow. Only gradually had the Western farmer become a distinct figure for the imagination and his role in an essentially classless society recognized. The old attitude of upper-class condescension toward the plowman made it difficult for even sympathetic observers to become fully aware of the social revolution that was taking place in the interior. As late as 1819, the surveyor and gazetteer Edmund Dana, who knew his subject first hand, remarked casually in his *Geographical Sketches* that "The main business of common laborers, constituting the great mass of population in the west, will be the cultivation of the lands." [Charles J.] Faulkner himself, whose allusions to independent yeomen are a far cry from the unconscious snobbery of Dana's phrase "common laborers," could nevertheless refer to the "peasantry west of the Blue Ridge" in a way that would have been inconceivable ten years later. The Western yeoman had to work as hard as a common laborer or a European peasant, and at the same tasks. Despite the settled belief of Americans to the contrary, his economic status was not necessarily higher. But he was a different creature altogether because he had become the hero of a myth, of *the* myth of mid-nineteenth-century America. He no longer resembled even the often-praised English yeoman, darling of poets and social theorists. The very word had changed its meaning in American speech. The Western yeoman had become a symbol which could be made to bear an almost unlimited charge of meaning. It had strong overtones of patriotism, and it implied a far-reaching social theory. The career of this symbol deserves careful attention because it is one of the most tangible things we mean when we speak of the development of democratic ideas in the United States.

The beginning of it can be observed in James K. Paulding's early poem *The Backwoodsman,* published in 1818. Paulding's story begins in [St. John de] Crèvecœur's country, the Hudson Valley, but a single generation has brought a lamentable change there in the condition of the agricultural laborer. Instead of the Arcadian bliss which Crèvecœur had described on the eve of the Revolution, poverty and even starvation threaten Paulding's hero, the worthy but unfortunate Basil. The hardest toil and the most unremitting frugality cannot now earn independence for the agricultural laborer without inherited capital. There is no longer any land for him. After a week of desperate exertion in the fields—another man's fields—he spends his Sundays trying to find game or fish to keep his family from starvation, but to no avail, and when he falls ill the household faces absolute despair. If Paulding has darkened the shadows for dramatic effect, the picture still stands in impressive contrast with that presented in the *Letters from an American Farmer.*

Paulding's theme is the opportunity waiting in the West for such unfortunates. The crux of the matter is the ownership of land, which constitutes independence. As long as he must till another's land, Basil can never rise above grinding poverty. This will forever be the miserable destiny of "old Europe's hapless swains," but in America the great virgin West offers land for all who will cultivate it:

> Hence comes it, that our meanest farmer's boy
> Aspires to taste the proud and manly joy
> That springs from holding in his own dear right
> The land he plows, the home he seeks at night;
> And hence it comes, he leaves his friends and home,
> Mid distant wilds and dangers drear to roam,
> To seek a competence, or find a grave,
> Rather than live a hireling or a slave.

Basil accordingly gathers his family together and joins the throngs heading westward.

Settled beyond the Ohio on land bought from a benevolent landlord with liberal terms of credit, Basil is transformed. He now has that blessed independence which is the basis at once of physical comfort and moral virtue. Where free or virtually free land is available Crèvecœur's Utopia can flourish again. It is worth noting, incidentally, that Paulding's version of an ideal society in the West likewise has a strong tinge of that delight in the village which distinguished the stream of New England influence (as expressed for example in Dwight's *Greenfield Hill*) from the Southern frontier pattern of settlement in scattered clearings. Basil and his family had wept to leave behind the village church and tolling bell and the smoke of rural hamlets in their old home, but the backwoodsmen immediately create "a little rustic village" on the bank of the Ohio:

> To cultivated fields, the forest chang'd,
> Where golden harvests wav'd, and cattle rang'd;
> The curling smoke amid the wilds was seen,
> The village church now whiten'd on the green,
> And by its side arose the little school,
> Where rod and reason, lusty urchins rule,
> Whose loud repeated lessons might be heard,
> Whene'er along the road a wight appear'd.

The white church and the school are of New England but we must also make allowance for British influence. Paulding's

acknowledged master, Thomas Campbell, had already transplanted a very literary village to the Pennsylvania frontier in his *Gertrude of Wyoming* (1809). And back of Campbell was, among others, the Goldsmith of *The Deserted Village* (1770).

The sturdy plowman . . . is the mainstay of his country in war as well as in peace. The mettle of the Ohio emigrants is soon tested by Indian troubles arising from the War of 1812. Paulding points out that the hardy peasantry in Germany and Spain had stood to defeat Napoleon after kings and nobles had fled: Freedom's band, the militia of the West, are warriors even more formidable than the downtrodden slaves of the Old World. When Basil and his companions confront the Indians at Tippecanoe they have become "our bold yeomen."

At this stage of Basil's development Paulding's failure to grasp the implications of his material is strikingly evident. Like many later writers who dealt with the settlement of the West, he means to depict the "rise of the common man." But there are two ways of thinking about this rise. The political ideology of the 1830's and 1840's assumed that the common man had risen to dominate, or at least to share control of the government without ceasing to be the common man; it was a process whereby power in the state passed from one class to another. If this theory were analyzed rigorously, it would probably appear that the transfer of power to a new class was believed to have been accompanied by a decided weakening of all lines between classes. Certainly the myth of the garden as it had matured by the middle of the century interpreted the whole vast West as an essentially homogeneous society in which class stratification was of minor importance.

But *The Backwoodsman* was written before these changes had become apparent. Furthermore, Paulding was a prisoner of literary convention. Although Campbell, closer to the centers from which technical innovation was radiating, had written of the American frontier in Spenserian stanzas, the provincial Paulding was not up to this revolutionary daring and felt incapable of managing anything beyond the heroic couplet. But this choice of a measure committed him to linguistic and social conventions thoroughly unsuited to his theme. There was a basic impropriety in trying to write about the fluidity of classes in a measure which proclaimed with every caesura that order was Heaven's first law. In this dilemma Paulding resorted to irony:

> My humble theme is of a hardy swain [he began],
> The lowliest of the lowly rural train . . .
> Simple the tale I venture to rehearse,
> For humble is the Muse, and weak her verse;
> She hazards not, to sing in lofty lays,
> Of steel-clad knights, renown'd in other days,
> For glorious feats that, in this dastard time,
> Would on the gallows make them swing sublime . . .

We are to understand that the theme seems humble only when looked at from the standpoint of an indefensible code of aristocracy; the hardy swain appears degraded to those who venerate the knight, but a true scheme of values would make the swain the hero and consign the knight to the gallows.

Yet Paulding is not prepared either intellectually or technically for the reversal of social values which his irony implies; he is not really convinced that the hardy swain is superior to the upper classes. The rise of the common man is for him not a destruction of the class system but the rise of an individual member of the lower class in a social scale which itself is not changed. It is therefore not enough that Basil should be elevated to the rank of a bold and independent yeoman; he must be promoted out of his class. At the end of the poem he is something quite different from either a backwoodsman or a yeoman:

> Old BASIL—for his head is now grown gray—
> Waxes in wealth and honours every day;
> Judge, general, congressman, and half a score
> Of goodly offices, and titles more
> Reward his worth, while like a prince he lives,
> And what he gains from heav'n to mortals gives. . . .

Timothy Flint's efforts to depict Western life in fiction are even more instructive than Paulding's. A Massachusetts clergyman who went West in 1816 as a missionary and became a leading Western man of letters, he was in theory committed to the dream of a democratic agrarian Utopia. If his New England background led him to emphasize the recreation of the pattern of the village in the West, the villages of his imagination were very close to the soil and represented no alien element in a basically agricultural economy. In his *Recollections of the Last Ten Years,* published in 1826, he apostrophizes the Missouri River in prophecy of an ideal Western society much like Paulding's:

> anticipation, rapt away,
> Forestalls thy future glory, when thy tide
> Shall roll by towns, and villages, and farms,
> Continuous, amidst the peaceful hum
> Of happy multitudes, fed from thy soil;
> When the glad eye shall cheer at frequent view
> Of gilded spires of halls, still vocal with the task
> Of ripening youth; or churches sounding high,
> Hosannas to the Living God.

On occasion Flint could do full justice to a very Jeffersonian yeoman, and like Jefferson he saw the problem of American society as a choice between an agrarian and an industrial order. He defined his position in attacking the apologists for industry who were developing a theory of protective tariffs. Reviewing Alexander Hill Everett's *America* in 1827, Flint refused to accept either the Boston Brahmin's glowing description of New England mill towns or the pathetic picture of the sufferings of farmers who had escaped to the West:

> Thousands of independent and happy yeomen [he declared], who have emigrated from New England to Ohio and Indiana,—with their numerous, healthy and happy families about them, with the ample abundance that fills their granaries, with their young orchards, whose branches must be propped to sustain the weight of their fruit, beside their beautiful rivers, and beech woods, in which the squirrels skip, the wild deer browse, and the sweet red-bird sings, and with the prospect of settling their dozen children on as many farms about them,—would hardly be willing to exchange the sylvan range of their fee simple empires, their droves of cattle, horses, and domestic animals, and the ability to employ the leisure of half of their time as they choose, for the interior of square stone or brick walls, to breathe floccules of cotton, and to contemplate the whirl of innumerable wheels for fourteen hours of six days of every week in the year. . . . While there are uncounted millions of acres of fertile and unoccupied land, where farmers can rear their families in peace, plenty and privacy, under the guardian genius of our laws, we hope, that farms will continue to spread to the bases of

the Rocky mountains. Farmers and their children are strong, and innocent and moral almost of necessity. Compare the cheeks of the milk maid with the interesting, but pale faces in the great manufactories. The rigid laws, the stern rules of young associations, the extreme precautions that regulate the intercourse, the moral schools of discipline in these establishments, prove, after all, what the wise and provident superintendents think of the natural tendency of things in them. It is only a besieged city, that requires martial law, and the constant guard of armed sentinels.

The fee-simple empire on this familiar pattern appears again and again in Flint's nonfictional writings. He describes Ohio, for example, as a perfect realization of the ideal, which for him means that it reproduces the bucolic New England of the age before the coming of the cotton mills—a land of small farms, as he had described it in 1815 before he left, cultivated by independent and virtuous owners; of frequent and neat schoolhouses; of village churches standing as emblems of law, justice, order, industry, and temperance. Ohio, Flint wrote admiringly in 1833, "seems to have invited a hardy and numerous body of freeholders to select themselves moderate and nearly equal-sized farms, and to intersperse them over its surface." Like Faulkner of Berkeley County he points the contrast between this picture of social happiness and the landscape presented by the slave states. Under the plantation system, flourishing villages and a compact population of small farmers cannot develop. Isolated mansions inhabited by intelligent and hospitable families rise here and there, at great distances from one another, but the mansions are surrounded by squalid Negro cabins, and "the contrast of the hovels and the mansion can never cease to be a painful spectacle to the eye."

Yet if Flint took pleasure in the yeoman society of the free Northwest, he was unable to use the yeoman in fiction. His only novel laid in the Mississippi Valley shows that he was even more handicapped by ingrained class feeling than Paulding had been. *George Mason, The Young Backwoodsman,* published in 1829, is in part autobiographical. The Reverend George Mason, father of the hero, like Flint resigns his pastorate in a New England village because of factional strife in his congregation, and takes his family to the Southwest. They settle on a small claim in the forest—probably a reminiscence of Flint's experiences near Jackson, Missouri, although the setting of the story is ostensibly Mississippi. After great hardships which stand in marked contrast to Flint's generalizations about peace and plenty in the West, the father dies, but the eldest son George succeeds in becoming owner of a steamboat and at the end of the book the Mason family is installed with a comfortable income in a village on the Upper Ohio. The son and the eldest daughter Eliza have meanwhile been provided with suitable mates.

Flint's feeling about this material is confused. He announces at the outset that he will deal with "the short and simple annals of the poor," who comprise nine-tenths of the human race. His thesis is that a noble heart can swell in a bosom clad in the meanest habiliments, and that "incidents, full of tender and solemn interest, have occurred in a log cabin in the forests of the Mississippi." Certain slaveowners are depicted as illiterate and rude, the coarse and vulgar rich. But no instance of nobility in natives of the West is exhibited except in the benevolent slave Pompey. The Masons, although destitute, encounter no person in the backwoods whom Flint considers their social equal. The mates provided for the son and daughter are as wealthy as Cooper would have made them. One is a New Englander, the other a Pennsylvanian. Near the end of the book George's prospective wife turns pale at the thought of having to travel on the deck of the river steamboat with the poor families, instead of in the cabin with the first-class passengers.

The lesson of Flint's novel . . . is that the literary imagination moved very slowly toward acceptance of the democratic principles so glowingly embodied in agrarian theory. This was doubtless due in part to the fact that even bad fiction comes out of a deeper level of the personality than conceptual thought. It owes something also to the inertia of literary forms, a force . . . operating in the Leatherstocking tales. (pp. 135-42)

The abstractions of the agrarian tradition were applied with little change to successive areas in the Northwest as settlement advanced into them. James B. Lanman, for example, a native of Connecticut who lived in Michigan for two years in the late 1830's at the height of the land boom, contributed articles to the influential *Hunt's Merchants' Magazine* celebrating the intelligent plowman who, as he followed his harrow over the mellow land, his own land, was filled with "the spirit of independence, always arising in the mind of every freeholder." In a later article Lanman invokes the memory of Jefferson and recites all the themes of the myth of the garden:

> If, as has been remarked by a distinguished statesman, cities are the sores of the political body, where the bad matter of the state is concentrated, what healthful habitudes of mind and body are afforded by agricultural enterprise! The exhilarating atmosphere of a rural life, the invigorating exercise afforded by its various occupations, the pure water, the abundance of all the necessaries of subsistence, leading to early and virtuous marriages, all point to this pursuit as best adapted to the comfort of the individual man. Its beneficial bearing upon the state is no less obvious. The agriculturist, removed from the pernicious influences that are forever accumulated in large cities, the exciting scenes, which always arise from large accumulations of men, passes a quiet and undisturbed life, possessing ample means and motives thoroughly to reflect upon his rights and duties, and holding a sufficient stake in the soil to induce him to perform those duties both for himself and his country. It is to the true-hearted and independent yeomen of a nation that we look, in times of national danger, to uphold its institutions, and to protect themselves in preserving the principles of the state. It is to them that we refer for the support of sound legislation, and from their ranks that we derive the best soldiers when the horrors of war overspread a land. While other branches of human enterprise are protected in their due measure, it can scarcely be denied that agricultural enterprise, the basis of almost every form of human pursuit, should be encouraged as the safeguard of a country, the promoter of its virtue, and the solid foundation of its permanent happiness and most lasting independence.

(pp. 142-43)

Henry Nash Smith, "The Garden of the World and American Agrarianism" and "The Yeoman and the Fee-Simple Empire," in his Virgin Land: The American West as Symbol and Myth, *Cambridge,*

Mass.: Harvard University Press, 1950, pp. 123-32, 133-44.

ALFRED HABEGGER

[*In the following excerpt, Habegger examines three types of protagonists in nineteenth-century American humor.*]

One of the most important and persistent effects of the frontier was to relax the social contract by allowing frontiersmen to revert to the life of a hunter. The sophisticated French republican, Crèvecoeur, writing shortly before the Revolutionary War, considered frontiersmen an unhappy instance of cultural regression:

> By living in or near the woods, their actions are regulated by the wildness of the neighbourhood. The deer often come to eat their grain, the wolves to destroy their sheep, the bears to kill their hogs, the foxes to catch their poultry. This surrounding hostility immediately puts the gun into their hands; they watch these animals, they kill some; and thus by defending their property, they soon become professed hunters; this is the progress; once hunters, farewell to the plough. The chase renders them ferocious, gloomy, and unsociable.

Many other observers, such as William Byrd of Westover, complained about the laziness of settlers on or near the frontier. But these cultivated men—Crèvecoeur with his physiocratic ideology based on the independent landholder, Byrd with his investments in land and aristocratic values—were hardly in a good position to appreciate the siren song that drifted out of the forested wilderness and caught the ears of so many American men. What that song promised was free land, abundant game, no taxes, no oppression—the illusion, in other words, of total independence. The frontier would be the place where you would be left alone to do just what you wanted. The appeal of this siren song was very deep. Primatologists, paleo-archaeologists, and anthropologists are converging on a more detailed view of how humans survived for at least one million years by means of hunting and gathering—men doing most of the hunting, women most of the gathering. In late eighteenth- and early nineteenth-century America, the civilized overlay grew sufficiently thin that the conditions were met for European colonials to come out of culture in a very odd way, to acquire a new kind of self-knowledge. Our peculiar American masculinity originated in a discovery made again and again on the moving frontier by men who had begun life thinking of themselves as Europeans or colonials or Americans—the discovery that they were more wild than domestic, that civilized folks had been laboring under some pretty fancy mistakes about the nature of mankind. The frontier allowed the heady pleasure of a reversion to a savage state and released an enormous amount of masculine aggression.

I believe that one of the things that happened to many trappers, hunters, and casual wanderers and homesteaders was that they rediscovered those aboriginal, species-specific human traits that a mere 10,000 years of civilized life had not been able to expunge. Yet it would be naive to conclude that frontiersmen managed to become true savages. True savages grow up in particular cultures along with other members of a band. Because there is no such thing as a primitive human apart from any particular culture, there can be no such thing as a complete reversion to a savage state. This seems to me to be the basic illusion in the myth that is the subject of Richard Slotkin's stimulating book *Regeneration through Violence* [see excerpt above]. Slotkin argues that John Filson's 1784 narrative of the life of Daniel Boone was the definitive American myth. This narrative told the story of a civilized man who turned into an archetypal hunter and settler. For Slotkin, the key element was violent combat. When Daniel Boone entered the wilderness, he joined an Indian in mortal combat, killing the Indian. But in the very act of doing so, he submitted to the wilderness order and acquired an Indian identity. One may accept the idea that frontier violence entered deeply into American masculinity, and yet remain skeptical of Slotkin's myth and symbol formulations. The question is this: how can you become an Indian in any sense without growing up in or living with a tribe? Many American men no doubt thought of themselves as in some way Indian. But that was an illusion.

There were a number of other illusions about the frontier, one of the biggest being that it was in some way the Land of Cockayne, a place where one could at last find the good life without having to work very hard. From the very beginning, in other words, the idea of the frontier was exceedingly cloudy, and this cloudiness has persisted down to our own time. Some people seem to believe that the first backwoodsmen habitually spoke in half-horse, half-alligator braggadocio. Others, such as Charlton Laird, accept Charles Dickens' version of Western life in 1842:

> There never was a race of people who so completely gave the lie to history as these giants, or whom all the chroniclers have so libelled. Instead of roaring and ravaging about the world, constantly catering for their cannibal larders, and perpetually going to market in an unlawful manner, they are the meekest people in any man's acquaintance: rather inclining to milk and vegetable diet, and bearing anything for a quiet life.

A partial solution to the fearfully contradictory evidence is to recognize that the frontier was enveloped from the beginning by a rich cluster of lies, illusions, myths, and golden dreams, and that practically everybody who went there did so very self-consciously, with certain very definite and strongly held opinions.

One of the primary reasons for insisting on the haze of illusions surrounding the frontier—and in particular on its siren song of ease and independence—is to reach an understanding of one of the oddest of native American products, tall talk. This term was used to designate several different, though equally hyperbolic, kinds of speech or writing—the use of preposterous Latinate language ("if 'taint, I hope I may be teetotaciously exfluncted"), the telling of a farfetched story, or the uttering of an absurd brag. Tall talk seems to have originated in conjunction with a certain stereotype, the Kentuckian, a person who lived only to drink, gamble, boast, and fight. It was the Kentuckian Dickens actually hoped to see. Walter Blair has found an early description of this creature, of two of them in fact, from an 1810 travel book:

> One said, "I am a man; I am a horse; I am a team. I can whip any man *in all Kentucky*, by G-d." The other replied, "I am an alligator, half man, half horse; can whip any man *on the Mississippi*, by G-d." The first one again, "I am a man; have the best horse, best dog, best gun, and the handsomest wife in all Kentucky, by G-d." The other, "I am a Mississippi snapping turtle: have bear's claws, alligator's teeth, and the devil's tail; can whip *any*

man, by G-d." This was too much for the first, and at it they went like two bulls.

The behavior exhibited in this scene is so interesting that it is easy to understand why Dickens made a point of looking for instances of it. It was this kind of braggadocio, exaggerated to the point of becoming fantastic and suicidal, that hightoned Europeans first learned to think of as "American humor." Christian Schultz, Jr., the traveler who brought home this particular gem, apparently presented it as fact.

But the anecdote was not factual, it was literary. Only if this is understood can our earliest American humor come into focus. Like most of the pieces belonging to later Southwestern humor, this anecdote was originally told by someone very different from the two characters who end up fighting like bulls. Essentially, the piece is a burlesque of the raw independence of men on the frontier. The kind of tall talk the two men exchange has a simple social meaning—it makes them look more impressive—taller—than they really are. Each man is using speech to make himself look big, and one of the reasons each man does this is that he is affirming that archetypal and indomitable savage masculinity that was supposed to be attainable on the frontier. Their ritual boasts are the comic expression of the male ideal of total self-reliance and personal supremacy. Furthermore, each man recognizes that the other's boast is a challenge to combat that cannot go unanswered. Each man *must* answer the challenge. If he does not, it means he is admitting the lie on which he has staked his life—the lie that he has in some way managed to escape human limitations, relative status, mortality. Yet the authors of pieces like this one were not jeering at or in any way satirizing the combatants. Men living in a culture that called forth enormous respect for displays of courage, good marksmanship, political oratory, and shrewd Yankee trading could hardly bring themselves to belittle any form of challenging male prowess. Yet they could not get rid of their sense of the unreality of the masculine ideal. So they laughed. It was by means of a humorous burlesque of the fool within that men stayed sane.

Male behavior in the first half-century of the Republic often exhibited the same weird combination of enormous inflation and enormous comic deflation. Several poets tried to write heavy Miltonic epics about our national independence, but the only good long poems to emerge from our revolutionary political history were mock-epics, *M'Fingal* and *The Hasty Pudding*. Aside from Charles Brockden Brown's novels, our first long fiction with a native flavor was the debunking *Modern Chivalry* by Hugh Henry Brackenridge. Strangest of all is the song that by all rights is the real national anthem, "Yankee Doodle." This song was written by an Englishman in derision of colonial Americans, who then took it as their own marching song. This combination of revolutionary assertiveness and humorous self-deflation was deeply imbedded in the American character. It appears everywhere in *Walden,* even on the title page, which gives a polite printed form of the rooster's crow that backwoodsmen theoretically uttered: "I do not propose to write an ode to dejection, but to brag as lustily as chanticleer in the morning, standing on his roost, if only to wake my neighbors up." For a man to crow like a rooster was to utter a defiant challenge—and also to play the fool. It makes sense that American humor became the distinctive nineteenth-century literary genre for men.

The backwoods boaster was inevitably associated with a wild place that had not yet been tamed, but the men who wrote about him were inevitably associated with newspapers or law offices or army forts or the stage. In 1840 a Florida newspaper gave a brief account of a bragging speech by a backwoodsman named Little Billy. In this account, tall talk as a burlesque mode of speech has begun to crystallize into one of the narrative forms characteristic of Southwestern humor (1830-1855).

> As we were passing by the court-house, a real "screamer from the Nob," about six feet four in height, commenced the following tirade: "This is *me,* and no mistake! Billy Earthquake, Esq., commonly called Little Billy, all the way from the No'th Fork of Muddy Run! I'm a small specimen, as you see, a remote circumstance, a mere yearling; but cuss me if I ain't of the true imported breed, and can whip any man in this section of the country. Whoop! won't *nobody* come out and fight me? . . .
>
> "Maybe you don't know who Little Billy is? I'll tell you. I'm a poor man, it's a fact, and smell like a wet dog; but I can't be run over. I'm the identical individual that grinned a whole menagerie out of countenance, and made the ribbed-nose baboon hang down his head and blush. W-h-o-o-p! I'm the chap that towed the Broad-horn up Salt River, where the snags were so thick that the fish couldn't swim without rubbing their scales off!—fact, and if any denies it, just let 'em make their will! Cock-a-doodle-doo!"

Little Billy's tall tale about towing a boat up a river is not intended to amuse or distract a group of idlers, let alone readers, but to make somebody stand up and fight. And unless the bystander pretends to swallow every word, he'll have to risk getting hurt. But of course there are no bystanders, only a silent courthouse. Little Billy is out of place, or out of time, and partly because of that, comic. He aims his challenge at the courthouse, the symbol of the law's arrival on the frontier and the sign of his own obsolescence. Frustrated by the refusal of anyone to answer him like a man, Little Billy stalks out of town, "walking off in disgust." He may not know it, but he has just lost the main event.

The fact that so incredibly many of the early tall talk anecdotes consist of a burlesque of male belligerence constitutes a weighty piece of evidence for viewing early nineteenth-century American humor as a very important masculine social institution. It of course was also a literary institution, and in the light of later writers like Mark Twain and William Faulkner, a very influential and valuable one. But because it emerged out of concrete historic circumstances, it is difficult not to yield to the temptation to wonder to what extent the burlesque boast mirrored actual behavior. Unable to resist temptation, I see at least five ways in which the chest-thumping wild man reflected male behavior.

First, I think this humorous figure bespeaks the centrality of bluffing in male encounters in that period. One of Augustus Baldwin Longstreet's sketches is narrated by a man who hears dreadful boasts and signs of battle in the woods. On investigating, he finds that it is only a boy playing at being a man: "I was jist seein' how I could 'a' fout." Beadle's second *Book of Fun* (1860) reprinted an amusing story, "Bears in Arkansas," told by a hunter who happened to be standing near a bear tree when a small bear walked up to leave his mark. According to the narrator, bears mark trees because "it's a great satisfaction to an old he bar to have the highest mark

on the tree." To his surprise, the narrator sees the young bear carry a "big clunk" up to the tree and by standing on it leave a mark "a foot above the highest." These two anecdotes neatly point out the element of deception involved in ordinary masculine bluffing.

Another way the half-horse, half-alligator reflects the men who enjoyed laughing at this type is that it articulated their own sense of suppressed but latent animality. Here, we get a first-rate piece of evidence from *Huckleberry Finn,* where a roomful of men derive enormous enjoyment out of the spectacle of the Royal Nonesuch. Another novel in which a man impersonates a beast in order to amuse an audience, a mixed one in this instance, is *Kate Beaumont* by John William De Forest. A church fair organized to raise money for a steeple entertains the crowd with a howling gyascutus: "He ran at the shins of his keeper; he stood five feet eight in his boots, and pawed the kerosene-lit air; he howled in his virile fashion until the blood of small urchins curdled with horror." This almost uncontrollable beast is indeed remarkably virile. Later, after the impersonator takes off the costume and joins the audience, his sister says: "How could you make such a guy of yourself! But, really, it *was* funny."

To make a guy of oneself—this phrase originally meant to make an object of ridicule of oneself. The dictionaries of American English do not cite De Forest's passage, which seems to me extremely suggestive in the way it brings together *guy* and *gyascutus.* De Forest may have seen a connection between these words. Could the connection be etymological? Could the casual American word for boy or man be identical in its origins with the word for a mythical virile beast?

But the gyascutus was not entirely mythical, and sometimes he got loose from his keeper. There is abundant evidence that it was anything but unusual for American men to go on a rampage when they drank too much. It is well to remember that drunkenness is shaped by culture as much as loving or fighting. Mark Twain gave a chilling portrait of a violent drunk in the *Adventures of Huckleberry Finn,* where Pap very nearly kills his own son. But this episode was not purely realistic; the satiric quality of Pap's speech suffices to prove that Mark Twain was doing much more than simply reporting behavior. Silas Lapham's drunkenness is much more realistic. Significantly, what Lapham does, before his wife finally succeeds in dragging him home, is to utter a challenging brag: "Ten years ago he, Silas Lapham, had come to Boston a little worse off than nothing at all, for he was in debt for half the money that he had bought out his partner with, and here he was now worth a million, and meeting you gentlemen like one of you." One of the magnificent aspects of this novel is the way Howells reveals a wild, chest-thumping brother hidden under the outer layers of personality. But the most revealing portrait of the inner gyascutus is, once again, in De Forest's *Kate Beaumont,* in the character of the gentlemanly Randolph Armitage:

> "It seemed so absurd that any human being could become demented enough to beat and belabor inanimate things till he gasped with fatigue . . . The man was more like a crazy monkey than like a human being. His pranks surpass all description."

This is his wife's description of Randolph, and we see it verified:

> "You bear a hand somewhere else," screamed Randolph, all at once beside himself with an insane

rage, approaching to *delirium tremens.* "You bear a hand out of this house. You leave. It's my house."

The master passion expressing itself in this drunk man seems to be a rage at the temerity of someone's invading his castle. Was this raging territoriality the passion of which our early American humor was a (relatively) polite masquerade? After all, the hope of getting free land of one's own was precisely what drew many men to the frontier.

Although it would be naive to read those early half-horse, half-alligator boasts as literal reporting of actual events, art surely influenced life in the last century as much as it seems to do today, and many men may have playfully or self-consciously squared off in the approved fashion. Even the cowboy who rides into town to shoot 'em up was not simply relieving his pent-up feelings but following an old, half-obligatory scenario. There is a passage in A. J. Sowell's *Rangers and Pioneers in Texas* that suggests the ritual element in this kind of male violence:

> Occasionally in some Western village you will hear a voice ring out on the night air in words something like these: "Wild and wooly," "Hard to curry," "Raised a pet but gone wild," "Walked the Chisholm Trail backwards," "Fought Indians and killed buffalo," "Hide out, little ones," and then you may expect a few shots from a revolver. It is a cowboy out on a little spree, but likely he will not hurt anyone, as some friend who is sober generally comes to him, relieves him of his pistol, and all is soon quiet again.

Finally, the ring-tailed roarer to some extent really did reflect a kind of criminal bullying that emerged on the frontier. Here and there men terrorized entire neighborhoods, though they generally acted in consort with their brothers or cronies or gangs of outlaws. A case in point is the Sullivan family in the Piney Woods section of southern Mississippi known as Sullivan's Hollow. One of the Sullivans once made a couple of passing strangers dance and whoop with him, until he found out that one of them was related by marriage. Another once got in a fight and had his abdominal wall slashed so badly his intestines spilled out on the sand. He washed them in a creek and had himself sewed up. Then, "some said, he went out into the yard climbed upon a stump, flapped his arms like a rooster's wings, and crowed." In time the Sullivans spread elsewhere, one of them becoming notorious throughout the East Lawrence highlands of Kansas for his rough practical joking.

But it is time to return to literary history and attempt to sketch the literary evolution through the nineteenth century of the backwoods boaster and his characteristic form of speech, tall talk. Bearing in mind that this boaster was a burlesque of an ideal male gender role—the self-reliant, world-defying man—one sees a certain inevitability in the sequence of development.

1) 1800-1830. The ringtailed roarer and his boast. This early stage looks more like folklore than it really was. It shows up in travel books, newspapers, and the occasional literary character such as Nimrod Wildfire in James K. Paulding's *The Lion of the West* (1830).

2) Southwestern Humor. This phase ran from 1830 to 1855. Most of the pieces were sketches published in newspapers, books, and a New York magazine with a national circulation, *The Spirit of the Times.* The authors of many sketches never identified themselves. Known authors were generally profes-sional men—lawyers, newspapermen, doctors, actors, artists, and army officers. These writers frequently introduced their low-life humor by using a cultivated and ironic bystander, narrator, or narrative voice.

3) Literary Comedians of the 1860s. This phase began just before the Civil War, when Charles Farrar Browne took the persona of Artemus Ward and David Ross Locke that of Petroleum V. Nasby. Their humor not only circulated through newspapers but, miraculously, came to life on the stage. Samuel L. Clemens turned into Mark Twain and made paying audiences of gold miners laugh. The literary comedians wrote books, yet they were also public figures and were closely associated with their comic masks.

4) Boy Books. This phase came and went in the 1870s and 80s. What happens in the boy books is that a young practical joker, or more often a gang of mischievous and enterprising boys, torments a stable adult order.

These successive phases were four very widespread trends, each of which became an easily recognized mode in its time, gained a certain fashionable quality, and, except for the first phase, attracted many writers. Of course, there were numerous humorists who didn't fit into these modes, especially the Down East humorists, and there were some phases that would persist well into the twentieth century in the Mountain West. The reason for stacking these four phases in their order of development is to reveal the degeneration of an ideal type—the burlesque form of the mythic autonomous male. In the initial phase, he was already funny but still seen as bigger than life, a tall Kentuckian or six-foot-four Little Billy. In Southwestern humor he was still a boasting hunter or rowdy, but his adventures were more artistic and often framed by a far more civilized storyteller. With the literary comedians, the confident fighter turned into a humorless and incompetent oldtimer, a frontiersman collapsed into a hayseed. Finally, in *Tom Sawyer* and the other boy books, the central character was not even a man but simply a mischievous boy. Each phase of nineteenth-century American humor focused on a certain male type, and these types were the successively degenerate sons of Daniel Boone, the archetypal macho hero. Their decreasing stature, power, and wildness reveal what was happening to the ideal male self that was brought to birth by the vision of an apparently unlimited wilderness. Some cultures have made great epics out of defeat. We preferred to go the American way, laughing, with a great big guffaw. It is tempting to see in this shrinking devolution nothing but the harmful effects of industrialization and urbanization. That view, however, overlooks the falsity in the idealized male view of the frontier—the illusion that there one might finally achieve an archaic and self-reliant way of life. Even more, such a view overlooks the unreality of the whole idea of self-reliance or total autonomy.

Thus, the humor of the literary comedians represents an inevitable stage in a long socio-literary process. The harmless, easygoing old duffer who got center stage in so much humor of the 1860s and early 70s is what six-foot-four Little Billy inevitably turned into, after the courthouse was built and nobody would fight with him anymore. The literary comedians created the new ineffective type by actively impersonating him. Except for George Washington Harris, the Southwestern humorists had carefully distinguished between themselves and the backwoods ruffian, who was so rude and threatening they had to keep him at arm's length. One of the ways they did this was by framing his rough assertiveness in an artificial prose that was warranted to be safely civilized. But the humorists of the 1860s were able to take the risk of dissolving this distinction because the old bully had passed his prime. Thus, they transformed themselves into Artemus Ward, Petroleum V. Nasby, Bill Arp, Mark Twain, founding their mask in every case upon a man who was a countrified survival from the past, an oldtimer who hadn't been able to adjust to the present. This man was a loser, a failure, and that was why men laughed at him.

The connection between failure and funniness is apparent in a trick of speech used by most of the literary comedians—their drawl. Of course, the drawl reflected a rural origin at a time when everyone knew the future lay in the city, but more than that the drawl revealed a leisurely and unfashionable spirit, one that would not be hurried or bothered. It was the sign of a man caught in the backwaters and content to stay there. It was a token of social or professional failure. In its countrified slowness, drawling was the oral equivalent to leaning back in your chair and propping your feet on the table. Drawling meant that you weren't going to worry about a thing and also that you weren't ever going to get ahead.

The most famous trademark of the comedians of the sixties, their deadpan delivery, was also a token of failure. Deadpan is not blankness of expression so much as a humorlessness charged with helpless sorrow. Artemus Ward spoke with "the melancholy earnest manner of a man completely unconscious that there is anything grotesque in what he says." One of Mark Twain's first listeners recollected "his slow deliberate drawl, the anxious and perturbed expression of his visage, the apparently painful effort with which he framed his sentences, and, above all, the surprise that spread over his face when the audience roared with delight." W. D. Howells' best American humorist, a Wyoming rancher in *Doctor Breen's Practice,* speaks "lifelessly," with "no gleam of insinuation in his melancholy eye." When he finishes a monologue, he gives "a sort of weary sigh, as if oppressed by experience." He utters his boasts "with a wan, lack-lustre irony, as if he were burlesquing the conventional Western brag and enjoying the mystifications of his listener." And there it is: the literary comedians were not bragging like Little Billy but doing something sadder and more civilized. The deadpan comedian spoke with the sad sincerity of a man who had failed to get ahead and would never understand why. In Orpheus C. Kerr's Civil War letters, a solemn incompetent named Bob tried to fight a duel:

> "Gaul darn ye!" screamed Samyule, turning purple in the face, "you've gone and shot all the rim of my cap off."

> "I couldn't help it," says Bob, looking into the barrel of his pistol with great intensity of gaze.

The whole deadpan mode is summed up in that great intensity of gaze—Bob's sober melancholy absorption in his own failure. What a far cry he is from a comic superman like Little Billy!

Suddenly men were more interested in victims and losers than in the confidence men and Yankee peddlers that had always been stock characters on the American scene. In Mark Twain's *Roughing It* we learn about a greenhorn who buys a bad horse, a "genuine Mexican plug." About the seller, we learn nothing. Similarly, "The Great Jumping Frog of Calaveras County" tells us about the dupe, Jim Smiley, but not the anonymous trickster who fills the bullfrog full of shot. In

a country where the ability to drive a shrewd bargain had been a classic test of manhood, men in the sixties seemed to be most interested in those who failed this ritual confrontation.

In Southwestern humor the distinctive way of talking was the extravagant spread-eagle boast of the proverbial scrappy frontiersman. Men laughed at this, but a generation later, when the literary comedians spoke with the born loser's flat literalism, they laughed a lot harder. Machismo had been trampled on in a vital spot. The old violent and self-sufficient masculine ideal had suffered a devaluation. The frontier was farther away than ever now, and men were beginning to suspect it would never come back. The Combine was consolidating its power. The 1860s, the decade of war and rapid industrialization, exacted a terrible cost from the men who made it all hum. As they moved from farms and small towns to the army, the factory, the city, they had to conform to a new masculine ethos, put on a new identity. Now they had to look sharp, get up and go, keep in step with large impersonal systems, acquire a new and mechanical sense of time.

The fourth phase in the life of the incredible shrinking American man arrived in the 1870s and 80s, in an outpouring of boy books. In most of these books, the boy lived in an old-fashioned place, relatively untouched by urbanization or industrialization. He was "bad," though often only in play, like Tom Sawyer and his gang pretending to be marauders. The boy never had to work, he often skipped school, and his most distinctive act was the practical joke. In *The Story of a Bad Boy* he set off the town cannons or pushed an old carriage into the Fourth of July bonfire; in *Tom Sawyer* he fooled the town into thinking he was dead and then strode down the church aisle at his own funeral. The butt of his jokes was the community, the whole adult order of things, particularly its pieties and annual rituals, which he assaulted for the same reason that Little Billy assaulted the courthouse. The boy waged a careless, undeclared war against civilization and its discontents. He ran off to the river or the woods whenever he could—the very places that were once wilderness—and the games he played there imitated the exploits of a prior generation of men, the frontiersmen. The boy, in fact, was the remains of the man who had once found a new identity, or rather, a few pieces of a very, very old identity, in the wilderness. (pp. 127-39)

Alfred Habegger, "Taking Down the Big One: From Frontier Boaster to Deadpan Loser to Boy," in his Gender, Fantasy, and Realism in American Literature, *Columbia University Press, 1982, pp. 126-39.*

PORTRAYALS OF NATIVE AMERICANS

ROY HARVEY PEARCE

[*An American educator and critic, Pearce has written on American literature and intellectual history and is perhaps best known for his* The Savages of America (*1953; revised edition published in 1965 as* Savagism and Civilization), *in which he examined white society's assumptions about native Americans and about their own civilization. In the following excerpt, he views the captivity narrative, a chronicle of the experiences of settlers captured by native Americans, as a reflection of American popular culture.*]

The Narrative of Indian captivity has long been recognized for its usefulness in the study of our history and, moreover, has even achieved a kind of literary status. Generally it has been taken as a sort of "saga," something which somehow is to be understood as expressive of the Frontier Mind—whatever that may be. But this is to make of the captivity narrative a kind of composite, abstracted thing; this is to make a single genre out of the sort of popular form which shapes and reshapes itself according to varying immediate cultural "needs." Certainly there is a natural basic unity of content in the many narratives which we have; but variation in treatment of content, in specific form, and in point of view is so great as to make for several genres, for several significances. Here matters of pure historical fact (a purity which is often suspect, as we shall see) and ethnological data—that is, of content abstracted from treatment—are beside the point; what is important is what the narrative was for the readers for whom it was written. The significances of the captivity narrative vary from that of the religious confessional to that of the noisomely visceral thriller. The distance between the two sorts of narratives is great; over that distance can be traced the history of the captivity narrative taken as a popular genre—or, more properly, genres. As popular genre, or genres, it comes to have a kind of incidental literary value, enters literary history proper in *Edgar Huntly,* and functions as a popular vehicle for various historically and culturally individuated purposes. And it is as such that I propose to consider it here.

The first, and greatest, of the captivity narratives are simple, direct religious documents. They are for the greater part Puritan; and their writers find in the experience of captivity, "removal," hardships on the march to Canada, adoption or torture or both, the life in Canada which so often seemed to consist in nothing but resisting the temptations set forth by Romish priests, and eventual return (this is the classic pattern of the captivity), evidences of God's inscrutable wisdom. Thus Increase Mather in the *Essay for the Recording of Illustrious Providences* (1684) prefaces Quintin Stockwell's story of his captivity with these words:

> Likewise several of those that were taken Captive by the *Indians* are able to relate affecting Stories concerning the gracious Providence of God, in carrying them through many Dangers and Deaths, and at last setting their feet in a large place again. A Worthy Person hath sent me the Account which one lately belonging to *Deerfield* (his name is *Quintin Stockwell,*) hath drawn up respecting his own Captivity and Redemption, with the Providence attending him in his distress, which I shall here insert in the Words he himself expresseth. . . .

Thus too, John Williams, in dedicating his *Redeemed Captive Returning to Zion* (1707) to Joseph Dudley, indicates that he tells his story because "The wonders of divine mercy, which we have seen in the land of our captivity, and been delivered therefrom, cannot be forgotten without incurring the guilt of blackest ingratitude." The Puritan narrative is one in which the details of the captivity itself are found to figure forth a larger, essentially religious experience; the captivity has symbolic value; and the record is made minute, direct, and concrete in order to squeeze the last bit of meaning out of the experience.

The Stockwell and the Williams narratives, along with Jonathan Dickenson's Quaker *God's Protecting Providence Man's Surest Help and Defense* (1699), are in the pattern of the best known (and deservedly so) of the narratives, Mrs. Rowlandson's *Soveraignty and Goodness of God* (1682). Here, it will be recalled, there is the fusion of vivid immediacy and religious intensity. At the very beginning Mrs. Rowlandson writes: "Now away we must go with those barbarous creatures, with our bodies wounded and bleeding, and our hearts no less than our bodies." And later she pictures the Indians' triumphant celebrations: "This was the dolefullest night that ever my eyes saw. Oh the roaring and singing and dancing and yelling of those black creatures in the night, which made the place a lively resemblance of hell. . . . " Constantly she prays and considers her life one long terrifying religious adventure. There is even in the Rowlandson narrative, as in the others which I have instanced, a certain aesthetic quality which derives from the freshness and concreteness of detail with which the narrator explores her experience. Here we have the quality of the diary and that of, say, Edwards's *Personal Narrative* at their best. Here we have the captivity as a direct statement of a frontier experience, an experience which is taken as part of the divine scheme.

Such narratives were popular in their appeal when they first appeared and so continued. But gradually the quality of directness, of concern with describing an experience precisely as it had affected the individual who underwent it, of trying somehow to recapture and put down what were taken as symbolic psychic minutiae, began to disappear. Other interests predominated. The propagandist value of the captivity narrative became more and more apparent; and what might be termed stylization, the writing up of the narrative by one who was not directly involved, came to have a kind of journalistic premium.

Cotton Mather propagandizes. He presents in the *Magnalia* (1702) the direct, religiously intense narratives of Hannah Swarton and Mrs. Duston (Book VI, Chapter II, and Book VII, Appendix, Article XXV) and four "Relations" of *"The Condition of the* Captives *that from time to time fell into the Hands of the* Indians; with some very Remarkable Accidents" (Book VII, Appendix, Article VII). He concludes the "Relations" thus:

> In fine, when the *Children* of the *English Captives* cried at any time, so that they were not presently quieted, the manner of the *Indians* was to dash out their Brains against a *Tree.*
>
> And very often, when the *Indians* were on or near the Water, they took the small *Children,* and held 'em under Water till they had near Drowned them, and then gave 'em unto their Distressed Mothers to quiet 'em.
>
> And the *Indians* in their Frolicks would Whip and Beat the small *Children,* until they set 'em into grievous Outcries, and then throw 'em to their amazed Mothers for them to quiet 'em again as well as they could.

This was *Indian Captivity!*

If the *Magnalia* is the record of godly New England's triumph over the wilderness, part of that record is of a triumph over the evil dwellers in the wilderness. Even as Mather rejoices over Christianizing the Indian (Book VI, Chapter VI), so he promotes hatred of the Indian. And in the *Magnalia* the captivity begins to become explicitly a vehicle of Indian-hatred.

The development of variant texts of *God's Mercy surmounting Man's Cruelty, Exemplified in the Captivity and Redemption of Elizabeth Hanson* (1728) indicates clearly the pattern of what I have termed stylization of the captivity narrative. The edition of 1728 is direct and colloquial, in the pattern of Mrs. Rowlandson's narrative. The nominal reprint of this (1754) is somewhat more "correct." And the *Account of the Captivity of Elizabeth Hanson* which first appeared (so far as I have been able to discover) in 1760 as "Taken in Substance from her own Mouth, by Samuel Bownas," although it still is in the first person, is made into something even more acceptably "literary"; freshness and direct emotional value have all but disappeared. The beginnings of the three versions will illustrate satisfactorily this matter of stylization:

1728:

> As soon as they discovered themselves (having as we understood by their Discourse, been sculking in the Fields some Days watching their Opportunity when my dear Husband, with the rest of our Men, were gone out of the way) two of the barbarous Salvages came in upon us, next Eleven more, all naked, with their Guns and Tomahawks came into the House in a great Fury upon us, and killed one Child immediately, as soon as they entered the Door, thinking thereby to strike in us the greater Terror, and to make us more fearful of them.

> Then in as great Fury the Captain came up to me; but at my Request, he gave me Quarter; there being with me our Servant, and Six of our Children, two of the little Ones being at Play about the Orchard, and my youngest Child but Fourteen Days old, whether in Cradle or Arms, I now mind not: Being in that Condition, I was very unfit for the Hardships I after met with, which are briefly contained in the following Pages.

1754:

> As soon as the Indians discovered 'emselves (having as we afterwards understood, been sculking in the fields some days watching their opportunity when my dear husband, with the rest of our men, were gone out of the way) two of them came in upon us, and then eleven more, all naked, with their guns and tomahawks, and in a great fury killed one child immediately as soon as they entered the door, thinking thereby to strike in us the greater terror, and to make us more fearful of them.

> After which, in like fury the captain came up to me; but at my request, he gave me quarter. There was with me our servant, and six of our children; two of the little ones being at play about the orchard, and my youngest child but fourteen days old, whether in cradle or arms, I now remember not; being in this condition, I was very unfit for the hardships I after met with, which I shall endeavor briefly to relate.

1760:

> On the 27th of the Sixth Month, called August, 1725, my husband and all our men-servants being abroad, eleven Indians, armed with tomahawks and guns, who had some time been skulking about the fields, and watching an opportunity of our mens absence, came furiously into the house. No sooner

had they entered, than they murdered one of my children on the spot; intending no doubt, by this act of cruelty, to strike the greater degree of terror into the minds of us who survived. After they had thus done, their captain came towards me, with all the appearance of rage and fury it is possible to imagine; nevertheless, upon my earnest request for quarter, I prevailed with him to grant it.

I had with me a servant-maid and six children; but two of my little ones were at that time playing in the orchard. My youngest child was but fourteen days old; and myself, of consequence, in a poor weak condition, and very unfit to endure the hardships I afterwards met with, as by sequel will appear.

And so it goes throughout the entire narrative. Bownas, as a traveling, ministering Quaker, has reworked the Hanson narrative into something which, although its main intent is still to illustrate "the many deliverances and wonderful providences of GOD unto us, and over us," is essentially a journalistic piece, and as such prefigures the stylistic form of the later captivity narrative.

What one sees developing in Cotton Mather's use of the captivity narrative and in Bownas's version of the Hanson narrative became formally characteristic of the genre by the mid-

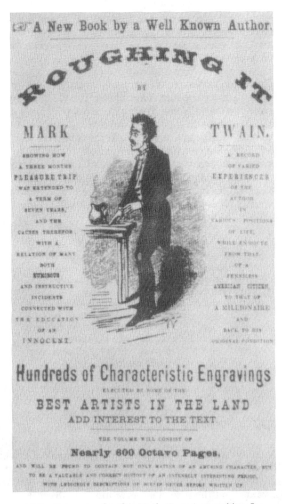

Advertising circular for Mark Twain's Roughing It, *1872.*

eighteenth century. Religious concerns came to be incidental at most; the intent of the typical writer of the narrative was to register as much hatred of the French and Indians as possible. In order to accomplish this, he produced a blood-and-thunder shocker. Hence the captivity narrative was shaped by the interests of the popular audience towards which it was directed; French and Indian cruelty, not God's Providences, was the issue. The writing of the hack and the journalist, not the direct outpourings of the pious individual, became the standard of, and the means to, this new end. By 1750 the captivity narrative had become the American equivalent of the Grub Street criminal biography. To say all this is not to deny the fact of suffering and hardship and tremendous courage on the part of captives. It is only to record the cultural significance of what the captives had to say about their experiences and of the way in which they said it.

So William Fleming in his *Narrative of the Sufferings and Surprizing Deliverances of William and Elizabeth Fleming* (1750) records in adventurous detail how he was taken captive on his Pennsylvania farm and was forced by the Indians to guide them to his wife, how she was taken captive, and how after seeing others tortured and killed, the two of them managed to escape. For all of this, he is willing to exculpate the Indians; hence the subtitle of the Narrative reads: "A NARRATIVE necessary to be read by all who are going in the Expedition [against the French], as well as by every BRITISH subject. Wherein it fully appears, that the Barbarities of the *Indians* is owing to the *French,* and chiefly their Priests." The French, their priests, and the French-inspired Indians are the objects of the hatred of many others, among them Nehemiah How (*A Narrative of the Captivity of Nehemiah How* [1748]), John Gyles (*Memoirs of the Odd Adventures, Strange Deliverances, . . in the Captivity of John Gyles, Esq.* [1736]), Joseph Bartlett (*A Narrative of the Captivity of Joseph Bartlett among the French and Indians* [1807], written ca. [1754]), Robert Eastburn (*The Dangers and Sufferings of Robert Eastburn* [1758]), and Thomas Brown (*A Plain Narrative of the Uncommon Sufferings, and Remarkable Deliverance of Thomas Brown* [1760]).

The natural shift from this sort of narrative is to the out-and-out sensational piece. Here the problem for the historian who would wish to make use of such information as the narratives contain would be one of verification. For these stories are truly wild and woolly. One of the best is the immensely popular *French and Indian Cruelty Exemplified, in the Life and Various Vicissitudes of Fortune, of Peter Williamson* (1757). According to his narrative, Williamson was kidnaped "when, under the years of pupillarity" and taken from his native Scotland to America. There he was sold as a bond servant and eventually, falling into all sorts of good fortune, acquired a wife, a wealthy father-in-law, and a fine frontier Pennsylvania farm. But then came captivity.

He recounts in great and gory detail his struggles, his marches with his captors, and his being tortured. But he adds: " . . . yet what I underwent was but trifling, in comparison to the torments and miseries which I was afterwards an eyewitness of being inflicted on others of my unhappy fellow creatures." As the Indians proceed, they murder and pillage and scalp; such prisoners as they take they torture mercilessly. Then Williamson makes his point:

> From these few instances of savage cruelty, the deplorable situation of these defenseless inhabitants, and what they hourly suffered in that part of the globe, must strike the utmost horror to a human soul, and cause in every breast the utmost detestation, not only against the authors of such tragic scenes, but against those who through perfidy, inattention, or pusillanimous and erroneous principles, suffered these savages at first, unrepelled, or even unmolested, to commit such outrages and incredible depradations and murders: For no torments, no barbarities that can be exercised on the human sacrifices they get into their power, are left untried or omitted.

He continues, giving a simple illustration of what he means. He describes three persons whom the Indians decided to torture. They were tied to a tree "where one of the villains, with his scalping knife, ript open their bellies, took out their entrails, and burnt them before their eyes, whilst others were cutting, piercing, and tearing the flesh from their breasts, hands, arms, and legs with red hot irons, till they were dead." Since one was still alive, however, he was buried so that only his head remained above ground; then he was scalped, still alive, and fire put to his head so that "his brains were boiling." Then, "inexorable to all his plaints, they continued the fire, whilst, shocking to behold! his eyes gushed out of their sockets; and such agonizing torments did the unhappy creature suffer for near two hours, till he was quite dead." On such details Williamson lovingly dwells. Later he even points out that it is an Indian custom to let children train themselves for warfare by beating out the brains of the useless old people of the tribe!

Williamson continues his own story in this vein. Eventually he escapes, enlists to fight the French and the Indians, records his rejoicing when the soldiers were "cutting, hacking, and scalping the dead Indians" and when they quarreled over possession of Indian scalps. Williamson says that he fought all over the colonies in the middle fifties; he seems to have been in on every major campaign; one wonders how he got around so handily. At any rate, the bulk of his story exists only to exemplify French and Indian cruelties. And its significance here is mainly vulgar, fictional, and pathological.

Other narratives of the type of Williamson's seem also to be mélanges of fact and fiction. To point this out is not to indulge in a kind of historical sophistication, not to forget that captivity and torture and death were hard facts of frontier life. Rather it is to suggest that the writers of these later narratives are not concerned with working up accurate records of their (or others') captivities, but with the salability of penny dreadfuls. Thus the blood-and-thunder *History of the Life and Sufferings of Henry Grace* (1764) records a ten-year captivity in which Grace was carried back and forth from Canada to the Mississippi country and saw all tribes from the St. John's Indians to the Cherokees. *A Brief Narration of the Captivity of Isaac Hollister* (1767) has as its high point Hollister's detailing how he cut off five or six pounds of a recently dead fellow-prisoner; one is left to assume that Hollister was thus kept from starving. The *Narrative of Mr. John Dodge* (1779), in which hatred is shifted from the French- to the British-inspired Indian, is marked by a minute description of the "thoughts that must have agitated the breast of a man, who but a few minutes before saw himself surrounded by Savages," and who now was being saved in proper melodramatic style. Thus, too, finally, it is with *A Narrative of the Capture of Certain Americans* (1780?), with William Walton's *Captivity and Sufferings of Benjamin Gilbert and His Family* (1793), and with *The Remarkable Adventures of Jackson Johonnot*

(1793); all are most likely at bottom true, but are built up out of a mass of crude, sensationally presented details.

The journalistic extremity of language and style of these later narratives is typified by that of *A True Narrative of the Sufferings of Mary Kinnan* (1795). Here, however, it is sensibility which takes over. She begins thus:

> Whilst the tear of sensibility so often flows at the unreal tale of woe, which glows under the pen of the poet and the novelist, shall our hearts refuse to be melted with sorrow at the unaffected and unvarnished tale of a female, who has surmounted difficulties and dangers, which on a review appear to be romantic, even to herself?

In this vein she goes on, relating how her captivity broke the pattern of her happy, pastoral life in Virginia: "Here I would mark nature progressing, and the revolutions of the season; and from these would turn to contemplate the buds of virtue and of genius, sprouting in the bosoms of my children." In the Indian attack her children and her husband were killed:

> Gracious God! What a scene presented itself to me! My child, scalped and slaughtered, smiled even then; my husband, scalped and weltering in his blood, fixed on me his dying eye, which, though languid, still expressed an apprehension for my safety, and sorrow at his inability to assist me; and accompanied the look with a groan that went through my heart. Spare me the pain of describing my feelings at this scene, this mournful scene, which racked my agonizing heart, and precipitated me on the verge of madness.

Nevertheless, throughout the narrative she continues to dwell on Indian horror and cruelty and on her own torn sensibilities.

Tales of barbarity and bloodshed, however true at base and however "serious" in intent, were everywhere the thing. Hugh Henry Brackenridge, one of our great Indian haters, edited and caused to be published in the 1780's the garish narratives of Knight and Slover (*Narrative of a Late Expedition*, 1783). These are particularly interesting because of their verifiable authenticity. Knight and Slover describe their adventures as members of Crawford's expedition into the Ohio country in 1782. The story of their capture and of Crawford's being horribly tortured while Simon Girty looked on is too well known to require retelling here. It is sufficient to note that the narratives are printed mainly to point up Brackenridge's firm belief in the necessity of eliminating entirely those "animals, vulgarly called Indians." The purpose of the publication of the narratives is put straightforwardly in the prefatory note "To the Public":

> . . . these Narratives may be serviceable to induce our government to take some effectual steps to chastise and suppress them; as from hence they will see that the nature of an Indian is fierce and cruel, and that an extirpation of them would be useful to the world, and honorable to those who can effect it.

So, too, the *Affecting History of the Dreadful Distresses of Frederic Manheim's Family* (1793?) is a hodgepodge of journalistic horrors aimed at proving that the Indians exercise "dreadful cruelties" on "persons so unfortunate as to fall into their hands." The *Affecting History* is actually a little anthology of choice bits of captivity narratives, each bit selected for its blood-chilling potentialities. In the edition of 1794, issued by commercially wise Matthew Carey, there is a crude engraving, portraying Manheim's daughters, nude at the stake, while Indians dance madly about them. And even such narratives as Luke Swetland's *Narrative* (ca. 1780) and James Smith's *Account of Remarkable Occurrences* (1799), although they contain little of Indian horrors (their authors indeed were admittedly rather well treated), are aimed at giving Americans some practical ways of dealing with the Indian on the frontiers.

The various states of the narrative of Mercy Herbeson will sum up the fate of the captivity narrative towards the end of the eighteenth and at the beginning of the nineteenth century. Mrs. Herbeson's captivity came as an aftermath of the failure of St. Clair's expedition against the Indians of the Ohio country, who were now dangerously self-confident and daring. They had waited until her husband and the other men of the neighborhood were gone, awakened her in her sleep, murdered one of her children as they left the cabin, and killed another as they journeyed. She managed to escape on the third day out and, after great suffering, finally reached a settlement, almost naked, starving, with thorns driven all the way through her unshod feet. And the next morning, as she writes, "a young man employed by the magistrates of Pittsburgh came for me to give in my deposition, that it might be published to the American people."

We have two versions of the deposition, both dated 1792; one of these (*Capture and Escape of Mercy Harbison*) is a direct, semi-literate narrative in the first person, the quality of which reminds one of the earliest captivity narratives; the other is a third person recounting of this, virtually a summary. This last forms one of the choice bits which is included in the Manheim *Affecting History*, described above. Then in 1825 the narrative was published as *A Narrative of the Sufferings of Massy Harbison*. Here the 1792 deposition is expanded into something like the Kinnan narrative. The editor ("J. W.") points out in his introduction that Mrs. Herbeson is now a poor widow, that she has suffered heroically, and that it is the duty of every good American to keep her memory green. The narrative proper is still in the first person, but it is shot through with pleasantly sentimental bits. Mrs. Herbeson is made to make such comments as this: "Some seem to pass over the seasons of life, without encountering those awfully agitating billows which threaten their immediate destruction; while to others, the passage to the tomb is fraught with awful tempests and overwhelming billows." Generally sensibility and melodrama take the place of simplicity and directness. Much miscellaneous material on the nature of the savage and on the Indian wars is added. And in the fourth edition (1836) of this version, the "editor's" name, John Winter, appears, the miscellaneous material has practically smothered the original narrative, and there is little or no pretense at authenticity. is little or no pretense at The publication of a captivity narrative had become an occasion for an exercise in blood and thunder and sensibility.

Moreover, it becomes apparent that towards the end of the eighteenth century American readers were not taking the captivity narrative very seriously. Even for a popular genre, it was quite old and quite tired. In 1796 Mrs. Susannah Willard Johnson felt it necessary to apologize for the publication of her recollections of her captivity in 1749:

> Our country has so long been exposed to Indian Wars, that recitals of exploits and sufferings, of escapes and deliverances have become both numer-

ous and trite.—The air of novelty will not be attempted in the following pages; simple facts, unadorned, is what the reader must expect; pity for my sufferings, and admiration at my safe return, is all that my history can excite.

If this prefatory note is genteel, Mrs. Johnson's *Narrative* is not. Taken captive while pregnant, giving birth to her child while on the march, adopted into an Indian family, and finally sold to the French and then ransomed by her family—she still cannot expect that her experiences will be taken as seriously as they should be.

And something analogous to this also seems to have been the experience of Mrs. Jemima Howe. For, objecting to the polished-up and hence commercially acceptable version of her captivity published by David Humphreys in his *Essay on the Life of the Honourable Major-General Israel Putnam* (1788), she allowed the Reverend Bunker Gay to edit a *Genuine and Correct Account* of her captivity in 1792; truth was more important than the journalistic appeal demanded by American readers. And later, to take another sort of example, Matthew Bunn, apparently finding that his *Narrative* (1806) was not being swallowed whole, appended a truth-swearing affidavit to editions of his story appearing after 1826. By 1800, then, the captivity narrative had all but completed its decline and fall.

It is as the eighteenth-century equivalent of the dime novel that the captivity narrative has significance for the history of our literature. We have already seen how in the latter half of the eighteenth century it had become more and more customary to work up the narrative into something exciting and journalistically worth while by stylizing and by adding as much fictional padding as possible. There are, of course, narratives which are out-and-out fakes—for example, *A Surprizing Account of the Captivity and Escape of Philip M'Donald & Alexander M'Leod* (1794), "Abraham Panther's" *A Very Surprising Narrative of a Young Woman Discovered in a Rocky Cave* (1788?), *The Surprising Adventures and Sufferings of John Rhodes* (1799), and "Don Antonio Descalves's" *Travels to the Westward* (1794?). But these narratives differ from such as those of Peter Williamson and Mrs. Kinnan only in the degree of their absurdity; and they are published as genuine and authentic accounts. What I should like to consider here are two specifically "literary" pieces, Ann Eliza Bleecker's *History of Maria Kittle* (1793) and Charles Brockden Brown's *Edgar Huntly* (1799), both of which were intended to achieve much of their effects as they related to the captivity genre of the 1790's.

The History of Maria Kittle is simply a captivity narrative turned novel of sensibility. This, Mrs. Bleecker says, is a "true" story:

> However fond of novels and romances you [she is addressing the novel to a Miss Ten Eyck] may be, the unfortunate adventures of one of my neighbours, who died yesterday, will make you despise that fiction, in which, knowing the subject to be fabulous, we can never be so truly interested.

The "unfortunate" adventures are the stock materials of the captivity, conditioned, as I have indicated, by female sensibility. Horror is piled on horror. The Indian raiders come, shoot Maria's brother-in-law (her husband is away, of course), tomahawk that brother-in-law's pregnant wife, and tear Maria's infant son from her arms and "dash his little forehead against

the stones." Her daughter hides herself in a closet and is burned alive when the Indians set fire to the house. Maria and another brother-in-law are taken prisoner; and the march begins. On all this she soliloquizes:

> O barbarous! surpassing devils in wickedness! so may a tenfold night of misery enwrap your black souls as you have deprived the babe of my bosom, the comfort of my cares, my blessed cherub, of light and life—O hell! are not thy flames impatient to cleave the center and engulph these wretches in thy ever burning waves? are there no thunders in Heaven—no avenging Angels—no God to take notice of such Heaven defying cruelties?

Pitched thus, the *History* goes on through suffering, struggling, and bloodshed to eventual rescue, ransom, and reunion. Mrs. Bleecker delights in gruesomeness—in, as she says, opening the sluice gates of her readers' eyes. She is interested, most of all, in—and this again is her phrasing—the luxury of sorrow. And she finds that this is to be achieved by actualizing the potentialities of the captivity narrative as novel of sensibility. Still, the distance between the two was, as we have already seen, really not very great.

Charles Brockden Brown similarly is interested in the luxury of horror and, perhaps more seriously, in the workings of a mind under abnormal stress. This American Gothicism he points up in *Edgar Huntly* by making marauding Indians representative of the terrors of existence on the frontier, thus attempting to domesticate the English genre from which his novel stems:

> One merit the writer may at least claim: that of calling forth the passions and engaging the sympathy of the reader by means hitherto unemployed by preceding authors. Puerile superstitions and exploded manners, Gothic castles and chimeras, are the materials usually employed for this end. The incidents of Indian hostility, and the perils of the Western wilderness, are far more suitable; and for a native of America to overlook these would admit of no apology.

This, of course, is from Brown's famous preface. If English writers were to use medieval materials for their romances, American writers were to tap native Gothic sources.

It will be recalled that in Chapter XVI Huntly finds himself in an underground pit, with no knowledge of how he got there or how he is to get out. After a series of storm-and-stress adventures, he does find his way to a cave which will lead him out; but the cave is occupied by a party of raiding Indians with a girl captive. Huntly manages to kill the Indian sentinel and to escape with the girl to the deserted hut of an Indian crone whom he calls Queen Mab. Indians come to the hut, and Huntly kills them, meantime being wounded himself. When a rescue party arrives, Huntly is thought to be dead and is left alone. But his Indian adventures continue. And in the process of these adventures he kills another Indian, gets lost trying to make his way home through the wilds, is mistaken for an Indian and pursued, and finally discovers that the Indian raiders have killed the uncle with whom he has lived.

Brown does not reproduce the captivity narrative as such; but he capitalizes on all that such narratives had come to mean for American readers—a meaning which rose out of emphasis on physical terror, suffering, and sensationalism. He is careful to account exactly for Huntly's fascination by and fear of the Indians: They had murdered his parents. As he has Huntly say:

> Most men are haunted by some species of terror or antipathy, which they are, for the most part, able to trace to some incident which befell them in their early years. You will not be surprised that the fate of my parents, and the body of this savage band, who, in the pursuit that was made after them, was overtaken and killed, should produce lasting and terrific images in my fancy. I never looked upon or called up the image of a savage without shuddering.

Brown was thus doing little that was new. He was simply legitimizing much that was part of the captivity narrative and its sensational offshoots in the 1790's.

The captivity narrative continued to be a popular journalistic, terroristic vehicle through the first three quarters of the nineteenth century. New episodes came with new frontiers; yet patterns and themes were reproduced again and again. There is little need of detailing these, I think; for they simply define and redefine the captivity as we have seen it produced in the 1780's and 1790's. I have seen some forty narratives printed between 1813 and 1873, all of which seem to stem from real enough experiences, but all of which have been worked up into something terrible and strange. Their language is most often that of the hack writer gone wild. Even when they appear to be genuine productions of the nominal narrator, they tend to be formed according to the pattern of the captivity narrative as pulp thriller.

As is to be expected, the problem of authenticity in some of the narratives of the first half of the nineteenth century is hopelessly confused. Thus the *Narrative of the Captivity and Extreme Sufferings of Mrs. Clarissa Plummer* (1839) seems to be worked up from *A Narrative of the Captivity of Mrs. Horn* and the *Narrative* of Mrs. Rachel Plummer, both of the same year. The writer of the first of these three simply put together the best (and wildest) parts of the second and third. The *Narrative of the Capture and Providential Escape of Misses Frances and Almira Hall* (1832) is basically true, but the captives' names were Sylvia and Rachel and the details of the actual captivity have been highly colored in the narrative. And in *An Affecting Narrative of the Captivity and Sufferings of Mrs. Mary Smith* (1818), which is a tale of the Creek War and of Mrs. Smith's being rescued by a detachment of Jackson's army, the torture episode is lifted verbatim from the title narrative in the *Affecting History of the Dreadful Distresses of Frederic Manheim's Family* (1793). Faced with such a confusion of fact and fiction, the twentieth-century reader can only wonder.

Already, however, the captivity narrative had been looked on from something of a scholarly point of view. Certainly, if the coming of a document into the province of antiquarian scholarship and pseudo scholarship means that that document is no longer immediately vital, that its vitality has to be recovered, as it were—then the captivity narrative as a significant popular form was all but dead in the second quarter of the nineteenth century. The problem now was to "use" the captivity narrative, to see what it revealed about the frontier and the frontiersman, to broaden the scope of the American historical imagination.

In short, such narratives were collected and anthologized for what their editors (rather self-consciously, to be sure) insisted were scholarly reasons. The earlier collections seem to be equally sensational, propagandist, and academic. Archibald Loudon calls his two-volume collection (1808) *A Selection of Some of the Most Interesting Narratives of Outrages Committed by the Indians in Their Wars, with the White People.* He is proud that his is the first genuinely scholarly collection of such narratives and intends it for historians: "The historian, will here find materials to assist him in conveying to after ages, an idea of the savages who were the primitive inhabitants of this country; and to future generations of Americans, the many difficulties, toils, and dangers, encountered by their fathers, in forming the first settlement of a land, even at this day so fair, so rich, in every kind of cultivation and improvement." And beyond this: "The philosopher who speaks with delight, of the original simplicity, and primitive innocence of mankind, may here learn, that man, uncivilized and barbarous, is even worse than the most ferocious wolf or panther of the forest." Finally, Loudon quotes, approvingly of course, Brackenridge on the ignoble savage.

Significantly, Loudon includes in his collection only narratives and anecdotes which support his thesis; but all these, he indicates, are "compiled from the best authorities." Included are the Knight and Slover narratives, the whole of the Manheim *Affecting History* compilation, the narrative of Mrs. Herbeson, and many another such. Here Loudon sets the pattern for three other editors who follow him, Samuel Metcalf (*A Collection of Some of the Most Interesting Narratives of Indian Warfare in the West* [1821]), Alexander Withers (*Chronicles of Border Warfare* [1831]), and John A. M'Clung (*Sketches of Western Adventure* [1832]).

Later collections are somewhat more objective than these. So Samuel Gardner Drake refrains from comment when he includes two New England captivity narratives in his vastly popular *Indian Biography* (first printed in 1832 and reprinted many times thereafter in various versions under various titles). His large-scale work with the captivity narrative, however, is to be found in his *Indian Captivities* (1839), a collection which may be called truly scholarly in intent. As Drake indicates, he prints only "entire Narratives," and he has not "taken any liberties with the language of any of them, which would in the remotest degree change the sense of a single passage. . . ." He realizes that these narratives will shock some of his readers, but he reminds them that the stories are only "pages of Nature"; and the fashion of studying those pages "has now long obtained, and pervades all classes." And he points out that there is much to be learned incidentally about the Indian and his nature and customs in these narratives. Thus they are worth the study of historians and scientists.

Interestingly enough, Drake takes time out to attack other "collections of Indian Narratives of a similar character to this." They are similar in title only, he insists; for their editors tamper with the original texts. Drake will let the captives speak for themselves and thus preserve the integrity of their narratives. And then he presents his narratives, some twenty-nine of them, including those of Mrs. Rowlandson, Mrs. Hanson, Mrs. Howe, How, Williamson, Colonel Smith, and Manheim. Others he prints from manuscripts which he apparently obtained from local historical societies. He offers little comment on the individual narratives. He takes his task as editor very seriously.

So, too, one J. Pritts, following largely Withers's *Chronicles* of 1831, published in 1839 his *Incidents of Border Life, Illustrative of the Times and Conditions of the First Settlements in*

Parts of the Middle and Western States. He indicates that he is publishing this collection as the result of a

> determination on our part to collect as many of the printed fragments of that part of our country's history as a diligent research might enable us to procure; and from the collection, and such additional resources as might fall within our reach, to compile a volume embracing whatever might seem interesting and suitable to the design and scope of the desired work.

Although this collection is localized, in form and intent it closely parallels that of Drake.

Finally, even the great Schoolcraft appended to his much reprinted *The American Indians, Their History, Condition, and Prospects* (first issued in 1844-1845 under the title *Onéata, or The Red Race of America*) an "Appendix, containing Thrilling Narratives, Daring Exploits, Etc. Etc." And there is serious editorial treatment of single captivity narratives in Edwin James's *A Narrative of the Captivity and Adventures of John Tanner* (1830) and in Lewis Henry Morgan's notes to editions of Seaver's *Narrative of the Life of Mary Jemison* appearing after 1847 (which, incidentally, contrast greatly with the materials and manner of the narrative itself). Thus, even as sensational narratives were being produced, the older narratives—sensational or not—were being considered for their possible historical and ethnological value.

From Mrs. Rowlandson through Williamson and Mrs. Kinnan and Mrs. Smith to Dr. Drake is indeed a long, long way. The captivity narrative as a popular genre varies with the quality of the cultural milieu in which it is produced; it comes finally into the province of historical scholarship, for the immediate cultural "need" for it is gone, or almost gone. Certainly, so long as the narrative continues to be produced, the experience which it records is at core vital; but to say this is only partially to describe both experience and narrative. For an experience and a narrative, as we have seen, can be vital for many different reasons. And the captivity narrative is interesting and valuable to us, I submit, not because it can tell us a great deal about the Indian or even about immediate frontier attitudes towards the Indian, but rather because it enables us to see more deeply and more clearly into popular American culture, popular American issues, and popular American tastes. As religious confessional, as propaganda, and as pulp thriller, the captivity narrative gives us sharp insight into various segments of popular American culture. Only a properly historical view, a consideration of form, impact, and milieu as well as of content, will enable us to see what the captivity narrative really was and came to be. (pp. 1-20)

Roy Harvey Pearce, "The Significances of the Captivity Narrative," in American Literature, Vol. 19, No. 1, March, 1947, pp. 1-20.

ANDREW WIGET

[*Wiget is an American educator and critic who is especially interested in native American oral literature and in the literature that developed from the contact between European settlers and native Americans. In the following excerpt, he examines changing images of the wilderness presented in captivity narratives.*]

The task of westering not only taxed the settlers' economic and physical resources to the limit, forcing innovations in finance, technology, and social systems; it also forced changes in their imaginative perception of the wilderness, a continual revaluation of the meaning of the unknown land beyond the margins of civilization. The captivity narrative enduring as a genre throughout the frontier experience, reflects at various moments in its development those critical turning points at which the social and imaginative forces which stirred in the contemporary mind changed the image of the wilderness from Desert to Garden. As the Puritan providential view of history disintegrated in the last decades of the eighteenth century under the impact of new ideas, especially sentimentalism and a growing interest in various aspects of the Romantic vision, narrators of the Indian captivities began to separate the Indian from his forest or plains background. The providential perspective which had served for over a hundred years as a frame to hold the foreground and the background of the desert portrait of the hostile and alien wilderness together and in focus was broken. This effective dissolution of the ties between native and nature permitted narrators to continue to malign the Indian while marvelling at the wonders of the visible world. Americans began to represent the wilderness landscape as the source of wonder, the ground of possibilities, even a potential Garden.

Though the Puritans came to America to escape religious persecution, they mortgaged their way on the promised benefits of the fur trade. Abuses in the New England trade, its ultimate failure, and the tension produced by steady encroachment on Indian lands, precipitated the early forest wars of the sixteenth century, a conflict aggravated by the involvement of colonies in the European wars that carried France and England into the eighteenth century. But the Puritans were possessed of a peculiar ideology whose imaginative energy colored not only their interpretation of these events, but their vision of the Indian and the wilderness landscape through which he roamed. In the words of William Hubbard, chief chronicler of King Philip's War, the New World wilderness was a "howling desert." He described the Plimoth forces, who abandoned chasing the Indians into the infamous Poccasset swamps, as unwilling

> to run into the mire and dirt after them in a dark swamp being taught by late experience how dangerous it is to fight in such dismal woods, when their eyes were muffled with the leaves, and their arms pinioned with the thick boughs of trees, as their feet were continually shackled with the roots spreading every way in those boggy woods.

Nathaniel Saltonstall, another war reporter, also featured the wilderness landscape as one vast tract of forest and swamp. In 1682 when her classic captivity narrative was published, Mary Rowlandson, too, described the wilderness as "vast and howling," filled with snow, cold, wild rivers, vast swamps, dense forest, and inhabited by "wild beasts." By 1699, when Cotton Mather published his history of the wars, *Decennium Luctuosum,* the descriptive language was already stereotyped. Recounting the captivity of Sarah Gerish, Mather describes her

> terrible march through the Thick Woods, and a thousand other Miseries, till they came to the Norway-Plains. From thence they made her go to the end of Winno-pisseag Swamps, where sometimes they must Scramble over huge Trees fallen by Storm or Age for a vast way together, and some-

times they must Climb up long, steep, tiresome, and almost Inaccessible Mountains. . . .

A Long and sad Journey she had of it, thro' the midst of an hideous Desart, in the midst of a dreadful Winter.

Mather continues, urging the reader to imagine the captive's fear when the Indians had abandoned her: "What Agonies you may imagine she was in, to find herself left a prey for Bear and Wolves, and without any sustenance, in a howling Wilderness many Scores of Leagues from any Plantation?"

The emotional energy necessary to sustain the violence of this wilderness imagery was rooted in the Puritans' inability to separate the landscape from its Indian inhabitants with whom they were forever involved in a real and bloody war. In this howling desert, the Indian was naturally a wild beast, the most ferocious animal, literally a man-eater; the imagery of the landscape was inextricably bound to this image of the Indian. Of the Poccasset swamp, Hubbard remarks, "it is ill fighting with a wild beast in his own den." And Saltonstall notes the Indian's uncanny, almost supernatural mastery of that swamp:

This Pocassit Swamp, is judged about seven or eight Miles long, and so full of Bushes and Trees, that a Parcel of Indians may be within the Length of a Pike of a Man, and He cannot discover them; and besides, this as well as all other Swamps, is so soft Ground, that an Englishman can neither go nor stand thereon, and yet these bloody savages will run along over it, holding their Guns cross their Arms (and if Occassion be) discharge them in that Posture.

Mather emphasizes the Indian's peculiar, yet natural, relationship to the wilderness by using animal images. The forests were "The Dark places of New-England, where Indians had their Unapproachable Kennels, were Habitations of Cruelty"; and the Indian was variously portrayed in his den or lair as a dragon, tiger, werewolf, bear, adder, wolf, and finally, as the Devil.

The Puritans, of course, considered themselves God's chosen people. In the battle to carve a New Israel out of the heathen Canaan to which He had led them, they were His army and the Indians were the heathen oppressors of Israel and allies of the devil. The land could be made clean only through blood; it had to be wrested in mortal and immortal combat from the hands of the implacable savage demons that possessed it. As long as this providential perspective persisted, the colonial mind could never see the wilderness as a land of promise, a native Eden. The wilderness continued to be imaged as hell in the minds of some individuals until the end of the nineteenth century. However, this hellish *wilderness* of the Puritans and of the Rowlandson-Mather narratives, though it persisted in the popular imagination and was reflected in captivity narratives through the period following the French and Indian war, began very early to be undermined by the seeds of sentimentalism.

The seeds had been planted in the captivity narrative genre from the first; the Puritan narratives consistently displayed a white heroine, often with babe in arms. Rowlandson, for instance, finds herself alone in the wilderness with only her "poor wounded babe, and it seemed a present worse than death that it was in such pitiful condition, bespeaking compassion." Elizabeth Hanson in her 1724 narrative complains

of "being tender and weakly," since it had been "but fourteen days since my lying in." By the end of the eighteenth century the Madonna of the Wilderness had become a captivity narrative motif. When the Indians attack the house of Mrs. Frances Scott, the editor of her 1786 narrative describes the parent-child relationship in clearly sentimental terms:

the eldest, a beautiful girl of eight years old, awoke and escaped out of the Bed, and ran to the Parent, and, with the most Plaintive Accents, cried, 'O Mamma! Mamma! Save Me! The Mother, in the deepest anguish of spirit and with a Flood of Tears, entreated the Savages to spare her child; but with brutal Fierceness they tomahawked and stabbed her in the Mother's Arms.

Melodrama, of course, was inherent in such situations. In her narrative of 1792, Jemima Howe, describing her winter captivity, notes that "The lips of my own child were sometimes so benumbed that when I put it to my breast, it could not, till it grew warm, embibe the nourishment requisite for its support." The *fictional* captivity narrative exploited these incidents more frequently; in the narrative of Maria Kittle, written by Ann Eliza Bleecker in 1797, Maria's daughter, the "smiling Anna," wins the affection of everyone; including the Indians who bring her, "the earliest strawberries, the scarlet plumb and other delicate wild fruits in painted baskets." Under such circumstances the audience appeal of the narrative drifted away from religious concerns with Providence towards an emotional involvement with the Heroine.

This change in attitude is made clear by a subtle and distinctive shift in the stock opening of captivity narratives. The standard motivation of Puritan narratives was the sin of pride; a proud person was made subject to the test of God's wrath, his "refining fire." Rowlandson explains the Indian attack by remarking, "The Lord hereby would make us the more to acknowledge his hand, and see that our help is always in him." John Gyles strikes a similar note in the opening of his narrative, published in 1736, as does Peter Williamson in his narrative of 1757. But by the last third of the century, under the impact of sentimentalism, the situation which precipitated the attack in both fictional and nonfictional narratives was not the would-be captive's pride but his idyllic pastoral and nuptial happiness. The fictional narratives written by Miss Bleecker (1797) and by the pseudonymous Abraham Panther (1787) begin similarly. Panther's captive tells of spending with her husband "many happy evenings vowing mutual love and fondly anticipating future happiness." Bleecker's Mrs. Kittle and her husband, visited and loved by everyone, occupied a "small, neat" farm; and Mr. Kittle, out hunting with his brother, exults in the outdoors, his wife and his children, exclaiming "I anticipate my heaven." Sentimentalized bliss rather than pride went before the fall in nonfictional captivities as well; Mary Kinnan, in her 1795 narrative described her pre-captivity state thus: "Happiness smiled on our cottage;—content spread her influence around;—the voice of grief was not heard." Even John Filson, in his 1784 narrative of the captivity of Daniel Boone, describes the tranquil, Edenic qualities of the Kentucky wilderness just before the Indians attack.

The sentimental appeal of the fictional narrative was often made openly. Panther's captive, awakening from a swoon, begins with the ingenuous disclaimer that it "cannot be very interesting or entertaining—yet it may possibly excite your pity, while it gratifies your curiosity." Maria Kittle's "smiling

Anna" asks her father, when he leaves the day before their captivity, "who will tend me when my papa, my mama's papa is gone?" This overt sentimental appeal in sentimental language colored nonfictional narratives as well. The impassioned Mary Kinnan began her 1795 narrative in this manner:

> Whilst the tear of sensibility so often flows at the unreal tale of woe, which glows under the pen of the poet and the novelist, shall our hearts refuse to be melted with sorrow at the unaffected and unvarnished tale of a female, who has surmounted difficulties and dangers which on a review appear romantic, even to herself.

Susannah Johnson (1807), while remarking that "The air of novelty will not be attempted in the following pages; simple facts, unadorned, is what the reader must expect," added that "pity for my sufferings and admiration for my safe return is all that my history can excite." And when Mrs. Johnson is "Taken with the pangs of childbirth," she urges "The compassionate reader to drop a fresh tear, for my inexpressible distress."

Perhaps the most dramatic element in this deterioration of the Puritan perspective was the secularization of the wilderness experience. This is most marked by the decline in the use of Biblical quotation. The numerous quotations, complete with textual references, served to create for the Puritan a wilderness experience that was a nearly-allegorical "type" of the Babylonian captivity, investing the narrative with the religious themes of the test of faith, the chosen people in the land of the heathen, and the intervention of Providence. Almost all the references in Rowlandson, for instance, come from the Psalms and prophetic books written during or about the Babylonian captivity. The Puritan captivity narrative was perhaps the highest New World embodiment of a grace rather than works theology of salvation. Extensive and exact quotation from the Bible seems to have been a function of the closely circumscribed Puritan religious community; as the frontier moved westward out of New England into the Appalachians and the eighteenth century, such exact quotations diminish considerably. Bartlett (1807) uses them extensively in his anti-Catholic captivity narrative of the French and Indian War, as does Zadock Steele (1818); notably, both are New Englanders. Paraphrasings appear in the place of exact quotations in Eastburn (1758) and Marrant (1785), the last making open reference to Whitfield's preaching; hymns of Watts and Wesley are often quoted in place of Biblical quotations. More common are general references to Providence, beginning with Hanson (1724) and persisting, though becoming fewer and fewer, into the nineteenth century. By the end of the century, many narratives had dispensed with religious allusions almost entirely, supplanting them with literary allusions to Shakespeare and later Romantic poets.

Even the "remarkable Providences" which so characterize the Puritan perspective were considerably secularized. In 1783, John Slover, about to be burned at the stake, found himself the gracious recipient of a sudden cloudburst out of a clear sky which drenched the fire and saved him: Slover does not emphasize his particular salvation, but seems more taken, as the reader is, by the wonder of it. Mrs. Frances Scott, lost in the wilderness, is also the recipient of a miracle, but in her case no mention is made of Providence:

> Our Wanderer now left the River, and after proceeding a good distance, she came to where the val-

ley parted in two, each leading a different Course. Here a painful Suspense again took place: A forlorn Creature almost exhausted, and certain, if she was far led out of the Way, she should never see a human Creature. During this Soliloquy, a beautiful Bird passed close by her, fluttering along the Ground, and went out of sight up one of the Vallies. This drew her Attention, and whilst considering what it might mean, another Bird of the same Appearance, fluttered past her, and took the same Valley the other had done. This determined her choice of the Way.

Two days later, having chosen the right path, Mrs. Scott left the wilderness behind. Lacking divine reference, Providence has been reduced to chance. This is emphasized in Mary Kinnan's 1795 narrative. Planning to rendezvous in the woods with her brother who has come to rescue her, she misses him, each "having gone to different trees." The following night they are reunited, presumably under the right tree, though no reference to the tree or Providence is made in the text.

Perhaps nothing illustrates more clearly the change in attitude that led to the destruction of the Providential perspective than a small passage in John Slover's narrative. Slover experiences a change of heart "sudden and perceivable as lightning, an assurance of my peace made with God," while he is at the stake awaiting the fire. But he prefaces the revelation of that experience with a statement that, "I knew myself to have been a regular member of the church and to have sought repentance for my sins." It is clear that his "confidence in mind" about his salvation does not depend wholly upon that sudden grace from God, but also upon some sense of his own worth. The focus of the writer's as well as the reader's attentions here moves away from the arbitrary intervention of transcendent Deity to the interior life of the man.

This emphasis on sentimentalism and the personal ego perspective of the narrator also affected the treatment of the landscape. While Puritan narratives had used very emotional language to describe the wilderness, the source of that language was ultimately the peculiar communal, religious perspective furnished by their ideology. The appearance in the last third of the eighteenth century of a new Romantic aesthetic served to focus attention on the human source of wilderness imagery.

Beginning with the resurrection of Longinus' treatise, *On the Sublime,* at the beginning of the eighteenth century, English essayists began to pay attention to the capacity of the wilderness landscape to stir our emotions. In an important series of essays in the *Spectator,* Joseph Addison addressed himself to "The Pleasures of the Imagination," asserting that they arose primarily from "the Sight of what is Great, Uncommon, or Beautiful." The scenes of storms, whitewater, and mountains which he used to exemplify his thesis were quickly appropriated by many who saw in the grandeur of nature the highest kind of beauty. MacPherson's *Ossian,* so often quoted in the eighteenth century as the highest expression of the sublime, is filled with such rugged, misty landscapes. In America, Jefferson, it appears, knew both the *Spectator* essays and *Ossian* and accepted that vision of the landscape. His description of the magnificence of the Natural Bridge or of the grandeur of the Blue Ridge reveal his interest in the wilderness landscape; even Filson's Boone cannot describe the region with such open pleasure and excitement.

But if landscape influenced emotions, elevating the soul in "a proud flight," it was also true that one's emotional state could affect the vision of the landscape. Hugh Blair, perhaps Ossian's greatest apologist in the eighteenth century, pointed this out, revealing the sentimentalism inherent in such a perspective; Ossian's poetry, Blair wrote, "deserves to be styled, The poetry of the heart. It is . . . a heart that is full, and pours itself forth." Implicit in this aesthetic, in Ossian's poetry, and even in Jefferson's agrarianism, is an incipient primitivism which postulates a correspondence between the landscape and the soul. This primitivism is founded on the ambiguity of the relationship between the viewer and the landscape, an ambiguity Longinus perceived when he wrote that the soul "is filled with joy and vaunting, as if it had itself produced what it has heard."

This ambiguity had a lasting effect on the captivity narrative: man could be depressed and see the wilderness as hostile and oppressive, while in fact the wilderness may be exceedingly beautiful. Bleecker makes this clear in her fictitious narrative of Maria Kittle:

> When our souls are gloomy, they seem to cast a shade over the objects that surround us, and make nature correspondent with our feelings. So Mr. Kittle thought the night fell with a deeper gloom than usual.

And elsewhere she describes Maria waking:

> As the sun began to exhale the crystal glories of morning, . . . half rising, and reclining on her elbow, [Maria] surveyed the lonely landscape with a deep sigh; they were on an eminence that commanded an unlimited prospect of the country every way. The birds were cheerful; the deer bounded fearless over the hills; the meadows blushed with the enamel of Flora; but grief had saddened every object in her sight; the whole creation seemed a dark blank to the fair mourner.

The ambiguity between objective and subjective landscape was not restricted to fictional narratives, though it was certainly more prominent there. Mary Kinnan, in her narrative of 1795, implies that there are two landscapes when she says: "Nature too *seemed* to conspire against me." (My emphasis) And in 1872, Fanny Kelly wrote of the Plains, "with a mind free from fear and anxiety, the whole picture would have been a dream of delight." Her mood, however, precluded any enjoyment.

The belief that there were two landscapes, one in the imagination and one in reality, wrought havoc with the Puritan landscape. Rachel Plummer could write in 1839, "Notwithstanding my sufferings, I could not but admire the country," but for Mather, Hubbard, and Rowlandson such a distinction was impossible. The Puritan wilderness landscape of the mind was the real landscape, the only landscape, and it was hell. However, the doctrine of correspondence between soul and nature with its two landscapes opened the door to new treatments of the wilderness. The landscape could be both hell, reflecting the tortured state of the narrator's mind and emotions, and an Eden in and of itself.

In terms of the landscape as hell, a persistent motif in the captivity narrative from Rowlandson (1682) to Kelly (1872) is the belief that man can only be dehumanized in the wilderness. This is most clearly indicated by his being forced to eat "uncivilized" food and, out of sheer hunger, actually to like it; such food might be horsemeat, roots, grubs, the entrails

of animals, even human flesh. Tortures and treachery persist; new levels of savage Indian inventiveness seem to be uncovered in each succeeding narrative. In Peter Williamson's narrative (1757) a captive is buried with only his head exposed and a fire built around him just enough distance away that his brains slowly boil and eyes gush out. The heightened emotional state of the narrator is often mentioned, even in the most objective treatments; Charles Johnston (1827) felt horror "thrill through his frame." Such heightened states often induced forebodings, visions, and other psychological phenomena. Jemima Howe (1793) imagined she saw the tortured "Carcasses" of her children hanging in a tree; John Tanner (1830) had a vision of where he would kill a bear come true; Rachel Plummer (1839) saw a ministering angel who visited her in a cave; Mary Jemison (1842) saw a white sheet loom before her menacingly, seeming to obliterate her vision, and imagined very graphically possible tortures she might suffer; and Fanny Kelly (1872) was convinced she heard the voices of her husband and child crying out to her in the darkness.

This Gothic strand of tortures, animalism, forebodings, and visions was linked closely with sentimentalism and the emotional state of the narrator. These events served as a kind of "objective correlative" by which the depths of the narrator's emotional suffering could be meaningfully communicated to the reader. It is clear, however, that the terror resides in the imagination of the narrator and is not an inherent quality of the wilderness environment. For it is in some of these same narratives which exacerbate earlier Gothic tendencies that the seeds of the wilderness Garden first bloom. Picturesque imagery of violent, but thrilling storms abound; the landscape is often treated in picturesque, even sublime images; curiosity about great natural wonders increases; fertility rather than sterility is a common theme; and an Eden of beauty, enchantment, even of plenty, is pictured for the reader.

Those thrilling but threatening storms that Romantic landscape artists in paint and prose found so attractive and which seem to represent so ideally the ambivalence of the landscape, its sublime but fearful aspect, abound. Jemima Howe (1793) describes a violent lightning storm and an earthquake; Mary Kinnan (1795) found, "the rain descended in torrents, the lightnings flashed dreadfully, and almost without intermission; whilst the thunder rolled awfully on high." The fullest elaboration of these terrible but sublime storms in a captivity narrative appears in one of the first Beadle dime novels, the fictional *Seth Jones: or, The Captives of the Frontier* (1861) by Edward S. Ellis:

> The heavy clouds, growing darker and more awful, poured forward until they seemed to concentrate in the western sky, where they towered aloft like some old embattled castle. The thunder grew heavier, until it sounded like the rolling of chariot wheels over the courts of heaven, and the red streams of liquid fire streamed down the dark walls of Storm Castle.

A similarly awesome thunderstorm was described less poetically by Fanny Kelly in her 1872 narrative.

Though in their sublimity both were attractive to man, the grandeur of the frontier storms was more than matched by the grandeur of the frontier landscape itself. The "landscaping" tradition took two courses: on the one hand, the frontier was almost idyllically imagined, pastoral images abound and lead inevitably to the ultimate description of the wilderness as Garden; on the other hand, the picturesque tradition is less concerned with pastoral aspects of the wilderness than it is with descriptions of the natural wonders.

Picturesque scenery prevailed in captivity narratives by the end of the eighteenth century. Mrs. Frances Scott wanders through a pass in the Great Laurel Mountains amidst huge upheavals of rock, "numerous high craggy cliffs along the Water-Edge." Brown describes a similar picture of the Wilderness in *Edgar Huntly:*

> The hollows are single, and walled round by cliffs, ever varying in shape and height . . . The streams that burst forth from every crevice are thrown, by the irregularities of the surface, into numberless cascades, often disappearing in mists or in chasms, and emerge from subterranean channels and, finally, either subside into lakes, or quietly meander through lower and more level grounds.
>
> Wherever nature left a flat it is made rugged and scarcely passable by enormous and fallen trunks, accumulated by the storms of ages . . .

The grandiose scenery and picturesque sights that fill the pages of the narratives of Rachel Plummer (1839) and Fanny Kelly (1872) take on the character of natural wonders. Knowing quite clearly that the water she is seeing was a mirage—she indicates this in a footnote to her readers—Plummer's description emphasizes wonderment, and she remarks, "Is there anything like magic in this." This wonderment continues as she discovers sea shells on the plains and concludes the land must have been covered by a great sea; when she finds "thousands of bushels of salt—yea, millions—resembling ice"; and when she describes the burning springs, yellow earth and thorny trees of the desert. Some of her accounts border on the fabulous. She describes a "man-tiger" which inhabits the Rockies, is eight or nine feet tall, has the features of a man and claws instead of fingers; as well, she asserts, "a species of human beings live in caves" in the mountains; in both cases she is reflecting the mythology of her Comanche captors, the first in reference to the grizzly bear, the second to a race of dwarfs that occur frequently in myth. Her most elaborate and extensive description she reserves for the Rocky Mountains: "so incredibly high, and perpendicular are they in many places, that is impossible to ascend them." In some places, Fanny Kelly's narrative (1872) approaches the same sense of the sublime and picturesque. She describes in extensive detail and in vivid language a prairie fire and a redrock canyon, imagining the latter as huge "carved columns supporting a mighty ruin."

But by far the most noticeable change in wilderness imagery is the development of Edenic motifs in late eighteenth century captivity narratives. The rescuers of "The beautiful lady" in Abraham Panther's tale (1787) are amazed at the scene that they view after two weeks march in the wilderness:

> The land we found exceedingly rich and fertile, everywhere well watered, and the variety of berries, nuts, ground-nuts, &c., afforded a very comfortable living.
>
> On the fourteenth day of our travels, while we were observing a high hill, at the foot of which, ran a beautiful stream, which passing through a small plain, after a few windings, lost itself in a thicket—and observing the agreeable picturesque prospect, which presented itself on all sides, we were surprised at the sound of a voice, which seemed at no great distance.

And Maria Kittle describes a landscape where "birds were cheerful; the deer bounded fearless over the hills; the meadows blushed with the enamel of Flora;. . . . and spotted trout, and other fish, dart sportively across the water." Both Maria Kittle and the "beautiful lady" also describe contrastive, menacing scenery, but it is clear that the wilderness also includes Garden imagery.

Writers of "factual" captivity narratives also developed this Garden image, though tentatively at first. As early as 1785, Frances Scott began developing the image of the wilderness as a land of plenty by providing the first cataloging of flora and fauna found beyond the frontier. Mary Kinnan (1795) was taken by the Indians "into a fine country, [Ohio] where we had venison, and other game." Kinnan's observation was supported by Mary Jemison (1842), who described Indian life in the Ohio region:

> The town where they lived was pleasantly situated on the Ohio, at the mouth of the Shenanjee; the land produced good corn; the woods furnished plenty of game, and the waters abounded in fish.

And Charles Johnston (1827) wrote of the same region, "During the whole march, we subsisted on bear's meat, venison, turkeys, and racoons, with which we were abundantly supplied, as the ground over which we passed afforded every species of game." Filson's narrative of Boone's captivity (1784) and Morrow's narrative of the daughters' (1833) draw a similar Edenic picture of Kentucky.

As the frontier moved westward across the Mississippi towards the Rockies, there were those who automatically saw this new wilderness as Garden and so recorded their images for others back East to read. Rachel Plummer (1839) for instance, seeing natural wonders, a profusion of timber and game, openly admired the landscape. She described the vast slope of the southern Rockies as "being prairie and timber, and very rich with many fine springs. . . . a very diversified country; abounding with small prairies, skirted with timber of various kinds——oak, of every description, ash, elm, hickory, walnut, and mulberry. . . . [and] the purest atmosphere I ever breathed." She then proceeded to catalogue all the game animals of the region. Forty years later, Fanny Kelly did a similar service for the High Plains, describing a flower-covered landscape crossed with streams. Her description of the Powder River Valley is an open challenge to Eastern farmers:

> Between these ranges [Bighorn and Cloud Peak], that culminate in the queenly, shining crowned height that takes its name from the clouds it seems to pierce, are fertile valleys, in which game abounds, and delicious wild fruits in great variety, some of which cannot be surpassed by cultivated orchard products in the richness and flavor they possess. . . .
>
> Between these ranges [Bighorn and Wind River], and varying in breadth from twelve to twenty-five miles, are fine hunting grounds, abounding in noble orchards of wild fruit of various kinds, and grapes, as well as game of the choicest kind for the huntsman.

Because writing is an art and a material form of communication, it is one thing to describe and explain the change in wilderness imagery from desert to Garden on an ideological level and another thing to illustrate how it may have come about in practice. Three factors materially contributed to altering the image of the wilderness in captivity narratives.

First, the lag between the time of the captivity and the publication of the narrative seems to have increased. Originally timely pieces reflecting current positions toward the Indian, British, or French, the narratives were usually published within one year after the experience. This changed, however. Though Frances Scott's 1784 captivity was published in 1785, Jemima Howe's 1755 experience was not printed until 1792; Susannah Johnson (1744) published her narrative in 1807, and Zadock Steele (1780) published his in 1818. The span of time between Joseph Bartlett's 1708 captivity and its 1807 publication was nearly a century. Therefore, as the time lag between experience and publication became common, the record of the experience was subject to a greater variety of social and ideological influence.

Also, by the end of the eighteenth century, writers of some note began concerning themselves with the captivity experience. The narrative written by the pseudonymous Abraham Panther may hardly merit anthologizing, but nevertheless it was reprinted twenty-five times and became something of an early American bestseller. On the other hand, Ann Eliza Bleecker, whose fictional Maria Kittle is the subject of a novel length captivity narrative, moved in a circle of New York literati that included her husband, Anthony, William Dunlap, and Charles Brockden Brown. The latter's fictional *Edgar*

Lydia Maria Child

Huntly draws heavily on captivity narrative materials. In the nineteenth century, James Fenimore Cooper's *The Prairie* and *The Last of the Mohicans* feature Indian captivities prominently. In the last half of the nineteenth century, minor writers like Edward Ellis and Joseph Badger consciously exploited the captivity experience in dime novels.

The impact of conscious literary effort and elevated style must have been felt most heavily by the editors of later captivity narratives. Editors are creatures of their time, often homogenizing unique experiences told in an original manner by imposing a language and tone foreign to the captive himself on the material. The editors of Frances Scott's 1786 narrative felt compelled to add a preface to her narrative which included several handfuls of Biblical quotations. She had included very few in her narrative, perhaps because it was 1786; but, because the book was published in Boston, the quotation-riddled preface was mandatory. The publishers of Mary Jemison's classic narrative reacted strongly against the Gothic elements that had filled narratives at the turn of the century; they assured their readers that "no extraneous or equivocal matter has been introduced, for the purpose of exciting the wonder of a visionary imagination, or of ministering to the cravings of a morbid appetite." The author of the biography added that, "No circumstance has been intentionally exaggerated by the paintings of fancy, nor the fine flashes of rhetoric." Disclaimers aside, Jemison's narrative has its share of rhetorical flash and fancy, though it is supposedly a verbatim record of what was told to the author by Jemison who was nearing one hundred years of age and had lived with the Shawnee, out of regular contact with English-speaking Americans, for seventy-eight years. The weight of probability suggests that it was the editor, closer to the literary and intellectual currents of his age than the settler and his wife, who introduced sentimental language into the narrative, exaggerated incidents of terror and pathos, shaped the theme and moral sentiment of the tale, and eventually contributed most to the changing image of the wilderness.

Clearly the Garden image of the wilderness, like the Desert image, developed in response to emotional, imaginative, and material needs. The "desert" had assisted in the development of closely-defined, stable communities; it prevented a too quick dissipation of spiritual and material resources. But the burgeoning population of a new nation needed, at the end of the eighteenth century, to get to the other side of the mountains, and half a century later to the other side of a great river. The Garden image developed to resolve the conflict between a wilderness foreign to man and man's need for water, timber, rich soil and open range. That it developed in the captivity narrative, the most unlikely of genres, is a reflection of the flexibility of the human imagination. Under the impact of social and intellectual forces focussed on the genre by its editors, the captivity narrative created an ambiguous wilderness, one both fruitful and attractive yet peopled with savages. Then only the extermination of the Indians stood between the farmer and the peaceful cultivation of his soil.

But the Indians did not die alone, and the wilderness Garden was not created without an additional price. The vitality of the captivity narrative, with its ability to stir our imaginations in great moments of real drama through coherent and powerful drawing of wilderness life, also dies. When sentimentalism undermined the savage wilderness, it also undermined the dramatic situation of the heroine. No longer fighting for her life in an alien and hostile land, she was reduced to an interested observer at best, to a whining female at worst, and her sufferings seemed the stuff of melodrama, arbitrary and meaningless. Two hundred years of a vital genre disappeared in tears and exclamation points, but not without radically changing our image of the wilderness. (pp. 69-80)

> Andrew Wiget, "Wonders of the Visible World: Changing Images of the Wilderness in Captivity Narratives," in The Westering Experience in American Literature: Bicentennial Essays, *edited by Merrill Lewis and L. L. Lee, Western Washington University, 1977, pp. 69-84.*

LOUISE K. BARNETT

[In the following excerpt, Barnett discusses the portrayal of native Americans and the expression of American nationalism in the frontier romance.]

By the beginning of the nineteenth century, when a substantial amount of fiction using Indian characters began to appear, the initial shock of confrontation between two disparate cultures was long over in the settled regions which produced the nation's first authors. While the drama would be reenacted repeatedly on the moving frontier in the first half of the coming century, it would not deviate from the pattern imposed by the pilgrims upon the seaboard Indians. Only with the complete passing of autonomous Indian tribes in the generation after the Civil War would any change take place in either history or fiction.

For this reason, the body of fiction containing Indian characters and written between 1790 and 1860 constitutes a distinct and coherent genre which will be referred to in this study as the frontier romance. To quote Hugh Henry Brackenridge's Indian treaty-maker [in *Modern Chivalry,* ed. Lewis Leary], it can be said of the contributions to this genre: "These things are now reduced to a system: and it is so well known to those who are engaged in the traffic, that we think nothing of it." Conventions were quickly established and little questioned: a standard plotting device, stereotyped characters, and a racist-nationalistic philosophy of white-Indian relations are shared by almost all authors who use Indians in their fiction.

The prevailing attitude of the frontier romance is aptly expressed by Francis Parkman [in *The Oregon Trail*]:

> For the most part, a civilized white man can discover very few points of sympathy between his own nature and that of an Indian. With every disposition to do justice to their good qualities, he must be conscious that an impassable gulf lies between him and his red brethren. Nay, so alien to himself do they appear, that, after breathing the air of the prairie for a few months or weeks, he begins to look upon them as a troublesome and dangerous species of wild beast.

A few notable writers believed Indians to be "much more like ourselves than unlike" [*The Journal of Henry David Thoreau*], but those who wrote within the genre of the frontier romance exemplify Parkman's position. Whatever their good intentions, the "impassable gulf" intervened and negated them. Unable to perceive a common humanity shared by Indian and white, and thus bound by a concept of the Indian as both Other and Inferior, these writers could not achieve the insight into their Indian characters necessary for valid aesthetic creation. Like Benjamin West's portrait of Colonel Guy Johnson, their fiction points up the splendor of the pre-

possessing white man in the foreground and consigns the Indian to a shadowy and implicitly inferior background. As literature, the frontier romance exemplifies the clash of aesthetic and nonaesthetic demands within a fictive construct and the problem of writing fiction about a radically different culture. As cultural document, it reflects the racism and nationalism characteristic of the society which produced it. (pp. 17-18)

Between the American Revolution and the emergence of the frontier romance as a recognizable genre in the 1820s, a number of demands for cultural emancipation from England were made. An independent literature was especially wanted because, as Noah Webster wrote: "We shall always be in leading strings till we resort to original writers and original principles instead of taking upon trust what English writers please to give us." What these "original principles" might be, or what elements of American life might be fashioned successfully into a national literature, were not at first clearly defined; what mattered in the earliest period of nationhood was to call for action. Thus, Samuel Woodworth's prefatory remarks to his venture into the frontier romance in 1816 anticipate approval simply on the grounds of being American: "*The Champions of Freedom* cannot fail of being patronised by Americans, even though dressed in homespun uniform, coarse and inelegant. It is of domestic manufacture, and cannot displease the eye of a patriot." Still earlier, in the preface to *Edgar Huntly* (1801), Charles Brockden Brown had asserted a more substantive claim:

> that of calling forth the passions and engaging the sympathy of the reader by means hitherto unemployed by preceding authors. Puerile superstition and exploded manners, Gothic castles and chimeras, are the materials usually employed for this end. The incidents of Indian Hostility, and the perils of the Western wilderness, are far more suitable; and for a native of America to overlook these would admit of no apology.

At the time, however, neither Brown nor other writers of prose fiction were ready to utilize this frontier subject matter.

Before the 1790s, in effect before the American Revolution had been assimilated by writers, the captivity narratives provided a sufficient treatment of the conflict of cultures. After the Revolution, the impulse of nationalism began to find expression in a demand for both American-authored imaginative literature, including fiction, and native themes. For all their simple virtues, captivity narratives were inadequate as vehicles for nationalism and as art: whatever the embellishments and exaggerations which came to be incorporated into these accounts during the latter half of the eighteenth century, they remained purportedly authentic chronicles of limited scope.

As sentiment for a national literature increased, given impetus by a second victory over the British in the War of 1812, Indians naturally received further scrutiny as a possible subject for fiction. Theodore Dehon, in his Phi Beta Kappa address, "Upon the Importance of Literature to Our Country" (1807), proposed the Indian as "the chief hope for an original American literature." William Tudor, Jr.'s Phi Beta Kappa address of 1815, which appeared in the *North American Review,* compared Indians to Homeric heroes at length: the original Indians, uncontaminated by white association, "possessed so many traits in common with some of the nations of antiquity, that they perhaps exhibit the counterpart of what the Greeks were in the heroick ages, and particularly the Spartans during the vigour of their institutions." In another issue of the *North American Review,* he advances as worthy of literary treatment "the important part played by the various Indian tribes, particularly the Six Nations, whose history is abundantly interesting."

What very likely translated the academic speculation into the first wave of frontier romances was the availability of an adaptable pattern in Scott's *Waverley* novels and the popularity of *Yamoyden,* a long romantic poem about King Philip's War which was published in 1820. The separate success of historical romance and Indian subject matter made the union of this form and content irresistible. John G. Palfrey's enthusiastic review of *Yamoyden* in the prestigious *North American Review* concludes by particularly commending the white-Indian encounter to writers of fiction: "Whoever in this country first attains the rank of a first rate writer of fiction, we venture to predict, will lay his scene here. The wide field is ripe for the harvest, and scarce a sickle has yet touched it." William Howard Gardiner's review of *The Spy,* which also appeared in the *North American Review,* similarly suggests the writing of romance built around Indian characters:

> We are confident that the savage warrior, who was not less beautiful and bold in his figurative diction, than in his attitude of death . . . patiently enduring cold, hunger, and watchfulness, while he crouched in the night-grass like the tiger expecting his prey, and finally springing on the unsuspicious victim with that war-whoop, which struck terror to the heart of the boldest planter of New England in her early day, is no mean instrument of the sublime and terrible of human agency.

Obviously enamoured of the same savage menace that Gardiner promotes, R. C. Sands, a year later, commends the American aborigine to the attention of native literature:

> If scenes of unparalleled torture and indefatigable endurance, persevering vengeance and unfailing friendship, hair-breadth escapes and sudden ambush; if the horrors of the gloomy forests and unexplored caverns, tenanted by the most terrible of banditti; if faith in wild predictions and entire submission of the soul to the power of ancient legends and visionary prophecies, are useful to the poet or romancer, here they may be found in abundance and endless variety.

Even after frontier romances had inundated the country, literary figures continued to expatiate on the fitness of the Indian for romance: such well-known writers as John Greenleaf Whittier and N. P. Willis in the thirties and Edgar Allan Poe and William Gilmore Simms in the forties reiterated the Indians' literary virtues. Poe's review of Cooper's Indian romance *Wyandotté* praised its theme, life in the wilderness, as "one of intrinsic and universal interest, appealing to the heart of man in all phases." Simms proclaimed that the fate of the Indian "may be wrought into forms as nobly statuesque as any that drew a nation's homage to the splintered summits of Olympus." Elsewhere he recommends the stories of such Indians as Osceola, Tecumseh, and Logan as subjects which "in a community even partially civilized would have been worthy of all fame and honour in succeeding times."

Not everyone agreed that Indians constituted a valuable resource for American literature. Most of the dissenters deemed it a narrow and quickly exhausted vein, one unsuited to the literary needs of an advanced people. At a time when little use of Indians had been made by fiction, John Bristed predicted that "a novel describing these miserable barbarians, their squaws, and papooses, would not be very interesting to the present race of American readers." Seven years later a review of *Escalala,* a poem about Indians, opens with the flat assertion that "the character of the North American Indian affords but a barren theme for poetry." The disparity between primitive and civilized which Bristed had considered detrimental to possible Indian fiction is also remarked by the *Escalala* reviewer:

> The Indian has a lofty and commanding spirit, but its deeply marked traits are few, stern, and uniform, never running into those delicate and innumerable shades, which are spread over the surface of civilised society, giving the fullest scope to poetic invention, and opening a store of incidents inexhaustible, and obedient to the call of fancy.

After a substantial number of frontier romances had been written, reviewers still invoked the cultural gulf between reader and subject as a prime obstacle to its success. Apropos of Cooper's first two Leatherstocking novels, Granville Mellen wrote:

> It appears certain to us that there is a barrenness of the novelist's peculiar circumstance in the life of a savage . . . and it must necessarily be a troublesome tax upon the ingenuity to throw a moderate share of interest round a narrative founded upon events connected with these simple, silent creatures. . . . There is not enough in the character and life of these poor natives to furnish the staple of a novel.

The focus of critical disdain for the literary Indian was centered in the paucity of interesting activities to be found in his primitive way of life and in the boredom which enforced repetition would presumably generate in civilized readers. As early as 1826, one writer complained that Indians were so limited as a subject that "almost every production into which they are introduced partakes more or less of the same character and abounds in incidents and sentiments that are similar, and evidently copies of one common original."

In the same year a reviewer of *The Last of the Mohicans* queried: "How many novels can he [Cooper] afford to write? How many changes can he ring upon scalping, shooting, tomahawking, etc.?" Constantly turning from his review of *The Red Rover* to consider Cooper's frontier romances, Mellen similarly objects: "Once done, it is, comparatively, done for ever; and our complaint is, that we are overdoing the matter." Significantly, he concluded: "The Indians as a people, offer little or nothing that can be reasonably expected to excite the novelist, formed as his taste must be on a foreign standard." Although he failed to see its implications, Mellen's observation was accurate: having no interest in Indians *per se,* novelists would only concern themselves with Indians in contact with whites; having little or no firsthand experience with Indians and many preconceptions about them, they would invariably create lifeless and narrowly conceived stereotypes in their works.

Critics who saw no literary potential in the Indian thus failed to perceive what supporters and writers of the frontier romance seemed to know instinctively: that the genre would not only be written by white authors for a white audience; it would also be about whites, and especially their superiority to Indians. Tudor, for example, enthusiastically commends the Indian to the novelist for "perilous and romantick adventures, figurative and eloquent harangues, strong contrasts and important interests," but the incidents he employs to illustrate these generalities are all white-Indian episodes which glorify whites. As the modern critic Benjamin T. Spencer states: "The Indian was to appear only as grist for the conqueror's mill, not as a sensitive being fit for tragic, epic, or lyric treatment in his own right."

The unfriendly reviewer of *Escalala* had some inkling of this state of affairs when he noted that "seemingly aware of these difficulties [the barrenness of the Indian theme], the author of *Escalala* has employed the agency of civilised men, in filling up some of the most important parts of his poem." By the time of Simms the formulation was more forthright: the native writer must "learn to dwell often upon the narratives of the brave fathers who first broke ground in the wilderness, who fought or treated with the red men." As Harriet V. Cheney wrote in her early novel *A Peep at the Pilgrims* (1824):

> The Indians continued their hostilities, which were marked by the most atrocious cruelties that ever harrowed the feelings of humanity. . . . Nothing but that persevering energy and unwavering confidence in divine protection, which so remarkably characterized the venerable pilgrims of New-England, could have enabled them to endure such complicated trials.

The title of Mrs. Cheney's book accurately indicates her subject, but many a work given the name of an Indian focuses largely upon the white characters. John Shecut's *Ish-Noo-Ju-Lut-Sche,* for example, is dedicated to the "honored and truly respected descendants of the venerated Knickerbockers, or primitive settlers of 'Der Nieu Niederlands' . . . designed to transmit to posterity the integrity, virtue, and patriotism of those illustrious personages."

Writers who failed to give the white side its due in the confrontation with Indians were taken to task by critics. Palfrey's landmark review of *Yamoyden* praises "the very happy use which the writers have made of their reading in the antiquities of the Indians," but faults the role assigned to whites in the poem: "But we doubt whether poetically, and we do not doubt whether historically speaking it was best to represent the settlers as entirely in the wrong, and the Indians as wholly in the right." Palfrey's own attitude is revealed by a disquisition on history which precedes the discussion of the poem. "We are glad," he begins, "that somebody has at last found out the unequalled fitness of our early history for the purposes of a work of fiction." This leads not to a consideration of *Yamoyden's* noble red men, the subject of the poem, but to a long paean on the white settlers:

> The men who stayed by their comfortable homes to quarrel with the church and behead the king, were but an inferior race to those more indignant if not more aggrieved, who left behind them all that belongs to the recollections of infancy and the fortunes of maturer life . . . to lay the foundations of a religious community in a region then far less known to them than the North Western Coast of our continent is now to us. . . . Wrong or right, every thing about these men was at least prominent and high-toned.

The early colonists appear to be ideal types: "Consummate gentlemen and statesmen, like Winthrop, . . . soldiers, in-trepid and adventurous like Standish and Church." Opposed to these heroes are the Indians: "Phlegmatic but fierce, inconstant though unimpassioned, hard to excite and impossible to soothe, cold in friendship and insatiable in revenge." Elsewhere the debunker of Philip's greatness, Palfrey castigates the views of the authors of *Yamoyden* as more romantic than historical, more likely derived "from Mr. Irving's life of Philip . . . than from any graver authority." Both the nature of his treatment of whites and Indians and the small amount of space he devotes to the latter in proportion to the former more clearly presage the frontier romance than anything *Yamoyden* itself does.

As Palfrey envisioned, the most obvious way in which American literature can serve as a vehicle for nationalism is in depicting the triumph of whites who were willing to become a new people and to wrest the land by violence from the native inhabitants and from those whites who held to their Old World identities. Thus, fiction which takes place during the French and Indian Wars shows the colonists defeating the French and their Indian allies; fiction of the Revolution shows them defeating the British and their Indian allies. When no foreign whites are involved in the action, the American settlers are victorious over Indians alone: Indians exist in the frontier romance primarily to be killed by whites.

At the beginning of *The Prairie Flower,* the work of one of the least reflective of frontier romancers, Emerson Bennett, one young man proposes to another that they go West to " 'hunt, fish, trap, shoot Indians, anything, everything, so we manage to escape ennui, and have plenty of adventure!' " The distinctively American rite of Indian-killing is not so openly acknowledged by James Kirke Paulding, who refers to an encounter with Indians as the initiation ritual into manhood:

> Young men bordering on the frontiers were accustomed almost universally to commence the business of this world with a trading voyage among the savages of the borders. Previous to assuming the post and character of manhood, it was considered an almost indispensable obligation to undertake and complete some enterprise of this kind, replete with privations and dangers. (*The Dutchman's Fireside*)

The vague allusion at the end of the passage covers the possibility which is always actualized in the frontier romance: the proof of manhood not by the unglamorous activity of trading with the Indians but by killing them. More explicitly, a frontiersman tells an uninitiated stranger in Robert Montgomery Bird's *Nick of the Woods:* " 'When you kill an Injun yourself, I reckon . . . you will be willing to take all the honor that can come of it, without leaving it to be scrambled after by others.' " The patriotic aspect of Indian-killing is asserted by another frontiersman in the same novel: " 'I go for the doctrine that every able-bodied man should save his country and his neighbors, and fight their foes; and them that does is men and gentlemen, and them that don't is cowards and rascals, that's my idear.' " The large numbers of Indians killed in frontier romances indicate that such a credo was subscribed to by the writers in the genre.

In spite of their endless avowals to do justice to the Indian, these authors could not put aside history, which showed the white man's triumph over the native inhabitants, or their own feelings or racial and cultural superiority. They saw themselves as the measure of man, and the Indians, by this standard, were sadly deficient. Most of the frontier romancers make some statement like the one which opens the anonymous *Christian Indian*: "It must always be a subject of regret to the true-hearted American, that the soil he now possesses was the price of a plunder, and persecution, and bloodshed, to its original owners." But none were willing to place the Indians' claims to the continent above the white man's: the same book ends on a note of satisfaction that "cultivated fields and thronged city have replaced trackless deserts and barren moors. . . . We compare again and again the past and the present, and see in our own superior blessings, the realization, almost of all the glowing and bright anticipations of the early sage."

From the earliest settlement, apologists had advanced some version of justification by cultivation to rationalize the expropriation of the Indian, an argument which continued to have great appeal in the nineteenth century. As William Henry Harrison demanded rhetorically: "Is one of the fairest portions of the globe to remain in a state of nature, the haunt of a few wretched savages, when it seems destined by the Creator to give support to a large population and to be the seat of civilization?" At the end of the century Theodore Roosevelt answered: "The settler and pioneer have at bottom had justice on their side; this great continent could not have been kept as nothing but a game preserve for squalid savages." Saved from starvation by Indian corn, the first colonists had reason to know that some Indians did cultivate the land, but even had this been true of all, the cultivation pronouncements made by Harrison and Roosevelt contained an equally potent underlying argument: the Indians were savages whose failure to cultivate was simply a convenient indicator of their great inferiority to the white man. When in the early 1770s colonists broke the crown law by settling on Indian lands, Governor Dunmore of Virginia observed: "Nor can they be easily brought to entertain any belief of the permanent obligation of Treaties made with those People, whom they consider as but little removed from the brute Creation." More than a century later, in pondering why "the Phoenician factory . . . fostered the development of the Mediterranean civilization, while in America the trading post exploited the natives," Frederick Jackson Turner concluded: "The explanation of this difference is to be sought partly in race differences, partly in the greater gulf that separated the civilization of the European from the civilization of the American Indian as compared with that which parted the early Greeks and the Phoenicians."

Living in an intensely nationalistic and progressive period, those members of the conquering race who elected to write frontier romances could hardly be expected to solve the historical dilemma, to find even a literary way of doing justice to the Indian. The noble savage might display virtues in a remote primitive milieu, but once he was juxtaposed to the white man, he had to be judged inferior. As the authors of *Yamoyden* were reminded, sympathy for the Indian must be subordinated to a celebration of the American achievement.

The cultivation rationale, with its concomitant assumption of white superiority, quickly found its way into the frontier romance, not only through the dramatized successes of the white characters, but also through authorial comment. At either the beginning or end of a work, or in both places, the writer is apt to compare past and present. Thus, M. C. Hodges's *The Mestico* concludes: "The restless, indolent, discontented Indians have been removed to their western reserve; and much of the fertile land that was wasting under

their miserable tillage, now blooms under the industry of the whites." Making the same point, but less obtrusively, Mrs. Cheney has the hero of *A Peep at the Pilgrims* observe "where the wilderness of nature had yielded to the hand of cultivation, villages were arising, and the soil teemed with all the rich and varied bounties which could spring up to reward the labours of the husbandman." Characters, too, are apt to express this view. Earth, the frontiersman in James Strange French's *Elkswatawa*, defends his position to the more idealistic hero, Rolfe: " 'I believe I think as most of the whites do, and that is, that these lands are too good for them; they should be cultivated instead of lying waste for them to prowl over.' " Even the Indians are expected to appreciate the reasonableness of this argument in James McHenry's *The Wilderness*. To persuade them to free their captive, George Washington, the prophet Tonnaleuka tells the Indians: " 'The whole of this waste wilderness will yet bloom and flourish, in consequence of his great deeds and heroic virtues.' "

Another variation on the defense of white dispossession of the Indian by cultivation is Charles Fenno Hoffman's short story "Queen Meg." In the midst of a "long settled and highly cultivated district," a few boat hours from New York City, the author comes upon a household of squatter Indians: "A more wretched-looking set of objects I never saw." Evidently the matriarch of the family is of high Indian lineage: owing to "her confused ideas of what she deemed her natural rights," she haughtily rejects the idea of her progeny working as day laborers. Authorial disapproval comes down heavily on Queen Meg and her shiftless brood. Here is, in Hoffman's eyes, an excellent exemplification of why whites deserve the land: they settle and cultivate; the Indians squat and degenerate. Hawthorne or Melville might have found irony in the relative positions of Indians and whites, the transformation of rightful possessors into squatters and vice versa, but to Hoffman, Queen Meg's refusal to accept the change is merely ludicrous.

Karl Postl is more candid in exposing the reality behind the cultivation rationale. In his *Tokeah*, although Indians have been industriously cultivating the land, white hostility toward them is undiminished: "Already in those early times they began to look with an unfriendly eye upon the lawful possessors of these lands, whom they considered as a sort of nuisance that could not be too soon removed." Regardless of what use Indians make of it, whites want the land for themselves.

As James Hall admitted in his short story "The War Belt," the white acquisition of Indian land was never a historical issue:

> That the enterprising and intelligent population of the United States would spread out from the seaboard over the wilderness; that the savage must retire before civilized man . . . were propositions too evident to be concealed or denied. But it never was intended that the Indian should be driven from his hunting grounds by violence; and while a necessity, strong as the law of nature, decreed the expulsion of the mere hunter, and gave dominion to art, industry, and religion, it was always proposed that the savage should be removed by negotiation, and a just price given for the relinquishment of his possessory title.

However accurate Hall's assessment of white intentions to

purchase the land, fictive and nationalistic purposes conjoined to require that the land be bought, as historically it often was, primarily by bloodshed. Beginning with the established captivity narrative sequence, author after author describes an unprovoked Indian attack which makes some whites captives. Departing from the authentic captivity narratives, they then show white retaliation: the captives must be restored and the civilized community freed from future threat. By the work's conclusion the Indians have been soundly defeated, and, as a result, the white characters will be able to "make the wilderness bloom."

Because it placed the Indians totally in the wrong, such a formula was infinitely more satisfying than the land purchase policy. The Indians forfeited their right to the land by shedding the first blood; more compelling than their failure to cultivate or their other primitive characteristics, this gratuitous demonstration of innate wickedness justified not only the white claims to the continent but the extermination of the Indian. As David Brion Davis explains: "Writers had a certain justification for dwelling upon the ritual [of killing Indians], since it signified the free white man's possession of the rights and privileges of his civilization, a racial eucharist, granting secular freedom and wealth after the sacrifice of a red man's flesh and blood." By slaying the Indian, European whites killed Cotton Mather's serpent in the New World garden, a rite of passage from which they emerged a new people.

Although the conventions of English literature which the frontier romance relied on dictated the aristocratic lineage of the white hero and heroine, these children of nobility invariably became permanent citizens of the New World. While large portions of Susannah Rowson's *Reuben and Rachel* are set in England, for example, the ending upholds an American residency in the most telling terms: those of property. Reuben is unable to inherit his English estate: "His dark complextion, the nature of his father's marriage to Oberea [an Indian] which in law would have been termed illegal, all militated against success." The hindrances of the Old World are not found in the new: in the novel's conclusion, Reuben takes possession of his father's Pennsylvania estate, marries, and settles down there. More openly didactic is the ending of *A Peep at the Pilgrims:* "Major Atherton, in the following year, revisited his native land, but the ties which once bound him to it were weakened by absence. . . . He disposed of his paternal inheritance, and returned to America, where his affections were entirely concentrated." As it is described in the frontier romance, the Old World is a place where difficulties like the failure to obtain one's rightful inheritance or religious persecution are experienced. Several works use lovers who are separated in England and reunited in America.

Should a white villain be part of the plot, he is typically British, often aristocratic, and usually involved in anti-American activities. Such is the case in Gideon M. Hollister's *Mount Hope,* where the villain not only kidnaps the heroine but pursues the regicides Goffe and Whalley. In Catharine Maria Sedgwick's *Hope Leslie,* the evil Sir Philip similarly combines anti-Puritan policy with an attempted abduction of the heroine. In the more modern time of the War of 1812 the villain of Anna L. Snelling's *Kabaosa* is a British officer who has betrayed his Indian friend by seducing his wife. He plots against the American side in general, and in particular, with appropriate rant, against the white heroine: " 'When once I have her in my power, I'll make her rue this hour of insult.' "

Needless to say, both the New World and the heroine are preserved from these intended British villainies.

A certain restraint and decorum are evident in intrawhite conflicts of this sort which are absent from the clash of whites and Indians. Although on opposing sides, whites share a common Western culture; they remain gentlemanly. In Eliza Lanesford Cushing's *Saratoga,* for example, the British partisan Major Courtland is gradually won over to a high opinion of the rebels by demonstrations of their fighting ability. For most of the novel's two volumes he withholds his approval of his daughter's American suitor, but after she has refused the preferred British aspirant, he acquiesces gracefully. Mutual respect for each other's country prevails between Major Courtland and the American Colonel Grahame.

On a larger scale the same kind of understanding obtains between the English and French in James Fenimore Cooper's *The Last of the Mohicans.* When Fort William Henry is forced to surrender, General Montcalm shows the English "unusual and unexpected generosity"; all is arranged in accordance with military honor. As the Munro sisters leave the fort, "the French officers, who had learned their rank, bowed often and low, forbearing, however, to intrude those attentions which they saw, with peculiar tact, might not be agreeable." In contrast to this deference, the Indian allies of the French treacherously attack the English:

> More than two thousand raving savages broke from the forest at the signal, and threw themselves across the fatal plain with instinctive alacrity. We shall not dwell on the revolting horrors that succeeded. Death was everywhere, and in his most terrific and disgusting aspects. Resistance only served to inflame the murderers, who inflicted their furious blows long after their victims were beyond the power of their resentment. The flow of blood might be likened to the outbreaking of a torrent; and, as the natives became heated and maddened by the sight, many among them even kneeled to the earth, and drank freely, exultingly, hellishly, of the crimson tide.

Groups of whites in the frontier romance are never guilty of such wanton and seemingly irrational atrocities. At times they may be forced to take harsh measures against the Indians, like the burning alive of hundreds of Pequots at Mystic, but these are depicted as rational and necessary acts, never as gratuitous barbarism.

Undoubtedly, part of the overembellishment in battle descriptions like Cooper's can be attributed to the defensiveness which American authors often displayed about the worth of their native materials. It might be true, as Palfrey asserted, that "compared with some of ours, Scottish rivers are but brooks, and Scottish forests mere thickets," but scenery was of little help. The writer needed huge deeds more than huge rivers. For the settler to reap the maximum glory, he had to overcome a foe of the first magnitude: unable to compete with the armies of Europe in size or magnificence, Indians had to excel in gruesome accomplishment—hence Cooper's hellish blood drinkers. In *Tom Hanson, the Avenger,* Samuel Young defiantly challenges the Old World to equal the horror of Indian warfare:

> Talk, ye philanthropists, of barbarity in the Dark Ages: tell of the tyranny of superstition, of the horrors of civil wars: tell of France and her bloody scenes, when frantic with revolutionary frenzy.

Yea, summon more, and let all fail in rendering a comparison to those terrible scenes of bloodshed and havoc perpetrated in the New World, amid a wilderness infested with devils in human shape.

Taking a different tack, Mrs. Cheney points out somewhat apologetically that the battle of Mystic was disproportionately significant to the small numbers involved in the fighting:

> This memorable, but almost forgotten contest,—however trifling it may appear in comparison with the more brilliant conquests of Europe, which have so often convulsed her fairest kingdoms and deluged her fields with the blood of thousands of victims to her ambition or revenge,—was notwithstanding productive of the most important consequences, and strikingly exhibits the firmness and courage of the early settlers of New-England. (*A Peep at the Pilgrims*)

Where whites are victorious, the author stresses their valor, although "the laurels of the conqueror were unhappily stained with the blood of the innocent and defenceless."

Even should an author regard an action like the attack on Mystic as white cruelty, he could scarcely reject the major assumption that the development of the American continent for white civilization was a desideratum. Daniel Thompson's *The Doomed Chief,* a romance set in the time of King Philip's War, is sympathetic to the Indians and strongly censorious of the Puritans. The white characters who hate Indians are at worst scheming hypocrites, at best honest tools of the unscrupulous villains. In contrast, the hero is a vigorous partisan of Philip's nobility. In the trial of the three Indians, which led to the outbreak of war, Thompson sums up the Puritan defects:

> Great was the displeasure of the court functionaries and their supporters, at Williams' triumphant vindication of King Philip, the great Diabolus of their prejudice, fear and hatred; at his fearless unmasking of their disguised policy for the subjugation of the Indians, and especially at his ungracious exposure of the weakness of their testimony against the already death-doomed prisoners.

Their corrupt system of justice, secret machinations against an Indian policy established by treaty, and warped feeling make the Puritans singularly unattractive, but immediately after this harsh indictment, Thompson is forced to partially recant: in spite of their failings, the Puritans contributed to "the still more beneficent fabric of our present American liberty." And in spite of the praises heaped upon the Indians, they become the familiar "infernal scamps" and "murderous hounds," pursued by the hero, among others, when the war gets under way. The best that Thompson can do for his Indians is to allow them to die as they want on their home ground rather than being sold into slavery.

An analogous situation exists in *Mount Hope,* which treats the same historical events as *The Doomed Chief.* Its author, Gideon M. Hollister, is a partisan of the noble savage as long as he is not in direct conflict with the white man. Although he professes "sympathies . . . almost equally divided" between the two sides, in battle he portrays the standard savage of the captivity narrative tradition, a barbaric scalper and mutilator of the wounded who is no match for the intrepid white sharpshooters. The Indians' nobility ultimately resides in their death, and here Hollister is generous: "The records of Spartan and Roman fame do not contain a sentiment more worthy of a hero when passing to the land where his religion has taught him that valour shall be rewarded, than the last word of the son of Miantunnamoh."

However reluctantly, writers of the frontier romance learned the lesson which Palfrey sought to impart in his review of *Yamoyden.* Should they espouse the Indian cause too ardently, they faced the consequences predicted by Irving in his discussion of the prospects of the Indian in American literature:

> Should he [the poet] venture upon the dark story of their wrongs and wretchedness; should he tell how they were invaded, corrupted, despoiled; driven from their native abodes and the sepulchres of their fathers; hunted like wild beasts about the earth; and sent down with violence and butchery to the grave; posterity will either turn with horror and incredulity from the tale, or blush with indignation at the inhumanity of their forefathers.

Horror and incredulity, or the blush of shame, would have been unpleasant reactions to elicit from a reading public. Nor could they comfortably coexist with a number of ideas sacred to nineteenth-century Americans: the inevitability of an advanced people supplanting a primitive one, the appropriateness of a Christian supplanting a heathen society, and the greatness of the country's pioneer forebears. If writers believed, like Thompson, that white dealing with the Indians constituted a "damning record . . . of turpitude and wrong," they also had to believe that the best of all possible choices had been made. As James Kirke Paulding piously appraised the situation: "The red man is gone, and the white man is in his place. Such are the mutations of the world! Shall we lament them? No. It is the will and the work of Him that made all, governs all, disposes all; and it is all for the best." Mrs. Snelling, in contrast, entertains the shadow of a doubt: "It is *almost* with feelings of self-reproach that we look back upon the past" [emphasis added]. More than counterbalancing the destruction of the Indians was the creation of the mighty nation of which Thompson and his literary confreres were part.

Although the desirability of white dispossession of the Indian and the necessity of doing so violently were assumptions shared by most writers of the frontier romance, it did not follow that they should be utterly heedless of the Indian's passing. Sympathy for the foreign powers expelled from the North American continent was uncalled for; the French, Dutch, Spanish, and British had nation-states in Europe to retreat to. Indians, on the other hand, were only able to leave America feet first; already virtually exterminated along the Eastern seaboard, they seemed in the first half of the nineteenth century to face rapid and complete extinction. As Cooper wrote in *The Redskins:*

> We white men are so occupied with ourselves, and our own passing concerns, look on all other races of human beings as so much our inferiors, that it is seldom we have time or inclination to reflect on the consequences of our own acts. Like the wheel that rolls along the highway, however, many is the inferior creature that we heedlessly crush in our path. Thus has it been with the red-man, and . . . thus will it continue to be.

Writers of the frontier romance accepted the process as inevitable; what whites could do, Cooper vaguely suggests, is pause for a moment and contemplate what they had done. It was thus a minor motif of nationalism in the frontier romance to have, in James Hall's words, "sympathy for the fallen fortune of those who once flourished and are now no more."

As a chapter in the continent's past, the aboriginal inhabitants warranted preservation in literature (if not in actuality); indeed, one argument advanced by critics who called for the literary treatment of the Indian was the importance of memorializing him:

> Gradually receding before the tread of civilization, and taking from it only the principle of destruction, they seem to be fast wasting to utter dissolution, and we shall one day look upon their history, with such emotions of curiosity and wonder, as those with which we now survey the immense mounds and heaps of ruin in the interior of our continent.

Given the repeated failure of attempts to halt the rapid degeneration of Indians in contact with whites, writers of the frontier romance believed that Indians would soon exist only in their pages: "The memory of the race is destined to be saved, if saved at all, only by a miracle. Already the flame flickers in its socket;—its fading rays linger only on the pages of romantic fiction. The night will come, and the sun will go down upon the Indian forever" (*Miriam Coffin*).

The flourishing cities and fields which were ritualistically invoked at the end of the tale presupposed a disappearing wilderness, and along with it, the vanishing Indian figure. At times the new and more advanced literally replaces the old and primitive; as Mrs. Cheney notes: "The houses of the European planters arose on the ashes of their humble wigwams." In keeping with the white man's superior ability to change the natural environment, and perhaps to emphasize the finality of the Indians' tragedy, authors often remarked that Indians left no trace of their one-time presence. As Joseph C. Hart writes about Nantucket: "Nothing now remains to indicate their locality [the Indian towns], but deep beds of ashes, mixed with seashells, which unerringly point out the hearths of the wigwams of the Indian." John Davis's *The First Settlers of Virginia* concludes in a more philosophical vein: "No vestige is left behind of a powerful nation, who once unconscious of the existence of another people, dreamt not of invasions from foreign enemies, or inroads from colonists, but believed their strength invincible, and their race eternal."

If the historical Indians of precolonial times believed their race eternal, those of the frontier romance do not. Rather than making statements in their own person, authors sometimes elect to have Indian characters themselves comment upon their declining fortunes. Joseph Brant, for example, refers to himself in Charles Fenno Hoffman's *Greyslaer* as one of nature's "doomed children that must soon pass away." In another Revolutionary War novel in which Brant appears, the doom is already accomplished. An Indian making a treaty with the Tories asks rhetorically:

> "Where are now those dwellings of the brave? They have vanished like the blossoms that are beautiful when fanned by the gale of spring, but that wither and fade away when the fierce summer bursts upon them with the relentless scorching of his beams. So have our people faded before the wrath of the children of your father."

Indians are apt to be prescient in foreseeing the outcome of their encounter with the white man. In Davis's *The First Settlers of Virginia,* an Indian attributes his tribe's attack on the exploratory expedition of Captain John Smith to a suspicion that the English "were a people come from under the world to take their world from them."

After *The Last of the Mohicans,* a number of authors embodied the elegiac theme in a "last red man" character, usually a chief who is the last of his tribe or line. In an anonymous tale, "The First and Last Sacrifice," a dying warrior laments: " 'I had a father, I had a mother; I had a wife, I had children. I have no father, I have no mother; I have no wife, I have no children. I am the last of my race. I have no kindred.' " Some of these lonely figures think to journey into the wilderness beyond the reach of the white man, but by the time most frontier romances were written, it was apparent that no western removal could permanently appease the white man's desire for land. As Cooper's Trackless describes the Indian's situation in *The Redskins:* " 'The red-man keeps on his trail, and the pale-face is never far behind. . . . When that other lake is seen, the red-man must stop, and die in the open fields, where rum, and tobacco, and bread are plenty, or march on into the great salt lake of the west and be drowned.' " The dying out of the race is the end which Uncas also envisions in the anonymous romance *The Witch of New England:* " 'A little longer and the whitemen will cease to persecute us,—for we shall have ceased to exist and the great names of our fathers will have no tongue to repeat them.' "

Generally, a sympathetic understanding of the Indian's untenable position in the unequal struggle with the white man is found in the hero of a full-length frontier romance. The bringer of civilized values and humane feelings into the wilderness milieu, he can see the conflict more objectively than the hate-ridden frontiersmen. Nevertheless, action and attitude are often at variance. When fighting occurs, the hero must perform bravely on the right side, but he refuses to commit, and is often repulsed by, the excesses of wanton killing and scalping which characterize the frontiersman's behavior. This contrast in white attitudes is brought out in a number of hero and frontiersman couples: Rolfe and Earth in *Kabaosa,* Sumner and Luke in *Elkswatawa,* Herrick and Adherbal in *The Hawk Chief,* and Greyslaer and Balt in *Greyslaer.* While the old, experienced hunter pleads frontier necessity, the novice-hero displays a conscience about the Indian which appears to be a luxury in the wilderness environment.

At times, set debates about Indian character take place in the frontier romance in which the hero defends the aborigine as a noble savage. Edward Bradley, in *The Witch of New England,* extols the character of the American Indian to a skeptical friend: " 'He is brave, hospitable, a faithful friend and kind husband according to the habits of his people. . . . The catalogue of his virtues far out-vies the list of his vices.' " Colonel Grahame, the hero of *Saratoga,* is equally certain that "even in their savage state, they possess many virtues, and those the noblest that can dignify humanity." Most eloquent of all is that atypical frontiersman Natty Bumppo, who praises and sympathizes with the Indians of his choice throughout the Leatherstocking Tales.

Most frontier romances were produced between the War of 1812 and the Civil War, a period of high nationalistic consciousness. Secure in having twice defeated the British, the young nation saw a glorious future for itself. As G. Harrison Orians describes the period: "The eighteenth century with its chain-of-being and its concept of a fixed universe had partly given way before a vision of a world whose limits were constantly expanding and whose denizens had a passion for physical progress." Indians, with their stubborn adherence to a primitive way of life, could have no place in the progressive and materialistic American world of the nineteenth century; whether or not they actually became extinct, as the writers of the frontier romance expected, their meaning for white Americans was clearly linked to the country's past, to the transient frontier situation. In this context they played a vital part: like the ancient dragon guarding the treasure, Indians were the evil enemy who must be slain before whites could possess the land. As the painted devils and formidable foes of white settlement whose image had already been widely disseminated by the popular captivity narratives, Indians lived on into fiction. By overcoming them, whites demonstrated those superior qualities which writers never grew tired of praising; moreover, they suffered hideous tortures, scalpings, and massacres, which consecrated their cause. Through the loss of their own blood and the shedding of the Indians', "the brave pioneers who led the van of civilisation" felt that they had paid the price for their new world inheritance. Having established their right by conquering the original inhabitants, Americans could then eject the strongest foreign claimant—the mother country.

Opposed to the success story which dominates the pages of the frontier romance is the fate of the defeated and dispossessed. As civilized life replaced frontier survival conditions, the brutal aspects of white conquest assumed greater prominence. The victor could not repudiate the victory, nor genuinely repent what he yet enjoyed, but he could express an appreciation of the Indian's life and character—as exhibited apart from white contact—and a regret that the white man's inevitable triumph had so utterly destroyed him. A concern with the tragedy of the Indians was a legitimate manifestation of nationalism, for from that tragedy, what promised to be the greatest example of Western civilization took its being. (pp. 21-43)

Louise K. Barnett, "The White Fantasy World of the Frontier Romance," and "Nationalism and the Frontier Romance," in her The Ignoble Savage: American Literary Racism, 1790-1890, *Greenwood Press, 1975, pp. 17-19, 21-47.*

FEMINIST READINGS OF FRONTIER LITERATURE

LELAND S. PERSON

[*In the following excerpt, Person explains ways in which narratives written by women contradict the Adamic myth of the frontier and provide an alternative view of the frontier experience.*]

In the past three decades critics of American frontier literature have emphasized the myth of the American Adam, "standing alone, self-reliant and self-propelling," in some western virgin land [R. W. B. Lewis, *The American Adam: Innocence, Tragedy, and Tradition in the Nineteenth Century;* see Further Reading]. Leslie Fiedler only slightly modified the male exclusivity of the myth by citing the "archetypal relationship" of "two lonely men, one dark-skinned, one white . . . [who] have forsaken all others for the sake of the austere, almost inarticulate, but unquestioned love which

binds them to each other and to the world of nature which they have preferred to civilization" [*Love and Death in the American Novel*]. Joel Porte revealed the myth's misogynist tendency in his comments upon Cooper's *The Pathfinder* [in his *The Romance in America: Studies in Cooper, Poe, Hawthorne, Melville, and James*]: the "American Adam [Natty Bumppo] knows intuitively how to avoid the error of his archetypal ancestor: he can only hope to retain possession of his American Eden if he makes a pact with the devil [Chingachgook, the Big Serpent] and they jointly exclude women from the virgin forest." All three comments, of course, imply that in these critics' views frontier fiction is a predominantly male genre. If included at all, women play negative roles as projections of male fantasies, as symbols of what Adam must leave behind or banish from his virgin land. The frontier is appealing, in Fiedler's words, because it offers escape from the "tyranny of home and woman."

Although it certainly describes many frontier novels, the Adamic myth has three weaknesses: it obscures the often heroic roles that women actually played on the frontier, it oversimplifies women's roles in many novels, and, most important, it ignores the possibility of a female-centered frontier myth. In her recently published *The Land Before Her,* Annette Kolodny has gone a long way toward redressing the balance, demonstrating through discussions of many little-known narratives and popular novels the existence of a woman's wilderness myth: a fantasy of the land as a domesticated garden [see excerpt below]. My purpose in this essay is to explore another aspect of women's fantasies, by contrasting male and female attitudes toward miscegenation in a number of stories and novels. Kolodny has pointed the way, although, as she notes, her emphasis on women's attitudes toward the land has precluded much discussion of attitudes toward Indians. As we shall see, however, nowhere are differences between male and female attitudes toward Indians more sharply defined than in their views on intermarriage. Most importantly, the successful marriages between white women and Indian men (in works by Catharine Maria Sedgwick and Lydia Maria Child) suggest terms for an alternative, female, frontier fantasy—a pact between Indians and women, an Eden from which Adam rather than Eve has been excluded.

Examining the rise of frontier fiction as a popular genre, furthermore, supports the view that the male-authored tradition of men alone in nature was by no means seminal. The first two American novels to use Indians and Indian captivity, for example, were both written by women: Ann Eliza Bleecker's *The History of Maria Kittle* (1793) and Susannah Rowson's *Reuben and Rachel* (1798). During the 1820s, the period of frontier fiction's initial popularity, four more important novels by women appeared (compared to eleven by men). In fact, while 1823 can be considered to mark the beginning of the genre's popularity, with the publication of Cooper's *The Pioneers,* James McHenry's *The Spectre of the Forest* and *The Wilderness,* and James Kirke Paulding's *Koningsmarke,* 1824 marks the inception of an admittedly short-lived female alternative. Harriet V. Cheney's *A Peep at the Pilgrims,* Lydia Maria Child's *Hobomok,* and Eliza Cushing's *Saratoga* found competition only from John Brainard's brief *Fort Braddock Letters* and the anonymously published *The Witch of New England.* During the genre's heyday in the 1830s and 1840s, on the other hand, only one of over forty fictional works—Anna L. Snelling's *Kabaosa, or, The Warriors of the West*—was written by a woman, while male writers such as Cooper,

Simms, Bird, Paulding, Hall and Bennett solidified the genre's popularity. Arguably, the increasing popularity of the masculine adventure story devoted to exploration, hunting, and Indian fighting intimidated female authors.

Cooper suggests as much in his 1826 preface to *The Last of the Mohicans.* Sure that readers who expected an "imaginary and romantic picture of things which never had an existence" would be disappointed by his narrative, he explained that it "relates . . . to matters which may not be universally understood, especially by the more imaginative sex"—that is, by women. Given the relative balance between male- and female-authored texts at that point in the genre's history, Cooper might have spared his female readers such patronization. Yet he did anticipate the increasing alienation of women from the frontier as it was depicted in male-authored novels during the next two decades. And if women, in Cooper's view, required help in understanding the esoteric materials in *The Last of the Mohicans,* subsequent male authors made it clear that women in their novels needed even more male help— especially in combating the threat of an Indian assault.

Besides their ideal of men alone in nature, many male-authored frontier novels establish triangular, doubly exploitive relationships among Indian and white males and white women that reinforce male fantasies of chivalrous protection, rescue, and revenge. In scenes that bring to fictional life the characters in Vanderlyn's *Death of Jane McCrea,* women in the wilderness are repeatedly placed in jeopardy. Threatened with captivity, forced marriage, rape, or murder by savage Indian males, they must be protected by male heroes; if captured, they must be rescued by men, and if killed, they must have their deaths avenged by their distraught husbands, who often use their deaths as excuses to wage war on all Indians.

However repugnant such pogroms may be in fiction, they do conform to the historical record. Susan Brownmiller has pointed out [in *Against Our Will: Men, Women, and Rape*] that frontiersmen often used such stories about the assault or rape of white women by Indians "as an inflammatory excuse for their own behavior," and Susan Armitage has argued that the "projection of the urge to violence onto the Indian provided a splendid rationale for white retaliation. Protection of white women, the symbols of civilization, and the extermination or removal of Indians went hand-in-hand" [see excerpt below]. To reinforce their view that women in the wilderness required male protection from Indians, frontier novels typically exploit the stereotyped figure of the Bad Indian, the "bloodthirsty savage, seeking vengeance or just malicious fun at the expense of innocent Whites, especially women." [Robert F. Berkhofer, Jr., *The White Man's Indian: Images of the American Indian from Columbus to the Present*]. Or as Natty Bumppo says in *The Last of the Mohicans* (1826), thereby codifying the opposition which his presence makes triangular, he must " 'save these tender blossoms from the fangs of the worst of sarpants.' "

At their most benign, frontier novels simply expose women to the threat of Indian assault, not upon their lives, but upon their imaginations. The "threat" involves the idea of marriage to an Indian. When Magua proposes to Cora Munro in *The Last of the Mohicans,* for example, he does so with such "fierce looks" that Cora's "eyes sank with shame, under an impression that . . . they had encountered an expression that no chaste female might endure." Similarly, after being captured by the Sioux in *The Prairie* (1827), both Inez Middleton and Ellen Wade become objects of covetous looks by the chief Mahtoree: "There was something so startling in the entrance, and so audacious in the look of their conqueror, that the eyes of both sunk to the earth under a feeling of terror and embarrassment." And in *The Pathfinder* (1840) Cooper expresses Mabel Dunham's fear of captivity simply by having her recall the legends she has heard: "Our heroine well knew that the Indians usually carried off to their villages, for the purposes of adoption, such captives as they did not slay, and that many instances had occurred, in which individuals of her sex had passed the remainder of their lives in the wigwams of their conquerors. Such thoughts as these, invariably drove her to her knees, and to her prayers."

In these and other cases a miscegenation phobia accompanies the American Adam's image of women in the wilderness. However legitimate his concern about the prospect of attack and assault, it is the *idea* of interracial marriage that often concerns him. When Cora Munro reports Magua's proposal to Duncan Heyward, the Major's response succinctly expresses the male attitude toward miscegenation. " 'Cora! Cora!' " he exclaims. " 'You jest with our misery! Name not the horrid alternative again; the thought itself is worse than a thousand deaths.' " Heyward's view is echoed by Mark Heathcote in Cooper's *The Wept of Wish-Ton-Wish* (1829), which Fiedler terms the "first anti-miscegenation novel in our literature." Speaking of his kidnapped sister's marriage to the Narragansett chief, Conanchet, Heathcote comments, " 'But be she what hardships and exposures have made her, still must Ruth Heathcote be far too good for an Indian wigwam. Oh! 'tis horrible to believe that she is the bond-woman, the servitor, the wife of a savage!' " In *The Prairie* Cooper is

Davy Crockett

so concerned about his heroine's protection from the very idea of marriage to an Indian that he does not even allow Natty Bumppo to translate Mahtoree's very gracious proposal to Inez Middleton. "The trapper had not lost a syllable of the speech," Cooper notes, "and he now prepared himself to render it into English, in such a manner as should leave its principal idea even more obscure than in the original."

One of the best fictional treatments of the captivity-miscegenation-revenge theme is James Hall's "The Pioneer" (1835), a first-person narrative that underscores the miscegenation phobia that motivates the Indian hater. After his uncle and mother are killed by Indians and his sister kidnapped, William Robinson begins a systematic program of revenge: "I believed that in killing a savage I performed my duty as a man, and served my country as a citizen." But the turning point of Robinson's tale is his discovery of his sister, her Indian husband, and two children. Although everything indicates that she has adapted to her situation, and she "coldly" refuses his invitation to return to "civilised life," Robinson simply cannot accept his sister's condition. "I could not look at the Indian husband of my sister without aversion," he says, "and her children, with their wild dark eyes, and savage features, were to me objects of inexpressible loathing." To his imagination, his sister has been irreparably deformed, and her present appearance entirely eclipses his fond memories of her. "I had seen her," he continues, "and the illusion was destroyed. Instead of the lovely woman, endued with the appropriate graces of her sex, I found her in the garb of the wilderness, and the voluntary companion of a savage, the mother of squalid imps, who were destined to a life of rapine; instead of the gentle and rational being, I saw her coarse, sunburned, and ignorant—without sensibility, without feminine pride, and with scarcely a perception of the moral distinctions between right and wrong." Although Robinson's narrative is meant to explain his "reformation" from Indian hater to preacher, that reformation does not extend to his sister nor to his attitude toward miscegenation. From that point of view, the story finally depicts an unbridgeable imaginative gap—echoed in Robinson's parting thoughts as he leaves his sister: "I had secretly resolved never to see her again."

At their most misogynist, frontier novels depict women physically threatened with assault, rape or murder. One of the most forthright examples is Robert M. Bird's *Nick of the Woods* (1837). When Edith Forrester is captured by Indians, Bird introduces a new character, the white renegade Richard Braxley, to clarify the threat Edith faces. Braxley covets Edith's property and has been plotting to bring her under his power, but when she refuses his proposals, he threatens to turn her over to the Indians. " 'Death is a boon the savages may bestow, when the whim takes them,' " he warns. " 'But before that, they must show their affection for their prisoner. There are many that can admire the bright eyes and ruddy cheeks of the white maiden; and some one, doubtless, will admit the stranger to a corner of his wigwam and his bosom!' " Braxley is a stock villian from whose grasp Edith will be climactically rescued by her brother Roland, but in using him as he does, Bird highlights the "pact" that many male novelists forge between white and Indian males—at the expense of women. It is the white man who threatens the captured maiden with rape *by Indians,* thereby demonstrating a willingness to use both Indians and women to fulfill his own designs.

In most cases, male-authored frontier novels merely subject

women to the *threat* of such "horrid alternatives"; at their worst, they linger over the spectacle of a woman's jeopardy. In *The Yemassee* (1835), when Bess Matthews encounters a huge rattlesnake in the forest, William Gilmore Simms unabashedly exploits his heroine's terror and the sexual symbolism of the snake's "assault." [The critic adds in a footnote: A single passage from *The Yemassee* will exemplify Simms's seemingly perverse delight in his heroine's plight: "She sees him approach—now advancing, now receding;—now swelling in every part with something of anger, while his neck is arched beautifully like that of a wild horse under the curb; until, at length, tired as it were of play, like the cat with its victim, she sees the neck growing larger and becoming completely bronzed as about to strike—the huge jaws unclosing almost directly above her, the long tubulated fang, charged with venom, protruding from the cavernous mouth."] Although Bess is saved by the son of the Yemassee chief, the late-arriving hero Gabriel Harrison assumes that, instead of rescuing her, Occonestoga is assaulting her. While Harrison's mistake is understandable, the scene clearly locates the Indian threat to women in its hero's imagination. Except for its conclusion (Bess's rescue), the scene brings to literary life the implications of Vanderlyn's *Death of Jane McCrea.* The emphasis in the foreground is on the maiden's plight, while the white male remains in the background, rushing in at the climactic moment to punish the Indian for what he thinks he has done.

Harrison's mistake is rectified, but Simms further subjects Bess to the threat of assault when the renegade Ishiagaska invades her bedroom, creeping through the window and, Simms implies, out of her dreams: "in her dreams there floated images of terror; and vague aspects that troubled or threatened, caused her to moan in her sleep, as at a danger still to be apprehended or deplored." The scene is a veritable archetype of the triangle I have identified, and Simms invests it with such an emotional charge that each character in the triangle is transfigured. Ishiagaska "stood, silent for awhile, surveying at his ease the composed and beautiful outline of his victim's person. . . . " he writes. "Never did her beauty show forth more exquisitely than now, when murder stood nigh, ready to blast it for ever." Bess's awakening only exacerbates her predicament and emphasizes her beautiful passivity. The "broad blade was uplifted, shining bright in the moonlight, and the inflexible point bore down upon that sweet white round, in which all was loveliness, and where all of life;—the fair bosom, the pure heart, whence the sacred principles of purity and vitality had at once their abiding place." Although Harrison again saves Bess from her expected fate, she is nonetheless victimized. Simms stops the action at the moment of greatest danger, filling the interval between the knife's descent and the expected completion of its movement with an apostrophe to the helpless and beautiful maiden. Rhetorically, that is, Simms consummates that act of violation even as he prevents it. The Indian character is sacrificed to the author's purpose as well, intensifying the sensual appeal of the woman in the act of threatening it, the two character types—Eve and Satan—conjoined in a conventional tableau that only Adam can decompose.

It certainly can be argued that the prevalence of such scenes in frontier novels reflects the real and present danger of women's lives on the frontier, and it is clear that most pioneer women were afraid of Indians. Kolodny has argued that the captivity narrative served women as a vehicle by which they could displace and thus relieve various fears about life in the wilderness. In some of the later narratives, she maintains, captivity is little more than a "pretext for establishing . . . the central drama of the story: the woman's suffering in the wilderness." It is all the more remarkable then that the male narratives we have examined should repeatedly figure the danger to women in the wilderness in sexual terms. Moreover, even during the period of the early captivity narratives, the historical record does not support the emphasis we have seen in male novels on forced marriage, assault, and rape. J. Norman Heard, for example, concludes [in his *White into Red: A Study of the Assimilation of White Persons Captured by Indians*] that "forcible rape of white females by Indians east of the Mississippi was rare or non-existent, [although] women captured as adults in that region frequently became the wives of warriors." James Axtell draws a similar conclusion [in his "The White Indians of North America"] and offers three explanations for the Indians' lack of sexual interest in their female captives: aesthetic preference for darker-skinned women, strong incest taboos preventing sexual relations with women meant for adoption into their families, and a "religious ethic of strict warrior continence." Axtell points out, in fact, that captives were not forced into marriage because "any form of compulsion would have defeated the Indians' purpose in trying to persuade the captives to adopt their way of life." "Not only were younger captives and consenting adults under no compulsion, either actual or perceived, to marry, but they enjoyed as wide a latitude of choice as any Indian." Indeed, "so free from compulsion were the captives that several married fellow white prisoners."

Not only was Indian treatment of white women less violent than frontier novels would imply, but women's attitudes toward miscegenation were less hostile. This is not to say, of course, that women looked forward to captivity or that capture was any less terrifying, but frontier women do seem to have been more adaptable than male novelists would suggest. Marriages between captured white women and Indian males were not unusual on the actual frontier, nor were the refusals of such women to be redeemed from "captivity." As David Haberly notes, some of the most popular captivity narratives (e.g., those of Eunice Williams, Mary Jemison, Frances Slocum, and Cynthia Ann Parker) included such marriages ["Women and Indians: *The Last of the Mohicans* and the Captivity Tradition," *American Quarterly,* 28 (1976)]. One of the reasons was the intolerance of the society to which a captive might return. "In the case of the adult white woman," Brownmiller says, "to replace a relatively secure status as an Indian wife with a questionable future in white society as a 'defiled' woman could be reason enough to choose to remain with the Indians." Although her captivity occurred after the publication of the novels in question and in the West (Kansas, 1896), it seems reasonable to consider Anna Brewster Morgan's experience as representative. "An Indian chief proposed to me and I married him," she recalls, "thereby choosing the least of two evils and never expecting to see a white person again. . . . I began to think much of him for his kindness to me, and when they brought the news that there were two white men in the camp, I did not care to see them."

Even though recent scholarship contradicts the stereotype of the rapacious savage and the pale maiden who feels shamed by the very thought of the "horrid alternative," there is no reason that nineteenth-century frontier novels should conform to the historical record. That they do not, however, supports the view that such stereotypes are rooted in male fantasies. And it is not only the historical record that casts doubt upon the male-centered, doubly exploitive triangle I have cited. Even the literary record offers examples of willing marriages between white women and Indians. Besides *Hope Leslie* (1827) and *Hobomok*, there is Susannah Rowson's *Reuben and Rachel* and James Everett Seaver's *Narrative of the Life of Mrs. Mary Jemison* (1824). According to Kolodny, Jemison's *Life* "represented the first text in American literature to move a real-world white woman beyond the traditional captivity pattern to something approaching the *willing* wilderness accommodation of Daniel Boone." Jemison lived for over forty years among the Seneca Indians, was married twice, and had eight children. But as Kolodny also shows, the "revolutionary" aspects of the narrative occur largely in spite of its male amanuensis. Especially notable is the tension between Jemison's story and Seaver's desire to mold it in the captivity tradition. "But every now and then," Kolodny notes, "what seems authentically to have been Jemison's story breaks out of the molds to which Seaver and his backers would consign it, evading the narrative conventions of captivity and sentimental romance alike and becoming, instead, the story of a woman who, in the forested wilderness of upstate New York, knew how to 'take my children and look out for myself.' "

Jemison's narrative, *Hope Leslie,* and *Hobomok* were all published in the 1820s, before many of the novels that have since formed the Adamic tradition. In other words, literary, as well as historical, evidence existed that could have formed the basis of an alternative tradition that was more sympathetic to women and Indians—and to their intermarriage. This is not to say, however, that women viewed the frontier or Indians through rose-colored glasses. Novels by women do include acts and threats of violence and the ever-present danger of captivity.

In Ann Eliza Bleecker's *History of Maria Kittle* (1793), for example, Maria is kidnapped after a vicious Indian attack; her brother-in-law is killed, his corpse mangled and scalped. Even more graphically, the Indians split her sister-in-law's head open, deform her "lovely body with deep gashes," and tear her unborn baby away in order to dash it against a stone wall. But even though the woman is viciously assaulted, Bleecker's description exhibits none of the verbal indulgence we observed in a novel such as *The Yemassee*. The "rape" is simply an act of terrible violence, a grotesque violation of a woman's body and of her motherhood.

In *A Peep at the Pilgrims,* Harriet V. Cheney expresses special hostility toward the Pequod tribe, depicting and justifying their extermination by the English settlers in 1637. No less a historical personage than Miles Standish assures the hero, Edward Atherton, that the " 'savages are so perfidious, that no treaty can bind them; and so jealous of us, as to aim continually at our total ruin.' " Later, when the heroine, Miriam Grey, is captured by the Pequods in Weathersfield, Connecticut, Atherton is distraught because he has heard of the Pequods' penchant for cold-blooded murder and even cannibalism. Interestingly, Cheney never even alludes to fears of rape or forced marriage. In fact, even though Pequod barbarity reaches epic proportions (at least in rumor), Miriam's captivity involves no cruelty at all. She is temporarily adopted by Chief Mononotto and cared for very kindly by his wife, Mioma, before being traded to the Dutch for several Pequod warriors.

Similarly, in *Saratoga* Mrs. Eliza Cushing is not unaware of Indian atrocities, nor does she allow her heroine to be. When

Catherine Courtland first encounters Ohmeina, an "instinctive horror froze [her] blood" because she has heard of the "barbarous excesses" which savages have committed. Catherine's fear in fact is caused by her knowledge of the recent murder of Jane McCrea, who was "bound, by two ferocious savages, to a tree, and cruelly scalped and murdered. Without a hand to aid, or a voice to soothe her, she fell victim to the wanton fury of monsters, only human in outward form." *Saratoga,* however, is designed to revise such views of the Indian by demonstrating—admittedly, with considerable condescension—his potential for civilization. Ohmeina, Catherine assures her cousin, "is not a savage. He is humanized by the influence of that same religion, which we have been taught to reverence, and I would rather trust myself with him, than with many a boasting hero, who has less cause for triumph, and fewer virtues to ennoble him, than fall to the lot of this poor Indian." Cushing's comparison of white and Indian males, to the advantage of the latter, suggests a sympathetic attitude toward Indians that other female novelists shared. In both *Hope Leslie* and *Hobomok* marriage to an Indian is an acceptable alternative to a conventional marriage in a white patriarchal society.

In depicting such a marriage, however, Sedgwick and Child were anticipated by almost thirty years by Susannah Rowson, most famous as the author of *Charlotte* (1791). In a brief but pivotal episode in *Reuben and Rachel,* Rowson describes William and Rachel Dudley's nineteen years with an Indian tribe in New Hampshire between 1661 and 1680. Rowson's view of captivity is benign indeed. Adopted by Otooganoo and his wife, William becomes the chief's tutor, teaching him (and Rachel) to speak English. After marrying Otooganoo's daughter, Oberea (who bears him a son), William even succeeds his adoptive father as chief. Rachel, moreover, falls in love with the warrior Yankoo. When he dies in a raid against the English settlements before marriage can occur, Rachel returns with her mother to England. Although she attracts many suitors, she remains true to Yankoo's memory. " 'I may . . . find men more accomplished, who will talk with more eloquence, are more polished in their manners,' " she explains; " 'but where shall I find the equal to Yankoo for sincerity?' " Rowson, in short, treats Rachel Dudley's betrothal to Yankoo with marked sympathy and respect—as the result of genuine love rather than of environmental conditioning or coercion—and thus offers a prototype that both Sedgwick and Child would develop in the 1820s.

Published just a year after *The Last of the Mohicans,* Catharine Sedgwick's *Hope Leslie* contradicts several assumptions of works in the Adamic tradition. Sedgwick's revisionist purpose is most evident in her comparison of Indian culture and a Puritan community near Springfield, Massachusetts, and in the contrasting careers of the two sisters, Faith and Hope Leslie. During an Indian attack in which her foster mother and stepsisters are killed, Faith is taken captive. During her seven years' captivity, she marries an Indian (Oneco), and adapts so well to Indian life that she cannot even imagine a return to civilization. Hope Leslie, though in love with Everell Fletcher, is pursued and nearly abducted by the Lovelacian villain, Sir Philip Gardiner, before her expected marriage to Fletcher. By doubling her heroine, Sedgwick offers her readers an interesting dichotomy. Hope Leslie has far more to fear from the white, civilized male than her sister has to fear from her Indian abductor (whom she has known since childhood). If Hope's experience is any indication, in fact,

Faith's captivity and marriage to Oneco is a rescue, a liberation from the designs of a patriarchal society.

Although Sedgwick never suggests that English civilization is inferior to a life in the forest, she does criticize the Puritans' intolerance and injustice and, while not justifying Indian atrocities, sympathizes with the Pequods' motivation. The attack on the Fletcher home, for example, avenges the Puritans' destruction of their village and enables the chief to rescue the son and daughter whom the English had taken prisoner. Sedgwick is especially severe in depicting the status of women and their relationship to male authority embodied in the church, society and family. To Governor Winthrop's view, for instance, Hope Leslie lacks "that passiveness that, next to godliness, is a woman's best virtue." To correct her wildness, he says, she wants only the "authority of a husband." Such authority confers inordinate privilege, illustrated by the familiar theme of seduction, a kidnap plot, and the threat of forced marriage.

These issues culminate in volume two of the novel when the Leslie sisters are temporarily reunited. After seven years, Faith does not even speak English and refuses Hope's pleas to return home. When their reunion is interrupted by the Governor's militia, Faith is recaptured (along with an Indian girl, Magawisca), while Hope is taken prisoner by Oneco and the Chief, Mannonotto (the same benevolent chief Cheney depicts in *A Peep at the Pilgrims*). The scene represents the closest Sedgwick comes to employing the threat of an Indian assault. As the one who arranged the reunion, Hope expects to be blamed by the Indians for the ambush and its consequences: "all that she had heard or imagined of Indian cruelties was present to her imagination; and every savage passion seemed to her to be embodied in the figure of the old chief." Sedgwick, however, immediately shows Hope's fears of *Indian* assault to be groundless, for her imprisonment is shortlived. But no sooner is she free than she encounters a group of drunken British sailors, one of whom advances toward her "with a horrid leer on his face." Rather than project the threat of assault upon an Indian character, Sedgwick attributes it to the British—to the genteel rake, Gardiner, or to his lower-class counterparts, the sailors. Gardiner, moreover, poses the greatest danger to the Indians as well, at one point trying to enflame a crowd against Magawisca by accusing her of Devil worship.

Despite obvious flaws in plotting and excessive reliance on the conventions of sentimental fiction, *Hope Leslie* represents an interesting alternative to more famous frontier novels, particularly in its comparison of women's treatment in Pequod and Puritan societies. The novel suggests very clearly that the threat of assault or forced marriage inheres in cultural attitudes of possession and authority—in a view of women as objects. If the experiences of Hope and Faith Leslie are credible examples, Sedgwick seems to have realized that the most serious threat to frontier women did not necessarily proceed from Indians.

Like *Hope Leslie,* Lydia Maria Child's earlier *Hobomok* features a marriage between a white woman (Mary Conant) and an Indian male. Whereas Sedgwick represents marital choices for the frontier woman by using two female characters, Child uses a single character who marries twice. But like Sedgwick, Child sets her novel in a Puritan New England (Naumkeak, or Salem) characterized by the authority of fathers and ministers. On the day when the organization of the church is being celebrated, Mr. Higginson confirms in his sermon that all individual freedom must be suppressed. " 'Liberty of conscience,' " he warns, " ' is the gilded bait whereby Satan has caught many souls. The threshold of hell is paved with toleration.' " In a letter to her grandfather, Mary herself notes that in New England the "heartes of men are as harde and sterile as their unploughed soil," and Mary's friend Sally Oldham forthrightly observes that Mary's own father is " 'overfond of keeping folks in a straight jacket.' "

By contrast, both the Indian and the wilderness are characterized by tolerance and freedom. Early in *Hobomok* Child includes a remarkable scene in which Mary Conant steals into the forest at night to perform a ceremony which she hopes will reveal her husband-to-be. Cutting her arm with a knife, she writes in blood upon a piece of white cloth, marks a "magic circle" upon the ground with a stick, and then attempts to conjure her future husband (the Episcopalian Charles Brown) into joining her. But just before Brown can do so, Hobomok leaps into the circle. The scene has many characteristics of a dream, an escape from oppressive social order into an imaginative wilderness where repressed desires can be liberated.

As such, the scene should be compared to the rattlesnake scene in *The Yemassee*. Both scenes reveal the authors' ideas about women's fantasies, and both depict at least a momentary triangle involving white women and white and Indian males. But the implications of the scenes and particularly the nature of the women's desires are very different. Simms subjects a passive Bess Matthews to the prolonged threat of assault and then identifies the threat with an Indian. Conversely, Child puts Mary Conant in charge of her dream and implies that her desires originate in a context of repression and, most important, include no trace of violence. Indeed, Hobomok worships Mary, is interested only in seeing her to safety, and is never mistaken for an assailant. He is "cast in nature's noblest mould," warns the English settlement of impending attack, and often supplies game and furs to his English friends.

When Charles Brown is banished for his heretical beliefs, Mary intends to remain unmarried and to await his return. When he is reported drowned, however, she is grief-stricken, suffers what Child calls a "partial derangement," and abruptly agrees to marry Hobomok. She is motivated by a "sense of sudden bereavement, deep and bitter reproaches against her father, and blind belief in fatality [i.e., that the earlier conjuration has fated her to marry Hobomok]." The motives Child attributes to Mary offer interesting examples of unacknowledged desires competing with social sanctions. Torn by grief at the deaths of a lover whom her father has helped banish and of the mother to whom she might turn for solace, Mary reacts violently against her father's authority and offers herself to a suitor even less acceptable. More positively, in a society which offers little in the way of prospective husbands, Mary simply wants to be loved, and "in the desolation of the moment, she felt as if [Hobomok] was the only being in the wide world who was left to love her." Although Child casts some doubt upon Mary's motives and sanity, the marriage is unquestionably successful. Gradually, Mary's affection for Hobomok increases, and she gives birth to a son. In a statement that anticipates Anna Brewster Morgan's experience and demonstrates women's adaptability, Mary admits to Sally Oldham, " 'I speak truly when I say that every day I live with that kind, noble-hearted creature, the better I love him.' "

For reasons that remain unclear, however, Child does not allow the marriage to last. When Charles Brown reappears (he did not drown after all), Hobomok abruptly bows out of the novel, heading "far off among some of the red men in the west." Not even pausing to say good-bye, his only gesture is a last look at Mary and young Hobomok. Despite its rather weak motivation, Hobomok's leaving makes sense in the fantasy Child has created. His departure and replacement by Charles Brown enable Mary to fulfill two dreams: marriage to a socially tabooed male who loves her and who "gives" her a son (named by tribal custom Charles Hobomok Conant) in whom he barely claims a patronymic stake, and then a second marriage to a now socially approved husband. To complete the substitution, Brown adopts Hobomok's son, who receives half of Mary's legacy from her grandfather, matriculates at Harvard, and then finishes his education in England. "His father was seldom spoken of; and by degrees his Indian appellation was silently omitted." All that remains of Hobomok is a letter announcing his "divorce" from Mary. . . . (pp. 668-83)

Hobomok, then, does depend upon a female fantasy, but that fantasy is not so much sexual as emotional and social, and omits the threatened violence of forced marriage we observed in the novels by men. Neither Child nor Sedgwick considers "savagism" preferable to civilization, but each clearly rebels against the arbitrary authority of Puritan society, particularly as that authority is exercised by fathers in determining their daughters' fates in marriage. The Indian male, reverential and loving rather than possessive and authoritarian, offers a romantic contrast. In that respect, both *Hope Leslie* and *Hobomok* mark at least a potential beginning of an alternative—feminist—tradition within the frontier genre, in which miscegenation is hardly a "horrid alternative."

As Kolodny has argued, reading frontier narratives by women should at least qualify critical emphasis on the Adamic tradition and its fantastical image of the solitary man in nature. In addition to revising our view of the landscape as subject to "mastery and possession," women's narratives modify the conventional triangle involving women and white and Indian males, in which miscegenation figures as a nightmarish "evil worse that death." Instead of facing threats of Indian assault, forced marriage, or rape, women depict themselves as being offered a choice between white and Indian males and societies. And far from being "horrid," marriages to Indians are shown in some fictions to offer women a preferable alternative to the traditional status of a wife in a patriarchal and authoritarian society. In general, women's narratives lend literary support to James Axtell's view that many captives "found Indian life to possess a strong sense of community, abundant love, and uncommon integrity—values that the English colonists also honored, if less successfully."

Although I haven't the space to do so in detail, I should like to suggest a reason for the different attitudes toward miscegenation in male- and female-authored novels. Attempting to explain the "universal fact of female devaluation," anthropologist Sherry B. Ortner argues that all cultures identify women with nature and men with culture itself: "Since it is always culture's project to subsume and transcend nature, if women were considered part of nature, then culture would find it 'natural' to subordinate, not to say oppress, them." On the surface, of course, frontier fiction seems to contradict Ortner's thesis, since women are so often identified not with nature but with the culture men are trying to escape. Ortner's more general principle of female devaluation offers an answer. Universally, she says, women are identified with "something that every culture devalues, something that every culture defines as being of a lower order of existence than itself." Most commonly, that "something" is nature, but if, as in frontier literature by men, nature is more highly valued than culture, then women become likely symbols of the latter.

As Kolodny has shown in *The Lay of the Land,* moreover, male novelists typically pre-empt any rightful place for women in their exclusive "nature-culture" by personifying the landscape itself as feminine. Making women symbols of the false culture they are escaping, men doubly purge "real" women from their new Edens, denying them significant relationships with the frontier hero—and with nature. Although Ortner points out that, universally, women have "reached culture's conclusions" and accepted their own devaluation, the frontier fiction by women we have examined suggests that some writers rebelled against their culture's conclusions. Recognizing the Puritans' suitability as symbols of patriarchal authority, recognizing women's common exclusion from men's nature-culture, Child and Sedgwick turned the tables on male-dominated culture and found their own place in nature; they "married" nature in the form of an Indian male.

Male characters often did that, too, though more commonly in the mountain man novels of the twentieth century than in the frontier fiction of the nineteenth (e.g., Vardis Fisher's *Mountain Man* [1948] and A. B. Guthrie's *The Big Sky* [1962]). But more typical is the response of Natty Bumppo in *The Deerslayer,* who twice refuses the chance to take his place in Indian society by marrying the widow of a warrior he has killed. Natty refuses Judith Hutter's offer of marriage as well, sending her off to the settlements and to "culture," while he and Chingachgook (and the latter's bride) remain in "nature." Natty's "sweetheart," he tells Judith, is "in the forest"—leaving her to wonder, "where is the man to turn this beautiful place into . . . a Garden of Eden for [her]." If she (or Cooper) had read *Reuben and Rachel, Hobomok,* or *Hope Leslie,* Judith might have found an answer to her question. In exploring possibilities of marriage rather than antagonism between races, in relying on fantasies of love rather than assault, Rowson, Sedgwick, and Child suggest an alternative to the Adamic myth Natty embodies—an incipient myth of an American Eve, in which, like Natty's, women's "sweethearts" are also "in the forest." (pp. 683-85)

> Leland S. Person, "The American Eve: Miscegenation and a Feminist Frontier Fiction," in American Quarterly, Vol. 37, No. 5, Winter, 1985, pp. 668-85.

SUSAN H. ARMITAGE

[*An American critic and historian who specializes in women's literature, Armitage is particularly interested in oral histories and in women's experiences in the American West. In the following excerpt, she emphasizes the contribution of writings by women to a fuller understanding of the frontier, especially the relations between white settlers and native Americans.*]

The frontier myth is the great American myth, the story of how we made this land "our land." The stages of the process are familiar to us all: the encounter with wilderness, the risk, challenge and commitment, the final slow surrender of freedom to advancing civilization. In the west, even today, our frontier heritage is always present, as near as the stark and beautiful landscape which surrounds us.

The frontier myth *is* evocative, but it contains some deeply disturbing elements. The frontier myth is a male myth, preoccupied with stereotypically male issues like courage, physical bravery, honor, and male friendship. While these are important themes, they by no means encompass the reality and complexity of the frontier experience.

The frontier, Frederick Jackson Turner said, was the boundary between savagery and civilization. In the frontier myth, these two extremes are represented by the Indian, symbol of savagery, and the white woman, symbol of civilization. Usually, however, they remain secondary characters, for the white male hero occupies the space between them. As Leslie Fiedler formulates it [in his *The Return of the Vanishing American*], the white male himself becomes the boundary between the Indian-occupied "Wilderness" on the one side, and the woman-occupied "Clearing" on the other. The conflict between savagery and civilization is played out in the persona of the white male hero. Because of this persistent focus on the white male, Indians and women rarely achieve full, authentic stature in frontier literature.

Nor is this all. At its deepest level, the frontier myth is concerned with violence and conquest—over the land, over the native inhabitants of that land, over fear of the unknown—and finally, over the temptation to succumb to wilderness and revert to savagery. To justify this violence, the historical reality of Indians and women has been distorted.

According to the frontier myth, the confrontation between savagery—Indians—and civilization—white women—was violent and terrible. Captivity narratives, a major form of popular literature dating from Puritan times, told and retold the gruesome story. The Indians attacked fiercely and without cause, pillaging, burning and killing. The survivors, helpless women and children, were taken off into captivity. Few captives escaped or were rescued—many died, were lost, or, interestingly enough, became so assimilated to Indian culture that they didn't want to return.

The captivity narrative was originally preoccupied with the religious question of God's grace for those who escaped the wilderness. In addition, the early narratives often expressed interest in, and attraction to, Indian culture. As early as 1800, authentic captivity narratives had been replaced by immensely popular, melodramatic literature, full of hatred of Indians. These accounts, often totally fabricated, told of savage, irrational Indian violence against ever more helpless white women. As the frontier expanded, this projection of the urge to violence onto the Indian provided a splendid rationale for white retaliation. Protection of white women, the symbols of civilization, and the extermination or removal of Indians went hand-in-hand.

The frontier myth, then, quite deliberately dramatized the stark dichotomy between savage Indians and civilized white women. But in so doing, the myth seriously misrepresented the frontier reality.

What was the reality? To answer that question, let us go directly to women's sources—to the diaries, letters, memoirs and novels women wrote about their experience on the trans-Mississippi frontier. These sources tell us of a very different confrontation between Indians and women.

The woman and her children are alone and "unprotected"—because the white man is elsewhere—when the Indians arrive. The result is not a massacre. The Indians want food, not scalps. The woman, while afraid of the Indians, is even more afraid to refuse their demands. She cooks the requested item, or regretfully offers up a scarce store-bought food. The Indians leave peacefully. When the white man returns home, he praises the woman for her courage and commonsense.

This same scene appears again and again in women's writings. Clearly, this anxious domestic encounter was much more common than the notorious, popularized stories of massacre and captivity. Why, then, has the reality been so ignored?

To answer that question, let us return to our female sources and look at the domestic encounter in more detail. First, women were alone, and thrown upon their own resources. Mollie Dorsey Sanford's first encounter with Indians came on the wagon train from Nebraska to Colorado. She was alone, driving the family wagon, happily enjoying a respite from incompatible fellow-travellers, when a band of passing Indians saw her. They threatened her, apparently playfully—they gestured at cutting off her braids, and she feared scalping. Then they demanded food. Her fear was palpable: she let them have all of her precious, irreplaceable sugar, and drew from the episode the lesson that she could never again seek personal independence from the wagon train [*Mollie: The Diary of Mollie Dorsey Sanford*].

Other, more settled and experienced women responded differently to Indian demands. Amelia Buss, settled in Fort Collins, Colorado, in 1866, was frightened but exasperated, and peremptorily told the local Indians that she had no more food to spare [Western History Archives, Boulder, Colorado]. Flora Hunter of Nebraska, aware that an entire tribe was camped around her cabin, at first fearfully gave two Indian braves six loaves of newly-baked bread, and then lost her temper at her wasted work, and shooed them out of her kitchen [Berna Hunter Chrisman, *When You and I Were Young, Nebraska!*]. Other women resorted to cunning and doctored the food, adding something so unpleasant that the Indians never came back for more.

Initially, of course, most women were afraid for their lives, for they all knew massacre and captivity stories. Significantly, in the female sources I have consulted, there is not a hint of sexuality. There are no fears of rape—although there are of scalping—and there is not the slightest suggestion of sexual interest in the "noble red man." The common female response to male Indians was one of repugnance, not of attraction. To most women, Indians remained frighteningly alien—dirty and smelly, incomprehensible and annoyingly inquisitive.

Some few women moved beyond fear to observation and even sympathy. Flora Hunter was interested and amazed to see that her six loaves of bread were divided and shared among the entire tribe, from the smallest baby to the most elderly [*When You and I Were Young, Nebraska!*]. Nannie Alderson of Montana, who lived in close proximity to the once-fearsome Northern Cheyenne, became very friendly with several members of the tribe, and pitied the once self-reliant people who were now reduced to begging for food.

Nannie's sympathetic presence was elsewhere on the unfortunate day when a hired hand decided to brag about his marksmanship by shooting off the hat of the tribal chieftain. For this insult, the Indians promptly turned against their erstwhile friends and burned the cabin to the ground [Nannie T.

Alderson and Helena Huntington Smith, *A Bride Goes West*].

Women reacted to Indians with fear and anxiety, for very female reasons. Their fears were not sexual, but stemmed instead from new strains on their traditional female role. The Indians walked right into the kitchen. On the frontier, not even the domestic sphere, woman's special space, was private. Women were indeed very vulnerable. Although they usually had guns, they could not use them because they were alone and outnumbered. Finally, Indian demands for food could jeopardize the entire family.

The complaint of Caddie Woodlawn's mother now seems merely amusing: "Johnny, my dear . . . those frightful savages will eat us out of house and home" [Carol Ryrie Brink, *Caddie Woodlawn*]. The Woodlawns lived on a settled frontier (Wisconsin) and did indeed have food to spare. However, an inconvenience on a settled frontier was a major deprivation on a new frontier. Laura Ingalls Wilder recalled that, when her family lived on the Kansas-Oklahoma border, visiting Indians took all of the family's cornmeal and tobacco, which could not be replenished without a four-day round-trip journey to the nearest store. Nevertheless, when informed of the Indian visit, Mr. Ingalls reassured his wife, "You did the right thing . . . We don't want to make enemies of any Indians" [*Little House on the Prairie*].

Here is one major source for the anxious female response to Indians. The pioneer woman's major role was that of domestic provider and sustainer. She was responsible for feeding and clothing her children and her husband. For her, the Indian demands posed a frightful choice: between the needs of her immediate family and the wider social demand for peace with the Indians. She had to silence her domestic instincts and training and give away scarce, often irreplaceable food supplies. She had to adapt her role to the new reality.

It is a fact, of course, that Indians did occasionally kill and capture, and white men and women were always afraid of that possibility. The frontier myth dealt with this fear by emphasizing the white response, glorifying the violent, individual conflict with wilderness. While the frontier myth had great psychological appeal, it was not a guide for action, for the reality was much more complex and ambiguous than the myth admitted. Let us summarize the ways in which the female version complements the myth with the authenticity of real experience.

First, actual contact demonstrated that not all Indians were brutal, irrational savages. Certainly they were frightening and unpredictable. But they could also be pitiful: they begged for food. It was impossible to regard all Indians as vicious, implacable, inevitable enemies.

But this potential understanding was largely vitiated for women because the nature of the cultural contact provoked such great anxiety. Indian demands for food underlined the precariousness of white frontier existence. White families were not yet self-sufficient in food, nor close enough to other settlers to form new interdependent communities. The Indian demand for food was thus a constant reminder to whites that their frontier experiment might fail.

Furthermore, the domestic encounter demonstrated that violence was seldom an appropriate response to Indian demands. The adaptive, accommodating responses of women had the full support of their husbands. Realistically, frontier homesteaders were too isolated and outnumbered to risk violence against the Indians, as the Alderstons learned to their regret. The Indian presence was often irritating. Nevertheless, the individual violence celebrated by the frontier myth was inappropriate to the circumstances. The only possible answer was adaptation. Although women might be frightened, white men could not always be present to protect them from the Indians. Women had to learn how to cope on their own, and men had to learn to support them.

Frederick Jackson Turner understood that his famous "frontier as process" was in fact two processes, not only the famous recreation of civilization (i.e. the defeat of "savagery") but an earlier, more informal process of adaptation to a new reality. This process of adaptation, which was not heroic, and not violent, included the anxious response to Indians which I have described. In most frontier areas, the early uncertain period of settlement was quite short. Crops grew, new settlers moved in, the Indians were killed or confined to reservations by soldiers. But the memoirs of the early days remained, and are rediscovered today in women's literature.

The frontier myth glorifies the deepest, most violent emotions aroused by the encounter with the new land and the unknown—that is why it is myth. Myths begin with reality, although they eventually transcend that reality. As I have shown, the frontier myth does not accurately reflect the reality for women and Indians, and therefore misrepresents the experience of the families who settled on the boundary between savagery and civilization, the frontier.

The foregoing brief analysis of the domestic encounter is just one small example of the ways in which women's literature can begin to complement our understanding of the frontier myth. Women's literature will illuminate the private, domestic, interior side of the frontier experience which the myth has ignored. Women's literature will have much to tell us about other non-heroic aspects of the encounter with wilderness: responses to isolation, to hardship and failure, and more positively, about informal, cooperative efforts at community building. (pp. 5-10)

> *Susan H. Armitage, "Women's Literature and the American Frontier: A New Perspective on the Frontier Myth," in* Women, Women Writers, and the West, *edited by L. L. Lee and Merrill Lewis, The Whitston Publishing Company, 1979, pp. 5-13.*

ANNETTE KOLODNY

[*A leading theorist of feminist criticism, Kolodny is the author of the influential essay "Dancing through the Minefield: Some Observations on the Theory, Practice, and Politics of a Feminist Literary Criticism." In the following excerpt from her* The Land before Her: Fantasy and Experience of the American Frontiers, 1630-1860, *the second volume of a projected trilogy on the mythology of the frontier, she examines the positive portrayal of the frontier in domestic fiction written by women in the mid nineteenth century.*]

"The story of feminine trials and triumphs," which Nina Baym observes [in her *Woman's Fiction: A Guide to Novels by and about Women in America, 1820-1870*] "dominated woman's writing in the 1850s," must . . . be seen as a literary response born of the anxiety attendant upon rapidly changing role expectations and accelerating technological transitions. In the face of increasingly restricted employment opportunities for middle-class women, "slave wages" for working-class

women, quickened industrialization, spreading urbanization, and still carrying with it the memory of the economic upheavals following the Panic of 1837, the domestic fiction of mid-century America sought solace and security in the image of the home "as a moral repository in an immoral society . . . [and] a bastion of stability in a changing, fragmentary world."

The very factors that produced such a fiction also conspired to make the frontier west an attractive setting for its fantasy. To begin with, current wisdom pictured the west—and especially the frontier—as largely agricultural. For most Americans, this implied not only the absence of mills and factories but the absence of those glaring disparities in wealth that had begun to mark the northeast; for novelists like E. D. E. N. Southworth and Mary Hayden Pike, moreover, the small farms of the frontier promised a society untouched by the blot of slavery. In an age that looked with suspicion on the phenomenal fortunes apparently made overnight by factory and mill owners, the west suggested an escape from superfluity, an escape from wealth gained only by investment, and an escape from the exploited labor of the poor. In an era when fewer than 2 percent of the rich were not born rich, the raw frontier could still be fantasized as a realm that might nurture that quintessential American hero, the self-made man.

Above all else, however, the frontier west gave these novelists the chance to displace the gilded mansions and sordid tenements of New York, the dormitory dwellings of the New England mills, and the columned plantation houses of the south with the "very comfortable and pleasant . . . log cabin home." No novel missed the chance to extol its virtues or ignored the opportunity to picture the happy family gathered cozily "about the hearthstone." "Yes, very comfortable and pleasant was that log cabin home," these novels all averred, "and seldom in the splendid parlors of our Atlantic cities does a happier [family] gather about the hearthstone, than that which, after the supper was over, drew around that ample fire-place." In this scene from Caroline Soule's *The Pet of the Settlement* (1860), the daughter of the house is pictured "knitting" clothes that are essential—not merely ornamental—for the family, while her father tends both the fire and a baby, "trotting [the child] on his foot 'to Banbury Cross.'"

It is an image of relaxed domesticity. But it is an image with a point. The domesticity that these novelists pictured in the new west was a domesticity in which women and men alike played important (if different) roles. The father who once spent all his evenings away from home in the counting houses of the city now delights in entertaining children by the hearthside and in taking his family for picnics on the flowering prairies. At the same time, the women in these cabins are given real, but never arduous, work to perform. Theirs is a role that keeps them happily and usefully "busy from early dawn to twilight."

Significantly, the "three departments" that Catherine Beecher had entrusted to women ["the training of the mind in childhood, the nursing of infants and of the sick, and all the handicrafts and management of the family state"] are only played out in these novels once the family removes to the west. While the family remains in the east, by contrast, we rarely see the women characters work (unless they are poor), and more often than not, we see them wasting their time in frivolous social pursuits. To the functioning of the log cabin home, however, the woman is essential—as essential as the "ample fire-place" where she does her cooking or boils water for washing, and around which (like herself) the family gathers. Thus, in an age when many middle-class women experienced themselves increasingly displaced from any real responsibility in running a household, the domestic novel of western relocation claimed contemporaneity through the frontier setting, but all the while harked back to patterns symbolic of earlier times—patterns that reestablished women's meaningful centrality in the domestic scene.

No less important, the supposedly unformed frontier settlements offered these novelists a chance to project their idealized notions of community itself. It was, needless to say, a community informed by the domestic ethos in which the values of home and hearth, rather than the market economy, organized the larger social structure. When a small child is found abandoned on the Iowa prairie in Caroline Soule's *The Pet of the Settlement,* for instance, it is not a single household but the settlement as a whole that adopts her, with all the "men, women and children" crying out, " 'I'll do my part, I'll do my part'." Older widows and single men in these novels are similarly adopted by neighboring families who offer them not only a room of their own but the affectionate appellation of "grandmother" or "uncle." Exploiting the familial metaphors inherent in women's promotional writings, novelists like Caroline Soule thus sought to portray communities in which the inhabitants gave palpable meaning to [Eliza W.] Farnham's description of westerners acting together as "the sons and daughters of this land"; and the characters in these novels repeatedly bear out [Mary Austin] Holley's description of pioneer Texans as "universally kind and hospitable."

The urgent need for such fantasies, of course, explains these writers' penchant for ignoring what Caroline Kirkland had earlier tried to teach [in writings based on her experiences on the Michigan frontier], or what the daily newspapers everywhere declared about the west. Land speculators, absentee landlords, or moneylenders charging anywhere from 30 to 60 percent annual interest do not appear in the westernized domestic fictions. Their representations of the west are never informed by the fact that, as early as 1836, President Andrew Jackson was expressing his alarm at the growing "monopoly of the public lands in the hands of speculators and capitalists, to the injury of the actual settlers in the new States, and of emigrants in search of new homes." Nor did they hint that Jackson's alarm had been well grounded: of the 38,000,000 acres of public lands sold between 1835 and 1837, 29,000,000—that is, almost three-quarters of the whole—were acquired by speculators. Absentee landlords and exploited tenants became the rule, rather than the exception, in places like the prairie counties of central Illinois. And by 1846 an Indiana farmer observed that one-third of the voters in his state were "tenants or day laborers or young men who have acquired no property." In the novels of the domestic fantasists, by contrast, the families relocated westward are universally prosperous, and most characters reap "golden harvests."

Refusing also to acknowledge the stark reality of a crude first cabin, constructed of "logs and nothing else, the fire made on the ground, or on a few loose stones, and a hole in the roof for the escape of the smoke," these writers instead adhered to the further fantasy of the "very comfortable and pleasant . . . log cabin home." Lydia Hunt Sigourney captured its essence in her enormously popular, "The Western Home" (a poem which first saw magazine publication at the beginning of the decade and then titled a collection of her

poems in 1854). Here, Kirkland's reports of tight quarters and rough puncheon floors are superseded by the prettier picture of a "new home in greenwood fair":

> [The] humble roof was firmly laid,
> Of jointed logs the building made,
> Yet more of space, and comfort too,
> Was there than met the careless view;
> For well these walls the storm could quell,
> And tyrant cold or heat repel.

Discounting Kirkland's descriptions of the sheer drudgery of first settlement, these novelists joined with Sigourney to picture the frontier housewife working "with harmonizing will," finding only "pleasure in her duties." Discounting Kirkland's anger at the dishonest practices of western bankers and land speculators, the novelists asserted, along with Sigourney, that the western home implied "an Eden refuge, sweet and blest." And, like her, they asked their readers to believe that the western "home's secluded bound" offered a sure haven from the exploitations of a capitalist economy and the uncertainties of the marketplace. Caroline Soule, for example, portrayed moneylending as a local affair based wholly on benevolence. In *The Pet of the Settlement,* her displaced easterner, Mr. Belden, recoups the fortune earlier lost in the counting-houses of New York by virtue of "patient, honest industry, and not by skin-flint usury," she insists. In turn, as Soule depicts him, Belden helps others to prosper in Iowa. " 'If ye ever happen to get hard up for cash and need a loan to lift ye,' " one of the older pioneers boasts to a prospective newcomer to the settlement, " 'there's Belden'll help you along, and won't ask you forty per-cent either, and if he sees ye'r industrious and steady-like, he'll wait till the heavens open before he'll foreclose any mortgage he may have agen ye.' "

If Soule's portrait of the honorable Belden bore little resemblance to the actuality of eastern-financed moneylending on the western frontier, it nonetheless testified to the underlying motives of her story. In *A New Home,* Kirkland may have aimed at "a veracious history of actual occurrences." The women who followed her lead to western materials, however, wanted only to escape the circumstances that gave rise to what Margaret Fuller had described as "those painful separations, which already desecrate and desolate the Atlantic coast." The domestic fictionists, in short, wanted to believe— as Fuller had wanted to believe—that on the uncrowded and fertile tracts of the western prairies "whole families might live together" in a kind of extended domestic Eden, the sons returning "from their pilgrimages to settle near the parent hearth" and the daughters finding "room near their mother." As a result, though their novels never shied away from depicting the squalor of the urban poor or the mind- and body-numbing labor of an impoverished New England farm, only rarely did these women even approach Kirkland's description of "the tenant of a log-cabin whose family, whatever be its numbers, must burrow in a single room, while a bed or two, a chest, a table, and a wretched handful of cooking utensils, form the chief materials of comfort."

Precisely because these writers were committed to a fantasy and not to any specific geography or agrarian economic organization, moreover, their novels exhibit a peculiar tension that goes beyond the purposeful masking of historical reality. The reversion to familial configurations from an earlier period, made possible by the isolated border setting, stands side by side in their texts with assertions of development and centrality. For, without ever owning up to the contradiction, the domestic fictionists who turned to western materials generally applaud the change "from a straggling, border village into a populous and central town." The point must therefore be made that just because writers like Maria Susanna Cummins and Caroline Soule chose to regenerate their broken and ruined city families in the agricultural west did not mean that they were inveterately opposed to cities, manufacturing, or even to class distinctions. It was only the squalor and corrupting influences of the city, the meaner exploitations of poor laborers by factories, and the vicious disparities of class to which these writers objected. They wanted to evade certain consequences attendant upon an accelerated industrialized urbanization because they saw those consequences ravaging families and destroying the domestic ideals to which they held; but industry and urbanization themselves they did not reject. (Only Mary Hayden Pike and E. D. E. N. Southworth actually rejected on ideological and philosophical grounds the plantation society premised on slavery.)

Needless to say, to preserve the fantasy, the domestic fictionists took great pains to distinguish their fictional western towns from the "crowded, cramped and choked" environments of the older settlements. *This* town, they assure readers, is "spacious, broad and airy." Caroline Soule declares that the fifteen-year period of development she catalogues in *The Pet of the Settlement* represents "only a bright, beautiful change." But her language subtly suggests otherwise:

> Years have come and gone . . . changing [the little Settlement] from a straggling, border village into a populous and central town; not crowded, cramped and choked though, but spacious, broad and airy. The arching trees that line each avenue, giving it a picture-look, with their cool and waving shadows, while the ample parks, with their green and tasteful hedges, their closely shaven lawns, their clustering shrubs, their gorgeous flowers, their sparkling fountains, singing birds, tame forest pets, and chattering, dancing little children, are a sweet relief to the dim [sic: din] and bustle of its thoroughfares, and give to its busiest denizen a taste of that dear country life for which his heart is panting.

Now so disassociated is the town from its frontier origins that, within its precincts, the busy "denizen" *pants* for even a "taste of that dear country life" that had gone before. To a genre originally conceived in nostalgia, that sentiment is here again introduced—though, again, it is never named as such.

The reason such contradictions go unacknowledged is that most of these novelists did not so much want to abandon the east as to offer an idealized alternative by which it might be regenerated. The west merely provided an appropriate stage set for elaborating the ideal. Thus, though many a heroine is said to be "held . . . spell-bound" by "the sudden glory of the extended landscape," none of these writers invoked either irony or regret when they pictured "hundreds of glorious old forest trees falling only to rise again, not as the green and leafy bowers of singing birds, but . . . as the spacious marts of trade, [or] the dusty, noisy workshop."

The point, after all, was not to suggest that the informing values of hearth and home could only take hold in the relatively unsophisticated settlements at the edges of society. The reformist impulse of this fiction needed to demonstrate that such values could flourish even in the face of accelerating development and thus serve as a model by which the nation as a whole might be transformed. Displacing the uglier realities of the older regions, the idealized fictional west was to become central to a new national self-image. And to that end, even the new technology might be useful. As one of the Iowa pioneers in Soule's *The Pet of the Settlement* confidently predicts, in the near future " 'there'll come puffin' and blowin' and snortin' along, that . . . iron horse . . . and then ye see, why we shan't be out west a bit, but jist in the very centre of creation, with all the world a-coming in to see how we git along'."

Though the bulk of its story line is usually played out on some prairie frontier, the domestic novel of western relocation was nonetheless a response to eastern—and not western—concerns. And although the fantasy demands of the genre produced an idealized west onto which women readers might project otherwise threatened visions of home and hearth, writers like Cummins, Southworth, and Soule did not conceive themselves as promotionalists for westward migration. Even so, constrained by the need to make their western idylls persuasive as well as attractive, the domestic fictionists had to offer palliative resolutions to the fears and anxieties that their women readers traditionally associated with westward migration. As a result, following promotionalists like Mary Austin Holley and Eliza Farnham, and adapting many of their happier metaphors as plot structures, the domestic fictionists (even if inadvertently) succeeded in creating a sort of collective "emigrants' guide" that spoke specifically to women.

When Elisabeth Adams wrote from Iowa to her sister in Ohio, in 1846, complaining that "if I could only have mother or a sister here I should be very glad," she testified to women's general distress at family separations—and to their particular distress at isolation from female relatives. The domestic fictions set in the west, which began to appear just a few years after Adams's arrival in Davenport, responded to this familiar complaint by inventing an ingenious pattern of surrogates. In *Mabel Vaughan,* Cummins provided her heiress heroine with a surrogate sister in the person of a neighboring minister's daughter. And when the Widow Symmes becomes ill in Soule's *The Pet of the Settlement,* the motherless Margaret Belden took her home and "nursed her as a daughter would a mother." Upon her recovery, the old woman is urged to remain on in the Belden household and is given a room that, thereafter, all "called . . . affectionately, grandmother's room."

Responding to women's reluctance to exchange comfortable household arrangements for primitive conditions—"I miss many of the conveniences of home," Elisabeth Adams admitted in a letter to her sister—the domestic fictionists hinted at a speedy transition from original log cabin to framed house or charming cottage. The fear of geographical isolation to which Elisabeth Adams gave voice soon after her arrival in Iowa—"I am alone tonight, the wind sounds so mournful and the house is so still that I am almost sad"—called forth other devices. To these plaintive chords the domestic fictionists responded with promises of " 'the iron horse' " putting their western settlements, soon enough, " 'jist in the very centre' " of things. Even the rigors of the journey were minimized, as most of these novelists depicted their characters traveling in relative comfort on steamboats, canalboats, and railroads; and since they generally restricted their settings to frontiers well east of the Missouri River, arduous travel by wagon only rarely figured in their pages.

Perhaps the most tenacious anxiety to which these books responded was the lingering suspicion that women became dessicated or masculinized (or both) on the frontier. Writing from Kansas in 1859, Sarah Everett thanked a sister-in-law in western New York State for sending dress trimmings. She then added: "It was two or three weeks before I could make up my mind to wear anything so gay as that lining and those strings." "I am a very old woman," Sarah explained, "my face is thin sunken and wrinkled, my hands bony withered and hard—I shall look strangely I fear with your nice undersleeves and the coquettish cherry bows." The Sarah Everett who wrote those lines was twenty-nine years old. Whether we take her protests as exaggerations or, more probably, as accurate assessments of the physical toll of pioneering, one crucial fact emerges: Sarah Everett's fear of growing old before her time, of losing the capacity for feminine coquetry, was a fear that most women (and men) associated with westward emigration.

With unerring precision, Cummins directed herself to these fears in *Mabel Vaughan.* To the dread of physical dessication, Cummins offered categorical denials. At twenty-five, now having spent six years in Illinois, Mabel is said to enjoy a "complexion [that] has lost nothing of its fairness; the full brown eye glows with as soft a light; the smile which plays around the mouth is as spontaneous and attractive; and the chestnut hair . . . is as rich and glossy as ever." To the fear "that Mabel's manners would lose something of their delicacy . . . [or] her mode of expression, would become masculine and harsh," Cummins opposed fully one-third of her novel. Portrayed throughout the book as stereotypically patient and passive, though always acutely sensitive to the needs of those around her, Mabel's capacity for "unfailing cheerfulness and sympathy with others' joy" is especially emphasized once she removes to Illinois.

These novels exhibited their greatest ingenuity for altering contemporary belief and perception, however, in their strategies for making the prairie landscape seem both inviting and familiar. Only Southworth, in *India,* played upon American women's habitual fear of entrapment within an isolated wooded landscape. She allowed her heroine one fearful night in a log cabin located within an "old primeval forest," where she is menaced by a pack of hungry wolves. Denominated " 'a small, cowardly race,' " though, the wolves are quickly dispatched by the heroine's husband and, thereafter, the young bride is pictured wandering safely and happily in a wilderness garden where, like a latter-day Eve, she gathers "a rich harvest . . . of ripe fruit." For the most part, however, the landscapes of these novels involve the open spaces of the prairies. And even Southworth describes the prairie stands of trees as "dotted groves" or "like oases in [a] desert."

In fact, by 1850, the cutting edge of settlement had for so long been identified with the prairie that heavily wooded landscapes no longer figured prominently as emblems of the frontier. Instead, Americans imagined the parklike expanses made famous by Holley and Farnham: unimpeded prospects across rolling and flowered prairies with, here and there, a river and a stand of trees. By the end of the decade, when *The Pet of the Settlement* appeared, the alternations of closed and open spaces had become almost schematic. Soule's characters encounter "on the one side a ten-mile prairie stretching its emerald hues to the golden horizon, . . . on the other, a dense forest." And everywhere in these novels, the prairies

are said to be carpeted with wild strawberries and "multitudes of roses and pinks."

If the prairie frontier was thus made inviting, it was also denuded of its strangeness. " 'Well, really now,' " declares a maiden aunt, newly arrived in Illinois, " 'I don't see such a great difference, after all, between this country and what I've been used to at the East.' " The domestic novels of western relocation were full of such statements, though none as fully articulated as that of Aunt Sabiah in Cummins's *Mabel Vaughan:*

> "That 'ere great field, prairie, or whatever you call it, is pretty much like our meadows at home, only it ain't fenced off; and rivers are rivers anywhere, and always will run down hill, and trees are trees, and sky's sky, and as to the people, you say they're most all New England settlers so I don't see there's anything heathenish about the place after all."

The comparison of prairies to meadows—a frequent comparison in these novels—without any acknowledgment of the tall prairie grasses unique to the west is trivializing and inadequate, as are the statements about rivers, trees, and sky. But then this was precisely the purpose of the passage: it was intended to trivialize real topographical differences. The closing reference to "New England settlers" then successfully completes the imputation of the customary. And a recognizable social community is thereby transposed to a landscape that has now been reclaimed as familiar.

With strategies such as these, aided by a vocabulary and a symbolic system evocative of Eden, the westernized domestic fictions encouraged women readers to claim the new frontier as a garden of their own—as men had always done—but, at the same time, they followed the promotionalists in redefining what the garden signified. No longer the realm of the isolate Adamic male adventurer, the frontier in these novels came to embrace home, family, and a social community informed by their values. If few pioneer women actually encountered such idealized configurations as daily reality, this does not diminish the fact that the novelists' domesticated western fantasy represented a historically important creative act. For it provided prospective female emigrants with a set of images through which to forge some kind of acceptable anticipatory relationship to an unfamiliar landscape.

To fully appreciate the crucial significance of that contribution, we need only recall that it was not simply deteriorating conditions in the east that made the domestic novel turn westward in the 1850s. The nation as a whole had turned its eyes and imagination in that direction. As financial institutions recovered from the Panic of 1837, the two decades preceding the Civil War counted American emigrants and European immigrants, in unprecedented numbers, pushing out to the borderlands along the Missouri River. Beyond the Missouri, lengthening wagon trains began crossing the Great American Desert, heading overland to a fabled Pacific paradise. What made the domestic novel unique in this context was its single-minded insistence upon *women's* participation in the westward movement.

Of course, as the historian Elizabeth Fries Ellet pointed out, women had always been part of these migrations, even if her 1852 *Pioneer Women of the West* was among the first studies devoted to demonstrating that fact. The promotional writings of Mary Austin Holley and Eliza Farnham and Caroline Kirkland's successive volumes on her experience in Michigan notwithstanding, the emigrants' guides upon which most families depended for their dreams and facts about the west still largely continued to ignore women's presence. Almost as an afterthought, following paragraphs of detailed advice concerning clothing and gear for men and boys, one popular overland guide of 1846 commented briefly, "All [women and girls] can do, is to cook for camps . . . nor need they have any wearing apparel, other than their ordinary clothing at home." It was an inaccurate statement of women's many trail duties, and it was bad advice. Worse than that, it all but edited women out of the great westward adventure.

In the face of this kind of repeated refusal to formally prepare women for their role in the westering process, the domestic novels of western relocation fulfilled a vital—if unintentional—function. As always in women's fiction, they offered their readers practical advice about housekeeping on a frontier (since some of these authors knew the west firsthand), and they provided symbolic constructs where more conventional sources of information were lacking. These westernized domestic fictions thus represented unique guide-books to uncharted territories and, as such, they offered comforting and familiar image systems that could serve as templates for the organization of experience. Ten years after her arrival in Iowa, for example, Elisabeth Adams still clung to images lifted directly out of the domestic fictionists' pages. "Sometimes," she wrote her husband, "a vision of a pleasant home with a garden and flowers and creeping vines, and children and husband dear all at home, no more to roam, comes over me, and I confess I look forward to its reality with anticipated pleasure." (pp. 167-77)

> Annette Kolodny, "The Domestic Fantasy Goes West," in her The Land Before Her: Fantasy and Experience of the American Frontiers, 1630-1860, The University of North Carolina Press, 1984, pp. 161-77.

TWENTIETH-CENTURY REACTION AGAINST FRONTIER LITERATURE

MARK VAN DOREN

[*Van Doren was one of the most prolific men of letters in twentieth-century American writing. His work includes poetry (for which he won the Pulitzer Prize in 1940), novels, short stories, drama, criticism, social commentary, and the editing of a number of popular anthologies. He has written accomplished studies of William Shakespeare, John Dryden, Nathaniel Hawthorne, and Henry David Thoreau, and served as the literary editor and film critic for the* Nation *during the 1920s and 1930s. Van Doren's criticism is aimed at the general reader, rather than the scholar or specialist, and is noted for its lively perception and wide interest. In the following excerpt, he analyzes a counter-frontier movement in American literature in the early decades of the twentieth century.*]

We are in the midst of a movement in American thought which will turn out to be of immense importance. An understanding of it, and of what lies beneath it, requires an understanding of the whole past of America as well as the power to foresee something of the future, and an appreciation of it will bring a comprehension of the most interesting literature

being produced in the United States today. To use the word movement to describe a series of scattered statements and points of view is perhaps unjustified; yet I am convinced that the historian of twentieth-century American letters will discern something like a movement here, and that he will find it explanatory of much to come which we now know nothing about. It is a movement against the frontier, an effort to cast out of ourselves the last remaining vestiges of the thing we have been in the habit of honoring—the pioneer spirit.

It has long been the custom to pride ourselves upon being the sons and grandsons of pioneers, and we have fallen into the practice of imputing to those forebears the highest, indeed the only, human virtues. That these were purely moral virtues has not been so clearly seen, nor has it often been realized that there are other virtues worthy of praise. Ruggedness, restlessness, adaptability, and practicality, joined with a simple sense of duty and an inclination to avoid scrutiny of the orthodox rules—these are the virtues of the pioneer as we have celebrated them. Near to us as he necessarily is, he is naturally dear to us in consequence; and while we may have been aware of his limitations from time to time, we have hastily discovered excuses for him, insisting that his hardihood in existing at all under certain conditions quite wiped out his shortcomings. There he has stood—a gaunt, hard figure facing the West with courage and resolution born of a life dedicated entirely to action. He has been our free spirit, our guide, our model, our silent censor. Whether he has appeared to us in the form of a Puritan conquering the New England forest, a citizen with a rifle pushing across the Alleghenies to open up a great wide world of river and prairie, a temporary settler on the plains, a pilgrim in a covered wagon, a maker of western trails, or a seeker after California gold, he has seemed to us sufficient in himself. If there were other qualities than those he had, they would come later of their own will and in their due order; enough that he had cleared the ground.

Well, the ground is clear. There are no more physical worlds to subdue. The pioneer has done his work. And what is there now for us to do? That is the question which is being asked, and it is being asked with a nervousness which comes from a conviction that the pioneer was not so temporary after all. He did his work of subduing our physical world, and did it very well; but then he did not disappear. He lives in us too much still. His failings are too much our failings; we have not yet got his blood out of our veins, the disease of his dryness out of our minds. For the movement of which I speak treats him as a dry, inadequate man, and charges us with having lazily accepted dryness and inadequacy as our national characteristics—covering them up, of course, with a great show of activity and a restless passion for multiplying the details of our lives.

"The movement into backwoods America turned the European into a barbarian," says Lewis Mumford in *The Golden Day*, one of the most interesting contributions so far made to the criticism I am considering. "The truth is that the life of the pioneer was bare and insufficient: he did not really face Nature, he merely evaded society. . . . Man is, after all, a domestic animal; and though he may return to unbroken nature as a relief from all the sobrieties of existence, he can reside for long in the wilderness only by losing some of the essential qualities of the cultivated human species." The picture painted by Mr. Mumford, who incidentally is a penetrating critic of American architecture as well as of American manners and letters, is a picture of man suddenly transplanted out of a difficult social environment and set down in one wholly material. The new environment had its difficulties, and these were met with that technique which we understand under the term "the conquest of Nature"; but in one sense it was fatally easy. Cut off from the roots of an immemorial culture, the American man—who by selection anyway had been a European disposed to place a high value upon material success— kept no equipment wherewith to fashion another culture of his own. And so, according to Mr. Mumford, he tended to relapse into barbarism—or, in other words, into intolerance, industrialism, and Americanism.

John Crowe Ransom, a distinguished southern poet, says:

> The pioneering life is not the normal life, whatever some Americans may suppose. The lesson of each of the major European cultures now extant is in this, that European opinion does not make too much of the intense practical enterprises, but is at pains to define rather narrowly the minimum of practical effort which is prerequisite to the reflective and aesthetic life. It is the European intention to live materially along the inherited line of least resistance in order to put the surplus of energy into the free life of the mind. . . . It is hard for Americans to see that it is normal for the mind in its maturity to renounce the materialistic dreams of its youth.

Mr. Ransom is one of those southerners today who hope to discourage the thought that the South, in order to "advance," must become like the North. They would have it advance by standing still and considering itself, not by plunging into the stream of perfectly heedless progress toward an unexamined and uncriticized goal. Mr. Ransom's picture, then, like Mr. Mumford's, is of a people which has forgotten its aim—if indeed it ever had any beyond the subjugation of a physically hostile environment. His attack is against a species of human being marked at the same time by ambition and by sterility. And it is against what is believed to be the sterility of the American mind that the whole movement of which I speak directs its force.

Van Wyck Brooks, the herald of the new attitude, in books published as long ago as 1915 and as recently as his *Emerson and Others* last year, has never relaxed in his prosecution of the theory which Mr. Mumford and Mr. Ransom have touched upon. He has been called a man with one idea, and he is; but the idea may prove to be one worthy of the devotion he has given it. He has expressed it in many ways—among others in the form of a commentary on the failure of Mark Twain to be quite the master of literature he might have been. Mr. Brooks's thesis in *The Ordeal of Mark Twain* is that a man born with unequaled gifts as a satirist and humorist was held in check by an American environment insufficient to the needs of a first-rate artist in these fields. The American people, Mr. Brooks has said, know how to make a living—none better—but they do not know how to live. There is something thin about them, some lack of wholeness and passion, some barrenness of spirit; and these deficiencies take the form of petty intolerance, resentment against originality, disinclination to hear free spirits talking. There have been others to say this also; Waldo Frank has said it in *Our America,* Sinclair Lewis in his series of satirical novels; Sherwood Anderson in his studies of the American machine age; and H. L. Mencken in his hoarse cries against *homo Americanus.* Edwin Arlington Robinson, Eugene O'Neill, and Theodore Dreiser in their respective fields of poetry, drama, and fiction have given us

a long list of characters baffled and defeated by an empty world about them. It is the prevailing note in our literature, or at any rate it has been so during most of the period since 1900.

Lucy Lockwood Hazard, in a recent volume called *The Frontier in American Literature,* shows how Mark Twain may be taken as an epitome of the whole movement toward depression and self-doubt. Beginning to write in the expansive mid-nineteenth-century West, he was then a loud and happy spokesman of the pioneer spirit, which he glorified in books like *Roughing It,* and which later on he was to romanticize in books like *Huckleberry Finn* and *Life on the Mississippi.* But as time wore on and the American experiment produced in his eyes less courage than corruption, less principle than predatoriness, less exploration than exploitation, he wrote *The Gilded Age* to show that American money had its shoddy, counterfeit side. And he ended up as complete a misanthrope as America has yet produced—significantly enough, however, being prevented by the pressure of his public and his publishers from displaying this latest phase before he died. Such a career is indeed an epitome of our literary development over the last seventy-five years. The writers of what Mr. Mumford calls our "golden day," notably Emerson, Melville, and Whitman, were successfully and beautifully expansive; the country they worked in seemed to them to have infinite promise, and they shouted in no uncertain accents their affirmation of the American creed. Only in Melville lay the seed of that decay which attacked him in his prime and rendered him so curiously silent during the last forty years of his life. The story in its later chapters is the story of a literature over which has steadily crept the shadow of self-doubt and self-blame, until now we have the spectacle of satires becoming best sellers.

There are signs, fortunately, that we are about done hearing all this. Not that it was not good to hear while it was pertinent and necessary; not that it ever is a bad thing to face the truth about one's self. But it has been enough, perhaps, simply to get the thing said, and certainly there are those who tire of it as the third decade of the century draws to a close. One of the more brilliant of the younger American critics has been complaining that his generation no longer cares to be told what America is not. The frontier for him is so completely vanished that he has no revenge to take upon it; it has left no marks on his soul. He is interested—no, not in what America is, but in what we can say here about human nature as such, and in the ways that remain to be devised for setting this human nature forth in fiction, poetry, drama, or what not. He dismisses Dreiser, Anderson, Lewis, and O'Neill as representatives of a great stammering generation of writers who were necessary but are no longer interesting, and finds in them indeed a childish simplicity such as is to be found in boys who have just stumbled upon an awkward truth. He looks hopefully to Ernest Hemingway, Conrad Aiken, Thornton Wilder, and others now appearing on the horizon, expects of them some fresh and penetrating and permanent commentary on human life. He and his contemporaries seem not to be interested in America as a literary problem; America is as good or as bad as any other portion of the globe. An artist may function here or not at all. The question is simply this: What shall he say and how shall he say it?

Thornton Wilder, for instance, has written a Pulitzer Prize novel about some people of Peru, and the wide reception he has got may be indicative of a tendency in the American public generally to have done with the gloomy sociology of his predecessors in fiction. The interest taken in *The Bridge of San Luis Rey* is very likely an interest in complications arising out of love, religion, and parenthood—universal, not American, themes. So with Ernest Hemingway, in whose novels and short stories we get the most severely pruned growths of human situation, reared without theory and presented without commentary. And so perhaps with a whole new generation of writers, most of whom are not even names to us now. They will have learned the lesson of the sociological novelists; they will never return to the America that had not achieved self-consciousness. But they will wear their own self-consciousness with a difference; they will not parade it, or even let us know that they possess it. And they will go on to produce works of art.

It might be objected that an equally significant number of writers are dealing directly with the American soil, are reviving rather than slaying our interest in the frontier and the pioneer. But they too are doing what they do with a difference. There is a school of mid-western and trans-Mississippi novelists whose concern is with elemental matters having to do with the forces of nature at work upon man. Admitted. Their emphasis, however, is upon other features than those once dominant. Their studies are studies of the impress made upon the unchangeable stuff of human nature by wind and drouth and endless prairie. In other words, they are treating a certain situation under its own aspect, in obedience to its own laws, and—interestingly enough—with much of the same technique as has been employed for several years in an exceedingly old European country by Knut Hamsun.

The outstanding novelist in this class is Willa Cather, and there is perhaps no better in the United States today. But I do not think that this is so for the reason that she treats of American subjects primarily. She is first of all an artist; she is scrupulous; she works deliberately; she learns from each book she writes how to make the next one richer and deeper; she is immersed in her own problems. And so I would say that she might have made the same success with other materials; it only happened that these interested her. It only happened that she was born and educated in Nebraska, and that she was powerfully impressed by the personalities of certain natives and immigrants whom she observed there. *My Ántonia, O Pioneers, The Song of the Lark,* and those still subtler books that have come since are great novels; and they are great because they possess the qualities that great novels have always possessed, no matter in what country they have been written—the qualities, namely, of luminousness, solidity, patience, reality, richness, and rounded beauty. Someone has pointed out that when she does not take pioneers for her characters she takes artists, which means that she is interested solely in free minds. I think it is the freedom that interests her rather than the pioneering or the careering through art. Freedom happens to be her material—freedom together with all the obstacles that challenge it and so force it into play. And freedom is not a uniquely American theme.

What the movement against the pioneer will come to is, as I have suggested, something to be determined by time. Certainly it will have to spread farther than it has already spread in order to be fundamentally effective; for it is still confined to a comparatively slender group of sophisticated critics. But this is not of necessity a handicap. Changes of even greater importance have had their start in two or three minds, and Emerson once said that "it all goes on in half a dozen." Its

progress will depend on the amount of truth there is in it and upon the readiness of the American people to understand it and therefore profit by it. The chances are that the American people will not be swift in their acceptance of the notion that it is time to forget their youth. Oscar Wilde let one of the characters in his plays say that "America's youth is her oldest tradition." Possibly a number of centuries have still to pass before this tradition is dead of old age.

The movement is none the less interesting. Never before has emphasis been placed so clearly upon our need of maturity. Never before have we had so fresh a start waiting for us as a nation. "The golden day" was in a sense premature, since there were still worlds to conquer in the West. Now that we are fairly compact as a people, and stand facing a future which will not excuse us if we fail to be interesting, it is our privilege—I do not say it is our duty—to be interesting. We can do this by ceasing to harp upon our pioneering past, by bothering no longer about our origins, our character, our destiny, and by settling down to produce a number of grown-up, independent interpretations of the universe. Unity will not be necessary or desirable in the new literature to come. There is no unity in any of the really great literatures, and it is to be hoped that we shall soon stop talking about the Americanism of our books. Let them be simply books. Their Americanism will take care of itself. (pp. 616-23)

Mark Van Doren, "The Repudiation of the Pioneer," in English Journal, *Vol. XVII, No. 8, October, 1928, pp. 616-23.*

FURTHER READING

I. Anthologies

Davidson, Levette Jay, and Botswick, Prudence, eds. *The Literature of the Rocky Mountain West, 1803-1903.* Caldwell, Idaho: Caxton Printers, 1939, 449 p.

Contains a variety of documents about the West, including fiction, explorers' reports, personal reminiscences, and humorous sketches by such writers as Mary Hallock Foote, Washington Irving, Meriwether Lewis and William Clark, Francis Parkman, and Mark Twain. The volume includes an introductory essay for each section and a bibliography of works that were not excerpted.

Durham, Philip, and Jones, Everett L., eds. *The Frontier in American Literature.* New York: Odyssey Press, 1969, 393 p.

Collection of excerpts intended "to sample the rich variety of fiction and poetry inspired by unique American experiences." Organized by regions, the volume includes works by Stephen Vincent Benét, Willa Cather, James Fenimore Cooper, Nathaniel Hawthorne, Washington Irving, Jack London, Mark Twain, Walt Whitman, and others.

Flanagan, John T., ed. *America Is West: An Anthology of Middle-western Life and Literature.* Minneapolis: University of Minnesota Press, 1945, 677 p.

Selected short stories, essays, and novel excerpts on such subjects as the frontier, native Americans, explorers, the Mississippi River, folklore and legends, and midwestern small-town life. Featured authors include Alice Cary, Hamlin Garland, Caroline Kirkland, Edgar Lee Masters, Abraham Lincoln, Sinclair Lewis, Carl Sandburg, and Mark Twain.

Major, Mabel, and Smith, Rebecca W., eds. *The Southwest in Literature: An Anthology for High Schools.* New York: Macmillan, 1929, 370 p.

Contains fiction, poetry, and songs about the American Southwest by such writers as Mary Austin, Willa Cather, John Gould Fletcher, John G. Neihardt, and Mark Twain.

Richmond, Robert W., and Mardock, Robert W., eds. *A Nation Moving West: Readings in the History of the American Frontier.* Lincoln: University of Nebraska Press, 1966, 366 p.

Excerpts from first-person accounts of events and experiences during the settlement of the American West, including relations with native Americans, the hardships of pioneering, the construction of railroads, and the celebration of frontier holidays. Contributors include Timothy Dwight, John C. Frémont, and Washington Irving.

Trent, William P., and Wells, Benjamin W., eds. *Colonial Prose and Poetry.* New York: Thomas Y. Crowell, 1901, 331 p.

Selections of colonial American writing, including works by William Bradford, Anne Bradstreet, Captain John Smith, Roger Williams, and John Winthrop.

II. Secondary Sources

Allen, Gay Wilson. "How Emerson, Thoreau, and Whitman Viewed the 'Frontier.' " In *Toward a New American Literary History,* edited by Louis J. Budd, Edwin H. Cady, and Carl L. Anderson, pp. 111-28. Durham, N.C.: Duke University Press, 1980.

Examines the positions of Ralph Waldo Emerson, Henry David Thoreau, and Walt Whitman on the relationship between society and the wilderness.

Billington, Ray A. "The Plains and Deserts through European Eyes." *The Western Historical Quarterly* X, No. 4 (October 1979): 467-87.

Surveys the view of the American West presented by European novelists, asserting that "the West for them was a horror-land of torture and sudden death where the hero could demonstrate the ability of man to conquer savagery—and the taste of the readers for sadistic sensationalism could be satisfied." Billington asserts the importance of these images in shaping Europeans' attitudes toward the United States well into the twentieth century.

Bold, Christine. "The Voice of the Fiction Factory in Dime and Pulp Westerns." *Journal of American Studies* 17, No. 1 (April 1983): 29-46.

Traces the development of the conventions of commercial Western fiction by examining the changing relationship between writers and editors of the genre.

Bryant, James C. "The Fallen World in *Nick of the Woods.*" *American Literature* XXXVIII, No. 3 (November 1966): 352-64.

Analyzes the depiction of the wilderness and of the struggle between white settlers and native inhabitants in the novel by Robert Montgomery Bird, concluding "all members of the human race appear to be fallible sons of Adam in a fallen world."

Davis, Robert Murray. "The Frontiers of Genre: Science-Fiction Westerns." *Science-Fiction Studies* 12, No. 35 (March 1985): 33-41.

Compares various aspects of the science-fiction and the Western genres, then examines John Jakes's *Six-Gun Planet* (1970) and John Boyd's *Andromeda Gun* (1974) as examples of "the ways in which conventions from the two genres have been combined in order to create a doubled, ironic perspective by which to evaluate, judge, and grudgingly testify to the power of the two forms and of the values which they embody."

Doyle, James. "From Conservative Alternative to Vanishing Frontier: Canada in American Travel Narratives, 1799-1899." *The Canadian Review of American Studies* V, No. 1 (Spring 1974): 26-35.

Examines attitudes toward Canada expressed by nineteenth-century American writers, including Hamlin Garland, William

Dean Howells, Henry David Thoreau, and Walt Whitman. Doyle notes that this "range of opinion is a virtual summary of nineteenth-century American political and social thought."

Dwyer, Richard A., and Lingenfelter, Richard E. *Lying on the Eastern Slope: James Townsend's Comic Journalism on the Mining Frontier.* Miami: University Presses of Florida, 1984, 167 p.

Study of "Lying Jim" Townsend and his role in Western comic journalism. The volume includes selections of Townsend's writings, a biographical account, and an examination of the relationship among editors of mining camp journalism during the nineteenth century.

Fairbanks, Carol. *Prairie Women: Images in American and Canadian Fiction.* New Haven: Yale University Press, 1986, 300 p.

Surveys fiction written by American and Canadian women about life on the prairies. Fairbanks states, "I would argue . . . that in the last quarter of the nineteenth century when prairie women began to publish their own stories about the frontier, they wanted to undermine or, at a minimum, modify the public's image of the lives of women on the frontier."

Fiedler, Leslie A. *The Return of the Vanishing American.* New York: Stein & Day, 1968, 192 p.

Discusses the portrayal of native Americans in American literature in an effort to "define the myths which give a special character to art and life in America."

Gurian, Jay. *Western American Writing: Tradition and Promise.* De-Land, Fla.: Everett/Edwards, 1975, 153 p.

Collection of essays in which Gurian examines fiction, journalism, poetry, history, and film about the West in order to "discover a continuing and fundamental tradition which has had a crucial effect on western American writing of every type since the beginning of settlement."

Haberly, David T. "Women and Indians: *The Last of the Mohicans* and the Captivity Tradition," *American Quarterly* XXVIII, No. 4 (Fall 1976): 431-43.

Analyzes ways in which the conventions of captivity narratives influenced structural and thematic elements of James Fenimore Cooper's *The Last of the Mohicans.*

Hall, Joan Joffe. "*Nick of the Woods*: An Interpretation of the American Wilderness." *American Literature* XXXV, No. 2 (May 1963): 173-82.

Discusses the significance of the portrayal of Nathan Slaughter, the protagonist of Robert Montgomery Bird's *Nick of the Woods,* and draws several comparisons with James Fenimore Cooper's Leatherstocking Tales.

Hall, Roger Allan. "Frontier Dramatizations: The James Gang." *Theatre Survey* XXI, No. 2 (November 1980): 117-28.

Examines various dramatizations of the story of the James brothers and discusses contemporary criticism of the productions.

Hazard, Lucy Lockwood. *The Frontier in American Literature.* New York: Thomas Y. Crowell, 1927, 308 p.

Traces the "pioneering spirit" in frontier literature of various regions and periods of significance in American history, including seventeenth-century Puritan society, the antebellum South, the California Gold Rush, and the industrial era of the late nineteenth century.

Humphrey, William. *Ah, Wilderness! The Frontier in American Literature.* El Paso: Texas Western Press, 1977, 29 p.

Discusses the American frontier hero and his desire to escape from civilization into primitivism. Humphrey asserts, "Ours is a bachelor literature and it exalts the bachelor life, more particularly, the backwoods bachelor life. It has done so from the start."

Jones, Howard Mumford. *The Frontier in American Fiction: Four*

Lectures on the Relation of Landscape to Literature. Jerusalem: Magness Press, 1956, 95 p.

Includes an introductory essay on the depiction of the American landscape in European and American writing and chapters devoted to the frontier fiction of Willa Cather, James Fenimore Cooper, and Mark Twain.

Karolides, Nicholas J. *The Pioneer in the American Novel, 1900-1950.* Norman: University of Oklahoma Press, 1967, 324 p.

Examines subjects and themes in novels about the frontier written during the first half of the twentieth century. Karolides asserts, "an analysis of the conception of the pioneer in the novel will aid in comprehending how Americans see their past and how they see themselves in relation to their heritage of a way of life and a national character."

Kolodny, Annette. *The Lay of the Land: Metaphor as Experience and History in American Life and Letters.* Chapel Hill: University of North Carolina Press, 1975, 185 p.

Explores the "repetition of the land-as-woman symbolization in American life and letters" from the documents of sixteenth-century explorers to twentieth-century novels.

Krieg, Joann Peck. "The Transmogrification of Faerie Land into Prairie Land." *Journal of American Studies* 19, No. 2 (August 1985): 199-223.

Analyzes the influence of Edmund Spenser's *The Faerie Queene* on the depiction of the wilderness in the paintings of Benjamin West and Thomas Cole and in the fiction of James Fenimore Cooper. Krieg concludes: "As a moral allegory *The Faerie Queene* is a romance of fallen man in a fallen world striving to reclaim both himself and it; as such it proved the basis for a moral view of landscape peculiarly suited to the American experience."

Lewis, R. W. B. *The American Adam: Innocence, Tragedy, and Tradition in the Nineteenth Century.* Chicago: University of Chicago Press, 1955, 201 p.

Examines the writings of prominent authors of New England and the Atlantic seaboard during the mid nineteenth century, including James Fenimore Cooper, Nathaniel Hawthorne, Oliver Wendell Holmes, Herman Melville, Francis Parkman, and Walt Whitman, in order to explore "the beginnings and the first tentative outlines of a native American mythology."

Littlefield, Daniel F., Jr., and Parins, James W. "Short Fiction Writers of the Indian Territory." *American Studies* XXIII, No. 1 (Spring 1982): 23-38.

Biographical and critical sketches of William Jones, John Milton Oskison, and Alexander Lawrence Posey.

McDermott, Douglas. "The Development of Theatre on the American Frontier, 1750-1890." *Theatre Survey* XIX, No. 1 (May 1978): 63-78.

Defines a three-phase process through which frontier theatre developed in order to discuss "the nature and significance of the frontier and its theatre for the overall history of theatre in America."

Meldrum, Barbara. "Images of Women in Western American Literature." *The Midwest Quarterly* XVII, No. 3 (Spring 1976): 252-67.

Outlines several approaches with which to study the depiction of women in western American literature, citing examples from late nineteenth- and early twentieth-century fiction.

———, ed. *Under the Sun: Myth and Realism in Western American Literature.* Troy, N. Y.: Whitston Publishing Co., 1985, 230 p.

Collection of essays on such topics as the definition of "myth" and "reality" in writing about the American West, the meaning of Western "primitivism," and the portrayal of madness in fictional and nonfictional accounts of the midwestern pioneer experience, and on the works of individual writers, including Willa Cather, Stephen Crane, and Thomas Hornsby Ferril.

Meyer, Roy W. "The Outback and the West: Australian and American Frontier Fiction." *Western American Literature* VI, No. 1 (Spring 1971): 3-19.

Compares subjects, themes, and characters in Australian and American frontier fiction. Meyer concludes that despite some similarities, "Australian fiction about the outback differs from American Western fiction both in specifics and in its broad contours."

Morgan, Anne Hodges. "Oklahoma in Literature." In *Oklahoma: New Views of the Forty-Sixth State,* edited by Anne Hodges Morgan and H. Wayne Morgan, pp. 175-203. Norman: University of Oklahoma Press, 1982.

Examines novels and plays depicting events in Oklahoma from the 1890s through World War I, the period of the region's transition to statehood.

Paine, Gregory. "The Frontier in American Literature." *The Sewanee Review* XXXVI, No. 2 (April 1928): 225-36.

Surveys criticism on frontier literature written during the early decades of the twentieth century. Paine argues that the frontier should be viewed "as a fact rather than as a symbol or a spirit" and suggests "perhaps the frontier as a factor in American literature will prove less important than, in our first enthusiasm, we have thought."

Pearce, Roy Harvey. *The Savages of America: A Study of the Indian and the Idea of Civilization.* Baltimore: Johns Hopkins Press, 1953, 252 p.

Examines white society's assumptions about native Americans and about its own civilization. Pearce explains, "I have tried to recount how it was and what it meant for civilized men to believe that in the savage and his destiny there was manifest all that they had grown away from yet still had to overcome."

Peck, H. Daniel. "James Fenimore Cooper and the Writers of the Frontier." In *Columbia Literary History of the United States,* edited by Emory Elliott, pp. 240-61. New York: Columbia University Press, 1988.

Compares the frontier fiction written by Robert Montgomery Bird, James Fenimore Cooper, and William Gilmore Simms, asserting that Cooper made the most significant contribution to the genre.

Raymond, Elizabeth. "Learning the Land: The Development of a Sense of Place in the Prairie Midwest." In *Midamerica XIV: The Yearbook of the Society for the Study of Midwestern Literature,* edited by David D. Anderson, pp. 28-40. East Lansing, Mich.: Midwestern Press, 1987.

Explores the "distinctive regional identity" evident in the literature of the Prairie Midwest.

Rubin, Louis D., Jr. "The Romance of the Colonial Frontier: Simms, Cooper, the Indians, and the Wilderness." In *American Letters and the Historical Consciousness: Essays in Honor of Lewis P. Simpson,* edited by J. Gerald Kennedy and Daniel Mark Fogel, pp. 112-36. Baton Rouge: Louisiana State University Press, 1987.

Compares characterizations and themes in William Gilmore Simms's *The Yemassee* and James Fenimore Cooper's *The Last of the Mohicans.*

Seelye, John. "Ugh!" *Seventeenth-Century News* XXXIV, Nos. 2-3 (Summer-Fall 1976): 37-41.

Analyzes strengths and weaknesses of Richard Slotkin's *Regeneration through Violence: The Mythology of the American Frontier, 1600-1860* [see excerpt above].

Simonson, Harold P. *The Closed Frontier: Studies in Literary Tragedy.* New York: Holt, Rinehart & Winston, 1970, 160 p.

Studies the works of Ole Rölvaag, Mark Twain, and Nathanael West as illustrations of "the tragedy inherent in the closed frontier."

Turner, Frederick Jackson. *The Frontier in American History.* 1920. Reprint. Tuscon: University of Arizona Press, 1986, 375 p.

> Collection of essays including the influential paper "The Significance of the Frontier in American History."

Tuska, Jon, Piekarski, Vicki, and Blanding, Paul J., eds. *The Frontier Experience: A Reader's Guide to the Life and Literature of the American West.* Jefferson, N.C.: McFarland & Co., 1984, 434 p.

> Annotated bibliography of nonfiction books about the West, including introductory essays, a chronology of important events, and lists of suggested fiction and films to supplement the study of a particular event, region, or era. The editors state that they intend their book to "assist and guide a general reader through the vicissitudes of studying the American frontier and the Westward expansion."

VanDerBeets, Richard. "A Surfeit of Style: The Indian Captivity Narrative as Penny Dreadful." *Research Studies* 39, No. 4 (December 1971): 297-306.

> Traces the evolution of the captivity narrative from the later decades of the eighteenth century. VanDerBeets asserts, "the infusion of melodrama and sensation in the narratives, motivated by a profitable and growing pulp thriller market, demonstrably altered the character of the genre."

————. "The Indian Captivity Narrative as Ritual." *American Literature* 43, No. 4 (January 1972): 548-62.

> Likens the structure of captivity narratives to archetypal mythic journeys, from "Separation" through "Transformation" to "Return." VanDerBeets suggests that the "shared ritual features" of captivity narratives unite them as one genre.

Von Frank, Albert J. *The Sacred Game: Provincialism and Frontier Consciousness in American Literature, 1630-1860.* Cambridge: Cambridge University Press, 1985, 188 p.

> Considers the ways in which various American writers, including Anne Bradstreet, Timothy Dwight, Ralph Waldo Emerson, Margaret Fuller, and Washington Irving, "illustrate, in their different historical settings, different aspects of American literary provincialism."

Wasserstrom, William. "The Lily and the Prairie Flower." *American Quarterly* IX, No. 4 (Winter 1957): 398-411.

> Examines the portrayal of women and sexuality in literature about the West, suggesting that this literature reflects "a native effort to resolve the old, old conflict between lust and love."

Webb, Walter Prescott. "The Great Frontier and Modern Literature." *Southwest Review* 59, No. 4 (August 1974): 381-401.

> Traces the effect of the concept of the frontier on imagination and literature from the fifteenth through the twentieth centuries.

Williams, Kenny J. *Prairie Voices: A Literary History of Chicago from the Frontier to 1893.* Nashville: Townsend Press, 1980, 529 p.

> Surveys fiction, journalism, and the publishing industry in Chicago from the late seventeenth century through the 1890s. The volume contains extensive appendices detailing selected newspapers, magazines, novels, and publishing houses in nineteenth-century Chicago.

English Decadent Literature of the 1890s

INTRODUCTION

English Decadent literature was the product of a loosely affiliated coterie of writers and artists of the 1890s who manifested in both their lives and works a highly stylized manner, a fascination with morbidity and perversity, and an attitude of world-weariness. Principal figures of the period include Oscar Wilde, Aubrey Beardsley, Max Beerbohm, Hubert Crackanthorpe, John Davidson, Ernest Dowson, John Gray, Lionel Johnson, and Arthur Symons. The often brief and troubled lives of many of these writers encouraged the kind of retrospective mythologizing that led William Butler Yeats to characterize them as "The Tragic Generation."

Works of English literary Decadence evince neither an explicitly articulated philosophy nor a unified body of artistic goals, but derive from common sources and share stylistic and thematic features. Chiefly influenced by poets associated with the earlier movements of Decadence and Symbolism in France, including Charles Baudelaire, Paul Verlaine, and Stéphane Mallarmé, English decadent writers adhered to the doctrine of "art for art's sake," which eliminated concern with moral, didactic, or social considerations in art. English Decadent literature also reflects French models in displaying a desire for novel sensation (the *frisson nouveau,* or "new thrill"), a preoccupation with both mysticism and nihilism, and the assertion of an essential enmity between art and life. Further inspiration for writers of the 1890s derived from English essayist Walter Pater, who presented an example of perfectionism and artificiality in his prose style, as well as from the melancholy themes and sensuous style characteristic of the Pre-Raphaelites, an earlier movement in English art and literature which included poets Dante Gabriel Rossetti and Algernon Swinburne and painter Edward Burne-Jones. Themes and subjects explored in Decadent literature included ennui, despair, degeneration, alienation, and states of altered awareness as a result of extreme emotion, religious fervor, or drug or alcohol use. Perhaps the most representative work of English Decadent literature is Oscar Wilde's novel, *The Picture of Dorian Gray,* in which the protagonist's pursuit of sensation is inspired by *A rebours* (1884; *Against the Grain*), by Joris-Karl Huysmans, the seminal novel of French Decadence. Nevertheless, poetry was the most usual vehicle for Decadent themes, and, determined to test the limits of social acceptability in their art, Decadent poets routinely violated recognized moral and ethical standards. In Ernest Dowson's "Non Sum Qualis Eram Bonae sub Regno Cynarae," for example, the narrator seeks solace in "madder music and . . . stronger wine" and the sweet kisses of a "bought red mouth." Wilde's "The Harlot's House" describes the transmutation of love to lust. The titles of Arthur Symons's "Maquillage," "The Opium Smoker," "The Absinthe-Drinker," and "White Heliotrope"; Lionel Johnson's "Nihilism"; Lord Alfred Douglas's "Ennui"; and Dowson's "Dregs" epitomize Decadent concerns.

In 1895 Wilde's conviction on charges of gross indecency, stemming from commerce with male prostitutes, effectively ended the vogue for English Decadent literature as public censure of Wilde and his work extended to other writers and artists associated with the movement. Satires on the dress, behavior, and literature of Decadents and Aesthetes that had filled the popular press were replaced by humorless condemnations, and Decadent works could not find publishers. The *Yellow Book,* a journal with which many Decadent writers were associated, failed in 1897, and the *Savoy,* a magazine edited by Symons and art directed by Beardsley, barely lasted through 1896. Further, many of the most prominent Decadent writers died young: Hubert Crackanthorpe committed suicide at twenty-six in 1896; Beardsley, whose striking black and white illustrations are considered the perfect visual complement of literary decadence, died of tuberculosis at twenty-six in 1898; Ernest Dowson, thirty-two, and Wilde, forty-six, both died in 1900; Lionel Johnson, whose ill health has been blamed on excessive drinking, died of a stroke at thirty-four in 1902.

The powerful personalities and often tragic lives of principal figures of the English Decadent movement continue to exert a strong appeal, and individual works of Decadent literature are often considered among the finest of their time. Moreover, English literary Decadence is often credited with popularizing French literary conventions in England, and is recognized as an important transitional phase between Victorian and Modernist literature.

REPRESENTATIVE WORKS

Beardsley, Aubrey
    "The Three Musicians" (poem) 1896; published in journal *The Savoy*
    Under the Hill [censored edition] (unfinished novel); published in journal *The Savoy,* 1896; also published as *The Story of Venus and Tannhäuser* [uncensored edition], 1907
Beerbohm, Max
    The Works of Max Beerbohm (essays) 1896
    The Happy Hypocrite (short story) 1897
Crackanthorpe, Hubert
    Wreckage (short stories) 1893
    Vignettes: A Miniature Journal of Whim and Sentiment (essays) 1896
    Collected Stories 1893-1897 (short stories) 1969
Davidson, John
    Fleet Street Eclogues (poetry) 1893
Douglas, Lord Alfred
    The Collected Poems of Lord Alfred Douglas (poetry) 1919
Dowson, Ernest
    The Pierrot of the Minute (drama) 1897
    The Poems of Ernest Dowson (poetry) 1905
Gray, John
    Silverpoints (poetry) 1893

Johnson, Lionel
"The Cultured Faun" (essay); published in journal *The Anti-Jacobin,* 1891
Poems (poetry) 1895
Post Liminium (essays and criticism) 1911
Le Gallienne, Richard
English Poems (poetry) 1892
Rolfe, Frederick
Tarcissus: The Boy Martyr of Rome in the Diocletian Persecution (poetry) 1880
Stories Toto Told Me [as Frederick Baron Corvo] (short stories) 1898
Symons, Arthur
Days and Nights (poetry) 1889
Silhouettes (poetry) 1892; revised edition, 1896
London Nights (poetry) 1895
Amoris Victima (poetry) 1897
Wilde, Oscar
Intentions (essays and criticism) 1891
Lord Arthur Savile's Crime, and Other Stories (short stories) 1891
The Picture of Dorian Gray (novel) 1891
Salomé (drama) [first publication] 1893
The Ballad of Reading Gaol, and Other Poems (poetry) 1898
*De Profundis

*(This work was not published in its entirety until 1949.)

FIN DE SIECLE: THE DECADENT PERIOD

BERNARD BERGONZI

[*Bergonzi is an English novelist, essayist, and critic. In the following excerpt, he discusses literary Decadence as one of the manifestations of a fin-de-siècle sensibility.*]

Towards the end of the nineteenth century many writers felt that literature and art had moved into a new phase, and that even though Queen Victoria continued to be very much alive, the Victorian era was already passing away. Although there was, and is, agreement that the change took place, critics remain divided about the best way of describing this phase of cultural history, and about the point in time when it began to emerge. To talk simply of the 'nineties' is tempting: the period was indeed remarkably compact, with a very characteristic literary flavour, and its mythology has survived for over seventy years. The 'nineties', whether qualified as 'naughty' or 'mauve' or 'yellow', can still exert a striking appeal, as is evident in the recent vogue for Beardsley prints and *art nouveau* decoration. And yet to refer to a single decade in this way can be misleading, since many of the essential attitudes of the nineties had their roots in the eighties or even the seventies; specifically, the Aesthetic Movement, which is sometimes referred to as though it were synonymous with the innovations of the nineties, was essentially a manifestation of the previous decade; as early as 1881 Oscar Wilde was caricatured in the Gilbert and Sullivan opera, *Patience.* The word 'Decadence' has a broader application, but suffers from its ambiguity; some of the time it suggests a combination of physical lassitude and psychological and moral perversity—

as exemplified for instance in J. K. Huysman's novel, *A Rebours,* which was much admired in the nineties—although more properly it should refer only to language. Arthur Symons wrote in the Introduction to *The Symbolist Movement in Literature* (1899): 'the term is in its place only when applied to style; to that ingenious deformation of the language, in Mallarmé, for instance, which can be compared with what we are accustomed to call the Greek and Latin of the Decadence.' A few years before, Symons had been happy to use 'decadence' in the broader and looser sense, as in his poem, 'Intermezzo', which describes the dancer 'Nini Patteen-l'Air' as the 'Maenad of the Decadence'.

I have decided in this essay to use the phrase *fin de siècle,* which clearly points to the preoccupations of the last years of the nineteenth century, without being limited to a single decade, and which can cover such particular manifestations as 'aestheticism' and 'decadence'. From the early nineties onward, *fin de siècle* was something of a catch-phrase; there is a characteristic instance in Wilde's *The Picture of Dorian Gray,* published in 1891:

'*Fin de siècle,*' murmured Lord Henry.

'*Fin du globe,*' answered his hostess.

'I wish it were *fin du globe,*' said Dorian with a sigh. 'Life is a great disappointment.' (chapter xv)

In the poem just referred to, Symons attributes to Nini Patteen-l'Air

The art of knowing how to be
Part lewd, aesthetical in part
And *fin-de-siècle* essentially.

Holbrook Jackson quotes various other entertaining instances of the phrase in his book, *The Eighteen Nineties* [excerpted below] (first published in 1913 and still an indispensable guide to the period). It occurs most portentously in Max Nordau's *Degeneration,* of which the English translation appeared in 1895; writing with ponderous, pseudo-scientific assurance, Nordau uses the phrase *fin de siècle* to define and dismiss practically everything that was significant in late nineteenth-century art and literature: Wagner, Ibsen, Zola, the French symbolists, were all seen as symptomatic of a prevalent mental and physical degeneration. The English translation of *Degeneration* was something of a *succès de scandale;* it ran through several impressions in 1895, no doubt because it coincided with the trials of Oscar Wilde, but was quickly forgotten. Bernard Shaw attacked the book at length in *The Sanity of Art.*

The phrase *fin de siècle* was applied to a wide range of trivial behaviour, provided it was sufficiently perverse or paradoxical or shocking. Yet in so far as *fin de siècle* refers to a serious and consistent cultural attitude, it has two essential characteristics: the conviction that all established forms of intellectual and moral and social certainty were vanishing, and that the new situation required new attitudes in life and art; and the related belief that art and morality were separate realms, and that the former must be regarded as wholly autonomous; hence, the aesthetic doctrine of 'art for art's sake'. As I have remarked, it is difficult to define the point at which these attitudes begin clearly to emerge. If the *fin de siècle* represented a break with established Victorian attitudes, then the break was not particularly clean: in a literary sense there are lines of development that link the *fin de siècle* poets with the major Romantics; with Blake, with Coleridge and with Keats. Arthur Hallam's review of Tennyson's early poems—whose influence was acknowledged by Yeats—was an important intermediary: Hallam praised a poetry of pure images, without any admixture of rhetoric, in a thoroughly proto-symbolist fashion. One writer has attempted to pin down the emergence of the doctrine of aestheticism:

> The actual doctrine appears first in Swinburne's review of Baudelaire's *Fleurs du mal* in the *Spectator* for September 6th, 1862 (reprinted in Swinburne's *Works,* volume XIII, p. 419) and in Pater's essay on Winckelmann, which was published in the *Westminster Gazette* in 1867. Swinburne's *William Blake* (1868) gave prominence to the phrase 'art for art's sake' and five years later the phrase was embodied in the provocatively enigmatic conclusion to Pater's *Renaissance* [Ian Fletcher, "Bedford Park: Aesthete's Elysium?" in *Romantic Mythologies,* Ian Fletcher, ed.].

The mention of Walter Pater takes us clearly within the ambience of the *fin de siècle.* For over thirty years Pater was one of the most influential of English writers, both for his manner of writing and for what was supposed to be his essential message. Oscar Wilde, in *De Profundis,* refers to reading Pater's *The Renaissance* (originally entitled, in the first edition of 1873, *Studies in the History of the Renaissance*) in his first term at Oxford, calling it 'that book which has had such a strange influence over my life'. Arthur Symons, in a memorial essay written after Pater's death, said that *The Renaissance* 'even with the rest of Pater to choose from, seems to me sometimes the most beautiful book of prose in our literature'. James Joyce, in many passages in his early books, *Dubliners* and *A Portrait of the Artist as a Young Man,* reveals a consciousness that has been saturated in Pater's prose. W. B. Yeats, looking back in the 1920s to his companions of the nineties, wrote [in his *Autobiographies* (1955)]:

> If Rossetti was a subconscious influence, and perhaps the most powerful of all, we looked consciously to Pater for our philosophy. Three or four years ago I re-read *Marius the Epicurean,* expecting to find I cared for it no longer, but it still seemed to me, as I think it seemed to us all, the only great prose in modern English. . . .

Such valuations are hard for the present-day reader to accept, since he is accustomed to a prose that is expressive rather than musical, and he is likely to echo Max Beerbohm's complaint about Pater [in his *Works and More* (1946)], with its illustrative parody.

> I was angry that he should treat English as a dead language, bored by that sedulous ritual wherewith he laid out every sentence as in a shroud—hanging like a widower, long over its marmoreal beauty or ever he could lay it at length in his book, its sepulchre.

Beerbohm's point is well taken, and yet it is in a sense unfair to Pater; his prose makes its effects cumulatively, and its appeal can grow with familiarity; one also becomes aware of a curious counterpointing between Pater's elaborately cadenced, ritualistic prose, and his sceptical, relativistic, even iconoclastic intelligence. (pp. 17-20)

From an art-historical point of view, *The Renaissance* is an important work, since Pater was one of the first English writers to deal in an analytical and historically conscious fashion with some of the major artists of the Italian Renaissance, thus anticipating the later, more systematic research of Berenson and other scholars. At the same time Pater ranges widely, in a way that illustrates the cultural time-travelling and eclecticism that typified the Aesthetic Movement of the seventies and eighties. At one end of the scale he writes about two thirteenth-century French stories, and at the other he discusses the eighteenth-century German antiquarian, Johann Winckelmann. The most famous lines in *The Renaissance*—indeed, in all Pater's work—form the celebrated purple passage about the Mona Lisa, which Yeats rather perversely arranged in *vers libre* to print as the first exhibit in the *Oxford Book of Modern Verse.* It is unfortunate that this passage has come to be regarded merely as a virtuoso stylistic exercise; it occurs as the climax of Pater's essay on Leonardo, and is carefully led up to and prepared for by the developing strategy of the essay. Furthermore, what Pater says about the Mona Lisa is at least as important as the way he says it. For him she is a symbol of the modern consciousness that is burdened by a multiplicity of knowledge and experience; she is an embodiment of the timeless frequenting of many cultures that modern historical knowledge has made possible; she anticipates *The Waste Land* and the *Musée Imaginaire:*

> She is older than the rocks among which she sits; like the vampire, she has been dead many times, and learned the secrets of the grave; and has been a diver in deep seas, and keeps their fallen day about her; and trafficked for strange webs with Eastern merchants: and, as Leda, was the mother of Helen of Troy, and, as Saint Anne, the mother of Mary; and all this has been to her but as the sound of lyres and flutes, and lives only in the delicacy with which it has moulded the changing lineaments, and tinged the eyelids and the hands. The fancy of a perpetual life, sweeping together ten thousand experiences is an old one; and modern philosophy has conceived the idea of humanity as wrought upon by, and summing up in itself, all modes of thought and life. Certainly Lady Lisa might stand as the embodiment of the old fancy, the symbol of the modern idea.

In the almost equally celebrated 'Conclusion' to *The Renaissance,* Pater continues to stress the 'modern idea': 'to regard all things and principles of things as inconstant modes or fashions has more and more become the tendency of modern thought'. Here we see the authentically *fin de siècle* note. As a historical relativist, Pater was sceptical about the possibility of ultimate values and truths; human life was fleeting and uncertain, and instead of pursuing abstractions, man should constantly strive to refine and purify his sensations and impressions:

> Every moment some form grows perfect in hand or face; some tone on the hills or the sea is choicer than the rest; some mood of passion or insight or intellectual excitement is irresistibly real and attractive to us,—for that moment only. Not the fruit of experience, but experience itself, is the end. A counted number of pulses only is given to us of a variegated, dramatic life. How may we see in them all that is to be seen in them by the finest senses? How shall we pass most swiftly from point to point, and be present always at the focus where the greatest number of vital forces unite in their purest energy?
>
> To burn always with this hard, gemlike flame, to maintain this ecstasy is success in life. In a sense it might even be said that our failure is to form habits:

Max Beerbohm caricature "Some Persons of 'The Nineties'." Left to right: Richard Le Gallienne,
W.R. Sickert, Arthur Symons, George Moore, John Davidson, Henry Harland, Charles Conder,
Oscar Wilde, William Rothenstein, Max Beerbohm, W.B. Yeats, and Aubrey Beardsley.

for, after all, habit is relative to a stereotyped world, and meantime it is only the roughness of the eye that makes any two persons, things, situations, seem alike. While all melts under our feet, we may well grasp at any exquisite passion, or any contribution to knowledge that seems by a lifted horizon to set the spirit free for a moment, or any stirring of the senses, strange dyes, strange colours, and curious odours, or work of the artist's hands, or the face of one's friend. Not to discriminate every moment some passionate attitude in those about us, and in the very brilliancy of their gifts some tragic dividing of forces on their ways is, on this short day of frost and sun, to sleep before evening.

The traditional *carpe diem* theme is reinforced by a profound, modern scepticism which rejects any 'theory or idea or system which requires of us the sacrifice of any part of this experience'. The moral antinomianism that Pater's 'Conclusion' seemed to be advancing was found deeply subversive; and Pater, who in his personal life was an orderly, withdrawn, somewhat timid scholar, removed it from the second edition of *The Renaissance:* 'As I conceived it might possibly mislead some of those young men into whose hands it might fall.' He finally restored the 'Conclusion', slightly modified, to the

third edition of his book, with the added comment: 'I have dealt more fully in *Marius the Epicurean* with the thoughts suggested by it.'

Marius the Epicurean, published in 1885, is nominally a novel, but Pater's talents for fiction were limited, and there is little sense of character or dramatic interplay in *Marius.* The central figure is a Roman gentleman living in the second century A.D., a conscientious, rather solemn young man, who attempts to live according to the best principles of paganism, as outlined in the Epicurean philosophy. *Marius the Epicurean* is sub-titled 'His Sensations and Ideas', and although Marius' attitude to life is continuous with that presented in the 'Conclusion' to *The Renaissance,* his Epicureanism is a very high-minded affair, far removed from mere sensuous hedonism; Marius cultivates the pleasures of the mind and spirit rather than of the senses. But the insufficiency of Epicureanism weighs increasingly on Marius, and he is drawn to an enchanting community of early Christians. He is captivated by the beauty of their ritual, and the sweetness and light of their beliefs, and he dies in their care, without having been formally converted. Provided one does not expect the normal satisfactions of fiction from *Marius,* and gives oneself time to adapt to its infinitely leisurely cadences, *Marius* can be read as a work of a genuine if muted charm, where action is at a minimum, but where the reader is slowly borne along by the billowing movement of Pater's prose and caught up by degrees into Marius' unfolding consciousness. Although Pater endeavours to make the historical detail correct, it is evident that an earnest nineteenth-century inquirer lies beneath Marius' Roman exterior, and that the Roman Empire of the Antonines thinly conceals the late-Victorian British Empire. The book develops at length the historical superimpositions hinted at in the description of the Mona Lisa.

Pater's major writings reveal another crucial element in the *fin de siècle* state of mind: the mistrust of theory and system, and the corresponding stress on sensation and impression, led in the nineties to a taste for the brief, concentrated lyric, and, in prose, for the short story. In the twentieth century the tendency became more systematic, in the 'images' and 'epiphanies' and other moments of fragmentary illumination in the literature of the Modern Movement. *Marius* had a more immediate effect in projecting the attractiveness of ritual as a way of life, independently of religious affiliation. Yeats remarked of it:

> I began to wonder if it, or the attitude of mind of which it was the noblest expression, had not caused the disaster of my friends. It taught us to walk upon a rope tightly stretched through serene air, and we were left to keep our feet upon a swaying rope in a storm [*Autobiographies*].

There was one writer who absorbed Pater's lesson not wisely but too well, who achieved a tragic celebrity with relatively slender talents, and whose name is still a veritable symbol for the whole *fin de siècle* period and state of mind. This, of course, is Oscar Wilde: he is difficult to place in literary history, since, as he admitted, he devoted his genius to his life rather than his art. Wilde survives as a figure of pure and fascinating mythology, where the works inevitably seem secondary to the legend of the man. The essential judgements were made, sharply but justly, soon after Wilde's death [in *Studies in Prose and Verse* (1904)] by Arthur Symons, who was the finest critic of his day:

> His intellect was dramatic, and the whole man was not so much a personality as an attitude. Without being a sage, he maintained the attitude of a sage; without being a poet, he maintained the attitude of a poet; without being an artist, he maintained the attitude of an artist, and it was precisely in his attitudes that he was most sincere.

Admittedly, Wilde wrote copiously in verse and prose, but the more one reads through his collected works, the more one is conscious of its largely derivative quality. Most of the verse draws heavily on a variety of Victorian poets, while his most famous piece of fiction, *The Picture of Dorian Gray,* though a lively story, is a pale imitation of Huysman's *A Rebours.* The dialogues first published in Wilde's book, *Intentions,* 'The Critic as Artist' and 'The Decay of Lying', offer a witty and accessible source of ideas about art that were fundamental to symbolist aesthetics, and which have been developed in the literature and criticism of the twentieth century. Yet they are all taken over from other critics: 'Reading *Intentions* one finds here a bit of Arnold, here a patch of Pater or William Morris and, in this unlikely company, even Carlyle' [Ruth Z. Temple, 'The Ivory Tower as Lighthouse,' in *Ed-*

wardians and Late Victorians; see Richard Ellman, ed. in Further Reading].

If one wishes to find what is most enduring in Wilde's work, one is likely to turn to his comedies, *Lady Windermere's Fan, A Woman of No Importance, An Ideal Husband* and *The Importance of Being Earnest,* which were produced between 1892 and 1895. All are excellent pieces of theatre and splendidly witty. Yet the first three tend to be melodramatic and contain a rather uneasy mixture of farce and morality; *The Importance of Being Earnest* is Wilde's comic masterpiece, and indeed one of the great comedies of the English theatre. Its qualities have been well described by Ian Gregor in an important article on Wilde's comedies ["Comedy and Oscar Wilde," *The Sewanee Review* LXXIV (1966)]; he says of this play: 'what he gives us is a completely realised idyll, offering itself as something irrevocably *other* than life, not a wish-fulfilment of life as it might be lived'. For the rest, some of Wilde's shorter tales preserve their self-conscious charm; and among the poems, 'The Ballad of Reading Gaol' stands out as an impressive achievement, although it is over-long and suffers from Wilde's tendency to turn the elements of tragedy into a repetitive decoration. To quote Symons again:

> In this poem, where a style formed on other lines seems startled at finding itself used for such new purposes, we see a great spectacular intellect, to which, at last, pity and terror have come in their own person, and no longer as puppets in a play.

Symons himself was one of the most interesting figures of the *fin de siècle* period. He was born in 1865 and emerged in the eighties as a self-taught but learned young literary man, who was widely read in several languages. In addition to his distinction as a critic, he was a prolific minor poet, a translator, an essayist on all forms of art and an entrepreneur of foreign literary influences. In this last respect Symons was of crucial importance, notably as the author of *The Symbolist Movement in Literature* (1899), a book which discussed the work of such French poets as Rimbaud, Verlaine, Laforgue and Mallarmé. This book had a decisive influence on the development of twentieth-century poetry in English. It was dedicated to Yeats, who became a close friend of Symons in the nineties; Symons, who was very much at home in Paris literary circles, introduced Yeats to Mallarmé and other French symbolists, and to their work, thereby expanding and reinforcing Yeats's existing interest in poetic symbolism, which he had developed from his reading of Blake and his dabblings in magic and the occult. Yeats himself influenced Symons away from mere 'decadence' as a literary concept, towards a quasi-occult understanding of symbolism, reinforced with a Paterian sense of ritual; in the introduction to *The Symbolist Movement,* Symons wrote that literature 'becomes itself a kind of religion, with all the duties and responsibilities of the sacred ritual'. A few years later T. S. Eliot, as an undergraduate at Harvard, was to find Symons's book extremely fruitful:

> I myself owe Mr Symons a great debt. But for having read his book I should not, in the year 1908, have heard of Laforgue and Rimbaud; I should probably not have begun to read Verlaine, and but for reading Verlaine, I should not have heard of Corbière. So the Symons book is one of those which have affected the course of my life [quoted in F. O. Matthiessen, *The Achievement of T. S. Eliot* (1959)].

Yeats and Symons were associated in a group of poets calling themselves the Rhymers' Club that met during the nineties; in Yeats's words, the Club 'for some years was to meet every night in an upper room with a sanded floor in an ancient eating-house in Fleet Street called the Cheshire Cheese'. The Rhymers, as their name denoted, aimed at the unpretentious pursuit of pure song, purged of Victorian rhetoric or moralising, and their habit of meeting regularly in such surroundings was an attempt to combine French literary café life with Johnsonian conviviality. These poets were later to be mythologised by Yeats as the 'tragic generation': two of the Rhymers, Ernest Dowson and Lionel Johnson, were to die in their thirties, and another, John Davidson, committed suicide in 1909 at the age of forty-three. Symons, although he lived to be nearly eighty, was afflicted by madness in his later years. The Rhymers did not have the temper of literary revolutionaries, but they aimed to break with the recent past in a way that has been memorably described by Yeats [in his introduction to *The Oxford Book of Modern Verse* (1936)]:

> The revolt against Victorianism meant to the young poet a revolt against irrelevant descriptions of nature, the scientific and moral discursiveness of *In Memoriam*—'When he should have been brokenhearted,' said Verlaine, 'he had many reminiscences'—the political eloquence of Swinburne, the psychological curiosity of Browning, and the poetical diction of everybody. Poets said to one another over their black coffee—a recently imported fashion—'We must purify poetry of all that is not poetry', and by poetry they meant poetry as it had been written by Catullus, a great name at that time, by the Jacobean writers, by Verlaine, by Baudelaire. Poetry was a tradition like religion and liable to corruption, and it seemed that they could best restore it by writing lyrics technically perfect, their emotion pitched high, and as Pater offered instead of moral earnestness life lived as 'a pure gem-like flame' all accepted him for master.

As I have remarked, the brief concentrated lyric could serve as the literary crystallisation of a Paterian sensation; the most obvious stylistic influences at work in such poetry were the Elizabethan lyric and the short poems of Verlaine. Even now, so long after they wrote, it is not easy to get the poets of the nineties in critical focus. It is tempting to mythologise them as men, as Yeats did, and to regard their verses as infinitely poignant human records; alternatively, one can dismiss them as *poseurs* of patently limited talent, whose literary achievement is minuscule, when it is not wholly unnoticeable. Looked at as objectively as possible, the poets of the nineties do have certain definable qualities in their favour. They were at their best extremely skilful craftsmen, who could bring off subtle and striking rhythmic effects, and who were surprisingly successful in importing a Verlainian music into their poems. And by following the example of Baudelaire they were able to enlarge the subject-matter of poetry, even though Baudelaire was systematically misunderstood in the nineties as a romantically decadent celebrant of 'sin' rather than as the tormented Catholic moralist that he was later to appear to T. S. Eliot. At all events, the sensibility of the nineties was inclined to write about prostitutes, or other sources of casual amour: 'the chance romances of the streets, the Juliet of a night', in Symons's words. However much the poets may have romanticised these matters, by touching on them at all they were acknowledging an element in the social reality of Victorian London that had not, so far, received much literary recognition. Despite the narrowness of their poetic means, poets such as Dowson and Symons broadened the spectrum

of poetic material in a way that anticipates Eliot, and which shows the influence not merely of French poetry, but of French fiction. Where they were weakest was in the resources of their diction. Dowson's well-worn (and hard-wearing) anthology favourite, 'Non Sum Qualis Eram Bonae sub Regno Cynarae', illustrates these considerations:

> Last night, ah, yesternight, betwixt her lips and mine
> There fell thy shadow, Cynara! thy breath was shed
> Upon my soul between the kisses and the wine;
> And I was desolate and sick of an old passion,
> Yea, I was desolate and bowed my head:
> I have been faithful to thee, Cynara! in my fashion.
>
> All night upon mine heart I felt her warm heart beat,
> Night-long within mine arms in love and sleep she lay;
> Surely the kisses of her bought red mouth were sweet;
> But I was desolate and sick of an old passion,
> When I awoke and found the dawn was gray:
> I have been faithful to thee, Cynara! in my fashion . . .

It is evident that Dowson's Swinburnian or Pre-Raphaelite diction is strained to breaking-point in his attempt to convey a novelistic complexity of the erotic life. But I would argue that the poem's achievement is that it can take the strain: Dowson's intentions are reinforced by a remarkable verbal energy that underlies the seemingly debilitated surface of the poem, and by his virtuoso manipulation of rhythm.

Symons treats of a similar theme, more succinctly and equally musically, in 'Leves Amores II', a poem which conveys an intensely 'realistic' experience with all the immediacy demanded by twentieth-century poetics:

> The little bedroom papered red,
> The gas's faint malodorous light,
> And one beside me in the bed,
> Who chatters, chatters, half the night.
>
> I drowse and listen, drowse again,
> And still, although I would not hear,
> Her stream of chatter, like the rain,
> Is falling, falling on my ear.
>
> The bed-clothes stifle me, I ache,
> With weariness, my eyelids prick;
> I hate, until I long to break,
> That clock for its tyrannic tick.

Symons was an intensely visual poet, who often anticipates the effects demanded by the Imagists of *c.* 1912; as, for instance, in 'At Dieppe: After Sunset', written in 1890:

> The sea lies quieted beneath
> The after-sunset flush
> That leaves upon the heaped grey clouds
> The grape's faint purple blush.
>
> Pale, from a little space in heaven
> Of delicate ivory,
> The sickle-moon and one gold star
> Look down upon the sea.

Symons was a passionate frequenter of the music-halls of London and Paris, and he constantly celebrates them in his verse. His interest in ballet-girls was not merely amorous; he was a great exponent of the *fin de siècle* interest in the dance as a momentary fusion of art and ritual, a pure expressive image lifted out of discourse and the flux of everyday life. This topic has been discussed by Frank Kermode in *Romantic Image* and pursued in detail in 'Poet and Dancer before Diaghilev', an essay which combines theatrical and literary history (included in Kermode's *Puzzles and Epiphanies,* 1962).

Another of the Rhymers, Lionel Johnson, has left an unflattering comment both on Symons's proto-Imagist methods and his propensity for sordid subjects [quoted in *The Literary Essays of Ezra Pound,* T. S. Eliot, ed. (1960)]:

> [Symons] is a slave to impressionism, whether the impression be precious or not. A London fog, the blurred, tawny lamplights, the red omnibus, the dreary rain, the depressing mud, the glaring gin-shop, the slatternly shivering women: three dexterous stanzas telling you that and nothing more. And in nearly every poem, one line or phrase of absolutely pure and fine imagination. If he would wash and be clean, he might be of the elect.

Johnson was a poet of more austere temperament than Dowson or Symons; his indulgence was alcohol rather than harlots. Like his contemporaries Johnson was a disciple of Pater, but he followed the implications of *Marius the Epicurean* to their logical conclusion and joined the Roman Catholic Church. Catholicism was very much in the air in the nineties: Dowson also became a Catholic, of an intensely aesthetic, wistful kind, though he does not seem to have shared Johnson's attachment to reading the Fathers of the Church and otherwise speculating on doctrinal niceties (graphically described by Yeats in the *Autobiographies*). Aubrey Beardsley was converted to Catholicism towards the end of his short life, and Oscar Wilde became a Catholic on his death-bed. Another convert was the poet John Gray, not one of the Rhymers, who was a close friend of Wilde and who was falsely alleged to be the original of Dorian Gray: he interestingly broke the *fin de siècle* pattern of the 'tragic generation' by becoming a priest and not dying young. Gray ended his days in 1934 at the age of sixty-eight as a well-loved parish priest in Edinburgh. The temper of this aesthetic Catholicism is well illustrated in two poems on the same theme by Dowson and Johnson, which also serve to contrast the temperaments of the two poets:

'Benedictio Domini'

Without, the sullen noises of the street!
The voice of London, inarticulate,
Hoarse and blaspheming, surges in to meet
The silent blessing of the Immaculate.

Dark is the church, and dim the worshippers,
Hushed with bowed heads as though by some old spell.
While through the incense-laden air there stirs
The admonition of a silver bell.

Dark is the church, save where the altar stands,
Dressed like a bride, illustrious with light,
Where one old priest exalts with tremulous hands
The one true solace of man's fallen plight.

Strange silence here: without, the sounding street
Heralds the world's swift passage to the fire:
O Benediction, perfect and complete!
When shall men cease to suffer and desire?

Dowson

'The Church of a Dream'

Sadly the dead leaves rustle in the whistling wind,
Around the weather-worn, gray church, low down the vale:
The Saints in golden vesture shake before the gale;

The glorious windows shake, where still they dwell enshrined;
Old Saints by long dead, shrivelled hands, long since designed:
There still, although the world autumnal be, and pale,
Still in their golden vesture the old saints prevail;
Along with Christ, desolate else, left by mankind.

Only one ancient Priest offers the Sacrifice,
Murmuring holy Latin immemorial:
Swaying with tremulous hands the old censer full of spice,
In gray, sweet incense clouds; blue, sweet clouds mystical:
To him, in place of men, for he is old, suffice
Melancholy remembrances and vesperal.

Johnson

Both poems convey a Paterian feeling for liturgy, but where Dowson is fervid and aspiring, Johnson is cold and melancholy. Johnson was, if anything, a more accomplished verbal artist than Dowson or Symons, but compared with theirs, his poetry, which dwells on religious topics or fragments of Celtic legend (although born a Welshman, Johnson transformed himself into an honorary but patriotic Irishman), is somewhat stiff and lacking in human interest. He is seen at his best in such accomplished anthology pieces as 'By the Statue of King Charles at Charing Cross' and 'The Dark Angel'.

In attacking Symons for his taste for low urban subjects, Johnson was drawing attention to another poetic preoccupation of the *fin de siècle:* if a tormented eroticism was one way of extending the range of poetry, a fascination with the multifarious life of the modern city was another. London was not, of course, a completely untouched poetic subject; Tennyson momentarily caught the anomic quality of urban life in a superb image in *In Memoriam:*

> He is not here; but far away
> The noise of life begins again,
> And ghastly thro' the drizzling rain
> On the bald street breaks the blank day.

Wordsworth treated London positively in 'Sonnet Written on Westminster Bridge' and negatively in the middle books of the *Prelude;* and there are dark visions of London life in Blake and the Augustan satirists. Yet the great exemplar for the *fin de siècle* poets was Baudelaire, whose poems about Paris had shown the intense but sombre poetic possibilities of the huge modern metropolis. A more romantic source of urban imagery was Whistler and other painters; Wilde wrote in 'The Decay of Lying':

> Where, if not from the Impressionists, do we get those wonderful brown fogs that come creeping down our streets, blurring the gas-lamps and changing the houses into monstrous shadows? To whom, if not to them and their master, do we owe the lovely silver mists that brood over our river, and turn to faint forms of fading grace curved bridge and swaying barge?

He had already shown a similar response in his poem, 'Impression du Matin', published in 1881:

> The Thames nocturne of blue and gold
> Changed to a Harmony in grey:
> A barge with ochre-coloured hay
> Dropt from the wharf: and chill and cold
>
> The yellow fog came creeping down
> The bridges, till the houses' walls
> Seemed changed to shadows and St Paul's

Loomed like a bubble o'er the town.

Among the Rhymers there were similarly romantic treatments of the urban scene; Richard Le Gallienne's 'A Ballad of London' indulges in the characteristic *fin de siècle* preference for the artificial over the natural:

> Ah, London! London! our delight,
> Great flower that opens but at night,
> Great City of the midnight sun,
> Whose day begins when day is done.
>
> Lamp after lamp against the sky
> Opens a sudden beaming eye,
> Leaping alight on either hand
> The iron lilies of the Strand . . .

Symons wrote copiously about London—his third book of poems, published in 1894, is appropriately called *London Nights*—and his treatment ranges between the romantic and the intensely realistic; he is usually most effective when he is most purely descriptive:

> The grey and misty night,
> Slim trees that hold the night among
> Their branches, and, along
> The vague Embankment, light on light.

One of the most striking of the poets associated with the Rhymers was John Davidson, a melancholy Scotsman of philosophical inclinations—he was one of the first people in England to be interested in Nietzsche—whose treatment of urban themes was realistic to the point of grimness. Perhaps Davidson's best-known poem is 'Thirty Bob a Week', the monologue of an impoverished clerk hopelessly struggling to keep up appearances and make ends meet:

> For like a mole I journey in the dark,
> A-travelling along the underground
> From my Pillar'd Halls and broad Suburbean Park,
> To come the daily dull official round;
> And home again at night with my pipe all alight,
> A-scheming how to count ten bob a pound.

T. S. Eliot wrote interestingly about his admiration for this poem:

> I am sure that I found inspiration in the content of the poem, and in the complete fitness of content and idiom: for I also had a good many dingy urban images to reveal. Davidson had a great theme, and also found an idiom which elicited the greatness of the theme, which endowed this thirty-bob-a-week clerk with a dignity that would not have appeared if a more conventional poetic diction had been employed. The personage that Davidson created in this poem has haunted me all my life, and the poem is to me a great poem for ever.

Davidson coldly appraised the newer aspects of the spreading metropolis in 'A Northern Suburb':

> In gaudy yellow brick and red,
> With rooting pipes, like creepers rank,
> The shoddy terraces o'erspread
> Meadow, and garth, and daisied bank.
>
> With shelves for rooms the houses crowd,
> Like draughty cupboards in a row—
> Ice-chests when wintry winds are loud,
> Ovens when summer breezes blow.

In such poems as these Davidson suggests a poetic equivalent

to the fiction of George Gissing. In a late poem, written not long before he died, Davidson turned to the fairly well-worn subject of the Thames and treated it in a way that is both realistic and richly textured:

> As gray and dank as dust and ashes slaked
> With wash of urban tides the morning lowered;
> But over Chelsea Bridge the sagging sky
> Had colour in it—blots of faintest bronze,
> The stains of daybreak. Westward slabs of light
> From vapour disentangled, sparsely glazed
> The panelled firmament; but vapour held
> The morning captive in the smoky east.
> At lowest ebb the tide on either bank
> Laid bare the fat mud of the Thames, all pinched
> And scalloped thick with dwarfish surges. Cranes,
> Derricks and chimney-stalks of the Surrey-side,
> Inverted shadows, in the motionless,
> Dull, leaden mirror of the channel hung.

The poets associated with the Rhymers were not the only ones who expressed a *fin de siècle* sensibility. I have already referred to John Gray, the author of *Silverpoints* (1893), a slender volume designed with infinite preciousness by the artist Charles Ricketts; Gray's poetry was of a matching preciousness—Lionel Johnson dismissed him as a 'sometimes beautiful oddity'—although some of it has a curious distinction; like Symons, Gray was very familiar with the French symbolists, and translated some of their verse, usually in a more restrained and laconic fashion than Symons. Another Catholic, Francis Thompson, continues to be well-known, at least on the strength of his 'Hound of Heaven': Yeats remarked of him in relation to the Rhymers, 'Francis Thompson came once but never joined'. Thompson's life of indignity and suffering makes him a signal embodiment of the late nineteenth-century myth of the *poète maudit,* and his Catholicism was more existential and less Paterian or aesthetic than that of his contemporaries. In literary respects, too, his perspective was somewhat different from theirs; his models were the Metaphysicals, particularly Crashaw, and Shelley, whom he saw, curiously, as fulfilling their promise. The influence of these poets is evident in 'The Hound of Heaven', which remains a vigorous if over-forceful record of spiritual adventure. In 'In No Strange Land' Thompson writes more calmly of mystical experience:

> O world invisible, we view thee,
> O world intangible, we touch thee,
> O world unknowable, we know thee,
> Inapprehensible, we clutch thee!
>
> Does the fish soar to find the ocean,
> The eagle plunge to find the air—
> That we ask of the stars in motion
> If they have rumour of thee there?

Another poet chiefly remembered as the author of a famous anthology piece is W. H. Henley; the poem is, of course, 'Invictus':

> Out of the night that covers me,
> Black as the Pit from pole to pole,
> I thank whatever gods may be
> For my unconquerable soul.

The rhetoric now seems a little stagey and unconvincing, though the poem's defiant spirit reflects Henley's own life-long struggle against physical disability. His most interesting work is the early sequence of poems called 'In Hospital', which dates from the 1870s; its exact descriptive realism gives it a surprisingly modern flavour. Henley also experimented with *vers libre,* and in his 'London Voluntaries' he treated a familiar topic, although in a more rhapsodic spirit than most of the Rhymers would have thought appropriate. Although his verse reflected something of the *fin de siècle,* in his role as publicist, critic and editor Henley was decidedly out of sympathy with anything that smacked of aestheticism or decadence. He favoured a robust, extravert attitude in literary matters, and in politics he was a vehement imperialist. Henley was a friend of R. L. Stevenson, with whom he collaborated in several works, and as editor of the *Scots Observer,* the *National Observer* and the *New Review* he sponsored such new arrivals on the literary scene as Kipling and Wells. The nineties was a great period for literary magazines: the *Yellow Book,* which ran from 1894 to 1897, is generally regarded as the quintessential expression of the *fin de siècle* spirit, although this was only true, if at all, of the first four numbers, of which Aubrey Beardsley was art editor; after the débâcle of Wilde in 1894, Beardsley was removed from his post, and the *Yellow Book,* although unchanged in appearance, became a sober middle-of-the-road publication. The spirit of the nineties was better captured in the *Savoy,* which was edited by Arthur Symons, and although it ran for only a few months during 1896, it was described by Holbrook Jackson [in his *The Eighteen Nineties*] as 'the most ambitious and, if not the most comprehensive, the most satisfying achievement of *fin de siècle* journalism in this country', Beardsley's drawings were prominent in the *Savoy,* which also published one of his occasional ventures into literature, the consciously decadent romance, *Under the Hill.* A prominent contributor to the early *Yellow Book* was Max Beerbohm; his love of witty paradox and his preference for the artificial as against the natural—his essay, 'The Pervasion of Rouge', is characteristic—made him thoroughly *fin de siècle,* but he always wrote in a spirit of ironical, mocking detachment, and his essays have lasted better than the work of his more fervid contemporaries. The wealth of literary periodicals in the nineties meant that the short story as a literary form was encouraged, and excellent work was done in this medium by Kipling and Wells and James. Closer to the *fin de siècle* spirit were English disciples of Maupassant like Hubert Crackanthorpe and Ella D'Arcy.

Considered as a literary period the 1890s was rich and various, and much of its best work was written outside the ambience of the *fin de siècle* mood. A comprehensive survey of the period would certainly acknowledge, for instance, in poetry, Kipling's *Barrack-room Ballads,* Housman's *A Shropshire Lad* and Alice Meynell's *Poems,* as well as the poets I have discussed. In fiction, the major achievements of the nineties include Gissing's *New Grub Street,* Stevenson's *Weir of Hermiston,* George Moore's *Esther Waters,* James's *Spoils of Poynton* and *The Awkward Age,* and Hardy's *Tess of the D'Urbervilles* and *Jude the Obscure.* The last-named of these does, in fact, embody a good deal of the *fin de siècle* state of mind, notably in the presentation of the neurasthenic 'new woman', Sue Bridehead, and in the grotesque child, 'Father Time'. H. G. Wells's *The Time Machine* is a highly distinguished piece of fiction which . . . is pervaded by *fin de siècle* feelings, little as one would normally associate them with Wells. And the picture would need to be completed by some consideration of Shaw's achievement in *Plays: Pleasant and Unpleasant.*

Yet to concentrate on what I have tried to isolate, however imperfectly, as the *fin de siècle* mentality is to stress what from Pater onward was known as the 'modern', and to emphasise those elements in late nineteenth-century literary theory and practice that were to be picked up by the Modern Movement in the early twentieth. In one sense the activity exemplified by the Rhymers did not last beyond the end of the century. As Yeats put it [in his introduction to *The Oxford Book of Modern Verse*]:

> Then in 1900 everybody got down off his stilts; henceforth nobody drank absinthe with his black coffee; nobody went mad; nobody committed suicide; nobody joined the Catholic church; or if they did I have forgotten.

(Yeats, in his habitual mythologising, *had* forgotten: Symons went mad and Davidson committed suicide.) And yet, in a deeper sense, the continuities between Pater and Joyce, and between Symons or Davidson and Eliot, are apparent. Yeats himself, who has appeared in this essay as a commentator rather than a creative participant, is the supreme example of a great writer of our century who was nurtured in the nineties, and who transcended the *fin de siècle* spirit without abandoning it. (pp. 20-39)

> *Bernard Bergonzi, "'Fin de Siècle',"* in his The Turn of a Century: Essays on Victorian and Modern English Literature, *Barnes & Noble Books, 1973, pp. 17-39.*

HOLBROOK JACKSON

[*An English essayist, editor, and literary historian, Jackson was closely associated with a number of London periodicals during his career, among them the* New Age, *T. P. O'Connor's* Weekly *and* Magazine, *and* To-Day, *his own journal which featured contributions from such prominent writers as Walter de la Mare, John Drinkwater, T. S. Eliot, and Ezra Pound. He is best remembered for his* The Eighteen Nineties: A Review of Art and Ideas at the Close of the Nineteenth Century, *a comprehensive study of late nineteenth-century arts and letters which is regarded as an invaluable documentation of that era. In the following excerpt from that work, Jackson discusses fin-de-siècle English culture.*]

In the year 1895 Max Beerbohm announced, how whimsically and how ironically it is not necessary to consider, that he felt himself a trifle out-moded. "I belong to the Beardsley period," he said. The Eighteen Nineties were then at their meridian; but it was already the afternoon of the Beardsley period. That very year Aubrey Beardsley's strange black and white masses and strong delicate lines disappeared from the *Yellow Book,* and he only contributed to the first few numbers of the *Savoy,* which began in 1896. Fatal disease was overtaking him, and remorse. Aubrey Beardsley actually abandoned his period in the evening of its brief day, and when he died, in 1898, the Beardsley period had almost become a memory. But, after all, Aubrey Beardsley was but an incident of the Eighteen Nineties, and only relatively a significant incident. He was but one expression of *fin de siècle* daring, of a bizarre and often exotic courage, prevalent at the time and connected but indirectly, and often negatively, with some of the most vital movements of a decade which was singularly rich in ideas, personal genius and social will. Aubrey Beardsley crowded the vision of the period by the peculiarity of his art rather than by any need there was of that art to make the period complete. He was, therefore, not a necessity of the Eighteen Nineties, although his appearance in the decade was inevitable; indeed he was so essentially *fin de siècle* that one can say of him with more confidence than of any other artist of the decade that his appearance at any other time would have been inopportune.

The Eighteen Nineties were so tolerant of novelty in art and ideas that it would seem as though the declining century wished to make amends for several decades of intellectual and artistic monotony. It may indeed be something more than coincidence that placed this decade at the close of a century, and *fin de siècle* may have been at one and the same time a swan song and a death-bed repentance. (pp. 17-18)

Max Nordau, the Jeremiah of the period, linked up his famous attack on what were called "*fin de siècle* tendencies" with certain traditional beliefs in the evil destiny of the closure of centuries [see Further Reading]. "The disposition of the times is curiously confused," he said;

> a compound of feverish restlessness and blunted discouragement, of fearful presage and hang-dog renunciation. The prevalent feeling is that of imminent perdition and extinction. *Fin de siècle* is at once a confession and a complaint. The old northern faith contained the fearsome doctrine of the Dusk of the Gods. In our days there have arisen in more highly developed minds vague qualms of the Dusk of the Nations, in which all suns and all stars are gradually waning, and mankind with all its institutions and creations is perishing in the midst of a dying world.

All of which sounds very hectic and hysterical now, nearly twenty years after it was first written, when many of the writers and artists he condemned have become harmless classics, and some almost forgotten. But it is interesting to remember Nordau's words, because they are an example of the very liveliness of a period which was equally lively in making or marring itself. The Eighteen Nineties, however, were not entirely decadent and hopeless; and even their decadence was often decadence only in name, for much of the genius denounced by Max Nordau as degeneration was a sane and healthy expression of a vitality which, as it is not difficult to show, would have been better named regeneration.

At the same time the fact must not be overlooked that much of the vitality of the period, much even of its effective vitality, was destructive of ideas and conventions which we had come to look upon as more or less permanent; and one cannot help feeling, at this distance, that not a little of *fin de siècle* attractiveness was the result of abandonment due to internal chaos. But this is no cause for condemnation on our part, still less for self-complacency; for, as we have been told by Friedrich Nietzsche, himself a half-felt motive force, in this country at least, behind the tendencies of the times: "Unless you have chaos within you cannot give birth to a dancing star." More than one dancing star swam into our ken in the last decade of the nineteenth century, and the proof of the regenerative powers of the period are to be found most obviously, but perhaps even more certainly, if not quite so plainly, in the fact that those who were most allied with its moods and whims were not only conscious of the fact, but in some cases capable of looking at themselves and laughing. *Fin de siècle* was a pose as well as a fact, a point not realised by Nordau. John Davidson, among others, was able to smile at its extravagances, and in *Earl Lavender,* his burlesque novel of the decadence, one of the characters, a garrulous Cockney dame with a smattering of French, reveals the existence of power to cast what Meredith would have called "the oblique ray" upon the

doings of the time. "It's *fang-de-seeaycle* that does it, my dear," says this lady, "and education, and reading French."

It is obvious, then, that people felt they were living amid changes and struggles, intellectual, social and spiritual, and the interpreters of the hour—the publicists, journalists and popular purveyors of ideas of all kinds—did not fail to make a sort of traffic in the spirit of the times. Anything strange or uncanny, anything which savoured of freak and perversity, was swiftly labelled *fin de siècle,* and given a certain topical prominence. The term became a fashion, and writers vied one with another as to which should apply it most aptly. At least one writer emphasised the phrase in an attempt to stigmatise it. "Observe," wrote Max Beerbohm, "that I write no fool's prattle about *la fin de siècle.*" And Max Nordau gives a useful list illustrating the manner in which the term was used in the country of its birth. A king who abdicates but retains by agreement certain political rights, which he afterwards sells to his country to provide means for the liquidation of debts contracted by play in Paris, is a *fin de siècle* king. The police official who removes a piece of the skin of the murderer Pranzini after execution and has it tanned and made into a cigarcase, is a *fin de siècle* official. An American wedding ceremony held in a gasworks and the subsequent honeymoon in a balloon is a *fin de siècle* wedding. A schoolboy who, on passing the gaol where his father is imprisoned for embezzlement, remarks to a chum: "Look, that's the governor's school," is a *fin de siècle* son. These are only a few from among innumerable examples illustrating the liveliness of the people of the Nineties to their hour and its characteristics. A further indication of the way in which the phrase permeated the mind of the period is found in its frequent occurrence in the books and essays of the day. It appears fittingly enough in Oscar Wilde's *The Picture of Dorian Gray,* that typical book of the period, as a reflection upon an epigram afterwards used in *A Woman of No Importance.* Lady Narborough is saying:

> "If we women did not love you for your defects, where would you all be? Not one of you would ever be married. You would be a set of unfortunate bachelors. Not, however, that that would alter you much. Nowadays all the married men live like bachelors and all the bachelors like married men!"
>
> "*Fin de siècle,*" murmured Sir Henry.
>
> "*Fin du globe,*" answered his hostess.
>
> "I wish it were *fin du globe,*" said Dorian, with a sigh. "Life is a great disappointment."

A reviewer of the novel, in the *Speaker* of 5th July 1890, describes Lord Henry Wotton as "an extremely *fin-de-siècle* gentleman." And another book of the period, *Baron Verdigris: A Romance of the Reversed Direction,* by Jocelyn Quilp, issued in 1894, with a frontispiece by Beardsley, is prefaced by the following inscription:—

> *This Book is Dedicated equally to Fin-de-Siècleism, the Sensational Novel, and the Conventional Drawing-Room Ballad.*

But side by side with the prevailing use of the phrase, and running its popularity very close, came the adjective "new"; it was applied in much the same way to indicate extreme modernity. Like *fin de siècle,* it hailed from France, and, after its original application in the phrase *l'art nouveau* had done considerable service in this country as a prefix to modern pictures, dresses and designs, our publicists discovered that other things were equally worthy of the useful adjective. Grant Allen wrote of "The New Hedonism"; H. D. Traill, of "The New Fiction," opening his essay with the words: "Not to be *new* is, in these days, to be nothing." In August 1892 William Sharp designed and produced one number, and one only, of the *Pagan Review,* which was written entirely by himself under various pseudonyms, to promote the "New Paganism," described as "a potent leaven in the yeast of the 'younger generation,' and which was concerned only with the *new* presentment of things." And again, in the famous attack on *The Picture of Dorian Gray,* in the *St James's Gazette,* on the first appearance of the novel in the pages of *Lippincott's Monthly Magazine* for July 1890, reference is made to "The New Voluptuousness" which "always leads up to bloodshedding." Oscar Wilde himself wrote on "The New Remorse," in the *Spirit Lamp,* in 1892. The range of the adjective gradually spread until it embraced the ideas of the whole period, and we find innumerable references to the "New Spirit," the "New Humour," the "New Realism," the "New Hedonism," the "New Drama," the "New Unionism," the "New Party," and the "New Woman." The popular, and what we should now call "significant," adjective was adopted by publishers of periodicals, and during the decade there was the *New Age,* a penny weekly with a humanitarian and radical objective, which, after many vicissitudes and various editorial changes, still survives; while William Ernest Henley, coming under the spell of fashion and carrying his modernism from the eighties, on the death of the *National Observer* started the *New Review.*

A decade which was so conscious of its own novelty and originality must have had some characteristics at least which distinguished it from the immediately preceding decade, if not from all preceding decades. The former is certainly true: the Eighteen Nineties possessed characteristics which were at once distinctive and arresting, but I doubt whether its sense of its own novelty was based in changes which lacked their counterparts in most of the decades of the nineteenth century—pre-eminently a century of change. The period was as certainly a period of decadence as it was a period of renaissance. The decadence was to be seen in a perverse and finicking glorification of the fine arts and mere artistic virtuosity on the one hand, and a militant commercial movement on the other. The one produced the *Yellow Book* and the literature and art of "fine shades," with their persistent search for the "unique word" and the "brilliant" expression; the other produced the "Yellow Press," the boom in "Kaffirs," the Jameson Raid, the Boer War and the enthronement of the South African plutocrat in Park Lane. But this decadent side of the Nineties must not be looked upon as wholly evil. Its separation from a movement obviously ascendant in spirit is not altogether admissible. The two tendencies worked together, and it is only for the sake of historical analysis that I adopt the method of segregation. Taken thus the decadence reveals qualities which, even if nothing more than "the soul of goodness in things evil," are at times surprisingly excellent. The decadent vision of an Aubrey Beardsley introduced a new sense of rhythm into black and white art, just as the, on the whole, trivial masters of "fine shades," with their peacock phrases, helped us towards a newer, more sensitive and more elastic prose form. The "Yellow Press," with all its extravagances, was at least alive to the desires of the crowd, and the reverse of dull in the presentment of its views; and if it gave Demos the superficial ideas he liked, it was equally prepared to supply a better article when the demand arose. And, withal, a wider publicity was given to thought-provoking ideas and imaginative themes, although adjusted, and often very

much adjusted, to the average taste, than had hitherto been possible. (pp. 18-23)

[The] chief characteristics of the Eighteen Nineties proper, although dovetailed into the preceding decade, may be indicated roughly under three heads. These were the so-called Decadence; the introduction of a Sense of Fact into literature and art; and the development of a Transcendental View of Social Life. But again, it must not be assumed that these characteristics were always separate. To a very considerable extent they overlapped, even where they were not necessarily interdependent. Oscar Wilde, for instance, bridged the chasm between the self-contained individualism of the decadents and the communal aspirations of the more advanced social revolutionaries. His essay, *The Soul of Man under Socialism,* has been acclaimed by recognised upholders of Socialism. And even his earlier aestheticism (which belonged to the Eighties) was an attempt to apply the idea of art to mundane affairs. Bernard Shaw, rationalist and anti-romantic apostle of the sense of fact, openly used art to provoke thought and to give it a social, as distinct from an individualist, aim; just as other and more direct literary realists, such as Emile Zola and Henrik Ibsen, had done before him, either avowedly or by implication. The more typical realists of the Nineties, George Gissing and George Moore, seem to be devoid of deliberate social purpose, but the prevalent didacticism of the period is strikingly pronounced in the work of H. G. Wells, who has contrived better than any other writer of his time to introduce reality into his novels without jeopardising romance, to hammer home a theory of morality without delimiting his art. But apart from such obvious resemblances between types of *fin de siècle* genius, the popular idea of the period looked upon one phase of its thought as no less characteristic than another. The adjective "new" as an indicator of popular consciousness of what was happening, was, as we have seen, applied indifferently to all kinds of human activity, from art and morals to humour and Trade Unionism. (pp. 26-7)

The Eighteen Nineties was the decade of a thousand "movements." People said it was a "period of transition," and they were convinced that they were passing not only from one social system to another, but from one morality to another, from one culture to another, and from one religion to a dozen or none! But as a matter of fact there was no concerted action. Everybody, mentally and emotionally, was running about in a hundred different directions. There was so much to think about, so much to discuss, so much to see. "A New Spirit of Pleasure is abroad amongst us," observed Richard Le Gallienne, "and one that blows from no mere coteries of hedonistic philosophers, but comes on the four winds." The old sobriety of mind had left our shores, and we changed from a stolid into a volatile nation. (p. 31)

The movement of the Eighteen Nineties . . . which has most engaged the attention of writers, the movement called "Decadent," or by the names of Oscar Wilde or Aubrey Beardsley, the movement Max Nordau denounced in Europe generally, and recently summed up by the *Times* under the epithet "The Yellow Nineties," does even now dominate the vision as we look backwards. And, indeed, though only a part of the renaissance, it was sufficiently "brilliant," to use one of its own *clichés,* to dazzle those capable of being dazzled by the achievements of art and letters for many years to come. For a renaissance of art and ideas which in literature had for examplars Oscar Wilde (his best books were all published in the Nineties), Bernard Shaw, H. G. Wells, Rudyard Kipling,

John Davidson, Hubert Crackenthorpe, W. B. Yeats, J. M. Barrie, Alice Meynell, George Moore, Israel Zangwill, Henry Harland, George Gissing, "John Oliver Hobbes," Grant Allen, Quiller Couch, Max Beerbohm, Cunninghame Graham, Fiona Macleod (William Sharp), Richard Le Gallienne, Ernest Dowson, Arthur Symons, Lionel Johnson, and A. B. Walkley; and in pictorial art, James Pryde, William Nicholson, Phil May, William Orpen, Aubrey Beardsley, E. E. Hornel, Wilson Steer, Charles Ricketts, J. J. Shannon, Charles Shannon, John Lavery, John Duncan Fergusson, J. T. Peploe, Charles Conder and William Rothenstein could not have been other than arresting, could not, indeed, be other than important in the history of the arts. For, whatever may be the ultimate place of these workers in literature and painting in the national memory, and whatever value we set upon them, then and now, few will deny that even the least of them contributed something of lasting or of temporary worth to the sensations and ideas of their age, or its vision of life, and to its conception of spiritual or mental power.

As to what individuals among these writers and painters were the peculiar products of the Eighteen Nineties—that is, those who could not, or might not, have been produced by any other decade—it is not always easy to say. In dealing with the writers the book-lists of John Lane, Elkin Mathews and Leonard Smithers are useful guides in any process of narrowing-down; and further guidance may be found by a perusal of the files of the *Yellow Book* and the *Savoy,* for these two publications were the favourite lamps around which the most bizarre moths of the Nineties clustered. There were few essential writers of the Nineties who did not contribute to one or the other, and the very fact that Henry Harland, who edited the former, and Arthur Symons, who edited the latter, were able to gather together so many writers and artists who were at once novel and notable, emphasises the distinction of the artistic activities of the time. But that emphasis should not be taken as indicating merely an awakening of virtuosity during the Nineties; the many definite artistic movements, embracing both writers and painters and craftsmen, could not have occurred had there not been a considerable receptivity among the people of the time. A renaissance of art depends equally upon artist and public: the one is the complement of the other. The Eighteen Nineties would have been unworthy of special notice had there not been a public capable of responding to its awakening of taste and intelligence. (pp. 34-6)

> *Holbrook Jackson, in his* The Eighteen Nineties: A Review of Art and Ideas at the Close of the Nineteenth Century, *1913. Reprint by Humanities Press, 1976, 304 p.*

ANDREW LANG

[Lang was one of England's most powerful men of letters during the closing decades of the nineteenth century, and is remembered today as the editor of the "color fairy books," a twelve-volume series of fairy tales introduced with The Blue Fairy Book *(1889) and ending with* The Lilac Fairy Book *(1910). A romantic vision of the past imbued Lang's writings, coloring his work as a translator, poet, and revisionist historian. Among the chief proponents of Romanticism in a critical battle that pitted late nineteenth-century revivalist Romanticists against the defenders of Naturalism and Realism, Lang espoused his strong preference for romantic adventure novels throughout his literary criticism and found little to comment from among the works of Realists or Naturalists. In the follow-*

ing essay, Lang responds to an article by Arthur Symons on the death of Ernest Dowson, Fortnightly Review, *June 1900, and denounces the fashion for Decadence in England.]*

What is a "Decadent," in the literary sense of the word? I am apt to believe that he is an unwholesome young person, who has read about "ages of decadence" in histories of literature, likes what he is told about them, and tries to die down to it, with more or less of success. Not pretending to have studied the subject much, I conceive that the later poets of the Greek mythology were decadents. They lived in a time when many things were on the wane, and they wrote little pieces, pretty and profane, morbid, maudlin, and, occasionally, loathsome. But Mimnermus, about a thousand years earlier, when Greece had not nearly reached her highest pitch of glory, was as decadent a writer as anybody. It was his nature so to be. His decadence was unconnected with national decay. Therefore, if decadence is "in" now, we need not think that all society is corrupt. Some rather cleverish persons wish to be thought up to what they regard as a decadent date, and that is all.

In the *Fortnightly Review* for June [1900] appears an article on a young gentleman recently dead, whom I shall call X. His name is given by the writer, Mr. Symons, but that is no reason why I should give the name. X, we learn, "was undoubtedly a man of genius"—in the decadent line, I venture to presume. The songs of poor X are "evasive immaterial snatches," expressive of "a life which had itself so much of the swift, disastrous, and suicidal impetus of genius." Unlucky genius! But why these epithets? Were Plato, Shakespeare, Voltaire, Scott, Sir Isaac Newton, Goethe, Wordsworth, or Sophocles, persons of "swift, disastrous, and suicidal" tendencies? Not they, and if Burns, Byron, Poe, Musset were certainly "fast," and more or less disastrous and suicidal, that proves nothing to the detriment of genius. There are thousands of rapid and disastrous young men who have no genius at all.

X was educated (more or less) at Queen's College, Oxford, where Mr. Symons thought he took haschisch, then "his favorite form of intoxication," but where he certainly did not take a degree.

Probably X had read Gautier's essay on haschisch, and tried it for fun, or to astonish the other Queen's men. Coleridge and De Quincey had genius, and ate opium. X took haschisch; it does not follow that he had genius. He had never read Dickens, but many persons, with no recognized claim to renown, are equally unfortunate. X belonged to a Rhymer's Club, apparently formed for the purpose of enabling the members to find somebody who would let them read their verses aloud. This acquiescence is very rare: speaking as a poet myself, I do not think I ever knew anybody who would stand it. But it is long since I made the experiment. X had "the face of a demoralized Keats," a friendly posthumous remark by Mr. Symons. His manner was "refined"; his appearance "dilapidated." "Without a certain sordidness in his surroundings he was never quite comfortable." By kicking holes in his boots, crushing in his hat, and avoiding soap, any young man may achieve a comfortable degree of sordidness, and then, if his verses are immaterial, and his life suicidal, he may regard himself as a decadent indeed. But whether, to get so little, it is worth while to endure so much, every poet must ask himself. Into the details of X's exquisitely evanescent love story, I do not go. 'T was not a market-gardener, but a waiter (perhaps a "plump headwaiter") that *she* married. "Did it ever mean very much to her to have made and to have killed a poet?" Mr. Symons asks. Probably she neither made a poet, nor killed one. Beginning with haschisch, at Queen's, and going on to "readier means of oblivion," poor X killed himself, if any one killed him. Again, into the chapter of "means of oblivion" I do not care to go, "the poisonous liquors of those pot-houses which swarm about the Docks." Were all these excesses due to the young woman who decided on the waiter? Probably not: beginning with haschisch a man soon comes to the dregs of the butt, to the lees of the wine.

In the matter of work, X wrote two novels, in collaboration, "both done under the influence of Mr. Henry James." This does not look like genius: a lad of genius, why should he put himself under the influence of Mr. Henry James? In another book the influence of Mr. Wedmore was combined with that of Mr. James. All this was extremely up to date. X had not read Dickens, but he had carefully studied Mr. Wedmore. In verse, "his obligation to Swinburne, always evident, increased as his own inspiration failed him." Clearly, X did not "draw fire from the fountains of the past," but of the present. Where are the signs of genius? Mr. Swinburne, I think, from his boyhood, wrote mainly under the influence of Mr. Swinburne. I dare swear Mr. James has been the chief influence in the writings of Mr. James.

> Surely the kisses of her bright red mouth were sweet,

wrote X [*sic;* the line, from Dowson's "Non Sum Qualis Eram Bonæ sub Regno Cynaræ," is "Surely the kisses of her bought red mouth were sweet"]. Perhaps they were, but the line is mere Mr. Swinburne. I remember as fine a line, on old cigar-ends:

> The ashes of the weeds of thy delight.

The poet's name is unknown. Again, X writes:

> I have forgot much, Cynara, gone with the wind,
> Flung roses, roses, passionately with the throng,
> Dancing, to put thy pale lost lilies out of mind.

Yes, but we are put in mind of Mr. Browning:

> It was roses, roses, all the way;

and of Mr. Swinburne:

> Lilies and languors of virtue,
> And roses and raptures of vice.

Without having read all X's poems, and with only a fragment or two, in the *Fortnightly* article, before me as examples, I express no opinion about the genius of X. Only it does not seem to be made very manifest unto men. Little imitative things, sad *épaves* ["wrecks"] of a life wasted on ideals out of Murger and Baudelaire: old, old, outworn fallacies, and follies, and affectations, these appear to be what is left. The story is a worn piece of pathos. The ideas of life on which X ruined himself have been the ideas of hundreds of boys, of whom the majority laugh at their past selves in a year of two. If this kind of existence, if these sorts of productions, be decadent, surely even boys must see that decadence is rather a mistake.With all its faults, there is more to be said for muscular Christianity. However, on this head one need not preach to the Anglo-Saxon race, which is already converted. (pp. 171-73)

Andrew Lang, "Decadence," in The Critic, *New York, Vol. XXXVII, No. 2, August, 1900, pp. 171-73.*

PAUL ELMER MORE

[*More was an American critic who, along with Irving Babbitt, formulated the doctrines of New Humanism in early twentieth-century American thought. The New Humanists were strict moralists who adhered to traditional conservative values in reaction to an age of scientific and artistic self-expression. In regard to literature, they believed a work's implicit reflection of support for the classic ethical norms to be of as much importance as its aesthetic qualities. More was particularly opposed to Naturalism, which he believed accentuated the animal nature of humans, and to any literature, such as Romanticism, that broke with established classical tradition. In the following excerpt from a review of Holbrook Jackson's* The Eighteen Nineties, *excerpted above, More offers a negative assessment of English Decadent literature of the 1890s.*]

Mr. Jackson has written a book [*The Eighteen Nineties,* excerpted above] that is at once excellent in understanding and perverted in its conclusions; nor, if one considers his theme, is this paradox as singular as it might appear, for it is a common mark of the condition which he expounds as apologist. His subject, with some excursions into alien matters, is the irruption of a sort of decadence into English art and literature in the closing years of the nineteenth century; and his quotations are so apt and abundant, his characterizations so clear and well-instructed, that one scarcely needs to go outside of his pages to form an independent judgment of the school, while the confusion of his own ideas when he tries to interpret the facts is an added document in evidence.

The movement, whose influence to-day is concealed because it has put on a new disguise, may be said to have opened with the publication of Oscar Wilde's "Decay of Lying" and *Picture of Dorian Gray* in 1890, and to have closed with his pitiful death in 1900. By the little band who were working so feverishly in the midst of the surrounding British philistinism it was thought to be the dawn of a new era for art—"a great creative period is at hand," wrote William Sharp. While at the same time it was felt to be the end of all things, and the phrase *fin de siècle* was whispered as a kind of magic formula. "It's *fang-de-seeaycle* that does it," says one of John Davidson's burlesque characters, "and education, and reading French." As one goes back to the productions of these men now, and particularly as one turns over the effusions in the early volumes of the *Yellow Book,* one is likely to be impressed mainly by a note of amateurishness running through their work. In comparison with the decadents of the Continent whom they attempted to imitate, they appear rather like truant boys who need to be spanked and sent again to their lessons. In the first issue of the *Yellow Book,* the "incomparable" Max Beerbohm prints "A Defence of Cosmetics," wherein he observes sententiously that "the Victorian era comes to its end and the day of sancta simplicitas is quite ended." The essay seems to us today, with the reek of Broadway in our nostrils, as childlike a piece of extravagance as could well be imagined; yet it succeeded in rousing a little storm of protest, and one solemn critic wrote it down as "the rankest and most nauseous thing in all literature." Another contributor, Lionel Johnson, asks, in surprise at his own naughtiness: "What would the moral philosophers, those puzzled sages, think of me? An harmless hedonist? An amateur in morals, who means well, though meaning very little?" And one is inclined to answer: "My dear sir, be comforted; the puzzled sages would not have thought of you at all."

Yet however we may, and do, pass by these books as largely factitious imitations, there is an aspect of the revolt that is serious enough in all conscience. The disease from which it sprung was no jest, and beneath the antic contortions of their wit these men were suffering the very real pangs of physical disorganization. It is in fact like a nightmare to read their lives. The hectic decay of Aubrey Beardsley is almost health in comparison with the state of most of those who gave to the movement its tone. Of the living we speak not: but there is Lionel Johnson, the best artist of them all, a victim of absinthe, found in the gutter with his skull crushed; there is John Davidson, with his vision of a new universe ended in mad suicide; there are Ernest Dowson and Francis Thompson, mingling their religion with the fumes of alcohol and opium; there are others whose tainted lives and early deaths need not be examined; and, above all, is the hideous tragedy in Reading Jail. These men, who appeared to be treading so fantastically in "the variant by-paths of the uncertain heart," knew also in the flesh the certain terrors of organic decay.

No, we shall do these men less than justice if we merely smile at their mopping and mowing as at the gestures borrowed of a jackanapes. They are worthy of condemnation. They had a real driving motive in the flesh, and they had their ideal philosophy. Through all their works, now in the form of direct argument, now implied in the symbol of verse or picture, you will find running the ambitious design of making life itself into a fine art, of welding life and art into one indistinguishable creation. As Oscar Wilde says of his hero in the book which is the completest manifesto of the school,

> There were many, especially among the very young men, who saw, or fancied that they saw, in Dorian Gray the true realization of a type of which they had often dreamed in Eton or Oxford days—a type that was to combine something of the real culture of the scholar with all the grace and distinction and perfect manner of a citizen of the world. To them he seemed to be of the company whom Dante describes as having sought to "make themselves perfect by the worship of beauty."

And with this coalescence of art and life, as its very source and purpose, was to be joined the garnering of sensations, in a manner which these young enthusiasts caught up from Rossetti and Walter Pater and the other virtuosos of the vibrating nerve. Thus, to the confusion of the Philistine, the Puritan, and the votary of common-sense, they were to create for the world a new Hedonism: "It was to have its service of the intellect, certainly; yet it was never to accept any theory or system that would involve the sacrifice of any mode of passionate experience. Its aim, indeed, was to be experience itself, and not the fruits of experience, sweet or bitter as they might be."

In this longing after the fulness of experience, without consideration of the lessons of experience, we come close to the heart of the movement, and we also see how it was no vagary of a few isolated youths, but was the product of the most characteristic evolution of the age. "It was," as our present guide rightly observes,

> the mortal ripening of that flower which blossomed upon the ruins of the French Revolution, heralding not only the rights of man, which was an abstraction savoring more of the classical ideal, but the rights of personality, of unique, varied, and varying men.

Personality was to assert itself in the direction of unlimited and unquestioned expansiveness, in the claim of the individual to be purely and intensely himself, in the free pursuit of those emotions and sensations which are the root of division among mankind, while denying those rights of man, in the classical sense, which mean the subordination of the individualizing desires to the commonalty of the law of reason. And, as life and art were to proceed hand in hand, personality was to manifest itself in a symbolism which should endeavor, in the words of Arthur Symons, "to fix the last fine shade, the quintessence of things; to fix it fleetingly; to be a disembodied voice, and yet the voice of a human soul. The final marriage of life and art was to be in the swooning ecstasy of music. There was nothing discordant between the toil of the artist to fix the quintessence of things in fleeting form and the insatiable curiosity of a chaotic egotism. Nietzsche had said it: "Unless you have chaos within, you cannot give birth to a dancing star"—an idea which Mr. Jackson has developed at hazardous length, thus:

> Indeed, when wrought into the metal of a soul impelled to adventure at whatever personal hazard, for sheer love of expanding the boundaries of human experience and knowledge and power, they [this egotism and curiosity] become, as it were, the senses by which such a soul tests the flavor and determines the quality of its progress. In that light they are not decadent, they are at one with all great endeavor since the dawn of human consciousness. What, after all, is human consciousness when compared with Nature but a perversity—the self turning from Nature to contemplate itself? . . . Not even a child has curiosity until it has experienced something; all inquisitiveness is in the nature of life asking for more, and all so-called decadence is civilization rejecting, through certain specialized persons, the accumulated experiences and sensations of the race.

There is no need to illustrate this philosophy by examples. Any one who has read Oscar Wilde's *Picture of Dorian Gray* may waive the pleasure or pain of going through the other productions of the school. Most of these writers, in fact, had a perfectly clear knowledge of what they desired to be and to accomplish. And not seldom they knew the fruits of their philosophy and experience, as any one may discover by turning over the pages of Mr. Jackson's book. The root of the whole matter lay in a febrile satiety of the flesh, in a certain physical lesion, which the sufferers, having no philosophy of moral resistance to oppose to it, translated into a moral fatigue. "It was as though they had grown tired of being good, in the old accepted way; they wanted to experience the piquancy of being good after a debauch." In this mood the literature of exquisite curiosity, whether veiled under the English cant of Epicurean austerity or announced more boldly from across the Channel, fell upon the dryness of their souls like a spark of fire upon parched grass. The consequence is set forth in Dorian Gray's discovery of *A Rebours:*

> It was the strangest book that he had ever read. It seemed to him that in exquisite raiment, and to the delicate sound of flutes, the sins of the world were passing in dumb show before him. . . . There were in it metaphors as monstrous as orchids, and as subtle in color. The life of the senses was described in the terms of mystical philosophy. One hardly knew at times whether one was reading the spiritual ecstasies of some mediæval saint or the morbid confessions of a modern sinner. It was a poisonous book. The heavy odor of incense seemed to cling about its pages and to trouble the brain. The mere

cadence of the sentences, the subtle monotony of their music, so full as it was of complex refrains and movements elaborately repeated, produced in the mind of the lad, as he passed from chapter to chapter, a form of reverie, a malady of dreaming.

There could not be a better description of the way in which art revealed itself to all the men of the group as a kind of narcotic for the torture of tired nerves, evoking under brush or pen the images of artificial dreaming, whether they displayed "the wan and saintly amorousness" of Burne-Jones's figures for "The Romaunt of the Rose," or waxed "fat with luxury" in the illustrations of Aubrey Beardsley, or flaunted the ghastly cosmetic rictus of Arthur Symons's creatures of the stage. Almost always behind the veil, and too often stalking wantonly into view, is the horror of an impotent sex-inquisitiveness and perversion. The subject is not agreeable to touch on, but any one who thinks such a statement too strong may satisfy himself by the frank confessions of their apologist. Beardsley, for instance, "loved the abnormal, and he invented a sort of phallic symbolism to express his interest in passionate perversities. His prose work, *Under the Hill,* is an uncompleted study in the art of aberration." The spectacular disaster of Reading Jail has so impressed our imagination that we are apt to regard its victim as a monster among his fellows, whereas in his heart of hearts he was probably less perverted than were many of those who went through life unscathed by public opinion. But if the author of *Dorian Gray* carried the outer brand, the wages of an evil mind fell upon them all. It is said of Aubrey Beardsley that he "introduced into art the desolation of experience, the *ennui* of sin." That is to take him, perhaps, a trifle too gravely, but there is something in the conduct of his later years that may at least remind us of Poe's decrepit "Man of the Crowd." "His restlessness," observes his friend, Max Beerbohm, "was, I suppose, one of the symptoms of his malady. He was always most content where there was the greatest noise and bustle, the largest number of people, and the most brilliant light." And that, adds Mr. Jackson, "is a picture of the age, as well as of its epitome, Aubrey Beardsley." The right of personality to reject "the accumulated experience" of the race, and to expand indefinitely in the search of sensations, turns out in reality to be in no wise "at one with all great endeavor," but to be in the main the unfruitful restlessness of satiety and impotence. (pp. 566-67)

Paul Elmer More, "A Naughty Decade," in The Nation, *New York, Vol. 98, No. 2550, May 14, 1914, pp. 566-68.*

G. K. CHESTERTON

[*Regarded as one of England's premier men of letters during the first half of the twentieth century, Chesterton is best known today as a colorful bon vivant, a witty essayist, and creator of the Father Brown mysteries and the fantasy* The Man Who Was Thursday (1908). *Much of Chesterton's work reveals his childlike joie de vivre and reflects his pronounced Anglican and, later, Roman Catholic beliefs. His essays are characterized by their humor, frequent use of paradox, and chatty, rambling style. In the following essay, he offers a retrospective assessment of literary and artistic Decadence, focusing on sterility and finality as qualities that led to the demise of the Decadent movement.*]

Most of us would agree in talking of that queer period called "The Eighteen Nineties" that, in spite of some very different

elements, it may justly be called the age of the decadents. The critic who would write truly of that age must be just severe and fastidious enough to smell poison in the period, but not too severe or fastidious to appreciate it in small doses. There are some for whom the unmanly moral antics in which that age ended are so horrible that they can have no patience with the quaint and harmless accessories. They have come to dread every dandy as a possible criminal; they think the praise of emeralds can only be a prelude to the drinking of absinthe; the praise of rubies only a prelude to the shedding of blood. I am not of such a temper. I think the jokes of the decadents extremely good—as long as they were jokes. I derived, and still derive a very positive literary pleasure from such fantasies as *The Sphinx.* I like fantastic moons to shiver in some stagnant lake. I positively request a scarlet snake to dance to fantastic tunes. I am very much gratified to hear that there is a hole "left by some torch or burning coal on Saracenic tapestries"; partly because it is such fun to think that the tapestries are spoilt. A small but strong pleasure is really given by these fancies; and can do no harm as long as we know they are fanciful. The mistake of these people was that they tried to turn dolls into idols.

> Sometime a horrible marionette
> Came out and smoked his cigarette
> Upon the steps like a live thing.

You are all right if you never fall into the error of thinking it is a live thing.

One can, I think, be genuinely interested in the arabesques of that artistic age; one need not be impatient with them; no nation which has to govern Oriental peoples should ever be impatient with arabesques. One should, I think, appreciate, for instance, the real delicacy (yes, and humility) of a man like Mr. Max Beerbohm—who is in a very true sense the "town" and all that is best in the town. But while we sympathize with these small things, we must also sympathize with some big things. We must realize that in *The Ballad of Reading Gaol* there is, after all, very little of the *bizarre* which its author generally pursued.

Fin de siècle is a phrase much used, and, I think, rightly so used, to describe the period of the Eighteen Nineties; tho one must, of course, see its lack of logic. A century has no hair; and it cannot whiten. A century has no teeth, and they cannot fall out. It was an arithmetical coincidence that the decay of the Victorian comfort and conviction occurred at the end of one hundred arbitrarily selected years. Yet, as I say, the phrase, tho not logical, is really significant; and for this reason: that the authors and artists in question were not only coming to the end of the century but to the end of everything. There was an element in their work not easy to define except by some simile of death. They were "the last word in art," or "the last word in criticism," not only in the general sense of being the newest, but in the literal sense that there was no more to be said. Their self-emancipation was suicide. If I may presume to imagine or imitate their literary method, it is not difficult to conceive their talking about it under the image of suicide. One might have said, "I would fling myself into the fire, if I knew it was of burning roses"; or one might say, "Haman was the most enviable of human beings. I would willingly hang myself, but my gallows must be higher than the stars"; or another might say, "If I commit the hara-kari I should not be thinking of the sanguinary pattern on the floor, but of the silvery pattern on the sword." One may like that style or dislike it; it is still true to point out that whether

Title page and first text page of Oscar Wilde's The Sphinx, *designed by Charles S. Ricketts.*

you burn yourself or hang yourself or stab yourself, your next stage of development is being what is known as "dead"; and, except in theological hypotheses, done with. *Qualis artifex pereo* is your last epigram; any other would be an anti-climax; and there are neither epigrams nor climaxes nor flatterers nor foolish ladies nor sycophants of the intellect in the grave, whither thou goest.

There was this sterility and finality in all their criticism. To take a case at random, one of them defined a woman as a sphinx without a secret. Given this, we can only say that the remark is interesting—and the woman isn't. In so far as a word can kill a sentence, or a sentence can kill a book, he will merely be acting like a barbarian who burned the library of Alexandria. If he is wrong, he has missed the secret; and even if he is right he has not increased the interest. If there is no secret there is no sphinx. As I have said, I warmly second the motion that a scarlet snake be induced to dance to fantastic tunes. But if it be finally settled that there are no snakes in Iceland, I will not go to Iceland and play fantastic tunes for indefinite periods to stimulate a snake who I know isn't there. The same killing of all further interest in the topic can be seen in the parallel pictures of women by a man like Beardsley. The portrait of a lady by Gainsborough or Romney may suggest almost any shade of morals or manners between Lady Hamilton and Mrs. Siddons. But every touch of the brush on dress or distance somehow suggests that the sitter, like the painter, had a thing called a heart, whether it led her right or wrong. Therefore she is still alive, and Meredith might have written a novel about her, or Shaw a play. But Beards-

ley, in black and white (both literally and symbolic) in lines as clear as fine print, does succeed in suggesting a woman without a heart. And to me looking at a heartless lady is as boring as talking to a headless lady. A headless lady (to borrow the ladies' phrase) has no expression.

What produced this, then, in all this period is the sense of the word "Finis"; with a Beardsley tail-piece. Despite the pure note of Francis Thompson, the purer element does not predominate. Thompson's words increased and multiplied to replenish the earth and subdue it. His thoughts *bred;* because he began with a thought that he really thought. But of most of them one thinks as of those terminal figures that Beardsley could draw. The head on the pedestal might laugh like Pan; and not merely leer like Priapus. But it is in every sense a terminal figure. It stands and smiles at the limit of our lives; and beyond it there is no road.

G. K. Chesterton, *"Writing 'Finis' to Decadence,"* in The Independent, *Vol. 89, No. 3554, January 15, 1917, p. 100.*

DEFINITIONS

ARTHUR SYMONS

[*While Symons initially gained notoriety as a member of the English Decadent movement of the 1890s, he eventually established himself as one of the most important critics of the modern era. In the following excerpt, he characterizes Decadent literature of the 1890s.*]

The latest movement in European literature has been called by many names, none of them quite exact or comprehensive—Decadence, Symbolism, Impressionism, for instance. It is easy to dispute over words, and we shall find that Verlaine objects to being called a Decadent, Maeterlinck to being called a Symbolist, Huysmans to being called an Impressionist. These terms, as it happens, have been adopted as the badge of little separate cliques, noisy, brainsick young people who haunt the brasseries of the Boulevard Saint-Michel, and exhaust their ingenuities in theorizing over the works they cannot write. But, taken frankly as epithets which express their own meaning, both Impressionism and Symbolism convey some notion of that new kind of literature which is perhaps more broadly characterized by the word Decadence. The most representative literature of the day—the writing which appeals to, which has done so much to form, the younger generation—is certainly not classic, nor has it any relation with that old antithesis of the Classic, the Romantic. After a fashion it is no doubt a decadence; it has all the qualities that mark the end of great periods, the qualities that we find in the Greek, the Latin, decadence: an intense self-consciousness, a restless curiosity in research, an oversubtilizing refinement upon refinement, a spiritual and moral perversity. If what we call the classic is indeed the supreme art—those qualities of perfect simplicity, perfect sanity, perfect proportion, the supreme qualities—then this representative literature of to-day, interesting, beautiful, novel as it is, is really a new and beautiful and interesting disease.

Healthy we cannot call it, and healthy it does not wish to be considered. The Goncourts, in their prefaces, in their *Journal,* are always insisting on their own pet malady, *la névrose* ["neurosis"]. It is in their work, too, that Huysmans notes with delight "le style tacheté et faisandé"—high-flavored and spotted with corruption—which he himself possesses in the highest degree. "Having desire without light, curiosity without wisdom, seeking God by strange ways, by ways traced by the hands of men; offering rash incense upon the high places to an unknown God, who is the God of darkness"—that is how Ernest Hello, in one of his apocalyptic moments, characterizes the nineteenth century. And this unreason of the soul—of which Hello himself is so curious a victim—this unstable equilibrium, which has overbalanced so many brilliant intelligences into one form or another of spiritual confusion, is but another form of the *maladie fin de siècle.* For its very disease of form, this literature is certainly typical of a civilization grown over-luxurious, over-inquiring, too languid for the relief of action, too uncertain for any emphasis in opinion or in conduct. It reflects all the moods, all the manners, of a sophisticated society; its very artificiality is a way of being true to nature: simplicity, sanity, proportion—the classic qualities—how much do we possess them in our life, our surroundings, that we should look to find them in our literature—so evidently the literature of a decadence?

Taking the word Decadence, then, as most precisely express-

ing the general sense of the newest movement in literature, we find that the terms Impressionism and Symbolism define correctly enough the two main branches of that movement. Now Impressionist and Symbolist have more in common than either supposes: both are really working on the same hypothesis, applied in different directions. What both seek is not general truth merely, but *la vérité vraie,* the very essence of truth—the truth of appearances to the senses, of the visible world to the eyes that see it; and the truth of spiritual things to the spiritual vision. The Impressionist, in literature as in painting, would flash upon you in a new, sudden way so exact an image of what you have just seen, just as you have seen it, that you may say, as a young American sculptor, a pupil of Rodin, said to me on seeing for the first time a picture of Whistler's, "Whistler seems to think his picture upon canvas—and there it is!" Or you may find, with Sainte-Beuve, writing of Goncourt, the "soul of the landscape"—the soul of whatever corner of the visible world has to be realized. The Symbolist, in this new, sudden way, would flash upon you the "soul" of that which can be apprehended only by the soul—the finer sense of things unseen, the deeper meaning of things evident. And naturally, necessarily, this endeavor after a perfect truth to one's impression, to one's intuition—perhaps an impossible endeavor—has brought with it, in its revolt from ready-made impressions and conclusions, a revolt from the ready-made of language, from the bondage of traditional form, of a form become rigid. In France, where this movement began and has mainly flourished, it is Goncourt who was the first to invent a style in prose really new, impressionistic, a style which was itself almost sensation. It is Verlaine who has invented such another new style in verse.

The work of the brothers De Goncourt—twelve novels, eleven or twelve studies in the history of the eighteenth century, six or seven books about art, the art mainly of the eighteenth century and of Japan, two plays, some volumes of letters and of fragments, and a *Journal* in six volumes—is perhaps, in its intention and its consequences, the most revolutionary of the century. No one has ever tried so deliberately to do something new as the Goncourts. . . . And in the preface to *Chérie,* in that pathetic passage which tells of the two brothers (one mortally stricken, and within a few months of death) taking their daily walk in the Bois de Boulogne, there is a definite demand on posterity. "The search after *reality* in literature, the resurrection of eighteenth-century art, the triumph of *Japonisme*—are not these," said Jules, "the three great literary and artistic movements of the second half of the nineteenth century? And it is we who brought them about, these three movements. Well, when one has done that, it is difficult indeed not to be *somebody* in the future." Nor, even, is this all. What the Goncourts have done is to specialize vision, so to speak, and to subtilize language to the point of rendering every detail in just the form and color of the actual impression. M. Edmond de Goncourt once said to me—varying, if I remember rightly, an expression he had put into the *Journal*—"My brother and I invented an opera-glass: the young people nowadays are taking it out of our hands." (pp. 858-60)

What Goncourt has done in prose—inventing absolutely a new way of saying things, to correspond with that new way of seeing things which he has found—Verlaine has done in verse. In a famous poem, "Art Poétique," he has himself defined his own ideal of the poetic art:

> Car nous voulons la Nuance encor,
> Pas la Couleur, rien que la Nuance!
> Oh! la Nuance seule fiance

Le rêve au rêve et la flûte au cor!

Music first of all and before all, he insists; and then, not color, but *la nuance,* the last fine shade. Poetry is to be something vague, intangible, evanescent, a winged soul in flight "toward other skies and other loves." (p. 860)

Joris Karl Huysmans demands a prominent place in any record of the Decadent movement. His work, like that of the Goncourts, is largely determined by the *maladie fin de siècle*—the diseased nerves that, in his case, have given a curious personal quality of pessimism to his outlook on the world, his view of life. Part of his work—*Marthe, Les soeurs vatard, En ménage, À vau-l'eau*—is a minute and searching study of the minor discomforts, the commonplace miseries of life, as seen by a peevishly disordered vision, delighting, for its own self-torture, in the insistent contemplation of human stupidity, of the sordid in existence. Yet these books do but lead up to the unique masterpiece, the astonishing caprice of *A Rebours,* in which he has concentrated all that is delicately depraved, all that is beautifully, curiously poisonous, in modern art. *A Rebours* is the history of a typical Decadent—a study, indeed, after a real man, but a study which seizes the type rather than the personality. In the sensations and ideas of Des Esseintes we see the sensations and ideas of the effeminate, over-civilized, deliberately abnormal creature who is the last product of our society: partly the father, partly the offspring, of the perverse art that he adores. Des Esseintes creates for his solace, in the wilderness of a barren and profoundly uncomfortable world, an artificial paradise. His Thébaïde raffinée is furnished elaborately for candle-light, equipped with the pictures, the books, that satisfy his sense of the exquisitely abnormal. He delights in the Latin of Apuleius and Petronius, in the French of Baudelaire, Goncourt, Verlaine, Mallarmé, Villiers; in the pictures of Gustave Moreau, the French Burne-Jones, of Odilon Redon, the French Blake. He delights in the beauty of strange, unnatural flowers, in the melodic combination of scents, in the imagined harmonies of the sense of taste. And at last, exhausted by these spiritual and sensory debauches in the delights of the artificial, he is left (as we close the book) with a brief, doubtful choice before him—madness or death, or else a return to nature, to the normal life.

Since *A Rebours,* M. Huysmans has written one other remarkable book, *Là-Bas,* a study in the hysteria and mystical corruption of contemporary Black Magic. But it is on that one exceptional achievement, *A Rebours,* that his fame will rest; it is there that he has expressed not merely himself, but an epoch. And he has done so in a style which carries the modern experiments upon language to their furthest development. Formed upon Goncourt and Flaubert, it has sought for novelty, *l'image peinte,* the exactitude of color, the forcible precision of epithet, wherever words, images, or epithets are to be found. Barbaric in its profusion, violent in its emphasis, wearying in its splendor, it is—especially in regard to things seen—extraordinarily expressive, with all the shades of a painter's palette. Elaborately and deliberately perverse, it is in its very perversity that Huysmans' work—so fascinating, so repellent, so instinctively artificial—comes to represent, as the work of no other writer can be said to do, the main tendencies, the chief results, of the Decadent movement in literature.

Such, then, is the typical literature of the Decadence—literature which, as we have considered it so far, is entirely French. But those qualities which we find in the work of Goncourt, Verlaine, Huysmans—qualities which have permeated literature much more completely in France than in any other country—are not wanting in the recent literature of other countries. In Holland there is a new school of Sensitivists, as they call themselves, who have done some remarkable work—Couperus, in *Ecstasy,* for example—very much on the lines of the French art of Impressionism. In Italy, Luigi Capuana (in *Giacinta,* for instance) has done some wonderful studies of morbid sensation; Gabriele d'Annunzio, in that marvellous, malarious *Piacere,* has achieved a triumph of exquisite perversity. In Spain, one of the principal novelists, Señora Pardo-Bazan, has formed herself, with some deliberateness, after Goncourt, grafting his method, curiously enough, upon a typically Spanish Catholicism of her own. In Norway, Ibsen has lately developed a personal kind of Impressionism (in *Hedda Gabler*) and of Symbolism (in *The Master-Builder*)—"opening the door," in his own phrase, "to the younger generation." And in England, too, we find the same influences at work. The prose of Mr. Walter Pater, the verse of Mr. W. E. Henley—to take two prominent examples—are attempts to do with the English language something of what Goncourt and Verlaine have done with the French. Mr. Pater's prose is the most beautiful English prose which is now being written; and, unlike the prose of Goncourt, it has done no violence to language, it has sought after no vivid effects, it has found a large part of mastery in reticence, in knowing what to omit. But how far away from the classic ideals of style is this style in which words have their color, their music, their perfume, in which there is "some strangeness in the proportion" of every beauty. The *Studies in the Renaissance* have made of criticism a new art—have raised criticism almost to the act of creation. And *Marius the Epicurean,* in its study of "sensations and ideas" (the conjunction was Goncourt's before it was Mr. Pater's), and the *Imaginary Portraits,* in their evocations of the Middle Ages, the age of Watteau—have they not that morbid subtlety of analysis, that morbid curiosity of form, that we have found in the works of the French Decadents? A fastidiousness equal to that of Flaubert has limited Mr. Pater's work to six volumes, but in these six volumes there is not a page that is not perfectly finished, with a conscious art of perfection. In its minute elaboration it can be compared only with Goldsmith's work—so fine, so delicate is the handling of so delicate, so precious a material.

Mr. Henley's work in verse has none of the characteristics of Mr. Pater's work in prose. Verlaine's definition of his own theory of poetical writing—"sincerity, and the impression of the moment followed to the letter"—might well be adopted as a definition of Mr. Henley's theory or practice. In *A Book of Verses* and *The Song of the Sword* he has brought into the traditional conventionalities of modern English verse the note of a new personality, the touch of a new method. The poetry of Impressionism can go no further, in one direction, than that series of rhymes and rhythms named *In Hospital.* The ache and throb of the body in its long nights on a tumbled bed, and as it lies on the operating-table awaiting "the thick, sweet mystery of chloroform," are brought home to us as nothing else that I know in poetry has ever brought the physical sensations. And for a sharper, closer truth of rendering, Mr. Henley has resorted (after the manner of Heine) to a rhymeless form of lyric verse, which in his hands, certainly, is sensitive and expressive. Whether this kind of *vers libre* can fully compensate, in what it gains of freedom and elasticity, for what it loses of compact form and vocal appeal, is a difficult question. It is one that Mr. Henley's verse is far from solving in the affirmative, for, in his work, the finest things, to my mind, are rhymed. In the purely impressionistic way, do not the *London Voluntaries,* which are rhymed, surpass all the unrhymed vignettes and nocturnes which attempt the same quality of result? They flash before us certain aspects of the poetry of London as only Whistler had ever done, and in another art. Nor is it only the poetry of cities, as here, nor the poetry of the disagreeable, as in *In Hospital,* that Mr. Henley can evoke; he can evoke the magic of personal romance. He has written verse that is exquisitely frivolous, daintily capricious, wayward and fugitive as the winged remembrance of some momentary delight. And, in certain fragments, he has come nearer than any other English singer to what I have called the achievement of Verlaine and the ideal of the Decadence: to be a disembodied voice, and yet the voice of a human soul. (pp. 865-67)

> *Arthur Symons, "The Decadent Movement in Literature," in* Harper's New Monthly Magazine, *Vol. LXXXVII, No. DXXII, November, 1893, pp. 858-67.*

CLYDE DE L. RYALS

[*Ryals is an American educator and critic. In the following essay, he defines Decadence as essentially a Romantic movement.*]

It is no longer fashionable to use the epithet *decadent* as a critical term for literature; indeed, when it is used at all, it generally indicates a critical stricture. Perhaps it has been so often employed by politicians to refer to practices not approved by the government in power that the modern critic would hesitate to use it at all. But there is, however, a definite need, in literary criticism at least, for such a term; and since the word is already part of our language, we might as well retain that term.

Let us immediately admit that the word, like such critical terms as *classical* and *romantic,* can only be an approximate label: it can—and does—mean many things to many men. But the fact that it does not have an exact one-sentence definition does not obviate its usefulness in critical writing. The epithet *decadent* does have a definite value, for some critical term is needed to differentiate further between the labels *classical* and *romantic.*

The debate over the meanings of these two terms has been a long and involved one ever since they were introduced by Goethe and Schiller, and it is too complicated for us to enter into here. We need only remind ourselves that the sole object in employing such terms is to keep in mind the characteristics of a period in which a certain work was produced and also to help us remember the tendencies of the period which influenced the particular work. Most of us will agree that when we speak of classicism we mean a culture which has achieved a synthesis of form and ideas in which there is almost perfect balance of forces, and that when we speak of romanticism we mean a culture in which the classical synthesis has begun to disintegrate and one force has outbalanced another. For example, we speak of Pope and Johnson as classicists and Wordsworth and Coleridge as romanticists, and by applying such terms to these writers we have more or less informed our readers of something of the culture which caused these men to write as they did. But if we restrict ourselves to this nomenclature concerning the writers of the eighteenth and nineteenth centuries, we have no approximate term by which to designate such writers as Walter Pater, Oscar Wilde, or Er-

nest Dowson; in fact, we have no term to indicate a whole phase, a phase which existed *sotto voce* to be sure, of the entire Romantic Movement.

With the exception of such poets as Gerard Manley Hopkins who were atypical of their time, modern criticism seems almost to have forgotten the poetry of the last quarter of the nineteenth century. Whenever it is mentioned at all, critics, even though they hesitate to use the term, refer to it sneeringly as "decadent." But almost no one has seen fit to define what the word *decadent* as applied to English literature of the late nineteenth century means. If it is to be used as a term of opprobrium, then it must mean, as dictionaries usually indicate, a deterioriation or a decline. But the decadence of the eighteen-eighties and nineties was not, as most critics are willing to admit, a decline from some classical standard. If it was a deterioration, then what was it a deterioration of? If we examine this question, we can, I think, see that the term, so loosely bandied about by the decadents themselves, is appropriate for the literature of the closing years of the nineteenth century.

The definition of decadence that I should like to advance is that decadence, as far as the literature of the nineteenth century is concerned, is but a subphase of romanticism and exists, in varying degrees of course, wherever the romantic impulse exists; that is, if romanticism is the state which results when the classical synthesis has begun to disintegrate, then decadence is the result of the complete disintegration.

Romanticism is itself an effort to achieve a synthesis: as Walter Pater pointed out [in *Appreciations* (1910)], romanticism finds its essence in a blending of strangeness and beauty, a mixing of unlikely elements; and this, of course, is the basis for decadence. Decadence undertakes not only to mix unlikely elements; it also seeks to mix them in ever more unlikely proportions, so that in a decadent work of art all sense of proportion is lost. The differences between Coleridge's *Christabel* and Wilde's *Salome,* for example, are only differences of degree. Both were born of that curious mixture of unlikely elements combined with the desire for beauty. But Wilde's play has gone further in its expression of the strange and the bizarre than has Coleridge's poem. Coleridge managed to keep these elements under control, maintaining a delicate balance between the simple and the complex, the plain and the grotesque; as an artist, Coleridge maintained control over his imagination. When he describes the strange transformation that Christabel undergoes, he assuredly is dealing with the bizarre:

> A snake's small eye blinks dull and shy,
> And the lady's eyes they shrunk in her head,
> Each shrunk up to a serpent's eye.

But Coleridge does not dwell on the grotesqueness of Christabel's snake-like appearance; immediately he shifts his attention back to the fair Geraldine, and thus the reader is never fully aware how grotesque the isolated passage quoted above really is.

Wilde, on the other hand, did not maintain a proper balance between the simple and the complex. In *Salome* Wilde is not content with simply showing the horror of the situation; he dwells upon it until it becomes grotesque. Salome takes the head of Iokanaan and goes through a long amorous monologue addressed to the horrible object. In seeking to add the element of strangeness to art, Wilde has allowed his imagination to run rampant and thus to distort his art by its very grotesqueness. And here we find the difference between romantic and decadent art: whereas romanticism expressed itself by maintaining an equilibrium between the natural and the grotesque, decadence found expression in distorting this balance and placing value on the grotesque at the expense of the natural. That is why there is no impression of spontaneity in decadent art, why decadent poetry is more complex than romantic poetry.

In both romanticism and decadence there is something of the unhealthy, of, if you will, the diseased; but this quality is so much more apparent in decadent art. Seeking always to find the curious, to mix strangeness and beauty in ever more unlikely proportions, the decadent turned to the pathological for expression. In all sorts of sexual aberrations he found subjects for his art. With Lionel Johnson the decadent seemed to feel that

> . . . all the things of beauty burn
> With flames of evil ecstasy.
>
> ("The Dark Angel")

And here the search for curious sensation led out of the sunlight of romanticism and into the shadows of decadence.

For a comparison of romanticism and decadence we need turn only to the different treatments of that poetic figure the Fatal Woman. Fatal Women have always existed in literature, but during the late romantic period, as Professor Mario Praz in his *The Romantic Agony* has made abundantly clear, English poets took her as their very own, Keats, of course, providing the prototype for the whole group. The figure, one might say, is the decadent equivalent of the Byronic Hero. If we compare the Fatal Woman with the Byronic Hero, we may be able to see the essential difference between romanticism and decadence. Romanticism, of which Childe Harold and Manfred were the outgrowth, was essentially a masculine state of mind. Occasionally a poet such as Shelley might hysterically proclaim, "I fall upon the thorns of life! I bleed!" but generally the mood of the romantic poet was one of virile, egotistic determination. Admittedly, romanticism, as we have suggested, contained something of sexual pathology, of the macabre and the diabolical; but working against all this there was a striving for humanistic ideals, which for the most part dominated the romantic impulse. Decadence, on the other hand, marked the virescence of a more feminine sensibility, characterized by a withdrawal from masculine reality. The decadent poet no longer writes about life, but rather about his withdrawal from life. "I broider the world upon a loom," wrote Arthur Symons,

> I broider life into the frame,
> I broider my love, thread upon thread;
> The world goes by with its glory and shame,
> Crowns are bartered and blood is shed;
> I sit and broider my dreams instead.
> And the only world is the world of dreams.
>
> ("The Loom of Dreams")

It is not surprising, therefore, that the romantic hero, symbol of masculinity, was replaced by the decadent heroine, the Belle Dame Sans Merci. Instead of the male dominating the female, as Byron's protagonists had ruthlessly done, the situation was reversed to the point where the female, the beautiful but sterile Eternal Woman, predominated over the male. As we follow the decadence from its roots in romanticism, we can see in an unbroken line the growing importance of the Fatal Woman, until at last she reaches her apotheosis in Pater's La Gioconda and in Wilde's Salome and Sphinx.

The interest shown in the androgynous and in such sexual aberrations as sadism was but another method for expressing self, and this expression of self is characteristic of the whole literature of the nineteenth century in England. Self-consciousness, or egotism, is part of both the romantic and decadent attitude. Byron's Manfred, the arch romantic hero, as well as Wilde's Dorian Gray, the typical decadent hero, could only proceed from an intense egotism. The romantic and decadent personality could never project beyond itself. All of Wordsworth's characters, for instance, are but different sides of Wordsworth's own nature, "an intense intellectual egotism . . . swallowing up everything," said Hazlitt. With the decadent, however, egotism developed into a more subtle self-consciousness, the result of which was an intense search for sensations, with special emphasis on what those sensations mean to the individual. Like Pater's Marius, the decadent personality sought for a life

> of various yet select sensation. . . . From the maxim of *Life as the end of life,* followed, as a practical consequence, the desirableness of refining all the instruments of inward and outward intuition, of developing all their capacities, of testing and exercising one's self in them, till one's whole nature became one complex medium of reception, towards the vision—the "beatific visions," if we really cared to make it such—of our actual experience in the world.

The romantic, however, managed to keep his egotism subordinated in some measure to the ideals of romanticism; that is, in romantic art, besides self there is always something other than self. In the case of Wordsworth it was the subordination of self to humanitarian ideals. The decadent, on the contrary, always keeps self in the foreground in his art; the self becomes the center of interest and the standard of value. Experience is valued for its own sake, the more varied the better. The decadent forgets that he is part of the universe and ignores his relationship to other forms of life. This in itself is decadence. C. E. M. Joad, in [*Decadence* (1947)], the only book-length work devoted to a study of decadence, says:

> Decadence, then, is a sign of man's tendency to misread his position in the universe, to take a view of his status and prospects more exalted than the facts warrant and to conduct his societies and to plan his future on the basis of this mis-reading. The mis-reading consists in a failure to acknowledge the non-human elements of value and deity to which the human is subject.

If we accept Joad's statement, we can see that romanticism in the early nineteenth century was always on the border of becoming decadent. The romantic hero like Manfred is ever verging on misreading his position in the universe; like Villier de l'Isle Adam's Axel, he withdraws in contempt from the world of men and retreats into a world of his own making. But even though the romantic hero is continually bordering on becoming a decadent hero, he somehow restrains his impulses and subordinates them to something other than himself.

The conflict between humanitarianism and self-oriented aestheticism is apparent in romantic poetry if we examine the poems of Keats. In *The Fall of Hyperion* the hero seeks to reach the summit of poetic knowledge, but before he can continue his quest he is questioned and told that

> None can usurp this height . . .
> But those to whom the miseries of the world
> Are misery, and will not let them rest.
> All else who find a heaven in the world,
> Where they may thoughtless sleep away their days,
> If by a chance into this fane they come,
> Rot on the pavement where thou rotted'st half.

Already romanticism was beginning to lose its humanistic ideals.

Often it is difficult to draw the line between romanticism and decadence. When Keats, for example, writes such lines as

> Dark, nor light,
> The region; nor bright, nor sombre wholly,
> But mingled up, a gleaming melancholy;
> A dusky empire and its diadems;
> One faint eternal eventide of gems.
>
> (*Endymion*)

It is almost impossible to believe that he has not crossed the boundary towards decadence. But despite his interest in the opulence of a "faint eternal eventide of gems," his fascination with such grotesque figures as the Lamia who became "convuls'd with scarlet pain," he still does not give his poetry over entirely to the bizarre. He might, as he says in the "Ode to a Nightingale," be "half in love with easeful death," but there is still the qualification "half."

Perhaps the difference between the early stages of romanticism and romanticism as it turned into decadence can be accounted for if we take into consideration the social situation of the nineteenth century. At the beginning of the century romanticism was a new force in English literature, and its advocates took to it with all the passion and frenzy which any new movement engenders. Romanticism heralded a brave new era. Men cried out for personal freedom, for the rights of man, for the cause of social justice; theirs was a striving for a new ideal. With the reform bills much of that which the romanticists had been seeking was accomplished; their ideals were transformed into realities. The problem then was to use this new power to bring about an even more ideal situation, and thus the emphasis changed from a romantic idealism to a more practical point of view. The individual champion of man's rights gave way to the committee.

Coming at the end of a long period of conflict and struggle, the decadents of the last quarter of the century had not these ideals to cling to. Humanitarianism had been taken over as the function of various agencies, which in their fervor had defended social justice as the practical ideal of a commercial society—the better off the worker was, the more money he would have to purchase the output of the industrial machine. The humanitarian function of romantic art had been usurped by the pragmatist. The writer of the eighties and nineties could no longer accept the humanistic ideal of romanticism, but yet he found himself still incurably romantic. He shared the romantic's distrust of reason, his concepts of beauty, his philosophical idealism; but he could not share his ideals. The only solution for the *fin de siècle* artist, therefore, was to accept the methods and basic concepts of romanticism without its ideals. This is why decadent art so often appears as a parody of romantic art, for romanticism devoid of ideals and taken to excess must necessarily result in an art which few modern readers can take seriously; in nearly every case it must appear to be factitiously contrived.

As a way of viewing man, romanticism in literature was the equivalent of liberalism in politics. Yet the so-called Decadent Movement was highly conservative, if not outright reactionary. The decadent of the nineties thought of his era not as the beginning of a new way of life, as the romantics had done, but as the culmination of the past. Such a sentiment was expressed by Ernest Dowson when he wrote that he was "only tired / Of everything I ever desired" ("Spleen") and by Arthur Symons, who cried "I tire of all but swift oblivion" ("Satiety"). Weary of his own time, the decadent longed for a former age, for tradition and traditional values. If the romantics turned from time to time to the past for some of their subjects, they did so as spectators of history, not with the desire to recapture the past for their own time. They were like English tourists off on a holiday to some exotic country, viewing the customs and dress-habits of the natives but not going so far as to don the exotic costumes themselves. With the men of the last decades of the century, however, this was not the case. Feeling the desolateness of their own age, they developed a nostalgia for other places and other times; they had, to quote Pater, "that inversion of homesickness . . . , that incurable thirst for the sense of escape, which no actual form of life satisfies, no poetry even, if it be merely simple and spontaneous." But this nostalgia itself was born of a romanticism which had ceased to be a truly creative force in art. Of this, Yeats, who so appropriately labeled the men of the nineties the "tragic generation," spoke when he wrote:

> We were the last romantics—chose for theme
> Traditional sanctity and loveliness.
>
> ("Coole Park and Ballylee, 1931")

This recoil from the contemporary world can be followed from the end of the Romantic Movement as such throughout the century in the works of Ruskin, Morris, Rossetti, and Pater until it reaches fruition in the cult of inaction in the nineties.

As long as romanticism maintained its ideals it was a positive force and a creative element; but stripped of its ideals, it became merely a method of escape from the world, destroying the ties which bind man to the universe. The romantic poet might cry out against the works of the gods, but he knew that he was subject to their rule and to natural laws; or if like the Titans he decided to war against and attempt to make himself the equal of the gods, he knew it was the gods who would win. Thus, the romantics placed their faith in hope:

> to hope till Hope creates
> From its own wreck the thing it contemplates.
>
> (*Prometheus Unbound*)

But the decadent poet has not this view. He has the arrogance to think himself not part of the universe; he is guilty of *hubris;* he does not cooperate with the moral machinery; and he has neither hope nor consolation. He seeks out experience not for its meaning in relation to other experiences, but experience as an end in itself. He cannot coordinate his experiences; he cannot order his own way. The results of such a philosophy account for that wistfulness and life-weariness of decadent poetry. Ernest Dowson put his finger on the cause when he wrote:

> we cannot understand
> Laughter or tears, for we have only known
> Surpassing vanity; vain things alone

Have driven our perverse and aimless band.
                                        ("A Last Word")

This was decadence, but essentially it was romanticism which had grown weary of itself and had turned back on itself.

Decadence in the literature of the nineteenth century was well characterized by Arthur Symons when he said that it possessed the qualities of "an intense self-consciousness, a restless curiosity in research, an over-subtilising refinement upon refinement, a spiritual and moral perversity." Symons was not accurate, however, when he wrote that decadence is "certainly not classic, nor has it any relation to that old antithesis of the classic, the romantic." Decadence is not only related to romanticism; it is an integral part of it. It is all too evident, if one goes searching for the origins of the Decadent Movement, that decadence had its roots in the Romantic Movement and was the logical outgrowth of romanticism, and also, insofar as romanticism itself was but an outgrowth of classicism's own discontent with itself, derived in part from the classic. It was a romanticism which, having grown tired of itself, inverted those values, for the large part humanistic values, which earlier romantics like Wordsworth had maintained to be the essence of romanticism. An aesthetic which sought the curious, the bizarre, and the strange and which placed value on revolt from the accepted order of things and the cultivation of the individual personality at the expense of social endeavor—all of which romanticism certainly advocated—could only lead to another aesthetic in which those searchings and those values would be taken to their logical ends.

Decadent, then, as a label applied to British literature of the latter part of the nineteenth century is not necessarily a term of critical stricture. Decadence, let us repeat, is simply a condition inherent in romanticism that proceeds from romanticism when the romantic impulse is not held in check. Once the romantic blending of strangeness and the desire for beauty ceases to be a perfect blending, that is, when the strange turns into the grotesque, then decadence must necessarily be the result. (pp. 85-92)

> Clyde de L. Ryals, "Toward a Definition of 'Decadent' as Applied to British Literature of the Nineteenth Century," in The Journal of Aesthetics and Art Criticism, Vol. XVII, No. 1, September, 1958, pp. 85-92.

RUSSELL M. GOLDFARB

[*Goldfarb is an American educator and critic whose studies of nineteenth-century literature include* Sexual Repression and Victorian Literature *(1970) and* Spiritualism and Nineteenth-Century Letters *(1977). In the following excerpt, he examines contemporary and modern applications of the term "decadence" as applied to English literature of the 1890s.*]

It is my purpose to give an account of how the word "decadence" has been used and what it has meant in descriptions of Victorian *fin de siècle* literature, the poetry and prose of the eighteen-nineties. Although occupying critics in the past, questions such as the following will here be ignored because they are tangential to definition: Is decadent literature indicative of moral insanity or what Max Nordau in *Entartung* [*Degeneration* (see Further Reading)] called *sittlicher wahnsinn?* Did decadence have the strength of a literary movement? Is decadence merely an imitation or weakened repetition of superior art forms? Does Victorian decadence have roots in

French or English literature? These questions have engendered much controversy, controversy that has perhaps obscured agreement among critics as to the fundamental meaning of decadence. If one is to understand what people do mean by the term, it is necessary to determine its significance by looking closely at only relevant accretions. The simplest way to do this is to isolate the separate traits various writers have attributed to decadence.

Popular contemporary impressions were revealed in satires written during the nineties. Max Beerbohm's essay in the first volume of the *Yellow Book* [April 1894], "A Defence of Cosmetics," is a case in point. Using a traditional satiric device whereby he says one thing and means another, Beerbohm begins his essay with the remark, "Nay, but it is useless to protest. Artifice must queen it once more in the town. . . ." Beerbohm means to protest about artifice because he thinks it to be the decadent instrument of insincerity, imposture, and artificiality. "And, truly, of all the good things that will happen with the full renascence of cosmetics, one of the best is that surface will finally be severed from soul." Artifice makes a woman "blush for you, sneer for you, laugh or languish for you." That is to say, artifice helps to create a pose; it hides all natural emotions. Beerbohm thought the most distinctive quality of decadent literature was artifice.

Better known than Beerbohm's essay, and probably the best known of the satires written about the eighteen-nineties is Robert Hitchens' *The Green Carnation*. To Hitchens, decadence was unconventional and exhibitionist behavior. One of his characters says, "I have been an aesthete. I have lain upon hearth-rugs and eaten passion flowers. I have clothed myself in breeches of white samite, and offered my friends yellow jonquils instead of afternoon tea." The same person exclaims:

> Eleven! I had no idea it was so early. I am going to sit up all night with Reggie, saying mad scarlet things, such as Walter Pater loves, and waking the night with silver silences. . . . Let me be brilliant, dear boy, or I feel that I shall weep for sheer wittiness, and die, as so many have died, with all my epigrams still in me.

It is noteworthy that Hitchens' attention is also engaged by the beliefs that art is independent of morality and that art is more important than morality: "There is nothing good and nothing evil. There is only art. . . . Forget your Catechism and remember the words of Flaubert and of Walter Pater." But although Hitchens says decadence is amoral, one of his contemporaries said that people who are opposed to decadence think it is immoral.

John Davidson expresses this notion in his burlesque novel, *A Full and True Account of the Wonderful Mission of Earl Lavender, which lasted One Night and One Day.* A character says, "I knew a woman who read French, and she ran away from her husband, and died of consumption. For it's in the language. My husband says it's rotten and corrupt, and he ought to know, being a chemist by examination." Another character is of the same opinion, "It's fang-de-seeaycle that does it, my dear, and education, and reading French."

The immorality of decadent literature especially concerned Jocelyn Quilp, whose *Baron Verdigris: A Romance of the Reversed Direction* is dedicated "equally to Fin-de-Siecyl-ism, the Sensational Novel, and the Conventional Drawing-Room Ballad." Probably with Oscar Wilde's defense of *The Picture of Dorian Gray* in mind, Quilp declares in the introduction to his satire, "My great object in this book, as in life, is to be Very Moral." Then with true satiric exaggeration Quilp goes on to draw a character, the Baron Verdigris, who is more criminal and more perverse than Dorian Gray. The Baron even pushes decorum to its extreme, for he has "a passion for having all the surroundings of his crimes thoroughly artistic and in harmony with one another."

Not one of these satirists' decadent heroes conforms to conventional patterns of Victorian thought and behavior. G. S. Street clearly considered the lust for unusual experience one of the most characteristic attributes of the decadent. Tubby, the hero of Street's *The Autobiography of a Boy,* has a theory of life which compels him to be sometimes drunk; he is wearily indifferent to all things, and he desires to be regarded as a man to whom no chaste woman should be allowed to speak; he feels old, sad, and weary, and distrusts people who are artistic because his own devotion to art goes far deeper than theirs. When Tubby's father tells him either to settle down or go to Canada, Tubby decides to hunt game in Canada. He remarks, "I have never killed a man, and it may be an experience—the lust for slaughter." Rather than marry, settle down, and take a share in the world's work, Tubby chooses to pursue a quest for unusual experience.

Many of the ideas held by *fin de siècle* satirists were extensions of impressions which were current in the eighteen-seventies and eighties about certain kinds of literature. For instance, Max Beerbohm's opinion of decadence as dependent upon artifice, insincerity, and imposture was an echo of Robert Buchanan's opinion concerning Pre-Raphaelite fleshly mysticism [*The Fleshly School of Poetry* (1872)]. Robert Hichens' satire of decadent eccentricity and exhibitionism was a continuation of the ridicule established in the eighties by George Du Maurier's caricatured aesthetes in *Punch* and Gilbert and Sullivan's *Patience* (1881). These ideas about Pre-Raphaelitism and aestheticism were intensified in the nineties when they were connected with decadence, which was more important in terms of popular appeal than either of its immediate predecessors.

But there is a sharp distinction between decadence as a popular and as a literary term. The authors of satires with market appeal had no use for the vocabulary and standards of formal criticism. They concerned themselves with exploiting popular ideas about whatever single quality of decadence best suited their purposes. To Max Beerbohm, decadence was artifice; to Robert Hichens, it was unconventional and exhibitionist behavior; to John Davidson and Jocelyn Quilp, it was immorality; to G. S. Street, the lust for unusual experience. After 1900 most of the people who wrote about decadence defined the term for use as a standard of literary criticism. They put together several attributes common to decadent literature and formed a definition. Two essays written in the nineties, however, did anticipate the transfer of popular ideas about decadence into what shall be called its critical idea.

In a letter published in the second volume of the *Yellow Book* [July 1894], Max Beerbohm explains the satirical intent of "A Defence of Cosmetics." He explains his intentions, Beerbohm says, because his essay on cosmetics was not signed D. Cadent or Parrar Docks and it was thought to be a defense instead of a condemnation of decadent values. Beerbohm has to "assure the affrighted mob that it [was] the victim of a hoax," that his essay, "so grotesque in subject, in opinion so flippant, in style so widely affected, was meant for a burlesque

upon the 'precious' school of writers." In his explanatory letter Beerbohm writes,

> There are signs that our English literature has reached that point, when, like the literature of all nations that have been, it must fall at length into the hands of the decadents. The qualities that I tried in my essay to travesty—paradox and marivaudage, lassitude, a love of horror and all unusual things, a love of argot and archaism and the mysteries of style—are not all these displayed, some by one, some by another of *les jeunes écrivains?*

Vague as he is in use of a phrase such as "mysteries of style," Beerbohm considers decadence a term descriptive of certain literary qualities.

Arthur Symons clearly illuminates the contemporary impression of decadence in an essay of 1893 entitled "The Decadent Movement in Literature" [excerpted above]:

> If what we call the classic is indeed the supreme art—those qualities of perfect simplicity, perfect sanity, perfect proportion, the supreme qualities—then this representative literature of today, interesting, beautiful, novel as it is, is really a new and beautiful and interesting disease.

Decadent literature was neither simple, nor sane, nor perfectly proportioned; it was rather the expression of "an intense self-consciousness, a restless curiosity in research, an oversubtilizing refinement upon refinement, a spiritual and moral perversity." Six years later, in *The Symbolist Movement in Literature,* Symons wrote that decadence was merely an interlude, a novelty of style. Whereas he once considered decadence the newest movement in literature, he now writes, "something which is vaguely called Decadence [has] come into being." Symons changed his mind because he thought the early literature of the nineties was only preparatory to a serious attempt "to spiritualize literature" under the banner of Symbolism; but he had once been eloquent in propagandizing decadence:

> To fix the last fine shade, the quintessence of things; to fix it fleetingly; to be a disembodied voice, and yet the voice of a human soul: that is the ideal of Decadence.

Both Max Beerbohm and Arthur Symons interpreted decadence as a literary term in the eighteen-nineties. Beerbohm's interpretation was somewhat murky: he thought decadent literature was unusual and mysterious. Of Arthur Symons, Holbrook Jackson has said, "during the earlier phase his vision of the decadent idea was certainly clearer than it was some years later, when he strove to differentiate decadence and symbolism." Later critics who have dealt with decadence have been largely influenced by Symons' earlier remarks.

The chapter of Holbrook Jackson's *The Eighteen-Nineties* entitled "The Decadence" is an extended description of Symons' early definition of decadence, a definition which is highly praised: "with the passing of time the term has come to stand for a definite phase of artistic consciousness, and that phase is precisely what Arthur Symons described it to be. . . ." Jackson presents the chief characteristics of decadence in summary fashion as (1) Perversity (2) Artificiality (3) Egoism, and (4) Curiosity. Decadent literature, he observes, was studded with the literary jewelry of purple patches and fine phrases. The decadents wrote of London rather than of the country because the city represented their love of the artificial. They adored the color white because white was symbolic of the debauchee's love of virginity. Jackson adds that the decadents also loved the cleanliness in unclean things and presented the sweetness of unsavoury alliances in volumes of "hot verse" or ornate prose—"hot verse" being used in the modern sense of poems dealing passionately with sexual themes.

Other ideas are dealt with by Samuel Chew in "Aestheticism and 'Decadence' " [see Further Reading]. He has this to say about Arthur Symons' verse, which he considers representative of English decadence: "In [Symons'] poetry there is a remoteness from contemporary society that expresses the point of view of the entire group of 'Decadents.' " Social problems did not concern the *fin de siècle* writers whose poetry was characterized by "the substitution of suggestion for statement; the effects of 'correspondence' of words and music and color; the dim sadness and misty unwholesomeness; the profound sensuality; and the reliance upon symbols." These characteristics, supplemented by qualities of morbidity, perversity, and "ephemeral sensualities," comprise Chew's notion of decadence.

The "misty unwholesomeness" of which Chew speaks is a reference to decadent immorality or amorality. C. E. M. Joad takes a stand on the issue of morality in *Decadence* [see Further Reading]: "Once the preoccupation with sexual morality is transcended, the alleged correspondence between decadence and lack of morality ceases to have any very obvious meaning. Writers who seem decadent are not immortal; the authors of books in which morality is 'loose' are not decadent." Exclusive of sexual morality, to be decadent is not to be immoral. And it would be absurd to call a man decadent solely because he goes to bed with somebody else's wife or with nobody's wife.

The chief tenet of decadence, Joad feels, is that "experience is valuable or is at least to be valued for its own sake, irrespective of the quality or kind of the experience." As a Christian, Joad thinks the doctrine deplorable, for if the flux of the experience becomes an end value in life, and if everything changes and dissolves at a touch, then there can be no absolute truth, no absolute beauty, and no timeless deity. A sign of decadent literature is praise of experience rather than praise of a timeless deity.

To say of decadence that aesthetic values prevail over moral values is to agree with Joad. Aaotos Ojala expresses this thesis in Part One of *Aestheticism and Oscar Wilde*. There is something static, narcissistic, satanic, and horrible in the decadent scheme of values, and the romantic castle of *Dorian Gray* in particular gives expression to this. "The spirit which inhabits Wilde's Romantic Castle is the spirit of Decadence. Romantics still recognize the values of moral and ethical ideas, but to the decadents art and intellect are the supreme realities." Jerome Hamilton Buckley carries this idea further; he says decadent literature was "animated by a conscious will to explore the dark underside of experience, with which the Decadent himself associated immorality and evil" [see excerpt below]. The chapter entitled "The Decadence and After" in *The Victorian Temper* is Buckley's attempt to characterize the literature of Wilde and his later disciples, Beardsley and his friends, the members of the Rhymers' Club, and the contributors to the *Yellow Book*. He says that the decadents, who were aware of their attributes and proud of their title, suffered world-weariness, emphasized the artifice of art,

looked to art rather than nature for their images and themes, sought the rarer enticements of sin, stressed all that was artificial, and were markedly addicted to imposture (in the sense that they lacked sincerity). Buckley's analysis of decadence is very similar to analyses presented in two unpublished doctoral dissertations—Robert D. Brown's "Joris-Karl Huysmans and the Bodley Head Decadents," submitted in 1952 at Indiana University, and Clyde de L. Ryals' "Decadence in British Literature Before the *Fin de Siècle*," submitted in 1957 at the University of Pennsylvania.

Brown contends that English decadence can be identified by the serious use of diabolism and artificiality. The typical decadent registers literary sophistication, boredom, lassitude, an unquenchable desire for new sensations, perversity, and neurotic interests. Ryals says much the same thing: decadence is characterized by "an emphasis on the pleasure of the senses; a fascination with the morbid, the strange, and the unnatural; the tendency to remain passive in the face of action and to preconceive reality." Having echoed so many critics, it is indeed difficult to understand why three years ago Ryals wrote, "Almost no one has seen fit to define what the word *decadent* as applied to English literature of the late nineteenth century means" [see excerpt above].

Fortunately, several people have seen fit to describe decadence and their repetitive descriptions clearly indicate fundamental agreement among them as to the meaning of the word. Thus, when any given critic uses the term, he can be assured a fairly knowledgeable audience. We understand that late Victorian decadence refers to poetry and prose which does not emphasize philosophical, historical, or intellectual concerns, but which does emphasize the value to be gained

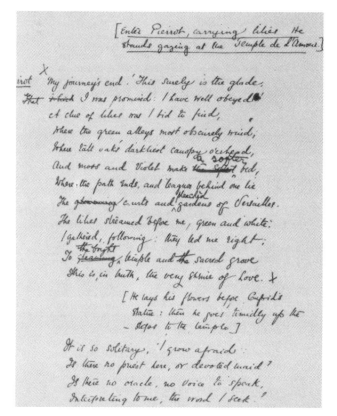

Manuscript page from Ernest Dowson's verse drama The Pierrot of the Minute.

both from experience of all sorts and from indulgence in a life of sensations. Because of this emphasis, decadent literature is animated by the exploration of immoral and evil experiences; never does it preach morality, nor does it strongly insist upon ethical responsibilities. Decadent literature is characterized by artistic concern for the morbid, the perverse, the sordid, the artificial, the beauty to be found in the unnatural, and the representation of the cleanliness in unclean things; it is characterized by a self-conscious and weary contempt for social conventions such as truth and marriage, by an acceptance of Beauty as a basis for life. (pp. 369-73)

> Russell M. Goldfarb, "Late Victorian Decadence," in The Journal of Aesthetics and Art Criticism, Vol. XX, No. 3, Spring, 1962, pp. 369-73.

R. K. R. THORNTON

[In the following excerpt, Thornton examines the use of Decadence as a critical term in nineteenth-century English literary criticism.]

The term [Decadence], although accepted even by the 'best writers' of the mid century, would perhaps not have had the popularity it did had it not been for Walter Pater. He used the term and was interested in many associated ideas, and he was the one man who claimed the respect of the new generation of the nineties as a whole. In 1873 he wrote of the poems of du Bellay that the Renaissance was 'thus putting forth in France an aftermath, a wonderful later growth, the products of which have to the full that subtle and delicate sweetness which belongs to a fine and comely decadence, just as its earliest phases have the freshness which belongs to periods of growth in art.' Again, when writing of 'Mr Gosse's Poems' in the *Guardian* in 1890:

> for a writer of his peculiar philosophic tenets, at all events, the world itself, in truth, must seem irretrievably old or even decadent. Old, decadent, indeed, it would seem with Mr Gosse to be also returning to the thoughts, the fears, the consolations, of its youth in Greece, in Italy.
>
> (*Essays from the Guardian*, 1901)

More significant than these comments, Pater praises the late Roman age in his seminal book *Marius the Epicurean* (1885), the golden book of many writers for some time. Here his carefully cadenced and delicately phrased sentences inevitably associate the ideas of style and decadence. (pp. 35-6)

Beerbohm's definition of Decadent qualities in his 'A Letter to the Editor' of the second *Yellow Book* depends on Wilde:

> There are signs that our English literature has reached that point, when, like the literatures of all the nations that have been, it must fall at length into the hands of the decadents. The qualities that I tried in my essay to travesty—paradox and marivaudage, lassitude, a love of horror and all unusual things, a love of argot and archaism and the mysteries of style—are not all these displayed, some by one, some by another of *les jeunes écrivains*? Who knows but that Artifice is in truth at our gates and that soon she may pass through our streets? Already the windows of Grub Street are crowded with watchful, evil faces.

There is indeed an increasing self-consciousness, and an interest in artificiality and the creations of man, that would lead to the literariness of Lionel Johnson, the poems on paintings,

the increasing concentration on form as subject, and the criticism of the *Yellow Book* within its own pages.

It was before the publication of Wilde's book [*The Picture of Dorian Gray*] that a newer interpretation of the word 'decadence' was brought into English, perhaps its earliest appearance being in an essay by Havelock Ellis in the *Pioneer* for October 1889. Swinburne and other Francophiles would have been familiar with the beliefs and names of French groups, but I know of no reference to Decadence in Swinburne. For his generation as a whole, reference to German writers, to Heine and Goethe, is far more common than mention of French authors, Gautier or Baudelaire. In October of 1889 Ellis wrote 'A Note on Paul Bourget'; Bourget . . . was the author of two books on contemporary writers, *Essais de Psychologie Contemporaine* (1881) and *Nouveaux Essais de Psychologie Contemporaine* (1885), which have a scientific approach which would attract Ellis. In them he studies authors who particularly embody various aspects of modern writing, Baudelaire, Leconte de Lisle, Tourguéniev, Amiel, Renan, Flaubert, Taine, Stendhal, Dumas fils, Edmund and Jules de Goncourt. He comes to the melancholy conclusion that all their work is profoundly pessimistic, a later expression of *le mal du siècle* (just as Symons was to see things as the results of the *maladie fin de siècle*), a result of tiredness with life and an attitude that all effort is vain. In the essay on Baudelaire, Bourget discusses the *Théorie de la Décadence*, and this section forms the point of departure for Ellis's comments. Bourget had stated that: 'Par le mot de décadence, on désigne volontiers l'état d'une société qui produit un trop petit nombre d'individus propres aux travaux de la vie commune' (*Essais de Psychologie Contemporaine*). Ellis translates the whole passage when he writes of decadence:

> Bourget uses this word as it is generally used (but, as Gautier pointed out, rather unfortunately) to express the literary methods of a society which has reached its limits of expansion and maturity—'the state of society,' in his own words, 'which produces too large a number of individuals who are unsuited to the labours of common life. A society should be like an organism. Like an organism, in fact, it may be resolved into a federation of smaller organisms, which may themselves be resolved into a federation of cells. The individual is the social cell. In order that the organism should perform its functions with energy it is necessary that the organisms composing it should perform their functions with energy, but with a subordinated energy, and in order that these lesser organisms should themselves perform their functions with energy, it is necessary that the cells comprising them should perform their functions with energy, but with a subordinated energy. If the energy of the cells becomes independent, the lesser organisms will likewise cease to subordinate their energy to the total energy and the anarchy which is established constitutes the *decadence* of the whole. The social organism does not escape this law and enters into decadence as soon as the individual life becomes exaggerated beneath the influence of acquired well-being, and of heredity. A similar law governs the development and decadence of that other organism which we call language. A style of decadence is one in which the unity of the book is decomposed to give place to the independence of the page, in which the page is decomposed to give place to the independence of the phrase, and the phrase to give place to the independence of the word'.
>
> (*Views and Reviews, First Series*, 1932)

The italicizing of the word, and Ellis's whole tone of explaining some concept new to the language, gives some basis for the suggestion that this may indeed be the first time the word is used with this application in English. Summing up Bourget's ideas, Ellis emphasizes style rather than subject, and includes some more names in the heterogeneous collection of writers who at one time or another fall into that category:

> A decadent style, in short, is an anarchistic style in which everything is sacrificed to the development of the individual parts. Apuleius, Petronius, St Augustine, Tertullian, are examples of this *decadence* in ancient literature; Gautier and Baudelaire in French literature; Poe and especially Whitman (in so far as he can be said to have a style) in America; in English literature Sir Thomas Browne is probably the most conspicuous instance; later De Quincey, and, in part of their work, Coleridge and Rossetti.
>
> *(Views and Reviews)*

Like Pater and like his friend Arthur Symons, Ellis insists on the style of Decadence rather than its content, but he does note the difficulty of the word when he notes that 'the style of decadence sometimes tends to represent what Baudelaire calls "la phosphorescence de la pourriture".'

Ellis, like most of the men who were to write on the topic, was familiar with France; not so Lionel Johnson, whose knowledge of France was largely academic, but who in April 1891 wrote an article for volume VI of the *Century Guild Hobby Horse*, 'A Note upon the Practice and Theory of Verse at the Present Time Obtaining in France', an article subtly illuminated by the appearance opposite its final page of Dowson's 'Cynara' (the same volume had as its frontispiece a reproduction of G. F. Watts's painting 'A Roman Lady in the Decadence of the Empire'). Johnson first identifies in France a 'spirit of excellent curiosity' (Arnold's term soon to be used by Symons) and, having spoken of older French schools, goes on to write of the new, again with the manner of explaining new ideas and relying heavily on French sources:

> But we have now to say the few words, possible to an English writer, upon the last, the newest, of the French schools: and it cannot be without great caution, great deference, great submission, that I must speak. So sincerely do I feel this; so well do I recognize the difficulty of criticism and the peril of wrong judgment, incident to writers upon a foreign literature: that I will stand aside, and let a more competent writer define the schools, to which belong, not, it may be thought, too happily, the names of *décadence* or of *symbolisme*.
>
> (pp. 37-40)

In English, *décadence* and the literature thereof, mean this: the period, at which passion, or romance, or tragedy, or sorrow, or any other form of activity or of emotion, must be refined upon, and curiously considered, for literary treatment: an age of afterthought, of reflection. Hence come one great virtue, and one great vice: the virtue of much and careful meditation upon life, its emotions and its incidents: the vice of over subtilty and of affectation, when thought thinks upon itself, and when emotions become entangled with the consciousness of them.

In English, *symbolisme,* and its literature, mean this: a recognition, in things, of a double existence: their existence in nature, and their existence in mind. The *sun sets:* what is the impression of that upon your mind, as you say the words? Clearly, that is the 'true truth' of the thing; its real and eternal significance: not the mere natural fact, but the thing, as it is in thought. So, literature is the evocation of truth from the passing show of things: a view, curiously like many philosophical views, from the days of Heraclitus to the days of Kant.

Now, in either of these schools, poetry becomes a matter of infinite pains, and of singular attention; to catch the precise aspect of a thing, as you see or feel it; to express, not the obvious and barren fact, but the inner and fruitful force of it; this is far from easy, far from trivial.

This is a fascinating article, written at a time when Johnson was looked up to as the theoretician of a group of young poets and one of their most able critics. From a purely verbal point of view, it is noticeable that he uses the French forms of Decadence and Symbolism, though one should not make too much of that since Johnson is rather a conservative writer. From the point of view of content, one must note the clarity of his definitions, his stress on the 'deliberate *science*' of the French poets, and his insistance on the need for technique. The magazine may well have had a small circulation, but it would have reached most of those writers who would be significant in the nineties.

About the same time as this article was published, another contributor to the *Century Guild Hobby Horse* showed the horror with which some Victorians looked at Decadence. In 'Michael Field's' diary for 1891, the fervent comment on the evening of Census Sunday, 5 April, was 'For oneself the prayer From decadence, Good lord deliver us!' It is probable then that the term was becoming popular a little before Johnson's article.

The conjunction of English and French traditions can be seen in Johnson's final paragraph, which may derive from his reading in French, but could equally well derive from Pater, who had written in the Preface to the *Renaissance* that

> To define beauty, not in the most abstract, but in the most concrete terms possible, to find, not a universal formula for it, but the formula which expresses most adequately this or that special manifestation of it, is the aim of the true student of aesthetics.
>
> 'To see the object as in itself it really is,' has been justly said to be the aim of all true criticism whatever; and in aesthetic criticism the first step towards seeing one's object as it really is, is to know one's own impression as it really is, to discriminate it, to realise it distinctly.

It is not far from here to Symons's description of Decadence, nor is it far from here to Eliot's 'objective correlative' which he defines in the penultimate paragraph of his 1919 essay on *Hamlet* as a 'set of objects, a situation, a chain of events which shall be the formula of that *particular* emotion.'

The two or three years after 1891 saw an explosion in the popularity of the word itself, though the ideas described as Decadent look familiar. Bourget had said the Decadents were pessimistic; *Punch* depicted 'Post Prandial Pessimists':

Scene—*The Smoking-room at the Decadents*

FIRST DECADENT. *(M. A. Oxon)* After all, Smythe, what would life be without coffee?

> SECOND DECADENT. *(M. A. Camb.)* True, Jeohnes,
> true! And yet, after all, what is life *with* coffee?
> (15 October 1892)

Obviously Decadence comes with an education, but by December of 1892 it is just part of the battle of the sexes in 'Snubbing a Decadent':

> HE. A—don't you find existence an awful bore?
>
> SHE. A—well, *some* people's existence—most decidedly!

Punch in fact drew a great deal of copy from Decadent poets in these years, among which Owen Seaman's satires, later published as *The Battle of the Bays* (1894), must stand high. The highest concentration of references to Decadence was in 1894. On 7 July 'Our Decadents' in the person of Flipbutt, a famous young art-critic, mistook a child's drawing for an impressionist work. On 14 July 'Our Female Decadents' preferred to sit out dances with an energetic but clumsy dancer. In the same issue, a playlet called 'Select Passages from a Coming Poet' contained pieces called 'Disenchantment' and 'Abasement'. It is not difficult to see the poetry being satirized here:

> My love has sickled into Loath,
> And foul seems all that fair I fancied—
> The lily's sheen a leprous growth,
> The very buttercups are rancid

or in 'Abasement':

> With matted head a-dabble in the dust,
> And eyes tear-sealèd in a saline crust,
> I lie all loathly in my rags and rust—
> Yet learn that strange delight may lurk in self-disgust.

To this last a character remarks, 'I rather like that—it's so very decadent!' On 27 October 'Our Decadents' (obviously a popular series) stand rather aesthetically saying:

> ALGY. What's the matter, Archie? You're not looking well!
>
> ARCHIE. *You* wouldn't look well, if you'd been suffering from insomnia every afternoon for a week!

And the Christmas number rounded off the year with its 'Britannia à la Beardsley *(By our 'Yellow' Decadent)*'.

While *Punch* was making fun, the discussion about Decadence went on. Richard Le Gallienne expanded the discussion of the subject in the *Century Guild Hobby Horse* in 1892. Indeed, in 1892 and 1893 he was often occupied with the topic. In letters to the pages of the *Daily Chronicle,* he (among nearly 2,000 correspondents) discussed Christianity and Decadence, and from these letters came his *Religion of a Literary Man* (1893) in which there is a violent attack on *'décadent'* art. Le Gallienne keeps the French word, as he had done in the poem 'The Décadent to his Soul', which he published in his *English Poems* (1892), obviously in an attempt to keep the blight away from English poetry. The introductory poem 'To the Reader' complains that

> Art was a palace once, things great and fair,
> And strong and holy, found a temple there:
> Now 'tis a lazar-house of leprous men.

'The Décadent to his Soul' makes a more specific attack. At one time the *Décadent* had thought that

> The body were enough,
> The body gives me all.

But seeing the attractive soul, he smiled evilly and

> dreamed of a new sin:
> An incest 'twixt the body and the soul.

So the *Décadent*

> used his soul
> As bitters to the over dulcet sins,
> As olives to the fatness of the feast—
> She made those dear heart-rending ecstasies
> Of minor chords amid the Phrygian lutes,
> She sauced his sins with splendid memories,
> Starry regrets and infinite hopes and fears;
> His holy youth and his first love
> Made pearly background to strange-coloured vice.

The accuracy of Le Gallienne's analysis is obvious if one puts this poem against Dowson's work, especially 'Cynara' which Le Gallienne knew. He quite rightly points to the tension between ideal and real, but sees it as perverse rather than tragic:

> Sin is no sin when virtue is forgot.
> It is so good in sin to keep in sight
> The white hills whence we fell, to measure by—
> To say I was so high, so white, so pure,
> And am so low, so blood-stained and so base;
> I revel here amid the sweet sweeet mire
> And yonder are the hills of morning flowers:
> So high, so low; so lost and with me yet;
> To stretch the octave 'twixt the dream and deed,
> Ah, that's the thrill!

Finally, Le Gallienne wishes to keep the soul and body separate, weeping for both because

> The man was once an apple-cheek dear lad,
> The soul was once an angel up in heaven.
>
> O let the body be a healthy beast,
> And keep the soul a singing soaring bird;
> But lure thou not the soul from out the sky
> To pipe unto the body in the sty.

Le Gallienne does not write a good poem, but it is perceptive of important features of Decadent writing, in particular the Decadent paradox.

Unfortunately he does not notice the paradox in his own book, between his stolidly English attitude in poems like the two I have mentioned and the Decadent view in 'Beauty Accurst'. E. K. Chambers brought this out among other points in a review of Le Gallienne's book for the *Academy,* which places Decadence effectively:

> The title of Mr Le Gallienne's book is designed, one gathers, to be a protest against certain latter-day tendencies in literature; and the protest is amplified in an address 'To the Reader', and in a very striking, clever poem called 'The Décadent to his Soul'. Mr Le Gallienne wishes us clearly to understand that he is on the side of the angels, and that he is not tarred with the brush of Verlaine, that his inspiration is manly and normal, not abnormal and morbid. . . . But whom is Mr Le Gallienne attacking? Is the note of decadence so strong in our younger poets, in those in whose hands the future of our poetry rests? If Mr Le Gallienne will look for a moment beyond the borders of the Rhymers' Club, he will surely see that it is not. Mr Robert Bridges, Mr William Watson, Mr Alfred Austin, Mrs Woods—

they are sane and healthy and 'English' enough; they have not made Cayenne pepper of their souls. And what has Mr Le Gallienne to say for 'Beauty Accurst'—la très belle *Beauté maudite?* Then again, the antithesis of 'English' and 'Décadent' is not a true one.

(*Academy,* 19 November 1892)

Le Gallienne rather weakly replied to this review, claiming he had in mind 'the tendency of modern English letters' rather than the 'work of any particular poet, the influences in the air, mainly critical as yet, which will inevitably, one may fear, affect the youngest generation of poets.'

Certainly he was frequently concerned with those influences in his criticism, attempting in a variety of reviews to define Decadence to his own liking. His usual argument was that Decadence failed to 'see life steadily and see it whole', though his poem had complained of remembering virtue in the midst of sin. In his 'Considerations suggested by Mr. Churton Collins' "Illustrations of Tennyson"' in the *Century Guild Hobby Horse* (vol. VII, 1892), Le Gallienne took up the argument from Lionel Johnson earlier in the same magazine, and tried to think out the question of literary Decadence.

> But what is decadence in literature? It seems largely to be confused with a decadence in the style of literature, which is not quite the same thing. Even that decadence is continually misunderstood—euphuism and quite proper organic refinements of style being continually confused with each other. Mr. Collins, and many others, continually assume that the mere exercise of conscious art in literature, the care of the unique word, the use of various literary means to literary ends, as alliteration and onomatopoeia, constitute decadence. To say this is to be forced to the absurd conclusion that the nearer an instrument approaches perfection, the more it becomes adapted to the uses for which it is designed, the less its value. The only decadence in style are euphuism and its antithesis, slang. . . .
>
> But decadence in literature is more than a question of style, nor is it, as some suppose, a question of theme. It is in the character of the treatment that we must seek it. In all great vital literature, the theme, great or small, is always considered in all its relations near and far and above all in relation to the sum total of things, to the infinite, as we phrase it; in decadent literature the relations, the due proportions, are ignored. One might say that decadence consists in the euphuistic expression of isolated observations. Thus disease, which is a favourite theme of *décadents,* does not in itself make for decadence: it is only when, as often, it is studied apart from its relations to health, to the great vital centre of things, that it does so. Any point of view, seriously taken, which ignores the complete view, approaches decadence.
>
> To notice only the picturesque effect of a beggar's rags, like Gautier; the colour-scheme of a tipster's nose, like Mr. Huysmans; to consider one's mother merely prismatically, like Mr. Whistler—these are examples of the decadent attitude.
>
> At the bottom, decadence is merely limited thinking, often insane thinking.

It may be the result of answering Lionel Johnson's attitude that this article is French orientated, but the same attack on French models is implicit in Le Gallienne's *The Religion of a Literary Man* (1893), especially since *décadence* is still set apart by its accent and italics as an unwanted import from France.

Speaking of the religious senses, he says that

> The Sense of Beauty, however, is not necessarily a religious sense—save in so far as it gives birth to the sense of wonder, of love, of gratitude. Curiously enough, in our own day, among what we call *décadent* artists, we find its influence not, as one would have expected, as a spiritualising, but as a materialising, an actually degrading, influence. Even when, as I make bold to say of its worst forms, *décadent* art is not merely the expression of moral mental and spiritual disease, lusts that dare no other operation finding vent in pictorial and literary symbolism, even when it retains a certain innocence and health, it does its best to limit its appeal to what we call the sensual faculties. It merely addresses the sensual eye and ear the more obviously, and endeavours desperately to limit beauty to form and colour, scornfully ignoring the higher sensibilities of heart and spirit.

It is an accurate enough description of certain theories of art then current to say that they are concerned with the sensual faculties. The 'Conclusion' to the *Renaissance,* about which Le Gallienne is so enthusiastic elsewhere, states that life itself is only realized through these faculties, and implies that symbols would be useless if there were no means of apprehending them. On the question of the morality of art, Le Gallienne is a little confused, wishing for the moral and yet understanding the need for the art of his day to be free from the restraint of conventional morals.

> Not, of course, that I mean for a moment that art must be definitely moral or didactic. It has nothing to do with morals—only, so to say, with spirituals. Many people seem to confuse the moral and the spiritual. As a matter of fact the spiritual must often of necessity be the immoral. A man's subject may be as so-called 'immoral' as he pleases so that he is able to treat it spiritually, or shall we say symbolically, in its relation to the whole of life.

He continues to argue that artists may claim to be dealing only with form and colour, but they cannot hope to paint a person without implying more than form and colour, as in the case of Whistler's portrait of his mother, because 'In the empire of life, art is but a province, and, like the artist, is subject to greater laws than its own'.

The arguments may be a little lacking in sharpness, but Le Gallienne had a good nose for a popular subject, and this was a popular book, running to over 5,000 copies. His main claim is something of a reiteration of his *Hobby Horse* article about the lack of proportion:

> This *décadence* is simply the result of that modern disregard of proportion of which I shall have to speak again. It would almost seem that the relative spirit has carried us so far that we have come to deny not only ultimates, but relations also. *Décadence* is founded on a natural impossibility to start with. It attempts the delineation of certain things and aspects *in vacuo,* isolated from all their relations to other things and their dependence on the great laws of life. Its position is as absurd as that of an artist who should say: I will paint this figure in but two dimensions, and will give it no length; or one who would say: I will paint this summer

landscape, but omit all reference to sunlight. So hardly less vainly does the *décadent* attempt to ignore certain conditions of his theme, which, actually, it is impossible to ignore.

And so we are treated to Baudelaire's prismatic hues of corruption once again. Le Gallienne fails to notice that the impossibility of the task is recognized by Decadent writers and is itself a cause of much of the parody and the anguish in Decadent writing.

Because of Le Gallienne's popularity, let me reproduce two further sections from his book which are not so commonly reprinted as his other versions of Decadence. First, he acknowledges that his book will be rejected by

> the typical literary man of the period, who sips his absinthe (with a charmingly boyish sense of sin), and reads Huysmans. To discuss such antiquated matters as God, Love, and Duty, when one might be wrangling over Degas, or grappling with a sonnet by Mallarmé!

Obviously the Decadent again, who is further analysed in a section called 'The Dream of the Décadent':

> But in other guises, that dog-fighter is still with us. His latest evangel has been that of the demi-monde and the music-hall. Soon, he has prophesied, 'domesticity' with all its irksome restraints, shall be no more. Repent, for a Walpurgis night is at hand when men and women shall once more run on all fours as dogs, and revel in the offal of the streets. O happy era of liberty, when the talon is free of the sheath for ever, and lust may run without his muzzle; when every one may be as indecent as his heart wishes, and he who loves the gutter may lie therein without reproach; when no man takes off the hat to a woman or a church, but all may wear it jauntily on one side, through the length and breadth of the land, may smoke and drink unmoved before the sacred passion-play of life, and expectorate with a fine carelessness, none daring to make them afraid! Such is the dream of the poor little sensual 'dog-fighter' of our days. Instead of dogs he sells us beastly and silly novels, poetry he dare not expose for sale at Farringdon market, and pathetic 'advanced' science which runs thus: 'It is a sad mission to cut through and destroy with the scissors of analysis the delicate and iridescent veils with which our proud mediocrity clothes itself. Very terrible is the religion of truth. The physiologist is not afraid to reduce love to a play of stamens and pistils, and thought to a molecular movement. Even genius, the one human power before which we may bow the knee without shame, has been classed by not a few alienists as on the confines of criminality, one of the tetralogic forms of the human mind, a variety of insanity.' But shall we despair of man's soul because, forsooth! a Lombroso cannot find it, or of love because Paul Verlaine is a satyr, of religion and law because a mad poet fires his little pistol at Westminster. I think not. What are all these men but dirty children building their mud-pies, and soon oblivion, like an indignant mother, shall send them all to bed.
>
> The spring of a new era is in the air—an era of faith. That prophesied Walpurgis night is already behind us; and except in the imagination of a handful of ill-conditioned writers, artists, and 'thinkers', who have written and painted and 'thought' for each other, it never had even any potential existence.

The passage is interesting for its detail, and for placing Le Gallienne against both Verlaine and Lombroso—where would he stand when he read Nordau's Lombroso-inspired attacks on Verlaine?

Le Gallienne is himself trapped in the Decadent dilemma, writing on obviously Decadent themes in his 'Beauty Accurst' and 'A Ballad of London', while longing for religious acceptability and expressing his faith in a separate book on religion and Literature. How appropriate then for him to review John Gray, a poet who expressed the opposing sides of his character in his *Silverpoints* and his *Spiritual Poems* (1896). Reviewing the former when it came out in 1893, Le Gallienne found it not Decadent, a curious conclusion when one considers that it is often regarded as the epitome of Decadent book-production, that it imitates and translates from Decadent poets like Baudelaire and Verlaine, and even uses the line from the Decadent poem 'Langueur' to set the tone. Le Gallienne reiterates his earlier ideas about proportion, and gives a detailed picture of what he associates with Decadence:

> Mr Gray's poems are not so decadent as he would have us suppose. They are luxurious to the last degree, they are subtly cadenced as the song the sirens sang, they will dwell over-unctuously on many forbidden themes—'many whisper things I dare not tell'—they are each separately dedicated to every more or less decadent poet of Mr Gray's acquaintance, and their *format;* an adaptation of the Aldine italic books, is of a far-wrought deliciousness.
>
> But in spite of his neo-Catholicism and his hot-house erotics, Mr Gray cannot accomplish that gloating abstraction from the larger life of humanity which marks the decadent.
>
> (*Retrospective Reviews,* 1896)

And having quoted a stanza ending 'What bonny hair our child will have!' he concludes 'Is this not absurdly domestic in a decadent? Really Mr Gray must check these natural impulses.' The luxuriousness of the poem, the perhaps literally deathly pallor of the lady, seem to have escaped him. The lady is another of those attractive and impossible women—'Bud and fruit are always ripe' as Gray has it—of the Decadent ideal.

Le Gallienne follows the general pattern of writers who were both involved in the controversy of the 1890s and wrote of it later, in that he is less willing in 1926 to have the writers of the period gathered under the flag of Decadence. In his *The Romantic '90s* (1926) he says that

> The *Yellow Book* has become the symbol of the period, and the two or three writers and artists to whom the word 'decadence' may perhaps be applied have been taken as characteristic of a time which was far from being all 'yellow', or 'naughty', or 'decadent'.

In the end, all that he sees the group of writers most closely associated with Decadence to have in common is a publisher, John Lane. Vincent O'Sullivan, who published books in the nineties with the imprint of Leonard Smithers and designs by Beardsley, shares this rejection of the label in his *Opinions,* blaming it all on Arthur Symons who, he says, 'though he was perhaps the only decadent in London . . . has managed to pass into history as the leader of a definite movement called Decadent'.

Symons is unquestionably the central Decadent writer. Intimate with Havelock Ellis, whose early essay on Bourget may have introduced the topic to this country, Symons went to Paris in 1889 and 1890 and consolidated his ideas about contemporary French schools of literature. Ellis, with whom he went, was finding out what was going on in medical and anthropological quarters, while Symons was getting first-hand information on trends in art and literature, but they must have shared each other's interests (there is an intriguing possibility of close links between medical and scientific discoveries and the vocabulary of Decadence). During their stay, they met many of the leaders of the Decadent movement, and others associated with it, Verlaine, Mallarmé, Rodin and Odilon Redon, and Huysmans, to whom they were introduced by Remy de Gourmont.

It was thus with first-hand knowledge of the facts and with Havelock Ellis's comments on Bourget's interpretation of Decadence that Symons began to use the term, but he is by no means whole-heartedly in support of either '*Décadents*' or '*Symbolistes*' in these early days, as one can see from his review of Verlaine's *Bonheur:*

> He has done what Goncourt has done in his prose: he has contributed to the destruction of a classical language, which, within its narrow limits, had its own perfection. But how great a gain there has been, along with this inevitable loss! In the hands of the noisy little school of *Décadents*, the brain-sick little school of *Symbolistes,* both claiming Verlaine as a master, these innovations have of course been carried to the furthest limits of caricature.
>
> (*Academy,* 18 April 1891)

Edmund Gosse defends this position of Symons's in the *Academy* for 7 January 1893, saying that 'if the school has had a single friend in England, it has been Mr. Arthur Symons, one of the most brilliant of the younger poets; and even he has been interested, I think, more in M. Verlaine than in the Symbolists and Décadents proper'. But in 1893 Symons seems more disposed to accept the title of Decadent, although he still makes reservations about the extremes, in his article on 'The Decadent Movement in Literature' [excerpted above].

This article, more than any other, whether by Le Gallienne, Johnson or Ellis, has had the most far-reaching effect on subsequent accounts and criticisms of the Decadent movement in England. For the first time the movement was not merely described, but vigorously defended and praised, and the movement was seen as a European rather than a merely French phenomenon. Walter Pater was linked with the school and, in more detail, W. E. Henley was praised for doing in English the things that the French Decadents had done. Again the controversialist of the nineties developed into a less partial observer in the twentieth century, for when the essay was reprinted in *Dramatis Personae* (1925), all matter describing the Decadence in England is omitted. Perhaps after the response to the Wilde trial, Henley could hardly be said to deserve the name of Decadent.

I make no apology for quoting at length from this central statement of Decadent ideas. It is the most extended, authoritative and influential statement and, more important, it dates from the central years of the movement. Symons explains his terms in the opening paragraphs:

> The latest movement in European literature has been called by many names, none of them quite exact or comprehensive—Decadence, Symbolism,

Impressionism, for instance. It is easy to dispute over words, and we shall find that Verlaine objects to being called a Decadent, Maeterlinck to being called a Symbolist, Huysmans to being called an Impressionist. These terms, as it happens, have been adopted as the badge of little separate cliques, noisy, brainsick young people who haunt the brasseries of the Boulevard Saint-Michel, and exhaust their ingenuities in theorizing over the works they cannot write. But, taken frankly as epithets which express their own meaning, both Impressionism and Symbolism convey some notion of that new kind of literature which is more broadly characterized by the word Decadence.

The last sentence is a little unhelpful, but, probably deriving his ideas about classical Decadences as much from Lionel Johnson as from his own reading in those Decadent authors, Symons does give some particular qualities that help to define Decadence:

> The most representative literature of the day—the writing which appeals to, which has done so much to form, the younger generation—is certainly not classic, nor has it any relation with that old antithesis of the Classic, the Romantic. After a fashion it is no doubt a decadence: it has all the qualities that mark the end of great periods, the qualities that we find in the Greek, the Latin, decadence: an intense self-consciousness, a restless curiosity in research, an over-subtilizing refinement upon refinement, a spiritual and moral perversity. If what we call the classic is indeed the supreme art—those qualities of perfect simplicity, perfect sanity, perfect proportion, the supreme qualities—then this representative literature of to-day, interesting, beautiful, novel as it is, is really a new and beautiful and interesting disease.

For Symons at this time, Decadence is both a style and an attitude towards content, both characterized by their newness, their lack of relation to what has gone before, although he does pick up and express forcibly that idea which had been present in Baudelaire which associates corruption both of language and subject with Decadence: 'Healthy we cannot call it, and healthy it does not wish to be considered.' Diseased or not, Symons defends Decadent art against the classic, since it depicts what it must, life as it is around it:

> For its very disease of form, this literature is certainly typical of a civilization grown over-luxurious, over-inquiring, too languid for the relief of action, too uncertain for any emphasis in opinion or in conduct. It reflects all the moods, all the manners, of a sophisticated society; its very artificiality is a way of being true to nature: simplicity, sanity, proportion—the classic qualities—how much do we possess them in our life, our surroundings, that we should look to find them in our literature—so evidently the literature of a decadence?

He takes the word Decadence as 'most precisely expressing the general sense of the newest movement in literature' and defines its qualities as novelty, artificiality, self-consciousness, over-subtlety, complexity and a spiritual and moral perversity.

Decadence he divides into the two branches of Symbolism and Impressionism, both of which seek *la vérité vraie,* Impressionism by representing things as they appear to the senses, and Symbolism by penetrating the surface to reach the inner meaning of things. In order to keep pace with these searching theories, which demand an endeavour after the perfect expression and a rejection of the ready-made in both language and form, a new style had to be developed. (pp. 41-53)

In 1899 in *The Symbolist Movement in Literature,* [Symons] repudiates the term Decadent, and explains away the whole movement as merely preparing the way for something more important:

> Meanwhile, something which is vaguely called Decadence had come into being. That name, rarely used with any precise meaning, was usually either hurled as a reproach or hurled back as a defiance. It pleased some young men in various countries to call themselves Decadents, with all the thrill of unsatisfied virtue masquerading as uncomprehended vice. As a matter of fact, the term is in its place only when applied to style; to that ingenious deformation of the language, in Mallarmé, for instance, which can be compared with what we are accustomed to call the Greek and Latin of the Decadence. No doubt perversity of form and perversity of matter are often found together, and, among the lesser men especially, experiment was carried far, not only in the direction of style. But a movement which in this sense might be called Decadent could but have been a straying aside from the main road of literature. Nothing, not even conventional virtue, is so provincial as conventional vice; and the desire to 'bewilder the middle-classes' is itself middle-class. The interlude, half a mock-interlude, of Decadence, diverted the attention of the critics while something more serious was in preparation. That something more serious has crystallised, for the time, under the form of Symbolism, in which art returns to the one pathway, leading through beautiful things to the eternal beauty.

This is the language of Yeats in the Preface to *Poems* (1895). Decadence is almost a scapegoat, but the dismissal highlights the rapid rise and fall of the popularity of Decadence even with its central figure.

Not that the word dropped out of use. Symons had disclaimed its application to matters other than style, but it had occurred with other applications in his own writing. In an essay 'On English and French Fiction' reprinted in *Dramatis Personae* (1925), he speaks of the 'subtle decadence of *Dorian Gray*' while concentrating on the subject of the book. In the essay 'Confessions and Comments' he writes of the novels of George Moore that they are 'entertaining, realistic, and decadent; and certainly founded on modern French fiction'. Nine pages later he writes of 'that perverse, decadent, delicately depraved study of the stages in the education of the young Parisian girl, *Chérie.*' The subject matter is of some relevance when he takes Sir Richard Burton as his subject:

> Certainly Burton leaves out nothing of the nakedness that startles one in the verse of Catullus: a nakedness that is as honest as daylight and as shameless as night. When the text is obscene his translation retains its obscenity; which, on the whole, is rare: for the genius of Catullus is elemental, primitive, nervous, passionate, decadent in the modern sense and in the modern sense perverse.

The self-consciousness, a characteristic of Decadent literature, marks this criticism and its use of the term. Even in 1897 Symons had realized that Decadence had ceased to express the main trend in literature, significantly in an essay on

W. E. Henley called 'Modernity in Verse' (reprinted in *Studies in Two Literatures,* 1924). For Symons, modernity had taken the place of Decadence as the quality of Henley's work, and the essay amounts to a retraction of his earlier position in the *Harper's* article. From a position where he tentatively accepted Decadence as a description of content and style, Symons retreated to using the term only of style, and then abandoned it as a temporary phase, only half serious.

Max Beerbohm was never wholly serious, but does confirm the bias towards style and the debt to Pater in his essay 'Be it Cosiness' in the *Pageant* in 1896:

> Not that even in those more decadent days of my childhood did I admire the man [Pater] as a stylist. Even then I was angry that he should treat English as a dead language, bored by that sedulous ritual where-with he laid out every sentence as in a shroud—hanging, like a widower, long over its marmoreal beauty or ever he could lay it at length in his book, its sepulchre.

Beerbohm's self-conscious style is both criticism and parody at once. In the first *Yellow Book,* in April 1894, Beerbohm had connected Decadence and artifice, in particular the artifice of make-up, while making that uncomfortable comparison between the end of the Victorian era and the decline of Rome:

> For behold! The Victorian era comes to its end and the day of sancta simplicitas is quite ended. The old signs are here and the portents to warn the seer of life that we are ripe for a new era of artifice. Are not men rattling the dice-box and ladies dipping their fingers in the rougepot? At Rome, in the keenest time of her degringolade, when there was gambling even in the holy temples, great ladies (does not Lucian tell us?) did not scruple to squander all they had upon unguents from Arabia.

This essay, 'a bomb thrown by a cowardly decadent' in the eyes of its critics and in Max's eyes a flippant burlesque, is almost the swan-song of the movement. Telescoping his view of history, Max viewed 1880 and his youth as the distant past and, while Beardsley was yet working, said farewell to the 'Beardsley period'. And the *Yellow Book,* commonly held to be the epitome of the Decadence, changed drastically after volume IV. (pp. 55-7)

The English translation [of Max Nordau's *Entartung*], *Degeneration* (1895), and the vigorous attacks and defences that it occasioned, form the centrepiece of the nineties controversy about the subject. Not only does it range over the whole of Europe to glean its examples of Decadent artists, but it also makes use of medical theories in much the same way as some of the French realistic novelists had done. It contained most of the conventional responses to Decadent art, but it provided the moral judgments with a backing of medical and psychological theory that seemed formidable. Critics who were slightly biased against Decadence in art were immediately won over. An extreme view can be seen in the reviewer in the *World,* quoted in advertisements before Nordau's *Conventional Lies of Our Civilization* (1895):

> That the melancholy phenomena exhibited by the 'mystics' and 'symbolists', the 'décadents' and the 'ego-maniacs' of latter-day literature and art have been due to some strange epidemic of mental declension, was evident to most thinking persons before Nordau turned the pitiless searchlight of his

analytical genius upon those several orders of art eccentrics.

What is most effective about the book is that almost all except the opinion is accurate; there is no comparable review of Decadent European literature, and certainly not at that early date. But it is not surprising that such a damning view of literature, one that promises that literature's place in society will grow less and less significant, should have found opponents, and not necessarily among the Decadent writers. Bernard Shaw, for example, would not normally be classed as Decadent (although his review first appeared in the American Anarchist paper *Liberty* on 27 July 1895, under the heading 'A Degenerate's View of Nordau'), but his defence, or rather his attack on Nordau's methods and conclusions, is convincing. Yet even his *The Sanity of Art* does not dismiss finally one of Nordau's major themes, that of the insanity of genius.

Symons, as in his essay on de Nerval, would make the question. Rimbaud had wished for a systematic derangement of all the senses. Macaulay had written in 1825 that 'Perhaps no person can be a poet, or even enjoy poetry, without a certain unsoundness of mind.' And Wilde even tried to make use of it, pleading in a letter to the Home Secretary that sexual misdemeanours are diseases and 'In the works of eminent men of science such as Lombroso and Nordau, to take two instances out of many, this is specially insisted on with reference to the intimate connection between madness and the literary and artistic temperament', and Wilde seeks justification from the book that helped in the case against him by pointing out that Nordau had 'devoted an entire chapter to the petitioner as a specially typical example of this fatal law.' Havelock Ellis, in *The New Spirit* (1890), says that 'it may be that what we call "genius" is something abnormal and distorted, like those centres of irritation which result in the pearls we likewise count so precious. It is a commonplace of Romantic theory. (pp. 63-4)

Nordau's book views Decadence as merely a small part of the whole field of ego-mania. Of course in a post-Romantic period Nordau has little difficulty in finding writers who seem interested in themselves. So the Parnassians in France, the Diabolists, Ibsen and Nietzsche are all lumped together with Decadents and Aesthetes as Ego-maniacs. Nordau follows the history of Decadence more accurately than most of his predecessors had, through Baudelaire, Gautier, and Huysmans, and he ridicules quite rightly the supposed parallels with the Roman Decadence. He approves Bourget's interpretation of Decadence, but he includes Bourget among the Decadents because he can admire Baudelaire while realizing that the Decadent is not concerned with social aims. In fact, after a lengthy examination of *A Rebours* Nordau comes to a conclusion not unlike [A. E. Carter's in *The Idea of Decadence in French Literature: 1830-1900* (1958)] that the Decadent seeks exactly the opposite of what the multitude seeks, he is 'an ordinary man with a *minus* sign'. Nordau spends some time on a diatribe against Maurice Barrès and his *culte du moi* ["cult of the self"] before he comes to the English Decadents, whom he equates with the Aesthetes as A. J. Farmer would do in his *Le mouvement esthétique et 'Décadent' en Angleterre*. Swinburne would probably have been the starting point in this section but for his 'mysticism' and his place among the PreRaphaelites, and the honour goes to Wilde:

> The ego-mania of decadentism, its love of the artificial, its aversion to nature, and to all forms of activity and movement, its megalomaniacal contempt

for men and its exaggeration of the importance of art, have found their English representative among the 'Aesthetes', the chief of whom is Oscar Wilde.

Wilde's chief offence seems to be his personal eccentricity, particularly his clothing, since his plays and poems 'are feeble imitations of Rossetti and Swinburne, and of dreary inanity. His prose essays, on the contrary, deserve attention, because they exhibit all the features which enable us to recognise in the "Aesthete" the comrade in art of the Decadent'. And from these essays Nordau draws up his list of Decadent characteristics in Wilde: the way he despises nature; his egomania; his despising popular opinion; his ideal of the inactive life; his admiration for immorality, sin and crime, as in the essay on Wainwright; his 'slight mysticism in colours'; his central glorification of art; and perhaps most damning from Nordau's point of view, the idea that 'Aesthetics are higher than ethics' (quoting from Wilde's *Intentions*).

Nordau shows up the weakness in his earnestness when he writes of Wilde's theories. Wilde seems for once to agree with him on the point that life imitates art, but Nordau staunchly refuses to see the tone of Wilde's assertions and takes him quite literally:

> Wilde does not refer to the fact, long ago established by me, that the reciprocal relation between the work of art and the public consists in this, that the former exercises suggestion and the latter submits to it. What he actually wished to say was that nature—not civilized men—develops itself in the direction of forms given in by the artist.

And so Nordau takes Wilde's assertion that painters have changed the climate and created London fogs as a statement 'so silly as to require no refutation. It is sufficient to characterize it as artistic mysticism'. In general, Nordau's attitude, his insensitivity, his literalness, and his willingness to make any characteristic represent degeneracy without proof that it is a necessary and not accidental characteristic, combine to vitiate his conclusions. He quite rightly notes the antinatural tendencies of the groups of writers he discusses, but in his insistence on the morality of art he heavily underscores the emphasis placed by its critics on the content of Decadent art. He is not ashamed of mixing art and life himself and insists in his conclusions on the actual degeneracy of these writers:

> Insensible to its tasks and interests, without the capacity to comprehend a serious thought or a fruitful deed, they dream only of the satisfaction of their basest instincts, and are pernicious—through the example they set as drones, as well as through the confusion they cause in minds insufficiently forwarned, by their abuse of the word 'art' to mean demoralization and childishness. Ego-maniacs, Decadents and Aesthetes have completely gathered under their banner this refuse of civilized peoples, and march at its head.

The book's influence can be gauged from its popularity, seven editions in a year, but there was an aptness in its time of publication that may well have boosted its sales, for it came out in the year of Wilde's trials. The attack on Wilde, accusing him of perverting the young and innocent, can scarcely have made his case easier when he was brought to trial in April. The book came out on 22 February, four days after the Marquis of Queensberry had left his libellous card at the Albermarle, and five editions of the book had been printed before the end of the second trial. Nordau's ideas and accusations are heard again, more shrilly, in the *National Observer* of 6 April 1895, in an article possibly written by Charles Whibley, and obviously endorsed by the editor, W. E. Henley. This is before the second trial:

> There is not a man or woman in the English-speaking world possessed of the treasure of a wholesome mind who is not under a deep debt of gratitude to the Marquess of Queensberry for destroying the High Priest of the Decadents. The obscene impostor, whose prominence has been a social outrage ever since he transferred from Trinity Dublin to Oxford his vices, his follies, and his vanities, has been exposed, and that thoroughly at last. There must be another trial at the Old Bailey, or a coroner's inquest—the latter for choice; and the Decadents, of their hideous conceptions of the meaning of Art, and of their worse than Eleusinian mysteries there must be an absolute end.

Decadence was by now more than style; and more than content; it had become life. Montgomery Hyde adds other details which prove that the persecution of Wilde was more than artistic, and more than theoretic:

> Meanwhile messages of congratulation were pouring in on Queensberry. On being informed by one of the Sunday newspapers that a further pile of messages was waiting for him, the delighted Marquess said: 'You know, I have not much to do with distinguished people, but I had a very nice letter from Lord Claud Hamilton, and a kind telegram from Mr Charles Denby, the actor, with "Hearty Congratulations", et cetera. Various clubs have telegraphed also. Here is a message: "Every man in the City is with you. Kill the — !" '

The weight of feeling against anything associated with the name of Decadence made it impossible for any movement with the name to continue. Symbolism was there to take its place as it had done with no prompting in France; and, although many writers stuck by Wilde both in ideas and deeds, the Decadent movement had received a mortal blow.

The strength of feeling against Wilde can be seen by the comments quoted above, written the day after his first arrest. Before he was committed for trial, *Punch* of 13 April 1895 had printed some verses 'Concerning a Misused Term':

viz., 'Art' as recently applied to a certain form of Literature.

Is this, then, 'Art'—ineffable conceit,
Plus worship of the Sadi-tinted phrase,
Of pseud-Hellenic decadence, effete,
Unvirile, of debased Petronian ways?

Is *this* your 'Culture', to asphyxiate
With upas-perfume sons of English race,
With manhood-blighting cant-of-art to prate,
The jargon of an epicene disgrace?

Shall worse than pornographic stain degrade
The name of 'Beauty', Heav'n imparted dower?
Are *they* fit devotees, who late displayed
The symbol of a vitriol-tainted flower?

And shall the sweet and kindly Muse be shamed
By unsexed 'Poetry' that defiles your page?
Has Art a mission that may not be named,
With 'scarlet sins' to enervate the age?

All honour to the rare and cleanly prints,
Which have not filled our homes from day to day

With garbage-epigrams and pois'nous hints
How aesthete-hierophants fair Art betray!

If such be 'Artists', then may Philistines
Arise, plan sturdy Britons as of yore,
And sweep them off and purge away the signs
That England e'er such noxious offspring bore!

Wilde may be said to have been judged before he was tried, but the whole Decadent movement was on trial with him.

The trial and the accompanying adverse publicity for Decadence were devastatingly effective. By 11 May *Punch* could see degeneration as a thing of the past. 'A Philistine Paean' sang of the change of atmosphere:

At last! I see signs of a turn in the tide,
And O, I perceive it with infinite gratitude,
No more need I go with a crick in my side
In attempts to preserve a non-natural attitude.
Something has changed in the season, *somewhere*:
I'm sure I can feel a cool whiff of fresh air!

After Nordau, the poem discovered that 'Egomania is *not* the last word of latter-day wisdom', and that High Art was maudlin, not decent, mad, unclean, impure. At last the Philistine did not feel obliged to admire the literature of the egomaniac, mystical High Art school, though he did feel a little baffled at the inclusiveness of the condemnation:

I am not *quite* sure that I *quite* understand
How they've suddenly found all our fads are degenerate;
Why MAETERLINCK, IBSEN, VERLAINE, SARAH
 GRAND, TOLSTOI, GRANT ALLEN, ZOLA, are
 'lumped'—but, at any rate,
I know I'm relieved from one horrible bore,—
I need not admire what I hate any more.

With all this feeling concentrated against the ideas for which Decadence had been held to stand, it is not unnatural that the writers who still subscribed to some of those ideas should seek a new label which would describe their beliefs without the overtones of moral scorn and censure which inevitably attached themselves to Decadence. It is difficult to find after 1895 any example of the term used with the approval it had before, as with Lionel Johnson, or even as an approximate label as Symons had used it.

In the *Savoy,* which inherited from the *Yellow Book* the unfortunately implicated Beardsley, many of the interesting writers, and much of the unsavoury reputation, it was necessary to deny association with Decadence, though Symons staunchly defended its theories elsewhere. Symons's statements in the *Savoy* of November 1895 make the position clear:

> We have no formula and we desire no false unity of form or matter. We have not invented a new point of view. We are not Realists or Romanticists or Decadents. For us, all art is good which is good art.

And even *Punch* seems to have lost interest in the idea of Decadence under the pressure of more important items on the international field.

The rise and fall of the Decadent movement in England was in the main confined to the years from 1889 to 1897; it was certainly over by the end of the century. Some of the chief figures of that movement died with the century, setting a permanent seal on that sense of an ending: Dowson, Wilde, John-

Max Beerbohm, 1901.

themselves unable to abandon it because it fits something, whether works, writers, attitudes, or merely the need of the time. It will always be an approximation, a label rather than a definition. . . . (pp. 65-70)

R. K. R. Thornton, in his The Decadent Dilemma, *Edward Arnold, 1983, 216 p.*

MAJOR FIGURES: "THE TRAGIC GENERATION"

GRANVILLE HICKS

[*Hicks was an American literary critic whose famous study* The Great Tradition: An Interpretation of American Literature since the Civil War *(1933) established him as the foremost advocate of Marxist critical thought in Depression-era America. After 1939, Hicks sharply denounced communist ideology, which he called a "hopelessly narrow way of judging literature," and in his later years adopted a less ideological posture in critical matters. In the following excerpt, he considers Oscar Wilde's importance as a central symbol of literary Decadence and discusses other major figures of the movement.*]

In spite of their various kinds of non-conformity, the great Victorians were accepted by the middle-class reading public as spokesmen rather than enemies, and some of them, notably Tennyson and Dickens, were not merely accepted but idolized. With the sixties and seventies, however, with Ruskin's attack on laissez-faire economics and with Swinburne's flouting of evangelical morality, writers and readers found themselves in opposing trenches. The warfare continued in the eighties, with Morris, Hardy, Gissing, Moore, and Butler rushing to the attack, each with his own particular weapons and his own particular battle-cry. And each was met with vituperation.

No one, however, was denounced so promptly and hysterically as Oscar Wilde. As soon as his first collection of verse appeared, the late Victorian reading public identified him as an intolerable threat to the home, the church, and the state. The scandal that Wilde's *Poems* created in 1881 was perhaps no greater than that which Swinburne's *Poems and Ballads* had aroused in 1867, but, thanks to Wilde's gifts for self-advertising, more persons were aware of the affront he had offered them. And the indignation was given no chance to die down, but steadily accumulated force from 1881 to 1895. At first the defenders of Victorianism satirized Wilde, masking their fury with an affectation of playfulness, but soon their viciousness was undisguised, and in the end they had a cruel revenge.

The kind of panic Wilde's work inspired was intensified by the appearance of a group of writers and artists who appeared to be his disciples. There was more and more talk in the eighties about estheticism, and in the nineties a disturbing word became current—decadence. The *Yellow Book* in 1894 and the *Savoy* in 1896 gave the word a certain content. Arthur Symons, Ernest Dowson, Max Beerbohm, and especially Aubrey Beardsley were held to be exponents of decay, with such writers as Lionel Johnson, John Davidson, Henry Harland, Richard Le Gallienne, and W. B. Yeats under suspicion. A certain number of self-constituted guardians of the British Empire and all its institutions found it easy to con-

son, Crackanthorpe, Beardsley, Beerbohm retired from the struggle, and even Symons renounced the name. The novelty of Decadence had worn off, and Symbolism took its place.

One can put some order into the subject of Decadence apart from the historical order by seeing the discussion tending towards distinct polarities. First there is the pole of the critic, who equates modern literature with that of Roman Decadence as a way of showing tendencies to be avoided; the attitude is a moral one, and attacks largely on the grounds of subject, though with occasional criticisms of style, especially when the vocabulary in which that style is defended implies decay or disease. Second there is the pole of the writer, who sees a Decadent literature as appropriate to a time of Decadence, but, maintaining the irrelevance of art to morality, concentrates on matters of style and technique. Nordau is the culmination of the first type, though he no longer makes the parallel with Rome, and founds his arguments on Darwinian models and an extension of Lombroso's work. Symons is the epitome of the second type. Unfortunately, the adherents of the movement made their case difficult by using a name which implied a degeneracy which was, without need of proof, an undesirable state; and the case was made worse by the continued hints of immorality or disease in their subjects. The built-in moral overtones of Decadence finally invalidated the term, and the writers moved towards the available and less loaded notion of Symbolism.

The term had never been completely satisfactory, nor had it ever been completely clear. But it had provided a useful focus and has gone on providing a focus ever since. Despite a willingness to acknowledge its inadequacy, critics have found vince sections of the reading public that England's greatness was seriously threatened, and Victorianism fought back.

Though Wilde was not in fact the leader of the decadent cult, the public thought he was, and resentment concentrated on him, so that work for which he had no responsibility contributed to his downfall, which in turn affected writers who were in no sense his associates. The ostentatious worship of beauty in the eighties and nineties brought into action all the intolerance and meanness of the middle-class mind, and Wilde had the undeserved honor and pain of bearing the full brunt of this attack.

"I was a man," Wilde wrote in *De Profundis,*

> who stood in symbolic relations to the art and culture of my age. I had realized this for myself at the very dawn of my manhood, and had forced my age to realize it afterwards. Few men hold such a position in their own lifetime, and have it so acknowledged. It is usually discerned, if discerned at all, by the historian, or the critic, long after both the man and his age have passed away. With me it was different. I felt it myself and made others feel it.

What is most extraordinary about this statement is that, by and large, it is true. Wilde did, quite consciously, make himself a symbol, a symbol of the artistic mind in a Philistine civilization. That he was an adequate symbol may be doubted; that he compelled the acceptance of his symbolic quality is undeniable. (pp. 217-19)

It is dangerous to speak of "the esthetic movement" without quotation marks, for it seems largely a creation of Wilde's ambition, but, in a vague sense, it did exist, and even had an historian. Walter Hamilton, who wrote about it as early as 1882 [in *The Aesthetic Movement in England*], traced it to the Pre-Raphaelite Brotherhood. It had become talked about through various notorious quarrels, beginning with Whistler's suit against Ruskin. Ruskin, because of his championing of the Pre-Raphaelites and his insistence on the necessity of beauty, was one of the godfathers of the movement, but Whistler, who repudiated Ruskin's ethical preoccupations, was closer to the younger men. So far as the public was concerned, two brands of estheticism were at war, and the public learned that there were issues even if it did not try to understand them.

Robert Buchanan's attack on Rossetti in "The Fleshly School of Poetry," with the long controversy that followed, also helped to give estheticism notoriety. But chiefly it was *Punch* that, with Wilde's collaboration, created the esthetic movement out of flimsy materials. For nearly a generation sound men—readers of *Punch*—had been dismayed by all the talk about beauty. It was effeminate, absurd, and un-British. Everybody knew that Ruskin and Morris were crackpots, and Swinburne and Rossetti made no attempt to conceal their depravity. And yet there were Englishmen who took the esthetic movement seriously. People went to Grosvenor Gallery and pretended to be impressed by the Pre-Raphaelite paintings; women tried to look like Rossetti's tubercular models; homes were furnished in what was believed to be Morris' style; there was even a suburb for esthetes, the Bedford Park Estate, where esthetic wallpapers, tapestries, and painted tiles were as common as whatnots in the homes of *Punch's* readers.

Concerned to resist this subversive influence, *Punch* had been ridiculing the esthetes before Wilde left Oxford. Quite aware

of the emotions that were troubling the editors of *Punch* and their right-minded fellow-citizens, Wilde made himself the symbol they were looking for. His costumes, his mannerisms, his flowers, his sayings, his ostentatious tributes to Lily Langtry, his sonnets to Ellen Terry, his rhapsodies on Sarah Bernhardt, all lent themselves, with a perfection that can only have been intentional, to the needs and the by no means subtle wit of the staff of *Punch. Punch* wanted a butt for its resentment, and Wilde wanted to be talked about. Both were satisfied.

What surprises one, looking at the cartoons and parodies that appeared, is the bitterness. There is, moreover, a kind of innuendo that would be inconceivable, given Great Britain's libel laws, in this day when knowledge of sexual abnormality is general. This was no mere foible that *Punch* was attacking, but a danger to the social system, and the dirtier the stick, the more effective the beating. Wilde might well have taken alarm if he had not been blindly self-confident and in his own way quite fearless.

For the moment the beneficent result of the onslaught was a sale for the *Poems,* which, privately published in June, 1881, was in its fifth edition within six months. Wilde, who did not have a low opinion of the merits of his poetry, knew well enough that it was the merits of his publicity that gave the volume its circulation. He also knew that the poems would add to the legend. The three longest and most pretentious, "The Garden of Eros," "The Burden of Itys," and "Charmides," were not quite what *Punch* called them, "Swinburne and water," but they had almost exactly the qualities that had shocked and titillated readers of *Poems and Ballads.* Almost any well-read person could see that the poems were imitative; the marks of Swinburne, Arnold, Tennyson, and, in at least one poem, Thomas Hood were unmistakable. More derivative even than most first volumes, *Poems* made it difficult to say where, in the mass of influences, the author was to be found. But the ideas were disturbing, even if they were somebody's else, and the rhetorical passages, Swinburnian though they were, satisfied a public that was looking for sensationalism. (pp. 221-23)

Seven years after *Poems* [Wilde] published his second volume, *The Happy Prince,* and, though a collection of fairy stories was scarcely what had been anticipated, his admirers found in the tales proof that he was a master of prose. The following year, 1889, brought forth "The Decay of Lying," one of his more pretentious essays, and "The Portrait of Mr. W. H.," Shakespearean criticism in the form of fiction. 1890 was the year of *Dorian Gray,* which appeared in *Lippincott's Magazine,* and "The Critic as Artist." In 1891 came the publication in book form of *Dorian Gray, Lord Arthur Saville's Crime, Intentions,* and *A House of Pomegranates,* the magazine publication of *The Soul of Man Under Socialism,* and the sixth edition of *Poems.* The first performance of *Lady Windermere's Fan* was on February 20, 1892.

Here, then, were five fruitful years, culminating in the kind of success Wilde had longed for. After his youthful clowning he had remained unproductive just long enough to convince his enemies that he was wholly a fraud, and then had dazzled them with fairy tales, humorous short stories, critical essays, a novel, a sociological essay, and a play. Almost everything he wrote, moreover, was bizarre enough to add to his legend. What, for example, could the average Englishman make of "The Decay of Lying" and "Pen, Pencil and Poison" except to conclude that they were written in defense of crime? Why should an esthete write fairy tales if not to convey doctrines of a subtle immorality? Was not "The Portrait of Mr. W. H." an attack on the greatest of British authors, *The Soul of Man under Socialism* an assault on the political and economic bases of national life, and *Dorian Gray* an affront to every decent Englishman?

Wilde believed in the policy of shocking people, and it had been so successful that he seldom considered the damage to himself. Yet certain passages in "The Portrait of Mr. W. H." and *Dorian Gray* indicated either ignorance on his part or a complete faith in the ignorance of his contemporaries. The age was ignorant; he was right about that. Though it has been said on good evidence that homosexuality was common, it was not understood. Mr. Justice Wills, for example, obviously believed that there were different levels of sensuality: a good man lived in matrimonial fidelity; a bad man had illicit relations with women; a worse man had illicit relations with men. In the course of human degradation, he apparently held, one form of sensuality led to another and lower form. This was the general belief, and consequently there was not only a good deal of injustice but also a curious kind of innocence. Much that would today seem evidence of homosexuality was then regarded as merely bizarre or effeminate.

If it had not been for this confusion, Wilde would not have been likely to write the passage in "The Portrait of Mr. W. H." in praise of the higher love between man and man, with its direct allusion to Plato's *Symposium,* nor would he have indicated quite so frankly the relationship between Dorian Gray and Basil Hallward and that between Gray and Lord Henry, who is so obviously Wilde himself. We cannot help assuming that Wilde did not want to flaunt his homosexuality as such, for he went to some pains to deny the charge even among friends. He had done much talking about secret and splendid sins, but it was not his intention to be too specific. The trouble was that it was easy to provide details from his own experience and to depend on the general ignorance. What he did not anticipate was that, though readers of *Dorian Gray* seldom knew exactly what was bothering them, they were troubled, and they did feel that Wilde had somehow betrayed himself. The critic in the *Saturday Review* failed, in the course of his long diatribe, to define his objections to the book, but the strength of his emotion was unmistakable and ominous. He seemed to feel, moreover, as did other critics, that Wilde was providing evidence that could eventually be used to destroy him.

In spite of the gathering opposition, Wilde was entering his period of triumph. It is worth noticing that three of his plays were problem-plays, and that in all three conventional morality is satisfied. *Lady Windermere's Fan* inquires whether, when lovely woman has stooped to folly, she should tell her daughter, and it reaches its climax in the redeeming self-sacrifice of the sinner. *An Ideal Husband* poses the problem of the early misdeeds of a successful man and the self-righteousness of his wife. *A Woman of No Importance* tells the old story of wronged innocence, and ends with the triumph of the victim over her betrayer. All three of them plead for tolerance for the sinner, but only within limits long established by literary convention. (pp. 225-28)

An Ideal Husband was produced on January 2, 1895, and *The Importance of Being Earnest* on February 14. Four days later the Marquis of Queensberry, father of Lord Alfred Douglas, left for Wilde at the Albemarle Club a visiting card with an illiterate but libelous message. The resulting trial, which

Wilde insisted on against the advice of most of his friends, was held in April, and Wilde's case collapsed in three days. Almost immediately he was arrested on charges of gross indecency. The first jury disagreed, but at a second trial he was found guilty, and on May 25 he was sentenced to two years' imprisonment at hard labor.

"The gods had given me almost everything," Wilde wrote in *De Profundis.*

> I had genius, a distinguished name, high social position, brilliancy, intellectual daring; I made art a philosophy and philosophy an art; I altered the minds of men and the colors of things; there was nothing I said or did that did not make people wonder. I took the drama, the most objective form known to art, and made it as personal a mode of expression as the lyric or sonnet; at the same time I widened its range and enriched its characterization. Drama, novel, poem in prose, poem in rhyme, subtle or fantastic dialogue, whatever I touched, I made beautiful in a new mode of beauty: to truth itself I gave what is false no less than what is true as its rightful province, and showed that the false and the true are merely forms of intellectual existence. I treated art as the supreme reality and life as a mere mode of fiction. I awoke the imagination of my century so that it created myth and legend around me. I summed up all systems in a phrase and all existence in an epigram. . . .

It does not matter how much of this is true. It is what Wilde, as he lay in Reading Gaol, wanted others to believe and must at moments have believed himself. It is easy to argue after the event that only catastrophe could have been a fitting climax for Wilde's life. Perhaps the argument is false, but how else could his life have ended? He had made himself, as he said, a symbol, and what he symbolized was hated by many men. That they would have their revenge no one but he could have doubted.

Quite possibly it was Wilde's habit of seizing every opportunity for publicity that prompted the fatal challenge to Queensberry. Having won the position he had planned for himself, he thought any kind of triumph easy, and a triumph over the Marquis of Queensberry would have been particularly dear. As it was, it was Queensberry who did the celebrating, after the stupid trial and the shocking sentence and the rejoicing in the streets. The forty gentlemen who honored the Marquis at dinner were sound citizens, who could understand a man's abusing his wife, as Queensberry was said to have done, and probably were tolerant of perversion in the sniggering way that men of the world often are. What they hated in Wilde was his insolent defiance of their whole carefully arranged scheme of life.

Wilde was a symbol, then, when he went to prison, and a symbol when he came out. He might have used his symbolic status to make a victory of his defeat, and "The Ballad of Reading Gaol" suggested that he was about to do this. He cast himself, as *De Profundis* shows, in a new part. "Tired of being on the heights," he wrote, "I deliberately went to the depths in the search for new sensation. What the paradox was to me in the sphere of thought, perversity became to me in the sphere of passion. . . . I allowed pleasure to dominate me. I ended in horrible disgrace. There is only one thing for me now, absolute humility."

In prison Wilde had seen for the first time something of the world that lay outside the narrow circle of London society and its hangers-on, and he had reached in "The Ballad of Reading Gaol" for a subject and a form that had wide appeal. Perhaps his humility would have been only one more pose, but it could have been a pose that would have rescued his reputation. What one realizes now, however, reading the suppressed passages of *De Profundis,* is that Wilde was no longer capable even of posing. The gross years of prosperity, the trial, and the prison term had broken the ambition that had pushed him so steadily onward. He made an effort immediately after his release, but he lapsed into self-indulgence and the miserable meannesses of his last years. The promise, such as it was, of "The Ballad of Reading Gaol" was illusory. Wilde's literary life had ended with the trial, and the only question was how long it would take for him to find his way to the grave. (pp. 229-31)

For the public Wilde symbolized a whole literary movement, but he was not in reality its leader. His disciples were men of rather slight talents: Lord Douglas, Robert Sherard, Robert Ross, and Reggie Turner. He knew, of course, all of his literary contemporaries, and was on friendly terms with many of them, but the more distinguished men were not in the circle closest to him, and several were a little scornful of both his personality and his work. They rallied, with some exceptions, to his defense when he was on trial, and they paid tribute to him after his death, but they never called him master.

The literary movement of the nineties, variously called esthetic and decadent and impressionistic, found its center in the *Yellow Book* and the *Savoy,* not in Oscar Wilde, and, as Osbert Burdett has said, Aubrey Beardsley rather than Wilde was its representative figure. The *Yellow Book* grew out of the meeting of three men: Beardsley, Henry Harland, and John Lane. (pp. 242-43)

In these three men were the forces that made the *Yellow Book* what it was. Lane was practical enough, in spite of his willingness to publish young poets. Harland was an increasingly popular practitioner of the romanticism that Wilde had hailed in "The Critic as Artist," and though one scarcely finds Beauty walking with slim, gilded feet in his tales, his preoccupation with style and his scorn for moral preaching made him acceptable to the other young men of his generation. Beardsley, however, was the only one of the trio to whom the label "decadent" could be applied with any meaning. It was the indefinable perversity of his drawings that impressed the purchasers of the *Yellow Book* and led them to see in the volume as a whole qualities that were not there.

For Beardsley did not set the tone of the quarterly. The leading contribution in the first number was Henry James's "The Death of the Lion," and James, who could be associated with the decadence only because the younger men united in admiring his craftsmanship, remained a frequent contributor. William Watson, Edmund Gosse, Arthur Waugh, and Richard Garnett gave respectability to the issue, and Leighton, Pennell, and Laurence Housman were among the illustrators. There was, it is true, a rather fleshly poem by Arthur Symons, and John Davidson, Max Beerbohm, and Hubert Crackanthorpe were included, but the advance-guard was in the minority.

As the *Yellow Book* had begun, so it continued, for Lane had achieved a formula that served his purpose. James continued to give distinction. Harland, Austin Dobson, Kenneth Gra-

hame, Richard Le Gallienne, and various mediocrities provided charm and romance; Hubert Crackanthorpe, Ella D'Arcy, and others served up slices of life; Watson was often present for decorum's sake; Symons, Dowson, Lionel Johnson, Beerbohm, Davidson, Conder, and especially Beardsley furnished novelty and sometimes the sensationalism readers wanted. Four issues appeared edited according to this formula, and then, so the story goes, just at the time of the Wilde trial, Mrs. Humphry Ward persuaded William Watson to issue an ultimatum against Beardsley's drawings, and Lane capitulated. The *Yellow Book* continued for two years more, but it became less and less representative of anything except the taste for romantic fiction. Most issues opened with a story by Henry Harland and closed with one by Ella D'Arcy. Crackanthorpe and Miss D'Arcy and later Arnold Bennett were its realists, but Harland, Le Gallienne, Harold Frederic, Baron Corvo, and John Buchan brought down the scales on the romantic side. Many of the more distinguished authors and artists departed with Beardsley.

They were, most of them, contributing to the new magazine, the *Savoy.* After his break with Lane, Beardsley had found himself a new publisher in the somewhat disreputable figure of Leonard Smithers. Smithers launched the *Savoy* in January, 1896, with Arthur Symons as editor, and thus a new triumvirate was formed. The first issue of the *Savoy* was more impressive than the *Yellow Book* had ever been. Shaw, Beerbohm, Dowson, Yeats, and Havelock Ellis wrote for it, and C. H. Shannon, Charles Conder, and William Rothenstein joined Beardsley as the magazine's artists. Beardsley contributed an amusing poem and the first installment of *Under the Hill* as well as a dozen drawings. "We have no formulas," an editorial note ran, "and we desire no false unity of form or matter. We have not invented a new point of view. We are not Realists, or Romanticists, or Decadents. For us, all art is good which is good art. . . . We could scarcely say more, and we are content to think we can scarcely say less."

The second issue was as good and as successful as the first, and with the third the *Savoy* became a monthly. This, as Symons subsequently admitted, was a mistake. There were, he pointed out, fewer persons than he had hoped who "really cared for art, and really for art's sake," and he might have added that there was not enough first-rate work to fill twelve issues a year. Furthermore, a large bookseller, responding to the general uneasiness, banned the magazine from his stores, ostensibly because of a drawing by William Blake. The last issue, published in December, 1896, was devoted entirely to stories, poems, and essays by Symons and drawings by Beardsley.

When the *Savoy* suspended publication, the movement it had expressed was near its end. It was short-lived, but the remarkable thing is that, in a country in which writers have been notably individualistic, there had been a movement. And even more remarkable is the fact that the movement was made up of men who wanted to raise individualism to a new pitch. They had come together to defend their various individualisms against the assaults of an age of conformity. Most of them either lived in London or frequently visited the city. They went to music-halls and bars together, and the majority belonged to the Rhymers' Club. Though they issued no manifestoes, they constituted a movement, and they had created two magazines.

There is also a common pattern in their lives. Aubrey Beardsley, even if he had not some claim to literary reputation because of his fragment of a rococo novel and his two poems, would have to be included in any discussion of the literary movement, since to most readers of the *Yellow Book* and the *Savoy* his drawings seemed to express what the movement was trying to say. Unwell from early childhood, he had begun to suffer from hemorrhages when he was seventeen. That was in 1889, when he was working in the insurance office. Encouraged by Burne-Jones and by Morris' disciple, Aymer Vallance, he studied art for a time in a night school, and then began his extraordinary career. As soon as John Lane had issued his edition of the *Morte d'Arthur,* he was offered many commissions. His style changed rapidly as he came under various influences, but, whatever models he chose, his work was always his. He was so persistently bawdy, in his drawings as in his speech, that Lane examined his work with a magnifying glass for hidden obscenities. But Beardsley did not have to be obscene in any ordinary sense to attract attention. His masculine women and feminine men, the expressions of malice or terror or secret knowledge that are on most of the faces he drew, the lines that are so pure in execution and so ambiguous in intent, these were sufficient to excite alarm as well as admiration.

He spared himself neither in his work nor in his diversions. He was often interrupted by hemorrhages, and in the last years he knew that the fatal attack might come at any time, but that did not lessen his exertions. In March, 1897, he became a Catholic, but, though his sincerity is not to be doubted, his work shows little change of attitude until his final, pitiful plea to Smithers to destroy his obscene drawings. The last year of his life was spent in France, where he died on March 16, 1898.

Ill health may have made him reckless, but his defiance went deeper than that. Whatever else his drawings contained, there was always contempt in them and disillusionment. He was seldom pornographic, except perhaps in privately published work, and if he was obscene, it was in ways not calculated to arouse desire. His respectable contemporaries pretended to be shocked, but actually they were bewildered and unnerved. He was even more hated than Wilde, who before his trial could be dismissed as a clown and afterwards as a pervert. Some passion of indignation burned within Beardsley, and there were many who feared the flames.

Ernest Dowson could never have upset the bourgeoisie as Beardsley did, for the bourgeoisie scarcely knew he existed. Unlike Beardsley, he was brought up in a family with literary interests, and he went to Oxford. Like Beardsley, he was ill from childhood, refused to consider his health, and died young. He was motivated by no intense hatred; his was a simpler relationship to a society he could not tolerate, a relationship based on shy indifference. In his life he sought the relief of drink and occasionally of drugs. In his poetry he celebrated the unhappy love affair in which, by some inner necessity, he was involved. When, Symons tells us, he had to leave the restaurant in which his inamorata worked, he would begin drinking and spend the night in some house of prostitution. Then, at a later stage there might be a sonnet or a villanelle—"for Adelaide."

Whatever it was that drove him to squalid excesses, it did not speak in his poetry. In that respect Dowson resembled another member of the Rhymers' Club, Lionel Johnson. Johnson did not indulge in sexual excesses—he was, according to Yeats, incapable of them—but he did drink heavily, and thus shortened his life. He, too, was an Oxford man, and had been

under the influence of Pater and Symonds. Even earlier, while at Winchester, he had shown a serious interest in religion, and he had joined the Catholic Church in 1891. During the early nineties he wrote critical essays for London papers, erudite essays with an eighteenth century ponderousness. Excited by Yeats's Irish literary movement, he created an imaginary Irish ancestry for himself so that he might participate in it. He died in 1902.

There are, as Yeats points out, one or two poems in which Johnson symbolizes his inner struggle, but most of his poetry is that of a scholar and a Christian, just as Dowson's is that of a romanticist and a man of quiet melancholy. Dowson, with his echoes of Horace and the nice perfection of his lines, seems much of the time to be writing exquisite exercises upon themes assigned by some amiable schoolmaster. Johnson's poetry affects strength rather than delicacy, but it is unconvincing in the same way. Even without knowing the facts of his life, one would expect them to be somehow at variance with his verse. With both poets premature death is overshadowed by a greater tragedy.

John Davidson also belonged to the Rhymers' Club, but he was ten years older than most of the members, brought different experiences to his work, and found his way to a different—if parallel—conclusion. Born in Scotland, he went to work when he was thirteen. In 1890 he came to London, and for several years supported himself by hack work. He had rejected in youth the strict Calvinism in which he was brought up, but he was not tempted, as so many of his contemporaries were, by Catholicism. Instead he accepted the rigid materialism of the century, and in time he became a disciple of Nietzsche. While still in Scotland he had written a number of unactable verse plays that showed his ebullience and unconventionality and his admiration for the Elizabethans, but it was in *Fleet Street Eclogues* that he first spoke for himself. For a time his ballads had some success, but in the first years of the century he abandoned the form and wrote a series of philosophical poems he called testaments. He grew more and more bitter towards society, and in 1909 he committed suicide.

If it were not ridiculous to suggest that writers of this or any other period can be classified, the question might legitimately be raised whether Davidson belongs with the writers of the decadence or with the school of energetic manliness and imperialism. He believed in the superman, opposed social reform, emphasized the will, and was unafraid of violence in his verse. He was a member of the Rhymers' Club, but he damned his fellow-members as lacking "blood and guts." Though he objected as strongly as they did to the accepted Victorian authors, he resisted the influence of the French symbolists and sought a new basis for poetry. He did not follow Beardsley, Johnson, and Harland into the Catholic Church, nor had he any sympathy with Yeats's kind of mysticism. Yet one can see why he was a member of the Rhymers' Club, and certainly "The Ballad of a Nun" was not out of place in the *Yellow Book*. If he quarreled with the symbolists and decadents, he fought side by side with them against the prevailing convictions of the middle class, and by his suicide he accepted the pattern that belongs to the group.

Hubert Crackanthorpe also committed suicide, as did Francis Adams and Laurence Hope. Beardsley died in his twenties, Dowson and Johnson in their thirties, Charles Conder, Henry Harland, Oscar Wilde, and Francis Thompson in their forties. The death of each, except possibly Harland, might have been postponed. It is no wonder that some critics have talked of a death-will and associated it with the literary aims and conceptions of the movement.

Richard Le Gallienne, Arthur Symons, Max Beerbohm, and W. B. Yeats were the principal survivors. Le Gallienne quickly proved himself to have been nothing but a romantic hanger-on, a self-made man of letters with the face and manners of a poet. Beerbohm continued as he had begun, but the more he wrote and the more he drew, the clearer it became that his association with the group was accidental. Symons lived on, but his mind was periodically clouded, and he did little important work after the appearance of *Images of Good and Evil* in 1899. Yeats continued to grow and change, until finally he took his place in the front rank of living poets.

Yeats's career, more strikingly than Beerbohm's, helps us to understand why it is so comparatively easy and so approximately just to give definite boundaries to the literary movement of the nineties. We do not think of Yeats as representative of that movement because he means so much more than that. But the majority of the writers died before they could mean more. Perhaps they never would have done anything better or anything very different, just as Symons never did. That we cannot know. But it is clear that, in the history of British literature, the movement was a passing phase, sharply marked because so many of the writers passed with it.

"I was born," Arthur Symons wrote [in his *Dramatis Personae*], " 'like a fiend hid in a cloud,' cruel, nervous, excitable, passionate, restless, never quite human, never quite normal, and, from the fact that I have never known what it was to have a home, as most children know it, my life has been in many ways a wonderful, in certain ways a tragic one: an existence, indeed, so inexplicable even to myself, that I cannot fathom it. If I have been a vagabond, and have never been able to root myself in any one place in the world, it is because I have no early memories of any one sky or soil. It has freed me from many prejudices in giving me its own unresting kind of freedom, but it has cut me off from whatever is stable, of long growth in the world."

Wilde could have said somewhat the same thing. Dowson, who in his youth had drifted about the Continent with his family, divided his later years between France and England, and his *nostalgie de boue* [literally, "nostalgia for mud;" the phrase has been taken by William Gaunt to signify a craving for abjection] so eminently in the decadent tradition, grew out of his homelessness. Davidson, Harland, and Yeats were all expatriates, and Yeats was the only one who thought of rooting his poetry in his homeland. Lionel Johnson pathetically envied Yeats his country, and tried to make himself an Irish poet. Max Beerbohm came from a solid enough British family, but nothing about him so impressed his contemporaries at Oxford as his utter detachment. As for Beardsley, he seemed to friends a changeling, quite unrelated to the mother and sister with whom he lived.

There is perhaps nothing unusual in this, for the artist often has few obvious ties to contemporary society. Yet most writers do become spokesmen for groups that are bound together by more than merely literary tastes. That is true of all the major Victorians and of William Morris. It is true in a sense of Hardy and Butler and for a time of George Gissing. It is true of the writers of the nineties only to the extent that restlessness and disillusionment were not rare in the decade. What they had in common with each other and with a certain number of their contemporaries was a centrifugal impulse.

Few of them succeeded in coming to terms with society—even the kind of terms that are represented by a consistent opposition. One can see, for example, that Lionel Johnson conceived of himself as a Catholic gentleman and scholar, not as a chronic alcoholic. Dowson would have chosen to live not in the mud but on a high romantic level. Yeats did in some measure achieve his desired identification with Ireland, but, instead of becoming a bard for the masses, became one of the most abstruse and difficult poets of his generation. Beardsley could not restrain his pen from blasphemy, the while he sincerely professed Catholicism. Symons, it is true, seemed to be what he wanted to be, but a psychologist would point to the mental crises of his middle years as proof of conflict. Davidson remained wholeheartedly a rebel, but he broke under the strain.

It does not distinguish these writers to say they were in revolt against the age in which they lived; so were Morris and Hardy and Butler and Gissing; so were Shaw and Wells and a score of the younger authors. Yeats admits this in *The Trembling of the Veil.* "As time passed," he writes, "Ibsen became in my eyes the chosen author of very clever young journalists, who, condemned to their treadmill of abstraction, hated music and style; and yet neither I nor my generation could escape him because, though we and he had not the same friends, we had the same enemies." Again, he says of Shaw: "He could hit my enemies and the enemies of all I loved, as I could never hit, as no living author that was dear to me could ever hit." Yeats and his friends hated greed and hypocrisy as much as Shaw did. Yeats even, for a time, accepted Morris' Socialism because he shared so completely his distaste for contemporary ugliness. If Socialism would bring what he wanted, then Yeats felt, just as Wilde did when he wrote *The Soul of Man,* that he was for Socialism.

But the more obvious way was to leave the bourgeoisie to its ugliness and to go about the creation of beauty. The writers of the nineties might feel their hopes rise when there was a strong popular movement against capitalism, but they could not believe that it was their duty to initiate or nourish such a revolt. They were, for the most part, men of unusual sensitivity, men who shuddered at the turmoil and the rawness of industrial and commercial life. When one remembers how many of them were weakened by disease, one cannot wonder that they were incapable of offering any direct resistance to the evils they were so conscious of. They were readily convinced of the impregnability of ugliness and greed, and they sought what they wanted wherever they could, even if fleetingly, find it.

Here, then, were a dozen men coming from all parts of the British Isles to London, though they felt no particular loyalty to the city. They had none of the faith of the early romantics in nature, and little of their faith in man. They hated the social order of which they were part, but they were powerless to change it and ready to believe that it could not be changed. If their sensitiveness might be called abnormal, they could say with some reason that normality was no virtue in an age such as theirs. They had no respect for Victorian morality and, except for Davidson, no confidence in Victorian science. They believed in beauty as artists of all ages have done, but they believed in it more intensely, for it was all they believed in.

Naturally they turned, as writers have always done, to those of their predecessors and older contemporaries who had seen life somewhat as they saw it. With the majority of the Victorian spokesmen they had no sympathy. Yeats has told how Huxley, Tyndall, Carolus Duran, and Bastien-Lepage represented for him the unimaginativeness he hated. What they set forth as reality was to him an illusion. His friends agreed, and they also condemned, even more vigorously, every writer who could be suspected of supporting Victorian morality. That left, in England, the Pre-Raphaelites and Pater. The Pre-Raphaelites had refused to regard art as a branch of pedagogy, and, while insisting on precision in detail, had tried to give the imagination freedom. Pater had done more, and he remained a force in the literature of the nineties after the Pre-Raphaelites were accorded only appreciative sympathy. The famous preface to *The Renaissance,* with its emphasis on the isolated sensation, made the younger men understand what life and poetry and art meant to them. They understood, as Yeats put it, "that Swinburne in one way, Browning in another, and Tennyson in a third, had filled their work with what I called 'impurities,' curiosities about politics, about science, about history, about religion; and that we must create once more the pure work."

They turned to France, where "pure work" was being created. They had no difficulty in doing so, for Paris was as much their home as London, and they were more at ease with French than with British contemporaries. Insular British literature, as we have seen, was once more reaching out to the literature of a foreign land. Certain French writers had already traveled or were traveling the path that the young men of England and Ireland saw stretching before them: Baudelaire, Verlaine, Barbey d'Aurevilly, Huysmans, Villiers de l'Isle-Adam, and others.

It is no surprise that both George Moore and Oscar Wilde paid tribute to Huysmans' *Against the Grain* and imitated it, for it was the perfect bible of the decadence. Soberer and perhaps more significant authors might, even on first contact with its glamor, sense its defects, finding in it the tawdriness that was so obvious in the imitations, but it remained for many a "wonderful" and "poisoned" book, and its central theme, the superiority of the neurotic personality, was a powerful consolation. Its autobiographical hero, des Esseintes, did not merely feel himself set apart from his times; that isolation was made his claim to greatness. He could not endure works of literature, art, and music that had "the approbation of the general voice," and his quest for the esoteric sent him to decadent Latin authors and the least appreciated of his contemporaries. The shudder that he felt at all contact with the public and that led him to take refuge in "a refined Thebaid," was proof to him that he was of a higher race. He could not find pleasure where others found it: sexual indulgence had to have some element of perversion, and the artificial was always preferable to the natural. "Nature has had her day," Huysmans wrote, in phrases Wilde was to copy; "she has definitely and finally tired out by the sickening monotony of her landscapes and skyscapes the patience of refined temperaments." Des Esseintes cared only for "the distillation of overwrought and subtle brains." He abandoned real for artificial flowers, and then wanted "natural flowers imitating the false." The search for the unique, the confusion of the senses, the breaking down of all barriers between the imaginary world and the real—the qualities, in short, of symbolism—were given an intensely melodramatic form.

For us *Against the Grain* is important less because of its direct influence, which was considerable, than because of its revelation of the animus of the decadence. Huysmans' hatred for

mankind reduced itself, again and again, to a hatred for the bourgeoisie.

> Nobility was utterly decayed, dead; aristocracy had fallen into idiocy or filthy pleasures! . . . The least scrupulous, the least dull-witted, threw all shame to the winds; they mixed in low plots, stirred up the filth of base finance. . . . After the aristocracy of birth, it was now the turn of the aristocracy of money; it was the Caliphate of the counting-house, the despotism of the Rue du Sentier, the tyranny of commerce with its narrow-minded, venal ideas, its ostentatious and rascally instincts. . . . More nefarious, more vile than the nobility it had plundered and the clergy it had overthrown, the bourgeoisie borrowed their frivolous love of show, their decrepit boastfulness, which it vulgarized by its lack of good manners, stole their defects which it aggravated into hypocritical vices. Obstinate and sly, base and cowardly, it shot down ruthlessly its eternal and inevitable dupe, the populace, which it had itself unmuzzled and set on to spring at the throat of the old castes. Now the victory was won. Its task once completed, the plebs had been for its health's sake bled to the last drop, while the bourgeois, secure in his triumphs, throned it jovially by dint of his money and the contagion of his folly. The result of his rise to power had been the destruction of all intelligence, the negation of all honesty, the death of all art; in fact, the artists and men of letters, in their degradation, had fallen to their knees and were devouring with ardent kisses the unwashed feet of the high-placed horse-jockeys and low-bred satraps on whose alms they lived.

Would Beardsley or Dowson or Johnson or Davidson or Symons or Yeats have quarreled with this statement? It was the bourgeoisie that they hated and either openly attacked or harried with flamboyant proclamations of their own dissidence. Baudelaire's hostility to the bourgeoisie had sent him to the barricades in forty-eight, though his sympathies with the proletariat had not survived their defeat. In the eighties and nineties the bourgeoisie, both in France and in England, seemed more firmly entrenched than ever. The signs of a break in bourgeois power that Morris could see were scarcely visible to the London and Paris poets, and insofar as they were recognized at all, they were regarded as evidences of bourgeois misrule, proof of bourgeois stupidity and not of bourgeois weakness. The only thing to do was to secede. Art must be taken away from the bourgeoisie and from the artists who kissed the unwashed bourgeois foot. And if that meant the rejection of much that had once seemed to be art but now was irremediably sullied by the admiration of the uncritical, then the decadents were prepared to limit themselves to the esoteric. Art, by their theory, true art, could appeal only to the chosen few, and to prove their membership in the elect they rejected as "a thing polluted, commonplace, almost repulsive" any work that the middle class liked.

Against the Grain defined the new attitude. Romanticism had earlier been part of a great expansive movement of the human mind. The decadents were romantic in their scorn of the conventional and their preference for the indefinite, but romanticism was now a movement of contraction. Politics, science, history, religion, Yeats said, did not properly belong to art. "No preferences, no prejudices, no particular feelings of any kind," said Wilde. The decadents did not—perhaps could not—practice all that they preached, but the limitations they did accept would never have been tolerated by the first generation of romantics.

Against the Grain also exhibited, in however exaggerated a form, the personality of the decadent artist. Des Esseintes could stand, *mutatis mutandis,* for Baudelaire, Verlaine, and Mallarmé, as well as for Huysmans himself. He could stand, too, for Dowson, Symons, Johnson, Beardsley, Wilde, Conder. It may be that all the conflicts that grew out of the creation of an industrial civilization had increased the number of neurotic personalities. But whether that is true or not, the conditions under which an artist worked in the eighties and nineties could only intensify any antecedent instability of character. Yeats, more firmly rooted than most of his contemporaries, nevertheless had a long struggle to achieve stability, and his success was almost unique. The notion not unnaturally flourished that sanity was a bourgeois trait and therefore to be condemned. Unable to overcome their vices, the decadents made virtues of them, dramatizing in their works the tragic consequences exhibited in their lives.

In political life anarchism is the refuge of the hopeless, and the decadence was anarchistic. Yet its writers had a deep passion for order. In Huysmans this was shown by the attraction, to which he eventually yielded, that Catholicism had for him. *Against the Grain* shows Huysmans haunted by the dread that none of his acts has any significance, and wondering what in that case becomes of his vaunted superiority over the masses of mankind. Even his sins are merely the whims of unstrung nerves and a depleted digestion if there is no absolute standard by which they can be judged. That is the attraction, for him as for Barbey d'Aurevilly, of demonolatry, and it is no wonder that d'Aurevilly said of *Against the Grain,* "After such a book, it only remains for the author to choose between the muzzle of a pistol or the foot of the cross."

Huysmans chose the cross, and so did many of his contemporaries in England. Both Lionel Johnson and Francis Thompson turned to Catholicism and made themselves Catholic poets. Beardsley was converted to the faith, in part by the persuasions of John Gray, a delicate if imitative symbolist poet, himself a convert. Robert Ross became a Catholic and was presumably responsible for the presence of the priest at Wilde's deathbed, and two other disciples of Wilde, Sherard and Lord Alfred Douglas, subsequently adopted that faith. And, to complete the list of converts, there were Henry Harland and Ernest Dowson.

One cannot help suspecting that the doctrine of art for art's sake was not enough in itself to support these men. In their rebellion against contemporary society they needed some sort of bulwark. The church, of course, did not sanction their way of life or even their doctrine of art, but underneath both lay their distrust of contemporary society, and it was precisely at that point that the church could sustain them. For, especially in England, where its position was always difficult, the church stood apart from the progress of capitalism. Not only was it the one organization that could look back to a precapitalist past; not only did it set its values against the values of a competitive world; it was relatively unpolluted by the vulgarity that had overcome the representative churches of the British middle class. Yeats and Davidson felt the same need for support as did the converts, but Yeats found his mysticism adequate to sustain him, and Davidson told himself he was a superman and committed suicide when he could no longer believe it.

"No poem," said Baudelaire, "can be so grand, so noble, so truly worthy of the name of poem as that which is written solely for the pleasure of writing a poem." And again: "I say that, if the poet has pursued a moral end, he has diminished his poetic force, and it is not rash to predict that his work will be bad. Poetry cannot, under pain of death or decay, be assimilated to science or morality. It does not have truth for its object, but only itself." A dozen British writers would at one time or another have subscribed to that doctrine, but not one was consistent in adherence. All of them felt the need of relating their art to a philosophy of life.

Indeed, their work had always rested on a non-literary principle, that is, on hatred of the bourgeoisie. As Wilde's career has already made plain to us, the doctrine of art for art's sake was a protest against contemporary standards and a way of escaping from bourgeois controls. It was an attempt to fight the old battle on a new front, one on which the artists had at least a momentary advantage. But if there were strategic gains, there were creative losses, and the position had to be abandoned.

The mortality rate was so high that a literary generation simply vanished. Moreover, it left few disciples and had little enduring influence. In the general battle to free British writers from the demands of an outworn and therefore stultifying moral code, the esthetes played a part, but otherwise it is hard to see how they have affected the course of English literature. Later writers learned much from the symbolists, but learned it direct from the French, not from their English disciples and inferiors. Wilde's reputation persisted because he was a symbol. Other reputations, with the exception of Beardsley's, quickly dwindled. Yeats's prestige continued to grow, but after his Irish experiments and his pre-occupation with the "Great Wheel," it became increasingly difficult to remember what he had stood for—or had been thought to stand for—in the nineties.

The Wilde incident and the episode of the *Yellow Book* and the *Savoy* are almost unique in English literary history, and it is impossible to understand them apart from the tensions of the closing decade of the century. Slight as their literary results seem to have been, their effect upon the public was incalculable. If the esthetes thought to escape bourgeois criticism by repudiating bourgeois standards, they were mistaken, for Wilde and Beardsley, and to a lesser extent their associates, were attacked with unprecedented virulence. But it was precisely the feverishness of the attack that gave the decadents their measure of victory, since it resulted in a closer scrutiny of prevailing standards than had been effected by any of the more direct critics. The writers were ill-equipped for survival in the struggle, and few of them survived, but they had their revenge, for Victorianism was dying too. It took a longer time to die than the delicate poets of the eighties and nineties, but its doom was just as sure. (pp. 243-60)

Granville Hicks, "Oscar Wilde and the Cult of Art," in his Figures of Transition: A Study of British Literature at the End of the Nineteenth Century, *Macmillan Publishing Company, 1939, pp. 217-60.*

WILLIAM BUTLER YEATS

[*The leading figure of the Irish Literary Renaissance and a major poet in twentieth-century literature, Yeats was also an active critic of his contemporaries' works. As a critic he judged the works of others according to his own poetic values of sinceri-*

ty, passion, and vital imagination. In the following excerpt, Yeats characterizes English Decadent authors and artists as a "tragic generation" and speculates as to why many did not survive the period.]

Shaw and Wilde, had no catastrophe come, would have long divided the stage between them, though they were most unlike—for Wilde believed himself to value nothing but words in their emotional associations, and he had turned his style to a parade as though it were his show, and he Lord Mayor.

I was at Sligo again and I saw the announcement of his action against Lord Queensberry, when starting from my uncle's home to walk to Knocknarea to dine with Cochrane of the Glen, as he was called, to distinguish him from others of that name, an able old man. . . . I remember that I spoke that night of Wilde's kindness to myself, said I did not believe him guilty, quoted the psychologist Bain, who has attributed to every sensualist "a voluminous tenderness," and described Wilde's hard brilliance, his dominating self-possession. I considered him essentially a man of action, that he was a writer by perversity and accident, and would have been more important as soldier or politician; and I was certain that, guilty or not guilty, he would prove himself a man. I was probably excited, and did most of the talking, for if Cochrane had talked, I would have remembered an amusing sentence or two; but he was certainly sympathetic. A couple of days later I received a letter from Lionel Johnson, denouncing Wilde with great bitterness. He had "a cold scientific intellect"; he got a "sense of triumph and power, at every dinner-table he dominated, from the knowledge that he was guilty of that sin which, more than any other possible to man, would turn all those people against him if they but knew." He wrote in the mood of his poem, "To the Destroyer of a Soul," addressed to Wilde, as I have always believed, though I know nothing of the circumstance that made him write it.

I might have known that Wilde's fantasy had taken some tragic turn, and that he was meditating upon possible disaster, but one took all his words for play—had he not called insincerity "a mere multiplication of the personality" or some such words? I had met a man who had found him in a barber's shop in Venice, and heard him explain, "I am having my hair curled that I may resemble Nero"; and when, as editor of an Irish anthology, I had asked leave to quote "Tread gently, she is near under the snow," he had written that I might do so if I pleased, but his most characteristic poem was that sonnet with the lines

> Lo! with a little rod
> I did but touch the honey's romance—
> And must I lose a soul's inheritance.

When in London for my play I had asked news from an actor who had seen him constantly. "He is in deep melancholy," was the answer. "He says that he tries to sleep away as much of life as possible, only leaving his bed at two or three in the afternoon, and spending the rest of the day at the Café Royal. He has written what he calls the best short story in the world, and will have it that he repeats to himself on getting out of bed and before every meal. 'Christ came from a white plain to a purple city, and as he passed through the first street, he heard voices overhead, and saw a young man lying drunk upon a window-sill, "Why do you waste your soul in drunkenness?" He said. "Lord, I was a leper and You healed me, what else can I do?" A little further through the town he saw a young man following a harlot, and said, "Why do you dissolve your soul in debauchery?" and the young man answered, "Lord, I was blind, and You healed me, what else can I do?" At last in the middle of the city He saw an old man crouching, weeping upon the ground, and when He asked why he wept, the old man answered, "Lord, I was dead and You raised me into life, what else can I do but weep?"' "

Wilde published that story a little later, but spoiled it with the verbal decoration of his epoch, and I have to repeat it to myself as I first heard it, before I can see its terrible beauty. I no more doubt its sincerity than I doubt that his parade of gloom, all that late rising, and sleeping away his life, that elaborate playing with tragedy, was an attempt to escape from an emotion by its exaggeration. He had three successful plays running at once; he had been almost poor, and now, his head full of Flaubert, found himself with ten thousand a year:—"Lord, I was dead, and You raised me into life, what else can I do but weep." A comedian, he was in the hands of those dramatists who understand nothing but tragedy.

A few days after the first production of my *Land of Heart's Desire,* I had my last conversation with him. He had come into the theatre as the curtain fell upon my play, and I knew that it was to ask my pardon that he overwhelmed me with compliments; and yet I wonder if he would have chosen those precise compliments, or spoken so extravagantly, but for the turn his thoughts had taken: "Your story in "the National Observer, "The Crucifixion of the Outcast," is sublime, wonderful, wonderful." (pp. 188-91)

Cultivated London, that before the action against Lord Queensberry had mocked his pose and his affected style, and refused to acknowledge his wit, was now full of his advocates, though I did not meet a single man who considered him innocent. One old enemy of his overtook me in the street and began to praise his audacity, his self-possession. "He has made," he said, "of infamy a new Thermopylæ." I had written in reply to Lionel Johnson's letter that I regretted Wilde's downfall but not that of his imitators, but Johnson had changed with the rest. "Why do you not regret the fall of Wilde's imitators"—I had but tried to share what I thought his opinion—"They were worthless, but should have been left to criticism." Wilde himself was a martyr in his eyes, and when I said that tragedy might give his art a greater depth, he would not even grant a martyr's enemies that poor merit, and thought Wilde would produce, when it was all over, some comedy exactly like the others, writing from an art where events could leave no trace. Everywhere one met writers and artists who praised his wit and eloquence in the witness-box, or repeated some private saying. (pp. 192-93)

The Rhymers had begun to break up in tragedy, though we did not know that till the play had finished. I have never found a full explanation of that tragedy; sometimes I have remembered that, unlike the Victorian poets, almost all were poor men, and had made it a matter of conscience to turn from every kind of money-making that prevented good writing, and that poverty meant strain, and for the most part, a refusal of domestic life. Then I have remembered that Johnson had private means, and that others who came to tragic ends, had wives and families. Another day I think that perhaps our form of lyric, our insistence upon emotion which has no relation to any public interest, gathered together overwrought, unstable men; and remember, the moment after, that the first to go out of his mind had no lyrical gift, and that we valued him mainly because he seemed a witty man of the world; and that a little later another who seemed, alike as man and writer, dull and formless, went out of his mind, first burning poems which I cannot believe would have proved him as the one man who saw them claims, a man of genius. The meetings were always decorous and often dull; some one would read out a poem and we would comment, too politely for the criticism to have great value; and yet that we read out our poems, and thought that they could be so tested, was a definition of our aims. "Love's Nocturne" is one of the most beautiful poems in the world, but no one can find out its beauty, so intricate its thought and metaphor, till he has read it over several times, or stopped several times to re-read a passage, and the *Faustine* of Swinburne, where much is powerful and musical, could not, were it read out, be understood with pleasure, however clearly it were read, because it has no more logical structure than a bag of shot. I shall, however, remember all my life that evening when Lionel Johnson read or spoke aloud in his musical monotone, where meaning and cadence found the most precise elocution, his poem suggested "by the Statute of King Charles at Charing Cross." It was as though I listened to a great speech. Nor will that poem be to me again what it was that first night. For long I only knew Dowson's "O Mors," to quote but the first words of its long title, and his "Villanelle of Sunset" from his reading, and it was because of the desire to hold them in my hand that I suggested the first *Book of The Rhymers' Club.* They were not speech but perfect song, though song for the speaking voice. It was perhaps our delight in poetry that was, before all else, speech or song, and could hold the attention of a fitting audience like a good play or good conversation, that made Francis Thompson, whom we admired so much—before the publication of his first poem I had brought to The Cheshire Cheese the proof sheets of his "Ode to the Setting Sun," his first published poem—come but once and refuse to contribute to our book. Preoccupied with his elaborate verse, he may have seen only that which we renounced, and thought what seemed to us simplicity, mere emptiness. To some members this simplicity was perhaps created by their tumultuous lives, they praised a desired woman and hoped that she would find amid their praise her very self, or at worst, their very passion; and knew that she, ignoramus that she was, would have slept in the middle of "Love's Nocturne," lofty and tender though it be. Woman herself was still in our eyes, for all that, romantic and mysterious, still the priestess of her shrine, our emotions remembering the *Lilith* and the *Sybilla Palmifera* of Rossetti; for as yet that sense of comedy, which was soon to mould the very fashion plates, and, in the eyes of men of my generation, to destroy at last the sense of beauty itself, had scarce begun to show here and there, in slight subordinate touches among the designs of great painters and craftsmen. It could not be otherwise, for Johnson's favourite phrase, that life is ritual, expressed something that was in some degree in all our thoughts, and how could life be ritual if woman had not her symbolical place?

If Rossetti was a subconscious influence, and perhaps the most powerful of all, we looked consciously to Pater for our philosophy. Three or four years ago I re-read *Marius the Epicurean,* expecting to find I cared for it no longer, but it still seemed to me, as I think it seemed to us all, the only great prose in modern English, and yet I began to wonder if it, or the attitude of mind of which it was the noblest expression, had not caused the disaster of my friends. It taught us to walk upon a rope, tightly stretched through serene air, and we were left to keep our feet upon a swaying rope in a storm. Pater had made us learned; and, whatever we might be elsewhere, ceremonious and polite, and distant in our relations to one another, and I think none knew as yet that Dowson,

who seemed to drink so little and had so much dignity and reserve, was breaking his heart for the daughter of the keeper of an Italian eating house, in dissipation and drink; and that he might that very night sleep upon a six-penny bed in a doss house. It seems to me that even yet, and I am speaking of 1894 and 1895, we knew nothing of one another, but the poems that we read and criticised; perhaps I have forgotten or was too much in Ireland for knowledge, but of this I am certain, we shared nothing but the artistic life. Sometimes Johnson and Symons would visit our sage at Oxford, and I remember Johnson, whose reports however were not always to be trusted, returning with a sentence that long ran in my head. He had noticed books on political economy among Pater's books, and Pater had said, "Everything that has occupied man, for any length of time, is worthy of our study." Perhaps it was because of Pater's influence that we with an affectation of learning, claimed the whole past of literature for our authority, instead of finding it like the young men in the age of comedy that followed us, in some new, and so still unrefuted authority; that we preferred what seemed still uncrumbled rock, to the still unspotted foam; that we were traditional alike in our dress, in our manner, in our opinions, and in our style.

Why should men, who spoke their opinions in low voices, as though they feared to disturb the readers in some ancient library, and timidly as though they knew that all subjects had long since been explored, all questions long since decided in books whereon the dust settled—live lives of such disorder and seek to rediscover in verse the syntax of impulsive common life? Was it that we lived in what is called "an age of transition" and so lacked coherence, or did we but pursue antithesis?

All things, apart from love and melancholy, were a study to us; Horne already learned in Botticelli had begun to boast that when he wrote of him there would be no literature, all would be but learning; Symons, as I wrote when I first met him, studied the music halls, as he might have studied the age of Chaucer; while I gave much time to what is called the Christian Cabbala; nor was there any branch of knowledge Johnson did not claim for his own. When I had first gone to see him in 1888 or 1889, at the Charlotte Street house, I had called about five in the afternoon, but the man-servant that he shared with Horne and Image, told me that he was not yet up, adding with effusion "he is always up for dinner at seven." This habit of breakfasting when others dined had been started by insomnia, but he came to defend it for its own sake. When I asked if it did not separate him from men and women he replied, "In my library I have all the knowledge of the world that I need." He had certainly a considerable library, far larger than that of any young man of my acquaintance, so large that he wondered if it might not be possible to find some way of hanging new shelves from the ceiling like chandeliers. That room was always a pleasure to me, with its curtains of grey corduroy over door and window and book case, and its walls covered with brown paper, a fashion invented, I think, by Horne, that was soon to spread. There was a portrait of Cardinal Newman, looking a little like Johnson himself, some religious pictures by Simeon Solomon, and works upon theology in Greek and Latin and a general air of neatness and severity; and talking there by candlelight it never seemed very difficult to murmur Villiers de L'Isle Adam's proud words, "As for living—our servants will do that for us." Yet I can now see that Johnson himself in some half-conscious part of him desired the world he had renounced. I was often puzzled as to when and where he could have met the famous men or beautiful women, whose conversation, often wise, and always appropriate, he quoted so often, and it was not till a little before his death that I discovered that these conversations were imaginary. He never altered a detail of speech, and would quote what he had invented for Gladstone or Newman for years without amplification or amendment, with what seemed a scholar's accuracy. His favourite quotations were from Newman, whom, I believe, he had never met, though I can remember nothing now but Newman's greeting to Johnson, "I have always considered the profession of a man of letters a third order of the priesthood!" and these quotations became so well known that at Newman's death, the editor of *The Nineteenth Century* asked them for publication. Because of his delight in all that was formal and arranged he objected to the public quotation of private conversation even after death, and this scruple helped his refusal. Perhaps this dreaming was made a necessity by his artificial life, yet before that life began he wrote from Oxford to his Tory but flattered family, that as he stood mounted upon a library ladder in his rooms taking a book from a shelf, Gladstone, about to pass the open door on his way upstairs to some college authority, had stopped, hesitated, come into the room and there spent an hour of talk. Presently it was discovered that Gladstone had not been near Oxford on the date given; yet he quoted that conversation without variation of a word until the end of his life, and I think believed in it as firmly as did his friends. These conversations were always admirable in their drama, but never too dramatic or even too polished to lose their casual accidental character; they were the phantasmagoria through which his philosophy of life found its expression. (pp. 199-204)

He wanted us to believe that all things, his poetry with its Latin weight, his religion with its constant reference to the Fathers of the Church, or to the philosophers of the Church, almost his very courtesy were a study and achievement of the intellect. Arthur Symons' poetry made him angry, because it would substitute for that achievement, Parisian impressionism, "a London fog, the blurred tawny lamplight, the red omnibus, the dreary rain, the depressing mud, the glaring gin shop, the slatternly shivering women, three dexterous stanzas telling you that and nothing more." I, on the other hand, angered him by talking as if art existed for emotion only, and for refutation he would quote the close of the Aeschylean Trilogy, the trial of Orestes on the Acropolis. Yet at moments the thought came to him that intellect, as he conceived it, was too much a thing of many books, that it lacked lively experience. "Yeats," he has said to me, "you need ten years in a library, but I have need of ten years in the wilderness." When he said "Wilderness" I am certain, however, that he thought of some historical, some bookish desert, the Thebaid, or the lands about the Mareotic sea. Though his best poetry is natural and impassioned, he spoke little of it, but much about his prose, and would contend that I had no right to consider words made to read, less natural than words made to be spoken; and he delighted in a sentence in his book on Thomas Hardy, that kept its vitality, as he contended, though two pages long. He punctuated after the manner of the seventeenth century and was always ready to spend an hour discussing the exact use of the colon. "One should use a colon where other people use a semi-colon, a semi-colon where other people use a comma," was, I think, but a condescension to my ignorance for the matter was plainly beset with many subtleties.

Not till some time in 1895 did I think he could ever drink too much for his sobriety—though what he drank would certainly be too much for that of most of the men whom I knew—I no more doubted his self-control, though we were very intimate friends, than I doubted his memories of Cardinal Newman. The discovery that he did was a great shock to me, and, I think, altered my general view of the world. (pp. 204-05)

I began now to hear stories of Dowson, whom I knew only at the Rhymers, or through some chance meeting at Johnson's. I was indolent and procrastinating, and when I thought of asking him to dine, or taking some other step towards better knowledge, he seemed to be in Paris, or at Dieppe. He was drinking, but, unlike Johnson, who, at the autopsy after his death, was discovered never to have grown, except in the brain, after his fifteenth year, he was full of sexual desire. Johnson and he were close friends, and Johnson lectured him out of the Fathers upon chastity, and boasted of the great good done him thereby. But the rest of us counted the glasses emptied in their talk. I began to hear now in some detail of the restaurant-keeper's daughter, and of her marriage to the waiter, and of that weekly game of cards with her that filled so great a share of Dowson's emotional life. Sober, he would look at no other woman, it was said, but drunk, desired whatever woman chance brought, clean or dirty.

Johnson was stern by nature, strong by intellect, and always, I think, deliberately picked his company, but Dowson seemed gentle, affectionate, drifting. His poetry shows how sincerely he felt the fascination of religion, but his religion had certainly no dogmatic outline, being but a desire for a condition of virginal ecstasy. If it is true, as Arthur Symons, his very close friend, has written, that he loved the restaurant-keeper's daughter for her youth, one may be almost certain that he sought from religion some similar quality, something of that which the angels find who move perpetually, as Swedenborg has said, towards "the day-spring of their youth." Johnson's poetry, like Johnson himself before his last decay, conveys an emotion of joy, of intellectual clearness, of hard energy; he gave us of his triumph; while Dowson's poetry is sad, as he himself seemed, and pictures his life of temptation and defeat,

> Unto us they belong
> Us the bitter and gay,
> Wine and women and song.

Their way of looking at their intoxication showed their characters. Johnson, who could not have written "Dark Angel" if he did not suffer from remorse, showed to his friends an impenitent face, and defeated me when I tried to prevent the foundation of an Irish convivial club—it was brought to an end after one meeting by the indignation of the members' wives—whereas the last time I saw Dowson he was pouring out a glass of whiskey for himself in an empty corner of my room and murmuring over and over in what seemed automatic apology "The first to-day." (pp. 207-08)

At eleven one morning I met [John Davidson] in the British Museum reading-room, probably in 1894, when I was in London for the production of *The Land of Heart's Desire,* but certainly after some long absence from London. "Are you working her?" I said; "No," he said, "I am loafing, for I have finished my day's work." "What, already?" "I work an hour a day—I cannot work longer without exhaustion, and even as it is, if I meet anybody and get into talk, I cannot write the next day; that is why I loaf when my work is finished." No one had ever doubted his industry; he had supported his wife and family for years by "devilling" many hours a day for some popular novelist. "What work is it?" I said. "I am writing verse," he answered. "I had been writing prose for a long time, and then one day I thought I might just as well write what I liked, as I must starve in any case. It was the luckiest thought I ever had, for my agent now gets me forty pounds for a ballad, and I made three hundred out of my last book of verse."

He was older by ten years than his fellow Rhymers; a national schoolmaster from Scotland, he had been dismissed, he told us, for asking for a rise in his salary, and had come to London with his wife and children. He looked older than his years. . . . He had endured and was to endure again, a life of tragic penury, which was made much harder by the conviction that the world was against him, that he was refused for some reason his rightful position. (pp. 210-11)

He saw in delicate, laborious, discriminating taste, an effeminate pedantry, and would, when that mood was on him, delight in all that seemed healthy, popular, and bustling. Once when I had praised Herbert Horne for his knowledge and his taste, he burst out, "If a man must be a connoisseur, let him be a connoisseur in women." He, indeed, was accustomed, in the most characteristic phrase of his type, to describe the Rhymers as lacking in "blood and guts," and very nearly brought us to an end by attempting to supply the deficiency by the addition of four Scotsmen. He brought all four upon the same evening, and one read out a poem upon the Life Boat, evidently intended for a recitation; another described how, when gold-digging in Australia, he had fought and knocked down another miner for doubting the rotundity of the earth; while of the remainder I can remember nothing except that they excelled in argument. He insisted upon their immediate election, and the Rhymers, through that complacency of good manners whereby educated Englishmen so often surprise me, obeyed, though secretly resolved never to meet again; and it cost me seven hours' work to get another meeting, and vote the Scotsmen out. A few days later I chanced upon Davidson at some restaurant; he was full of amiability, and when we parted shook my hand, and proclaimed enthusiastically that I had "blood and guts." I think he might have grown to be a successful man had he been enthusiastic instead about Dowson or Johnson, or Horne or Symons, for they had what I still lacked, conscious deliberate craft, and what I must lack always, scholarship. They had taught me that violent energy, which is like a fire of straw, consumes in a few minutes the nervous vitality, and is useless in the arts. Our fire must burn slowly, and we must constantly turn away to think, constantly analyse what we have done, be content even to have little life outside our work, to show, perhaps, to other men, as little as the watch-mender shows, his magnifying glass caught in his screwed-up eye. Only then do we learn to conserve our vitality, to keep our mind enough under control and to make our technique sufficiently flexible for expression of the emotions of life as they arise. A few months after our meeting in the Museum, Davidson had spent his inspiration. "The fires are out," he said, "and I must hammer the cold iron." When I heard a few years ago that he had drowned himself, I knew that I had always expected some such end. With enough passion to make a great poet, through meeting no man of culture in early life, he lacked intellectual receptivity, and, anarchic and indefinite, lacked pose and gesture, and now no verse of his clings to my memory.

Gradually Arthur Symons came to replace in my intimate friendship, Lionel Johnson from whom I was slowly separated by a scruple of conscience. If he came to see me he sat tongue-tied unless I gave him the drink that seemed necessary to bring his vitality to but its normal pitch, and if I called upon him he drank so much that I became his confederate. Once, when a friend and I had sat long after our proper bed-time at his constantly repeated and most earnest entreaty, knowing what black melancholy would descend upon him at our departure, and with the unexpressed hope of getting him to his bed, he fixed upon us a laughing and whimsical look, and said:—"I want you two men to understand that you are merely two men that I am drinking with." That was the only time that I was to hear from him an imaginary conversation that had not an air of the most scrupulous accuracy. He gave two accounts of a conversation with Wilde in prison; in one Wilde wore his hair long, and in the other it had been cropped by the prison barber. He was gradually losing, too, the faculty of experience, and in his prose and verse repeated the old ideas and emotions, but faintly, as though with fading interest. I am certain that he prayed much, and on those rare days that I came upon him dressed and active before mid-day or but little after, I concluded that he had been to morning Mass at Farm Street.

When with Johnson I had turned myself to his mood, but Arthur Symons, more than any man I have ever known, could slip as it were into the mind of another, and my thoughts gained in richness and in clearness from his sympathy, nor shall I ever know how much my practice and my theory owe to the passages that he read me from Catullus and from Verlaine and Mallarmé. (pp. 211-13)

It seems to me, looking backward, that we always discussed life at its most intense moment, that moment which gives a common sacredness to the Song of Songs, and to the Sermon on the Mount, and in which one discovers something supernatural, a stirring as it were of the roots of the hair. He was making those translations from Mallarmé and from Verlaine, from Calderon, from St. John of the Cross, which are the most accomplished metrical translations of our time, and I think that those from Mallarmé may have given elaborate form to my verses of those years, to the later poems of *The Wind among the Reeds,* to *The Shadowy Waters,* while Villiers de L'Isle Adam had shaped whatever in my *Rosa Alchemica* Pater had not shaped. (p. 214)

Hitherto when in London I had stayed with my family in Bedford Park, but now I was to live for some twelve months in chambers in the Temple that opened through a little passage into those of Arthur Symons. If anybody rang at either door, one or other would look through a window in the connecting passage, and report. We would then decide whether one or both should receive the visitor, whether his door or mine should be opened, or whether both doors were to remain closed. I have never liked London, but London seemed less disagreeable when one could walk in quiet, empty places after dark, and upon a Sunday morning sit upon the margin of a fountain almost as alone as if in the country. I was already settled there, I imagine, when a publisher called and proposed that Symons should edit a Review or Magazine, and Symons consented on the condition that Beardsley were Art Editor—and I was delighted at his condition, as I think were all his other proposed contributors. Aubrey Beardsley had been dismissed from the Art editorship of the *Yellow Book* under circumstances that had made us indignant. He had illustrated Wilde's *Salome,* his strange satiric art had raised the popular press to fury, and at the height of the excitement aroused by Wilde's condemnation, a popular novelist, a woman who had great influence among the most conventional part of the British public, had written demanding his dismissal. "She owed it to her position before the British people," she had said. Beardsley was not even a friend of Wilde's—they even disliked each other—he had no sexual abnormality, but he was certainly unpopular, and the moment had come to get rid of unpopular persons. The public at once concluded—they could hardly conclude otherwise, he was dismissed by telegram—that there was evidence against him, and Beardsley, who was some twenty-three years old, being embittered and miserable, plunged into dissipation. We knew that we must face an infuriated press and public, but being all young we delighted in enemies and in everything that had an heroic air.

We might have survived but for our association with Beardsley; perhaps, but for his *Under the Hill,* a Rabelaisian fragment promising a literary genius as great maybe as his artistic genius; and for the refusal of the bookseller who controlled the railway bookstalls to display our wares. The bookseller's manager, no doubt looking for a design of Beardsley's, pitched upon Blake's *Antaeus setting Virgil and Dante upon the verge of Cocytus* as the ground of refusal, and when Arthur Symons pointed out that Blake was considered "a very

Max Beerbohm caricature of Aubrey Beardsley.

spiritual artist," replied, "O, Mr. Symons, you must remember that we have an audience of young ladies as well as an audience of agnostics." However, he called Arthur Symons back from the door to say, "If contrary to our expectations the *Savoy* should have a large sale, we should be very glad to see you again." As Blake's design illustrated an article of mine, I wrote a letter upon that remarkable saying to a principal daily newspaper. But I had mentioned Beardsley, and I was told that the editor had made it a rule that his paper was never to mention Beardsley's name. I said upon meeting him later, "Would you have made the same rule in the case of Hogarth?" against whom much the same objection could be taken, and he replied with what seemed to me a dreamy look, as though suddenly reminded of a lost opportunity—"Ah, there was no popular press in Hogarth's day." We were not allowed to forget that in our own day there was a popular press, and its opinions began to affect our casual acquaintance, and even our comfort in public places. At some well-known house, an elderly man to whom I had just been introduced, got up from my side and walked to the other end of the room; but it was as much my reputation as an Irish rebel as the evil company that I was supposed to keep, that excited some young men in a railway carriage to comment upon my general career in voices raised that they might catch my attention. I discovered, however, one evening that we were perhaps envied as well as despised. I was in the pit at some theatre, and had just noticed Arthur Symons a little in front of me, when I heard a young man, who looked like a shop-assistant or clerk, say, "There is Arthur Symons. If he can't get an order, why can't he pay for a stall?" Clearly we were supposed to prosper upon iniquity, and to go to the pit added a sordid parsimony. At another theatre I caught sight of a woman that I once liked, the widow of some friend of my father's youth, and tried to attract her attention, but she had no eyes for anything but the stage curtain; and at some house where I met no hostility to myself, a popular novelist snatched out of my hand a copy of the *Savoy,* and opening it at Beardsley's drawing, called *The Barber,* expounded what he called its bad drawing and wound up with, "Now if you want to admire really great black and white art, admire the *Punch* cartoons of Mr. Lindley Sambourne." Our hostess, after making peace between us, said, "O, Mr. Yeats, why do you not send your poems to the *Spectator* instead of to the *Savoy?*" The answer, "My friends read the *Savoy* and they do not read the *Spectator,*" called up a puzzled, disapproving look.

Yet, even apart from Beardsley, we were a sufficiently distinguished body: Max Beerbohm, Bernard Shaw, Ernest Dowson, Lionel Johnson, Arthur Symons, Charles Conder, Charles Shannon, Havelock Ellis, Selwyn Image, Joseph Conrad; but nothing counted but the one hated name. I think that had we been challenged we might have argued something after this fashion: "Science through much ridicule and some persecution has won its right to explore whatever passes before its corporeal eye, and merely because it passes: to set as it were upon an equality the beetle and the whale though Ben Jonson could find no justification for the entomologist in *The New Inn,* but that he had been crossed in love. Literature now demands the same right of exploration of all that passes before the mind's eye, and merely because it passes." Not a complete defence, for it substitutes a spiritual for a physical objectivity, but sufficient it may be for the moment, and to settle our place in the historical process. (pp. 215-18)

W. B. Yeats, "The Trembling of the Veil (1922),"

in his Autobiographies, *Macmillan & Co., Ltd.,*
1955, pp. 73-254.

FRENCH LITERATURE AND ENGLISH LITERARY DECADENCE

ENID STARKIE

[*Starkie was an English literary critic and the author of nu-*
merous studies of nineteenth- and twentieth-century French lit-
erature. Her works include important studies of Charles Bau-
delaire, Arthur Rimbaud, André Gide, and Gustave Flaubert.
In the following excerpt, she examines seminal French influ-
ences on English Decadent literature of the 1890s.]

In the eighteen-nineties interest in French literature amongst
English writers developed very rapidly. The way had been
prepared, twenty years before, by Swinburne and Pater, and
they were followed by others—especially by George Moore.
However, as the influence of France spread, the exponents of
the new art came more frequently into clash with the forces
of philistinism. The middle-class had been growing more
prosperous since the middle of the century, since the Exhibition of 1851, and their accumulated wealth added weight and
force to their opposition to an art which did not support their
ideal of goodness allied to riches.

After George Moore, the next writer significant in the propagation of the aesthetic ideal from France was Oscar Wilde,
who did not doubt that it would ultimately prevail. 'The future belongs to the Dandies,' he said. 'It is the exquisites who
are going to rule!' He became the perfect and supreme example of the aesthete in England. Like George Moore he was an
Irishman; he was born in Dublin in October 1854, a few days
before Arthur Rimbaud, and he was two years younger than
George Moore. He seemed, however, very much more than
that his junior, for he postponed his attainment of adult status by taking degrees at two universities. He obtained a First
Class in Greek and Latin in Final Honour Moderations at
Trinity College, Dublin, and also the Berkeley Gold Medal
for Greek. After that he went up, as a young graduate of
twenty, to Magdalen College, Oxford, with a Demyship. He
obtained a First Class in Honour Moderations in Classics in
1876, and a First in Litterae Humaniores in 1878. At Oxford
he made the acquaintance of Walter Pater, and fell forthwith
under his sway. He read his *Renaissance* with passionate admiration, and spoke of it in terms very similar to those used
by Swinburne about *Mademoiselle de Maupin*. 'It is my golden book! I never travel without it, but it is the very flower
of decadence; the last trumpet should have sounded the moment it was written.'

Oscar Wilde, more fortunate than Swinburne, won the
Newdigate Prize, in 1878, for his poem entitled 'Ravenna,'
and read a portion of it at the Encaenia in the Sheldonian
Theatre, in June that year—his first taste of public fame and
acclamation, and he enjoyed it!

Shortly after taking his degree he went to London to embark
on the career of a man of letters. His first collection of poems
appeared in 1881 when he was twenty-seven—the same year
as Moore's *Pagan Poems*—resplendent in a white vellum

parchment binding, with a cover device of gold prune blossoms designed by himself. They are not very distinguished or
original poems, and are very much influenced by the poets of
the Art for Art's Sake Movement in France, by Baudelaire
and Gautier in particular. Baudelaire's 'L'Héautontimor-
ouménos,' the self-torturer, is reflected in the following lines:

Being ourselves the sowers and the seeds,
The night that covers and the lights that fade,
The spear that pierces and the side that bleeds,
The lips betraying and the life betrayed.

Gautier's 'Symphonie en blanc majeur,' from *Émaux et*
camées, is echoed in 'A Symphony in Yellow':

An omnibus across the bridge
Crawls like a yellow butterfly,
And here and there, a passer-by
Shows like a little restless midge.

Big barges full of yellow hay,
Are moored against the shadowy wharf
And like a yellow silken scarf,
The thick fog hangs along the quay.

The yellow leaves begin to fade,
And flutter from the Temple elms;
And, at my feet, the pale green Thames
Lies like a rod of rippled jade.

While 'Harmony in the Gold Room' recalls Verlaine's poem,
'Le piano que baise une main frêle' from *Romances sans pa-*
roles.

Between 1881 and 1883 Oscar Wilde paid several visits to
Paris, and met some of the well-known poets of the time. In
1882 he went to the United States to lecture and, even then,
had already formed the habit of shocking those whom he met.
When asked, at the customs examination, whether he had
anything to declare, he answered: 'Nothing but my genius!'
Everywhere he went, on this lecture tour, he was taken as the
symbol of the Decadent—and this is interesting as it was two
years before this figure became crystallized in France in the
person of Des Esseintes.

Between 1880 and 1890 Oscar Wilde was training to be the
aesthetic leader of English literature. Writing in the *Yellow*
Book, in January 1895, Max Beerbohm said that, before
Wilde, there had been poets and painters, but that no one, before him, had spoken of the quality of beauty:

It would appear that it was to him that Art owed
the great social vogue she enjoyed at this time. Peacock feathers and sunflowers glittered in every
room, the curio shops were ransacked for furniture
of Queen Anne's days, and men and women, fired
with the fervid words of the young Oscar, threw
their mahogany into the streets. A few smart
women even dressed themselves in suave draperies
and unheard of greens. Into whatever ballroom you
went you would surely find, among the women in
tiaras and fops and the distinguished foreigners,
half a score of comely ragamuffins in velveteens,
murmuring sonnets, posturing, waving their hands.
The craze was called Aestheticism.

At first Oscar Wilde followed very closely the poets of the Art
for Art's Sake Movement, those who had been dead for many
years now—Baudelaire and Gautier. In 1883 he wrote his
first play, *The Duchess of Padua*, in 1885 another collection
of verse entitled *The Harlot's House*, the name poem of which
recalls Baudelaire. Next came, in 1888, a collection of short

stories, *The Happy Prince and Other Tales,* and, in 1891, a further collection of tales, *The House of Pomegranates.* In these the influence of Flaubert is predominant, and Wilde wished to produce in English what the French novelist had achieved in his *Trois contes.* In the second collection, *The Star Child* recalls *Saint Julien l'Hospitalier,* and *The Birthday of the Infanta* is reminiscent of the style of *Hérodias. The House of Pomegranates* is vastly superior to *The Happy Prince* and is, in fact, one of the most successful examples of Wilde's achievement in prose.

However, far more important than the poems or the short stories are the articles of aesthetic criticism, written between 1889 and 1890—though one of them, 'The Truth of Masks', had appeared under the title 'Shakespeare and Stage Costume' in 1885—and published under the title *Intentions* in 1891. 'Pen, Pencil and Poison' appeared in the *Fortnightly Review* in 1889; 'The Decay of Lying' in 1889 and 'The Critic as an Artist' in 1890—both in the *Eighteenth-Century Review.*

The ideas contained in these essays are largely borrowed from Baudelaire's aesthetic criticism, but Wilde has added a touch of blasé humour and flippancy, not present in the French author. They are the most extreme expression of the Art for Art's Sake doctrine, and Wilde declared that 'art never expresses anything but itself. All bad art comes from returning to life and Nature'. Like Gautier and Baudelaire, he raises art to the highest pinnacle, far higher than Nature, and he says: 'The more we study art, the less we care for Nature. What art really reveals is Nature's lack of design.' This is taken straight out of Baudelaire's *Salon* of 1846, as well as: 'There is no variety in Nature. It resides in the imagination, or fancy, of the man who looks at her. It is fortunate for us that Nature is so imperfect, as otherwise we should have had no art at all.' As for the imitation of Nature, he says: 'It is, on the contrary, Nature that copies art. A great artist invents a new type and life tries to copy it!'

> Nature is no great mother who has borne us. She is our creation. It is in our brain that she quickens to life. Things are because we see them, and what we see, and how we see it, depends on the arts that have influenced us. To look at a thing is very different from seeing a thing. One does not see anything until one sees its beauty. Then, and then only, does it come to existence. At present people see fogs, not because there are fogs, but because poets and painters have taught them the mysterious loveliness of such effects. There may have been fogs for centuries in London. But no one saw them, and so we do not know anything about them. They did not exist until Art invented them.

Eighteen-ninety-one was an important year for Oscar Wilde for, as well as *The House of Pomegranates* and *Intentions,* he published *Lord Arthur Savile's Crime* and *The Picture of Dorian Gray.* As a story *Lord Arthur Savile's Crime* is not very interesting for the plot is weak and the characterization poor, but its style is brilliant, and it contains passages which resemble prose poems by Baudelaire from his *Spleen de Paris*—one might call them, perhaps, *Spleen de Londres!* One such describes Lord Arthur's walk, at dawn, through London:

> Where he went he hardly knew. He had a dim memory of wandering through a labyrinth of sordid houses, of being lost in a great web of sombre streets, and it was bright dawn when he found himself, at last, at Piccadilly Circus. As he strolled home towards Belgrave Square, he met the great waggons on their way to Covent Garden. The white-smocked carters, with their pleasant sunburnt faces and coarse curly hair, strode sturdily on, cracking their whips, and calling out now and then to each other; on the back of a huge grey horse, the leader of a jangling team, sat a chubby boy, with a bunch of primroses in his battered hat, keeping a tight hold of the mane with his little hands, and laughing; and the great pile of vegetables looked like masses of jade against the morning sky, like masses of green jade against the pink petal of some marvellous rose. Lord Arthur felt curiously affected, he could not tell why. There was something in the dawn's delicate loveliness that seemed to him inexpressibly pathetic, and he thought of all the days that break in beauty and that set in storm. It was now a London free from the sin of night and the smoke of day, a pallid ghost-like city, a desolate town of tombs.

The Picture of Dorian Gray, which was inspired by *A Rebours,* became for England what Huysmans' novel had been for France, its aesthetic Bible, the book which gave the most perfect picture of the Decadent. There is no doubt that the 'yellow book' which leads Dorian Gray to perdition is *A Rebours.* 'Dorian Gray had been poisoned by a book' and, through it, he had learnt 'to look on evil simply as a mode through which he could realize his conception of the beautiful'. He procured from Paris no less than nine large-paper copies of the first edition, and had them bound in different colours, so that they might suit his various moods, and the changing fancies of a nature over which he seemed, at times, to have almost entirely lost control. The hero, the wonderful young Parisian, in whom the romantic and the scientific temperaments were so strangely blended, became to him a kind of 'prefiguring type of himself'. Indeed the whole book seemed to him to contain the story of his own life, written before he had lived it.

He proceeded then to make it true about his own life. Just as des Esseintes had enjoyed his symphonies of perfume and taste, so did Dorian Gray in like manner:

> And so he would now study perfumes, and the secrets of their manufacture, distilling heavily-scented oils, and burning odorous gums from the East. He saw that there was no mood of the mind that had not its counterpart in the sensuous life, and set himself to discover their true relations.

That is Baudelaire's theory of *correspondances,* and so is the following:

> What was there in frankincense that made one mystical, and in ambergris that stirred one's passions, and in violets that woke the memory of dead romances, and in musk that troubled the brain, and in champak that stained the imagination; and seeking often to elaborate a real psychology of perfumes, and to estimate the several influences of sweet-smelling roots, and scented pollen-laded flowers, or aromatic balms, and of dark and fragrant woods, of spikenard that sickens, of hovenia that makes men mad, and of aloes that are said to be able to expel melancholy from the soul?

The Preface is composed of aphorisms borrowed from Flaubert's correspondence. 'To reveal art and to conceal the artist is art's aim.' Or: 'There is no such thing as a moral or an immoral book. Books are well written, or badly written. That is all.' Or again: 'No artist has ethical sympathies. An ethical sympathy in an artist is an unpardonable mannerism of style.' Or, from Gautier: 'All art is useless.'

The Picture of Dorian Gray was very badly received by most of the daily papers, and it was pronounced very immoral, for did the author not say: 'The only way to get rid of a temptation is to give in to it.' The *Daily Chronicle* wrote, on 13 April 1891, that the book had been produced by 'the leprous literature of the French Decadents'. 'Leprous' was the favourite term of abuse used against any literature coming from France.

Salome, which appeared in 1893, was first written in French by Oscar Wilde himself, but it was said to have been revised and corrected by Vielé-Griffin. The subject, and some of the details, were taken from Flaubert's 'Hérodias' in *Trois contes,* but the emphasis has been moved from Herodias herself to Salome, the psychology has been made more decadent and morbid—especially in the case of Herod—and the style more luscious and unctuous.

The years from 1891 and 1895 were the most brilliant in Oscar Wilde's life, and they marked the zenith of his literary and social career. This fame was achieved largely on the stage, but the influence of the French theatre is not very great on his plays. Then in 1895, in the midst of success, came the bombshell of his trial, followed by his conviction and imprisonment. This killed him as a writer. He wrote nothing more except *De Profundis* and *The Ballad of Reading Gaol,* works in which the inspiration of France is absent. He was then trying only to be himself, and not to shock public opinion or to outrage philistine susceptibilities.

In the eighteen-nineties Arthur Symons was more responsible than any other writer for the propagation of French influence in England. Although, in his earlier days, he was, as everyone else, influenced by French Decadence, he eventually introduced the Symbolist Movement to his fellow-countrymen.

He was born in Wales in 1865 of Cornish parents, and so was a Celt, as were most of the writers who had affinities with French culture. He was privately educated and went up to Oxford, where he formed a friendship with Walter Pater, who was at the height of his popularity, and whom he so greatly admired that he dedicated to him his first book, a collection of poems, published in 1889, entitled *Days and Nights.* They are not very original and in 1906, when publishing a collected edition of his verse, he preserved only nine poems from them. The most important influence found in this collection is that of Baudelaire—in such poems as 'The Opium-Smoker,' 'Satiety,' and 'The Street-Singer.' In 'The Opium-Smoker' occur these lines which recall Baudelaire's theory of *correspondances:*

> I am engulfed, and drown deliciously.
> Soft music like a perfume, and sweet light
> Golden with audible odours exquisite,
> Swathe me with cerements for eternity.
> Time is no more. I pause and yet I flee.
> A million ages wrap me round with night.

In 1890 he went to Paris, and met Mallarmé at the 'Mardis' of the Rue de Rome. He writes of them in his *Symbolist Movement in Literature:*

> Invaluable, it seems to me, those Tuesdays must have been to the young men of two generations who have been making French literature; they were

unique, certainly in the experience of the young Englishman who was always so cordially received there, with so flattering a cordiality. Here was a house in which art, literature, was the very atmosphere, a religious atmosphere; and the master of the house, in his just a little solemn simplicity, a priest. . . . Here, in this one literary house, literature was unknown as a trade. And, above all, the questions that were discussed were never, at least, in Mallarmé's treatment, in his guidance of them, other than essential questions, considerations of art in the abstract, of literature before it coagulates into a book, of life as its amusing and various web spins the stuff of art.

In Paris Symons made the acquaintance of Verlaine, who was to be one of the most important influences on his poetry; and he read the works of Villiers de l'Isle Adam, but he was too late to meet him in person, since he had died the previous year.

In 1891, on his return to London, Symons, with some fellow Celts, founded The Rhymers' Club. The founders were W. B. Yeats, Rolleston and Lionel Johnson, Irishmen or of Irish stock; Symons and Ernest Rhys, Welshmen; John Davidson, a Scot; and Le Gallienne, in spite of his Gallic name an Englishman. Several other poets joined them later—Ernest Dowson, John Gray, and Wratislaw.

Walter Pater was their master and idol—Ernest Dowson, Lionel Johnson and Symons had known him as undergraduates at Oxford. Le Gallienne was to say later, in *The Romantic Nineties,* that Pater was to English literature what Flaubert had been to French literature, and that all the men of letters considered that *Marius the Epicurean* was the most beautiful book in the English language. Pater for them was the magician who had brought beauty back to earth, and had shown that the only wisdom was its pursuit.

The Rhymers' Club succeeded in interesting a publisher in their cause, John Lane, who, in 1892, published *The First Book of the Rhymers' Club,* in which most of the poets attached to the club were represented. The collection is very typical of the mood of the time, with its Decadence, and its fin de siècle pessimism.

That same year Symons published his second collection of verse, *Silhouettes,* where the most important influence is Verlaine, though traces of Baudelaire are still found in such poems as 'Du Maquillage,' 'Perfume,' and others. He follows Verlaine in his little songs like 'Pastel,' 'In Carnival,' and others of similar inspiration. He resembles him also in describing the London scene, as in the section entitled 'City Nights':

> The trains through the night of the town,
> Through a blackness broken in twain
> By the sudden finger of streets;
> Lights, red, yellow and brown,
> From curtain and window-pane,
> The flashing eyes of the streets.
>
> Night and the rush of the train,
> A cloud of smoke through the town,
> Scarring the life of the streets;
> And the leap of the heart again,
> Out into the night, and down
> The dazzling vista of the streets!

Wratislaw, a follower of Symons, shows similar French affinities. His first collection, *Love's Memorial,* is only a parody of Baudelaire, but his *Caprices,* published in 1895, is of a higher quality. It borrows its title from Verlaine, and he is the chief influence on poems such as 'A Moment,' 'Silhouettes,' and 'On the Embankment:'

> A mist on the darkened river
> Falls; in the rippled stream
> The yellow lights shake and quiver,
> The red lights quiver and gleam.
>
> For us in the maze of error,
> More weak than the wind-swept foam,
> The lights in the stream's dark mirror
> Seem lights of a perfect home.
>
> The tranquil river is going
> Down to the tranquil sea,
> And oh that its waves were flowing
> Silently over me!

The Rhymers certainly fostered an interest in contemporary French literature, and one of their number, John Gray, translated many French poems in his collection entitled *Silverpoints,* published in 1893.

Symons, at this time, was a Decadent in inspiration and in 1893 he published an article entitled 'The Decadent Movement in Literature' [excerpted above] which appeared in *Harper's Magazine* in November. There is nothing very original or new in it, as it consists of a boiling down of the aesthetic theories of Gautier, Baudelaire, and Huysmans—indeed his tastes in literature are exactly the same as those of des Esseintes. The article was, however, important as being the clear statement, in English, of the French Decadent position.

The Second Book of the Rhymers' Club appeared in 1894, and this was the final volume, for, shortly afterwards, the Club was disbanded.

The next group of writers, very similar to the first, was that associated with the *Yellow Book,* founded in 1894, and which further exemplified the Decadent ideals formulated by Symons. As Hubert Crackanthorpe said, in July 1894, in his article entitled 'Reticence in Literature': 'Decadence, decadence: you are all decadent nowadays!' And, in the same volume, Max Beerbohm wrote:

> There are signs that our English literature has reached that point when, like the literatures of all nations that have been, it must fall at length into the hands of the decadents. Who knows but that artifice is in truth at our gates and that soon she may pass through our streets? Already the windows of Grub Street are crowded with watchful evil faces. They are ready, the men of Grub Street, to pelt her, as they have pelted all that came near her. Let them come down while there is still time, and hang their houses with colours, and strew the road with flowers. Will they not, for once, do homage to a new queen? By the time this letter appears, it may be too late!

The ideal of the *Yellow Book* was that of Artifice and Artificiality, and Beerbohm wrote, in an article called 'In Defence of Cosmetics'—which recalls Baudelaire's 'Du maquillage'—in April 1894:

> For behold! The Victorian era comes to its end and the day of *sancta simplicitas* is quite ended. The old signs are here and the portents warn the seer of life that we are ripe for a new epoch of artifice. . . . Artifice is the strength of the world, and in that same mask of paint and powder, shadowed with vermeil tinct and most trimly pencilled, is woman's strength.

John Lane was the publisher of the *Yellow Book,* as he had been of *The Rhymers' Club,* and its flaming yellow was intended as a kind of flag. Henry Harland was appointed editor, and the artistic direction was entrusted to Aubrey Beardsley, who had illustrated Oscar Wilde's *Salome* for the edition published by John Lane in 1894. These illustrations, which Wilde himself had not liked, had made Beardsley the most notorious draughtsman of the day.

The first volume of the *Yellow Book,* with its so-called immoral French influence, was severely criticized by most of the papers, and a poem by Symons which it contained, *Stella Maris,* shocked the public on account of its outspoken evocation of the physical aspect of love.

Decadence was not so well established in England that it was parodied by Robert Hichens in his *Green Carnation,* published in 1894, and which is a satire especially on *The Picture of Dorian Gray.* It is written in a style which is scarcely an exaggeration, and it preaches what was called 'the higher philosophy, the philosophy to be afraid of nothing, to dare to live as one wishes to live, not as the middle-class wish us to live; to have the courage of one's desires, instead of only the cowardice of other people's'. The hero, Esmé Amarinth, says: 'I am going to sit up all night with Reggie, saying mad scarlet things. The shadows of the lawns are violet, and the stars wash the spaces of the sky with primrose and crimson.' The sentiments which the novel expresses are an exaggeration of the ideals of Art for Art's Sake. 'Nothing that is beautiful can possibly be wrong' or again 'there is nothing in the world worth having except youth, youth with its perfect sins, sins with the dew upon them like red roses—youth with its purple passions and its wild and wonderful tears. To sin beautifully, as you sin, Reggie, and as I have sinned for years, is one of the most complicated of arts. . . . Sin has its technique, just as painting has its technique. Sin has its harmonies and its dissonances, as music has harmonies and dissonances.'

The trial of Oscar Wilde in 1895 finished the *Yellow Book*—and also Decadence—although it lingered on until April 1897.

While the fifth volume of the *Yellow Book* was in preparation, the trial started, and John Lane and Harland took especial precautions with this volume, but they were nervous on account of the impression which might be created, in the circumstances, by Beardsley's drawings, which had always been considered amongst the worst aspects of the Decadents. Suddenly William Watson, aided and abetted by Mrs. Humphry Ward and Alice Meynell, sent an ultimatum to the editors, declaring that, if Beardsley's drawings were not withdrawn from the volume in preparation, they would contribute nothing further to the periodical. Harland and Lane, frightened of what might happen, omitted the drawings from the issue, without consulting Beardsley. When he heard what had occurred he resigned from the paper, and Lane then decided to make a complete break with the Decadents, and henceforth to publish only works like those of William Watson and of Mrs. Humphry Ward.

There was sanctimonious satisfaction in some quarters at the result of Oscar Wilde's trial, and many talked of the need of purifying the atmosphere, now that the most pernicious influence had been removed, and was held safely under lock and key. When Symons published his *London Nights* in 1895, he was severely reprimanded for continuing the nefarious fashion from France. His *Stella Maris,* which was reprinted here, and other poems of similar inspiration—as for instance 'Idealism'—were singled out for special condemnation:

> I know the woman has no soul, I know
> The woman has no possibilities
> Of soul or mind or heart, but merely is
> The master piece of flesh: well, be it so.
> It is her flesh that I adore; I go
> Thirstying afresh to drain her empty kiss;
> I know she cannot love; 'tis not for this
> I run to her embraces like a foe.

This is debased Baudelaire, and so is 'To One in Alienation':

> As I lay on the stranger's bed,
> And clasped the stranger-woman I had hired,
> Desiring only memory dead
> Of all that I had once desired;
>
> It was then that I wholly knew
> How wholly I had loved you, and, my friend,
> While I am I, and you are you,
> How I must love you to the end.

(pp. 101-12)

Most of the former Decadents were now turning against the Movement—amongst them Lionel Johnson, Max Beerbohm, and Le Gallienne. The latter had indeed published, in his *English Poems,* an attack against the influence of France, in the poem addressed 'To the Reader':

> Art was a palace once, things great and fair
> And strong and holy, found a temple there;
> Now 'tis a lazar-house of leprous men!
> O shall we hear an English song again!
> Still English larks mount in the merry morn,
> And English May still brings an English thorn,
> Still English daisies up and down the grass,
> Still English love for English lad and lass—
> Yet youngsters blush to sing an English song.
>
> Thou nightingale that for six hundred years
> Sang to the world—O art thou husht at last!
> For, not of thee this new voice in our ears,
> Music of France that once was of the spheres;
> And not of thee these strange green flowers that spring
> From daisy roots and seem to bear a sting.

The green flowers are the flowers of Decadence, the 'green carnation' of Robert Hichens' novel.

It looked indeed as if the Decadent Movement were over in England. Then the *Savoy* came along and, for a short time, gave it a new lease of life. This was founded by Leonard Smither in 1895, after John Lane had discarded the Decadents, and he appointed Arthur Symons as editor, who invited Beardsley to join the staff as arts director. The first number appeared in January 1896, but it was received by the critics with indifferent contempt and irony, and, by the third number, it had ceased arousing any interest at all. It lingered on until the end of the year, and finally expired through lack of funds. Symons wrote a valedictory article for its final number, entitled 'By Way of Epilogue', in which he complained that England was devoid of any interest in the arts.

The *Savoy* had lasted a bare year, and its aim had been to further interest in contemporary French literature, to discuss modern French poetry and its technique. It published articles on contemporary French poetry, with translations, and it dealt with further modern French poets, which the Rhymers

and the *Yellow Book* group had not yet considered—poets such as Émile Verhaeren, the great poet of the Belgian renaissance in French literature.

The year 1896 saw, as well as the *Savoy,* the publication of the collected poems of Ernest Dowson, one of the most characteristic of the Decadent poets, and one whose interest in French literature was deepest, for he had lived a great deal in France, in Normandy, Brittany, and Paris, and it was his favourite country. He had a special fondness for the poetry of Verlaine which he followed closely, and he deals with the same climate and moods—the last days of autumn, twilight, the damp of dark woods, the fogs of London, and nostalgia for the past. In such a mood is 'Amor Profanus,' which recalls Verlaine's 'Colloque sentimental':

> Beyond the pale of memory,
> In some mysterious dusky grove,
> I dreamed we met when day was done,
> And marvelled at our ancient love.
>
> Met there by chance, long kept apart,
> We wandered through the darkling glades,
> And that old language of the heart
> We sought to speak; alas poor shades!

This is a reflection of Verlaine's 'Colloque sentimental' from *Fêtes galantes.* . . .

Dowson also wrote a poem with the title 'Chanson sans paroles' which recalls Verlaine's 'Romances san paroles'; there is also one called 'Spleen,' reminiscent of Baudelaire's poems of the same name, in mood as well as title:

> I was not sorrowful, I could not weep,
> And all my memories were put to sleep.
>
> I watched the river grow more white and strange,
> All day till evening I watched it change.
>
> All day till evening I watched the rain
> Beat wearily upon the window pane.
>
> I was not sorrowful, but only tired
> Of everything that ever I desired.

While 'Ad Manus Puellae' must have been inspired by Gautier's 'Etudes de mains' from *Émaux et camées:*

> I was always a lover of ladies' hands!
> Or ever mine heart came here to tryst,
>
> For the sake of your carved white hands' commands;
> The tapering fingers, the dainty wrist;
> The hands of a girl were what I kissed.
>
> I remember an hand like a fleur-de-lys
> When it slid from its silken sheath, her glove;
>
> With its odorous passing ambergris;
> And that was the empty husk of a love.
> Oh! how shall I kiss your hands enough?
>
> They are pale with the pallor of ivories;
> But they blush to the tips like a curved sea-shell;
>
> What treasure, in kingly treasuries,
> Of gold, and spice for the thurible,
> Is sweet as her hands to hoard and tell?

And, finally, there is the Cynara poem, one of the best known and most characteristic poems of the Decadent Movement in England, a parable of the Movement, a symbol of the unattainable. It is written in the French metre, the Alexandrine

Last night, ah! yesternight, betwixt her lips and mine,
There fell thy shade, Cynara, thy breath was shed
Upon my soul betwixt the kisses and the wine;
And I was desolate and sick of an old passion,
Yea I was desolate and bowed my head;
I have been faithful to thee, Cynara, in my fashion.

Ernest Dowson's collection of poems, and that of Lord Alfred Douglas—published in the same year, in Paris, with the text in both French and English—are the last poems of the Decadents in England, and the second edition of Symons' *London Nights,* published in 1897, marks the end of the Movement.

His next collections—*Amoris Victima* of 1897 and *Images of Good and Evil* of 1899—show a change towards a new inspiration, for they are far less in the Baudelairean mood.

The result of the change is seen in his next work, *The Symbolist Movement in Literature,* published in 1899. In the dedicatory epistle to Yeats he writes:

> I speak often in this book of Mysticism, and that I, of all people, should venture to speak, not quite as an outsider, of such things, will probably be a surprise to many. It will be no surprise to you, for you have seen me gradually finding my way, uncertainly but inevitably in that direction, which has always been to you your natural direction.

There is more idealism here than in any of his previous works, and the influence of Villiers de l'Isle Adam and Maeterlinck have taken the place of that of Baudelaire. Discussing Decadence in the Introduction, Symons says:

> Meanwhile, something which is vaguely called Decadence had come into being. . . . It pleased young men in various countries to call themselves Decadents, with all the thrill of unsatisfied virtue masquerading as uncomprehended vice. . . . But a movement which in this sense might be called Decadent could but have been a straying aside from the main road of literature. Nothing, not even conventional virtue, is so provincial as conventional vice; and the desire to "bewilder the middle-class" is itself middle-class. The interlude, half a mock-interlude, of Decadence, diverted the attention of the critics while something more serious was in preparation. That something more serious has crystallized, for the time, under the form of Symbolism, in which art returns to the one pathway, leading through beautiful things to the eternal.

The Decadents, on the whole, had been a doomed generation—as Yeats called them in his *Autobiographies*—and nearly all of them ended tragically. Most of them had delicate constitutions—it is hard to imagine a Decadent enjoying robust health—and generally their intemperate habits did not improve matters. Beardsley was an alcoholic who died in penury in 1898; Dowson took hashish and also died in poverty in 1900; Lionel Johnson died an alcoholic in 1902; and John Davidson, after writing his *Testament* in 1908, committed suicide in 1909. (pp. 112-16)

Enid Starkie, "The Yellow Nineties," in her From Gautier to Eliot: The Influence of France on English Literature, 1851-1939, *Hutchinson & Co. (Publishers) Ltd., 1960, pp. 101-28.*

RUTH ZABRISKIE TEMPLE

[*Temple is an American critic and educator specializing in English literature of the late-Victorian and Edwardian periods. Her critical history* The Critic's Alchemy: A Study of the Introduction of French Symbolism into England *is an informative and illuminating guide to French sources of English Decadent literature. In the following excerpt from that work, Temple discusses the transitional role of English Decadents in rendering French Symbolism acceptable to English audiences and in preparing the way for further developments in modern literature.*]

French poetry has not been generally liked in England. Greek and Latin poetry have been extolled, German and Italian poetry have had their warm admirers, but for a variety of reasons and for many centuries English critics have deplored the poetry of their neighbors across the Channel. To the ordinary Englishman, from the Renaissance on, the alexandrine has seemed monotonous, the French language too weak for poetic intensity, French metaphors so abstract as to convict French poets of inadequate imagination. The chorus of denunciation reached its height with the Romantics. Then Hazlitt, inventing a monologue for Coleridge, makes the great talker say: "French poetry is just like chopped off logic; nothing comes of it. . . . It is all patchwork, all sharp points and angles, all superficial." This is what both Coleridge and Hazlitt believed about French poetry. Yet Symbolism, the great movement in modern poetry, had its origin in France. And thus the whirligig of time brings in his revenges.

For Symbolism exalts just that concept of the poem which the English critic and poet have thought peculiarly their own. Symbolism is not easy to define—no easier than Romanticism, of which, indeed, it is the child. As Romanticism, being complex, multitudinous, even contradictory, is better described than defined, and best described by the fragmentary professions of Romantics—the renascence of Wonder, Strangeness allied to beauty—so Symbolism yields something of its essence in the phrases of its practitioners: evocative sorcery, suggestive magic, pure poetry, the alchemy of the word. Fundamental to its aesthetic is the notion of an alchemical or magic transformation. The commonplace materials of the ordinary world—the objects of sensory experience—are transmuted in the poet's vision, for the poet is the "parfait magicien ès lettres," and language itself, the vehicle of everyday communication, takes on as the poet's medium a new dimension, becomes opaque, is translated into incantation, "those wavering, meditative, organic rhythms which are the embodiment of the imagination. . . ." Thus, Yeats tells us [in "The Symbolism of Poetry," *The Dome* (April 1900)], the poet makes the word his instrument, and by the poet's word the world itself is transformed. "Solitary men in moments of contemplation receive, as I think, the creative impulse from the lowest of the nine Hierarchies, and so make and unmake mankind, and even the world itself, for does not 'the eye altering alter all'." So the poem is a miracle, and Valéry, who calls it that, explains [in "Poetry and Abstract Thought," *Essays on Language and Literature,* J. L. Hevesi, ed. (1947)]:

> And when I say *miraculous* I use the word in the sense we give to it when we think of the spells and wonders of ancient magic. It should never be forgotten that the poetic form has been enlisted, down the ages, in the service of enchantment. Those who gave themselves up to the strange activities of magic must have believed in the power of the word. . . .

Baudelaire in the mid-nineteenth century was the first master of these mysteries. After him, adopting and modifying his theory and sometimes evolving more hermetic techniques, came Verlaine, Rimbaud, Laforgue, and Mallarmé. These were the poets of the French Decadence. In France of the twentieth century they have their great disciples, Claudel and Valéry, and so inescapable has been their influence that it was possible in a recent survey of French poetry for the author to group all the living poets as derivatives of either Rimbaud or Mallarmé. Moreover—and here is the novelty—their names are well known in England and even on "the cloudy and poetical side of the Channel" they have their devotees. "With Baudelaire," writes Valéry [in "The Position of Baudelaire," *Variety: Second Series* (1938)], "French poetry at length passes beyond our frontiers. It is read throughout the world; it takes its place as the characteristic poetry of modernity; it encourages imitation, it enriches countless minds."

To discover how and when this transformation came about in England we must turn to a period in English letters unhonored though by no means unsung, the Decadence. It has been fashionable to convict this period of futility and triviality, to dismiss it as the producer of nothing more distinguished than the Tragic Generation. The fashionable estimate is, I think, in need of re-examination. We have come to take for granted much that the Tragic Generation did for us, and, forgetting our indebtedness, we patronize our creditors. The British symbolist poets, however, have not been unmindful of their debt. Yeats tells us that he wrote down the memories he has called *The Trembling of the Veil* " . . . that young men to whom recent events are often more obscure than those long past, may learn what debts they owe and to what creditor." Notable among his own creditors is Arthur Symons. During the years when both young men lived in the Temple, Yeats, who had less French than Symons, came to know Mallarmé's poems and aesthetic theory through conversations with his friend, just then absorbed in the materials of his book *The Symbolist Movement in Literature.* And to this crucial book T. S. Eliot also has professed indebtedness.

> I myself owe Mr. Symons a great debt. But for reading his book I should not, in the year 1908, have heard of Laforgue and Rimbaud; I should probably not have begun to read Verlaine, and but for reading Verlaine, I should not have heard of Corbière. So the Symons book is one of those which have affected the course of my life [quoted by F. O. Matthiessen in *The Achievement of T. S. Eliot* (1947)].

This is an admirable execution of literary justice. But the tale is not complete.

"Good art," Ezra Pound says, "cannot possibly be palatable all at once." If the Decadence helped to shape the genius of the two greatest modern British poets, it also helped to prepare their audience. And this it did by in some sense domesticating French symbolist poetry in England. In the nineties, literary England enjoyed a visitation of what Baudelaire called the divine grace of cosmopolitanism. Verlaine and Mallarmé published in English periodicals and addressed English audiences; Baudelaire, Verlaine, and Mallarmé found not only apologists but sympathetic translators. The change in the climate of opinion was effected through the "alchemy" of criticism.

Notable among the critics were George Moore, Swinburne, and Arthur Symons. . . . Other critics might have been in-cluded—for example, Pater and George Saintsbury, but Saintsbury's contribution to the cause of French literature in England is so extensive and so diverse as to require separate treatment, and Pater, since he had little to say of French poetry, is most important for the theory and the method he passed on to Swinburne and to Symons.

All these were "aesthetic" critics. The term is now pejorative in connotation, and that it should be seems to me another of our failures in filial piety, for at least one school of modern criticism appears to share much of the theory and the method of its unacknowledged forebears. The New Critics, even in the moment of enunciating a similar doctrine, insist upon their difference from those for whom they fear to be mistaken—devotees of "the vapid doctrine known as Art for Art's sake." Perhaps the time has come to define and to reappraise the aesthetic critic.

Pater, the fountainhead, provides a definition [in his preface to *The Renaissance*].

> The aesthetic critic . . . regards all the objects with which he has to do, all works of art . . . as powers or forces producing pleasurable sensations, each of a more or less peculiar or unique kind. This influence he feels, and wishes to explain, analysing it, and reducing it to its elements. . . . The function of the aesthetic critic is to distinguish, analyse, and separate from its adjuncts, the virtue by which a picture, a landscape, a fair personality in life or in a book, produces this special impression of beauty or pleasure, to indicate what the source of that impression is, and under what conditions it is experienced. His end is reached when he has disengaged that virtue, and noted it, as a chemist notes some natural element, for himself and others.

Art, then, is distinguished by producing pleasure. The critic must discern the unique character of the work of art by which this end is achieved. Pater's followers made explicit much that is implicit here, and, supplementing Pater with Gautier and Baudelaire, they asserted that the critic's business, like the artist's, is with art alone, not with considerations of utility or morality. The critic will thus avoid the didactic heresy. The phrase is Poe's contribution, but it was taken over, in the glamour of foreign dress, by way of Baudelaire.

Baudelaire's critical doctrine reinforced Pater's for the aesthetic critics. His method can be summed up in his own phrase: "Je résolus de m'informer du pourquoi, et de transformer ma volupté en connaissance." Here, too, pleasure precedes knowledge, but the critic must analyze his pleasure until he knows its source; he must bring to bear on the work all the resources of intelligence as well as sensibility.

Now let us see how John Crowe Ransom, distinguished exponent of the New Criticism, defines the critic's function [in "Criticism as Pure Speculation," *The Intent of the Critic,* Donald A. Stauffer, ed. (1941)]:

> The intent of the critic may well be, then, first to read his poem sensitively, and make comparative judgments about its technical practice . . . Beyond that, it is to read and remark the poem knowingly; that is, with an esthetician's understanding of what a poem generically "is."

Two "readings," he goes on to say, are to be avoided, the psychologistic and the moralistic.

Ransom's description, being more compressed, is a little

harder, perhaps, to understand than Pater's, but do not the two passages say substantially the same thing? As in Baudelaire, too, there is the twofold response which the critic owes his material: sensitivity (the experience of pleasure) and knowledge. Enemies of the New Criticism can scarcely be blamed if they detect a similarity between its doctrine and that of the devotees of Art for Art. Friends should be pardoned if they do.

And indeed the common ancestor of these critics, New and aesthetic, is a man of utmost literary respectability, Samuel Taylor Coleridge. He too believed that poetry proposed as its immediate end pleasure. Insisting on a special relation of parts to whole in a poem and on the need for isolating "specific symptoms of poetic power," he anticipated Pater's search for the *virtue* or active principle of a poet's work. Also, he provided the rationale for the aesthetic critic's scrupulous attention to formal qualities and the New Critic's useful emphasis on textual explication.

Why, then, do the New Critics dismiss as "vapid" the doctrine of Art for Art's Sake? Among current beliefs about the nature of art, surely not the most difficult to defend—or the most repugnant to New Critics—is the belief that it is an end in itself: art is art and nothing more—or less. To make out a case for this point of view is on the whole less taxing than to defend art as a substitute for religion or the vehicle of truth or the handmaid of a political faith or even as all things to all men. There was no grave danger that art would be mistaken for any of these things in earlier ages when the universe seemed to present a coherent system in which man had his secure place. With the fragmentation of the world picture, artist and consequently critic became ill at ease. Their discomfiture was expressed in the various modes of Romanticism, and of these one of the most plausible is the "aesthetic" attitude. If all values are called in question, as they are today, then it is intelligent and intelligible for the artist to create his own values and to defend the autonomy of his province. Surely we may hope for a new synthesis, a new metaphysic in which art will have its respectable place and stand in a significant relation to other enterprises of the human spirit; in which it will be meaningful to say that art should instruct by pleasing. I do not think it can be maintained that such a synthesis has been achieved.

Meanwhile, though we may agree with Allen Tate that no good criticism will be produced until a metaphysic is restored, we may also legitimately prefer the criticism that takes art for nothing more or less than art—which the best art still tries to be. But to say this is of course to lay oneself open to the charge of defending that notorious structure the Ivory Tower.

Its history is a commonplace. The artist by mid-nineteenth century had come to feel his isolation. In a mercantile and democratic society he found himself deprived alike of audience and of prestige. He concluded that "The artist has throughout his career to fight the Philistine" [Osbert Sitwell, *Great Morning* (1947)], and, as the warriors of the Middle Ages fought from their castles, so the embattled artist withdrew to his ivory tower. Since the invention of the phrase by Sainte-Beuve, the tower has come to be a potent symbol in modern art. The towers of Vigny and Yeats are secure and separate, lifting their residents above the *fourmillante cité* ["teeming city"], above the crowd of bourgeois or of populace. From these elevated vantage points the poet is supposed, if he looks out at all, to look up, but, being insulated from the

sordid world of everyday, he is more apt to fix his gaze within and so to voyage on strange seas of thought, alone. Thus he incurs the opprobrium of escapism. But the tower may also be a lighthouse. Baudelaire has used the figure for the rôle of the great artists throughout the world's history. The lighthouse is plainly a useful building. Its guardians endure loneliness and privation—for which they are rewarded with the average citizen's admiring compassion—and they tend the light. When the poet is in residence, it is the light that never was on sea or land, the consecration and the poet's dream. Even this light has often been thought useful.

If the aesthetic critics must be associated with a tower, I think it should be the lighthouse. For no better illustration can be found of the tower's usefulness than their achievement in international relations. Looking across the Channel, as their more utilitarian contemporaries were not free to do, they descried the new French poets and made known the new poetry in all its esoteric particularity.

On the authority of the great modern critic Sainte-Beuve, we have it that correct evaluation of the new is the prime test of the critic's merit. . . . And by this test the aesthetic critic comes off very well. (pp. 13-19)

> *Ruth Zabriskie Temple, "The Alchemy of the Word," in her* The Critic's Alchemy: A Study of the Introduction of French Symbolism into England, *Twayne Publishers, Inc., 1953, pp. 13-19.*

THEMES

JEROME HAMILTON BUCKLEY

[*Buckley is an American educator and critic who has written extensively on English literature of the Victorian period. In the following excerpt, he examines some characteristic themes of English Decadent literature.*]

As the nineteenth century drew at last to its close, many a late Victorian pulpit rang with apocalyptic warnings. To the ardent Evangelical the end of all things was at hand; the old order, it seemed, could hardly long survive the faith that had made possible its dominance. By the early nineties, one Reverend Mr. Baxter was, therefore, quite convinced that the day of final doom, fast approaching, would be presaged by the ascent to Heaven, at an appointed hour in 1896, of some one hundred and forty-four thousand selected Christians. But when the hour arrived, most of the chosen, apparently, preferred to linger on earth for at least another year, that they might join in the festivities of Victoria's Diamond Jubilee. For the true-born Englishman, in fact, grown less and less responsive to every Evangelical appeal, was finding more immediate forms of emotional release in the imperial concerns of his Empress-Queen.

Ever since the collapse of British agriculture in the seventies, the middle classes, despite an ingrained insularity of outlook, had been no longer able to think wholly in terms of an island economy, self-sufficient and inviolate. Driven alike by the demands of trade and a mistrust of Continental competitors, industrial Britain had become increasingly dependent upon the resources and markets of her wide empire. From the imperial fervor of Disraeli—in its time as "realistic" as it had been visionary—there had arisen a bellicose jingoism which concealed in its foolish boast the practical purposes it was designed to serve. Clearly by the end of the eighties, the creed of the jingo had usurped much of the authority of the old religion. And the new Press, ready to exploit every popular sentiment to its own devious ends, had turned resolutely from the condition of England, which the "radicals" and the socialists were intent upon reforming, to the fortunes of Englishmen abroad, whose adventures actual or imaginary furnished the foreign correspondent sensational copy.

More guileless in their worship of things British, the poets of imperialism sought to reassert the basic values of their national heritage. In the best—at any rate—of their patriotic verses, Kipling, Henley, William Watson, even Henry Newbolt, all transcended the frantic bluster of the mere jingo. Hymning "England My Mother," Watson begged a deeper reverence for the literary culture which must certainly outlive any material disasters of an ominous future, for

> Nations are mortal,
> Fragile is greatness;
> Fortune may fly thee,
> Song shall not fly.

Similarly Newbolt, recalling to his countrymen the splendors of a storied past, asked earnestly, on the very eve of the African war,

> England! wilt thou dare tonight
> Pray that God defend the Right?
>
> ["The Vigil"]

And Henley, during the long-drawn conflict, came to dread that the "faith" which had guided the "master-work" of England, his England, might not necessarily "endure" forever; and repeatedly, in despair, he strove to overwhelm his own doubt with the resonance of hysteric doggerel. But his fears were by no means unique. All through the nineties there lay behind the cult of empire a half-hushed uneasiness, a sense of social decline, a foreboding of death as deep as Baxter's conviction, though far less precise in its prophecy. And it was therefore quite appropriate that Kipling, the true imperial laureate, should close the great Jubilee pageant itself with an eloquent reminder of the fate that had befallen the kindred pomps of Nineveh and Tyre.

Present in even the high imperial symphony, the note of world-fatigue dominated altogether the tenuous music of Decadence. To Wilde and his later disciples, to Beardsley and his friends of the *Yellow Book,* to the Rhymers whose youth was their age, *fin de siècle* meant more than the death of a century; it connoted a time of lulled disenchantment when Joy's hand was ever at his lips bidding adieu. Aware of their attributes and proud of their title, the Decadents suffered—or affected to suffer—the ineffable weariness of strayed revelers lost in a palace of fading illusion. Dowson, the most delicate lyrist among them, described in languid couplets their common ailment, "spleen," an antique English malady which Baudelaire had refined into a quite French and thoroughly modern malaise:

> I was not sorrowful, I could not weep,
> And all my memories were put to sleep.
>
> I watched the river grow more white and strange,
> All day till evening I watched it change.

> All day till evening I watched the rain
> Beat wearily upon the window pane.
>
> I was not sorrowful but only tired.
> Of everything that ever I desired.
>
> ["Spleen"]

And Arthur Symons, more deliberately, made the sigh of a lost lover the complaint of his whole "aesthetic" generation:

> Trouble has come upon us like a sudden cloud,
> A sudden summer cloud with thunder in its wings.
> There is an end for us of old familiar things
> Now that this desolating voice has spoken aloud.
>
> ["The Pause"]

So the artist, spiritually dispossessed, alienated from the life of old familiar things, might experience the defeat of desire, a private doom less remote than the larger death threatening all Victorian culture.

Yet the Decadents, for all their disillusion, were not so completely the victims of "spleen," of "that terrible *taedium vitae*" ["weariness with life"], as to approach with mere indifference the uncommon delights of art. For even to savor the weariness of self, they had had first to regard their own creative individuality as the one certain value in a disintegrating civilization. Sedulously, therefore, they strove to proclaim, by their very dress and speech and gesture, a full aesthetic autonomy. Like Dorian Gray, whose "chiselled lips curled in exquisite disdain" of all that was commonplace and vulgar, they struck the pose of the perfect dandy, self-sufficient and ironic, silhouetted in solemn black against the arc lamps of the London night, contemptuous of the busy grayness that scurried abroad in the sun. As writers and as draftsmen, they struggled to make a highly personal style the ultimate expression of their highly stylized personalities. Their prose glittered self-consciously with paradox and epigram fashioned to invert every bourgeois platitude. Their poems, moving lightly through unoriginal stanza patterns, turned a conventional poetic diction to new and sometimes startling effect. And their drawings and sketches, often as overwrought as Byzantine mosaics, imposed a kind of diseased vitality upon the fixed traditions of a fragile rococo.

In their various media they carefully emphasized rather than concealed the necessary artifice of art; and they looked not to nature but to art itself for their images and themes. Hubert Crackanthorpe, for instance, in a story "staged" like a one-act play, could describe his heroine's face as "a subtle harmony of tired colour" ["Yew-Trees and Peacocks"]. Beardsley could declare the pretty Princess of his ballad "as lyrical and sweet / As one of Schubert's melodies." And Symons could adapt to his verse the languid swirl of a Javanese dance, or, again, repeatedly play a weary passion against the painted backdrops of the theater or the lurid *décor* of a gas-lit café as chalked by the *décadent* Toulouse-Lautrec. Wilde, with similar intent, designed his single novel to demonstrate that the natural has significance only insofar as Nature may succeed in imitating Art. Thus the sky in *Dorian* becomes "an inverted cup of blue metal," the clouds are "like ravelled skeins of glossy white silk," and the chimney smoke ascends as "a violent riband, through the nacre-coloured air"; Sybil attains "all the delicate grace" of a Tanagra figurine; and Dorian holds through the years the untarnished glory of Hallward's first impression, while his career follows the course of Huysmans' wonderful fiction, which is virtually "the story of Dorian's life, written before he had lived it."

Dedicated as a whole to a determined artificiality, the novel flaunted the faith of the English Decadence that Art must transcend the actual, must indeed represent "man's gallant protest against Nature." But the gallantry of Decadent art demanded no courage of action, no true boldness of execution; it was a passive gallantry of style, precious, effeminate, effete. At odds forever with Victorian "manliness," the Decadent hero might well like Dorian bury "his rebellious curls" in the perfume of "great cool lilac-blossoms"; for he could never, on principle, face the social realities of his time. And before he yielded quite to overpowering ennui, he might escape to a world of unnatural sensation, presided over by some malign spirit of beauty, perhaps even Conder's androgynous Fairy Prince, masked, brocaded, and sinister.

"There is no such thing," wrote Wilde [in his preface to *The Picture of Dorian Gray*], "as a moral or an immoral book. Books are well written, or badly written. That is all." But the most overwritten literature of Decadence was nonetheless animated by a conscious will to explore the dark underside of experience, with which the Decadent himself associated immorality and evil. At a time when all normal objects of desire seemed weary and stale, smutched indeed by the rude hands of the Philistine, the artist might yet seek a fresh titillation, a genuine *frisson nouveau,* in the rarer enticements of sin, or at least in a lingering glance at sinful pleasures. Accordingly, like the George Moore who had penned his purple *Confessions* (1888), many a young Decadent prided himself on his love of "almost everything perverse" and his fierce "appetite for the strange, abnormal and unhealthy in art." There were moments, we read, when Dorian—and so, perhaps, Dorian's creator—"looked on evil simply as a mode through which he could realise his conception of the beautiful," moments when "the coarse brawl, the loathsome den, the crude violence of disordered life, the very vileness of thief and outcast, were more vivid, in their intense actuality of impression, than all the gracious shapes of Art, the dreamy shadows of Song."

Symons, apparently, understood Dorian's impulse; for though he remained in fact a conscientious and quite respectable craftsman, he declared in verse his surrender to the "multitudinous senses," and he found inspiration for lyric and sonnet in the outcast children of passion—the fallen woman in "the villainous dancing-hall" or the distraught opium smoker, with "soul at pawn," brooding in his rat-ridden garret. Crackanthorpe, likewise, through his several slender volumes, followed at a discreet distance the careful experiments with sex of the sadistic dandy or the "morbid craving for self-inflicted torture" of the duped lover. And Richard Le Gallienne, who in soberer mood decried Decadence as "limited thinking, often insane thinking" [*Retrospective Reviews* (1896)], acknowledged, in a rhyme called "Beauty Accurst," the dread fascination of the lustful lady, the *femme fatale* whose kiss was death. Few of the Decadents achieved in their private lives a more than vicarious knowledge of the wickedness that flowered egregiously in their poems and stories. And very few indeed merited the humorless, hysterical indictment of Max Nordau, whose *Degeneration* (1895) [see Further Reading], purporting to explore the pathology of *fin de siècle,* discovered in the Decadent artist an insane criminal type as yet unclassified by the great criminologist Lombroso. If a mysterious Baron Corvo hovered on the periphery of aesthetic London, not many young writers could even imagine the scope of his infamous adventures. Wilde himself, whose falling from grace when publicized was to shock most of his disciples, indulged but a commonplace and

Oscar Wilde and Lord Alfred Douglas.

tawdry perversion far beneath the nameless exotic sins upon which Dorian was wont to speculate. As it appeared in artistic form, Decadent "evil" was actually for the most part, like Decadent style, an artificial growth, the calculated product of a curious sensibility; and as such it reflected not the terrors of the objective world but the spiritual isolation of the artist, striving too deliberately to transcend the moral values of a middle-class convention.

Studiously unnatural in their aesthetic emotions, the Decadents, naturally, attracted many a satirist intent upon measuring all "specialized" subject matter by the broad perspectives of humor. Himself a nonchalant dandy on intimate terms with the best of the new minor poets, Max Beerbohm, for example, smiled urbanely at their most shocking productions, "the lurid verses written by young men, who in real life, know no haunt more lurid than a literary public-house" ["Be it Coziness"]. Less familiar with the objects of Decadent art, Owen Seaman rhymed off his direct reprimand "To a Boy-Poet of the Decadence," ridiculing the "dull little vices" of which the precocious worldling sang so wickedly. And G. S. Street in his prose *Autobiography of a Boy* (1894) invoked the indirection of irony to demolish the Decadent Tubby, a youth who, despite his conceit, enjoyed a certain popularity for his alleged sins and "the supposed magnificence of his debts," and who aspired as author of a "Ballad of Shameful Kisses" to be considered "a man to whom no chaste woman would be allowed to speak, an aim he would mention wistfully, in a manner inexpressibly touching, for he never achieved it."

But of all the anti-Decadent wits, Robert Hichens achieved through parody the gayest and subtlest attack. In *The Green Carnation* (1894) he allowed his determined dilettantes, Mr. Amarinth and Lord Reggie Hastings, each wearing most conspicuously "the arsenic flower of an exquisite life," to expose, by their every word and sigh and gesture, absurdities of thought and sentiment no less artfully cultivated than the exotic boutonniere itself. Lord Reggie, in whom the knowing might have seen a sharp resemblance to the young Lord Alfred Douglas, defended against all rational argument the creed of the Decadent life-taster, "the philosophy to be afraid of nothing, to dare to live as one wishes to live, not as the middle-classes wish one to live; to have the courage of one's desires, instead of only the cowardice of other people's." And Mr. Amarinth, clearly a caricature of Wilde, maintained a Decadent love of artifice and Whistler and his own brilliance and a loathing of the very word "natural," which meant to him "all that is middle-class, all that is of the essence of jingoism, all that is colourless, and without form, and void." Acquainted like Wilde with the principle of sensory "correspondences," Mr. Amarinth could befuddle an unaesthetic curate with his appreciation of a brown Gregorian chant—for all combinations of sounds, he explained, conveyed "a sense of colour to the mind" and Gregorians were "obviously of a rich and sombre brown, just as a Salvation Army hymn [was] a violent magenta." Or, again, recalling perhaps the preface to *Dorian,* he might exhort the simple-souled children of the village to cherish a dubious amorality: "There is nothing good and nothing evil. There is only art. Despise the normal, and flee from everything that is hallowed by custom as you would flee from the seven deadly virtues. Cling to the abnormal. . . . Forget your Catechism, and remember the words of Flaubert and of Walter Pater, and remember this, too, that the folly of self-conscious fools is the only true wisdom." Yet the burlesque, for all its cleverness, scarcely matched in sheer hilarity Wilde's own bright farce which adapted to the glory of nonsense the paradox of a Wildean Ernest and the aimless ennui of an effete Algernon. For the Decadents, in fact, required no parodist to remind them of their departures from the sober norms of reason. Quite self-conscious in their folly, they successfully anticipated all contemning laughter.

Not indeed until it was too late did Wilde himself actually realize the importance of being earnest. "I was, " he wrote truly, if rather defiantly, from prison [in *De Profundis*], "—I was a man who stood in symbolic relations to the art and culture of my age." This much he had known almost from the beginning. Yet as artist he was never able throughout his career, except perhaps in the powerful "Ballad of Reading Gaol" (1898), to achieve the intensity, the self-effacement, the high seriousness, required to produce the "one beautiful work of art" of which he dreamed. For all his apparent egotism, he lacked an essential faith in his own creations; he failed always to sustain for long any willing suspension of disbelief. Though he felt that a great literature must be born of a passionate sensibility rather than an overcurious, analytic brain, he somehow feared his own Decadent fancy, and he perversely allowed his disillusioned intellect to mock his aesthetic emotion. His best books are, therefore, vitiated, as well as enlivened, by his own ambivalence. His plays, for example, draw heavily upon the conventions of the concealed identity, the wronged woman, the barriers of caste—in short, upon all the stock in trade of the sentimental comedy; yet their abiding life lies in the free range of an intellectual wit which impedes the action and, long before the contrived finale, almost destroys the sentiment. On occasion, to be sure, we may suspect the playwright of deliberately burlesquing the distress of his heroines; but we can hardly assume that he would have us regard his most calculated pathos as completely ironic. For

Wilde's intentions as dramatist are far more confused than his obvious fluency might indicate; and it is, after all, not impossible to see how, in a Soviet Russia grown conservative under the pressures of war, *An Ideal Husband* (1895) could one day be revived as a serious vindication of the stability of the cultured home.

Not even in *Dorian Gray* (1890), despite its avowed amorality, are his purposes at all clearly defined. The novel, perhaps the most representative product of the Decadence in England, oscillates precariously between the two styles born of the artist's inner conflict. As a reworking of the familiar Faust theme, its allegory was fashioned to explore the terrors of evil that the soul yielding to the temptations of hedonistic desire must ultimately experience. But the overwrought prose which describes in deliberate detail all the furniture of Dorian's pleasure palace establishes no illusion of aesthetic truth; the "dreadful places near Blue Gate Fields," blurred by fog or ignorance, remain far more ludicrous than dreadful; and the whole sentimental melodrama which carries Dorian, the lovely "son of Love and Death," far from "the stainless purity of his boyish life" through "the sanguine labyrinth of passion" lacks both psychological depth and emotional conviction.

The prose, on the other hand, which enshrines the wit of Lord Henry, attains an apparently spontaneous ease and vivacity; it springs crisp and clear from Wilde's artificial second nature which became to him more natural than his original passionate impulse. As tempter, Lord Henry is detached and urbane, like the Spirit of Clough's *Dipsychus,* ironic rather than malevolent; "enthralled by the methods of natural sciences," he is the analyst of sin whose own worst vice is passivity, the rationalist whose diffident virtue hides in paradox. He represents, in fact, the more reasonable Wilde who, suspicious of his own perverse sensibilities, restrained *Dorian Gray* from the complete Decadence of the Huysmans novel which inspired its most lurid pages. And his shadow falls across even the pitiful *De Profundis* (1905), where the sinner, weary of time, can scarcely make convincing the will—tragic and intense, were it wholly earnest—to seek the Spiritual Newbirth of the high Victorians, to believe—in their terms—that as "the sea . . . washes away the stains and wounds of the world" so at last may Nature "cleanse me in great waters and with bitter herbs make me whole."

Though less striking than Wilde as personalities, and generally less eager to melodramatize their private emotions, the Decadents of the *Yellow Book* experienced in varying degrees the same conflict between the amoral dictates of a deliberate aesthetic creed and the unwelcome compulsions of a moral or social conscience. Symons, for instance, while probably the most serious and worshipful defender of the French literary *décadence,* could not but admit [in "Huysmans," *Figures of Several Centuries* (1916)] that the perfect *décadent,* Des Esseintes of Huysmans' *A Rebours,* seemed "half-pathological" in his misanthropy and altogether morbid in his quest for exotic sensation. And it was hardly strange that Symons' own verse "Credo," demanding of every full life "a strenuous virtue or a strenuous sin," should echo not the inhuman music of Verlaine, whose "disembodied voice" he admired, but the quite human message of "The Statue and the Bust" and indeed the whole far-from-Decadent assertion of the Browning who was his first master.

Intricate in its arabesques of line and overlaid everywhere with the suggestion of evil, Aubrey Beardsley's subtle art might appear at first glance a more complete expression of the Decadent spirit. Yet his best drawings betrayed a satiric purpose stronger than any delight in a perversely wicked *décor;* they were, in part at least, as his publisher John Lane insisted, the work of a "modern Hogarth . . . lampooning the period and its customs" [quoted by J. Lewis May; see Further Reading]. And among his writings, the notorious fragment *Under the Hill* (1896) was actually designed to rework with semi-ironic elaboration the legend of Tannhäuser, which remained in effect the tragic moral history of all the Decadents damned by the uncontrolled senses; and the grim "Ballad of a Barber" was surely intended to convey a complete allegory of Decadence itself through the tale of the artist-barber Carrousel, whose amoral art for art's sake crumbled forever on the intrusion of insane desire.

Crackanthorpe, who lacked Beardsley's talent for satire, sought to emulate in his brief fictions the cool objectivity of Maupassant. Yet he found a soulless naturalism quite unable to satisfy his own deeper emotional impulse; and he yielded again and again, in spite of his struggle for detachment, to an ethical commentary, sometimes oblique, but always more or less incompatible with the dispassionate method. In an unguarded moment he confessed that "all great art is moral in the wider and the truer sense of the word" ["Reticence in Literature," *The Yellow Book* II (1894)]. But, failing to discover for his own art any moral sanction that he might accept with his whole intellect, he turned in despair to the Decadent "pursuit of experience," which he called, self-consciously, "the refuge of the unimaginative" [quoted by Richard Le Gallienne in "Hubert Crackanthorpe," *Sleeping Beauty and Other Prose Fancies* (1900)], until eventually, defeated in all calmer efforts to escape, he plunged from a Paris bridge to his death in the cold impassive river.

Whatever his attitude towards Crackanthorpe's last defiant gesture, Lionel Johnson apparently regarded with due skepticism the suicidal gloom of many another late Victorian; for he proceeded in an amusing satire entitled "Incurable" (1896) to ridicule a typical young Decadent who resolved to "live his poetry . . . by dying, because he could not write it." Still, Johnson himself had to do battle with the Dark Angel that had desecrated the bright world of art, that had turned the Muses to Furies and had made

all things of beauty burn
With flames of evil ecstasy.

["The Dark Angel"]

And it was only after painful contest that he could reassert his essential faith in the moral will of the artist.

Even Ernest Dowson, who was perhaps never so certain of his adversary, sensed the inadequacies of the Decadent aesthetic and the hollowness of all the self-conscious posturing that passed for Decadent intensity. For even in Dowson, who more sweetly than any of his fellow poets sang the dark disillusions of the *fin de siècle,* the spirit of Decadence was not sufficiently strong to stifle a longing for ethical direction or to mitigate greatly the sincerity of an ultimate confession:

we cannot understand
Laughter or tears, for we have only known
Surpassing vanity: vain things alone
Have driven our perverse and aimless band.

["A Last Word"]

Among the more serious Decadents there thus persisted some capacity for a contrition which was neither perverse nor aim-

less nor in fact particularly "Decadent." But there was at the same time, throughout their works and days, so marked an addiction to pose that a knowing young man like Richard Le Gallienne, suspicious of their remorse, might charge them with invoking the long-neglected soul merely to serve as "bitters to the over dulcet sins" ["The Décadent to His Soul"]. Few literary critics could see, looking beyond the artifice of Crackanthorpe or Symons or Dowson, much more than a dim shadow of the positive emotion, the "moral" intensity, the objective human drama that they had learned to expect of the great writer. And many, therefore, waited rather impatiently, after the deaths of Browning and Tennyson, for the arrival of a new major poet, capable of transcending his own self-conscious moods. (pp. 226-38)

> Jerome Hamilton Buckley, "The Decadence and After," in his The Victorian Temper: A Study in Literary Culture, *Cambridge, Mass.: Harvard University Press, 1951, pp. 226-46.*

POETRY

DEREK STANFORD

[*Stanford is an English critic, poet, and biographer known for his insightful studies of nineteenth- and twentieth-century authors. His special area of critical interest is English art and literature of the 1890s. In the following excerpt from his introduction to* Poets of the 'Nineties, *he provides an overview of English Decadent poetry.*]

There are two things to remark in the poets of the 'nineties: the distinction of their work and the tragedy of their lives. The first is a fact, a critical commonplace; the second, a mystery still, a problem.

Utterly unlike, in their fevered existence, those 'bards who died content on pleasant sward, / Leaving great verse unto a little clan', the poets of the 'nineties did leave their own clear record: 'a few evasive . . . snatches of song'—output of a 'delicate . . . discriminating taste'. Mallarmé had spoken of the artists' need to 'purify the dialect of the tribe' and this was what the 'nineties poets effected. They took the heterogenous speech of Victorian poetry and sought to refine it. Yeats has commented that 'in the Victorian era the most famous poetry was often a passage in a poem of some length, perhaps of great length, a poem full of thoughts that might have been expressed in prose' ['Modern Poetry'; see Further Reading]. It was this prose element in verse that these poets desired to eliminate.

To the leading Victorian figures 'a short lyric had seemed an accident, an interruption amid more serious work'—the poet's expression on the problems of the day, on social, religious, or political issues. To the poets of the 'nineties, the lyric became the paradigm of all poetry. Its short highly cultivated span of perfection seemed to measure all that was mixed or unpoetic. 'We tried', recalled Yeats, 'to write like the poets of the Greek Anthology, or like Catullus, or like the Jacobean lyricists, men who wrote while poetry was still pure.' Verlaine had spoken of Victor Hugo as 'a supreme poet, but a volcano of mud as well as of flame'. The 'nineties poets wished to be all flame, happy to settle for a light-weight perfection. 'Their poems seemed to say', as Yeats remarked, 'you will remember us the longer because we are very small, very unambitious.' 'Yet my friends', continued Yeats, 'were most ambitious men; they wished to express life at its intense moments, those moments that are brief because of their intensity, and at those moments alone.'

Was there, one wonders, any occult connection between the nature, the distinction of this work, and the tragedies which their authors enacted? Yeats, who lived and moved among these poets, asked the question, and commented on a paradox. 'Why should men', he inquired [in 'The Tragic Generation'; see excerpt above], 'who spoke their opinions in low voices, as though they feared to disturb the readers in some ancient library, and timidly as though they knew that all subjects had long since been explored, all questions long since decided in books whereon the dust settled—live lives of such disorder . . . ?'

Certainly the casualty figures are impressive. 'I have known twelve men who killed themselves', Arthur Symons, veteran and doyen of the decade, reflected in later life. Symons, himself a prey to madness in middle years, had perhaps his heightened way of putting things; yet sober statistics all point in the same direction. Ernest Dowson, dead of consumption at thirty-two; Lionel Johnson, dying from a stroke, a confirmed dipsomaniac, at thirty-five; John Davidson, a suicide, at fifty-three; Oscar Wilde, disgraced and imprisoned at the height of his career, then dying after three years' barren exile, aged forty-six; Aubrey Beardsley (poet as well as artist), consumptive and dying at twenty-six.

And these were only the front-rank figures. Other casualties, among the friends of these men, would include William Theodore Peters, actor and poet, who died of starvation in Paris; Hubert Crackanthorpe, short-storyist, who threw himself into the Seine; Francis Adams, novelist and essayist, who died by his own hand; Henry Harland, editor of the *Yellow Book,* who died of consumption at forty-three; Francis Thompson, kept alive on opium, who died of the same disease at forty-eight; Charles Conder, rococo fan-painter, who died in an asylum, aged forty-one.

To this asylum, in 1908, Arthur Symons was sent after the attack of madness which came upon him in Italy. From its effects he never fully recovered. Yeats, alone almost, lived on to seventy-four, grand chronicler of all these 'luckless men'; and he, as Dorothy Wellesley once observed, looked as if he had never enjoyed a good day's health in his life.

Mortality and melancholy marked the poetry of this period. Dowson, in his later poem 'A Last Word,' writes what is clearly a requiem, a swan-song for a group attitude.

> Let us go hence: the night is now at hand;
> The day is overworn, the birds all flown;
> And we have reaped the crops the gods have sown:
> Despair and death; deep darkness o'er the the land,
> Broods like an owl; we cannot understand
> Laughter or tears, for we have only known
> Surpassing vanity: vain thoughts alone
> Have driven our perverse and aimless band.
>
> Let us go hence, somewhere strange and cold,
> To Hollow Lands where just men and unjust
> Find end of labour, where's rest for the old,
> Freedom to all from love and fear and lust.
> Twine our torn hands! O pray the earth enfold
> Our life-sick hearts and turn them into dust.

What was the reason for this vast pervading sadness?

During the last sixty years we have become so accustomed to think of tragedy as something politically imposed from outside—from war, oppression, and persecution—that we may incline to doubt the validity of Yeats' description of his colleagues of the 'nineties as 'the tragic generation'. For us, it is war that appointed two young generations to play the role of tragic heroes; and to us the young men of those earlier years seemed to enjoy an enviable position: heirs to security and peace. The Boer storm which shook the decade at its end was responsible for no such mortality rate amongst artists and men-of-letters as those of the 1914 and 1939 wars. Unlike the Spanish affair, the Boer War was not an intellectual's war.

To begin, then, to understand the fate which somehow involved these men of the 'nineties, we have to adapt our idea of tragedy to fit a quite dissimilar situation. The two key words most often bandied are 'decadence' and 'degeneration'. The second term had been employed as the title for a book which Max Nordau published in 1895. The author, an artistically insensitive German, with a pseudoscientific lack of humour, believed that from the time of Wagner and the Pre-Raphaelites European culture was the product of sick men. He diagnosed, in elaborate terms, a state of neurasthenia in the arts. Saintsbury, that hard-hitting no-nonsense Scot found 'too much of [Nordau's] book a silly . . . exaggeration, not at all ill-exemplifying the very weaknesses he discussed'. Bernard Shaw, provoked by the book into replying with his own work *The Sanity of Art* (1895), described Nordau's theory as 'at bottom, nothing but the familiar delusion that the world is going to the dogs'. There is no doubt that Nordau's label, stuck by him on to all and sundry, represented no objective approach. Yet even so, the pathological element is to be reckoned with when dealing with these poets. We shall note this element when we come to look at their individual lines. For the moment, we might say, that one aspect of 'decadence' is a pursuit of intensity beyond the strength of the organism.

Yeats, in seeking to solve the mystery of 'the tragic generation', appears to have entertained this notion at least once. 'Perhaps', he wrote, 'our form of lyric, our insistence upon emotion . . . gathered together overwrought, unstable men.' The moment after, he doubts this conjecture: 'I remember that the first to go out of his mind had no lyrical gift, and that we valued him mainly because he seemed a witty man of the world.'

'I have never', he tells us, 'found a full explanation of that tragedy.' His most original hints at a solution interpret it in cultural terms. Part of this interpretation has to do with the greater focussing of the poet's mind on purely aesthetic elements. 'When Edmund Spenser', he tells us, 'described the islands of Phaedria and of Acrasia he aroused the indignation of Lord Burleigh . . . and Lord Burleigh was in the right if morality were our only object. In these islands certain qualities of beauty, certain forms of sensuous loveliness were separated from all general purposes of life, as they had not been hitherto in European literature. . . . I think that the movement of our thought has more and more so separated certain images and regions of the mind, and that these images grow in beauty as they grow in sterility. Shakespeare leaned, as it were, even as craftsmen, upon the general fate of men and nations, had about him the excitement of the playhouse; and all poets . . . until our age came, and when it came almost all, had some propaganda or traditional doctrine to give companionship with their fellows.' The 'nineties dispensed with this companionship. They worked in a solitude of private feelings, removed from emotions of national public life. In this, they were thrown back upon themselves, on resources psychologically insufficient.

> What part in the world can the artist have,
> Who has awakened from the common dream,
> But dissipation and despair?

inquires Yeats knowing how in the last two so many of 'the tragic generation found their answer'.

Intellectually, he inclines to put the blame on Walter Pater. No work of prose was more admired by Yeats than *Marius, the Epicurean;* and yet, he confesses 'I began to wonder if it or the attitude of mind of which it was the noblest expression, had not caused the disaster of my friends. It taught us to walk upon a rope tightly stretched through serene air, and we were left to keep our feet upon a swaying rope in a storm.'

Pater's dangerous doctrines had been broached, of course, in his first book *The Renaissance: Studies in Art and Poetry* (1873). There, he at least came near to substituting sensation for wisdom as the wise man's ultimate aim. Experience, in and for itself, not the fruit of experience was what he recommended. 'The theory or idea or system which requires of us the sacrifice of any part of this experience, in consideration of some interest into which we cannot enter, or some abstract theory we have not identified with ourselves, or of what is only conventional has no real claim upon us.'

Unlike the thinkers of Balliol who were busy proclaiming a public philosophy, Pater's teaching was morbidly subjective. This cult of intensity—namely, that success in life consisted of burning always with a 'hard gem-like flame'—carried with it two corollaries, adopted by the poets of the 'nineties. Both of these were persuasively expressed, both went enveloped in the beauty of pathos.

The first was the notion that life is constituted of flux and that wisdom consists in accepting the fact. 'Not to discriminate every moment some passionate attitude in those about us, and in the very brilliancy of their gifts some tragic dividing of forces on their ways is, on this short day of frost and sun, to sleep before evening.'

The pathos of transience is written across the poetry of the 'nineties. Predominantly, in Yeats' words, it is the expression of men 'whose hearts perish every moment, and whose bodies melt away like a sigh' ['Rosa Alchemica,' *The Secret Rose* (1897)].

The second corollary is the idea of the inevitable solitariness of the individual. 'Experience', Pater declares, 'is ringed round for each one of us by that thick wall of personality through which no real voice has ever pierced on its way to us, or from us to that which we can only conjecture to be without. Every one of these impressions is the impression of the individual in his isolation, each mind keeping as a solitary prisoner its own dream of the world.' This privately enclosed impressionism (a word we shall have much trafficking with later) is a characteristic of 'nineties poetry. Usually, it is nothing more than a drifting flock of images, but sometimes as in the Epilogue to Arthur Symons' *London Nights* (1895) it attains to the dignity of philosophic statement.

Credo

> Each, in himself, his hour to be and cease
> Endures alone, but who of men shall dare
> Sole with himself, his single burden bear,
> All the long day until the night's release?
> Yet ere night falls, and the last shadows close,
> This labour of himself is each man's lot;
> All he has gained of earth shall be forgot,
> Himself he leaves behind him when he goes.
> If he has any valiancy within,
> If he has made his life his very own,
> If he has loved or labour'd, and has known
> A strenuous virtue, or a strenuous sin;
> Then, being dead, his life was not all vain,
> For he has saved what most desire to lose,
> And he has chosen what the few must choose,
> Since life, once lived, shall not return again.
> For of our time we lose so large a part
> In serious trifles, and so oft let slip
> The wine of every moment, at the lip
> Its moment, and the moment of the heart.
> We are awake so little on the earth,
> And we shall sleep so long, and rise so late,
> If there is any knocking at that gate
> Which is the gate of death, the gate of birth.

Looking back to those *fin-de-siècle* years from the changed climate of 1914, Yeats wrote his great verse epitaph on 'the tragic generation'. Speaking of those 'Companions of the Rhymers Club . . . poets from whom I learned my trade' [in 'The Grey Rock', *Responsibilities* (1914)], he recalled both their tragic lives and their artistic heroism.

> You had to face your ends when young—
> 'Twas wine or women, or some curse—
> But never made a poorer song
> That you might have a heavier purse,
> Nor gave loud service to a cause
> That you might have a troup of friends.
> You kept the Muses' sterner laws,
> And unrepenting faced your ends.

The Rhymers' Club was, indeed, the chief distillery of 'nineties poetry. Through its two anthologies it gave the tyro poets a hearing, providing them with a common cause and the conversation of their kind. Founded in the winter of 1891, the group lasted for three years, meeting 'in an upper room with a sanded floor in an ancient eating-house in the Strand [sic] called "The Cheshire Cheese"'. Yeats recalls the part he played in the inception of the Club with Ernest Rhys, a Welsh ex-mining engineer, poet, editor, translator. 'I had', he tells us, 'already met most of the poets of my generation. I had said to the editor of a series of shilling reprints, who had set me to compile tales of the Irish fairies, "I am growing jealous of other poets and we will all grow jealous of each other unless we know each other and so feel a share in each other's triumphs"' ['Four Years: 1887-1891', *The Trembling of the Veil*].

If it was this sentiment which led to the meetings and readings of the Club, the idea of producing an anthology together probably derives from the following letter: 'Thank you', wrote Edmund Gosse, already established as a critic, to Ernest Rhys who had sent him a sheaf of poems,

> for letting me read your very beautiful lyric 'A London Rose' . . . I wish I could suggest something sensible about the publishing of your book. It seems more difficult than ever to sell verse. I have been trying to find a publisher for Arthur Symons, alas, without success. It seems to me that it would be rather a good plan if four or five of the very best of

you young poets would club together to produce a volume, a new Parnassus, and so give the reading public a chance of making your acquaintance.

Many accounts have been given of the Club's make-up and meetings. Yeats, as often, is picturesque but inaccurate as to names and dates. The most conscientious and vivid record is that left by Victor Plarr, himself a Rhymer, in the story of his friend *Ernest Dowson, 1888-1897.* Among the list of members and guests these names of importance are included: Lionel Johnson, Ernest Dowson, Arthur Symons, John Davidson, Richard Le Gallienne, John Gray, Francis Thompson, and Oscar Wilde. (pp. 17-26)

In most of these men was a dedicatory passion; a belief in something, a striving towards it. Yet present in each was an antithetical self—a force leading not to attention and achievement, but one which dispersed the concentrative effort; and against it the powers of resistance were too small.

Perhaps the quality singularly lacking in both the lives and work of these men was a strain of toughness, of coarseness even. Yeats, watching Alfred Jarry's symbolist-expressionist farce *Ubu Roi* in company with Symons at the end of the century, seemed to feel the art of the Rhymers judged and sentenced by some harsh new manifestation:

> The players are supposed to be dolls, toys, marionettes, and now they are all hopping like wooden frogs, and I can see for myself that the chief personage, who is some kind of king, carries for sceptre a brush of the kind that we use to clean a closet . . . That night at the Hotel Corneille I am very sad. . . . I say, 'After Stéphane Mallarmé, after Paul Verlaine, after Gustave Moreau, after Puvis de Chevannes, after our own verse, after all our subtle colour and nervous rhythm, after the faint mixed tints of Conder, what more is possible? After us the Savage God.'
>
> (pp. 30-1)

The date of the first *Book of the Rhymers' Club* [1892] is itself significant. In the same year, seven months later, Tennyson—the star Victorian poet—died. Great and popular laureate, as he was, to these young men Tennyson represented the triumph of a mixed and middle-class art. With the famed practitioner of this old mode of poetry dead, the way was open for a fresh style in verse.

In place of a poetry of ideas, we were now to have poetry for poetry's sake. The Rhymer figures deliberately chose to emulate the pure art of fine minor poets rather than the often impure work of major ones. In his 'Toast' to the Rhymers, printed in their first *Book,* Ernest Rhys acknowledged these new adherences:

> As once Rare Ben and Herrick
> Set older Fleet Street mad,
> With wit not esoteric,
> And laughter that was lyric,
> And roystering rhymes and glad.
>
> As they, we drink defiance
> Tonight to all but Rhyme,
> And most of all to Science,
> And all such skins of lions
> That hide the ass of Time.

In this century of Science and Progress, little respect was accorded to the former by these poets. Yeats tells us how he 'detested' Huxley and Tyndall, feeling that they had deprived him of 'the simple-minded religion of my childhood' ['Four Years: 1887-1891']. Along with science as a demonological subject, in Yeats' mind, went Ibsenism, comedy, objectivity, and G. B. Shaw. 'I had a nightmare', Yeats wrote of the latter, 'that I was haunted by a sewing machine, that clicked and shone, but the incredible thing was that the machine smiled, smiled perpetually.'

Among the Bohemian élite of the Rhymers, progressive opinion was often unwelcomed. Symons found colourful romantic reasons against the Suffragette movement; while Dowson showed how wide was the gulf between himself and the affairs of the age when he said that, for himself, he was most led to fear an invasion by the Red Indians.

Greatest of this company as he was later to become, Yeats in the first half of the 'nineties was way behind many of them on points of inventiveness, modernity, and technique. 'Dowson, Johnson . . . or Symons,' he admitted, 'had what I still lacked, conscious deliberate craft, and what I must lack always, scholarship' [in 'Modern Poetry'; see Further Reading]. 'What I wanted from the poets of the 'nineties', T. S. Eliot has told us [in his preface to *John Davidson: A Selection of his Poems* (1961)], 'was what they did not have in common with the pre-Raphaelites, but what was new and original in their work.' There was, at this time, little beyond Pre-Raphaelitism in Yeats' poetry, the clear fixed colours of the earlier poets merging beneath an obscuring Celtic twilight. Some few shades of Spenser and Shelley, 'a fardel of old [Irish] tales', the recollection of certain folk-songs, and a dominant emotional immaturity—such was Yeats' stock-in-trade in those days. Even so, such a poem as 'The Lamentation of the Old Pensioner' has some of the aggressive naturalness we associate with his later poems:

> I spit into the face of Time
> That has transfigured me.

Yeats' contemporary instructor was Symons, a great importer of French styles into England. He was himself a poet of many poses, but his verse does succeed in delineating 'the décor which is the town equivalent of the great natural décor of fields and hills'. Urbane, in the original and derivative sense, his poetry naturalises aspects of 'the variable, most human, and yet most factitious town landscape' [*Silhouettes* (1896)]. Symons' poetry, along with that of Laforgue, is behind T. S. Eliot's early compositions: his *Preludes* and 'The Love Song of J. Alfred Prufrock.' 'I also had a good many dingy urban images to reveal', Eliot has told us. It is even easy to see how

> The feverish room and that white bed,
> The tumbled skirts upon a chair,
> The novel flung half-open where
> Hat, hair-pins, puffs, and paints are spread

of [Symon's 'White Heliotrope'] becomes the décor and belongings of 'the typist home at tea-time' from Eliot's disseminated masterpiece *The Waste Land:*

> Out of the window perilously spread
> Her drying combinations touched by the sun's last rays,
> On the divan are piled (at night her bed)
> Stockings, slippers, camisoles, and stays.

Yeats spoke of Symons as 'a writer who has carried further than most . . . that revolt against the manifold, the impersonal, the luxuriant, and the eternal'—by which four qualities he refers to the moralising, sermonising verse of the Victorians with its descriptive, idealistic, over-literary bias. Victorian poetry was often an art of argument: for the 'nineties, all abstract issues in verse were justified only as expressive instruments of subjective feeling. 'Literature', wrote Yeats in 1895, 'differs from explanatory and scientific writing in being wrought about a mood, or a community of moods . . . and if it uses argument, theory, erudition, observation, and seems to grow hot in assertion or denial, it does so merely to make us partakers at the banquet of the moods' [in 'The Moods', *Essays and Introductions*].

Mood was a key word with the critics of the 'nineties in the way that *temperament* had been the *Open Sesame* in Pater's writing. Symons' poetics bear indeed a striking resemblance to those of D. H. Lawrence, who said that he sought not 'the infinite or the eternal' but 'the incarnate moment . . . the immediate present, the Now' [in *New Poems* (1920)]. Place beside this Symons' description of his own poetry as 'a sincere attempt to render a particular mood which has once been mine, and to render it as if, for the moment, there was no other mood for me in the world' [*Studies in Prose and Verse* (1904)], and the insistence upon the present—the exclusive personal present—in both these poets is remarkable. How well, too, D. H. Lawrence's description of his own verse as 'unrestful, ungraspable' applies to the elusive verse of Symons. A 'Herrick of the Music-Halls', as he was called, he pursued an aesthetic of the fleeting, the fine fugitive beauty of transience. His is a poetry of mutability, an art of whatever flickers mysteriously into attraction at the very moment, almost, of its exit:

> Her face's wilful flash and glow
> Turned all its light upon my face
> One bright delirious moment's space,
> And then she passed . . .
>
> ['On the Heath']

Or take this even more abbreviated morse impressionism—a poem on the coming of the London dark—which Ernest Rhys quotes as characteristic of the poet:

> Next moment! Ah! it was—was not!
> I heard the chilliness of the street.
> Night came. The stars had not forgot.
> The moonlight fell about my feet.
>
> ['Everyman Remembers']

Without the range of Symons, but with a greater purity of artistic intention was Ernest Dowson. Translator of Verlaine, as were others of these poets, he set before himself the precept of 'la musique / Avant toutes choses'—'Music before all things'—possessing, in fact, little talent for anything save music. 'He used the commonplaces of poetry frankly' and 'sang one tune over and over again'. The song was a sad one, and today we regret that the poet lacked wit in his unrequited love. At his best, however, he does achieve a fastidious economy of self-pity which, serving rather to preserve than dissipate the obsession, results in an elegant confessional statement, such as we find in the poem headed 'O Mors! quam amara est memoria tua homini pacem habenti in substantiis suis.'

It is the very slenderness of Dowson's resources—a 'pure lyric gift, unweighted or unballasted by any other quality of mind or emotion'—which gave him his real distinction as a poet. His art is as far removed as is possible from the 'omniorum' poetry of the great Victorians. It is so thin, so fragile, it is hardly there, and yet that thinness conserves its purity.

The poetry of Lionel Johnson, beside that of these other two, seems a stiff and formal thing. It lacks both Dowson's lyric simplicity—the semblance of the heart uttering its feelings—and Symons' sophisticated inquiry. There is little adventurousness, little inventiveness in his verses; and they are burdened by a greater residue of Victorian diction than those of the other poets.

An essentially lonely man, he developed in his life a ritual of friendship to which the individual dedication of his several poems bears witness. It is certainly the intimate friendly tone—of a friend with a love of niceties and manners—which introduces an element of the easy and familiar into such poems as 'Plato in London' and 'Oxford Nights.' To Johnson, books were friends, and most of his friends were bookish. His old-fashionedness in literary etiquette was, in fact, a conscious reaction to both Decadent emancipation and to Victorian Philistinism. The latter fashion he parodied in a handful of brief pieces, of which 'A Decadent's Lyric' is the best. His short story 'Incurable' contains, among others, the following little skit:

> Ah, day by swift malignant day,
> Life vanishes in vanity:
> Whilst I, life's phantom victim, play
> The music of my misery.
> Draw near, ah dear delaying Death!
> Draw near, and silence my sad breath!

As Johnson's young poet in the story remarks, 'It was good, but Shakespeare and Keats, little as he could comprehend why, had done better.'

Johnson's own poetry seeks to revive memorials of 'a gracious age'. (Like Dowson, he was a member of the White Rose League which commemorates the Stuarts.) His art is that of the born bookman, more a matter of libraries than of life. Even so, to read him today is still an education in manners. And when his classic control finds some familiar subject on which it can work, the resultant poem has charm, ease and grace:

> On me and mine
> Clear candlelights in quiet shine:
> My fire lives yet! nor have I done
> With *Smollett,* nor with *Richardson.*
>
> ['Oxford Nights']
> (pp. 31-7)

The senior of these poets in age and reputation, Wilde was not a member of the Rhymers' Club, although he had attended as a guest. His first volume of poems had appeared in 1881, and his style in general was lush and prolix—a kind of Victorian baroque. There were, however, exceptions to this. 'The Harlot's House', written in tercets, has directness, tempo, economy which few of the poets of the 'nineties could equal.

> We caught the tread of dancing feet,
> We loitered down the moonlit street,
> And stopped beneath the harlot's house.
>
> Inside, above the din and fray,
> We heard the loud musicians play
> The 'Treues Liebes Herz' of Strauss.

Plagiarising Gautier and Whistler, he produced a number of poems which he spoke of as 'harmonies' or 'impressions'. These compositions are skillful arrangements of the poet's visual data—made up by someone with a window-dresser's eye.

They look towards Imagism, and possibly influenced Arthur Symons:

> The yellow fog came creeping down
> The bridges, till the houses' walls
> Seemed changed to shadows and St. Paul's
> Loomed like a bubble o'er the town.
> ['Impression du Matin']

But these pieces belong to the 'eighties, the years during which he wrote nearly all his verse. In 1895 had come his disgrace, and in 1898 there was published a work in a new manner, 'The Ballad of Reading Gaol.' Wilde, in his suffering was still the actor. Impressive as it is, 'The Ballad' is marked with histrionic affectation. Parallelism, repetition, antitheses liberally bestrew its verses. Its pitch is often over-strained; the declaiming voice is too frequently heard. Even so, there are passages where a new intimacy of tone is present. And these passages, in the speaking voice, are the best thing in all Wilde's poetry. Their natural quietness is the more penetrating:

> I never saw a man who looked
> With such a wistful eye
> Upon that little tent of blue
> Which prisoners call the sky.
> ['Impression du Matin']

When all his rhetoric was hushed, Wilde spoke superbly with a still small voice.

To speak of the poets of the 'nineties as essentially modern might appear a paradox. That *fin-de-siècle* decade, with its contrived naughtiness, may seem to many a period-piece epoch. Its ethics were largely a pose, its sentiments part of a decorative pattern. The 'nineties has been called the 'Beardsley Period', but to think of the art and literature of that era as consisting solely, in the illustrator's own words, of 'strange hermaphrodite creatures wandering about in Pierrot costumes' [J. Lewis May; see Further Reading] is to take the part for the whole. Speaking of his early days at Harvard, T. S. Eliot has told us that 'the poets of the 'nineties . . . were the only poets . . . who at that period of history seemed to have anything to offer me as a beginner . . . One was Arthur Symons . . . another was Ernest Dowson . . . and the third was [John] Davidson . . . from these men I got the idea that one could write poetry in an English such as one would speak oneself. A colloquial idiom. There was a spoken rhythm in some of these poems.'

This emancipation from '*tutti frutti* Tennysonian afflatus' and an all-too-conventional and bookish grandiloquence was the English counterpart of Verlaine's decision to take rhetoric and wring its neck. The French poet did indeed visit London, lecturing at Barnard's Inn and Oxford, as the guest of Arthur Symons in 1893. 'Music before all things . . . and, as far as that goes, choose rather the imperfect accord . . . the twilight tune where the precise and the indefinite join hands. Let your poem be a gay adventure . . . Fresh with the morning smells of mint and thyme. And all the rest is literature', Verlaine had written quizzically in *Art Poétique,* the manifesto of a new verbal freedom, which was also, of course, a new discipline.

All too few of the English poets were able to lift their diction out of the rut of Victorian heaviness.

> The touches of man's modern speech
> Perplex her unacquainted tongue

complained Francis Thompson in "The Singer Saith of His Song." Lionel Johnson described the style of his second book of poems as 'hopelessly in the would-be austere and hieratic manner'. This regulation rhetoric of the nineteenth century certainly took some breaking down; but here and there, from time to time, a number of the more forward poets made the break-through into a style more simple, precise, and urbane. Arthur Symons, critical spokesman of the era, mapped out the new direction in a magazine article in 1893. Linking together the gospels of Impressionism, Symbolism, and Decadence, he spoke of 'this endeavour after a perfect truth to one's impression, to one's intuition . . . [which] has brought with it, in its revolt from ready-made impressions and conclusions, a revolt from the ready-made of language, from the bondage of traditional form, of a form become rigid' [see excerpt above].

The poets of the 'nineties reacted in fact against the pomposities of convention in general. The reign of the ponderous sage, of Ruskin and Carlyle, was over. If Pater was venerated by these young men it was because his Cause was that of Art and because he taught that 'a certain shade of unconcern' is the mark of a complete culture in the handling of great issues and abstract questions. Victorianism, with its top-heavy excess of seriousness was on its way out. Matthew Arnold's 'seriousness' might well by himself be described as 'high'—but 'high' and 'heavy' are not the same thing, and Arnold's airy skirmishings with the British philistine, on behalf of sweetness and light, were conducted with a cavalier nonchalance and irony. With Pater and Arnold, then, as mentors the poets of the 'nineties renounced the Abyss of the Ethical Commonplace which so often darkly beckoned the Victorian masters.

In the 'nineties, Victorian middle-class verse gave way to an aristocratic poetic. Manners took precedence over morality. Irony and wit replaced philosophizing. (pp. 37-41)

> *Derek Stanford, "Poets of the 'Nineties," in his* Poets of the 'Nineties: A Biographical Anthology, *John Baker, 1965, pp. 17-46.*

DONALD DAVIDSON

[Davidson, with John Crowe Ransom, Allen Tate, and Robert Penn Warren, was a member of the Fugitive group of Southern poets from 1915-28. The stated aim of the Fugitives was to create a literature utilizing the best qualities of modern and traditional art. After 1928, the four major Fugitives joined with eight other writers, including Stark Young and John Gould Fletcher, to form the Agrarians, a group dedicated to the preservation of the Southern way of life and traditional Southern values. Davidson promoted the values of the Agrarians throughout his career. In the following excerpt, he discusses characteristic attitudes and themes in the works of major Decadent poets.]

[The Decadents] were not a group in any organized sense, though they had some harmony of purpose and attitude. They were brilliant individuals, each moving in an imaginatively created world of his own. Aside from a rather shifting agreement on aesthetic matters, they had in common chiefly an inner knowledge that Victorian romanticism had faded, with their arrival, into a season of autumn twilight.

But though the group was miscellaneous enough, their activity was dramatized for the public, and for a while sharply centralized, in the *Yellow Book* and its short-lived contemporary, the *Savoy.* There were other periodicals, such as the *Hobby Horse, Pageant,* and *Dome,* spiritual ancestors of the "little magazines" of the Nineteen-Twenties; but they did not last long enough to count. (p. xxix)

Such periodicals furnished outlets of publication. They did not establish real coteries or furnish rallying-grounds. The Rhymers' Club was a move in this latter direction. The poets of the Rhymers' Club did not agree on anything except that poetry was important. They wanted to write poetry and to discuss it. Into the English surroundings of the Cheshire Cheese, where they met, they tried to introduce the Gallic disinterestedness that Symons had found at Mallarmé's house or in the cafés of Paris, where a Verlaine could be heard discussing poetry—or possibly even be seen writing it—without any implications being drawn as to the oddity of his manners or the obliquity of his morals. They cultivated French intellectuality honestly enough, but the effort was a little strained and furtive, since the Cheshire Cheese was a retreat from an indifferent world, and not, like the Mermaid Tavern, a centre from which poetry radiated along with joviality. Nevertheless, Yeats's statement that the Rhymers' meetings were for him a school of poetry is assurance that their conversations were fruitful; and this assurance is supported by the fact that their two small publications—*The Book of the Rhymers' Club* and *The Second Book of the Rhymers' Club*—introduced, if only to a small public, many poems that have since become famous. But no group that contained such individual contrarieties as were represented in Davidson, Yeats, Johnson, and Symons could hold together very long. It was no more likely to become an Academy of Letters than the *Savoy* was likely to receive a subsidy from the Crown.

The years when this poetic activity was under way were years of a revival of fine printing, and of the arts of decoration and illustration. The tradition of William Morris and the Kelmscott Press was carried on, and the graphic arts, like the literary arts, felt the influence of French Impressionism. Whistler was fighting the battle of the fine arts and startling the public with his *Ten O'Clock* lectures and *The Gentle Art of Making Enemies.*

At the same time G. B. Shaw in *The Quintessence of Ibsenism* and in his own early plays, Arthur Morrison in *Tales of Mean Streets,* and Gissing in *New Grub Street* were charting the direction that fiction and drama were to take. Zola and the new naturalism were being imported from France. Hardy was about to end his career as novelist with *Jude the Obscure.* The most lasting feature of this prose literature was to be its social direction; for diligently though the novelist might try to be naturalistic, or scientific, naturalism kept getting mixed up with social protest.

But this quality was almost entirely lacking in the poetry of the Tragic Generation. It was their fate not to reform society but to be broken by it. Their disinterestedness was to be their doom. For clever as they were, they were not clever enough, or, like Shaw, charlatan enough, to mix their aesthetic notions up with a preachment for better plumbing or an argument to prove that Mrs. Warren's profession was somehow just as nice as Queen Victoria's. In short, they were not propagandists. And their doom, in time, became their theme. They were more deeply sunken than Shelley, for they were not quite romantic enough to think of themselves as the lyre of the west wind. They had nothing left but an appeal to Beauty—which, alas, in a way that nobody was quite clear about, had somehow got allied with sin. Osbert Burdett ex-

plains this situation as follows [in his *The Beardsley Period;* see Further Reading]:

> Almost a century of peace had given to English society the stability of a machine, and the routine of life on which it throve had little for the imagination, so that the convention and the period, working together, began to identify any protest with sin; and since the imagination was protesting, and beneath the surface human instincts remained unchanged, art and scandal began to be associated and the imaginative life began to take vice for its province and to praise forbidden fruits.

But Pater, in the "Postscript" to his *Appreciations,* had already written invitingly about "the addition of strangeness to beauty" and had added, dangerously: "Its [the romantic spirit's] desire is for a beauty born of unlikely elements, by a profound alchemy, by a difficult initiation, by the charm which wrings it even out of terrible things."

Now, to Pater's aestheticism were added the fascinations of French symbolist poetry. Baudelaire had published his *Fleurs du mal* in 1857 and uttered a doctrine that was the essence of Decadence:

> Poetry . . . has no purpose but itself; it can have no other purpose, and no poem will be so great, so noble, so truly worthy of the name of poem as that which has been written simply for the pleasure of writing a poem.

Such a dictum, as elaborated and applied by the French poets of the second half of the Nineteenth Century, and as interpreted by the English poets of the Decadence, perhaps simplified itself a little too easily. If a poet wanted to write about the most evil or obscene subject, what was there to stop him? Nothing, if he only made the poem beautiful—and beauty was a matter of technique. Thus it happened that the more "disinterested" the poet became—the more he tried to purify his verse by weeding out moral intrusions along with Victorian triteness—the more impure (in quite another sense) his poetry often became.

Strangely enough, this new aesthetics, perhaps unconsciously, appropriated a certain amount of justification from science, which was also purging itself of moral considerations and telling people to look bravely at the "facts" of life. Thus naturalistic fiction and symbolist poetry were two aspects of the same movement. The one relied upon reportorial honesty, the other upon exquisiteness and upon exactness of technique. The two aspects are illustrated in the single person of George Moore, who tried out naturalistic fiction in *Esther Waters* and who also, in his *Confessions of a Young Man* (1886)—first written in French and published in Paris—anticipated by more than a decade Arthur Symons's championship of Rimbaud, Verlaine, and other French poets in *The Symbolist Movement in Literature.*

The poetry of Decadence may have been, as Symons argued in his introduction to this book, "an interlude, half a mock-interlude," in the more general trend which he called the Symbolist movement. So far as Symbolism provides a technique through which the poet may apprehend and express the aesthetic qualities of an object, while merging with them naturally the religious or philosophical meanings which, in a materialistic civilization, become ever more difficult to rediscover, the Symbolist approach undoubtedly has merit. But for the poet of the Eighteen-Nineties this larger view was out of the question. The meaning of Decadence is that at the moment when style reached a point of subtlest refinement, the poet was made aware of the futility of his own utterance, and had nothing really worth declaring. His highly developed sense of form had nothing to play upon but his highly developed sense of frustration and death. His artistic integrity allowed him to make no evasion—what was wrong with the Victorians, he thought, was their evasion! The result was a poetry that spoke now in weariness, now in impudent defiance, and now—when it presumed to be "objective"—in fragments of harsh realism or impressionistic word-painting. Lacking ethical principle, the Decadent poet arrived at a quite understandable confusion between the sacred and profane, between saint and sinner. Often enough he felt that his most sinful moments were his most saintly ones. The religion of art, which bade him deal with the aesthetic impressions in the situation where they were keenest, drove him into writing about the desolate peace that came from defilement.

The poetry of Ernest Dowson, above all others, shows this paradox. His famous "Non Sum Qualis Eram Bonae sub Regno Cynarae" is a complete expression of Decadence in one of its most passionate and desperate moments. The lines echo, with a kind of tired nobility of utterance, the manner of Catullus and of the finest English love-lyrics from Shakespeare down to Keats and Poe. But there is no longer any romantic gusto—only a bewildered acceptance of an unnamed tragedy, a sordid romance. From such poetry it is but a step to the mocking, intellectualized irony of Beardsley's "The Three Musicians" or the staged eroticism of Symons's *London Nights*.

But these men found an escape which Dowson refused. It is ridiculous to say of Dowson, as Symons observes, that "he had the pure lyric gift, unweighted or unballasted by any other quality of mind or emotion; and a song, for him, was music first, and then whatever you please afterwards, so long as it suggested, never told, some delicate sentiment, a sigh or a caress." For Dowson's poetry is a poetry of continual regret and desolation. His "pure lyric gift" is coloured always with a doubt of the reality of his own joy, and the "quality of mind" which praises with an equal fastidiousness of verse the loves of harlots and the passionless peace of the monastery is only the disillusioned and confused mind of the true Decadent. It was a tragic situation, to which one cannot say that Dowson was at all reconciled.

Clearly Arthur Symons was reconciled or hardened to the situation; or perhaps he did not find it tragic. Boldly, a little blandly, he accepted the principle that art is all that is left. He rationalized it by adding, in effect, that art is all that matters. On the critical side he brilliantly elaborated his theories; in poetry he illustrated them. All that Symons proposed to do was to give play to the "religion of the eyes"; and the eyes, of course, were the sophisticated eyes of the cosmopolitan more interested in nuances than in statements. His aim was, to quote his biographer, T. Earle Welby, "with utmost economy, to suggest momentary impressions, transient moods; the impressions to be, by preference, those of one gazing at things themselves artificial or seen under an artificial light, the moods to be not only fleeting but frivolous or perverse." This intent led Symons into strange paths, but to the reviewer who objected that his verses were "unwholesome" and had "a faint smell of Patchouli about them," Symons had a ready retort [in his preface to the second edition of *Silhouettes*]:

> Patchouli! Well, why not Patchouli? Is there any

> "reason in nature" why we should write exclusively about the natural blush, if the delicately acquired blush of rouge has any attraction for us? Both exist; both, I think, are charming in their way; and the latter, as a subject, has, at all events, more novelty . . . There is no necessary difference in value between a good poem about a flower in a hedge and a good poem about the scent in a sachet.

It was a stout defence, but the poems seem often to be only highly finished exercises done to prove a point. Symons seems to haunt music halls, stage doors, and fashionable beaches simply in order to experience sensations that may be put into suitable poems. Within his range of artificially selected experiences, one sensation is as good as another so long as it is aesthetically enjoyed.

The poetry of Symons, like the poetry of the Imagists later on, is precise but abstract. He controls the irregular and rebellious material of human life like an artist in a studio arranging a "still life." Just as the modernistic painter abstracts from a landscape a "design" of colours and masses for the sake of an "interesting" effect, so Symons abstracts a pattern of sensational experience from an amorous rendezvous, a girl's face, the interior of a boudoir. His lyrics are studies or "silhouettes." Even the most erotic of his poems are a little cold. The poet is watching too analytically—he is making another "study."

Yet his poetry is important because Symons, far more consciously and more thoroughly than his contemporaries, broke with Victorian tradition and drew with firm hand the outline of a new method in verse. Deliberately he tried to give English verse the quality of the French verse he admired, and in so doing enlarged the range of the poetic instrument. With all its artifice, it has the peculiar rapture of the Nineties, and in the later poems it takes on a graver tone.

Stronger spirits like Lionel Johnson and John Davidson could not pass by the tragic issues as lightly as did Symons. In "Mystic and Cavalier" and "The Dark Angel" Lionel Johnson defined, more clearly and grimly than any other poet of his generation, the sense of fatality and brooding evil that plagued them all. These poems are, on a small scale, the *Waste Land* of the Tragic Generation; and Johnson, like T. S. Eliot in the Nineteen-Twenties, strove to find a consolation, if not a solution, in authoritative religion and reverence for the classics. His intellect told him that the pure aesthetic principle was not enough, and he therefore had less interest than his contemporaries in poetic experiments. In his private life he could not achieve the unity that he desired. It was impossible to practise the creed that "Life is ritual" in anything but a sheltered alcove where a man could shut himself up with his books and friends. London had no place for a brilliant and learned poet like Johnson, who believed in the dignity of letters and was unwilling either to pose or to propagandize in behalf of his art—or to evade the issue. In his private life the principle of disorder (the "dark angel" of his poem) could not be downed, even by his acceptance of Catholicism.

But from his poetry he banished it, with a firmness that made his verse intellectual and at times severe. If Milton had lived in the Nineties, he might have written English verse as Johnson wrote it; and Johnson, like Milton, wrote Latin verse. There are no finer poems of the decade than those in which Johnson celebrates the Greek and Latin classics and the Catholic saints who were his masters, or the historic glories of Winchester and Oxford, or the charm of the English countryside, or the love of Ireland that allied him for a few years with the poets and patriots of the Celtic Renaissance. Yet there was, too, something of the dandy in Johnson. Critical integrity, classic austerity of style, and the Catholic religion were not enough to expel the taint of Decadence wholly from his verse. His solution was too intellectual, as Dowson's was too emotional and Symons's too cosmopolitan. The end for him, in poetry, was a limited performance, and, in life, a tragic and early death.

Where Johnson was both courageous and articulate in his revolt, John Davidson was courageous and inarticulate. A Tennessee mountaineer would feel as little at home at a Greenwich Village tea as did the indomitable Scot in the Decadent circle; for their impulse was to prettify and refine—his, to roar at the world. Restraining, for a while, his desire to roar, Davidson dallied with the saintliness of sin in "A Ballad of a Nun" and "A Ballad of Hell." These and other ballads are counted among his most successful works, but they have an air of the *tour de force.* His hand was too heavy for that particular medium, and he turned from one form to another in an enormous striving for the form and the subject that would best carry his sense of indignation against the world. Of his many attempts, *Fleet Street Eclogues* perhaps availed best to give tongue to the conflicting voices that tore the soul of John Davidson between romance and realism, between a delicate lyricism and a Carlylean frenzy to denounce. When Decadence had had its day, he began the series of "Testaments," written in blank verse, which anticipated by a quarter of a century the *Testament of Beauty* of the more orderly-minded Robert Bridges. Like Bridges, Davidson wanted to come to grips with science. Somewhat like Bridges, though with a confused Nietzschean energy and afflatus of prophecy, he proposed to make an adjustment by taking over science.

> The world [he wrote] is in danger of a new fanaticism, of a scientific instead of a religious tyranny. This is my protest. In the course of many ages the mind of man may be able to grasp the world scientifically; in the meantime we can know it only poetically; science is still a valley of dead bones till imagination breathes upon it.
> [Quoted in Jackson's *The Eighteen Nineties*].

In such striving for a large affirmative Davidson had some kinship with Henley and Rudyard Kipling; but in his cloudy bitterness he was with the Decadents. His ideas were too vague and his equipment was too faulty for the tasks that his courage prompted him to essay.

Of the Rhymers' Club group also was Richard Le Gallienne, whose poetry grew out of a blithe excitement over the new literary modes rather than out of any genuine compulsion toward poetry. His was a kind of light verse with a Decadent stamp, and very little more. His gentle lyricism mirrored back a diminished image of whatever was going on. On the fringe of the movement, Laurence Binyon was able, in *London Visions,* to catch a few of the lights and shadows of the great metropolis. Stephen Phillips enjoyed a considerable vogue in his day, especially for his poetic dramas and dramatic monologues, but his poetry now seems a little hollow and overly pretentious. In Italy, Eugene Lee-Hamilton, on his invalid's couch, wrote bitter-sweet sonnets that were outcries of a physical rather than a spiritual frustration. And Victor Plarr and many others wrote magazine verse with an eager kind of facility. In any age, these would simply have copied whatever there was to copy. (pp. xxxi-xl)

Donald Davidson, in an introduction to British Poetry of the Eighteen-Nineties, *edited by Donald Davidson, Doubleday, Doran & Co., Inc., 1937, pp. xix-lii.*

JOHN M. MUNRO

[*Munro is an English educator and critic. In the following excerpt, he notes some principal influences on and characteristics of English Decadent poetry.*]

The impulse to categorize has long been a besetting sin of literary historians, and though one can understand and to some extent condone the practice of grouping a number of writers behind a seemingly appropriate banner, it is obvious that such a habit frequently lends itself to over-simplification and distortion. Nowhere is this more clearly demonstrated than among the writers who made their reputations during that period loosely referred to as the eighteen-nineties.

If, for example, one considers only the poets who were writing during the last decade of the nineteenth century, it is clear that far from constituting a neat, relatively homogeneous unit about which one may generalize with some assurance, they exhibit such a variety of beliefs and attitudes, to say nothing of techniques, that the conscientious literary historian if he wishes to present a true image of the decade must abandon his impulse to categorize. Even if we dismiss Tennyson, Swinburne, Christina Rossetti, William Morris and Coventry Patmore, all of whom lived beyond the year 1890, on the grounds that they rightly belong to an older generation, what is one to make of such widely different poets as Oscar Wilde, William Watson, Arthur Symons, Thomas Hardy, Alfred Austin, George Russell (AE), A. E. Housman, Rudyard Kipling, Ernest Dowson, W. E. Henley, W. B. Yeats, Robert Bridges, John Davidson, Alice Meynell, Henry Newbolt, Lionel Johnson, Wilfred Scawen Blunt and Francis Thompson? Some of them subscribed to the more orthodox forms of religious belief, some were agnostics, and at least one was an atheist; some were intensely patriotic, others were not; some sang of the country, some of the town; some proclaimed the glories of their age, and others found little in contemporary life worth praising; some were cheerful, and some were melancholy; some were content to utilize traditional English forms, while others looked to France for their models, and Kipling was criticised for not writing poetry at all. Indeed, all that one can say of these poets as a whole is that they demonstrate the impossibility of attributing to them anything which could be regarded as a common unifying force.

Thus the word "decadent" when used in relation to the literature of the late nineteenth century should be used with caution. Nevertheless, like all catch-words, "decadent" has sufficient truth in it at least partially to justify its use in describing the character of the period, and though one should always remember that the Nineties probably produced as many aggressive, righteous, sober and God-fearing men as any other decade, there were also a fairly numerous group whose beliefs and attitudes seemed to run counter to what we have come to regard as typically Victorian.

However, even if we recognise two main streams in the literature of the Nineties, which for convenience we may call "Decadent" and "Counter-Decadent," there are still problems, for Oscar Wilde, Richard Le Gallienne, John Davidson, W. E. Henley and Robert Louis Stevenson all wrote poems which belong some in one group and some in the other, while Lionel Johnson, though usually included among the Decadents, also parodied them. Furthermore, the Rhymers' Club, that informal group of poets which began to meet in an upstairs room of the Cheshire Cheese in 1891, and included among its members such notable *fin-de-siècle* poets as Arthur Symons, Ernest Dowson and Richard Le Gallienne, was far from being the rallying point of the Decadent Movement, as is popularly supposed. Their two anthologies, *The Book of the Rhymers' Club* (1892) and *The Second Book of the Rhymers' Club* (1894), contained poetry which ranged from the most melancholy, introspective expressions of dispirited malaise to resounding, energetic exhortations to work for a better world.

Finally, to confuse the situation still more, there is the difficulty in determining what the word "decadent" means when applied to late nineteenth-century literature. Generally the word "decadent" was bandied about in the Nineties as a term of opprobrium or approval, by the self-appointed spokesmen for public morality on the one hand, and by the daring young sophisticates on the other. Occasionally, however, there was an attempt to take stock and discover what the term really meant. For example, in a review of Churton Collins' *Illustrations of Tennyson,* included in the first volume of Richard Le Gallienne's *Retrospective Reviews: A Literary Log* (1896), the writer drew a sharp distinction between decadence in style and decadence in literature. The former he took to be "Euphuism—and its antithesis, slang," while the latter was, as he put it, "the euphuistic expression of isolated observations," that is to say, "limited thinking, often insane thinking." In July 1894, in the second number of the *Yellow Book,* Max Beerbohm offered his definition of decadence, suggesting that it was characterized by "paradox and marivaudage, lassitude, a love of horror and all unusual things, a love of argot and archaism and the mysteries of style."

Perhaps the neatest description of the qualities of a decadent was provided by Lionel Johnson in an essay entitled "The Cultured Faun," which appeared in the *Anti-Jacobin,* March 1891:

> Take a young man, who had brains as a boy, and teach him to disbelieve everything that his elders believe in matters of thought, and to reject everything that seems true to himself in matters of sentiment. He need not be at all revolutionary; most clever youths for mere experience's sake will discard their natural or acquired convictions. He will then, since he is intelligent and bright, want something to replace his earlier notions. If Aristotle's *Poetics* are absurd, and Pope is no poet, and politics are vulgar, and Carlyle is played out, and Mr. Ruskin is tiresome, and so forth, according to the circumstances of the case, our youth will be bored to death by the nothingness of everything. You must supply him with the choicest delicacies, and feed him upon the finest rarities. And what so choice as a graceful affectation, or so fine as a surprising paradox? So you cast about for these two, and at once you see that many excellent affectations and paradoxes have had their day. A treasured melancholy of the German moonlight sort, a rapt enthusiasm in the Byronic style, a romantic eccentricity after the French fashion of 1830, a "frank, fierce," sensuousness à la jeunesse Swinburnienne; our youth might flourish them in the face of society all at once, without receiving a single invitation to private views or suppers of the elect. And, in truth, it requires positive genius for the absurd to discover

Lionel Johnson, 1885.

a really promising affectation, a thoroughly fascinating paradox. But the last ten years have done it. And a remarkable achievement it is.

Externally, our hero should cultivate a reassuring sobriety of habit, with just a dash of the dandy. None of the wandering looks, the elaborate disorder, the sublime lunacy of his predecessor, the "apostle of culture." Externally, then, a precise appearance; internally, a catholic sympathy with all that exists, and "therefore" suffers, for art's sake. Now art, at present, is not a question of the senses so much as of the nerves. Botticelli, indeed, was very precious, but Baudelaire is very nervous. Gautier was adorably sensuous, but M. Verlaine is pathetically sensitive. That is the point: exquisite appreciation of pain, exquisite thrills of anguish, exquisite adoration of suffering. Here comes in a tender patronage of Catholicism: white tapers upon the high altar, an ascetic and beautiful young priest, the great gilt monstrance, the subtle-scented and mystical incense, the old-world accents of the Vulgate, of the Holy Offices; the splendour of the sacred vestments. We kneel at some hour, not too early for our convenience, repeating that solemn Latin, drinking in those Gregorian tones, with plenty of modern French sonnets in memory should the sermon be dull. But to join the Church! Ah, no! better to dally with the enchanting mysteries, to pass from our dreams of delirium to our dreams of sanctity with no coarse facts to jar upon us. And so these refined persons cherish a double "passion," the sentiment of repentant yearning and the sentiment of rebellious sin.

To play the part properly a flavor of cynicism is recommended: a scientific profession of materialist dogmas, coupled—for you should forswear constancy—with gloomy chatter about "The Will to Live." If you can say it in German, so much the better; a gross tongue, partially redeemed by Heine, but an infallible oracle of scepticism. Jumble all these "impressions" together, your sympathies and your sorrows, your devotion and your despair; carry them about with you in a state of fermentation, and finally conclude that life is loathesome yet that beauty is beatific. And beauty—ah, beauty is everything beautiful! Isn't that a trifle obvious, you say? That is the charm of it, it shows your perfect simplicity, your chaste and catholic innocence. Innocence of course: beauty is always innocent, ultimately. No doubt there are "monstrous" things, terrible pains, the haggard eyes of the *absintheur,* the pallid faces of "neurotic" sinners; but all that is the portion of our Parisian friends, such and such a "group of artists," who meet at the Café So-and-So. We like people to think that we are much the same, but it isn't true. We are quite harmless, we only concoct strange and subtle verses about it. And, anyway, beauty includes everything; there's another sweet saying for you from our "impressionist" copybooks. Impressions! that is all. Life is mean and vulgar, Members of Parliament are odious, the critics are commercial pedants; we alone know Beauty, and Art, and Sorrow, and Sin. Impressions exquisite, dainty fantasies; fiery-coloured visions; and impertinence struggling into epigram, for "the true," criticism; *c'est adorable!* And since we are scholars and none of your penny-a-line Bohemians, we throw in occasional doses of "Hellenism": by which we mean the Ideal of the Cultured Faun. That is to say, a flowery Paganism, such as no "Pagan" ever had: a mixture of "beautiful woodland natures," and "the perfect comeliness of the Parthenon frieze," together with the elegant languors and favourite vices of (let us parade our "decadent" learning) the *Stratonis Epigrammata.* At this time of day we need not dilate upon the equivocal charm of everything Lesbian. And who shall assail us?—what stupid and uncultured critic, what coarse and narrow Philistine? We are the Elect of Beauty: saints and sinners, devils and devotees, Athenians and Parisians, Romans of the Empire and Italians of the Renaissance. *Fin de siècle!* Literature is a thing of beauty, blood and nerves . . .

In "The Cultured Faun" Johnson effectively enumerates those qualities typical of those poets whom we call Decadent; but it would be wrong to conclude that the English Decadence was no more than a rather unhealthy, ludicrous literary fad. Le Gallienne, Beerbohm and Johnson dismiss the movement with contempt, but to Arthur Symons literary decadence deserved sympathetic consideration, and in his important essay, "The Decadent Movement in Literature" [excerpted above], published in *Harper's New Monthly Magazine* (November 1893), he set out to justify this kind of writing, endeavoring to show that it was a serious literary movement not unlike that of the Greek and Latin Decadence. It is characterised, he wrote, "by an intense self-consciousness, a restless curiosity in research, an over-subtilising refinement upon refinement, a spiritual and moral perversity." And, he continued, "if what we call the classic is indeed the supreme art—those qualities of perfect simplicity, perfect sanity, perfect proportion, the supreme qualities—then this representative literature of today, interesting, beautiful, novel as it is,

is really a new and beautiful and interesting disease." Nevertheless, such literature is typical of our civilisation, which has grown "over-luxurious, over-inquiring, too languid for the relief of action, too uncertain for any emphasis in opinion or conduct." It reflects all the moods and manners of a sophisticated society, and just as we lack "simplicity, sanity, proportion" in our lives, we should not expect to find them in our literature.

Apart from defining what the English Decadence was, there is, then, another problem in deciding whether it deserves to be taken seriously as a definite, if somewhat ill-defined, literary movement, or simply as an amusing interlude of no real literary or historical value. Neither problem admits of an easy solution. In general terms, however, we may say that the English Decadence, as defined by contemporaries, was concerned with the exploration of abnormal psychology; it professed to be concerned with Beauty, but with a beauty so bizarre and unconventional that one might feel more justified in calling it ugliness; it was self-conscious to the point of artificiality; it was generally at odds with the prevailing notions of decency and morality; it was somewhat precious and formal in style, sometimes betraying more concern with expression than subject matter; it was contemptuous of popular movements and attitudes; and it was imbued with a tone of lassitude and regret. Furthermore, it was associated with the young and was sometimes regarded as symptomatic of the age, but unlike the Imagist Movement of a decade or so later, it had no definite program and, apart from Symons in his *Harper's Magazine* article, no real spokesman. For some it was an intensely serious affair, while for others, usually those who stood outside the movement, it was a rather distasteful exhibition of misguided intelligence. In short, it is only in the most general terms that we may speak of a "Decadent Movement." Even then we should be cautious of ascribing to it precisely determined characteristics. (pp. 1-8)

[The] art for art's sake movement as a whole came to be looked upon both in France and in England as simply the rallying cry for those who sought to excuse their excessive interest in subjects abnormal and vicious. Yet Pater seems to have had in mind the correct meaning of the term when in the Conclusion to his *Studies in the History of the Renaissance* (1873) he expressed his belief in the supremacy of art over all other forms of human activity. At first, though, he appears to be advocating little more than a rather crude *carpe diem* approach to life. He tells us, for example, that "not the fruit of experience, but experience itself " is the proper end of existence. We are on this earth for so little time, therefore it behoves us to live intensely, "to burn always with [a] hard gem-like flame." Some spend their lives in "listlessness," others in the "high passions," but, says Pater, "the wisest spend it in art and song":

> For our one chance lies in expanding that interval, in getting as many pulsations as possible into the given time. Great passions may give us this quickened sense of life, ecstasy and sorrow of love, the various forms of enthusiastic activity, disinterested or otherwise, which come naturally to many of us. Of such wisdom, the poetic passion, the desire of beauty, the love of art for its own sake, has most. For art comes to you proposing frankly to give nothing but the highest quality to your moments as they pass, and simply for those moments' sake.

Read out of context it appears that Pater is recommending to his readers that they gather their rosebuds while they may.

Read in context it is clear that this was not Pater's intention at all. What he really said was that art can, as it were, confirm one's own conception of morality. We have so little time "to make theories about those things we see and touch." Furthermore, "any theory or ideal or system which requires of us the sacrifice of any or part of this experience, in consideration of some abstract theory we have not identified with ourselves, or of what is only conventional, has no real claim on us." A far more reliable guide is art, which evokes a "quickened and multiplied consciousness" and widens man's sensibilities. Philosophy, said Pater, in the essay on Winckelmann, simply serves culture, "not by the fancied gift of absolute or transcendental knowledge, but by suggesting questions which help one to detect the passion, and strangeness, and dramatic contrasts of life." Art, however, is superior because it alone can communicate the fullness of the world; hence its supreme importance.

Although this seems to have been Pater's philosophy, many writers of the Nineties either misunderstood or willfully ignored the fact that his theories were based on traditional ethics. Oscar Wilde, for example, who in *De Profundis* (1897) declared that the *Renaissance* had exerted a tremendous influence on his life, interpreted its conclusion quite simply as a plea for liberty in all matters of experience and expression, as evidenced by his glorification of the "new hedonism" in *Dorian Gray* and the details of his personal career.

It is tempting to blame Wilde entirely for his misreading of Pater, but the older critic certainly left himself open to misinterpretation. The voluptuous, slow-moving cadences of his prose, his rich and suggestive imagery, exude a seductive and not altogether wholesome charm which activates the libido rather than stimulates the brain. Neither is Pater's precise meaning always clear. Specifically, in the essay on Winckelmann his comments on the nature of the Hellenic ideal could, and indeed did, suggest that he sanctioned sexual inversion. (pp. 19-21)

There is . . . ample evidence for regarding the Decadent poets of the Nineties as heirs to an English Romantic tradition, fortified with borrowings from Gautier, and Baudelaire, and sanctified by the aesthetic theorizing of Walter Pater. In the 'eighties and 'nineties, however, the influence from France became even more marked, giving the Decadent poetry at the end of the century a distinct exoticism. Thus it may be argued that the English Decadence was not so much a new departure as an intensification of existing practices. Later poets still paid lip service to the cult of art for art's sake, they still took inspiration from Baudelaire, but to these were added imitation of prevailing French techniques.

It is obvious, for example, that towards the end of the century a number of English poets followed the technical precepts associated with that group of French writers known as the Parnassians. . . . Gautier had insisted that art had little or nothing to do with the transitory, mundane matters associated with man's social and political institutions, that the only permanency in an impermanent world is art. If followed, therefore, that the artist should strive to make his creations as perfect as possible, for only by so doing could he hope to achieve a measure of eternity. For the writer, Gautier stressed the relationship he felt should exist between literature and the plastic arts, and demanded that the poet lavish his craftsman's skill on the achievement of perfect form and clarity of outline, as a sculptor would hew a shape from a block of marble. This theory he embodied in a collection of poems called

Emaux et camées (1853), the very title of which indicates the poet's intentions, and in the last poem of the 1857 edition of that volume set forth his credo under the title "L'art," which Austin Dobson freely translated in 1876 under the title "Ars Victrix":

> Yes: when the ways oppose—
> When the hard means rebel,
> Fairer the work out-grows,—
> More potent far the spell.
>
> O Poet, then, forbear
> The loosely-sandalled verse,
> Choose rather thou to wear
> The buskin—strait and terse;
>
> Leave to the tiro's hand
> The limp and shapeless style,
> See that thy form demand
> The labour of the file.
>
> Sculptor, do thou discard
> The yielding clay,—consign
> To Paros marble hard
> The beauty of thy line;—
>
> Model thy Satyr's face
> For bronze of Syracuse;
> In the veined agate trace
> The profile of thy muse.
>
> Painter, that still must mix
> But transient tints anew,
> Thou in the furnace fix
> The firm enamel's hue;
>
> Let the smooth tile receive
> Thy dove-drawn Erycine;
> Thy sirens blue at eve
> Coiled in a wash of wine.
>
> All passes. ART alone
> Enduring stays to us;
> The bust outlasts the throne,—
> The Coin, Tiberius;
>
> Even the gods must go;
> Only the lofty Rhyme
> Not countless years o'erthrow,—
> Not long array of time.
>
> Paint, chisel, then, or write;
> But, that the word surpass,
> With the hard fashion fight,—
> With the resisting mass.

Gautier's artfully chiseled lyrics and sharply defined images inspired, first, several poets in France who, calling themselves Parnassians, attempted to follow Gautier's precepts in verses of their own. Later, a number of poets in England—notably Andrew Lang, Austin Dobson and Edmund Gosse—followed suit. None of these poets could properly be called Decadents, but other poets of the time who have greater claim to the title, were also influenced by the Parnassian example, most notably Lionel Johnson. Johnson published in the *Hobby Horse* of 1891 an essay entitled "A Note Upon the Practice and Theory of Verse at the Present Time Obtaining in France," in which he contrasted the grand but technically sloppy effects of such great English poets as Shakespeare and Robert Browning with the more precise artistry of the Parnassians. In his poetry, also, he strove to emulate the Parnassians, writing verse which Ezra Pound in his introduction to *The Poetical Works of Lionel Johnson* (1915) compared to "small slabs of ivory, firmly combined and contrived," as for example in "Dead," singled out by Pound for special praise:

> In Merioneth, over the sad moor
> Drives the rain, the cold wind blows:
> Past the ruinous church door,
> The poor procession without music goes.
>
> Lonely she wandered out her hour, and died.
> Now the mournful curlew cries
> Over her, laid down beside
> Death's lonely people: lightly down she lies.
>
> In Merioneth, the wind lives and wails,
> On from hill to lonely hill:
> Down the loud, triumphant gales,
> A spirit cries *Be strong!* and cries *Be still!*

Though Parnassianism exerted a powerful influence on the poetry of the English Decadence, a number of poets of the time were equally intoxicated by the more nebulous effects and delicate half-tones of Paul Verlaine, Baudelaire's spiritual successor. Like Baudelaire, Verlaine found the world a depressing place, and though he did not rail as loudly, he too looked upon life as a melancholy *danse macabre.* Unlike Baudelaire, however, whose preoccupation with the artificial was justified in terms of his aesthetic doctrine, Verlaine seems to have been drawn to it by a pathological fascination. His poetic sensibility responded to the melancholy half-tones of the twilit city and encouraged him to seek always for *la nuance* rather than for the color itself. For Verlaine, in so far as he was interested in the spirit world, a transcendental state was not so much to be perceived through the objects of physical reality as evoked by the music of poetry. As he wrote in "Art Poétique," as translated by Symons:

> Music first and foremost of all!
> Choose your measure of odd not even,
> Let it melt in the air of heaven,
> Pose not, poise not, but rise and fall.
>
> Choose your words, but think not whether
> Each to other of old belong:
> What so dear as the dim grey song
> Where clear and vague are joined together?
>
> 'Tis veils of beauty for beautiful eyes,
> 'Tis the trembling light of the naked noon
> 'Tis the medley of blue and gold, the moon
> And stars in the cool of autumn skies.
>
> Let every shape of its shade be born;
> Colour, away! come to me, shade!
> Only of shade can the marriage be made
> Of dream with dream and of flute with horn.
>
> Shun the Point, lest death with it come,
> Unholy laughter and cruel wit
> (For the eyes of the angels weep at it)
> And all the garbage of the scullery-scum.
>
> Take Eloquence, and wring the neck of him!
> You had better, by force, from time to time,
> Put a little sense in the head of Rhyme:
> If you watch him not, you will be at the beck of him.
>
> O, who shall tell us the wrongs of Rhyme?
> What witless savage or what deaf boy
> Has made for us this twopenny toy
> Whose bells ring hollow and out of time?
>
> Music always and music still!
> Let your verse be a wandering thing
> That flutters in flight from a soul on the wing
> Towards other skies at a new whim's will.
>
> Let your verse be the luck of the lure
> Afloat on the winds that at morning hint
> Of the odours of thyme and the savour of mint—
> And all the rest is literature.

Verlaine, then, cultivated the vague and avoided direct statement in favor of indirect moods and sensations. For him the "impression" mattered: only through the impression could the spirit of beauty be experienced. His views were followed by a number of the Decadent poets of the Nineties, by Ernest Dowson, John Gray and in particular by Arthur Symons, whose "Music and Memory," from *Silhouettes* (1892), is one of the most typical "impressionist" poems of the period:

> Across the tides of music, in the night,
> Her magical face,
> A light upon it as the happy light
> Of dreams in some delicious place
> Under the moonlight in the night.
>
> Music, soft throbbing music in the night,
> Her memory swims
> Into the brain, a carol of delight;
> The cup of music overbrims
> With wine of memory, in the night.
>
> Her face across the music, in the night,
> Her face a refrain,
> A light that sings along the waves of light,
> A memory that returns again,
> Music in Music, in the night.

Unlike Parnassianism, however, which was well entrenched before the end of the century, and endured through the early years of the twentieth to become an essential part of the Imagists' creed, Impressionism was something of a fad which all but expired with the Decadence. During the Nineties, however, it was very much in vogue, and Verlaine himself came to be regarded as a martyred saint who died in the cause of beauty, the victim of a crass and unfeeling bourgeoisie who were deaf to his music and saw only the sordidness of his life.

Gautier and the Parnassians, Baudelaire and Verlaine all left their mark on the English Decadence, but the most important foreign influence of all was not a poet but the novelist Joris-Karl Huysmans, whose *A rebours* (1884), described by Symons as the "breviary" of the Decadent Movement, gave many of the Decadents their *raison d'être.* It was one thing to subscribe to the theory of art for art's sake or to copy the technical idiosyncrasies of certain French writers; but to model oneself on the spectacular career of des Esseintes, the hero of Huysmans' notorious novel, became almost obligatory for those who sought membership among the Decadent élite. In *A rebours,* des Esseintes, wearied and disgusted by life, withdraws from society, preferring the seclusion of his sumptuously furnished apartment on the outskirts of Paris to the hubbub of the city. There, in this solitary retreat, he systematically cultivates his passion for the bizarre and the exotic, reading the works of the Greek and Latin Decadence, fondling jewels, composing "symphonies of perfumes," and tending rare and exotic plants, hoping to find in these pursuits some justification for existence. At last, his nervous system on the point of collapse, he is forced to recognize that he has reached a crisis, where only two alternatives remain open to him: a choice in Barbey d'Aurevilly's words, between the muzzle of a pistol or the foot of the Cross.

Although Huysmans' novel achieved a certain *succès de scandale,* it was not intended simply as a celebration of the perverse and the unnatural. It was, on the contrary, a serious, if ironic, exploration of all the sensuous pleasures life has to offer in the hope of finding in them some justification for existence. Yet, to many, the novel's main attraction was its exhaustive inventory of abnormal pleasures (a catalogue made doubly attractive by the artificial prose style in which it was written), which served as a stimulus to those who aspired to the Decadent ideal. Certainly these were the qualities which appealed most readily to Dorian Gray, and, we may infer, to Wilde himself. In *Dorian Gray* Wilde alludes to Husymans' *A rebours,* and describes it in some detail:

> It was the strangest book Dorian had ever read. It seemed to him that in exquisite movement, and to the delicate sound of flutes, the sins of the world were passing in dumb show before him. Things of which he had never dreamed were gradually revealed.
>
> It was a novel without a plot, and with only one character, being indeed, simply a psychological study of a young Parisian who spent his life trying to realise in the nineteenth century all the passions and modes of thought that belonged to every century except his own, and to sum up, as it were, in himself the various moods through which the world spirit had ever passed, loving for their mere artificiality those renunciations that men have unwisely called virtue as those natural rebellions that wise men call sin. The style in which it was written was that curious jewelled style, vivid and obscure at once, full of argot and archaisms, of technical expressions and of elaborate paraphrases, that characterises the work of some of the finest artists of the French School of symbolists. There were in it metaphors as monstrous as orchids and as evil in colour. The life of the sense was described in the terms of the mystical philosophy. One hardly knew at times whether one was reading the spiritual ecstasies of some medieval saint or the morbid confessions of a modern sinner. It was a poisonous book. The heavy odour of incense seemed to hang about its pages and trouble the brain. The mere cadence of the sentences, the subtle monotony of the music, so full it was of complex refrains and movements elaborately repeated, produced in the mind of the lad, a form of reveries, a malady of dreaming, that made him unconscious of the falling day and the creeping shadows.

In Wilde's description of *A rebours* we have the essential difference between the French and English Decadence. For all their insistence on the separation of art and life and their preoccupation with abnormal subjects, the French were not altogether irresponsible. Their literature was concerned with the possibility of an ideal state which would be of greater value than the bourgeois, materialistic world of conventional behavior and morality. They were, in fact, not so much "Decadents" as "Symbolists," writers who intended to evoke a superior state of being, writers dedicated to "le Beau et l'Idéal." Verlaine himself in an interview with Jules Huret in 1891 dismissed the term "Decadent" as meaningless, complaining that its use gave entirely the wrong idea about his own work and that of his contemporaries.

One cannot say that many of the English Decadents were concerned with ideal values. Certainly a number of them professed to be concerned solely with beauty, and one or two of them seem genuinely to have aspired to a spiritual world which they deemed more satisfying than life here below. W. B. Yeats, for example, in the Nineties at least, though he was to modify his position later, believed that poetry would become a "poetry of essences, separated one from another in little and intense poems," the result of "an ever more arduous search for an almost disembodied ecstasy." He also believed that the poet "should seek out those wavering, meditative, organic rhythms, which are the embodiment of the imagination, that neither desires nor hates, because it has done with time, and only wishes to gaze upon some reality, some beauty." Lionel Johnson, similarly dissatisfied with a purely earthbound existence, looked to the Roman Catholic Church to provide him with spiritual sustenance. For most of their contemporaries, however, it was not so much transcendence they sought as escape. Thus, when Ernest Dowson at the close of his "Nuns of the Perpetual Adoration" reminded us that "our roses fade, the world is wide; / But there, beside the altar, there is rest," he voiced an imperfectly conceived death-wish rather than a strenuously held belief in the spirit. By contrast, Baudelaire, Huysmans, and perhaps even Verlaine, for all their evident concern with sensuality and eroticism, were nonetheless fundamentally mystical in their approach to life.

Indeed, for all their enthusiasm for contemporary French literature, the English Decadents failed almost completely to appreciate its ultimate intentions. They acknowledged the French writers' emphasis on style, and sought to embody the same technical precision in their own work, sometimes attempting to reduplicate the finely wrought, sculptured images of Gautier and the Parnassians, and at other times, fortified by the example of the painter Whistler's hazy "nocturnes," strove for the vague imprecision of Verlaine. They leaned heavily towards Verlaine's idea of the supreme value of music, and sought to imitate his rhythms, often with success. Most obviously, however, they took inspiration from those subjects exploited by Verlaine and Baudelaire: the charm of the artificial; the attraction of the city in all its aspects; the fascination of mysterious and beautiful women. Finally, the melancholy of Verlaine, and the *weltschmerz* of Baudelaire were adopted, but mainly as an artistic pose. While there are plenty of sighs and similar expressions of despair in English Decadent poetry, the general effect is more of a petulant moan than the cry of deeply experienced disillusionment.

The English Decadence is a very feeble echo of the plaintive cry across the Channel. Unlike the French Decadence, which had matured over a period of seventy years or so and had been dedicated for the most part to definite artistic ideals, the majority of the writers in the English Decadent tradition were prompted mainly by a spirit of revolt, and lacking an aesthetic of their own, simply copied what they regarded as the salient characteristics of a similar movement in France.

Thus, although most of the English Decadents professed to share the Continental writers' belief in the importance of music in relation to poetry, they seem not to have been fully aware of the doctrine's implications. In France, both Verlaine and Mallarmé had stressed the significance of "music" in literature. For Verlaine, as A. G. Lehmann has pointed out in *The Symbolist Aesthetic in France* (1948), music seems to have meant little more than audible harmony, mellifluous cadences which fall pleasingly on the ear, while Mallarmé seems to have understood the word to refer to an inaudible harmony, a sort of music of the spheres, a Platonic ideal to which all poetry aspired. In short, Mallarmé's conception of music seems to have been close to Pater's, as he described it in his essay on "The School of Giorgione" in *Studies in the History of the Renaissance*. There Pater had suggested that "although each art has . . . its own specific order of impressions and an untranslatable charm . . . it is noticeable that, in its special mode of handling its given material, each art may be observed to pass into the condition of some other art, by what German critics call *Anders-Streben*—a partial alienation from its own limitations, through which the arts are able, not indeed to supply the place of each other, but reciprocally to lend each other new forces." Thus, "some of the most delightful music seems to be always approaching to figure, to pictorial definition," and "sculpture aspires out of the hard limitation of pure form towards colour, or its equivalent," while "French poetry generally with the art of engraving." But most important:

> *All art constantly aspires to the condition of music.* For while in all other kinds of art it is possible to distinguish the matter from the form, and the understanding can always make this distinction, yet it is the constant effort of art to obliterate it.

To this aesthetic doctrine the majority of the English Decadents paid only partial allegiance. They acknowledged Pater's belief in the ability of the various arts "to lend each other new forces," for Gautier had shown them that poetry could aspire to sculpture; Whistler had demonstrated that painting had affinities with music; and more generally, Baudelaire, in his poem "Correspondances," had asserted the complex interrelation between all things on this earth and those above, a theory which led Swinburne, and after him a few of the Decadents, to explore cautiously the possibilities of synesthesia. Poets such as Wilde and Symons made efforts to capture the pictorial effects of such painters as Whistler, Degas and Watteau in their poetry, and in the following poem called "The Opium Smoker" from *Days and Nights* (1889), Symons handles synesthetic techniques with some assurance:

> I am engulfed and drown deliciously.
> Soft music like a perfume, and sweet light
> Golden with audible odours exquisite,
> Swathe me with the cerements for eternity.
> Time is no more. I pause and yet I flee.
> A million ages wrap me round with night.
> I drain a million ages of delight.
> I hold the future in my memory.
>
> Also I have this garret which I rent,
> This bed of straw, and this that was a chair,
> This worn-out body like a tattered tent,
> This crust, of which the rats have eaten part,
> This pipe of opium; rage, remorse, despair;
> This soul at pawn and this delirious heart.

Yet the English Decadents seem not to have grasped fully what Mallarmé and Pater had meant by music. Dowson strove to write poems in which the words had been chosen more for their musical qualities than for their sense, and Symons wrote airs for the lute, in which he tried to capture the simplicity of that instrument's tone as well as its melancholy plangency. Perhaps most interesting of all, A. B. Miall prefaced the four sections of his volume *Nocturnes and Pastorals* (1896) with several bars of music from Chopin and Schubert, evidently intending that the music should set the tone for the verse that followed. But almost always the Decadents seem

to have had in mind audible music rather than the harmonious interdependence of form and content, which blended together comprise one beautiful, indivisible whole. It was Verlaine rather than Mallarmé they chose as their model, and though both John Gray and Arthur Symons translated the latter with considerable success, and W. B. Yeats was for a time attracted to him too, he was never very popular among the English Decadents, it being left to the generation of T. S. Eliot and Ezra Pound to explore more fully the possibilities of the Mallarméan aesthetic.

A poetry as heavily derivative as that of the English Decadence reveals, not surprisingly, uncertainty of direction; it has, most noticeably, a curiously factitious air. One rarely feels that it has been genuinely inspired, that it is the product of a passionately held conviction or attitude. Indeed, it would be strange if one felt otherwise, for most of the poets associated with the movement seem to have lacked a clearly defined identity of their own. For many, it seems to have been *de rigueur* to ape the attitudes of French literary bohemia. Others aspired to the courtly insouciance of a bygone age, Herbert Horne, for example, looking to the Restoration, and Aubrey Beardsley to the France of Louis XV, for guidance in matters of conduct and also for poetic inspiration. Those who were—or liked to consider themselves—Celts, that is to say W. B. Yeats, Ernest Rhys, Lionel Johnson, Victor Plarr, John Todhunter, regarded Ireland, Wales and even Brittany as their spiritual homes, seeing themselves as nineteenth-century reincarnations of the great mythic bards of the past. But almost without exception the Decadent poets seem to have been intent on establishing suitable identities for themselves rather than developing their own personalities.

Although the Decadents sought everywhere for suitable *personae,* one attitude they all seem to have held in common: they believed that they were the unacknowledged aristocracy of letters. They felt they were above the crowd, aesthetically more refined than their fellows, to whom they refused to pander or conform. Most of them had little contact with the masses, and were antagonistic to the popular movements of the time, desiring to keep the unpleasant realities of everyday life at a distance. The few who did concern themselves with contemporary social problems tended to be social outcasts themselves, impractical idealists with Utopian visions whose reformatory schemes met with little success. Prone to manic depression, their lives were invariably unhappy, when they were made to realise the discrepancy between their dreams for a better world and social reality. (pp. 32-63)

For the Decadents, withdrawal was almost axiomatic. Their enthusiasm for the elaborate ritual of the Roman Catholic Church, lovingly portrayed in a number of poems by Lionel Johnson, is of course symptomatic of this attitude, and so is the fact that many of the Decadents were confirmed drugtakers, alcoholics or homosexuals. Indeed, the kind of sex that is most frequently celebrated by the Decadents is of a peculiarly negative kind. The object of affection is either a member of the poet's own sex, a sterile androgyna, a child of infinite purity, or a prostitute whose depravity precludes the likelihood of natural human love, and whenever a normal relationship is described, it is usually to record its passing. It is in this psychological context that we should consider the Decadents' love of artifice, whether it takes the form of a painted chorus-girl, the city, or the elaborate and sometimes recondite imagery which some of them affected. Even their poems of seeming artlessness are so self-consciously simple that they frequently appear more artificial and contrived than some of their more elaborate verses.

The Decadents were unable to approach life unless they could cloak it with mystery, or veil it with garments woven from their fanciful dreams. Almost always we sense that their interest in writing poetry is to create dream worlds wherein they can lose themselves and so avoid facing reality. It is hardly surprising, therefore, that the setting of many of the Decadents' poems is the East, the orient of romantic legend, Burton's *Arabian Nights* suffused with exotic perfumes, brilliant with opulent decoration, and peopled by beautiful and delicate young men and maids, who stroll langorously through a melancholy, scented twilight. (pp. 63-4)

> John M. Munro, in his The Decadent Poetry of the Eighteen-Nineties, *American University of Beirut, 1970, 78 p.*

JEAN WILSON

[*In the following excerpt, Wilson suggests that works by major writers of the Decadent movement, including Oscar Wilde, John Davidson, Lionel Johnson, and Ernest Dowson, do not typify poetry of the 1890s.*]

> Let us accept the fact so well pointed out by Mr W. G. Blaikie Murdoch in *The Renaissance of the Nineties,* that the output of the nineties was 'a distinct secession from the art of the previous age . . . , in fact the eighties, if they have a distinct character, were a time of transition, a period of simmering for revolt rather than of actual outbreak; and it was in the succeeding ten years that, thanks to certain young men, an upheaval was really made'.

The quotation is from Bernard Muddiman's *Men of the Nineties* (1920) [see Further Reading], but it could have come from almost any writer on the period. Nevertheless, I do not think it true. A great many critics have written of a 'Nineties' movement, but few of them have attempted clearly to define what they meant by it. Of those who do Authur Symons is pleading a cause, Holbrook Jackson is rather general, and so too is Osbert Burdett [see Further Reading for Burdett; see Jackson and Symons excerpts above]. The most recent and detailed definition, by Derek Stanford [in his *Poets of the 'Nineties,* excerpted above], shows that certain popular myths about the nineties, which distort our own view of the period, have persisted to the present day. Stanford, many of whose ideas are derived from Arthur Symons, says that 'the exclusively *fin-de-siècle* verse' was marked by 'decadence, impressionism and aestheticism'. He emphasizes the influence of French poets, Baudelaire and Verlaine in particular, and that of certain Latin lyricists like Catullus. Pater's theories, he argues, encouraged the nineties poets to write 'poetry for poetry's sake', which meant that they gave up didactic or metaphysical aims in an attempt to capture 'the pathos of transience'. This more 'aristocratic poetic' made them rebel, in Arthur Symons's words, against 'the ready-made of language, from the bondage of traditional form, of a form become rigid'. Like Verlaine, Stanford says, they tried to 'wring rhetoric's neck' by rejecting the 'tutti frutti Tennysonian afflatus'. This desire to refine or purify poetry led them to see the lyric as 'the paradigm of all poetry'. Their lyrics contained a strong feeling of 'mortality and melancholy', which was expressed in 'images of fevered living'. Stanford believes that there is a 'connection between the nature, the distinction

of this work and the tragedies which their authors enacted' in their lives, and in saying this he hints at the source of the 'Nineties' myth. For, like nearly every other critic of the period, he seems unable to distinguish between a social and an aesthetic movement.

There was certainly a well defined social grouping of young writers in London in the late eighteen eighties. They patronized the same pubs and cafés and formed societies, such as the Rhymers' Club, among themselves. Many of them had been at Oxford, a high proportion of them were Catholics, a number came from upper-class backgrounds, and several died young of tuberculosis, drink, or suicide. But as poets they have relatively little in common. Even B. Ifor Evans, who argues that the nineties remains 'one of the most compact movements of modern times', concedes that 'poetry had only a limited share in its significance' [see Further Reading].

There is a certain convenience in shorthand terms, but this particular set are not very helpful, and even misleading. To talk about 'decadence', for instance, is to confuse art and life. As Edgar Jepson, a young poet of the period, points out [in his *Memoirs of a Victorian* (1933)], the adjective 'decadent' had a specific reference when it first came into use, which it quickly lost: 'When in the nineties we talked of the decadent poets we did not mean exactly what the journalists of today mean when they write with shocked pens of the decadents of the nineties. We were speaking of a French school of poets, of whom Verlaine was the chief, in whose verse there was a certain fall, a *Décadence . . .*'. As Jepson implies, 'decadent' is now used in a moral, not critical sense, and applied mainly to choice of subject matter rather than technique. Defiance of 'Victorian' conventions, especially the reference to illicit love, is often given as proof that a new movement was under way in the nineties. The fact that this kind of subject matter and attitude were already current at the very height of Victorianism, in the poetry of Swinburne and Meredith, for instance, is either ignored or forgotten.

What is also forgotten is that the influence of French poetry was felt long before the nineties, again by Swinburne, who modelled himself partly on Gautier and partly on Baudelaire. Even within the decade its influence was not confined to the 'decadents', for traditional poets like Henley, Lang, and Dobson were using French forms in their verse too, though they sometimes preferred fourteenth- to nineteenth-century models.

One distinctive feature of the French *symbolistes* is their fascination with the exotic, the bizarre, and the grotesque, and many critics give this as a common factor of 'Nineties' poetry. But English writers had been drawn to exotic themes since Dr Johnson wrote *Rasselas,* and their love of the grotesque and bizarre had already emerged in the Gothic novel and 'graveyard' poetry. What does perhaps differentiate the 'decadents' from other English writers with similar tastes is the themes they chose to express this interest. They turned to the city, which had been virtually ignored since the eighteenth century, and described its streets, music-halls, and theatres. But B. Ifor Evans exaggerates the situation when he says that among all this 'nineties paraphernalia of music-hall, ballet, warm elegant interiors and furtive shabbiness' there is 'never a glimpse of a tree or natural light of the sun'.

As for the 'aestheticism' that Stanford mentions, this too has been exaggerated. Most of the poets did certainly believe in the 'Art for Art's sake' doctrine of Walter Pater, but their self-conscious adherence was largely theoretical, as the work of Oscar Wilde, one of its most uncompromising exponents, shows. In spite of his pronouncement that 'there is no such thing as a moral or immoral book. Books are well written or badly written. That is all', *The Ballad of Reading Gaol,* his finest and best-known poem, is much more didactic than many of the poems of Robert Bridges, for instance. Even when Wilde and his companions were trying to 'capture the pathos of transience', as Derek Stanford puts it, they were doing no more than Bridges, who wrote several lyrics on the transience of spring, youth, and love, as most poets will. They differ from most of their contemporaries, however, in the quality of lyric poetry they produced in proportion to 'poetry of ideas', but in a century which had known Shelley, Tennyson, and Rossetti this is insufficient to distinguish them as a separate movement.

Yeats, who called them the 'last romantics' also described them as the 'tragic generation' and the tragedy of their personal lives is often given as proof of their common identity as poets. Even if we accept this assumption, a life like Stephen Phillips's, with its sudden rise to fame and just as rapid descent into obscurity, shows that some of their contemporaries led equally 'tragic' existences. But I believe that the 'tragedy' of their lives is only relevant if it can be seen to have affected their poetry. Here again I differ from Stanford, who implies that their melancholy had a direct effect on their work. His only proof of the difference their 'sadness' makes to their poetry, however, is to point to their choice of melancholy themes; but he seems to have forgotten groups like the 'graveyard' poets and individuals such as Keats, Rossetti, and Hardy, who express comparable feelings in similar themes.

A. J. A. Symons's claim that the attempt to follow Pater's injunction to 'fix the last fine shade' of emotion led to a corresponding 'elaboration of technique' [*An Anthology of 'Nineties' Verse* (1928)], is the most serious argument for the existence of a separate 'Nineties' group discussed so far. Pater had written at some length of the importance of style, in Flaubert particularly, and his disciples are supposed to have concentrated far more than their predecessors or contemporaries on *le mot juste.* I can only repeat that they were not as exceptional in their 'conscious deliberate craft' as their propagandists make out. Sir William Watson, usually considered the most traditional poet of the period, was so concerned with technique that he would spend an entire day revising a single line, and he is merely one example.

Not only are the nineties poets supposed to have taken 'the heterogeneous speech of Victorian poetry and sought to refine it' into 'pure' poetry, they are also believed to have 'wrung rhetoric's neck' (Stanford). According to Stanford their pursuit of 'pure' poetry attracted them to minor poets, particularly Latin ones like Catullus, Propertius, and Lucretius. I suspect that Stanford himself is not very clear what he means by 'pure' poetry; to me it suggests something far too deliberate to be unrhetorical. An examination of their poetry shows that a great deal of it contains as much rhetoric as Watson's intentionally rhetorical 'public' verse. They may have intended, as Arthur Symons says, to break away from 'the ready-made of language' and the 'bondage of traditional form', but most of them were far less successful than their non-'Ninetyish' contemporaries, Henley, Kipling, and Housman, whose colloquial idioms came far nearer to the spoken language.

I do not wish to suggest that none of the features mentioned

are to be found in nineties poetry. Many of them are. I am arguing rather that they are less prevalent than has been imagined, that they are nearly all inclusive not exclusive, and that they do not therefore justify the use of a separate label. What is perhaps most misleading about this label is the implication that the poets it describes are the most significant ones of the period. Yet none of the major poets of the decade follows in this supposedly central tradition. The only possible exception is the early Yeats. Even in his first phase, however, there are signs of a very different future development:

> The Woods of Arcady are dead,
> And over is their antique joy;
> Of old the world on dreaming fed;
> Gray Truth is now her antique toy.
>   ['The Song of the Happy Shepherd']

His later verse, with its rejection of 'dreaming', and more colloquial rhythms, is much nearer to 'Gray Truth' than anything one expects to find in 'Nineties' poetry. The same refusal to dream is obvious in Thomas Hardy's work from the beginning. With the publication of *Wessex Poems* in 1898, he establishes himself as a highly individual poet, whose only link with the 'Nineties' group is a prevailing sense of melancholy. A. E. Housman, too, shares little with them beyond this weariness of spirit. The outstanding features of his first book, *A Shropshire Lad* (1896), are the use of colloquial speech and homely subject matter, both of which are directly contrary to the 'decadent' tradition. Francis Thompson comes nearer to it in one or two of his poems. In 'Memorat Memoria', for instance, which Symons evidently thought typical enough to include in his anthology, he shows a longing to recapture the past, a secret enjoyment of shame, and a sense of the 'hateful horror' of love; there is something slightly grotesque in the line: 'I shall never feel a girl's soft arms without horror of the skin'. However, this type of poem is fairly exceptional; the majority of his poems treat of his relationship to God, and have more in common with seventeenth-century mystical poetry than with any contemporary verse. There is nothing whatever that could be called 'Ninetyish' in Rudyard Kipling. His use of colloquial speech rhythms, his predominantly hopeful tone, his almost aggressive patriotic verse, and his deliberately 'popular' appeal quite definitely set him apart from any such tradition.

There is also a large group of minor poets, who do not fit the definition. Men like William Watson, Stephen Phillips, Alfred Austin, Aubrey de Vere, Austin Dobson, and Lord de Tabley, for instance, could in no sense be seen as part of a rebellion against the Tennysonian tradition. Yet, if we are to judge by numbers and homogeneity, there is just as strong a case for arguing that they characterize the period as the supposedly representative 'Nineties' men.

Even within their own chosen area—the two *Books of the Rhymers' Club* and the various anthologies—those who talk of a 'central nineties tradition' can be questioned. Stanford describes the Rhymers' Club as 'the chief distillery of nineties poetry' and its two anthologies as 'a stamping-ground for the formation of a *fin-de-siècle* style', but one glance at these books, and his own and Symons's collections, will show that many of the minor poets included, such as Edwin Ellis, G. A. Greene, and Richard Le Gallienne, are scarcely distinguishable from the poets just mentioned. Le Gallienne, for instance, in 'The Decadent to his Soul' actively satirizes the tradition he is supposed to represent:

> Then from that day, he used his soul

As bitters to the over dulcet sins,
As olives to the fatness of the feast—
She made those dear heart-breaking ecstasies
Of minor chords amid the Phrygian lutes,
She sauced his sins with splendid memories,
Starry regrets and infinite hopes and fears;
His holy youth and his first love
Made pearly background to strange-coloured vice.

His most characteristic work fits into a more permanent English tradition of light nature and love lyrics. . . . (pp. 160-64)

Other minor poets included in these selections, however, do have certain 'Ninetyish' features. Olive Custance, for instance, has all the necessary ingredients in her work. In 'The Masquerade', the first of four poems printed in Symons's anthology, life is likened to a dance in which most people must participate, however 'wearily' they do so. The note of resignation and defeat is sounded at the end of the second stanza: 'We sing, and few will question if there slips / A sob into our singing'. The next poem, 'Mélisande', deals with the hopeless love of this 'pale little princess passionate and shy' for Pelleas, and her early death as a result. Its ornate vocabulary and exotic imagery, both reminiscent of the Pre-Raphaelites, also mark the two remaining pieces, 'Peacocks' and 'Black Butterflies'. In the first the peacock's 'gorgeous plumage' is compared to the poet's 'gay youth', which:

Tempts with its beauty that disastrous day
When in the gathering darkness of despair
Death shall strike dumb the laughing mouth of song.

In 'Black Butterflies', the significance attached to capturing each fine shade of feeling implies a belief in Pater's aesthetic theory of art. The combination of 'black butterflies', 'a tomb', and a 'strange sphinx' gives the poem a hot-house odour of artificiality. 'Evelyn Douglas', whose real name was John Barlas, shows the same love of the exotic in three out of the four poems chosen by Symons—'Dreamland', 'The Memphian Temple', and 'The Palace of Pleasure'. In the last, love and melancholy are combined, with very 'decadent' results:

And from recesses more aloof
Soft viols aching with desire
Prolonged a sad delicious sound,
Voluptuous melancholy notes
That round the soul like silence wound.

Eugene Lee-Hamilton, another poet included in Symons's anthology, also has the requisite *nostalgie de la vie,* as the very titles of his poems suggest: 'Lost Years', 'Meeting the Ghosts', 'By the Fire'. He shows a fascination with decay and a love of the exotic and the bizarre. He explicitly links these to his reading of French nineteenth-century poets by calling one of his exercises in the macabre 'Baudelaire':

A Paris gutter of the good old times,
Black and putrescent in its stagnant bed,
Save where the shamble oozings fringe it red,
Or scaffold trickles, or nocturnal crimes.

It holds dropped gold; dead flowers from tropic climes;
Gems true and false, by midnight maskers shed;
Old pots of rouge; old broken phials that spread
Vague fumes of musk, with fumes from slums and slimes.

And everywhere, as glows the set of day,
There floats upon the winding fetid mire
The gorgeous iridescence of decay:

A wavy film of colour, gold and fire,
Trembles all through it as you pick your way,
And streaks of purple that are straight from Tyre.

These three poets are undeniably 'Ninetyish', but (looking back on the decade from a distance of seventy years) it is hard to see why the second-rate work of a few obscure poets should be taken to represent its central tradition. For it is only in some of the minor poets that any homogeneity is to be found. The five leading poets of the group have very little in common with each other, and three of them—Oscar Wilde, Lionel Johnson, and John Davidson—do not even write 'Ninetyish' verse.

As Oscar Wilde admitted to Gide, he put his talent into art and his genius into life. He lived the part and symbolized the type of the 'Nineties' poet, but there is little in his poetry to justify the image. Apart from his long poem 'The Sphinx', with its baroque profusion of ancient gods, exotic names, and strange legends, one or two short lyrics, 'Panthea', which preaches the gospel of free love, and 'Charmides', which illustrates it, there is hardly anything 'decadent' in it.

On the contrary, his first collection of verses, 'Eleutheria', consists largely of political poems full of responsible social comment. In 'Ave Imperatrix', for example, he argues that affluence can never compensate for the horrors of war:

Go! crown with thorns thy gold-crowned head,
Change thy glad song to song of pain;
Wind and wild wave have got thy dead,
And will not yield them back again.

Other poems in the same collection are concerned with the French Revolution, democracy, Louis Napoleon, and the massacre of Christians in Bulgaria. His next book, *The Garden of Eros,* is a long narrative poem devoted more to nature and the praise of English poets than to love, in spite of its title. Wilde specifically acknowledges his debt to Keats, Shelley, Swinburne, Morris, Rossetti, and Spenser in verses packed with classical allusions: his description of summer in the garden abounds with references to Persephone, Herakles, Hylas, Juno, and other mythical figures. A similar kind of heavily-weighted nature poetry is to be found in 'The Burden of Itys', 'Panthea', and 'Humanitad', though in the last there is far more personally observed detail; he notices, for example, that 'a few thin wisps of hay / Lie on the sharp black hedges'.

The love poetry, which is not abundant, is generally lyrical and tender, whether personal, as in 'Apologia' and 'Quia Multum Amavi', or cast in dramatic form, as in 'Her Voice' and 'His Voice'. Other lyrics are collected together under the titles 'Wind Flowers' and 'Impressions'. The most touching lyric of all, written about his sister, who died in childhood, is to be found in 'Rosa Mystica', a group of religious poems:

Tread lightly, she is near
Under the snow,
Speak gently, she can hear
The daisies grow.

The rest of the 'Rosa Mystica' collection records Wilde's reaction on first seeing Italy. Although ostensibly travel poems, their real theme is his sense of being at the centre of the Roman Catholic faith. The 'Sonnet Approaching Italy', for example, ends:

But when I knew that far away at Rome
In evil bonds a second Peter lay,
I wept to see the land so very fair.

'Ravenna', for which he was awarded the Newdigate Prize at Oxford, in 1878, although again ostensibly a travel poem, is more of a reflection on the lives of great poets, Dante and Byron in particular.

Wilde's poetry is, on the whole, rather didactic; definite moral judgement is passed, for instance, in the following lines from 'The Harlot's House', superficially a 'decadent' poem:

> Sometimes a clockwork puppet pressed
> A phantom lover to her breast,
> Sometimes they seemed to try to sing.
>
> Sometimes a horrible marionette
> Came out, and smoked its cigarette
> Upon the steps like a live thing.
>
> Then turning to my love, I said,
> 'The dead are dancing with the dead,
> The dust is whirling with the dust.'

'The Ballad of Reading Gaol', his best-known poem, has an even more definite moral, based as it is on the assumption that justice is important, and should be seen to be done.

The most obvious influences in Wilde's poetry are not the French nineteenth-century poets, but Greek and Roman writers, Dante, Spenser, Keats, and the Pre-Raphaelites, all well-established models. Wilde's forms, too, are predominantly traditional. He does use French forms, like the *villanelle* or the *ballade,* at times, but on the whole he prefers the sonnet and simple four-, five-, or six-line stanzas. In 'The Sphynx' he uses Tennyson's 'In Memoriam' quatrain with a subtle difference, by writing it out in two-line stanzas, and thus creating internal rhyme.

So that, though a few of Wilde's poems fit the popular definition of 'Nineties' verse, and though he is considered typical enough to be represented by five poems in Symons's anthology, his poetry is both more and less than the definition implies.

John Davidson is even less of a 'Nineties' poet, except, again, for his life, or rather his death. For the public interpreted his suicide in 1909 as the gesture of yet another melancholy aesthete, whereas he had, in fact, given up the struggle against external hardships only after a determined fight. His poetry falls into three distinct phases: the apprentice work in Scotland on romantic plays and nature lyrics, the more 'realistic', socially responsible eclogues and ballads written after his move to London, and finally the metaphysical and somewhat didactic 'Testaments' of the early twentieth century. The middle period falls neatly within the nineties. The main works in it are: *In a Music Hall* (1891), *Fleet Street Eclogues* (1893), *Ballads and Songs* (1894), *Fleet Street Eclogues, Second Series* (1895), *New Ballads* (1896), *The Last Ballad* (1898). Davidson's preoccupation with the city rather than the countryside, hinted at in the title of *Fleet Street Eclogues,* his first successful work, gives him his only claim to the epithet 'Ninetyish'. (pp. 164-67)

Davidson also writes a small amount of love poetry, but again he is non-'Ninetyish' in his treatment of it, for there is very little wistfulness or intensity in it. 'A Ballad of Hell', for instance, an account of a suicide pact between two lovers, one of whom fails to keep it, does not fulfill the intensity promised in the theme, and the woman's journey into hell and her eventual escape to heaven are given far greater emphasis than the feelings of either of the lovers. 'The Ballad of Lancelot' is an-

other potentially powerful love story which never fully develops. Lancelot's madness, a result of his hopeless love for Guinevere, is described in convincing detail, but, again, there is no attempt to portray the passion between the two lovers.

Davidson is far more concerned with questions of social justice (as in 'Waiting'), the difficulties of religious belief (as in 'The Man Forbid'), and the problems of the artist ('A Ballad of Heaven'). Although he shows an occasional interest in medievalism (as in 'The Ordeal'), which links him with the Pre-Raphaelites and their successors, his overriding concern is with a totally different kind of subject matter.

His metaphysical bent, though not fully developed in this middle period, is nevertheless apparent. The young man in 'A Ballad in Blank Verse', for instance, forced to make a choice between Christianity and 'creedlessness', exclaims:

> Henceforth I shall be God; for consciousness
> Is God: I suffer; I am God: this self,
> That all the universe combines to quell,
> Is greater than the universe; and *I*
> Am that I am. To think and not be God?—
> It cannot be.

Davidson is rarely an optimistic writer, in fact often the reverse, but his poetry reveals a vitality and a belief in life that again disqualifies him from the title 'Ninetyish'. 'The Ballad of a Nun', for example, though it does not suggest that there is much hope for the recreant nun, enters enthusiastically into her joys, brief as they are:

> I am sister to the mountain now,
> And sister to the sun and moon.

There may be despair in his poetry; there is never *ennui.*

As I have already suggested, Davidson could not be mistaken for a disciple of 'Art for Art's sake'. On the contrary, the moral of his poems is often all too obvious. In 'A Ballad of a Coward', for instance, he states categorically that a retreat into 'love' or 'art' is no answer to the challenge of life; only by facing it unafraid can it be met. His 'message' is clothed in allegorical form here and in other poems, like 'A Ballad of an Artist's Wife', where he argues that great art is produced only at the expense of great suffering.

Besides the ballad, one of his favourite forms, Davidson also writes in quatrains, sestets, and blank verse, all traditional English measures. He does occasionally imitate French forms, such as the *rondeau,* the *rondel,* and the *villanelle,* but he is not influenced by French poetry in any other respect.

Finally, his love of the classics, which might appear to qualify him as a 'Nineties' poet, only emphasizes how far he is from being so. Whereas the genuine 'decadent' turns to Propertius, Catullus, and Lucretius for themes and attitudes, Davidson is content to remain with Virgil, as the title of his *Fleet Street Eclogues* suggests. In fact, rather than trying to fit him into a nineteenth-century movement at all, it would be more fruitful to compare him with the eighteenth-century poets, with whom he has more than a love of the major classics in common. They too chose mainly city themes, had an obvious sense of moral and social responsibility, and wrote bitter satire.

Lionel Johnson is another poet who has more in common with classic English traditionalists than with the 'decadents' he is supposed to represent. He has the same reverence for sanity, proportion, and *ordonnance.* His reverence for authority often leads him to echo or imitate older established poets, and he shares their fondness for poetic literary criticism (Johnson wrote elegies on Matthew Arnold, Lamb, and many others). He uses mainly traditional English forms, such as the sonnet, the couplet, the quatrain, and regular five- and six-line stanzas. When he does experiment, it is with his own, not French models.

Johnson's love of the classics is all-embracing, limiting him neither to the major nor the minor writers. Besides nine poems composed in Latin, there are others on Virgil, Lucretius, Plato, and the Greek and Latin authors generally. But, much as he admired the classics, in 'Men of Assisi', a poem celebrating the two famous natives of that town, Propertius and St Francis, Johnson rejects the man of letters in favour of the saint. Thus he epitomizes one of his recurring themes and dilemmas—the conflict between the religious and aesthetic life. Contrary to what is expected of a 'Nineties' poet, he invariably decides in favour of religion. In 'Dark Angel', for example, a poem which is supposed to refer to Wilde, he records a strong temptation and his ultimate victory over it:

> Thou art the whisper in the gloom,
> The hinting tone, the haunting laugh:
> Thou art the adorner of my tomb,
> The minstrel of mine epitaph.
>
> I fight thee, in the Holy Name!
> Yet, what thou dost, is what God saith:
> Tempter! should I escape thy flame,
> Thou wilt have helped my soul from Death . . .

Like Davidson, Johnson devotes a comparatively small amount of poetry to the theme of romantic love. Except for a few early poems, such as 'To Morfydd', 'Gwynedd', 'The Last Music', he is more concerned with love of God, or friendship (see especially 'Friends'). There is hardly any passion in his verse, though there are occasional nature lyrics, some of which have great charm:

> I hear the woodland folks,
> Each well-swung axe's blow:
> And boughs of mighty oaks,
> Murmuring to and fro.
>
> My step fills, as I go,
> Shy rabbits with quick fears:
> I see the sunlight glow
> Red through their startled ears.
>
> ('In England')

Again like Davidson, Johnson is increasingly concerned with political questions. Home Rule for Ireland, for example, is his subject in 'Parnell', 'Ireland's Dead', 'Ireland'. Since most of this political verse and the religious also, is didactic in tone, very little of his work is 'Art for Art's sake'. As B. Ifor Evans puts it, his life may have been influenced by 'the aestheticism of the close of the century . . . but his poetry is far removed from the schools with which such thought is associated'. However, A. J. A. Symons must have had some grounds for including nine of Johnson's poems in his anthology of 'Nineties' verse. It may have been because of certain Pre-Raphaelite traits in the early work, the rather florid style of 'In Memoriam', for instance, with its impressionistic vocabulary:

> Sea-gulls, wheeling, swooping, crying,
> Crying over Maes Garmon side!
> Cold is the wind for your white wings' flying:
> Cold and dim is our gray springtide.

or the exotic imagery of 'Gwynedd':

> Pale with great heat, panting to crimson gloom
> Quiver the deeps of the rich fire: see there!
> Was not that your fair face, in burning bloom
> Wrought by the art of fire? O happy art!
> That sets in living flames a face so fair . . .

None of these are permanent features of his style, however, and the only way in which Johnson's verse fits the prescribed category, is in its sustained sense of melancholy. It was doubtless this which dictated Symons's choice of 'The Precepts of Silence', with its mournful stanza:

> I know you: solitary griefs,
> Desolate passions, aching hours!
> I know you: tremulous beliefs,
> Agonized hopes, and ashen flowers!

'Mystic and Cavalier', with its solemn injunction:

> Go from me: I am one of those, who fall.
> What! hath no cold wind swept your heart at all,
> In my sad company? Before the end,
> Go from me, dear my friend!

and 'Nihilism', where his longing for death is voiced:

> Only the rest! the rest! Only the gloom,
> Soft and long gloom! The pausing from all thought!
> My life, I cannot taste: the eternal tomb
> Brings me the peace, which life has never brought . . .

But melancholy as it is, this tone is not sufficient justification for labelling Johnson a 'Nineties' poet.

With Ernest Dowson the case is different. Besides showing this same world-weariness, he possesses most of the other requisite features. Romantic love, for instance, is his main theme. The majority of his poems are addressed to Adelaide Foltinowicz, who was twelve when he first met her. His frustration at her inability or refusal to return his love over the years provokes him to write some passionate lyric poetry. Apart from the well-known 'Non Sum Qualis Eram Bonae sub Regno Cynarae', with its haunting refrain, 'and I was desolate and sick of an old passion', there are 'Ad Domnulam Suam', 'Exile', 'Vain Hope', 'Terre Promise', and many others. The conflict between the desire to worship from afar and the desire to possess is perfectly embodied in 'Flos Lunae':

> I would not alter thy cold eyes;
> I would not change thee if I might,
> To whom my prayers for incense rise,
> Daughter of dreams! my moon of night!
> I would not alter thy cold eyes.
>
> I would not alter thy cold eyes,
> With trouble of the human heart:
> Within their glance my spirit lies,
> A frozen thing, alone, apart;
> I would not alter thy cold eyes.

Another recurring and related theme is that of the transience of things, with its accompanying *carpe diem* implications:

> They are not long, the weeping and the laughter,
> Love and desire and hate:
> I think they have no portion in us after
> We pass the gate.
>
> They are not long, the days of wine and roses:
> Out of a misty dream
> Our path emerges for a while, then closes

Within a dream.

Dowson would have found these themes constantly reiterated in the work of his two favourite Latin poets, Propertius and Catullus, both of them minor poets in agreement with the definition. Also in agreement is his admiration for the French *symbolistes* Baudelaire, Rimbaud, and Verlaine whose interest in the grotesque and bizarre aspects of life may have encouraged Dowson to write a poem such as 'To One in Bedlam'.

He is also indebted to French literature for some of his forms, chiefly the *villanelle,* the *rondel,* and the *rondeau.* His verse reveals a far greater willingness to experiment in non-traditional English forms than any discussed so far. At the same time, he does not despise the simple quatrain which he can put to striking use:

> Calm, sad, secure; behind high convent walls,
> These watch the sacred lamp, these watch and pray:
> And it is one with them when evening falls,
> And one with them the cold return of day.
> ('Nuns of the Perpetual Adoration')

Dowson's interest in form does not mean that he is not equally concerned with style. This, in turn, links up with his adherence to the 'Art for Art's sake' creed. The didactic element rarely enters his poetry. Even the religious verse (and Dowson, like Johnson, was a Roman Catholic convert) has little or no 'message', but is yet one more means of expressing his sense of melancholy and touching on his favourite theme of unhappy love: 'For, Lord, I was free of all thy flowers, but I chose the world's sad roses' ('Impenitentia Ultima'). Longaker, in his introduction to the poetry, concludes: 'There is no doubt that Dowson was a painstaking craftsman, but he pondered *le mot juste* at length'. The first eight lines of 'To One in Bedlam' show how meticulously he chose his adjectives, to catch 'the last fine shade':

> With delicate, mad hands, behind his sordid bars,
> Surely he hath his posies, which they tear and twine;
> Those scentless wisps of straw, that miserably line
> His strait, caged universe, whereat the dull world stares,
>
> Pedant and pitiful. O, how his rapt gaze wars
> With their stupidity! Know they what dreams divine
> Lift his long, laughing reveries like enchaunted wine,
> And make his melancholy germane to the stars'?

Again, in keeping with the popular definition, Dowson does not write much pure nature poetry. Nature, when it is described, is so treated, not for its own sake, but in order to set a particular mood, as in 'My Lady April', for instance:

> Say, doth she weep for very wantonness?
> Or is it that she dimly doth foresee
> Across her youth the joys grow less and less,
> The burden of the days that are to be:
> Autumn and withered leaves and vanity,
> And winter bringing end in barrenness.

Dowson's lack of nature poetry is not balanced by a great deal of city poetry, and there are a few other ways in which he fails to fit the 'Nineties' image. He writes some 'occasional' poems for instance and, what is more surprising, some relatively cheerful ones:

> So shall we not part at the end of day,
> Who have loved and lingered a little while,
> Join lips for the last time, go our way,
> With a sigh, a smile?
> ('April Love')

On balance, however, Dowson is the only good poet considered so far who could be called 'Ninetyish', not only in his life, but in his work. His best and most typical verses are those imbued with a spirit of weariness and despair. Unlike many mediocre poets of the period, this tone is a sincere expression of his personality. There is not the trace of a pose, for instance, in this, his most hopeless poem of all, where even love becomes meaningless:

> I was not sorrowful, I could not weep,
> And all my memories were put to sleep.
>
> I watched the river grow more white and strange,
> All day till evening I watched it change.
>
> All day till evening I watched the rain
> Beat wearily upon the window pane.
>
> I was not sorrowful, but only tired
> Of everything that ever I desired.
>
> Her lips, her eyes, all day became to me
> The shadow of a shadow utterly.
>
> All day mine hunger for her heart became
> Oblivion, until the evening came,
>
> And left me sorrowful, inclined to weep,
> With all my memories that could not sleep.
> ('Spleen')

It is significant that Dowson dedicated this poem to Arthur Symons, for when his first book of verse came out in 1896, he was accused of having imitated him slavishly. Symons was regarded by the general public as the 'decadent' *par excellence,* and not without cause, for he is the only other writer of the decade who has a claim to be called both a poet and 'Ninetyish' at the same time. Though not of the stature of Dowson he produced some good poetry with the necessary ingredients. As an avowed disciple of 'Art for Art's sake', he was led to compose mood poetry of every kind, from descriptions of natural phenomena, such as sunsets and storms, to those of the ecstasies of love. In his anxiety to depict as many different aspects of love as possible he did not limit himself to what the Victorian public considered 'respectable' and a poem like 'Bianca' shocked them profoundly at its first appearance:

> Through her closed lips that cling to mine,
> Her hands that hold me and entwine,
> Her body that abandoned lies,
> Rigid with sterile ecstasies,
> A shiver knits her flesh to mine.
>
> Life sucks into a mist remote
> Her fainting lips, her throbbing throat;
> Her lips that open to my lips;
> And, hot against my finger-tips,
> The pulses leaping in her throat.

In 'Her Eyes' he also described the tender side of love and in 'In the Oratory' and 'A Clymene' its mysterious aspects. In 'The Last Exit' and 'From Romances sans Paroles' he touches, as might be expected, on the pains of unrequited love. He was fascinated by the exotic, the grotesque and the bizarre, and explored all three in his poem on Salome, a favourite topic of the period:

> Black-haired and garbed in long black garments, John
> With hand revulsed and eyes that ache with hate,

Equal in height with her, a dagger-thrust
Between them divides from him her raging lust,
Lust in her naked breasts that have two eyes,
Lust in her flesh, the flesh he looks upon,
Lust that makes her whole body undulate,
Lust on her lips; the lust that never dies,
Between the hollow of her breasts, a sign
Sinister of that hell that lives within
Her limbs that long for him; her mouth like wine,
Wine, that she gives to spirits more malign
Than hers . . .

('Studies in Strange Sins')

The influence of the nineteenth-century French poets is obvious, not only in this obsession with the bizarre, nor even in his confessed translations and imitations—for example 'Fêtes Galantes' and 'After Paul Verlaine'—but also in his fondness for city themes, which range from the sympathetic analyses of the causes of prostitution in 'Emmy' and 'Emmy at the Eldorado', to the detailed descriptions of London and Parisian night-life (music-halls and cafés in particular) in 'In Bohemia', 'At the Cavour', and 'In the Haymarket'.

Symons was fond, too, of the minor Latin poets. Like Dowson, he appreciated their *carpe diem* philosophy and their treatment of illicit love. In contrast to Lord Alfred Douglas and John Gray, who renounced their early work, he became more obviously 'decadent' the older he got. In his 1923 collection, *Love's Cruelty,* for instance, he devoted an entire section to 'Studies in Strange Sins', whereas in his 1896 volume he had dealt with less sensational topics.

But though Symons and Dowson conform closely to the popular concept of 'Nineties' poets, they are exceptions among the outstanding writers of the period and two poets can scarcely be said to constitute a movement. In short, the decade from 1890 to 1900 is one of the most highly individualistic periods in English literature. Besides poets like Hardy, who do not fit easily into any school, there are those like Yeats and Kipling who anticipate various new developments, those like Johnson, Bridges, and Watson who accept the established conventions of English verse, and those like Dowson and Symons who reject them. Holbrook Jackson writes:

> The Eighteen Nineties was the decade of a thousand 'movements'. People said it was a 'period of transition', and they were convinced that they were passing not only from one social system to another, but from one morality to another, from one culture to another, and from one religion to a dozen or none! But as a matter of fact there was no concerted action. Everybody, mentally and emotionally, was running about in a hundred different directions.
>
> (*The Eighteen Nineties*)

The only possible sense in which the so-called 'decadents' could be seen as the central 'movement' is in their common rejection of 'Tennysonian ideals'. As J. Fineman puts it [in his *John Davidson* (1916)]: 'The younger writers of the nineties, whether aesthetes, symbolists, realists, impressionists or Celts, agreed clearly in one respect—in reviling the taste that prevailed in the Victorian England of the second and third quarters of the nineteenth century.' (pp. 167-74)

Jean Wilson, "The 'Nineties' Movement in Poetry: Myth or Reality?" in The Yearbook of English Studies, *Vol. 1, 1971, pp. 160-74.*

PERIODICALS

FRASER HARRISON

[*In the following excerpt, Harrison offers an account of the publication history of the* Yellow Book, *discusses editors and major contributors, and comments on the fiction and artwork featured in the magazine.*]

The idea of the *Yellow Book* was initially conceived by Aubrey Beardsley and Henry Harland, both of whom in January 1894 were looking for new opportunities to exploit their own respective talents. They approached John Lane and suggested that he launch a magazine that was to be "representative of the most cultural work which was then being done in England . . . with no hall-mark except that of excellence and no prejudice against anything except dullness and incapacity". Lane eagerly encouraged them and agreed with his partner Elkin Mathews to finance and publish their brain-child.

By March a characteristically brash announcement was issued, decorated by a Beardsley drawing which depicted an exotically behatted lady casting a hungry eye over a bin of books outside a bookshop; the bookseller was clad, unaccountably, in Pierrot costume.

> The aim . . . of the *Yellow Book* is to depart as far as may be from the bad old traditions of periodical literature, and to provide an Illustrated Magazine which shall be beautiful as a piece of bookmaking, modern and distinguished in its letter-press and its pictures, and withal popular in the better sense of the word. It is felt that such a Magazine, at present, is conspicuous by its absence . . .

> Amongst the artists who will contribute drawings are SIR FREDERICK LEIGHTON, P.R.A., AUBREY BEARDSLEY, R. ANNING BELL, CHARLES W. FURSE, L. B. GOOLD, MAURICE GREIFFENHAGEN, WILLIAM HYDE, LAURENCE HOUSEMAN, J. T. NETTLESHIP J. BERNARD PARTIDGE, JOSEPH PENNELL, WILL ROTHENSTEIN, WALTER SICKERT, WILSON STEER, ALFRED THORNTON, and others . . .

The following is an incomplete list of those who will contribute articles, stories, and poems to the *Yellow Book.*

E. TRELAWNY BACKHOUSE
MAX BEERBOHM
A. C. BENSON
HUBERT CRACKANTHORPE
ELLA D'ARCY
JOHN DAVIDSON
AUSTIN DOBSON
MENIE MURIEL DOWIE
ERNEST DOWSON
GEORGE EGERTON
LANOE FALCONER
MICHAEL FIELD
JEAN DE FRANCE
NORMAN GALE
RICHARD GARNETT
EDMUND GOSSE
KENNETH GRAHAME
FREDERICK GREENWOOD
HENRY HARLAND
FRANK HARRIS
JOHN OLIVER HOBBES
SELWYN IMAGE

HENRY JAMES
LIONEL JOHNSON
RICHARD LE GALLIENNE
STANLEY V. MAKOWER
THEO MARZIALS
GEORGE MOORE
WALTER PATER
ELIZABETH ROBINS PENNELL
RICHARD PRYCE
ERNEST RHYS
GEORGE SAINTSBURY
CHARLES SIBLEY
OSWALD SICKERT
F. M. SIMPSON
ARTHUR SYMONS
NETTA SYRETT
BEERBOHM TREE
WILLIAM WATSON
ARTHUR WAUGH
CHARLES WHIBLEY
W. B. YEATS
I. ZANGWILL

. . . In many ways its contributors will employ a freer hand than the limitations of the old-fashioned periodical can permit. It will publish no serials; but its complete stories will sometimes run to a considerable length in themselves . . . And while the *Yellow Book* will seek always to preserve a delicate, decorous, and reticent mien and conduct, it will at the same time have the courage of its modernness, and not tremble at the frown of Mrs Grundy.

Altogether, it is expected that the *Yellow Book* will prove the most interesting, unusual, and important publication of its kind that has ever been undertaken. It will be charming, it will be daring, it will be distinguished. It will be a *book*—a book to be read, and placed upon one's shelves, and read again; a book in form, a book in substance; a book beautiful to see and convenient to handle; a book with style, a book with finish; a book that every book-lover will love at first sight; a book that will make book-lovers of many who are now indifferent to books.

The *Yellow Book* will contain no advertisements other than publishers' lists'

As events turned out some of the names on the list never appeared in the magazine, but the list is in itself indicative of Lane's taste and ambitions. As Arthur Waugh, Evelyn's father, later wrote in his autobiography:

> There was no sort of hint that the *Yellow Book* was to be the oriflamme of decadence; indeed, if any such suggestion had been made to its publisher, he would have become inarticulate on the spot. For Lane was dreadfully afraid of offending the proprieties, or indeed causing any annoyance to any person of importance . . . So the table of contents for the first number of the *Yellow Book* was an ingenious study in compromise; there was in point of fact no real Yellow Book atmosphere; the sly newcomer intended to be all things to all men.

John Lane had already established himself as one of London's leading *avant-garde* publishers. He had a shrewd eye for talent, particularly talent that was potentially fashionable, and he had suggested Beardsley to Wilde when in 1893 they were looking for an artist to illustrate Wilde's play, *Salomé*. Beardsley (1872-98) was then a mere twenty years old, but

his drawings for Dent's edition of Malory's *Morte D'Arthur* had already won him a measure of fame.

He and Wilde enjoyed an uneasy friendship. Beardsley had been piqued when Wilde, not surprisingly, chose Alfred Douglas in favour of him to translate *Salomé* from its original French, but he took typical revenge by caricaturing his benefactor no less than four times in his *Salomé* drawings. Wilde appears at first to have been fascinated by Lane's consumptive protégé: "He has a face like a silver hatchet adorned by grass green hair." Later he dismissed him as not flesh and blood, but rather "a monstrous orchid", and claimed to have invented him. He disliked Beardsley's illustrations for his play: "They are too Japanese, while my play is Byzantine . . . They are like the scribbles a precocious boy makes on the margins of his copybooks." But the drawings made the play famous, and Beardsley fashionable.

Association with the most famous playwright of the day—*A Woman of No Importance* was then running at The Haymarket—had put Beardsley in the limelight, but when he, Lane and Harland laid their plans for the *Yellow Book* he insisted that Wilde should never be a contributor. Neither of his colleagues demurred.

In the astonishingly brief period of four months this team succeeded in putting together the first volume. . . . (pp. 3-7)

Publication day was 15 April 1894. London suddenly turned yellow, and naturally the boldest display was at the Bodley Head's Vigo Street office where the little bow window was filled with copies "creating such a mighty glow of yellow at the far end of Vigo Street that one might have been forgiven for imagining for a moment that some awful portent had happened, and that the sun had risen in the West!" [J. Lewis May, *John Lane and the Nineties;* see Further Reading.]

The phenomenon was not, however, kindly received. The *National Observer* delivered a broadside of insults: "bizarre, eccentric, uncomfortably heavy to the hand . . . the audacious vulgarity and the laborious inelegance of the cover . . . a misarrangement in orpiment . . . nonsensical and hysterical matter". The *Times* condemned it as "a combination of English rowdiness with French lubricity." "The cover" (by Beardsley) it said "may be intended to attract by its very repulsiveness and insolence." *Punch* pithily summed up its attitude in the epigram "uncleanliness is next to Bodliness". Most reviewers echoed this tone of outrage and disgust, but the *Westminster* hit the highest note of indignation. Having dismissed Max Beerbohm's essay "A Defence of Cosmetics" as pernicious nonsense, it turned its attention to one of Beardsley's drawings and declared: "We do not know that anything would meet the case except a short act of Parliament to make this kind of thing illegal."

With publicity like this the magazine could not fail. A second printing was rushed out during that week, and a third was on the press by the weekend. The critics had concentrated their fire on Beerbohm, who remarked later, "as far as anyone in literature is lynched, I was", on Symons, whose poem "Stella Maris" celebrated a night spent with a prostitute, and on Beardsley. All three were gratified, and Beardsley positively revelled in his notoriety. *Punch* wittily dubbed him "Weirdsley Daubery", "Awfully Weirdly" and "Daubaway Weirdsley"; Beerbohm became "Max Mereboom" and their work was supposed to issue from "The Bogey Head".

Other contributors were less amused. Sir Frederick Leighton, the then President of the Royal Academy, whose drawing of two grey figures, muffled in drapery, posing meditatively against a grey background, had received pride of place among the illustrations, provoked the *Times*'s commiseration: "Leighton . . . finds himself cheek by jowl with such advanced and riotous representatives of the new art as Mr Aubrey Beardsley and Mr Walter Sickert." He immediately informed Lane that he had been reprimanded by his friends for embarrassing serious art, and thus the *Yellow Book* lost a valuable contributor.

Henry James too found the company he was obliged to keep unattractive. "I haven't sent you the *Yellow Book* on purpose," he wrote to his brother William, "and indeed I have been weeks and weeks receiving a copy of it myself. I say on purpose because although my little tale . . . appears to have had, for a thing of mine, an unusual success, I hate too much the horrid aspect and company of the whole publication. And yet I am to be intimately, conspicuously associated with the second number. It is for gold and to oblige the worshipful Harland." In fact he obliged the worshipful Harland with three stories and an essay in all.

The next three volumes were published with equal *éclat;* the press remained hostile but grew less vituperative.

This carefree era came, however, to an abrupt end on 5 April 1895. Oscar Wilde, following the failure of his libel case against the Marquess of Queensbury, Lord Alfred Douglas's father, was arrested on morals charges at the Cadogan Hotel, and removed in a four-wheeler to Bow Street police station. On his way out, Wilde, according to the press, "grasped his suede gloves in one hand and seized his stick with the other. Then he picked up from the table a copy of the *Yellow Book* which he placed in security under his left arm."

John Lane was on his way to America at the time, but when his ship docked he was handed a newspaper with the headline: "Arrest of Oscar Wilde, *Yellow Book* under his arm." Meanwhile crowds had gathered at Vigo Street and stoned the bow window under the sign of The Bodley Head. Lane had more than one reason to be nervous, for Wilde, a few months previously, had enjoyed a minor affair with one of the Bodley Head clerks, Edward Shelley. The poet had flattered the boy, encouraged his literary aspirations, and then dropped him. Shelley had fallen into disconsolate despair, and had been sacked. Lane cabled Frederick Chapman, his assistant, instructing him to withdraw all Wilde's publications. He in his turn received cables from London. Goaded by Mrs. Humphrey Ward, several of his authors expressed their horror and demanded Beardsley's dismissal. William Watson summed up the situation: WITHDRAW ALL BEARDSLEY'S DESIGNS OR I WITHDRAW MY BOOKS. The fifth volume was at the printers, but after a day or two of hesitation, Chapman recalled it and expunged all trace of Beardsley. Two weeks late, on 30 April 1895, the new, emasculated version was published. "It turned grey overnight," E. F. Benson remarked.

Apart from the fact that at the time Beardsley and Wilde were scarcely on speaking terms, the extraordinary irony was that the fatal volume under Wilde's arm was not the *Yellow Book* at all, but a French novel, *Aphrodite* by Pierre Louys, which happened to be bound in yellow. Beardsley may have been foppish and affected but there is no evidence that he was a homosexual. Indeed, in Stanley Weintraub's excellent biography there is no suggestion that he had a single romantic ex-

perience, far less a sexual one. But in the mind of Mrs Humphrey Ward and the like, Wilde and Beardsley were indistinguishable. She presumably saw Beardsley as a threat to common decency and from her point of view she was perhaps right, for during the remaining three years of his life, his work, free of Lane's vigilant restraint, became increasingly erotic.

Lane had always sailed close to the moral wind, but he had a genius for calculating just how far he could go without alienating respectable opinion. The magazine had been his most *risqué* venture, and one of his most successful, but, through no fault of his and despite his never-failing caution, it blew up in his face. He said later that the Wilde scandal "killed the *Yellow Book,* and it nearly killed me!" In point of fact they both survived: he to the age of seventy, the *Yellow Book* for nine more volumes. These nine "grey" volumes, although often derided, contain the bulk of the best contributions. Beardsley was certainly irreplaceable, but, with the significant exception of Symons, none of the contributors to the first four volumes felt obliged, as a matter of principle, to leave with him or because of him. James, Beerbohm, Grahame and many of the other original contributors remained loyal, and they were joined, in succeeding volumes, by, among others, Gissing, Wells, Bennett, Buchan, Baron Corvo and Yeats. Admittedly its demeanour after Beardsley's departure was more subdued, but for two more years it proceeded to flourish and maintain its standards.

Beardsley, after a period of drunken melancholy, collaborated with Arthur Symons and launched another magazine, the *Savoy,* which in its turn became a *succés de scandale,* to its editors' delight. It was published by Leonard Smithers, who could not have been more different to Lane. Part-pornographer, part-publisher, he prided himself on publishing what other, more conventional publishers dared not touch. Wilde described him in a letter to Reggie Turner: "He loves first editions, especially of women: little girls are his passion. He is the most learned erotomaniac in Europe. He is also a delightful companion, and a dear fellow, very kind to me."

Wilde also called him "the owner of Beardsley". With Smithers' encouragement, Beardsley went on to produce more brilliant work, and as his health grew worse his preoccupation with the erotic developed into an obsession, culminating in his unequivocally pornographic drawings for Smithers' edition of *Lysistrata.*

The series of coincidences linking Beardsley with Wilde was not quite complete, for it was Smithers who published Wilde's only book after his imprisonment, *The Ballad of Reading Gaol,* in February 1898. Beardsley died a month later at the age of twenty-five years, seven months. His last letter was to Smithers:

> Jesus is our Lord and Judge
>
> Dear Friend
>
> I implore you to destroy *all* copies of Lysistrata & bad drawings. Show this to Pollitt & conjure him to do the same. By all that is holy—*all* obscene drawings.
>
> Aubrey Beardsley
>
> In my death agony.

Aubrey Beardsley's cover for the first issue of the Yellow Book.

Shortly after Beardsley's death Wilde wrote to Smithers:

> I was greatly shocked to read of poor Aubrey's death. Superbly premature as the flowering of his genius was, still he had immense development, and had not sounded his last stop. There were great possibilities always in the cavern of his soul, and there is something macabre and tragic in the fact that one who added another terror to life should have died at the age of a flower.

On 30 November 1900 Wilde himself died, aged fifty-seven. Four years later Henry Harland also died, of tuberculosis.

Ever since those first, infuriated reviews, the *Yellow Book* has taken its place, along with Wilde, in the mythology of the nineties; it seems even now to represent some quintessential characteristic of its times. In 1914 Wyndham Lewis wrote in his manifesto for the magazine *Blast,* "The spirit and purpose of the Arts and Literature of Today are expressed in BLAST. No periodical since the famous *Yellow Book* has so comprehended the artistic movement of its decade. The artistic spirit of the Eighteen Nineties was the *Yellow Book.*" It was a fitting obituary, and, like all obituaries, it was a little less than disinterested, and a little kinder than it was accurate.

In March 1894, after sixty-one years in the House of Commons, Gladstone, the Prime Minister, resigned. It was during the same month that John Lane and Elkin Mathews, with notable panache, announced the imminent publication of the *Yellow Book.*

The coincidence, no doubt, lacks profound significance, but

to the *Yellow Book* devotee there is something revealing about this little conjunction of events. It would be fanciful to imagine that simply because the numerical chronology of a century was nearing its end, history would dutifully take note of the calendar and throw herself into a frenzy of termination. And yet one of the oddest characteristics of the 1890s is that they did indeed witness an eerily disproportionate number of beginnings and ends, births and deaths. This union of calendar and history is unnerving and lends foundation to the over-exploited phrase *fin de siécle.* The question which exercises the devotee is, however, to whose age did the *Yellow Book* truly belong: Gladstone's or Asquith's? Was it the last, bizarre throw of moribund Victorian sensibility, or was it instead a harbinger, in Victorian disguise, of what was to come?

A curious feature of critical and biographical writing devoted to the arts of the period is that the surrounding historical landscape is often obscured, even obliterated. This is particularly true of accounts of Wilde, the protagonists in his melodrama, and his literary colleagues. Their era is depicted as having its existence in some theatrical limbo, peopled exclusively by witty and/or tragic aesthetes and fulminating representatives of the bourgeoisie. Wilde himself is generally seen as the willing victim of his own noble folly, while his judge and prosecutor, together with a vindictive public, are seen as ogres of hypocrisy and cant. Though the stuff of legend, such an interpretation is hardly the truth of the matter.

The *Yellow Book* has suffered a similar fate: isolating it from its literary and publishing context, critics have tended to regard it solely as a product of the decadent movement. Hesketh Pearson, in his celebrated biography of Oscar Wilde, shares his hero's opinion, and curtly condemns it: "This quarterly publication . . . has in some curious way become associated with the forward movement of the nineties in arts and letters. It is supposed to have expressed the daring and rebellious spirit of youth, straining at the leash of Victorian respectability. It did nothing of the sort. It favoured no movement, it displayed no tendency . . . The only startling note was provided by Beardsley, who, however, was only permitted to alarm the readers for four numbers." In other words, The *Yellow Book* is contemptible because it is not what it pretended to be; it was a piece of low fraud which fortunately has been detected and exposed.

The other accusation most commonly thrown at the magazine's head is that after the Wilde debacle and Beardsley's dismissal it suffered a near-fatal stroke from which it recovered only to linger on its death-bed, frail and tame, until, nine volumes later, it finally expired, unmourned by readers and editorial staff alike.

Both this criticism, and the suggestion that the magazine was a manifesto of a movement whose members never signed it, stem from the assumption that the *Yellow Book* is in the mainstream of decadent writing. Since this is by no means the case, it is hardly surprising that many people have found it a disappointing example of a breed to which it never belonged. Rebutting these attacks does not necessarily involve the dramatic unmasking of hitherto unrecognized nuggets of literary gold; it does, however, involve placing the magazine in a new context, a context prescribed by the social conditions in which it flourished and foundered. (pp. 10-18)

The magazine's design and lay-out which [Beardsley] inaugurated remained unchanged after his departure and the later covers were more or less pale imitations of his style. The illustrations, which varied between thirteen and twenty-six in any one volume, were scattered seemingly at random between the stories and poems, although some attempt was made to place them more pointedly while Beardsley was Art Editor: the conjunction of Arthur Symons' poem "Stella Maris" and Beardsley's own "Night Piece" can hardly have been a coincidence. Sheets of tissue paper were inserted to protect the illustrations. . . . (p. 20)

Each volume terminated in a series of publishers' advertisements and John Lane's own Belles Lettres list, which included the back numbers of the *Yellow Book.* Those reproduced in this collection are taken from Volume VIII. The Lane list demonstrates how vigorously he led the field during this period, for most of the famous nineties' names are represented. A number of Wilde's books were published by The Bodley Head, mostly in limited editions: *The Sphinx* (a poem), *The Story of Mr W. H.,* both decorated by Charles Ricketts, *Lady Windermere's Fan, A Woman of No Importance, The Duchess of Padua,* all with bindings designed by Charles Shannon, and *Salomé,* with illustrations and cover design by Beardsley. All these were removed immediately after Wilde's arrest from the advertisement to be carried in Volume V and never reappeared. Although Beardsley himself was dismissed, it was evidently deemed acceptable that his *Story of Venus and Tanhauser* should continue to be advertised. *Salomé* shared the fate of Wilde's other work. The advertisements for Harland's *Grey Roses* and Ella D'Arcy's *Monochromes* gives an indication, even allowing for the highly selective bias with which all publishers compose such advertisements, of their considerable critical reputation at the time. The Belles Lettres list also contains the work of most of the *Yellow Book*'s regular contributors.

The length of the volumes varied between 256 pages (Volume IX) and 406 (Volume VIII); of the literary contents anything between a third and a half consisted of poetry, but, since none of the poems was longer than seven pages (John Davidson's "The Ballad of a Nun"), and most barely occupied a page, the prose predominated.

Fearing a reputation for excessive flippancy, and keen to demonstrate that their magazine had its serious side, Lane and Harland solicited a number of essays on literary and historical topics, designed to indicate an underlying spirit of editorial dignity and responsibility. Each volume contained one essay of this kind; some contained two or three. On the whole they are earnest, worthy, and dull. Max Beerbohm's essays "1880", "A Note on George the Fourth" and "A Defence of Cosmetics" are exceptions.

Lane felt it would be an amusing and stimulating idea to include in each volume an article examining the virtues and failings of the previous volume. Consequently the distinguished and, presumably, incorruptible man of letters and art critic Philip G. Hamerton was invited to pronounce mercilessly on Volume I. His critique duly appeared in Volume II. It has the embarrassing air of a fix, which it certainly was not, for he found next to nothing to condemn and much to commend. Apart from "regretting" the publication of "Stella Maris" and asking plaintively, "why should poetic art be employed to celebrate common fornication?", he was full of praise, going so far as to defend Beerbohm and to declare Beardsley "a man of genius", an extravagance which only earned him and the magazine fresh outcries from other critics. The experiment was not repeated.

Hamerton died shortly after, and will be remembered, perhaps unfairly, as the man who inquired in the *Saturday Review* why a picture with many colours in it should be called "A Symphony in White", which provoked from Whistler, its creator, the crushing reply: "And does he then, in his astounding consequence, believe that a Symphony in F contains no other note, but shall be a continued repetition of F F F? . . . Fool!"

This strain of complacent masochism was revived by Harland himself in three pseudonymous letters he wrote to the editor from "The Yellow Dwarf". Purporting to be the scourge of pretension, and of the *Yellow Book*'s pretensions in particular, the Dwarf jauntily surveyed the literary scene with what is supposed to be a sharp, unblinkered eye. While continually threatening to castigate the magazine for its mildest fault, Harland in fact used the letters as a thin excuse for lavishing shameless praise on his own contributors. Impudent and arch in tone, they presumably provide an insight of sorts into his character, although they can hardly have done the magazine a service. The Yellow Dwarf's Birthday Letter which appeared in Volume IX (April 1896) provides a good example:

> . . . The real truth is that in spite of many faults (I'll speak of them again in a minute), in spite of many faults, the *Yellow Book* has been from the commencement a very lively sort of *Yellow Book* indeed; in literary and artistic interest, and in mechanical excellence, far and far and far-away superior to any other serial in England—though that to be sure, you may object, isn't saying much. Consider, for an instant, your first number alone: the printing of it, the binding, the shape of its page, the proportion of text and margin; the absence of advertisements, so that we could approach its contents without being preoccupied by a consciousness of Eno's Fruit Salt and Beecham's Pills; and the pictures, and the care with which they were reproduced and then—and then the Literature! There was Mr. Henry James, a great artist at his best, in *The Death of a Lion . . .* etc., etc.

A page and a half of this impartial and objective commentary follows before he finally comes to his promised description of the magazine's faults:

> Brilliant as your first number was, brilliant as on the whole all your numbers have been, each and every one of them, if the truth must be told, has contained more than a delicate modicum—yea, even an unconscionable deal—of rubbish. Why do you do it, sir? As a concession to public taste. Bother the public taste! Because better stuff you can't procure? You could hardly procure worse stuff than some of the stuff I have in mind. I won't specify; 'twould be invidious to do so . . . And drop, drop—ah, how I should like to tell you whom to drop; but you wouldn't print it.

Not satisfied with being both editor and critic, Harland was also the magazine's most prolific contributor. Every volume contained at least one story by him under his own name, and, apart from The Yellow Dwarf, he used two other pseudonyms. His behavior was not however as vainglorious as it might appear today, for although none of his work is now in print, he was then a novelist of some standing and considerable experience. He was also by no means the only editor who consistently printed his own work: Beardsley and Symons created the *Savoy* specifically in order to provide an alternative outlet to the *Yellow Book* for their own material.

As a young man in New York, Harland had written a number of novels about the Jewish community, which had been highly praised, and had adopted a suitably Jewish-sounding pseudonym: Sydney Luska. When later he came to Europe, fell under the spell of French writers and began to write in their vein, he resumed his real name. But throughout his life his origins and background were shrouded in exotic mystery: he laid claim, in no less an organ than the *Dictionary of National Biography,* to St Petersburg as his birthplace, and to an aristocratic ancestry. Rumour, no doubt assiduously fed by him, had it that he was the natural son of the Emperor Franz Joseph. He was in fact born in New York, the son of a businessman.

These colourful eccentricities seem only to have endeared him to his contemporaries, for by the time he was editor of the *Yellow Book* he was a respected and popular literary figure. Beerbohm described him as "the most joyous of men and the most generous of critics." He appears to have been indefatigable in his efforts to help other writers, particularly unknown or young ones; he was devoted to his work—"Art, with him," said Le Gallienne, "was a life and death matter"; and no one can have campaigned as hard or as imaginatively to promote the short story as an acceptable and significant literary form. De Maupassant, Daudet and Merimée were his masters, and the *Yellow Book* was both his tribute to them, and his attempt to establish their genre on an equal footing in England.

Next to Harland, Ella D'Arcy was the *Yellow Book*'s most prolific contributor, with eleven stories to her name. She also acted as Harland's part-time editorial assistant and it is perhaps thanks to her that women writers provided such a substantial proportion of the magazine, for more than a third of the poems and stories are written by them. The illustrated pages remained, however, a male preserve.

Richard Le Gallienne, who was also a close friend of Harland, had more titles to his name than any other contributor—three poems, fifteen prose fancies and one story—but they are all short, and do not amount to anything like the number of words contributed by Harland, Ella D'Arcy or Henry James, whose three stories were very long, (the longest, "The Coxon Fund", is seventy pages). The prose fancy, or prose poem as Wilde called it, was a very typical nineties' form, and of all the *Yellow Book* pieces Le Gallienne's come closest to sounding the authentic decadent note. His pose of poet incarcerated in a grubby, vulgar world, whose infinitely sensitive soul yearns for transcendent mystery and beauty, gives him the opportunity both to mock and indulge the more effete absurdities of decadence.

"Variations upon Whitebait" (Volume VIII) is a typical example:

The author and his girl-friend are dining in a restaurant; she asks him how the whitebait they are eating "get their beautiful little silver water-proofs".

> "Electric Light of the World," I said, "it is like this. While they are still quite young and full of dreams, their mother takes them out in picnic parties of a billion or so at a time to where the spring moon is shining, scattering silver from its purse of pearl far over the wide waters, silver, silver, for every little whitebait that cares to swim and pick it up. The mother, who has a contract with some such big restaurateur as ours here, chooses a convenient area

> of moonlight, and then at a given sign they all turn over on their sides, and bask and bask in the rays, little fin pressed lovingly against little fin—for this is the happiest in the young whitebait's life: it is at these silvering parties that matches are made and future consignments of whitebait arranged for. Well, night after night, they thus lie in the moonlight, first on one side then on the other, till by degrees, tiny scale by scale, they have become completely lunar plated. Ah! how sad they are when the end of that happy time has come."

A number of other writers and poets contributed regularly to the magazine: Max Beerbohm, Hubert Crackanthorpe, William Watson, H. B. Marriot Watson, his wife Rosamund Marriot Watson, Evelyn Sharp, Olive Custance and Henry James. Among the artists who contributed regularly were Walter Sickert, Will Rothenstein, Charles Condor, Patten Wilson and Wilson Steer. Beardsley, during his short tenure of office, besides designing covers and title pages, drew sixteen illustrations for the magazine, two under the pseudonyms Philip Broughton and Albert Foschter for Volume III, which to his glee, were warmly praised. (pp. 20-7)

Among so many contributors of differing backgrounds and ages, it would be surprising if any one theme or preoccupation was found to be held in common. The identity of woman, and, more specifically, her sexuality were, however, issues that dominated, either overtly or by implication, an enormous number of *Yellow Book* stories. This can hardly have been the result of editorial policy, nor was it the result of Harland's commissioning so many women writers, for these themes obsessed both the men and the women alike, and neither group displays more or less radicalism or conservatism than the other.

"Marcel: An Hotel Child" by Lena Milman (Volume XII), provides an example of a story in which female sexuality was, as it were, the unconscious theme underlying the apparent one.

The narrator, an English gentleman on his travels, makes the acquaintance in Venice of a small boy, one Marcel Van Lunn, son of Mrs Van Lunn, a wealthy American widow. Mama and her son, it transpires, eke out an arid if expensive existence by traipsing round the pleasure haunts of Europe at the whim of Mama's lover, who is cryptically referred to as "Monsieur". Mama, not unreasonably, is keener on spending her time with "Monsieur" than with her lonely but forbearing son. The more she neglects the boy, the more he turns to the Catholic Church, focussing his unrequited filial affection on the Virgin Mary. His real mother, meanwhile, is gadding about the canals, making an exhibition of herself with her lover.

The narrator is informed by a resident gossip that Mrs Van Lunn has put herself beyond the social pale, for "Monsieur Casimir Portel is neither her first, nor likely to be her last 'travelling companion'." "I cared not at all," the narrator reports, "as far as Mrs Van Lunn was concerned, but, as I listened to the sordid story, I saw again the pathetic profile of Marcel, and felt gloomily conscious of my impotence to avert the misery which I saw threaten." He has, as it turns out, good grounds for these despondent ruminations for, some six months later, he once again runs into the Van Lunns only to discover that his young friend has caught a mysterious fever. The boy languishes in bed for some days—he lacks "recuperative force"—and then, to everyone's relief, appears to be on the mend. Mrs Van Lunn immediately departs for Palermo, claiming to have been called there on urgent business, although the narrator makes it clear that he, for one, is not fooled by this trumpery and knows lechery when he sees it.

On his mother's disappearance Marcel suffers a relapse. He overhears some people in the next door room accuse her of neglecting him, staggers in, passionately defends her and expires shortly after with the word "mother" on his lips. "Was it," the narrator muses, "a vision of the blue-robed, star-crowned Madonna that he had so greeted, or one of Mrs Van Lunn, in her *Doucet* travelling suit, as he had seen her last, as he had so longed to see her again?"

Six months later the narrator reads an announcement of Mrs Van Lunn's marriage to M. Portel. "So Mrs. Van Lunn was *rangée*. The obstacle had been removed!"

Mrs Van Lunn's neglect of her child, though reprehensible, hardly merits the cruel punishment it receives. Her real crime is, of course, her shameless devotion, in the face of society's open disapproval, to a man not her husband; the fact that both of them are foreigners with funny names only makes matters worse. Although she presumably loved her M. Portel, and may even have lived happily and respectably ever after with him, her story is described as squalid, and so it was, in 1894. She chose to flout a sacred convention and, consequently, she was obliged to endure not merely the indignity of a sullied reputation but also the death of her son. Not that his decease is depicted as a direct, moral effect of her misbehaviour, but it is unequivocally seen as a well-deserved repercussion.

Fatal repercussions of this kind occur again and again in *Yellow Book* stories when women attempt to take the initiative, particularly in marriage, or attempt to assert themselves emotionally.

In, for instance, "The Elsingfords" by Henry Harland, a dowdy and absurd woman, notorious for the tedium of her tea-parties, succeeds in marrying, much to the astonishment and amusement of his friends, a celebrated artist. After the wedding she insists on their living in America, her homeland, and reveals that she hates England and the English. When, four years later, they return to Europe, she refuses to live in London and they take up residence in Paris. He complains the climate is bad for his health; she derides what she calls his hypochondria: "Be a man! Get up and go out. Don't stick at home molly-coddling yourself like an old woman." Although the husband rises heroically to the challenge, soon enough he contracts a sinister cough and is confined to his bed. A doctor advises him to leave immediately for Egypt if he wants to save his life. His wife is prostrated: "If I had dreamed—if I had dreamed that it was anything serious."

Death, in this case, is cheated of its victim, but Harland makes it clear that when wives, particularly feather-headed wives manifestly inferior to their husbands, start to dictate terms in a marriage the consequences can only be regrettable, if not fatal.

Ella D'Arcy's bleakly entitled story "A Marriage" (Volume XI), . . . contains the same elements, although they are painted in far more macabre colours. The hero of her story, against the advice of his friend, the narrator, decides to do the decent thing by his mistress, even though this involves a drop in class status. Prior to the marriage the girl is thought by her lover to be a model of domestic modesty, but, once

married, this paragon transforms herself into a virago of pretension and intolerance. The scales fall from the husband's eyes, and as his wife glides implacably up the ladder of social advancement, he is left behind to brood bitterly on his folly—and the folly of marriage generally. Sure enough, he too contracts the sinister cough, and dies.

Neither neglect nor carelessness killed this husband; the poor fellow simply succumbed to his wife's superior psychological strength. She was invincibly selfish and he was unequal to the struggle.

Netta Syrett's "Thy Heart's Desire" (Volume II) seems to suggest that even the contemplation of infidelity on the part of a wife is sufficient to loosen her husband's frail grasp on life. The couple in this case are living in a tent in a remote corner of India; the wife finds their isolation hard to bear, she is not cut out for colonial exile and she misses her books and friends. Her husband, a bluff, good-hearted chap, but "not much of a reader", positively relishes their rugged existence and fails to appreciate how much she is suffering. Into their camp rides a dashing friend of the husband, bearing a packing case full of books; friend and wife experience mutual attraction; he makes a pass, but, after a moment's passionate hesitation, her better self triumphs and she resists temptation. The damage is, however, done; within two days her husband is dead. No romantic cough for him, he is bluntly declared defunct.

Perhaps the most revealing example of death at the hands of insurgent femininity is H. B. Marriot Watson's "The Dead Wall" (Volume VI). . . . The wife in this instance does not obliquely provoke her husband's death, she actually drives him to suicide.

The very quality of melodrama inherent in so many of these stories is an indication of the terror that the possibility of female liberation, in the modern sense of heightened consciousness, must have struck in the hearts of husbands and wives alike during this decade. The middle-class wife who found her repressed situation irksome must have also feared the consequences of her liberty, regardless of whether or not her husband was sympathetic. She not only had to bear and combat the prejudice, hostility and ridicule of society at large, she not only had to put into perspective the propaganda of a century, but she also had to come to terms with the prospect of disastrously upsetting the balance of her domestic life. It is at the centre of this dilemma that the *Yellow Book* stories stand. Few of them unequivocally champion either the male or female cause, but all of them are concerned with accounting the price that must be paid when a woman interferes with the marital *status quo*. Women, no less than men, must have feared, however unconsciously, that their right to assert themselves could only be obtained by sacrificing their husband's manliness. By challenging the concept of male supremacy they automatically questioned their husband's virility.

Convention, to say nothing of John Lane, prevented the *Yellow Book* writers describing their characters' sex lives, but most of the stories, particularly Marriot Watson's, are fraught with sexual tension. The narrator in "Marcel", for instance, says he feels "impotent" in the face of Mrs Van Lunn's behaviour. Mrs Elsingford in Harland's story is constantly urging her husband to "be a man". Much reference is made, in "Thy Heart's Desire", to the husband's pipe, which, at moments of especial poignancy, his wife fills for him. The husband in "The Dead Wall" when threatening suicide in front of his wife, "handles" a revolver and "cocks it" to lend conviction to his threat; she reduces him, however, to such a pitch of emasculation that instead of using the revolver he poisons himself with "a little phial". And many of the stories are set abroad, particularly in Paris, where sexual liaisons could not only exist but be seen to exist.

The deaths which occur so frequently and which are used so predictably in order to resolve emotional deadlocks, are, on the whole, sketchily and unconvincingly described; but then they are more symbolic than real. Unconsciously the writers of these bizarre stories must have felt that death provided the only euphemism sufficiently powerful and portentous to substitute for the situations they actually wanted to talk about; death was capable of standing for castration, impotence, etiolation or just plain spinelessness, in short, any of the states to which, they feared, a woman might reduce a man if she took up arms against the sexual hierarchy of the day.

Who was this terrifying and destructive New Woman?

To *Punch* she was, naturally, a huge joke. Determined to reassure its largely male readership, it was constantly cracking rib-ticklers at her expense:

> "I say, Tibbins, old man, is it true that your wife has been asked to resign at the Omphale club?"

> "Well, yes; you see the Committee found that she was guilty of ungentlemanly behaviour." (5 January 1895)

> "By the way Doctor, the 'new Woman', don'tcher-know—what'll she be like, when she's grown old?"

> "My dear Colonel, she'll never grow old."

> "Great Scott! You don't mean she's going to last for ever!"

> "She won't even last the century! She's got every malady under the sun!" (13 April 1895)

If jokes could kill, the nineteenth century would be strewn with *Punch*'s victims, all brutally clubbed to death. As a barometer of middle-class prejudice it must be unsurpassed, but like all registers of prejudice, as fast as it dispensed disapproval it advertised its fears. Although suffering from no gentlemanly inhibitions when it came to vilifying the New Woman, it was clearly rattled by her. With more optimism than accuracy, it depicted her as a normal, wholesome girl, with all her mother's normal, wholesome instincts, who had, alas, been subverted, evilly influenced and generally led astray. The *Yellow Book* was frequently pointed to as the kind of pernicious propaganda likely to poison the pure well of womanhood.

Husbands and admirers of the screaming sisterhood were regarded as particularly preposterous. In, for example, "She Notes" (10 March 1894) by Borgia Smudgiton with Japanese Fan de Siécle Illustrations by Mortarthurio Whiskersly, the following piece of domestic dialogue is overheard:

> "Off your pipe, old chappie. Feel a bit cheap?" (It is her husband who speaks this way.)

> "Yes, beastly, thanks old man!" (He dispenses a restorative whisky—neat, of course; "soda's for boys".)

> "What's your book?"

> "O, one of Wilde's little things. I like Wilde; he shocks the middle classes. Only the middle classes are so easily shocked!"

The joke, presumably, lies in seeing what happens when you allow things to go to extremes: the man solicitously attends to his gruff mate, administers soothing drinks, and attempts to take an interest in her reading, which is of course well above his pretty head. She is moody, domineering and dissatisfied; Wilde, in her view, does not go nearly far enough. The joke, however, smacks more of fear than satire.

In the 28 April issue of 1894, *Punch* put its point of view earnestly and directly in the form of a poem entitled Donna Quixote:

> You shake your lifted latch-key like a lance!
> And shout "in spite of babies, bonnets, tea,
> Creation's heir, I must, I will be—Free!"
> Therefore, dear Donna Quixote, be not stupid
> Fight not with Hymen, and war not with Cupid
> Run not amuck 'gainst Mother Nature's plan,
> Nor make a monster of your mate, poor Man,
> Or like La Mancha's cracked, though noble, knight,
> You'll find blank failure in mistaken fight.

One can only hope that the New Woman was reassured by finding herself one of *Punch*'s regular targets—it was after all an honour she shared with most of the nineteenth century's trail-blazing men and women—and that the magazine's sententious advice and clod-hopping jokes only spurred her on to greater efforts in her quest for identity. Inherent in these jokes are, however, the same fears that permeate the *Yellow Book* stories, and their effect on any woman who regarded herself as New must, once her initial indignation had abated, have been highly disturbing. She, no less than *Punch,* did not wish to see her husband transformed into the pathetic creature so vividly envisioned by Borgia Smudgiton, and yet in 1894 this must have seemed to be precisely the risk she was taking.

Fortunately their morbid literary preoccupations did not in any way repress the women contributors to the *Yellow Book,* most of whom led vigorous, passionate lives, wrote prolifically and successfully and survived to ripe old ages. They conducted their lives according to the most *avant-garde* principles, and their behaviour seems to radiate none of the fearful caution that characterises their *Yellow Book* fiction.

"Graham Tomson", for instance, deserted her husband, Arthur Tomson, artist and member of the New English Art Club, for H. B. Marriot Watson with whom she lived in order to provide grounds for divorce. In time she married Marriot Watson, and poems by her appear in the *Yellow Book* under both names. Mènie Muriel Dowie was both writer and explorer; she too abandoned her husband for another man, who, fittingly enough, was also an explorer. Netta Syrett, who died in 1940, and Ethel Colburn Mayne, who died in 1941, both published innumerable novels. Ethel Sharpe, who died in 1945, became a suffragette at the turn of the century and fought indefatigably for that and many other causes throughout her long life; she also wrote regularly for the *Guardian.* Ada Leverson has passed into legend as Wilde's Sphinx, the woman who protected and housed him when he was on bail before his trial, and more or less a fugitive. She contributed two stories to the magazine and wrote a number of novels. Most of the other women displayed a similar energy and an admirable capacity for maintaining emotional stability within unconventional relationships despite the prevailing moral disapproval of the day.

These achievements, mundane enough in themselves, provide a startling contrast to the pattern of failure and inadequacy that typified the lives of so many of the male contributors. Compared to the vitality and productivity of the women, the debility of the men looks positively eerie, and almost suggests that everyone's worse fears, including *Punch*'s, did come true and that the women did indeed suck their new-found vigour from the veins of their men.

Punch found the Decadent poets supremely ridiculous and contemptible:

> Algie: What's the matter Archie? You're not looking well.
>
> Archie: You wouldn't look well, if you'd been suffering from insomnia every afternoon for a week. (27 October 1894)

Not content with jokes it committed its scorn to verse:

> "To Any Boy-Poet of the Decadence"
>
> For your dull little vices we don't care a fig,
> It is *this* we deeply deplore;
> You were cast for a common or usual pig,
> But you play the invincible bore.

Cartoon decadents are depicted as weak-chinned, wilting youths whose pipe-stem necks are barely capable of upholding their ludicrous bow-ties.

Physical frailty and "petty vice" do in fact characterize the so-called decadent writers, and the roll-call of their deaths makes grim reading. Yeats referred to his friends of the Rhymers' Club days as The Tragic Generation, and not without reason.

Tuberculosis killed both Beardsley and Harland. Hubert Crackanthorpe drowned himself at the age of twenty-six in the Seine after his wife had left him for another man, although, typically, he had spent the same night discussing the situation with friends and family and had defended her behaviour. John Davidson drowned himself in the Cornish Sea, at the age of forty-two, leaving a suicide note: "The time has come to make an end. There are several motives. I find my pension not enough; I have therefore still to turn aside and attempt things for which people will pay. My health also counts. Asthma and other annoyances I have tolerated for years; but I cannot put up with cancer . . . " Charles Conder, also tubercular, died at the age of forty-one, drunk and melancholic. Lionel Johnson died at thirty-five. Ernest Dowson died of self-neglect as much as anything at the age of thirty-two. Arthur Symons lived to the exceptional age of eighty, but spent many years in an asylum, the same one in which Conder died. Symons has written that he knew twelve men who killed themselves.

Physical enfeeblement, a savage need for self-abasement and a devastating inability to establish and sustain sexual relationships compound the uniform misery of their lives. Ernest Dowson, for example, permanently destitute and frequently drunk, developed a passion for the twelve-year-old daughter of a Soho restaurant owner, Adelaide Foltinowicz, known as Missie. Night after night he played chess with her father in order to be near his beloved. He did all he could to impress her mother with his eligibility as a suitor. He dedicated verses

to her (1896): "For Adelaide. To you who are my verses, as on some future day, if you ever care to read them, you will understand." She never did understand, and, prosaically enough, gave her heart instead to a tailor who had once worked in the restaurant, and married him. In his story "Apple Blossom in Brittany" (Volume III), he idealized his hopeless romance: an English critic falls in love with his teenage French ward, proposes marriage, but cannot bring himself to persuade her when she voices her doubts, and finally returns her to her convent. "Any other ending to his love," he reflects, "had been an impossible grossness, and that to lose her in just that fashion was the only way in which he could keep her always. And his acquiescence was without bitterness, and attended only by that indefinable sadness which to a man of his temper was but the last refinement of pleasure." His life was one of unrelieved tragedy; his father poisoned himself, his mother put a noose round her neck, and he himself died of tuberculosis in 1900, penniless, starved and alcoholic.

George Gissing fell victim to another neurosis, typical of this blighted generation: he was obsessed by prostitutes. He was dismissed from Owen's College, Manchester, and imprisoned for stealing money which he had given to a street-walker. He subsequently married her and lived unhappily with her for six years until she left him and went back to the streets. He saw her once again, in 1888, when he was summoned to a room in a Lambeth slum where she had been found dead. His second wife was a servant girl whom he picked up in Regent's Park. He was no happier with her and finally left her for a Frenchwoman with whom he lived, more or less contentedly, until he died of pneumonia in 1903 at the age of forty-six. His second wife ultimately went mad. Throughout his life he consistently befriended and helped prostitutes, and through them he seemed to be trying to find a way of coming to terms with the erotic conditions and confusions of his day. He was not interested in the comparatively respectable "mistresses" who served the bourgeoisie and lived in lucrative seclusion in St John's Wood, but was fascinated by the ragged, impoverished, gin-addicted waifs on whom Jack the Ripper preyed in 1887. Their wretchedness both appalled and excited him and he was realistic enough to offer them what they needed most, not religious solace or rustic exile, but hard cash.

In France the prostitute was, if not respected, at least acknowledged; she was licensed by the police and protected from many of the humiliations her English sister was obliged to endure; she was painted by many of the Impressionists, notably Toulouse-Lautrec, and writers like the de Goncourt brothers, Balzac, Baudelaire, Dumas Fils, and Zola elevated her to the status of heroine. Conditions were, however, very different in England, where an enormous army of unmentionable prostitutes daily marched the streets catering for every class and taste, where a huge but clandestine trade in pornography flourished, but where the prostitute as a literary subject was virtually taboo. In Victorian literature it is almost impossible to find a novel in which such a woman plays an important role. The double standard imposed a stern regime and the artist who dared to challenge it did so at his peril. When, for instance, Bernard Shaw attempted to produce his play *Mrs Warren's Profession,* in which his heroine decided that to turn prostitute was preferable to working in a white lead factory, the Lord Chamberlain refused to grant a licence.

Bearing in mind the sinister comparison with their female contemporaries, it is impossible not to feel that these men found the conventions which were supposed in their day to govern and maintain sexual relationships totally inadequate and treacherous. The confident, measured stride of Victorian manhood had, by the nineties, begun to falter and trip. The threats and demands represented by the ever accelerating movement towards female emancipation on all fronts, seems to have unnerved and unbalanced this group of men and driven them to seek comfort and oblivion in homosexuality, prostitution, addiction to alcohol and opiates, sterile relationships with children, and, in some cases, forlorn celibacy.

In this context, it is difficult to regard the Decadents as a band of daring and iconoclastic rebels; they look far more like refugees fleeing in the face of bewildering social evolutions. Their output, by Victorian standards, was diminutive and pale. Their poems were short and their emotional range extremely limited; their prose is largely confined to essays, short stories, fragments and prose fancies; their leading artist worked exclusively in black and white; their work is often narcissistic and precious. And yet it is in this paleness that their fascination lies, for it represents a desperate and feverish attempt to escape both from the hideousness of industrialized Victorian England and from the very developments that were putting an axe to the root of the world they found so insupportable.

It is curious, but somehow fitting, that the decade should be dominated by Beardsley, a consumptive in his twenties whose *oeuvre* consisted entirely of black and white drawings. In his *Yellow Book* illustrations women predominate as subjects and his attitude to female sexuality was far more direct and provocative than any of the other contributors, which perhaps explains why the reviewers condemned his work so venomously. They not only attacked him personally but also dismissed his drawings as evil, ugly and plain bad. "Who wants these fantastic pictures," asked the *World*, "like Japanese sketches gone mad, of a woman with a black tuft for a head, and snake-like fingers starting off the key-board of a piano; of Mrs Patrick Campbell with a black sticking-plaister hat, hunchy shoulders, a happily impossible waist, and a yard and half of indefinable skirt . . . " Beardsley's women, declared *The National Observer* critic, "resemble nothing on the earth, nor in the firmament that is above the earth, nor in the water under the earth, with their lips of a more than Hottentot thickness, their bodies of a lath-like flatness, their impossibly pointed toes and fingers, and their small eyes which have the form and comeliness of an unshelled snail."

The world inhabited by his figures is essentially artificial; the clothes they wear are elaborate, preposterous, and, above all, suggestive; their rooms and gardens are sheer masquerade; men and women alike wear masks, cosmetics, beauty spots and absurdly elaborate coiffures; their bodies are often unnaturally elongated, and their feet reduced to miniatures; they keep company with satyrs, pierrots, embryos and grotesques. His scenes are lit by candles, foot-lights, gas-lights, or an unearthly twilight, but, whatever the source, shadows are never cast.

Although none of the *Yellow Book* drawings are explicitly erotic, they all emanate an erotic nuance, and this insinuating quality, together with the indiscriminate and shameless hints of lesbianism, homosexuality, transvestism, and of other, more shadowy vices, must have particularly aggravated the critics. His women in no way conform to the conventions of Victorian feminity: they are not pure or sweet or noble; they are not motherly or infantile; they do not remotely represent

chastity, innocence or sanctity. Nudity in art was acceptable, indeed positively welcome to the Victorians, but Beardsley's women are seldom nude; on the contrary they are deliberately dressed to attract and provoke. His women are eager to be observed. They seem to take the viewer into their confidence, inviting him to share their intimacies; they tease, they challenge, and occasionally they even wink at the onlooker. Above all, his women are knowing. They know about sex, and are manifestly keen to indulge their knowledge.

His title *"L'Education Sentimentale"*, for example, makes it clear, not that the drawing needs any clarification, that the subject is erotic: the taller figure of the crone on the left is obscenely raddled; the young girl on the left is winking mischievously and making it obvious that there is not much the older woman can teach her. Her pose, a piece of calculated insolence on Beardsley's part, is a wicked caricature of the conventional concept of little-girl innocence. Nothing, it must have seemed to the critics, was sacred to this monster. The scene is rendered totally theatrical by the curving line that separates the two figures and culminates in a loose fold of drapery—a typical Beardsley gesture.

"Nightpiece", the drawing which immediately precedes Symon's "Stella Maris" is also deliberately provocative. The drawing is entirely black except for a grey building looming in the background and the stark white of the girl's face, bosom and foot. She is on the streets, unaccompanied and luridly dressed. Her expression is enigmatic and private. If she is a prostitute, and that seems to be the implication, she clearly feels no guilt or embarrassment. She is doing precisely what Victorian women were meant not to do, particularly in the pages of a fashionable literary quarterly: she is advertising her sexuality.

Holbrook Jackson, in his masterly account of the 1890s [see excerpt above], said of Beardsley that he was an intellectual artist, "drawing the thing as he *thought* it". Beardsley, he maintained, was "the most literary of all modern artists; his drawings are never the outcome of observation—they are always the outcome of thought; they are thoughts become pictures. And even then they are rarely if ever the blossoming of thought derived from experience; they are the hot-house growths of thought derived from books, pictures and music. Beardsley always worked indoors, without models and by artificial, generally, candle, light." Presumably the *National Observer* critic would have quarrelled with none of this, but it was those very "thoughts become pictures" that so revolted him and confirmed his worst suspicions regarding the Decadents. By giving flesh to decadent fantasy Beardsley not only made a brazen mockery of decency and morality, he also advanced a monstrously perverted vision of womanhood, a vision doubly damnable for its uncomfortable similarity to the portrait proposed by certain extremists among women themselves. It is not surprising that *Punch* felt obliged to warn its lady readers against the malignant consequences of dabbling in the *Yellow Book*.

A cynic might be entitled to ask why the magazine folded. If, he might enquire, it was so fascinating and sold so well, if it was so beloved by those in the fashionable know, and so loathed by those critics whose vilification could be relied on to further recommend it to the *avant-garde,* if it was so compelling even when it was bad, why then did it peter out after only thirteen volumes?

The answer must be pure conjecture since Lane and Harland were understandably tight-lipped on the subject.

Beardsley's dismissal cannot be accounted the reason. It is true that whatever he did was news, and that his drawings, along with other controversial contributions, provoked just the kind of publicity that a publisher hopes for when launching a new venture. But by the fifth volume the magazine had been in existence for more than a year and its reputation must have been firmly established. It is also true that Lane's experience during the Wilde scandal had taught him that pulling the bourgeois tail was a lucrative business until the victim chose to retaliate, and thereafter he probably discouraged any potentially lubricous contributions. He certainly never found another artist of Beardsley's calibre. The standard however of many of the later nine volumes is just as high, if anything higher, than the first four: Henry James, Arnold Bennett, H. G. Wells, Baron Corvo, John Buchan, George Gissing, Edmund Gosse and W. B. Yeats for instance all appear in the later so-called grey volumes.

There is, on the other hand, no question that editorial inspiration seems to flag badly towards the end; the same writers reappear again and again, Harland's own contributions increase in number and length, and the volumes begin to fall into a disappointingly predictable pattern. This was not necessarily Harland's fault, who appears to have been conscientious and industrious throughout; the reason lies perhaps in the very nature of the magazine itself. There is no contemporary magazine with which to compare it, but if a progressive publisher, say Jonathan Cape, decided to launch a quarterly incorporating work by its leading authors—Kingsley Amis, Doris Lessing, John Fowles, Paul Bailey, Patrick White, Luis Borges, Philip Roth, Pablo Neruda, Roger McGough, Leonard Cohen, etc., and work by equally distinguished authors usually attached to other publishers' lists, with designs and illustrations by, say, Allan Jones, David Hockney, Graham Sutherland, the result would no doubt be a formidable success, and would add considerably to the prestige of the publisher concerned. But it would be surprising if the success of such a publication were sustained. Authors and publishers alike, after the initial excitement, would soon revert their energies and attention to their real job, the prime source of their livelihood, that of writing and publishing full-scale books. Such was the fate of the *Yellow Book.* Four times a year Harland was required to produce a lengthy volume comprising prose, verse and illustrations of the highest quality; it was a feat beyond even his exceptional capability.

At the funeral, John Lane remarked that the magazine had failed to pay dividends, a direct reference presumably to declining sales figures. The magazine's design and production were lavish, and in the early volumes positively extravagent, and its price—five shillings—was by no means exorbitant; healthy sales therefore were certainly needed to cover costs alone. But Lane was probably also referring to dividends of another kind. He had backed the magazine in order to advertise his list and attract new authors; the Wilde scandal had rebounded badly on him and given rise to publicity of the most damaging kind, from which he only recovered by playing safe with both his list and the *Yellow Book;* new authors, whose work appeared in the magazine, certainly joined his list—Wells and Bennett among them—but he must have concluded that Harland's ability to recruit new blood was no better than his own, a conclusion which automatically jeopardized the magazine's continuing existence. The *Yellow Book*

was terminated not because of any inherent inadequacy in its contents but largely because it had ceased to command the enthusiasm of its proprietor and had ceased to serve his interests.

The volume dated April 1897 was the last to appear. It was published late and the *Times* did not miss its opportunity: "the *Yellow Book,* though it has outlived its youthful wildness keeps up a reputation for eccentricity by producing its April number . . . in May." No announcement of the magazine's decease was made; no explanation was offered. (pp. 27-48)

Fraser Harrison, in an introduction to The Yellow Book: An Illustrated Quarterly, *edited by Fraser Harrison, St. Martin's Press, 1974, pp. 3-48.*

ROBERT M. BOOTH

[*In the following excerpt, Booth provides an account of the publication history of the* Savoy, *examining the contents and reception of each volume and assessing its achievement.*]

In 1891 Leonard Charles Smithers, a Sheffield solicitor, had come to London and set up as a bookseller and publisher. Not a great deal is known about him, and what accounts there are differ considerably. Some people thought him repulsive and promiscuous; others said that he was faithful to one woman, and very amiable. It seems probable, however, that for the most part he was a scandalous person. He seems to have risen in the world quickly by selling pornographia which he kept in Gladstone bags under his counter, in case of a police raid. If a raid seemed imminent the bags would be hurried away to a railway station and there deposited until all was safe again. Starting as a secondhand book seller, Smithers soon had enough money to start his own publishing business, and declared his policy: 'I'll publish anything that the others are afraid of.' In 1898 he had occasion to prove himself, for he was the only publisher in London who would publish Wilde's *The Ballad of Reading Gaol.* He had talent and discrimination, and published some of the most beautiful books ever produced in any country, designing them himself. He was a genuine artist and bibliophile.

One day Smithers called on a certain Arthur Symons—whose *London Nights* he had published in June 1896—and proposed that Symons should edit for him a review or magazine such as the *Yellow Book* had been originally. Symons consented only on condition that Beardsley should be art editor. (He had himself contributed to the *Yellow Book* until Beardsley was dropped from it.) Smithers agreed, and went to see Beardsley, whom he found lying on a pile of cushions and so horribly white that he thought he was dying. Hurriedly he told him of the project, all the while fearing that he had come too late; but the thought of editing a rival to the *Yellow Book* brought colour to Beardsley's cheeks, and it seems that he immediately suggested: 'Why not call it the *Savoy?*' Vincent O'Sullivan (1860-1940: Irish-American poet, author of *Aspects of Wilde*) says that the name was derived from the Savoy Hotel. Here began a new lease of life for Beardsley; he left his bed and worked as never before.

Thus the *Savoy* was born.

Arthur Symons, poet and critic (1865-1945) was one of the literary pillars of the eighteen nineties. An editor of rare genius, he had first learned of beauty from Pater, and was greatly influenced by the French decadents. He understood them, and the influences that made for their modernity. A great admirer of Baudelaire, Mallarmé, and Verlaine, he rendered their poetry into good English verse. He knew Verlaine well, and persuaded him to leave hospital to lecture for a short while in England. His love of Verlaine is manifested by frequent reference to him in the *Savoy.*

Symons's choice for the *Savoy* was not always decadent, but always modern; he could discriminate without prejudice or predilection; but only with a conviction that beauty justified its own existence. Thus 'he culled for the *Savoy* the finest flowers in the fields of literature and art'. He states his policy for the magazine in the editorial note to volume I:

> It is hoped that the *Savoy* will be a periodical of an exclusively literary and artistic kind. To present Literature in the shape of its letter press, Art in the form of its illustrations, will be its aim. For the attainment of that aim we can but rely on our best endeavours and on the logic of our belief that good writers and artists will care to see their work in company with the work of good writers and artists. Readers who look to a new periodical for only well-known or very obscure names must permit themselves to be disappointed. We have no objection to a celebrity who deserves to be celebrated, or to an unknown person who has not been seen often enough to be recognized in passing. All we ask from our contributors is good work, and good work is all we offer our readers. This we offer with some confidence. We have no formulas, and we desire no false unity of form or matter. We have not invented a new point of view. We are not Realists, or Romanticists, or Decadents. For us, all art is good which is good art. We hope to appeal to the tastes of the intelligent by not being original for originality's sake, or audacious for the sake of advertisement, or timid for the convenience of the elderly-minded. We intend to print no verse which has not some close relationship with poetry, no fiction which has not a certain sense of what is finest in living fact, no criticism which has not some knowledge, discernment, and sincerity in its judgement. We could scarcely say more, and we are content to think we can scarcely say less.

Symons was dissatisfied with the uneven editing, fin de siècle pose, and apparent readiness to compromise, of the *Yellow Book.* He made sure the *Savoy* did not degenerate, and in fact produced a magazine that throughout its eight volumes easily surpassed the *Yellow Book.* (pp. 74-6)

Beginning as a quarterly, [the *Savoy's*] first volume appeared in January 1896. Symons and Beardsley had chosen for the magazine a format that would show off Beardsley's drawings to advantage. It was crown quarto (10″ x 8″)—larger than the *Yellow Book.* Like the *Yellow Book* it had a hard cover, but pink, not yellow. The price was half a crown—half that of the *Yellow Book.* Beardsley supplied a cover design and a title page, as he did for the seven subsequent volumes. The two mysterious veiled figures on the title page invite the reader into a mirrored recess, through curtains spangled with roses. As well as contributing eleven drawings (one of which is a Christmas card loosely inserted—a novel idea and a collector's curse), Beardsley contributed the first three chapters of his romantic novel *Under the Hill.*

Under the Hill is an amazingly successful experiment in rococo art and promises a literary genius as great as the writer's artistic genius. In reading it one is reminded of passages from

Huysmans's *A Rebours* and Wilde's *The Picture of Dorian Gray* (so much influenced by the former). For example:

> It was taper-time; when the tired earth puts on its cloak of mists and shadows, when the enchanted woods are stirred with light footfalls and slender voices of the fairies, when all the air is full of delicate influences, and even the beaux, seated at their dressing-tables, dream a little.
>
> A delicious moment, thought Fanfreluche, to slip into exile.
>
> The place where he stood waved drowsily with strange flowers, heavy with perfume, dripping with odours. Gloomy and nameless weeds not to be found in Mentzelius. Huge moths, so richly winged they must have banquetted upon tapestries and royal stuffs, slept on the pillars that flanked either side of the gateway, and the eyes of all the moths remained open and were burning and bursting with a mesh of veins. The pillars were fashioned in some pale stone and rose up like hymns in the praise of pleasure, for from cap to base, each one was carved with loving sculptures showing such a cunning invention and such a curious knowledge, that Fanfreluche lingered not a little in reviewing them . . .
>
> The frockless Helen and Fanfreluche, with Mrs Marsuple and Claude and Clair, and Farcy, the chief comedian, sat at the same table. Fanfreluche, who had doffed his travelling suit, wore long black silk stockings, a pair of pretty garters, a very elegant ruffled shirt, slippers and a wonderful dressing-gown; and Farcey was in ordinary evening clothes. As for the rest of the company, it boasted some very noticeable dresses, and whole tables of quite delightful coiffures. There were spotted veils that seemed to stain the skin, fans with eye-slits in them, through which the bearers peeped and peered; fans painted with figures and covered with the sonnets of Sporion and the short stories of Scaramouch; and fans of big, living moths stuck upon mounts of silver sticks.

The similarity of words and illustrations is amazing.

The rest of the contents is of an equally high standard. There are several essays: Bernard Shaw's "On Going to Church," Selwyn Image's "On Criticism and the Critic," Havelock Ellis's "Zola, the Man and his Work," and an article on "English Art from 1860-1870" by Joseph Pennell. There are poems by Yeats, Dowson, and Beardsley; short stories by Max Beerbohm, Dowson, and Yeats; while Symons himself contributes a poem, a translation from the *Fêtes galantes* of Verlaine and a study of the charms and delights of a stay at Dieppe in 1895. Apart from the drawings of Beardsley, the art side contains reproductions of the work of most of the distinguished artists of the day: Charles Shannon, Charles Conder, Will Rothenstein, Frederick Sandys, James McNeill Whistler, and Max Beerbohm, all of which, though of a high standard, are somewhat dwarfed by Beardsley's extraordinary designs.

Altogether, this first number contains much excellent and varied work; but in spite of this its reception by the public was for the most part unfavourable.

Punch, for example, devoted half a page to an elaborate satire on "The Book of the Week, the *Saveloy*", which begins: 'Very refreshing it is to turn from the morbid philosophy of the Besantine School of literature [a reference to the writings of Sir

Walter Besant] to the sweet fresh air of the new world to which Mr Weirdsley and his colleagues take us.' *Punch's* first dig is at Symons: "An Idyll of the Seaside: Margate 1895 by Simple Symons"; then Beerbohm: "A Fine Child by Max Mereboom"; and last but not least Beardsley is satirized.

> *Under Ludgate Hill* is a novel rather of character than of adventure. It is chiefly remarkable for its terse vigorous style, its absolute truthfulness to nature, and—more important than all the rest—its high moral tone. The character of the excellent Mrs Marsuple is superbly developed, while Claud and Clair are creations—they seem to live. This book should be on every school room table; every mother should present it to her daughter, for it is bound to have an ennobling and purifying influence. Here is a powerful description of the refreshment bar of Messrs Spiers and Pond:—

> 'The refreshment table was freighted with the most exquisite and shapely delicacies, sufficient to make Buzzard's a place of naught. On quaint pedestals of every sort stood bottles of cherry brandy, of ginger-beer, of lime-juice cordial. Marmalade and jam were in frail porcelain pots. There were jam-tarts that seemed to stain the table, bath-buns baked to the utmost, and flecked with tiny dead flies, macaroons of all sorts, and sandwiches cut like artificial flowers. There were seed-cakes sown with caraway seeds, gingerbread twisted into cunning forms, and sausage-rolls so beautiful that the teeth might have no pleasure until they had closed upon them . . . Some of the bar-maids had put on delightful little fringes dyed in reds and yellows, and some wore great white aprons after the manner of the New Magdalen. They were silenced by the approach of the Bovril that was served by waiters dressed in black.'

> Have I not said enough about the *Saveloy* to show that no family should be without it?

There is, of course, no mention in *Punch* of George Bernard Shaw or Havelock Ellis!

The *Savoy,* however, cleverly hit back at *Punch* in volume II. Among Leonard Smithers's advertisements at the back there are extracts from the press notices of volume I. *Punch's* sarcasm is ingeniously cut, and selected to read as a thoroughly favourable criticism.

Symons replies to the press in general in his editorial note to this volume.

> In presenting to the public the second number of The Savoy I wish to thank the critics of the press for the flattering reception which they have given to No. I. That reception has been none the less flattering because it has been for the most part unfavourable. Any new endeavour lends itself, alike by its merits and by its defects, to the disapproval of the larger number of people. And it is always possible to learn from any vigorously expressed denunciation, not, perhaps what the utterer of that denunciation intended should be learnt. I confess cheerfully that I have learnt much from the newspaper criticisms of the first number of the *Savoy*. It is with confidence that I anticipate no less instruction from the criticisms which I shall have the pleasure of reading on the number now issued.

Volume II appeared in April 1896 and kept up the standard of volume I. The printing had been transferred from H. S. Nichols to the Chiswick Press, and consequently the printing and paper were of a much higher standard. Yeats, Dowson, Symons, Havelock Ellis, Gosse, Image, and Beardsley contribute stories, poems, or essays. The art section is as distinguished as in the first volume. The work of a new artist, William T. Horton, shows the influence of Beardsley in his use of masses of black and white. It is interesting to see that the press notices for this volume are much more favourable, although it contains a much higher proportion of what would have been called 'decadent' work than volume I. Here are a few specimens. '. . . quite a galaxy of really excellent writers'; 'The new *Yellow Book* just out is stale and humdrum, and not to be compared to the *Savoy* in interest and attractiveness'; 'Mr Symons professes himself delighted with the "flattering" reception accorded to the first number. It is to be feared therefore that he will be less pleased with the reception likely to be given to the second, which is in so many ways better than the first; for it runs a great risk of being praised and bought.' 'The best things in it are Mr Aubrey Beardsley's pictures in black and white . . . all extraordinary in the daring with which they sail so near the grotesque without ever stepping across the line of beauty.'

Punch remained sarcastic. 'What has the Baron to say of the *Saveloy*—no, beg pardon, the *Savoy*—No. II for April, edited by Arthur Symons, and illustrated by one Aubrey Beardsley—Weirdsley? "Wonderful—most wonderful! But as it takes my breath away", says the Baron, "and paralyses my writing hand, I am compelled to reserve my criticism." ' Perhaps this slightly different approach indicates that they too found some good in the *Savoy,* but would not admit it. Anyhow, this is the last time the *Savoy* is mentioned in *Punch.*

With volume III the *Savoy* becomes a monthly instead of a quarterly; the price goes down to two shillings, and instead of pink boards it appears in blue paper covers with the magazine's title in red letters, giving it a distinguished and eye-catching appearance. In an editorial note Symons promises a serialised novel by George Moore—a promise which was never fulfilled—and reassures the public by telling them that the *Savoy* is 'A Periodical whose only aim is to offer its readers letterpress which is literature and illustrations which are art'.

The editorial note and the volume's size show great optimism about the magazine's future. The contents include a good short story by Hubert Crackanthorpe, the second of two articles on Nietzsche by Havelock Ellis, poems by Dowson and Yeats, a translation from Mallarmé by George Moore, and drawings by Beardsley, Beerbohm, and Charles Shannon. But it is an article by W. B. Yeats on William Blake and his illustrations to *The Divine Comedy* that is the cause of a great blow. The firm of W. H. Smith and Son, who even then controlled all the main railway bookstalls, banned the magazine. It seems that the head manager, looking for a Beardsley design, picked upon Blake's Antaeus setting Virgil and Dante on the verge of Cocytus as grounds for refusal. When Arthur Symons pointed out that Blake was considered 'a very spiritual artist' the manager replied: 'Oh Mr Symons, you must remember that we have an audience of young ladies as well as an audience of agnostics.' He called Symons back from the door as he was leaving, and added: 'If, contrary to our expectation, the *Savoy* should have a large sale we should be very glad to see you again.'

Those who were against the *Savoy* and its circle showed their fury and disapproval with an almost blind ardour. A gentleman to whom Yeats was introduced one evening got up and walked to the other side of the room. A. E. (the Irish poet George William Russell, who wrote under this style) denounced the *Savoy* as 'the organ of the Incubi and Succubi'. Yeats recounts how someone else to whom he was introduced said of Beardsley's drawing The Coiffing that it was simply 'bad', and offered the work of the *Punch* artist Linley Sambourne as 'great black and white art'—a judgement that was, to say the least, unreasonable and irresponsible.

Yeats wrote a letter to a national daily paper about W. H. Smith's ban on the *Savoy,* in the course of which he naturally referred to Aubrey Beardsley. He was told that the editor had made it a rule that this name was never to be mentioned in his paper.

The press notices for volume III were mainly descriptive and non-commital. The *Saturday Review,* however, spoke of Beardsley's 'supreme position as a draughtsman'.

With volume IV we see the vital importance to the *Savoy* of Beardsley's contributions. But he was suffering from consumption, and this often prevented him from working. *Under the Hill* had to be discontinued after chapter IV; and to this fourth volume he was able to contribute only a cover design. This meant that the art section consisted mainly of reproductions of drawings by William Blake. The literary content is of the usual high standard and includes three sonnets by Lionel Johnson, who had not previously contributed. There is also a charming essay by Symons on an un-named poet (in fact Ernest Dowson).

The absence of Beardsley is also noticeable in volume V, but is somewhat made up for by the best cover he ever did for the magazine. This was from an illustration to the 'Colloque Sentimental' of Verlaine. But Beardsley's influence can be seen in the work of K. Womrath which appears in this volume. The *Savoy* still seems to be thriving; but with the appearance of volume VI we can detect the beginning of the end.

An analysis of the contents shows that it was not an expensive issue. Funds were running low. It contains ten articles or poems: four are by Symons; one of the poems is by Theodore Wratislaw, from a book which Smithers was about to publish; another is by Ernest Dowson, who at this time was extremely poor and depressed and was paid a pittance by Smithers for any original work or translations he might produce. The illustrations consist mainly of work by Beardsley, D. G. Rossetti (these of course could be obtained free of charge), and two eighteenth century bookplates. But because the *Savoy* was being produced cheaply it does not mean that quality was being sacrificed. To anyone not looking for signs of failure the magazine must have appeared as good as ever.

It seems that Smithers, counting himself personally responsible for the magazine, was by this time raising money on his furniture to keep it going. In a note (dated October) to the November issue he announced the end. It was to be discontinued after the next volume. In his editor's note Symons says:

> The *Savoy* has done something of what I intended it to do: it has made warm friends and heated enemies: and I am equally content with both. It has in the main conquered the prejudices of the press; and I offer the most cordial thanks to those newspaper critics who have had the honesty and the courtesy to allow their prejudices to be conquered. But it has not conquered the general public, and, without the florins of the general public no magazine such as

the *Savoy,* issued at so low a price, and without the aid of advertisements, can expect to pay its way. We therefore retire from the arena, not entirely dissatisfied, if not a trifle disappointed.

The literary contents of this last number are as good as ever. They are mainly by Symons, Yeats, Beardsley, Dowson, and Havelock Ellis; and there is a short story, "The Idiots," by Joseph Conrad. It is unlikely that the inclusion of a drawing by Beardsley called *Ave Atque Vale* and of a very sad portrait of Arthur Symons by Jacques E. Blanche was accidental.

For the last issue the letters of the title on the cover were changed from red to black. Funds were so low that Beardsley and Symons were forced to produce the whole magazine themselves. All the text is by Symons and the drawings by Beardsley. It was a remarkable feat. There are two poems, a short story, an essay on Walter Pater, a translation from Mallarmé, and an article on the Isles of Arran, all by Symons; and there are no less than fourteen drawings by Beardsley.

Arthur Symons comments in the Epilogue:

> It is a little difficult to remember the horrified outcry—the outcry for no reason in the world but the human necessity of making a noise—with which we were first greeted. I look at those old press notices sometimes, in my publisher's scrap-book, and then at the kindly and temperate notices which the same papers are giving us now; and I find the comparison very amusing. For we have not changed in the least, we have simply gone our own way.

He goes on to say:

> Worst of all, we assumed there were very many people in the world who cared for art, and really for art's sake. Comparatively few people care for art at all, and most of these care for it because they mistake it for something else.

On this somewhat bitter note, and with a promise to reappear—less frequently, but in a larger and better edition—the *Savoy* retired from the scene.

Why did the *Savoy* fail? For it to have survived at all there must have been a certain receptivity among the public. There must therefore be internal as well as external reasons for its failure. Firstly, only once—in the first volume—were there any advertisements, except for those of its publisher Leonard Smithers. Secondly, converting it from a quarterly to a monthly increased expenditure; yet the price was lowered to two shillings. This meant that a great deal was being given for very little money. These are factors which to a certain extent could have been avoided; but the public which bought the *Savoy* could not be changed. The price charged was well within the means of the fairly numerous cultured class, but there was simply not a large enough demand for a 'decadent' periodical of this fine type. Also, the action of W. H. Smith and Son went a long way towards causing the failure.

It has been suggested that Beardsley's health was a factor contributing to the defeat of the *Savoy;* but this is not so. We have seen that it kept up a good standard when work from Beardsley was not available, and it seems that his health remained much the same, sometimes good, sometimes bad, until his death in 1898. Beardsley as Beardsley may certainly have had something to do with it. We have seen the sort of reaction that was shown to him by the press. Even without him the *Savoy* was distinguished; but nothing counted save the one hated name.

To Aubrey Beardsley the end of the *Savoy* was a great blow. After its collapse he was often heard to say, 'Now, if the *Savoy* were going, *there* would be a picture.'

Neither Beardsley, the decadence, nor the price of the magazine, was entirely to blame. There was simply no permanent public for such a venture. There is no doubting the excellence of the contents: a great deal has survived reprinting. To found a noncommercial magazine or review and gain enough support to maintain it still needs a widespread change in public taste. It was the uneasy sense that this moment might be arriving, that disinterested work might be able to enter the commercial field and appropriate a corner of it, that contributed to the excitement the *Savoy* aroused. But the rising force of patriotism at the end of the Victorian era also partially submerged the *Savoy*. It was the final eddy of an ebbing tide.

What were the achievements of the *Savoy?* In a single year it went far towards realising the editor's ideal; it never admitted anything that could not be recommended on artistic grounds alone. It was admittedly art for art's sake, and it maintained its fin de siècle tone.

The decadents found it difficult to see why they were so shocking. Later they defend and explain themselves. Symons does so in a sentence which in its beauty hides its own dangers. 'To fix the last fine shade, the quintessence of things, to fix it however fleetingly, to be a disembodied voice and yet the voice of a human soul, that is the ideal of decadence.' Yeats too is able to justify it [see excerpt above]: 'Science has won the right to explore whatever passes before its corporeal eye. Literature now demands the same right of exploration of all that passes before the mind's eye merely because it passes.' He admits that this is not a complete defence since it substitutes a spiritual for a physical objectivity. It is, however, sufficient to settle the place of the decadents in English literature.

The decadence (and the *Savoy*) could be described as 'one of those hours that might have been and might not be'. Nevertheless, it has left us something. The work of this 'kid glove' school has a certain subtlety of emotion, a note of refinement, and a distinction of utterance. All its work, good and bad, is marked by an obsession with art. It was just unfortunate that, with their violent love for a strangeness in proportion, for the abnormal and bizarre and for the pursuit of the unattainable, the decadents should have found themselves fighting against the high principled and conservative late Victorians. This, however, was probably the cause of much in their movement, which could not have been born without it.

These men believed that the desire for perfection was an end in itself. This desire gives to work, however limited in scope, a worth beyond its own nature that survives the mode in which it is done. This quality, like the desire that went to its making, is rare; and it is the rareness of a body of men intent upon it that has given the *Savoy* its historical place among literary reviews.

The *Savoy* stood boldly and alone—outstanding in the world of periodicals. It easily surpassed the *Yellow Book* as an exponent of fin-de-sièclism. It was indeed the most vital manifestation of the movement. It stood for the modern note without fear or wavering of purpose; hence it represents the most ambitious and most satisfying achievement of fin de siècle journalism in England. (pp. 76-85)

Robert M. Booth, "Aubrey Beardsley and 'The Savoy'," in The Aylesford Review, *Vol. VIII, No. 2, Autumn, 1966, pp. 71-85.*

FURTHER READING

I. Anthologies

Aldington, Richard, ed. *The Religion of Beauty: Selections from the Aesthetes.* London: William Heinemann, 1950, 364 p.
    Includes poetry and excerpted prose by Aubrey Beardsley, Max Beerbohm, Austin Dobson, Lord Alfred Douglas, Ernest Dowson, Lionel Johnson, John Addington Symonds, Arthur Symons, and Oscar Wilde, among others. Aldington discusses principal writers, works, and events connected with English Decadent literature of the 1890s in an introduction.

Beckson, Karl, ed. *Aesthetes and Decadents of the 1890s: An Anthology of British Poetry and Prose.* New York: Vintage Books, 1966, 310 p.
    Anthology of art, poetry, and prose, including illustrations by Aubrey Beardsley and literary works by Beardsley, Max Beerbohm, Lord Alfred Douglas, Ernest Dowson, Lionel Johnson, Richard Le Gallienne, Arthur Symons, Oscar Wilde, and others. Beckson supplies an introduction surveying English Aesthetic and Decadent literature, appendices featuring excerpts from seminal Aesthetic and Decadent works as well as notable contemporary satires of Aesthetic and Decadent literature, biographical sketches of the authors represented, and a bibliography of works devoted to individual writers of the 1890s.

The Book of the Rhymers' Club. London: Elkin Mathews, 1892, 94 p.
    Collection of poetry from Rhymers' Club members, including Ernest Dowson, Edwin John Ellis, George Arthur Greene, Lionel Johnson, Richard Le Gallienne, Victor Plarr, Ernest Radford, Ernest Rhys, Thomas William Rolleston, Arthur Symons, John Todhunter, and William Butler Yeats.

Davidson, Donald, ed. *British Poetry of the Eighteen-Nineties.* Garden City, N.Y.: Doubleday, Doran & Co., 1937, 420 p.
    Includes poetry by Aubrey Beardsley, John Davidson, Ernest Dowson, Lionel Johnson, Richard Le Gallienne, Arthur Symons, and Oscar Wilde in an anthology that includes many poets not associated with English Decadent literature. Davidson's introduction is excerpted above.

Engelberg, Edward, ed. "Symbolist and Decadent Poetry." In *The Symbolist Poem: The Development of the English Tradition*, pp. 195-266. New York: E. P. Dutton & Co., 1967.
    Includes poetry by Aubrey Beardsley, Ernest Dowson, George Moore, Arthur Symons, and Oscar Wilde.

Secker, Martin, ed. *The Eighteen-Nineties: A Period Anthology in Prose and Verse.* London: Richards Press, 1948, 616 p.
    Prose and poetry from the 1890s, focusing on English Decadent literature. In an introduction, John Betjeman offers the following suggestion for invoking the period: "Draw the curtains, kindle a joss-stick in a dark corner, settle down on a sofa by the fire, light an Egyptian cigarette and sip a brandy and soda, as you think yourself back to the world which ended in prison and disgrace for Wilde, suicide for Crackanthorpe and John Davidson, premature death for Beardsley, Dowson, Lionel Johnson, religion for some, drink and drugs for others, temporary or permanent oblivion for many more."

The Second Book of the Rhymers' Club. London: Elkin Mathews John Lane, 1894, 136 p.
  Collection of poetry from Rhymers' Club members, including all the contributors to the original volume.

Stanford, Derek, ed. *Poets of the 'Nineties: A Biographical Anthology.* London: John Baker, 1965, 225 p.
  Selection of poetry by writers whom Stanford considers representative of English literary Decadence. The editor provides a general introduction, which is excerpted above, as well as biographical and critical commentary on each poet.

————, ed. *Short Stories of the 'Nineties: A Biographical Anthology.* New York: Roy Publishers, 1968, 253 p.
  Includes short stories by Hubert Crackanthorpe, Ernest Dowson, Henry Harland, Richard Le Gallienne, and Arthur Symons, among others. Stanford supplies an introduction discussing the chief characteristics, principal influences, and primary themes of the short fiction of the period.

————, ed. *Critics of the 'Nineties.* London: John Baker, 1970, 244 p.
  Representative collection of critical writing, primarily by English authors of the 1890s associated with Decadent literature. In an introduction Stanford identifies characteristics of the literature and criticism of the period.

————, ed. *Writing of the 'Nineties: From Wilde to Beerbohm.* London: Dent, 1971, 230 p.
  Selection of late nineteenth-century English essays, sketches, manifestos, short fiction, poetry, and criticism. In an introduction Stanford suggests that the lives and works of Oscar Wilde and Max Beerbohm representatively encompass the period. A bibliography lists primary and secondary sources for further reading.

————, ed. *Three Poets of the Rhymers' Club: Ernest Dowson, Lionel Johnson, John Davidson.* Cheshire: Carcanet Press, 1974, 177 p.
  Collects poetry of Davidson, Dowson, and Johnson. Stanford includes biographical and critical discussion of each poet and a list of suggested further reading about the Rhymers' Club and its members.

Symons, A. J. A., ed. *An Anthology of 'Nineties' Verse.* London: Elkin Mathews & Marrot, 1928, 176 p.
  Anthology including poetry by principal Decadent poets and an introduction by the editor.

Thornton, R. K. R., ed. *Poetry of the 'Nineties.* Harmondsworth: Penguin Books, 1970, 272 p.
  Thematically arranged collection that includes works of English Decadent poetry and an introduction by the editor.

Wallis, Nevile, ed. *Fin de Siècle: A Selection of Late 19th Century Literature and Art.* London: Allan Wingate, 1947, 94 p.
  Includes prose and poetry by Max Beerbohm, Hubert Crackanthorpe, John Davidson, Lord Alfred Douglas, Ernest Dowson, Lionel Johnson, Richard Le Gallienne, and Oscar Wilde; and illustrations by Aubrey Beardsley, Beerbohm, and William Rothenstein. "A Note on the Period," by Holbrook Jackson, prefaces the collection.

Weintraub, Stanley, ed. *The "Yellow Book": Quintessence of the Nineties.* Garden City, N.Y.: Anchor Books, 1964, 373 p.
  Reprints selections from the *Yellow Book* from 1894 through 1897. In an introduction Weintraub examines the reputation and publication history of the *Yellow Book* and describes the contents of each issue.

————, ed. *The "Savoy": Nineties Experiment.* University Park: Pennsylvania State University Press, 1966, 294 p.
  Reprints selections from the eight issues of the *Savoy* (1896). An introduction offers a detailed account of the magazine's inception and publication history and discusses its editors and contributors.

II. Secondary Sources

Alexander, Calvert, S. J. "Fin de Siècle—Wilde, Beardsley, Dowson." In his *The Catholic Literary Revival: Three Phases in Its Development from 1845 to the Present,* pp. 89-112. 1935. Reprint. Port Washington, N.Y.: Kennikat Press, 1968.
  Suggests that the personal tragedies that befell some central figures of English Decadent literature filled a cautionary function in the course of the Catholic Literary Revival.

Aslin, Elizabeth. *The Aesthetic Movement: Prelude to Art Nouveau.* New York: Frederick A. Praeger, 1969, 192 p.
  Profusely illustrated history focusing on the impact of the Aesthetic movement, primarily on decor and clothing. Aslin includes chapters on "Oscar Wilde and America," detailing Wilde's 1882-83 American lecture tour, during which he spoke on aestheticism; and "Satire and Comment," outlining reaction to the Aesthetic movement, including satires of prominent figures of English Decadent literature.

Bargainnier, Earl F. "Fog and Decadence: Images of the 1890's." *Journal of Popular Culture* XII, No. 1 (Summer 1978): 19-29.
  Includes discussion of the popular perception of the 1890s as an era of literary Decadence.

Batho, Edith, and Dobrée, Bonamy. *The Victorians and After: 1830-1914.* London: Cresset Press, 1938, 370 p.
  Offers discussion of English Decadent writers in an overview of the literature of the period. Approximately half of the volume comprises bibliographies of representative works organized by genre.

Beckson, Karl. "A Mythology of Aestheticism." *English Literature in Transition* 17, No. 4 (1974): 233-49.
  Examines "a central mythology" of fin-de-siècle Aestheticism: "The Religion of Art and Beauty."

Beerbohm, Max. "Enoch Soames." In his *Seven Men,* pp. 9-51. New York: Alfred A. Knopf, 1920.
  Witty account of the fictional "Enoch Soames"—an ineffectual English poet who embodies characteristic attributes of the fin-de-siècle Decadents.

————. *Max's Nineties: Drawings, 1892-1899,* by Max Beerbohm, edited by Osbert Lancaster. Philadelphia: J. B. Lippincott Co., 1958, unpaged.
  Selection of Beerbohm's drawings that includes caricatures of literary figures of the 1890s. In an introduction, Lancaster discusses Beerbohm's life and career.

————. "Aesthetes and Decadents." In *Beerbohm's Literary Caricatures: From Homer to Huxley,* edited by J. G. Riewald, pp. 151-69. Hamden, Conn.: Archon Books, 1977.
  Includes caricatures of John Davidson, Henry Harland, Richard Le Gallienne, James Whistler, and Oscar Wilde. The editor supplies biographical information and anecdotes about the subject of each caricature.

Bradley, William Aspenwall. "What Is Decadence?" *The Bookman* (New York) XXXVII, No. 4 (June 1913): 431-38.
  Explores the origins and currency of the term Decadence.

Briggs, Julia. "Diabolism and Decadence: The Mood of the Nineties." In her *Night Visitors: The Rise and Fall of the English Ghost Story,* pp. 76-97. London: Faber, 1977.
  Examines ways that literary Decadence found expression in the supernatural literature of the 1890s.

Brisau, A. "The *Yellow Book* and Its Place in the Eighteen-Nineties." *Studia Germanica Gandensia* VIII (1966): 135-72.
  Examines the principal themes of prose fiction and poetry published in the *Yellow Book* and discusses the chief contributors to the magazine.

Burdett, Osbert. *The Beardsley Period: An Essay in Perspective.* New York: Boni and Liveright, 1925, 302 p.
    Lively chronicle of English literary Decadence of the 1890s, offering commentary on the origins and development of English Decadent literature and some of the central figures of the movement.

Campos, Christophe. "From Café to Studio (George Moore and the Nineties)." *The View of France: From Arnold to Bloomsbury,* pp. 139-92. London: Oxford University Press, 1965.
    Examines the vogue of French bohemianism with English Decadent writers of the 1890s.

Casford, E. Lenore. *The Magazines of the 1890's: A Chapter in the History of English Periodicals.* Eugene, Ore.: University Press, 1929, 39 p.
    Surveys principal magazines associated with English Decadent literature, including the *Albemarle,* the *Yellow Book,* the *Savoy,* the *Anti-Philistine,* the *Butterfly,* the *Dome,* the *Hobby-Horse,* the *Pageant,* and the *Quarto.* In an introductory essay Casford discusses "The Decadent Writers of the 1890's."

Charlesworth, Barbara. *Dark Passages: The Decadent Consciousness in Victorian Literature.* Madison: University of Wisconsin Press, 1965, 155 p.
    Discusses the lives and works of Lionel Johnson, Walter Pater, Dante Gabriel Rossetti, Algernon Swinburne, Arthur Symons, and Oscar Wilde, concluding that in their pursuit of varied experience, "the Decadents failed in their lives and in their art."

Chew, Samuel C. "Aestheticism and 'Decadence'." In *A Literary History of England,* edited by Albert C. Baugh, pp. 1475-84. New York: Appleton-Century-Crofts, 1948.
    Outlines the origin and development of late nineteenth-century literary Aestheticism and Decadence.

Clarke, Austin. "The Nineties." In his *The Celtic Twilight and the Nineties,* pp. 9-30. Dublin: Dolmen Press, 1969.
    Includes discussion of English Decadent literature in an overview of various literary movements that flourished at the time of the Celtic Twilight.

Croft-Cooke, Rupert. *Feasting with Panthers: A New Consideration of Some Late Victorian Writers.* London: W. H. Allen, 1967, 309 p.
    Seeks to demythologize figures of "the Naughty, the Romantic or the Yellow Nineties, the Beardsley period," principally by focusing on their aberrant sexuality.

Cruse, Amy. "The Decadents of the 'Nineties." In her *After the Victorians,* pp. 44-55. London: George Allen & Unwin, 1938.
    Discusses some seminal works and principal figures of English literary Decadence.

Decker, Clarence R. "The Aesthetic Revolt against Naturalism in Victorian Criticism." *PMLA* LIII, No. 3 (September 1938): 844-56.
    Considers Aestheticism largely a reaction against literary Naturalism.

Dowling, Linda C. *Aestheticism and Decadence: A Selective Annotated Bibliography.* New York: Garland Publishing, 1977, 140 p.
    Annotated bibliography of works devoted to literary Aestheticism and Decadence. In an introduction Dowling discusses common myths about and oversimplifications of English Decadent literature of the 1890s.

Ellmann, Richard, ed. *Edwardians and Late Victorians.* New York: Columbia University Press, 1960, 246 p.
    Includes essays on English literature of the 1890s by Helmut E. Gerber, Graham Hough, Ruth Z. Temple, and others.

Evans, Ifor. "Oscar Wilde, Ernest Dowson, Lionel Johnson and the Poetry of the Eighteen-Nineties." In his *English Poetry in the Later Nineteenth Century,* pp. 390-420. Rev. ed. London: Methuen & Co., 1966.
    Biographical and critical commentary on the three poets listed.

Fletcher, Ian, ed. *Romantic Mythologies.* London: Routledge & Kegan Paul, 1967, 297 p.
    Features several essays that treat English Decadent literature of the 1890s, including "Pierrot and Fin de Siècle," by A. G. Lehmann; and " 'Aubrey Beardsley, Man of Letters'," by Annette Lavers.

——, ed. *Decadence and the 1890s.* London: Edward Arnold, 1979, 216 p.
    Collection of essays on English Decadent literature that includes " 'Decadence' in Later Nineteenth-Century England," by R. K. R. Thornton; " 'Decadent Spaces': Notes for a Phenomenology of the *Fin de Siècle,*" by Jan B. Gordon; "Swinburne's Circle of Desire: A Decadent Theme," by Chris Snodgrass; "Fierce Midnights: Algolagniac Fantasy and the Literature of the Decadence," by Jerry Palmer; "The Decadent Writer as Producer," by John Goode; "From Naturalism to Symbolism," by John Lucas; "The Legend of Duse," by John Stokes; and "Decadence and the Little Magazines," by Ian Fletcher.

Frierson, William C. "The Eighteen-Nineties: Generalities on Its Fiction." In his *The English Novel in Transition: 1885-1940,* pp. 116-24. Norman: University of Oklahoma Press, 1942.
    Summarizes some salient characteristics of English fiction of the 1890s.

Garbáty, Thomas Jay. "The French Coterie of the *Savoy:* 1896." *PMLA* LXXV, No. 5 (December 1960): 609-15.
    Comments on the Gallic temperament of the *Savoy:* and its contributors and editors, who divided their time between England and France and conceived of the publication in France following Oscar Wilde's trial and conviction.

Gardiner, Bruce. *The Rhymers' Club: A Social and Intellectual History.* New York: Garland Publishing, 1988, 250 p.
    Account of the Rhymers' Club, which included English Decadent poets among its loosely organized membership.

Gaunt, William. *The Aesthetic Adventure.* New York: Harcourt, Brace and Co., 1945, 269 p.
    Account of literary and artistic Decadence that includes discussion of England during the 1890s.

Gilman, Richard. *Decadence: The Strange Life of an Epithet.* New York: Farrar, Straus and Giroux, 1979, 179 p.
    Includes discussion of English Decadent literature of the 1890s in an examination of the various uses of the term "decadent" as applied to cultural phenomena of the late nineteenth and the twentieth centuries.

Guérard, Albert. "Symbolism and Decadence." In his *Art for Art's Sake,* pp. 69-84. Boston: Lothrop, Lee and Shepard Co., 1936.
    Examines Symbolism and Decadence in the literature of the 1890s.

Harris, Wendell V. "Innocent Decadence: The Poetry of the *Savoy.*" *PMLA* LXXVII, No. 5 (December 1962): 629-36.
    Distinguishes between the perverse and violent themes of French Decadent poetry and the melancholy lassitude that Harris finds characterizes English Decadent poetry, a representative selection of which appeared in the *Savoy.*

——. "John Lane's Keynotes Series and the Fiction of the 1890's." *PMLA* 83, No. 5 (October 1968): 1407-13.
    Surveys the nineteen volumes of John Lane's Keynotes Series, which Harris considers "offers a significant sample from the heart of the 1890's which is particularly illustrative of what happened to fiction at the time."

Held, George. "The Second Book of the Rhymers' Club." *The Journal of the Rutgers University Library* XXVIII, No. 2 (June 1965): 15-21.
    Offers bibliographic information about *The Second Book of the Rhymers' Club* (1894), surveys the volume's contents, and discusses principal contributors.

Hepburn, James G. "Transition, Decadence, and Estheticism: Some Notes." *English Literature in Transition* 6, No. 1 (1963): 16-17.
   Considers literary Decadence as a primarily transitional literary phenomenon, not indicative of "absolute decline."

Hichens, Robert Smythe. *The Green Carnation.* New York: M. Kennerley, 1894, 211 p.
   Satirical novel lampooning the behavior of the Decadents and Aesthetes of the 1890s. Following its publication, a number of Decadent authors, including Oscar Wilde, adopted the green carnation as an emblem.

Hough, Graham. "Fin-de-Siècle." In his *The Last Romantics,* pp. 175-215. London: Gerald Duckworth & Co., 1949.
   Discusses the contributions of Lionel Johnson, James Whistler, and Oscar Wilde, the writers of the French Decadence, and those of the Rhymers' Club, to the development of fin-de-siècle Aestheticism in nineteenth-century English art and literature.

Hyde, H. Montgomery. *The Trials of Oscar Wilde.* London: William Hodge and Co., 1948, 384 p.
   Includes transcripts of Wilde's three trials in 1895, commentary on the proceedings, and an account of reaction in London literary circles.

Joad, C. E. M. "Applications: Decadence in Our Time." In his *Decadence: A Philosophical Inquiry,* pp. 247-424. London: Faber and Faber, 1948.
   Discusses decadence in literature, art, and society.

Le Gallienne, Richard. "What's Wrong with the Eighteen-Nineties?" *The Bookman* (New York) LIV, No. 1 (September 1921): 1-7.
   Discussion of 1890s literature and culture that includes commentary on literary Decadence.

————. *The Romantic '90s.* London: Putnam & Co., 1951, 162 p.
   Reminisces about the period, recalling the writers and artists of the 1890s.

Lester, John A., Jr. *Journey through Despair, 1880-1914: Transformations in British Literary Culture.* Princeton, N.J.: Princeton University Press, 1968, 211 p.
   Examines loss of faith as a characteristic theme in late nineteenth- and early twentieth-century English literature.

Long, Richard A., and Jones, Iva G. "Towards a Definition of the 'Decadent Novel'." *College English* 22, No. 4 (January 1961): 245-49.
   Defines some essential characteristics of the Decadent novel.

May, J. Lewis. *John Lane and the Nineties.* London: John Lane, 1936, 272 p.
   Anecdotal biography of the publisher who produced the *Yellow Book* as well as lavish editions of many English Decadent works.

Mégroz, R. L. "Decadence." In his *Modern English Poetry: 1882-1932,* pp. 37-60. London: Ivor Nicholson & Watson, 1933.
   Examines "the tendency to moral and spiritual disorder in [the] style and mood" of some English Decadent poets of the 1890s.

Mix, Katherine Lyon. *A Study in Yellow: The "Yellow Book" and Its Contributors.* Lawrence: University of Kansas Press, 1960, 325 p.
   Account of the magazine's publication history and of the principal editors, authors, and artists who contributed to it.

Morland, M. A. "Nietzsche and the Nineties." *Contemporary Review* 193 (April 1958): 209-12.
   Examines Friedrich Nietzsche's influence on prominent English authors of the 1890s.

Muddiman, Bernard. *The Men of the Nineties.* London: Henry Danielson, 1920, 145 p.

Account of 1890s literary London as "essentially the age of young men."

Murdoch, W. G. Blaikie. *The Renaissance of the Nineties.* London: Alexander Moring, 1911, 83 p.
   Overview of the literature of the 1890s.

Nalbantian, Suzanne. *Seeds of Decadence in the Late Nineteenth-Century Novel: A Crisis in Values.* New York: St. Martin's Press, 1983, 144 p.
   Includes examination of specific literary applications of the term "decadence" to works of fin-de-siècle Aestheticism.

Nelson, James G. *The Early Nineties: A View from the Bodley Head.* Cambridge: Harvard University Press, 1971, 387 p.
   Account of the bookshop and publishing firm that includes discussion of many of the authors and artists connected with the Bodley Head.

————. "The Nature of Aesthetic Experience in the Poetry of the Nineties: Ernest Dowson, Lionel Johnson, and John Gray." *English Literature in Transition* 17, No. 4 (1974): 223-32.
   Examines the aesthetic experience—a moment of apprehension of great beauty—that is central to the poetry of Dowson, Gray, and Johnson.

Nordau, Max. *Degeneration.* 1895. Reprint. New York: Howard Fertig, 1968, 566 p.
   Attack that purports to explore the pathology of late nineteenth-century cultural trends. Following the methods of criminologist Cæsar Lombroso, Nordau suggests that "the tendencies of the fashions in art and literature . . . have their source in the degeneracy of their authors, and . . . the enthusiasm of their admirers is for manifestations of more or less pronounced moral insanity, imbecility, and dementia."

O'Sullivan, Vincent. "The Eighteen-Nineties." In his *Opinions,* pp. 192-205. London: Unicorn Press, 1959.
   Recollections of English literature and authors of the 1890s.

Perkins, David. "*Ars Victrix:* The London Avant-Garde." In his *A History of Modern Poetry: From the 1890s to the High Modernist Mode,* pp. 30-59. Cambridge, Mass.: Harvard University Press, 1976.
   Includes commentary on literary Aestheticism, Decadence, Symbolism, and Impressionism, as well as discussion of individual British poets of the 1890s.

Peters, Robert C. "Toward an 'Un-Definition' of Decadent as Applied to British Literature of the Nineteenth Century." *Journal of Aesthetics and Art Criticism* XVIII, No. 2 (December 1959): 258-64.
   Suggests that Ryals's proposed definition of Decadence (excerpted above) is insufficient.

Pondrom, Cyrena N. "A Note on the Little Magazines of the English Decadence." *Victorian Periodical Newsletter,* No. 1 (January 1968): 30-1.
   Finds that periodicals preceding the *Yellow Book,* including the *Dial,* the *Spirit Lamp,* and the *Chameleon,* reveal the growth of English interest in French literary Decadence.

Reed, John R. *Decadent Style.* Athens: Ohio University Press, 1985, 274 p.
   Includes references to English Decadent literature of the 1890s and defines Decadent literature as that which treats themes of social and physical decay and examines sexual and psychological perversities.

Ryskamp, Charles, ed. *Wilde and the Nineties: An Essay and an Exhibition.* Princeton, N.J.: Princeton University Press, 1966, 64 p.
   Memorial booklet commemorating an exhibition of Wilde memorabilia at the Princeton University Library. Includes the essay "The Eighteen Nineties: Perspectives," by E. D. H. Johnson.

Sims, George. "Leonard Smithers: A Publisher of the Nineties." *The London Magazine* 3, No. 9 (September 1956): 33-40.

>   Biographical sketch of the publisher and book dealer who issued the *Savoy* and advanced the careers of several notable artists of the period, including Aubrey Beardsley, Max Beerbohm, and Charles Conder.

Stein, Joseph. "The New Woman and the Decadent Dandy." *Dalhousie Review* 55, No. 1 (Spring 1975): 54-62.

>   Explores the enmity between the "new woman" of the 1890s and the Decadent aesthete who enjoyed a synchronous vogue, and suggests that dandyism declined with the rise of feminism.

Symons, Arthur. *Studies in Prose and Verse.* New York: E. P. Dutton & Co., 1922, 291 p.

>   Includes chapters devoted to English Decadent authors, including Hubert Crackanthorpe, Austin Dobson, Ernest Dowson, and John Addington Symonds.

Temple, Ruth Z. "Truth in Labelling: Pre-Raphaelitism, Aestheticism, Decadence, Fin de Siècle." *English Literature in Transition* 17, No. 4 (1974): 201-22.

>   Suggests that the designations Pre-Raphaelite, Aesthetic, Decadent, and fin de siècle are often misused, and offers new interpretations of the terms.

Thatcher, David S. "Nietzsche and the Literary Mind." In his *Nietzsche in England, 1890-1914: The Growth of a Reputation,* pp. 121-37. Toronto: University of Toronto Press, 1970.

>   Examines instances of English authors and artists of the period drawing from Nietzschean thought.

Turquet-Milnes, G. "The Baudelairian Spirit in England." In his *The Influence of Baudelaire in France and England,* pp. 219-64. London: Constable and Co., 1913.

>   Includes discussion of Baudelaire's influence on English Decadent literature of the 1890s.

Whissen, Thomas Reed. *The Devil's Advocates: Decadence in Modern Literature.* New York: Greenwood Press, 1989, 130 p.

>   Discussion of English Decadent literature of the 1890s is included in an examination of the theme of decadence in European and American literature of approximately the last hundred years.

Yeats, William Butler. "Modern Poetry." In his *Essays and Introductions,* pp. 491-508. New York: Macmillan Co., 1961.

>   Transcript of a 1936 radio broadcast including Yeats's discussion of the lives and works of Ernest Dowson and Lionel Johnson.

English Romantic Poetry

INTRODUCTION

Dating from the final decade of the eighteenth century, the Romantic period in English poetry lasted nearly forty years and is considered one of the richest eras in poetry, primarily for the writings of William Blake, William Wordsworth, Samuel Taylor Coleridge, John Keats, Percy Bysshe Shelley, and George Gordon, Lord Byron. Although these poets never regarded themselves as a movement, commentators define English Romantic poetry in terms of several characteristics, including a reverence for nature; a belief in the innate goodness of the individual; a tendency toward idealism and then melancholy when ideals have failed; and an attraction to things beyond human knowledge: the spiritual, the supernatural, the mythical, and the mystical. In general, the English Romantic poets exalted imagination and feeling over intellect and rationality. For this reason, their work is perceived as a revolt against eighteenth-century Neoclassicism. Most critics consider this reaction to have been inspired by the radical political and social climate in the years following the French Revolution, an event that instilled in the poets a belief in the unlimited potential and freedom of the individual. In addition to an ideological reaction, the Romantic revolt involved the structure and style of poetry. Believing that poetic structure should grow out of the subject matter rather than be imposed by poetic conventions, the Romantics rejected the formulaic heroic couplet frequently used by Alexander Pope, Samuel Johnson, and other Neoclassicists, and adopted poetic forms that allowed them greater freedom of expression, such as the ode and the verse narrative. Whereas Neoclassical poetry is generally dispassionate and descriptive, Romantic verse is subjective, visionary, and suggestive, abounding in seemingly trivial details from which the poets derived great symbolic meaning. While critics consider Romantic poetry revolutionary, they also point out that it was firmly based in intellectual and literary tradition. Its ideological underpinnings have been traced to the idealism of Plato and the eighteenth-century philosophers John Locke, David Hume, and Jean Jacques Rousseau, while the poetry itself has been found to manifest the influence of William Shakespeare, John Milton, and Edmund Spenser. Although their work was severely attacked in the early twentieth century by many prominent writers, including T. S. Eliot, T. E. Hulme, and Cleanth Brooks, the Romantics remain among the most esteemed poets in world literature, and their writings—preeminently such poems as Wordsworth's "Ode: Intimations of Immortality through Recollections of Early Childhood," Coleridge's "Rime of the Ancient Mariner," and Keats's "Ode to a Nightingale"—have had a pervasive influence on nineteenth- and twentieth-century literature.

REPRESENTATIVE WORKS

Blake, William
Poetical Sketches (poetry) 1783

The Book of Thel (poetry) 1789
Songs of Innocence (poetry) 1789
The Marriage of Heaven and Hell (poetry and prose) 1790-93?
The French Revolution (poetry) 1791
America: A Prophecy (poetry) 1793
Visions of the Daughters of Albion (poetry) 1793
Europe: A Prophecy (poetry) 1794
The First Book of Urizen (poetry) 1794
Songs of Innocence and Experience (poetry) 1794
The Book of Ahania (poetry) 1795
The Book of Los (poetry) 1795
The Song of Los (poetry) 1795
Milton (poetry) 1804-08?
Jerusalem (poetry) [written 1804-09?] 1818
Vala: or, The Four Zoas (poetry) [written 1796-1807?] 1893
The Complete Writings of William Blake (poetry, prose, drama, marginalia, and letters) 1968
Byron, Lord (George Gordon)
Hours of Idleness (poetry) 1807
English Bards and Scotch Reviewers (poetry) 1809
Childe Harold's Pilgrimage (poetry) 1812
The Bride of Abydos (poetry) 1813
The Giaour (poetry) 1813
The Corsair (poetry) 1814
Lara (poetry) 1814
Ode to Napoleon Buonaparte (poetry) 1814
Hebrew Melodies (poetry) 1815
Childe Harold's Pilgrimage: Canto the Third (poetry) 1816
Parisina (poetry) 1816
The Prisoner of Chillon, and Other Poems (poetry) 1816
The Siege of Corinth (poetry) 1816
The Lament of Tasso (poetry) 1817
Manfred (verse drama) 1817
Beppo (poetry) 1818
Childe Harold's Pilgrimage: Canto the Fourth (poetry) 1818
Mazeppa (poetry) 1819
Don Juan, Cantos I-XVI. 6 vols. (poetry) 1819-24
Cain (verse drama) 1821
Marino Faliero, Doge of Venice (verse drama) 1821
Heaven and Earth (verse drama) 1823
The Vision of Judgment (poetry) 1823
The Deformed Transformed (verse drama) 1824
Letters and Journals. 11 vols. (letters and journals) 1975-81
The Complete Poetical Works of Byron. 3 vols. (poetry and verse dramas) 1980-81
Coleridge, Samuel Taylor, and Wordsworth, William
Lyrical Ballads, with a Few Other Poems (poetry) 1798; also published as *Lyrical Ballads, with Other Poems* [revised edition], 1800
Coleridge, Samuel Taylor
Poems on Various Subjects (poetry) 1796; also published as *Poems* [revised edition], 1797

OVERVIEWS AND REPUTATION

DAVID PERKINS

[*Perkins is an American critic and educator. In the following excerpt, he provides an overview of the English Romantic period, focusing on the poetry as "the supreme achievement of the age."*]

The half-century from approximately 1775 to 1830 saw the American Revolution and the emergence of the United States, the French Revolution and Napoleon, the spread throughout Europe and America of democratic and egalitarian ideals, the origin or intensification in every European country of a sentiment of national identity, and, especially in England, the first important development of the industrial system. At the same time, virtually every realm of thought and art underwent a profound modification of which we still feel the impact. Three famous names in Germany alone—Kant, Goethe, Beethoven—may briefly suggest something of the scope of this cultural achievement and transition.

The term "Romantic," which is conventionally applied to the last thirty years of this period (1800-30), is far from adequate. All historical labels are, of course, simplifications and fail to suggest the diversity of life, thought, and art in the period to which they are applied. And this particular era, which in many respects ushered in the modern world, was at least as diverse as any previous thirty-year period. As a qualitative or descriptive term, the word "Romantic"—in its traditional and popular sense—is strictly applicable to only some aspects of the intellectual and cultural character of these thirty years. To begin with, the word still carries overtones it acquired in the early and middle eighteenth century, when it was connected with one of several reactions against neoclassical taste. In contrast to the rational order, regularity, and generalization associated with neoclassical art, "Romanticism"—largely because it was associated with the art and literature of the Middle Ages—suggested the "irregular," "picturesque," "wild," and distant. Of course interest in these qualities was strong in the early nineteenth century. But if the literature of the "Romantic" era was concerned with the remote or the distant, it was also concerned, in a new and vital way, with the concrete and the directly familiar; and in it we find the beginnings of modern naturalism and realism. If it was idealistic, it was also at times directly empirical, and it flourished contemporaneously with a rapid development of historical study and psychological analysis. If it was attracted to the Middle Ages, it was equally drawn to classical antiquity; and its critical values both encouraged and profited from a resurgent and more informed study of the classical.

Beginning in 1798 the word "Romantic" was caught up by the influential German critics Friedrich and August Wilhelm von Schlegel, who gave it a deeper and more specific group of meanings; and throughout the nineteenth century the term became more widely used for the simple reason that nothing better appeared. The Schlegel brothers were interested in defining a contrast between the art and literature of the classical world and that of the Middle Ages and Renaissance (which they called "modern" in antithesis to "ancient"). According to the Schlegels, the "modern" is relatively indifferent to artistic form and seeks instead "fullness and life"—a complete expression of all life in its dynamism and its endless variety and particularity. Because this ideal is infinite, the spiritual quality of "modern" or "Romantic" art differs totally from the classical. The "Romantic" refuses to recognize restraints in subject matter or form and so is free to represent the abnormal, grotesque, and monstrous and to mingle standpoints, *genres,* modes of expression (such as philosophy and poetry), and even the separate arts in a single work. Ultimately it mirrors the struggle of genius against all limitation, and it leads to a glorification of yearning, striving, and becoming and of the personality of the artist as larger and more significant that the necessarily incomplete expression of it in his work. In this antithesis the Schlegels exalted the Romantic over the classical, but, it may be repeated, they applied the term to medieval literature and to such figures as Cervantes and Shakespeare and did not, on the whole, have in mind the writers of their own day. Nevertheless, they defined an ideal with which men of their time could identify, and it is especially as a result of their writings that the word "Romantic," as Goethe said in 1830, "goes over the whole world and causes so many quarrels and divisions . . . everyone talks about classicism and romanticism—of which nobody thought fifty years ago."

Even this more comprehensive use of the term is frequently attacked. It is argued that English writers did not think of themselves as "Romantic" or as constituting a "movement"; even in Germany the group that called itself "Romantic" did not include most of the figures now embraced by that generalization. Furthermore, as a critical term it tends to equivocate between the Romantic considered as a recurring type of personality and as a particular historical era. Moreover, even as the name of a cultural epoch the term constantly shifts meaning. Romanticism was not the same phenomenon in literature, fine arts, music, philosophy, historiography, and science; nor did it fall within the same span of time in the separate lines of endeavor and in the several nations. Hence, the argument goes, Romanticism is a name without a corresponding object, and it should either be used in the plural ("Romanticisms") or scrapped. On the other hand, it can be urged that the era under consideration, however variously delimited, was relatively short, and that within it one can identify widespread, though not necessarily harmonious, ideals, concepts, tastes, interests, and feelings. The term will be used here to refer to leading aspects of this cultural era, keeping in mind the era's variousness and distinctness.

The Historical Background

In discussing the historical background of the brilliant achievement of this period, one must begin with the French Revolution. For us, after nearly two centuries of revolution in various parts of the world, it is almost impossible to imagine the shock and awakening that swept over Europe when in 1789 the Bastille, a prison that symbolized royal power, was stormed by a Paris mob and a great popular uprising broke out in France. With the possible exception of the Reformation, which had developed much more slowly, there was nothing like it within historical memory. Two of its myriad

effects may be noted at once. With the dissolution of social and class barriers—or even the hope of it—individual energies were released and it seemed that no limit needed to be set to personal ambition. . . . A few years later the prime example was, of course, the rise of Napoleon, but well before this the Revolution had an effect throughout Europe in stimulating the soaring aspiration that is so marked in the major figures of the age. In the second place, to sympathizers everywhere it appeared that society was about to be established on a rational and democratic basis, or even on a basis of fraternal love. "Nothing," said Southey long afterward, "was dreamt of but the regeneration of the human race." "Bliss was it in that dawn to be alive," remembered Wordsworth, "France standing on the top of golden hours / And human nature seeming born again." Throughout Europe the example of France intensified the already widespread questioning of social and political institutions, and, with the possibility of a transformation before their eyes, men set themselves with a new excitement and determination to seek ultimate principles—what is justice? human nature? the rights of man? whence derived?—and the quickening challenge of fundamental rethinking touched intellectual life at all points. There was, said Hazlitt, "a mighty ferment in the heads of statesmen and poets, kings and people." A "new impulse had been given to men's minds" and "philosophy took a higher, poetry could afford a deeper range." (pp. 1-3)

During the Revolution and subsequent war with France, the English upper classes lived in terror of a similar outbreak at home. To what extent this was a likelihood is not easy to say. Certainly English political and social institutions were unlike those of France and most of Europe. In the first place, power, instead of being concentrated in the monarch and his appointees, was more widely distributed. England was an aristocracy in which the lords and gentry controlled most positions of influence—they sat in Parliament, officered the army and navy, held the high places in the Anglican Church, and, as Justices of the Peace, dispensed law throughout the countryside. But they were not a closed group; middle class persons of talent or wealth could be assimilated into the governing class. In the second place, the ideals of the Revolution did not have the same impact in England as in the rest of Europe, partly because—with their traditional insular complacence—Englishmen viewed foreign ideology with suspicion and partly because of the widespread religious revival that began with the Methodist movement in the later part of the eighteenth century. This revival both distracted and consoled the suffering poor and made the "atheist" Jacobin an object of horror. The feeling was reinforced a few years later by the patriotic sentiment (powerfully expressed in Wordsworth's sonnets of 1802) that united the nation against France during the most dangerous period of the war. Finally, there was the continuing, pervasive effect of the oratory and pamphlets of the Whig statesman Edmund Burke, who attacked the Revolution. Then, as since, Burke was able, as one writer put it, to "sway the intelligent as a demagogue sways a mob." Nevertheless, the Revolution and its principles had active partisans, such as Tom Paine, who published his *Rights of Man* in 1791-92. Most of the Romantic writers of the first generation—notably Blake, Wordsworth, Coleridge, Southey, Lamb, and Hazlitt—were at first sympathetic to the Revolution, but, except for Blake and Hazlitt, they gradually adopted a more conservative position as their hopes were disappointed by events: the fall from power in France of the more moderate revolutionary party, the Girondins, and the rise of the extreme radicals, or Jacobins; the massacre in September, 1792, of more than a thousand prisoners by the Paris mob; the English war against France, which produced an acute conflict of emotions in these writers, setting love of country against revolutionary hope for mankind; the Reign of Terror in Paris (May, 1793-July, 1794), when thousands of supposed counterrevolutionaries were guillotined by the government of Robespierre; the French aggression against republican Switzerland in 1798; and the *coup d'état* of November, 1799, by which Napoleon siezed power and established a military dictatorship.

Except for one brief peace, England was at war with France for twenty-two years (1793-1815), and for part of this time was without allies and in daily fear of invasion. Thanks to the national ardor and, later, to the genius of Napoleon the French armies usually won on land. England and her allies eventually triumphed because of superior financial strength, control of the sea (confirmed by Nelson's victory at Trafalgar, 1805), Napoleon's insatiable ambition that caused him to overextend himself, and the overwhelming numerical preponderance of the allied armies in the closing years of the war. After Napoleon's abdication the Bourbon kings were restored in France, and the monarchs of Prussia, Russia, and Austria formed an alliance which gradually became an instrument for the suppression of liberal sentiments throughout Europe. For several years English statesmen uneasily cooperated with this policy and thereby earned the hatred of liberals such as Byron and Shelley, who experienced Austrian rule firsthand in Italy. After 1822 English foreign policy wore a more liberal aspect, and the government supported the revolt of the South American republics against Spain and of Greece against Turkey.

Particularly during the early years of the war the Tory government was reactionary and repressive. Liberal and reform movements were blackened with the cry "Jacobin," and their proponents were in jeopardy of prison. Though supported by philosophic radicals, factory workers, wealthy industrialists, and Dissenters (Protestant sects outside the established Anglican Church), proposals to reform Parliament by making it more representative came to nothing. Collective bargaining was outlawed (1799) and mass public meetings of any kind could be held only with permission of the magistrates. Suspected persons were sometimes kept in prison indefinitely without being brought to trial, a procedure that became possible only by suspending *habeas corpus.* Writers in such journals as Francis Jeffrey's liberal *Edinburgh Review* or Leigh Hunt's radical *Examiner* had to be cautious for fear of prosecution under the libel or sedition laws. Government spies and informers—"Satan's Watch-fiends," Blake called them—were active. Coleridge tells how one such eavesdropper reported that he and Wordsworth were discoursing on "Spy Nozy" (actually the philosopher Spinoza). This atmosphere, in which the government feared revolution and the liberals the government, naturally intensified passions and helps to explain, for example, how Blake could be tried for sedition on the word of a soldier and why the Tory journals *Blackwood's Edinburgh Magazine* and *The Quarterly Review* vilified Keats's poetry simply because Keats was associated with Hunt. It also helps to explain the bitterness of liberals such as Hazlitt toward the later conservatism of Southey, Coleridge, and Wordsworth.

Meanwhile, profound social and economic changes were taking place. The Industrial Revolution—the transition from hand and home manufacture of goods to the machine and factory system—meant that people were moving from the country villages to the new factory towns that sprang up, especially in the midlands. Local governments made little provision for the needs of this population for law, health, education, religion, or diversion. Life in the towns was grim and often vicious. The hardships inevitable in such a dislocation were further exacerbated by the reigning economic doctrine of *laissez faire.* It was held that the cheapest production of goods and thus the largest sum of national wealth would be secured if the government did not interfere in the operation of economic laws through the free market. Thus, except to outlaw collective bargaining, the government did nothing to adjust relations between the new capitalists and their employees, and workers had no protection against a sudden loss of employment or reduction of wages. In the countryside other developments resulted in similar distress among the poor. The members of a village had traditionally used some land in common, and for the marginal rural class the opportunity to pasture animals or raise crops on the common land had often made the difference between a meager sufficiency and pauperism. But throughout the eighteenth century improvements brought about by scientific agriculture made it increasingly profitable for private owners to "enclose" and farm these common lands for themselves. The process of enclosure was further accelerated by shortages of food during the war. At the same time, the loss of cottage industries—notably spinning and weaving, which now migrated to the factories—further impoverished the rural poor. During the war the price of food, like all other prices, fluctuated wildly but generally rose because European grain could not be imported. The high price of bread was artificially continued by the Corn Law of 1815 that protected English farmers from foreign competition. Because of the Industrial and Agricultural Revolutions England's wealth and productivity increased enormously during the Romantic Period, and it is probable that even the poor enjoyed, on the whole, a higher standard of living than previously. The cost was a more distant relationship between rich and poor, employers and employees, and a new resentment in the poor, who both in industry and agriculture now felt themselves dependent and insecure.

The Literary Scene

A sketch of the literary milieu may begin with the publishing trade itself. Literacy in Britain had been growing steadily since the Renaissance, and acquaintance with current books was to some degree a social obligation. As a result a large public was willing to pay the relatively high prices of from six shillings to one pound for a volume. (A pound at that time was worth approximately five to seven pounds, or about fifteen to twenty dollars, in present-day purchasing power.) A popular writer could earn a fortune for himself and his publisher. John Murray sold 10,000 copies of Byron's *The Corsair* on the day of publication, and Byron later demanded £2,625 for the fourth canto of *Childe Harold.* Sir Walter Scott may have received from writing as much as £80,000 in his lifetime. But, except for Byron, Scott, and Wordsworth in his later years, the major poets of the age sold very little.

The leading magazines and reviews also had a wide audience. The first of these, *The Edinburgh Review,* was founded in 1802 and became an organ of liberal thought. It included articles on history, politics, and science as well as on imaginative literature, and its influence was considerable. In fact, it was partly because of the structures and ridicule of its editor, Francis Jeffrey, that Wordsworth's reputation advanced so slowly. *The Quarterly Review* was established in 1809 as a

Tory counterpart to *The Edinburgh Review,* and two other prominent journals were the Tory *Blackwood's Edinburgh Magazine,* founded in 1817, and *The London Magazine,* which dates from 1820. *The London Magazine* printed some poems of Keats, Clare, and Hood and first published De Quincey's *Confessions of an English Opium Eater,* portions of Hazlitt's *Table Talk,* and Lamb's *Essays of Elia.* The journals paid contributors well, usually between ten and twenty guineas per sheet; and without the stimulus they provided, less nonfictional prose would have been written. Yet the familiar essays, criticism, and miscellaneous prose of Lamb, Hazlitt, Southey, and De Quincey—all written chiefly for the journals—are among the enduring achievements of the age.

Another outlet, especially for criticism, was public lectures, usually paid for by subscription and given as a series. Most of Coleridge's influential Shakespearean criticism was delivered as such lectures. He spoke from notes, trusting to inspiration, and what he said survives chiefly in fragments. A different method was adopted by Hazlitt, who wrote out his lectures and later published them as books: *Lectures on the English Poets* (1818), *The English Comic Writers* (1819), and *The Dramatic Literature of the Age of Elizabeth* (1820). The first of these series was attended by the young Keats and, with other writings of Hazlitt, helped to waken his moral and poetic ideals of disinterestedness and the sympathetic imagination.

The age produced much drama, but little of value. There are many explanations, including the intimidation the Romantics felt before the examples of Shakespeare and the Elizabethans and their effort to imitate too exclusively the more external aspects of the Elizabethan drama. To this we could add the cramping effect of censorship, which precluded serious discussion of religion or politics. But most important was the state of the acting profession, the theaters, and the audience. The star system prevailed and created a tendency to conceive plays with one or two overwhelming characters. Acting style was declamatory. The theaters were large, so that most playgoers were relatively far from the stage. (Covent Garden Theater had a proscenium approximately forty-three feet wide and thirty-five high and could seat 3,044.) Production costs were high. The audience was noisy and undiscriminating. In these circumstances the theater managers, striving to fill their capacious houses, vied with one another in producing spectacular scenic effects. One piece packed Drury Lane Theater for three weeks by offering such excitements as a burning forest and a lady on horseback riding up the cataract of the Ganges. The possibility and prevalence of such effects may indicate that Shelley's *Prometheus Unbound,* or more especially Byron's *Manfred,* though closet drama, were not so remote from the stage as they now seem. Certainly they show the influence of the contemporary theater. When Byron requires that Arimanes be seated on a "Globe of Fire" or Shelley brings on stage a rushing, whirling sphere of "Ten thousand orbs involving and involved," they are only slightly straining the resources of the theater managers, and the opening of *Prometheus Unbound* in "A Ravine of Icy Rocks in the Indian Caucasus" was routine.

By the early years of the nineteenth century the novel at least rivaled poetry and certainly outstripped the drama as the most popular of literary forms. A swarm of hacks engendered yearly broods for the circulating libraries. At a higher level Ann Radcliffe specialized in gothic novels of terror such as *The Mysteries of Udolpho* (1794) and *The Italian* (1797), the latter presenting as a main attraction the sinister monk Schedoni. To Jane Austen the gothic and sentimental cast of mind was an object for parody, and her portraits of the life of the gentry were worked with a conscious artistry and irony that make her now the most highly esteemed novelist of the period. In the judgment of the age, however, the leading novelist by far was Sir Walter Scott. A mine of antiquarian and historical information, he virtually invented the historical novel in a series of works set in the Middle Ages and in different eras and locales of the Scottish past and present. The charm of local custom and manners was reinforced by picturesque landscape, memorable characters, and rapid adventure. His fame and popularity spread throughout Europe and is one of the important cultural phenomena of the period.

The Romantic Mode

Nevertheless, the supreme achievement of the age was in poetry. From the standpoint of literary history, many of the common themes and styles of the Romantic poets are a development of the efforts of forerunners in the eighteenth century, poets who came after Pope and who, despite their admiration of him, tried to explore new possibilities. From another point of view, the Romantic mode concretely expresses underlying premises as to the nature of reality (which are taken up in a separate section below).

Among the most obvious general features of Romantic poetry are persistent reference to nature and natural objects, intimate self-revelation of the poet, and direct expression of strong, personal emotion. These aspects are so obvious that they are often cited reductively, and some preliminary qualifications are in order. The prominence of landscape and natural objects in this poetry does not necessarily involve a flight from wider concerns to the simplicities of the countryside. For the greater poets, the description of landscape and natural objects was not only a theme but a vehicle, a medium in which intellection was expressed. As Schiller pointed out in his famous essay "On Naive and Sentimental Poetry" (1795-96), the poet in the modern world does not depict nature for its own sake but to convey the "ideal." Similarly, the *étalage du moi* ("display of the self") in this poetry need not reflect egoistic self-absorption but arises partly in the struggle of thinking men to ground speculation and belief in what seemed the most certain facts of experience. So also with the emphasis on feeling, manifested in frequent exclamatory interjections, weighted use of names of emotions together with descriptions of emotional states, and a tendency through the course of a poem to trace not so much the sequence of logical argument or of narration, but rather the evolution and turn of feeling. Wordsworth's formula that "poetry is the spontaneous overflow of powerful feelings" boldly sums up one general presupposition that influenced poets and critics throughout the period. But neither this nor countless similar statements justifies an easy antithesis between the classical and the Romantic by equating it with such antitheses as reason and passion or control and release. Nor does it inevitably imply a supposition that feeling is of itself a good. The essential meaning of the Romantic emphasis on feeling is not cultivation of one quality or power at the expense of others but the pursuit of an ideal of unity or completeness of being.

The imagery of the English Romantic poets reflects, in one of its aspects, a living attention to concrete particulars. "To Generalize," declared Blake in a marginal note, "is to be an Idiot. To Particularize is the Alone Distinction of Merit." The frequent result is a full, vivid, and exact realization of objects. In "This Lime-Tree Bower My Prison," for example, Coleridge devotes three lines to a detailed description of a "Broad and sunny leaf" dappled by the "shadow of the leaf and stem above." Through four lines of "Resolution and Independence" Wordsworth describes a hare running on a moor and raising a mist about her from the "plashy earth." From some of the enthusiastic comments in Keats's letters, it might be inferred that the principal aim of poetry is to catch and render each thing of this world in its full individuality, and his own work provides memorable examples: "The hare limped trembling through the frozen grass," in *The Eve of St. Agnes,* or the "wailful choir" of "small gnats" in the ode "To Autumn":

> Then in a wailful choir the small gnats mourn
> Among the river sallows, borne aloft
> Or sinking as the light wind lives or dies.

In each of these examples objects are seen in a context of other objects and circumstances, and the context gives a further particularity to the image. This vision of things in context informs much Romantic imagery. It has an ontological meaning, but for the moment a more purely literary effect may be noticed, namely, the impression it gives of actual observation and immediate experience.

Yet with this "purchase on matter," as Hazlitt called it, this keeping to "natural bones or substance," the Romantics seldom sought or achieved the detached, scientific objectivity that was held as an ideal in the "realism" of the later part of the century. Keats especially valued a responsiveness so keen and massive that it brings about a sympathetic identification. This state of mind, which Hazlitt characterized as "gusto," manifests itself in an imagery of densely intertwined impressions, often taking the form of synaesthesia (the interpretation of one sense by another, as in the phrase "soft incense") and often including a dynamic, even organic participation in the life of the thing portrayed. More commonly, Romantic poetry renders things not as they are "in themselves" (supposing that were possible) but as they are modified in perception by the thoughts and feelings of the poet. In this process objects and scenes, though present in thick, substantial being, also become outward expressions of human insight and feeling.

To this must be added the pervasive reliance on the quality of suggestion. For the whole context of any event or object might be specified to some degree, but it could not possibly be exhausted descriptively or known completely. Hence the Romantics prized a use of language that would remain open to all that could not be said and, at the same time, summon the imaginative energies of the reader. "The power of poetry," said Coleridge, lecturing on Shakespeare's *The Tempest,*

> is, by a single word perhaps, to instil that energy into the mind, which compels the imagination to produce the picture. Prospero tells Miranda,

> "One midnight,
> Fated to the purpose, did Antonio open
> The gates of Milan; and i' the dead of darkness,
> The ministers for the purpose hurried thence
> Me, and thy *crying* self."

> Here, by introducing a single happy epithet, "crying," in the last line, a complete picture is presented to the mind, and in the production of such pictures the power of genius consists.

Most Romantic poets believed in the reality of a supersensuous or noumenal realm of being. The intuition of this could be expressed only by suggestion, and thus suggestive uses of language often appear in poems or passages that, for readers in the period, belonged to the widely recognised category of the "sublime." The term, popularized throughout the eighteenth century, had referred to objects of overwhelming vastness or power, or to the state of mind felt in their presence; in the Romantic age it came also to designate more particularly that state of mind arising in contact, either direct or through analogy, with the transcendent and infinite. Thus "the grandest efforts of poetry," Coleridge said,

> are when the imagination is called forth, not to produce a distinct form, but a strong working of the mind, still offering what is still repelled, and again creating what is again rejected; the result being what the poet wishes to impress, namely, the substitution of a sublime feeling of the unimaginable for a mere image.

Often the quest for the "unimaginable" through suggestion took another form in evoking the mysterious, occult, and supernatural. This became something of a fad and was often pursued for its own sake, but of such poems as Keats's "La Belle Dame sans Merci" and Coleridge's "The Ancient Mariner," "Christabel," and "Kubla Khan" with its famous lines

> A savage place! as holy and enchanted
> As e'er beneath a waning moon was haunted
> By woman wailing for her demon-lover!

the most general meaning lies in the reminder of what Wordsworth called "unknown modes of being," of a reality beyond the limited, empirical one that comes to us through our senses and understanding. It was from reading the *Arabian Nights,* said Coleridge, and similar tales of "Giants & Magicians, & Genii" that his mind "had been habituated *to the Vast*—& I never regarded *my senses* in any way as the criteria of my belief."

Some of the aspects of imagery already mentioned—the involvement of the mind in the object, the reliance on suggestion—approximate what would ordinarily be called symbolism. Certainly both the term and the way of thinking and writing it describes have a large place in poetic theory of the period, especially that of Coleridge and Shelley, and in the practice of all the major poets. There was, however, no one theory or practice, and perhaps the chief general statement that can be made is simply that the Romantics did not possess a traditional symbolism of which the meaning or reference is determined by convention. In them one finds instead what has become more explicit and conscious in contemporary poets such as Yeats and T. S. Eliot, who adopted it as the chief technique of the *Four Quartets:* images recur in the work of a writer and bring associations from the poems or passages in which they had been used before; these images thus acquire increasing depth of implication and in them the writer gradually develops a personal symbolism. This appears in its most systematic form in Blake's "prophetic" poems and is perhaps least apparent in Keats. However, Keats's odes are the finest examples in the period of what may be called the poetry of symbolic debate. In these poems a central symbolism—the nightingale, the Grecian urn—enables the poet to engage conflicting values and attitudes concretely and to achieve at least an *ad hoc* resolution. A special type of Romantic symbolism arises in what may be called visionary poetry. This is found in poems presenting superhuman beings in a dreamlike realm, as in Shelley's *Prometheus Unbound* or Keats's "The Fall of Hyperion," and also in the use of an imagery wrenched out of natural contexts and relations. For example, Blake's "The Tyger" shows a blacksmith creating a tiger, and Shelley for symbolic purposes in "The Witch of Atlas" sends an open boat beneath the surface of a river. Visionary symbolism often implies a belief that ultimate truth lies beyond nature rather than in it, and that to reflect the supernatural and eternal, a poet must articulate images in total freedom.

The diction and syntax of Romantic verse, like much else besides, were strongly influenced by ideals of spontaneity or naturalness. When in the Preface to the *Lyrical Ballads* Wordsworth asked himself the crucial question "What is a Poet?" he gave the revolutionary though not unprecedented answer that a poet is a "man speaking to men." The traditional view had been that a poet is a "maker," and this implied a more detached relation between the poet and his work and also between the poet and his readers. As a "speaker" the Romantic poet was likely to avoid the appearance and to some degree the fact of predeliberating artistry, partly because this might seem insincere and partly because spontaneity, immediacy, or naturalness were thought to have an inherent value in bringing us closer to the poet and to actual experience. Thus in "Hyperion" Keats produced the most brilliant of the many Miltonic imitations, yet he quickly abandoned the style: "Miltonic verse cannot be written but in an artful or rather artist's humour." One of his "Axioms" was that "if Poetry comes not as naturally as the Leaves to a tree it had better not come at all." In this spirit Wordsworth's Preface to the *Lyrical Ballads* specifically condemned poetic diction, periphrasis, and "personifications of abstract ideas"— conventions in the poetry of the previous hundred years— and affirmed that one "principal object" was "as far as is possible, to adopt the very language of men." Though this intention applied *in toto* only to some poems in the *Lyrical Ballads,* an ideal of easy naturalness modified the phrasing of Wordsworth and Coleridge throughout their careers—one may think of Wordsworth's "Michael," for example, where a child herding sheep is "Something between a hindrance and a help"—and this ideal was caught up and carried further by the second generation of poets: Keats, Shelley, and especially Byron. In syntactical arrangement the Romantics (except Byron in his satires) strove to avoid the balance and antithesis they especially associated with Pope and judged "mechanical." Instead their sentence structure is often unpremeditated, digressive, and accumulative as it enacts the drama of the mind's free movement. "My thoughts," said Coleridge, "bustle along like a Surinam toad, with little toads sprouting out of back, side and belly, vegetating while it crawls."

Intellectual Background

British Empiricism

The most influential English philosopher throughout the eighteenth century was John Locke, two of whose assertions may be noticed here. In the first place, Locke put in a new form the old argument that only particular, concrete things exist. General terms such as "man," "freedom," and so forth name ideas that we have abstracted from experience, and such ideas have no counterpart in reality. (For example, there is no essence or substance "man" but only individual men.) In the second place, denying the existence of innate ("inborn") ideas, Locke held that the mind at birth may be compared to a *tabula rasa* (smoothed tablet) on which impres-

sions are engraved as we grow up. These impressions are always sensory, and thus sensations are the ultimate source of all our ideas.

This analysis, or rather the whole tradition of British empirical psychology and philosophy that flowed from it, profoundly supported tendencies and premises in Romantic literature that were also developing from other sources. For one thing, if real things are always particular, it might easily be argued that they are always unique. Thus, especially in the criticism of Hazlitt, "truth" as the aim of art might shift its traditional meaning. No longer referring to permanent, universal forms or types, truth might now require that an object be presented with full concreteness and with a highlight on what peculiarly characterizes or differentiates it. An art thus bringing forth distinct individualities or identities was, for Hazlitt, "expressive," and in his estimates of books and paintings the criterion of "expressiveness" usually predominates. In this sense, British empiricism strongly reinforced the particularist and circumstantial bias in Romantic poetry.

The same tradition also encouraged a literature of self-expression and the subjective exploration of the writer's mind and feelings. One stimulus was simply the attention given by Locke and his followers to facts and processes of mind. This of itself promoted introspection. There were, however, more urgent considerations. If all ideas, including general ones, come ultimately from concrete experience and refer back to it, that experience is by definition personal and differs from one individual to another. Moreover, psychological theory in the later eighteenth century usually explained the unity of the mind by the association of ideas. It was held that when two or more ideas are linked together, as by succession in time, simultaneity in space, and so forth, one idea will thereafter recall the other. Thus gradually a system of associative links is set up such that the whole mind is latently present at any moment. But in any particular mind what associative links are actually established is to some degree accidental. To this must be added the disturbing arguments of David Hume, in whose philosophy the empirical tradition led to a throughgoing scepticism. To Hume it seemed that since we have cognizance only of the contents of our own minds, we can never know that our sensations or ideas correspond to what exists outside us. For example, we can never know that one thing is the cause of another, for we experience only the succession of two ideas, not those realities in which the supposed principle of cause and effect may or may not operate. Hume thus denied the possibilities either of directly knowing the real world or of making any necessary inferences concerning it. While this extreme position was not generally adopted, there was a widespread assumption that one's hold upon objective truth is uncertain and that opinions and assertions can be spoken only from a personal point of view, that is, with reference to one's own experience and consciousness. It was perhaps with some such recognition that Coleridge resolved "to write my metaphysical works, as my Life, & in my Life, intermixed with all the other events or history of the mind & fortunes of S. T. Coleridge," a project partly fulfilled in *Biographia Literaria.*

A further inducement to self-expression developed from the premise of the unique character of each individual. Just as art, looking outward, might strive to disclose the particular identity of other objects or persons, so the poet might legitimately disclose his own identity, and readers might welcome intimacy with a being both unique and exceptionally gifted.

1795 portrait of Samuel Taylor Coleridge by P. Vandyke.

"Poetry without egotism," Coleridge remarked, is "comparatively uninteresting." Thus originality, which had once implied merely novel inventiveness or had been applied as a cant term to "natural" or untaught poets such as Burns and Clare, came to be regarded as the inevitable result of successful self-expression, and at the same time it acquired the peculiar sanction it still to some degree retains. "Points have we all of us," said Wordsworth, "where all stand single,"— "Something within which yet is shared by none." The effort of the poet is to impart his special dower, "Heaven's gift . . . that fits him to perceive / Objects unseen before." In an extreme espousal of Romantic views, the development and expression of one's originality might seem almost a sacred duty. It was a dynamic cooperation with the creating, proliferating energies of the cosmos, in which the cosmos itself was enriched and at the same time reflected from a novel point of view.

Transcendentalism

Romantic transcendentalism arose as a direct reaction against the emppirical tradition. In the philosophy of Kant "transcendental" refers to the *a priori* element in experience—that is, the way in which the mind determines and orders its own contents through its own laws—and the term "transcendent" refers to ideas, such as freedom of the will, God, and immortality, that cannot become objects of knowledge. More generally, transcendentalism is the belief in the existence of a timeless realm of being beyond the shifting, sensory world of common experience. It was nourished in the Romantic Period from many sources—Plato and the Neopla-

tonic philosophers, contemporary German idealism, occult and theosophical writings, and, at least in Blake, Wordsworth, and Shelley, from personal experiences sometimes called mystical. (Transcendentalism as an element in the Romantic philosophy of organicism will be discussed later.) In Shelley especially, however, the cosmos is conceived less as an organic whole and more as divided between the actual, concrete, present world and the ideal or transcendent that lies beyond. The first has an inferior degree of reality, while the second is the goal of aspiration and the true home of the human spirit. At moments one may intuit or, as Keats said, "guess at" the realm of timeless and perfect being, and to express or convey such moments, with their overwhelming impact on thought and feeling, is the highest aim of poetry.

Time, History, and Nostalgia

As a third influence on Romantic literature, in addition to empirical and transcendental premises, one may note the more modern consciousness of time and history that had been emerging throughout the eighteenth century. This may be described in brief as a shift toward a genetic and historically relative point of view. Increasingly the assumption was that both social institutions and personal character could be understood only by examining the historical circumstances that shaped their origin and growth. For example, Wordsworth's *Prelude* is a long, introspective, biographical account of his own development, the purpose of which was to interpret his present character and to determine, he says, his qualifications for writing a major philosophic poem. Human nature, which classical and neoclassical thinkers had presumed to be essentially the same in all times and places, now appeared to be molded by history and therefore susceptible of fundamental change. Supposedly universal standards could not so readily be invoked, for it could be argued that moral and literary rules lose validity and pertinence with the passage of time. (pp. 4-14)

The historical point of view induced a tendency to balance progress against loss. But however mindful of present advantages one might strive to be, it was not easy to think of the times forever gone without also sliding into regret. Unquestionably the consciousness that time brings fundamental change and that the past is irrecoverable was a principal source of Romantic nostalgia, a state of mind so pervasive that it is often said to be the essence of Romanticism. With respect to what may be called cultural nostalgia, however, it should be stressed that at least in England it rarely involved a genuine assumption that some past age or alien state was more to be valued than the present. Thus "primitivism," the glowing description of the virtues of the "state of nature" as it might be imagined in prehistoric man, American Indians (the "noble savage"), Scotch Highlanders, children, or (notably by Wordsworth) the peasantry of England, did not usually express a wish to go back or away but was rather a wistful sense of loss, a reaction against urban complexity and artifice, and a potent means of criticizing contemporary society. So also with the attraction to the Middle Ages, as in Scott's novels and poems or Keats's *The Eve of St. Agnes,* or to the Renaissance, as in Hunt's "Story of Rimini" or Keats's *Isabella,* or to ancient Greece dreamily conceived, as in Keats's *Endymion,* or to the contemporary Near East as with Byron. In all these instances the nostalgia was partly for a setting that contrasted with the present by allowing color, adventure, mystery, sincerity, simplicity, passion, and beauty.

Nostalgia toward one's own past was naturally more intense

and less manageable. The changes that time brings in the self and its world are a major theme of Romantic literature, and, though Wordsworth tried to do so in such poems as "Intimations of Immortality" and "Elegiac Stanzas on . . . Peele Castle," it was not easy to find in adult maturity a compensation for the loss of youth. Most especially is this true with such writers as Wordsworth and Shelley, who felt that childhood or youth had been marked by moments of profound intuition or visionary insight no longer experienced. But the same thing was felt by writers who lay no claim to moments of special illumination. Nostalgia—the vivid, tender, descriptive cherishing and sorrow for the past—dominates the familiar essays of Lamb and Hazlitt, and, with the implication of a heart now jaded and guilt-hardened, it sweeps through much of Byron: "No more—no more—Oh! never more on me / The freshness of the heart can fall like dew."

Organicism

Romantic organicism was an attempt to reconcile in a profounder conception the several premises already discussed. The opposition of empiricism and transcendentalism was itself one ramification of questions that had been taken up in philosophy at least since Plato and that Descartes (1596-1650) had formulated in a way that challenged thinkers for the next hundred and fifty years. According to Descartes reality is comprised of three principles or substances—matter, mind, and God—and the difficulty was to show how these are interconnected. By the early nineteenth century the issue was usually posed in terms of such dualisms as matter and mind, the real and the ideal, or nature and God. One might, with Spinoza, adopt a pantheist solution by arguing that matter and mind are both modifications of the one substance, God, or one might, as was often the case in British empiricism (especially as it was taken over and developed by French writers), strive to show that the mind is not a separate substance but a mode of physical or material activity. In Kant and his successors throughout the nineteenth century, on the other hand, the philosophy of idealism stressed the mental or ideal as a distinct component of reality and maintained that the mind, instead of depending on impressions from without, has the prime role in the creation of what we know as experience. The idealists argued, for example, that values such as beauty or goodness are real but not learned from experience. Instead they are either determined by the mind in an *a priori* way, or, as in Plato, they exist in a transcendent realm that is at least partially disclosed to human beings. Through his free will (the existence of which empiricists often denied) man then strives to express these values in his own acts—in other words, to bring value into the realm of concrete phenomena. Organicism abandons these dualisms by conceiving the cosmos (reality) as a process rather than as a substance, an activity in which the material world, the mental or ideal, and the Divine mutually involve or interpenetrate each other.

Among philosophers the concept of organicism was especially developed by the German idealists and, in an entirely different way in our own century, in the brilliant, difficult metaphysics of Alfred North Whitehead. In the English Romantic writers it is present as a basic conception of reality that is often expounded abstractly (especially by Wordsworth and Coleridge) but still more frequently manifests itself as it guides critical interpretation and poetic vision. This poetry, as Whitehead said, could be described as a "protest on behalf of the organic view of nature," and the protest based itself on "the concrete facts of our apprehension." That is, in immedi-

ate awareness we do not distinguish what the mind has contributed from what comes from without. Values, for example, such as beauty or goodness are felt as aspects of concrete experience, and it is only by a secondary act of abstraction that we say they have their source only in the mind or only in the transcendent or empirical realms. Unless, therefore, by analysis we chop an experience into separate aspects ("we murder to dissect," as Wordsworth put it), we will not argue that values are any more or less "real" than whatever other aspect or object we may discriminate in the wholeness of the immediate event. Objects themselves, moreover, emerge in actual perception with an infinite background of which we are always to some extent aware. So in Wordsworth, said Whitehead, it is

> the brooding presence of the hills which haunts him. His theme is nature *in solido*, that is to say, he dwells on that mysterious presence of surrounding things, which imposes itself on any separate element that we set up as an individual for its own sake. He always grasps the whole of nature as involved in the tonality of the particular instance.

And we should add that, for Wordsworth, the "whole of nature" involves also the Divine.

The organicist vision of nature thus had a profound impact on poetic theory and critical values. The implications were articulated chiefly by Coleridge in the concept of "organic form," which is, in many respects, a rationale of the working procedures of Romantic poetry. The argument was that a poem manifests a process that is at least analogous to that of reality itself. It fuses, Coleridge said, the universal with the particular, the idea with the image, the part with the whole; it exists both as a unity and as an activity that develops through time; it reconciles spontaneity with inevitability and law. A model or analogy often proposed was a growing tree. One may say that the universal principle or form of a tree is implicit in the seed, yet it declares itself only through time. The form does not exist independent of the concrete manifestation, and it expresses itself in each part, as also the existence of each part presupposes the whole. Coleridge often contrasted organic with "mechanical" form. The "mechanical," he said (paraphrasing A. W. Schlegel), is predetermined and subsequently impressed on whatever material we choose, as when "to a mass of wet clay we give whatever shape we wish it to retain when hardened." The organic form, on the other hand, "shapes as it develops itself from within, and the fullness of its development is one and the same with the perfection of its outward form." Each exterior thus becomes a "true image" of "the being within." The concept of organic form provided a fundamental justification for art, which could be regarded as a means of concretely knowing or even participating in reality as process. It also gave rise to an approach to art that stressed sympathetic identification rather than analysis from a critical distance. And it stimulated a criterion of evaluation that rests on the extent to which all the "parts" of a work of art (plot, character, emotion, theme, image, and the like) interconnect and sustain one another. This relationship was, however, to be sensed immediately, and it is doubtful whether Coleridge would have approved much of the criticism of our own time that applies this criterion by piecemeal analysis.

The Imagination

In the Romantic Period much of the speculation outlined above centers around the term "imagination." Until the later eighteenth century the term had usually denoted the faculty by which we form mental images of things not present to our senses or held in memory. This faculty could also combine ideas in ways not warranted by experience, as when the idea of supernatural power is joined to the shape and passions of man in order to produce the gods of Greek mythology. As the example suggests, the imagination thus described was thought to have a large role in poetry, but it was far from being the essential power of poetry simply because it was not necessarily or even probably directed to reality or truth. As conceptions of reality changed, however, a new way of knowing it had to be described, and the term "imagination" gradually extended its meaning. There was, however, no single interpretation of the imagination, for this varied with the general context of thought in the different writers. (pp. 15-17)

In its most general significance, "imagination" denoted a working of the mind that is total, synthetic, immediate, and dynamic. In this sense, the theory of the imagination was a reaction not only against empirical analysis but also against the traditional faculty psychology, of which the vocabulary, at least, persisted throughout the nineteenth century. This psychology conceived the mind as exhibiting separate powers or functions (sensation, memory, reason, emotion, and so forth), and not all of these functions were necessarily engaged in any particular act of the mind. Thus mathematics was thought to involve a step-by-step proceeding of just one faculty, and similarly emotion might be disengaged from reason or sensation from emotion. Granting that the mind can indeed work this way, the Romantic writers held that in doing so it loses touch with the fullness of reality. If this reality inheres in concretely individuated particulars, then the imagination may be described, with Hazlitt, as the immediate response of all faculties at once to the particular object, and also the coalescence or synthesis of the impressions thus received into a unified mental construct that corresponds in every way to its object. One should stress the concrete richness of the image thus created, for it may be so distinct and vivid that one forgets one's own separate identity and lives in the object. Thus the imagination in its highest working becomes "sympathetic," freeing one from self-consciousness and self-interest and enabling one to enter into the experience and feelings of other persons and even into animals and inanimate objects. "If a sparrow come before my window," said Keats, "I take part in its existence and pick about the gravel," and Byron proclaimed, "I live not in myself, but I become / Portion of that around me." The same sympathy could also be given, Keats reminds us, to "creations of my own brain"; this further explains Keats's conception, derived from Hazlitt, of the poet of "Negative Capability" whose own identity never appears in his work, a type of poetic character of which Shakespeare was clearly the supreme example. Moreover, the same loss of self in sympathetic identification could be felt before the landscape as a whole, as is often the case in Wordsworth and Byron, and sometimes in Shelley.

However, the term could also designate a power able to commune with transcendent reality. In Shelley it is sometimes identified with the Platonic reason (*nous*). In connection with organicism, on the other hand, the imagination, as the active coalescing of all faculties of the mind, involves faculties empirically directed to the outer world, as the senses, faculties through which we have access to our own human nature, as the emotions, and a faculty of transcendent intuition (which Coleridge, at least, usually called reason). Thus only through the imagination can we apprehend reality in its organic

wholeness and process. Especially in Wordsworth, however, the term is invested with so much significance that different implications are highlighted in different contexts. Sometimes it appears that when the imagination is most fully roused the senses fail ("the light of sense goes out"), and the imagination achieves a direct intuition of one's own nature and of transcendent truth inwardly possessed. More frequently, however, Wordsworth describes imagination as a "modifying" power by which the mind imposes itself in the act of perception, thereby immediately endowing the thing perceived with passion and with symbolic meaning.

The Figure of the Poet

"A man may write at any time," said Dr. Johnson, "if he will set himself doggedly to it." As for genius, it is nothing more than general and capacious power of mind. These opinions, like so many of Johnson's, express an instinctive recoil from what he regarded as cant, and they help measure the distance between the classical position (for which Johnson is in many ways the greatest English spokesman) and the oncoming Romantics, standing in awe before what Coleridge called "the creative, productive life-power of inspired genius." The difference, however, lay not in reverence for poets (or rather, for the ideal figure of the poet, since living writers profited little from the emotion). This had always been felt. The point is that it was now felt with an intensity that itself distinguished the Romantic Period. And it was based on different concepts. Creation, for example, had earlier been the prerogative of God; artists aspired to reproduce or "imitate" His works, not His way of working, and thereby to express the general and permanent truths of nature and the moral law. Throughout the eighteenth century, however, there was a growing tendency to understand the artist's creative act by analogy with that of God. A poet, it seemed, might bring forth a new nature; and his works, or even a single work, might be regarded as his independent universe, complete in itself, harmonious, and obedient to its own laws. The analogy, which still influences criticism, naturally reorganized emotions along with conceptions.

In Plato the image of the inspired poet is that of a man suddenly possessed by a god who speaks through him. Coming after a hundred years of empirical, psychological speculation, the Romantics seldom claimed divine seizure (though there are versions of this view, especially in Shelley and Blake), but they nevertheless stressed that a poet is inspired. This was interpreted either as an invasion of the conscious mind from the unconscious or, more frequently, as a peculiarly rapid and total mental functioning, a sudden and more intense degree of what was described above in connection with the imagination. Inspiration implied that poetry was to some degree involuntary—according to Shelley, "A man cannot say, 'I will compose poetry' "—and also that poetry allows readers access to moments of peculiarly heightened intellection. To quote Shelley again, "Poetry is the record of the best and happiest moments of the happiest and best minds." A mind thus creative and inspired characterized "genius," which was often contrasted with mere talent. Where the man of talent may note only a few premises, proceed step-by-step, and stay within the boundaries of tradition and convention, the working of genius is original, comprehensive, immediate, and unerring. For Hazlitt, Coleridge was "the only person I ever knew who answered to the idea of a man of genius. . . . His thoughts did not seem to come with labour and effort; but as if borne on the gusts of genius, and as if the wings of his imagination lifted him from off his feet." In *The Prelude* Wordsworth looks back to the strength of imagination in childhood and youth with the same Romantic awe:

> Of genius, power,
> Creation and divinity itself
> I have been speaking, for my theme has been
> What passed within me
>
> [III. 173-76].

Inevitably the figure of the poet or artist was likely to be presented in strongest contrast with the rest of mankind, the "trembling throng," Shelley called them, "Whose sails were never to the tempest given." The poet is on a quest, and as such he is a dedicated and heroic being. For this reason, he may be lonely among other men who cannot share his insight or his quest. To the generality of mankind, Wordsworth acknowledged in *The Prelude,* the poet may appear mad. Even if he were, reverence would still be due him, for he would have been

> crazed
> By love and feeling, and internal thought
> Protracted among endless solitudes
>
> [V. 145-47].

But the truth is, Wordsworth adds, that even "in the blind and awful lair / Of such a madness" dwells a power of insight inconceivable to others. Moreover, the intense self-commitment of the poet to his quest justifies him in casting off the lesser responsibilities of littler men:

> Enow there are on earth to take in charge
> Their wives, their children, and their virgin loves,
> Or whatsoever else the heart holds dear;
> Enow to stir for these;
>
> [V. 153-56].

and Wordsworth, like most of the Romantic poets, could think of himself as a "Pilgrim of Eternity"—Shelley's phrase for Byron.

The quest pursues an infinite, perhaps unknown ideal—complete being, final truth—and therefore the poet's life is endless striving. In this, however, as in many other respects, he is not distinguished from other men so far as they are sensitive and aware. Perhaps at death, Shelley felt, "the pure spirit shall flow / Back to the burning fountain whence it came," but while we live in time we are trapped in a hopeless wish for the inaccessible—"the desire of the moth for the star." Or perhaps, as sometimes in Wordsworth, a man through his infinite striving participates in the open, endless process of becoming that characterizes reality itself:

> Our destiny, our being's heart and home,
> Is with infinitude, and only there;
> With hope it is, hope that can never die,
> Effort, and expectation, and desire,
> And something evermore about to be
>
> [XI. 604-08].

Or perhaps man's infinite desire is simply to undergo all experience. In this sense, greatness may be fatal, a fever, Byron said, that drives him ever onward without rest or satisfaction.

In the quest of the infinite the poet-hero might be represented not only as great but as guilty. Even in Keats's conception of the Shakespearean poet of "negative capability," the imagination, as it seeks to encompass the whole of reality, is not limited by moral allegiances and "has as much delight in conceiving an Iago as an Imogen." More generally, to seek ulti-

mate truth implies that it is not already possessed, and thus the poet might figure as the rejecter or defier of tradition, convention, law, religion, and the collected social or even supernatural powers that seek to chain the human spirit. Thus the poet could be seen as creative in metaphysical insight and moral conduct, redeeming men from error and empty guilt and awakening in them a higher ideal. Or he could be seen as disclosing the existential loneliness of man in a vast cosmos without meaning or purpose. Or, finally, he could be seen as a guilty transgressor, stepping beyond the legitimate boundaries of knowledge and morality. Many of the major, recurrent figures of what one might call the Romantic legendry are heroic rebels—Prometheus, Napoleon, Satan, Don Juan, Cain—but the implications of this rebellion are often ambiguous, and they vary from one writer to another, reflecting tensions in the writers themselves and in the period. (pp. 18-21)

> *David Perkins, in an introduction to* English Romantic Writers, *edited by David Perkins, Harcourt Brace Jovanovich, 1967, pp. 1-24.*

J. B. PRIESTLEY

[*A highly prolific English man of letters, Priestley is the author of numerous popular novels that depict the world of everyday, middle-class England. In this respect, Priestley has often been likened to Charles Dickens, a critical comparison that he dislikes. His most notable critical work is* Literature and Western Man *(1960), a survey of Western literature from the invention of movable type through the mid-twentieth century. In the following excerpt from the chapter "The English Romantics" in that work, Priestley discusses the major Romantic poets.*]

The 'English' in the [chapter title 'The English Romantics'] really refers to the language in which these romantic authors wrote, not to their nationality. True, most of them were English in both senses of the term, but not all. Indeed, Robert Burns, who cannot be ignored, was not only a Scot but also wrote almost all his best verse in a broad Scots dialect, almost a separate language. He is entirely an eighteenth-century figure, and stands outside the Romantic Movement, though there are romantic elements in his work. He is very much of his country, which even today regards him affectionately as a national representative figure rather than as one of its authors. He passionately proclaims what almost every Scot, from lords at the head of ancient clans to peasant ploughmen, have thought and felt. The Scots are an odd people, more sharply divided than most between an austere piety and a rather grim devotion to knowledge, on the one side, and, on the other, a violent and reckless love of wine, woman and song, that no poet has celebrated more lustily than Burns, though he was equally capable of praising the industriousness, frugality and innocent family life of the opposite party. He was not concerned about having a fixed attitude and being consistent; he was a poet of the people, both the virtuous and the wicked, conscientious peasant proprietors and jolly beggars on the road, understood them all, having shared their lives, their toil and frugality and their debauchery; and it is all there, expressed with frankness and gusto, in his narrative poems and songs, especially in his songs, which have both satirical sharpness and lyrical beauty. Burns has the wide range of sympathy, the balance of classical and romantic elements, of a great poet, all the breadth if not (except to the Scots) all the height and depth; he might be described as one of the humbler and more limited master singers.

Another poet who is outside the Romantic Movement—and

one who could never be included in any movement—is William Blake, artist, writer and seer. He lived and died in poverty and obscurity, and his complete originality of outlook and a few personal eccentricities encouraged those who knew him only slightly to believe he was insane. And no doubt those who believe that the society we have created during the last hundred and fifty years is essentially sound and healthy will continue to believe, if they ever think about him, that Blake was insane. But there is more profit for mind and soul in believing our society to be increasingly insane, and Blake (as the few who knew him well always declared) to be sound and healthy. And as doubt about our mechanical progress has grown, so has Blake's stature both as a poet and thinker, and it has not stopped growing yet. He was born in 1757 but decisively rejected everything that the eighteenth century upheld, and even a rebel like Rousseau was among his dislikes. He looks back to Böhme, to the strange and obscure sects of Germany in the sixteenth century and of England in the mid-seventeenth century, and forward to the analytical psychology of Jung and his school in our time, men whose criticism of our society he would have applauded; and the only contemporary to whom he can be linked at all is that odd and strongly original Scandinavian religious philosopher and mystic, Swedenborg. Both men boldly described their visions, but Blake was better equipped for the task, being both poet and painter. His writing consists of his poems, largely lyrical and, in spite of occasional faulty diction and careless phrasing, blazing with genius; his aphorisms and critical notes in prose, frequently very profound and always lively reading; and his 'prophetic books', highly symbolic and very obscure and often rather repellent narrative poems. In his early *Songs of Innocence*—and the contrast between innocence and experience was one of Blake's great themes—he seems to recapture an Elizabethan freshness, zest, careless ecstasy, as no other lyrical poet has done before or since his time. And between these early songs and the mysterious craggy 'prophetic books' he produced a small number of poems, usually lyrical in style, equally remarkable for their force, bold originality, and the haunting beauty of their symbolic imagery.

We have seen how ever since the high Middle Ages, when Western Man achieved a complete religious basis and framework to his life, men had felt the loss of this basis and framework. The secret of William Blake, and the key to both his strength and his weakness as a poet, is that he recreated this basis and framework for himself. He can be called a one-man religious revival. But it is the fundamental religious attitude, not the beliefs and dogma, forms and ceremonies, once associated with it, he is reviving. He makes this very plain:

> I must Create a System, or be enslav'd by another Man's;
> I will not Reason and Compare: my business is to Create.

At the centre of his system is the creative imagination, which he associates with Christ, as against the Jesus who belongs to mere ecclesiasticism, to the accusers and judges of sin. He was the enemy of eighteenth-century Reason, which he recognized, with profound intuition, as the analytical intellect, losing itself in lifeless abstractions, entangling us more and more in the opposites, destroying the natural balance and the interplay of psychic energy between consciousness and the unconscious. One of his strongest pieces, *The Marriage of Heaven and Hell,* not only anticipates the discoveries of depth psychology but also reveals how close his thought came to the profoundest Oriental philosophy, then unknown. Again, his understanding of sex, his mistrust of the growing demands of

collective organisations on the individual, his dislike of the Industrial Revolution (his "dark satanic mills") then in its first phase, his equation of all serious art with the religious attitude, help to explain why a man once regarded as a harmless lunatic, or an eccentric with lyrical genius, is now more and more carefully studied as a man of prophetic insight and deep natural wisdom. And even among English-speaking readers he has not yet arrived at his full stature. Here, in this steady growth and deepening of interest, is the proof of his strength. His weakness, when he is considered as anything except the author of a few enchanting lyrics, is that the religious basis and framework are of his own creation; he had to discover and use his own symbols, so that much of his work seems almost as obscure as if it had been written in a private language. His drawings, which often illustrate his poems, are of some help, but too often they are filled with figures from his own personal mythology. There are some men, of great personality and power, who seem by some mistake of the divinities to have been dropped on the right planet but at the wrong time, or to have arrived at the right time but on the wrong planet; and Blake is one of them. His work, ranging from pure song to obscure epics of unconscious processes, at its best blazes with genius and at its worst still flickers with it, the genius of a seer who looks beyond the immediate ages of Reason and Romance, and cannot be adequately interpreted in terms of either. Probably his own time has still to come.

This period in English literature, giving it some of its finest poetry, is often called the Romantic Revival. But this is misleading, for nothing in fact was revived. The typical eighteenth-century judgments on the value of medieval and Elizabethan literature were sharply reversed, and so was that century's opinion of itself. Much from the more distant past was rediscovered, both by the romantic poets and by the few critics, notably Hazlitt, Lamb and Leigh Hunt, who were in sympathy with them. But they were not returning in spirit to these earlier ages, were not attempting to revive them; they were consciously expressing a new age, a new spirit and outlook. These Romantics were the up-to-date men; it was their hostile critics, the spokesmen of the ponderous official reviews, still drearily trying to maintain eighteenth-century standards, who were old-fashioned, out of date. But these English poets and the few critics and essayists who admired them did not see themselves co-operating in a definite movement, conducting an æsthetic campaign. Unlike the French and Germans and other continentals, the English never have such campaigns. There has always been in English writers a strong individualistic strain that discourages any such concerted action, and the Romantics were individualists to a man. Again, English society is neither fiercely hostile to new literary ideas nor enthusiastic about them; it is blandly indifferent to any æsthetic problems. How the English, who mostly care less about literature than other peoples, have contrived to produce such an astounding array of literary genius is one of the mysteries of this life. What is certain is that what was elsewhere a definite Romantic Movement, as in Germany complete with periodicals and publishers, philosophers and courses of university lectures, was in England a mere drift towards romantic writing.

This drift, however, produced some of the great literature of the language. Not the greatest, though, and not great at all in some forms of literature. This age failed in the drama, though not from want of trying. Apart from the incomparable Jane Austen, who had no more to do with the Romantics than if they had been on the moon, and whose whole tone and quality are exquisitely classical, it failed in the novel proper. Its history and biography show us nothing to compare with Gibbon's *Decline and Fall* or Boswell's immortal *Life of Johnson*. But it is great and triumphant in its poetry and its miscellaneous prose, the essay and very personal occasional criticism. And being a highly individualistic age, even for this nation of individualists, it is particularly rich in authors who are fascinating personalities, around whose lives scores of volumes have been written. The political differences of the time were sharply challenging, especially during the years immediately following the French Revolution and then later during the reaction that followed the defeat of Napoleon; but it is typical of this English period that the romantic writers cannot be found all in one political camp, that they too were divided in their opinions and sympathies. Thus Hazlitt, as literary critic, stoutly championed the work of Wordsworth and Coleridge, but, in his polemics, fiercely attacked them for what he considered their apostasy to the principles of the French Revolution. Byron and Scott, though the two greatest romantic influences in Europe, were poles apart in politics. Shelley was too extreme for anybody's agreement. The aristocrats among them became the revolutionaries; the poor young men gradually transformed themselves into High Tories. The period is as rich in contradictions, ironies, absurdities, as it is in personalities.

One of its ironies, more important to us here than the rest, is that its two most influential figures, Scott and Byron, who for many years dominated the Romantic Movement throughout the Western world, were not themselves the kind of Romantics that Rousseau produced, and at heart did not belong to the Movement at all. Let us take Walter Scott, the older man, first. His narrative verse had its day—he survives as a poet through a few short pieces in the manner of the Border ballads—but of course it was his Waverley novels or historical romances that made him famous both at home and abroad. Their immediate success was stupendous; they were read with enthusiasm by all classes of readers in all civilised countries, and very soon imitated: Scott is the father of nineteenth-century romantic and historical prose fiction. . . . That he was over-estimated throughout the nineteenth century is certain; but that he has been under-valued by criticism since then is equally certain. (pp. 139-44)

Too often, however, his work has not been examined in the right light. He has been accepted, and then criticised, too often simply as a medieval romancer, the author of *Ivanhoe* or *The Talisman*. But his strongest work belongs, as his own upbringing did, to the eighteenth century. And too little has been made, as breadth and sanity and a certain generosity of temperament have themselves gone out of fashion, of his genuinely rare massive virtues, his feeling for character in all but its most subtle and tormented aspects, his command of a wide scene in almost any period, his ability to present a great action in all its greatness, his masculine breadth and sweep and generous force. In spite of his romantic influence, he is in fact one of the supreme extroverted writers, with a boyish passion for historically picturesque and gallant action and for famous characters larger than life, but never losing the cool shrewd judgment of men and affairs that belonged to the Edinburgh advocate that he was trained to be, and that he never quite ceased to be, among all his romancing. And the irony of his position, as one of the great influences of the Romantic Movement, is that at heart he belonged far more to the old eighteenth century than he did to this new age, that in the narrower but truer psychological sense of the term he was not

a Romantic at all. He owes nothing whatever to Rousseau, whom he would certainly have detested, and is completely different in temperament and attitude from those writers who obviously stem from Rousseau. Scott is the great romancer who does not belong to romanticism.

Now for Byron, a harder nut to crack. We find him, at the age of twenty, writing to his mother: "I do not know that I resemble Jean Jacques Rousseau. I have no ambition to be like so illustrious a madman . . . " In one of his later journals, he repeats that he cannot see any point of resemblance, gives a score of examples of the ways in which he and Rousseau differed, and concludes: " . . . Rousseau's way of life, his country, his manners, his whole character were so very different, that I am at a loss to conceive how such a comparison could have arisen . . . " But, as he admits, it was frequently being made. If Rousseau was the prophet of the Romantic Age, Byron became its hero. Europe accepted him as the archetypal and symbolic figure of romance. It was as if one of Rousseau's day-dreams came to life. Byron had every qualification the for role of leading man in the drama of the Romantic Age. He was a prolific, impassioned and glorious poet; he was an aristocrat and as beautiful as Apollo; he was misunderstood and abused by his fellow-countrymen; he was wickedly amorous, a satanic philanderer, though capable— or so a million women dreamed—of being reformed by the love of a good woman; when weary of brittle gaiety and debauchery, he retired, a solitary exile, to various picturesque places, and there, wrapped in a cloak, with the clear-cut, pale, sad face of a young Lucifer, he composed immortal stanzas to the ocean, the mountains, thunder-and-lightning; he worshipped the wild beauty of Nature and strange women and man's liberty, for which he fought and died at last in Greece. This was his legend; he wrote it in one poetic tale or drama after another, in sparkling lyrics by the hundred; and he lived it. Only Goethe, forty years older, loomed larger. The advantages Byron possessed over his companion English poets were immense. Not only did he look and behave like every romantic reader's idea of a poet; he had all the prestige of a rich English milord, with the further prestige of having quarrelled with all the other milords; he took the centre of the international stage doubly illuminated by literary glory and scandal; and most of his verse could be easily enjoyed in its original English and lost little or nothing in translation. No wonder that his legend captured Europe, from the great ladies ready to lose their hearts to him down to wistful young clerks, with a taste for romantic verse, who tried to imitate his appearance. The very Age turned Byronic.

Let us admit that Byron's real character was far from simple, containing many conflicting elements, and innumerable close studies have been made of it, producing many different judgments of him. Any account of him within the limits imposed on us here must be inadequate. But it can be said at once that his legend, turning him into the supreme European figure of romance, grossly exaggerates one aspect of his real nature, a side of him deliberately turned toward the public, like that of a man of action—and Byron might be described as a romantic man of action—who knows he has a role to play. (Had he lived another twenty years, it is more than likely that he would have destroyed the whole romantic-poetical legend and created a very different public Byron.) He was quite right when he saw himself in the sharpest contrast to Rousseau, who was at the mercy of his unconscious as Byron never was. There was in fact securely held in Byron much of that eighteenth century against which Rousseau rebelled. Byron among his close friends, and in his journals and letters, never appears like a man abandoning himself to his dreams; he has much wit, humour, common-sense and shrewd judgment; he is essentially masculine and often appears insensitive to feminine values, and, for all his famous amours, he seems happier in male than in female company. He has far more of the conventional mind of his time than the other romantic poets. As Hazlitt, who did not like him, pointed out, there is in him a strong element of mere dandyism. He never forgets his rank. Much of his misanthropy, world-weariness, dust and ashes of despair, is part of the romantic-poetic performance, for in his longer poems especially he is a highly-skilled and astute entertainer, knowing exactly what mixture of the picturesque, the historical, the dramatic, the amorous, the grandly misanthropical, will hold his readers. Not that everything is false: the melancholy satiety is probably true enough, and the injured pride, and the dislike of obvious tyranny and stifling conventions, and the feeling of guilt left him by his relation with his half-sister, Augusta Leigh. But except in a few splendid lyrics, quite different in poetic quality from his large performances, he is not at heart a romantic poet at all. *Don Juan,* his best work, which shows us his strong masculine intellect, his witty impertinence, his rhetorical gusto, all at their best, is, only in its time and not in its spirit, one of the great romantic poems. There was much of the eighteenth century living on in Byron, together with some occasional flashes that make him suddenly seem startlingly modern. But this magnificent king of the Romantics was never at heart one of their company.

England's nearest approach to a romantic movement was in 1798 when William Wordsworth and Samuel Taylor Coleridge together produced *Lyrical Ballads.* It contains several poems long recognised to be masterpieces, but the critics at that time disliked it. The official critics, who contributed anonymous reviews to the quarterlies, continued to dislike and misunderstand the new poetry for the next thirty years, and as they enjoyed being offensive, to be reviewed by them was something of an ordeal. This probably explains why Wordsworth postponed the publication of his long poem, *The Prelude,* and never completed its philosophical companion, *The Excursion.* Shortly after the publication of *Lyrical Ballads* Wordsworth returned to his own countryside, the Lake District, and there spent the rest of his long life. He and Coleridge and Robert Southey were frequently called 'The Lake Poets'. (Southey, once thought to be the poetic equal of the other two, his monumental epics greatly impressing his contemporaries, is now chiefly remembered for one or two of his prose works, notably his *Life of Nelson.*) But Wordsworth's poetry is quite unlike that of his friends; he is an original. Once past his rebellious youth, he sternly rejected much of what romanticism offered—nobody could have been more unlike Lord Byron—but he retained and even heightened Rousseau's passion for solitude and communion with Nature. Indeed, Wordsworth is the supreme poet of this passion. Deliberately discarding the usual romantic stage effects, avoiding the use of a tinselled-and-spangled poetic vocabulary and largely expressing himself in plain language, making no attempt to be entertaining in the Byronic manner, he created his own kind of poetry.

A good deal of it, perhaps most of it, is very dull, like a long walk on a grey day. But just as somewhere on that walk there might be a sudden and superb flash of beauty, so in Wordsworth's poetry there are short passages, perhaps only a line or so, that are miraculous. An apparently simple unadorned phrase will suddenly blaze in the reader's imagination. These great moments of his, once experienced, are never forgotten, and we never entirely lose our response to them. Wordsworth is essentially a poet of such moments, and there can be no doubt that on his endless walks among the bleak fells, as he brooded in solitude, the familiar but ever-changing scene spread wide before him, he was in search of these moments, when the mountains and the bare trees and the grass would seem to be lit up from within, when simple words in some magical arrangement of the unconscious would rise to consciousness. There are times known to most of us when, the conscious mind having been quietened and slowed down by hours of solitary walking and brooding, we suddenly relate ourselves to the natural scene through our unconscious, return to the enchanted unity with it which we knew in childhood, seem to lose the ego and our separateness; and of these times Wordsworth is the prophet and high priest. One of his greatest poems is his "Intimations of Immortality". But in almost all his heightened moments, suddenly soaring out of the dull page, he is revealing such intimations. He is not a pantheist; he does not see Nature as God but as the symbol of God, making a sign, when we are ready to receive it, of our immortality. His essential poetry, as distinct from his uninspired verse-making, can be reduced to a very small volume, containing ecstatic moments of communion expressed in lines unlike those of any other poet, apparently simple in language and structure but curiously haunting, necromantic, as if brought from some depth of ancient incantation. So this long-faced, priggish trudger, meditating his dreary Ecclesiastical Sonnets as he does his twenty miles a day, must be included among the great Romantics.

Of the other two Lake Poets we might say that the industrious Southey had character without genius and Coleridge had genius without character. The promise of Coleridge in youth was boundless; it is agreed by all his contemporaries that the range and the force of his mind were extraordinary—"A hooded eagle among blinking owls", Shelley calls him; but years of opium encouraged him to meditate, dream and talk—he was the greatest talker of the age—and discouraged him from sitting down regularly at a desk to work. When we consider his unequalled reputation in his own time and the extent of his influence, we seem to inherit from him only mere fragments, a few terraces, pillars and broken statues representing a vast empire. But these fragments easily justify that reputation. His finest poetry was written while he was still young and the close friend of the two Wordsworths, William the poet and his remarkable sister, Dorothy. Later, when he had turned to prose, he was able to complete his *Biographia Literaria,* but the astonishing breadth and depth of his mind are best discovered in the various volumes, edited long after his death, that collect for us his scattered essays and notes and passages from his lectures. In his youth he learnt much from German criticism and philosophy, especially that of Schelling, but the criticism of his mature years surpasses the finest German criticism of his time both in its range and its remarkable insight. Though he swung over, like Wordsworth, from youthful rebellion to what looks painfully like High Tory and Church reaction, his perception and understanding of what is important in great literature remained with him, and in his own fragmentary fashion he must be considered the finest critic in this whole European Age of Romance. All his poetry worth cherishing could be printed in a very small volume, giving us *The Ancient Mariner,* "Kubla Khan" and "Christabel" (both unfinished), and a few shorter poems. But their quality more than redeems the lack of quantity. *The Ancient Mariner* is the most wonderful romantic narrative poem in the English language, one of the supreme triumphs of the romantic imagination, unforgettable in its horrors, marvels and lyrical beauty. Coleridge has described for us how he came to write "Kubla Khan", that elixir distilled from the very essence of romance, a poetic fragment that is as mysterious, evocative, vague and yet charged with meaning, as a piece of great music. He fell asleep while reading the old traveller's tales in *Purchas's Pilgrimage,* dreamt the poem or at least experienced it as a succession of dream images, and on waking "instantly and eagerly" wrote down what he remembered, immediately composing the poem. He could not finish it, he tells us, because he was interrupted by somebody coming to see him on business. There could be no better example of the contribution of the unconscious to poetry of this order: it is the whole romantic process dramatically demonstrated. Professor Irving Babbitt, who detested Rousseau and romanticism, quotes Coleridge's line "O Lady! we receive but what we give" as an example [in his study *Rousseau and Romanticism*], 1919, following Rousseau, of the false 'Arcadian imagination' turning us away from reality; but in these very chapters of his, Babbitt shows how close to reality Coleridge's observation is, how a profound psychological truth is expressed in it, for being prepared to give little to Rousseau, Coleridge, the whole Romantic Age, Babbitt receives equally little from them. Had Coleridge possessed the will-power, conscious purpose, ethical severity, that Babbitt recommends to literature and its authors, he would undoubtedly have left us a much larger body of work. But it would not have included *The Ancient Mariner* and "Kubla Khan".

Shelley, who saw Coleridge as "a hooded eagle", was drowned at the age of thirty, and, perpetually young himself, he is one of the supreme poets of and for impetuous and enthusiastic youth. He combines in himself and his work two very different things that are often found together in the young. The foundation of his thought is the ultra-rational atheism and philosophical anarchy not uncommon in the later eighteenth century and expressed at length by William Godwin, the desiccated Prospero to whom Shelley was the Ariel. (Godwin's daughter, Mary, was Shelley's second wife. She ought to be remembered, if not by readers then by film-goers, as the creator of *Frankenstein.*) Using this foundation merely as its runway, Shelley's poetic imagination took off into the blue. It is an imagination differing in degree but not in kind from that of many enthusiastic romantic young people, to whom this poet always had—and let us hope always will have—a very special attraction. More mature readers are apt to note a lack of ordinary human feeling, a remoteness from common interests, in this poetry; and when it is below its highest level, a certain gaseous quality, a blurring of images, a use of words too reminiscent of the absurd philosophical romances the poet read (and wrote) in his early youth. And Shelley, a rapid and prolific writer, is too often well below his highest level.

But when he is in full high flight—and he is a poet we associate with air and fire, not earth and water—his poetry is marvellous in its innocence and loveliness, its swiftness and grace, its opalescent colouring and shifting lights; as if it already belonged to—and is indeed celebrating—some future Golden Age, when men have rid themselves of their heavy bodies and iron laws, when the imagination can dissolve and recompose any scene, when all are Ariels free of their last tasks and Prometheus is unbound for ever. What any generous youth, preferably in rebellion against tyranny and injus-

tice, imagines for a few minutes, losing himself in excited fancies, goes soaring and glittering and singing through volume after volume of Shelley. But though neither the beautiful melancholy nor the high and sometimes shrill ecstasies, the vague music and perfume and multi-coloured transformations of these lyrics, are quite of this world; there are signs here and there, flashes of psychological insight, notably in his drama, *The Cenci,* that had Shelley lived longer and come to the end of his urge to soar and sing (for even his narrative and dramatic poems are lyrical in feeling), he might have broken the spell condemning so many of the English romantic poets to try, and fail, in the theatre, and so restored the tradition of poetic drama. As it is, he remains a lyrical genius, a romantic figure of eager revolt and poetry that, at certain ages and always for some readers, completely captures the imagination.

John Keats was the youngest of these great romantic poets, but he was the first to die, in 1821 at the age of twenty-six. His first book, containing the long narrative poem, *Endymion,* was denounced with such ferocity by the official reviewers, who did not begin to understand what they were reading, that it was widely believed, by Byron among others, that out of sheer disappointment and mortification his health failed him and so he died young. This is completely untrue. He met this savage criticism in the manliest spirit. "The imagination of a boy is healthy, and the mature imagination of a man is healthy; but there is a space of life between, in which the soul is in a ferment, the character undecided, the way of life uncertain, the ambition thick-sighted: thence proceeds mawkishness . . . " This is well said, but it was said by Keats and not by one of his critics. Indeed, this young surgeon's apprentice had more wisdom and a finer understanding of the arts than could be discovered in a total muster of the *Quarterly Review*'s contributors. His letters, more mature in thought and feeling than most of his poems, make us appreciate what must have been lost to literature by his early death. A handful of the poems he left us, the great odes and the best of the sonnets, gives him a place of equality beside Wordsworth, Coleridge, Byron, Shelley; but before his last fatal illness he developed and matured so quickly, adding to his poetry the high spirits, good sense, flashes of unusual insight, of his letters, that potentially he seems the greatest of these poets, promising to be master of almost any form of literature.

The suggestion, often made, that here cut off in youth was a poet possibly of Shakespearean stature is not at all absurd, even if the poems alone are considered and the wider promise in the letters is ignored. For there is a likeness to the younger Shakespeare of the poems, in this work of Keats. There is the same wide and deep sensuality, the same richness, the same attempt to express fairly common thoughts and moods with the utmost felicity. What is being expressed is neither very original nor profound—Keats is at the opposite extreme from a poet like Blake—but the poetry achieves its own originality, and even profundity, through this richness, this wonderful felicity of image and phrase, its unusual evocative quality, its undertones and overtones. Keats's great lines, like Shakespeare's, haunt the memory, and he soon became one of the most frequently quoted of English poets. Though the themes he chose, the moods he expressed, are extremely romantic, belonging to a day-dreaming youth, the mind behind the strongest poems, the mind deliberately enriching the lines like a composer using the full resources of his orchestra, is a mind already finely balanced between consciousness and the unconscious, that of a major artist, far removed from the pathetic figure of boyish romance that Keats is sometimes assumed to be. He is indeed too often considered in terms of his tragi-comic love-affair, his tuberculosis, his melancholy flight to Italy, his grave in Rome, as if he were a sentimental schoolgirl's idea of a romantic poet. But the poetry itself, his letters, his life in its factual details, show us a very different sort of man, immense if shadowy in his promise, solid and enduring in his performance, brief though it was. And there is not a more attractive figure in all the annals and legends of this Romantic Age than young, for ever young, John Keats. (pp. 144-53)

J. B. Priestley, "The English Romantics," in his Literature and Western Man, *Harper & Brothers, 1960, pp. 139-58.*

NORTHROP FRYE

[*Frye has exerted a tremendous influence in the field of twentieth-century literary scholarship, mainly through his study* Anatomy of Criticism *(1957). In this seminal work, Frye makes controversial claims for literature and literary critics, arguing that judgments are not inherent in the critical process and asserting that literary criticism can be "scientific" in its methods and its results without borrowing concepts from other fields of study. Literary criticism, in Frye's view, should be autonomous in the manner that physics, biology, and chemistry are autonomous disciplines. For Frye, literature is schematic because it is wholly structured by myth and symbol. The critic becomes a near-scientist, determining how symbols and myth are ordered and function in a given work. The critic need not, in Frye's view, make judgments of value about the work; a critical study is structured in that the components of literature, like those of nature, are unchanging and predictable. Frye believes that literature occupies a position of extreme importance within any culture. Literature, as he sees it, is "the place where our imaginations find the ideal that they try to pass on to belief and action, where they find the vision which is the source of both the dignity and the joy of life." The literary critic serves society by studying and "translating" the structures in which that vision is encoded. In the following excerpt, Frye describes the revolutionary artistic and philosophical changes that occurred during the Romantic period.*]

Any such conception as "Romanticism" is at one or more removes from actual literary experience, in an inner world where ten thousand different things flash upon the inward eye with all the bliss of oversimplification. Some things about it, however, are generally accepted, and we may start with them. First, Romanticism has a historical center of gravity, which falls somewhere around the 1790-1830 period. This gets us at once out of the fallacy of timeless characterization, where we say that Romanticism has certain qualities, not found in the age of Pope, of sympathy with nature or what not, only to have someone produce a poem of Propertius or Kalidasa, or, eventually, Pope himself, and demand to know if the same qualities are not there. Second, Romanticism is not a general historical term like "medieval": it appears to have another center of gravity in the creative arts. We speak most naturally of Romantic literature, painting, and music. (p. 1)

Third, even in its application to the creative arts Romanticism is a selective term, more selective even than "Baroque" appears to be becoming. We think of it as including Keats, but not, on the whole, Crabbe; Scott, but not, in general, Jane Austen; Wordsworth, but not, on any account, James Mill. As generally used, "Romantic" is contrasted with two other terms, "classical" and "realistic." Neither contrast seems sat-

isfactory. We could hardly call Wordsworth's preface to the *Lyrical Ballads* anti-realistic, or ignore the fact that Shelley was a better classical scholar than, say, Dryden, who, according to Samuel Johnson, translated the first book of the *Iliad* without knowing what was in the second. Still, the pairings exist, and we shall have to examine them. And yet, fourth, though selective, Romanticism is not a voluntary category. It does not see Byron as the successor to Pope or Wordsworth as the successor to Milton, which would have been acceptable enough to both poets: it associates Byron and Wordsworth, to their mutual disgust, with each other.

Accepting all this, we must also avoid the two traps in the phrase "history of ideas." First, an idea, as such, is independent of time and can be argued about; an historical event is not and cannot be. If Romanticism is in part an historical event, as it clearly is, then to say with T. E. Hulme: "I object to even the best of the Romantics" [see Further Reading] is much like saying: "I object to even the best battles of the Napoleonic War." Most general value-judgments on Romanticism as a whole are rationalizations of an agreement or disagreement with some belief of which Romantic poetry is supposed to form the objective correlative.

This latter is the second or Hegelian trap in the history of ideas, which we fall into when we assume that around 1790 or earlier some kind of thesis arose in history and embodied itself in the Romantic movement. Such an assumption leads us to examining all the cultural products we call Romantic as allegories of that thesis. These have a way of disagreeing with each other, and if we try to think of Romanticism as some kind of single "idea," all we can do with it is what Lovejoy did: break it down into a number of contradictory ideas with nothing significant in common. In literature, and more particularly poetry, ideas are subordinated to imagery, to a language more "simple, sensuous, and passionate" than the language of philosophy. Hence it may be possible for two poets to be related by common qualities of imagery even when they do not agree on a single thesis in religion, politics, or the theory of art itself.

The history of imagery, unlike the history of ideas, appears to be for the most part a domain where, in the words of a fictional Canadian poetess, "the hand of man hath never trod." Yet we seem inexorably led to it by our own argument, and perhaps the defects in what follows may be in part excused by the novelty of the subject, to me at least. After making every allowance for a prodigious variety of technique and approach, it is still possible to see a consistent framework (I wish the English language had a better equivalent for the French word *cadre*) in the imagery of both medieval and Renaissance poetry. The most remarkable and obvious feature of this framework is the division of being into four levels. The highest level is heaven, the place of the presence of God. Next come the two levels of the order of nature, the human level and the physical level. The order of human nature, or man's proper home, is represented by the story of the Garden of Eden in the Bible and the myth of the Golden Age in Boethius and elsewhere. Man is no longer in it, but the end of all his religious, moral, and social cultivation is to raise him into something resembling it. Physical nature, the world of animals and plants, is the world man is now in, but unlike the animals and plants he is not adjusted to it. He is confronted from birth with a moral dialectic, and must either rise above it to his proper human home or sink below it into the fourth level of sin, death, and hell. This last level is not part of the order of nature, but its existence is what at present corrupts nature. A very similar framework can be found in classical poetry, and the alliance of the two, in what is so often called Christian humanism, accounts for the sense of an antagonism between the Romantic movement and the classical tradition, in spite of its many and remarkable affinities with that tradition.

Such a framework of images, however closely related in practice to belief, is not in itself a belief or an expression of belief: it is in itself simply a way of arranging images and providing for metaphors. At the same time the word "framework" itself is a spatial metaphor, and any framework is likely to be projected in space, even confused or identified with its spatial projection. In Dante Eden is a long way up, on top of the mountain of purgatory; heaven is much further up, and hell is down, at the center of the earth. We may know that such conceptions as heaven and hell do not depend on spatial metaphors of up and down, but a cosmological poet, dealing with them as images, has to put them somewhere. To Dante it was simple enough to put them at the top and bottom of the natural order, because he knew of no alternative to the Ptolemaic picture of the world. To Milton, who did know of an alternative, the problem was more complex, and Milton's heaven and hell are outside the cosmos, in a kind of absolute up and down. After Milton comes Newton, and after Newton ups and downs become hopelessly confused.

What I see first of all in Romanticism is the effect of a profound change, not primarily in belief, but in the spatial projection of reality. This in turn leads to a different localizing of the various levels of that reality. Such a change in the localizing of images is bound to be accompanied by, or even cause, changes in belief and attitude, and changes of this latter sort are exhibited by the Romantic poets. But the change itself is not in belief or attitude, and may be found in, or at least affecting, poets of a great variety of beliefs.

In the earlier framework, the disorder of sin, death, and corruption was restricted to the sublunary world of four elements. Above the moon was all that was left of nature as God had originally planned it before the fall. The planets, with their angel-guided spheres, are images of a divinely sanctioned order of nature which is also the true home of man. Hence there was no poetic incongruity in Dante's locating his Paradiso in the planetary spheres, nor in Milton's associating the music of the spheres with the song of the angels in the "Nativity Ode," nor in using the same word "heaven" for both the kingdom of God and the sky. A post-Newtonian poet has to think of gravitation and the solar system. Newton, Miss Nicolson has reminded us, demanded the muse, but the appropriate muse was Urania, and Urania had already been requested by Milton to descend to a safer position on earth for the second half of *Paradise Lost.*

Let us turn to Blake's poem *Europe*, engraved in 1794. *Europe* surveys the history of the Western world from the birth of Christ to the beginning of the French Revolution, and in its opening lines parodies the "Nativity Ode." For Blake all the deities associated with the planets and the starry skies, of whom the chief is Enitharmon, the Queen of Heaven, are projections of a human will to tyranny, rationalized as eternal necessity and order. Christianity, according to this poem, had not abolished but confirmed the natural religion in the classical culture which had deified the star-gods. The doom of tyranny is sealed by the French Revolution, and the angel who blows the last trumpet as the sign of the final awakening of

liberty is Isaac Newton. The frontispiece of *Europe* is the famous vision of the sky-god Urizen generally called the Ancient of Days, holding a compass in his left hand, and this picture is closely related to Blake's portrait of Newton, similarly preoccupied with a compass and oblivious of the heavens he is supposed to be studying.

Blake's view, in short, is that the universe of modern astronomy, as revealed in Newton, exhibits only a blind, mechanical, subhuman order, not the personal presence of a deity. Newton himself tended to think of God still as "up there," even to the extent of suggesting that space was the divine sensorium; but *what* was up there, according to Blake, is only a set of interlocking geometrical diagrams, and God, Blake says, is not a mathematical diagram. Newtonism leads to what for Blake are intellectual errors, such as a sense of the superiority of abstractions to actual things and the notion that the real world is a measurable but invisible world of primary qualities. But Blake's main point is that admiring the mechanisms of the sky leads to establishing human life in mechanical patterns too. In other words, Blake's myth of Urizen is a fuller and more sophisticated version of the myth of Frankenstein.

Blake's evil, sinister, or merely complacent sky-gods, Urizen, Nobodaddy, Enitharmon, Satan, remind us of similar beings in other Romantics: Shelley's Jupiter, Byron's Arimanes, the Lord in the Prologue to *Faust.* They in their turn beget later

Life mask of William Blake, age sixty-six.

Romantic gods and goddesses, such as Baudelaire's female "froide majesté" ["cold majesty"], Hardy's Immanent Will, or the God of Housman's "The chestnut casts his flambeaux," who is a brute and blackguard because he is a sky-god in control of the weather, and sends his rain on the just and on the unjust. The association of sinister or unconscious mechanism with what we now call outer space is a commonplace of popular literature today which is a Romantic inheritance. Perhaps Orwell's *1984,* a vision of a mechanical tyranny informed by the shadow of a Big Brother who can never die, is the terminal point of a development of imagery that began with Blake's Ancient of Days. Not every poet, naturally, associates mechanism with the movements of the stars as Blake does, or sees it as a human imitation of the wrong kind of divine creativity. But the contrast between the mechanical and the organic is deeply rooted in Romantic thinking, and the tendency is to associate the mechanical with ordinary consciousness, as we see in the account of the associative fancy in Coleridge's *Biographia* or of discursive thought in Shelley's *Defence of Poetry.* This is in striking contrast to the Cartesian tradition, where the mechanical is of course associated with the subconscious. The mechanical being characteristic of ordinary experience, it is found particularly in the world "outside"; the superior or organic world is consequently "inside," and although it is still called superior or higher, the natural metaphorical direction of the inside world is downward, into the profounder depths of consciousness.

If a Romantic poet, therefore, wishes to write of God, he has more difficulty in finding a place to put him than Dante or even Milton had, and on the whole he prefers to do without a place, or finds "within" metaphors more reassuring than "up there" metaphors. When Wordsworth speaks, in *The Prelude* and elsewhere, of feeling the presence of deity through a sense of interpenetration of the human mind and natural powers, one feels that his huge and mighty forms, like the spirits of Yeats, have come to bring him the right metaphors for his poetry. In the second book of *The Excursion* we have a remarkable vision of what has been called the heavenly city of the eighteenth-century philosophers, cast in the form of an ascent up a mountain, where the city is seen at the top. The symbolism, I think, is modeled on the vision of Cleopolis in the first book of *The Faerie Queene,* and its technique is admirably controlled and precise. Yet surely this is not the real Wordsworth. The spirits have brought him the wrong metaphors; metaphors that Spenser used with full imaginative conviction, but which affect only the surface of Wordsworth's mind.

The second level of the older construct was the world of original human nature, now a lost paradise or golden age. It is conceived as a better and more appropriate home for man than his present environment, whether man can regain it or not. But in the older construct this world was ordinarily not thought of as human in origin or conception. Adam awoke in a garden not of his planting, in a fresh-air suburb of the City of God, and when the descendants of Cain began to build cities on earth, they were building to models already existing in both heaven and hell. In the Middle Ages and the Renaissance the agencies which helped to raise man from the physical to the human world were such things as the sacraments of religion, the moral law, and the habit of virtue, none of them strictly human inventions. These were the safe and unquestioned agencies, the genuinely educational media. Whether the human arts of poetry and painting and music were genuinely educational in this sense could be and was dis-

puted or denied; and the poets themselves, when they wrote apologies for poetry, seldom claimed equality with religion or law, beyond pointing out that the earliest major poets were prophets and lawgivers.

For the modern mind there are two poles of mental activity. One may be described as sense, by which I mean the recognition of what is presented by experience: the empirical, observant habit of mind in which, among other things, the inductive sciences begin. In this attitude reality is, first of all, "out there," whatever happens to it afterwards. The other pole is the purely formalizing or constructive aspect of the mind, where reality is something brought into being by the act of construction. It is obvious that in pre-Romantic poetry there is a strong affinity with the attitude that we have called sense. The poet, in all ages and cultures, prefers images to abstractions, the sensational to the conceptual. But the pre-Romantic structure of imagery belonged to a nature which was the work of God; the design in nature was, as Sir Thomas Browne calls it, the art of God; nature is thus an objective structure or system for the poet to follow. The appropriate metaphors of imitation are visual and physical ones, and the creative powers of the poet have models outside him.

It is generally recognized that Rousseau represents, and to some extent made, a revolutionary change in the modern attitude. The primary reason for his impact was, I think, not in his political or educational views as such, but in his assumption that civilization was a purely human artifact, something that man had made, could unmake, could subject to his own criticism, and was at all times entirely responsible for. Above all, it was something for which the only known model was in the human mind. This kind of assumption is so penetrating that it affects those who detest Rousseau, or have never heard of him, equally with the small minority of his admirers. Also, it gets into the mind at once, whereas the fading out of such counter assumptions as the literal and historical nature of the Garden of Eden story is very gradual. The effect of such an assumption is twofold. First, it puts the arts in the center of civilization. The basis of civilization is now the creative power of man; its model is the human vision revealed in the arts. Second, this model, as well as the sources of creative power, are now located in the mind's internal heaven, the external world being seen as a mirror reflecting and making visible what is within. Thus the "outside" world, most of which is "up there," yields importance and priority to the inner world, in fact derives its poetic significance at least from it. "In looking at objects of Nature," says Coleridge in the Notebooks, "I seem rather to be seeking, as it were *asking* for, a symbolical language for something within me that already and forever exists, than observing anything new." This principle extends both to the immediate surrounding world which is the emblem of the music of humanity in Wordsworth and to the starry heavens on which Keats read "Huge cloudy symbols of a high romance."

Hence in Romantic poetry the emphasis is not on what we have called sense, but on the constructive power of the mind, where reality is brought into being by experience. There is a contrast in popular speech between the romantic and the realist, where the word "romantic" implies a sentimentalized or rose-colored view of reality. This vulgar sense of the word may throw some light on the intensity with which the Romantic poets sought to defy external reality by creating a uniformity of tone and mood. The establishing of this uniformity, and the careful excluding of anything that would dispel it, is one of the constant and typical features of the best Romantic poetry, though we may call it a dissociation of sensibility if we happen not to like it. Such a poetic technique is, psychologically, akin to magic, which also aims at bringing spiritual forces into reality through concentration on a certain type of experience. Such words as "charm" or "spell" suggest uniformity of mood as well as a magician's repertoire. Historically and generically, it is akin to romance, with its effort to maintain a self-consistent idealized world without the intrusions of realism or irony.

For these reasons Romanticism is difficult to adapt to the novel, which demands an empirical and observant attitude; its contribution to prose fiction is rather, appropriately enough, a form of romance. In the romance the characters tend to become psychological projections, and the setting a period in a past just remote enough to be re-created rather than empirically studied. We think of Scott as within the Romantic movement; Jane Austen as related to it chiefly by her parodies of the kind of sensibility that tries to live in a self-created world instead of adapting to the one that is there. Marianne in *Sense and Sensibility,* Catherine in *Northanger Abbey,* and of course everybody in *Love and Friendship,* are examples. Crabbe's naturalistic manifesto in the opening of *The Village* expresses an attitude which in itself is not far from Wordsworth's. But Crabbe is a metrical novelist in a way that Wordsworth is not. The soldier in *The Prelude* and the leech-gatherer in "Resolution and Independence" are purely romantic characters in the sense just given of psychological projections: that is, they become temporary or epiphanic myths. We should also notice that the internalizing of reality in Romanticism proper develops a contrast between it and a contemporary realism which descends from the pre-Romantic tradition but acquires a more purely empirical attitude to the external world.

The third level of the older construct was the physical world, theologically fallen, which man is born into but which is not the real world of human nature. Man's primary attitude to external physical nature is thus one of detachment. The kind of temptation represented by Spenser's Bower of Bliss or Milton's Comus is based on the false suggestion that physical nature, with its relatively innocent moral freedom, can be the model for human nature. The resemblances between the poetic techniques used in the Bower of Bliss episode and some of the techniques of the Romantics are superficial: Spenser, unlike the Romantics, is consciously producing a rhetorical set piece, designed to show that the Bower of Bliss is not natural but artificial in the modern sense. Man for pre-Romantic poets is not a child of Nature in the sense that he was originally a primitive. Milton's Adam becomes a noble savage immediately after his fall; but that is not his original nature. In Romanticism the cult of the primitive is a by-product of the internalizing of the creative impulse. The poet has always been supposed to be imitating nature, but if the model of his creative power is in his mind, the nature that he is to imitate is now inside him, even if it is also outside.

The original form of human society also is hidden "within." Keats refers to this hidden society when he says in a letter to Reynolds: "Man should not dispute or assert but whisper results to his neighbour . . . and Humanity . . . would become a grand democracy of Forest Trees!" Coleridge refers to it in the *Biographia* when he says: "The medium, by which spirits understand each other, is not the surrounding air; but the *freedom* which they possess in common." Whether the Ro-

mantic poet is revolutionary or conservative depends on whether he regards this original society as concealed by or as manifested in existing society. If the former, he will think of true society as a primitive structure of nature and reason, and will admire the popular, simple, or even the barbaric more than the sophisticated. If the latter, he will find his true inner society manifested by a sacramental church or by the instinctive manners of an aristocracy. The search for a visible ideal society in history leads to a good deal of admiration for the Middle Ages, which on the Continent was sometimes regarded as the essential feature of Romanticism. The affinity between the more extreme Romantic conservatism and the subversive revolutionary movements of fascism and nazism in our day has been often pointed out. The present significance for us of this fact is that the notion of the inwardness of creative power is inherently revolutionary, just as the pre-Romantic construct was inherently conservative, even for poets as revolutionary as Milton. The self-identifying admiration which so many Romantics expressed for Napoleon has much to do with the association of natural force, creative power, and revolutionary outbreak. As Carlyle says, in an uncharacteristically cautious assessment of Napoleon: "What Napoleon *did* will in the long-run amount to what he did *justly;* what Nature with her laws will sanction."

Further, the Romantic poet is a part of a total process, engaged with and united to a creative power greater than his own because it includes his own. This greater creative power has a relation to him which we may call, adapting a term of Blake's, his vehicular form. The sense of identity with a larger power of creative energy meets us everywhere in Romantic culture, I think even in the crowded excited canvases of Delacroix and the tremendous will-to-power finales of Beethoven. The symbolism of it in literature has been too thoroughly studied in Professor Abrams's *The Mirror and the Lamp* and in Professor Wasserman's *The Subtler Language* for me to add more than a footnote or two at this point. Sometimes the greater power of this vehicular form is a rushing wind, as in Shelley's Ode and in the figure of the "correspondent breeze" studied by Professor Abrams. The image of the Aeolian harp, or lyre—Romantic poets are apt to be sketchy in their orchestration—belongs here. Sometimes it is a boat driven by a breeze or current, or by more efficient magical forces in the "Ancient Mariner." This image occurs so often in Shelley that it has helped to suggest my title; the introduction to Wordsworth's *Peter Bell* has a flying boat closely associated with the moon. Those poems of Wordsworth in which we feel driven along by a propelling metrical energy, *Peter Bell,* "The Idiot Boy," *The Waggoner,* and others, seem to me to be among Wordsworth's most central poems. Sometimes the vehicular form is a heightened state of consciousness in which we feel that we are greater than we know, or an intense feeling of communion, as in the sacramental corn-and-wine images of the great Keats odes.

The sense of unity with a greater power is surely one of the reasons why so much of the best Romantic poetry is mythopoeic. The myth is typically the story of the god, whose form and character are human but who is also a sun-god or tree-god or ocean-god. It identifies the human with the nonhuman world, an identification which is also one of the major functions of poetry itself. Coleridge makes it a part of the primary as well as the secondary imagination. "This I call *I,*" he says in the *Notebooks,* "identifying the percipient and the perceived." The "Giant Forms" of Blake's prophecies are states of being and feeling in which we have our own being and feeling; the huge and mighty forms of Wordsworth's *Prelude* have similar affinities; even the dreams of De Quincey seem vehicular in the same sense. It is curious that there seems to be so little mythopoeic theory in Romantic poets, considering that the more expendable critics of the time complained as much about the obscurity of myth as their counterparts of today do now.

One striking feature of the Romantic poets is their resistance to fragmentation: their compulsion, almost, to express themselves in long continuous poems is quite as remarkable as their lyrical gifts. I have remarked elsewhere that the romance, in its most naive and primitive form, is an endless sequence of adventures, terminated only by the author's death or disgust. In Romanticism something of this inherently endless romance form recurs. *Childe Harold* and *Don Juan* are Byron to such an extent that the poems about them can be finished only by Byron's death or boredom with the *persona. The Prelude,* and still more the gigantic scheme of which it formed part, has a similar relation to Wordsworth, and something parallel is beginning to show its head at once in Keats's "Sleep and Poetry" and Shelley's *Queen Mab.* We touch here on the problem of the Romantic unfinished poem, which has been studied by Professor Bostetter [see Further Reading]. My present interest, however, is rather in the feature of unlimited continuity, which seems to me connected with the sense of vehicular energy, of being carried along by a greater force, the quality which outside literature, according to Keats, makes a man's life a continual allegory.

We have found, then, that the metaphorical structure of Romantic poetry tends to move inside and downward instead of outside and upward, hence the creative world is deep within, and so is heaven or the place of the presence of God. Blake's Orc and Shelley's Prometheus are Titans imprisoned underneath experience; the Gardens of Adonis are down in *Endymion,* whereas they are up in *The Faerie Queene* and *Comus;* in *Prometheus Unbound* everything that aids mankind comes from below, associated with volcanoes and fountains. In *The Revolt of Islam* there is a curious collision with an older habit of metaphor when Shelley speaks of

A power, a thirst, a knowledge . . . below
All thoughts, like light beyond the atmosphere.

The "Kubla Khan" geography of caves and underground streams haunts all of Shelley's language about creative processes: in *Speculations on Metaphysics,* for instance, he says: "But thought can with difficulty visit the intricate and winding chambers which it inhabits. It is like a river whose rapid and perpetual stream flows outwards. . . . The caverns of the mind are obscure, and shadowy, or pervaded with a lustre, beautifully bright indeed, but shining not beyond their portals."

In pre-Romantic poetry heaven is the order of grace, and grace is normally thought of as descending from above into the soul. In the Romantic construct there is a center where inward and outward manifestations of a common motion and spirit are unified, where the ego is identified as itself because it is also identified with something which is not itself. In Blake this world at the deep center is Jerusalem, the City of God that mankind, or Albion, has sought all through history without success because he has been looking in the wrong direction, outside. Jerusalem is also the garden of Eden where the Holy Word walked among the ancient trees; Eden in the unfallen world would be the same place as England's green

and pleasant land where Christ also walked; and England's green and pleasant land is also Atlantis, the sunken island kingdom which we can rediscover by draining the "Sea of Time and Space" off the top of the mind. In *Prometheus Unbound* Atlantis reappears when Prometheus is liberated, and the one great flash of vision which is all that is left to us of Wordsworth's *Recluse* uses the same imagery.

> Paradise, and groves
> Elysian, Fortunate Fields—like those of old
> Sought in the Atlantic Main—why should they be
> A history only of departed things,
> Or a mere fiction of what never was? . . .
> —I, long before the blissful hour arrives,
> Would chant, in lonely peace, the spousal verse
> Of this great consummation.

The Atlantis theme is in many other Romantic myths: in the Glaucus episode of *Endymion* and in De Quincey's *Savannah-la-Mar,* which speaks of "human life still subsisting in submarine asylums sacred from the storms that torment our upper air." (pp. 2-18)

In *The Pilgrim's Progress* Ignorance is sent to hell from the very gates of heaven. The inference seems to be that only Ignorance knows the precise location of both kingdoms. For knowledge, and still more for imagination, the journey within to the happy island garden or the city of light is a perilous quest, equally likely to terminate in the blasted ruin of Byron's "Darkness" or Beddoes's "Subterranean City." In many Romantic poems, including Keats's nightingale ode, it is suggested that the final identification of and with reality may be or at least include death. The suggestion that death may lead to the highest knowledge, dropped by Lucifer in Byron's *Cain,* haunts Shelley continually. A famous passage in *Prometheus Unbound* associates the worlds of creation and death in the same inner area, where Zoroaster meets his image in a garden. Just as the sun is the means but not a tolerable object of sight, so the attempt to turn around and see the source of one's vision may be destructive, as the Lady of Shalott found when she turned away from the mirror. Thus the world of the deep interior in Romantic poetry is morally ambivalent, retaining some of the demonic qualities that the corresponding pre-Romantic lowest level had.

This sense that the source of genius is beyond good and evil, that the possession of genius may be a curse, that the only real knowledge given to Adam in Paradise, however disastrous, came to him from the devil—all this is part of the contribution of Byron to modern sensibility, and part of the irrevocable change that he made in it. Of his Lara Byron says:

> He stood a stranger in this breathing world,
> An erring spirit from another hurl'd;
> A thing of dark imaginings, that shaped
> By choice the perils he by chance escaped;
> But 'scaped in vain, for in their memory yet
> His mind would half exult and half regret . . .
> But haughty still and loth himself to blame,
> He call'd on Nature's self to share the shame,
> And charged all faults upon the fleshly form
> She gave to clog the soul, and feast the worm;
> Till he at least confounded good and ill,
> And half mistook for fate the acts of will.

It would be wrong to regard this as Byronic hokum, for the wording is very precise. Lara looks demonic to a nervous and conforming society, as the dragon does to the tame villatic fowl in Milton. But there is a genuinely demonic quality in him which arises from his being nearer than other men to the unity of subjective and objective worlds. To be in such a place might make a poet more creative; it makes other types of superior beings, including Lara, more destructive.

We said earlier that a Romantic poet's political views would depend partly on whether he saw his inner society as concealed by or as manifested in actual society. A Romantic poet's moral attitude depends on a similar ambivalence in the conception of nature. Nature to Wordsworth is a mother-goddess who teaches the soul serenity and joy, and never betrays the heart that loves her; to the Marquis de Sade nature is the source of all the perverse pleasures that an earlier age had classified as "unnatural." For Wordsworth the reality of Nature is manifested by its reflection of moral values; for De Sade the reality is concealed by that reflection. It is this ambivalent sense (for it is ambivalent, and not simply ambiguous) of appearance as at the same time revealing and concealing reality, as clothes simultaneously reveal and conceal the naked body, that makes *Sartor Resartus* so central a document of the Romantic movement. We spoke of Wordsworth's Nature as a mother-goddess, and her psychological descent from mother-figures is clearly traced in *The Prelude*. The corn-goddess in Keats's "To Autumn," the parallel figure identified with Ruth in the "Ode to a Nightingale," the still unravished bride of the Grecian urn, Psyche, even the veiled Melancholy, are all emblems of a revealed Nature. Elusive nymphs or teasing and mocking female figures who refuse to take definite form, like the figure in *Alastor* or Blake's "female will" types; terrible and sinister white goddesses like La Belle Dame sans Merci, or females associated with something forbidden or demonic, like the sister-lovers of Byron and Shelley, belong to the concealed aspect.

For Wordsworth, who still has a good deal of the pre-Romantic sense of nature as an objective order, nature is a landscape nature, and from it, as in Baudelaire's *Correspondances,* mysterious oracles seep into the mind through eye or ear, even a bird with so predictable a song as the cuckoo being an oracular wandering voice. This landscape is a veil dropped over the naked nature of screaming rabbits and gasping stags, the nature red in tooth and claw which haunted a later generation. Even the episode of the dog and the hedgehog in *The Prelude* is told from the point of view of the dog and not of the hedgehog. But the more pessimistic, and perhaps more realistic, conception of nature in which it can be a source of evil or suffering as well as good is the one that gains ascendancy in the later period of Romanticism, and its later period extends to our own day.

The major constructs which our own culture has inherited from its Romantic ancestry are also of the "drunken boat" shape, but represent a later and a different conception of it from the "vehicular form" described above. Here the boat is usually in the position of Noah's ark, a fragile container of sensitive and imaginative values threatened by a chaotic and unconscious power below it. (pp. 18-22)

I give an example from Auden . . . to show that the Romantic structures of symbolism are still ours. In Freud, when the conscious mind feels threatened by the subconscious, it tries to repress it, and so develops a neurosis. In Marx, the liberal elements in an ascendant class, when they feel threatened by a revolutionary situation, develop a police state. In both cases the effort is to intensify the antithesis between the two, but this effort is mistaken, and when the barriers are broken down we reach the balanced mind and the classless society

respectively. "For the Time Being" develops a religious construct out of Kierkegaard on the analogy of those of Marx and Freud. The liberal or rational elements represented by Herod feel threatened by the revival of superstition in the Incarnation, and try to repress it. Their failure means that the effort to come to terms with a nature outside the mind, the primary effort of reason, has to be abandoned, and this enables the Paradise or divine presence which is locked up inside the human mind to manifest itself after the reason has searched the whole of objective nature in vain to find it. The attitude is that of a relatively orthodox Christianity; the imagery and the structure of symbolism is that of *Prometheus Unbound* and *The Marriage of Heaven and Hell.*

In Romanticism proper a prominent place in sense experience is given to the ear, an excellent receiver of oracles but poor in locating things accurately in space. This latter power, which is primarily visual, is associated with the fancy in Wordsworth's 1815 preface, and given the subordinate position appropriate to fancy. In later poetry, beginning with *symbolisme* in France, when there is a good deal of reaction against earlier Romanticism, more emphasis is thrown on vision. In Rimbaud, though his *Bateau Ivre* [*Drunken Boat*] has given me my title, the poet is to *se faire voyant* ["to make himself a seer"], the *illuminations* are thought of pictorially; even the vowels must be visually colored. Such an emphasis has nothing to do with the pre-Romantic sense of an objective structure in nature: on the contrary, the purpose of it is to intensify the Romantic sense of oracular significance into a kind of autohypnosis. . . . Such an emphasis leads to a technique of fragmentation. Poe's attack on the long poem is not a Romantic but an anti-Romantic manifesto, as the direction of its influence indicates. The tradition of *symbolisme* is present in imagism, where the primary of visual values is so strongly stated in theory and so cheerfully ignored in practice, in Pound's emphasis on the spatial juxtaposing of metaphor, in Eliot's insistence on the superiority of poets who present the "clear visual images" of Dante. T. E. Hulme's attack on the Romantic tradition is consistent in preferring fancy to imagination and in stressing the objectivity of the nature to be imitated; less so in his primitivism and his use of Bergson. The technique of fragmentation is perhaps intended to reach its limit in Pound's publication of the complete poetical works of Hulme on a single page.

As I have tried to indicate by my reference to Auden, what this anti-Romantic movement did not do was to create a third framework of imagery. Nor did it return to the older construct, though Eliot, by sticking closely to Dante and by deprecating the importance of the prophetic element in art, gives some illusion of doing so. The charge of subjectivity, brought against the Romantics by Arnold and often repeated later, assumes that objectivity is a higher attribute of poetry, but this is itself a Romantic conception, and came into English criticism with Coleridge. Anti-Romanticism, in short, had no resources for becoming anything more than a post-Romantic movement. The first phase of the "reconsideration" of Romanticism . . . is to understand its continuity with modern literature, and this phase is now well developed in the work of Professor Kermode and others. All we need do to complete it is to examine Romanticism by its own standards and canons. We should not look for precision where vagueness is wanted; not extol the virtues of constipation when the Romantics were exuberant; not insist on visual values when the poet listens darkling to a nightingale. Then, perhaps, we may see in Romanticism also the quality that Melville found in Greek architecture:

> Not innovating wilfulness,
> But reverence for the Archetype.

(pp. 22-5)

Northrop Frye, "The Drunken Boat: The Revolutionary Element in Romanticism," in Romanticism Reconsidered: Selected Papers from the English Institute, *edited by Northrop Frye, Columbia University Press, 1963, pp. 1-25.*

STEPHEN SPENDER

[*Spender is an English man of letters who rose to prominence during the 1930s as a Marxist lyric poet and as an associate of W. H. Auden, Christopher Isherwood, C. Day Lewis, and Louis MacNeice. Like many other artists and intellectuals, Spender became disillusioned with communism after World War II, and although he occasionally makes use of political and social issues in his work, he is more often concerned with aspects of self-knowledge and depth of personal feeling. His poetic reputation declined in the postwar years, while his stature as a prolific and perceptive literary critic has grown. Spender believes that art contains "a real conflict of life, a real breaking up and melting down of intractable material, feelings and sensations which seem incapable of expression until they have been thus transformed. A work of art doesn't say 'I am life, I offer you the opportunity of becoming me.' On the contrary, it says: 'This is what life is like. It is even realer, less to be evaded, than you thought. But I offer you an example of acceptance and understanding. Now, go back and live!'" In the following essay, Spender tests Romantic poetry against what he calls the "Romantic Gold Standard," the criteria by which the Romantics judged poetry.*]

Romantic: an idea irremediably vague. Used in a general sense, it suggests a landscape which, in turn, suggests an atmosphere. Forests, cliffs, mountains, torrents, caves, icebergs, the wide expanses of sea or plains, the horror of moon-lit graveyards: such vastnesses of solitude are the Romantic setting. And yet it is a spiritualized, a civilized, a communicable, a voluble solitude. It is the solitude of the Ancient Mariner, in his bones, burning from his eyes, fastening on the listener.

The inhuman, fierce, untamed jungle or desert, the cold immensity of the scientific universe expressed in measurements which cannot be grasped by the imagination—these are even more alien to the Romantic than to the classic temperament. For Romanticism is not chaos—it is a programme for conquering all conquerable worlds with the enforced wild life of the imagination.

The classic landscape is nature tamed to be garden. The Romantic is garden in which the flowers are forced to grow wild.

In the late eighteenth century, features of the tamed and untamed gardens could be spliced in what one might term the Romantic-classic object—torrent, grotto, fountain, cavern, Folly—the consciously Romantic effect in the classic setting.

Recent English taste, shown in the work of some young poets, in one outstanding anthology—Geoffrey Grigson's *The Romantics*—and in the paintings of John Piper, Graham Sutherland and others, shows a connoisseur's judgment of Romantic effects. This certainly widens our conception of what is Romantic: and yet it seems to miss the Romantic centre. Lines like these by William Shenstone—with which Mr.

Grigson opens his selection—show more of the taste for Romantic effects than of the Romantic intensity:

> My banks they are furnish'd with bees,
> Whose murmur invites one to sleep;
> My grottoes are shaded with trees,
> And my hills are white-over with sheep.

This shows the late eighteenth-century *penchant* towards Romantic effects—and yet that very verb 'furnish' is, surely, of the vocabulary the Romantics were to rebel against.

The search for Romantic foreshadowing results in delightful discoveries: especially since we easily forgive poets for being romantic before the Romantics. All the same, it may distract us from understanding what is the very intense and concentrated passion essential to Romanticism.

The Romanticism of the Romantics is by no means the same thing as a certain mood which is one of the permanent aspects of poetry. Keats, looking for ancestors, found them in Chaucer, Spenser, the Shakespeare of *A Midsummer Night's Dream* and *The Tempest,* the Milton of *Comus* and *Il Penseroso.* Nor is it just the gilded or glade-shadowed and moon-lit past atmosphere which provided his ancestry. There is violence, exoticism, and desperation of solitude in Webster and Tourneur to overshadow their nineteenth-century offshoot—*The Cenci.*

Thus an impassable gulf divides the mood of the Romanticism of the early nineteenth century from that of earlier, and later, periods. In Chaucer and Shakespeare, the Romantic effect is ornamental or atmospheric. And if the late Elizabethan and Jacobean playwrights were 'out of joint' with their time in a way which reminds us of Byron, nevertheless their despair—however violent and strange—has the impersonality of one history raging against another. It is closer to the *saeva indignatio* of Swift, or of the later, unromantic Yeats, than to the earlier, Keatsian Yeats.

'Much have I travell'd in the realms of gold', expresses Keats's view of the poetry of the past, and his exhortation to Shelley that every line must be loaded with ore, his programme for the present. Middleton Murry has drawn attention to the way in which Keats's poetic life was so completely identified with a phase of Shakespeare's poetry as to amount to an identification of Keats with Shakespeare. But if in one sense this makes Keats like Shakespeare, in another sense it makes him very un-Shakespearean indeed: for Shakespeare was immersed in life in his time, and not in the poetic life of some past poet. He did not, like the Romantics, go to the past for a blood transfusion.

The Romantic line is the *crème de la crème* of Chaucer, Spenser, certain passages of Shakespeare and Milton, by-passing the eighteenth century and the Metaphysical poets. An idea of a stream of poetry flowing through and merging completely with the stream of life several centuries ago, provided the Romantics with the idea of poetry as be-all and end-all: just as the pre-Raphaelite painters were to turn back to an earlier time for subject-matter, manner and technique of painting—by way of the poetry of Keats. What makes Romantic poetry so hypnotic is surely this identification of the idea of poetry with the most poetic moments of past poetry and of history. The result is a kind of poetry which passes judgement on other poetry by virtue of its intense preoccupation with a poetic subject-matter and the poetic being of the writer himself; while, at the same time, on account of the Romantic tendency to identify poetry with the poetic task, it evades criticism. To point out that Shelley is often very prosy indeed seems sacrilege. It is so unlike Shelley's—and, indeed, one's own—idea of Shelley in his work. We judge Shelley by Shelley and his aims.

Until recently we have—for a hundred years—accepted the Romantic Gold Standard and considered much other poetry as pure, or alloy, or devalued currency, according to it. Anthologies like Palgrave's *Golden Treasury* and *The Oxford Book of English Verse* are not—as is often assumed—just examples of Victorian Taste: they are acts of homage to the Romantic power which produces the hallucination that English poetry after Milton leads up to Keats, and then down from him.

One of the best things that can be said for modern analytic criticism is that, with its cold-blooded instruments of examination, it has dispelled the idea that all poetry must submit to the test of the lines of Romantic poetry written out of poetic situations by people who lead poetic lives. We have come to see that poetry may not altogether benefit from the poet's life and mind being so poetic: that a certain distance between the created work and the poet's existence, intentions and intellectual interests, may give poetry a vigour coming from seemingly unpoetic things—which are amongst the most living things.

Judging English poetry by the Romantic Gold Standard, this is the kind of picture we get:

(1) The gilded pre-Romantics—passages of Spenser, parts of Shakespeare, the Elizabethan song writers, the anonymous ballad-makers, the poets whom Keats, with his infallible instinct for this particular kind of gold, loved. Milton—a fatal influence—he did not so much love as succumb to.

(2) The golden Romantics: Wordsworth, Coleridge, and Byron in certain poems; Shelley and Keats in all their poems that were not failures; Blake in *The Bard*.

(3) The Victorians. They issued a paper currency still tied to the Romantic Gold Standard—which was followed by the serious devaluation of the '80's and '90's, and, lastly, by Inflation with the Georgians.

Gilded Romanticism is atmosphere in the Ballad-makers, fancy in Shakespeare and the other Elizabethans, desperation in the Jacobeans, the grottoesque in Pope. The currency of the Victorians is the result of their enthralment by the Romantic attitude and (perhaps still more) the Romantic vocabulary, and of their divided attitude towards the age in which they lived. They lacked the Romantic intensity and yet were incapable of attaching their poetry to any dogma. There was nothing else for the Victorian poet to be but Romantic.

Tennyson's Romanticism is peripheral, because, although for him the poetic line was the Romantic one, he lacked the Romantic vocation. He attempted to argue with his age on its own terms, and, in doing so, accepted its standards. 'Vex not thou the poet's mind, with thy shallow wit.' The difference between the mind of the poet and that of the sophist whom Tennyson is here addressing is one of degree, rather than of kind: and ultimately, it is perhaps social. Tennyson despises the 'fool lord', the bloated rich, the scientific materialist. It may seem cheap to point out that he himself became a peer, and rich, and that he attempted to use the arguments of scientists in poetry, yet to do so is to illustrate the difference be-

tween his attitude to the poet as poet and that of Keats for whom the poet was 'Seated on Elysian lawns, / Brows'd by none but Dian's fawns.'

For the Romantic, the poet has become the only interpreter of the absolute, and eventually his poetry, and his own being as poet, become absolute. At the same time, he is expected to be a poet in every line he writes. By this test the Romantics themselves of course often fail, yet their successes in writing out of a poetic experience in which poetry seems the inevitable language of the Romantic life have caused an impressive confusion of poetry *with* life: so that past acres of worldly, courtierly, witty, scholarly, philosophic, intellectual and religious poetry seem anti-poetic, because they contain material or ideas not intrinsic to the fusion of poetry with life.

In a Romantic poem the subject often appears to be invested by the poetry with a greater virtue within the poem than it would have outside it. For the Romantics, poetry is not a mirror held up to an illuminating—but making us look back at—nature (as it is in poems as different as *Venus and Adonis* and *The Rape of the Lock*). It encloses and magnifies the specially poetic original experience. Romantic love is the more love through being a subject for Romantic poetry, religion is the less Romantic because it is attached to rules, dogmas and arguments appealing to reason, and therefore—in Romantic poetry—the more dogmatic the belief, the less it seems poetically religious. Nature is transcended in Romantic poetry. The reader of the lake poets goes to Cumberland to see a landscape which has been transformed into Wordsworth:

> And I have felt
> A presence which disturbs me with the joy
> Of elevated thoughts; a sense sublime
> Of something far more deeply interfused
> Whose dwelling is the light of setting suns,
> And the round ocean and the living air,
> And the blue sky, and in the mind of man. . . .

This presence is the poetic imagination. Since Wordsworth is the only person capable of communicating this supranatural experience of nature, this is Wordsworth's world, not nature's.

Thus the Romantic poet becomes the centre of his own universe. For his readers, he is the one who offers a key which will open a lock transforming all experience into a world of poetic imagination richer than any real experience.

The golden Romantic poet then is more than life-enhancer, more than critic of life, more than upholder of a past tradition, more even than mystic—he is the magician who, at a time when faiths are weakened and the new material environment is beginning to set up impassable barriers between the individual and shared spiritual life, turns all his experience, of past literature, philosophic ideals, and untouched nature, into molten imagination. Whatever his poetry touches, it scores a victory of the imagination over the world: religion, politics, love, all can be transmuted into a poetic experience where the poetry outweighs the creed or dogma, the vision the politics, the emotion, the person. At the same time it selects from past poetry only that which it can transform into its own gold. Everything not from realms of gold is eschewed, expelled from the poetic universe.

Romanticism arose, of course, from a real crisis in human affairs, and had its origin in the works of philosophers and emancipators, though most of the Romantics—in their poetry at least—are independent of those who emancipated them.

Nevertheless, there is a real need for the members of this school to justify and explain themselves to outsiders. Keats's poetry is inseparable from his idea of the poetic as the truly sensuous life, Byron's is attached to the Byronic legend, Shelley's is the imagined central vision of a democratic philosophy. The golden Romanticism has relations with the past, alliances in the present, opponents, and a powerful diplomacy rationalizing its claims to set up a super-realistic reality. This comes partly from the need of all inhabitants of shut-off inner worlds to keep open paths leading back to the outside world, if only to avoid complete introversion and perhaps insanity (neither of which was always prevented), partly also from the need to answer that question about poetry which the Movement gave rise to very urgently: If the poet can invent within his poetry a self-sufficient world of imagined truth and beauty, then what relation if any does this have to the outside world of science, religion and politics?

Surely, the Romantics all suffered from the temptation to influence and attack the whole contemporary scene from the centre of the Romantic vision. They disagreed, however, on important points of tactics: whether poetry should attempt to change the world; whether it was the secret cult of an élite; whether it invented a life of the imagination which could replace all other life; or whether it called back 'the lapséd Soul' to 'The Holy Word / That walked among the ancient trees', and could the 'fallen, fallen light renew'.

Shelley believed in a revolution through poetry which had read science and learned Godwinian philosophy. For Keats poetry was the imaginary fruit, more delicious, more lasting, and without the evil of real fruit. For Byron, it was the mask of his own life. Wordsworth and Coleridge, of course, matured beyond the ideas of their youth. Still, in them, Romanticism remains centered on the omnipotence in their lives of imagination; and when, as happened, they abandoned this, they ceased to be Romantics. For what the Romantics have in common is the belief in the potentiality of the poet to create in his poetry a centre around which other forms of life would crystallize. But in this Coleridge and Wordsworth were Romantics only at certain periods of their lives, and by no means in all their poems.

Shelley's political utopianism is so crude that it is easy to overlook the fundamental identity of his claim 'Poets are the unacknowledged legislators of mankind' with other Romantic statements. Yet 'Beauty is truth, truth beauty—that is all / Ye know on earth, and all ye need to know', is a statement of essentially the same nature. For in a passive way Keats is simply asserting what Shelley claims—that the core of life is the image created by the poetic imagination—though he does not claim that this truth legislates. Matthew Arnold's 'poetry is a criticism of life' comes out of the same hat.

If Romanticism has diplomatic relations with the world of life, it has far more intimate relations with death. The Romantic dream was that reality should be life transformed into some sequence of images of the imagination, whether the Beauty that is truth, or the procession of Byron's bleeding heart, or the imaginative centre of a poetic justice at the centre of democracy. But when the imagination was confronted by irreducible facts that cannot be controlled or altered by the transcendent imaginative faculty, then the poet often turned to death rather than to life. In his book *The Romantic Agony,* Mario Praz analyses this fatal Romantic death-wish, together with much else that is perverse, violent and abnormal.

The early deaths of Byron, Shelley and Keats have it in common that they occurred at a time when the Romantic system had broken down in each poet's own life, and when, in order to live, he would have had to take some of those major decisions in accepting and dealing with reality which mark the transition from one stage of life and of work to another.

Keats is the most honest, the least self-deceiving, the most human and sympathetic of the Romantics, the one in whom the Romantic aim of creating an interior world of poetry was most clearly expressed. At the same time, he is the one with the least desire to reform or change the external world through an interior poetry, the one in whom the Romantic experience is most purely and lucidly gone through. Romanticism with him becomes something almost modest, and in his letters he states his views with perfect good faith:

> Now it appears to me that almost any Man may like the spider spin from his own inwards his own airy Citadel—the points of leaves and twigs on which the spider begins her work are few, and she fills the air with a beautiful circuiting. Man should be content with as few points to tip with the fine Web of his Soul, and weave a tapestry empyrean—full of symbols for his spiritual eye, of softness for his spiritual touch, of space for his wandering, of distinctness for his luxury.

He set out in his poetry to create this world where the poet who has renounced worldly ambition, opinions, public thoughts, and certitude of faith, makes for his soul—and perhaps also for the senses of his body—a dwelling, through the power of the imagination. In these early epistles to his brothers and his friends he is led on from thought to thought, from rhyme to rhyme by a fairy chain, from link to link of images and ideas associated only by poetry:

> Just like that bird am I in loss of time,
> Whene'er I venture on the sea of rhyme;
> With shattered boat, oar snapt, and canvas rent,
> I slowly sail, scarce knowing my intent;
> Still scooping up the water with my fingers,
> In which a trembling diamond never lingers.

There is intensity in this free, wandering, purposeless pursuit of an objective which is purely Beauty. Heaping delight on delight, he arrives at an image which turns out to be a goal, as it were at the edge of a cliff, or in a clearing at the centre of a wood. His early poems often take the reader for a gentle walk through groves or shrubs where one catches sight of nymph or goddess. He justifies the long poem *Endymion* as 'a week's stroll for the summer'.

Each of his Odes is a picture, self-sufficient within its frame that cuts it off from the outside world. Each is a concentration of sensations satisfying in life, transformed in poetry into something more satisfying than life. They are a world where voices from outside remind the poet that the world is a place where 'men sit and hear each other groan' but within the poetry 'it seems rich to die'. The Odes are dwelling places of pure sensation equipped with every faculty of imagination-transformed material to delight the soul and body:

> And in the midst of this wide quietness
> A rosy sanctuary will I dress
> With the wreath'd trellis of a working brain,
> With buds, and bells, and stars without a name,
> With all the gardener Fancy e'er could feign,
> Who, breeding flowers, will never breed the same:
> And there shall be for thee all soft delight

That shadowy thought can win,
A bright torch, and a casement ope at night,
To let the warm Love in!

The world of Keats's Romanticism, the sanctuary of Psyche, is perhaps the chamber of maiden thought, of one of his most famous letters:

> I compare human life to a large Mansion of Many Apartments, two of which I can only describe, the doors of the rest being as yet shut upon me. The first we step into we call the infant or thoughtless Chamber, in which we remain so long as we do not think—We remain there for a long while, and notwithstanding the doors of the second Chamber remain wide open, showing a bright appearance, we care not to hasten to it; but are at length imperceptibly impelled by the awakening of this thinking principle within us—we no sooner get into the second Chamber, which I shall call the Chamber of Maiden-Thought, than we become intoxicated with the light and the atmosphere, we see nothing but pleasant wonders, and think of delaying there for ever in delight: However among the effects this breathing is father of is that tremendous one of sharpening one's vision into the heart and nature of Man—of convincing one's nerves that the world is full of Misery and Heartbreak, Pain, Sickness and oppression—whereby this Chamber of Maiden-Thought becomes gradually darken'd and at the same time on all sides of it many doors are set open—but all dark—all leading to dark passages—We see not the ballance of good and evil. We are in a Mist. We are now in that state—We feel the 'burden of the Mystery'. To this point was Wordsworth come, as far as I can conceive, when he wrote 'Tintern Abbey' and it seems to me that his Genius is explorative of those dark Passages. Now if we live, and go on thinking, we too shall explore them—

We, who read this, see how difficult it was for Keats to live and explore them, with the identity of his dying brother Tom pressing on him so that he could work only with difficulty. Could the Romantics, Keats, Byron and Shelley, ever have pressed through those dark passages, had they survived?

Was not the Romantic Movement simply an assortment of varied situations into which a number of poets, who were really the heirs of the eighteenth-century tradition, had been forced by the French Revolution, the growth of English industrialism, the beginnings of the decay of rural life? Can one imagine an alternative to this magnificently varied attempt to build centre and fortress of the imagination, from which poetry would gradually advance into the world through dark underground passages?

Perhaps the answer is to be found in certain poems of Blake, and others of Coleridge. Both sometimes write in a diction different from that of the Romantics, and from their own Romantic poems, and much nearer to what today we think of as fulfilling the requirements of a modern diction.

With Blake there is a directness, an immediacy, and a faith in both the body and the spirit, which reminds us of a writer like D. H. Lawrence. There is a density of experience and particularity of belief in his poems, which makes the productions of the genteel though revolutionary literary class of other Romantics seem generalized attitudes and emotions. To read "London" is to feel that Victorian poetry is a sensuous, rich, prolific divagation from the direct pure line of a submerged tradition, at once human and intensely visionary. Blake can no more than Lawrence be claimed as a 'proletarian' writer, and yet both were strengthened in every line they wrote through their work not being part of the stream of literature coming from the ruling class. The weakness of Shelley is that he only has his own Eton and Oxford education, and Godwin's philosophy, with which to attack his own class. He does not derive organic strength from another kind of life with which to attack the life to which he himself is habituated. But Blake does write out of another life, the continuity of a tradition of artisans, handworkers, non-conforming cranks. "London" opens with the lines:

> I wander thro' each charter'd street,
> Near where the charter'd Thames does flow,
> And mark in every face I meet
> Marks of weakness, marks of woe.
>
> In every cry of every Man,
> In every Infant's cry of fear,
> In every voice, in every ban,
> The mind-forg'd manacles I hear.

Compare these famous lines with Shelley's equally famous opening of the most direct of all his political poems, *The Mask of Anarchy:*

> i
>
> As I lay asleep in Italy
> There came a voice from over the Sea,
> And with great power it forth led me
> To walk in the visions of Poesy.
>
> ii
>
> I met murder on the way—
> He had a mask like Castlereagh—
> Very smooth he looked, yet grim;
> Seven blood-hounds followed him.

Nothing could be more apparent than the difference between the two poems. With Blake one feels that he writes with his own blood about the blood that he knows: 'And the hapless soldier's sigh / Runs in blood down Palace walls.' Shelley writes as a member of a ruling class about other members of this ruling class, rumours of whose oppressive acts reach him in Italy, where he is living abroad. Politically speaking, Shelley is the revolutionary; but poetically speaking, it is in Blake that we feel the revulsion of life at the oppression of life—the true subject of such a poetry, which lies far deeper than—and might be directed against—any politics.

All the same, as T. S. Eliot has pointed out, Blake had the disadvantages as well as the advantages of his self-education. His alternative to the aristocratic tradition that had turned bad on itself in the Romantics was too narrow, too provincial, too home-made, too cranky, to save the Romantic Movement from becoming swamped by the ideas of the time in the Victorian era.

Coleridge, in certain poems, provides another alternative to the Romantic cubing of poetry by the poetic situation and the poet himself. In poems like "Dejection: an Ode," and "Human Life or the Denial of Immortality," he writes a poetry which is open to discuss the ideas of prose, and which in rhythm and imagery reflects intellectual reasons in a way which—although in an entirely different idiom—recalls the eighteenth century:

> If dead, we cease to be; if total gloom

Swallow up life's brief flash for aye, we fare
As summer-gusts, of sudden birth and doom,
Whose sound and motion not at all declare,
But are their whole of being!

This has rhythm and diction based on speech; intellectual strength able to meet, in poetry, philosophic ideas; a vital interest which is not only of poetry, but of the intellectual questions which most concern us. Blake and Coleridge, different as they are, meet today across the Victorian gulf, in poetry that speaks very directly to us.

But by the Romantic Gold Standard, these attempts of Coleridge seemed a falling back into the prosaic. The movement which had begun with politically Republican sympathies became so much involved with the problem of the poet and of poetry in the world, that finally its achievement was to declare something which might be called the Autonomous Republic of Poetry which had its own religion, its own politics, its own currency, protected by mountain barriers from everything in life which could be put into prose. (pp. 97-110)

Stephen Spender, "The Romantic Gold Standard," in his The Making of a Poem, *second edition, W. W. Norton & Company, Inc., 1962, pp. 97-110.*

RICHARD HARTER FOGLE

[*An American critic and educator, Fogle has written extensively on English Romantic poetry. In the following excerpt, he summarizes and challenges the opinions of the New Critics, whose influential attacks damaged the reputation of the Romantic poets in the early to mid twentieth century.*]

New Critics share an absolutism which in intention is worthy of praise, but open to many objections in practice. It is praiseworthy insofar as it endeavors to supply objective, permanent, and invariable standards for the evaluation of literature. It is objectionable when it leaps to conclusions without first examining the evidence; when it short-circuits due process of law and becomes judge, jury, prosecuting attorney—and finally executioner—all at once. The New Critical standards which are appropriate to this discussion are called Irony and Organic Unity. As applied to the Romantic poets they are used as weapons, or as yardsticks to demonstrate the failures of Romantic poetry. The intention of this essay is to maintain that they are misapplied, and consequently that the judgments based upon them are erroneous and unjust.

The attitude of the New Critics toward the Romantics is foreshadowed in T. E. Hulme's tentative but important "Romanticism and Classicism" [see Further Reading], an opening shot against nineteenth-century poetry. Hulme takes the essence of Romanticism to be the Rousseauistic belief that man is good and a creature of infinite possibilities. This belief obviates the necessity of formal religion, the faith in the existence of a Supernatural Being. Belief in God, however, is deeply ingrained in human nature. If it is abandoned there must be some kind of compensating substitution. What happens in Romanticism, then, is this:

You don't believe in Heaven, so you begin to believe in a Heaven on earth. In other words, you get romanticism. The concepts that are right and proper in their own sphere are spread over, and so mess up, falsify and blur the clear outlines of human experience. It is like pouring a pot of treacle over the dinner table. Romanticism then . . . is spilt religion.

The Romantic is always talking about the infinite, because he believes that man is infinite, and this leads to extravagance of speech and empty rhetoric. In contrast, the classic has his feet always on the ground; he is faithful to "the concept of a limit." Romantic poetry, thinks Hulme, is for this reason at last on the point of death, and a very good thing, too. But while romantic verse has passed away, the attitude of mind which demands romantic qualities in verse lives on.

I object [he says] even to the best of the romantics. I object still more to the receptive attitude. I object to the sloppiness which doesn't consider that a poem is a poem unless it is moaning or whining about something or other. I always think in this connection of the last line of a poem of John Webster's which ends with a request I cordially endorse:

'End your moan and come away.'

The thing has got so bad now that a poem which is all dry and hard, a properly classical poem, would not be considered poetry at all.

Luckily, however, Romanticism is dying, to be succeeded by "a period of dry, hard classical verse." For this Hulme suggests a new aesthetic and theory of imagery. Aesthetic pleasure, in his opinion, lies in the communication of experience; and poetry, which is a "visual, concrete" language, "a compromise for a language of intuition which would hand over sensations bodily," is the ideal vehicle for this communication. In this fact is the sufficient justification for poetry.

In this account there are several points of special significance. First to be noticed is the sweeping contemptuousness of Hulme's attitude toward Romanticism. He formulates a narrow and rigid definition, epigrammatic and denunciatory. Although at the outset he warns the reader that he is using the terms "Romanticism" and "Classicism" in a limited and special sense, he permits them throughout his essay to assume a general significance. He confesses that there are other things in the poetry of the Romantics besides the qualities which he condemns, but the general effect of his remarks is implicitly damaging to it.

Of interest, too, is his assertion that the justification of poetry lies in its accurate delineation of things and experiences, almost a substitute for the intuition of the things and experiences themselves. Clearly here is the germ of a theory of poetry as knowledge, which as formulated by Hulme one need not be very far gone in idealism to question. In the first place, he assumes that all sensory images are visual: an assumption obviously false. Second, and more important, he thoroughly confuses poetry and life. If poetry is a substitute for consciousness itself, by which we intuit things and experience, on what ground can poetry exist? It can in that case only do poorly what we ourselves can do supremely well. A word is not, after all, equivalent to a thing.

The implications of this theory of imagery are that poetry should occupy itself with objects: small objects, with definite limits, so as to present a minimum of difficulty to perception. Hulme predicts that the new poetry will "be cheerful, dry and sophisticated," in keeping with the finite quality of its subject matter.

It is noticeable that Hulme's distaste for Romanticism is in some measure due to what he regards as its Monism. The classicist will not seek to impose a factitious unity upon the natural world. In the brilliant series of detached aphorisms collected under the name of "Cinders" he declares that there is no cosmos, that all is flux, and that "only in the fact of consciousness is there a unity of the world." Taken together with his explicit utterances upon imagery, this pronouncement suggests an artistic preoccupation with the single image and a relative indifference to the unity of the whole, in keeping with his general *Weltanschauung.*

Hulme expresses an attitude and a set of beliefs about Romanticism, poetry, and imagery which recur in a greater or less degree in the criticism of all his successors. His attitude toward the Romantics, for example, his love of definiteness and concreteness in imagery, and his desire for "a period of dry, hard, classical verse," are all apparent in the essays of T. S. Eliot.

This attitude is faithfully reproduced in Eliot's superbly supercilious judgment:

> . . . the only cure for Romanticism is to analyze it. What is permanent and good in Romanticism is curiosity . . . a curiosity which recognizes that any life, if accurately and profoundly penetrated, is interesting and always strange. Romanticism is a short cut to the strangeness without the reality, and it leads its disciples only back upon themselves . . . there may be a good deal to be said for Romanticism in life, there is no place for it in letters [*The Sacred Wood*, 1920].

In Eliot is the same narrowness of definition, the same epigrammatic brilliance, the same over-aweing certainty that one finds in Hulme. So confident is the tone, so nervous and close-packed the expression, that one is inclined to take this statement for far more than it actually is. Mr. Eliot has failed to inform us what, where, and how extensive is the Romanticism of which he is thinking. (pp. 243-48)

Eliot's greatest contribution to the New Criticism, "the unified sensibility," is, however, a complete departure from the ideas of Hulme. In his important essay on "The Metaphysical Poets" Eliot suggested a view of literary history and a standard for poetry which have been extended and systematized by others. The metaphysical poets of the seventeenth century, along with many of the late Elizabethan and Jacobean dramatists, possessed a unity of sensibility, "a mechanism of sensibility which could devour any kind of experience." Through the influence of two powerful poets, Milton and Dryden, this unity was lost. The metaphysicals, however, were in the direct current of English poetry, not those who followed. Judged by this standard of sensibility, the eighteenth and nineteenth centuries were found wanting. Thought and feeling were separated. "The poets revolted against the ratiocinative, the descriptive; they thought and felt by fits, unbalanced; they reflected" [*Homage to John Dryden,* 1924]. To a poet like Donne, however, "A thought . . . was an experience; it modified his sensibility."

At this point Eliot proposes a definition of the poet's psychology which we find reflected again and again in later critics:

> When a poet's mind is properly equipped for its work, it is constantly amalgamating disparate experience; the ordinary man's experience is chaotic, irregular, fragmentary. The latter falls in love, or reads Spinoza, and these two experiences have nothing to do with each other, or with the noise of the typewriter or the smell of cooking; in the mind of the poet these experiences are always forming new wholes.

Closely allied to this statement is his shrewd remark on Johnson's condemnation of the metaphysical poets for "yoking the most heterogeneous ideas by violence together."

> The force of this impeachment [says Eliot] lies in the failure of the conjunction, the fact that often the ideas are yoked but not united. . . . But a degree of heterogeneity of material compelled into unity is omnipresent in poetry.

He observes of the poetry of the future that it will probably be difficult and complex:

> Our civilization comprehends great variety and complexity, and this variety and complexity, playing upon a refined sensibility, must produce various and complex results. The poet must become more and more comprehensive, more allusive, more indirect, in order to force, to dislocate if necessary, language into his meaning.

Poetic imagery, then, is likely to be heterogeneous in material, comprehensive, and difficult, but unified by the amalgamating power of the poet's mind.

Mr. Eliot has offered a number of acute and suggestive generalizations, which have taken deep root in modern criticism. But the merely tentative and suggestive quality of his pronouncements contrasts remarkably with the rigidly dogmatic structures which have been reared upon them. The notion of "the unified sensibility," for example, of which its creator has modestly said that it has had a success in the world astonishing to him, seems a slender basis for a new and revolutionary theory of the history of English poetry. . . . [To] a reader of the Romantics it looks like a streamlined modern version of Coleridge on the Imagination, or Wordsworth on the Poet in the 1800 *Preface;* and therefore, since it obviously is intended to exclude Romantic poetry, needs to be more fully differentiated from Romantic theory. (pp. 248-51)

The doctrine of poetry and of imagery which appears in Eliot as "unified sensibility" or "heterogeneity of material compelled into unity by the operation of the poet's mind" is more elaborately formulated by I. A. Richards, to whose work all of the New Critics are indebted. Mr. Richards divides poetry into the "Synthetic" and the "Exclusive," a classification roughly corresponding to the "unified" and "dissociated" sensibility of Eliot. In Synthetic Poetry there is an "equilibrium of opposed impulses, which we suspect to be the groundplan of the most valuable aesthetic responses." The distinction between Exclusive and Synthetic Poetry runs thus:

> A poem of the first group is built out of sets of impulses which run parallel, which have the same direction. In a poem of the second group the most obvious feature is the extraordinary heterogeneity of the distinguishable impulses. But they are more than heterogeneous, they are opposed. They are such that in ordinary, non-poetic, non-imaginative experience, one or other set would be suppressed to give as it might appear freer development to the others [*Principles of Literary Criticism,* 1924].

From this distinction Richards evolves his theory of Irony. Exclusive Poetry is sentimental poetry, incomplete in its view of life and open to attack by Irony. Synthetic poetry, being itself ironic, is invulnerable:

> Irony in this sense consists in the bringing in of the opposite, the complementary impulses; that is why poetry which is exposed to it is not of the highest

Percy Bysshe Shelley

order, and why irony itself is so constantly a characteristic of poetry which is.

This principle of irony is apotheosized under the name of synaesthesis as the ultimate aesthetic experience, as Beauty itself, in *The Foundations of Aesthetics.* Synaesthesis is an equilibrium and harmony of various impulses, bringing into play all the faculties. By this equilibrium and harmony "we are enabled to appreciate relationships in a way which would not be possible under normal circumstances. Through no other experience can the full richness and complexity of our environment be realized."

Richards, then, elaborates a conception of poetry and of poetic imagery which is parallel to the more tentative and fragmentary notions of Eliot. Although he is not concerned to assay individual poets, his illustrations are so chosen as to be implicitly damaging to the Romantics, especially to Shelley. (pp. 252-54)

Richards' Irony is deeply indebted to Coleridge's theory of the Imagination, in which opposite or discordant qualities are reconciled, a more than usual state of emotion is conjoined with more than usual order, and judgment and self-possession are combined with enthusiasm and feeling. There is, however, a significant difference of emphasis. Coleridge would reconcile opposites in an organic synthesis of emotion and order, judgment and feeling. In Richards the synthesizing agent is slighted, the discordant and opposing materials

stressed. It is the opposition and heterogeneity itself upon which his attention is focussed, and the balancing and harmonizing are in the main left to take care of themselves.

The concept of Irony, or heterogeneity, or "unified sensibility," is a basic tenet for most of the New Critics, and I believe accepted in practice even when, as by John Crowe Ransom, the theory itself is repudiated. Richards' semantic emphasis upon the flexibility and variety of words according to their context and situation has had a like effect. Richards also, like Hulme and Eliot, prefers verse to be urbane, social, and easy in tone: a preference which has had its influence upon later critics. I think I do not distort his intention in saying that this urbanity of tone is with him at least implicitly a standard of judgment. It is very close to Eliot's "wit," and closely linked also with the theory of irony. It implies a certain dandyism and imperturbability, a refusal to be disturbed by inconvenient emotions. Like Eliot, Mr. Richards finds this quality absent in the Romantics.

In the criticism of John Crowe Ransom and Allen Tate one finds . . . the same love of heterogeneity as in Eliot and Richards; the same demand for dry urbanity of tone. One finds in them also, however, a preoccupation with form unexampled even in Eliot, an exclusive and intransigent aestheticism. Poetry to them is an absolute substance, related to the affairs of the world only at several removes. It "finds its true usefulness in its perfect inutility" [Tate, *Reactionary Essays,* 1936]. It is "the art of apprehending and concentrating our experience in the mysterious limitations of form." The objective reality of poetry is in its formal qualities, which it is therefore the chief business of the critic to examine. Poetry, however, gives us the only complete knowledge of the world, "that unique and formed intelligence of the world of which man alone is capable" [Tate, *Reason in Madness,* 1941].

To Ransom and Tate Romantic poetry is imperfect poetry because it attempts to communicate ideas; because it employs mass language, the only effective means of communication; and because it is "associationist," vaguely musical, cloudy, and "pretty" [Ransom, *The World's Body,* 1938]. The best poetry, and the best imagery, is complex and ironic, "metaphysical." In the words of Tate, "The poet attains to a mastery over experience by facing its utmost implications. There is the clash of powerful opposites." Ransom approves of the deliberate obscurity of Tate's poem, "Death of Little Boys." A poem is "nothing short of a desperate ontological or metaphysical manoeuvre." The antithesis of this poetry is Romanticism. "The poetry I am disparaging is . . . the poetry written by romantics, in a common sense of that term." Romantic poetry is also to be condemned because it is "Platonic." It is "allegory, a discourse in things, but on the understanding that they are translatable at every point into ideas."

Applied specifically to the problem of poetic imagery, the theories of Ransom and Tate correspond roughly to the ideas of Hulme and Eliot, and in a lesser degree to those of I. A. Richards. Their view of Poetry as Knowledge is very close to Hulme's "poetry of things," and would seem to be open to the same objections. Ransom, in commenting upon Aristotle, declares, like Hulme, that the accurate description of things is enough for poetry, that the end of art is an infinite degree of particularity. The realism of technique thus to be employed is not "photographic," but "psychological." The value and the distinction of the artistic process lie in the pains lavished by the artist upon technique. But this technique, by Mr. Ransom's account of it, is an isolated entity related neither to subject or object. He tells us nothing either of the mind of the artist by which the thing is perceived or in what manner words are able to express the thing itself. Tate comparably asserts that poetry is *complete* knowledge, knowledge of whole objects, unlike the limited knowledge which science offers us, but also fails to furnish a psychological or metaphysical rationale.

The flaw in the criticism of Ransom and Tate, in their approach specifically to Romanticism and particularly to Shelley, is its absolutism. They transform a set of interesting but incompletely grounded and provisional insights into critical absolutes. They mistake their own speculations, acute but limited in validity, for truths of universal application. They establish categories, and these categories suddenly become independent, fixed, and permanent. They generalize with astounding haste. Like T. E. Hulme, they formulate a definition of Romanticism, for example, which is at first limited to a single context, but which is later applied indiscriminately to vast tracts of poetry and legions of poets. (pp. 254-58)

In Cleanth Brooks' *Modern Poetry and the Tradition* [see Further Reading] the doctrines of the New Criticism become a developed and explicit system. The true "tradition," as one might guess, is the tradition of metaphysical wit and complexity. Like Eliot and Basil Willey he traces its downfall to Hobbes and the scientific rationalism of the late seventeenth century and hails its resurgence in the moderns of the twentieth. Romanticism he finds unsatisfactory, both in theory and in practice. The Romantics attempted to break loose from the bonds of eighteenth-century neoclassicism, but failed to go far enough. Instead of repudiating completely the eighteenth-century belief in the inherent beauty and poetic value of certain types of objects, they merely substituted other objects. By denying the importance of the intellect in favor of emotion and spontaneity they fell into the fallacy of dissociating the elements of poetic sensibility. The modern poet and theorist, on the other hand, reposes his confidence in the power of his imagination, which fuses and harmonizes disparate, incongruous, and apparently unattractive materials into unity. He does not make the error of distinguishing Fancy from Imagination, wit from high poetry.

In ["What Does Modern Poetry Communicate?" *American Prefaces*, 1940] Mr. Brooks joins Ransom and Tate in condemning "the fallacy of communication." the poem itself is "the linguistic vehicle which conveys the thing most clearly and accurately"; therefore it is fallacious to abstract its ideas in order to understand it. The poet employs the methods characteristic of poetry: indirection, "the use of symbol rather than abstraction, suggestion rather than explicit pronouncement, metaphor rather than direct statement." In a later article [*The Language of Poetry*, 1942] he declares that paradox is the very stuff of poetry. (pp. 267-69)

He attributes to the Romantics a doctrine of the inherent beauty of poetic objects which he has found in Addison, relating it to Romanticism on the strength of a statement from Wordsworth: "Fancy depends upon the rapidity . . . with which she scatters her thoughts and images; trusting that their number, and the felicity with which they are linked together, will make amends for the want of individual value."

Now the phrase "poetic objects" presents its difficulties: it seems to suggest a confusion of life and art which one cannot believe has ever been literally accepted by any group; in any event, the citation from Wordsworth will hardly support its

implications, since his "thoughts and images" are psychological, and related to "objects" only at many removes. Mr. Brooks does, however, hit at a vital issue. One may confidently repel the suggestion that any Romantic poet has believed that good material makes good poetry by some simple transference from life to paper; it is highly probable, on the other hand, that the great majority of poets of every period and allegiance have believed that some objects were more beautiful than others, and some subjects more promising to poetry. The greatest source of possible confusion lies in the meaning of "beauty." Mr. Brooks, if I interpret him properly, is in this context thinking of beauty as sentimentality, as false and oversimplified idealization; and for him it is a reproach to the Romantics that they desired to express the beautiful. The general imputation, of course, I flatly deny; but it would be senseless and humorless to attempt a systematic rebuttal.

One might, however, suggest that Mr. Brooks has fallen into the very trap he has prepared for Romanticism; that he proposes an absolute distinction of content and form, material and art. Thus by a shift from the theory of Romanticism to its poetry he has it performing the easy task of molding inherently beautiful materials into what one supposes must be beautiful poetry. Metaphysical poetry is more virtuous; apparently it deliberately sets itself a more difficult problem, on the theory that it is less laudable to shoot a bear than to kill it with your hands. Yet it could be considered that with successful execution the result will be the same; while by the second method the chance that the bear may win is largely increased. The imagination of the poet may be concerned with the choice of subject as well as the shaping of it; psychologically it may be that the two processes are simultaneous and indistinguishable. Mr. Brooks, like other New Critics, is deeply concerned to find trustworthy, objective standards of value. Will he then, when he judges the finished statue, estimate the cost of the stone, and have a preference for the cheapest?

If one accepts the implications of the literary history sketched in *Modern Poetry and the Tradition,* to which I presume most New or Metaphysical Critics would assent, the eighteenth century becomes a kind of poetic nadir, above which the Romantics strove to rise with poor success. The underlying reason for this failure is not wholly clear. Mr. Brooks sometimes seems to feel that if they had taken thought, had been better men, had read more Donne, they too might have been Metaphysicals, and that their failure to be so was a flat dereliction of duty. One wonders by what mysterious providence the twentieth century has been blessed, that its poets alone have been privileged to see the light long lost; and why this providence so signally ignored meanwhile so many. One wonders further what justice can condemn the Romantic and Victorian outcasts; how in this case the ways of God shall be justified to the errant. Could this providence be named the Time Spirit? And if so, what becomes of our absolute, objective, and universal standards?

Mr. Brooks conceives of metaphysical poetry as a norm, or as a whole compared to which Romantic poetry is an imperfect part. Romantic poetry is the product of a divided; metaphysical of a unified sensibility. I suggest that this may well be a fallacy. Speaking frankly as a Romantic partisan, I am yet unwilling to attempt a reversal, to suggest that Mr. Brooks has confused the terms and should put them in their proper places. On the other hand, I am quite willing to assert that the Metaphysical whole is not less but more confined than the Romantic whole; that the area of reality governed by it has shrunk, and not expanded.

On such issues as this it is useless to argue at length; no one will be converted, and the chapter-and-verse would be another book. But let us take as a part of the argument what may stand as an emblem of the whole. That is, the statement of Mr. Brooks that the Romantics dissociated the elements of poetic sensibility by stressing the importance of emotion and spontaneity.

The Romantics were fully aware of the problem, and considered themselves not to be over-stressing, but rather reinstating emotion, as a real factor in the poetic complex which had been badly neglected. Wordsworth, defining poetry as "a spontaneous overflow of emotion," continued immediately, ". . . Poems to which any value can be attached were never produced on any variety of subjects but by a man who, being possessed of more than usual organic sensibility, had also thought long and deeply." His "emotion recollected in tranquillity" epitomizes a psychological theory of poetic creation which strives to do justice to conscious and unconscious, intellect and emotion, idea and sensation. The *Prelude* is the fullest examination ever made of the organic unity of the poetic mind, an immense and subtle synthesis of widely differing forces. It is almost superfluous to speak of Coleridge's theory of Imagination, the unifying power in which all faculties are reconciled and none are slighted. Shelley, with his Platonic Inspiration theory, manages to employ an extremely acute intellect in the substantial bulk of his considerable poetry. As a matter of fact Mr. Brooks himself, with his doctrine of imaginative as opposed to logical unity, might by fault-finding critics be charged with having effected this baneful separation. He may very well plead that in his use of the terms he has intended no simple opposition or dissociation; but then so with at least equal reason may the Romantics absolve themselves.

The application of these statements to Shelley follows. Shelley, in the opinion of Mr. Brooks, occupies much too high a place in the ranks of the English poets.

> The traditional historian hardly sees Shelley as a very unsatisfactory poet greatly inferior to Keats. A more considered view must surely hold him so. Shelley is not merely guilty of poor craftsmanship—slovenly riming, loosely decorative and sometimes too gaudy metaphor. Consideration of the two poets on the basis of tone and attitude will reveal more important differences. Keats is rarely sentimental, Shelley frequently so. Keats is too much the artist to risk Shelley's sometimes embarrassing declarations—"I die, I faint, I fail," or "I fall upon the thorns of life! I bleed!"

Two charges in this passage are possible to discuss—Shelley's "loosely decorative metaphor" and his sentimentality. They may be translated into the assertion that he fails to measure up to Mr. Brooks' basic poetic standards—organic unity and irony. Irony Mr. Brooks has most recently defined, in the terms of Eliot, as "that which the mind of the reader can accept as coherent, mature, and founded on the facts of experience," and alternatively from I. A. Richards as

> . . . "poetry of synthesis"—that is, it is a poetry which does not leave out what is apparently hostile to its dominant tone, and which, because it is able to fuse the irrelevant and discordant, has come to terms with itself and is invulnerable to irony.

Organic unity, or "the concept of the poem as organism," which for Mr. Brooks is of such importance that "the best hope that we have for reviving the study of poetry and of the humanities generally" rests upon it, means that "Each part—image, statement, metaphor—helps build the total meaning of a poem and is itself qualified by the whole context."

Now, insofar as Mr. Brooks has made it possible to measure Shelley by these standards, I should maintain that of the two poems which he cites "The Indian Serenade" is "sentimental" but possesses organic unity, while I should passionately deny that the "Ode to the West Wind" is either sentimental or inorganic. In regard to the "Indian Serenade," Mr. Brooks has so underrated the poet that he supposes him to be talking quite literally about himself; if the lover, the "I" of the lyric, is to be translated as it were bodily into Shelley, this lyric is indeed open to irony. But the title itself would indicate that this is not so, that the love affair is a matter of imagination and in a sense dramatic. "The Indian Serenade" is slight and quite frankly of no great consequence. It seems to me artistic and well integrated in design. (pp. 269-74)

Here we must note an important difficulty in using the concept of organic unity as a critical weapon. If one commences, as does Mr. Brooks, by speaking of the poem as "organism," one makes a statement about the nature of poetry and poetic creation. This statement has nothing to do with judicial or evaluative criticism; it is descriptive and leads to explanation rather than judgment. Criticism which begins with the assumption of the organic will not question the existence of meaningful relationships within the poem, but will proceed to look for them, in the full confidence that they are there to be found. Such a criticism will look for the master-principle of the organism within the poem itself; it will regard the importation of principles from without as irrelevant. As soon, in fact, as judicial criticism commences, the concept of the poem as organism ceases to have validity.

The practical consequences of this position are extensive. They lead me from my point of view to reject organic unity as a tool of evaluation, on the grounds that with good will one can find it in any poem whatever. It is not a reliable criterion, and if used as a criterion can be manipulated at will. If organic unity itself becomes a critical absolute, the grounds for distinction are wiped out. All poems which possess organic unity are equally good—if my contention is correct, and all poems may be shown to have organic unity, the result is soul-destroying.

A comparable, although perhaps a lesser source of difficulty, occurs in the use of the concept of irony. One can accept it as a standard for poetry, defined as does Eliot as "that which the mind of the reader can accept as coherent, mature, and founded on the facts of experience," or in the Coleridgean formulation of "the reconciliation of opposites"; but the application must vary with the critic. Whether rightly or wrongly, I cannot permit the decision as to what constitutes coherence and maturity in the individual work to be made for me; I must make it myself, and will resist any formulation which seems to me to be arbitrary, distorted, tactless, ignorant—in any way incomplete, in fine. I am likely, then, to find Mr. Brooks's descriptions of the Ironic unsatisfactory, as presumably he would mine. His irony I am likely to find a mere attitude without a situation, or a rigid, predetermined formula, or sometimes a new invention to enable you to go wading without getting your feet wet. I find irony, within the present meaning of the term, in the studious understatement of the conclusion of "Michael," in the self-realization which under-lies the apparent breaking-off of "Kubla Khan," in the breadth of understanding beneath the excitement of the "Ode to the West Wind." Mr. Brooks would be unlikely to agree.

In his most recent book, *The Well Wrought Urn,* Mr. Brooks has devoted an appendix to an eloquent and persuasive de-fense of absolutist criticism. Here he avouches the very wor-thy aim of applying a single objective standard to poetry of every age and type. The explications with which he illustrates his method and point of view are often distinguished and al-ways interesting. One may hazard the opinion, however, that the method, which accentuates the similarities between good poems of all ages and ignores the differences, fails to complete the process of criticism. For the essential qualities which make good poetry can only be adequately discussed after the differences have been accounted for, after the poems have been identified in their uniqueness. To use the metaphor of organic unity, by his method we get too quickly from the parts to the whole; we are likely to be overhasty in passing judgment and slight the complexity of the relationship.

In his appendix Mr. Brooks maintains that by standards alone can we avoid a disastrous relativism in which all judg-ments are dissolved and the study of literature itself is doomed. And we may safely agree. But it does not follow that we must accept a single standard; still less does it follow that this standard must be that of Mr. Brooks. Alternatives pre-sumably are possible. One might suggest that . . . the ideal criticism is composed of the "participant" *plus* the "specta-tor" attitude. Observe the poem in its own terms and its own relationships, and only then proceed to evaluation by external standards.

Standards are undoubtedly essential; without them we can-not have rational or even intelligible criticism. We can be grateful to Mr. Brooks for many skilful and illuminating ex-plications, and understand their bases from his statements of principle. Only thus, of course, can we hope to agree or dis-agree with judgment, and come at last to whatever truth we are qualified to see. But if he asks us to accept, let us say, "metaphysical poetry," as a norm, forsaking all others, we must reply that he has not sufficiently considered other poet-ry to convince us that he has really examined all its possibili-ties; that we must combat our own limitations, attempt to transcend them, and arrive at our own synthesis. Mr. Brooks has somewhere expressed the fear that critical relativism may lead us to confuse Edgar A. Guest and Shakespeare; critical absolutism, one may feel, has already confused Edgar A. Guest and Shelley, in an almost equal failure of values. (pp. 275-78)

> *Richard Harter Fogle, "Romantic Bards and Meta-physical Reviewers," in his* The Imagery of Keats and Shelley: A Comparative Study, *1949. Reprint by Archon Books, 1962, pp. 241-78.*

JOHN CLUBBE

[*An American educator and critic, Clubbe specializes in nineteenth-century English literature. In the following excerpt, he surveys what he considers to be critical misrepresentations of English Romanticism and upholds a humanist view of Ro-mantic poetry.*]

The history of literary criticism, it must be said, is in part a history of man's folly, dullness, blindness, even dishonesty when confronted with some of man's greatest artistic achieve-ments. If, as Hazlitt observed, "the arts are not progressive," it is certainly true that we have had little progress in the art of criticism, although fads come and go. The present over-whelming tidal wave of academic writing about literature provides the evidence, and nowhere is that evidence more vis-ible than in "critical" writing about the basic nature of En-glish Romanticism. Some notable progressions in our under-standing of the subject have been made, to be sure, but these we pay for at the cost of a rising tide of misinformation rolling from the presses. And a certain part of this gets reprinted, presumably because the authors have become well-known, and thus their misrepresentations become part of the ever more influential folklore of Romanticism.

"Romanticism is still the most vexing problem in literary his-tory," wrote Morse Peckham in 1965, "even more irritating than the problem of the Renaissance" [see Further Reading]. The situation has not changed since then. If anything, Ro-manticism gets even more attention than when Peckham wrote. It seems worthwhile, then, once more to investigate the folklore that has grown up around the subject, to discover what relationship past criticism of Romanticism has to pres-ent, and to pinpoint a few of the problems that the plethora of current writing on the subject poses. With all the wealth of critical intelligence that has been devoted to the English Romantic poets in recent decades, we are in many ways fur-ther than ever from understanding them within the humanis-tic perspective they themselves desired. (pp. 95-6)

So stunning is the achievement of the Romantic poets, begin-ning with *Songs of Innocence* in 1789 and continuing through the mid-1820s with the later cantos of *Don Juan,* that it left even astute contemporaries or near-contemporaries both be-wildered and awed. Macaulay, not usually identified as a par-tisan of Romanticism and never thinking to apply the term "Romantic" to particular poets, recognized the unity of the movement when as early as 1830 he spoke of it as "the most enlightened generation of the most enlightened people that ever existed" ["Southey's Colloquies on Society," in *Macau-lay: Selected Writings,* 1972]. De Quincey, looking back in 1838 on what he had lived through, thought it "a revolution more astonishing and total than ever before happened in liter-ature or in life" ["Recollections of Charles Lamb," in *Collect-ed Writings,* 14 Vols., 1896-97]. Another decade, and Char-lotte Brontë in *Jane Eyre* has St. John Rivers (not, one would have thought, a friend to the Romantics) recall the earlier part of the century as "the golden age of modern literature." But coming to terms with this literature has proved a difficult task. Neither Macaulay, De Quincey, nor Brontë viewed it with perspective sufficient to grasp the nature of its effort.

It is Matthew Arnold who provides the first sustained evalua-tion of the Romantics, an evaluation that is also a misreading, one that was enormously influential and lasted through T. S. Eliot and the New Critics. Over the course of his life Arnold grappled with the poetry of the two generations preceding his own to which he owed, as he well knew, so much. Like Eliot after him, he wrote out of the biases of an artistic sensibility and of an essentially romantic temperament. A disillusioned child of Romanticism, he rebelled uneasily against his inheri-tance. Objectivity escaped him because these poets, more even than he realized, had shaped him, indeed had enabled him to forge his own identity as a creative writer. In "Memo-rial Verses" (1850) Arnold remembers that his soul had *"felt"* Byron "like the thunder's roll"; Wordsworth's "healing power" had taught him (and his generation) how to cope with emotional turmoil. Although in the Preface to his 1853 *Poems* he disapproved of the Romantics' concentration on contemporary life and on subjective states, he looked back, nonetheless, with intense longing upon the energy they had displayed. In "Stanzas from the Grande Chartreuse" (1855) he recalls Byron, Shelley and the *Obermann* of Senancour, before closing the poem with a vision of a future age of poetic greatness. Then poets—by banner and bugle accompanied—will make the blood dance and chain the eyes. Is not this, in effect, a vision of a new age of *Romantic* poetry?

In "The Function of Criticism at the Present Time" (1865) Arnold expressed the opinion that Romantic literature "had about it something premature," and that most of "its productions are doomed . . . to prove hardly more lasting than the productions of far less splendid epochs." "This prematureness" came about, Arnold believed, because Romantic literature did not have "sufficient materials to work with." It lacked substantial ideas, ideas tested by time and thus of perennial interest to the human mind. "In other words," he continued, "the English poetry of the first quarter of this century, with plenty of energy, plenty of creative force, did not know enough." When the Romantics thought, they were children. Arnold found Byron "empty of matter," Shelley "incoherent," and Wordsworth (whom he had known personally) "wanting in completeness and unity." In other ages of poetic greatness, Arnold conceived that the poet lived "in a current of ideas in the highest degree animating and nourishing to the creative power; society was, in the fullest measure, permeated by fresh thought, intelligent and alive." But England in the early nineteenth century had "neither a national glow of life and thought, such as we had in the age of Elizabeth, nor yet a culture and a force of learning and criticism such as were to be found in Germany."

The main weakness in Arnold's critique of Romanticism is that he does not adequately grasp the nature and dimensions of the societal upheaval during the decades in which the Romantics wrote. Actually, students of Romanticism today, however divergent their points of view, would agree that Arnold's depiction of Elizabethan England tallies point by point with most estimates of the England of the Romantics. Because Arnold undervalued the cultural impact upon literature of the French Revolution, he did not comprehend that it had fostered a national glow as vital in its way as that of Elizabethan England and that this glow had nurtured the Romantic poets.

In his later writings on Romanticism Arnold let biographical considerations influence (in all cases, adversely) his opinion of the poets and, consequently, of their poetry: Shelley was an ineffectual angel with a "lovely wail" who abandoned his first wife to prostitution, Byron a forceful personality but a profligate, Keats a dreamer who wrote too passionate love-letters, Coleridge a man who moved in mists of opium. Blake he never considered. Wordsworth, it is true, remained for him a major poet whom he continued to admire selectively and with reservations, yet one wonders what Arnold, who disliked *Vaudracour and Julia,* would have thought finally of Wordsworth had he known that Wordsworth had in this poem (then published separately from *The Prelude*) recreated his liaison with Annette Vallon.

For Arnold, early and late, poetry, to afford "consolation and stay" must embody a "criticism of life." He never quite realized that within the poetry of the early nineteenth century

there existed a cluster of ideas as rich and substantial as in the finest poetry of earlier ages, and that it was as a criticism, or evaluation, of life that Romantic poetry excels. In "Wordsworth" (1879) Arnold asks us to contemplate the word *"life* until we learn to enter into its meaning," but he did not perceive that the essence of Romantic poetry *is* the principle of life itself. Though he valued detachment and wrote in a style that (like Eliot's in the next century) suggests this virtue, Arnold did not achieve it in dealing with the literature of the early nineteenth century. In "The Study of Poetry" (1880) he admitted that in approaching the Romantic poets he trod on "burning ground" and that his "estimates [were] so often not only personal, but personal with passion."

T. S. Eliot in the twentieth century accentuates Arnold's ambivalences with respect to the Romantics. He was, first of all, ambivalent about Arnold himself and severely qualifies whatever praise he allots him. Arnold, says Eliot, "we go to . . . for refreshment and for the companionship of a kindred point of view to our own, but not as disciples." To him, then, "Arnold is rather a friend than a leader" ["Arnold and Pater," in *Selected Essays,* 1950]. Much as had Arnold, Eliot felt he had to shake off the influence of an earlier generation. He found Arnold's as impressive but inhibiting an achievement as Arnold had found that of the two Romantic generations.

Still, as he explains in *The Use of Poetry and the Use of Criticism,* Arnold for all his deficiencies was a man of the world *"qui sait se conduire"* ["who knows how to: conduct himself"]. Eliot conceived of himself as filling, indeed fulfilling, Arnold's role as conscience to his age and arbiter of its literary past. When he points out the need for criticism every century or so to "set the poets and the poems in a new order," i.e., the need for literary history, he justifies his own as well as Arnold's endeavor. But the "period of apparent stabilization" that we come to with Arnold was, in Eliot's view, "shallow and premature"—almost the exact words that Arnold had used to characterize the Romantics. Thus Eliot would do what Arnold had not (it "was not the time in which it could be done"), and he would do it better than Arnold could have done it.

In *The Sacred Wood* (1920) Eliot picked up Arnold's comment, already cited, that had Byron "empty of matter," Shelley "incoherent," and Wordsworth lacking "completeness and unity." He finds that "this judgment of the Romantic Generation has not, so far as I know, ever been successfully controverted." Returning to the Romantics in *The Use of Poetry,* he denounces their "prophetic frenzies" and observes that one turns to Arnold with relief "after associating with the riff-raff of the early part of the century." He was needed in the wake of the Romantic excesses, Eliot writes, because "it was desirable after the surprising, varied and abundant contribution of the Romantic Period that [the] task of criticism should be undertaken again."

The adjectives "surprising, varied and abundant" should, in turn, surprise us; had not Eliot earlier in the essay characterized the Romantics as "riff-raff"? What do we make of this? Is Old Possum teasing his sober academic audience? Can *The Use of Poetry* be a far more ironic book than several generations of scholars who grew up taking Eliot's every pronouncement with utmost seriousness care to recognize? Still, regardless of how we interpret the tone of "riff-raff," the word itself leaves no doubt that Eliot's distaste for the Romantics was fostered, as Arnold's was before him, by the unease he felt in contemplating their personal lives. Despite the negativism of his public pronouncements, he was clearly, as was Arnold, of two minds about them. However loosely they had lived, however flabby their ideas and self-indulgent their poetry, their contribution had been "surprising, varied and abundant."

Eliot's views on individual Romantics vary slightly from decade to decade, but remain basically those expressed in *The Use of Poetry*. There Shelley comes off, as he had for Arnold, worst: his ideas were those of "adolescence" (Arnold had found them "incoherent"), the man was "self-centered," "sometimes almost a blackguard," and the poetry fatally flawed by the ideas—though Eliot exempts from this judgment *The Triumph of Life*, different in tone from anything else Shelley wrote and for which Eliot had a lifelong admiration. "The attractive Keats" comes off best, particularly in the Odes; his letters are "certainly the most notable and the most important ever written by any English poet." Wordsworth's Preface is a superb statement, his poetry has impressive moments, but Eliot finds his personality unendearing. Coleridge the critic has little appeal to "a practical mind like mine," and his best criticism emerges when he writes out of his own experience and away from German influence. Though Eliot did not consider Blake in *The Use of Poetry*, in the earlier *Sacred Wood* he found him (while admitting his genius) "terrifying" and "eccentric." Byron, whom he wrote about in 1937, he thought had a genius for tale-telling, had verve and force, but was also flatulent and careless (he must be read not by the line but by the paragraph); yet such weaknesses do not prevent *Don Juan* from being a virtually unqualified success.

Several of these poets, Shelley and Byron in particular, had been youthful favorites, and even less successfully than had Arnold, did Eliot distance himself from them. As he matured, he overreacted, mainly against Shelley, but also against the other Romantics. He denounced them for traits that he, temperamentally a Romantic himself, had tried to suppress in his own work. When Eliot disliked the ideas of a poet, no more than Arnold could he respond favorably to that poet's writings. Not surprisingly, then, does he decide in *The Use of Poetry* that Arnold's position on the Romantics was "well-balanced and well-marshalled," for in large part certainly he had made it his own. He points out—correctly for his time—that "the valuation of the Romantic poets, in academic circles, is still largely that which Arnold made." His own critical endeavor he viewed as one that would reinforce that evaluation by grounding it on firmer principles.

Four years after Eliot published his *Use of Poetry*, F. L. Lucas came out with a witty book entitled *The Decline and Fall of the Romantic Ideal*. In it Lucas made fun of a number of major Romantic works and predicted that their day had now passed. Forty and more years later we have undergone several further evolutions in critical taste, have seen the New Humanists succeeded by the New Critics, who have, in turn, been superseded by the various critical modes of the '60s and '70s. Lucas, like Eliot, wrote at a time when Romantic poetry generated little interest and less criticism. Today the circle has come full cycle: hardly another subject in literary history arouses the controversy that swirls around Romanticism. (pp. 97-101)

The present diversity of viewpoints has spawned, in turn, exciting theoretical criticism. But much of this criticism, though evidencing intelligence and insight, has avoided larger questions about the poets and their poems. It has especially avoided consideration of the poets' basic ideas and assumptions from a humanistic perspective. Poets and poems tend to disappear under an avalanche of theory. Or the critic views the literary artifact as a hermetically-sealed off preserve on which to exercise his skill, the subtlety of his performance outweighing the value of the text. Despite or because of this flood of theorizing and bravura personal criticism, we may be further away than before from understanding the Romantics in a comprehensive, humanistic sense.

Two standard collections of the modern folklore of Romanticism—each a gathering of flowers already more or less faded—are *Romanticism: Points of View,* edited by Robert F. Gleckner and Gerald E. Enscoe, and *Romanticism and Consciousness,* edited by Harold Bloom, both published in 1970 [see Further Reading]. . . . These reprinted essays, many of them originally parts of books, afford a fair sample of the present state of knowledge of English Romanticism and tell us something of its history in the twentieth century. Several are significant contributions to the study of the subject. Others are based on insufficient knowledge. A few—such as the essays by Babbitt and Christopher Caudwell—are simply polemics. Written from a New Humanist and a Marxist perspective respectively, they are replete with deliberate and perverse misreadings calculated to prove the author's particular thesis. No serious student of literature today, however hostile he may be to Romanticism, would accept them as responsible critiques. A number of the other essays erect a discussion of Romanticism upon a shockingly inadequate base, with little or no reference to the six major poets, or to poems, in support of their contentions. As documents in the later history of Romanticism they have a certain interest; as guides to understanding Romantic poetry their value is slight.

But I wish now to focus upon three essays that typify some of the major tendencies in criticism of Romantic poetry since Eliot's time: one from 1939 by Cleanth Brooks, one from 1969 by Harold Bloom, and one from 1951 by Morse Peckham. All three essays at least mention poets and poems.

In *Modern Poetry and the Tradition* (1939) [see *Further Reading*] Brooks argues that "the romantic poets, in attacking the neo-classic conception of the poetic, tended to offer new poetic objects rather than to discard altogether the conception of a special poetical material." But this conception did not exist in the eighteenth century any more than it did in the nineteenth. In Pope's *Rape of the Lock,* for example, we have an elaborate description of a woman putting on her make-up in the morning; in Swift we have various references to the fact that women may "stink" and must "shit"—words he actually uses. What Brooks regards as unpoetic flourished both in eighteenth- and in early nineteenth-century satire. He writes further:

> Moreover, as a reaction to neoclassicism, the [Romantic] movement was too much centered in the personal and the lyrical, and it has a cult of simplicity of its own. It substituted romantic subjectivism for neoclassic objectivism instead of fusing the two as they were fused in a great dramatic period such as the Elizabethan. Wordsworth has as little of the dramatic as does Shelley, and where we find an overt attempt at the dramatic; it is the personal self-dramatization of Byron—the self-conscious actor, not the objectifying dramatist. Keats, oddly enough, comes closest to giving us dramatic poems—in the great odes.

Here Brooks damns an entire genre—the lyric (traditionally but not necessarily defined as "personal" because it often uses a first-person persona). But, as Brooks recognizes, it is possible to achieve the dramatic—as Keats did—in terms of an "I." So also did Wordsworth achieve the dramatic in *The Prelude* (to say nothing of Eliot in *Ash Wednesday* and the *Quartets*). A personal letter may be "dramatic." As for Shelley, he wrote *The Cenci*. Byron is damned for being a "self-conscious actor" dramatizing himself, but this aspect of his poetry is evident *only* if we know Byron from biographies or from his letters. We do not learn from Brooks that he wrote *Manfred, Cain* and other plays. Brooks presumably means that Byron had limited ability to produce a host of different dramatic characters. It is true that the Romantic age was not a great age of drama, but we have had few of these—the age of Greek tragedy, the Elizabethan, perhaps the twentieth century.

Brooks writes subsequently: "Most of all, the poets distrusted the intellect." Again, this is too simple, ultimately quite false. Blake in *The Marriage* thought of "Reason as the bound or outward circumference of Energy" (and his Urizen is an incomplete figure); Wordsworth in *The Prelude* identified "intellectual Love" with Imagination, which is "Reason in her most exalted mood" (XIV, 206-07, 192)—*loss* of faith in the power of reason is the abyss into which he falls in *The Prelude,* the lowest point of his depression, and from which he recovers. The only one of the major Romantics who may be said to have distrusted the intellect is the only true skeptic among them—Byron, who frequently doubted the possibility of real knowledge about important things (see *Don Juan*, IX, 16-17, 20). Three paragraphs later Brooks claims that Wordsworth's "finest effects—as in 'Michael'—are usually the result of a cumulative process rather than the use of a few, carefully selected dramatic symbols." The effect of "Michael" is certainly cumulative, but the poem *also* makes use of a few carefully selected dramatic symbols—among them, the cottage, the oak and the unfinished sheepfold.

Brooks's "more considered view" of Shelley, obviously influenced by Arnold and Eliot, holds him to be "a very unsatisfactory poet greatly inferior to Keats." Yet in his discussion he quotes only two lines from the entire body of Shelley's work and does not refer, even indirectly, to one of the great poems. Brooks's charges are merely affirmed and, in fact, left wholly unsupported. For Brooks, "under the general principles of symbolist-metaphysical poetry" Shelley "comes off rather badly." No evidence for this statement is given. It cannot apply to a poem such as *Epipsychidion,* where the flower imagery, which *is* the poem itself, is transformed toward the end into a world of "fruits and flowers," warmed and given life by the light imagery, sharpened and specified as the sun (Emily) that inspires the poetic production of the poet.

Brooks's insensitivity to what Shelley is doing manifests itself also by inaccurate quotation and misleading commentary. He speaks of "the formula employed by Shelley in his 'Ode to a Skylark'—lush imagery followed by the abstract

> Our sweetest songs are those that tell
> of saddest thought . . . "

Here the title is misquoted and the Alexandrine is printed as if it were two lines, depriving it of its soaring effect and ignoring its contrast with the preceding trimeter lines, which echo playfully one of Hamlet's soliloquies (IV, iv, 36-39). Brooks follows by referring to Wordsworth's "rather flat generaliza-

tion" in "Expostulation and Reply," of which he quotes two stanzas (beginning " 'The eye—it cannot choose but see' "). His quotation ignores the dramatic conflict suggested by a title he does not mention, ignores the image of the "I" as Adam in a newly-created garden, ignores the intensity of effect achieved (within the limits of the ballad stanza) in the next, penultimate stanza.

Harold Bloom's contributions to Romantic studies pose a different kind of problem. A stimulating, at times brilliant theorist of literature, Bloom, unlike Brooks, writes as an enthusiastic partisan of Romanticism, which he conceives of as embracing most nineteenth- and twentieth-century literature. His combination of massive generalization, unqualified statement ("definitive" becomes the favorite word), and confident tone tends to bowl over the unwary. The result can be a distortion of Romantic poetry as great as Brooks's. "The most searching critique of Romanticism that I know is Van den Berg's critique of Freud," Bloom tells us in "The Internalization of Quest Romance." Van den Berg's work [*The Changing Nature of Man (Metabletical),* 1961]. interesting as it is, does not upon examination even *mention* the six major English Romantic poets or their writings. One can thus, it appears, cite as "searching" a critique of Romanticism without that critique having to refer to the subject matter in question. Needless to say, no student of Romanticism since Bloom has found it necessary to take up Van den Berg.

Another example. A few pages earlier, Bloom had informed us that "behind continental Romanticism there lay very little in the way of a congenial native tradition of major poets writing in an ancestral mode." Aside from wondering what exactly Bloom means by "ancestral mode," I find this statement, like much else in Bloom's work, an over-simplification. Though generally valid for German Romanticism, it does not hold true for French and Italian. Scholars of English Romanticism are notoriously innocent or misinformed about the development of continental Romanticism, and statements such as the above will keep them innocent or add to their stock of misinformation.

Many of Bloom's observations upon individual poets are no less unfortunate. We read, for instance, that "Wordsworth's Copernican revolution in poetry is marked by the evanescence of any subject but subjectivity." This observation is true neither of Wordsworth's own early or later poetry, nor of much poetry after Wordsworth. Bloom presumably refers to the "egotistical sublime" of such a poem as *The Prelude* (he mentions Keats's phrase in the previous sentence), but his statement fails to distinguish between the lyrical ballads of low or humble life and the very different *Prelude,* and it disregards such poems as the classical story of *Laodamia,* written in 1814.

Bloom states further that "The Romantics tended to take Milton's Satan as the archetype of the heroically defeated Promethean quester." Blake in Plate 6 of *The Marriage* did claim that Milton was "a true poet and of the Devil's party without knowing it," but Coleridge in *The Statesman's Manual* damned Milton's Satan for engendering "Satanic pride and rebellious self-idolatry," Byron in the Preface to *Cain* treated him with skeptical amusement, and Shelley in the Preface to *Prometheus Unbound,* although he recognized a similarity between Prometheus and Satan, deplored the "pernicious casuistry" produced by the latter character in the reader's mind. In the next paragraph Bloom tells us that "most simply, Romantic nature poetry . . . was an antinature poetry." Without denying, for example, the internalization of nature in Wordsworth, this is another dramatically misleading simplification, phrased for its shock value. Three sentences further on we learn (in Bloom's characteristic minatory language) that Shelley "attacked" Wordsworth in *Mont Blanc.* But Shelley never said he did, the poem neither mentions nor quotes Wordsworth, and its view of nature is in some ways compatible with Wordsworth's, in other ways incompatible.

One last example of Bloom's grandly careless misreadings of Romantic poetry: "If Wordsworth . . . was not questing for unity with nature, still less were Blake, Shelley, and Keats." But the Romantics *did* seek unity with nature. Here, most obviously, we may recall the great "spousal verse" of Wordsworth's "Prospectus." Blake, it is true, deplored "the Delusive Goddess Nature & her Laws," but he has in mind here the Newtonian mechanical universe of single vision. Once man's senses are cleansed he will see the infinite in all things; there will be a new earth and a new heaven, and it will be within the perceiving mind of man, even though Blake recognized that all men do not see alike. Similarly, when Shelley's Prometheus is bound, all nature becomes fallen; when he is unbound, nature is redeemed (I,1. 152 ff). Keats's chameleon poet is "continually in for[ming?]—and filling some other Body—the Sun, the Moon, the Sea and Men and Women." "Coleridge and Byron," Bloom continues, "were oddly closer . . . to pantheism or some form of nature-worship, but even their major poems hardly approximate nature poetry." But Coleridge in "Dejection: An Ode" laments the failed marriage of Nature and the shaping spirit of his imagination, and he goes on to write "Hymn before Sunrise in the Vale of Chamouni," whereas Byron in the third canto of *Childe Harold* becomes "portion" of all that is around him (stanza 72).

Morse Peckham, in his various writings on Romanticism over the years, rarely stoops to discuss a poet, much less a poem, in search of a theory or in support of a generalization. When he does, the results can be unhappy. In section III of "Toward a Theory of Romanticism," he introduces the term "negative romanticism" in an effort to fit Byron into his theory. "Briefly, Negative Romanticism is the expression of the attitudes, the feelings, and the ideas of a man who has left static mechanism but has not yet arrived at a reintegration of his thought and art in terms of dynamic organicism." For Peckham, "Byron's Romantic view of nature as an organism with which man is unified organically by the imagination is equally fitful and limited to the period of Shelleyan influence." It manifests itself in *Childe Harold's* third canto, "written and published in 1816, when Byron was temporarily under Wordsworth's influence through Shelley." Peckham finds "not very convincing" "Wellek's suggestion that Byron is a symbolist. . . . To be sure, Byron uses symbols; but he uses them compulsively, as everyone else does, not as a conscious principle of literary organization and creation."

On the whole, Peckham does not deal adequately with Byron. Basically, Byron is a deist, though he can express an organic view of nature. The Byronic quest of *Childe Harold,* like the Wordsworthian, is not only a quest for a spiritual home but also one in which the persona strives to achieve or complete the perfected thing that is the poem. *Childe Harold* is a poem about the creation of itself and of its protagonist, a poem that forges its own reality as it moves from stanza to stanza, scene to scene. It is not trying to arrest process but to create the illusion of it, to achieve life and joy out of a Coleridgean dejec-

tion. Peckham speaks of the third canto as being written under Wordsworthian influence, and in a sense this is true, but all men are under many influences. The more one reads Byron's poetry the more influences one finds—and the more original a poet he appears.

In *Don Juan* Byron regularly satirizes rigidity and restraint; just as regularly he celebrates freedom, change and movement. Diversity is a virtue for him. At the house party at Norman Abbey, he satirizes the bored sameness of the frozen Englishmen assembled there, and more than once he laments the loss of the Romantic or creative imagination. As for symbolism, it is the product of the imagination, and for Peckham "the unconscious is really a postulate to the creative imagination." Therefore, it is irrelevant that Byron uses symbols "compulsively" in his poems. They are there, and Byron's poetry everywhere evidences a *conscious* interest in the workings of the poetic mind. To the extent that *Don Juan* is a poem about the evolving self, it is a poem of process. Basically, then, Peckham's view of Byron, like that of a number of critics of Romanticism, is incomplete. Both here and elsewhere in his essay his views must be qualified, for they place too great emphasis on the dark and negative side of Byron, which could and did exist with his positive side.

In his "Introduction" to a special issue of *Studies in Romanticism* [Fall, 1970], "The Concept of Romanticism," Peckham more often attacks or supports other theorists on Romanticism than he discusses the subject in terms of its writers. He writes with the glee of a social scientist who has learned a German word that explains it all (*"aufgehoben"* in his case) and leaves the impression of a man who cannot make up his mind whether to become a sociologist or the presiding bishop of South Carolina. He concludes his "Introduction" thus: "Interim reports are all I have ever offered, though apparently some scholars still take seriously what I have myself rejected, publicly." So now, it appears, we must study and master the development of Peckham, along with that of Wordsworth and the other poets. By his successive recantations and dramatic turn-abouts since the original statement of 1951, Peckham apparently wishes to impress his readers as a man who constantly thinks new thoughts and fearlessly voices them, whatever the cost in denying earlier positions. He calls attention to his previous essays, trumpets their classic status, proclaims their significance as "interim reports." One can, however, draw conclusions other than he may wish us to. Someone who has thought through a subject thoroughly and remains fascinated by it—might he not publish modifications, additions, elaborations, to the earlier work rather than start anew each time around?

It remains now to deal briefly with the recent situation. Despite a number of honorable exceptions, much criticism of the 1970s exacerbates earlier tendencies. A humanistic perspective on the Romantic poets seems, at times, even further away than before. Language, which began to cause difficulties in Bloom's "Internalization of Quest Romance" and in Peckham's studies, has now emerged as the major problem facing Romantic scholarship today. Adherents of traditional approaches sharply demarcate their positions from those of the Yale group. Two instances only. I take them from a recent number of the *Keats-Shelley Journal,* but they could have come from any of a number of other periodicals in recent years. Carl Woodring, reviewing Thomas Weiskel's *The Romantic Sublime* in 1978, pointed out that "This book will be intelligible in later years, only if students of literature who encounter it have first read Lacan, Hartman, and Bloom in addition to Freud and whatever critics set the pace between now and then. If critical terminology proves endlessly cumulative, what student can save time for the poets? When terminology accumulates, each critic writes in a language previously unknown but requiring a knowledge of all the languages subsumed in the new one." In the same issue, Robert Ryan, reviewing Stuart Ende's *Keats and the Sublime,* writes: "The difficulty lies in the specialized vocabulary that is employed throughout. . . . Three-quarters of the way through the book Ende is still laboriously defining and redefining the words he is using, his initial hope 'that the contexts will define the terms' never being fully realized." These observations neatly pinpoint a major problem—essentially a problem of communication and human sympathy—facing Romantic studies today. Language, Woodring and Ryan imply, has a direct relationship to meaning—and to the critic's audience.

In his Preface of 1800 Wordsworth grasped this relationship between language and audience more sensitively than we have since: "The Poet thinks and feels in the spirit of human passions," he wrote. "How, then, can his language differ in any material degree from that of all other men who feel vividly and see clearly?" Wordsworth insisted that "poets do not write for poets alone, but for men." Substitute "critics" for "poets" and we confront the impediment posed by modern critics who write, not for others or to elucidate literary texts, but for themselves.

In recent years a number of writers on Romanticism—a number by no means large though influential beyond numerical proportion—have lapsed into cryptograms that inhibit communication except to others of like persuasion. It may be argued that the question of language affects all areas of English studies and so it does, but some of the more notorious practitioners of the Obscure Arcane, for reasons not altogether evident, focus their main efforts on Romantic poetry. A colleague of mine, many years a careful student of Romanticism, recently read a new study of the subject by someone of comparable credentials. Every so often, he said, he came across a sequence of three or four paragraphs that after repeated rereadings yielded no discernible meaning to him. The experience, I suspect, is not unusual today, and if I do not name names, it is because everyone can supply his own. (pp. 101-08)

If professional students of Romanticism cannot understand what their peers write, what must be the reaction of less advanced students of literature, of interested students in other disciplines, or even of that perhaps not-so-mythical bird, the general reader? We fondly seal ourselves off in our little realms and signal to each other in code at a time when more than ever before we need to communicate with others, others including our students. If we are not to dull whatever willingness our audience still has to respond to literature, we must return to basic English. And to the poetry itself.

Modern pundits of Romanticism exhort students to approach the subject via a course of study in Hegel or Plotinus, or through phenomenological or structuralist or consciousness criticism, or through the eyes of whatever guru is currently à la mode. But our academic training already leads us, in many cases, to over-intellectualize our response to poetry. After reading Hegel or the structuralists or the latest wonder, we fail to react imaginatively to the lines of poetry before our eyes or to relate these words to our own humanity and to what we know of that of others. (p. 108)

Although Romantic literature probably will never cease to stimulate reinterpretation, approaches that isolate this literature from its human and social context ultimately distance it from us. Rather than interpose the opinions of literary theoreticians and philosophers between the texts and us, we need to keep close to the texts themselves and to the personal, historical and cultural situation out of which they arose. (pp. 108-09)

We neglect in our onanistic, intellectual analyses the *intelligence du coeur* that the Romantics all felt and expressed. The literature they wrote is too good to have it distorted by the latest critical fad or jargon, however popular. We respond most deeply to Wordsworth, as to the other poets, in human terms. If we cannot do that as a first step, no second step will be worth much.

The six major poets—Blake, Wordsworth, Coleridge, Byron, Shelley, Keats—evinced in their lives and art the richness of their humanity. They are read today in large part because they thought and wrote deeply about significant areas of human endeavor and art. "For poetry to be great," Donald Davie has written [in his *Articulate Energy: An Inquiry into the Syntax of English Poetry,* 1955], "it must reek of the human, as Wordsworth's poetry does. This is not a novel contention; but perhaps it is one of those things that cannot be said too often." Literature was important for the Romantics, but more important than literature was life. The reason we keep returning to their works is that they knew so much about humanity, both the particular humanity that was themselves and that of others whom they observed, were curious about, and learned from. "Our very words 'human' and 'humanity,' and all the words that have developed from them," Walter Jackson Bate has reminded us [in *The Burden of the Past and the English Poet,* 1971], "come from the [Latin] word meaning 'earth' (*humus*)." Out of this concern with *humus,* with the ways human beings are—and can be—emerges a poetry suffused with imaginative empathy into human emotions and into the human mind. We need to consider freshly not over-subtle nuances of interpretation but elemental questions about the ethical, esthetic and spiritual qualities of life that the Romantics raise in their poetry. We need to understand why we should still read Romantic literature, what its basic assumptions and characteristics are, what values it embodies.

Modern critics of Romanticism thus need to embody a perspective that takes its stand not in a chosen methodology but in a regard for human life in all its bewildering complexity. "I hate all mystery," wrote Byron in *Don Juan,* "and that air of clap-trap, which your recent poets prize" (II, 124). The mystery and claptrap that so annoyed him among his contemporaries has yielded, as we have seen, to the mandarin prose and convoluted argument of some recent practitioners of Romantic criticism—with, alas, no Byron to guy them. Romanticism is, after all, what it is because poets wrote poems—poets who lived at a particular time in history and within particular human and social contexts—and not because subsequent literary historians have organized these poets and poems into a movement, labeled it and developed theories about it. Thus, if we wish to grapple with the larger subject of Romanticism, we should move outward from the poets, not, as often in the recent interpretations, inward from Romanticism to the poets, a procedure that scants works in favor of theory. Whatever English Romanticism may signify, its meaning derives validity chiefly when it emerges from sustained contemplation of the six major poets who are its glory. (pp. 109-10)

John Clubbe, "The 'Folklore' of English Romanticism," in Mosaic: A Journal for the Interdisciplinary Study of Literature, Vol. XIV, No. 3, Summer, 1981, pp. 95-112.

MAJOR SUBJECTS AND THEMES

C. M. BOWRA

[*An English critic and literary historian, Bowra was considered among the foremost classical scholars of the first half of the twentieth century. He also wrote extensively on modern literature, particularly modern European poetry, in studies noted for their erudition, lucidity, and direct style. In the following excerpt, Bowra examines the conception of the imagination held by various Romantic poets.*]

If we wish to distinguish a single characteristic which differentiates the English Romantics from the poets of the eighteenth century, it is to be found in the importance which they attached to the imagination and in the special view which they held of it. On this, despite significant differences on points of detail, Blake, Coleridge, Wordsworth, Shelley, and Keats agree, and for each it sustains a deeply considered theory of poetry. In the eighteenth century imagination was not a cardinal point in poetical theory. For Pope and Johnson, as for Dryden before them, it has little importance, and when they mention it, it has a limited significance. They approve of fancy, provided that it is controlled by what they call "judgment," and they admire the apt use of images, by which they mean little more than visual impressions and metaphors. But for them what matters most in poetry is its truth to the emotions, or, as they prefer to say, sentiment. They wish to speak in general terms for the common experience of men, not to indulge personal whims in creating new worlds. For them the poet is more an interpreter than a creator, more concerned with showing the attractions of what we already know than with expeditions into the unfamiliar and the unseen. They are less interested in the mysteries of life than in its familiar appearance, and they think that their task is to display this with as much charm and truth as they can command. But for the Romantics imagination is fundamental, because they think that without it poetry is impossible.

This belief in the imagination was part of the contemporary belief in the individual self. The poets were conscious of a wonderful capacity to create imaginary worlds, and they could not believe that this was idle or false. On the contrary, they thought that to curb it was to deny something vitally necessary to their whole being. They thought that it was just this which made them poets, and that in their exercise of it they could do far better than other poets who sacrificed it to caution and common sense. They saw that the power of poetry is strongest when the creative impulse works untrammelled, and they knew that in their own case this happened when they shaped fleeting visions into concrete forms and pursued wild thoughts until they captured and mastered them. (pp. 1-2)

The Romantic emphasis on the imagination was strength-ened by considerations which are both religious and metaphysical. For a century English philosophy had been dominated by the theories of Locke. He assumed that in perception the mind is wholly passive, a mere recorder of impressions from without, "a lazy looker-on on an external world." His system was well suited to an age of scientific speculation which found its representative voice in Newton. The mechanistic explanation which both philosophers and scientists gave of the world meant that scanty respect was paid to the human self and especially to its more instinctive, though not less powerful, convictions. Thus both Locke and Newton found a place for God in their universes, the former on the ground that "the works of nature in every part of them sufficiently evidence a diety" [*The Reasonableness of Christianity*, 1695], and the latter on the principle that the great machine of the world implies a mechanic. But this was not at all what the Romantics demanded from religion. For them it was a question less of reason than of feeling, less of argument than of experience, and they complained that these mechanistic explanations were a denial of their innermost convictions. So too with poetry. Locke had views on poetry, as he had on most human activities, but no very high regard for it. For him it is a matter of "wit," and the task of wit is to combine ideas and "thereby to make up pleasant pictures and agreeable visions in the fancy" [*An Essay Concerning Human Understanding*, 1690]. Wit, in his view, is quite irresponsible and not troubled with truth or reality. The Romantics rejected with contumely a theory which robbed their work of its essential connection with life.

Locke is the target both of Blake and of Coleridge, to whom he represents a deadly heresy on the nature of existence. They are concerned with more than discrediting his special views on God and poetry: they are hostile to his whole system which supports those views and, even worse, robs the human self of importance. They reject his conception of the universe and replace it by their own systems, which deserve the name of "idealist" because mind is their central point and governing factor. But because they are poets, they insist that the most vital activity of the mind is the imagination. Since for them it is the very source of spiritual energy, they cannot but believe that it is divine, and that, when they exercise it, they in some way partake of the activity of God. Blake says proudly and prophetically:

> This world of Imagination is the world of Eternity; it is the divine bosom into which we shall all go after the death of the Vegetated body. This World of Imagination is Infinite and Eternal, whereas the world of Generation, or Vegetation, is Finite and Temporal. There Exist in that Eternal World the Permanent Realities of Every Thing which we see reflected in this Vegetable Glass of Nature. All Things are comprehended in their Eternal Forms in the divine body of the Saviour, the True Vine of Eternity, The Human Imagination. [*A Vision of the Last Judgment*]

For Blake the imagination is nothing less than God as He operates in the human soul. It follows that any act of creation performed by the imagination is divine and that in the imagination man's spiritual nature is fully and finally realized. Coleridge does not speak with so apocalyptic a certainty, but his conclusion is not very different from Blake's:

> The primary IMAGINATION I hold to be the living Power and prime Agent of all human Perception, and as a repetition in the finite mind of the eternal

act of creation in the infinite I AM. [*Biographia Lite-raria*]

It is true that he regards poetry as a product of the secondary imagination, but since this differs only in degree from the primary, it remains clear that for Coleridge the imagination is of first importance because it partakes of the creative activity of God.

This is a tremendous claim, and it is not confined to Blake and Coleridge. It was to some degree held by Wordsworth and Shelley and Keats. Each was confident not only that the imagination was his most precious possession but that it was somehow concerned with a supernatural order. Never before had quite such a claim been made, and from it Romantic poetry derives much that is most magical in it. The danger of so bold an assumption is that the poet may be so absorbed in his own private universe and in the exploration of its remoter corners that he may be unable to convey his essential experience to other men and fail to convert them to his special creed. The Romantics certainly created worlds of their own, but they succeeded in persuading others that these were not absurd or merely fanciful. Indeed, in this respect they were closer to earth and the common man than some of their German contemporaries. They have not the respect for unsatisfied longing as an end in itself or the belief in hallucination and magic which play so large a part in the mind of Brentano, nor have they that nihilistic delight in being detached from life, of which Novalis writes to Caroline Schlegel:

> I know that imagination is most attracted by what is most immoral, most animal; but I also know how like a dream all imagination is, how it loves night, meaninglessness, and solitude.

This was not what the English Romantics thought. They believed that the imagination stands in some essential relation to truth and reality, and they were at pains to make their poetry pay attention to them.

In doing this they encountered an old difficulty. If a man gives free play to his imagination, what assurance is there that what he says is in any sense true? Can it tell us anything that we do not know, or is it so removed from ordinary life as to be an escape from it? (pp. 2-5)

The Romantics face this issue squarely and boldly. So far from thinking that the imagination deals with the non-existent, they insist that it reveals an important kind of truth. They believe that when it is at work it sees things to which the ordinary intelligence is blind and that it is intimately connected with a special insight or perception or intuition. Indeed, imagination and insight are in fact inseparable and form for all practical purposes a single faculty. Insight both awakes the imagination to work and is in turn sharpened by it when it is at work. This is the assumption on which the Romantics wrote poetry. It means that, when their creative gifts are engaged, they are inspired by their sense of the mystery of things to probe it with a peculiar insight and to shape their discoveries into imaginative forms. Nor is this process difficult to understand. Most of us, when we use our imaginations, are in the first place stirred by some alluring puzzle which calls for a solution, and in the second place enabled by our own creations in the mind to see much that was before dark or unintelligible. As our fancies take coherent shape, we see more clearly what has puzzled and perplexed us. This is what the Romantics do. They combine imagination and truth because their creations are inspired and controlled by a pecu-

Manuscript page of stanzas 47-8 from Percy Shelley's "The Witch of Atlas."

liar insight. Coleridge makes the point conclusively when he praises Wordsworth:

> It was the union of deep feeling with profound thought; the fine balance of truth in observing, with the imaginative faculty in modifying the objects observed; and above all the original gift of spreading the tone, the *atmosphere,* and with it the depth and height of the ideal world around forms, incidents, and situations, of which, for the common view, custom had bedimmed all the lustre, had dried up the sparkle and the dew drops. [*Biographia Literaria*]

So long as the imagination works in this way, it cannot fairly be accused of being an escape from life or of being no more than an agreeable relaxation.

The perception which works so closely with the imagination is not of the kind in which Locke believed, and the Romantics took pains to dispel any misunderstanding on the point. Since what mattered to them was an insight into the nature of things, they rejected Locke's limitation of perception to physical objects, because it robbed the mind of its most essential function, which is at the same time to perceive and to create. On this Blake speaks with prophetic scorn:

> Mental Things are alone Real; what is call'd Corpo-

real, Nobody Knows of its Dwelling Place: it is in Fallacy, and its Existence an Imposture. Where is the Existence Out of Mind or Thought? Where is it but in the Mind of a Fool? [*A Vision of the Last Judgment*]

[In a letter] Coleridge came to a similar conclusion for not very different reasons:

> If the mind be not *passive,* if it be indeed made in God's image, and that, too, in the sublimest sense, the *Image of the Creator,* there is ground for the suspicion that any system built on the passiveness of the mind must be false as a system.

When they rejected the sensationalist view of an external world, Blake and Coleridge prepared the way to restoring the supremacy of the spirit which had been denied by Locke but was at this time being propounded by German metaphysicians. Blake knew nothing of them, and his conclusions arose from his own visionary outlook, which could not believe that matter is in any sense as real as spirit. Coleridge had read Kant and Schelling and found in them much to support his views, but those views were deprived less from them than from his own instinctive conviction that the world of spirit is the only reality. Because he was first a poet and only secondly a metaphysician, his conception of a universe of spirit came from his intense sense of an inner life and from his belief that the imagination, working with intuition, is more likely than the analytical reason to make discoveries on matters which really concern us.

In rejecting Locke's and Newton's explanations of the visible world, the Romantics obeyed an inner call to explore more fully the world of spirit. In different ways each of them believed in an order of things which is not that which we see and know, and this was the goal of their passionate search. They wished to penetrate to an abiding reality, to explore its mysteries, and by this to understand more clearly what life means and what it is worth. They were convinced that, though visible things are the instruments by which we find this reality, they are not everything and have indeed little significance unless they are related to some embracing and sustaining power. Nor is it hard to see what this means. Most of us feel that a physical universe is not enough and demand some scheme which will explain why our beliefs and convictions are valid and why in an apparently mechanistic order we have scales of values for which no mechanism can account. Locke and Newton explain what the sensible world is, but not what it is worth. Indeed, in explaining mental judgements by physical processes they destroy their validity, since the only assurance for the truth of our judgements is the existence of an objective truth which cannot be determined by a causal, subjective process. Such systems embody a spirit of negation, because in trying to explain our belief in the good or the holy or the beautiful they succeed only in explaining it away. That is why Blake dismissed atomic physicists and their like as men who try in vain to destroy the divine light which alone gives meaning to life, and proclaimed that in its presence their theories cease to count:

> The Atoms of Democritus
> And Newton's Particles of light
> Are sands upon the Red sea shore,
> Where Israel's tents do shine so bright.
> ["Mock on, Mock on, Voltaire, Rousseau"]

The Romantics were concerned with the things of the spirit and hoped that through imagination and inspired insight they could both understand them and present them in compelling poetry.

It was this search for an unseen world that awoke the inspiration of the Romantics and made poets of them. The power of their work comes partly from the driving force of their desire to grasp these ultimate truths, partly from their exaltation when they thought that they had found them. Unlike their German contemporaries, who were content with the thrills of *Sehnsucht,* or longing, and did not care much what the *Jenseits,* or "beyond," might be, so long as it was sufficiently mysterious, the English Romantics pursued their lines of imaginative enquiry until they found answers which satisfied them. Their aim was to convey the mystery of things through individual manifestations and thereby to show what it means. They appeal not to the logical mind but to the complete self, to the whole range of intellectual faculties, senses, and emotions. Only individual presentations of imaginative experience can do this. In them we see examples of what cannot be expressed directly in words and can be conveyed only by hint and suggestion. The powers which Wordsworth saw in nature or Shelley in love are so enormous that we begin to understand them only when they are manifested in single, concrete examples. Then, through the single cases, we apprehend something of what the poet has seen in vision. The essence of the Romantic imagination is that it fashions shapes which display these unseen forces at work, and there is no other way to display them, since they resist analysis and description and cannot be presented except in particular instances.

The apprehension of these spiritual issues is quite different from the scientific understanding of natural laws or the philosophical grasp of general truths. Such laws and truths are properly stated in abstract words, but spiritual powers must be introduced through particular examples, because only then do we see them in their true individuality. Indeed, only when the divine light of the imagination is on them do we begin to understand their significance and their appeal. That is why Blake is so stern on the view that art deals with general truths. He has none of Samuel Johnson's respect for the "grandeur of generality," and would disagree violently with him when he says, "nothing can please many and please long, but just representation of general nature." Blake thought quite otherwise:

> To Generalize is to be an Idiot. To Particularize is the Alone Distinction of Merit. General Knowledges are those Knowledges that Idiots possess.

> What is General Nature? is there Such a Thing? what is General Knowledge? is there such a Thing? Strictly Speaking All Knowledge is Particular. [Blake's Marginalia to Sir Joshua Reynolds's *Discourses*]

Blake believed this because he lived in the imagination. He knew that nothing had full significance for him unless it appeared in a particular form. And with this the Romantics in general agreed. Their art aimed at presenting as forcibly as possible the moments of vision which give to even the vastest issues the coherence and simplicity of single events. Even in "Kubla Khan," which keeps so many qualities of the dream in which it was born, there is a highly individual presentation of a remote and mysterious experience, which is in fact the central experience of all creation in its Dionysiac delight and its enraptured ordering of many elements into an entrancing pattern. Coleridge may not have been fully conscious of what he was doing when he wrote it, but the experience which he portrays is of the creative mood in its purest moments, when boundless possibilities seem to open before it. No wonder he felt that, if he could only realize all the potentialities of such a moment, he would be like one who has supped with the gods:

> And all should cry, Beware! Beware!
> His flashing eyes, his floating hair!
> Weave a circle round him thrice,
> And close your eyes with holy dread,
> For he on honey-dew hath fed,
> And drunk the milk of Paradise.

It was in such experience, remote and strange and beyond the senses, that the Romantics sought for poetry, and they saw that the only way to convey it to others was in particular instances and examples.

The invisible powers which sustain the universe work through and in the visible world. Only by what we see and hear and touch can we be brought into relation with them. Every poet has to work with the world of the senses, but for the Romantics it was the instrument which set their visionary powers in action. It affected them at times in such a way that they seemed to be carried beyond it into a transcendental order of things, but this would never have happened if they had not looked on the world around them with attentive and loving eyes. One of the advantages which they gained by their deliverance from abstractions and general truths was a freedom to use their senses and to look on nature without conventional prepossessions. More than this, they were all gifted with a high degree of physical sensibility and sometimes so enthralled by what they saw that it entirely dominated their being. This is obviously true of Wordsworth and of Keats, who brought back to poetry a keenness of eye and of ear which it had hardly known since Shakespeare. But it is no less true of Blake and Coleridge and Shelley. The careful, observing eye which made Blake a cunning craftsman in line and colour was at work in his poetry. It is true that he was seldom content with mere description of what he saw, but, when he used description for an ulterior purpose to convey some vast mystery, his words are exact and vivid and make his symbols shine brightly before the eye. Though Coleridge found some of his finest inspiration in dreams and trances, he gave to their details a singular brilliance of outline and character. Though Shelley lived among soaring ideas and impalpable abstractions, he was fully at home in the visible world, if only because it was a mirror of eternity and worthy of attention for that reason. There are perhaps poets who live entirely in dreams and hardly notice the familiar scene, but the Romantics are not of their number. Indeed, their strength comes largely from the way in which they throw a new and magic light on the common face of nature and lure us to look for some explanation for the irresistible attraction which it exerts. In nature all the Romantic poets found their initial inspiration. It was not everything to them, but they would have been nothing without it; for through it they found those exalting moments when they passed from sight to vision and pierced, as they thought, to the secrets of the universe.

Though all the Romantic poets believed in an ulterior reality and based their poetry on it, they found it in different ways and made different uses of it. They varied in the degree of importance which they attached to the visible world and in their interpretation of it. At one extreme is Blake, who held that the imagination is a divine power and that everything real comes from it. It operates with a given material, which is nature, but Blake believed that a time would come when nature will disappear and the spirit be free to create without it. While it is there, man takes his symbols from it and uses them to interpret the unseen. Blake's true home was in vision, in what he saw when he gave full liberty to his creative imagination and transformed sense-data through it. For him the imagination uncovers the reality masked by visible things. The familiar world gives hints which must be taken and pursued and developed:

> To see a World in a Grain of Sand
> And a Heaven in a Wild Flower,
> Hold Infinity in the palm of your hand
> And Eternity in an hour.
>
> ["Auguries of Innocence"]

Through visible things Blake reached that transcendent state which he called "eternity" and felt free to create new and living worlds. He was not a mystic striving darkly and laboriously towards God, but a visionary who could say of himself:

> I am in God's presence night and day,
> And he never turns his face away.
>
> [a fragment]

Of all the Romantics, Blake is the most rigorous in his conception of the imagination. He could confidently say, "One Power alone makes a Poet: Imagination, The Divine Vision," because for him the imagination creates reality, and this reality is the divine activity of the self in its unimpeded energy. His attention is turned towards an ideal, spiritual world, which with all other selves who obey the imagination he helps to build.

Though Blake had a keen eye for the visible world, his special concern was with the invisible. For him every living thing was a symbol of everlasting powers, and it was these which he wished to grasp and to understand. Since he was a painter with a remarkably pictorial habit of mind, he described the invisible in the language of the visible, and no doubt he really saw it with his inner vision. But what he saw was not, so to speak, an alternative to the given world, but a spiritual order to which the language of physical sight can be applied only in metaphor. What concerned him most deeply and drew out his strongest powers was the sense of a spiritual reality at work in all living things. For him even the commonest event might be fraught with lessons and meanings. How much he found can be seen from his "Auguries of Innocence," where in epigrammatic, oracular couplets he displays his sense of the intimate relations which exist in reality and bind the worlds of sight and of spirit in a single whole. His words look simple enough, but every word needs attention, as when he proclaims:

> A Robin Red breast in a Cage
> Puts all Heaven in a Rage.

Blake's robin redbreast is itself a spiritual thing, not merely a visible bird, but the powers which such a bird embodies and symbolizes, the free spirit which delights in song and in all that song implies. Such a spirit must not be repressed, and any repression of it is a sin against the divine life of the universe. Blake was a visionary who believed that ordinary things are unsubstantial in themselves and yet rich as symbols of greater realities. He was so at home in the spirit that he was not troubled by the apparent solidity of matter. He saw something else: a world of eternal values and living spirits.

Keats had a more passionate love than Blake for the visible world and has too often been treated as a man who lived for sensuous impressions, but he resembled Blake in his conviction that ultimate reality is to be found only in the imagination. What it meant to him can be seen from some lines in "Sleep and Poetry" in which he asks why the imagination has lost its old power and scope:

> Is there so small a range
> In the present strength of manhood, that the high
> Imagination cannot freely fly
> As she was wont of old? prepare her steeds,
> Paw up against the light, and do strange deeds
> Upon the clouds? Has she not shown us all?
> From the clear space of ether, to the small
> Breath of new buds unfolding? From the meaning
> Of Jove's large eye-brow, to the tender greening
> Of April meadows?

Keats was still a very young man when he wrote this, and perhaps his words are not so precise as we might like. But it is clear that he saw the imagination as a power which both creates and reveals, or rather reveals through creating. Keats accepted the works of the imagination not merely as existing in their own right, but as having a relation to ultimate reality through the light which they shed on it. This idea he pursued with hard thought until he saw exactly what it meant, and made it his own because it answered a need in his creative being.

Through the imagination Keats sought an absolute reality to which a door was opened by his appreciation of beauty through the senses. When the objects of sense laid their spell upon him, he was so stirred and exalted that he felt himself transported to another world and believed that he could almost grasp the universe as a whole. Sight and touch and smell awoke his imagination to a sphere of being in which he saw vast issues and was at home with them. Through beauty he felt that he came into the presence of the ultimately real. The more intensely a beautiful object affected him, the more convinced he was that he had passed beyond it to something else. In *Endymion* he says that happiness raises our minds to a "fellowship with essence" and leaves us "alchemized and free of space":

> Feel we these things? that moment we have stept
> Into a sort of oneness, and our state
> Is like a fleeting spirit's. But there are
> Richer entanglements, enthralments far
> More self-destroying, leading by degrees
> To the chief intensity.

The beauty of visible things carried Keats into ecstasy, and this was the goal of his desires, since it explained the extraordinary hold which objects of sense had on him and justified his wish to pass beyond them to something permanent and universal. Keats' notion of this reality was narrower than Blake's, and he speaks specifically as a poet, whereas Blake included in the imagination all activities which create or increase life. Moreover, while Blake's imagination is active, Keats suggests that his is largely passive and that his need is to feel the "chief intensity." But he is close to Blake in the claims which he makes for the imagination as something absorbing and exalting which opens the way to an unseen spiritual order.

Coleridge, too, gave much thought to the imagination and devoted to it some distinguished chapters of his *Biographia Literaria*. With him it is not always easy to disentangle theories which he formed in later life from the assumptions upon which he acted almost instinctively before his creative faculties began to fail. At times he seems to be still too aware of the sensationalist philosophy of his youth. From it he inherits a conception of a world of facts, an "inanimate cold world," in which "objects, *as* objects, are essentially fixed and dead." But as a poet he transcended this idea, or turned it to an unexpected conclusion. Just because the external world is like this, the poet's task is to transform it by the imagination. Just as "accidents of light and shade" may transmute "a known and familiar landscape," so this dead world may be brought to life by the imagination. Coleridge justified this [in a letter] by a bold paradox:

> Dare I add that genius must act of the feeling that body is but a striving to become mind—that is mind in its essence.

What really counted with him was his own deep trust in the imagination as something which gives a shape to life. What this meant to him in practice can be seen from the lines in "Dejection" in which he explains that nature lives only in us and that it is we who create all that matters in her:

> Ah! from the soul itself must issue forth
> A light, a glory, a fair luminous cloud
>   Enveloping the Earth—
> And from the soul itself must there be sent
>   A sweet and potent voice, of its own birth,
> Of all sweet sounds the life and element!

Coleridge does not go so far as Blake in the claims which he makes for the imagination. He is still a little hampered by the presence of an external world and feels that in some way he must conform to it. But when his creative genius is at work, it brushes these hesitations aside and fashions reality from a shapeless, undifferentiated "given." In the end he believes that meaning is found for existence through the exercise of a creative activity which is akin to that of God.

Coleridge advanced no very definite view of the ultimate reality which poetry explores. If we may judge by "Kubla Khan," he seems to have felt, at least in some moods, that the mere act of creation is itself transcendental and that we need ask for nothing more. But perhaps the evidence of "Kubla Khan" should not be pressed too far. Indeed, if we turn to "The Ancient Mariner" and "Christabel," it seems clear that Coleridge thought that the task of poetry is to convey the mystery of life. The ambiguous nature of both poems, with their suggestion of an intermediate state between dreaming and waking, between living people and unearthly spirits, gives an idea of the kind of subject which stirred Coleridge's genius to its boldest flights. Whatever he might think as a philosopher, as a poet he was fascinated by the notion of unearthly powers at work in the world, and it was their influence which he sought to catch. Of course, he did not intend to be taken literally, but we cannot help feeling that his imaginative conception of reality was of something behind human actions which is more vivid than the familiar world because of its sharper contrasts of good and evil and the more purposeful way in which it moves. This conception was developed only in poetry, and even then only in two or three poems. Coleridge seems to have been forced to it by a troubled and yet exciting apprehension that life is ruled by powers which cannot be fully understood. The result is a poetry more mysterious than that of any other Romantic, and yet, because it is based on primary human emotions, singularly poignant and intimate.

Wordsworth certainly agreed with Coleridge in much that he said about the imagination, especially in the distinction between it and fancy. For him the imagination was the most important gift that a poet can have, and his arrangement of his own poems shows what he meant by it. The section which he calls "Poems of the Imagination" contains poems in which he united creative power and a special, visionary insight. He agreed with Coleridge that this activity resembles that of God. It is the divine capacity of the child who fashions his own little worlds:

> For feeling has to him imparted power
> That through the growing faculties of sense
> Doth like an agent of the one great Mind
> Create, creator and receiver both,
> Working but in alliance with the works
> Which it beholds.
>
> [*The Prelude*]

The poet keeps this faculty even in maturity, and through it he is what he is. But Wordsworth was fully aware that mere creation is not enough, that it must be accompanied by a special insight. So he explains that the imagination

> Is but another name for absolute power
> And clearest insight, amplitude of mind,
> And Reason in her most exalted mood.
>
> [*The Prelude*]

Wordsworth did not go so far as the other Romantics in relegating reason to an inferior position. He preferred to give a new dignity to the word and to insist that inspired insight is itself rational.

Wordsworth differs from Coleridge in his conception of the external world. He accepts its independent existence and insists that the imagination must in some sense conform to it. Once again he sees the issue illustrated by childhood:

> A plastic power
> Abode with me; a forming hand, at times
> Rebellious, acting in a devious mood;
> A local spirit of his own, at war
> With general tendency, but, for the most,
> Subservient strictly to external things
> With which it communed.
>
> [*The Prelude*]

For Wordsworth the imagination must be subservient to the external world, because that world is not dead but living and has its own soul, which is, at least in the life that we know, distinct from the soul of man. Man's task is to enter into communion with this soul, and indeed he can hardly avoid doing so, since from birth onward his life is continuously shaped by nature, which penetrates his being and influences his thoughts. Wordsworth believed that he helped to bring this soul of nature closer to man, that he could show

> by words
> Which speak of nothing more than what we are

how exquisitely the external world is fitted to the individual mind, and the individual mind to the external world. This, it must be admitted, was not to Blake's taste, and he commented [in an annotation to Wordsworth's *Excursion*]: "You shall not bring me down to believe such fitting and fitted." But for Wordsworth this was right. Nature was the source of his inspiration, and he could not deny to it an existence at least as powerful as man's. But since nature lifted him out of himself, he sought for a higher state in which its soul and the

soul of man should be united in a single harmony. Sometimes he felt that this happened and that through vision he attained an understanding of the oneness of things.

Though Shelley's mind moved in a way unlike that of his fellow Romantics, he was no less attached to the imagination and gave to it no less a place in his theory of poetry. He understood the creative nature of his work and shows what he thought of it when in *Prometheus Unbound* a Spirit sings of the poet:

> He will watch from dawn to gloom
> The lake-reflected sun illume
> The yellow bees in the ivy-bloom,
> Nor heed nor see, what things they be;
> But from these create he can
> Forms more real than living man,
> Nurslings of immortality!

Shelley saw that though the poet may hardly notice the visible world, he none the less uses it as material to create independent beings which have a superior degree of reality. Nor did he stop at this. He saw that reason must somehow be related to the imagination, and he decided, in contradistinction to Wordsworth, that its special task is simply to analyse the given and to act as an instrument for the imagination, which uses its conclusions to create a synthetic and harmonious whole. He calls poetry "the expression of the Imagination," because in it diverse things are brought together in harmony instead of being separated through analysis. In this he resembles such thinkers as Bacon and Locke, but his conclusion is quite different from theirs, since he insists that the imagination is man's highest faculty and through it he realizes his noblest powers.

In his *Defence of Poetry* Shelley controverted the old disparaging view of the imagination by claiming that the poet has a special kind of knowledge:

> He not only beholds intensely the present as it is,
> and discovers those laws according to which present things ought to be ordered, but he beholds the future in the present, and his thoughts are the germs of the flower and the fruit of latest time . . .
> A poet participates in the eternal, the infinite, and the one.

For Shelley the poet is also a seer, gifted with a peculiar insight into the nature of reality. And this reality is a timeless, unchanging, complete order, of which the familiar world is but a broken reflection. Shelley took Plato's theory of knowledge and applied it to beauty. For him the Ideal Forms are a basis not so much of knowing as of that exalted insight which is ours in the presence of beautiful things. The poet's task is to uncover this absolute real in its visible examples and to interpret them through it. It is spiritual in the sense that it includes all the higher faculties of man and gives meaning to his transient sensations. Shelley tried to grasp the whole of things in its essential unity, to show what is real and what is merely phenomenal, and by doing this to display how the phenomenal depends on the real. For him the ultimate reality is the eternal mind, and this holds the universe together:

> This Whole
> Of suns, and worlds, and men, and beasts, and flowers,
> With all the silent or tempestuous workings
> By which they have been, are, or cease to be,
> Is but a vision;—all that it inherits
> Are motes of a sick eye, bubbles and dreams;
> Thought is its cradle, and its grave, nor less

The future and the past are idle shadows
Of thought's eternal flight—they have no being:
Nought is but that which feels itself to be.

[Hellas]

In thought and feeling, in consciousness and spirit, Shelley found reality and gave his answer to Prospero's nihilism. He believed that the task of the imagination is to create shapes by which this reality can be revealed.

The great Romantics, then, agreed that their task was to find through the imagination some transcendental order which explains the world of appearances and accounts not merely for the existence of visible things but for the effect which they have on us, for the sudden, unpredictable beating of the heart in the presence of beauty, for the conviction that what then moves us cannot be a cheat or an illusion, but must derive its authority from the power which moves the universe. For them this reality could not but be spiritual, and they provide an independent illustration of Hegel's doctrine that nothing is real but spirit. In so far as they made sweeping statements about the oneness of things, they were metaphysicians, but, unlike professional metaphysicians, they trusted not in logic but in insight, not in the analytical reason but in the delighted, inspired soul which in its full nature transcends both the mind and the emotions. They were, too, in their own way, religious, in their sense of the holiness of reality and the awe which they felt in its presence. But, so far as their central beliefs were concerned, they were not orthodox. Blake's religion denied the existence of God apart from men; Shelley liked to proclaim that he was an atheist; Keats was uncertain how far to accept the doctrines of Christianity. Though later both Coleridge and Wordsworth conformed almost with enthusiasm, in their most creative days their poetry was founded on a different faith. The Romantic movement was a prodigious attempt to discover the world of spirit through the unaided efforts of the solitary soul. It was a special manifestation of that belief in the worth of the individual which philosophers and politicians had recently preached to the world.

This bold expedition into the unknown, conducted with a scrupulous sincerity and a passionate faith, was very far from being an emotional self-indulgence. Each of these poets was convinced that he could discover something very important and that he possessed in poetry a key denied to other men. To this task they were prepared to devote themselves, and in different ways they paid heavily for it, in happiness, in self-confidence, in the very strength of their creative powers. They were not content to dream their own dreams and to fashion comforting illusions. They insisted that their creations must be real, not in the narrow sense that anything of which we can think has some sort of existence, but in the wide sense that they are examples and embodiments of eternal things which cannot be presented otherwise than in individual instances. Because the Romantics were poets, they set forth their visions with the wealth that poetry alone can give, in the concrete, individual form which makes the universal vivid and significant to the finite mind. They refused to accept the ideas of other men on trust or to sacrifice imagination to argument. As Blake says of Los,

I must Create a System or be enslav'd by another Man's.
I will not Reason and Compare: my business is to Create.

[Jerusalem]

The Romantics knew that their business was to create, and through creation to enlighten the whole sentient and conscious self of man, to wake his imagination to the reality which lies behind or in familiar things, to rouse him from the deadening routine of custom to a consciousness of immeasurable distances and unfathomable depths, to make him see that mere reason is not enough and that what he needs is inspired intuition. They take a wider view both of man and of poetry than was taken by their staid and rational predecessors of the eighteenth century, because they believed that it is the whole spiritual nature of man that counts, and to this they made their challenge and their appeal. (pp. 7-24)

C. M. Bowra, "The Romantic Imagination," in his The Romantic Imagination, Cambridge, Mass.: Harvard University Press, 1949, pp. 1-24.

STEPHEN PRICKETT

[*In the following excerpt, Prickett explains the Romantic concept of nature and its relation to the poetic imagination.*]

And as imagination bodies forth
The forms of things unknown, the poet's pen
Turns them to shapes and gives to airy nothing
A local habitation and a name.

It is a commonplace that Shakespeare is an anachronism—but nowhere is that extraordinary timeless quality of his thought and language better illustrated than in these lines from *A Midsummer Night's Dream* (v.i.). His use of 'imagination' in this sense was not to be recaptured until the time of the Romantics, and in the intervening centuries the idea of the imagination as a creative and interpretative power was largely lost. By the beginning of the eighteenth century it was another low-status word like 'romantic' and 'gothic', with connotations either of madness or deception. . . . [However], 'imagination' became an increasingly important word in philosophy as the century went on. A closely parallel development was also taking place in literature, so that by the early nineteenth century 'imagination' had regained much of its Shakespearean force, but within a quite new intellectual context, becoming a key word in the critical vocabulary of the age.

Nevertheless it would be a mistake to assume the word had a single meaning for poets any more than it had for the philosophers of the period. Broadly speaking, uses of the word fall into two distinct groups. On the one hand, there were those like Wordsworth and Coleridge who employed 'imagination' principally in connexion with sense-perception; on the other were those who, like Blake and Keats, seemed to use the word to describe various forms of transcendent, visionary and supersensual experiences. Though these two ways of using it look in theory as if they are fundamentally incompatible, we shall see that both positions have blurred edges and even, at times, seem to meet and overlap. (p. 209)

[Nature] too is a key word, yet it is a word of such blanket meaning that all attempts at definition seem to founder at the onset. It can, for instance, mean any one of the following:

1 The 'cosmos': the sum total of everything is clearly 'nature' in its broadest sense, but in fact the word is more normally used as *a contrast* with something else. For example:
2 The 'world of sense-perception' (as distinct from the 'supernatural');
3 The 'country' (as distinct from the town);
4 'What grows organically' (as distinct from an artifact that is made by man);

5 'What happens spontaneously' (as distinct from what is 'unnatural', either because it is laboured as contrived, or, as in 'unnatural vices', because it is held to be denying, perverting or thwarting a quality or instinct believed to be innate).

As we shall see, the last three notions—the 'rural', the 'organic' and the 'spontaneous'—are central to some aspects of Romanticism, and play a key part in the poetry of Wordsworth, for example. All three conceptions are what we might call inarticulate value words: that is, we have come to think of them somewhat vaguely as Good Things without, perhaps, having any very clear reason why. Indeed, poets as diverse as Pope, Wordsworth, Hopkins, Hardy and Lawrence all claimed they were in accordance with 'nature'.

Yet 'nature' can also be thought of in a much more active and manipulative role, as in:

6 'The life-force': This is a very ancient meaning indeed, going back to classical times and the Greek mystery cults. Two Latin tags bring out an ambiguity that has always haunted the word.
   (a) *Natura naturans:* literally 'nature naturing'. Nature is here experienced as an active, dynamic power in a constant process of change and renewal. It is in complete contrast with
   (b) *Natura naturata:* literally 'nature natured'. Here nature is frozen, is laid out on a slab for dissection and scientific investigation. The observer does not participate. It is against this view that Wordsworth was reacting in his famous line from 'The Tables Turned': 'We murder to dissect.'

Very often this idea of 'nature' as a dynamic power is personified:

7 'The Goddess': sometimes this is no more than old Mother Nature; sometimes she is further personified as in Kingsley's Mother Carey in *The Water Babies* (1863); sometimes she is felt to be dignified, awe-inspiring, and remote; sometimes she is downright evil, as in certain classical nature-cults of Pan involving human sacrifice, the worship of Baal in Palestine, or, in Tennyson's modern evolutionary version, 'Nature red in tooth and claw'.

It is here, when we approach human responses to nature, that the latent ambiguity of the word becomes most apparent. It can be seen as morally neutral, as in:

8 'The thing in itself': from the clear-cut position where it is the 'nature' of wind to blow, rain to fall, or snow to be cold, this rapidly shades off through things like 'it is the nature of cats to play with mice' into implied moral judgement, especially in the case of
9 Human 'nature': here we find now fully developed a moral polarity between:
   (a) Man as fundamentally good. This is the view for instance of Rousseau, the early Wordsworth and Shelley.
   (b) Man as fundamentally bad. This section can again be divided between the religious pessimists, such as St Paul, Calvin, Dr Johnson, Coleridge and T. S. Eliot, and the atheistical pessimists, including Hobbes, perhaps Peacock, and Thomas Hardy.

We could go on. A. O. Lovejoy claims to have distinguished more than sixty separate meanings of the word 'nature' [in 'On the Discrimination of the Romanticisms,' *English Romantic Poets;* M. H. Abrams, ed., 1960], but the complexity of the word and its connotations are apparent. Though we have somewhat arbitrarily divided Romantics into optimists and pessimists over human nature, it is clear, of course, that such a classification is far too simple. Both Wordsworth and Coleridge, for instance, were optimists in their youth, believing in human perfectibility and in the ideals of the French Revolution, but they later came, through experience, to believe in original sin and adopt a much more 'conservative' position. Wordsworth, however, turned towards nature (i.e. in the sense of meanings 2, 3 and 4) as he lost faith in human nature (9a) in the aftermath of the French Revolution. In Book X of *The Prelude* (1805) he speaks of how he was restored and made a poet through the influence of his sister, Dorothy, his friendship with Coleridge,

> And, lastly, Nature's self by human love
> Assisted, through the weary labyrinth
> Conducted me again to open day,
> Revived the feelings of my early life.

Here, as so often for Wordsworth, nature is a semi-personified force, extended to man and possessed of healing powers (i.e. meaning 7).

Elsewhere, however, Wordsworth seems to think of nature not so much as an external power to man, but as proof of his involvement with his environment. In one of the now famous passages in 'Tintern Abbey' he concludes:

> Therefore am I still
> A lover of the meadows and the woods,
> And mountains; and of all that we behold
> From this green earth; of all the mighty world
> Of eye and ear, both what we half-create,
> And what perceive; well pleased to recognise
> In nature and the language of the sense,
> The anchor of my purest thoughts, the nurse,
> The guide, the guardian of my heart, and soul
> Of all my moral being.

This clearly starts with meaning 2. But if we want to see what he means by 'half-create' we need look no further than a little poem he wrote in March 1802:

> My heart leaps up when I behold
> A rainbow in the sky;
> So was it when my life began;
> So is it now I am a man:
> So be it when I shall grow old
> Or let me die!
> The child is father of the man;
> And I could wish my days to be
> Bound each to each by natural piety.

In choosing the example of the rainbow as his touchstone of beauty, Wordsworth took his place in a controversy that had been raging ever since Newton had first explained what caused the optical phenomenon itself. In Lockean terms a rainbow is peculiar in that it consists *entirely* of secondary qualities: there is no quantifiable object there, merely the refraction of sunlight by water drops. For some, such as Addison and Thompson, it was a reminder of the 'pleasing delusion' under which we live our lives; for others, including Keats, it was rather a reminder of how science had destroyed beauty by explaining it away. Wordsworth bypassed both parties. He was interested in the rainbow precisely because it *does* consist only of secondary qualities. The rainbow can exist only if there are certain conditions present in the atmosphere, *and* if there is an observer present. Without Wordsworth, the observing eye, there would be *no* rainbow. It is for him a perpetual reminder that nature, in all our senses, is something in which we participate, in the most literal manner. As Hopkins was to put it fourteen years after Wordsworth's death:

> It was a hard thing to undo this knot.
> The rainbow shines, but only in the thought
> Of him that looks. Yet not in that alone,
> For who makes rainbows by invention?
> And many standing round a waterfall
> See one bow each, yet not the same to all
> But each a hand's breadth further than the next.
> The sun on falling waters writes the text
> Which yet is in the eye or in the thought.
> It was a hard thing to undo this knot.

But in the passage we quoted from 'Tintern Abbey' there was another very different attitude to nature coupled with this sense of participation. If nature is Wordsworth's own half-creation, how can it also be the 'soul' of all his 'moral being'? This was something that puzzled Blake as well. In Wordsworth's *Poems* of 1815 there is a poem with the long-winded but significant title: 'The Influence of Natural Objects in Calling forth and Strengthening the Imagination in Boyhood and Early Youth.' Blake first read it in 1826 and scribbled furiously in the margin of his edition, 'Natural Objects always did and now do weaken, deaden and obliterate imagination in Me. Wordsworth must know that what he writes Valuable is Not to be found in Nature.'

This was a point on which Blake was very clear. One of his earliest pieces, written in 1788, ten years before the *Lyrical Ballads,* is entitled *There is No Natural Religion.* Nature, he points out, being perceived by the senses, is subject to the limits of sense-perception. It cannot, by Locke's definition, point beyond itself to anything greater: 'From a perception of only 3 senses or 3 elements none could deduce a fourth or fifth.' To put it simply, our senses of touch, taste or hearing would tell us nothing about sight if we were born blind. There is nothing cumulative about the senses. How much less then, can nature, the creature of sense (meaning 2), point towards the 'infinite' which lies at the heart of religious experience? On the contrary, it is what Blake (apparently following Lowth) calls the 'Poetic' or 'Prophetic' which mediates revelation to man, showing him that his perceptions are *not* finally bounded by the limitations of sense, but as his desire is infinite (and ultimately *for* the infinite), so the possession of that desire and he himself, the possessor, are 'infinite'. Religion, by its very nature (meaning 7) is opposed to nature (meaning 2).

Blake thus came to see the 'imagination' not as Wordsworth did, as the power that links man to nature (meaning 2), but as analogous to an extra sense reaching *beyond* sense-perception:

> Vision or Imagination is a Representation of what Eternally Exists, Really & Unchangeably. Fable or Allegory is Form'd by the daughters of Memory. Imagination is surrounded by the daughters of Inspiration. . . . The Hebrew Bible & the Gospel of Jesus are not Allegory, but Eternal Vision or Imagination of All that Exists.

Though there are clearly Platonic elements in this, it is not classic Platonism or even Neoplatonism. Blake is not interest-

ed here in particular philosophic systems (although . . . he did have a good grasp of current philosophical problems) but in trying to describe a power that embraces nature by *transcending* it. Values are not things that we find in nature, they are what we approach nature with.

This meaning of the word 'imagination' is in some ways extraordinarily close to Kant's 'Reason'. Not, it is true, as Kant himself intended the word, but as subsequent German Idealists and Coleridge came to use it. In spite of Kant's warnings that Reason was regulative only, they seem to have interpreted him to mean that it was possible to perceive God by direct mystical intuition. This power of Reason they described as being fundamentally 'poetic' in character. As Carlyle put it with characteristic enthusiasm;

> Not by logic or argument does it work; yet surely and clearly may it be taught to work; and its domain lies in that higher region whither logic and argument cannot reach; in that holier region where Poetry and Virtue and Divinity abide, in whose presence Understanding wavers and recoils, dazzled into utter darkness by that 'sea of light', at once the fountain and the termination of true knowledge.

Yet there is a fundamental difference between this and Blake. For Carlyle and Coleridge, the world of Reason is fundamentally separate from the material and sensual world of the understanding. For Blake, the imagination, though it transcends nature, encompasses it. Another of Blake's marginalia to Wordsworth's 1815 *Poems* reads 'One Power alone makes a Poet: Imagination, The Divine Vision.' On this point Blake is, interestingly, more Kantian than the Kantians—though we have no evidence that he knew Kant at all.

Imagination is not a part of nature (meaning 2); it is, rather, the precondition with which we approach it. 'As a man is, so he sees.' Or, more explicitly: 'A fool sees not the same tree that a wise man sees.' Thus, for Blake, Wordsworth's claim to find *in* nature (presumably still meaning 2) values that belong to a different order of things is both puzzling and disturbing. Coleridge, similarly, showed an increasing distrust of nature (presumably 2 and 3) as a *source* of joy and inspiration, although he never ceased to take a delight in it. Some modern critics, David Ferry [in *The Limits of Mortality,* 1959] and Geoffrey Hartman [*Wordsworth's Poetry 1787-1814,* 1967] for instance, claim to have detected a similar disillusion and even terror of nature in Wordsworth (meanings 2, 3, 4 and even 5). Yet, as we have seen, tension and paradox are of the essence of Romantic poetry.

Wordsworth is essentially a dialectical poet, reconciling in his poetry what Coleridge called 'opposite and discordant qualities'. Thus, though I have so far been indicating which meanings of 'nature' seem most appropriate in each case, the reader will no doubt have noticed that part of Wordsworth's peculiar effectiveness lies in his ability to play off one shade of meaning against the next. His relationship with nature is not merely one of part-creation, but one that grows *through* creation. In Book II of *The Prelude* (1805 version) he described this process of growth as one of active interchange between the self and external world:

> Emphatically such a Being lives,
> An inmate of this *active* universe:
> From nature largely he receives: nor so
> Is satisfied, but largely gives again,
> For feeling has to him imparted strength,

And powerful in all sentiments of grief,
Of exultation, fear, and joy, his mind,
Even as an agent of the one great Mind,
Creates, creator and receiver both,
Working but in alliance with the works
Which it beholds.—Such, verily, is the first
Poetic spirit of our human life . . .

This growth of the mind, we notice, is described as 'poetic', which, for Wordsworth is a way of saying that it involves the whole person, intellect and feelings alike. Man's participation in nature is, of course, at a perceptual level entirely unconscious, but at a conceptual level—at the stage at which we begin to think about 'nature'—it involves both intellect and feeling. It is at this level that the discovery of values comes in. It is neither a process of simple 'projection', nor one of passive receptivity, but one of progressive and ever more complex confirmation and discovery.

Though, for some, this was no more than the 'naturalism' Blake feared he had detected in Wordsworth, for others, no less concerned with a transcendent vision than Blake, this was the source of one of Wordsworth's greatest strengths. For instance, George MacDonald (1824-1905), the poet, novelist, literary critic and mystic argued that:

> The very element in which the mind of Wordsworth lived and moved, was Christian pantheism. . . . This world is not merely a thing which God hath made, subjecting it to laws; but is an expression of the thoughts, the feeling, the heart of God himself. . . .
>
> You will find that he sometimes *draws* a lesson from nature, seeming almost to force a meaning from her. I do not object to this, if he does not make too much of it as *existing* in nature. It is rather finding a meaning in nature that he brought to it. The meaning exists, if not there.

We have a good example of this 'discovery' of meaning in nature in a later book of *The Prelude*. At the beginning of Book XIII (1805) Wordsworth describes how he, with some friends, set out to climb Snowdon by moonlight. At first the mountain was covered in thick fog, but at last near the summit they suddenly burst through the 'sea of mist' into brilliant moonlight:

> A hundred hills their dusky backs upheaved
> All over this still ocean; and beyond,
> Far, far beyond, the vapours shot themselves,
> In headlands, tongues, and promontory shapes,
> Into the sea, the real sea, that seemed
> To dwindle, and give up its majesty,
> Usurped upon as far as sight could reach.
> Meanwhile, the Moon looked down upon this show
> In single glory, and we stood, the mist
> Touching our very feet; and from the shore
> At distance not the third part of a mile
> Was a blue chasm; a fracture in the vapour,
> A deep and gloomy breathing-place through which
> Mounted the roar of waters, torrents, streams
> Innumerable, roaring with one voice!
> The universal spectacle throughout
> Was shaped for admiration and delight,
> Grand in itself alone, but in that breach
> Through which the homeless voice of waters rose,
> That deep dark thoroughfare, had Nature lodged
> The soul, the Imagination of the whole.

The description of the mountain in moonlight, and the dark rift in the clouds is strikingly vivid, but, more than that, Wordsworth's final comment, linking 'Nature' and 'Imagina-tion', suggests that the whole scene holds a special significance. It formed for him, he tells us in the next few lines, 'The perfect image of a mighty mind.' This image of a mountain, all but its moonlit summit shrouded in mist, provides the model he has been in search of throughout *The Prelude*—the model by which he can describe the human mind. It corresponds in remarkable detail to the later (no less speculative) models offered by such clinical psychiatrists as Freud and Jung. The tiny illuminated area of consciousness is surrounded by the 'huge sea of mist' concealing what Wordsworth called 'an underpresence' (the words 'unconscious' or 'subconscious' belong to later psychiatry). The model is a familiar one: what is astonishing is to discover the detail with which Wordsworth has worked it out, and his feeling that nature had in some way put it there:

> above all
> One function of such mind had Nature there
> Exhibited by putting forth, and that
> With circumstance most awful and sublime,
> That domination which she oftentimes
> Exerts upon the outward face of things,
> So moulds them, and endues, abstracts, combines,
> Or by abrupt and unhabitual influence
> Doth make one object so impress itself
> Upon all others, and pervade them so
> That even the grossest minds must see and hear
> And cannot choose but feel.

Here Wordsworth is describing existentially a certain type of experience of discovery. Kekule's discovery of the 'Benzine ring' is another example which comes to mind. Wordsworth did not (I think) believe that nature had actually staged a miracle for him: he saw the occurrence as perfectly normal. He was, however, able to see in in the answer to his problem of how to describe the intuitively observed fact that so many of our most influential mental processes are hidden from us. In one sense, I suppose, it was 'projection' on Wordsworth's part, but that was not how he felt it. He experienced it as an overwhelming discovery *outside* himself. Moreover he gives us a clue as to how this might be in his description of the gap in the clouds as the 'Imagination' of the whole. It represents, in his psychological model, the meeting point of the conscious and unconscious areas of the mind—and, by a brilliant piece of reflexive metaphor, it is by just such an 'imaginative' gap that his conscious mind is able to 'discover' in nature what his unconscious in some sense already 'knows'. In Coleridge's perceptive phase, Wordsworth receives 'The light reflected, as a light bestowed.'

This definition of imagination is, of course, very similar to Coleridge's own. His famous description of the imagination in chapter XIII of the *Biographia Literaria* is in many ways parallel to Wordsworth's:

> THE IMAGINATION then, I consider either as primary or secondary. The primary IMAGINATION I hold to be the living Power and prime Agent of all human perception, and as a repetition in the finite mind of the eternal act of creation in the infinite I AM. The Secondary Imagination I consider as an echo of the former, coexisting with the conscious will, yet still as identical with the primary in the *kind* of its agency, and differing only in *degree,* and in the mode of its operation. It dissolves, diffuses, dissipates, in order to recreate; or where this process is rendered impossible, yet still at all events it struggles to idealize and to unify. It is essentially

vital, even as all objects (as objects) are essentially fixed and dead.

More ink has perhaps been spilled over this passage than any other piece of Romantic theory. Much of it need not detain us here. The actual formulation is taken from Schelling, but Coleridge has made one or two important changes. The first is that it is fundamentally egalitarian. The 'Secondary Imagination', the creative power of the poet or artist (what Wordsworth in the Snowdon passage called 'That Glorious faculty / Which higher minds bear with them as their own') is of the same *kind* as the Primary: the unconscious process of what has been called 'making and matching', by which *all* perception takes place. In other words, the peculiar power of the artist is not something unique, but is an exaggerated or heightened form of something we *all* possess to some degree.

Second, Coleridge contrasts imagination with fancy. Fancy, for him, is no more than a scissors-and-paste job of the mind. 'The Fancy is indeed no other than a mode of Memory emancipated from the order of Time and Space.' It is, in short, Locke's 'imagination'. Coleridge is attempting to distinguish between mere passive reproduction, and the active power of the 'shaping spirit of imagination' which is a divine gift, reflecting the creative powers of God. Nevertheless, in spite of this association between poetic creativity and the divine, Coleridge's 'Imagination' remains very much a thing of this world, concerned with nature (in meaning 2) and sense-perception.

Perhaps the most thorough-going claim for the creative powers of the imagination, however, came from Keats. On 22 November 1817, in a letter to his friend Benjamin Bailey (afterwards a friend of Wordsworth), he wrote:

> I am certain of nothing but of the holiness of the Heart's affections and the truth of the Imagination—What the imagination seizes as Beauty must be truth—whether it existed before or not—for I have the same idea of all our Passions as of Love they are all in their Sublime, creative of essential Beauty. The Imagination may be compared to Adam's dream—he awoke and found it truth.

The reference to Adam's 'dream' is to *Paradise Lost,* Book VIII, lines 460-90, where Adam is cast into a trance by God while he takes one of Adam's ribs to create Eve. Adam dreams of Eve, and then awakes and finds her real. As with the Knight at Arms 'alone and palely loitering' in 'La Belle Dame Sans Merci', Adam's dream was more 'real' to him than his waking surroundings, and had he not found Eve on awakening, life would thenceforth have been barren and meaningless. Clearly, therefore, though Keats's 'Imagination' is in some sense Platonic, like Blake's, its function is to transform our vision of *this* world rather than point to another.

This suggestion is reinforced by Keats's remark only a couple of lines later in the same letter: 'O for a life of Sensations rather than Thoughts!' Though this is sometimes quoted as being anti-intellectual, in context it has a quite different flavour: 'I have never yet been able to perceive how any thing can be known for truth by consequitive [*sic*] reasoning—and yet it must be. Can it be that even the greatest Philosopher ever arrived at his goal without putting aside numerous objections. However it may be, O for a life of Sensations rather than Thoughts!'

What Keats is saying here is very close to Blake's conclusion to *There is No Natural Religion:* 'If it were not for the Poetic or Prophetic character the Philosophic and Experimental would soon be at the ratio of all things, and stand still, unable to do other than repeat the same dull round over again.' Logical reasoning, in the Lockean sense, is completely enclosed. It is unable *either* to provide values *or* to provide certainty. Without imagination, or what Blake here calls 'the Poetic or Prophetic', it is sterile and useless. It cannot create, it cannot innovate, it cannot satisfy.

Though they reached their conclusions by very different paths, it is clear that for all the Romantics the role of the 'poet' is crucial to human existence. Both religion and philosophy are ultimately dependent on it. Without the poetic imagination nature itself is dead. (pp. 209-21)

> Stephen Prickett, "Romantic Literature," in The Romantics, *edited by Stephen Prickett, Methuen & Co. Ltd., 1981, pp. 202-61.*

W. K. WIMSATT, JR.

[*A prominent American literary theorist, Wimsatt is noted for his critical approach that views literature in isolation from both the intentions of the author and the emotional reactions of the reader. This theory is most notably articulated in his collection of essays* The Verbal Icon *(1954), from which the following study of Romantic nature imagery is taken.*]

Students of romantic nature poetry have had a great deal to tell us about the philosophic components of this poetry: the specific blend of deistic theology, Newtonian physics, and pantheistic naturalism which pervades the Wordsworthian landscape in the period of "Tintern Abbey," the theism which sounds in the "Eolian Harp" of Coleridge, the conflict between French atheism and Platonic idealism which even in *Prometheus Unbound* Shelley was not able to resolve. We have been instructed in some of the more purely scientific coloring of the poetry—the images derived from geology, astronomy, and magnetism, and the coruscant green mystery which the electricians contributed to such phenomena as Shelley's Spirit of Earth. We have considered also the "sensibility" of romantic readers, distinct, according to one persuasive interpretation, from that of neoclassic readers. What was exciting to the age of Pope, "Puffs, Powders, Patches, Bibles, Billet-doux" (even about these the age might be loath to admit its excitement), was not, we are told, what was so manifestly exciting to the age of Wordsworth. "High mountains are a feeling, but the hum of cities torture." Lastly, recent critical history has reinvited attention to the romantic theory of imagination, and especially to the version of that theory which Coleridge derived from the German metaphysicians, the view of poetic imagination as the *esemplastic* power which reshapes our primary awareness of the world into symbolic avenues to the theological.

We have, in short, a *subject*—simply considered, the nature of birds and trees and streams—a *metaphysics* of an animating principle, a special *sensibility,* and a *theory* of poetic imagination—the value of the last a matter of debate. Romantic poetry itself has recently suffered some disfavor among advanced critics. One interesting question, however, seems still to want discussion; that is, whether romantic poetry (or more specifically romantic nature poetry) exhibits any imaginative *structure* which may be considered a special counterpart of the subject, the philosophy, the sensibility, and the theory—

and hence perhaps an explanation of the last. Something like an answer to such a question is what I would sketch.

For the purpose of providing an antithetic point of departure, I quote here a part of one of the best known and most toughly reasonable of all metaphysical images:

> If they be two, they are two so
>   As stiff twin compasses are two,
> Thy soul the fixed foot, makes no show
>   To move, but doth, if th' other do.

It will be relevant if we remark that this similitude, rather far-fetched as some might think, is yet unmistakable to interpretation because quite overtly stated, but again is not, by being stated, precisely defined or limited in its poetic value. The kind of similarity and the kind of disparity that ordinarily obtain between a drawing compass and a pair of parting lovers are things to be attentively considered in reading this image. And the disparity between living lovers and stiff metal is not least important to the tone of precision, restraint, and conviction which it is the triumph of the poem to convey. Though the similitude is cast in the form of statement, its mood is actually a kind of subimperative. In the next age the tension of such a severe disparity was relaxed, yet the overtness and crispness of statement remained, and a wit of its own sort.

> 'Tis with our judgments as our watches, none
> Go just alike, yet each believes his own.

We may take this as typical, I believe, of the metaphoric structure in which Pope achieves perfection and which survives a few years later in the couplets of Samuel Johnson or the more agile Churchill. The difference between our judgments and our watches, if noted at all, may be a pleasant epistemological joke for a person who questions the existence of a judgment which is taken out like a watch and consulted by another judgment.

But the "sensibility," as we know, had begun to shift even in the age of Pope. Examples of a new sensibility, and of a different structure, having something to do with Miltonic verse and a "physico-theological nomenclature," are to be found in Thomson's *Seasons*. Both a new sensibility and a new structure appear in the "hamlets brown and dim-discovered spires" of Collins' early example of the full romantic dream. In several poets of the mid century, in the Wartons, in Grainger, or in Cunningham, one may feel, or rather see stated, a new sensibility, but at the same time one may lament an absence of poetic quality—that is, of a poetic structure adequate to embody or objectify the new feeling. It is as if these harbingers of another era had felt but had not felt strongly enough to work upon the objects of their feelings a pattern of meaning which would speak for itself—and which would hence endure as a poetic monument.

As a central exhibit I shall take two sonnets, that of William Lisle Bowles "To the River Itchin" (1789) and for contrast that of Coleridge "To the River Otter" (1796)—written in confessed imitation of Bowles. Coleridge owed his first poetic inspiration to Bowles (the "father" of English romantic poetry) and continued to express unlimited admiration for him as late as 1796. That is, they shared the same sensibility—as for that matter did Wordsworth and Southey, who too were deeply impressed by the sonnets of Bowles. As a schoolboy Coleridge read eagerly in Bowles' second edition of 1789 (among other sonnets not much superior):

> Itchin, when I behold thy banks again,

Portrait of Samuel Taylor Coleridge at age forty-two by Washington Allston.

> Thy crumbling margin, and thy silver breast,
> On which the self-same tints still seem to rest,
> Why feels my heart the shiv'ring sense of pain?
> Is it—that many a summer's day has past
> Since, in life's morn, I carol'd on thy side?
> Is it—that oft, since then, my heart has sigh'd,
> As Youth, and Hope's delusive gleams, flew fast?
> Is it—that those, who circled on thy shore,
> Companions of my youth, now meet no more?
> Whate'er the cause, upon thy banks I bend
> Sorrowing, yet feel such solace at my heart,
> As at the meeting of some long-lost friend,
> From whom, in happier hours, we wept to part.

Here is an emotive expression which once appealed to the sensibility of its author and of his more cultivated contemporaries, but which has with the lapse of time gone flat. The speaker was happy as a boy by the banks of the river. Age has brought disillusion and the dispersal of his friends. So a return to the river, in reminding him of the past, brings both sorrow and consolation. The facts are stated in four rhetorical questions and a concluding declaration. There is also something about how the river looks and how its looks might contribute to his feelings—in the metaphoric suggestion of the "crumbling" margin and in the almost illusory tints on the surface of the stream which surprisingly have outlasted the "delusive gleams" of his own hopes. Yet the total impression is one of simple association (by contiguity in time) simply asserted—what might be described in the theory of Hume or Hartley or what Hazlitt talks about in his essay "On the Love of the Country." "It is because natural objects have been associated with the sports of our childhood, . . . with our feelings in solitude . . . that we love them as we do ourselves."

Coleridge himself in his "Lines Written at Elbingerode in 1799" was to speak of a "spot with which the heart associates Holy remembrances of child or friend." His enthusiasm for Hartley in this period is well known. But later, in the *Biographia Literaria* and in the third of his essays on "Genial Criticism," he was to repudiate explicitly the Hartleyan and mechanistic way of shifting back burdens of meaning. And already, in 1796, Coleridge as poet was concerned with the more complex ontological grounds of association (the various levels of sameness, of correspondence and analogy), where mental activity transcends mere "associative response"—where it is in fact the unifying activity known both to later eighteenth century associationists and to romantic poets as "imagination." The "sweet and indissoluble union between the intellectual and the material world" of which Coleridge speaks in the introduction to his pamphlet anthology of sonnets in 1796 must be applied by us in one sense to the sonnets of Bowles, but in another to the best romantic poetry and even to Coleridge's imitation of Bowles. There is an important difference between the kinds of unity. In a letter to Sotheby of 1802 Coleridge was to say more emphatically: "The poet's heart and intellect should be *combined,* intimately combined and unified with the great appearances of nature, and not merely held in solution and loose mixture with them." In the same paragraph he says of Bowles' later poetry: "Bowles has indeed the *sensibility* of a poet, but he has not the *passion* of a great poet . . . he has no native passion because he is not a thinker."

The sententious melancholy of Bowles' sonnets and the asserted connection between this mood and the appearances of nature are enough to explain the hold of the sonnets upon Coleridge. Doubtless the metaphoric coloring, faint but nonetheless real, which we have remarked in Bowles' descriptive details had also something to do with it. What is of great importance to note is that Coleridge's own sonnet "To the River Otter" (while not a completely successful poem) shows a remarkable intensification of such color.

> Dear native Brook! wild Streamlet of the West!
> How many various-fated years have past,
> What happy and what mournful hours, since last
> I skimmed the smooth thin stone along thy breast,
> Numbering its light leaps! yet so deep imprest
> Sink the sweet scenes of childhood, that mine eyes
> I never shut amid the sunny ray,
> But straight with all their tints thy waters rise,
> Thy crossing plank, thy marge with willows grey,
> And bedded sand that veined with various dyes
> Gleamed through thy bright transparence! On my way,
> Visions of Childhood! oft have ye beguiled
> Lone manhood's cares, yet waking fondest sighs:
> Ah! that once more I were a careless Child!

Almost the same statement as that of Bowles' sonnet—the sweet scenes of childhood by the river have only to be remembered to bring both beguilement and melancholy. One notices immediately, however, that the speaker has kept his eye more closely on the object. There are more details. The picture is more vivid, a fact which according to one school of poetics would in itself make the sonnet superior. But a more analytic theory will find it worth remarking also that certain ideas, latent or involved in the description, have much to do with its vividness. As a child, careless and free, wild like the stream-

let, the speaker amused himself with one of the most carefree motions of youth—skimming smooth thin stones which leapt lightly on the breast of the water. One might have thought such experiences would sink no deeper in the child's breast than the stones in the water—"yet so deep imprest"—the very antithesis (though it refers overtly only to the many hours which have intervened) defines imaginatively the depth of the impressions. When he closes his eyes, they *rise* again (the word *rise* may be taken as a trope which hints the whole unstated similitude); they rise like the tinted waters of the stream; they gleam up through the depths of memory—the "various-fated years"—like the "various dyes" which vein the sand of the river bed. In short, there is a rich ground of meaning in Coleridge's sonnet beyond what is overtly stated. The descriptive details of his sonnet gleam brightly because (consciously or unconsciously—it would be fruitless to inquire how deliberately he wrote these meanings into his lines) he has invested them with significance. Here is a special perception, "invention" if one prefers, "imagination," or even "wit." It can be explored and tested by the wit of the reader. In this way it differs from the mere flat announcement of a Hartleian association, which is not open to challenge and hence not susceptible of confirmation. If this romantic wit differs from that of the metaphysicals, it differs for one thing in making less use of the central overt statement of similitude which is so important in all rhetoric stemming from Aristotle and the Renaissance. The metaphor in fact is scarcely noticed by the main statement of the poem. Both tenor and vehicle, furthermore, are wrought in a parallel process out of the same material. The river landscape is both the occasion of reminiscence and the source of the metaphors by which reminiscence is described. A poem of this structure is a signal instance of that kind of fallacy (or strategy) by which death in poetry occurs so often in winter or at night, and sweethearts meet in the spring countryside. The tenor of such a similitude is likely to be subjective—reminiscence or sorrow or beguilement—not an object distinct from the vehicle, as lovers or their souls are distinct from twin compasses. Hence the emphasis of Bowles, Coleridge, and all other romantics on spontaneous feelings and sincerity. Hence the recurrent themes of One Being and Eolian Influence and Wordsworth's "ennobling interchange of action from within and from without." In such a structure again the element of tension in disparity is not so important as for metaphysical wit. The interest derives not from our being aware of disparity where likeness is firmly insisted on, but in an opposite activity of discerning the design which is latent in the multiform sensuous picture.

Let us notice for a moment the "crossing plank" of Coleridge's sonnet, a minor symbol in the poem, a sign of shadowy presences, the lads who had once been there. The technique of this symbol is the same as that which Keats was to employ in a far more brilliant romantic instance, the second stanza of his "Ode to Autumn," where the very seasonal spirit is conjured into reality out of such haunted spots—in which a gesture lingers—the half-reaped furrow, the oozing cider press, the brook where the gleaners have crossed with laden heads. To return to our metaphysics—of an animate, plastic Nature, not transcending but immanent in and breathing through all things—and to discount for the moment such differences as may relate to Wordsworth's naturalism, Coleridge's theology, Shelley's Platonism, or Blake's visions: we may observe that the common feat of the romantic nature poets was to read meanings into the landscape. The meaning might be such as we have seen in Coleridge's sonnet, but it might more characteristically be more profound, concerning the spirit or soul of things—"the one life within us and abroad." And that meaning especially was summoned out of the very surface of nature itself. It was embodied imaginatively and without the explicit religious or philosophic statements which one will find in classical or Christian instances—for example in Pope's "Essay on Man":

> Here then we rest: "The Universal Cause
> Acts to one end, but acts by various laws,"

or in the teleological divines, More, Cudworth, Bentley, and others of the seventeenth and eighteenth centuries, or in Paley during the same era as the romantics. The romantic poets want to have it and not have it too—a spirit which the poet himself as superidealist creates by his own higher reason or esemplastic imagination. Here one may recall Ruskin's chapter of *Modern Painters* on the difference between the Greek gods of rivers and trees and the vaguer suffusions of the romantic vista—"the curious web of hesitating sentiment, pathetic fallacy, and wandering fancy, which form a great part of our modern view of nature." Wordsworth's *Prelude,* from the cliff that "upreared its head" in the night above Ullswater to the "blue chasm" that was the "soul" of the moonlit cloudscape beneath his feet on Snowdon, is the archpoet's testament, both theory and demonstration of this way of reading nature. His "Tintern Abbey" is another classic instance, a whole pantheistic poem woven of the landscape, where God is not once mentioned. After the "soft inland murmur," the "one green hue," the "wreaths of smoke . . . as . . . Of vagrant dwellers in the houseless woods" (always something just out of sight or beyond definition), it is an easy leap to the "still, sad music of humanity," and

> a sense sublime
> Of something far more deeply interfused,
> Whose dwelling is the light of setting suns.

This poem, written as Wordsworth revisited the banks of a familiar stream, the "Sylvan Wye," is the full realization of a poem for which Coleridge and Bowles had drawn slight sketches. In Shelley's "Hymn to Intellectual Beauty" the "awful shadow" of the "unseen Power" is substantiated of "moonbeam" showers of light behind the "piny mountain," of "mist o'er mountains driven." On the Lake of Geneva in the summer of 1816 Byron, with Shelley the evangelist of Wordsworth at his side, spoke of "a living fragrance from the shore," a "floating whisper on the hill." We remark in each of these examples a dramatization of the spiritual through the use of the faint, the shifting, the least tangible and most mysterious parts of nature—a poetic counterpart of the several theories of spirit as subtle matter current in the eighteenth century, Newton's "electric and elastic" active principle, Hartley's "infinitesimal elementary body." The application of this philosophy to poetry by way of direct statement had been made as early as 1735 in Henry Brooke's "Universal Beauty," where an "elastick Flue of fluctuating Air" pervades the universe as "animating Soul." In the high romantic period the most scientific version to appear in poetry was the now well recognized imagery which Shelley drew from the electricians.

In such a view of spirituality the landscape itself is kept in focus as a literal object of attention. Without it Wordsworth and Byron in the examples just cited would not get a start. And one effect of such a use of natural imagery—an effect implicit in the very philosophy of a World Spirit—is a tendency in the landscape imagery to a curious split. If we have not only the landscape but the spirit which either informs or vis-

its it, and if both of these must be rendered for the sensible imagination, a certain parceling of the landscape may be the result. The most curious illustrations which I know are in two of Blake's early quartet of poems to the seasons. Thus, "To Spring":

> O thou with dewy locks, who lookest down
> Thro' the clear windows of the morning, turn
> Thine angel eyes upon our western isle,
> Which in full choir hails thy approach, O Spring!
>
> The hills tell each other, and the list'ning
> Vallies hear; all our longing eyes are turned
> Up to thy bright pavillions; issue forth,
> And let thy holy feet visit our clime.
>
> Come o'er the eastern hills, and let our winds
> Kiss thy perfumed garments; let us taste
> Thy morn and evening breath; scatter thy pearls
> Upon our love-sick land that mourns for thee.

And "To Summer":

> O thou, who passest thro' our vallies in
> Thy strength, curb thy fierce steeds, allay the heat
> That flames from their large nostrils! thou, O Summer,
> Oft pitched'st here thy golden tent, and oft
> Beneath our oaks hast slept, while we beheld
> With joy thy ruddy limbs and flourishing hair.
> Beneath our thickest shades we oft have heard
> Thy voice, when noon upon his fervid car
> Rode o'er the deep of heaven; beside our springs
> Sit down, and in our mossy vallies, on
> Some bank beside a river clear, throw thy
> Silk draperies off, and rush into the stream.

Blake's starting point, it is true, is the opposite of Wordsworth's or Byron's, not the landscape but a spirit personified or allegorized. Nevertheless, this spirit as it approaches the "western isle" takes on certain distinctly terrestrial hues. Spring, an oriental bridegroom, lives behind the "clear windows of the morning" and is invited to issue from "bright pavillions," doubtless the sky at dawn. He has "perfumed garments" which when kissed by the winds will smell much like the flowers and leaves of the season. At the same time, his *own* morn and evening breaths are most convincing in their likeness to morning and evening breezes. The pearls scattered by the hand of Spring are, we must suppose, no other than the flowers and buds which literally appear in the landscape at this season. They function as landscape details and simultaneously as properties of the bridegroom and—we note here a further complication—as properties of the land taken as lovesick maiden. We have in fact a double personification conjured from one nature, one landscape, in a wedding which approximates fusion. Even more curious is the case of King Summer, a divided tyrant and victim, who first appears as the source and spirit of heat, his steeds with flaming nostrils, his limbs ruddy, his tent golden, but who arrives in our valleys only to sleep in the shade of the oaks and be invited to rush into the river for a swim. These early romantic poems are examples of the Biblical, classical, and Renaissance tradition of allegory as it approaches the romantic condition of landscape naturalism—as Spring and Summer descend into the landscape and are fused with it. Shelley's Alastor is a spirit of this kind, making the "wild his home," a spectral "Spirit of wind," expiring "Like some frail exhalation; which the dawn Robes in its golden beams." Byron's Childe Harold desired that he himself might become a "portion" of that around him, of the tempest and the night. "Be thou, Spirit fierce," said Shelley to the West Wind, "My spirit! Be thou me."

An English student of the arts in the Jacobean era, Henry Peacham, wrote a book on painting in which he gave allegorical prescriptions for representing the months, quoted under the names of months by Dr. Johnson in his *Dictionary:*

> *April* is represented by a young man in green, with a garland of myrtle and hawthorn buds; in one hand primroses and violets, in the other the sign Taurus.

> *July* I would have drawn in a jacket of light yellow, eating cherries, with his face and bosom sunburnt.

But that would have been the end of it. April would not have been painted into a puzzle picture where hawthorn buds and primroses were arranged to shadow forth the form of a person. There were probably deep enough reasons why the latter nineteenth century went so far in the development of so trivial a thing as the actual landscape puzzle picture.

In his Preface of 1815 Wordsworth spoke of the *abstracting* and *"modifying* powers of the imagination." He gave as example a passage from his own poem, "Resolution and Independence," where an old leech gatherer is likened to a stone which in turn is likened to a sea beast crawled forth to sun itself. The poems which we have just considered, those of Coleridge, Wordsworth, and Blake especially, with their blurring of literal and figurative, might also be taken, I believe, as excellent examples. In another of his best poems Wordsworth produced an image which shows so strange yet artistic a warping, or modification, of vehicle by tenor that, though not strictly a nature image, it may be quoted here with close relevance. In the ode "Intimations of Immortality":

> Hence, in a season of calm weather,
> Though inland far we be,
> Our souls have sight of that immortal sea
> Which brought us hither;
> Can in a moment travel thither—
> And see the children sport upon the shore,
> And hear the mighty waters rolling evermore.

Or, as one might drably paraphrase, our souls in a calm mood look back to the infinity from which they came, as persons inland on clear days can look back to the sea by which they have voyaged to the land. The tenor concerns souls and age and time. The vehicle concerns travelers and space. The question for the analyst of structure is: Why are the children found on the seashore? In what way do they add to the solemnity or mystery of the sea? Or do they at all? The answer is that they are not strictly parts of the traveler-space vehicle, but of the soul-age-time tenor, attracted over, from tenor to vehicle. The travelers looking back in both space and time see themselves as children on the shore, as if just born like Venus from the foam. This is a sleight of words, an imposition of image upon image, by the *modifying* power of imagination.

Poetic structure is always a fusion of ideas with material, a statement in which the solidity of symbol and the sensory verbal qualities are somehow not washed out by the abstraction. For this effect the iconic or directly imitative powers of language are important—and of these the well known onomatopoeia or imitation of sound is only one, and one of the simplest. The "stiff twin compasses" of Donne have a kind of iconicity in the very stiffness and odd emphasis of the metrical situation. Neoclassic iconicity is on the whole of a highly or-

dered, formal, or intellectual sort, that of the "figures of speech" such as antithesis, isocolon, homoeoteleuton, or chiasmus. But romantic nature poetry tends to achieve iconicity by a more direct sensory imitation of something headlong and impassioned, less ordered, nearer perhaps to the subrational. Thus: in Shelley's "Ode to the West Wind" the shifts in imagery of the second stanza, the pell-mell raggedness and confusion of loose clouds, decaying leaves, angels and Maenads with hair uplifted, the dirge, the dome, the vapors, and the enjambment from tercet to tercet combine to give an impression beyond statement of the very wildness, the breath and power which is the vehicle of the poem's radical metaphor. If we think of a scale of structures having at one end logic, the completely reasoned and abstracted, and at the other some form of madness or surrealism, matter or impression unformed and undisciplined (the imitation of disorder by the idiom of disorder), we may see metaphysical and neoclassical poetry as near the extreme of logic (though by no means reduced to that status) and romantic poetry as a step toward the directness of sensory presentation (though by no means sunk into subrationality). As a structure which favors implication rather than overt statement, the romantic is far closer than the metaphysical to symbolist poetry and the varieties of postsymbolist most in vogue today. Both types of structure, the metaphysical and the romantic, are valid. Each has gorgeously enriched the history of English poetry. (pp. 103-16)

> *W. K. Wimsatt, Jr., "The Structure of Romantic Nature Imagery," in his* The Verbal Icon: Studies in the Meaning of Poetry, *1954. Reprint by The Noonday Press, 1958, pp. 103-16.*

HAROLD BLOOM

[*Bloom is one of the most prominent contemporary American critics and literary theorists. In* The Anxiety of Influence *(1973), he formulated a controversial theory of literary creation called revisionism. Influenced strongly by Freudian theory, Bloom believes that all poets are influenced by earlier poets and that, to develop their own voice, they attempt to overcome this influence through a process of misreading. This process involves a deliberate revision of what has been said by another so that it conforms to one's own vision: "Poetic influence—when it involves two strong, authentic poets—always proceeds by a misreading of the prior poet, an act of creative correction that is actually and necessarily a misrepresentation. The history of poetic influence . . . is a history of anxiety and self-serving caricature, of distortion, of perverse, willful revisionism." In this way the poet creates a singular voice, overcoming the fear of being inferior to poetic predecessors. Bloom's later books are applications of this theory, extended in* Kabbalah and Criticism *(1974) to include the critic or reader as another deliberate misreader. Thus, there is no single reading of any text, but multiple readings by poets or critics who understand a work only in ways that allow them to assert their individuality or vision. In addition to his theoretical work, Bloom is one of the foremost authorities on English Romantic poetry and has written widely on the influences of Romanticism in contemporary literature. In the following excerpt, he argues that the Romantic poets struggled to free their imaginations from the confines of nature and self-consciousness.*]

Freud, in an essay written sixty years ago on the relation of the poet to daydreaming, made the surmise that all aesthetic pleasure is forepleasure, an "incitement premium" or narcissistic fantasy. The deepest satisfactions of literature, on this view, come from a release of tensions in the psyche. That

Freud had found, as almost always, either part of the truth or at least a way to it, is clear enough, even if a student of Blake or Wordsworth finds, as probably he must, this Freudian view to be partial, reductive, and a kind of mirror-image of the imagination's truth. The deepest satisfactions of reading Blake or Wordsworth come from the realization of new ranges of tensions in the mind, but Blake and Wordsworth both believed, in different ways, that the pleasures of poetry were only forepleasures, in the sense that poems, finally, were scaffoldings for a more imaginative vision, and not ends in themselves. I think that what Blake and Wordsworth do for their readers, or can do, is closely related to what Freud does or can do for his, which is to provide both a map of the mind and a profound faith that the map can be put to a saving use. Not that the uses agree, or that the maps quite agree either, but the enterprise is a humanizing one in all three of these discoverers. The humanisms do not agree either; Blake's is apocalyptic, Freud's is naturalistic, and Wordsworth's is—sometimes sublimely, sometimes uneasily—blended of elements that dominate in the other two.

Freud thought that even romance, with its element of play, probably commenced in some actual experience whose "strong impression on the writer had stirred up a memory of an earlier experience, generally belonging to childhood, which then arouses a wish that finds a fulfillment in the work in question, and in which elements of the recent event and the old memory should be discernible." Though this is a brilliant and comprehensive thought, it seems inadequate to the complexity of romance, particularly in the period during which romance as a genre, however displaced, became again the dominant form, which is to say the age of Romanticism. For English-speaking readers, this age may be defined as extending from the childhood of Blake and Wordsworth to the present moment. Convenience dictates that we distinguish the High Romantic period proper, during which a half-dozen major English poets did their work, from the generations that have come after them, but the distinction is difficult to justify critically.

Freud's embryonic theory of romance contains within it the potential for an adequate account of Romanticism, particularly if we interpret his "memory of an earlier experience" to mean also the recall of an earlier insight, or yearning, that may not have been experiential. The immortal longings of the child, rather variously interpreted by Freud, Blake, and Wordsworth, may not be at the roots of romance, historically speaking, since those roots go back to a psychology very different from ours, but they do seem to be at the sources of the mid-eighteenth-century revival of a romance consciousness, out of which nineteenth-century Romanticism largely came.

J. H. Van den Berg, whose introduction to a historical psychology I find crucial to an understanding of Romanticism, thinks that Rousseau "was the first to view the child as a child, and to stop treating the child as an adult." Van den Berg, as a doctor, does not think this was necessarily an advance: "Ever since Rousseau the child has been keeping its distance. This process of the child and adult growing away from each other began in the eighteenth century. It was then that the period of adolescence came into existence." Granting that Van den Berg is broadly correct (he at least attempts to explain an apparent historical modulation in consciousness that few historians of culture care to confront), then we are presented with another in a series of phenomena, clustering around Rousseau and his age, in which the major change

from the Enlightenment to Romanticism manifested itself. Changes in consciousness are of course very rare, and no major synthesizer has come forth as yet, from any discipline, to demonstrate to us whether Romanticism marks a genuine change in consciousness or not. From the Freudian viewpoint, Romanticism is an "illusory therapy" (I take the phrase from Philip Rieff), or what Freud himself specifically termed an "erotic illusion." The dialectics of Romanticism, to the Freudians, are mistaken or inadequate, because the dialectics are sought in Schiller or Heine or in German Romantic philosophy down to Nietzsche, rather than in Blake or the English Romantics after him. Blake and Coleridge do not set intellect and passion against one another, any more than they arrive at the Freudian simplicity of the endless conflict between Eros and Thanatos. Possibly because of the clear associations between Jung and German Romanticism, it has been too easy for Freudian intellectuals to confound Romanticism with various modes of irrationalism. Though much contemporary scholarship attempts to study English and Continental Romanticism as a unified phenomenon, it can be argued that the English Romantics tend to lose more than they gain by such study.

Behind Continental Romanticism there lay very little in the way of a congenial native tradition of major poets writing in an ancestral mode, particularly when compared to the English Romantic heritage of Spenser, Shakespeare, and Milton. What allies Blake and Wordsworth, Shelley and Keats, is their strong mutual conviction that they are reviving the true English tradition of poetry, which they thought had vanished after the death of Milton, and had reappeared in diminished form, mostly after the death of Pope, in admirable but doomed poets like Chatterton, Cowper, and Collins, victims of circumstance and of their own false dawn of Sensibility. It is in this highly individual sense that English Romanticism legitimately can be called, as traditionally it has been, a revival of romance. More than a revival, it is an internalization of romance, particularly of the quest variety, an internalization made for more than therapeutic purposes, because made in the name of a humanizing hope that approaches apocalyptic intensity. The poet takes the patterns of quest-romance and transposes them into his own imaginative life, so that the entire rhythm of the quest is heard again in the movement of the poet himself from poem to poem. M. H. Abrams brilliantly traces these patterns of what he calls "the apocalypse of imagination" [see excerpt below]. As he shows, historically they all directly stem from English reactions to the French Revolution, or to the intellectual currents that had flowed into the Revolution. Psychologically, they stem from the child's vision of a more titanic universe that the English Romantics were so reluctant to abandon. If adolescence was a Romantic or Rousseauistic phenomenon of consciousness, its concomitant was the very secular sense of being twice-born that is first discussed in the fourth chapter of *Émile,* and then beautifully developed by Shelley in his visionary account of Rousseau's second birth, in the concluding movement of *The Triumph of Life.* The pains of psychic maturation become, for Shelley, the potentially saving though usually destructive crisis when the imagination confronts its choice of either sustaining its own integrity or yielding to the illusive beauty of nature.

The movement of quest-romance, before its internalization by the High Romantics, was from nature to redeemed nature, the sanction of redemption being the gift of some external spiritual authority, sometimes magical. The Romantic movement is from nature to the imagination's freedom (sometimes a reluctant freedom), and the imagination's freedom is frequently purgatorial, redemptive in direction but destructive of the social self. The high cost of Romantic internalization, that is, of finding paradises within a renovated man, tends to manifest itself in the arena of self-consciousness. The quest is to widen consciousness as well as intensify it, but the quest is shadowed by a spirit that tends to narrow consciousness to an acute preoccupation with self. This shadow of imagination is solipsism, what Shelley calls the Spirit of Solitude or "Alastor," the avenging daimon who is a baffled residue of the self, determined to be compensated for its loss of natural assurance, for having been awakened from the merely given condition that to Shelley, as to Blake, was but the sleep of death-in-life. Blake calls this spirit of solitude a Spectre, or the genuine Satan, the Thanatos or death-impulse in every natural man. Modernist poetry in English organized itself, to an excessive extent, as a supposed revolt against Romanticism, in the mistaken hope of escaping this inwardness (though it was unconscious that this was its prime motive). Modernist poetry learned better, as its best work, the last phases of W. B. Yeats and Wallace Stevens, abundantly shows. . . . (pp. 13-16)

Paul De Man terms this phenomenon the post-Romantic dilemma, observing that every fresh attempt of Modernism to go beyond Romanticism ends in the gradual realization of the Romantics' continued priority. Modern poetry, in English, is the invention of Blake and of Wordsworth, and I do not know of a long poem written in English since then that is either as legitimately difficult or as rewardingly profound as *Jerusalem* or *The Prelude*. Nor can I find a modern lyric, however happily ignorant its writer, that develops beyond or surmounts its debt to Wordsworth's great trinity of "Tintern Abbey," *Resolution and Independence,* and the "Intimations of Immortality" Ode. The dreadful paradox of Wordsworth's greatness is that his uncanny originality, still the most astonishing break with tradition in the language, has been so influential that we have lost sight of its audacity and its arbitrariness. In this, Wordsworth strongly resembles Freud, who rightly compared his own intellectual revolution to those of Copernicus and Darwin. Van den Berg quietly sees "Freud, in the desperation of the moment, turning away from the present, where the cause of his patients' illnesses was located, to the past; and thus making them suffer from the past and making our existence akin to their suffering. It was not necessary." Is Van den Berg right? The question is as crucial for Wordsworth and Romanticism as it is for Freud and psychoanalysis. The most searching critique of Romanticism that I know is Van den Berg's critique of Freud, particularly the description of "The Subject and his Landscape":

> Ultimately the enigma of grief is the libido's inclination toward exterior things. What prompts the libido to leave the inner self? In 1914 Freud asked himself this question—the essential question of his psychology, and the essential question of the psychology of the twentieth century. His answer ended the process of interiorization. It is: the libido leaves the inner self when the inner self has become too full. In order to prevent it from being torn, the I has to aim itself on objects outside the self; " . . . ultimately man must begin to love in order not to get ill." So that is what it is. Objects are of importance only in an extreme urgency. Human beings, too. The grief over their death is the sighing of a too-far-distended covering, the groaning of an overfilled inner self.

Wordsworth is a crisis-poet, Freud a crisis-analyst; the saving movement in each is backward into lost time. But what is the movement of loss, in poet and in analyst? Van den Berg's suggestion is that Freud unnecessarily sacrificed the present moment, because he came at the end of a tradition of intellectual error that began with the extreme Cartesian dualism, and that progressively learned to devalue contact between the self and others, the self and the outer world, the self and the body. Wordsworth's prophecy, and Blake's, was overtly against dualism; they came, each said, to heal the division within man, and between man and the world, if never quite between man and man. But Wordsworth, the more influential because more apparently accessible of the two (I myself would argue that he is the more difficult because the more problematic poet), no more overcame a fundamental dualism than Freud did. Essentially this was Blake's complaint against him; it is certainly no basis for us to complain. Wordsworth made his kind of poetry out of an extreme urgency, and out of an overfilled inner self, a Blakean Prolific that nearly choked in an excess of its own delights. This is the Egotistical Sublime of which Keats complained, but Keats knew his debt to Wordsworth, as most poets since do not.

Wordsworth's Copernican revolution in poetry is marked by the evanescence of any subject but subjectivity, the loss of what a poem is "about." If, like the late Yvor Winters, one rejects a poetry that is not "about" something, one has little use for (or understanding of) Wordsworth. But, like Van den Berg on Freud, one can understand and love Wordsworth, and still ask of his radical subjectivity: was it necessary? Without hoping to find an answer, one can explore the question so as to come again on the central problem of Romantic (and post-Romantic) poetry: what, for men without belief and even without credulity, is the spiritual form of romance? How can a poet's (or any man's) life be one of continuous allegory (as Keats thought Shakespeare's must have been) in a reductive universe of death, a separated realm of atomized meanings, each discrete from the next? Though all men are questers, even the least, what is the relevance of quest in a gray world of continuities and homogenized enterprises? Or, in Wordsworth's own terms, which are valid for every major Romantic, what knowledge might yet be purchased except by the loss of power?

Frye, in his theory of myths, explores the analogue between quest-romance and the dream: "Translated into dream terms, the quest-romance is the search of the libido or desiring self for a fulfillment that will deliver it from the anxieties of reality but will still contain that reality." Internalized romance, and *The Prelude* and *Jerusalem* can be taken as the greatest examples of this kind, traces a Promethean and revolutionary quest, and cannot be translated into dream terms, for in it the libido turns inward into the self. Shelley's *Prometheus Unbound* is the most drastic High Romantic version of internalized quest, but there are more drastic versions still in our own age, though they present themselves as parodistic, as in the series of marvelous interior quests by Stevens, that go from "The Comedian As the Letter C" to the climactic *Notes Toward a Supreme Fiction.* The hero of internalized quest is the poet himself, the antagonists of quest are everything in the self that blocks imaginative work, and the fulfillment is never the poem itself but the poem beyond that is made possible by the apocalypse of imagination. "A timely utterance gave that thought relief " is the Wordsworthian formula for the momentary redemption of the poet's sanity by the poem already written, and might stand as a motto for the history of the modern lyric from Wordsworth to Hart Crane.

The Romantics tended to take Milton's Satan as the archetype of the heroically defeated Promethean quester, a choice in which modern criticism has not followed them. But they had a genuine insight into the affinity between an element in their selves and an element in Milton that he would externalize only in a demonic form. What *is* heroic about Milton's Satan is a real Prometheanism and a thoroughly internalized one; he can steal only his own fire in the poem, since God can appear as fire, again in the poem, only when he directs it against Satan. In Romantic quest the Promethean hero stands finally, quite alone, upon a tower that is only himself, and his stance is all the fire there is. This realization leads neither to nihilism nor to solipsism, though Byron plays with the former and all fear the latter.

The dangers of idealizing the libido are of course constant in the life of the individual, and such idealizations are dreadful for whole societies, but the internalization of quest-romance had to accept these dangers. The creative process is the hero of Romantic poetry, and imaginative inhibitions, of every kind, necessarily must be the antagonists of the poetic quest. The special puzzle of Romanticism is the dialectical role that nature had to take in the revival of the mode of romance. Most simply, Romantic nature poetry, despite a long critical history of misrepresentation, was an antinature poetry, even in Wordsworth who sought a reciprocity or even a dialogue with nature, but found it only in flashes. Wordsworthian nature, thanks to Arnold and the critical tradition he fostered, has been misunderstood, though the insights of recent critics have begun to develop a better interpretative tradition, founded on A. C. Bradley's opposition to Arnold's view. Bradley stressed the strong side of Wordsworth's imagination, its Miltonic sublimity, which Arnold evidently never noticed, but which accounts for everything that is major in *The Prelude* and in the central crisis lyrics associated with it. Though Wordsworth came as a healer, and Shelley attacked him, in "Mont Blanc," for attempting to reconcile man with nature, there is no such reconciliation in Wordsworth's poetry, and the healing function is performed only when the poetry shows the power of the mind over outward sense. The strength of renovation in Wordsworth resides only in the spirit's splendor, in what he beautifully calls "possible sublimity" or "something evermore about to be," the potential of an imagination too fierce to be contained by nature. This is the force that Coleridge sensed and feared in Wordsworth, and is remarkably akin to that strength in Milton that Marvell urbanely says he feared, in his introductory verses to *Paradise Lost.* As Milton curbed his own Prometheanism, partly by showing its dangers through Satan's version of the heroic quest, so Wordsworth learned to restrain his, partly through making his own quest-romance, in *The Prelude,* an account of learning both the enormous strength of nature and nature's wise and benevolent reining-in of its own force. In the covenant between Wordsworth and nature, two powers that are totally separate from each other, and potentially destructive of the other, try to meet in a dialectic of love. "Meet" is too hopeful, and "blend" would express Wordsworth's ideal and not his achievement, but the try itself is definitive of Wordsworth's strangeness and continued relevance as a poet.

If Wordsworth, so frequently and absurdly called a pantheist, was not questing for unity with nature, still less were Blake, Shelley, and Keats, or their darker followers in later genera-

tions, from Beddoes, Darley, and Wade down to Yeats and Lawrence in our time. Coleridge and Byron, in their very different ways, were oddly closer both to orthodox Christian myth and to pantheism or some form of nature-worship, but even their major poems hardly approximate nature poetry. Romantic or internalized romance, especially in its purest version of the quest form, the poems of symbolic voyaging that move in a continuous tradition from Shelley's "Alastor" to Yeats's "The Wanderings of Oisin," tends to see the context of nature as a trap for the mature imagination. . . . If the goal of Romantic internalization of the quest was a wider consciousness that would be free of the excesses of self-consciousness, a consideration of the rigors of experiential psychology will show, quite rapidly, why nature could not provide adequate context. The program of Romanticism, and not just in Blake, demands something more than a natural man to carry it through. Enlarged and more numerous senses are necessary, an enormous virtue of Romantic poetry clearly being that it not only demands such expansion but begins to make it possible, or at least attempts to do so.

The internalization of romance brought the concept of nature, and poetic consciousness itself, into a relationship they had never had before the advent of Romanticism in the later eighteenth century. Implicit in all the Romantics, and very explicit in Blake, is a difficult distinction between two modes of energy, organic and creative (Orc and Los in Blake, Prometheus bound and unbound in Shelley, Hyperion and Apollo in Keats, the Child and the Man, though with subtle misgivings, in Wordsworth). For convenience, the first mode can be called Prometheus and the second "the Real Man, the Imagination" (Blake's phrase, in a triumphant letter written when he expected death). Generally, Prometheus is the poet-as-hero in the first stage of his quest, marked by a deep involvement in political, social, and literary revolution, and a direct, even satirical attack on the institutional orthodoxies of European and English society, including historically oriented Christianity, and the neoclassic literary and intellectual tradition, particularly in its Enlightenment phase. The Real man, the Imagination, emerges after terrible crises in the major stage of the Romantic quest, which is typified by a relative disengagement from revolutionary activism, and a standing-aside from polemic and satire, so as to re-center the arena of search within the self and its ambiguities. In the Prometheus stage, the quest is allied to the libido's struggle against repressiveness, and nature is an ally, though always a wounded and sometimes a withdrawn one. In the Real Man, the Imagination, stage, nature is the immediate though not the ultimate antagonist. The final enemy to be overcome is a recalcitrance in the self, what Blake calls the Spectre of Urthona, Shelley the unwilling dross that checks the spirit's flight, Wordsworth the sad perplexity or fear that kills or, best of all, the hope that is unwilling to be fed, and Keats, most simply and perhaps most powerfully, the Identity. Coleridge calls the antagonist by a bewildering variety of names since, of all these poets, he is the most hagridden by anxieties, and the most humanly vulnerable. Byron and Beddoes do not so much name the antagonist as they mock it, so as to cast it out by continuous satire and demonic farce. The best single name for the antagonist is Keats's Identity, but the most traditional is the Selfhood, and so I shall use it here.

Only the Selfhood, for the Romantics as for such Christian visionaries as Eckhart before them, burns in Hell. The Selfhood is not the erotic principle, but precisely that part of the erotic that cannot be released in the dialectic of love, whether between man and man, or man and nature. Here the Romantics, all of them, I think, even Keats, part company with Freud's dialectics of human nature. Freud's beautiful sentence on marriage is a formula against which the Romantic Eros can be tested: "A man shall leave father and mother—according to the Biblical precept—and cleave to his wife; then are tenderness and sensuality united." By the canons of internalized romance, that translates: a poet shall leave his Great Original (Milton, for the Romantics) and nature—according to the precept of Poetic Genius—and cleave to his Muse or Imagination; then are the generous and solitary halves united. But, so translated, the formula has ceased to be Freudian and has become High Romantic. In Freud, part of the ego's own self-love is projected onto an outward object, but part always remains in the ego, and even the projected portion can find its way back again. Somewhere Freud has a splendid sentence that anyone unhappy in love can take to heart: "Object-libido was at first ego-libido and can be again transformed into ego-libido," which is to say that a certain degree of narcissistic mobility is rather a good thing. Somewhere else Freud remarks that all romance is really a form of what he calls "Family-romance"; one could as justly say, in his terms, that all romance is necessarily a mode of ego-romance. This may be true, and in its humane gloom it echoes a great line of realists who culminate in Freud, but the popular notion that High Romanticism takes a very different view of love is a sounder insight into the Romantics than most scholarly critics ever achieve (or at least state). All romance, literary and human, is founded upon enchantment; Freud and the Romantics differ principally in their judgment as to what it is in us that resists enchantment, and what the value of that resistance is. For Freud it is the reality-principle, working through the great disenchanter, reason, the scientific attitude, and without it no civilized values are possible. For the Romantics, this is again a dialectical matter, as two principles intertwine in the resistance to enchantment, one "organic," an anxiety-principle masquerading as a reality-principle and identical to the ego's self-love that never ventures out to others, and the other "creative," which resists enchantment in the name of a higher mode than the sympathetic imagination. This doubling is clearest in Blake's mythology, where there are two egos, the Spectre of Urthona and Los, who suffer the enchantments, real *and* deceptive, of nature and the female, and who resist, when and where they can, on these very different grounds. But, though less schematically, the same doubling of the ego, into passive and active components, is present in the other poets wherever they attempt their highest flights and so spurn the earth. The most intense effort of the Romantic quest is made when the Promethean stage of quest is renounced and the purgatorial crisis that follows moves near to resolution. Romantic purgatory, by an extraordinary displacement of earlier mythology, is found just beyond the earthly paradise, rather than just before it, so that the imagination is tried by nature's best aspect. Instances of the interweaving of purgatory and paradise include nearly everything Blake says about the state of being he calls Beulah, and the whole development of Keats, from *Endymion* with its den or cave of Quietude on to the structure of *The Fall of Hyperion* where the poet enjoys the fruit and drink of paradise just before he has his confrontation with Moneta, whose shrine must be reached by mounting purgatorial stairs.

Nothing in Romantic poetry is more difficult to comprehend, for me anyway, than the process that begins after each poet's renunciation of Prometheus; for the incarnation of the Real Man, the Imagination, is not like psychic maturation in poets

before the Romantics. The love that transcends the Selfhood has its analogues in the renunciatory love of many traditions, including some within Christianity, but the creative Eros of the Romantics is not renunciatory though it is self-transcendent. It is, to use Shelley's phrasing, a total going-out from our own natures, total because the force moving out is not only the Promethean libido but rather a fusion between the libido and the active or imaginative element in the ego; or simply, desire wholly taken up into the imagination. "Shelley's love poetry," as a phrase, is almost a redundancy, Shelley having written little else, but his specifically erotic poems, a series of great lyrics and the dazzling *Epipsychidion,* have been undervalued because they are so very difficult, the difficulty being the Shelleyan and Romantic vision of love.

Blake distinguished between Beulah and Eden as states of being, the first being the realm of family-romance and the second of apocalyptic romance, in which the objects of love altogether lose their object-dimension. In family-romance or Beulah, loved ones are not confined to their objective aspect (that would make them denizens of Blake's state of Generation or mere Experience), but they retain it nevertheless. The movement to the reality of Eden is one of recreation or better, of knowledge not purchased by the loss of power, and so of power and freedom gained *through* a going-out of our nature, in which that last phrase takes on its full range of meanings. Though Romantic love, particularly in Wordsworth and Shelley, has been compared to what Charles Williams calls the Romantic theology of Dante, the figure of Beatrice is not an accurate analogue to the various Romantic visions of the beloved, for sublimation is not an element in the movement from Prometheus to Man. There is no useful analogue to Romantic or imaginative love, but there is a useful contrary, in the melancholy wisdom of Freud on natural love, and the contrary has the helpful clarity one always finds in Freud. If Romantic love is the sublime, then Freudian love is the pathetic, and truer of course to the phenomenon insofar as it is merely natural. To Freud, love begins as ego-libido, and necessarily is ever after a history of sorrow, a picaresque chronicle in which the ever-vulnerable ego stumbles from delusion to frustration, to expire at last (if lucky) in the compromising arms of the ugliest of Muses, the reality-principle. But the saving dialectic of this picaresque is that it is better thus, as there is no satisfaction in satisfaction anyway, since in the Freudian view all erotic partners are somewhat inadequate replacements for the initial sexual objects, parents. Romantic love, to Freud, is a particularly intense version of the longing for the mother, a love in which the imago is loved, rather than the replacement. And Romantic love, on this account, is anything but a dialectic of transformation, since it is as doomed to overvalue the surrogate as it compulsively overvalues the mother. Our age begins to abound in late Romantic "completions" of Freud, but the Romantic critiques of him, by Jung and Lawrence in particular, have not touched the strength of his erotic pessimism. There is a subtly defiant attempt to make the imago do the work of the imagination by Stevens, particularly in the very Wordsworthian "The Auroras of Autumn," and it is beautifully subversive of Freud, but of course it is highly indirect. Yet a direct Romantic counter-critique of Freud's critique of Romantic love emerges from any prolonged, central study of Romantic poetry. For Freud, there is an ironic loss of energy, perhaps even of spirit, with every outward movement of love away from the ego. Only pure self-love has a perfection to it, a stasis without loss, and one remembers again Van den Berg's mordant observation on Freud: "Ultimately the enigma of grief is the libido's inclination toward exterior things." All outward movement, in the Freudian psychodynamics, is a fall that results from "an overfilled inner self," which would sicken within if it did not fall outward, and downward, into the world of objects and of other selves. One longs for Blake to come again and rewrite *The Book of Urizen* as a satire on this cosmogony of love. The poem would not require that much rewriting, for it now can be read as a prophetic satire on Freud, Urizen being a super-ego certainly over-filled with itself, and sickening into a false creation or creation-fall. If Romantic love can be castigated as "erotic illusion," Freudian love can be judged as "erotic reduction," and the prophets of the reality-principle are in danger always of the Urizenic boast:

> I have sought for a joy without pain,
> For a solid without fluctuation
> Why will you die O Eternals?
> Why live in unquenchable burnings?

The answer is the Romantic dialectic of Eros and Imagination, unfair as it is to attribute to the Freudians a censorious repressiveness. But, to Blake and the Romantics, all available accounts of right reason, even those that had risen to liberate men, had the disconcerting tendency to turn into censorious moralities. Freud painfully walked a middle way, not unfriendly to the poetic imagination, and moderately friendly to Eros. If his myth of love is so sparse, rather less than a creative Word, it is still open both to analytic modification and to a full acceptance of everything that can come out of the psyche. Yet it is not quite what Philip Rieff claims for it, as it does not erase "the gap between therapeutic rationalism and self-assertive romanticism." That last is only the first stage of the Romantic quest, the one this discussion calls Prometheus. There remains a considerable gap between the subtle perfection to which Freud brought therapeutic rationalism and the mature Romanticism that is self-transcendent in its major poets.

There is no better way to explore the Real Man, the Imagination, than to study his monuments: *The Four Zoas, Milton,* and *Jerusalem; The Prelude* and the *Recluse* fragment; "The Ancient Mariner" and "Christabel"; *Prometheus Unbound, Adonais,* and *The Triumph of Life;* the two *Hyperions; Don Juan; Death's Jest-Book;* these are the definitive Romantic achievement, the words that were and will be, day and night. What follows is only an epitome, a rapid sketch of the major phase of this erotic quest. The sketch, like any that attempts to trace the visionary company of love, is likely to end in listening to the wind, hoping to hear an instant of a fleeting voice.

The internalization of quest-romance made of the poet-hero not a seeker after nature but after his own mature powers, and so the Romantic poet turned away, not from society to nature, but from nature to what was more integral than nature, within himself. The widened consciousness of the poet did not give him intimations of a former union with nature or the Divine, but rather of his former selfless self. One thinks of Yeats's Blakean declaration: "I'm looking for the face I had / Before the world was made." Different as the major Romantics were in their attitudes toward religion, they were united (except for Coleridge) in *not* striving for unity with anything but what might be called their Tharmas or id component, Tharmas being the Zoa or Giant Form in Blake's mythology who was the unfallen human potential for realizing instinctual desires, and so was the regent of Innocence. Tharmas is a shepherd-figure, his equivalent in Wordsworth being

a number of visions of man against the sky, of actual shepherds Wordsworth had seen in his boyhood. This Romantic pastoral vision (its pictorial aspect can be studied in the woodcuts of Blake's Virgil series, and in the work done by Palmer, Calvert, and Richmond while under Blake's influence) is biblical pastoralism, but not at all of a traditional kind. Blake's Tharmas is inchoate when fallen, as the id or appetite is inchoate, desperately starved and uneasily allied to the Spectre of Urthona, the passive ego he has projected outward to meet an object-world from which he has been severed so unwillingly. Wordsworth's Tharmas, besides being the shepherd image of human divinity, is present in the poet himself as a desperate desire for continuity in the self, a desperation that at its worst sacrifices the living moment, but at its best produces a saving urgency that protects the imagination from the strong enchantments of nature.

In Freud the ego mediates between id and superego, and Freud had no particular interest in further dividing the ego itself. In Romantic psychic mythology, Prometheus rises from the id, and can best be thought of as the force of libido, doomed to undergo a merely cyclic movement from appetite to repression, and then back again; any quest within nature is thus at last irrelevant to the mediating ego, though the quest goes back and forth through it. It is within the ego itself that the quest must turn, to engage the antagonist proper, and to clarify the imaginative component in the ego by its strife of contraries with its dark brother. Frye, writing on Keats, calls the imaginative ego *identity-with* and the selfhood ego *identity-as,* which clarifies Keats's ambiguous use of "identity" in this context. Geoffrey Hartman, writing on Wordsworth, points to the radical Protestant analogue to the Romantic quest: "The terror of discontinuity or separation enters, in fact, as soon as the imagination truly enters. In its restraint of vision, as well as its peculiar nakedness before the moment, this resembles an extreme Protestantism, and Wordsworth seems to quest for 'evidences' in the form of intimations of continuity." Wordsworth's greatness was in his feeling the terror of discontinuity as acutely as any poet could, yet overcoming this terror nevertheless, by opening himself to vision. With Shelley, the analogue of the search for evidences drops out, and an Orphic strain takes its place, as no other English poet gives so continuous an impression of relying on almost literal inspiration. Where Keats knew the Selfhood as an attractive strength of distinct identity that had to be set aside, and Wordsworth as a continuity he longed for yet learned to resist, and Blake as a temptation to prophetic wrath and withdrawal that had to be withstood, Shelley frequently gives the impression of encountering no enchantment he does not embrace, since every enchantment is an authentic inspiration. . . . For Shelley, the Selfhood's strong enchantment, stronger even than it is for the other Romantics, is one that would keep him from ever concluding the Prometheus phase of the quest. The Selfhood allies itself with Prometheus against the repressive force Shelley calls Jupiter, his version of Blake's Urizen or Freud's superego. This temptation calls the poet to perpetual revolution, and Shelley, though longing desperately to see the tyrannies of his time overturned, renounces it at the opening of *Prometheus Unbound,* in the Imagination's name. Through his renunciation, he moves to overturn the tyranny of time itself.

There are thus two main elements in the major phase of Romantic quest, the first being the inward overcoming of the Selfhood's temptation, and the second the outward turning of the triumphant Imagination, free of further internalizations, though "outward" and "inward" become cloven fictions or false conceptual distinctions in this triumph, which must complete a dialectic of love by uniting the Imagination with its bride, a transformed, ongoing creation of the Imagination rather than a redeemed nature. Blake and Wordsworth had long lives, and each completed his version of this dialectic. Coleridge gave up the quest, and became only an occasional poet, while Byron's quest, even had he lived into middle age, would have become increasingly ironic. Keats died at twenty-five, and Shelley at twenty-nine; despite their fecundity, they did not complete their development, but their death-fragments, *The Fall of Hyperion* and *The Triumph of Life,* prophesy the final phase of the quest in them. Each work breaks off with the Selfhood subdued, and there is profound despair in each, particularly in Shelley's, but there are still hints of what the Imagination's triumph would have been in Keats. In Shelley, the final despair may be total, but a man who had believed so fervently that the good time would come, had already given a vision of imaginative completion in the closing act of *Prometheus Unbound,* and we can go back to it and see what is deliberately lacking in *The Triumph of Life.* What follows is a rapid attempt to trace the major phase of quest in the four poets, taking as texts *Jerusalem* and *The Prelude,* and the *Fall* and *Triumph,* these two last with supplementary reference to crucial earlier erotic poems of Keats and Shelley.

Of Blake's long poems the first, *The Four Zoas,* is essentially a poem of Prometheus, devoting itself to the cyclic strife between the Promethean Orc and the moral censor, Urizen, in which the endless cycle between the two is fully exposed. The poem ends in an apocalypse, the explosive and Promethean *Night the Ninth, Being The Last Judgment,* which in itself is one of Blake's greatest works, yet from which he turned when he renounced the entire poem (by declining to engrave it). But not before he attempted to move the entire poem from the Prometheus stage to the Imagination, for Blake's own process of creative maturation came to its climax while he worked on *The Four Zoas.* The entrance into the mature stage of the quest is clearly shown by the different versions of *Night the Seventh,* for the later one introduces the doubling of the ego into Spectre of Urthona and Los, Selfhood or *Identity-As,* and Imagination or *Identity-With.* Though skillfully handled, it was not fully clarified by Blake, even to himself, and so he refused to regard the poem as definitive vision. Its place in his canon was filled, more or less, by the double-romance *Milton* and *Jerusalem.* The first is more palpably in a displaced romance mode, involving as it does symbolic journeys downward to our world by Milton and his emanation or bride of creation, Ololon, who descend from an orthodox Eternity in a mutual search for one another, the characteristic irony being that they could never find one another in a traditional heaven. There is very little in the poem of the Prometheus phase, Blake having already devoted to that a series of prophetic poems, from *America* and *Europe* through *The Book of Urizen* and on to the magnificent if unsatisfactory (to him, not to us) *The Four Zoas.* The two major stages of the mature phase of quest dominate the structure of *Milton.* The struggle with the Selfhood moves from the quarrel between Palamabron (Blake) and Satan (Hayley) in the introductory Bard's Song on to Milton's heroic wrestling match with Urizen, and climaxes in the direct confrontation between Milton and Satan on the Felpham shore, in which Milton recognizes Satan as his own Selfhood. The recognition compels Satan to a full epiphany, and a subsequent defeat. Milton then confronts Ololon, the poem ending in an epiphany contrary to

Satan's, in what Blake specifically terms a preparation for a going-forth to the great harvest and vintage of the nations. But even this could not be Blake's final Word; the quest in *Milton* is primarily Milton's and not Blake's, and the quest's antagonist is still somewhat externalized. In *Jerusalem, The Prelude's* only rival as the finest long poem of the nineteenth century, Blake gives us the most comprehensive single version of Romantic quest. Here there is an alternation between vision sweeping outward into the nightmare world of the reality-principle, and a wholly inward vision of conflict in Blake's ego, between the Spectre and Los. The poet's antagonist is himself, the poem's first part being the most harrowing and tormented account of genius tempted to the madness of self-righteousness, frustrate anger, and solipsistic withdrawal, in the Romantic period. Blake-Los struggles on, against this enchantment of despair, until the poem quietly, almost without warning, begins to move into the light of a Last Judgment, of a kind passed by every man upon himself. In the poem's final plates (Blake's canonical poems being a series of engraved plates), the reconciliation of Los and his emanative portion, Enitharmon, begins, and we approach the completion of quest.

Though Blake, particularly in *Jerusalem,* attempts a continuity based on thematic juxtaposition and simultaneity, rather than on consecutiveness, he is in such sure control of his own procedure that his work is less difficult to summarize than *The Prelude,* a contrast that tends to startle inexperienced readers of Blake and of Wordsworth. *The Prelude* follows a rough, naturalistic chronology through Wordsworth's life down to the middle of the journey, where it, like any modern reader, leaves him, in his state of preparation for a further greatness that never came. What is there already, besides the invention of the modern lyric, is a long poem so rich and strange it has defied almost all description.

The Prelude is an autobiographical romance that frequently seeks expression in the sublime mode, which is really an invitation to aesthetic disaster. *The Excursion* is an aesthetic disaster, as Hazlitt, Byron, and many since happily have noted, yet there Wordsworth works within rational limits. *The Prelude* ought to be an outrageous poem, but its peculiar mixture of displaced genre and inappropriate style *works,* because its internalization of quest is the inevitable story for its age. Wordsworth did not have the Promethean temperament, yet he had absolute insight into it, as *The Borderers* already showed. In *The Prelude,* the initial quest phase of the poet-as-Prometheus is diffuse but omnipresent. It determines every movement in the growth of the child's consciousness, always seen as a violation of the established natural order, and it achieves great power in Book VI, when the onset of the French Revolution is associated with the poet's own hidden desires to surmount nature, desires that emerge in the great passages clustered around the Simplon Pass. The Promethean quest fails, in one way in the Alps when chastened by nature, and in another with the series of shocks to the poet's moral being when England wars against the Revolution, and the Revolution betrays itself. The more direct Promethean failure, the poet's actual abandonment of Annette Vallon, is presented only indirectly in the 1805 *Prelude,* and drops out completely from the revised, posthumously published *Prelude* of 1850, the version most readers encounter. In his crisis, Wordsworth learns the supernatural and superhuman strength of his own imagination, and is able to begin a passage to the mature phase of his quest. But his anxiety for continuity is too strong for him, and he yields to its dark enchant-

John Keats

ment. The Imagination phase of his quest does not witness the surrender of his Selfhood and the subsequent inauguration of a new dialectic of love, purged of the natural heart, as it is in Blake. Yet he wins a provisional triumph over himself, in Book XII of *The Prelude,* and in the closing stanzas of *Resolution and Independence* and the Great Ode. And the final vision of *The Prelude* is not of a redeemed nature, but of a liberated creativity transforming its creation into the beloved:

> Prophets of Nature, we to them will speak
> A lasting inspiration, sanctified
> By reason, blest by faith: what we have loved
> Others will love, and we will teach them how;
> Instruct them how the mind of man becomes
> A thousand times more beautiful than the earth
> On which he dwells, above this frame of things . . .

Coleridge, addressed here as the other Prophet of Nature, renounced his own demonic version of the Romantic quest (clearest in the famous triad of "Kubla Khan," "Christabel," and "The Ancient Mariner"), his wavering Prometheanism early defeated not so much by his Selfhood as by his Urizenic fear of his own imaginative energy. It was a high price for the release he had achieved in his brief phase of exploring the romance of the marvelous, but the loss itself produced a few poems of unique value, the "Dejection" Ode in particular. These poems show how Coleridge preceded Wordsworth in the invention of a new kind of poetry that shows the mind in

a dialogue with itself. The motto of this poetry might well be its descendant Stevens's "The mind is the terriblest force in the world, father, / Because, in chief, it, only, can defend / Against itself. At its mercy, we depend / Upon it." Coleridge emphasizes the mercy, Wordsworth the saving terror of the force. Keats and Shelley began with a passion closer to the Prometheus phase of Blake than of Wordsworth or Coleridge. The fullest development of Romantic quest, after Blake's mythology and Wordsworth's exemplary refusal of mythology, is in Keats's *Endymion* and Shelley's *Prometheus Unbound.* In this second generation of Romantic questers the same first phase of Prometheanism appears, as does the second phase of crisis, renounced quest, overcoming of the Selfhood, and final movement toward imaginative love, but the relation of the quest to the world of the reality-principle has changed. In Blake, dream with its ambiguities centers in Beulah, the purgatorial lower paradise of sexuality and benevolent nature. In Wordsworth, dream is rare, and betokens either a prolepsis of the imagination abolishing nature or a state the poet calls "visionary dreariness," in which the immediate power of the mind over outward sense is so great that the ordinary forms of nature seem to have withdrawn. But in Keats and Shelley, a polemical Romanticism matures, and the argument of the dream with reality becomes an equivocal one. Romanticism guessed at a truth our doctors begin to measure; as infants we dream for half the time we are asleep, and as we age we dream less and less, while we sleep. The doctors have not yet told us that utterly dreamless sleep directly prophesies or equals death, but it is a familiar Romantic conceit, and may prove to be true. We are our imaginations, and die with them.

Dreams, to Shelley and Keats, are not wish-fulfillments. It is not Keats but Moneta, the passionate and wrong-headed Muse in *The Fall of Hyperion,* who first confounds poets and dreamers as one tribe, and then overreacts by insisting they are totally distinct, and even sheer opposites, antipodes. Freud is again a clear-headed guide; the manifest and latent content of the dream can be distinct, even opposite, but in the poem they come together. The younger Romantics do not seek to render life a dream, but to recover the dream for the health of life. What is called real is too often an exhausted phantasmagoria, and the reality-principle can too easily be debased into a principle of surrender, an accommodation with death-in-life. We return to the observation of Van den Berg, cited earlier; Rousseau and the Romantics discovered not only the alienation between child and adult, but the second birth of psychic maturation or adolescence. (pp. 17-32)

The Promethean quest, in Shelley and in Keats, is from the start uneasy about its equivocal ally, nature, and places a deeper trust in dream, for at least the dream itself is not reductive, however we reduce it in our dissections. Perhaps the most remarkable element in the preternatural rapidity of maturation in Keats and Shelley is their early renunciation of the Prometheus phase of the quest, or rather, their dialectical complexity in simultaneously presenting the necessity and the inherent limitation of this phase. In "Alastor," the poem's entire thrust is at one with the poet-hero's self-destruction; this is the cause of the poem's radical unity, which C. S. Lewis rightly observed as giving a marvelous sense of the poet's being at one with his subject. Yet the poem is also a daimonic shadow in motion; it shows us nature's revenge upon the imagination, and the excessive price of the quest in the poet's alienation from other selves. On a cosmic scale, this is part of the burden of *Prometheus Unbound,* where the hero, who massively represents the bound prophet-ic power of all men, rises from his icy crucifixion by refusing to continue the cycles of revolution and repression that form an ironic continuity between himself and Jupiter. Demogor-gon, the dialectic of history, rises from the abyss and stops history, thus completing in the macro-cosmic shadow what Prometheus, by his renunciation, inaugurates in the micro-cosm of the individual imagination, or the liberating dream taken up into the self. Shelley's poetry after this does not maintain the celebratory strain of Act IV of his lyrical drama. The way again is down and out, to a purgatorial encounter with the Selfhood, but the Selfhood's temptations, for Shel-ley, are subtle and wavering, and mask themselves in the forms of the ideal. So fused become the ideal and these masks that Shelley, in the last lines he wrote, is in despair of any vic-tory, though it is Shelley's Rousseau and not Shelley himself who actually chants:

> . . . thus on the way
> Mask after mask fell from the countenance
> And form of all; and long before the day
>
> Was old, the joy which waked like heaven's glance
> The sleepers in the oblivious valley, died;
> And some grew weary of the ghastly dance,
>
> And fell, as I have fallen, by the wayside—

For Shelley, Rousseau was not a failed poet, but rather the poet whose influence had resulted in an imaginative revolu-tion, and nearly ended time's bondage. So, Rousseau speaks here not for himself alone, but for his tradition, and necessari-ly for Coleridge, Wordsworth, and the Promethean Shelley as well, indeed for poetry itself. Yet, rightly or wrongly, the image Shelley leaves with us, at his end, is not this falling-away from quest but the image of the poet forever wakeful amidst the cone of night, illuminating it as the star Lucifer does, fading as the star, becoming more intense as it narrows into the light.

The mazes of romance, in *Endymion,* are so winding that they suggest the contrary to vision, a labyrinthine nature in which all quest must be forlorn. In this realm, nothing nar-rows to an intensity, and every passionate impulse widens out to a diffuseness, the fate of Endymion's own search for his goddess. In reaction, Keats chastens his own Prometheus-ism, and attempts the objective epic in *Hyperion*. Hyperion's self-identity is strong but waning fast, and the fragment of the poem's Book III introduces an Apollo whose self-identity is in the act of being born. The temptation to go on with the poem must have been very great, after its magnificent begin-nings, but Keats's letters are firm in renouncing it. Keats turns from the enchantments of Identity to the romance-fragment, *The Fall of Hyperion,* and engages instead the demon of subjectivity, his own poetic ambitions, as Words-worth had done before him. Confronted by Moneta, he meets the danger of her challenge not by asserting his own Identity, but by finding his true form in the merged identity of the poethood, in the high function and responsibilities of a Wordsworthian humanism. Though the poem breaks off be-fore it attempts the dialectic of love, it has achieved the quest, for the Muse herself has been transformed by the poet's per-sistence and integrity. We wish for more, necessarily, but only now begin to understand how much we had received, even in this broken moment.

I have scanted the dialectic of love, in all of these poets. Ro-mantic love, past its own Promethean adolescence, is not the possessive love of the natural heart, which is the quest of Freudian Eros, moving always in a tragic rhythm out from and back to the isolate ego. That is the love Blake explicitly rejected:

> Let us agree to give up Love
> And root up the Infernal Grove
> Then shall we return and see
> The worlds of happy Eternity
>
> Throughout all Eternity
> I forgive you you forgive me . . .

The Infernal Grove grows thick with virtues, but these are the selfish virtues of the natural heart. Desire for what one lacks becomes a habit of possession, and the Selfhood's jeal-ousy murders the Real Man, the Imagination. All such love is an entropy, and as such Freud understood and accepted it. We become aware of others only as we learn our separation from them, and our ecstasy is a reduction. Is this the human condition, and love only its mitigation?

> To cast off the idiot Questioner who is always questioning,
> But never capable of answering . . .

Whatever else the love that the full Romantic quest aims at may be, it cannot be a therapy. It must make all things new, and then marry what it has made. Less urgently, it seeks to define itself through the analogue of each man's creative po-tential. But it learns, through its poets, that it cannot define what it is, but only what it will be. The man prophesied by the Romantics is a central man who is always in the process of becoming his own begetter, and though his major poems perhaps have been written, he as yet has not fleshed out his prophecy, nor proved the final form of his love. (pp. 33-5)

> *Harold Bloom, "The Internalization of Quest Ro-mance," in his* The Ringers in the Tower: Studies in Romantic Tradition, *The University of Chicago Press, 1971, pp. 13-35.*

J. R. WATSON

[In the following excerpt, Watson describes the significance that dreams held for the Romantic poets.]

Dreams are extraordinary examples of the private and unex-pected workings of the individual mind; they have a mysteri-ous and involuntary quality about them, an unpredictable and inconsequential mode of operation which suggests that the mind is stranger, freer, and more resourceful than any mechanical account would allow; and they operate in sym-bols. The symbolic operation of dreams links them with the working of the poetic imagination, which can allow one thing to stand for another, and can transform abstraction into sym-bol. It is not difficult to see why the Romantic poets were fas-cinated by dreams.

Their interest is related to the concern for the experience of childhood. According to Freud, dreams can involve a consid-erable degree of 'primary process thinking', the kind of men-tal activity found in babies, who are not sure where their own selves end and the outer world begins. As they develop into infants and change to 'secondary process thinking', the small child still has regressions into primary process thinking, tak-ing refuge in fantasy from the complexities of the world of re-ality. Gradually the attention to the outside world comes to dominate the conscious and waking mind, in a process of development which will be familiar to the readers of Wordsworth's 'Immortality Ode':

> Shades of the prison-house begin to close
>   Upon the growing Boy,
>   But He
> Beholds the light, and whence it flows,
>   He sees it in his joy;
> The Youth, who daily farther from the east
> Must travel, still is Nature's Priest,
>   And by the vision splendid
> Is on his way attended;
> At length the Man perceives it die away,
> And fade into the light of common day.

Wordsworth anticipates Freud's connection between the mental processes of infancy and the operation of dreams by describing the world of his first vision as

> Apparelled in celestial light,
> The glory and the freshness of a dream.

Dreams are precious evidence of an activity which is now impossible in the normal conditions of adult wakefulness. In the waking state the ego's censorship of fantasy takes over: there is a cognizance of space and time, of probability, and of cause and effect. Our whole perception of consciousness is involved with this process, as Erasmus Darwin (whom Coleridge read and met) wrote in *Zoonamia* (1794): 'we gain our idea of consciousness by comparing ourselves with the scenery around us; and of identity by comparing our present consciousness with our past consciousness'. *Zoonamia* has an important section on sleep, in which Darwin discusses dreams. He argues that the consciousness of our own existence is the result of the voluntary exertion of the mind; in dreams this voluntary exertion is suspended, and so 'we neither measure time, are surprised at the sudden changes of place, nor attend to our own existence, or identity'. The opposition here is between the waking consciousness, which is associated invariably with an awareness of time and place, and the unpredictable and unbounded dream-world. Blake used the same opposition between 'the sea of time and space', which he saw as deflecting him from the path of vision or truth, and the imagination:

> I am under the direction of Messengers from Heaven, Daily & Nightly; but the nature of such things is not, as some suppose, without trouble or care. Temptations are on the right hand & left; behind, the sea of time & space roars and follows swiftly; he who keeps not right onward is lost, & if our footsteps slide in clay, how can we do otherwise than fear & tremble?

So too Freud's 'primary process thinking' has been summed up as 'The direct expression of the unconscious instinctual drives' and as illogical, disregarding time and space. Secondary process thinking involves 'the processes used by the ego to deal with the demands of the real world and to modify the demands made by the instinctual drives. They are therefore based on logical thinking in contrast to the illogical pictorial thinking of the primary process.' Given these parallels, it is perhaps not surprising that the Romantics saw much in common between the dream-world and the world of the imagination, and that they were in consequence extremely interested in dreams. These could be either the dreams of sleep, or waking dreams; the latter were often described as 'reveries', for instance by Erasmus Darwin:

> whilst I am thinking over the beautiful valley,

through which I yesterday travelled, I do not perceive the furniture of my room: and there are some, whose waking imaginations are so apt to run into perfect reverie, that in their common attention to a favourite idea they do not hear the voice of the companion, who accosts them, unless it is repeated with unusual energy.

This contrast between yesterday's landscape and today's room uncannily anticipates Wordsworth's 'Tintern Abbey', written four years later, in which the poet remembers the landscape when he is 'in lonely rooms, and 'mid the din / Of towns and cities'; and it is noticeable that Wordsworth's language for such a reverie in which he sees the scenery of the Wye valley includes the image of sleep, so that

> we are laid asleep
> In body, and become a living soul:
> While with an eye made quiet by the power
> Of harmony, and the deep power of joy,
> We see into the life of things.

The idea that the soul awakes during these reveries is common in Romantic poetry. As we have seen, Blake associated them with visionary power; Keats describes a waking dream in the 'Ode to a Nightingale', and wonders which is real, the actual world of time and place, or the ideal world of the imagination in which the poet flies on the wings of poesy to a dark, sweet-smelling, and magic world of the nightingale.

Darwin emphasizes further points about dreams: he notes, for example, the great vivacity of dreams, whether sleeping or waking, and that this is accompanied by variety, novelty, and distinctness. There is an amazing 'rapidity of the succession of transactions in our dreams', but Darwin also believes that these have some relation to our waking lives (which puts him closer to Freud than to the Romantics): his observation that 'we recall the figure and the features of a long lost friend' in dreams is very close to the recorded experience of Coleridge, who frequently dreamed of his school desk-mate C. V. Le Grice. He noted that he was never astonished in these dreams to find himself back at Christ's Hospital, and his notebook entry says that his dreams were 'uncommonly illustrative of the non-existence of Surprize in sleep', another observation which echoes Darwin. Darwin observed two remarkable properties of dreams, their inconsistency and their total absence of surprise: he saw these as the result of the involuntary workings of the mind. During our conscious hours the mind can voluntarily reject inconsistencies, but in dreams the most unusual connection of ideas and images takes place.

Coleridge also read Andrew Baxter's *An Enquiry into the Nature of the Human Soul* (1733), which contains a long essay on dreaming. Writing in an age of mechanical philosophies of mind, Baxter boldly accepts that dreams are involuntary; they are 'chimerical and wild', and Baxter rejects all mechanical explanations for them, such as illness, heat, or cold. In so doing, he emphasizes not just the non-mechanical processes, but also the living excitement of dreams, 'in which there is so much *variety, action* and *life,* nay oftentimes *speech* and *reason'.* Baxter's problem is that dreams clearly happen, but are quite inexplicable in terms of normal eighteenth-century discourse. This is made clear in a footnote near the end, in which Baxter imagines an objector saying that his theories make dreams 'mere *enchantment* and *Rosicrucian-work,* which it is absurd to admit into philosophy and among natural appearances'; but, says Baxter,

> if it be a common and constant appearance in na-

ture, how can it be absurd to admit it into philoso-phy, or allow it a place among *natural phae-nomena?* . . . as to the accounting for it any other way, I am not able; let any one try it who pleases.

But, after all, do not *those* who are least willing to admit of *enchantment* and *Rosicrucian-work* among the *appearances* of *nature,* find themselves so *enchanted, deluded, imposed upon* every night?

So Baxter defends the originality and enchantment of dreams, seeing them as spontaneous and living, the product of an imagination which sounds curiously like Coleridge's:

If imagination be taken as something belonging to the soul, it is its own active power of voluntarily joining ideas together, without objects *ab extra* to cause them.

Baxter also anticipates Coleridge in an interesting association of atheism with deadness, which looks forwards to Cole-ridge's praise of the Hebrew poetry of the Scriptures as being alive—'in God they live and move and *have* their being':

Atheism is equally unentertaining to the *fancy,* and to the rational faculty; disagreeable to our nature in every respect; beginning and ending in *universal deadness;* a world of brute matter, tossed about by chance, without a governing mind, and living im-material beings in it, affords a lonely unpleasant prospect to the soul. If things were thus, we should want scope for the imagination, and even for ratio-nal enquiry; and must soon come to empty chance, or unsupported necessity, which extinguishes ideas, and puts an end to all pursuit.

So dreams, in the writings of Andrew Baxter, are evidence of a living soul, and of a marvellous and mysterious imagina-tion. The suggestion that a world of dead matter prevents the imagination from realizing its possibilities is very close to the Romantic view that the mind cannot be bound by circum-stances or by necessity. Dreams are evidence for this belief, against a mechanical world of cause and effect and against the despotism of the senses, especially the eye.

The 'marvellous poetry' of dreams (F. W. Hildebrandt's phrase) is important in the Romantic period, for several rea-sons. In the first place, dreams make new worlds, in which the imagination produces combinations and things previous-ly unthought of. The imagination is sovereign, untrammelled and unquestioned. Secondly, Freud recognized (belatedly) that dreams depend to a great extent on the use of symbols: two consequences of this are of considerable interest. One is the idea that things which are now symbolically related were probably united in earlier times by conceptual and linguistic identity. If we remember the widespread belief that in primi-tive times figurative language was the natural speech, it is clear that Freud and the Romantic poets were thinking along the same lines. The other concerns the infinite possibilities of symbols, and the many different levels on which they can be interpreted. The multi-layered, open text of the Romantics is strikingly akin to this: it is a poetry which does not provide a text which can be read in one way only, but which is sugges-tive, allowing a multiplicity of readings and reverberating in different ways in the mind. Finally in Freud's description we should observe the powerful distinction which he made be-tween dream-thoughts and dream-content. Dream-thoughts can be written down and analysed, whereas dream-content is always compressed and transformed. In this condensation, the content is often differently centred from the dream-

thoughts: Freud called this process 'dream-displacement', and linked it with dream-condensation as one of the deter-mining factors of dreams. At the centre of them is often some-thing deep and obscure, what Freud called 'the dream's navel, the spot which reaches down into the unknown' [*The Interpretation of Dreams*].

The construction of a dream, and its partial interpretation, have therefore much in common with their counterparts in art; once this is observed, or even suspected, it gives rise to a distinctive kind of poetry, concerned with the nature and processes of dreaming. A good example is Byron's 'The Dream', in which he philosophizes about dreams in a nicely antithetical way:

They leave a weight upon our waking thoughts
They take a weight from off our waking toils,
They do divide our being; they become
A portion of ourselves as of our time,
And look like heralds of eternity;

Sleep, he argues, has its own world, which is

A boundary between the things misnamed
Death and existence: Sleep hath its own world,
And a wide realm of wild reality.

He then goes on to make the significant leap between the mind in dream-work and the mind in its usual creative and active operations, seeing the two things as part of the same process:

They make us what we were not—what they will,
And shake us with the vision that's gone by,
The dread of vanished shadows—Are they so?
Is not the past all shadow?—What are they?
Creations of the mind?—The mind can make
Substance, and people planets of its own
With beings brighter than have been, and give
A breath to forms which can outlive all flesh.

Byron's poem is characteristically direct, tackling the ques-tion of the dream head-on. Other Romantic poets experience the dream-world as an integral part of their most important imaginative experience, and write about it without asking questions or rationalizing. They do so in several ways.

The first of these is the direct reporting of sleeping dreams, of which the most conspicuous examples are Wordsworth's account of the desert Arab in Book v of *The Prelude* and Coleridge's 'Kubla Khan'. Both poems contain examples of the mysterious and transforming power of dreams. In *The Prelude,* for example, the Arab upon a dromedary is also Don Quixote on Rosinante ('Of these was neither, and was both at once'). He has a stone and a shell, representing geometry and poetry respectively; they are symbols, and the poet re-cords his complete surrender to the imaginative vision in which they can be both books and stone or shell:

Strange as it may seem
I wondered not, although I plainly saw
The one to be a stone, th' other a shell,
Nor doubted once but that they both were books,
Having a perfect faith in all that passed.

The interpretation of this dream is not simple, although as editors have pointed out the description of the Arab or 'semi-Quixote' as 'an uncouth shape' associates him with the dis-charged soldier whom Wordsworth had befriended (as relat-ed in *The Prelude* at the end of Book IV, immediately before this dream). The displacement of the discharged soldier into the Arab underlines his strangeness: his progress in the dream suggests that he has become an embodiment of well-intentioned humanity, trying to preserve truth (in the form of geometric certainties) and beauty (in the form of poetry). He rides through the desert, the waste land of dryness (as it is, for example, in Ezekiel) but in his attempts to preserve geometry and poetry he seems likely to be overwhelmed by the uncontrollable, the great waters, by that which is magnificent but also totally beyond the control of mankind.

The matter is complicated by the dream's similarity to a dream of Descartes, dating from 1619. This may have been related to Wordsworth by Beaupuy, or possibly by Coleridge, and the fact that it is second hand may account for the 1805 text of *The Prelude*'s placing of the dream in the third person. In the revisions of 1839 Wordsworth changed it to become his own dream, and in a sense, imaginatively, he then took possession of it. The waters of destruction (if Beaupuy was the source) may have been the power and violence of the French Revolution, or so it can seem with hindsight; it is impossible to say. What remains is a curious and fascinating blend of possible starting-points for the dream: Beaupuy, the discharged soldier, the sufferings of the English destitute, the energies of the French Revolution, and the relation of all or some of these to the Quixote figure, who would preserve scientific truth and the wonder of poetry. These provide a characteristic dream set of possibilities, a multi-layered and elusive range of meanings, open to interpretations that are significantly different but often complementary; but in addition to these, what remains in the mind so remarkably is the imagery of the dream itself, that extraordinary sharp strangeness which the reader encounters at this point in *The Prelude*. It was, said De Quincey (who remembered it twenty years after reading it in manuscript), 'the very *ne plus ultra* of sublimity'.

There is no difficulty about the starting-point for 'Kubla Khan'. In the introductory note to the poem, Coleridge described how he had been taking opium, and fallen asleep while reading a sentence from a travel book, *Purchas's Pilgrimage,* concerning Kubla's palace and the wall around its gardens. The dream-poem which develops from this is an extraordinarily clear and sharp rendering of this into pictorial imagery, followed by the sharp contrasting section on the wild scenery outside; the two are connected by the same kind of random and chimerical association that is found in dreams. The mystery of the poem, its teasing lack of logic, is part of its fascination; although it took Coleridge a long time to pluck up courage to recognize this to the full and publish the poem. He first called it 'Of the Fragment of Kubla Khan', and published it only in 1816 (having written it in 1798) after Byron had encouraged him to do so. Even then it was sent into the world 'rather as a psychological curiosity, than on the ground of any supposed *poetic* merits.' In the well-known note to the poem, Coleridge claimed that it was unfinished because he had been interrupted during the writing down of the verse which had come to him in sleep; this account may or may not be substantially true, but the inability to remember dreams clearly is a common experience, unless they are written down immediately.

That Coleridge was interested in 'Kubla Khan' as a dream-poem is suggested by his note in the introduction to the poem which reminds the reader that are other dreams of pain and disease (as Erasmus Darwin had made clear), and drawing attention to his fragment 'The Pains of Sleep', published with 'Kubla Khan' and 'Christabel' in 1816. In this poem he describes three nights in succession of horrible dreams in which he saw

> a fiendish crowd
> Of shapes and thoughts that tortured me:
> A lurid light, a trampling throng,
> Sense of intolerable wrong,
> And whom I scorned, those only strong!

In this extract the nightmare seems to be associated with the poet's waking thoughts of fear, guilt, and shame. On the third night he wakes from the dream and weeps, and acknowledges a connection between his own sins and shortcomings and the horrors of the night.

In this way the dreams of sleep are interesting to the Romantics because they reveal something of the strange inner workings of the mind, its astonishing capacity for beauty and its fearful and dark terrors. This is closely connected with the second way in which the romantic imagination functions in relation to dreams: its reporting of waking dreams or reveries. As we have seen, Erasmus Darwin drew attention to the mind's capacity to wander from its present circumstances, and the visionary imagination is often seen at work in this way. Keats's 'Ode to a Nightingale' is a good example, as I have suggested: it is a poem which moves from a state in which it is aware of its circumstances and problems, enjoys a free-ranging imaginative encounter with the world of the nightingale, and then returns to its waking state at the end (although it is not sure which is the more 'real'). Another example of this movement, though it is described from the point of view of a *spectator ab extra* and is therefore in the third person, is Wordsworth's 'The Reverie of Poor Susan'. In the city, Susan hears the song of a captive thrush, and she sees her own country before her eyes:

> Green pastures she views in the midst of the dale,
> Down which she so often has tripped with her pail;
> And a single small cottage, a nest like a dove's,
> The one only dwelling on earth that she loves.

Then the vision disappears:

> She looks, and her heart is in heaven: but they fade,
> The mist and the river, the hill and the shade:
> The stream will not flow, and the hill will not rise,
> And the colours have all passed away from her eyes!

Often the dreams or reveries are like this: not only do they disappear, but they leave the poet uncomfortably aware of the dreariness of his surroundings relative to the beautiful world of his dreams. In both sleeping and waking dreams a contrast can be made between the ideal and the actual, between the beautiful possibility and the often undesirable reality. Blake uses this technique in 'The Chimney Sweeper' from *Songs of Innocence,* in which the little boy dreams of Heaven but wakes up to work on a dark morning.

The uncontrollable nature of dreams, together with their beauty and terror, leads us to the third way in which dreams are related to the Romantic imagination. This is when the word 'dream' is used as simile or metaphor, to indicate the blissful or strange nature of an experience:

> oh, then, the calm
> And dead still water lay upon my mind
> Even with a weight of pleasure, and the sky,
> Never before so beautiful, sank down
> Into my heart, and held me like a dream.
>
> (*The Prelude,* 1805)

Wordsworth's poetry often has such trance-states, and in the 'Immortality Ode' the winds come to him 'from the fields of sleep'. In the same way the word 'slumber' can be used to indicate a much longer period of time than just one night, a period in which the mind was relieved from the responsibility of considering (in this case) such things as death and ageing:

> A slumber did my spirit seal;
> I had no human fears:
> She seemed a thing that could not feel
> The touch of earthly years.
>
> No motion has she now, no force;
> She neither hears nor sees;
> Rolled round in earth's diurnal course,
> With rocks, and stones, and trees.
>
> ('A slumber did my spirit seal')

Here the speaker is living in a 'dream' of happiness from which he awakes in the second half of the poem. This use of dream, or sleep, or slumber, to indicate a trance-like or visionary state is indicative of a whole movement away from definiteness into something unfixed, mysterious, and unpredictable. In the passage from *The Prelude* above, Wordsworth describes the circumstantial detail of the boy playing his flute upon the rocky island, and then the verse turns away into the record of his own feelings, and so into the gradual mystery of a beautiful dream. This is no longer recording experiences, whether sleeping or waking, but seeing those experiences, and others, as dream-like. It is a short step from this to a point at which questions begin to be asked about the nature of life itself in relation to such moments, and about the kind of 'reality' that exists in it. Is the period of slumber, in the case of the 'Lucy' poem, more imaginatively and morally 'alive' than the period of awakening? Is the love for Lucy more potent and lasting than the knowledge of her death? In these ways, the enquiry into dreams produces a questioning of our waking lives themselves, as it does in *A Midsummer Night's Dream* and *The Tempest*:

> we are such stuff
> As dreams are made on, and our little life
> Is rounded with a sleep.
>
> (*The Tempest*, IV. i. 156-58)

Shelley, in particular, uses the image of a dream symbolically in pursuit of Platonic speculations about life as a semblance of reality rather than the reality itself. If life itself is a dream, we shall awake to a greater reality when the soul is freed from the body (as described by Plato in the *Phaedo*). The lovely ending of 'The Sensitive Plant' is an example. When all things in the garden go to rack and ruin, after the Lady's death, Shelley comments:

> Whether that Lady's gentle mind,
> No longer with the form combined
> Which scattered love, as stars do light,
> Found sadness, where it left delight,
>
> I dare not guess; but in this life
> Of error, ignorance, and strife,
> Where nothing is, but all things seem,
> And we the shadows of the dream,
>
> It is a modest creed, and yet
> Pleasant if one considers it,
> To own that death itself must be,
> Like all the rest, a mockery.
>
> That garden sweet, that lady fair,
> And all sweet shapes and odours there,

> In truth have never passed away:
> 'Tis we, 'tis ours, are changed; not they.
>
> For love, and beauty, and delight,
> There is no death nor change: their might
> Exceeds our organs, which endure
> No light, being themselves obscure.

If love, and beauty, and delight are the only permanent things, then human life is unreal and fleeting like a dream, and our lives are mysterious in their purpose and content.

The poet's duty is to celebrate those moments of life in which love, and beauty, and delight are found. If, when they happen, it seems like a dream, or a dream come true, then that is one of the functions of the imagination, as Keats realized when he told Benjamin Bailey that 'The imagination may be compared to Adam's dream—he awoke and found it truth.' In Book VIII of *Paradise Lost* Adam recounts his falling asleep and dreaming of the creation of Eve, and then waking to find her present in the flesh. Keats, characteristically, sees the imagination as making the dream become flesh, and certainly one of the functions of Romantic poetry is to do this. In its most characteristic mode, however, the process is not so simple as recording dreams or capturing the dream-like loveliness of a moment. There is often a teasing uncertainty about the nature of the experience which is being recounted, a difficulty in distinguishing the shadow from the substance; and it is in this indeterminacy that Romantic poetry often flourishes. In it strange, beautiful, and terrifying experiences occur, *as if* in dreams; and dreams take on the qualities of waking life. When Wordsworth meets the leech-gatherer, in 'Resolution and Independence', he has an abstracted period during the conversation, an example of what Erasmus Darwin would call 'reverie':

> The old Man still stood talking by my side;
> But now his voice to me was like a stream
> Scarce heard; nor word from word could I divide;
> And the whole body of the Man did seem
> Like one whom I had met with in a dream;

The transformation of dream into reality, or of reality into dream, is a vital activity of the Romantic imagination. It transforms strangeness into truth, as Coleridge saw: when describing the plan of *Lyrical Ballads,* he observed that his efforts were going to be directed to 'persons and characters supernatural, or at least romantic':

> yet so as to transfer from our inward nature a
> human interest and a semblance of truth sufficient
> to procure for these shadows of imagination that
> willing suspension of disbelief for the moment,
> which constitutes poetic faith.

We suspend our disbelief, and the shadows become real: the dream seems to be true. Whether it is literally or scientifically true does not matter; in fact it is better left uncertain. This is why 'The Rime of the Ancient Mariner' exercises such a spell over the reader; it is a 'poem of pure imagination', but it is told in a way which makes it seem urgently human and absolutely credible. If it is classified as a dream, its power immediately disappears, because it can be parcelled up and put away in a category. Lamb saw this clearly, when he opened the 1800 edition of *Lyrical Ballads:*

> I am sorry that Coleridge has christened his Ancient Marinere 'a poet's Reverie'—it is as bad as Bottom the Weaver's declaration that he is not a Lion but only the scenical representation of a Lion.

What new idea is gained by this Title, but one subversive of all credit, which the Tale should force
upon us, of its truth?

Lamb's invocation of *A Midsummer Night's Dream* is significant, for it reminds the reader of the play in which Shakespeare brilliantly teases the spectator with ideas of illusion
and reality. The action is magical and beautiful, terrifying
and sinister, a very midsummer madness; and madness and
dreams are closely allied, as David Simpson has pointed out.

Finally, the dream-like modes of Romantic poetry have consequences for its interpretation. There is often a dark and
mysterious centre to Romantic poetry, an inscrutable and
magical quality that exists in image and symbol, and in the
spaces between them. This is the poetic equivalent of Freud's
'the dream's navel, the spot which reaches down into the unknown': on the page there are infinite uncertainties in the
gaps within the text itself, forming what Wolfgang Iser calls
'a no-man's-land of indeterminacy' [in J. Hillis Miller, ed.,
Aspects of Narrative, 1971], and in the multi-layered possibilities of the images and symbols themselves. The reader has to
accept the mysterious and respect it. It is necessary to activate an imagination in order to receive the poem at all: not,
of course, to try to 'understand' it, to limit it to one interpretation, or to the confined edges of the reader's own mind, but
to experience its power and its mysterious magic. (pp. 56-67)

J. R. Watson, in his English Poetry of the Romantic
Period: 1789-1830, *Longman, 1985, 360 p.*

FREDERICK L. BEATY

[*In the following excerpt, Beaty discusses the Romantics' idea
of love.*]

The belief that Romantic writers introduced a radically new
approach to love is . . . myopic, for Denis de Rougemont,
C. S. Lewis, M. C. D'Arcy, Paul Kluckhohn, Maurice Valen-
cy, and J. B. Broadbent have demonstrated that the basic elements we call "romantic" have persisted in European literature since the twelfth-century Renaissance. Nevertheless,
there is also some truth to André Gide's assertion in *The
Counterfeiters* that every great school, other than the symbolist, has brought with it "a new way of looking at things, of
understanding love, of behaving oneself in life." What the
British Romantics inherited from native literary traditions of
the eighteenth century was by no means cast overboard,
though its elements were often used eclectically and reassembled into different patterns of thought. Chaste love, for example, that feeling grounded in spiritualized friendship and
leading to matrimony, continued to be admired, especially
among the middle classes, as much as it had been when
Thomson and Richardson advocated it. Nor did hedonistic
gratification, practiced in contempt of marriage by the heirs
of Restoration profligates, cease to exist after any given date,
as the novels of Smollett in particular show. Moreover, the
synthesis of tender esteem and passion, which the Romantics
are sometimes credited with having effected, had already
been cogently argued by Fielding both in the prefatory essay
to Book VI of *Tom Jones* and in the central character of that
novel. During the eighteenth century, doctrines of benevolence showing sympathy triumphant over self-love were so
extensively developed by sentimental philosophers like
Shaftesbury, Hutcheson, and Butler that Romantic writers
had only to select from various theories on universal love.
Even without a "renascence of wonder," amatory revenants,

at least in literature, survived the Age of Reason without any
effective exorcism by Newtonian physics or Lockian philosophy. And in contradistinction to the growing trends of sensibility, there was a depedestalization of insipid love by Sterne,
as well as the *comédie larmoyante,* sufficient to allow a comic
perspective. One might well ask, then, wherein Romantic attitudes toward love differed from preceding ones.

The answer to that query is best found in what the Romantics
refused to accept from their eighteenth-century heritage. A
revealing instance is Madame de Staël's attack on neoclassicists in *De l'Allemagne* (1813), which deplored their inability
to comprehend the "tender passion" as it had been convincingly depicted in chivalric romances. Indeed there was much
in the Gothic revival, including renewed interest in poetical
story-telling, that was congenial with the Romantics' anti-
intellectual acceptance of emotions so intense as to lead only
to death. Yet above all, British writers of the early nineteenth
century rejected the implicit assumption, associated with
both bourgeois-puritanical and aristocratic-epicurean traditions in their own country, that love and reason were necessarily incompatible. To understand what they most strenuously objected to one has only to examine some of Dr. Johnson's pronouncements on the detrimental effect of passion. In
his preface to Shakespeare (1765), he especially praised the
dramatist for a representation of love on the stage that accurately reflected its inconsequential role in the total scheme of
human affairs. According to the critic, Shakespeare was
aware that any emotion might produce either happiness or
misery depending on whether it was rationally controlled. By
the same principle, Johnson subsequently condemned Dryden's *All for Love; or, the World Well Lost* for its egregious
moral flaw of conceding passion's omnipotence. Particularly
in comparison with Shakespeare's redaction, as Johnson
compared them in his *Lives of the English Poets,* Dryden's
treatment of the love of Antony and Cleopatra appeared to
extol behavior that the good invariably associate with vice
and the bad with folly.

Contrary to such a rationalistic view, the Romantics wished
to reunite the physical and the spiritual in such a way that
reason and emotion would not confront each other destruc-
tively but would bolster one another in unison. In an idealized portrait of Byron as poetical redeemer, Shelley asserted
that Maddalo, instead of curbing his passions with his extraordinary intellectual powers, allowed each to strengthen
the other. Similarly Blake in *America* had his character Orc
imagine rejuvenated man with heart and head of the same
metal rather than, like the antecedents of that imaginary figure in the book of Daniel and Dante's *Inferno,* with a breast
inferior to his head. To justify this belief in emotions as a
valid guide to life it was necessary to formulate a new religion
as well as a new epistemology. Whereas Continental Romantics turned increasingly to authoritarian churches for solution of their personal dilemmas, those in Britain inclined toward individualistic faiths based primarily on love. Every independent thinker, without any mediation other than the
spirit of love itself, was expected to strive in Protestant fashion for direct contact between his own inner life and the Divine Being. Hence it was highly appropriate that virtually all
the British Romantics conceived of love as "light from heav-
en," and quotations incorporating that phrase can be found
in abundance.

In the tradition of Christian Platonism, of which Dante's *Paradiso* is possibly the most eloquent expression, earthly beau-

ty, since it could be perceived only through the eyes, was dependent upon the presence of light, metaphorically conceived as the nourishing principle of life itself. But whereas neoplatonists had been concerned with love primarily as a means of leading the human soul beyond corporeality to a perception of absolute beauty, goodness, and even immortality, the Romantics, without denying the validity of a spiritual quest, were interested in the light of love chiefly as a way of coping with problems in earthly existence. These converse orientations are strikingly revealed by the sun imagery of each period. As a symbol of God's love for his creation, the sun had been well established since early Biblical times, and even those, like Shelley, who denied a personal God employed it as an emblem of cosmic energy or human imagination. Though in purely physical terms the sun not only draws earth's moisture toward itself but also extends itself as warmth toward earth, the neoplatonists had used the celestial body primarily to illustrate the attracting force of the divine while the Romantics concentrated upon those powers that descended to the world of man. This latter view is especially obvious in the outright distrust of some early nineteenth-century authors toward a light that leads mortals beyond their natural habitat. Certainly in Shelley's "Alastor" the search for something not of this earth results in extinction rather than achievement, and the central theme of Keats's *Endymion* seems to be fulfillment (albeit a mixture of mortal and divine) upon earth itself.

The divergence in perspective is further revealed by the association of beauty with love in the earlier period and of poetic imagination with love in the later one. Although both beauty and imagination were included in the idealism of each age, the emphasis differed. Dante, while believing that poetic inspiration emanates from above, was overwhelmingly concerned with the combination of love and beauty that draws man *upward* into divinity, while the Romantics seemed more aware of the love and imagination that comes *down* from heaven. Thus Wordsworth might well exhort the poet to fulfill his mundane goals:

> If thou indeed derive thy light from Heaven,
> Then, to the measure of that heaven-born light,
> Shine, Poet! in thy place, and be content.

Possibly the neoplatonists' preoccupation with beauty, which by its very nature attracts *to* itself, accurately reflects a pre-Renaissance medieval otherworldliness; post-Renaissance humanism, on the other hand, would logically exalt that inspiration which reaches *from* itself to mortals below. Therefore the Romantics, in contrast to those earlier authors who delineated love as an ascending ladder or a spiral into the empyrean, quite properly described their concept as "light *from* heaven."

But even such basic terminology bore differing implications to highly individualistic thinkers, so that the supernal light was portrayed as having a variety of influences upon human beings. One of the most fervid expressions of Romantic hopes concludes Coleridge's "Religious Musings," in which the effect of God's love for man is likened to the result of warm sunlight on ice. Implicit in this comparison is not only the customary assumption that human response expresses a desire for the good and the beautiful but also that joy is one of its inherent components. In addition to its warming effects, the divine light of love was generally thought a means of expanding intellectual powers, as Keats's "Ode to Psyche" admirably demonstrates. Indeed warming and illuminating love

might be deemed the most exalted use of creative imagination. Accordingly, Shelley, in "Lines Written among the Euganean Hills," refers to the "love from Petrarch's urn" as "A quenchless lamp by which the heart / Sees things unearthly." Moreover, love could be a way of transcending the confinements of earthly existence, of achieving a union with some higher entity, or of effecting a justice beyond mortal laws, as shown in Coleridge's "Rime of the Ancient Mariner," Shelley's *Epipsychidion* and *The Triumph of Life,* Keats's *Endymion,* and a variety of spectral narratives.

Yet if love was truly a divine light in both the sensible and intelligible respects, it nevertheless entailed many problems to which the wisdom of the past offered no pat solutions. Assuming that the origin of such impetus was the Almighty Being, one might argue that adherence to its promptings represented a nobler obedience than submission to man-made law and therefore that the individual conscience would be the most valid criterion for moral judgment. Yet one might also contend that if spiritual illumination was not perfectly received in the human realm its guidance would not be infallible. Even if it shone unerringly on earth, it could be misunderstood by man's combined entity of body-and-soul. For while it might, as Byron suggests in *The Giaour,* lift "our low desire" above the earthly plane, it does not completely obliterate the animal in man. It might indeed become so weakened and distorted in the material world that its actual appearance is nothing more than a meteor-ray or will-o'-the-wisp. In this deceptive aspect it is impressively depicted by Shelley in "Lines Written in the Bay of Lerici." There the poet asserts that if he were a spirit drawn by starlight or an unthinking fish attracted to a fisherman's lantern (only to be speared), he might not worry about the effects of responding to the light of love. Unfortunately as a rational man he cannot "worship the delusive flame" without envisioning the dire consequences of such pleasure. Certainly Burns maintained that not only his susceptibility but the divine light itself had misled him, though Wordsworth, treating that assertion as blasphemy, retorted that if such impetus had truly come from heaven it could not possibly have led astray. Whatever the nature of the false inspiration—whether an influence of unheavenly origin or merely man's failure to comprehend the heavenly message—some Romantics felt that direct, unhindered apprehension of the true light would be possible only in the life beyond, a state of existence to which Shelley looked forward perhaps more than his contemporaries—

> some world far from ours,
> Where music and moonlight and feeling
> Are one. ("To Jane: 'The Keen Stars Were Twinkling' ")

In addition to these perplexing moral problems there was a more disturbing question of whether the light of love, like the imagination with which it was frequently identified, did actually emanate from an external, objective heaven or whether it was merely a projection of the inner eye. Could it indeed have been a "light that never was, on sea or land"—nothing more than a dream? A partial resolution to this problem, at least for some of the Romantics, apparently lay in their general belief that the god of love inheres not in the object of desire but rather in the very act of loving—in the *response* to some inspiring light, however evanescent it may be. Hence one need not know its ultimate source to profit from its benefits to the human soul. Or could the light perhaps be merely evidence of the soul's pre-existent mode of apprehension, fading in intensity as man grows farther from his unborn state? Indeed the theme of the "visionary splendour" with which youth invests the world is variously treated in Wordsworth's "Ode: Intimations of Immortality" and "Evening Voluntaries," Coleridge's "Dejection: An Ode," Shelley's "Lines Written among the Euganean Hills," and the first canto of Byron's *Don Juan.* Though in some instances it might be argued that loss of the gleam would be compensated by a deeper, more empathic, feeling for humanity, most Romantic artists believed that the light of imaginative love was tantamount to the life force itself. As a result, there was much discussion concerning the states of human existence most conducive to reception of its impetus.

But whatever the problems or the disagreements, writers attuned to the spirit of Romanticism proclaimed love's dominion over all other considerations, and this one belief distinguished them sharply from many of their predecessors and from the more circumspect Victorians who followed. Though every Romantic author interpreted love according to his individual personality and social background, each one— whether a peasant like Burns, an aristocrat like Byron, or a man of conventional morality like Scott—acknowledged fealty to that common ideal. Their treatments of subjects as diverse as incest, ghostly liaisons, and honorable wedlock can all be categorized as Romantic because they basically exalted love to such an extent that sacrifices in its behalf seemed worthwhile and even apparent misdeeds perpetrated in its pursuit became venial. As Scott asserted in his *Lay of the Last Minstrel* (1805),

> Love rules the court, the camp, the grove,
> And men below, and saints above,
> And love is heaven, and heaven is love.

Though some theologians still attributed man's fall to Adam's extraordinary affection for Eve, the Romantics generally preferred to regard that emotion less as a threat to divine edict than as a means of restoring the lost paradise or as salvation itself. Depending upon results, it could therefore (like Shelley's West Wind) be either destroyer or rejuvenator. But it was largely in the latter function that authors rebelling against a rationalistic world view preferred to consider love. The fact that they chose to identify the emotion with favorite speculations reveals the esteem in which it was ordinarily held. hence, in addition to its customary identification with human attachments, it became associated with appreciation of nature, empathic understanding, humor, imagination, and the regeneration of corrupt society. In a time of diverse cosmographies and increasingly complex interpretations of existence, human affection gave needed stability, providing a creativity myth to which the age could attach itself. Though love, like other manifestations of organic life, was constantly developing, it provided a norm countering whatever centrifugal forces threatened to hurl man farther from centrality. Moreover, it was a beneficial antidote to the solipsism and self-consciousness that beset highly introspective natures, breaking down barriers and divisions. For while creative imagination promoted the expression of individuality, there was ever present the danger of fragmentation; and love served as a means of restoring man's contact with his own kind, with social institutions, and with the supernatural. (pp. xiv-xx)

The Romantic movement constituted an exciting half-century of breaking through ideational barriers; and if some of the mental explorations appear to be unbalanced, one must accept them, without undue stress, as unavoidable by-products of the unfettered imagination combined with individuality. The bizarre and irrational elements, which some

critics have exploited as most characteristic of the period, are, I think, only to be expected among those relentlessly pursuing truth beyond the limits set by previous ages. In this regard there seems to be a definite parallel between the spirit of free scientific inquiry current in the period and the literary examination of human emotions—between man's external environment and his inner life; and the comparison logically extends to the trial and error method often necessary to search all possible avenues to knowledge.

Certainly the impetus toward freedom of thought and expression had never been stronger than in the Romantic age, but I am convinced that the results of this moving force were, as a whole, both positive and useful. It was the Romantics' intense belief in the overwhelming *power* of love which caused them to explore its potentialities to an almost limitless extent, so that no human relationship escaped their scrutiny. It was their devotion to the *truth* of love that caused them to question, and often defy, any religious beliefs, laws, and social customs which seemed to impede its implementation among men. Finally, it was their conviction in love's essential *goodness* that made them dare postulate mankind's salvation *upon earth*—not merely in some distant, spiritual afterworld. From Burns's declaration of brotherhood in "Is there, for honest Poverty" to Shelley's apocalyptic vision in *Prometheus Unbound* there was among the Romantic writers generally a profound faith in a better society. One cannot deny that by the time Romantic flights of fancy settled down into the more restrained Victorian age beneficial changes were beginning to occur in education, government, and social relations; and some credit for these advances is surely due to the position of love in the literature of the early part of the century. Indeed the ideas of Western man have never been quite the same since the Romantics began to explore uncharted regions of thought. Their new focus upon old problems and their shifted emphasis among old values shaped fresh points of view that still apply in the modern world.

But the Romantics voiced their recommendations not only in direct terms through their own words or those of fictional personalities; they spoke most impressively through the fundamental character of their literary heroes. Since idealistic movements especially tend to exalt human models who exemplify their beliefs, it is not surprising that hero-worship flourished in the Romantic age; but it seems to have taken a very different turn in England than it did elsewhere. While continental Europeans virtually created a cult by their glorification of the strong man associated with nationalism and worldly power, most English writers were drawn to another kind of personality. Though their willingness to challenge entrenched doctrines contributed to a certain admiration for Napoleon's energy, genius, and eagerness to overthrow dynastic authority, they generally saw his tyranny for what it was; hence, with the exception of Hazlitt, they did not share the extreme fascination with him felt by German philosophers such as Hegel, Fichte, and Nietzsche. If there was indeed any dominant hero among British Romantics, he was not primarily a military leader; neither was he merely a social misfit, an idealistic outlaw, or a malcontent striving for unattainable gratification, though all of these figures received some recognition. Basically he was an aspiring lover who, according to his own receptivity to light from heaven, became the instrument for working out divine will. Keats's Endymion was not atypical in rejecting a life of active leadership in favor of a higher calling—the fulfillment of love. In fact, most of the outstanding literary characters of the age—the poet whose mental growth Wordsworth detailed in *The Prelude*, Coleridge's Ancient Mariner, Byron's Don Juan, Shelley's Prometheus, and Keats's Lycius—achieved the status of great men largely by virtue of being imaginative lovers. Whereas the worldly empires of Napoleon and his twentieth-century imitators have crumbled, the literary dominion of love has survived. (pp. 276-78)

> *Frederick L. Beaty, in an introduction and afterword to his* Light from Heaven: Love in British Romantic Literature, *Northern Illinois University Press, 1971, pp. xiii-xx; 275-78.*

FORMS OF ROMANTIC POETRY

LIONEL STEVENSON

[*A respected Canadian literary critic, Stevenson was also the author of five biographies, all highly acclaimed for their scholarship, wit, and clarity. In the following excerpt, Stevenson illustrates how Romantic narrative poetry invokes the reader's imagination to supply details omitted by the poet.*]

An unacknowledged paradox inheres in many of the accepted definitions of the complex phenomenon known as Romanticism. Though varying as to other elements, the definitions usually agree in emphasizing that Romantic poetry is essentially subjective, and that for this reason none of the Romantic poets wrote in the objective genre of the novel (until Scott was belatedly impelled into it by circumstances), and all of them were inept when they attempted the most impersonal of genres, the drama. While this hypothesis is valid when confined to the achievements of the Romantic authors in the lyric and in poems of personal meditation, it ignores the conspicuous fact that many noteworthy poems by all the principal poets were in the primarily objective form of narrative.

It seems to be assumed that such poems are adequately marshaled under the Romantic banner because they present exotic settings or historical eras or exciting adventures or passionate love scenes or supernatural manifestations or humble rural tragedies; but exclusive reliance on subject-matter produces merely an elementary classification without much critical validity. A more sophisticated criterion is essential if narrative is to be regarded as a genuine and indeed eminent category of Romantic poetry.

The only extensive treatment of the subject, Karl Kroeber's *Romantic Narrative Art* (1960) [see Further Reading], is handicapped by the assumption that equal attention must be accorded to all narrative poems by Romantic (and pre-Romantic) writers. Scattered through the book are occasional hints of a valid definition, but they are obscured by the effort to deal exhaustively and indiscriminately with such unlike poems as "Tam O'Shanter," "Peter Grimes," *The Prelude, The Lady of the Lake,* "Christabel," *Don Juan,* "La Belle Dame Sans Merci," and *Miss Kilmansegg and her Precious Leg.* Hence, the book turns out to be a group of analyses of disparate poems rather than a unified study. I propose to differentiate among such poems and to eliminate a large proportion of them from the category of essentially Romantic art.

If it is legitimate to describe Romantic poetry as dominantly subjective, the concept has to apply equally to both sides of the artistic communication—not only to the author's creative impulse but also to the reader's response. Any sensitive reader not hopelessly shackled by text-book classifications must instinctively feel that some narratives by the Romantics possess a peculiar quality lacking in others by the same authors and their contemporaries. The quality can be designated by the term that Scott popularized, "glamour," or by Matthew Arnold's more sedate phrase, "natural magic"; but here again the mere use of a label does not suffice to distinguish an aesthetic effect. The prime necessity is to determine exactly what constitutes the exceptional impact of these quintessentially Romantic works.

If the reader's participation in the effect of a poem is to be enlisted, the only method is by stimulating his imagination to work independently. Watts-Dunton's old definition of the Romantic movement as "The Renascence of Wonder" can be applied, not as a superficial reference to supernatural marvels, but as an indication that the reader is led to wondering about elements in the story that are not explicitly set forth, and thereby to inventing them for himself. I do not imply, of course, that readers consciously undertake the function of expanding the story beyond the data provided by the author. The peculiar power of a successful poem in this mode is that it hypnotizes the reader into imagining events that he assumes to be in the poem though actually they are absent.

Literal-minded readers are apt to be impervious to such stimuli. This is the principal reason why so many critics in the Romantic era, conditioned by the rationality of the preceding century, dismissed poems by Coleridge or Keats as meaningless or mad. Demanding full and clear explanation as the first requisite of literary communication, they resisted any pressure upon the reader to cooperate in the creative process. For a similar reason, Bishop Percy, as a sound neoclassical intellectual, felt obliged to write additional stanzas to fill the gaps in his manuscript sources.

Two main methods are employed by the Romantic poets to ensure as far as possible that the reader will assume his fair share. One is to render the details so vivid that he perceives them fully with his mental senses. Settings, appearance of the characters, dialogue, maintenance of suspense, are all devices to simulate the experience of being in a theater and witnessing a play, with the consequent illusion of immediacy. This technique is entirely compatible with the Romantic preference for "specificity," in contrast with the insistence upon "generality" in neoclassical aesthetics. Nor is the use of sensuous detail in the Romantic poems confined to supplying materials for full visualization; it also can serve to induce a mood. The reader's matter-of-fact common sense is anesthetized by the poem's atmosphere, which renders him joyous or melancholy, hopeful or timorous, to a higher degree than the actual events of the poem require. When thus stimulated, the reader's imagination may possibly be capable of taking off on a short independent flight before relapsing into lethargy.

Preparing the reader to exert his creative power, however, is only the preliminary step. More subtle tactics are involved in pointing the direction in which it is to move. If such a poem is to communicate its overtones successfully, it must establish contact with some fairly general background that is likely to be deep in the reader's mind—usually fairy tales, mythology, or familiar works of earlier literature. Part of the value of this relationship between poet and reader is that it allows room for alternative assumptions. Depending on each reader's individual temperament and his patterns of association, he will extrapolate to suit himself.

Two possible sources may be suggested for this strategy of indirect suggestion. One of them is the folk ballad, with its stark condensation and its rigorous focus upon action. Thomas Gray observed this phenomenon when he remarked of "Gil Morice" in a letter to Mason: "You may read it two-thirds through without guessing what it is about; and yet, when you come to the end, it is impossible not to understand the whole story." Actually, Gray was reading an eighteenth-century "improved" version; the genuine folk versions as found in the Percy manuscript and elsewhere are far more cryptic. Nowadays it is generally believed that most folk ballads were adequately explicit when first composed and became eroded by oral transmission until only a fragmentary skeleton of the story remained; yet it is these mere shards of ballads that impress the reader most strongly. We do not know where Usher's Well is located, or the name of the Wife who lived there, or how her sons met their death, or why she understood the significance of their birch-bark hats; but by combining vivid detail with pregnant silence the forty-eight lines constitute one of the most unforgettable of the ballad tales.

The other probable source for the implicative method is Macpherson's Ossianic poems. In order to produce the illusion of ancient legends that have lost their historical context, he depicts his heroes as stalking phantom-like through misty Highland landscapes in an aura of eerie forebodings to engage in inexplicable battles. Unlike authentic folk-ballads, these pseudo-epic fragments remain remote from a modern reader's imagination through lack of the specific details that promote a sense of immediacy. The Romantic poets, however, found the elusiveness of *Fingal* and its sequels intensely suggestive.

It is time now to test these hypotheses by applying them to some representative poets of the Romantic age. When we begin with Wordsworth, we find that his narrative poems rate very low on the scale of imaginative suggestion. His earliest pieces, "An Evening Walk" and *Descriptive Sketches,* which are narrative only in that they report a series of observations chronologically, are in the neoclassical genre of topographical verse, with all its informative precision. "Guilt and Sorrow," still mainly neoclassical in manner, offers the sort of tale of humble life that later became Wordsworth's forte; but his method is not under control. The reader is indeed inadequately informed about some essential occurrences in the action, such as how the sailor lost his severance pay, how he murdered the traveler, and how the woman's family became impoverished; but we are not stimulated to invent fuller details. Rather, the summary of these crucial events merely exasperates us by its baldness. Though Wordsworth's later narrative poems are better proportioned, the stories are still recounted as explicitly as those of Crabbe. "Ruth," "Michael," and "Peter Bell," with their exhaustive biographical data, are typical. The technique of suggestion is to be found to a slight degree in only two of Wordsworth's narratives. In "The Thorn" it is achieved through the cautious innuendos of the narrator, a retired seaman who fancies himself superior to the gossip and superstitions of the villagers and who therefore scrupulously avoids asserting as positive fact that Martha Ray murdered her infant. In "The Idiot Boy" we have only Johnny's imbecile mumbling as a basis for inferring what happened to him during his ride. In both poems, however,

there is little demand upon the reader's inventiveness. Wordsworth's two narratives that use conventionally "Romantic" subjects, "Hart-Leap Well" and "The White Doe of Rylstone," are no less explicit than the tales of humble life.

In his long poems, Scott ranks almost as low as Wordsworth by the test of suggestive implication. In a few brief imitations of the folk ballad he proves that he can exert the evocative spell. We know nothing as to why Proud Maisie is doomed to an early and virgin death, but we reconstruct a whole tragic story from the seventy-five-word dialogue between the lady and the robin-redbreast. In the long narratives, however, this authentic Romantic power is totally obscured. In *The Lay of the Last Minstrel* even the Lady of Branksome's skill in black magic is prosaically attributed to her father's majoring in necromancy at the University of Padua, with a graduate course at St. Andrew's. The subsequent poems are so meticulously informative about every detail and so thorough in the analysis of character that we need not be astonished by the ease of Scott's transition to the writing of prose fiction. Incidentally, my hypothesis may help to demolish the still-surviving fallacy that Scott's prose stories are to be denied the name of "novels" and to be ignominiously classified as "romances." It is more appropriate to say that *Marmion* and *The Lady of the Lake* are not poetical romances but historical novels in rhyme.

The narrative technique of Coleridge is utterly different, as can be seen by contrasting *The Lay of the Last Minstrel* with "Christabel." The much-discussed similarities between the two poems in meter, setting, and theme only serve to emphasize the disparity. It seems indubitable that Coleridge's inability to finish the poem was due to his intuitive recognition that it had already achieved its full Romantic impact. Indeed, the laboriously written second canto is so inferior to the first that it seriously weakens the effect. The summary of the projected completion which Coleridge gave many years afterwards to the inquisitive Dr. Gillman is such a tissue of melodramatic absurdities that one must infer that he invented it on the spur of the moment as a mocking rebuke to an impertinent question. The first canto enthralls the reader by its sequence of hints that provoke curiosity. If Christabel wants to pray for her absent lover, why not in the castle chapel instead of under an oak on a cold night? If Geraldine was forcibly abducted and transported for two days tied on a horse's back, how can she be in a spotless white gown, with jewels entwined in her coiffure? What does Christabel see when Geraldine disrobes? If Geraldine is an evil witch, why does she seem to be suffering inner pangs? With these clues, as well as minor ones such as the mastiff's behavior, the fire's flaring, and Geraldine's collapse on the threshold, every reader can draw upon his private store of ideas about druidism, witchcraft, and perhaps lesbianism, and thus fill out the story as his taste dictates. At the same time, the visual details, from the last red leaf on the oak to the firelight glinting on Sir Leoline's shield and the lamp in Christabel's room fastened to an angel's feet by a two-fold silver chain, are so exact that even the weirdest supernatural conjectures become plausible. In the second part the interview with Sir Leoline and Bard Bracy's dream are disappointingly commonplace by comparison.

Coleridge's other attempt at a tale of chivalry, "The Ballad of the Dark Ladye," was abandoned even more abruptly, but I suspect for the opposite reason. The existing portion adheres so slavishly to the clichés of the folk ballad (or of eighteenth-century imitations of it) that there is scarcely any imaginative stimulus at all. My guess is that the last three stanzas of the fragment, wherein the Dark Ladye wistfully describes her longed-for wedding, set Coleridge's imagination off on a more rewarding scene,the opening of "The Ancient Mariner," and that he felt no impulse to return to the sterile ballad.

"The Ancient Mariner" is the only substantial narrative that Coleridge completed, and it seems clear and coherent enough to modern readers (except those whose minds have been obfuscated by a search for transcendental symbolism). It was regarded by Coleridge's contemporaries, however, as so obscure that in the revised version he provided the superfluous—indeed ludicrous—prose gloss as a contemptuous concession to obtuseness. In the poem such homely details as the diminishing view of kirk, hill, and lighthouse, and the presence of the mariner's brother and nephew in the crew combine to suggest that the setting is some little West-Country seaport (perhaps Dartmouth?), while the crossbow and the navigation by the position of the sun take us back before gunpowder and the compass to the time of Chaucer's Shipman, who was famous for

> his craft to rekene wel his tydes,
> His stremes, and his daungers hym bisides,
> His herberwe, and his moone, his lodemenage;

i.e., he navigated by soundings and landmarks and currents, around Western Europe from Hull to Carthage, from Gootland to Finistere, and would have been lost if out of sight of land.

Coleridge's nameless seaman on a nameless ship from a nameless port becomes the narrator through whom the reader observes vivid scenes of mast-high emerald icebergs or the tropical ocean burning green and blue and white. Such details induce imaginative identification, and yet we know perfectly well that the ship could not literally have been storm-driven as far as the Antarctic and then homeward across the Pacific. We are left to invent what might have been the actual events during his delirium. We summon up our geographical knowledge. Perhaps the ship encountered icebergs off Newfoundland and then drifted down to the Sargasso Sea. Even the mariner's later life is full of enigmas. How does he actually travel "from land to land"? How did he acquire his "strange powers of speech" (presumably, foreign languages)? We draw upon such legends as the Flying Dutchman and the Wandering Jew.

For many reasons, the most remarkable phenomenon of Coleridge's poetry is "Kubla Khan," and it is strange that Professor Kroeber should mention it in his book, since it tells no story at all. One is reminded of the old anecdote about a mad painter (a sort of super-Haydon) who exhibited a huge blank canvas as "The Passage of the Israelites," explaining that the Red Sea has just been driven back and the Israelites are about to arrive. In "Kubla Khan" the process of constructing the pleasure gardens has ended when the poem begins, and any adventures of Kubla Khan are yet to occur. Kroeber remarks that "an evanescent narrative" is "a disturbing element" in the poem. The fantastic landscape is so vivid that the reader feels impelled to populate it with characters and action, and therefore seizes on the "ancestral voices prophesying war" to create some episode of dire destruction, compounded out of Macpherson's gloomy soothsayers and the penalties for hubris in Greek tragedy.

In an attempt to forestall complaints about the non-narrative,

Coleridge gave it the subtitle "a vision in a dream," and provided the circumstantial preface in which he declares he "has frequently purposed to finish what had been originally, as it were, given to him" to the extent of "two or three hundred lines." As with "Christabel," one must feel that any such extension, presumably recounting Kubla Khan's downfall, would have destroyed the unique magic of the poem, which, as Lamb wrote to Wordsworth, "he repeats [*i.e.,* recites] so enchantingly that it irradiates and brings heaven and elysian bowers into my parlour when he sings or says it; but," Lamb goes on, "I fear lest it should be discovered by the lantern of typography and clear reducing to letters no better than nonsense or no sense." Like its author's other two truly Romantic poems, "Kubla Khan" avoids this disaster less by any inherent logic than by the reader's spontaneous provision of the missing data.

The second generation of Romantic poets displays the same sharp difference between imaginatively suggestive narratives and literally informative ones. Only in Byron's first oriental tale, *The Giaour,* does he leave much for the reader to infer, and so he attached the apologetic subtitle, "a fragment." A summary is required if we are to perceive the peculiar obliqueness of the narrative. After a long description of Aegean scenery in Byron's own voice, the point of view abruptly shifts to an unidentified onlooker, who understands nothing about what he observes and asks frequent questions, presumably addressed to a listener even less informed than himself. From a few hints we guess that he is a local fisherman, who catches a glimpse of a young Venetian galloping past. There follows a description of Hassan's deserted palace, contrasting its desolation with its former splendid luxury; and then occurs a brief episode in which the narrator's boat is commandeered by an emir for sinking an unidentified bundle in the sea. Only after one has read the whole poem can one infer that this episode must have preceded the glimpse of the agonized giaour and that both events occurred long before the devastation of Hassan's mansion. A narrator (perhaps not the same one) next mentions some conflicting rumors about Leila's disappearance from the harem. After an extended rhapsody over Leila's beauty, another specific episode suddenly begins: when Hassan and his henchmen are setting out on a journey—reportedly to find a new bride—they are waylaid by a robber band and Hassan is gorily slain, after which a survivor delivers his severed head to his mother (not previously mentioned in the tale). Though told with an observer's immediacy, these scenes can scarcely be accepted as reported by the fisherman who was present at the first events. Another interlude invokes hideous curses on the slayer without indication as to whether they are uttered by the bereaved mother or by someone else. Then a snatch of conversation indicates that many years have passed and that the scene has shifted to a Christian monastery (Mount Athos?). The Moslem who at the beginning saw the giaour riding by is now visiting the monastery and recognizes him among the cowled figures. One of the monks takes up the narrative (if so it may be designated), and the poem ends with an incoherent dying confession of the nameless giaour, which reveals a few clues to the story before he lapses into hallucinations.

This medley of uncoordinated glimpses, with abrupt flashbacks in time and shifts in point of view, in some respects foreshadows experimental techniques of the twentieth century. One might expect it to have been totally baffling to the reading public in the era that could not understand Wordsworth and Coleridge; but the violent emotions of revenge and remorse, the barbaric bloodshed and the sentimental rhapsodies, combined to achieve a sensational success.

Nevertheless, Byron did not continue to use the implicative technique. A trace of it remains in the abrupt transitions between scenes in *The Bride of Abydos,* but the point of view is consistently impersonal and the chronology is straightforward. *The Corsair,* though it begins *in medias res,* promptly cuts back to a factual chronicle of Conrad's previous life and an analysis of his character, after which the narrative advances smoothly. Only in *Manfred* is there any strong element of implication, since Manfred's unpardonable sin has to be left to the reader's imagination. It is in *The Giaour* and *Manfred,* then, that we find the quintessence of Byronic Romanticism; the other narratives move in the direction of *Beppo* and *Don Juan,* which are realistic (except for comic exaggeration) and explicit (except for sly innuendoes).

While Scott and Byron fall short of the subtle technique of imaginative suggestion, Shelley goes too far in the opposite direction. Dedicated to allegory and symbolism, he so overtly requires his readers to perceive esoteric meanings that his narratives lose much of their evocative power. In "Alastor" the young poet's frenetic roving through Europe, Asia, and North Africa is insistently a parable of the platonic search for ideal beauty, compounded with the death-wish. When compared with other accounts of wanderings, it lacks either the factual solidity of *Childe Harold's Pilgrimage* or the weird intensity of "The Ancient Mariner." There are improbabilities

George Gordon, Lord Byron.

aplenty: how can the shallop, whose sides "gaped wide with many a rift," sail on a stormy sea without leaking? how can the maelstrom act like an elevator to raise the boat several hundred feet upward? But we merely accept these unnatural phenomena passively as part of Shelley's dream world. The crucial mystery in the poem is the identity of the veiled maiden. Shelley indicates that she is no mere figment of an erotic dream, but an apparition of the spirit of solitude, or the creative imagination, or the muse of poetry, or the poet's inmost identity. To modern readers the vision has fascinating Freudian and Jungian implications, but this sort of analysis is totally different from imaginative response. Even the simple question as to whether the veiled maiden is to be regarded as good or evil is an abstract problem, unlike the imaginative one posed by Geraldine.

Similarly, "The Witch of Atlas" does not stimulate us to continue the story beyond the abrupt conclusion. The furniture of the cave, charmingly sensuous though it is, remains allegorical and therefore does not draw the reader into an illusion of actuality, as Tennyson, for example, does in his story of a similar magic tapestry-weaver, "The Lady of Shalott." Shelley apparently abandoned the poem before beginning to invent any adventures for the witch when she emerged from her cavern. *The Revolt of Islam* is a more elaborately developed narrative, but the exploits of Laon and Cythna are impenetrably enwrapped in cosmic personifications and revolutionary transports. In "Julian and Maddalo," the cryptic story of the maniac breaks off just when it ought to provide a few tangible clues, and is terminated with a perfunctory and ambiguous summary. Undeniably, Shelley himself is a highly Romantic figure, but he never mastered the elusive technique of Romantic narrative. We enjoy his poems by submerging our imagination in his rather than by proceeding to imagine anything for ourselves.

Between Byron, with his rationalistic bent for explicitness, and Shelley, with his ethereal obscurity, Keats stands as the paragon of Romantic narrative poets, rivaling Coleridge in his mastery of imaginative stimulation. *Endymion* is in some respects as elusive as "Alastor," which it resembles in much of its story; but Keats has the advantage of using familiar classical myths, so that his reader is able to rely on a few firm identifications. In this 'prentice work, however, Keats is so addicted to sensuous description for its own sake that the reader's imagination becomes cloyed by the sluggish flow of verbal honey. By the time Keats was ready to send *Endymion* to press, he was already outgrowing what he termed "a space of life . . . in which the soul is in a ferment, the character undecided, the way of life uncertain, the ambition thick-sighted; thence proceeds mawkishness." So far as narrative verse was concerned, the maturing experience was the writing of "Isabella," which is so unlike Keats's other poems that it is unduly scorned by some critics. Under the wholesome influence of the unromantic Boccaccio, Keats tells a straightforward story with realistic thoroughness, building up to a gruesome climax enhanced by its explicitness.

In his subsequent narratives he was firmly in control of the Romantic evocation. In writing "La Belle Dame Sans Merci" he submitted to the condensation and allusiveness of the folk ballad. One may profitably compare it with Coleridge's poem on the same theme, which is usually overlooked because the poet inexplicably imbedded it in another narrative under the title of "Love." The story of the narrator and his Genevieve is so sentimental that one scarcely recognizes the very different ballad hidden in the middle of it. When freed of its en-cumbrances, it becomes a minor masterpiece:

> I told her of the Knight that wore
> Upon his shield a burning brand;
> And that for ten long years he wooed
> The Lady of the Land. . . .
>
> But when I told the cruel scorn
> That crazed that bold and lovely Knight,
> And that he crossed the mountain-woods,
> Nor rested day nor night;
>
> That sometimes from the savage den,
> And sometimes from the darksome shade
> And sometimes starting up at once
> In green and sunny glade,—
>
> There came and looked him in the face
> An angel beautiful and bright;
> And that he knew it was a Fiend,
> This miserable Knight!
>
> And that unknowing what he did,
> He leaped amid a murderous band,
> And saved from outrage worse than death
> The Lady of the Land!
>
> And how she wept, and clasped his knees;
> And how she tended him in vain—
> And ever strove to expiate
> The scorn that crazed his brain;—
>
> And that she nursed him in a cave;
> And how his madness went away,
> When on the yellow forest-leaves
> A dying man he lay. . . .

There can be little doubt that Keats was familiar with this poem: the frame situation shows close resemblance to the epi-sode in "The Eve of St. Agnes" when Porphyro plays "an an-cient ditty, long since mute, / In Provence call'd 'La belle dame sans mercy.' " In Coleridge's poem it is described as "an old and moving story— / An old rude song."

In "La Belle Dame," even the metrical adaptation of ballad stanza, with the foreshortened last line, echoes Coleridge's. The shared elements are obvious—the crazed knight, the weeping lady, the cave, even the autumn leaves; but Keats has revised and tightened the story with consummate skill. The abrupt, violent fight with the murderous band is elimi-nated, the hard-hearted lady and the ambiguous angel-fiend of the wilderness are combined into a single female being; and instead of the pedestrian chronological order, the story is told retrospectively by the question-and-answer method—devices that Coleridge had used adeptly in "The Ancient Mariner." As a result, the reader of the Keats poem employs his own resources—stories of chivalric quests and fairy tales of na-ture-spirits striving for union with mortals—to flesh out the episode of the knight and the merciless lady. Acquaintance with the particular folk ballad of "Thomas the Rymer" may contribute, but it is not essential.

"The Eve of St. Agnes" is the very archetype of Romantic narrative, in that the story is conveyed almost wholly through setting and mood. The entire situation is little more than that of Coleridge's "Love," as noted above—the moon-light, the Gothic setting of ruined tower and "statue of the armed knight," the eager lover and shy but compliant maid-en. Regarded in terms of conventional narrative method, "The Eve of St. Agnes" flouts the basic rules. Suspense is

built up meretriciously and then flagrantly disappointed. An-gela's warnings lead us to expect a confrontation between Porphyro and his enemies, and the elaborate preparation of the supper seems like a foolhardy gesture that will ensure dis-covery. Instead, the lovers tiptoe out of the castle and escape unsuspected.

As peculiar as this anticlimax is the total absence of explicit beginning or conclusion. We have no information as to why Madeline's family hates Porphyro; there may have been a family feud or he may be of inferior birth. In view of the ha-tred, however, we must wonder how the lovers ever met each other. At the end, too, we are told only that "these lovers fled away into the storm." Some readers may put together the em-phasis upon intense cold, the absence of any reference to warm clothing, even the problem of transportation (did Por-phyro have a horse tethered conveniently nearby?) to infer that they soon perished of exposure, though happy in each other's arms. The morbid details in the last stanza reinforce this assumption. Sentimentalists, on the other hand, will in-sist that "they lived happy ever after" in the proper manner of fairy tales such as "The Sleeping Beauty," "Rapunzel," and many others with the same theme of a secluded heroine rescued by a venturesome lover.

The lack of substantive information in "The Eve of St. Agnes" can be made obvious by comparing it with *Romeo and Juliet,* which it resembles closely in situation and charac-ters. Writing for the objective medium of the stage, Shake-speare could leave nothing to be guessed at. We are fully in-formed as to the Montague-Capulet enmity and we witness the misdelivery of the invitation, which results in Romeo's first glimpse of Juliet. Romeo fights the inevitable duel with Paris, and at the end we are spared no pang of the lovers' deaths. Keats, in his poem, concentrates on Act III, scenes ii and v, of Shakespeare's play, and loads every rift with the ore of erotic suggestion through sense impressions.

After this high point, "Lamia" seems relatively informative; but the key issue is left ambiguous, to the confounding of crit-ics ever since. Like Geraldine, and Shelley's veiled maiden, and La Belle Dame, Lamia seems to be a malicious enchant-ress who is nevertheless inwardly tormented. Remembering the Wyf of Bathe's tale and other variants of the "loathly lady" theme, we tend to sympathize with her and condemn the heartlessness of her dismissal. On the other hand, Apollo-nius is the very embodiment of the wise and loyal mentor who so often protects rash youths from disaster. We are left to choose whichever interpretation suits our taste. (pp. 26-38)

Now that an array of evidence has been offered, it is possible to draw several conclusions about Romantic narrative. One is that, although many ultra-Romantic stories contain ele-ments of the supernatural, their distinctiveness does not re-side primarily in their remoteness from the material plane. The *Idylls of the King* are permeated with magic of many va-rieties, but it is treated in the matter-of-fact tone of epic expo-sition: the enslavement of Merlin by Vivien is utterly differ-ent in effect from that of Lycius or the Knight at Arms. The tech-nique of imaginative suggestion simply happens to function particularly well when applied to paranormal themes.

In a further respect, the poems I have discussed are particu-larly characteristic of the Romantic attitude. This is the mini-mizing of dramatic action, with its essential element of con-flict, in favor of passive surrender. Christabel is helplessly mesmerized by Geraldine; the Knight at Arms offers no resistance to La Belle Dame; Lycius is totally in the power of Lamia until the intervention of the rationalistic Apollonius. . . . The situations are suspended in a timeless void, unrelated to any wider context of human relationships or decisive action. Thus, they conform closely with the profound Romantic conviction of inwardness and isolation.

In conclusion, I wish to emphasize that my discussion is not intended to contribute to the current vogue of concern with symbolism and archetypal myths in poetry. The poems that I have mentioned may or may not convey transcendental significance. I have dealt solely with a matter of technique: the Romantic poets in some of their best narratives discovered a way of enhancing their readers' aesthetic satisfaction by enlisting a spontaneous imaginative participation. (p. 42)

> Lionel Stevenson, "The Mystique of Romantic Narrative Poetry," in Romantic and Victorian: Studies in Memory of William H. Marshall, edited by W. Paul Elledge and Richard L. Hoffman, Fairleigh Dickinson University Press, 1971, pp. 26-42.

ELIZABETH NITCHIE

[*In the following excerpt, Nitchie defends the formal excellence of Romantic poetry against the attacks of the New Critics.*]

[We] can say, with Virginia Woolf, that the poet is always our contemporary, that his work, being universal, is as alive in our own century as in his. It is in this second sense that I shall try to show that the Romantic poets, no matter how we respond to their ideas, are alive for us by reason of a formal excellence in their work that knows no restriction to time or place.

There is ample evidence that for modern critics as for modern readers Romantic poetry is alive. They are aware not only of breathing and heartbeat but of a vital energy that cannot be ignored, an energy not peculiar to the twentieth century but characteristic of all great poetry. Like all vital energy it rises from deep within the body and gives to it shape and action. Miss Edith Sitwell, quoting Blake ("Energy is the only life, and is from the Body"), says: "All technical achievement is, as it were, the Etheric Body of the poet" [*A Poet's Notebook,* 1943]. This Etheric Body cannot be denied to the Romantic poets.

Even the men commonly known as the new critics, who charge the Romantics with unreality and escapism, with adolescent thinking, especially with formlessness, recognize many of those technical virtues which they admire as they turn to examine individual poems. Cleanth Brooks includes Wordsworth's "Ode: Intimations of Immortality" and Keats's "On a Grecian Urn" among the well wrought works of art. And Keats's "To a Nightingale" Mr. Leavis says "has the structure of a fine and complex organism" [*Revaluations,* 1936]. . . . The attacks of the new critics are most often directed at those poems which, popular anthology pieces though they be, most scholars and critics would recognize as inferior. Shelley, for example, suffers under the analysis of "The Indian Serenade" or "When the Lamp Is Shattered." But what poet is always at his structural best? (pp. 3-4)

The modern critic's conception of form and its function differs little upon examination from that which we inherit from the Romantics. Form is a control—the "bridle of Pegasus," Mr. I. A. Richards calls it [in his *Coleridge on Imagination,*

1935]. Its function, says Mr. Ransom, is "to frustrate the natural man and induce the aesthetic one . . . ; it wants us to enjoy life, to taste and reflect as we drink" [*The World's Body,* 1938]. It controls also in the sense that it unifies all the diverse parts of the poetic structure, including the content, the meaning, the argument. "The composition of a poem is an operation in which the argument fights to displace the meter, and the meter fights to displace the argument," a fight in which the terms of peace "are the dispositions in the finished poem" [*The New Criticism,* 1941]. Indeed the moral intelligence gets into poetry "not as moral abstractions but as form, coherence of image and metaphor, control of tone and of rhythm, the union of these features" [Allen Tate, *Reason in Madness,* 1941].

We should not find anything shockingly new in these statements. They remind us of Wordsworth's

> function kindred to organic power,
> The vital spirit of a perfect form;

or of Coleridge's definition of a poem as "proposing to itself such delight from the *whole,* as is compatible with a distinct gratification from each component *part,*" and of his entire discussion of meter in the eighteenth chapter of the *Biographia Literaria.* Even Mr. Cleanth Brooks's insistence on paradox as the language of poetry should not startle those who remember Wordsworth's recognition of "the pleasure which the mind derives from the perception of similitude in dissimilitude" as a principle of the arts. In the familiar passage on the imagination in his *Biographia Literaria* Coleridge anticipated Mr. Brooks by more than a century:

> This power . . . reveals itself in the balance or reconcilement of opposite or discordant qualities: of sameness, with difference; of the general with the concrete; the idea with the image; the individual with the representative; the sense of novelty and freshness with old and familiar objects; a more than usual state of emotion with more than usual order; judgment ever awake and steady self-possession with enthusiasm and feeling profound or vehement; and while it blends and harmonizes the natural and the artificial, still subordinates art to nature; the manner to the matter; and our admiration of the poet to our sympathy with the poetry.

Indeed the modern critics often seem to have echoed the Romantic critics. Signor Croce, for example, sounds much like Wordsworth when he defines a poet or draws a distinction between imagination and fancy. They recognize their indebtedness. Miss Sitwell, the technician, fills her notebook with quotations from Blake, Coleridge, Wordsworth, and Shelley. The advocates of paradox and wit appeal to Coleridge by name and by quotation. Mr. I. A. Richards comments on a letter from Coleridge to Godwin: "I can think of no passage in which so many of the fundamental problems of what is now known as semasiology are so brought together or so clearly stated." Coleridge is, in fact, the father of many modern theories. (pp. 5-6)

Modern critics, as Mr. Barzun has pointed out [in his *Romanticism and the Modern Ego,* 1943], seem to contradict themselves by accusing Romantic poetry now of formlessness, now of too great concern for form. Yet the first charge is really implicit in the second. This second charge involves three alleged faults: too great insistence on conventional verse forms and on metrical rhythms for their own sake; too much use of language that is beautiful only by reason of sound or of vague suggestion and trite association; too frequent use of images and figures of speech for their individual beauty, so that the result in a poem is a failure in close-knit architectural structure.

If these things are so, the poets are untrue to their own critical theory. They furnish rebuttal in their statements on prosody, diction, imagery, and the organic structure of a poem.

Writing of prosody in his *Defence of Poetry,* Shelley said that "every great poet must inevitably innovate upon the example of his predecessors in the exact structure of his peculiar versification." Coleridge, explaining the variations in the meter of "Christabel," said that they occurred only "in correspondence with some transition, in the nature of the imagery or passion." Blake said of his septenaries: "Every word and every letter is studied and put into its fit place; the terrific numbers are reserved for the terrific parts, and the prosaic for the inferior parts; all are necessary to each other."

Similarly diction must be the organic outgrowth of thought. In "Style" DeQuincey recognized that Wordsworth was profoundly right in saying "that it is in the highest degree unphilosophic to call language or diction 'the *dress* of thoughts.' . . . [H]e would call it the '*incarnation* of thoughts.' " Blake wrote: "I have heard many people say, 'Give me the ideas, it is no matter what words you put them into.' . . . These people knew enough of artifice, but nothing of art. Ideas cannot be given but in their minutely appropriate words."

For Coleridge, "images, however beautiful . . . do not of themselves characterize the poet." The poetic image must have, among other qualities, "the effect of reducing multitude to unity, or succession to an instant." And Wordsworth has shown how the parts of a successfully imaginative figure of speech interact to produce the unity and concentration of poetic structure. For Keats the organization of imagery was that which gave shape and form to a poem. To him it is axiomatic that "Its touches of beauty should never be half-way, thereby making the reader breathless instead of content. The rise, the progress, the setting of Imagery should, like the sun, come natural to him, shine over him, and set soberly, although in magnificence, leaving him in the luxury of twilight." He wrote to Clarke of

> the sonnet swelling loudly
> Up to its climax, and then dying proudly.

On the whole matter of organic form one may quote Coleridge:

> The true . . . mistake lies in the confounding mechanical regularity with organic form. The form is mechanic, when on any given material we impress a pre-determined form, not necessarily arising out of the properties of the material; as when to a mass of wet clay we give whatever shape we wish it to retain when hardened. The organic form, on the other hand, is innate; it shapes, as it develops, itself from within, and the fullness of its development is one and the same with . . . its outward form.

Lest we think Coleridge unique in his generation, we can turn to DeQuincey on *Style*, or to Keats's third axiom, that like the leaves of a tree poetry must come from the poet's very lifesap.

Theory may be one thing, however, and practice another.

These principles should be considered in the light of Romantic poetry, not merely of Romantic criticism.

With a real concern for verse form and an unwillingness to be confined to the couplet the Romantic poets revived earlier English patterns—blank verse, the tetrameter couplet, the ballad stanza, the Spenserian stanza, the sonnet—and introduced from Italian verse the terza rima and the ottava rima. Of these strict forms the poets were not slavishly observant. Byron was unconventional in his occasional lyrical ottava rima and his freely overrunning Spenserian stanzas, as well as in his loose dramatic blank verse. Coleridge experimented with tetrameters in "Christabel," with the ballad stanza, with quantitative verse, and with rhythmic prose. Blake used blank verse in lyric poems, revived, with infinite variations and substitutions, the old fourteeners or septenaries in his prophetic books, and in many of his shorter poems achieved the kind of supple, clipped "prose" rhythms that we associate with modern innovators. Keats and Shelley both experimented with the sonnet. Keats developed his own form of the ode; Wordsworth freely adapted both the irregular and the regular patterns. Although, except for blank verse and Blake's septenaries, the emphasis is on end rhyme and regularly recurrent internal rhyme, there is no lack of assonance and suspension. And the sound patterns are as intricate and as highly unified in the work of Shelley or of Coleridge as in many poem by Archibald MacLeish or Dylan Thomas. The result is a rich variety of versification, with a range as wide as that of the twentieth century, except that the rhythms are those of music rather than of speech.

This music, though admittedly pleasing to the ear for its own sake, is primarily the music which belongs to the poem. The west wind sweeps through the terza rima; the cloud ever changes and shifts as the vowels and consonants shift, ever remains undying as the rhymes recur in Shelley's closely-patterned stanzas; the heavy, long-drawn sounds of grief wail for the world's wrong in "A Dirge." Biblical cadences dignify the blank verse in Wordsworth's tragic idyll of the Cumberland Abraham and Isaac. The visions in "Kubla Khan" melt one into another in hypnotic rhythms. The blank verse of *Hyperion* takes the shape of antique sculpture; the short lines of the "Ode to a Nightingale" have the sound of caught breath. The mocking colloquial tone of *Don Juan* is heard in the insistent, humorous reiterated rhymes of the ottava rima and the clinching finality of its couplet; a haunting regret lingers in the long vowels and feminine endings of "So We'll Go No More a-Roving." The lament for fleeting beauty sighs in the echoes of *The Book of Thel;* the exciting hammer strokes of the Creator sound in the stresses and repetitions of "The Tiger." (pp. 7-10)

The same principle applies also to language. To quote Wordsworth again, "Language is the *incarnation* of thought." The diction of the Romantic poet—when he is writing his great poems, of course—does not lose touch with reality. It is concrete—a quality which Mr. Albert Gerard says [in his essay "Coleridge, Keats, and the Modern Mind," *Essays in Criticism,* July, 1951] "a large section of the poetry-reading public of the present day chiefly values." It puts flesh on the objects upon which he steadily fixes his eye. Whether the poet looks at the dancing daffodils or the swift cloud shadows, the inner nature and the thoughts of Michael or of Prometheus, the world of classic art and literature or of contemporary politics and society, the drab and evil present or the ideal future, he sees what is real and he uses the "real language of men." This point is made especially clear for Wordsworth by a study of his first choices, the passages in the 1805 version of *The Prelude,* for example, instead of the 1850 version. And yet who has surpassed the reality of vision and of language in the 1850 lines about Newton's bust,

> The marble index of a mind for ever
> Voyaging through strange seas of thought, alone?

Romantic diction is not vague: it is precise.

Neither is it shallow or single: it is richly suggestive. "Ambiguity" was not unknown in the early nineteenth century, though Mr. Empson had not yet given it a name. What, for instance, of the two meanings of *closing* in the "Ode to the West Wind"—

> this closing night
> Shall be the dome of a vast sepulchre—

one, *enclosing,* related to *dome,* the other, *ending,* to *sepulchre?* The word pulls together the whole image and links it with the main theme of the poem: the enclosing cycle of death and rebirth. (pp. 10-11)

Like Romantic diction, the Romantic image is precise, often highly concentrated, wide in range, and structurally important to the poem.

The imagery of Shelley in particular is frequently said to be abstract and vague. There is perhaps some excuse for this charge. His images are often bewilderingly profuse: he slips, with a music which may lull the critical intelligence into inattention, from image to image, from metaphor to metaphor until, in terms of one of his favorite symbols, we ship our oars and float down the stream of sound. Yet upon the examination which the reader owes to good and difficult poetry, the images may prove to be as cunningly nested as Chinese boxes; or a series of metaphors is seen to be climaxed by a unifying line:

> Even as a vapor fed with golden beams
> That ministered on sunlight, ere the west
> Eclipses it, was now that wondrous frame—
> No sense, no motion, no divinity—
> A fragile lute, on whose harmonious strings
> The breath of heaven did wander—a bright stream
> Once fed with many-voiced waves—a dream
> Of youth, which night and time have quenched for ever—
> Still, dark, and dry, and unremembered now.

It should be clear too that images that seem abstract are the result of his expressed intention to draw them from the operations of the human mind: an avalanche is like a great truth loosened in a heaven-defying mind; the sun is like "thought-winged Liberty"; it is the spirits that come from the mind of humankind who comfort Prometheus and celebrate the millennium. His belief in "life's unquiet dream"—that mutability is the law of life and that men know only the imperfect, unreal, half-seen forms of ideal beauty—is expressed and reflected by his repeated images of things that shift and change and of the light of eternity stained by life or half-hidden, imperfectly revealed, behind a veil:

> Child of Light! thy limbs are burning
> Through the vest which seems to hide them;
> As the radiant lines of morning
> Through the clouds, ere they divide them;
> And this atmosphere divinest
> Shrouds thee wheresoe'er thou shinest.

This is the kind of precision which exactly expresses an idea. Shelley is capable also of the precision resulting from accurate observation: the "azure moss" submerged in the "intenser day" of the blue Mediterranean; the swift departure of Mercury over the eastern horizon:

> See where the child of Heaven, with winged feet,
> Runs down the slanted sunlight of the dawn.

The precision of Wordsworth, who looked steadily at his subject, is rarely questioned, or that of Coleridge, or of Keats, or of Byron, who, as Keats said, described what he saw.

Of himself in contrast Keats said that he described what he imagined, meaning, of course, that he exercised that abstracting and modifying power which Wordsworth ascribed to the imagination. The concentration that results from this activity is rare in Byron's poetry (though he occasionally startles us as by the image of the "arches on arches" of the Coliseum, where "the stars twinkle through the loops of time") and he is said to have asked Shelley what Keats meant by "a beaker full of the warm South." It is frequent in Keats's best poems. The development of an image can sometimes be traced from the lax assembling of details in the first draft to the poetic fusion in the published lines: from, for example,

> The Oaks stand charmed by the earnest stars

to

> Tall oaks, branch-charmed by the earnest stars.

As Robert Bridges said, Keats had "the power of concentrating all the far-reaching resources of language on one point, so that a single and apparently effortless expression rejoices the aesthetic imagination at the moment when it is most expectant and exacting, and at the same time astonishes the intellect with a new aspect of truth." Blake too knows the secret of creating the image that astonishes by its truth and rejoices by its fulfillment of aesthetic expectations and exactions:

> And the hapless soldier's sigh
> Runs in blood down palace walls.

These lines of Blake's show something of the range of Romantic imagery. Although many of the images of the period are drawn from what are commonly regarded as beautiful natural objects, they are by no means confined to bird songs and boughs breaking with honey-buds. Nature herself is not always beautiful: the dead wind stinks in Shelley's ruined garden. In the chartered streets of Blake's London are heard not only the soldier's sigh but the cries of the chimney-sweeper and the new-born infant, the curse of the harlot, the rumbling of the marriage-hearse. To these poets, as to those of other ages, the intellectual developments of the time furnished subject matter and images: new philosophical and psychological systems, innovations in social and political thinking, technological and scientific advances. As Lucretius used the atom, or Donne the compasses, or Tennyson the railroad, or our contemporaries the airplane or the bombsight, so Shelley, for example, that "Newton among poets," used electricity. (pp. 11-13)

The imaginal structure of the best poems of the Romantic period is tight and balanced and unified. It is no mere series of exquisite, flashing images. The sustained and intricate metaphor of "On First Looking into Chapman's Homer" determines and is determined by the structure of the Petrarchan sonnet. The images of death (Death and his brother Sleep) in the "Ode to a Nightingale," from the word *hemlock* in the first stanza to the word *buried* in the last, are interlocked with those of eternal life to culminate in the exaltation of the seventh stanza and be resolved in the fading uncertainty of the last. In "To a Skylark" images of the ascending bird and the overflowing, descending sound—the "rain of melody"—blend in the emotional identification of bird and poet. "The Solitary Reaper" is constructed on the contradictions in the girl's song which is both natural and mysterious, near and distant, symbolic of eternal beauty. The images of power and daring mount in "The Tiger" to a point where they explode in a heavenly cataclysm and return through the wondering contrast with the lamb to the slight modification of the first question. Often the images are symbols which hold the meaning of the poem: the light in Wordsworth's "Ode," the unfinished sheepfold in his "Michael," the albatross and the watersnakes in the *Ancient Mariner*—whether or not we accept them as symbols for Sara Coleridge and opium. These images fulfill the requirements of Keats's second axiom. They help the imagination to reveal itself in "the balance or reconcilement of opposite or discordant qualities." Through arching movement and often paradoxical tension they build the organically unified poem.

There is also in these poems a unity of logical or narrative structure. Even the reflective poems like "Tintern Abbey" or "Frost at Midnight" move along a line of somewhat free association to a conclusion which echoes the beginning and completes the circle of the poem. The structure is as strict as that of many similar contemporary poems, such as "The Love Song of J. Alfred Prufrock"—and infinitely clearer to the reader. The *Ancient Mariner* has in its very narrative that fine circular movement which Coleridge himself compared to the symbol of unity and eternity, the snake with its tail in its mouth. The Mariner's voyage begins and ends in reality, which both surrounds and is penetrated by the mystery. The albatross closes each arc of the circle as it closes each division of the poem. Even the moral, I believe, is part of the dynamic circle. Similar structure marks Keats's "Eve of St. Agnes." Youth and love and warmth and quiet are set in a frame of age and hate and cold and noise. Yet there is no sharp demarcation: old Angela ministers to youth and love; the noise of the revelry penetrates Madeline's chamber; the sleet patters against her window panes. The quiet of Madeline's azure-lidded sleep in blanched linen is in contrast with that of the Beadsman's eternal sleep among his ashes cold. Her vespers balance his thousand aves. All is fused in a rich intricate pattern and is set in a verse form which has always seemed perfect for the "golden broideries" on the pages of "legends old."

As Sir Herbert Grierson summarizes the Romantic theory of unity, "It is a harmony of all the elements, sensuous, intellectual, imaginative, none of which would be what it is apart from the others—diction, thought, imagery, rhythm, all are interdependent" [*Criticism and Creation,* 1949]. The Romantics—indeed all good poets—knew and acted upon the principle that Stephen Spender seems to have discovered, with some surprise, for himself, "that form does not lie simply in the correct observance of rules. It lies in the struggle of certain living material to achieve itself within a pattern" [*World within World,* 1951]. By imposing artistic discipline upon their living material and enabling it so to achieve itself, these poets attained "the inward balance and fulness which was, to a larger extent than is commonly realized, the ultimate ideal of English romanticism" [Albert Gérard, *Essays and Studies* I]. (pp. 14-16)

Elizabeth Nitchie, "Form in Romantic Poetry," in *The Major English Romantic Poets: A Symposium in Reappraisal, Clarence D. Thorpe, Carlos Baker and Bennett Weaver, eds., Southern Illinois University Press, 1957, pp. 3-16.*

R. A. FOAKES

[*In the following excerpt, Foakes analyzes the techniques the Romantics used to accomplish what he regards as their ultimate task: to impose a sense of order on a seemingly chaotic universe.*]

The Romantic poets wrote for a world which had changed greatly since the sixteenth, even since the early eighteenth century. Poets of these earlier times had been able to assume as their frame of reference a concept of an ordered and stable universe, organized in a system of degree ranging from God through angels, men and beasts to inanimate objects, a system in which man was the link between the natural and divine worlds, and in which the hierarchical structure of society corresponded to the ordered arrangement of the universe. This order did not exist in actuality, though it provided a prop or succedaneum for Tudor despotism, and might be seen as an ideal which society should attempt to fulfil; and indeed, much of the greatest literature of these centuries seems to grow out of the tensions between the ideal concept and the failure of life to correspond to it. (p. 39)

By the end of the eighteenth century the disparity between the ideal order and the world in which men lived had become so great, the ideal so meaningless, as to destroy its usefulness even as a myth. The growth of the middle class, of industry and trade, the decline of the monarchy and the aristocracy as representatives of power, and the approach of democracy were capped, for the early Romantic poets at any rate, by the French Revolution, Godwin's notions of a perfect society as a blithe anarchy, and pantisocracy. The old concept of an external order in the universe had gone, and was replaced by various ideas, which, like Godwin's theory, postulated the possibility of the self-fulfilment of the individual man as an ideal—the natural corollary to democracy; so Coleridge, welcoming the revolution, cried

And lo! the Great, the Rich, the Mighty Men,
The Kings and the Chief Captains of the World,
With all that fixed on high like stars of Heaven
Shot baleful influence, shall be cast to earth . . .
Return pure Faith! return meek Piety!
The kingdoms of the world are yours: each heart
Self-governed, the vast family of Love
Raised from the common earth by common toil
Enjoy the equal produce.

(*Religious Musings*)

The Romantic poets wrote for a society which could no longer be measured against a concept of order and degree, or by the standards of a mode of government fixed in a religious dispensation, one which was beginning to postulate the notion of self-government, of the equality of men. The destruction of an external frame of reference led them to seek a principle of order within the individual, within themselves, to write of man and the world largely in terms of their own inner life, or their own self-sought, self-created relationship with God. The point of reference in their poetry is the individual rather than society, or society seen as a collection of individuals, and not as an ordered hierarchy, and many of their greatest poems are documents of their own lives, *The Prelude, Don Juan, In Memoriam.*

The principle of order they sought was established not in terms of the external world and an appeal to reason, but in terms of the inner world of the individual, and an appeal to imagination. New critical attitudes and criteria were formulated to interpret and defend the new poetry, and received their finest expression in Coleridge's *Biographia Literaria* (1817). His theory of the imagination as the supreme unifying and creative power in the poet, was one aspect of a transcendentalism much less emphasized by modern writers who base their critical outlook on his; the imagination for Coleridge was that faculty which idealizes and unifies, the faculty by which we may perceive the unity of the universe, and apprehend God. It is not through Reason and self-knowledge that we approach the divine, but through the highest form of self-consciousness, which 'is for *us* the source and principle of all *our* possible knowledge'. It is through the individual consciousness, represented at its highest in the creative act of the imagination which repeats the eternal act of creation of God, that we perceive God;

> self-consciousness is not a kind of *being,* but a kind of *knowing,* and that too the highest and farthest that exists for *us.*

This highest form of knowledge is possible only to a few, and only those who

> can acquire the philosophic imagination, the sacred power of self-intuition,

will know and feel the 'potential' working in them, will be endowed with 'the ascertaining vision, the intuitive knowledge'. The best poetry will have the quality of intuitive perception of larger unities, and will represent the highest form of self-consciousness of the particular poet. It then becomes permissible to judge a poem critically as an expression of an individual mind, an inner experience, and to define critical values in terms of 'originality' or 'inspiration', concepts commonly used to acknowledge the presence of some mode of intuitive perception. So Coleridge said:

> What is poetry? is so nearly the same question with what is a poet? that the answer to one is involved in the solution of the other. For it is a distinction resulting from the poetic genius itself, which sustains and modifies the images, thoughts and emotions of the poet's own mind.

The Romantic poet employed the power of 'self-intuition' to restore order to a world which had ceased to afford ready-made images of order, in the way it had done for Shakespeare and for Pope. For Shakespeare the natural world (the macrocosm) was an extension of man's world (the microcosm), and the objects, beings, attributes of both could be used as touchstones of order and value, according to their place in the hierarchy. Just as the colour of a man's hair might indicate his character (for instance, the flaxen hair of Andrew Aguecheek), or his exclusion from the accepted order of society through deformity or bastardy make him a natural rebel (Richard III, Falconbridge, Edmund), so the natural world might also provide correspondences for temperament (as Othello, a native of a hot, tropical area, is passionate and hot-blooded), or accompany with appropriate disturbances men's disorderly acts (as night strangles day and the sun fails to rise after the murder of Duncan). Pope praised the 'amiable simplicity of unadorned nature' in his discourse on gardens, and

emphasized that art consisted in 'the imitation and study of nature', but his practice, like that of other landscape gardeners of his age, was to impose an order on natural scenery, even if it was an order, as in the contrived 'wilderness', derived from nature's wildness and not from geometry. In his poetry the natural world appears enamelled and painted as in a formal design, in which man's creations take their place, 'Rich industry sits smiling on the plains', and the 'ascending villas' on Thames-side suggest model planning. Nature is 'methodized' in accordance with an aristocratic scale of order and value in society, which in turn is given the sanction of divine law. In different ways, for both Shakespeare and Pope, the natural world was seen as providing a ready-made set of parallels for or images of human actions and attributes, as established in an order which reflected the order of human society.

The concept of ideal order in human society, the world of man, which had provided Shakespeare and Pope with a frame of reference, had collapsed and could no longer supply images of harmony for the Romantic poets; indeed, as stress was laid on self-intuition, self-consciousness and the individual imagination, human society became an image of waste, futility and ultimate disorder—so in Romantic and Victorian poetry the city becomes an image of spiritual exhaustion, or even an image of hell. The natural world also lost its order and its old emblematic function of providing a set of correspondences to the world of man, and took on a new aspect, offering in its wildness, as untainted by man, a refuge from disorder, and in its grandeurs, types of the sublime, images of aspiration. Natural objects, which seemed pure and permanent, or permanently recurring, in relation to the corruption of society and the transitoriness of life, were translated into symbols of the Romantic search for order, or into images of a spiritual harmony. Whereas for Shakespeare and Pope the natural world had reflected the order and values of man's world, of human society, an order attributed, it is true, to a divine dispensation, it now came to be used to embody the aspiration of the Romantic poet, to reflect directly a transcendental or spiritual order established by the imagination. Natural objects came to act as what Coleridge called 'conductors' of truths:

> the imagination . . . that reconciling and mediatory power . . . incorporating the reason in images of the sense, and organizing (as it were) the flux of the senses by the permanence and self-circling energies of the reason, gives birth to a system of symbols, harmonious in themselves, and consubstantial with the truths, of which they are the conductors.

Whereas Shakespeare and Pope could use an accepted frame of reference as a touchstone of values, the Romantic poet had to employ his imagination to create one, and he wrote his greatest poetry when he succeeded in giving birth to a 'system of symbols' conducting truths. These might not even be truths of the same kind as those which Shakespeare and Pope embody in poetry, for the natural order to which these refer was taken as a norm *from* which the world and society (man in his fallen state) deviate in error or rebellion; but the Romantic poet attempted to establish a harmony such as the individual isolated in an anarchic society might attain by the power of self-intuition, that is, a possible spiritual order in which the individual might find an ideal, find repose from the world, and *into* which he might deviate from the norm. Since there was no common frame of reference to which the Romantic poet's system of symbols could be related, the truths which they might conduct were not always apparent, as is instanced by the famous review of *The Rime of the Ancient Mariner* as 'the strangest story of a cock and a bull'. This difficulty was overcome in two ways, firstly by the use of images of impression, and secondly by the use of a vocabulary of value-words attached to these images.

By employing images of impression from the natural world, the poet could rely on traditional and common associations to enforce a symbolic value, and could use, to cite two simple examples, the rose as a type of beauty, mountains as emblems of aspiration. Inevitably some images proved so appropriate to the Romantic endeavour to tame chaos, to assert an ideal order, that they recur in the work of many poets. The most universal image is perhaps that of light, a fit symbol of spiritual illumination, of the transcendental vision, of the work of the imagination, or of the ideal to which the poet aspires. It takes many forms, but the sun, moon and stars are especially prominent because of their associations with heaven, their nature as permanent sources of light. So for instance, the sun and the moon are controlling influences on the voyage of the ancient mariner, and throughout Coleridge's poetry the moon in particular seems, as a light that shines in darkness, to symbolise the work of the imagination. In *The Prelude,* as elsewhere in Wordsworth's poetry, the sun and moon play their part, especially the 'deep radiance' of the setting sun,

> that deep farewell light by which
> The setting sun proclaims the love he bears
> To mountain regions.
>
> (VIII.117-19)

Again, in the climax of this poem it is the moon that reigns 'in single glory' over the grand vision in the last book. Keats wrote a long poem on the theme of *Endymion,* a human being spiritualized, made immortal, through his love for the moon, which again represents perhaps the power of the imagination; and the central figure of *Hyperion* is the sun-god. As Keats had appealed to a star as an emblem of permanence,

> Bright star, would I were steadfast as thou art!

so in "Adonais" Shelley's vision transmutes the dead poet into a fixed star, made immortal. One of the dominant images in *In Memoriam* is again light, and the restoration of faith in Tennyson is symbolized in the union of the evening and morning stars, Hesper and Phosphor (Section cxxi), both Venus, and both representing that love which had seemed destroyed with the death of Hallam, but is finally reborn in the morning light of a new assertion. All the heavenly bodies were types of 'that unchanging realm, where Love reigns evermore', and the pervasive image of light could well be made the basis of an anthology of Romantic poetry.

Light is one of many natural phenomena which provided images for the Romantic poets; indeed, all the forms of nature served as types of a permanence contrasting with the mutability of human life. So Coleridge said,

> all that meets the bodily sense I deem
> Symbolical, one mighty alphabet
> For infant minds; and we in this low world
> Placed with our backs to bright Reality,
> That we may learn with young unwounded ken
> The substance from its shadow.
>
> (*The Destiny of Nations*)

This 'bright Reality', of the light that is a symbol of love and the intuitive experience of harmony, and is associated with the beneficial forms of nature, with all that is fertile or helps

towards fertility, has its opposite in images of darkness, chaos and barrenness, amongst which the most important is perhaps that of the city. For the city-dweller became a type of the man isolated not only from his fellows, but from those forms of nature which might lead him to a transcendental sense of unity with the universe:

> A sordid solitary thing,
> Mid countless brethren with a lonely heart
> Through courts and cities the smooth savage roams
> Feeling himself, his own low self the whole;
> When he by sacred sympathy might make
> The whole one Self!
>
> (Coleridge, *Religious Musings*)

The city is peopled by savages, and the noble shepherds of Wordsworth's poetry are corrupted by contact with societies of men and cities. The poet called London a 'wide waste' in *The Prelude;* for the order, the harmony, which the Romantic poets assert is not one of society, but a transcendental harmony which the individual can attain only through communion with fit symbols, with what is beautiful and permanent, finding 'religious meanings in the forms of Nature'.

Another means these poets employed to establish this transcendental order was a vocabulary of assertion, of value-words representing concepts or feelings universally regarded as valuable, such as beauty, truth, liberty; words representative of the highest kind of bond between human beings, such as love, sympathy, harmony; words endowed by religious associations with a special sanctity, such as grace, ministry; or again, words expressive of the greatest human endeavour and aspiration, such as power, might, awful, sublime. These words and others which in their common use were associated with what men most value, with the loftiest hopes and ambitions, the greatest achievements, were used by the poets in connexion with images of impression. This vocabulary provided a context of values for the images, which take on a special character in terms of the value-words, for aspects of the natural world are endowed with the noblest human and religious attributes by their means. The effect is, in Wordsworth's phrase, to make

> The surface of the universal earth
> With triumph, and delight, and hope, and fear,
> Work like a sea.
>
> (*Prelude,* I.499-501)

Hence the forms of nature, the images of impression, become agencies by which these attributes may be transferred back to the poet's, and hence the reader's, aspiration, to the search for order. The process is again hinted at in the same book of *The Prelude:*

> Wisdom and Spirit of the Universe!
> Thou Soul that art the eternity of thought!
> That giv'st to forms and images a breath
> And everlasting motion! not in vain,
> By day or star-light thus from my first dawn
> Of Childhood didst Thou intertwine for me
> The passions that build up our human Soul,
> Not with the mean and vulgar works of Man,
> But with high objects, with enduring things,
> With life and nature, purifying thus
> The elements of feeling and of thought,
> And sanctifying, by such discipline,
> Both pain and fear, until we recognize
> A grandeur in the beatings of the heart.

The forms and images of nature are intertwined with human

passions so that by a reciprocal action they are endowed with human feelings and with values, and at the same time the poet's feelings and aspirations are purified and sanctified. The value-words and the images reinforce one another, so that the images are imbued with the poet's vision, and the words become representatives of the truths for which the images act as conductors.

This vocabulary helps to establish the images in a 'system of symbols', and the images fortify the value-words and give strength to them when, as frequently, they emerge in passages of affirmation. Images of impression such as those noted, of light, the sun and moon, or the city, the desert, are relatively static symbols, offering little possibility of development as a structural basis for a long substantial poem. While they sufficed for a lyric or a brief notation of a poet's assertion, the long poem demanded a framework to give coherence and force to the images, to give them relation as a system of symbols; and long poems were necessary for an adequate statement of the vision, the assertion, because only a long poem allowed a full deployment of images and value-words, a sufficient context for them to interact richly, and lend complete authority and scale to the poem's affirmation. So the larger Romantic poems are given a shape which is governed and informed by a structural image, an action or theme which provides a framework integrating image and value-word, creating a system of symbols, and becoming the vehicle of the poem's final statement. These structural images, like the other images of impression, and the value-words, are rooted in a traditional way of seeing the life of the individual, or in a common experience of life. The most important are the image of life as a journey in time, and the image of love between two individuals as a type of a higher union.

It is out of these elements, images of impression, including the larger structural images, and the vocabulary of assertion, that the Romantic vision is built. The language of Romantic poetry works in terms of these elements, the study of which is the best guide to the true nature and quality of its endeavour to make order out of chaos. (pp. 41-50)

> *R. A. Foakes, "Order Out of Chaos: The Task of the Romantic Poet," in his* The Romantic Assertion: A Study in the Language of Nineteenth Century Poetry, *Yale University Press, 1958, pp. 39-50.*

POLITICS, SOCIETY, AND ROMANTIC POETRY

M. H. ABRAMS

[*Abrams is an American critic best known for his writings on English Romanticism. In the following excerpt from his essay "English Romanticism: The Spirit of the Age," he asserts the importance of the radical political climate in the years following the French Revolution as an influence on Romantic poetry.*]

My title echoes that of William Hazlitt's remarkable book of 1825 [*The Spirit of the Age*], which set out to represent what we now call the climate of opinion among the leading men of his time. In his abrupt way Hazlitt did not stay to theorize, plunging into the middle of things with a sketch of Jeremy Bentham. But from these essays emerges plainly his view that

the crucial occurrence for his generation had been the French Revolution. In that event and its repercussions, political, intellectual, and imaginative, and in the resulting waves of hope and gloom, revolutionary loyalty and recreancy, he saw both the promise and the failures of his violent and contradictory era.

The span covered by the active life of Hazlitt's subjects—approximately the early 1790s to 1825—coincides with what literary historians now call the Romantic period; and it is Hazlitt's contention that the characteristic poetry of the age took its shape from the form and pressure of revolution and reaction. The whole "Lake school of poetry," he had said seven years earlier [in his *Lectures on the English Poets*, 1818], "had its origin in the French revolution, or rather in those sentiments and opinions which produced that revolution." Hazlitt's main exhibit is Wordsworth (the "head" of the school), whose "genius," he declares, "is a pure emanation of the Spirit of the Age." The poetry of Wordsworth in the period of *Lyrical Ballads* was "one of the innovations of the time."

> It partakes of, and is carried along with, the revolutionary movement of our age: the political changes of the day were the model on which he formed and conducted his poetical experiments. His Muse (it cannot be denied, and without this we cannot explain its character at all) is a levelling one.
>
> (pp. 26-7)

It seems to me that Hazlitt . . . [was] manifestly right: the Romantic period was eminently an age obsessed with the fact of violent and inclusive change, and Romantic poetry cannot be understood, historically, without awareness of the degree to which this preoccupation affected its substance and form. The phenomenon is too obvious to have escaped notice, in monographs devoted to the French Revolution and the English poets, singly and collectively. But when critics and historians turn to the general task of defining the distinctive qualities of "Romanticism," or of the English Romantic movement, they usually ignore its relations to the revolutionary climate of the time. (pp. 28-9)

It may be useful, then, to have a new look at the obvious as it appeared, not to post-Marxist historians, but to intelligent observers at the time. I shall try to indicate briefly some of the ways in which the political, intellectual, and emotional circumstances of a period of revolutionary upheaval affected the scope, subject-matter, themes, values, and even language of a number of Romantic poems. I hope to avoid easy and empty generalizations about the *Zeitgeist,* and I do not propose the electrifying proposition that "le romantisme, c'est la révolution." Romanticism is no one thing. It is many very individual poets, who wrote poems manifesting a greater diversity of qualities, it seems to me, than those of any preceding age. But some prominent qualities a number of these poems share, and certain of these shared qualities form a distinctive complex which may, with a high degree of probability, be related to the events and ideas of the cataclysmic coming-into-being of the world to which we are by now becoming fairly accustomed.

By force of chronological habit we think of English Romanticism as a nineteenth-century phenomenon, overlooking how many of its distinctive features had been established by the end of the century before. The last decade of the eighteenth century included the complete cycle of the Revolution in France, from what De Quincey [in his essay "William

Portrait of William Wordsworth at age twenty-eight by William Shuter.

Wordsworth"] called its "gorgeous festival era" to the *coup d'état* of November 10, 1799, when to all but a few stubborn sympathizers it seemed betrayed from without and within, and the portent of Napoleon loomed over Europe. That same decade was the period in which the poets of the first Romantic generation reached their literary maturity and had either completed, or laid out and begun, the greater number of what we now account their major achievements. By the end of the decade Blake was well along with *The Four Zoas;* only *Milton* and *Jerusalem* belong to the nineteenth century. By the end of the year 1800 Wordsworth had already announced the over-all design and begun writing the two great undertakings of his poetic career; that is, he had finished most of the first two books and a number of scattered later passages of *The Prelude,* and of *The Recluse* he had written "Home at Grasmere" (which included the extraordinary section he later reprinted as the "Prospectus of the design and scope of the whole poem") as well as the first book of *The Excursion.* Coleridge wrote in the 1790s seven-tenths of all the nondramatic material in his collected poems.

"Few persons but those who have lived in it," Southey reminisced [in a letter written] in his Tory middle age, "can conceive or comprehend what the memory of the French Revolution was, nor what a visionary world seemed to open upon those who were just entering it. Old things seemed passing away, and nothing was dreamt of but the regeneration of the human race." The early years of the Revolution, a modern commentator has remarked, were "perhaps the happiest in the memory of civilized man," and his estimate is justified by the ecstasy described by Wordsworth in *The Prelude*—"bliss was it in that dawn to be alive"—and expressed by many observers of France in its glad dawn. . . .

[It] seemed to many social philosophers that the revolution against the king and the old laws would cure everything and establish felicity for everyone, everywhere. In 1791 Volney took time out from his revolutionary activities to publish *Les ruines, ou méditations sur les révolutions des empires,* in which a supervisory Genius unveils to him the vision of the past, the present, and then the "New Age," which had in fact already begun in the American Revolution and was approaching its realization in France. "Now," cries the author, "may I live! for after this there is nothing which I am not daring enough to hope." Condorcet wrote his *Outline of the Progress of the Human Spirit* as a doomed man hiding from the police of the Reign of Terror, to vindicate his unshaken faith that the Revolution was a breakthrough in man's progress; he ends with the vision of mankind's imminent perfection both in his social condition and in his intellectual and moral powers. The equivalent book in England was Godwin's *Political Justice,* written under impetus of the Revolution in 1791-93, which has its similar anticipation of mankind morally transformed, living in a state of total economic and political equality.

The intoxicating sense that now everything was possible was not confined to systematic philosophers. In 1793, Hazlitt said, schemes for a new society "of virtue and happiness" had been published "in plays, poems, songs, and romances—made their way to the bar, crept into the church . . . got into the hearts of poets and the brains of metaphysicians . . . and turned the heads of almost the whole kingdom." Anyone who has looked into the poems, the sermons, the novels, and the plays of the early 1790s will know that this is not a gross exaggeration. Man regenerate in a world made new; this was the theme of a multitude of writers notable, forgotten, or anonymous. In the Prologue to his highly successful play, *The Road to Ruin* (1792), Thomas Holcroft took the occasion to predict that the Revolution in France had set the torrent of freedom spreading,

> To ease, happiness, art, science, wit, and genius to give
> birth;
> Ay, to fertilize a world, and renovate old earth!

"Renovate old earth," "the regeneration of the human race"—the phrases reflect their origin, and indicate a characteristic difference between French and English radicalism. Most French philosophers of perfectibility (and Godwin, their representative in England) were anticlerical skeptics or downright atheists, who claimed that they based their predictions on an inductive science of history and a Lockian science of man. The chief strength and momentum of English radicalism, on the other hand, came from the religious Nonconformists who, as true heirs of their embattled ancestors in the English Civil War, looked upon contemporary politics through the perspective of biblical prophecy. In a sermon on the French Revolution preached in 1791 the Reverend Mark Wilks proclaimed: "Jesus Christ was a Revolutionist; and the Revolution he came to effect was foretold in these words, 'He hath sent me to proclaim liberty to the captives.' " The Unitarians—influential beyond their numbers because they included so large a proportion of scientists, literary men, and powerful pulpit orators—were especially given to projecting on the empirical science of human progress the pattern and detail of biblical prophecies, Messianic, millennial, and apocalyptic. "Hey for the New Jerusalem! The millennium!" Thomas Holcroft cried out, in the intoxication of first reading Paine's *The Rights of Man* (1791); what this notorious atheist uttered lightly was the fervent but considered opinion of a number of his pious contemporaries. . . . In 1791 Joseph Priestley, scientist, radical philosopher, and a founder of the Unitarian Society, had written his *Letters* in reply to Burke's *Reflections,* in which he pronounced the American and French revolutions to be the inauguration of the state of universal happiness and peace "distinctly and repeatedly foretold in many prophecies, delivered more than two thousand years ago." Three years later he expanded his views in *The Present State of Europe Compared with Antient Prophecies.* Combining philosophical empiricism with biblical fundamentalism, he related the convulsions of the time to the Messianic prophecies in Isaiah and Daniel, the apocalyptic passages in various books of the New Testament, and especially to the Book of Revelation, as a ground for confronting "the great scene, that seems now to be opening upon us . . . with tranquillity, and even with satisfaction," in the persuasion that its "termination will be glorious and happy," in the advent of "the millennium, or the future peaceable and happy state of the world." Wordsworth's Solitary, in *The Excursion,* no doubt reflects an aspect of Wordsworth's own temperament, but the chief model for his earlier career was Joseph Fawcett, famous Unitarian preacher at the Old Jewry, and a poet as well. In Wordsworth's rendering, we find him, in both song and sermon, projecting a dazzling vision of the French Revolution which fuses classical myth with Christian prophecy:

> I beheld
> Glory—beyond all glory ever seen,
> Confusion infinite of heaven and earth,
> Dazzling the soul. Meanwhile, prophetic harps
> In every grove were ringing, "War shall cease."
>   . . . I sang Saturnian rule
> Returned,—a progeny of golden years
> Permitted to descend and bless mankind.
> —With promises the Hebrew Scriptures teem.
>   . . . the glowing phrase
> Of ancient inspiration serving me,
> I promised also,—with undaunted trust
> Foretold, and added prayer to prophecy.

The formative age of Romantic poetry was clearly one of apocalyptic expectations, or at least apocalyptic imaginings, which endowed the promise of France with the form and impetus of one of the deepest rooted and most compelling myths in the culture of Christian Europe.

In a verse-letter of 1800 Blake identified the crucial influences in his spiritual history as a series beginning with Milton and the Old Testament prophets and ending with the American War and the French Revolution. Since Blake is the only major Romantic old enough to have published poems before the Revolution, his writings provide a convenient indication of the effects of that event and of the intellectual and emotional atmosphere that it generated.

As Northrop Frye has said in his fine book on Blake [*Fearful Symmetry,* 1947], his *Poetical Sketches* of 1783 associate him with Collins, Gray, the Wartons, and other writers of what Frye later called "The Age of Sensibility." As early as the 1740s this school had mounted a literary revolution against the acknowledged tradition of Waller-Denham-Pope—a tradition of civilized and urbane verse, controlled by "good sense and judgment," addressed to a closely integrated upper class, in which the triumphs, as Joseph Warton pointed out [in *An Essay on the Genius and Writings of Pope,* 1782], were mainly in "the didactic, moral, and satiric kind." Against this tradition, the new poets raised the claim of a more daring, "sublime," and "primitive" poetry, represented in England by Spenser, Shakespeare, Milton, who exhibit the supreme virtues of spontaneity, invention, and an "enthusiastic" and "creative" imagination—by which was signified a poetry of inspired vision, related to divinity, and populated by allegorical and super-natural characters such as do not exist "in nature." [see Abrams, *The Mirror and the Lamp,* in Further Reading].

Prominent in this literature of revolt, however, was a timidity, a sense of frustration very different from the assurance of power and of an accomplished and continuing literary renascence expressed by a number of their Romantic successors: Coleridge's unhesitating judgment that Wordsworth's genius measured up to Milton's, and Wordsworth's solemn concurrence in this judgment; Leigh Hunt's opinion that, for all his errors, Wordsworth is "at the head of a new and great age of poetry" [*The Feast of the Poets,* 1814]; Keats's conviction that "Great spirits now on earth are sojourning"; Shelley's confidence that "the literature of England . . . has arisen, as it were, from a new birth." The poets of sensibility, on the contrary, had felt that they and all future writers were fated to be epigones of a tradition of unrecapturable magnificence. So Collins said in his "Ode on the Poetical Character" as, retreating from "Waller's myrtle shades," he tremblingly pursued Milton's "guiding steps"; "In Vain—

> Heaven and Fancy, kindred powers,
> Have now o'erturned the inspiring bowers,
> Or curtained close such scene from every future view.

And Gray:

> But not to one in this benighted age
> Is that diviner inspiration given,
> That burns in Shakespeare's or in Milton's page,
> The pomp and prodigality of Heaven.

So, in 1783, Blake complained to the Muses:

> How have you left the antient love
> That bards of old enjoy'd in you!

Besides *Poetical Sketches,* Blake's main achievements before the French Revolution were *Songs of Innocence* and *The Book of Thel,* which represent dwellers in an Eden trembling on the verge of experience. Suddenly in 1790 came *The Marriage of Heaven and Hell,* boisterously promulgating "Energy" in opposition to all inherited limits on human possibilities; to point the contemporary relevance, Blake appended a "Song of Liberty," which represents Energy as a revolutionary "son of fire," moving from America to France and crying the advent of an Isaian millennium:

> EMPIRE IS NO MORE! AND NOW THE LION AND
> WOLF SHALL CEASE.

In 1791 appeared Blake's *The French Revolution,* in the form of a Miltonic epic. Of the seven books announced, only the first is extant, but this is enough to demonstrate that Blake, like Priestley and other religious radicals of the day, envisioned the Revolution as the portent of apocalypse. After five thousand years "the ancient dawn calls us / To awake," the Abbé de Sieyès pleads for a peace, freedom, and equality which will effect a regained Eden—"the happy earth sing in its course, / The mild peaceable nations be opened to heav'n, and men walk with their fathers in bliss"; when his plea is ignored, there are rumblings of a gathering Armageddon, and the book ends with the portent of a first resurrection: "And the bottoms of the world were open'd, and the graves of archangels unseal'd."

The "Introduction" to *Songs of Experience* (1794) calls on us to attend the voice which will sing all Blake's poems from now on: "Hear the voice of the Bard! / Who Present, Past, & Future, sees," who calls to the lapsèd Soul and enjoins the earth to cease her cycle and turn to the eternal day. This voice is that of the poet-prophets of the Old and New Testaments, now descending on Blake from its specifically British embodiment in that "bard of old," John Milton. In his "minor prophecies," ending in 1795, Blake develops, out of the heroic-scaled but still historical agents of his *French Revolution,* the Giant Forms of his later mythical system. The Bard becomes Los, the "Eternal Prophet" and father of "red Orc," who is the spirit of Energy bursting out in total spiritual, physical, and political revolution; the argument of the song sung by Los, however, remains that announced in *The French Revolution.* As David Erdman has said, *Europe: A Prophecy* (1794) was written at about the time Blake was illustrating Milton's "On the Morning of Christ's Nativity," and reinterprets that poem for his own times. Orc, here identified with Christ the revolutionary, comes with the blare of the apocalyptic trumpet to vex nature out of her sleep of 1,800 years, in a cataclysmic Second Coming in "the vineyards of Red France" which, however, heralds the day when both the earth and its inhabitants will be resurrected in a joyous burst of unbounded and lustful energy.

By the year 1797 Blake launched out into the "strong heroic Verse" of *Vala, or The Four Zoas,* the first of his three full-scale epics, which recounts the total history of "The Universal Man" from the beginning, through "His fall into Division," to a future that explodes into the most spectacular and sustained apocalyptic set-piece since the Book of Revelation; in this holocaust "the evil is all consum'd" and "all things are chang'd, even as in ancient times."

No amount of historical explanation can make Blake out to be other than a phoenix among poets; but if we put his work into its historical and intellectual context, and alongside that of his poetic contemporaries of the 1790s, we find at least that he is not a freak without historical causes but that he responded to the common circumstances in ways markedly similar, sometimes even to odd details. But while fellow-poets soon left off their tentative efforts to evolve a system of "machinery" by which to come to terms with the epic events of their revolutionary era, Blake carried undauntedly on.

What, then, were the attributes shared by the chief poets of the 1790s, Blake, Wordsworth, Southey, Coleridge?—to whom I shall add, Shelley. Byron and Keats also had elements in common with their older contemporaries, but these lie outside the immediate scope of my paper. Shelley, however, though he matured in the cynical era of Napoleon and the English Regency, reiterated remarkably the pattern of his predecessors. By temperament he was more inclusively and extremely radical than anyone but Blake, and his early "principles," as he himself said, had "their origin from the discoveries which preceded and occasioned the revolutions of

America and France." That is, he had formed his mind on those writers, from Rousseau through Condorcet, Volney, Paine, and Godwin, whose ideas made up the climate of the 1790s—and also, it should be emphasized, on the King James Bible and *Paradise Lost.*

1. First, these were all centrally political and social poets. It is by a peculiar injustice that Romanticism is often described as a mode of escapism, an evasion of the shocking changes, violence, and ugliness attending the emergence of the modern industrial and political world. The fact is that to a degree without parallel, even among major Victorian poets, these writers were obsessed with the realities of their era. Blake's wife mildly complained that her husband was always in Paradise; but from this vantage point he managed to keep so thoroughly in touch with mundane reality that, as David Erdman has demonstrated, his epics are hardly less steeped in the scenes and events of the day than is that latter-day epic, the *Ulysses* of James Joyce. Wordsworth said that he "had given twelve hours thought to the conditions and prospects of society, for one to poetry"; Coleridge, Southey, and Shelley could have made a claim similarly extravagant; all these poets delivered themselves of political and social commentary in the form of prose-pamphlets, essays, speeches, editorials, or sermons; and all exhibit an explicit or submerged concern with the contemporary historical and intellectual situation in the greater part of their verses, narrative, dramatic, and lyric, long and short.

2. What obscures this concern is that in many poems the Romantics do not write direct political and moral commentary but (in Schorer's apt phrase for Blake) "the politics of vision," uttered in the persona of the inspired prophet-priest. Neoclassic poets had invoked the muse as a formality of the poetic ritual, and the school of sensibility had expressed nostalgia for the "diviner inspiration" of Spenser, Shakespeare, and Milton. But when the Romantic poet asserts inspiration and revelation by a power beyond himself—as Blake did repeatedly, or Shelley in his claim that the great poets of his age are "the priests of an unapprehended inspiration, the mirrors of gigantic shadows which futurity casts upon the present"—he means it. And when Wordsworth called himself "A youthful Druid taught . . . Primeval mysteries, a Bard elect . . . a chosen Son," and Coleridge characterized *The Prelude* as "More than historic, that prophetic Lay," "An Orphic song" uttered by a "great Bard," in an important sense they meant it too, and we must believe that they meant it if we are to read them aright.

The Romantics, then, often spoke confidently as elected members of what Harold Bloom calls "The Visionary Company," the inspired line of singers from the prophets of the Old and New Testaments through Dante, Spenser, and above all Milton. For Milton had an exemplary role in this tradition as the native British (or Druidic) Bard who was a thorough political, social, and religious revolutionary, who claimed inspiration both from a Heavenly Muse and from the Holy Spirit that had supervised the Creation and inspired the biblical prophets, and who, after the failure of his millennial expectations from the English Revolution, had kept his singing voice and salvaged his hope for mankind in an epic poem.

3. Following the Miltonic example, the Romantic poet of the 1790s tried to incorporate what he regarded as the stupendous events of the age in the suitably great poetic forms. He wrote, or planned to write an epic, or (like Milton in *Samson Agonistes*) emulated Aeschylean tragedy, or uttered visions

combining the mode of biblical prophecy with the loose Pindaric, "the sublime" or "greater Ode," which by his eighteenth-century predecessors had been accorded a status next to epic, as peculiarly adapted to an enthusiastic and visionary imagination. Whatever the form, the Romantic Bard is one "who present, past, and future sees"; so that in dealing with current affairs his procedure is often panoramic, his stage cosmic, his agents quasi-mythological, and his logic of events apocalyptic. Typically this mode of Romantic vision fuses history, politics, philosophy, and religion into one grand design, by asserting Providence—or some form of natural teleology—to operate in the seeming chaos of human history so as to effect from present evil a greater good; and through the mid-1790s the French Revolution functions as the symptom or early stage of the abrupt culmination of this design, from which will emerge a new man on a new earth which is a restored Paradise.

To support these large generalizations I need to present a few particulars.

Robert Southey, the most matter-of-fact and worldly of these poets, said that his early adoration of Leonidas, hero of Thermopylae, his early study of Epictetus, "and the French Revolution at its height when I was just eighteen—by these my mind was moulded." The first literary result came a year later, in 1793, when during six weeks of his long vacation from Oxford he wrote *Joan of Arc: An Epic Poem*—with Blake's *French Revolution,* the first English epic worth historical notice since Glover's *Leonidas,* published in 1737. Southey's Joan has been called a Tom Paine in petticoats; she is also given to trances in which "strange events yet in the womb of Time" are to her "made manifest." In the first published version of 1796, Book IX consists of a sustained vision of the realms of hell and purgatory, populated by the standard villains of the radicals' view of history. To Joan is revealed the Edenic past in the "blest aera of the infant world," and man's fall, through lust for gold and power, to this "theatre of woe"; yet "for the best / Hath he ordained all things, the ALL-WISE!" because man, "Samson-like" shall "burst his fetters" in a violent spasm not quite named the French Revolution,

> and Earth shall once again
> Be Paradise, whilst WISDOM shall secure
> The state of bliss which IGNORANCE betrayed.
> "Oh age of happiness!" the Maid exclaim'd,
> "Roll fast thy current, Time, till that blest age
> Arrive!"

To the second book of *Joan* Coleridge (then, like Southey, a Unitarian, and like both Southey and Wordsworth, considering entering the clergy) contributed what he called an "Epic Slice," which he soon patched up into an independent poem, *The Destiny of Nations: A Vision.* The vision, beamed "on the Prophet's purgèd eye," reviews history, echoes the Book of Revelation, and ends in the symbolic appearance of a bright cloud (the American Revolution) and a brighter cloud (the French Revolution) from which emerges "A dazzling form," obviously female, yet identified in Coleridge's note as an Apollo-figure, portending that "Soon shall the Morning struggle into Day." With the epomania of the age, Coleridge considered writing an epic of his own, laid out plans which would take twenty years to realize, and let it go at that. His ambition to be the Milton of his day was, in practice, limited to various oracular odes, of which the most interesting for our purpose is *Religious Musings,* his first long poem in blank

verse; on this, Coleridge said [in a letter], "I build all my poetic pretensions." The poem as published bore the title "Religious Musings on Christmas Eve. In the year of Our Lord, 1794," and Coleridge had earlier called it "The Nativity." The year is precisely that of Blake's *Europe: A Prophecy,* and like that poem, *Religious Musings* is clearly a revision for the time being of Milton's "On the Morning of Christ's Nativity," which had taken the occasion of memorializing Christ's birth to anticipate "The wakefull trump of doom" and the universal earthquake which will announce His Second Coming:

> And then at last our bliss
> Full and perfect is.

There is never any risk of mistaking Coleridge's voice for that of Blake, yet a reading of Coleridge's poem with Blake's in mind reveals how remarkably parallel were the effects of the same historical and literary situation, operating simultaneously on the imagination of the two poets.

Coleridge's opening, "This is the time," echoes "This is the Month" with which Milton begins his Prologue, as Blake's "The deep of winter came" reflects "It was the Winter wild" with which Milton begins the Hymn proper. (Blake's free verse is also at times reminiscent of the movement of Milton's marvelous stanza.) Musing on the significance of the First Advent, Coleridge says, "Behold a VISION gathers in my soul," which provides him, among other things, a survey of human history since "the primeval age" in the form of a brief theodicy, "all the sore ills" of "our mortal life" becoming "the immediate source / Of mightier good." The future must bring "the fated day" of violent revolution by the oppressed masses, but happily "Philosophers and Bards" exist to mold the wild chaos "with plastic might" into the "perfect forms" of their own inspired visions. Coleridge then presents an interpretation of contemporary affairs which, following his Unitarian mentor, Joseph Priestley, he neatly summarizes in his prose "Argument" as: "The French Revolution. Millennium. Universal Redemption. Conclusion." His procedure is to establish a parallel (developed in elaborate footnotes) between current revolutionary events and the violent prophecies of the Book of Revelation. The machinery of apocalypse is allegorical, with the "Giant Frenzy" given the function of Blake's Orc in "Uprooting empires with his whirlwind arm." In due course the "blest future rushes on my view!" in the form of humankind as a "vast family of Love" living in a communist economy. "The mighty Dead" awaken, and

> To Milton's trump
> The high groves of the renovated Earth
> Unbosom their glad echoes,

in the adoring presence of three English interpreters of millennial prophecy, Newton, Hartley, and Priestley, "patriot, and saint, and sage." (In Blake's *Europe,* not Milton but Newton had "siez'd the trump & blow'd the enormous blast"; as in Coleridge's poem, however, he seemingly appears not in his capacity as scientist but as author of a commentary on the Book of Revelation.)

Wordsworth thought the concluding section of *Religious Musings* on "the renovated Earth" to be the best in Coleridge's *Poems* of 1796. On this subject Wordsworth was an expert, for a year prior to the writing of the poem, in 1793, he had concluded his own *Descriptive Sketches* with the prophecy (precisely matching the prophecy he attributed to the Wanderer in his *Excursion*) that the wars consequent on the French Revolution would fulfill the predictions both of the Book of Revelation and of Virgil's Fourth Eclogue:

> —Tho' Liberty shall soon, indignant, raise
> Red on his hills his beacon's comet blaze . . .
> Yet, yet rejoice, tho' Pride's perverted ire
> Rouze Hell's own aid, and wrap thy hills in fire.
> Lo! from th' innocuous flames, a lovely birth!
> With its own Virtues springs another earth:
> Nature, as in her prime, her virgin reign
> Begins, and Love and Truth compose her train . . .
> No more . . .
> On his pale horse shall fell Consumption go.

"How is it," Blake was to ask in his conclusion of *The Four Zoas*, "we have walk'd thro' fires & yet are not consum'd? / How is it that all things are chang'd, even as in ancient times?"

Some two decades later Shelley recapitulated and expanded these poetic manifestations of the earlier 1790s. At the age of nineteen he began his first long poem, *Queen Mab*, in the mode of a vision of the woeful past, the ghastly present, and the blissful future, and although the concepts are those of the French and English *philosophes*, and the Spirit of Necessity replaces Providence as the agent of redemption, much of the imagery is imported from biblical millennialism. The prophecy is that "A garden shall arise, in loveliness / Surpassing fabled Eden"; when it eventuates, "All things are recreated," the lion sports "in the sun / Beside the dreadless kid," and man's intellectual and moral nature participates in "The gradual renovation" until he stands "with taintless body and mind" in a "happy earth! reality of Heaven!" the "consummation of all mortal hope!"

If I may just glance over the fence of my assigned topic: in Germany, as in England, a coincidence of historical, religious, and literary circumstances produced a comparable imaginative result. In the early 1790s the young Hölderlin was caught up in the intoxication of the revolutionary promise; he was at the time a student of theology at Tübingen, and immersed in the literary tradition of *Sturm und Drang* libertarianism, Schiller's early poems, and Klopstock's *Messias* and allegoric odes. A number of Hölderlin's odes of that decade (the two "Hymnen an die Freiheit," the "Hymne an die Menschheit," "Der Zeitgeist") are notably parallel to the English form I have been describing; that is, they are visionary, oracular, panoramic, and see history on the verge of a blessed culmination in which the French Revolution is the crucial event, the Book of Revelation the chief model, and the agencies a combination of Greek divinities, biblical symbols, and abstract personifications of his own devising. (pp. 29-52)

The visionary poems of the earlier 1790s and Shelley's earlier prophecies show imaginative audacity and invention, but they are not, it must be confessed, very good poems. The great Romantic poems were written not in the mood of revolutionary exaltation but in the later mood of revolutionary disillusionment or despair. Many of the great poems, however, do not break with the formative past, but continue to exhibit, in a transformed but recognizable fashion, the scope, the poetic voice, the design, the ideas, and the imagery developed in the earlier period. This continuity of tradition converts what would otherwise be a literary curiosity into a matter of considerable historical interest, and helps us to identify and interpret some of the strange but characteristic elements in later Romantic enterprises.

Here is one out of many available instances. It will have become apparent even from these brief summaries that certain terms, images, and quasi-mythical agents tend to recur and to assume a specialized reference to revolutionary events and expectations: the earthquake and the volcano, the purging fire, the emerging sun, the dawn of glad day, the awakening earth in springtime, the Dionysian figure of revolutionary destruction and the Apollonian figure of the promise of a bright new order. Prominent among these is a term which functions as one of the principal leitmotifs of Romantic literature. To Europe at the end of the eighteenth century the French Revolution brought what St. Augustine said Christianity had brought to the ancient world: hope. As Coleridge wrote [in "To William Wordsworth"], on first hearing Wordsworth's *Prelude* read aloud, the poet sang of his experience "Amid the tremor of a realm aglow,"

> When from the general heart of human kind
> Hope sprang forth like a full-born Deity!

and afterward, "Of that dear Hope afflicted and struck down. . . . " This is no ordinary human hope, but a universal, absolute, and novel hope which sprang forth from the Revolutionary events sudden and complete, like Minerva. Pervasively in both the verse and prose of the period, "hope," with its associated term, "joy," and its opposites, "dejection," "despondency," and "despair," are used in a special application, as shorthand for the limitless faith in human and social possibility aroused by the Revolution, and its reflex, the nadir of feeling caused by its seeming failure—as Wordsworth had put it, the "utter loss of hope itself / And things to hope for." (*The Prelude*, 1805, XI, 6-7.)

It is not irrelevant, I believe, that many seemingly apolitical poems of the later Romantic period turn on the theme of hope and joy and the temptation to abandon all hope and fall into dejection and despair; the recurrent emotional pattern is that of the key books of *The Excursion*, labeled "Despondency" and "Despondency Corrected," which apply specifically to the failure of millennial hope in the Revolution. But I want to apply this observation to one of those passages in *The Prelude* where Wordsworth suddenly breaks through to a prophetic vision of the hidden significance of the literal narrative. In the sixth book Wordsworth describes his first tour of France with Robert Jones in the summer of 1790, the brightest period of the Revolution. The mighty forms of Nature, "seizing a youthful fancy," had already "given a charter to irregular hopes," but now all Europe

> was thrilled with joy,
> France standing on the top of golden hours,
> And human nature seeming born again.

Sharing the universal intoxication, "when joy of one" was "joy for tens of millions," they join in feasting and dance with a "blithe host / Of Travellers" returning from the Federation Festival at Paris, "the great spousals newly solemnised / At their chief city, in the sight of Heaven." In his revisions of the 1805 version of *The Prelude*, Wordsworth inserted at this point a passage in which he sees, with anguished foreboding, the desecration by French troops of the Convent of the Chartreuse (an event which did not take place until two years later, in 1792). The travelers' way then brings them to the Simplon Pass.

Wordsworth's earlier account of this tour in the *Descriptive Sketches*, written mainly in 1791-92, had ended with the prophecy of a new earth emerging from apocalyptic fires, and a return to the golden age. Now, however, he describes a strange access of sadness, a "melancholy slackening." On the Simplon road they had left their guide and climbed ever upward, until a peasant told them that they had missed their way and that the course now lay downwards.

> Loth to believe what we so grieved to hear,
> For still we had hopes that pointed to the clouds,
> We questioned him again, and yet again;

but every reply "Ended in this,—*that we had crossed the Alps.*"

> Imagination . . .
> That awful Power rose from the mind's abyss
> Like an unfathered vapour that enwraps,
> At once, some lonely traveller; I was lost;
> Halted without an effort to break through;
> But to my conscious soul I now can say—
> "I recognise thy glory". . . .

Only now, in retrospect, does he recognize that his imagination had penetrated to the emblematic quality of the literal climb, in a revelation proleptic of the experience he was to recount in all the remainder of *The Prelude.* Man's infinite hopes can never be matched by the world as it is and man as he is, for these exhibit a discrepancy no less than that between his "hopes that pointed to the clouds" and the finite height of the Alpine pass. But in the magnitude of the disappointment lies its consolation; for the flash of vision also reveals that infinite longings are inherent in the human spirit, and that the gap between the inordinacy of his hope and the limits of possibility is the measure of man's dignity and greatness:

> Our destiny, our being's heart and home,
> Is with infinitude, and only there;
> With hope it is, hope that can never die,
> Effort, and expectation, and desire,
> And something evermore about to be.

In short, Wordsworth evokes from the unbounded and hence impossible hopes in the French Revolution a central Romantic doctrine; one which reverses the cardinal neoclassic ideal of setting only accessible goals, by converting what had been man's tragic error—the inordinacy of his "pride" that persists in setting infinite aims for finite man—into his specific glory and his triumph. Wordsworth shares the recognition of his fellow-Romantics, German and English, of the greatness of man's infinite *Sehnsucht* ["Yearning"]; his saving insatiability, Blake's "I want! I want!" Shelley's "the desire of the moth for the star"; but with a characteristic and unique difference, as he goes on at once to reveal:

> Under such banners militant, the soul
> Seeks for no trophies, struggles for no spoils
> That may attest her prowess, blest in thoughts
> That are their own perfection and reward. . . .

The militancy of overt political action has been transformed into the paradox of spiritual quietism: under such militant banners is no march, but a wise passiveness. This truth having been revealed to him, Wordsworth at once goes on to his apocalypse of nature in the Simplon Pass, where the *coincidentia oppositorum* of its physical attributes become the symbols of the biblical Book of Revelation:

> Characters of the great Apocalypse,
> The types and symbols of Eternity,
> Of first, and last, and midst, and without end.

This and its companion passages in *The Prelude* enlighten the

orphic darkness of Wordsworth's "Prospectus" for *The Recluse,* drafted as early as 1800, when *The Prelude* had not yet been differentiated from the larger poem. Wordsworth's aim, he there reveals, is still that of the earlier period of millennial hope in revolution, still expressed in a fusion of biblical and classical imagery. Evil is to be redeemed by a regained Paradise, or Elysium: "Paradise," he says, "and groves / Elysian, Fortunate Fields . . . why should they be / A history only of departed things?" And the restoration of Paradise, as in the Book of Revelation, is still symbolized by a sacred marriage. But the hope has been shifted from the history of mankind to the mind of the single individual, from militant external action to an imaginative act; and the marriage between the Lamb and the New Jerusalem has been converted into a marriage between subject and object, mind and nature, which creates a new world out of the old world of sense:

> For the discerning intellect of Man,
> When wedded to this goodly universe
> In love and holy passion, shall find these
> A simple produce of the common day.
> —I, long before the blissful hour arrives,
> Would chant, in lonely peace, the spousal verse
> Of this great consummation . . .
> And the creation (by no lower name
> Can it be called) which they with blended might
> Accomplish:—this is our high argument.

In the other Romantic visionaries, as in Wordsworth, naive millennialism produced mainly declamation, but the shattered trust in premature political revolution and the need to reconstitute the grounds of hope lay behind the major achievements—the shift to a spiritual and moral revolution which will transform our experience of the old world—is also the argument of a number of the later writings of Blake, Coleridge, Shelley, and, with all his differences, Hölderlin. An example from Shelley must suffice. Most of Shelley's large enterprises after *Queen Mab*—*The Revolt of Islam, Prometheus Unbound, Hellas*—were inspired by a later recrudescence of the European revolutionary movement. Shelley's view of human motives and possibilities became more and more tragic, and, like Blake after his *French Revolution,* he moved from the bald literalism of *Queen Mab* to an imaginative form increasingly biblical, symbolic, and mythic; but the theme continues to be the ultimate promise of a renovation in human nature and circumstances. In *Prometheus Unbound* this event is symbolized by the reunion of Prometheus and Asia in a joyous ceremony in which all the cosmos participates. But this new world is one which reveals itself to the purged imagination of Man when he has reformed his moral nature at its deep and twisted roots; and the last words of Demogorgon, the inscrutable agent of this apocalypse, describe a revolution of spirit whose sole agencies are the cardinal virtues of endurance, forgiveness, love, and, above all, hope—though a hope that is now hard to distinguish from despair:

> To suffer woes which Hope thinks infinite . . .
> To love, and bear; to hope till Hope creates
> From its own wreck the thing it contemplates . . .
> This is alone Life, Joy, Empire, and Victory!

"Two voices are there. . . . And, Wordsworth, both are thine." I have as yet said nothing about Wordsworth's *Lyrical Ballads* and related poems, although Hazlitt regarded these as the inauguration of a new poetic era and the close poetic equivalent to the revolutionary politics of the age. Yet the *Ballads* seem in every way antithetical to the poetry I have just described: instead of displaying a panoramic vision of present, past, and future in an elevated oracular voice, these poems undertake to represent realistic "incidents and situations from common life" in ordinary language and to employ "humble and rustic life" as the main source of the simple characters and the model for the plain speech.

Here are some of the reasons Hazlitt gives [in his *The Spirit of the Age,* 1825] for his claim that "the political changes of the day were the model on which [Wordsworth] formed and conducted his poetical experiments":

> His Muse (it cannot be denied, and without this we cannot explain its character at all) is a levelling one. It proceeds on a principle of equality, and strives to reduce all things to the same standard. . . .
>
> His popular, inartificial style gets rid (at a blow) of all the trappings of verse, of all the high places of poetry. . . . We begin *de novo,* on a tabula rasa of poetry. . . . The distinctions of rank, birth, wealth, power . . . are not to be found here. . . . The harp of Homer, the trump of Pindar and of Alcaeus, are still.

Making due allowance for his love of extravagance, I think that Hazlitt makes out a very plausible case. He shrewdly recognizes that Wordsworth's criteria are as much social as literary, and that by their egalitarianism they subvert the foundations of a view of poetry inherited from the Renaissance. This view assumed and incorporated a hierarchical structure of social classes. In its strict form, it conceived poetry as an order of well-defined genres, controlled by a theory of decorum whereby the higher poetic kinds represent primarily kings and the aristocracy, the humbler classes (in other than a subsidiary function) are relegated to the lowlier forms, and each poem is expressed in a level of style—high, middle, or low—appropriate, among other things, to the social status of its characters and the dignity of its genre. In England after the sixteenth century, this system had rarely been held with continental rigor, and eighteenth-century critics and poets had carried far the work of breaking down the social distinctions built into a poetic developed for an aristocratic audience. But Wordsworth's practice, buttressed by a strong critical manifesto, carried an existing tendency to an extreme which Hazlitt regarded as a genuine innovation, an achieved revolution against the *ancien régime* in literature. He is, Hazlitt said, "the most original poet now living, and the one whose writings could least be spared: for they have no substitute elsewhere." And Wordsworth has not only leveled, he has transvalued Renaissance and neoclassic aesthetics, by deliberately seeking out the ignominious, the delinquent, and the social outcast as subjects for serious or tragic consideration—not only, Hazlitt noted, "peasants, pedlars, and village-barbers," but also "convicts, female vagrants, gipsies . . . ideot boys and mad mothers." Hence the indignation of Lord Byron, who combined political liberalism with a due regard for aristocratic privilege and traditional poetic decorum:

> "Peddlers," and "Boats," and "Wagons"! Oh! ye shades
> Of Pope and Dryden, are we come to this?

In his Preface to *Lyrical Ballads* Wordsworth justified his undertaking mainly by the ultimate critical sanctions then available, of elemental and permanent "nature" as against the corruptions and necessarily short-lived fashions of "art." But Wordsworth also dealt with the genesis and rationale of *Lyrical Ballads* in several other writings, and in terms broader than purely critical, and these passages clearly relate his

poems of humble lives in the plain style to his concept and practice of poetry in the grand oracular style.

In the crucial thirteenth book of *The Prelude* Wordsworth describes how, trained "to meekness" and exalted by "humble faith," he turned from disillusionment with the "sublime / In what the Historian's pen so much delights / To blazon," to "fraternal love" for "the unassuming things that hold / A silent station in this beauteous world," and so to a surrogate for his lost revolutionary hopes:

> The promise of the present time retired
> Into its true proportion; sanguine schemes,
> Ambitious projects, pleased me less; I sought
> For present good in life's familiar face,
> And built thereon my hopes of good to come.

He turned, that is, away from Man as he exists only in the hopes of naive millennialists or the abstractions of the philosophers of perfectibility to "the man whom we behold / With our own eyes"; and especially to the humble and obscure men of the lower and rural classes, "who live / By bodily toil," free from the "artificial lights" of urban upper-class society, and utter the spontaneous overflow of powerful feelings ("Expressing liveliest thoughts in lively words / As native passion dictates"). "Of these, said I, shall be my song." But, he insists, in this new subject he continues to speak "things oracular," for though he is "the humblest," he stands in the great line of the "Poets, even as Prophets, each with each / Connected in a mighty scheme of truth," each of whom possesses "his own peculiar faculty, / Heaven's gift, a sense that fits him to perceive / Objects unseen before." And chief among the prophetic insights granted to Wordsworth is the discovery that Nature has the power to "consecrate" and "to breathe / Grandeur upon the very humblest face / Of human life," as well as upon the works of man, even when these are "mean, have nothing lofty of their own."

We come here to a central paradox among the various ones that lurk in the oracular passages of Wordsworth's major period: the oxymoron of the humble-grand, the lofty-mean, the trivial-sublime—as Hazlitt recognized when he said that Wordsworth's Muse "is distinguished by a proud humility," and that he "elevates the mean" and endeavors "(not in vain) to aggrandise the trivial." The ultimate source of this concept is, I think, obvious, and Wordsworth several times plainly points it out for us. Thus in *The Ruined Cottage* (1797-98) the Pedlar (whose youthful experiences parallel Wordsworth's, as the poet showed by later transferring a number of passages to *The Prelude*) had first studied the Scriptures, and only afterward had come to "*feel* his faith" by discovering the corresponding symbol-system, "the writing," in the great book of nature, where "the least of things / Seemed infinite," so that (as a "chosen son") his own "being thus became / Sublime and comprehensive. . . . Yet was his heart / Lowly"; he also learned to recognize in the simple people of rural life what Wordsworth in a note called "the aristocracy of nature." The ultimate source of Wordsworth's discovery, that is, was the Bible, and especially the New Testament, which is grounded on the radical paradox that "the last shall be first," and dramatizes that fact in the central mystery of God incarnate as a lowly carpenter's son who takes fishermen for his disciples, consorts with beggars, publicans, and fallen women, and dies ignominiously, crucified with thieves. This interfusion of highest and lowest, the divine and the base, as Erich Auerbach has shown, had from the beginning been a stumbling-block to readers habituated to the classical separation of levels of subject-matter and style, and Robert Lowth in the mid-eighteenth century still found it necessary to insist, as had Augustine and other theologians almost a millennium and a half earlier, that the style of the Bible had its special propriety and was genuinely sublime, and not, as it seemed to a cultivated taste, indecorous, vulgar, barbarous, grotesque. (pp. 53-66)

Wordsworth . . . in the period beginning about 1797, came to see his destiny to lie in spiritual rather than in overt action and adventure, and to conceive his radical poetic vocation to consist in communicating his unique and paradoxical, hence inevitably misunderstood, revelation of the more-than-heroic grandeur of the humble, the contemned, the ordinary, and the trivial, whether in the plain style of direct ballad-like representation, or in the elevated voice in which he presents himself in his office as recipient of this gift of vision. In either case, the mode in which Wordsworth conceived his mission evolved out of the ambition to participate in the renovation of the world and of man which he had shared with his fellow-poets during the period of revolutionary enthusiasm. Both the oracular and the plain poetry, in the last analysis, go back beyond Milton, to that inexhaustible source of radical thought, the Bible—the oracular poetry to the Old Testament prophets and their descendant, the author of the Book of Revelation, and the plain poetry to the story of Christ and to His pronouncements on the exaltation of the lowly and the meek. For the Jesus of the New Testament, as the Reverend Mark Wilks had said in 1791, was indeed "a revolutionary," though not a political one; and Wordsworth, in his long career as apologist for the Anglican Establishment, never again came so close to the spirit of primitive Christianity as in the latter 1790s when, according to Coleridge, he had been still "a Republican & at least a *Semi*-atheist." (pp. 71-2)

> *M. H. Abrams, "English Romanticism: The Spirit of the Age," in* Romanticism Reconsidered: Selected Papers from the English Institute, *edited by Northrop Frye, Columbia University Press, 1963, pp. 26-72.*

D. A. BEALE

[In the following excerpt, Beale analyzes the revolutionary, as distinct from radical, political implications of Romantic poetry.]

In 1946, Lionel Trilling lamented that the liberal humanism of his day found little or no expression in great imaginative literature, that there was no connection between the political ideas of liberal thinkers and 'the deep places of the imagination'. Given this, he insisted on the need 'to organise a new union between our political ideas and our imagination', because, since our fate is political, 'the only possibility of enduring it is to force into our definition of politics every human activity and every subtlety of every human activity'. Thirty years on and the new union between politics and imagination is still not achieved. Our growing distrust of politics and politicians produces merely 'protest' literature, which, however justified in its propagandas and protests, does not radically alter our apprehension of the world since it is frequently concerned to demonstrate a thesis rather than to explore the truths of human experience. 'Imagination' and 'Mind' in Trilling's sense seem still to have little to do with politics or our view of politics.

Fortunately, this division has not always existed. For the

great English Romantic poets such a divorce would have been unthinkable, for theirs is a politics deriving from an imaginative apprehension of Man's central humanness. In an age of Revolutionary fervour, it would have been difficult for any creature of imagination to be unaffected by that great turn of the human mind towards Freedom. What is striking, however, is not just the intensity of their sympathy for the upsurge of liberty and human brotherhood, but the range and profundity of their reaction. And it may be that Romanticism was that moment in Western cultural history when poetry and politics fused in a total imaginative sense of the nature of Man: that Freedom was the essential condition of Man's humanity. And this was a European phenomenon involving music, philosophy, religion, psychology, historiography, and fine art, as well as literature. The thrust of English Romanticism is revolutionary, and revolutionary in complex ways: it is not just revolutionary in politics alone, but revolutionary at a much deeper level, in terms of its exploration of the sources of any humanly valuable political revolution—namely in terms of a total revolution in consciousness and awareness; for unless Man's imaginative and conceptual apprehension of things is transformed, then there can be no possibility of political change of any substantial kind. And this attempt to transform the sensibilities of men is contingent upon the Romantic assertion of the inwardness of creative power, of the imagination as the central human faculty.

In the early 1790s, the Spirit of the Age was intoxicating: the phrase is Hazlitt's, and looking back later, he characterized the age as 'that glad dawn of the day-star of liberty; that spring-time of the world in which the hopes and expectations of the human race seemed opening in the same gay career with our own'. Wordsworth's exuberance is justly famous:

> Bliss was it in that dawn to be alive,
> But to be young was very Heaven!
> *The Prelude* (1805) Book X, 693-4

Behind such optimism lay the French Revolution, and, earlier, the American Revolution with its ringing affirmation, 'We hold these truths to be self-evident, that all men are created equal, that they are endowed by their Creator with certain unalienable Rights, that among these are Life, Liberty, and the Pursuit of Happiness'. Addressing the Society for the Commemoration of the Revolution in November 1789, Dr Richard Price exhorted,

> Be encouraged, all ye friends of freedom, and writers in its defence! The times are auspicious . . . Behold kingdoms admonished by you, starting from sleep, breaking their fetters, and claiming justice from their oppressors! Behold the light you have struck out, after setting AMERICA free, reflected to FRANCE, and there kindled into a blaze that lays despotism in ashes, and warms and illuminates all EUROPE!

Sentiments such as these, however, were not universally held, and, in Price's case, served to make him a *bête noire* in Burke's celebrated attack on the French Revolution. It is no part of my purpose here to repudiate Burke: his combination of intellectual power and sustained compassion reveals a mind actively engaged in politics in a profound way. His view is of society as an organic whole, growing organically out of its past,

> a partnership not only between those who are living, but between those who are living, those who are dead, and those who are to be born. Each con-

tract of each particular state is but a clause in the great primaeval contract of eternal society, linking the lower with the higher natures, connecting the visible and invisible world, according to a fixed compact sanctioned by the inviolable oath which holds all physical and all moral natures, each in their appointed place.

In some ways, a splendid vision, but it is, nevertheless, hierarchic and, within the society of Burke's time, social hardship and injustice were immense, partly as a consequence of increased industrialisation and rapid urban growth. For the disaffected, Burke's arguments were all very well, but why should there be an indulged aristocracy and a disenfranchised and deprived poor? Against Burke's affirmation of the prerogatives of class and wealth, Paine asserted the Rights of Man. Instead of Burke's view of the need for monarchy, Paine grumbled that 'the palaces of kings are built on the ruins of the bowers of paradise'. Intellectually, of course, Paine is very much Burke's inferior, but if we'd wanted a crushing answer to Burke, we could, in 1794, have opened a volume of poetry, uniquely presented in illuminated form, and found this, Blake's magnificent poem, 'London':

> I wander thro' each charter'd street,
> Near where the charter'd Thames does flow,
> And mark in every face I meet
> Marks of weakness, marks of woe.
>
> In every cry of every Man,
> In every Infant's cry of fear,
> In every voice, in every ban,
> The mind-forg'd manacles I hear.
>
> How the Chimney-sweeper's cry
> Every black'ning Church appalls;
> And the hapless Soldier's sigh
> Runs in blood down Palace walls.
>
> But most thro' midnight streets I hear
> How the youthful Harlot's curse
> Blasts the new born Infant's tear,
> And blights with plagues the Marriage hearse.

In these lines human suffering, repressive control, child-labour, the complacent theism of the churches, and the poisoning of man's sexual life are orchestrated into a massive vision of horror. The power of imagination, and the huge indignation at appalling social injustice derive here not from any pro/con party argument, but from a felt sense of lived human consequences. And these consequences, as Blake showed elsewhere, derived not from party *per se,* and not just from the traditional bases of typical government activity like order, law, religious orthodoxy, and control, but from the enduring hunger for an order of any kind, even if perverse and hostile to the human: in short, from a division in man related to the dominance of the rationalizing intellect. Amongst other things, what has happened in *The Songs of Innocence and Experience* is a shift from generalisations about men, to the truth of the individual life, the difference between considering man from the perspective of a national constitution, and considering man as man. And in the Romantic period, the condition of men in England was appalling. The English governing class, terrified that Jacobinism might spread to England, became enormously repressive: radicals agitating for parliamentary reform were regarded as subversive; even peaceful efforts to bring about social changes of a fundamental kind, and changes in institutions, were treated as high treason; some radicals were hanged, others imprisoned or transport-ed. The Combinations Acts proscribed trade unions, and, in 1819 for example, one James Watson was found guilty at the Manchester Assizes, and sentenced to twelve months jail 'for a conspiracy to raise the wages of those employed in the art, craft, or mystery of weaving'. 'In 1688 a member of the errant poor could be put to death for some fifty crimes; by 1819 his chances of capital felony had risen to an indeterminate height by the addition of 187 new capital statutes, each literally fascistic', according to Carl Woodring [see Further Reading]. More interest, apparently, was expressed in passing laws about hunting and poaching than about the poverty of the labouring classes.

In February 1812, Lord Byron, in the House of Lords, was in the minority in opposing the Framebreakers Bill designed to make the Luddites' smashing of weaving frames a capital offence. Working from the principle that mankind 'must not be sacrificed to improvements in mechanism', Byron spoke of the disaffected weavers as 'men liable to conviction, on the clearest evidence, of the capital crime of poverty', as a result of which the 'wretched mechanic was famished into guilt'. 'I have traversed the seat of war in the Peninsula, I have been in some of the most oppressed provinces of Turkey; but never under the most despotic of infidel governments did I behold such squalid wretchedness as I have seen since my return in the very heart of a Christian country . . . Is death the remedy for a starving and desperate populace? Will the famished wretch who has braved your bayonets be appalled by your gibbets? . . . will he be dragooned into tranquillity?' A few days later, in *The Morning Post,* Byron published 'An Ode to the Framers of the Frame Bill':

> Men are more easily made than machinery—
> Stockings fetch better prices than lives—
> Gibbets on Sherwood will heighten the scenery,
> Shewing how Commerce, how Liberty thrives!

Men were being sacrificed to a brutal and inhuman industrialism. On 16th August, 1819, a peaceful, orderly gathering of some 50,000 workers in St. Peter's Fields, Manchester, was broken up by yeomanry and the 15th Hussars with consequent loss of life, ironically called the Massacre of Peterloo, after Waterloo four years earlier. Shelley responded to this with *The Masque of Anarchy,* which attacked the hypocrisies and frauds of the Castlereagh administration, and advocated passive resistance as the way to triumph: 'Ye are many, they are few'.

Such a climate naturally provoked opposition, and it is in the difference between kinds of opposition that the revolutionary element in Romantic poetry is best seen. A direct assault on such injustices came from radical writers like Godwin, Holcroft, Bage, radical rather than revolutionary to the extent that they operated at the level of opposing institutions rather than going to the sources of the institutions' operations. The dangers for these men were considerable. Indeed, Godwin's *Political Justice* might have led to his arrest if it had not been for the fact that Pitt allowed it to be sold at three guineas, assuming that the poor and disaffected for whom it was intended would be unable to afford it. Pitt, however, was circumvented because workers contributed together, pooled their money, and bought copies which were passed around among them. These writers are hardly read now, and this may have something to do with the fact that their sphere of operations is local: their reforming zeal is directed against specific institutions and ideologies, and the conditions to which these give rise, the savagery of law, and the injustice of class. In comparison with Romantic poetry, these social protest/propaganda novels are limited to the extent that they are confined by the prominence of their specific antagonisms, so that the struggle is one of surfaces only. For the Romantics, the very existence of these abhorrent surface conditions was symptomatic of something deeper, forces of repressive and oppressive control which had become actualised in those specific forms which promoted the counterthrust of the radicals. Clearly, the radicals remain locked with the externals, so that the actuality of conditions/institutions not only gives rise to, but also determines the level of the radical attack. The root problem remains untouched.

The Romantic assault, on the other hand, is thoroughgoing, and incarnates a massive repudiation of orthodoxies, and it operates at multiple levels. In basic terms, the Romantic revolt is a break with those orthodoxies which, for them, resulted in fragmentation: hence they reject what they believed to be eighteenth-century notions of perception, of social mechanism, of abstract language, and evolve instead a different perspective which I propose to call mythic. At all levels, the emphases shift towards modes of greater wholeness, of unity, and mythic structures become an enacted mode of relationship and liberation. For the Romantics, the contemporary view of things was reductive, since it separated one thing from another, man from man; reduced nature to mechanical order, and split men from it. By its crude empiricist/associationist mechanics it split faculties of mind, dividing man within himself, crippling his instinctual life; and imposed the brutal formalities of state, religion, and law upon man.

For them, any mode of thinking which was divisive was to be deplored, because it resulted in division within man, and effected a split between man and man, man and nature, and so on. And to them, this was precisely what was happening; the horrors of oppression derived from man's alienation from his true role as part of a living, vital universe informed by love. The Locke tradition, involving Newton and Bacon (Blake's unholy trinity), had exalted Reason, Nature, and Law at the expense of value, resulting in a world of fact, a universe of death. . . . In a world of such denuded empiricism, the human consequences involved the enclosure of men within an illusion of fixed, unchangeable structures, mental, political, moral, religious: emotion and imagination were debased, and man's instinctual life splintered and shrivelled.

Blake's is probably the most comprehensive of all the Romantic attacks on this, for Blake saw that the consequences of the Lockean/Newtonian explanation of mind and universe, and their relationship, could only be an enclosing prison producing 'the cavern'd man' lit by the windows of the five senses, which are for Blake the limits of error. Blake celebrated the liberating possibilities of 'Eternal Science' and 'Sweet Science', setting them against the 'Self-Destroying Beast form'd Science' which enforces an unsatisfactory vision of man because the rigid conceptions inherent in scientific presuppositions were carried over into the moral life. And law, at this level, was devoid of humanness. In *The French Revolution,* Orleans says,

> . . . for fire delights in its form.
> But go, merciless man! enter into the infinite labyrinth of
>   another's brain
> Ere thou measure the circle that he shall run. Go, thou
>   cold recluse, into the fires

> Of another's high flaming rich bosom, and return uncon-
>   sum'd, and write laws.

II. 189-192

Again, Blake's attack on eighteenth-century limits of order is linked directly to those boundless energies of man divided and crippled by the harsh morality of a cruel law. His image of repressive force is the fallen god of the rationalising selfhood, Nobodaddy, or Urizen, who, in *The First Book of Urizen,* rejects the exuberance of the contraries of eternal life for the bogus repose of solidity, a stony law he calls holiness in his self-absorption:

> I have sought for a joy without pain,
> For a solid without fluctuation.
> Why will you die, O Eternals?
> Why live in unquenchable burnings?

II, 4:10-13

Out of the obsessions of his limited selfhood, he produces the iron laws of prudence which constitute the Net of Religion:

> One command, one joy, one desire,
> One curse, one weight, one measure,
> One King, one God, one Law.

II, 4:38-40

Such things were contingent upon a rigid repressive theist universe, deriving from orthodox Judaeo-Christian theology with its assumption of a hidden creator absent from the world, apart in a blinding cloud of holiness, manifesting his love in laws hostile to man's impulses because they mechanized him. Blake's view was that such laws had split mind from body, made the latter sinful, and consequently etiolated the human by the prohibition of moral law and the analytic abstractions of mind. Men were thus divided within themselves, split from the world, and progressively shrunken in isolation—for Blake, a system of slavery. Blake's principle of recovery, of course, is the figure of Los, the Imagination: 'I must Create a System or be enslav'd by another Man's'. But Los creates his own system 'to deliver Individuals from those Systems'; it is a system which dissolves.

Running through the Romantics is a revulsion from the formulations of abstract theory, from all attempts to fix experience in terms of definable, predictable laws of action, since these come to predominate over the individual life, and limit even the possibilities of experience. For the Romantics, the consequences of all this in art were depressing. The old rhetoric was inadequate since it functioned by locating words and meanings within long-established traditions of value and order, and the nature of its language was such that it precluded that imaginative, extensive reference which they sought as poets. What the Romantics sought was not a fixed order but a structure of meaning. Speaking generally, by the 1760s language was a discursive tool, a frame for analysis and abstraction rather than a poetic medium. What had been the rich doctrine of Concordia Discors, a vital harmony achieved by tension and contrariety, had become merely the balancing in stasis of similar and dissimilar, leading to crude analogies between man and nature. Instead of earlier modes of analogical thinking, analogies were now constructs lacking any interior correspondence.

As a consequence of such rigidity, however, orders were seen to interlock, religion, politics, society, class, culture, and so on, so that the Romantic shift is not just a shift in poetic alone, but at all levels of awareness. And it is essentially revolutionary, politically and poetically.

Portrait of William Wordsworth at age forty-eight by Benjamin Robert Haydon.

Against the universe of death, the divorce between mind and nature, the Romantics oppose their own felt, concrete experience of unity, of the point

> . . . when the light of sense
> Goes out, but with a flash that has revealed
> The invisible world . . .
> *The Prelude* (1850) Book VI, 600-602

or when

> . . . we are laid asleep
>
> In body, and become a living soul:
> While with an eye made quiet by the power
> Of harmony, and the deep power of joy,
> We see into the life of things.
> "Tintern Abbey," ll. 45-49

In other words, in the immediacy of unanalysed awareness. Clearly, such poetry is subjective, inevitably so, since, as in Coleridge's case, he'd *felt* the world differently to the way the eighteenth century insisted that it was; his mind 'feels as if it ACHED to be hold and know something GREAT—something ONE and INDIVISIBLE'.

Blake insists that 'if the doors of perception were cleansed, everything would appear to man as it is, infinite'. Blake, like Shelley after him, argues that man's attitude does not just reflect, but radically alters man's world, so that it lies in the state of the mind whether or not the universe will be paradisal, or 'a shape of error'. Wordsworth and Coleridge do the same in their metaphors of creative perception, especially in the recurring image of a wedding of man and nature leading to a new heaven and a new earth, discovering the power of renovating the universe of death in the imaginative act of creative perception. It is no accident, for example, that another word for the poet is 'seer'.

In *The Prelude,* Wordsworth speaks of the life of everyday renovated by a coalition of mind and nature in the act of perception, by an 'ennobling interchange / Of action from without and from within', between 'the object seen and eye that sees'. Perception is not just a creative sentient act, but also a unifying one: 'to behold' is a cooperative interaction of man and nature. To quote Coleridge, '—and this I call *I*—the identifying the Percipient and the Perceived'. Perception in this sense involves a complex relationship between man and nature. Quoting Coleridge again,

> —In looking at objects of Nature while I am thinking, as at yonder moon dim-glimmering thro' the dewy window-pane, I seem rather to be seeking, as it were ASKING, a symbolical language for something within me that already and forever exists, than observing any thing new. Even when the latter is the case, yet still I have always an obscure feeling as if that new phaenomenon were the dim Awaking of a forgotten or hidden Truth of my inner Nature / It is still interesting as a Word, a Symbol! It is *LOGOS,* the Creator! (and the Evolver!)

Out of this transaction, then, evolves the Symbol, not as if it were a picture of something else 'out there', but as something that implicates, and is part of, the complex nature of this relationship, opening up hitherto unknown levels of reality. And the Symbol as it functions in Romantic poetry is testament to the richness of experience in the organically creative encounter of mind and not-mind. In this sense, a Symbol is a configuration of relationship, of the dynamic unity of mind and nature. Coleridge's definition, for all its tortuousness, is nevertheless vitally illuminating:

> A symbol is characterised by a translucence of the Special in the Individual, or of the General in the Especial or of the Universal in the General. Above all by the translucence of the Eternal through and in the Temporal. It always partakes of the Reality which it renders intelligible; and while it enunciates the whole, abides itself as a living part in that Unity, of which it is the representative.

At the political level, perception and revolution are linked. Schiller, for example, in his *On the Aesthetic Education of Man* (1793), internalizes the chiliastic fervour of the French Revolution into aesthetic terms; 'If man is ever to solve that problem of politics in practice, he will have to approach it through the problem of the aesthetic, because it is only through Beauty that man makes his way to Freedom'. For Schiller, the Revolution had failed because it had neglected the need for a change of consciousness, 'the moral possibility is lacking', and he went on to point out that the aesthetic state can only be accomplished by a total revolution of man's consciousness, 'a complete revolution in his whole way of feeling is required'.

Both Wordsworth and Coleridge embody political implications in metaphors of man's relationship with nature; words such as 'despotism' and 'tyranny' are frequently used in their discussions of sense perception. This is partly why the 'spots of time' are so nourishing to Wordsworth, because in those earlier experiences 'the tyranny of the eye' over the mind did not exist. For him, there was then

> . . . the deepest feeling that the mind
> Is lord and master, and that outward sense
> Is but the obedient servant of her will.
> *The Prelude* (1805) Book XI, 271-273

The political implications are clear enough. Seeing the failure of the French Revolution, these poets transfer the focus from revolutionary war to liberation from imprisonment by any pre-cast view, which, consolidating over the act of individual perception, converts it into a merely habitual response. In other words, this is a shift to liberation in terms of the mind's experience in perception. In Coleridge's poem 'France: An Ode', we can see this shift, as the poem turns on the conversation of political elements (slavery and liberty) into metaphors of mind in relation to Nature. As France invades Switzerland, the high hopes of the poem fall away—freedom can neither be won, nor imposed by any external power. That is to say, a revolution conducted by those who are perceptually enslaved, whose minds are imprisoned by the most basic limits of the physical senses, merely replaces one slavery by another slavery:

> The Sensual and the Dark rebel in vain,
> Slaves by their own compulsion! In mad game
> They burst their manacles and wear the name
> Of Freedom, graven on a heavier chain!
> O Liberty! . . .
>
> ll. 85-89

As M. H. Abrams says [in *Natural Supernaturalism* (see Further Reading)]: 'The poem closes in an exemplary Romantic situation: the speaker alone on a windy cliff, fronting the open landscape, and experiencing essential liberty in the power of his being to unite with, and so to repossess, the scene before him, in an act of enfranchised perception which is an act of spontaneous love',—the emotion which in Romantic Poetry is called Joy. And it is clear here, in retrospect, why Blake's source of regenerative and revolutionary power shifted from the energy of Orc in the Lambeth Books to the creativity of Los building the city of Golgonooza, since only in creativity can the fall into division be transformed into the joy of unification.

Clearly the Romantic poets embody a greater density of awareness than the radical prose writers, since they go beyond the overt specifics of politics to the underlying configurations and patterns of human impulse; and this is to say, in part, that for as long as we confine our study of Romantic theories of the imagination within the limits of pure aesthetic theory we do the Romantics a profound disservice. The imagination, creative and unifying, reveals through its symbol-making power not only the vitalism and organicism of the universe and man's unity with it, but also the sense of men as a community—men united in common humanity, cherishing and respecting individuality within a communal framework: 'Love of Nature leads to Love of Man'.

Going further, a distinctive feature of the Romantics is their acute sense of the historical significance of their own time, and this issues, in their poetry, in a complex fusion of the contemporary and the symbolic. The keystone of the high Romantic political argument is, quite simply, Liberty—individual liberty, freedom of thought and feeling, national liberty; and since for them men could only achieve their full humanness if free, indeed, that freedom alone was the guar-

antee of that humanness, they repudiated those elements which threatened and destroyed liberty. Monarchy and government become for them a dehumanised and dehumanising power struggle leading to war, to self-interest, slaughter, and national suppression; at home in terms of taxes, law, and reactionary canting about patriotism, and abroad in terms of power exerted over the conquered. The Church, on the other hand, imposes the hypocrisies of charity, war, self-interested salvation, and so on, instead of nourishing the human, offering brutality and cruelty instead of Christ's great doctrine as Blake saw it: 'The spirit of Jesus is continual forgiveness of Sin'. We remember Blake's 'The Human Abstract',

> Pity would be no more
> If we did not make somebody poor . . .

The union of State and Church, Blake's 'Tree of Mystery', where the state becomes an object of near-religious veneration, and the church an object of state power, is thus morally and humanly culpable for the Romantics. With the exception of Keats, all the Romantics in their protests against these things were subjected in some way or other to secret police activity. The rigidities of habit and the structures of complacency, by the sheer fact that they seek to control and suppress rather than open things up to discussion, prove the end of any creative activity of mind. In real terms, such traditional ways of life are essentially ways of death. Against the self-justifying cant of an age of suppression, war and terror, the Romantics bring not a sword but peace. As Milton rejected the earlier epic conventions of war for the epic of the wayfaring Christian, so the Romantics evolve a new epic structure: no God, merely the mind of man and Nature; the three-term dialectic has become a two-term dialectic—Nature and Man in their reciprocal interchange take on the creative power of God. In our time, a poet like Wallace Stevens can tell us, 'We say God and the imagination are one'. And with the Romantics, the range spans the apocalyptic humanism of Blake and Shelley, and the agnostic humanism of Keats.

With Byron and Shelley, Liberty is of the essence in their politics; Byron's clarion-call was heard all over Europe:

> Yet, Freedom! yet thy banner, torn but flying,
> Streams like the thunder-storm AGAINST the wind!
> *Childe Harold's Pilgrimage*. Canto IV, XCVIII

As with Blake, for both of them, the American and French Revolutions, and industrial development in terms of mechanism were of crucial importance, but their revolt involves a metaphysical dimension also: on the one hand, Satan's rebellion against God as dramatised in Milton's *Paradise Lost,* coming from an earlier time when men had fought to achieve civil liberties; and on the other hand, the myth of Prometheus, the Titan rebel against Jupiter, incarnate in part in Blake's earlier giant form Orc, but becoming in the work of both Byron and Shelley a terribly ambiguous mythic symbol.

It may be useful to bear in mind that Robert Southey, a former radical turned Tory, branded Byron and Shelley as the Satanic school of poetry; Byron, of course, annihilated him in *The Vision of Judgement* and few people have really read Southey since. In their time, their poetry was subjected to much moral vituperation (largely on the part of Tory reviewers and Tory churchmen) based on already established orders of morality, whereas the Romantics were concerned to introduce the possibility of a more centrally humane ethic. In our time they have both been repudiated by some practitioners of close verbal criticism, Shelley as being obscure, facile, and having no grasp of the actual, Byron as having written much Romantic hokum and three satires of merit. Amongst other things, it is saddening to see solid orthodoxies built up by critics around writers whose whole drift was to repudiate orthodoxies, and to open the mind to a fresh liberated and liberating view of things. Blake, in the prose introduction to *Jerusalem,* argues that 'Poetry Fetter'd Fetters the Human Race': it is not just governments that fetter; critics might consider their fettering power as well. Given the limitations of time, I propose to confine myself to Shelley's poetry where the possibilities of myth are more immediately apparent than in Byron.

It should be clear by now that reform means different things to the radicals and to the Romantics. For the radicals, reform means the amelioration of conditions à la Robert Owen. For the Romantics, it is a question of RE-FORM, totally transforming man's view of the world. At the basest level of sense-experience, as we have seen, all is surface and separate: man is alienated from nature, men, and himself. There is no sense of living connection or unity except in the merest accidents of contingency. Opposing this with a kind of organic vitalism, the problem was to find a way of writing adequate to a vision of felt unity, and incarnating a felt sense of communion. Further, to find, as it were, a myth for the age, a structure capable of sustaining the new view, was of the essence. If the older orders were to be rejected, men still needed some kind of structure of meaning. As Coleridge put it, translating Schiller's *Die Piccolomini,* 'Still the heart doth need a language . . . .'.

In Shelley's greatest poetry, this attempt to find a new form issues in mythmaking. It was Shelley, of course, who was expelled from Oxford for writing a pamphlet, *The Necessity of Atheism,* and it was Shelley who distributed libertarian pamphlets in Dublin. Shelley reacted to political issues in various ways. His overtly social poems in 1819, for example *Song to the Men of England* and *Lines on the Castlereagh Administration,* were radical enough to be handed around as exhortatory literature among the Chartists later. On the other hand, his version of *Oedipus Tyrannus,* which he comically called *Swellfoot the Tyrant,* a satiric treatment of the 'green bag' incident of 1817, was yet another way of dealing with current political matters. *Queen Mab,* written in 1812, is in essence mid-way between the radical novelists and Shelley's own later myths, and though it is perverse and unsuccessful as poetry, it was extraordinarily influential as polemic, becoming, in this century, a handbook for the unemployed. But for Shelley seeking a more comprehensive mode, it was unsatisfactory. *Prometheus Unbound,* a myth structured in the form of a lyrical drama, is Shelley's unique artistic achievement: and moreover it is one of the central achievements of English Romanticism. At first sight, mythmaking may seem to have little to do with revolutionary politics, and such doubts arise possibly because the brute facts of our political life intrude upon us so obdurately. But for Shelley, as for Blake, mythmaking is politically crucial. In their earlier poetry, Blake and Shelley often grappled with the externals of the revolutionary situation, and this is gradually subverted by the recognition that it is the internal impulses which must be attacked since these bring about the abhorrent externals. Hence, in Blake, we find the shift from the Orc-Urizen cycle to the creative, transforming power of Los, the artist, the imagination. And this shift occurs also in Shelley from *Queen Mab* and *The Revolt of Islam* to *Prometheus Unbound.* And this represents a profound redirecting of revolutionary imper-

atives; and it is revolutionary, since it not only seeks to transform the mind, but to dramatise and incarnate that very transformation as something humanly possible. Instead of the surface radical attempt to transform something 'out there', the emphasis now is on realising something always possible within man, but which is habitually suppressed. In Blake's view, all men contain within themselves 'The Eternal Great Humanity Divine'. The point is to release it. So it is with Shelley. And in mythmaking, revolutionary ardour politically, and the revolutionary view of human perception run together.

The Romantics' way out of the dilemma of too close a focus on details is to turn from the realistic narrative of the radical prose writers to self-created mythologies, extended dramatisations of regenerated perception and a renovated world. Only by exploiting the imagination to the full could the reader's imaginative sympathies be transformed so that the overtly political could be seen in its widest human context, and the awareness generated kept clear of any specific ideology. To release human power is to join with the power of the cosmos, to heal the breach, and to restore man to his central, living implication in the world. Hence, in *Prometheus Unbound,* we have images of internal impulse breaking the aridities of the surface, images of springs, of fire, and the crucial, central, seismic image of the volcano.

If, as Rousseau had insisted, man's condition was man-made, then man could, and ought, to unmake it, and remake it. If he remade it in the old way, then the cycles of defeat could only continue. But if the imagination were transformed, then we could be pulled away from habitual structures, cut free from easy complacencies, and compelled to the more majestic struggle to become free. The mind is creative; reality is brought into being by experience, by a constructive act of mind. If, as Rousseau asserted, civilization's origin was human, based on human models, then we could create new models.

Surface politics is contingent upon the basest surface senses of crude empiricism, as I've tried to suggest, which, to reorientate Paine's argument about Burke, sees only the plumage and forgets the dying bird. The bare limits of the senses produce a world of surfaces like, say, the concentration on skin-colour, for example, which imprison us as well as the world, leading to a conceptual and imaginative slavery in a world of separateness, apartness, discreteness, where connections are of the cause and effect variety. Clearly, it is easy to control such an order since things are reduced to the lowest common denominators, notwithstanding the illusions of certainty and order. This leaves the human impoverished, and one of the measures of our shrunken humanity is the appalling state of politics, a thing of surfaces, of bogus order. If things are split apart then we get a world of aggregates not of union. 'As a man is, So he Sees', says Blake. If a man is spiritually dead, he deprives life of its vital power, converts men and flowers into things, and we are left with what Wallace Stevens calls 'the malady of the quotidian',

> . . . the dumbfounding abyss
> Between us and the object . . .

To assert union is one thing; to evolve an adequate language is another. Shelley, I think, solves the problem brilliantly. When language is used in terms of 'communication', union is mechanised; indeed, things remain separate and are, as in analogies lacking any interior correspondence, merely connected rather than unified. Even in terms of visual impression, the extra letters in the word 'communication' have sundered and mechanised the word 'communion'. If deprived of its capacity for communion, language declines in real terms; it possesses merely frozen formality, not shaping form. It lacks the adventure of a living encounter. In *Prometheus Unbound,* Prometheus

> . . . gave man speech, and speech created thought,
> Which is the measure of the universe . . .
>
> II, iv, 72-73

Clearly, speech unfetters man from silence: he creates words, and creates with words, and words, if we are truly alive, should not refetter us in the inert conventions of cliché, but should testify in their infinite capacity to all the vibrations of the imaginative and probing mind. This has its dangers. The Promethean figure is ambiguous in Romanticism; he represents revolt, endurance, heroism, but it is revolt into the problematic condition of freedom. The ambiguity of the Promethean figure insists that an increase in consciousness carries with it a corresponding increase in despair, something which Kierkegaard was to analyse in detail later in the nineteenth century.

However problematic, this is a higher condition than inertia. To quote Shelley in *Julian and Maddalo,*

> . . . it is our will
> That thus enchains us to permitted ill—
> We might be otherwise—we might be all
> We dream of happy, high, majestical.
> Where is the love, beauty, and truth we seek
> But in our mind? and if we were not weak
> Should we be less in deed than in desire?
>
> ll. 170-176

We must turn from the illusions of fixity and narrow certainty and enter the spiral of design with all its complexity and all its attendant hazards. And the unity achieved here is far greater than any imposed order, and is incarnated in the symbols of poetry. In *The Revolt of Islam,* Shelley speaks of language as

> Clear elemental shapes, whose smallest change
> A subtler language within language wrought:
> The key of truths . . .
>
> Canto VII, 3111-3113

In *A Defence of Poetry,* he speaks of poetic language as being 'vitally metaphorical; that is, it marks the before unapprehended relations of things and perpetuates their apprehension . . .'. Metaphor is unity, and language is thus the central articulation of human communion. Syntax is not so much a basic law of words, but a mysterious structure within which the rich meanings of words are drawn into relationship. And a human community is a human syntax, an order not imposed from without, but evolving in terms of holding in tension the multiplicity, diversity and ambiguity of individual men in their encounters with experience, and with each other. Language, and its form in poetry, thus incarnates the human imperatives of the poem. What had been formerly discrete and separate elements are compelled into a larger whole, eliciting a massive pattern of implication, wedding diversity into complex unity. In *Adonais,* Shelley insists on a cosmic 'plastic stress' which

> Sweeps through the dull dense world, compelling there,
> All new successions to the forms they wear . . .
>
> ll. 382-383

In *Prometheus Unbound,* he envisions another stress, adamantine, holding all men in a vast communion with themselves and with the universe:

> Man, oh, not men! a chain of linked thought,
> Of love and might to be divided not,
> Compelling the elements with adamantine stress . . .
> Man, one harmonious soul of many a soul,
> Whose nature is its own divine control,
> Where all things flow to all, as rivers to the sea . . .
>
> IV 394-402

So the creative mind creates and incarnates that energetic process in the act of poetic creation, and in its artefact. And by extension, this too is a paradigm of political action. To see, amidst the diversities of men, an underlying unity of enriching possibility, and to release its energies as directing forces for human good, is *the* political problem and obligation. The poet performs it. In this sense, politics is a creative release of all this manifold diversity into a harmonious becoming of possibility. And this is not Platonic idealism at all, since that sees reality as something beyond the human: Shelley sees this possibility in terms of dimensions of humanness buried and suppressed within man, requiring to be liberated. And just as the poet is concerned to release what is already within us, so the mythic structure of *Prometheus Unbound* releases that which is latent in man, mind, and nature, and which is habitually ignored. Myth here celebrates a new order and a new way of looking, a revolution in imaginative awareness.

[In his *Essay on Man,* 1925] Ernst Cassirer describes mythic thinking like this:

> Myth has, as it were, a double face. On the one hand it shows as a conceptual, on the other hand a perceptual structure. It is not a mere mass of unorganised and confused ideas. If myth did not PERCEIVE the world in a different way, it could not *judge* or *interpret* it in its specific manner. We must go back to the deepest stratum of perception to understand the character of mythical thought.

This applies to *Prometheus Unbound* very closely, and out of this mythmaking emerges Shelley's glowing vision of man irradiated by love, revealed in his true humanness:

> The loathsome mask has fallen, the man remains
> Sceptreless, free, uncircumscribed, but man
> Equal, unclassed, tribeless, and nationless.
> Exempt from awe, worship, degree, the king
> Over himself; just, gentle, wise . . .
>
> III iv 193-197

This springs from no facile optimism. Prometheus' triumph is achieved in terms of internal change, and the Jupiter he overthrows is not destroyed, merely subjugated—a symbolic dramatisation of man's ability to overcome his own self-destructive potentialities. But Jupiter is always there, always potential in the human soul, and unless man maintains his self-won integrity by love, Jupiter will rise again. Real integrity is created amidst tension, not apart from it.

At the end of *Hellas,* in the great final choric hymn of a renovated cosmos,

> The world's great age begins anew,
> The golden years return,
>
> ll. 1060-1061

Shelley counters the hope and optimism with a doubt which repudiates any accusations of naïve optimism:

Oh, cease! must hate and death return?
Cease! must men kill and die? . . .
The world is weary of the past,
Oh, might it die or rest at last!

                                        ll. 1096-1101

For Shelley, clearly, the break out of the cycle was not easy, and even at the end of the 'Ode to the West Wind', the unanswered question, and the implication of human revolution within the cycles of the seasons, suggest a hard road to freedom. There is no guarantee that his words will rekindle man into his fully liberated humanness—only the passionate hope that they may do so:

> Drive my dead thoughts over the universe
> Like withered leaves to quicken a new birth!
> And, by the incantation of this verse,
>
> Scatter, as from an unextinguished hearth
> Ashes and sparks, my words among mankind!
> Be through my lips to unawakened earth
>
> The Trumpet of a prophecy! O, Wind,
> If Winter comes, can Spring be far behind?
>
>   ll. 63-70

It was Shelley's profound belief that the imagination, as *the* creative faculty, was also the civilising force in society. In *A Defence of Poetry,* he makes this rhapsodic claim:

> The great secret of morals is love, or a going out of our own nature and an identification of ourselves with the beautiful which exists in thought, action, or person, not our own. A man, to be greatly good, must imagine intensely and comprehensively; he must put himself in the place of another and of many others; the pains and pleasures of his species must become his own. The great instrument of moral good is the imagination. . . .

In *Prometheus Unbound,* we hear of 'the unpastured sea hungering for calm'. Only in this kind of way, with a capacity for love informed by a civilising imagination, could that kind of fulfilling calm be achieved. But it is of the essence of the revolutionary thrust of Romantic poetry that the vision of a renovated world is not so much an achieved artefact as the power of bringing such a world into being in the first place. It is never finally accomplished, but is always an eternal and enduring possibility that might be achieved. As Fichte put it, 'To be free is nothing: to become free is very heaven'.

At the political level, Romantic poetry strives to bring within its orbit those elements which it is often more comfortable or convenient to omit; in this way it attempts to incarnate honestly the real complexity of revolutionary possibilities. And for as long as we continue to regard literature as a means of gratifying our personal sensibilities; for as long as we continue to dismiss Romantic poetry because, according to a narrow view of aesthetics, the quality of feeling in it may not be quite right, it may be that we are guilty of a culpable literacy, for we cannot and must not pretend that man's inhumanity to man 'is irrelevant to the responsible life of the imagination' [George Steiner, *Language and Silence,* 1969].

And for those who are disposed to dismiss the Romantic vision as a dream, it may be necessary to invoke Yeats, who says in four telling words, 'In dreams begins responsibility'. Responsibility, towards humanity and towards that liberty in which alone man realises his true humanness, is the unacknowledged apex of the Romantic mind. (pp. 47-65)

D. A. Beale, "The Trumpet of a Prophecy: Revolution and Politics in English Romantic Poetry," in Theoria, *Pietermaritzburg, Vol. XLVIII, May, 1977, pp. 47-67.*

RAYMOND WILLIAMS

[*Williams was an English critic whose literary theory is informed by his socialist ideology and his belief that a reader's perception of literature is directly related to cultural attitudes which are subject to change over the course of time. In the following excerpt, he discusses the changes that occurred during the Romantic period regarding conceptions of art and the artist's role in society.*]

Than the poets from Blake and Wordsworth to Shelley and Keats there have been few generations of creative writers more deeply interested and more involved in study and criticism of the society of their day. Yet a fact so evident, and so easily capable of confirmation, accords uneasily in our own time with that popular and general conception of the 'romantic artist' which, paradoxically, has been primarily derived from study of these same poets. In this conception, the Poet, the Artist, is by nature indifferent to the crude worldliness and materialism of politics and social affairs; he is devoted, rather, to the more substantial spheres of natural beauty and personal feeling. The elements of this paradox can be seen in the work of the Romantic poets themselves, but the supposed opposition between attention to natural beauty and attention to government, or between personal feeling and the nature of man in society, is on the whole a later development. What were seen at the end of the nineteenth century as disparate interests, between which a man must choose and in the act of choice declare himself poet or sociologist, were, normally, at the beginning of the century, seen as interlocking interests: a conclusion about personal feeling became a conclusion about society, and an observation of natural beauty carried a necessary moral reference to the whole and unified life of man. The subsequent dissociation of interests certainly prevents us from seeing the full significance of this remarkable period, but we must add also that the dissociation is itself in part a product of the nature of the Romantic attempt. Meanwhile, as some sort of security against the vestiges of the dissociation, we may usefully remind ourselves that Wordsworth wrote political pamphlets, that Blake was a friend of Tom Paine and was tried for sedition, that Coleridge wrote political journalism and social philosophy, that Shelley, in addition to this, distributed pamphlets in the streets, that Southey was a constant political commentator, that Byron spoke on the frame-riots and died as a volunteer in a political war; and, further, as must surely be obvious from the poetry of all the men named, that these activities were neither marginal nor incidental, but were essentially related to a large part of the experience from which the poetry itself was made. It is, moreover, only when we are blinded by the prejudice of the dissociation that we find such a complex of activities in any way surprising. For these two generations of poets lived through the crucial period in which the rise both of democracy and of industry was effecting qualitative changes in society: changes which by their nature were felt in a personal as well as in a general way. In the year of the French Revolution, Blake was 32, Wordsworth 19, Coleridge 17 and Southey 15. In the year of Peterloo, Byron was 31, Shelley 27, Keats 24. The dates are sufficient reminder of a period of political turmoil and controversy fierce enough to make it very difficult for even the least sensitive to be indifferent. Of the slower, wider, less observable changes that we call the Industrial Revolution, the landmarks are less obvious; but the lifetime of Blake, 1757 to 1827, is, in general, the decisive period. The changes that we receive as record were experienced, in these years, on the senses: hunger, suffering, conflict, dislocation; hope, energy, vision, dedication. The pattern of change was not background, as we may now be inclined to study it; it was, rather, the mould in which general experience was cast.

It is possible to abstract a political commentary from the writings of these poets, but this is not particularly important. The development of Wordsworth, Coleridge and Southey from differing degrees of revolutionary ardour in their youth to differing degrees of Burkean conservatism in their maturity is interesting. A distinction between the revolutionary principles of Shelley and the fine libertarian opportunism of Byron is useful. A reminder that Blake and Keats cannot be weakened to some ideal vagueness, but were, as men and poets, passionately committed to the tragedy of their period, is timely. In every case, however, the political criticism is now less interesting than the wider social criticism: those first apprehensions of the essential significance of the Industrial Revolution, which all felt and none revoked. Beyond this, again, is a different kind of response, which is a main root of the idea of culture. At this very time of political, social and economic change there is a radical change also in ideas of art, of the artist, and of their place in society. It is this significant change that I wish to adduce.

There are five main points: first, that a major change was taking place in the nature of the relationship between a writer and his readers; second, that a different habitual attitude towards the 'public' was establishing itself; third, that the production of art was coming to be regarded as one of a number of specialized kinds of production, subject to much the same conditions as general production; fourth, that a theory of the 'superior reality' of art, as the seat of imaginative truth, was receiving increasing emphasis; fifth, that the idea of the independent creative writer, the autonomous genius, was becoming a kind of rule. In naming these points, it is of course necessary to add at once that they are clearly very closely interrelated, and that some might be named as causes, and some as effects, were not the historical process so complex as to render a clear division impossible.

The first characteristic is clearly a very important one. From the third and fourth decades of the eighteenth century there had been growing up a large new middle-class reading public, the rise in which corresponds very closely with the rise to influence and power of the same class. As a result, the system of patronage had passed into subscription-publishing, and thence into general commercial publishing of the modern kind. These developments affected writers in several ways. There was an advance, for the fortunate ones, in independence and social status—the writer became a fully-fledged 'professional man'. But the change also meant the institution of 'the market' as the type of a writer's actual relations with society. Under patronage, the writer had at least a direct relationship with an immediate circle of readers, from whom, whether prudentially or willingly, as mark or as matter of respect, he was accustomed to accept and at times to act on criticism. It is possible to argue that this system gave the writer a more relevant freedom than that to which he succeeded. In any event, against the dependence, the occasional servility and the subjection to patronal caprice had to be set the direct relation of the act of writing with at least some part of society, personally known, and the sense, when relations were fortunate, that the writer 'belonged'. On the other hand, against the independence and the raised social status which success on the market commanded had to be set similar liabilities to caprice and similar obligations to please, but now, not liabilities to individuals personally known, but to the workings of an institution which seemed largely impersonal. The growth of the 'literary market' as the type of a writer's relations with his readers has been responsible for many fundamental changes of attitude. But one must add, of course, that such a growth is always uneven, both in its operations and in its effects. It is not perhaps until our own century that it is so nearly universal as to be almost dominant. By the beginning of the nineteenth century the institution was established, but it was nevertheless modified by many kinds of survival of earlier conditions. The important reactions to it were, however, laid down at this time.

One such reaction, evidently, is that named as the second point: the growth of a different habitual attitude towards the 'public'. Writers had, of course, often expressed, before this time, a feeling of dissatisfaction with the 'public', but in the early nineteenth century this feeling became acute and general. One finds it in Keats: 'I have not the slightest feel of humility towards the Public'; in Shelley: 'Accept no counsel from the simple-minded. Time reverses the judgement of the foolish crowd. Contemporary criticism is no more than the sum of the folly with which genius has to wrestle.' One finds it, most notably and most extensively, in Wordsworth:

> Still more lamentable is his error who can believe that there is anything of divine infallibility in the clamour of that small though loud portion of the community, ever governed by factitious influence, which, under the name of the PUBLIC, passes itself upon the unthinking, for the PEOPLE. Towards the Public, the Writer hopes that he feels as much deference as it is entitled to; but to the People, philosophically characterized, and to the embodied spirit of their knowledge . . . his devout respect, his reverence, is due.

It is, of course, easier to be respectful and reverent to 'the People, philosophically characterized', than to a Public, which noisily identifies itself. Wordsworth, in his conception of the People, is drawing heavily on the social theory of Burke, and for not dissimilar reasons. However the immediate argument went, whatever the reactions of actual readers, there was thus available a final appeal to 'the embodied spirit . . . of the People': that is to say, to an Idea, an Ideal Reader, a standard that might be set above the clamour of the writer's actual relations with society. The 'embodied spirit', naturally enough, was a very welcome alternative to the market. Obviously, such an attitude then affects the writer's own attitude to his work. He will not accept the market quotation of popularity:

> Away then with the senseless iteration of the word *popular* applied to new works in poetry, as if there were no test of excellence in this first of the fine arts but that all men should run after its productions, as if urged by an appetite, or constrained by a spell.

He will continue to insist, in fact, on an Idea, a standard of excellence, the 'embodied spirit' of a People's knowledge, as something superior to the actual course of events, the actual run of the market. This insistence, it is worth emphasizing, is one of the primary sources of the idea of Culture. Culture, the 'embodied spirit of a People', the true standard of excellence, became available, in the progress of the century, as the court of appeal in which real values were determined, usually in opposition to the 'factitious' values thrown up by the market and similar operations of society.

The subjection of art to the laws of the market, and its consideration as a specialized form of production subject to much the same conditions as other forms of production, had been prefigured in much late-eighteenth-century thinking. Adam Smith had written:

> In opulent and commercial societies to think or to reason comes to be, like every other employment, a particular business, which is carried on by a very few people, who furnish the public with all the thought and reason possessed by the vast multitudes that labour.

This is significant as a description of that special class of persons who from the 1820s were to be called 'intellectuals'. It describes, also, the new conditions of specialization of the artist, whose work, as Adam Smith had said of knowledge, was now in fact

> purchased, in the same manner as shoes or stockings, from those whose business it is to make up and prepare for the market that particular species of goods.

Such a position, and such a specialization of function, followed inevitably from the institution of commercial publishing. The novel, in particular, had quickly become a commodity; its main history as a literary form follows, as is well known, precisely the growth of these new conditions. But the effects were also obvious in poetry, on which the impact of a market relationship was inevitably severe. Alongside the rejection of the Public and of Popularity as standards of worth, increasing complaint was made that literature had become a trade. The two things, in fact, were normally treated together. Sir Egerton Brydges wrote in the 1820s:

> It is a vile evil that literature is become so much a trade all over Europe. Nothing has gone so far to nurture a corrupt taste, and to give the unintellectual power over the intellectual. Merit is now universally esteemed by the multitude of readers that an author can attract. . . . Will the uncultivated mind admire what delights the cultivated?

Similarly in 1834 Tom Moore spoke of the

> lowering of standard that must necessarily arise from the extending of the circle of judges; from letting the mob in to vote, particularly at a period when the market is such an object to authors.

He went on to distinguish between the 'mob' and the 'cultivated few'. It is obvious, here, how the adjective 'cultivated' contributed to the newly necessary abstractions, 'cultivation' and 'culture'. In this kind of argument, 'culture' became the normal antithesis to the market.

I have emphasized this new type of an author's relationship to his readers because I believe that such matters are always central in any kind of literary activity. I turn now to what is clearly a related matter, but one which raises the most difficult issues of interpretation. It is a fact that in this same period in which the market and the idea of specialist production received increasing emphasis there grew up, also, a system of thinking about the arts of which the most important elements

are, first, an emphasis on the special nature of art-activity as a means to 'imaginative truth', and, second, an emphasis on the artist as a special kind of person. It is tempting to see these theories as a direct response to the actual change in relations between artist and society. Certainly, in the documents, there are some obvious elements of compensation: at a time when the artist is being described as just one more producer of a commodity for the market, he is describing himself as a specially endowed person, the guiding light of the common life. Yet, undoubtedly, this is to simplify the matter, for the response is not merely a professional one. It is also (and this has been of the greatest subsequent importance) an emphasis on the embodiment in art of certain human values, capacities, energies, which the development of society towards an industrial civilization was felt to be threatening or even destroying. The element of professional protest is undoubtedly there, but the larger issue is the opposition on general human grounds to the kind of civilization that was being inaugurated.

Romanticism is a general European movement, and it is possible to relate the new ideas, as they arise, solely to a larger system of ideas in European thinking as a whole. The influence of Rousseau, of Goethe, of Schiller and of Chateaubriand can certainly be traced. Indeed, if we consider the ideas in abstraction, we can take the idea of the artist as a special kind of person, and of the 'wild' genius, as far back as the Socratic definition of a poet in Plato's *Ion.* The 'superior reality' of art has a multitude of classical texts, and, within our period, is an obvious relation with the German idealist school of philosophy and its English dilution through Coleridge and Carlyle. These relations are important, yet an idea can perhaps only be weighed, only understood, in a particular mind and a particular situation. In England, these ideas that we call Romantic have to be understood in terms of the problems in experience with which they were advanced to deal.

A good example is a definition in one of the early documents of English Romanticism, [Edward] Young's *Conjectures on Original Composition* (1759):

> An Original may be said to be of a *vegetable* nature; it rises spontaneously from the vital root of genius; it *grows,* it is not *made;* Imitations are often a sort of *manufacture,* wrought up by those *mechanics, art* and *labour,* out of pre-existent materials not their own.

This is a piece of very familiar Romantic literary theory: contrasting the spontaneous work of genius with the formal imitative work bound by a set of rules. As Young also writes:

> Modern writers have a *choice* to make . . . they may soar in the regions of *liberty,* or move in the soft fetters of easy *imitation.*

But what Young is saying when he defines an 'original' is, if we look at his terms, very closely linked with a whole general movement of society. It is certainly literary theory, but as certainly it is not being formulated in isolation. When he says of an original that 'it grows, it is not made', he is using the exact terms on which Burke based his whole philosophical criticism of the new politics. The contrast between 'grows' and 'made' was to become the contrast between 'organic' and 'mechanical' which lies at the very centre of a tradition which has continued to our own day. Again, when he defines an 'imitation', Young condemns it in terms of the very industrial processes which were about to transform English society: 'a sort of *manufacture, wrought up* by those *mechanics . . . out of pre-existent materials not their own'.* The point may or may not hold in literary theory; but these are certainly the terms and the implied values by which the coming industrial civilization was to be condemned.

Burke condemned the new society in terms of his experience (or his idealization) of the earlier society. But increasingly as the huge changes manifested themselves the condemnation became specialized, and, in a sense, abstract. One part of the specialization was the growth of the standard of Cultivation or Culture; another part, closely related to this and later in fact to combine with it, was the growth of the new idea of Art. This new idea of a superior reality, and even of a superior power, is strikingly expressed by Blake:

> 'Now Art has lost its mental charms
> France shall subdue the World in Arms.'
> So spoke an Angel at my birth,
> Then said, 'Descend thou upon Earth.
> Renew the Arts on Britain's Shore,
> And France shall fall down and adore.
> With works of Art their armies meet,
> And War shall sink beneath thy feet.
> But if thy Nation Arts refuse,
> And if they scorn the immortal Muse,
> France shall the arts of Peace restore,
> And save thee from the Ungrateful shore.'
> Spirit, who lov'st Britannia's Isle,
> Round which the Fiends of Commerce smile. . . .

In Blake, the professional pressures can be easily discerned, for he suffered badly in 'the desolate market where none come to buy'. He reminds us of Young, when he attacks

> the interest of the Monopolizing Trader who Manufactures Art by the Hands of Ignorant Journeymen till . . . he is Counted the Greatest Genius who can sell a Good-for-Nothing Commodity for a Great Price.

But, equally, Blake's criticism goes far beyond the professional complaint: the Imagination which, for him, Art embodies is no commodity, but

> a Representation of what Eternally Exists, Really and Unchangeably.

It is in such a light that the inadequacies of existing society and of the quality of life which it promotes are to be seen and condemned.

It is important to measure the strength of this claim, for we shall misunderstand it if we look only at some of the later divagations of the idea of Genius. The ambiguous word in Young's definition is 'Imitation', which in nearly all Romantic theory acquired a heavily derogatory sense. This is because 'imitation' was understood to mean 'imitation of works already done', that is to say conformity to a given set of rules. The eloquence deployed against the set of rules is both remarkable and, in the end, tedious. What was happening, technically, was no more than a change of convention, which when it is of any magnitude normally carries such eloquence as a by-product. To the degree that the change is more than a change in convention—and changes in convention only occur when there are radical changes in the general structure of feeling—the word 'Imitation' is particularly confusing. For indeed, in the best 'classicist' theory, Imitation is the term normally used to describe what Blake has just described, and what all the Romantic writers emphasized: 'a Representation of what Eternally Exists, Really and Unchangeably'.

Imitation, at its best, was not understood as adherence to somebody else's rules; it was, rather, 'imitation of the universal reality'. An artist's precepts were not so much previous works of art as the 'universals' (in Aristotle's term) or permanent realities. This argument, really, had been completed in the writings of the Renaissance.

The tendency of Romanticism is towards a vehement rejection of dogmas of method in art, but it is also, very clearly, towards a claim which all good classical theory would have recognized: the claim that the artist's business is to 'read the open secret of the universe'. A 'romantic' critic like Ruskin, for example, bases his whole theory of art on just this 'classicist' doctrine. The artist perceives and represents Essential Reality, and he does so by virtue of his master faculty Imagination. In fact, the doctrines of 'the genius' (the autonomous creative artist) and of the 'superior reality of art' (penetration to a sphere of universal truth) were in Romantic thinking two sides of the same claim. Both Romanticism and Classicism are in this sense idealist theories of art; they are really opposed not so much by each other as by naturalism.

What was important at this time was the stress given to a mode of human experience and activity which the progress of society seemed increasingly to deny. Wordsworth might hold with particular conviction the idea of the persecuted genius, but there is a more general significance in his attitudes to poetry, and indeed to art as a whole:

> High is our calling, Friend!—Creative Art . . .
> Demands the service of a mind and heart
> Though sensitive, yet in their weakest part
> Heroically fashioned—to infuse
> Faith in the whispers of the lonely Muse
> While the whole world seems adverse to desert.

These are the lines to the painter Haydon, in December 1815. They are significant for the additional reason that they mark the fusing into the common 'sphere of imaginative truth' of the two separate *arts,* or skills, of poetry and painting. While in one sense the market was specializing the artist, artists themselves were seeking to generalize their skills into the common property of imaginative truth. Always, this kind of emphasis is to be seen as a mode of defence: the defensive tone in Wordsworth's lines is very obvious, and in this they are entirely characteristic. At one level the defence is evidently compensatory: the height of the artists' claim is also the height of their despair. They defined, emphatically, their high calling, but they came to define and to emphasize because they were convinced that the principles on which the new society was being organized were actively hostile to the necessary principles of art. Yet, while to see the matter in this way is to explain the new emphasis, it is not to explain it away. What was laid down as a defensive reaction became in the course of the century a most important positive principle, which in its full implications was deeply and generally humane.

There are many texts from which this principle can be illustrated, but the most characteristic, as it is also among the best known, is Wordsworth's Preface of 1800 to the *Lyrical Ballads.* Here it is not only the truth but the general humanity of poetry which Wordsworth emphasizes: first, by attacking those

> who talk of Poetry as of a matter of amusement and idle pleasure; who will converse with us as gravely about a *taste* for poetry, as they express it, as if it

were a thing as indifferent as a taste for rope-dancing, or Frontiniac or Sherry.

The concept of *taste*—which implies one kind of relationship between writer and reader—is inadequate because

> it is a metaphor, taken from a *passive* sense of the human body, and transferred to things which are in their essence *not* passive—to intellectual *acts* and *operations.* . . . But the profound and the exquisite in feeling, the lofty and universal in thought and imagination . . . are neither of them, accurately speaking, objects of a faculty which could ever without a sinking in the spirit of Nations have been designated by the metaphor *Taste.* And why? Because without the exertion of a cooperating *power* in the mind of the Reader, there can be no adequate sympathy with either of these emotions: without this auxiliary impulse, elevated or profound passion cannot exist.

This states in another way an important criticism of the new kind of social relationships of art: when art is a commodity, taste is adequate, but when it is something more, a more active relationship is essential. The 'something more' is commonly defined:

> Aristotle, I have been told, has said, that Poetry is the most philosophic of all writing: it is so: its object is truth, not individual and local, but general and operative; not standing upon external testimony, but carried alive into the heart by passion; truth which is its own testimony, which gives competence and confidence to the tribunal to which it appeals, and receives them from the same tribunal. . . . The Poet writes under one restriction only, namely, the necessity of giving immediate pleasure to a human Being possessed of that information which may be expected from him, not as a lawyer, a physician, a mariner, an astronomer, or a natural philosopher, but as a Man. . . . To this knowledge which all men carry about with them, and to these sympathies in which, without any other discipline than that of our daily life, we are fitted to take delight, the Poet principally directs his attention. . . . He is the rock of defence for human nature; an upholder and preserver, carrying everywhere with him relationship and love. In spite of difference of soil and climate, of language and manners, of laws and customs: in spite of things silently gone out of mind, and things violently destroyed; the Poet binds together by passion and knowledge the vast empire of human society, as it is spread over the whole earth, and over all time.

This is the case which, in its essentials, was to be eloquently restated by Shelley in his *Defence of Poetry.* It is the case which extends through Ruskin and Morris into our own century, when Poetry, as Wordsworth would have approved, has been widened to Art in general. The whole tradition can be summed up in one striking phrase used by Wordsworth, where the poet, the artist in general, is seen as

> an upholder and preserver, carrying everywhere with him relationship and love.

Artists, in this mood, came to see themselves as agents of the 'revolution for life', in their capacity as bearers of the creative imagination. Here, again, is one of the principal sources of the idea of Culture; it was on this basis that the association of the idea of the general perfection of humanity with the practice and study of the arts was to be made. For here, in the work

of artists—'the first and last of all knowledge . . . as immortal as the heart of man'—was a practicable mode of access to that ideal of human perfection which was to be the centre of defence against the disintegrating tendencies of the age.

The emphasis on a general common humanity was evidently necessary in a period in which a new kind of society was coming to think of man as merely a specialized instrument of production. The emphasis on love and relationship was necessary not only within the immediate suffering but against the aggressive individualism and the primarily economic relationships which the new society embodied. Emphasis on the creative imagination, similarly, may be seen as an alternative construction of human motive and energy, in contrast with the assumptions of the prevailing political economy. This point is indeed the most interesting part of Shelley's *Defence:*

> Whilst the mechanist abridges, and the political economist combines, labour, let them beware that their speculations, for want of correspondence with those first principles which belong to the imagination, do not tend, as they have in modern England, to exasperate at once the extremes of luxury and want. . . . The rich have become richer, and the poor have become poorer; and the vessel of the state is driven between the Scylla and Charybdis of anarchy and despotism. Such are the effects which must ever flow from an unmitigated exercise of the calculating faculty.

This is the general indictment which we can see already forming as a tradition, and the remedy is in the same terms:

> There is no want of knowledge respecting what is wisest and best in morals, government, and political economy, or at least, what is wiser and better than what men now practise or endure. But . . . we want the creative faculty to imagine that which we know; we want the generous impulse to act that which we imagine; we want the poetry of life: our calculations have outrun conception; we have eaten more than we can digest. . . . Poetry, and the Principle of Self, of which Money is the visible incarnation, are the God and Mammon of the world.

The most obvious criticism of such a position as Shelley's is that, while it is wholly valuable to present a wider and more substantial account of human motive and energy than was contained in the philosophy of industrialism, there are corresponding dangers in specializing this more substantial energy to the act of poetry, or of art in general. It is this specialization which, later, made much of this criticism ineffectual. The point will become clearer in the later stages of our enquiry, where it will be a question of distinguishing between the idea of culture as art and the idea of culture as a whole way of life. The positive consequence of the idea of art as a superior reality was that it offered an immediate basis for an important criticism of industrialism. The negative consequence was that it tended, as both the situation and the opposition hardened, to isolate art, to specialize the imaginative faculty to this one kind of activity, and thus to weaken the dynamic function which Shelley proposed for it. We have already examined certain of the factors which tended towards this specialization; it remains now to examine the growth of the idea of the artist as a 'special kind of person'.

The word *Art,* which had commonly meant 'skill', became specialized during the course of the eighteenth century, first to 'painting', and then to the imaginative arts generally. *Artist,* similarly, from the general sense of a skilled person, in ei-

Manuscript of Ode to a Nightingale *by Keats.*

ther the 'liberal' or the 'useful' arts, had become specialized in the same direction, and had distinguished itself from *artisan* (formerly equivalent with *artist,* but later becoming what we still call, in the opposite specialized sense, a 'skilled worker'), and of course from *craftsman.* The emphasis on skill, in the word, was gradually replaced by an emphasis on sensibility; and this replacement was supported by the parallel changes in such words as *creative* (a word which could not have been applied to art until the idea of the 'superior reality' was forming), *original* (with its important implications of spontaneity and vitalism; a word, we remember, that Young virtually contrasted with *art* in the sense of skill), and *genius* (which, because of its root association with the idea of *inspiration,* had changed from 'characteristic disposition' to 'exalted special ability', and took its tone in this from the other affective words). From *artist* in the new sense there were formed *artistic* and *artistical,* and these, by the end of the nineteenth century, had certainly more reference to 'temperament' than to skill or practice. *Aesthetics,* itself a new word, and a product of the specialization, similarly stood parent to *aesthete,* which again indicated a 'special kind of person'.

The claim that the artist revealed a higher kind of truth is, as we have seen, not new in the Romantic period, although it received significant additional emphasis. The important corollary of the idea was, however, the conception of the art-

ist's autonomy in this kind of revelation; his substantive element, for example, was now not faith but genius. In its opposition to the 'set of rules', the autonomous claim is of course attractive. Keats puts it finely:

> The Genius of Poetry must work out its own salvation in a man: It cannot be matured by law and precept, but by sensation and watchfulness in itself. That which is creative must create itself.

Our sympathy with this rests on the emphasis on a personal discipline, which is very far removed from talk of the 'wild' or 'lawless' genius. The difference is there, in Keats, in the emphasis on 'the Genius of Poetry', which is impersonal as compared with the personal 'genius'. Coleridge put the same emphasis on law, with the same corresponding emphasis on autonomy:

> No work of true genius dares want its appropriate form, neither indeed is there any danger of this. As it must not, so genius cannot, be lawless; for it is even this that constitutes it genius—the power of acting creatively under laws of its own origination.

This is at once more rational and more useful for the making of art than the emphasis, at least as common in Romantic pamphleteering, on an 'artless spontaneity'. Of the Art (sensibility) which claims that it can dispense with art (skill) the subsequent years hold more than enough examples.

As literary theory, the emphases of Keats and Coleridge are valuable. The difficulty is that this kind of statement became entangled with other kinds of reaction to the problem of the artist's relations with society. The instance of Keats is most significant, in that the entanglement is less and the concentration more. If we complete the sentence earlier quoted from him we find:

> I have not the slightest feel of humility towards the public, or to anything in existence,—but the eternal Being, the Principle of Beauty, and the Memory of Great Men.

This is characteristic, as is the famous affirmation:

> I am certain of nothing but of the holiness of the Heart's affections, and the truth of Imagination. What the Imagination seizes as Beauty must be truth—whether it existed before or not—for I have the same idea of all our passions as of Love; they are all, in their sublime, creative of essential Beauty. . . . The Imagination may be compared to Adam's dream—he awoke and found it truth.

But the account of the artist's personality which Keats then gives is, in his famous phrase, that of 'Negative Capability . . . when a man is capable of being in uncertainties, mysteries, doubts, without any irritable reaching after fact and reason'. Or again:

> Men of Genius are great as certain ethereal Chemicals operating on the Mass of neutral intellect—but they have not any individuality, any determined Character—I would call the top and head of those who have a proper self, Men of Power.

It is certainly possible to see this emphasis on passivity as a compensatory reaction, but this is less important than the fact that Keats's emphasis is on the poetic *process* rather than on the poetic *personality.* The theory of Negative Capability could degenerate into the wider and more popular theory of the poet as 'dreamer', but Keats himself worked finely, in experience, to distinguish between 'dreamer' and 'poet', and if in the second *Hyperion* his formal conclusion is uncertain, it is at least clear that what he means by 'dream' is something as hard and positive as his own skill. It is not from the fine discipline of a Keats that the loose conception of the romantic artist can be drawn.

Wordsworth, in the 'Preface to *Lyrical Ballads*', shows us most clearly how consideration of the poetic process became entangled with more general questions of the artist and society. In discussing his own theory of poetic language, he is in fact discussing communication. He asserts, reasonably and moderately, the familiar attitude to the Public:

> Such faulty expressions, were I convinced they were faulty at present, and that they must necessarily continue to be so, I would willingly take all reasonable pains to correct. But it is dangerous to make these alterations on the simple authority of a few individuals, or even of certain classes of men; for where the understanding of an Author is not convinced, or his feelings altered, this cannot be done without great injury to himself: for his own feelings are his stay and support.

This has to be said on the one side, while at the same time Wordsworth is saying:

> The Poet thinks and feels in the spirit of human passions. How, then, can his language differ in any material degree from that of all other men who feel vividly and see clearly?

And so:

> Among the qualities . . . enumerated as principally conducing to form a Poet, is implied nothing differing in kind from other men, but only in degree. . . . The Poet is chiefly distinguished from other men by a greater promptness to think and feel without immediate external excitement, and a greater power in expressing such thoughts and feelings as are produced in him in that manner. But these passions and thoughts and feelings are the general passions and thoughts and feelings of men.

Of these chief distinctions, while the first is a description of a psychological type, the second is a description of a skill. While the two are held in combination, the argument is plausible. But in fact, under the tensions of the general situation, it became possible to dissociate them, and so to isolate the 'artistic sensibility'.

The matter is exceptionally complex, and what happened, under the stress of events, was a series of simplifications. The obstruction of a certain kind of experience was simplified to the obstruction of poetry, which was then identified with it and even made to stand for it as a whole. Under pressure, art became a symbolic abstraction for a whole range of general human experience: a valuable abstraction, because indeed great art has this ultimate power; yet an abstraction nevertheless, because a general social activity was forced into the status of a department or province, and actual works of art were in part converted into a self-pleading ideology. This description is not offered for purposes of censure; it is a fact, rather, with which we have to learn to come to terms. There is high courage, and actual utility, if also simplification, in Romantic claims for the imagination. There is courage, also, in the very weakness which, ultimately, we find in the special pleading of personality. In practice there were deep insights, and great

works of art; but, in the continuous pressure of living, the free play of genius found it increasingly difficult to consort with the free play of the market, and the difficulty was not solved, but cushioned, by an idealization. The last pages of Shelley's *Defence of Poetry* are painful to read. The bearers of a high imaginative skill become suddenly the 'legislators', at the very moment when they were being forced into practical exile; their description as 'unacknowledged', which, on the theory, ought only to be a fact to be accepted, carries with it also the felt helplessness of a generation. Then Shelley at the same time claims that the Poet

> ought personally to be the happiest, the best, the wisest, and the most illustrious of men;

where the emphasis, inescapably, falls painfully on the *ought*. The pressures, here personal as well as general, create, as a defensive reaction, the separation of poets from other men, and their classification into an idealized general person, 'Poet' or 'Artist', which was to be so widely and so damagingly received. The appeal, as it had to be, is beyond the living community, to the

> mediator and . . . redeemer, Time.

Over the England of 1821 there had, after all, to be some higher Court of Appeal. We are not likely, when we remember the lives of any of these men, to be betrayed into the irritability of prosecution, but it is well, also, if we can avoid the irritability of defence. The whole action has passed into our common experience, to lie there, formulated and unformulated, to move and to be examined. 'For it is less their spirit, than the spirit of the age.' (pp. 30-48)

Raymond Williams, "The Romantic Artist," in his Culture and Society: 1780-1950, *Columbia University Press, 1958, pp. 30-48.*

PHILOSOPHY, RELIGION, AND ROMANTIC POETRY

L. J. SWINGLE

[In the following essay, Swingle warns against approaching Romantic poetry with expectations of discovering simplistic norms and doctrines, arguing that the poets used verse to question the underlying assumptions and myriad possibilities of belief rather than to assert any specific doctrine.]

As the sad case of Othello reminds us, false assumptions often lead to the destruction of beloved objects. The reader of Romantic poetry, it seems to me, often plays Othello to that poetry's Desdemona. He approaches the poetry with false assumptions and, loving not wisely but too well, does the poetry in. The Iago figure in this drama is the idea of Romanticism. It whispers in the reader's ear, "Dynamism," "Organicism," a seductive tale of "Isms." Thus the reader is made to forget the obvious signs of a fundamental skeptical streak that runs through Romantic poetry. He falls into the simplistic assumption (often unconsciously, one suspects) that the Romantic poets seek predominantly to tell us things, that they write basically a poetry of doctrine, offering the "Isms" of Romanticism for reader consumption. So the reader approaches the poetry as if it were doctrinal or at least meant to be so; and in this way, like Desdemona, Romantic poetry is much abused.

This doctrinal assumption leads to two distinct types of error which appear frequently in criticism of Romantic poetry. The first is a creative error. Expecting the poetry to communicate doctrine, the reader makes it do so. He creates "messages." Coming to a poem like Blake's "The Tyger," for example, with its world of awed, agonizing questions, the reader feels the proper response must be to answer the questions. "Did he who made the Lamb make thee?"—Yes! (or, depending on quirks in the reader's psychology, No!). The reader addicted to this creative error burrows through Romantic poems, looking for the doctrines. He thinks that Keats is telling us, "Beauty is truth, truth beauty," and he believes that it is Coleridge who urges, "He prayeth well, who loveth well." Assuming that the poetry tells him things, he creates a satisfaction about his assumption. The second error is a condemnatory one. Here, too, the reader comes to the poetry looking for doctrine, but he does not proceed to create what is not there. Rather, seeing that the poetry does not fulfill his expectation, he condemns it for not doing so or, more frequently, for trying to do so and failing. It is this sort of reader who condemns Wordsworth's "Tintern Abbey," for example, for obscurity of language and phrasing. Expecting Wordsworth to offer him doctrines he cannot find, he simply decides that Wordsworth is not doing a good job.

Perhaps this merely suggests that the Iago figure needs reforming, that we need a more adequate theory of Romanticism. But I think not. The problem arises rather from the fact that many readers try to make a theory of Romanticism serve also for a theory of Romantic poetry—a service it cannot really perform. Romanticism has to do with a fundamental state of mind, with patterns of ontological and normative commitments. One can think of it as the state of mind out of which Romantic poetry is generated, or as the state of mind toward which Romantic poetry moves, or perhaps even as both. But Romantic poetry itself, while related in complex ways to this state of mind, is not identical with it. To come to terms with Romantic poetry, we have to deal with activities rather than with "states." Our concern is with immediate means and ends, with movements the poet attempts to accomplish, and ways in which he attempts to manipulate the reader. If things are working well, the poetry is like a drama which the reader becomes caught up in. To get into the poetry successfully, what is needed is not so much a theory of Romanticism but a theory of Romantic poetry, a model of the drama the poetry creates, something which explores the manipulations the poet exercises upon us as we read his poetry.

Like any poetry, Romantic poetry is full of doctrinal elements. But it is important to think about what part these elements play in the poems. A poem can be designed to communicate doctrine, explain its meaning or implications, convince the reader of the truth value or usefulness of a given doctrine—in which cases doctrine plays the leading role in the poem: it is what the poem is about. But doctrinal elements can also play a supporting role. They can be used to promote some end beyond themselves. For example:

    Work A: And, spite of pride, in erring reason's spite,
               One truth is clear: Whatever IS, is RIGHT.
    Work B: "One truth is clear," the White Rabbit said,
               "Whatever IS, is RIGHT."

    Work C: When I see the rising sun, then I know
               one truth is clear: Whatever IS, is
               RIGHT.

In Works B and C, character and situation are merged with doctrine, and in the resultant drama the doctrinal element plays a quite different role from the one it plays in Work A. The doctrinal element functions as part of a piece of data, and works to create questions in our minds. In B, for example, the White Rabbit *says* this, but does he think it is true, does he know it, how does he know it? And there are other kinds of questions: does this doctrine apply only to a White Rabbit's value system, or also to a man's? Likewise in C, questions are raised, centering most obviously on the problem of the relationship between experience and knowledge. What is important here is that the doctrinal element itself recedes into the background. It functions in these works as a means of raising questions not only about itself but about matters beyond itself. This, of course, is why it would be a mistake to lift the doctrinal element out of B and C, claiming that this element is what those works are about.

This is a simple point, but it is often lost sight of by readers who come to Romantic poetry looking for its doctrines. Readers feel a fatal temptation to isolate passages like, "O fret not after knowledge," or "Gentleness, Virtue, Wisdom, and Endurance, / These are the seals of that most firm assurance / Which bars the pit over Destruction's strength"—forgetting that the speakers here are not Keats and Shelley but a thrush and Demogorgon, and that these passages function in their poems to raise questions, just as in Work B. The same is true for passages like Wordsworth's often-quoted, "Knowing that Nature never did betray / The heart that loved her," which, in "Tintern Abbey," parallels Work C. Looking for the doctrines, readers forget what is going on in the poems.

Very few of the poems that we usually think of as "Romantic" parallel Work A. Blake's *Marriage of Heaven and Hell* comes to mind, and Wordsworth's "Prospectus" to *The Excursion,* also parts of *The Prelude* that seem to stand as plateaus in the narration, and some of Wordsworth's sonnets ("The World Is Too Much with Us," for example). One thinks of Keats's "To Autumn," some of Shelley's political pieces, such as the "Song to the Men of England," and Byron's "Prometheus." One is tempted to include poems like Coleridge's "France: An Ode," and especially Wordsworth's Immortality Ode, but these are really both poems of data (paralleling Work C). It is hard to arrive at a very extensive list, and I think this is significant in revealing the distinctive experience we undergo when we read Romantic poetry.

Most Romantic poetry follows the pattern of Works B and C. This poetry employs doctrine, but in a distinctive way. Rather than raising questions in order to move toward a presentation of doctrine, Romantic poetry tends to do quite the opposite: it employs doctrine in order to generate an atmosphere of the open question.

To take a case in point, consider Wordsworth's well-known little poem, "Lines Written in Early Spring." The body of this poem offers us plenty of doctrine: we learn how much the heart must grieve over "what man has made of man," and how "every flower/ Enjoys the air it breathes." This is the sort of thing befuddled students write down in their notebooks under "Wordsworth: His Doctrines." But one must look at the climax of the poem:

If this belief from heaven be sent,
If such be Nature's holy plan,
Have I not reason to lament
What man has made of man?

The poem closes with a question, and the emphasis in this last stanza (made clear by repetition) is on the "If." The poem does not end in resolution, offering answers, order, and a doctrinal position. Rather, ending in a question balanced precariously on the "If," the poem creates tension. It works to disturb the mind. What would serve to erase that "If"? What must man know, or choose to believe, in order to remove the "If" and arrive at the solid ground of confident statement? The poem forces questions like this upon us, and the questions expand, becoming a challenge to the bases of our own beliefs—*if* we are reading the poetry carefully. Many readers do not read it very carefully, and this is because they come to the poetry with the false expectations discussed earlier. They "know" that the Romantic poets believed many things, many "Isms," and they "know," therefore, that Romantic poetry must be *telling* them things, communicating doctrines. Given this, they do not quite see what they are actually reading. They do not really notice the "If," and so poems like this one become for them not question but statement.

I think that the first principle in reading Romantic poetry is to be alert for the "If," for those elements in the poetry which generate the question. Romantic poetry is predominantly a literature which asks rather than tells, which exposes problems rather than solves them. The main product of Romantic poetry is the question, and its main effect on a reader is disturbance.

It is helpful to compare our experience in reading Romantic poetry to the experience we enter into when we read Descartes' *Meditations*. In his *Meditations* Descartes leads us on a quest for certainty, for something not open to doubt—this in the context of an attempt to free man as much as possible from the errors which have traditionally plagued his efforts to understand himself and the cosmos. In this quest for certainty, Descartes adopts the tool of a radical skepticism, submitting to question established beliefs, exposing them to the test of doubt, breaking them down when they prove doubtable. The movement is "downward" in an attempt to uncover the assumptions that underlie beliefs, and finally to arrive at a solid ground, something that cannot be doubted. Descartes thought he found a solid ground in the realm of the mind's activity, in the famous *Cogito, ergo sum*.

The Romantic poet leads us on the same quest. Like Descartes, he is first of all a questioner who asks, poses negative examples, and explores the possibility of alternate hypotheses. He confronts the world of established belief-structures with the skeptic's eye, applying the test of doubt. His primary impulse is to move "downward," to explore the underpinnings of belief and reach down to a solid ground, some kind of *Cogito*. The Romantic's flirtation with both historical and cultural primitivism; Coleridge's almost obsessive concern with sources "far higher and far inward" and his interest in the certainty which is "itself the ground of all other certainty"; Keats's desire to follow Wordsworth and "think *into* the human heart"; Wordsworth's own concern with the "*Naked* dignity of man" and his attempt, through his poetry, to touch the "grand *elementary* principle of pleasure"—throughout the writings of the Romantic poets one encounters this impulse to uncover, to seek within, and search out a Cartesian-like *Cogito*.

In his *Meditations* Descartes asks, "How do I know that I am not myself deceived every time I add 2 and 3, or count the sides of a square, or judge of things yet simpler, if anything simpler can be suggested?" The Romantic poet asks,

How do you know but ev'ry Bird that cuts the airy way,
Is an immense world of delight, clos'd by your senses five?

"How do you know . . . ?"—the apparently solid world of established beliefs and order loses its stability, is called into question. The reader is forced backward, to a confrontation with his presuppositions, and beyond this to a reconsideration of the data of experience which underlie those presuppositions.

Such poetry involves a restructuring of traditional conceptions about what poetry is supposed to offer a reader. (Thus we often find the Romantic poet considering his work as "experiment.") True to tradition, this poetry seeks to offer a combination of instruction and delight. But the meaning of these terms has changed. Teaching does not mean offering answers to the reader's questions, playing Sherlock Holmes to the reader's Watson. And the delight offered is not the satisfaction that accompanies a resolution of tension. Quite the opposite: Romantic poetry teaches by questioning the reader's answers. It guides by producing rather than relieving tension. It does not present the result of a quest, but instead forces the reader to experience the act of questing himself. And the delight produced is that of a quest in process: the intellectual excitement of exposing false certainties, illuminating unconsidered complexities and new possibilities; the very opening out of intellectual horizons that accompanies the experience of grappling with uncertainties.

For purposes of analysis, we can make a somewhat overly precise distinction and speak of Romantic poetry as embodying two main movements, sometimes within a single poem, sometimes not. The first of these is an attempt to disrupt a reader's equilibrium, to break down his sense of order and cast doubt upon the doctrines he holds when he comes to the poetry. The effect is to gain a suspension of the reader's sense that the cosmos is well and solidly structured and that he has a good grasp of that structure. This is a preparatory movement, readying the reader for a serious consideration of the underlying world of unstructured data. The second movement leads the reader into an exploration of this data, attempting to grasp not doctrine but the "primal stuff" of experience with which one must deal in order to generate doctrine.

We may take note of several ways in which the poetry works to accomplish this first movement of breaking down the reader's sense of order. Most obvious is the technique of the direct question, posed strikingly and left to reverberate unanswered in the reader's mind. Blake's "Tyger" is the extreme example. One also thinks especially of such poems as Wordsworth's "Matthew," Keats's "Nightingale," and Shelley's "Mont Blanc." These poems are so structured that the question bursts in upon the reader's mind in the final lines, with the effect of rendering what came before hypothetical, fragile, or uncertain.

In "Mont Blanc," for example, the reader follows the mind's meditation upon the spectacle of Mont Blanc, out of which meditation is generated a pattern of intuitions about the nature of the cosmos. But the poem ends with a question:

And what were thou, and earth, and stars, and sea,

If to the human mind's imaginings
Silence and solitude were vacancy?

Our stability is undercut, as we are forced to consider the possibility that the intuitions just gained are not solid ground upon which one can build with confidence. Rather they are fragile constructs, functions of the fact that the mind perceives (or at the moment is perceiving?) the cosmos in certain ways. Again we confront the "If." The unanswered question echoes in our minds as we turn from the poem. The poem works to generate not doctrine and resolution but, quite the opposite, tension, as one is left to experience an expanding horizon of possibilities.

Often the technique operates less obviously. Rather than posing the question directly, the poetry works in such a way as to force the reader himself to pose questions. Wordsworth's "Anecdote for Fathers" and his "We Are Seven" offer variations on this technique. Both poems play upon the reader's expectation that poetry is "significant," that it grapples with important problems and comes up with significant answers. Both poems flirt with the inane, or what seems to be the inane, teasing the reader as he moves through the poem, leading him into a state of half-irritated suspense, waiting for the "point." But then both poems simply end, abruptly—the first offering only the information that some kind of "lore," as the poem puts it, has been learned, the second offering nothing at all except perhaps the vision of a little girl and an old narrator staring stubbornly at each other. The reader is forced back to the experience of the narrative itself, and now the poems begin to open out into possibility (in the same way that one of Blake's lyrics expands when one tries to grasp it). This is especially true of "Anecdote for Fathers." The poem may be simply a lesson in lying, but Wordsworth adds just enough symbolic touches (the "dry walk," the "gilded" weather vane, and so forth) to open the question of a possible intuition of truth in the child's assertions. Further, the narrative may suggest that human beings choose before discovering reasons for their choices; or it may be that children do so but, given the natural development of the organism, adults live a different mental life; or it may be that the relationship between choice and reasons is a function of education. The poem does not provide answers. Rather, it is designed to create questions, to work upon a reader's mind in such a way that certainties are replaced by possibilities.

The most subtle technique in this movement to break down a reader's sense of certainty is one in which the poetry builds toward and then actually produces a "point" or answer, which, in fact, is no answer at all when it is closely examined. An example is Keats's "La Belle Dame Sans Merci." Here the reader is offered a question at the poem's beginning: "O what can ail thee, knight-at-arms, / Alone and palely loitering?" At the poem's close, he receives what appears to be an answer: "And this is why I sojourn here, / Alone and palely loitering." But what does the "this" refer to? Perhaps the effect of the knight's dream: having been warned, the knight has awakened from La Belle Dame's web. But then, considering the knight's present sad condition, perhaps he is still in the web. Yet, stepping back to a more basic consideration, is there a web at all? The knight was warned in a dream: was it a true dream? We are forced back to the substance of the knight's adventure to see what can be known of the mysterious Dame. Now the poem, like Keats's image of the "large Mansion of Many Apartments," becomes a thing of many open but dark doorways. Certain words catch the eye. The

Dame "look'd at me *as* she did love" (italics mine): does this mean "as if " or "while"? "And *sure* in language *strange* she said" (italics mine): surely? We begin to realize that all one can know of La Belle Dame are her physical actions. The mind behind those actions, the intent, is beyond our grasp. It is unknown, and it can only become known *if* we can accept dream as a means of gaining knowledge of the world outside the self. Again we have to do here with a poem of possibility and tension, one which teases the mind and wavers on the "If." One begins to see that the poem is an exploration of the unanswerable questions underlying the commitments man makes when he relates himself to something unknown, a Something Out There.

This same technique of offering an answer which is not an answer is employed by Coleridge in his "Rime of the Ancient Mariner." The Mariner's advice to the Wedding-Guest, "He prayeth well, who loveth well," which readers traditionally have put down in their notebooks under "Coleridge: His Doctrines," is nothing more than a set of directions for praying. It tells one how to take the medicine, but leaves open the question of whether the medicine has any effect upon one's health. The atmosphere here is not unlike that produced in *Alice in Wonderland* when things are encountered which are marked, simply, "Eat Me!" Will there be any effect? What will the effect be? As in Keats's poem, one is driven back to the substance of the narrative itself. And here again, as in Keats's poem, one encounters those words which open doors but leave one in darkness:

O happy living things! no tongue
Their beauty might declare:
A spring of love gushed from my heart,
And I blessed them *unaware:*
Sure my kind saint took pity on me,
And I blessed them *unaware.*

(Italics mine)

At first we are tempted perhaps to see in these lines an instance of Romantic concern with processes of the subconscious mind, illustrating their speculation that somehow the subconscious may be more a source of health than the conscious mind. But then, thinking again, the questions begin to appear. If the Mariner blessed them "unaware," how do we know that he did in fact bless them? Is "sure" to be read as a confident "It is certain," or as a tense "It *must* be true that . . . "? As is the common experience in Romantic poetry, the poet catches the reader up in open-ended questions and expanding possibilities.

The second dominant movement in Romantic poetry is an attempt to grasp the experiential data that underlie the doctrinal constructs men impose upon the cosmos. The reader is prepared for this by the techniques discussed above, which question the reader's doctrinal constructs, making him view answers with suspicion and think in terms of possibilities rather than certainties. Having broken down the stability of what we "know," the poetry moves toward an examination of the fundamental mental experience out of which what we term "knowledge" is generated.

Descartes, pursuing certainty, was led back to the *Cogito*, which seemed to him a solid ground. Like Descartes, the Romantic poet is led back to the realm of the mind's activity, where he does not find solid ground, but merely another question: I think, yes, but *how* do I think? Descartes had finally been willing to forgo questions and to make the assumption that some kinds of thinking are better than others; upon that kind of thinking associated with "clear and distinct ideas" he was able to build upward again toward patterns of order. The Romantic poet, however, is cut off from this possibility by the Lockean philosophical tradition with its critical investigation of the notion of "idea." The great barrier here, of course, is the intense and rigorous skepticism of David Hume. Thus the Romantic poet is forced to be a more stubborn questioner than Descartes. Because of this, when he enters the realm of mind, he becomes caught up in the labyrinth of the mind's activity.

The question of how the mind *should* operate yields in Romantic poetry to the prior consideration of how the mind *does* operate. In what various ways do men actually think (using that term in the broadest possible sense), and what are the effects of these various ways of thinking? How do idiots, peasants, children, feeble old men think? And what sorts of things does one really think about, what strange thoughts come to a human being? Poetry must break down those old limits imposed by notions of decorum and try to grasp all the data which have never really been grasped before. Thus the idea that poetry should not do X is a sign to the Romantic poet that X is precisely what poetry should do: if poetry should be reasonable, impersonal, general, and deal with "significant" things, the Romantic poet will do his best to capture the nonrational, the ego, the minute particular, and the absolutely trivial. The important point to consider here, I think, is that the Romantic poet's basic concern is not to indoctrinate us into valuing the yin instead of the yang of things; rather it is to advance the case of whatever is antithetical to commonly accepted belief, thus to keep alive the possibility of an opposite belief.

Ultimate normative and ontological commitments are suspended. The poetry seeks to offer us the basic data of mental activity rather than final statements about what "should be" or what "really is." Thus Wordsworth argues in an essay:

> The appropriate business of poetry, (which, nevertheless, if genuine, is as permanent as pure science,) her appropriate employment, her privilege and her *duty,* is to treat of things not as they *are,* but as they *appear;* not as they exist in themselves, but as they *seem* to exist to the *senses,* and to the *passions.*
> (Italics his)

Wordsworth's reference to science here is significant. In Romantic poetry, as in science, the quest for certainty leads back to the raw data of experience, the evidence about the way the mind operates, upon which any stable doctrinal construct must be based.

This second movement in Romantic poetry works to get "beneath" traditional doctrinal constructs—patterns of "should" and "really"—and to test the data assumptions upon which they are based. Consider, for example, Sir Philip Sidney's famous sonnet which begins,

> Leave me o Love which reachest but to dust,
> And thou my mind aspire to higher things:
> Grow rich in that which never taketh rust:
> What ever fades, but fading pleasure brings.

Sidney's thinking here is based upon certain assumptions about the mind's activity in the presence of mutable and eternal things—the assumption, for example, that the relationship between the human mind and a mutable love is a "pleasure" experience. Romantic poetry offers us tests of such assumptions, such as Wordsworth's "Lucy" poems, a series of

poems seeking to expose how in fact the mind does relate to a love object which is mutable. We see in these poems the "strange fits of passion" to which the mind becomes subject, and we observe how the mind reacts to the death of the love object. In "A Slumber Did My Spirit Seal," we ourselves are forced to provide the data. The poem offers the phenomenon:

> No motion has she now, no force;
> She neither hears nor sees;
> Rolled round in earth's diurnal course,
> With rocks, and stones, and trees.

We ourselves are drawn into the experience of earthly love's mutability; our minds' reaction tests the validity of an order constructed upon the doctrine, "Leave me o Love." Is our reaction one of "fading pleasure"? If not, something is amiss at the basis of Sidney's conception. Other Romantic poems (one thinks especially of Keats's "Ode on a Grecian Urn") explore the mind's experience in the presence of eternal objects. Is the human mind able to "grow rich" in what "never taketh rust"? Can the mind in fact establish a relationship with something eternal? If not, if eternal objects in Keats's phrase only "tease us out of thought," then something is wrong with a conception of order based upon the assumption that the mind flourishes in the presence of eternity.

The Romantic poet's attempt to uncover this data of the mind's activity tends to express itself in three main types of poems. The first is a meditative poem, fairly simple in basic structure. The reader looks on as a narrator's mind confronts a particular object and strives to come to terms with it. We encounter many such "object" poems in Romantic poetry, poems about nightingales, skylarks, urns, harps, west winds, and the like. There are, of course, complex variations. The narrator's mind can become two minds engaged in dialogue about some object, as in Wordsworth's "The Thorn." Or the object can expand into a temporal-spatial situation, as in Wordsworth's "Tintern Abbey" or Coleridge's "Frost at Midnight."

The second main type is a narrative-dramatic poem. Here the reader, again an onlooker, watches a mind become involved in a series of events, a patterning of several objects and situations. He observes how the mind tries to deal with them, the ways it seeks to discover or to impose order. One thinks of such poems as Coleridge's "Ancient Mariner" or Byron's "Manfred" or "The Prisoner of Chillon."

The third main type is a poem in which the poet involves the reader himself. Objects, situations, and events are made to work directly upon the reader's mind rather than upon the mind of a narrator or dramatic character within the poem. The reader falls from his position as observer and becomes a participant. He is thus made to experience directly (with the poet acting as manipulator of stimuli) the ways in which the mind works to derive order and value constructs from experience. Wordsworth's "Slumber," discussed above, is a poem of this type. So also, I think, is Coleridge's "Christabel," a poem in which the narrator's inability to grasp what is going on forces the reader to enter the poem and involve his mind in the tangle of events. Blake's *Songs of Innocence and of Experience* (when considered as a single poem) is also of this type.

This second movement in Romantic poetry, like the one discussed earlier, makes special demands upon the reader. The reader encounters a line of poetry like "I fall upon the thorns of life! I bleed!"—and his reaction may well be to object that such stuff is overly sentimental, and so not suitable for poetry. This reaction, however, shows that the reader has not really grasped what goes on in Romantic poetry. The reader is insisting upon a poetry of doctrine rather than a poetry of data. He has carried over from his readings in other poetry the assumption that poetry presents the result of a quest, that it deals in how man *should* think. But in Romantic poetry, as I have suggested, the attempt is to get beneath this "should" and all its train of doctrinal assumptions. The attempt is to investigate, to uncover; one must conclude finally that these are the grounds upon which the poetry must be judged. The question is whether Shelley's often abused line does not in fact uncover a fundamental datum of the mind's activity, whether it reaches back into the Is behind the Ought To Be and grasps in words something of the dark world of man's private mental experience.

The major difficulty Romantic poetry presents to many readers is its open-endedness. The poetry offers questions, exposes problems, uncovers data. It casts doubt upon supposed certainties, and it suggests possible new directions for thought. Romantic poetry stirs the mind—but then it leaves the mind in that uneasy condition. Often a reader's temptation is to push the poetry further in order to arrive at certainties, statements of doctrine. As I suggested earlier, this generally results in one of two errors: either the reader creates his own poem, making it say things it does not say; or the reader condemns the poetry for not saying things, or for not saying them clearly. In reading Romantic poetry, one is perhaps tempted to ask: What is the poetry telling us? But usually one's question should rather be: What is the poetry asking us?

The Romantic poet's desire, certainly, was to move toward a poetry of doctrine. But his greater desire was to know that his doctrine was well-grounded, that it could make some claim to certainty. So the Romantic poet first had to move on a quest "downward," doubting, asking questions, exploring data, searching for a solid ground. Thus he was led into the labyrinth of the mind's activity, from which he never really emerged. It is significant that the great Romantic philosophical poem, *The Recluse,* was never completed, in fact was hardly begun. Rather it was the preparatory poem, *The Prelude,* which caught Wordsworth up and absorbed his energies. The "failure" of the Romantic poet, if one wishes to call it that, is that he was too rigorous in his search for a solid ground. He asked questions too well and explored data too thoroughly. He was never able to convince himself completely that an axiom could have the characteristic of necessity, so he continued to cut the ground from under himself. The quest and the questions continued. For the reader, however, this must come to be the success of Romantic poetry: it provides a strong challenge to man's ability to come up with answers, to construct patterns of doctrine out of the raw data of experience. (pp. 974-80)

> L. J. Swingle, *"On Reading Romantic Poetry,"* in
> PMLA, *Vol. 86, No. 5, October, 1971, pp. 974-81.*

EARL R. WASSERMAN

[*Wasserman was an American critic and educator. In the following excerpt, he argues that the English Romantics used poetry to explore the relationship between subjective and objective reality.*]

According to the Humpty Dumpty principle of semantic wages we owe the word "Romanticism" a good deal of extra pay; we have made it do such a lot of overtime work by meaning so many things. We even insist that, since the word exists, it must stand for something real prior to our isolation of that something, and we have labored to divine that arcane meaning. We generally lop off a period of time, variously and arbitrarily determined, presuming it to be infused with some identifying quality whose name is "Romanticism"; and we then set out, in fact, to constitute the *a priori* phantom by defining it, with little resulting agreement, usually by naming the common features in manifestations of what we assume must be "Romantic." The logic is that of the vicious circle: the definition assumes as existent and understood that which is to be defined and proved to exist. Since, like Humpty Dumpty, I'd rather not have the word come round of a Saturday night to exact such heavy wages of me, I ask permission to sack it. My subject, then, is Wordsworth, Coleridge, Keats, and Shelley. They share, of course, many features, but a catalogue of these would merely melt the four poets into an anonymous confection and filter out what is idiosyncratic; that is, it would destroy our essential reason for reading them and disregard their poetic motives. On the other hand, since the four belong to approximately the same era, what they obviously share is access to facets of a common culture. Ideally, therefore, it should be possible to relate them to that culture in such a way as not merely to preserve their individual uniqueness but indeed to locate it with some precision, for if anything is palpable it is that they vigorously disagreed on central issues and that their works differ in vastly more essential and interesting ways than they are similar.

The bulk of eighteenth-century descriptive poetry is so large as to suggest that the poets must have had a significant apprehension of the external world, or at any rate came to grips with it in profound ways. In point of fact nearly all this verse is, in these terms, trivial, and most of it betrays an uncertain or ineffectual conception of how one experiences the external nature which is its subject matter. Clearly the external world counted for much in that culture, and poetic representation of landscape was thought vaguely significant. But the problem of the transaction between the perceiving mind and the perceived world was either evaded or left uneasily indecisive in descriptive verse, where one might reasonably expect it to demand attention.

If eighteenth-century poetry hedged on this question, which I shall—very loosely—call epistemological, contemporary philosophy certainly did not, and it is highly likely that the subtleties of eighteenth-century epistemology both drove the poets to confront the external world and deterred them from confronting it in any important way. By its very nature British empiricism had long tended to unsettle any assurance of an external world whose existence and qualities are exactly as the senses report. Hobbes had recognized the disparity between sensible qualities and the object being perceived. Locke, building on Boyle's distinction, divided qualities into those which are attributes of the object and those in the perceiver's mind, such as sound and color; and by locating the former in a pure "substance," which is unknowable in itself, he left man convinced of the reality of his own mental impressions, but highly uncertain about the nature or reality of the external world. Berkeley then located both sets of qualities in the perceiver's mind and, destroying Locke's "substance," made God the cause of our perceptions and assigned the reality of the external world to the act of its being perceived: natural science becomes merely a study of the principles governing the uniform relations of our sensations. Hume then completed Berkeley's subversion of the "external" by sceptically concluding that we can have no real knowledge of the existence or nature of the external causes of our impressions. Well might a landscape poet like Richard Jago be uneasy lest "all this outward Frame of Things" be "unsubstantial Air, / Ideal Vision, or a waking Dream" (*Edge-Hill*). Meanwhile, the mechanists like Hartley and the French school tried to cut the epistemological knot by explaining both mind and nature as matter and motion; and the Scottish School took the coward's way out by eschewing theory and limiting itself to description of mental phenomena on the basis of unassailable, God-given common sense. The stage was set for Kant and the epistemology of transcendentalism.

To these whirlwinds of eighteenth-century epistemology the poets, outwardly, remained rather indifferent, as though their poetic valuing of the external world guaranteed it against philosophic doubts. Richard Jago was at least aware of the philosophic storm and saw that it was relevant to the descriptive poet. "Reason," he admitted, "strives in vain to tell / How Matter acts on incorporeal Mind / Or how . . . Imagination paints / Unreal Scenes." And he was conscious that some philosophers were questioning whether "All this outward Frame of Things / Is what it seems" so that "this World, which we material call," may be "A visionary Scene, like midnight Dreams, / Without Existence, save what Fancy gives." But apparently feeling that such questionings threatened, rather than enriched, his poetic enterprise, he settled them in the commonsensical Scottish way, by refusing to "renounce / Man's surest Evidence." "Quit we rather then / These Metaphysical Subtleties," he said, rather hoping they would go away and leave man confident his experiences are not imaginary. (pp. 17-19)

This lack of any significant epistemology can be taken as typical of the hundreds of eighteenth-century meditative-descriptive poems. When the poet is not merely organizing sense data into some picturesque, sublime, or beautiful distribution, he usually devotes himself to humanizing the external scene by associating it with some emotion, moral theme, historical episode, moving narrative, or autobiographical experience. The scene becomes significant only by stimulating the poet to link it with man by some loose association. Even when he directly considers the relation of the objective and subjective worlds he usually postulates nothing more intimate than analogy. According to Akenside, the imagination, working with sense data, gives the mind "ideas analogous to those of moral approbation and dislike." Almost all the "ornaments of poetic diction," he thought, arise from the analogy between the material and immaterial worlds and between "lifeless things" and man's thought and passion. Accordingly, the eighteenth-century poet is forever interrupting his scene-painting to find its moral or emotional analogue. A description of flickering sunlight must be paired with a note on the analogous emotion of gaiety; if the poet observes that "Those thorns protect the forest's hopes; / That tree the slender ivy props," he must add, "Thus rise the mighty on the mean! / Thus on the strong the feeble lean!" (F. N. C. Munday, *Needwood Forest,* 1776). . . . Such tenuous, inorganic bonds between inner man and outer world betray the impotence of later eighteenth-century poetic epistemology, just as the ubiquitous urge to find some moral or subjective analogue to the scene reveals the anxiety to internalize the external and integrate the spiritual with the phenomenal. The resort to analogy only dodges the problem, since it both pretends to a rela-

tion between subject and object and yet keeps them categorically apart. (pp. 20-1)

Though the eighteenth-century poets bid us behold nearly every hill and plain, their reasons and those of the aestheticians are largely adventitious and extrinsic to the unmediated encounter with the object. For example, Archibald Alison at the end of the century seems to promise a poetically viable epistemology by proposing that "As it is only . . . through the medium of matter, that, in the present condition of our being, the qualities of mind are known to us, the qualities of matter become necessarily expressive to us of all the qualities of mind they signify" (*Essays on the Nature and Principles of Taste,* 1790). What we might then expect is a system identifying perception with significant cognition and resolving the divorce between subject and object by making perception an act of self-knowledge. But the subject-object relations Alison develops are in fact no more than those employed by the descriptive poets: matter is the immediate sign of mental powers and affections; or it is the sign of mental qualities as a consequence of experience, analogy, and association. In sum, our "minds, instead of being governed by the character of external objects, are enabled to bestow upon them a character which does not belong to them" and to connect with the appearances of nature "feelings of a nobler or a more interesting kind, than any that the mere influences of matter can ever convey"; and Alison's system implies little more than the characteristic poetry in which the scene is understood as an independent entity that becomes significant through equally independent subjective values loosely linked to it. His theory of matter as aesthetic sign merely offers a fuzzy rationale for the established eighteenth-century descriptive mode instead of healing the dualism and leading to a more organic poetry. The unresolved dualism of the poets and aestheticians results in a dualistic poetry: the scene is perceived and then felt or associated or thought, but seldom, if ever, apprehended *in* the perception. It is therefore a poetry of hobbling simile, rather than symbol. And it is a poetry that never fulfills itself to allow the poet to withdraw from a self-supporting creation; rather, it ends only when the poet has spent himself, the poem being sustained as long as he continues to annotate his sensory data with significances.

One radical heritage of the early nineteenth century, then, was a deal of revolutionary epistemological speculation and a literary tradition to which these speculations should have been important, but were not. What Wordsworth, Coleridge, Keats, and Shelley chose to confront more centrally and to a degree unprecedented in English literature is a nagging problem in their literary culture: How do subject and object meet in a meaningful relationship? By what means do we have a *significant* awareness of the world? Each of these poets offers a different answer, and each is unique as poet in proportion as his answer is special; but all share the necessity to resolve the question their predecessors had made so pressing through philosophic and aesthetic concern and poetic neglect or incompetence. Even in 1796, when Coleridge had not advanced beyond a poetics in which "moral Sentiments, Affections, or Feelings, are deduced from, and associated with, the Scenery of Nature," he was conscious of a pressure to "create . . . [an] indissoluble union between the intellectual and the material world." Of course epistemologies involve ontologies and can, and did, interconnect with theologies; but the epistemological problem is radical to this poetry as poetry, since it determines the role the poet will assign his raw materials, how he will confront them, and how he will mold them into a poem. Nothing I have to say about each of the poets is less than familiar; but I believe it has not been customary to view them collectively in terms of what I have called epistemology or to see it as the common base on which their poetry rests.

Wordsworth's earliest descriptive poems, *An Evening Walk* and *Descriptive Sketches,* are strictly in the eighteenth-century mode and are dull in proportion as they merely organize images into picturesque and sublime configurations and propose moral analogues. The emergence of the radically different Wordsworth is marked by a primitive, childlike wonderment that he experiences the outer world *at all.* In a sense he is an ur-Romantic, celebrating unphilosophically the forgotten basic miracle that the self may possess the outer world in some telling way, and making fresh the wonder of the act. He seeks to convey, for example, the awe with which, when the boy of Winander tensely waited in the silence for the owls to return his hoot,

> a gentle shock of mild surprise
> Has carried far into his heart the voice
> Of mountain-torrents; or the visible scene
> Would enter unawares into his mind
> With all its solemn imagery, its rocks,
> Its woods, and that uncertain heaven received
> Into the bosom of the steady lake.
> (Prelude. V. 381-388)

Many poems, such as "Expostulation and Reply," are essentially delighted responses to the discovery that the external world *can* move into the consciousness. Stale and negligible as this fact had been to his predecessors, Wordsworth, by responding to it with almost naive amazement, cleared the ground for fresh poetic considerations of the transactions between things and mind. His "To a Highland Girl," for example, progressively transfers the perceived scene and girl into the poet's mind and memory, starting with the paradox, "Thee, neither know I, nor thy peers; / And yet my eyes are filled with tears." Subject is affected by object and yet is unrelated to it. Progressively the poet proposes more binding relationships: to pray for the girl after he is gone, to make a garland for her, to dwell beside her and adopt her ways, to share a common neighborhood, to be her brother, her father. For as an external object, finite and fixed in space, she is to him "but as a wave / Of the wild sea," a transient image on his senses and unrelated to his being. The poet's plea is, "I would have / Some claim upon thee," the subject yearning to possess the object in some absolute relationship, not merely to be transiently touched by it. How the object is transformed into the stuff of the mind Wordsworth does not here say; but it is incorporated into the memory so that he may part from the girl in space and time, and yet,

> till I grow old,
> As fair before me shall behold,
> As I do now, the cabin small,
> The lake, the bay, the waterfall;
> And Thee, the Spirit of them all!

Whereas the eighteenth-century poet took it for granted that we perceive and sought by collateral accretions to give percepts value, Wordsworth invested with value the very act of experience.

That Wordsworth had no philosophy in him has been widely suspected, and it is likely that Coleridge foisted on him the burden of appearing a systematic thinker. At any rate, formal epistemology was of prime importance to Coleridge; and

Wordsworth, trying to look like the philosophic poet Coleridge urged him to be, offers almost every variety of epistemological hypothesis. Associationism and analogy are there, and so, too, is mutual interdependence:

> an ennobling interchange
> Of action from without and from within;
> The excellence, pure function, and best power
> Both of the objects seen and eye that sees.
> (Prelude, XIII. 375-378)

So, too, is something of Coleridge's position: "thou must give, / Else never canst receive" (*Prelude,* XII. 276-277). Or he can postulate, to Blake's annoyance, the old teleological doctrine of the exquisite fittingness of subject and object, speaking of the relation, however, not as a meeting but as a wedding and of its result as a kind of biological creation, "which they with blended might / Accomplish" (*Recluse*). The power of the senses "to own / An intellectual charm" he attributed to "Those first-born affinities that fit / Our new existence to existing things" (*Prelude,* I. 552-556).

Varied and inconsistent though his many explanations are, they at least reveal how recurrently the poetic enterprise of the Romantic required attention to the negotiations between the senses and the mind. It was inescapable for a poet whose plan, as Coleridge outlined it, was "to treat of man as . . . a subject of eye, ear, touch, and taste, in contact with external nature, and informing the senses from the mind, and not compounding a mind out of the senses." But Wordsworth was honest enough to admit his tolerance for multiple views: "To every natural form, rock, fruit, or flower . . . I gave a moral life: I saw them feel, or linked them to some feeling" (*Prelude,* III. 127-130). Coleridge might well have thought of him as Dr. Johnson did of pliant Poll Carmichael: "I had some hopes for her at first, . . . but she was wiggle-waggle, and I could never persuade her to be categorical."

But when Wordsworth set about to shape a poetic union of the world and the mind, instead of theorizing about it, there tends to appear one dominant mode, which can be described by the following among his many formulations:

> . . . by contemplating these Forms [i.e., of nature]
> In the relations which they bear to man,
> He shall discern, how, through the various means
> Which silently they yield, are multiplied
> The *spiritual* presences of absent things.
> (Excursion, IV. 1230-1234)

"The Solitary Reaper," for example, ends with approximately the same detailed description of the singing reaper with which it began—but with an essential difference. In the intervening stanzas the girl's song is stretched out in space (by comparison with song among Arabian sands and in the farthest Hebrides) and in time (perhaps its burden is of long ago, today, or the future); and, by virtue of its being in a strange tongue, its content has no specificity. The boundaries around the specific song have been stretched thin, and when we return at length to the original scene the song, having nearly lost its finitude and become quasi-spiritual, has made its way into the poet's inner consciousness.

Perhaps the best account of such a process of experience is Coleridge's analysis of a partial, inadequate form of his own epistemology. Since Coleridge, adapting Schelling, held that in knowledge object and subject "are identical, each involving, and supposing the other" (*Biographia Literaria*), he rejected the possibility that either has precedence. Were the objective taken as prior, then we would "have to account for the supervention of the subjective, which coalesces with it." If the object were prior, as it is for Wordsworth, then it must "grow into intelligence." "The phaenomena (*the material*) must wholly disappear, and the laws alone (*the formal*) must remain. Thence it comes, that in nature itself the more the principle of law breaks forth, the more does the *husk* drop off, the phaenomena themselves become more spiritual and at length cease altogether in our consciousness." Coleridge rejected this position, but Wordsworth's poetic instincts led him to it: the object is perceived vividly, usually with great specificity; the husk is then dissolved; and when the phenomenon has at last become "spiritualized" it passes into the core of the subjective intelligence. Lucy Gray slips away from her defining surroundings, evaporates into footprints in the snow, which, in turn, vanish at the middle of the bridge between the phenomenal and spiritual worlds; and she becomes the living spirit of solitude. Of the cuckoo's twofold voice, "At once far off, and near," the song to the nearby is addressed to the physical scene, and first becomes subordinate to the far-off one that brings "a tale / Of visionary hours" and then is lost in it, so that the bird may be "No bird, but an invisible thing, / A voice, a mystery," a spirit in nature that binds the poet's past with his present, his far-off with his near. Or, in "Resolution and Independence" the poet oscillates between perception of the leach-gatherer and a dreamlike inner vision of him until at length the leach-gatherer has become an object of the "mind's eye" and moves into the poet's spirit as a moral force, instead of being only a visible exemplum.

To Coleridge the goal of art is "To make the external internal, the internal external, to make Nature thought and thought Nature" ("On Poesy or Art"); and Wordsworth occasionally echoed him: "All things shall live in us and we shall live / In all things that surround us." But in fact only the first half of this statement truly describes his poetic processes, and he was closer to the mark when he wrote that the imagination, "either by conferring additional properties upon an object, or abstracting from it some of those which it actually possesses," enables it to "re-act upon the mind which hath performed the process, like a new existence" (1815 Preface). The senses shuck off or greatly attenuate the materiality of the image, or the imagination transmutes sensory data into something quasi-immaterial so that, for Wordsworth, sound was "Most audible . . . when the fleshly ear . . . Forgot her functions, and slept undisturbed" (*Prelude*, II. 415-418): when "bodily eyes / Were utterly forgotten . . . what I saw / Appeared like something in myself, a dream, / A *prospect of the mind*" (*Prelude*, II. 349-352). This is why Keats, looking from the other side of the fence, could speak of Wordsworth's poems as "a kind of sketchy *intellectual landscape*" (to Bailey, October 1817) and why Shelley could describe Wordsworth's art as "Wakening a sort of thought in sense." Wordsworth's poetic experience seeks to recapture that condition of boyhood when, as he said, he was "unable to think of external things as having external existence, and I communed with all that I saw as something not apart from, but inherent in, my own immaterial nature."

It is notable that Wordsworth's major contemporaries—Coleridge, Keats, Hazlitt, De Quincey, and Shelley—all recognized that at the core of his thought and art is the tendency to assimilate the outer world to the mind, to absorb object into subject. Their vivid awareness of this suggests not only the epistemological center of Wordsworth's poetry but also

the overriding importance to his contemporaries of the epistemological problem. Shelley, who identified Wordsworth with Peter Bell, may speak for all of them:

> All things that Peter saw and felt
> Had a peculiar aspect to him;
> And when they came within the belt
> Of his own nature, seemed to melt,
> Like cloud to cloud, into him.
>
> And so the outward world uniting
> To that within him, he became
> Considerably uninviting
> To those who, meditation slighting,
> Were moulded in a different frame.
>
> . . . . .
>
> He had a mind which was somehow
> At once circumference and centre
> Of all he might or feel or know;
> Nothing went ever out, although
> Something did ever enter.
>
> . . . . .
>
> Yet his was individual mind,
> And new created all he saw
> In a new manner, and refined
> Those new creations, and combined
> Them, by a master-spirit's law.
>
> Thus—though unimaginative—
> An apprehension clear, intense,
> Of the mind's work, had made alive
> The things it wrought on; I believe
> Wakening a sort of thought in sense.
>
> But from the first 'twas Peter's drift
> To be a kind of moral eunuch,
> He touched the hem of Nature's shift,
> Felt faint—and never dared uplift
> The closest, all-concealing tunic.

Keats, who is Wordsworth's exact antithesis, had no such compunctions. For him significant experience absorbs the self into the essence of the object, and therefore he condemned Wordsworth's inversion of this relationship as the "egotistical sublime." The epistemological difference between the two is that which Coleridge drew between Milton and Shakespeare: Milton, like Wordsworth, "attracts all forms and things to himself, into the unity of his own IDEAL," and all "things and modes of action shape themselves anew" in his being; Shakespeare, like Keats, "darts himself forth, and passes into all the forms of human character and passion" and "becomes all things." The difference is also that between the two eighteenth-century traditions from which they stem. Wordsworth derives mainly from the empirical and associative doctrines which speculated on how the imagination transmutes sensation into the stuff of the mind; Keats belongs to the tradition of sympathy, largely by way of Hazlitt, who protested against an art in which some sentiment is forever "moulding everything to itself." But however widely they differ, they obviously share a deep-rooted concern with how the subjective and objective worlds carry on their transactions. It is the question their culture had made of prime importance to the poetic act; and much of their poetry is the act of answering it.

Rejecting Wordsworth's "egotistical" assimilation of object to subject, Keats assumed that everything has its own vital and immutable quintessence and that the fulfillment of experience is the absorption of the experiencing self into that essence through the intensity of the sensory encounter. The "Man of Genius," as opposed to the "Man of Power," has no "individuality," no "proper self," since he is "continually informing and filling some other Body" or, according to Hazlitt, losing his personal identity "in some object dearer to him than himself." When I am in a room full of people, Keats wrote, "then not myself goes home to myself: but the identity of every one in the room begins so to press upon me that I am in a very little time annihilated."

Consequently, whereas Wordsworth's major poetic process requires the dissolution of the object's sensory finitude, awakening "a sort of thought in sense," Keats's process requires that the self rise to increasingly more intense sensory ardor until it is of the order of the object's dynamic essence—just as his Porphyro must rise "Beyond a mortal man impassion'd far" in order to melt into his own immutable essence as it exists in Madeline's intense dream. For Keats the object becomes progressively sharper, richer, more vibrant—more, not less, itself—as the experiencing self is entangled, enthralled, destroyed, until, "Melting into its radiance, we blend, / Mingle, and so become a part of it" (*Endymion,* I. 798-811). Correspondingly, his images become symbols, not by becoming "sketchy intellectual Landscapes," but by achieving their most intense sensory nature, since, as he wrote, everything becomes valued by the ardor with which it is pursued. The poet, capable of ecstatically entering the essences of objects, finds his way to the instincts of the eagle and knows the tiger's yell "like mother-tongue"; he can explore "all forms and substances / Straight homeward to their symbol-essences." The first three stanzas of the "Ode on a Grecian Urn" are a full enactment of this process of empathic absorption, as the observer is progressively drawn to the urn, to the frieze within it, and to the perdurably ecstatic life in the frieze—a life which he at last experiences by being assimilated into it. Endymion's detested moments, on the other hand, are those when, after absorption into essence, he makes "the journey homeward to habitual self," self-conscious instead of other-conscious. This epistemology Keats anchored in a private faith that we create our own post-mortal existence, since in our final absorption into the ultimate essence we shall experience hereafter in a "finer tone" and immutably our transient earthly absorptions into essences; and most of Keats's poetry is an exploration of the ramifications of this belief. But the form and quality his poetic materials take and the role they play are determined by his epistemology of empathy.

Since for Coleridge the goal of art is "to make Nature thought and thought Nature," neither the Wordsworthian nor the Keatsian position is adequate. Starting with the dualism of nature and the self, Coleridge made the purpose of his epistemology such a reconciliation of the two that they may be "coinstantaneous and one." Ultimate knowledge is self-knowledge, for only in this act are subject and object identical. But in order to be an object the infinite subject must also be finite; and therefore the act of self-knowledge, whereby "a subject . . . becomes a subject by the act of constructing itself objectively to itself," is the reconciliation and identity of the finite and infinite, nature and self. All higher knowledge must be a mode of this act, since "every object is, as an *object,* dead, fixed, incapable in itself of any action, and necessarily finite"; it is vital only insofar as the self is viewing itself in the object. Hence such Coleridgean carousels as this: "to make the object one with us, we must become one with the object—*ergo,*

an object. *Ergo,* the object must be itself a subject—partially a favorite dog, principally a friend, wholly God, *the* Friend"—that is, either vehicles for the self or the total Selfhood. Consequently the Coleridgean imagination is the act of reconciling the phenomenal world of the understanding with the noumenal world of the reason. It incorporates "the reason in images of the sense" and organizes "the flux of the senses by the permanent and self-circulating energies of the reason" to give birth to symbols, which are both "harmonious in themselves, and consubstantial with the truths of which they are the conductors." Art, like the self-knowing subject, is "the middle quality between a thought and a thing, or . . . the union and reconciliation of that which is nature with that which is exclusively human"; and taste, a mode of imagination, "is the intermediate faculty which connects the active with the passive powers of our nature, the intellect with the senses; and its appointed function is to elevate the *images* of the latter [the Wordsworthian mode], while it realizes the *ideas* of the former." Wordsworth occasionally wished to say something of the sort:

> . . . his spirit drank
> The spectacle. Sensation, soul, and form
> All melted into him. They swallowed up
> His animal being; in them did he live
> And by them did he live. They were his life.

But this is both more than the epistemology that motivated him and far less than Coleridge's purpose, which is not merely to dissolve self and nature into each other, but, starting with "I am" instead of "it is," to develop the noumenal potential in the phenomenal.

With a single sentence Coleridge has preserved from embarrassment the critic who would make the transition from his metaphysics and poetics to his poetry: "I freely own that I have no title to the name of poet, according to my own definition of poetry." Frankly, it is not readily conceivable how Coleridge's epistemology could be translated into the life of a poem by shaping its matter, imparting a special quality to its imagery, or providing a process for the transformation of images into symbols. In other words, it is difficult to conceive of a poetry in which his epistemology and his theories of imagination and symbolism would be recognizable as shaping forces. But in fact he was not proffering a program; he was defining the ideal nature and role of poetry. As a practicing poet, for example, he performs no special act to cause his symbols to render intelligible the reality of which they partake; he merely deposits images which we are expected to conceive of as significant. Occasionally it is true, we find him making poetic statements that approximate his conception of a self constituting itself by constructing and viewing itself as object. Thus, of Mont Blanc he wrote:

> Thou, the meantime, wast blending with my Thought,
> Yea with my Life, and Life's own secret joy:
> Till the dilating soul, enrapt, transfused,
> Into the mighty vision passing—there
> As in her natural form, swelled vast to Heaven.
>   ("Hymn before Sunrise")

To the complaint of Wordsworth, expectedly unsympathetic on epistemological grounds, that this is the "Mock Sublime", Coleridge replied: "from my childhood I have been accustomed to *abstract* and as it were unrealize whatever of more than common interest my eyes dwelt on; and then by a sort of transference and transmission of my consciousness to identify myself with the object." And of course his epistemology is the necessary gloss on the Dejection ode to explain why the senses are inadequate and how the imagination develops subjective life in objects, which, as objects, are "dead, fixed":

> I may not hope from outward forms to win
> The passion and the life, whose fountains are within.
>
> O Lady! we receive but what we give,
> And in our life alone does Nature live:
> Ours is her wedding garment, ours her shroud!
> And would we aught behold, of higher worth,
> Than that inanimate cold world allowed . . .
> Ah! from the soul itself must issue forth
> A light, a glory, a fair luminous cloud
> Enveloping the Earth—
> And from the soul itself must there be sent
> A sweet and potent voice, of its own birth,
> Of all sweet sounds the life and element!

But the most important poetic role of Coleridge's epistemology is to provide the dramatic form for a group of poems which act out the principle that the self becomes a self by objectifying itself so as to identify finite and infinite. "This Lime-Tree Bower," which may be taken as typical, begins with the poet disconsolately imprisoned in the bower, isolated and unrelated to anything, like Keats detesting the journey homeward to habitual self, like Wordsworth unable to assert a claim on the Highland girl. Between him and his departing friend Charles Lamb is a dell, the divisive gulf separating the ego from the non-ego. In imagination he attends Lamb in his passage through the dell until the imagined friend emerges on the glowing plain with a freedom and joy that mock the gloom of the bower-shaded poet:

> So my friend
> Struck with deep joy may stand, as I have stood,
> Silent with swimming sense; yea, gazing round
> On the wide landscape, gaze till all doth seem
> Less gross than bodily. . . .

Escape from the prison of selfhood requires a union, through the imagination, with an object, an object that is itself a subject, a "friend," a Charles Lamb; and the self must "become one with the object" so that the poem ends with Coleridge watching the sunset and imagining Lamb watching the sunset as he himself had once watched it. The end is release from the prison, the freedom which is the ground of the willful act of imagination; and the end is the joy and vitality returned to the self by its evolving its own life in the object of experience.

Shelley's epistemology is so deeply embedded in an idiosyncratic ontology that it is difficult to disengage it, especially since he does not start with the usual distinction between autonomous subject and object. His grounds are two empirical axioms: "the mind cannot create, it can only perceive"; and "nothing exists but as it is perceived." The mental image results from perceiving something whose nature we cannot know, and consequently, with respect to the mind, the perception *is* the sole object. Shelley has cut the epistemological knot by putting aside an external world that stands against the self and by making the basic transaction one between the self and its mental impressions in all their combinations. The subject is what we are; the object, our percepts and feelings. But even this distinction is false, relevant only because of the whole falsity of our mortal condition. In childhood, Shelley writes, we "less habitually distinguished all that we saw and felt, from ourselves. They seemed, as it were, to constitute one mass." In the most vivid apprehension of being, men

"feel as if their nature were dissolved into the surrounding universe, or as if the surrounding universe were absorbed into their being. They are conscious of no distinction" ("On Life"). Only subsequently are we misled into supposing a dualism of subject and object and a categorical difference between things and thoughts. What we call a "thing," he said, is merely "any thought upon which any other thought is employed with an apprehension of distinction"; and the division between "external" and "internal" is merely nominal, so that "when speaking of the objects of thought, we indeed only describe one of the forms of thought" and, "speaking of thought, we only apprehend one of the operations of the universal system of beings." True phenomenal knowledge, then, does not consist in bridging the gap between self and nature, but in withdrawing these illusory entities to their common source. Consequently it is considerably less than a figure of speech when Shelley commands the West Wind: "Be thou, Spirit fierce, / My spirit! Be thou me. . . ." Or when, in "Mont Blanc," he *pretends* a distinction between thoughts and things, he can define reality only as a continuous mental act, a vain striving by the mind to identify its shadowy images with the corresponding but unknowable external world that has cast them.

Hence the curiously insubstantial, unrealized quality of Shelley's poetic imagery. Clouds, winds, vapors, skylarks, and flowers hover between thing and thought because his experiential reality is neither subjective nor objective, an irrelevant distinction if our being and our perceptions "constitute one mass." Insofar as, limited by time and space, we perceive a mutable world external to ourselves, we perceive what "seems," not what "is." Shelley's real, nonillusory world, unlike Wordsworth's or Keats's, is symbolic in its very nature, since it is not categorically different from other thoughts—or, more properly, since what we call the world is constituted of the mass of our thoughts, including our own nature. The West Wind *is* Necessity, the summit of Mont Blanc *is* the residence of the Power, its ravine *is* the Mind, and life *is* like a dome of many-colored glass, not because things are like thoughts, but because one order of thought differs from another, as Shelley said, only in force.

The four Romantics, it is clear, are sharply at odds with each other, in the terms I have been concerned with. But the very fact that their positions do clash so directly on these terms, instead of being merely unrelated, confirms that they all face the central need to find a significant relationship between the subjective and objective worlds. We may conceive of poetry as made up superficially *of* features, such as nature images, melancholy, or lyricism; but it is made *by* purposes, and epistemology is poetically constitutive. All the Romantics, it is true, give extraordinary value to a faculty they call the imagination because they must postulate an extraordinary faculty that bridges the gap between mind and the external world; but no two of them agree on a definition of this faculty, any more than they do on the mode of existence of the external nature they so commonly write about. Admittedly, all are symbolic poets, since the symbol is the marriage of the two worlds, but their kinds of symbolism are necessarily as widely diverse as the epistemologies that generate them. (pp. 21-34)

Earl R. Wasserman, "The English Romantics: The Grounds of Knowledge," in Studies in Romanticism, *Vol. IV, No. 1, Autumn, 1964, pp. 17-34.*

The Burning of Shelley's Body *by L.E. Fournier.*

ALBERT S. GERARD

[*Gérard is a Belgian educator and critic. In the following excerpt, he explores the ontological and ethical implications of the Romantics' belief in cosmic unity and its impact on the structure of their poetry.*]

Romantic poetry derived much of its revolutionary character from an intense and outspoken dissatisfaction with the dualistic world view which had prevailed during the eighteenth century. The young Coleridge and the young Wordsworth were persuaded that the established dichotomies—between spirit and matter in ontological thought, between subject and object in the theory of knowledge, between content and form in the sphere of art—were as unjustifiable and harmful as was the petrified division of society into an aristocratic ruling class and an oppressed majority; and once they had both settled into a more sedate—or, perhaps, more resigned—recognition of the limitations of the human mind and of the inherent imperfections of human society, they were stridently disavowed by Shelley, who, together with Keats, resumed the fight and the quest which the Lake poets had apparently relinquished. If one impulse can be singled out as central to the romantic inspiration, it is the *Sehnsucht,* the yearning toward the absolute, the aspiration to oneness and wholeness and organic unity, the dream of perfection. To many, both before and since the romantic period, this impulse has appeared juvenile. Nevertheless, it was the fountainhead of the intellectual and poetic activity of the romantics, in England as elsewhere. And it was taken seriously because its validity seemed to be guaranteed by visionary experiences which all young romantic poets found crucial, since they provided what appeared to them convincing evidence that such yearning was by no means illusory or utopian.

In these germinal experiences—such as those described in "The Eolian Harp" and "Tintern Abbey," not to mention *The Prelude,* or those that are allegorically conveyed in "Alastor" or *Endymion*—there were many individual variations. Each of England's four major romantic poets was a man of strong personal temperament. And of course, they belonged to two generations, one of which reached manhood while the French Revolution was in progress, and the other at the time of Waterloo. The younger writers were bound to be influenced by their elders and in some measure to react against them. Nor is it immaterial that Shelley and Keats died at an early age, which prevented them from developing as their predecessors did. While Wordsworth and Coleridge reinstalled themselves—somewhat smugly, as many think—in the main current of Christian tradition, Shelley and Keats did not live to reach the stage when a man begins to feel humble enough to seek the help and comfort of guidance from above. But in spite of this diversity, they all participated in a similar *Sehnsucht,* and the quasi-mystical experiences that stirred their imaginations had much in common.

It used to be said disparagingly that romantic poetry is poetry of feeling. It is indeed suffused in emotion. But the strong feelings which overwhelm the poet's soul, the joy, the sense of glory, should rather be considered a psychological consequence of the poetic experience, and the subjective proof of its vital importance. The experience itself is not only emotional; it is also, and indeed primarily, cognitive. It includes sensory and intellectual elements; it brings the whole soul into activity; as a result, it is rich in moral and metaphysical implications.

Basically the poetic experience is a form of knowledge. It is not a strictly sensory form of knowledge, like that which often inspires the Imagists, since through the particular and the sensuous it aspires to reach to the universal. But it does not reach the universal by way of abstractions, like the philosophical poetry of eighteenth-century neoclassicism. In fact, it is felt as an intuition of cosmic unity: the sudden realization that the universe is neither an unintelligible chaos, nor a well-regulated mechanism, but a living organism, imbued throughout with an idea which endows it with its unity, its life, its harmony, its ultimate significance. (pp. 3-5)

This intuition appears at its most explicit in the early major works of the English romantics. It is expressed in Coleridge's idea of the One Life and in Wordsworth's description of his blessed moods; in "Alastor," it underlies the Poet's endeavor to identify himself with the absolute; in *Endymion,* it accounts for the hero's hope to achieve the fusion of the ideal and the human. But it is through the formal features and structures into which the romantic inspiration spontaneously organized itself, rather than through explicit statements, that we can best realize its intensity and its concrete modes. The metaphors of totality, of prismatic refraction, of interconnection, of fusion, the abundance of which is one of the distinguishing features of romantic poetry, all suggest the coalescence of the One and the Many. (p. 239)

The romantic intuition of unity necessarily entailed the need to account for the apparent dualities of day-to-day experience, and so to clarify the relations between God and the created world, between man and society, between man and nature. The oscillating rhythm of many romantic poems is a spontaneous reflection of that preoccupation, and thus, on the structural plane, a symbol of the idea which provided their inspiration. The wanderings of the poet's attention, the expansion and contraction of its focus, its swift passage from self to non-self and back to self, are all the more revealing as they are certainly unpremeditated, flowing as they do from the very heart of his inspiration, from the all-dominating need to effect the fusion of what is apparently heterogeneous. Man, therefore, is not an isolated atom of being. He is enmeshed in a complex network of interactions, in which causality and analogy are necessarily connected. The inherent structure of the Wye landscape makes it appear to be an organized microcosm, and thus causes it to kindle thoughts about the highest ethical and metaphysical issues. The thorn has become a suitable correlative of human suffering because it too has been broken and distorted by the uncontrollable forces of a malignant fate. The west wind is both a power in its own right and an adequate image of the power inherent in the human mind.

This sense of universal kinship, of oneness, participation, and totality, is a well-known feature of romanticism. What is perhaps not so commonly realized is that it raised, for the poets themselves, problems which are both of an ontological and of an ethical nature.

The ontological problem lay in the need to test the truth of the central intuition and to define—supposing it were at all possible—the nature and the modes of the unity it revealed. For the romantic poets, this was by no means an academic exercise in pure cerebration. It was a question of vital import, since it was so clearly bound to authenticate or to invalidate their most urgent and most original experience, the core of their poetic inspiration and, consequently, their own appraisal of what they were worth as poets and as men.

The dialectical and dramatic element which constitutes the hidden design of much romantic poetry was due to the clash between the romantic intuition and a number of dogmatic and experimental elements. Of course, it contradicted the dualistic tenets of the traditional, "Newtonian" cosmology: but this was exactly what the romantics were reacting against. More important, at least to Coleridge and, later, to Wordsworth, was the fact that the pantheistic trend which the intuition of oneness seemed to involve was at variance with orthodox Christian transcendentalism. The attractive idea that, in ultimate reality, God and the world were one entailed an impious confusion of the Creator and his creature. . . . The systolic rhythm and the panoramic vision which characterize Coleridge's conversation poems testify, as eloquently as do the explicit statements, to the intensity of his sense of a fundamental kinship in which man, nature, and God are united. The misgivings kindled by the contradiction between intuition and dogma were ultimately solved through Coleridge's symbolic conception of nature. By considering nature to be not a deceitful counterfeit of infinity but a living and organized whole, bearing, in its vastness and all-inclusiveness, the stamp, and thus suggesting the idea, of the spiritual force that created it and ever animates it, he was able to account satisfactorily for his and his friend's most cherished insight without at the same time yielding to the temptation of pantheism. Neither Keats nor Shelley, brought up in a different intellectual climate and, as it were, emancipated by the early works of their elders, felt that need to accommodate their intuition of unity to the orthodox creed of Christianity.

The third challenge which the romantic *Sehnsucht* had to meet—apart, that is, from the challenge of eighteenth-century dualism and of Christian transcendentalism—was the much more formidable challenge of experiential evidence, which operated in various ways, both on the ontological and on the ethical planes.

The romantic revolution began in the eighteenth century with the revaluation of nature, and the status of nature remained one of the cruxes of mature romantic thought. Within an idealistic system, two possibilities first occur: either nature is the appropriate medium through which the infinite is revealed to man, or it is a material veil which prevents man from perceiving the absolute. The second view is that of the Poet in "Alastor"; the first is that of Coleridge and Wordsworth, and in "Alastor" it is that of Shelley in the introductory section and of the Poet previous to his enticing vision. In spite of all that has been said about pantheism, animism, and nature mysticism in romantic poetry, one thing stands out fairly clearly from a careful scrutiny of the texts: it is the extreme caution exercised by the poets in dealing with the extrasensory cognitive aspect of the experiences they describe. The meandering structure of "Tintern Abbey" is a reflection of its puzzled mood: the poet's attention oscillates between the two poles of certainty and speculation; while he feels assured that the contemplation of the forms of nature is a source of solace and moral improvement, he has no means of ascertaining whether his sense of a mystical insight into ultimate reality is valid, or whether it is a vain belief. Wordsworth knows that his ecstasies are transient, that they rest on a shaky foundation of subjectivity, that he is bound to lose them; and so, in "Tintern Abbey," he builds his hopes of happiness and betterment, not on them, but on the sensory apprehension of nature in which they are embedded—until he realizes, in "Resolution and Independence," that the shapes of the visible world may owe their influence on man to the grace of the benevolent God who transcends them. Similarly, Shelley shows, in "Alastor," what happens when the poet relinquishes his hold on the world of nature and of man, and abandons himself to the mystical quest of the unmediated vision: he becomes imprisoned in his subjectivity, his self-centeredness, and although his purpose is the loftiest that can be imagined, his doubt is never dispelled, and his fate is annihilation.

There is probably no finer expression of this intellectual dilemma so characteristic of romanticism than Keats's "Ode to a Nightingale," which, as E. R. Wasserman has observed [in his *The Finer Tone: Keats' Major Poems,* 1953], has its being in the "Purgatory blind" of the "Epistle to John Hamilton Reynolds." In his own way, Keats gives poetic shape to inner processes which are closely related to those of the Poet in "Alastor." He describes himself as "too" happy in his empathy with the nightingale's happiness, in the same way that Shelley's hero has "too" exquisite a perception of absolute beauty: the same hubris is at work. The ecstasy in the first stanza is parallel to the dream-vision of Shelley's poet, and is suitably accompanied by the same night of the senses ("a drowsy numbness") which characterizes Wordsworth's mystic moods and which, in "Alastor," takes the form of the hero's blindness to the beauty of nature and of the Arab maiden. The next stanzas recount the poet's attempt to recapture, to prolong and to intensify this ineffable bliss. But here again we find the characteristic pulsating rhythm which makes the poet's attention oscillate between blissful absorption into the ideal, and painful recognition of the real. That the poet's obsession with the world of sorrow and transitoriness takes the upper hand shows that wine, in stanza II, is only—in Wasserman's words—"a symbol of the misguided effort to engage in the sensory essence of nature without pain; a beguiling hope of penetrating to the inwardness of the sensory in such a way as to be at ease in empathy; a worldly illusion that fellowship with sensuous essence is only a distracting pleasure." It is only through imagination and poetry (of the luxurious kind) that Keats succeeds in restoring the visionary trance ("Already with thee"). But this merely recreates the condition of the first stanza, and the problem of perpetuating the visionary state remains entire: there is only one higher intensity, and that is death. The poet is now faced with the frightening mystery of death which had lured Shelley's hero to nothingness. But Keats realizes that it only *"seems"* "rich to die," and the ambiguity of death is intimated in the last two lines of the stanza:

> Still wouldst thou sing, and I have ears in vain—
> To thy high requiem become a sod.

Death would perpetuate forever the night of the senses which is part of the ecstasy; but at the same time, it would destroy the imagination, which had come alive in ecstasy; in death, the poet would become deaf not only to sensory music, but even to the bird's high requiem; like the hero of "Alastor," he would be no more than a sod. This realization of the vanity of the death-wish . . . is enhanced by the awareness that the bird, the emblem of the ideal, was "not born for death."

What the poet has learned by now is that, although he can enjoy brief moments of ecstasy, man cannot live in the ideal world, not even by seeking death. It is of the essence of such blessed moods that they should be transient, so that the poet is brought back, in stanza III, to "the weariness, the fever, and the fret," which he had hoped to evade altogether. The bird's song, which had started "in full-throated ease" presently fades away as a "plaintive anthem"; the bird itself was not born for death, but its voice is soon "buried" deep. And as the return pattern comes full circle, when the poet is tolled back to his "sole self," he is left to face the greatest loss of all. Not only is the ecstasy painfully short-lived, but its reality, as vision, is open to doubt. Like Wordsworth wondering whether his insight into the life of things may not be a vain belief, Keats asks himself whether he has not merely been cheated by his fancy, whether his flight into heavenly light

in the company of the nightingale might not be just a dream rather than a genuine vision, shadowy of truth:

> Was it a vision, or a waking dream?
> Fled is that music:—do I wake or sleep?

This ode, together with "Tintern Abbey" and "Alastor," throws a light of its own on what might be called the ontological skepticism of the romantics, a large portion of whose poetry results from their obstinate attempt to verify their seminal insights, to assess the significance of their intuition, to draw a firm line between what of it is objective perception and what wishful thinking, to determine as accurately as possible the concrete modalities of the cosmic unity. And although they were not as much concerned with the theory of the symbol as Coleridge was, their poetic practice tends in the same direction: toward a symbolic, rather than mystical, apperception of the world. The mechanism has been described in the simplest terms by Shelley, who wrote, in "Julian and Maddalo," that he loved all the places

> where we taste
> The pleasure of believing what we see
> Is boundless, as we wish our souls to be.

The distinction between "symbolic" and "mystical" appears in the word "believing." And in "Mont Blanc," after describing the snow-capped mountain as the seat of absolute Power, Shelley adds wistfully:

> And what were thou, and earth, and stars, and seas,
> If to the human mind's imaginings,
> Silence and solitude were vacancy?

The symbolical meaning with which Mont Blanc is loaded is the result of a subjective operation of the human imagination; it is nevertheless valid and significant: the mountain is not actually the supreme Power, but it is a suitable analogue of a power that really exists. As Coleridge had said, it is in this faith that created things legitimately counterfeit infinity.

But the symbolic apprehension of nature is not limited to this metaphysical analogy between the vastness, the harmony, the power of natural objects and the spiritual absolute. The idea of the oneness of being leads to that of the kinship of beings. Hence a psychological symbolism in which the outward forms of nature are seen as correlatives of human attitudes, situations, emotions. In the same way that the expanse of the landscape gives a feeling of infinity because its very amplitude is a product of the infinite spiritual force which organizes the original chaos of inert matter, so for Wordsworth the thorn is an appropriate emblem of human misery, not merely because of its tortured shape—this would be pathetic fallacy—but because its tortured shape is the result of the action of hostile forces, as is the misery of Martha Ray: it is in this sense that the thorn, as a symbol, "abides itself as a living part in that unity, of which it is the representative."

On the ontological plane, then, the romantic *Sehnsucht nach dem Unendlichen* ["yearning toward the absolute"], backed by the romantic intuition of cosmic oneness, managed to come to terms with the dualistic outlook which is built into the Western tradition. However strongly they were attracted at first toward the idea of a unity of essence, as formulated in the doctrines of pantheism, extreme idealism, or other forms of philosophical monism, the English romantics maintained their grasp upon the actual. What they did was to reinterpret and restate the relation between spirit and matter, man and nature, God and the created world, in such a way as to substitute organic relational patterns of causation and analogy for the simple mechanistic outlook against which they were reacting. Fundamentally, symbolism is the outcome of this process.

But the cosmic intuition and the infinite *Sehnsucht* were raising problems that were even more urgent on the ethical plane because they were bound to lead not only to a conception of the nature of the universe but also to a redefinition of the good life. Here, too, romantic poetry is the response to a challenge of contradiction, for the ontological intuition of cosmic oneness was necessarily accompanied by an ecstatic bliss which sought to perpetuate itself, by a feeling that the intrinsic harmony of the universal scheme should and could result in absolute happiness, and that it was possible to raise the actual to the sphere of the ideal by pursuing single-mindedly the life of the imagination in fellowship with essence. The romantics were caught between these great expectations and the experiential evidence of human frailty, of evil and suffering. And this awareness of cruelty and destruction, in its impact on the dream of perfection, had important implications for their conception of the principles of man's ethical behavior and entailed the necessity to revise their early ideas and immature hopes. This is Wordsworth's problem in "Resolution and Independence," and it is reflected in mythical terms in "Alastor" and in *Endymion.*

The antinomy between the ideal of harmony and happiness and the darker sides of human experience can lead to a number of attitudes, among the most extreme of which is to be counted the German *Ironie.* . . . While eighteenth-century enlightenment ignored the *Durst nach Ewigkeit* ["thirst for eternity"], German romanticism exacerbates it by constantly reminding itself that it is both *unmöglich* ["impossible"] and *notwendig* ["necessary"] to gratify it: *Ironie* thus appears as a kind of masochistic contemplation of the torturing incompatibility of life and the ideal. And if anything clearly divides English romanticism from its German counterpart, it is the former's determination to overcome the poisoned delight of such unresolved paradoxes and to achieve a meaningful synthesis.

The antinomy of ideal and actual can also be evaded through a denial of the impossibility of gratifying the *Sehnsucht.* This prompts the poet to reject life altogether and to escape, through the death-wish, to a dream world of absolute perfection. As Baudelaire was to say:

> Certes, je sortirai, quant à moi, satisfait
> D'un monde où l'action n'est pas la soeur du rêve.
> ["Certainly, I will be, as far as I'm concerned, satisfied
> With a world where action is not the sister of a dream."]

The English romantics do not appear to have been attracted for any length of time to the extreme idealism characteristic of many of their continental colleagues. . . . "Alastor" is to be understood as a warning against, rather than a plea for, the death-wish: it is the cathartic poem in which Shelley dramatized the absolute *Sehnsucht* and worked out to its ultimate absurdity the extreme idealism which was one of the temptations to which romanticism was bound to be subjected by the very nature and intensity of its spiritualistic assumptions. There is, of course, an unsolved contradiction in the attitude of the romantics to death, and it shows with what intensity they were thinking anew the perennial problems involved in the human predicament. On the one hand, for Shelley in "Alastor" and for Keats in the "Ode to a Nightingale,"

death in annihilation. But on the other hand, the romantics usually held the view that death is the gate to immortality. If we take them at their face value, such statements are of course irreconcilable. But their assertive form is misleading; it conveys an impression of confidence and certainty, whereas they are the outcome of hope, anxiety, and puzzlement. It is rather significant that most of Keats's dicta on death are couched in interrogative or optative terms:

> Can death be sleep, when life is but a dream,
> And scenes of bliss pass as a phantom by?

he wrote in an early sonnet, thus setting the tone for later utterances. "I long to believe in immortality," he wrote to Fanny Brawne in June 1820 and some time later, to Charles Brown: "Is there another Life? Shall I awake and find all this a dream? There must be we cannot be created for this sort of suffering." Neither Coleridge nor Wordsworth had tackled the problem in the same pathetic way: they were still too much immersed in the orthodox tradition of Christian dogma. But for men of a later generation, the mystery of the country from whose bourne no traveler returns was invested with fresh poignancy. Therefore, they could not yield to the temptation of the death-wish because they could not long for a death which might mean annihilation, and they could not possibly know whether death meant anything else. They could only hope, and long to believe, and meanwhile accept the common fate of man.

What the major romantic poets of England held in common, then, was a firm determination to solve their dilemma rather than evade it. Coleridge, of course, had a ready-made solution, defined in the argument prefixed to the "Ode to the Departing Year": "The Divine Providence . . . regulates into one vast harmony all the events of time, however calamitous some of them may appear to mortals." The very low poetic quality of the "Ode" intimates, however, that this highly orthodox and dogmatic view was a piece of dead knowledge, a mere abstraction which had not been proved upon the poet's pulse. Such facile confidence in the automatic action of providential benevolence is by no means representative. Wordsworth's case is quite different. With him, belief in divine grace is not an initial assumption blindly inherited from the orthodox tradition. It results from an organic widening of his apprehension of nature's influence, which is now provided with a proper metaphysical perspective. Nature does not only send blissful moods: she also sends trials, ordeals, sufferings, anxiety; but these too, when seen in the light of the divine grace that ordains everything, appear to be the instruments of moral improvement, and ways to surer happiness. This wider understanding of man's situation in the world is the outcome of a long and difficult inner process of moral growth, through recognition and acceptance, non-attachment and self-conquest. (pp. 240-50)

[The] major assumptions and experiences of the romantic poets organically embodied themselves in definable structural patterns. The panoramic perception of the world is a spatial correlative of the sense of infinity. The systolic rhythm of contraction and expansion is a direct outcome of the sense of kinship and interchange which presides over the poet's relation with nature. Likewise, the fundamental preoccupation of the romantics with becoming, growing, and maturing has its structural homologue in the upward spiral movement which modifies the return pattern in many romantic poems. Any definition of romantic egotism must carry two important qualifications. First, the romantics allow themselves to be self-centered because they regard themselves as suitable representatives of mankind; as Keats said, "A Man's life of any worth is a continual allegory." Furthermore, the self in which they seem to be absorbed is not given from the very first in a state of immutable perfection; its distinguishing feature is its flexibility, its capacity for change. In Germany, this dynamic principle of romanticism was connoted by the concept of *Werden* ["growth" or "development"]. But for the English romantics, there is no such thing as pure *Werden*: becoming is always purposive; it is moral growth. Whether the poet deals with the self directly—as is generally true with Coleridge and Wordsworth—or vicariously—as Keats does in *Endymion*—the self to which he returns is not the self with which he had started: it has been deepened and enriched by experience and meditation.

The combination of the return pattern with the systolic rhythm makes it possible further to define this process of growth, which seems to develop along the lines of a triadic—one might almost say Hegelian—scheme, in the sense that it is the resultant of the interaction of opposite forces. In Wordsworth's daffodil poem, the melancholy solitude ("lonely"), the grayness ("cloud"), the sedate aloofness ("floats on high") of the poet are successfully challenged by the colorful movement of the companionable daffodils ("crowd," "golden," "dancing"), so that he is drawn into their "jocund company"—an experience which, because it is an experience of communion with the otherness of nature, leaves him permanently changed and enriched ("wealth"). In some of the conversation poems, Coleridge's initial frustration is similarly relieved by his sense of humanitarian duty ("Reflections") or through vicarious enjoyment of the symbolic landscape ("This Lime-tree Bower"). But the pattern reveals itself to be more pregnant with ethical significance when it gives poetic shape to the impact of experience upon innocence: the mystic intuition stumbles on the humdrum experience of everyday life; the multifariousness of material forms, however beautiful, prevents any immediate perception of spiritual oneness; the dream of bliss and beauty seems to be nullified by the harsh facts of evil and sorrow; rational thought shakes the foundations of faith, whether it be faith in the spirit, or in nature, or in the imagination.

Most of the poems discussed [here] deal with this second stage, when the high expectations and the immeasurable hopes no longer reign unchallenged, but are thwarted by the uncomfortable awareness of the limitations of human nature. They are located in what Keats calls "the space of life between," where the idealistic assurance of untried innocence is shattered by a new and painful grasp of the actual, and where, consequently, perplexity is the dominant mood: the perplexity of Wordsworth in "Tintern Abbey," of the Poet in "Alastor," of Endymion, all of whom have to face their loss, the loss of the illusion that life can be lived in fellowship with essence, that imaginative bliss can become the daily routine, that the poet can spend his whole life "in pleasant thought, / As if life's business were a summer mood." The growth of the mind first involves the shattering of such expectations. The depth and the scope of this renunciation had been prophetically described by Keats, as early as 1816, in a passage of "Sleep and Poetry," the first half-line of which was to be significantly echoed later in the "Ode to a Nightingale":

> The visions are all fled—the car is fled
> Into the light of heaven, and in their stead
> A sense of real things comes doubly strong,
> And, like a muddy stream, would bear along

> My soul to nothingness: but I will strive
> Against all doubtings, and will keep alive
> The thought of that same chariot, and the strange
> Journey it went.
>
> (ll. 155-162)

It is the tragic irony of the Poet's odyssey in "Alastor" that in refusing to face the ordeal and to follow the muddy stream of real things, he embarks on another stream that will also lead him to nothingness. The common feature of the English romantics is their determination to face evil and sorrow, "the agonies, the strife of human life," while at the same time keeping alive the vision of the ideal which had first inspired them. The development of their ethical outlook is, therefore, parallel to that of their ontological insight. In "Tintern Abbey," Wordsworth strives against the corroding effect of doubt by falling back on his assurance that nature's beauteous forms, whether or not they are a revelation of the absolute, are at least the undoubted source of all goodness and bliss. In "Resolution and Independence," the problem is one not of knowledge but of moral behavior, and the function of restoring the poet's inner peace, of reconciling him with his new responsibilities and with the trials that are in store for him, is fulfilled not by nature but by the leech-gatherer. But in fact, the old man impersonates a new, more complex, stage in Wordsworth's idea of nature; that he is first presented in the semblance of a stone or a sea beast identifies him with nonhuman nature in the usual Wordsworthian manner; but he is also the repository of an articulate wisdom referring to purely human problems and experiences, with which nonhuman nature could not cope; moreover, his sudden appearance, then and there, is ascribed, however tentatively, to the effect of divine grace. A new element is thus introduced into Wordsworth's world view, which brings it into harmony with that of Coleridge: the idea of a transcendent godhead which, although distinct from the world it created, still acts in and through it, thus helping man to cope with an otherwise unmanageable experience.

There was nothing revolutionary in such ideas. But this growing perception of reality was vital knowledge, not inherited dogma. It was not merely conceptual but experiential, and it involved a change in the poet's ethical attitude to life. The importance of the romantic ethos has never been sufficiently realized. For this inner evolution, as we can follow it step by step in Wordsworth's poetry and in the last book of *Endymion*, results in a second reversal of values: a reversal of some of the most widely advertised attitudes of romanticism. The desire for mystical union with the ideal makes room for a humble perception of the proper bound of human nature; the romantic *Sehnsucht* is replaced by acceptance. Paradoxically, the net result of Endymion's flight "beyond his natural sphere," "beyond the seeming confines of the space / Made for the soul to wander in," is to make him renounce his early impulse to act or think beyond mankind, to share powers of body or of soul that his nature and his state cannot bear!

The conventional image of Shelley as an ineffectual angel, as an ethereal prophet engulfed in his escapist dream of perfection and in his refusal to face the evidence of human ignorance and to come to grips with the ugly complexity of the world, is due partly to his spiritualistic vocabulary and disembodied imagery, and partly to the idealistic indictment of life which certainly does inspire much of his poetry. There is considerable truth in D. G. James's comparison of Keats and Shelley [in his *The Romantic Comedy*, 1948]:

Shelley had nothing of the tender play of scepticism which distinguishes Keats, a scepticism which is also a humility. Scepticism of this kind neither kills nor debauches; it is completely free of any hardness of mind and heart; it deepens, steadies, enriches, and makes wise. Shelley might move from a dogmatic atheism to a dogmatic Platonism; he could not pursue his life acknowledging ignorance and submitting to uncertainty.

Close reading of the poetry, however, suggests that such a statement, which reflects a commonly held conception of both poets' personalities, needs some qualification. To a large extent, Keats's intellectual quality and the source of his modern appeal can be said to reside in his willingness to accept ignorance and submit to uncertainty; but they also reside in what we might call his "aesthetic approach," which prompted him to find the meaning of life, as far as man on earth can apprehend it, in beauty. On the other hand, skepticism was Shelley's basic attitude as well. In "Alastor" and in the second stanza of the "Hymn to Intellectual Beauty" we find him—like Keats in the "Epistle to Reynolds"—craving for answers to the questions raised by the "eternal fierce destruction" at work in the universe; and Shelley's alleged dogmatism becomes very doubtful when we recall how early he acknowledged that

> No voice from some sublimer world hath ever
> To sage or poet these responses given—

or ever will. For Shelley, as for Keats, the first lesson taught by experience was agnosticism.

Once this stage has been reached, it is of course possible to conceive a number of responses widely ranging between the two extremes of suicidal nihilism and thoughtless sybaritism. The Lake poets abolished the supremacy of experience and reason and reverted to religious idealism. Keats and Shelley attempted to make sense out of life's sorrow and evil in terms of the aesthetic approach: man's endeavors and frustrations, his revolt and his defeat are justified in the name of such intensity of beauty as may inhere in "the tempestuous loveliness of terror." In the "Ode to the West Wind," however, this is but a minor trend. The distinguishing feature of Shelley is perhaps his manly determination—which can certainly be construed as intellectual arrogance—to work out an acceptable positive philosophy on the basis of ontological ignorance. In the cosmos as man's limited senses can perceive it, the only enduring reality is the immanent, impersonal force of change. As an object, it is man's tragedy that he is bound to fall a victim of mutability. As a subject, it is man's greatness that he is sensitive to and aware of his fate; it is the poet's privilege that he can shape the human drama into a thing of beauty; and it is the prophet's glory that, in his recognition that evolution is a power within as well as an outside force, he can master its energy and actively curb it to alleviate the ills of mankind.

It is one of the recurring patterns of Western civilization that its wildest fits of idealism ultimately serve to deepen and enrich and revitalize a central tradition of positive acceptance of the human condition. As far as European romanticism is concerned, this has been generally acknowledged only in the case of German literature at the turn of the eighteenth and nineteenth centuries. German historians have a disconcerting habit of dividing the twin careers of Schiller and Goethe into a period of wild *Sturm und Drang* romanticism followed by a period of subdued and mature *Klassik*. What this implies is simply that both writers' youthful revolutionary idealism brought them back to a more sedate consideration of the universe and of the function of art in it. Their individualistic rebellion against constraints imposed by society led them to a renewed sense of social responsibility; their rejection of reality helped them toward a deeper understanding of it; and their emphasis on untrammeled self-expression in poetry ultimately resulted in a subtler perception of the function of formal values. . . . The same dialectical movement controlled the swift evolution of the major romantic poets of England. Their basic intuition of spiritual oneness combined with a recognition of the inescapable duality of spirit and matter to produce a far more subtle view of both the kind of unity which they felt and the kind of duality which they experienced. Their youthful dream of perfection coalesced with their experience of evil and grief to provide new meaning and new vitality for the traditional, Christian-Stoic ethos of acceptance and responsibility. The net result of the dialectical struggle between the ideal premise and the experiential premise is a synthesis which brings romanticism back to the scale of values which had dominated the Western mind for centuries; indeed, it was this agonizing struggle which made them perceive, through personal experience and individual meditation, the vital rationale of those values.

Nor is this development traceable only in the intellectual field of the romantic world outlook, or in the moral field of the romantic conception of the good life. It is also manifest in the sphere of poetic practice. The romantic revolt against rules of composition that were felt to have become mechanical was actuated by an urgent need for individual sincerity and total expressiveness, both emotional and intellectual. For the romantic poet, the highest value is authenticity. He is not concerned with teaching or pleasing, because he has no palpable design upon the reader. He does not set out to impress him with his wit and skill. His main purpose is to elucidate, to clarify, and to express his inner experiences, his hopes, his insights, his puzzlement, his anxieties, with maximum accuracy—a feat which can only be performed through symbolic statement. This need to rejuvenate poetry by bringing it back to the sources of genuine experience accounts for Wordsworth's early emphasis on the "spontaneous overflow of powerful feelings." It was, as we can now recognize, a somewhat dangerous trend. For men of lesser or of no genius, the criterion of sincerity was later taken to justify the most nauseating exhibitions of cheap sentimentality, the most incoherent ramblings oozing from the sulphurous depths of the unconscious, and the most hermetic ejaculations of unbridled egotism. But all this is part of the decay of romanticism. For the romantics themselves soon came to realize that sincerity is only a prerequisite, not the sufficient condition of art as they understood it. In their theory and in their poetry, the principle of sincerity is effectively and successfully counterbalanced by two other principles which were part and parcel of the very tradition against which they thought they were reacting.

One is the principle of general truth, in which Aristotle [in his *Poetics*] had seen a reason for regarding poetry as "a more philosophical and a more excellent thing than history: for poetry is chiefly conversant about general truth, history about particular. In what manner, for example, any person of a certain character would speak or act, probably or necessarily—this is general; and this is the object of poetry, even while it makes use of particular names. But what Alcibiades did, or what happened to him—this is particular truth." In his *Essay of Dramatic Poesy*, Dryden had accordingly described the object of a play as to give "a just and lively image of human nature"; and after him, Samuel Johnson had insisted on literature's duty to provide "just representations of general nature." Both in doctrine and in practice, the romantics upheld this principle, and its fusion with the premise of egotistic sincerity was achieved through the symbol concept in theory and through symbolic statement in poetry. This is probably one of those exceptional cases where doctrine ultimately reveals itself to have been more pregnant with consequences than actual practice. For in poetic practice, the romantic poets were innovators only in a very limited sense: writers have always made use of symbolic statement to explore areas of experience where rational logic is too coarse a tool. But it was not until Schiller and Goethe and Coleridge and Baudelaire that a valid definition of the symbol was framed, the reason being, in all probability, that a symbolic perception of the world was a necessary prerequisite for any symbolic conception of the work of art. (pp. 250-58)

The second principle which corrects the romantic premise of spontaneity is that of organized form. There was a time when this would have seemed a shocking statement to offer. Although the romantics had abundantly proclaimed that there is no such thing as lawless art, and although Coleridge had been the initiator of the theory of organic form in England, romantic poetry was felt to be diffuse, rambling, nebulous, and, as it were, boneless, because it seldom exhibited the strongly marked structure characteristic of neoclassical poetry. It must be admitted that although the romantic poets pondered at leisure and expatiated at considerable length on most of the problems pertaining to their art, nowhere in the vast scattered body of romantic theorizing can we find any concrete, detailed discussion of structure. Herbert Read's excellent definition of organic form [in his *Form in Modern Poetry,* 1932] will help us understand why this should be so: "When a work of art has its own inherent laws, originating with its very invention and fusing in one vital unity both structure and content, then the resulting form may be described as *organic.*" This implies that the creative process is primarily expressive rather than constructive. In other words, the purpose of the poet is not to fabricate an artifact according to a formal pattern preexisting in his mind; it is to provide a total and accurate rendering of the germinal idea which stirs his imagination. If this is the poet's main preoccupation, the part played by conscious artistry—at least with regard to the overall structure of the poem—is bound to be rather slight, for the work of art in its progress from beginning to end will strive to reflect as faithfully as possible the movements of the artist's mind. In the last analysis, it depends upon the quality of the poet's mind whether his poetry will turn out to be shapeless effusion or organized form. It was, I believe, some such idea that Wordsworth had in view when he stated, in his Preface of 1800, that "Poems to which any value can be attached were never produced on any variety of subjects but by a man who, being possessed of more than usual organic sensibility, had also thought long and deeply," and Coleridge, when he wrote to Sotheby, in 1802, "that a great Poet must be, implicitè if not explicitè, a profound Metaphysician."

In times of stress and change, the quality of a poet's mind will reveal itself in his refusal to be swayed by conventional ideas and attitudes, in his readiness to explore new areas of experience and to experiment with new forms of expression, and in his capacity to do so in an orderly way. This is how both thought and poetry renew themselves. The poets of the Renaissance rejected the fixed forms mechanically derived from

the organic forms of courtly poetry by late medieval versifiers, in favor of the Pindaric ode whose freedom and flexibility made it a more suitable medium for expressing their own original living vision. This is exactly what the romantic poets did. Apparently, they were unaware of the precise nature of the new formal patterns which they were creating—or they would have discussed them. Indeed, it is most probable that those patterns were not immediately perceptible because they did not correspond to the usual criteria of formal structure, the chief of which are regularity, uniformity, and symmetry. There are two carved scenes on Keats's urn, but he devotes three stanzas to one, and one to the other; the two main parts of "Resolution and Independence" are extremely unequal in length, and they can be subdivided in two different ways with different results according as the principle of division is topical or thematic.

It was to be expected that the principle of spontaneity would make havoc of external, static unity. This does not mean that it is destructive of any kind of unity. . . . [Much] of the profoundly satisfying quality of [Romantic] poetry lies in the fact that the romantic writers successfully resisted the temptation of shapelessness in the field of aesthetic creation in the same way that they resisted the temptation of extreme idealism in the ontological field and the temptation of sybaritic egotism or querulous self-pity in the ethical field. It is one of the life-giving paradoxes of literary history that the present-day revaluation of romanticism as a stage in the wider continuity of the Western tradition—not only moral and philosophical but also aesthetic—could not have been accomplished if the twentieth-century reaction against romanticism had not renewed critical interest in the classical problem of formal structure, just as we could not have become alive to the oxymoronic quality of romantic thought and poetry if it had not been for the rediscovery of the Metaphysicals and for the stress laid by modern anti-romantic critics on the significance of paradox and ambiguity. The reappraisal of romanticism in our time provides a rather fascinating example of the ways in which literary history and criticism combine to sift the work of the past and so to assess what is truly valuable in the vast storehouses of our literary inheritance. When Keats wrote that "a thing of beauty is a joy for ever," he was certainly unaware of all the possible implications of the phrase. But we know that only a thing which is a joy forever can truly be called a thing of beauty. And in order to be a joy forever, it must satisfy two timeless criteria. It must provide a genuine insight into the reality of man's condition; it must express man's hopes and fears, his doubts and perplexities; it must renew our perception of the miracle and the misery of the human predicament. And through the paradox of art, it must fix this image of the transient for so long as men can breathe or eyes can see, thus mastering the power which Endymion attributed to love: the power "to make / Men's being mortal, immortal.". . . The status now awarded to romantic poetry, after it has been submitted to the exacting tests of close critical analysis, shows that it too falls within the general definition of great poetry which Shelley had proposed in his *Defence:* "A great poem is a fountain for ever overflowing with the waters of wisdom and delight; and after one person and one age has exhausted all of its divine effluence which their peculiar relations enable them to share, another and yet another succeeds, and new relations are ever developed, the source of an unforeseen and an unconceived delight." (pp. 259-63)

Albert S. Gérard, in his English Romantic Poetry:

Ethos, Structure, and Symbol in Coleridge, Wordsworth, Shelley, and Keats, *University of California
Press, 1968, 284 p.*

JOSEPH A. WITTREICH, JR.

[*In the following excerpt, Wittreich places Romantic poetry in
the tradition of prophetic and apocalyptic literature.*]

Not since the Puritan Revolution had there been so much
prophesying [as during the Romantic period]—or so much
writing on the prophecies, secular and sacred, the focal point
of which always seemed to be the Apocalypse of St. John,
whose prophecy, it was thought, was now being brought to
fulfillment by the French Revolution. Robert Southey caught
something of this eschatological excitement when, in a letter
of 1824, reflecting back on those revolutionary years, he remarked, "Few persons, but those who lived in it, can conceive
or comprehend what the meaning of the French Revolution
was, nor what a visionary world seemed to open upon those
who were entering it. Old things seemed passing away, and
nothing new was dreamt of but the regeneration of the human
race." Wordsworth not only shared in but fueled this enthusiasm as he looked ahead to "a sublime movement of deliverance," declaring in *The Convention of Cintra,* "Let . . . the
human creature be rouzed; . . . let him rise and act. . . . Regeneration is at hand." In *Reply to Mathetes,* he represented
the poets as morning stars, awakening men from sleep and
mobilizing the energy of the multitudes for some glorious
end. The excitement was contagious; poets were caught up
in it; and Milton himself, along with John of Patmos, was regularly summoned to preside over this volatile phase of history
when the first paradise seemed ready to be lost in the splendors of a second.

The Romantics did not discover prophecy—they recovered
it—and, in the process, restored poetry to the once but no
longer secure foundations of Scripture. At different times, of
course, first this scriptural book, then that, predominated;
but during the Romantic period it was the prophetic books
that commandeered attention, and a specific one: the Book
of Revelation. That is not surprising, given Romanticism's
predisposition to use this book as a mirror of its own history
and its prompting of artists to use this same book as an aesthetic model or as the cipher for a poetics. What is surprising
is the extent to which Romantic poetry, allying itself with a
tradition of apocalyptic prophecy, often casting itself in this
mold, recoils from apocalypse, turning a tradition that had
always afforded a critique of culture into a tradition that
would now critique itself. And what is still more surprising,
perhaps, is the extent to which both St. John and Milton
themselves seem to authorize such an enterprise. Both seem
to comprehend that apocalyptic is but one of an array of attitudes a writer might assume while writing prophecy, which
credits the present with a responsibility for shaping the future
that apocalypse glimpses. Prophecy ascribes to man, to
human consciousness, the task of making the future that
apocalypse, in its despair, consigns to a God in whom it vests
the power of effecting what man is otherwise powerless to realize. If prophecy is an invasion of the mind, an agent in the
expansion of human consciousness, apocalypse (as it was
then widely understood) is an assault upon history, a deus ex
machina device for achieving what is humanly unattainable.

The very idea of apocalypse has been used, and abused, as a
code word for Romantic ideology, which exalts imagination

in poetry, symbol and myth in poetic style, and which perceives an integrated world in nature. As foundation stones of
Romanticism, apocalypse and prophecy are a joint presence
in its literature, revealing the extent to which that literature
is self-reflexive and furnishing in conjunction a critique of the
very ideology that literature would foster and of the self-
representations that it would promote. The ideological critique that some would perform from the outside, or that they
see being performed by the second generation of Romantics
upon the first, is more often than not an embedment within
Romantic literature itself, which summoning up commonplaces of prophetic and apocalyptic traditions also submits
those commonplaces to scrutiny, even sometimes to harsh interrogation. Jerome McGann says it best when he observes
that "Romantic poetry incorporates Romantic ideology as a
drama of contradictions which are inherent to that ideology.
In this respect Romantic poetry occupies an implicit—
sometimes even an explicit—critical position toward its subject matter" [see Further Reading]. And as McGann goes on
to observe:

> Changed circumstances . . . pushed the later Ro-
> mantics, in particular Byron and Shelley, into a
> more seriously problematic relation to the Roman-
> tic ideas of the poet-as-*vates* and the special privi-
> lege of art. In them the so-called Romantic Conflict
> went much deeper than anything by the earlier Ro-
> mantics, and this later problematic eventually con-
> tributed to the breakup of Romanticism as a coher-
> ent movement.

Plate from William Blake's The Book of Urizen.

Blake and Wordsworth may seem to be little more than purveyors of a modified, secularized apocalyptic tradition that in the poetry of Coleridge comes under a careful review, thus paving the way for the sharpening attention and deepening criticism of this tradition afforded by Byron, Keats, and the Shelleys. Even with Blake and Wordsworth, however, though more covertly, the commonplaces of prophetic and apocalyptic traditions, as well as commonplace attitudes toward both, are being interrogated from the inside with the result that such interrogation, as well as the critique that it engenders, may be seen—indeed *should* be seen—as an aspect of the dialectic playing itself out, with increasing intensity, within Romantic literature itself. (pp. 39-42)

The Apocalypse is a subversive book—and most subversive, as Vasily Rozanov has shown [in *The Apocalypse of Our Time, and Other Writings,* 1977] of its own supposed ideology. For once the stars are torn from the firmament and the world is in ruins, once weeping and lamentation have ceased, tears have been wiped away, and there is a reign of peace, what is brought forth is not life in heaven but life on earth: "the joy of living on earth, *precisely on earth.* . . . The Apocalypse presents, calls for, and demands a new religion. . . . It shouts 'at the end of time' . . . for 'the last age of humanity.' " The movement of the Apocalypse was not beyond but back into time and history, and in aligning themselves so closely with the prophetic Milton, the Romantics found an important conduit for John's "apocalyptic" message.

No evasion, no idealization of history, Romantic prophecy emerges from Miltonic prophecy, appropriating its tenets and discoveries. When, in *Milton,* Blake quips, "Say first! what mov'd Milton" he does so by way of remembering what Milton says first in *Paradise Lost,* that it was in response to an ancient prophecy in heaven that Satan moved against Adam and Eve and that Paradise was lost, and, remembering this, by way of playing upon the irony that Milton now moves in response to a prophecy which he understands, only gradually, and by which the lost paradise will be restored. Prophecy has often had negative consequences on history, a fact Milton himself underscores by ending *Paradise Lost* as it began, with a prophecy whose vision of history, not full of glad tidings, is fraught with the misery, fever, and fret of human existence; a prophecy in which the veil on coming centuries is rent, opening a window on the history of the poet's own time. Prophecy of the past masking as prophecy of the future is actually being written in the present tense. The example of Milton in old age, having fallen on evil days and evil tongues, compassed round by danger and darkness but not enslaved, dramatizes the situation of the prophet, one of exile and cultural alienation, provoking him into self-scrutiny and scrutiny of history and then into quarreling with both, and heightening his political concern and urgency, even if paradoxically such concern and urgency seem diminished by his self-reflection and analysis. Milton made clear to the Romantics, through the examples of both *Paradise Lost* and *Samson Agonistes,* first that prophecy which seems to be a revelation of the poet to the world is, in fact, a revelation of the world to itself, and second that even if poetic prophecy harbors apocalyptic desires (and perhaps *most* when it harbors such desires), the poet-prophet must tell the story of what went wrong, monstrously so, with the story itself seeming always to ravage the apocalyptic myth, distancing history from it and forcing a readjustment of expectations in the wake of damaged hopes and dashed promises.

In Milton's last poems, no less than in the Apocalypse itself, apocalypse is brought under scrutiny and becomes an object of criticism; it is represented as an irony curling back upon itself. That is, the Apocalypse presented itself to the Romantics as what we would call today a very Derridean, deconstructive book. . . . Both John and Milton appear to devise a system for delivering us from apocalyptic systems, and in such a way as to make the Apocalypse a very congenial book for those who felt, as Wordsworth did in "Home at Grasmere," that poetry should now divest itself of "all Arcadian dreams, All golden fancies of the golden age, / The bright array of shadowy thoughts from times / That were before all time, and are to be / Ere time expire."

What is distinctive about Romantic poetry is the disjunction of prophecy and apocalypse within it, together with its compulsion to move prophecy beyond poetics into the realm of ideology, where prophecy and apocalypse, losing their identity, acquire distinction; where in poetry there is now a dispersion of prophetic voices. Not all these voices sing of joy; some murmur ominously, and others, uttering odious truth, send forth songs of misery and woe. Some would exalt the English nation; others would shake her shores. In the great poetic prophecies of English Romanticism, these various voices are orchestrated, now with this and now with that one predominating; and of these prophecies *The Prelude* is still the premiere example. Long before its publication and immediately after hearing a recitation of it, Coleridge, in "To William Wordsworth" (1806), recognized *The Prelude* for what it is: a "prophetic Lay," more than historic, about the building up of the human spirit. Here Wordsworth joins with Blake in depicting the formation of the prophetic character—the same agonizing, arduous process unfolded in Blake's prophetic writings from *The Marriage of Heaven and Hell* through *Jerusalem.* As Byron and Shelley were later to do, he turns the prophetic poet into an oracle, making of him the image of a better time and making him issue a prophecy that begins and ends in the mind of man.

Not just Blake and Wordsworth, but all the Romantics, are preoccupied with the vatic stance and maintain ties with prophetic tradition—with what is, from their perspective, inseparable from the Milton tradition. Blake and Wordsworth are the most firmly bound to this tradition, exploring the possibilities for prophecy in the modern world. Shelley, however, particularly in *Prometheus Unbound,* manifests a tendency, also evident in the poetry of Coleridge and Byron, to investigate the limitations of prophecy by way of rendering more precisely its efficacy for the new age. And that same tendency is there, even more emphatically, in the poetry of Keats.

Of the Romantics, Keats is the poet least rooted in prophetic tradition; yet he is also the poet who gathers into sharpest focus the turns and counterturns of Romantic poetry, its fleeing from and then flying back into vision, as well as the perennial problem of whether the poet speaks oracularly or merely gives vent to his dreams: "Was it a vision, or a waking dream? / . . .—Do I wake or sleep?" That question is posted, not just here in "Ode to a Nightingale," but in *The Fall of Hyperion,* where visionaries and dreamers are identified only to be denigrated (ironically by the "High Prophetess") for not thinking of the earth. Subsequently, in lines Keats apparently meant to cancel, Moneta instructs the poet: "The poet and the dreamer are distinct, / Diverse, sheer opposite, antipodes. / The one pours out a balm upon the world, / The other vexes it." *The Fall of Hyperion* begins by distinguishing between

Poets and Fanatics, between those who are engaged by and disengaged from the world. What gnaws at Keats clearly is that those who fly after their visions may also be flying from social and political responsibility: the fanatic, paradoxically, surrenders the ideology of prophecy. In the very act of making such distinctions, though, Keats opens a gulf between poets and visionaries, between poetry and prophecy, that the other Romantics had sought to bridge. Coleridge called any distinction between the artist and the visionary a coldblooded hypothesis; and Shelley wrote his *Defence of Poetry,* in part, to argue for the interconnectedness of poetry and prophecy, his objective thus being to make "poetry an attribute of prophecy." But as with Keats, so with the rest of these poets: they are impelled to scrutinize prophecy, to examine its limitations; and they conclude that this tradition is cause both for celebration and for criticism.

Part of the allure of prophecy is that poetry could be fashioned to fit its outline without ever being circumscribed by it. Prophecy seemed to correlate with Blake's—with the Romantics'—idea of one central form containing all others; it was a mixed genre, a composite or global order. It was also a difficult order hammered out of a multiplicity of perspectives and organized around a system of synchronisms, a consequence of which was that prophecy was often plotless and always radically redundant. This mode was especially agreeable to poets like Wordsworth who were in constant search of new combinations of forms, who made an idealism of sundry forms commingling, and whose objective through form was to present the parts as parts with a feeling for the whole, to construct new patterns out of the elements of previous patterns and thereby reactualize the text within the text. Wordsworth does this in *The Prelude* by allowing the final episode on Mount Snowdon to recapitulate all of the poem's earlier hilltop and mountaintop experiences. The very logic of prophecy calls for the surrender of usual notions of sequence and succession, for their displacement by synchronic structures, and cajoles poets into searching for new and more intricate forms of intertextuality. Indeed, those new forms of intertextuality provide the principles for interleaving one's own poems and for integrating them into the one poem, which is the poet's own canon—Wordsworth's Gothic cathedral to which all his poems are architecturally significant and for which they are mutually supportive.

The special allure of the Revelation prophecy is that it posed the crucial questions for an aspiring poet-prophet. Was prophecy possible, and could it be profitable in the new age? Did the spirit of the age neuter or nurture prophecy? And what exactly are the literary activities of the prophet, hence of the poet who is an aspiring prophet? Is John simply a compositor, setting forth another's vision? If so, is he actually redacting another's prophecy, or is he rather editing it? If an editor, is it only another's prophecy that he is preparing; or does he instead stitch together various prophecies, making an anthology of the scattered fragments of many others' visions? Or, if John is the author of this prophecy, is he an active or passive recipient of his vision? Does he record here one continuous vision, or separate visions received at different times and even at times distant from another? The answers to these questions, in a very important way, determine the authenticity, as well as the authority, of any given prophecy and affect the form it will assume, as well as the truth claims made for it. But most important, perhaps, is the question of the relationship between prophecy and apocalypse and of the relationship of their own poetry to the traditions of both. Prophe-

cy may supply the form, the poetic casting; but apocalypse seems always to be the deep concern, functioning here as subtext and there as co-text. Prophecy may become self-reflexive; but its turn upon itself is usually preliminary to its turning against apocalypse, a tradition whose thrust was into future history and then beyond and whose subject, it seemed, was God, not man.

Witness the example of Coleridge, whose own dedication to the art of prophecy manifests itself in such poems as *Religious Musings,* which, referring to the Book of Revelation, itself culminates in a vision; or in "The Destiny of Nations," which Coleridge calls "A Vision" and in which he speaks of prophets as "Fit instruments and best, of perfect end"; and in "Ode to the Departing Year," which in its dedicatory letter allows that "among the Ancients, the Bard and the Prophet were one and the same character" and which also finds Coleridge explaining, "although I prophesy curses, I pray fervently for blessings." The prophetic role here assumed by Coleridge, the poem's epigraph makes clear, is that of a Cassandra; and the epigraph, as Coleridge explains, is there to remind us that "we see but *one* side, and are blind to noon day evidence on the other." Mankind, with its single vision, lets the prophets like Cassandra go unheeded. Still, the difficulties with prophesying are twofold: typically, prophecy is addressed to an audience without the eyes to see and the ears to hear; yet the prophet himself is thwarted by himself—by his failure to achieve vision despite his straining for and yearning after it, or by its loss, by the poet's own difficulty in articulating the vision and in creating the paradise the vision decrees. But the prophet is also thwarted by his medium, which is marked by both obscurity and fragmentariness. These limitations of prophecy offer the grounds for exploration in Coleridge's first collection of his poetry, *Sibylline Leaves* (1817). Through his title, Coleridge relates a whole gathering of poems to prophetic tradition and, furthermore, indicates his own comprehension of the problem of prophesying in the new age.

That enigmatic title brought notice to these Cumaean murmurs, seemingly tossed about by all the winds of heaven, and even sent one of Coleridge's [reviewers] to a dictionary, whereupon the following explanation was elicited from him:

> "Sibylline", says our Dictionary, means "of or belonging to a Sibyl or Prophetess": the word cannot therefore, we hope, be appropriated by Mr. Coleridge, who is not so humble a poet as to assume, voluntarily, the character of an old woman. But on refreshing our classic memory we grasp the very essence and soul of this mysterious title. The Sibyl wrote her prophecies on leaves; so does Mr. Coleridge his verses—the prophecies of the Sibyl become incomprehensible, if not instantly gathered; so does the sense of Mr. Coleridge's poetry; the Sibyl asked the same price from Tarquin for her books when in 9, 6, and 3 vols; so does Mr. Coleridge for his, when scattered over sundry publications, and now as collected into one—as soon as the Sibyl had concluded her bargain she vanished, and was seen no more in the regions of Cumae so does Mr. Coleridge assure us he will be seen no more on Parnassus—the Sibylline books were preserved by Kings, had a College of Priests to take care of them, and were so esteemed by the people, that they were seldom consulted; even so does Mr. Coleridge look to delight Monarchs, his book will be treasured by the Eleven Universities, and we venture to suppose that it will be treated by the public . . . pretty

much in the same way with the ravings of his Archetype.

However cunning, this explanation disregards the serious dimension of Coleridge's title: its intention of thrusting all these poems within the orbit of prophecy and, simultaneously, of identifying the problems felt by a poet who would now assume the role of prophet. In this regard, Coleridge's own note on his title is revelatory: "The following collection has been entitled *Sibylline Leaves,*" he says, "in allusion to the fragmentary and widely scattered state in which they have been long suffered to remain." It is the "fragmentary . . . state" of these poems, then, to which Coleridge draws our attention and which he thereby invites us to ponder. Doing just that [in his *"Kubla Khan" and the Fall of Jerusalem,* 1975], E. S. Shaffer notices that the preface to "Kubla Khan" "is not an excuse for a fragment, but a presentation of credentials for writing apocalyptic, for assuming the prophetic role. . . . The prefatory 'Vision in a Dream' becomes a kind of authenticator of the poet's right to present the prophetic lays of a 'John.' " Many of Coleridge's poems are, like "Kubla Khan," both "A Vision" and "A Fragment": they come forth, in the words of *Religious Musings,* "in fragments wild / Sweet echoes of unearthly melodies" and are all "Monads of the infinite mind," particles of the divine vision. Each poem is an atom belonging to one body, pursuing its own self-centered end while contributing at the same time to a larger totality. Just as in "The Destiny of Nations," the large vision is composed of "fragments many and huge," which, once assembled as in "The Picture," "Come trembling back, unite, and once more / The pool becomes a mirror." There is method in Coleridge's fragments.

Coleridge's title implies a theory of the fragment, inviting the reader to perceive these poems as deliberately fragmentary and to find in them a metaphor for evolving consciousness and being. Yet the title is also a reminder that the oracles of the sibyls were consulted on occasions of disaster, their purpose being not to predict the future but instead to counsel men in how to avert a national danger. Through his title, therefore, Coleridge also points to the legislative function of his poems, to their potentiality as a transforming power both on individual men and on national history. In this connection, Coleridge would probably expect us to recall something of the history of the sibylline oracles. The pagan sibyls were replaced first by Hebrew, then by Christian ones. In each moment of replacement, the old form is retained while the content is altered; the old form indicates the concern of the newer oracles (whether they be Hebrew or Christian) with a "pagan" audience and, furthermore, implies the oracles' purpose of conversion: they would bestow light on mankind and prepare a new way for him to follow. Always ethical and historical in their interest, the oracles, once Christianized, turn from the past to future history. In the process, sibylline literature merges into apocalyptic literature, prophecy and apocalyptics now joining together and remaining in early Romantic literature closely allied. They are irrevocably allied in Blake's poetry—in the correlation of *Milton* and *Jerusalem,* for example—and also in the early Coleridge as evidenced by the most startling of his prophetic poems, "The Rime of the Ancient Mariner." Yet by Wordsworth and Byron, prophecy and apocalypse are segregated, their long-enduring alliance broken, for purposes of redefining relationships and revising inflections. By the Shelleys, on the other hand, apocalyptics itself is distinguished from millenarianism: they reject the former, at least as an eschatological conception, while counte-

nancing the latter. Keats, for his part, deepens the Romantic critique of apocalyptics into a critique of the visionary ideology in which prophecy itself had established its moorings.

In various of her novels, Mary Shelley provides a link between Coleridge's thinking on prophecy and that of Byron and her poet-husband. Fragments of discourse, ostensibly edited by Victor Frankenstein, then by Captain Walton, and arranged by Mary according to the logic of her vision within a dream, *Frankenstein* has been described as "obviously and notoriously a 'prophetic' book"; and it clearly belongs to what was destined to become a tradition of the apocalyptic novel. More interesting for our purposes, however, is *Valperga,* which postulates that prophecy is about the self that is also the object of its contemplation and which, through two Cassandra-like heroines, explores the burden of prophecy. Mary Shelley concludes, it would seem, that it is a test of the true prophet that he should not be heard, that the prophecy itself go unheeded. In *The Last Man,* there is a reflection, in the introduction, on the 1818 visit of Mary and Shelley to the sibyl's cave; and that reflection, in turn, sets forth the idea that the leaves found in the cave are fragments of prophecy, the raw materials that require shaping into a unified and intelligible vision. (pp. 42-50)

What is important, Mary claims, is a decipherer—someone to integrate and explain and give continuity to the fragments. Prophetic works are, by definition, fragmentary, the particles of a vision that receives articulation and definition only to the extent that an author of prophecy is able to make its fragmentary parts cohere, each with the others. The journey into the cave is the journey into the self, into one's own mind; and the leaves are fragments of that mind which, once integrated, brings light out of darkness. The episode is another rendering of Byron's promotion of self-knowledge and of Shelley's proclamation that prophecy begins and ends in the human mind.

Byron's most conspicuous evocation of prophetic tradition occurs in his preface to *The Prophecy of Dante,* where he identifies as his literary models not just "the Prophecies of Holy Writ" but also "Cassandra of Lycophron, and the Prophecy of Nereus," having already explained in a letter to John Murray, dated 29 October 1819, that Dante, here speaking in his own person, will embrace "all topics in the way of prophecy—like Lycophron's Cassandra." Through these references to prophetic tradition, Byron implies a criticism of prophecy, thereby forging his own statement on the problems of prophesying in the modern world. Apollo had bestowed on Cassandra the spirit of prophecy; but in her prophesyings (first of the ruin of Troy and then of the death of Agamemnon) she was unheeded. Because it is not listened to, Byron is saying, prophecy makes nothing happen and, because of the failings of mankind, has never possessed the legislative power so often ascribed to it. The truth of prophecy, hence their acknowledgment of the prophet, steals upon men tardily, "strik[ing] their eyes through many a tear / And mak[ing] them own the prophet in his tomb." Byron's critique here is underscored by his reference to the prophecy of Nereus, who checks the waves, halts Helen's ship, and foretells her cruel fate. The point of this prophecy, as related in one of the Horatian poems—that Helen in her adultery will become the destroyer of a nation—is enlarged upon in a succeeding poem, where blame is affixed not so much to Helen as to the fury of the lion that exists in all men and that motivates them to run their ploughs over, and thereby destroy, the world.

With considerable calculation, Byron allows *Marino Faliero* and *The Prophecy of Dante* to front one another in the same poetic volume, where a cautious commitment to prophecy emerges out of a devastating critique of apocalypse; where a world of fallen vision is paradoxically redeemed by vision, by the emergence of a prophetic consciousness. Byron is reported to have had a highly particularized knowledge of the New Testament, especially of Revelation, and to have talked about the Apocalypse as a curiously perplexing book. Both poems use the Book of Revelation to deliver their pointedly prophetic message, which is a message against apocalypse, even in *The Prophecy of Dante* where "the hue / Of human sacrifice . . . / Troubles the clotted air," where "still Division sows the seeds of woe," but where all that is necessary is for the avenger to stop avenging. *Marino Faliero* climaxes in a Christian vision of apocalypse, with the avenging angel emptying the vials of wrath in the harlot city of Venice—climaxes in a violent swirl of largely negative apocalyptic imagery. Here apocalyptic impulses are shown defeating human freedom and leaving the poet on a rock of desolate despair. The apocalyptic vision at the end of *Marino Faliero* crowds upon the prophetic eye of Dante, the latter poem reinforcing the conclusion of the former one, that apocalypse, which often had been a device for tempering disillusion with hope, has become an instrument instead for intensifying despair with a sense of doom. If prophecy offers a potential release from the tragedy of history, apocalypse causes history to lean back again upon tragedy, making history indistinguishable from tragedy.

Apocalypse is an idea in and an illusion of history, which needs shattering, and is also a spirit in man, which needs restraining, an avenging passion which requires bridling. This, in turn, becomes Byron's highest hope for prophecy: that it may forestall an apocalypse in the world and become the principal agent in individual redemption, effecting those discoveries, first in *The Prophecy of Dante* and then in *Childe Harold's Pilgrimage,* which enable the poet, finally, to accede to the prophetic office and to enlighten mankind as an oracle. Byron's point here is like Wordsworth's in "Home at Grasmere:" the poet is not born into the consciousness of the prophet but must struggle to achieve it; he is not summoned by God but beckoned by history to prophesy. Both poets may be said to begin in the same attitude, the one Wordsworth assumes in "Home at Grasmere":

> No prophet was he, had not even a hope,
> Scarcely a wish . . .
> The lot of others, never could be his lot.

Like Wordsworth, Byron reaches the discovery that, indeed, he can be an oracle to his fellow man. Only gradually does the poet succeed to the prophetic office, and only then (and then, at least for Byron, in only a very limited sense) does he become an oracle and, like Wordsworth in *The Prelude,* an epic hero. This principle animates *Don Juan*—a poem that begins with the declaration "I want a hero" and that ends in the discovery that the poem's narrator *is* its hero.

It is too simple to conclude that, speaking "with an ironic countervoice," Byron "opens a satirical perspective on the vatic stance of his Romantic contemporaries" [M. H. Abrams, *Natural Supernaturalism,* 1971]. Rather, he foregrounds the undersong—its doubts, misgivings, suspicions—of all Romantic prophecy; but also, in admitting to the prophetic consciousness as a potentiality of the poet, Byron joins with Blake, Wordsworth, and the Shelleys in the Romantic

celebration of the artist as a culture-hero. Like Blake in *The Marriage of Heaven and Hell,* Byron exploits the radical possibilities of eschatological satire. But unlike Coleridge, Byron, in *Childe Harold's Pilgrimage,* claims no muse for his "lowly lay"; he dissociates himself from "the phrensy" of prophetic tradition and refuses "to soar," preferring instead to gaze beneath the "cloudy canopy" and to proclaim "the Muses' seat . . . their grave." On the face of things, Byron is doing just what Hazlitt accused him of doing, "reversing the laws of vision," in a poem whose "broken magnificence," in the words of John Wilson, is but the surface expression of a larger intention to assemble the "fragments of a dark dream of life" and stand them up against all the coherent visions of utopia made of hopes that have become like ashes in the mouth, and founded upon the supposition that man is becoming instead of that he is ceasing to be. It is not that Byron is simply anti-utopian; rather, he would exchange utopias of escape for those of realization.

Byron's strategy, both here and in *Don Juan,* is like Coleridge's: to present a poem whose parts are shattered fragments of a whole, a poem that will be like "a broken mirror, which the glass / In every fragment multiplies; and makes / A thousand images of one that was." That strategy Byron justifies through his explanation that man "seest not all; but piecemeal . . . must break, / To separate contemplation, the great whole." "Our outward sense," he says, "Is but of gradual grasp"; and so only if we grow with its growth can "we . . . dilate / Our spirits to the size of that they contemplate." And Byron's purpose, like Coleridge's, is conversion and liberation of a "race of inborn slaves, who wage war for their chains, . . . rather than be free." Yet that purpose in Byron's poetry becomes highly restricted. A poem like "The Rime of the Ancient Mariner," for example, couples prophecy and apocalypse; it is about the surrender of hope and betrayal of vision, about the consequences of not keeping faith in time of trouble. Betraying his vision, the mariner as false prophet consigns others to eternal death and himself to death-in-life; he keeps others from the marriage feast. Yet even if he has slain his vision, thereby deferring apocalyptic consummation, the whole experience survives to form a prophecy, a warning prophecy that, if heeded, will open upon the naturalized apocalypse of Wordsworth's "Tintern Abbey," with the alienation of the one poem giving way to the communion of the other. The love of nature leads to the love of man, and the apocalypse in nature prophesies an apocalypse in history. In contrast, a poem like *Childe Harold's Pilgrimage* not only makes prophecy an end in itself but tightens its compass so greatly that, while still encircling and so pertaining to the individual, it no longer contains and thus loses all contact with, all pertinence for, history.

In *The Ghost of Abel,* Blake chides Byron for this perversion of prophecy, for this denial of the eschatological possibilities implanted from the very beginning in that tradition. Implicit in Shelley's poems, which repeatedly enter into dialogue with Byron's, is this same criticism, in the infinitely more restrained formulation of his preface to *The Revolt of Islam:* "There is a reflux in the tide of human things which bears the shipwrecked hopes of men into a secure haven after the storms are past. Methinks, those who now live have survived an age of despair." Shelley's fine discrimination of history and eschatology may prevent him from restoring prophecy and apocalypse to union, but he does restore millennial expectations to prophecy. His poetry everywhere intones the counsel of *Prometheus Unbound:* "to hope till Hope creates

/ From its own wreck the thing it contemplates," although even here the prospect of a new Promethean man seems brighter than that for a new golden age in history. Demogorgon's words are reminiscent of those more prosaic lines in *The Prelude* where Wordsworth declares that "Man is only weak through his . . . / . . . want of hope where evidence divine / Proclaims to him that hope should be most sure." They recall, too, Byron's 1821 *Memoranda* statement, "What is Poetry?—The feeling of a Former world and Future"—a statement that causes the poet to invoke the prophets and thereupon to observe, "If it were not for Hope, where would the Future be? . . . in all human affairs it is Hope—Hope—Hope."

Prometheus Unbound, the greatest and surely the most hopeful of Shelley's prophetic utterances, seems to argue that for the great artist, for Prometheus, revolution is not enough: the great artist, of which Prometheus is the prototype and Shelley an ectype or copy, must also reconceive, create anew, the essential framework of the world. In Shelley's countermyth to Aeschylus's, Prometheus achieves his apotheosis as poet-prophet. He is the maker of the prophecy that, emanating from him, also ends in him. The archetypal prophet, like Blake's Los, Prometheus is also the emblem of prophecy: "He gave man speech, and speech created thought / . . . and the harmonious mind / Poured forth in all-prophetic song." The associations here exploited by Shelley are the same ones that Sidney, in his *Apologie for Poetrie,* had focused for the Renaissance: Prometheus is the prototypical poet, "the first light-giuer to ignorance"; he is a type of the poet as *vates* who is all that Prometheus's name, as Sidney interprets it, implies—"a diuiner, Fore-seer, or *Prophet*"—and who, considering what may be and should be, apprehends and thereupon paints for mankind a new ideal. "These bee they," says Sidney, "that, as the first and most noble sorte [of poet], may justly be called *Vates.*" Similar associations, of course, are developed by Byron in *The Prophecy of Dante,* where the poet is depicted as a prophet, a "new Prometheus . . . / Bestowing fire from heaven, and then, too late, / Finding the pleasures given repaid with pain"; they are also inferred by Mary Shelley and recorded in her notes to Percy's poem, where she describes Prometheus as "the prophetic soul of humanity" and the final act of his poem as a "rejoicing in the fulfillment of the prophecies."

Those associations may be inferred from *Prometheus Unbound* because they are embedded in its text, having first been gathered into focus by its epigraph. There reference is made to Amphiarus, who becomes the spokesman for Zeus, a false prophet who is a mouthpiece for and an upholder of orthodoxies; and that reference implies a contrast with Prometheus, who is the overthrower of Zeus, a prophet who, undermining orthodoxies, would remake the world. Myth opposes myth in *Prometheus Unbound,* where Shelley's supporting strategy is to create a new oracle, a new prophecy, that will subvert the old oracle, the old prophecy. Yet this new prophecy, for all its apocalyptic rumblings, is not an "apocalypse." What follows the appeal "Tear the veil!" and the declaration "It is torn" is a revelation; but that revelation promises nothing that is final, complete, conclusive. History may be brought to an apotheosis, but it may also slide back into its former self.

Early readers of *Prometheus Unbound* understood something of this, declaring the poem's subject to be "the *deliverance* of Prometheus"—his "transition . . . from a state of suffering

to a state of happiness; together with a corresponding change in the situation of mankind." Modern criticism has finely honed that perception, freeing Shelley of the charge of mindless millenarianism and aligning him with Swedenborg and Blake, for whom an apocalypse is, first of all, a mental event—man's summoning of himself to judgment—and possibly a causal, yet conditional, event whereby a man, through regeneration, may redeem the universe, even if only temporarily. The poem's revelation, as Harold Bloom acknowledges [in *Shelley's Mythmaking,* 1959], is "that apocalypse can roll over into the fallen state again"; or as Earl Wasserman says even more insistently [in *Shelley: A Critical Reading,* 1971], "Shelley has not promised an apocalypse for man." All he does do, through his invocation of the Book of Revelation, is to assure us that not John of Patmos's God, but only the human mind, once it becomes unbound, can suppress the serpent, seal the pit, and summon up a new heaven and a new earth in history. Insistently we are reminded by the Spirits of act I, as Prometheus is reminded, that they "bear the prophecy / Which begins and ends in thee." This is to say no more, and no less, than that prophecy is the creation of the human mind it both reflects and transforms; prophecy is a mirror of the very thing it contemplates and a model of that which it would create.

There is, moreover, an intricate and rich intertextuality joining *Prometheus Unbound* to *The Cenci* and jointing them as companion poems. The Book of Revelation is a vital part of that intertextuality, moving through the substratums of Shelley's tragedy and on the surface of his lyrical drama, serving the one poem as subtext and providing for the other a co-text, with Shelley seeming to insist that the Apocalypse, with its contrary perspectives and paradoxical formulations, furnishes both negative and positive images for history, even for post-Christian history, and that it also applies to history indefinitely, where its paradigmatic events occur over and over again, here with tragic and there with liberating consequences. If, as Byron thought, liberation is the poetry of politics, liberation is also the politics of prophecy out of which Romantic poetry is made. Here, inward commotions of the mind find their counterpart in the convulsive movements of history, the winning of inward freedom promising social betterment and prognosticating the improvement of history.

It has been said that prophecy is the central metaphor for *modern* poetry; prophecy is, in fact, the central metaphor for much poetry of the Western world, ancient and modern—Virgil's and Dante's, Ariosto's and Tasso's, Spenser's and Milton's. And more: prophecy is, arguably, the ur-form of most major poetry of English Romanticism. If the critical reorientation accomplished by an earlier generation of criticism made an orthodoxy of F. R. Leavis's proposition that the "Romantic poets have among themselves no attachments of the kind that link the poets in the line from Donne and Ben Jonson to Pope and the line from Pope to Crabbe" [*Revaluation: Tradition and Development in English Poetry,* 1936], the dominance of prophecy in Romantic poetry exposes the heresy in that "orthodoxy." Prophecy poses, against Leavis's "line of wit," a line of vision; and the Romantics' adoption of prophecy, sometimes viewed as a device for mystifying their poetry and for escaping history, is, more exactly, their instrument for the demystification of poetry and for encountering history.

The apocalyptic component in Romantic poetry is a deliberate factoring into it of error, a way of giving poetic presence to error. Historically, apocalypse was always subject to misreading, misinterpretation, egregious misrepresentation. No less than Milton, and as much to their credit, the Romantics, in aligning themselves with apocalyptic prophecy—with this tradition of misunderstanding—tie themselves to the possibility of error, all the while hoping, of course, to render the possibility less probable. In Romantic prophecy, as in Milton's last prophetic poems, apocalypse is a presence that the poetry evades until the dream can be internalized; yet such a strategy has also been misconstrued as revoking the promise of history by centering its promise in the self. What with Milton became the central concern of literary prophecy—and what Milton's poetry itself made the crucial issue for Romantic prophecy—was learning to perceive sequential apocalypses, of history and of individuals (usually in that order) as an inverted sequence, the elements of which were interdependent. Apocalypse could therefore continue its grip on poetic desire by marking the space, sometimes huge space, between expectation and fulfillment—the space "between" being the space of the poem and being filled with the realization that prophecy, which had always been a critique of culture, might also, and just as appropriately, become a critique of itself. Poetry, in the process, acquires a prophetic wisdom of its own and, in its encounter with and sometimes ravaging of the apocalyptic myth, yields up a Poets' Revelation.

It should come as no surprise that *The Prelude,* which Howard Nemerov describes [in his *Reflexions on Poetry and Poetics,* 1972] as "a series of mountain climbs, with vision at the top of each mountain, climaxed by the grand vision from Mount Snowdon," should also harbor what Nemerov presents as the essential prophetic wisdom of the poet, that he "doesn't foretell the future, he makes it, he brings it to pass, he sings it up." The true prophet, assuming he is a poet, need not hurl himself into the future; for his real concern will be with seeing the present clearly, with effecting an unveiling of it. In this refined sense, *The Prelude* is an apocalyptic poem, although, in this context, it must be allowed that one of the chief critical disputes involving this poem is whether it represents a false or true apocalypse, whether finally it portrays an apocalypse at all or, as Jonathan Wordsworth argues [in his *William Wordsworth: The Borders of Vision,* 1982], presents the poet as "a borderer . . . between the unregenerate present and the millenarian future." Even more than *The Prelude, The Recluse* displays apocalyptic hesitancy, with Wordsworth at once engaging and disengaging the apocalyptic myth in such a way as to make the Apocalypse a co-text of his poetry and, simultaneously, a subtext of history—in such a way as to produce an unveiling of the mind while leaving nature and the world of history still partially veiled. Blake is the only Romantic poet to present a united vision of apocalypse in the mind and in history. By Wordsworth and the other Romantics, such visions become progressively, explicitly disunited until by Shelley they are reintegrated in the vision of *Prometheus Unbound,* where the very idea of apocalypse is radically redefined. Wordsworth may have disclaimed the honor of being a poetic guide to the other poets of his age, but in matters of prophecy and apocalypse he was emphatically a guide, especially for the poets of the second generation, whose apocalyptic hesitancy is transferred to prophecy and who, even if they become regenerate, thus offering a hope that can be generalized to mankind, become increasingly tentative about their prophetic posture and claims, producing a poetry that is now rife with apocalyptic deferrals.

For pre-Miltonic poets, it may have been possible to use the

Apocalypse to hide the terrors of history and thereby evade eschatological despair, to temper the terrors of the present with the promises of a better future. Earlier ages, as Carl Jung observes [in *Psychologie und Religion,* 1939 (Eng. trans. 1958)], "could ignore the dark side of the Apocalypse, because the specifically Christian achievement was not to be frivolously endangered. But for modern man, the case is quite otherwise: We have experienced things so unheard of and so staggering that the question of whether such things are in any way reconcilable with the idea of a good God has become burningly topical. [The Apocalypse] is no longer a problem for experts in theological sermons, but a universal religious nightmare." Milton was not only the first of the modern poets but the first of them to feel compelled to justify God's ways to men. He made such efforts "burningly topical" in an age that made a nightmare of the Apocalypse, and Milton so represented it in *Samson Agonistes.*

We now know the history of apocalypse—and of the Apocalypse—in the post-Renaissance and modern world: of how that scriptural book, its total mythology and its eschatological visions, became historized and secularized, interiorized and humanized. Carl Becker records one phase of this history [in *The Heavenly City of the Eighteenth-Century Philosophers,* 1932]: the process whereby "the utopian dream of perfection, having been long identified with . . . life eternal in the heavenly city . . . was at last projected into the life of man on earth and identified with the desired and hoped-for regeneration of society." [In his *Natural Supernaturalism,* 1974] M. H. Abrams continues this story about how the heavenly city acquires earthly foundations by augmenting it with an account of how the Apocalypse becomes imploded in Romantic poetry. But there is also an episode in this tale that, omitting Byron and marginalizing Keats, Abrams does not relate. And it is a tale dear to the hearts of the Romantics who could not, or would not, laugh off "the trauma of history"; for whom, if I may continue to adapt David Roskies' chapter titles [for his *Against the Apocalypse: Responses to Catastrophe in Modern Jewish Culture*] as a shorthand, Jerusalem became a ruined city; whose poetry, in turn, made a "liturgy of destruction" and of "the self under siege." When the poet's homeland becomes a ruin, when its cities are places of nightmare, when the poet himself is a ruin among ruins, there is a new tale deriving from a narrowing of options: he may express blind faith or eschatological despair; he can implode history or watch it explode before his eyes.

In such a world, the apocalyptic myth and its eschatological visions exasperate; they do not edify. And not only are claims to vision submitted to scrutiny and often rendered suspect, but the myths encapsulated within vision come under review. Apocalypse, one of many forms of revelation, is wrenched away from prophecy, of which it is a species; and eschatological visions, when not made to clash with, are often wrested from their apocalyptic form. If not always, certainly by the time we reach the early years of the nineteenth century, poets comprehend the importance of distinguishing apocalyptic form from apocalyptic content and then of discriminating ideologically between apocalypse and prophecy.

In Romantic poetry, not only does eschatology come in for parody, but the visionary himself is reviled. It may be, as Bernard McGinn insists [in *The Apocalypse in English Renaissance Thought and Literature,* edited by C. A. Palrides and Joseph Wittreich, 1984], that without a pattern of crisis/judgment/vindication, there is no eschatology. That may be the very point of a symbolic structure like *Frankenstein,* where each of its three parts ends in judgment—of Justine, of the Monster, of Frankenstein himself—but where there is no accompanying vindication. In some Romantic literature, eschatological paradigms are invoked only to be eroded, while the visionary is censured rather than celebrated. Eventually, as Roskies remarks, all the redemptive ideologies (Judaic, Christian, even Marxist), each seen as an extension of the other, are discredited. Utopias become dystopias and then disappear from historical writings, redemptive ideologies flee from literature, and civilization moves into apocalyptic crisis. Yet even when the Romantics cannot embrace the Apocalypse and its eschatology, they call up both, not to crowd out, but to center, reality.

The Apocalypse can be used to departicularize history and, by identifying the present with the final days, can turn the present into a dead end. But the Apocalypse can also be used, as so often the Romantics did use it, to particularize the historical moment, to distance the present from the prophesied end and thereby make a future possible. Paradoxically, the Apocalypse, which could be used to blot out the present, could also be used to engender in the present a sense of belonging in time; it *could* be used to afford the present moment its fullness by imparting meaning to it in terms of the promised end.

One can always, it seems, under the pretense of lifting the veil, find encoded in present history a system of implied allusion that makes it coincide with the apocalyptic paradigm. But this is also an evasion, a reneging on responsibility. For as Roskies proposes of nineteenth- and twentieth-century writers (and what he says is not just true of *Jewish* writers), quite apart from creating an absolute identity between the present crisis and the apocalyptic end, they remember that the present occupies a place in the midst of time and allow it to gather meaning from an eschatological perspective. That perspective is enabling; for through it we may come, in Roskies' words, "to know the apocalypse, express it, mourn it, and transcend it" by fashioning catastrophe into something else, by turning images of destruction into new acts of creation. Such was the agenda of poetry in the Age of Wordsworth—an age that believed with the Wordsworth of *The Prelude* that poets must now exercise their skills "Not in Utopia . . . / Or some secreted island . . . / But in the very world, which is the world / Of all of us,—the place where, in the end, / We find our happiness, or not at all!" If the Apocalypse had been a book about and for achieving transcendence, if its myth had hitherto encapsulated a world beyond time, beyond its corruption and change, in its Romantic revision that book is brought down to earth, and in the process its myth, relieved of its illusions, is retrieved for, and newly accommodated to, history. (pp. 51-61)

Joseph A. Wittreich, Jr., " 'The Work of Man's Redemption': Prophecy and Apocalypse in Romantic Poetry," in The Age of William Wordsworth: Critical Essays on the Romantic Tradition, *edited by Kenneth R. Johnston and Gene W. Ruoff, Rutgers University Press, 1987, pp. 39-61.*

FURTHER READING

I. Anthologies

Heath, William, ed. *Major British Poets of the Romantic Period.* New York: Macmillan Co., 1973, 1140 p.
    Large selection from the poems and letters of the six major poets, with commentary, annotations, and a bibliography of secondary sources.

Mahoney, John L., ed. *The English Romantics: Major Poetry and Critical Theory with Selected Modern Critical Essays.* Lexington, Mass.: D. C. Heath and Co., 1978, 828 p.
    Includes writings by the six major poets and the essayist William Hazlitt, with introductions and notes by Mahoney and twenty-one essays by various other scholars, including M. H. Abrams, Cleanth Brooks, and Earl Wasserman.

Noyes, Russell, ed. *English Romantic Poetry and Prose.* New York: Oxford University Press, 1956, 1324 p.
    Represents all major and several minor poets and prose writers with essays, annotations, and a bibliography of secondary sources.

Perkins, David, ed. *English Romantic Writers.* San Diego: Harcourt Brace Jovanovich, 1967, 1265 p.
    Major and minor poets and prose writers, with essays by Perkins on the Romantic movement (excerpted above) and on each author.

II. Secondary Sources

Abrams, M. H. *The Mirror and the Lamp: Romantic Theory and the Critical Tradition.* New York: Oxford University Press, 1953, 406 p.
    Traces the development of Romantic poetic theory and examines its influence on modern critical thought.

——. *Natural Supernaturalism: Tradition and Revolution in Romantic Literature.* New York: W. W. Norton and Co., 1971, 550 p.
    Influential study that points out "some of the striking parallels" between Romantic writers in England and Germany, focusing on their "secularization of inherited theological ideas and ways of thinking."

——. *The Correspondent Breeze: Essays on English Romanticism.* New York: W. W. Norton and Co., 1984, 296 p.
    Collects several influential essays by Abrams, including "English Romanticism: The Spirit of the Age" (excerpted above).

——, ed. *English Romantic Poets: Modern Essays in Criticism.* London: Oxford University Press, 1960, 384 p.
    Reprints twenty-five essays by prominent scholars, including W. K. Wimsatt (excerpted above), Arthur O. Lovejoy, Harold Bloom, and Lionel Trilling.

Ball, Patricia, M. *The Central Self: A Study in Romantic and Victorian Imagination.* London: Athlone Press, 1968, 236 p.
    Studies the Romantic concept of the imagination and its influence on Victorian literature.

Bate, Jonathan. *Shakespeare and the English Romantic Imagination.* Oxford: Clarendon Press, 1986, 276 p.
    Examines "Shakespeare's influence on the minds and works of the major English Romantic poets."

Beach, Joseph Warren. *The Concept of Nature in Nineteenth-Century English Poetry.* New York: Pageant Book Co., 1956, 618 p.
    Explores the use and significance of nature in English and American poetry from the Romantic to the Modernist periods.

Bloom, Harold. *The Visionary Company: A Reading of English Romantic Poetry.* Garden City, N.Y.: Doubleday and Co., 1963, 495 p.

Detailed examination of the six major Romantic poets, concluding with a brief discussion of the minor Romantics.

———, ed. *Romanticism and Consciousness: Essays in Criticism.* New York: W. W. Norton and Co., 1970, 405 p.
Anthologizes theoretical, historical, and interpretive commentaries on Romanticism by such scholars as Harold Bloom (excerpted above), W. K. Wimsatt (excerpted above), M. H. Abrams, and Northrop Frye.

Bostetter, Edward E. *The Romantic Ventriloquists: Wordsworth, Coleridge, Keats, Shelley, Byron.* Seattle: University of Washington Press, 1963, 357 p.
Contends that the poetry of the Romantics reflects their failed struggle to affirm a philosophically invalid assumption: that the universe is a projection of the human imagination.

Brand, C. P. *Italy and the Romantics: The Italianate Fashion in Early Nineteenth-Century England.* Cambridge: Cambridge University Press, 1957, 285 p.
Discusses the depth and significance of the English Romantics' attraction to Italy and Italian culture.

Brinton, Craig. *The Political Ideas of the English Romantics.* New York: Russell and Russell, 1962, 242 p.
Analyzes the Romantics' political beliefs in relation to their period.

Brisman, Leslie. *Romantic Origins.* Ithaca, N.Y.: Cornell University Press, 1978, 410 p.
Asserts that two impulses are apparent in Romantic verse: to invent a mythic, idealized past and to acknowledge that past as a fabrication.

Brooks, Cleanth. "Metaphor and the Tradition" and "Notes for a Revised History of English Poetry." In his *Modern Poetry and the Tradition,* pp. 1-17, pp. 219-44. Chapel Hill: University of North Carolina Press, 1939.
Blames the influence of the Romantics for the slow acceptance of modern poetry and proposes a new view of poetic history based on the critical ideas of the modern poets. Throughout these chapters, Brooks expresses many of the New Critics' negative attitudes toward Romantic poetry.

Butler, Marilyn. *Romantics, Rebels and Reactionaries: English Literature and Its Background, 1760-1830.* Oxford: Oxford University Press, 1981, 213 p.
Overview of the English Romantic period.

Cantor, Paul A. *Creature and Creator: Myth-making and English Romanticism.* Cambridge: Cambridge University Press, 1984, 223 p.
Explores the interest in myths of creation among Blake, Byron, Keats, and Percy and Mary Shelley.

Clubbe, John, and Lovell, Ernest J., Jr. *English Romanticism: The Grounds of Belief.* London: Macmillan Press, 1983, 195 p.
Contends that, by acknowledging the fallen state of humankind and its need for redemption, the Romantics had a common ideological foundation in the Christian tradition.

Cooke, Michael G. *The Romantic Will.* New Haven: Yale University Press, 1976, 269 p.
Examines the significance of the will in English Romantic poetry.

Cooper, Andrew M. *Doubt and Identity in Romantic Poetry.* New Haven, Conn.: Yale University Press, 1988, 233 p.
Argues that Romantic poetry attempts to determine the legitimacy of two forms of doubt inherited from eighteenth-century sensationalist psychology: doubt about the existence of an external physical world and skepticism about the reality of minds other than one's own.

Curran, Stuart. *Poetic Form and British Romanticism.* New York: Oxford University Press, 1986, 265 p.

History of English Romantic poetry which contends that poetic "form, rather than being generally dismissed in the period, is a significant key to its character."

Dutt, Sukumar. *The Supernatural in English Romantic Poetry, 1780-1830.* 1938. Reprint. Folcroft, Pa.: Folcroft Library Editions, 1972, 415 p.
Studies the treatment of the supernatural by both major and minor Romantic poets.

Edwards, Thomas R. "The Revolutionary Imagination." In his *Imagination and Power: A Study of Poetry on Public Themes,* pp. 140-84. New York: Oxford University Press, 1971.
Explores how Blake, Shelley, and Wordsworth dealt with social and political matters in their poetry.

Elwin, Malcolm. *The First Romantics.* London: MacDonald and Co., 1947, 304 p.
Biographical study of Wordsworth, Coleridge, and Southey.

Enscoe, Gerald. *Eros and the Romantics: Sexual Love as a Theme in Coleridge, Shelley and Keats.* The Hague: Mouton, 1967, 178 p.
Argues that these three poets "examine the traditional association of the flesh with the devil" in the hope of redeeming "the flesh from this guilt by association."

Fairchild, Hoxie Neale. *The Romantic Quest.* New York: Columbia University Press, 1931, 444 p.
Attempts to provide "an interpretive analysis and synthesis of the chief tendencies" of the English Romantic period.

———. *Religious Trends in English Poetry, Vol. III: 1780-1830, Romantic Faith.* New York: Columbia University Press, 1949, 549 p.
Surveys the religious beliefs of the major Romantic poets.

Fogle, Richard Harter. *The Permanent Pleasure: Essays on Classics of Romanticism.* Athens, Ga.: University of Georgia Press, 1974, 225 p.
Reprints fifteen essays by Fogle on English and American Romanticism.

Fraistat, Neil. *The Poem and the Book: Interpreting Collections of Romantic Poetry.* Chapel Hill: University of North Carolina Press, 1985, 241 p.
Examines collections of poems published by the Romantics as distinct from isolated works.

Gleckner, Robert F., and Enscoe, Gerald E., eds. *Romanticism: Points of View.* Second edition. Detroit: Wayne State University Press, 1975, 346 p.
Reprints twenty-two important studies of Romanticism. Essays by Richard H. Fogle, W. K. Wimsatt, Northrop Frye, Raymond Williams, M. H. Abrams, Earl R. Wasserman, and Albert Gérard included in this collection are also excerpted above.

Gottfried, Leon. *Matthew Arnold and the Romantics.* Lincoln: University of Nebraska Press, 1963, 277 p.
Explores and evaluates "the full range of Arnold's reactions to the major Romantic poets over his whole career: the nature and extent of their poetic, critical, and personal influence upon him, and the quality and limits of his critical reaction to them."

Hancock, Albert Elmer. *The French Revolution and the English Poets: A Study in Historical Criticism.* 1899. Reprint. Port Washington, N.Y.: Kennikat Press, 1967, 197 p.
Early study tracing the influence of the French Revolution and French thought on Shelley, Byron, Wordsworth, and Coleridge.

Harvey, A. D. *English Poetry in a Changing Society, 1780-1825.* London: Allison and Busby, 1980, 195 p.
Focuses on the minor Romantic writers in order to provide a social and literary context for the study of the major poets.

Hayden, John O. *The Romantic Reviewers: 1802-1824.* Chicago: University of Chicago Press, 1968, 330 p.

Examines the contemporary critical reception of the English Romantics, including discussion of the reviewing periodicals and the practices, policies, and attitudes of the reviewers.

Hill, John Spencer, ed. *The Romantic Imagination: A Casebook.* London: Macmillan Press, 1977, 241 p.

Excerpts the Romantic poets' views on the imagination and reprints several modern critical studies of this topic by C. M. Bowra (excerpted above), Barbara Hardy, and W. J. Bate.

Hilles, Frederick W., and Bloom, Harold, eds. *From Sensibility to Romanticism: Essays Presented to Frederick A. Pottle.* New York: Oxford University Press, 1965, 585 p.

Festschrift on Augustan and Romantic poetry, including essays by Harold Bloom, M. H. Abrams, and E. D. Hirsch, Jr.

Hulme, T. E. "Romanticism and Classicism." In his *Speculations: Essays on Humanism and the Philosophy of Art,* edited by Herbert Read, pp. 111-40. London: Kegan Paul, Trench, Trubner, and Co., 1936.

Influential attack on Romanticism, predicting a revival of classical literary values.

Jackson, J. R. de J. *Poetry of the Romantic Period.* London: Routledge & Kegan Paul, 1980, 334 p.

History of English poetry from 1780 to 1835.

James, D. G. *The Romantic Comedy: An Essay on English Romanticism.* 1948. Reprint. London: Oxford University Press, 1963, 276 p.

Follows the evolution of the "Romantic spirit" throughout the period.

Jordan, Frank, ed. *The English Romantic Poets: A Review of Research and Criticism.* New York: Modern Language Association of America, 1985, 765 p.

Seven bibliographic essays, one covering the Romantic Movement in general and the rest devoted to the six major poets.

King-Hele, Desmond. *Erasmus Darwin and the Romantic Poets.* Houndsmills, England: Macmillan Press, 1986, 294 p.

Discusses the influence of Erasmus Darwin's diction, images, and ideas on the English Romantics.

Kipperman, Mark. *Beyond Enchantment: German Idealism and English Romantic Poetry.* Philadelphia: University of Pennsylvania Press, 1986, 242 p.

Attempts "to develop a vocabulary for discussing Romantic idealism" from Immanuel Kant's systematic exploration of self-consciousness and imagination in the *Critique of Pure Reason* and from the writings of German Idealists Johann Fichte and Friedrich Schelling.

Kroeber, Karl. *Romantic Narrative Art.* Madison: University of Wisconsin Press, 1960, 225 p.

Examines Romantic narrative poetry, considering such forms as the Romantic ballad, the visionary lyric, and the verse tale.

Kumar, Shiv K., ed. *British Romantic Poets: Recent Revaluations.* London: University of London Press, 1966, 327 p.

Gathers nineteen new and previously published essays: two on Romanticism and the remainder on major Romantic poets.

Levinson, Marjorie. *The Romantic Fragment Poem: A Critique of a Form.* Chapel Hill, N.C.: University of North Carolina Press, 1986, 268 p.

Structuralist study of poetic fragments by the Romantic poets.

McFarland, Thomas. *Romanticism and the Forms of Ruin: Wordsworth, Coleridge, and Modalities of Fragmentation.* Princeton, N.J.: Princeton University Press, 1981, 432 p.

Argues that the intensity of the Romantics' desire for systematic unity suggests that their actual condition was one of fragmentation and disharmony.

McGann, Jerome J. *The Romantic Ideology: A Critical Investigation.* Chicago: University of Chicago Press, 1983, 172 p.

Studies "Romantic poetry and Romantic criticism insofar as these phenomena have sought to define themselves to and within post-Romantic culture at large."

Metzger, Lore. *One Foot in Eden: Modes of Pastoral in Romantic Poetry.* Chapel Hill, N.C.: University of North Carolina Press, 1986, 274 p.

Examines the diverse ways the Romantics revitalized pastoral poetry.

Orel, Harold. *English Romantic Poets and the Enlightenment: Nine Essays on a Literary Relationship.* Banbury, England: Voltaire Foundation, 1973, 210 p.

Studies the effects of the French Revolution and of eighteenth-century attitudes, literary traditions, and political ideas on the Romantics.

Peckham, Morse. *The Triumph of Romanticism: Collected Essays.* Columbia: University of South Carolina Press, 1970, 462 p.

Diverse collection of essays by Peckham including four influential studies of Romantic poetic theory.

Powell, A. E. *The Romantic Theory of Poetry: An Examination in the Light of Croce's Æsthetic.* 1926. Reprint. New York: Russell & Russell, 1962, 263 p.

Discusses the theoretical underpinnings of Romantic poetry and criticism using Benedetto Croce's aesthetic theory as a point of reference.

Rajan, Tilottama. *Dark Interpreter: The Discourse of Romanticism.* Ithaca, N.Y.: Cornell University Press, 1980, 281 p.

Deconstructionist reading of Romantic poetry.

Read, Herbert. *The True Voice of Feeling: Studies in English Romantic Poetry.* New York: Pantheon Books, 1953, 382 p.

Traces the development of the idea of "organic form" in poetry from the Romantics to the Modernists.

Reed, Arden, ed. *Romanticism and Language.* Ithaca, N.Y.: Cornell University Press, 1984, 327 p.

Ten original essays by various scholars who focus on language in English Romantic literature.

Reiman, Donald H. *English Romantic Poetry, 1800-1835: A Guide to Information Sources.* Detroit: Gale Research Co., 294 p.

Selective annotated bibliography of criticism, including sections on the social, political, and literary background of the Romantic movement and the major and minor poets.

————. *Romantic Texts and Contexts.* Columbia: University of Missouri Press, 1987, 395 p.

In two parts, the first dealing with editing and textual problems encountered in the study of Romantic literature and the second examining the relationship between the Romantics' lives and their works.

————, Jaye, Michael C., and Bennett, Betty T., eds. *The Evidence of the Imagination: Studies of Interactions between Life and Art in English Romantic Literature.* New York: New York University Press, 1978, 409 p.

Gathers sixteen original essays by various scholars, including Carl Woodring, Aileen Ward, and David V. Erdman.

Rodway, Allan. *The Romantic Conflict.* London: Chatto & Windus, 1963, 256 p.

Studies Romantic and Pre-Romantic poetry, arguing that Romanticism "is more profitably approached as the product of a particular period than as the product of a particular kind of personality."

Ruoff, Gene W. *Wordsworth and Coleridge: The Making of the Major Lyrics, 1802-1804.* New Brunswick, N.J.: Rutgers University Press, 1989, 318 p.

Examines six early texts of "Ode: Intimations of Immortality from Recollections of Early Childhood," "Resolution and Independence," and "Dejection: An Ode," three works Ruoff considers necessary for understanding their authors, their age, and English poetry in general.

Schapiro, Barbara A. *The Romantic Mother: Narcissistic Patterns in Romantic Poetry.* Baltimore, Md.: Johns Hopkins University Press, 1983, 143 p.

Psychoanalytic investigation of the effects of the Romantics' relationships with women, especially their mothers, on the style, images, and themes of their poetry.

Simpson, David. *Irony and Authority in Romantic Poetry.* Totowa, N.J.: Rowman and Littlefield, 1979, 267 p.

Posits that "Romantic poetry is organized to make us confront the question of authority, especially as it pertains to the relationship between author and reader."

Stevenson, Warren. *The Myth of the Golden Age in English Romantic Poetry.* Salzburg: Institut für Anglistik und Amerikanistik, 1981, 109 p.

Discusses the treatment of the Edenic myth in Romantic poetry.

Swingle, L. J. "Romantic Unity and English Romantic Poetry." *Journal of English and Germanic Philology* LXXIV, No. 3 (July 1975): 361-74.

Points out several important concerns that Swingle feels M. H. Abrams neglects in the unifying theory of Romantic poetry presented in *Natural Supernaturalism* (see Further Reading entry above).

——. *The Obstinate Questionings of English Romanticism.* Baton Rouge: Louisiana State University Press, 1987, 211 p.

Attempts to determine whether the Romantics expressed a definite ideology or were more intent on questioning systems of belief in their writings.

Taylor, Anya. *Magic and English Romanticism.* Athens: University of Georgia Press, 1979, 278 p.

Examines the influence of the tradition of occultism on Romantic poetry.

Taylor, Beverly, and Bain, Robert, eds. *The Cast of Consciousness: Concepts of the Mind in British and American Romanticism.* New York: Greenwood Press, 1987, 249 p.

Collection of thirteen original essays, seven on the English and six on the American Romantics, with an introduction by the editors and an afterword by M. H. Abrams.

Thorslev, Peter L., Jr. "The Romantic Mind Is Its Own Place." *Comparative Literature* XV, No. 3 (Summer 1963): 250-68.

Studies the Romantics' revival of the Renaissance Satanic hero-villain character, the most influential of which is John Milton's Satan in *Paradise Lost.*

Twitchell, James B. *Romantic Horizons: Aspects of the Sublime in English Poetry and Painting, 1770-1850.* Columbia: University of Missouri Press, 1983, 232 p.

Defines the aesthetic and philosophical concept of the sublime as it is reflected in the poetry and art of the Romantic period.

Watson, J. R. *Picturesque Landscape and English Romantic Poetry.* London: Hutchinson Educational, 1970, 210 p.

Examines the influence of the eighteenth-century "cult of the picturesque" on the Romantics' depictions of landscape.

——, ed. *An Infinite Complexity: Essays in Romanticism.* Edinburgh: Edinburgh University Press, 1983, 248 p.

Festschrift containing essays on Wordsworth, Coleridge, Blake, Shelley, and minor poets John Clare, William Constable, and John Keble.

Wilkie, Brian. *Romantic Poets and Epic Tradition.* Madison: University of Wisconsin Press, 1965, 276 p.

Maintains that "the epic tradition was alive in the English Romantic age" and relates this tradition to major long poems of the period.

Wolfson, Susan J. *The Questioning Presence: Wordsworth, Keats, and the Interrogative Mode in Romantic Poetry.* Ithaca, N.Y.: Cornell University Press, 1986, 392 p.

Investigates Romantic poetry's ability to "provoke and sustain the mind's questionings" and to inspire diverse interpretations.

Woodhouse, A. S. P. "The Romantics: 1780-1840." In his *The Poet and His Faith: Religion and Poetry in England from Spenser to Eliot and Auden,* pp. 160-205. Chicago: University of Chicago Press, 1965.

Discusses the religious convictions and poetry of Blake, Coleridge, Wordsworth, Shelley, and two Oxford Movement writers, John Keble and John Henry Newman.

Woodring, Carl. *Politics in English Romantic Poetry.* Cambridge: Harvard University Press, 1970, 385 p.

Detailed examination of the influence of political theory on English Romantic poetry.

The Gothic Novel

INTRODUCTION

The Gothic novel—so called because many examples of the genre were set during the late-medieval, or Gothic, period—proliferated in England, Germany, and the United States during the late eighteenth and early nineteenth centuries. Critics date its inception to 1764, when English statesman and writer Horace Walpole published *The Castle of Otranto: A Gothic Story.* Walpole's novel enjoyed wide popularity and inspired a host of imitators who borrowed heavily from its essential features, thus establishing the conventions of the genre: an intricate plot, stock characters such as the naive maiden and the murderous or lascivious male villain, a ruined castle setting, and supernatural occurrences. According to Brendan Hennessy, the Gothic novel represents "one aspect of a general movement away from classical order in the literature of the eighteenth century, and towards imagination and feeling." Although the genre lost favor during the Victorian period, critics agree that both its mood and conventions exerted a marked influence on the development of English literature, evidenced by the brooding tone and use of the supernatural in novels by Charles Dickens and the Brontës, the emergence of horror, mystery, and detective fiction later in the nineteenth century, and the continuing fascination with the macabre and the bizarre in contemporary art forms. In addition, commentators have suggested that many examples of the Gothic novel transcend their function as popular fiction to reveal profound insights into the social and intellectual climate of their time.

REPRESENTATIVE WORKS

Beckford, William
   Vathek 1786
Brown, Charles Brockden
   Wieland; or, The Transformation 1798
Godwin, William
   *Things as They Are; or, The Adventures of Caleb
      Williams* 1794
Hogg, James
   Private Memoirs and Confessions of a Justified Sinner
      1824
Lee, Sophia
   The Recess: A Tale of Other Times 1785
Lewis, Matthew Gregory
   The Monk: A Romance 1796
Maturin, Charles Robert
   Melmoth the Wanderer 1820
Radcliffe, Ann
   *The Mysteries of Udolpho: A Romance Interspersed with
      Some Pieces of Poetry* 1794
   The Italian; or, The Confessional of the Black Penitents
      1797

Reeve, Clara
   The Champion of Virtue 1777; also published as *The
      Old English Baron: A Gothic Story,* 1778
Shelley, Mary Wollstonecraft
   Frankenstein; or, The Modern Prometheus 1818
Walpole, Horace
   The Castle of Otranto 1764

DEVELOPMENT AND MAJOR WORKS

HOWARD PHILLIPS LOVECRAFT

[*Lovecraft is considered one of the foremost modern authors of supernatural horror fiction. Strongly influenced by Edgar Allan Poe, Lord Dunsany, and early science fiction writers, he developed a type of horror tale that combined occult motifs, modern science, and the regional folklore of his native New England to produce the personal mythology on which he based much of his work. As is evident from his own fiction, Lovecraft was well versed in the history of Gothic writing, and his* Supernatural Horror in Literature *is one of the earliest and most comprehensive studies of this genre. From its opening statement—"the oldest and strongest emotion of mankind is fear"—to its concluding question—"who shall declare the dark theme a handicap?"—Lovecraft examines the literature of supernatural horror as an "essential branch of human expression." In the following excerpt from that work, Lovecraft traces the development of the Gothic novel by surveying the genre's major works.*]

The shadow-haunted landscapes of *Ossian,* the chaotic visions of William Blake, the grotesque witch dances in Burns's *Tam O'Shanter,* the sinister daemonism of Coleridge's *Christabel* and *Ancient Mariner,* the ghostly charm of James Hogg's *Kilmeny,* and the more restrained approaches to cosmic horror in *Lamia* and many of Keats's other poems, are typical British illustrations of the advent of the weird to formal literature. Our Teutonic cousins of the Continent were equally receptive to the rising flood, and Burger's *Wild Huntsman* and the even more famous daemon-bridegroom ballad of *Lenore*—both imitated in English by Scott, whose respect for the supernatural was always great—are only a taste of the eerie wealth which German song had commenced to provide. Thomas Moore adapted from such sources the legend of the ghoulish statue-bride (later used by Prosper Merimee in *The Venus of Ille,* and traceable back to great antiquity) which echoes so shiveringly in his ballad of *The Ring;* whilst Goethe's deathless masterpiece *Faust,* crossing from mere balladry into the classic, cosmic tragedy of the ages, may be held as the ultimate height to which this German poetic impulse arose.

But it remained for a very sprightly and worldly Englishman—none other than Horace Walpole himself—to give the growing impulse definite shape and become the actual founder of the literary horror-story as a permanent form. Fond of mediaeval romance and mystery as a dilettante's diversion, and with a quaintly imitated Gothic castle as his abode at Strawberry Hill, Walpole in 1764 published *The Castle of Otranto;* a tale of the supernatural which, though thoroughly unconvincing and mediocre in itself, was destined to exert an almost unparalleled influence on the literature of the weird. First venturing it only as a "translation" by one "William Marshal, Gent." from the Italian of a mythical "Onuphrio Muralto," the author later acknowledged his connection with the book and took pleasure in its wide and instantaneous popularity—a popularity which extended to many editions, early dramatization, and wholesale imitation both in England and in Germany.

The story—tedious, artificial, and melodramatic—is further impaired by a brisk and prosaic style whose urbane sprightliness nowhere permits the creation of a truly weird atmosphere. It tells of Manfred, an unscrupulous and usurping prince determined to found a line, who after the mysterious sudden death of his only son Conrad on the latter's bridal morn, attempts to put away his wife Hippolita and wed the lady destined for the unfortunate youth—the lad, by the way, having been crushed by the preternatural fall of a gigantic helmet in the castle courtyard. Isabella, the widowed bride, flees from this design; and encounters in subterranean crypts beneath the castle a noble young preserver, Theodore, who seems to be a peasant yet strangely resembles the old lord Alfonso who ruled the domain before Manfred's time. Shortly thereafter supernatural phenomena assail the castle in diverse ways; fragments of gigantic armour being discovered here and there, a portrait walking out of its frame, a thunderclap destroying the edifice, and a colossal armoured spectre of Alfonso rising out of the ruins to ascend through parting clouds to the bosom of St. Nicholas. Theodore, having wooed Manfred's daughter Matilda and lost her through death—for she is slain by her father by mistake—is discovered to be the son of Alfonso and rightful heir to the estate. He concludes the tale by wedding Isabella and preparing to live happily ever after, whilst Manfred—whose usurpation was the cause of his son's supernatural death and his own supernatural harassings—retires to a monastery for penitence; his saddened wife seeking asylum in a neighbouring convent.

Such is the tale; flat, stilted, and altogether devoid of the true cosmic horror which makes weird literature. Yet such was the thirst of the age for those touches of strangeness and spectral antiquity which it reflects, that it was seriously received by the soundest readers and raised in spite of its intrinsic ineptness to a pedestal of lofty importance in literary history. What it did above all else was to create a novel type of scene, puppet-characters, and incidents; which, handled to better advantage by writers more naturally adapted to weird creation, stimulated the growth of an imitative Gothic school which in turn inspired the real weavers of cosmic terror—the line of actual artists beginning with Poe. This novel dramatic paraphernalia consisted first of all of the Gothic castle, with its awesome antiquity, vast distances and ramblings, deserted or ruined wings, damp corridors, unwholesome hidden catacombs, and galaxy of ghosts and appalling legends, as a nucleus of suspense and daemoniac fright. In addition, it included the tyrannical and malevolent nobleman as villain; the saintly, long-persecuted, and generally insipid heroine who undergoes the major terrors and serves as a point of view and focus for the reader's sympathies; the valorous and immaculate hero, always of high birth but often in humble disguise; the convention of high-sounding foreign names, mostly Italian, for the characters; and the infinite array of stage proper-

ties which includes strange lights, damp trap-doors, extinguished lamps, mouldy hidden manuscripts, creaking hinges, shaking arras, and the like. All this paraphernalia reappears with amusing sameness, yet sometimes with tremendous effect, throughout the history of the Gothic novel; and is by no means extinct even today, though subtler technique now forces it to assume a less naive and obvious form. An harmonious milieu for a new school had been found, and the writing world was not slow to grasp the opportunity.

German romance at once responded to the Walpole influence, and soon became a byword for the weird and ghastly. In England one of the first imitators was the celebrated Mrs. Barbauld, then Miss Aikin, who in 1773 published an unfinished fragment called *Sir Bertrand,* in which the strings of genuine terror were truly touched with no clumsy hand. A nobleman on a dark and lonely moor, attracted by a tolling bell and distant light, enters a strange and ancient turreted castle whose doors open and close and whose bluish will-o'-the-wisps lead up mysterious staircases toward dead hands and animated black statues. A coffin with a dead lady, whom Sir Bertrand kisses, is finally reached; and upon the kiss the scene dissolves to give place to a splendid apartment where the lady, restored to life, holds a banquet in honor of her rescuer. Walpole admired this tale, though he accorded less respect to an even more prominent offspring of his *Otranto*—*The Old English Baron,* by Clara Reeve, published in 1777. Truly enough, this tale lacks the real vibration to the note of outer darkness and mystery which distinguishes Mrs. Barbauld's fragment; and though less crude than Walpole's novel, and more artistically economical of horror in its possession of only one spectral figure, it is nevertheless too definitely insipid for greatness. Here again we have the virtuous heir to the castle disguised as a peasant and restored to his heritage through the ghost of his father; and here again we have a case of wide popularity leading to many editions, dramatization, and ultimate translation into French. Miss Reeve wrote another weird novel, unfortunately unpublished and lost.

The Gothic novel was now settled as a literary form, and instances multiply bewilderingly as the eighteenth century draws toward its close. *The Recess,* written in 1785 by Mrs. Sophia Lee, has the historic element, revolving round the twin daughters of Mary, Queen of Scots; and though devoid of the supernatural, employs the Walpole scenery and mechanism with great dexterity. Five years later, and all existing lamps are paled by the rising of a fresh luminary order—Mrs. Ann Radcliffe (1764-1823), whose famous novels made terror and suspense a fashion, and who set new and higher standards in the domain of macabre and fear-inspiring atmosphere despite a provoking custom of destroying her own phantoms at the last through labored mechanical explanations. To the familiar Gothic trappings of her predecessors Mrs. Radcliffe added a genuine sense of the unearthly in scene and incident which closely approached genius; every touch of setting and action contributing artistically to the impression of illimitable frightfulness which she wished to convey. A few sinister details like a track of blood on castle stairs, a groan from a distant vault, or a weird song in a nocturnal forest can with her conjure up the most powerful images of imminent horror; surpassing by far the extravagant and toilsome elaborations of others. Nor are these images in themselves any the less potent because they are explained away before the end of the novel. Mrs. Radcliffe's visual imagination was very strong, and appears as much in her delightful landscape touches—always in broad, glamorously pictorial out-line, and never in close detail—as in her weird phantasies. Her prime weaknesses, aside from the habit of prosaic disillusionment, are a tendency toward erroneous geography and history and a fatal predilection for bestrewing her novels with insipid little poems, attributed to one or another of the characters.

Mrs. Radcliffe wrote six novels; *The Castles of Athlin and Dunbayne* (1789), *A Sicilian Romance* (1790), *The Romance of the Forest* (1792), *The Mysteries of Udolpho* (1794), *The Italian* (1797), and *Gaston de Blondeville*, composed in 1802 but first published posthumously in 1826. Of these *Udolpho* is by far the most famous, and may be taken as a type of the early Gothic tale at its best. It is the chronicle of Emily, a young Frenchwoman transplanted to an ancient and portentous castle in the Apennines through the death of her parents and the marriage of her aunt to the lord of the castle—the scheming nobleman, Montoni. Mysterious sounds, opened doors, frightful legends, and a nameless horror in a niche behind a black veil all operate in quick succession to unnerve the heroine and her faithful attendant, Annette; but finally, after the death of her aunt, she escapes with the aid of a fellow-prisoner whom she has discovered. On the way home she stops at a chateau filled with fresh horrors—the abandoned wing where the departed chatelaine dwelt, and the bed of death with the black pall—but is finally restored to security and happiness with her lover Valancourt, after the clearing-up of a secret which seemed for a time to involve her birth in mystery. Clearly, this is only the familiar material reworked; but it is so well reworked that *Udolpho* will always be a classic. Mrs. Radcliffe's characters are puppets, but they are less markedly so than those of her forerunners. And in atmospheric creation she stands preeminent among those of her time.

Of Mrs. Radcliffe's countless imitators, the American novelist Charles Brockden Brown stands the closest in spirit and method. Like her, he injured his creations by natural explanations; but also like her, he had an uncanny atmospheric power which gives his horrors a frightful vitality as long as they remain unexplained. He differed from her in contemptuously discarding the external Gothic paraphernalia and properties and choosing modern American scenes for his mysteries; but this repudiation did not extend to the Gothic spirit and type of incident. Brown's novels involve some memorably frightful scenes, and excel even Mrs. Radcliffe's in describing the operations of the perturbed mind. *Edgar Huntly* starts with a sleep-walker digging a grave, but is later impaired by touches of Godwinian didacticism. *Ormond* involves a member of a sinister secret brotherhood. That and *Arthur Mervyn* both describe the plague of yellow fever, which the author had witnessed in Philadelphia and New York. But Brown's most famous book is *Wieland; or, the Transformation* (1798), in which a Pennsylvania German, engulfed by a wave of religious fanaticism, hears "voices" and slays his wife and children as a sacrifice. His sister Clara, who tells the story, narrowly escapes. The scene, laid at the woodland estate of Mittingen on the Schuylkill's remote reaches, is drawn with extreme vividness; and the terrors of Clara, beset by spectral tones, gathering fears, and the sound of strange footsteps in the lonely house, are all shaped with truly artistic force. In the end a lame ventriloquial explanation is offered, but the atmosphere is genuine while it lasts. Carwin, the malign ventriloquist, is a typical villain of the Manfred or Montoni type. (pp. 23-9)

Horror in literature attains a new malignity in the work of Matthew Gregory Lewis (1773-1818), whose novel *The Monk* (1796) achieved marvelous popularity and earned him the nickname of "Monk" Lewis. This young author, educated in Germany and saturated with a body of wild Teuton lore unknown to Mrs. Radcliffe, turned to terror in forms more violent than his gentle predecessor had ever dared to think of; and produced as a result a masterpiece of active nightmare whose general Gothic cast is spiced with added stores of ghoulishness. The story is one of a Spanish monk, Ambrosio, who from a state of over-proud virtue is tempted to the very nadir of evil by a fiend in the guise of the maiden Matilda; and who is finally, when awaiting death at the Inquisition's hands, induced to purchase escape at the price of his soul from the Devil, because he deems both body and soul already lost. Forthwith the mocking Fiend snatches him to a lonely place, tells him he has sold his soul in vain since both pardon and a chance for salvation were approaching at the moment of his hideous bargain, and completes the sardonic betrayal by rebuking him for his unnatural crimes, and casting his body down a precipice whilst his soul is borne off for ever to perdition. The novel contains some appalling descriptions such as the incantation in the vaults beneath the convent cemetery, the burning of the convent, and the final end of the wretched abbot. In the sub-plot where the Marquis de las Cisternas meets the spectre of his erring ancestress, The Bleeding Nun, there are many enormously potent strokes; notably the visit of the animated corpse to the Marquis's bedside, and the cabbalistic ritual whereby the Wandering Jew helps him to fathom and banish his dead tormentor. Nevertheless *The Monk* drags sadly when read as a whole. It is too long and too diffuse, and much of its potency is marred by flippancy and by an awkwardly excessive reaction against those canons of decorum which Lewis at first despised as prudish. One great thing may be said of the author; that he never ruined his ghostly visions with a natural explanation. He succeeded in breaking up the Radcliffian tradition and expanding the field of the Gothic novel. Lewis wrote much more than *The Monk*. His drama, *The Castle Spectre*, was produced in 1798, and he later found time to pen other fictions in ballad form—*Tales of Terror* (1799), *Tales of Wonder* (1801), and a succession of translations from the German.

Gothic romances, both English and German, now appeared in multitudinous and mediocre profusion. Most of them were merely ridiculous in the light of mature taste, and Miss Austen's famous satire *Northanger Abbey* was by no means an unmerited rebuke to a school which had sunk far toward absurdity. This particular school was petering out, but before its final subordination there arose its last and greatest figure in the person of Charles Robert Maturin (1782-1824), an obscure and eccentric Irish clergyman. Out of an ample body of miscellaneous writing which includes one confused Radcliffian imitation called *The Fatal Revenge; or, the Family of Montorio* (1807), Maturin at length evolved the vivid horror-masterpiece of *Melmoth, the Wanderer* (1820), in which the Gothic tale climbed to altitudes of sheer spiritual fright which it had never known before.

Melmoth is the tale of an Irish gentleman who, in the seventeenth century, obtained a preternaturally extended life from the Devil at the price of his soul. If he can persuade another to take the bargain off his hands, and assume his existing state, he can be saved; but this he can never manage to effect, no matter how assiduously he haunts those whom despair has made reckless and frantic. The framework of the story is very clumsy; involving tedious length, digressive episodes, narratives within narratives, and labored dovetailing and coincidence; but at various points in the endless rambling there is felt a pulse of power undiscoverable in any previous work of this kind—a kinship to the essential truth of human nature, an understanding of the profoundest sources of actual cosmic fear, and a white heat of sympathetic passion on the writer's part which makes the book a true document of aesthetic self-expression rather than a mere clever compound of artifice. No unbiased reader can doubt that with *Melmoth* an enormous stride in the evolution of the horror-tale is represented. Fear is taken out of the realm of the conventional and exalted into a hideous cloud over mankind's very destiny. Maturin's shudders, the work of one capable of shuddering himself, are of the sort that convince. Mrs. Radcliffe and Lewis are fair game for the parodist, but it would be difficult to find a false note in the feverishly intensified action and high atmospheric tension of the Irishman whose less sophisticated emotions and strain of Celtic mysticism gave him the finest possible natural equipment for his task. Without a doubt Maturin is a man of authentic genius, and he was so recognized by Balzac, who grouped *Melmoth* with Moliere's *Don Juan,* Goethe's *Faust,* and Byron's *Manfred* as the supreme allegorical figures of modern European literature, and wrote a whimsical piece called *Melmoth Reconciled,* in which the Wanderer succeeds in passing his infernal bargain on to a Parisian bank defaulter, who in turn hands it along a chain of victims until a reveling gambler dies with it in his possession, and by his damnation ends the curse. Scott, Rossetti, Thackeray and Baudelaire are the other titans who gave Maturin their unqualified admiration, and there is much significance in the fact that Oscar Wilde, after his disgrace and exile, chose for his last days in Paris the assumed name of "Sebastian Melmoth."

Melmoth contains scenes which even now have not lost their power to evoke dread. It begins with a deathbed—an old miser is dying of sheer fright because of something he has seen, coupled with a manuscript he has read and a family portrait which hangs in an obscure closet of his centuried home in County Wicklow. He sends to Trinity College, Dublin, for his nephew John; and the latter upon arriving notes many uncanny things. The eyes of the portrait in the closet glow horribly, and twice a figure strangely resembling the portrait appears momentarily at the door. Dread hangs over that house of the Melmoths, one of whose ancestors, "J. Melmoth, 1646," the portrait represents. The dying miser declares that this man—at a date slightly before 1800—is still alive. Finally the miser dies, and the nephew is told in the will to destroy both the portrait and a manuscript to be found in a certain drawer. Reading the manuscript, which was written late in the seventeenth century by an Englishman named Stanton, young John learns of a terrible incident in Spain in 1677, when the writer met a horrible fellow-countryman and was told of how he had stared to death a priest who tried to denounce him as one filled with fearsome evil. Later, after meeting the man again in London, Stanton is cast into a madhouse and visited by the stranger, whose approach is heralded by spectral music and whose eyes have a more than mortal glare. Melmoth the Wanderer—for such is the malign visitor— offers the captive freedom if he will take over his bargain with the Devil; but like all others whom Melmoth has approached, Stanton is proof against temptation. Melmoth's description of the horrors of a life in a madhouse, used to tempt Stanton, is one of the most potent passages of the book. Stanton is at length liberated, and spends the rest of his life tracking down

Melmoth, whose family and ancestral abode he discovers. With the family he leaves the manuscript, which by young John's time is badly ruinous and fragmentary. John destroys both portrait and manuscript, but in sleep is visited by his horrible ancestor, who leaves a black and blue mark on his wrist.

Young John soon afterward receives as a visitor a shipwrecked Spaniard, Alonzo de Moncada, who has escaped from compulsory monasticism and from the perils of the Inquisition. He has suffered horribly—and the descriptions of his experiences under torment and in the vaults through which he once essays escape are classic—but had the strength to resist Melmoth the Wanderer when approached at his darkest hour in prison. At the house of a Jew who sheltered him after his escape he discovers a wealth of manuscript relating other exploits of Melmoth, including his wooing of an Indian island maiden, Immalee, who later comes into her birthright in Spain and is known as Donna Isidora; and of his horrible marriage to her by the corpse of a dead anchorite at midnight in the ruined chapel of a shunned and abhorred monastery. Moncada's narrative to young John takes up the bulk of Maturin's four-volume book; this disproportion being considered one of the chief technical faults of the composition.

At last the colloquies of John and Moncada are interrupted by the entrance of Melmoth the Wanderer himself, his piercing eyes now fading, and decrepitude swiftly overtaking him. The term of his bargain has approached its end, and he has come home after a century and a half to meet his fate. Warning all others from the room, no matter what sounds they may hear in the night, he awaits the end alone. Young John and Moncada hear frightful ululations, but do not intrude till silence comes toward morning. They then find the room empty. Clayey footprints lead out a rear door to a cliff overlooking the sea, and near the edge of the precipice is a track indicating the forcible dragging of some heavy body. The Wanderer's scarf is found on a crag some distance below the brink, but nothing further is ever seen or heard of him.

Such is the story, and none can fail to notice the difference between the moulded, suggestive, and artistically moulded horror and—to use the words of Professor George Saintsbury—"the artful but rather jejune rationalism of Mrs. Radcliffe, and the too often puerile extravagance, the bad taste, and the sometimes slipshod style of Lewis." Maturin's style in itself deserves particular praise, for its forcible directness and vitality lift it altogether above the pompous artificialities of which his predecessors are guilty. Professor Edith Birkhead, in her history of the Gothic novel [see Further Reading], justly observes that "with all his faults Maturin was the greatest as well as the last of the Goths." *Melmoth* was widely read and eventually dramatized, but its late date in the evolution of the Gothic tale deprived it of the tumultuous popularity of *Udolpho* and *The Monk.* (pp. 30-5)

Meanwhile other hands had not been idle, so that above the dreary plethora of trash like Marquis von Grosse's *Horrid Mysteries* (1796), Mrs. Roche's *Children of the Abbey* (1798), Mrs. Dacre's *Zofloya; or, the Moor* (1806), and the poet Shelley's schoolboy effusions *Zastrozzi* (1810) and *St. Irvine* (1811) (both imitations of *Zofloya*) there arose many memorable weird works both in English and German. Classic in merit, and markedly different from its fellows because of its foundation in the Oriental tale rather than the Walpolesque Gothic novel, is the celebrated *History of the Caliph Vathek* by the wealthy dilettante William Beckford, first written in the French language but published in an English translation before the appearance of the original. Eastern tales, introduced to European literature early in the eighteenth century through Galland's French translation of the inexhaustibly opulent *Arabian Nights,* had become a reigning fashion; being used both for allegory and for amusement. The sly humour which only the Eastern mind knows how to mix with weirdness had captivated a sophisticated generation, till Bagdad and Damascus names became as freely strewn through popular literature as dashing Italian and Spanish ones were soon to be. Beckford, well read in Eastern romance, caught the atmosphere with unusual receptivity; and in his fantastic volume reflected very potently the haughty luxury, sly disillusion, bland cruelty, urbane treachery, and shadowy spectral horror of the Saracen spirit. His seasoning of the ridiculous seldom mars the force of his sinister theme, and the tale marches onward with a phantasmagoric pomp in which the laughter is that of skeletons feasting under arabesque domes. *Vathek* is a tale of the grandson of the Caliph Haroun, who, tormented by that ambition for super-terrestrial power, pleasure and learning which animates the average Gothic villain or Byronic hero (essentially cognate types), is lured by an evil genius to seek the subterranean throne of the mighty and fabulous pre-Adamite sultans in the fiery halls of Eblis, the Mahometan Devil. The descriptions of Vathek's palaces and diversions, of his scheming sorceress-mother Carathis and her witch-tower with the fifty one-eyed negresses, of his pilgrimage to the haunted ruins of Istakher (Persepolis) and of the impish bride Nouronihar whom he treacherously acquired on the way, of Istakhar's primordial towers and terraces in the burning moonlight of the waste, and of the terrible Cyclopean halls of Eblis, where, lured by glittering promises, each victim is compelled to wander in anguish for ever, his right hand upon his blazingly ignited and eternally burning heart, are triumphs of weird colouring which raise the book to a permanent place in English letters. No less notable are the three *Episodes of Vathek,* intended for insertion in the tale as narratives of Vathek's fellow-victims in Eblis' infernal halls, which remained unpublished throughout the author's lifetime and were discovered as recently as 1909 by the scholar Lewis Melville whilst collecting material for his *Life and Letters of William Beckford.* Beckford, however, lacks the essential mysticism which marks the acutest form of the weird; so that his tales have a certain knowing Latin hardness and clearness preclusive of sheer panic fright.

But Beckford remained alone in his devotion to the Orient. Other writers, closer to the Gothic tradition and to European life in general, were content to follow more faithfully in the lead of Walpole. Among the countless producers of terror-literature in these times may be mentioned the Utopian economic theorist William Godwin, who followed his famous but non-supernatural *Caleb Williams* (1794) with the intendedly weird *St. Leon* (1799), in which the theme of the elixir of life, as developed by the imaginary secret order of "Rosicrucians," is handled with ingeniousness if not with atmospheric convincingness. This element of Rosicrucianism, fostered by a wave of popular magical interest exemplified in the vogue of the charlatan Cagliostro and the publication of Francis Barrett's *The Magus* (1801), a curious and compendious treatise on occult principles and ceremonies, of which a reprint was made as lately as 1896, figures in Bulwer-Lytton and in many late Gothic novels, especially that remote and enfeebled posterity which straggled far down into the nineteenth century and was represented by George W. M.

Horace Walpole

Reynold's *Faust and the Demon* and *Wagner the Wehr-Wolf. Caleb Williams,* though non-supernatural, has many authentic touches of terror. It is the tale of a servant persecuted by a master whom he has found guilty of murder, and displays an invention and skill which have kept it alive in a fashion to this day. It was dramatized as *The Iron Chest,* and in that form was almost equally celebrated. Godwin, however, was too much the conscious teacher and prosaic man of thought to create a genuine weird masterpiece.

His daughter, the wife of Shelley, was much more successful; and her inimitable *Frankenstein; or, the Modern Prometheus* (1817) is one of the horror-classics of all time. Composed in competition with her husband, Lord Byron, and Dr. John William Polidori in an effort to prove supremacy in horror-making, Mrs. Shelley's *Frankenstein* was the only one of the rival narratives to be brought to an elaborate completion; and criticism has failed to prove that the best parts are due to Shelley rather than to her. The novel, somewhat tinged but scarcely marred by moral didacticism, tells of the artificial human being moulded from charnel fragments by Victor Frankenstein, a young Swiss medical student. Created by its designer "in the mad pride of intellectuality," the monster possesses full intelligence but owns a hideously loathsome form. It is rejected by mankind, becomes embittered, and at length begins the successive murder of all whom Frankenstein loves best, friends and family. It demands that Frankenstein create a wife for it; and when the student finally refuses in horror lest the world be populated with such monsters, it departs with a hideous threat "to be with him on his wedding night." Upon that night the bride is strangled, and from that time on Frankenstein hunts down the monster, even into the wastes of the Arctic. In the end, whilst seeking shelter on the ship of the man who tells the story, Frankenstein himself is killed by the shocking object of his search and creation of his presumptuous pride. Some of the scenes in *Frankenstein* are unforgettable, as when the newly animated monster enters its creator's room, parts the curtains of his bed, and gazes at him in the yellow moonlight with watery eyes—"if eyes they may be called." Mrs. Shelley wrote other novels, including the fairly notable *Last Man;* but never duplicated the success of her first effort. It has the true touch of cosmic fear, no matter how much the movement may lag in places. Dr. Polidori developed his competing idea as a long short story, *The Vampyre;* in which we behold a suave villain of the true Gothic or Byronic type, and encounter some excellent passages of stark fright, including a terrible nocturnal experience in a shunned Grecian wood.

In this same period Sir Walter Scott frequently concerned himself with the weird, weaving it into many of his novels and poems, and sometimes producing such independent bits of narration as The "Tapestried Chamber" or "Wandering Willie's Tale" in *Red-gauntlet,* in the latter of which the force of the spectral and the diabolic is enhanced by a grotesque homeliness of speech and atmosphere. In 1830 Scott published his *Letters on Demonology and Witchcraft,* which still forms one of our best compendia of European witch-lore. Washington Irving is another famous figure not unconnected with the weird; for though most of his ghosts are too whimsical and humorous to form genuinely spectral literature, a distinct inclination in this direction is to be noted in many of his productions. The *German Student* in *Tales of a Traveller* (1824) is a slyly concise and effective presentation of the old legend of the dead bride, whilst woven into the cosmic tissue of *The Money Diggers* in the same volume is more than one hint of piratical apparitions in the realms which Captain Kidd once roamed. Thomas Moore also joined the ranks of the macabre artists in the poem *Alciphron,* which he later elaborated into the prose novel of *The Epicurean* (1827). Though merely relating the adventures of a young Athenian duped by the artifice of cunning Egyptian priests, Moore manages to infuse much genuine horror into his account of subterranean frights and wonders beneath the primordial temples of Memphis. De Quincey more than once revels in grotesque and arabesque terrors, though with a desultoriness and learned pomp which deny him the rank of specialist.

This era likewise saw the rise of William Harrison Ainsworth, whose romantic novels teem with the eerie and the gruesome. Capt. Marryat, besides writing such short tales as *The Werewolf,* made a memorable contribution in *The Phantom Ship* (1839), founded on the legend of the Flying Dutchman, whose spectral and accursed vessel sails for ever near the Cape of Good Hope. Dickens now rises with occasional weird bits like *The Signalman,* a tale of ghastly warning conforming to a very common pattern and touched with a verisimilitude which allied it as much with the coming psychological school as with the dying Gothic school. At this time a wave of interest in spiritualistic charlatanry, mediumism, Hindoo theosophy, and such matters, much like that of the present day, was flourishing; so that the number of weird tales with a "psychic" or pseudo-scientific basis became very considerable. For a number of these the prolific and popular Edward Bulwer-Lytton was responsible; and despite the large doses of turgid rhetoric and empty romanticism in his prod-

ucts, his success in the weaving of a certain kind of bizarre charm cannot be denied.

The House and the Brain, which hints of Rosicrucianism and at a malign and deathless figure perhaps suggested by Louis XV's mysterious courtier St. Germain, yet survives as one of the best short haunted-house tales ever written. The novel *Zanoni* (1842) contains similar elements more elaborately handled, and introduces a vast unknown sphere of being pressing on our own world and guarded by a horrible "Dweller of the Threshold" who haunts those who try to enter and fail. Here we have a benign brotherhood kept alive from age to age till finally reduced to a single member, and as a hero an ancient Chaldaean sorcerer surviving in the pristine bloom of youth to perish on the guillotine of the French Revolution. Though full of the conventional spirit of romance, marred by a ponderous network of symbolic and didactic meanings, and left unconvincing through lack of perfect atmospheric realization of the situations hinging on the spectral world, *Zanoni* is really an excellent performance as a romantic novel; and can be read with genuine interest by the not too sophisticated reader. It is amusing to note that in describing an attempted initiation into the ancient brotherhood the author cannot escape using the stock Gothic castle of Walpolian lineage.

In *A Strange Story* (1862) Bulwer-Lytton shows a marked improvement in the creation of weird images and moods. The novel, despite enormous length, a highly artificial plot bolstered up by opportune coincidences, and an atmosphere of homiletic pseudo-science designed to please the matter-of-fact and purposeful Victorian reader, is exceedingly effective as a narrative; evoking instantaneous and unflagging interest, and furnishing many potent—if somewhat melodramatic—tableaux and climaxes. Again we have the mysterious user of life's elixir in the person of the soulless magician Margrave, whose dark exploits stand out with dramatic vividness against the modern background of a quiet English town and of the Australian bush; and again we have shadowy intimations of a vast spectral world of the unknown in the very air about us—this time handled with much greater power and vitality than in *Zanoni.* One of the two great incantation passages, where the hero is driven by a luminous evil spirit to rise at night in his sleep, take a strange Egyptian wand, and evoke nameless presences in the haunted and mausoleum-facing pavilion of a famous Renaissance alchemist, truly stands among the major terror scenes of literature. Just enough is suggested, and just little enough is told. Unknown words are twice dictated to the sleep-walker, and as he repeats them the ground trembles, and all the dogs of the countryside begin to bay at half-seen amorphous shadows that stalk athwart the moonlight. When a third set of unknown words is prompted, the sleep-walker's spirit suddenly rebels at uttering them, as if the soul could recognize ultimate abysmal horrors concealed from the mind; and at last an apparition of an absent sweetheart and good angel breaks the malign spell. This fragment well illustrates how far Lord Lytton was capable of progressing beyond his usual pomp and stock romance toward that crystalline essence of artistic fear which belongs to the domain of poetry. In describing certain details of incantations, Lytton was greatly indebted to his amusingly serious occult studies, in the course of which he came in touch with that odd French scholar and cabbalist Alphonse Louis Constant ("Eliphas Levy"), who claimed to possess the secrets of ancient magic, and to have evoked the spectre of the old Grecian wizard Apollonius of Tyana, who lived in Nero's times.

The romantic, semi-Gothic, quasi-moral tradition here represented was carried far down the nineteenth century by such authors as Joseph Sheridan LeFanu, Wilkie Collins, the late Sir H. Rider Haggard (whose *She* is really remarkably good), Sir A. Conan Doyle, H. G. Wells, and Robert Louis Stevenson—the latter of whom, despite an atrocious tendency toward jaunty mannerisms, created permanent classics in *Markheim, The Body Snatcher,* and *Dr. Jekyll and Mr. Hyde.* Indeed, we may say that this school still survives; for to it clearly belong such of our contemporary horror-tales as specialise in events rather than atmospheric details, address the intellect rather than the impressionistic imagination, cultivate a luminous glamour rather than a malign tensity or psychological verisimilitude, and take a definite stand in sympathy with mankind and its welfare. It has its undeniable strength, and because of its "human element" commands a wider audience than does the sheer artistic nightmare. If not quite so potent as the latter, it is because a diluted product can never achieve the intensity of a concentrated essence.

Quite alone both as a novel and as a piece of terror-literature stands the famous *Wuthering Heights* (1847) by Emily Brontë, with its mad vista of bleak, windswept Yorkshire moors and the violent, distorted lives they foster. Though primarily a tale of life, and of human passions in agony and conflict, its epically cosmic setting affords room for horror of the most spiritual sort. Heathcliff, the modified Byronic villain-hero, is a strange dark waif found in the streets as a small child and speaking only a strange gibberish till adopted by the family he ultimately ruins. That he is in truth a diabolic spirit rather than a human being is more than once suggested, and the unreal is further approached in the experience of the visitor who encounters a plaintive child-ghost at a bough-brushed upper window. Between Heathcliff and Catherine Earnshaw is a tie deeper and more terrible than human love. After her death he twice disturbs her grave, and is haunted by an impalpable presence which can be nothing less than her spirit. The spirit enters his life more and more, and at last he becomes confident of some imminent mystical reunion. He says he feels a strange change approaching, and ceases to take nourishment. At night he either walks abroad or opens the casement by his bed. When he dies the casement is still swinging open to the pouring rain, and a queer smile pervades the stiffened face. They bury him in a grave beside the mound he has haunted for eighteen years, and small shepherd boys say that he yet walks with his Catherine in the churchyard and on the moor when it rains. Their faces, too, are sometimes seen on rainy nights behind that upper casement at Wuthering Heights. Miss Brontë's eerie terror is no mere Gothic echo, but a tense expression of man's shuddering reaction to the unknown. In this respect, *Wuthering Heights* becomes the symbol of a literary transition, and marks the growth of a new and sounder school. (pp. 36-44)

Howard Phillips Lovecraft, in his Supernatural Horror in Literature, *Ben Abramson Publisher, 1945, 106 p.*

DEFINITIONS

G. RICHARD THOMPSON

[*Thompson is an American educator and critic who specializes in the study of Gothic fiction and the works of Edgar Allan Poe. In the following excerpt, he identifies five different types of Gothic novels and discusses the four primary types.*]

Windswept castles, dim cathedrals, subterranean passages, creaking mansions, deserted churchyards. Dark forests, deep mountain gorges, sheer precipices, frozen wastes. Mysterious manuscripts telling stories within stories of vengeful villains, pursued maidens, murderous madmen; of rape, incest, torture, insanity, damnation; of pursuit by demons, ghosts, ghouls, resurrected corpses, vampires, werewolves. These are some of the stock-in-trade devices of Gothic fiction. But what do these elements have in common that we call them Gothic? How do they help to mark works as of a common genre? Is it because they connote sensationalism, terror, horror, fear of the supernatural, a foreboding sense of evil, perception of awesome and sinister mystery?

Since 1765, when Horace Walpole appended to the second edition of his supernatural romance *The Castle of Otranto* the subtitle "A Gothic Story," the word "Gothic" has been a convenient critical term to describe certain kinds of subject matter and effects in fiction. But the precise meaning of the word, like that of the word "Romantic," retains an ambiguous, even a contradictory quality. In history, Gothic refers to Northern European semi-barbaric tribes of the Dark Ages that picked the Roman Empire to pieces. Yet these so-called barbarians (Vandals, Visigoths, Ostrogoths) merged with Latin-speaking peoples to produce a Christian culture that unified all of Europe in the Middle Ages.

In art history, "Gothic" suggests the devotional quality of the elaborate architecture of cathedrals built by the peoples of Medieval Europe. Yet the word was used in the eighteenth century not only to mean Medieval in general but especially to indicate disapproval of the Middle Ages' "barbarous" forms of architecture, which were not in the Classical style. Modeling itself after what it conceived to be the high point of Classical culture in Rome under the rule of Augustus (63 B.C.-A.D. 14), the European eighteenth century saw itself as the Neo-Classical Age. Yet it was to produce a Neo-Gothic movement in literature that became an integral part of the Romantic movement by the end of the century.

In literature, the word "Gothic" was associated, via the popularity of Walpole's story, not only with the Medieval cathedral but also with various styles of Medieval castles as appropriate settings for the new "romantic" fiction that began to flood the presses in the 1780's and the 1790's. The Neo-Classicist critics, however, bemusedly disapproving of these tales of terror and adventure, seized on the word "Gothic" as a simple means of criticizing their lack of verisimilitude, their improbability and wild flights of fancy and imagination. Nevertheless, the Gothicism of these works was enthusiastically embraced by the reading public. In fact, the subtitle "A Gothic Tale," especially if a work also purported to be a translation, would stimulate greater sales than could be expected from the once popular sentimental and domestic tale. Didactic, satiric, and comic stories of domesticized people in a stable society were superseded by tales of mysterious, isolated personages committing vile deeds, then brooding on themselves—alternately indulging forbidden lusts and narcissistically feeling intense remorse, which, paradoxically, further fed the fires of the passion.

In fiction, such a conception of the hero can be traced back to the rapist and seducer villains of Samuel Richardson's *Pamela* (1740) and *Clarissa Harlowe* (1747-48). The main thrust of eighteenth-century fiction, however, had been toward the satiric social novel of Tobias Smollett, the "comic epic in prose" of Henry Fielding, and the droll narrative of Laurence Sterne. Oliver Goldsmith's genial *The Vicar of Wakefield* (1766) or Henry Mackenzie's sentimental *The Man of Feeling* (1771) dealt not with passion but with the more delicate feelings of gentle and good men and women. The Neo-Gothic mode in fiction blazed new trails. Reflecting the growing Romantic emphasis on the individual, on intense emotion (whether for good *or* evil), and on indulgence of the senses, the Gothic romance made a hero out of the feudal tyrant. The Gothic hero is typically an isolated villain who imprisons helpless maidens, culminates his eroticism, and maniacally destroys his enemies and friends. He struggles to use or overcome vague, malign forces just beyond his control—forces residing in the cosmos or in the mind—in the realm of the supernatural or of the irrational.

As the Romantic movement began to wane in the 1830's and 1840's, the emphasis on the Medieval past and on exotic settings lessened. But Gothic terror and horror and mystery continued as obsessive themes (even after Victoria ascended the British throne in 1837 and a new era of decorum settled over both Anglo-American and Continental culture) throughout the nineteenth century and into our own day. (pp. 1-3)

It is conventional to divide the British Gothic romance, which contains in its history a summation of Continental developments as well, into two basic types: the supernatural and the explained supernatural. Useful as this is, it is an oversimplification. Actually, in addition to a satiric mode, which we shall have to omit from discussion, we may distinguish several overlapping stages: principally, the historical mode, the explained mode, the supernatural mode, and the ambiguous mode. These represent the range of development from simple moralizing Gothic to what, for want of a better term, we may call philosophical Gothic. These distinctions are ontologically based; each mode displaces varying degrees of overt or covert concern for a world view, moving from certainty and stability toward ambiguity. The more complex a work, the less capable it is of being described fully by any category. For example, supernatural works that move toward metaphysical anxiety push the limits of the mode to the very border of the ambiguous mode. The most highly original works always alter or strain the genre.

1. *Historical Gothic.* The historical romance of "other times" is based on legend and superstition, with special, though not exclusive, reference to the Middle Ages. It is sometimes referred to as *Ritter* and *Räuber* (knight and robber) Gothic. It exhibits a strong tendency to moralize in conventional terms, and it may or may not include supernatural elements, which may or may not, haphazardly, imply a world view. Among these are Thomas Leland's *Longsword* (1752), Anne Lucy Barbould's *Sir Bertrand* (1773), Clara Reeve's *The Old English Baron* (1778), Sophia Lee's *The Recess; or, A Tale of Other Times* (1783-86), Anne Fuller's *Alan Fitz-Osborne* (1786), James White's *Earl Strongbow* (1789). These tales of other times culminate thirty to forty years later in the histori-

cal romances of Sir Walter Scott, in many of which the Gothic element is vividly present if not pervasive: *The Antiquary* (1816), *The Black Dwarf* (1816), *The Bride of Lammermoor* (1819), *The Monastery* (1820), *Woodstock* (1826), *Anne of Geierstein* (1829), and others.

Insofar as the supernatural is only an incidental element, the early historical mode of *Ritter* and *Räuber* Gothic is similar to the nonsupernatural tale of passionate crime or murderous pursuit such as William Godwin's *Caleb Williams* (1794). Indeed, the crime story and its allied genre, the detective story, develop principally from this form of Gothic modernized and urbanized. In early historical Gothic, the encounter of a character with a supernatural phenomenon may be irrelevant to the central world view of the work. The presence of an occasional witch, demon, or ghost implies no significant ontology shaping the themes of the work.

In some historical romances that are still recognizably Gothic but contain no supernatural elements, the sense of evil derives from purely human malevolence; the harmful consequences of the action result from such understandable human motives as greed or lechery. One thinks, for example, of the abusive anti-Catholic German novella *The Victim of Priestcraft* (trans. 1823), in which the good knight of the lofty Castle of Eagleeyric is degraded to a bloodthirsty robber by hypocritical priests. The book is representative of what might be called Protestant Gothic in its crude dramatization of the evils of the Romish Church, reflecting Protestant uncertainty about its own fragmentation of the once-unified theology of Catholicism at the same time that it conceives of Catholicism in terms of political and social oppression.

Other nonsupernatural Gothic works dramatize implacable, uncaused human malevolence and thereby move closer to the sense of cosmic dread without actually relying on a concept of the occult. Yet motiveless malevolence in the human psyche can suggest the presence of the demonic in the mind—a "depravity according to nature," to use Melville's phrase for Claggart in *Billy Budd* (1891), or the "longing of the soul to vex itself," to use Poe's definition in "The Imp of the Perverse" (1845). In Godwin's *Caleb Williams,* for example, the sense of dread derives from inversion of "righteous" pursuit of criminal by pursuer: the criminal pursues his accuser with a maniacal intensity akin to the demonic. In Poe's "The Cask of Amontillado" (1846), the malevolent threat derives from the disoriented mind of the murderer in an atmosphere wherein the imagery is strongly suggestive of a descent into hell. In tales of erotic aggression, the lover-murderer may be described in metaphors of the diabolic, but an actual realm of the occult is unnecessary to suggest the horror from the realm of the id. Yet the depths of cruelty and sickness in the human mind just may be a microcosm of a dark universe.

2. *Explained Gothic.* When the very world view of a story is centrally informed by the expectations of the ordinary day-to-day world, the effects of terror and horror derive largely from the tension generated by the insinuated existence of an occult realm threatening the stability of the everyday world. This quotidian stability is increasingly threatened until seemingly unnatural phenomena are "explained," usually at the end, and the rational world order is restored, though rather frayed at the edges. . . . Mrs. Radcliffe's romances of the 1790's gave a new dimension to the historical Gothic romance, especially the kind reliant upon the supernatural. The uses of setting are raised to a symbolic psychological level. Radcliffe less depicts the causes of terror and horror as im-

plies them through the responses of her trembling heroines. Reflecting Neo-Classical opposition to unrestrained force, passion, and superstition, there is little real violence in her works, and seemingly supernatural threats turn out to be misperceived natural phenomena or covert human machination. Mysterious voices echoing in castle corridors are revealed to be the garbled voices of pirates in the dungeon below, filtered up through crevices in the walls. The mysterious light on the lances of an advancing army is footnoted by a reference to "the Abbé Berthelon on electricity." In the explained mode, supernatural phenomena are reducible to misperception on the part of the characters with whom we journey the narrative, sharing their limited knowledge and their suspense. But the universe they inhabit is at last informed by conventional, unambiguous natural law and morality. Human motivation to evil, aggression, and malevolence is explainable in daylight terms—in rational formulas as simple as revenge or lust—rather than as uncaused human depravity possibly paralleling cosmic malevolence from the depths. In effect, instead of being antithetical to the supernatural, the explained mode is a natural, compatible development, concerned with the psychology of fear, though finally stopping short of full cosmic dread.

3. *Supernatural Gothic.* The supernaturalist mode of the Gothic romance, on the other hand, is centrally informed by a concept of the occult as an actual realm of phenomena that interpenetrates everyday reality. The supernatural tale, influenced by translations of German robber-bandit tales and exotic Oriental tales, flowered in Great Britain about the same time as the explained Gothic tale—that is, in the 1780's and 1790's. In supernaturalist tales, there tends to be less insinuation of mystery. More frequently, we have sudden shocks, blood and violence, colossal passions; actual demons, ghosts, witches, and monsters stalk through their pages, both threatening and reinforcing the conventional moral framework of their world.

A notorious example is William Beckford's *Vathek, an Arabian Tale* (1786), an Oriental romance of wild fantasy, surreal sexual violence, and nihilistic irony. Prince Vathek builds a palace of the senses; connected to it by an underground passage is a tower of fifteen hundred steps. The sensual palace, the tower of aspiration, and the subterranean depths constitute an iconography of the book's erotic and religious themes. Vathek's mother, Carathis, a necromancer, convinces him to deny Mohammed and set out in quest of the abode of subterranean fire. During the course of his journey, under the influence of a curse, he falls in love with the Princess Nouronihar, whom he takes with him to enjoy a few days of pleasure and power before they are doomed to an eternity of torture in the dark Hall of Eblis, where dwell the damned, their hearts afire within them. Despite the overt didacticism of the final punishment of evil, the moral character of the world of *Vathek* continually shifts, and the final impression is one of sickness and chaos.

A primary example of the supernaturalist mode is Matthew G. Lewis's *The Monk* (1796), which tells two interwoven stories. A long subplot deals with a young man, Don Raymond, who falls in love with a baroness's niece, Agnes, whom the baroness is forcing to enter a convent. Agnes seeks to escape by pretending to be the famous Bleeding Nun, the ghost of a holy sister who had murdered her lover a hundred years before. The ghost appears every five years, descends from the castle tower, and exits through the courtyard gates left open

Title page of the original French version of William Beckford's Vathek.

for her. At the appointed hour, Raymond meets a blood-splattered figure he thinks is Agnes (who actually has been sent to a convent in Madrid, where the novel's main character—Ambrosio, the monk—condemns her to the dungeon). There is a storm, Raymond's carriage overturns, he is rendered unconscious, and the nun is nowhere to be found. At least until the next night. At the stroke of one, the ghost of the Bleeding Nun appears to Raymond, lifts her veil, revealing a grinning skull face, and gives him an icy kiss. This horrible "erotic" scene is repeated each night while Raymond sinks in physical and mental health. Finally, a stranger—the Wandering Jew, who, for his cursing of Christ at the crucifixion, has himself been cursed with unending life—offers to help Raymond exorcise the ghost. On the stranger's advice, Raymond buries the murderess's bones, regains strength, and sets out to wander the earth in vain search of his imprisoned lover. In its chilling rendering of the repeated fleshless kiss and its introduction of the motif of endless wandering, the story provokes, in addition to bodily and mental pain, an element of religious anxiety. Raymond's ghostly punishment has no reference to any traditional moral transgression he has committed; it is an undeserved punishment for accidental encounter with the dark powers of the supernatural world.

This triple anxiousness is more intensely maintained in the

main plot, which concerns Ambrosio, abbot of the monastery of St. Clare. Initially a young man of high integrity and faith, he is seduced by Matilda, who has entered the monastery dressed as a monk. The seeds of degradation lie in Ambrosio's mind before Matilda's appearance. In a scene representative of how the Gothic world is a perversion of traditional ideals, Ambrosio moves from religious devotion before a painting of the Holy Virgin to near sexual climax. Ambrosio "fixed his eyes upon a picture of the Virgin. . . . Oh! if such a creature existed, and existed but for me! were I permitted to twine round my fingers those golden ringlets, and press with my lips the treasures of that snowy bosom!" (ch. 2). He succumbs to the thought that he might "barter for a single embrace" the reward he has hoped to gain by his thirty years' "piety."

After his actual physical seduction by Matilda, temporary surrogate for the unbearably unattainable Madonna, he revels in lust, violence, crime. The Virgin he now conceives of as an object of defilement. Eventually, in one of the most infamous scenes of early Gothic fiction, he will rape and murder his fifteen-year-old virgin sister among the rotting corpses of monks in the vaults of the monastery. The defilement Ambrosio yearns for includes acts of physical imprisonment, torture, and murder, psychologically sweetened by incestuous assault on a young girl, "spiritually" gratifying in the profanation of holy burial ground in semi-necrophiliac lust. Psychologically, his perversions indicate self-hate; spiritually, love-hate for a failed God. His rationalization for his act is to blame the girl for her innocent seductiveness—a characteristic male response to guilty sexual aggression. "What seduced me into crimes, whose bare remembrance makes me shudder? Fatal witch! was it not thy beauty?" As ever, his concern is finally with himself, with his own perdition, along with a triumphant Satanic pride in his description of his "pollution" of the virginal symbol of purity: "You will tell my judge, that you were happy, till *I* saw you; that you were innocent, till *I* polluted you!" (ch. 11).

Ambrosio's crimes are discovered, and he is delivered over to Spanish Inquisitors. At the last instant, he makes a pact with the devil to escape execution, and the novel concludes with a fantastic, apocalyptic scene. Amidst a wild storm, Satan snatches up his new victim, carries him to the mountaintop, and lets him fall headlong to die a lingering death, his body broken and his flesh torn, his wounds festering, until on the sixth day he is borne away by a flood. Although the conclusion offers a semblance of restored moral order, even the mystic religious quality of the conclusion is sensational and lurid; the work moves toward, but does not quite cross over into, moral and ontological ambiguity.

Other important works of the supernaturalist type include Mary Shelley's *Frankenstein* (1818) and Charles Maturin's *Melmoth the Wanderer* (1820), both of which create a fetid atmosphere of sickness at the same time that they illustrate the metaphysical dread of the high Gothic romance. Like *The Monk, Melmoth* is set against the background of the Spanish Inquisition and employs the legend of the Wandering Jew. The novel is complicated in structure, consisting of six main intertangled stories, each with several substories, one of which, the Wanderer's wooing and wedding the innocent girl Immalee, is one of the best demon-lover tales in the Gothic tradition. (pp. 13-20)

4. *Ambiguous Gothic.* The fourth mode of the Gothic romance would seem at first glance to be a combination, or fu-

sion, of the supernaturalist and the explained modes, though sometimes one or the other element dominates. In the ambiguous mode, as distinct from the supernaturalist, the tendency is not so much toward unattainable ultimate meanings as toward obsessive epistemological doubt in which the very medium of the narrative is called into question by unreliable narrators or interpreters. The threat of supernatural malevolence remains—but is it in the nature of the universe or in the mind? Or in an uncertain combination of both? Embedded in the form of the narrative are experiments with point of view and the tale within a tale that are more than literary devices; they reflect the sense of mystery and the undercurrent of anxiety in the Romantic Age.

The ambiguous mode represents the opposite end of the spectrum from the overt didacticism of historical Gothic and of certain simplistic works of supernatural and explained Gothic. As we have seen, an uncertain cosmos and metaphysical dread are often part of the effects of supernaturalist Gothic, and to a lesser extent, before the rational explanations are forthcoming, of the developing plot lines of explained Gothic. A distinction between forms of numinous dread, mystery outside and mystery inside, is not always easily made. Some supernaturalist works partake of epistemological anxiety, and a purely psychological work fits finally into the explained mode. But central to the ambiguous mode is heightened psychological and philosophical perplexity—so much so that such works may be considered not only as uncertain metaphysical texts, but fundamentally as epistemological texts.

For the Neo-Classical reader, explained Gothic seems to have been highly satisfying, since the explanation preserves everyday "probability." It also appeals to the problem- or puzzle-solving mind, as in a detective story, rather than to apprehension of what we may call a genuine "mystery." Partly for this reason, this technique was, for the Romantic mind, an unsatisfactory mode. Not only did it spoil unity of tone, but it also dissolved the philosophical basis of a genuine mystery. This dissatisfaction goes to the heart of the Romantic obsession with the ambiguous relationship of subjectivity and objectivity. A problem or puzzle aims at and is eliminated by a solution, is solved by a process of clarification, by reorganization of already available data, or by addition of further pertinent data. The solution is the hallmark of the detective story, which itself . . . developed out of the Gothic tradition. In a genuine mystery, however, one is faced with questions for which there is no objective context, no firm frame of reference, from within which to address the problem, puzzle, situation, question. The subject who apprehends a mystery is involved in, is part of, what he perceives. Theologically defined, the penetration of mystery constitutes a participation in the numinous, where distinctions between subject and object, between what is within the self and what is without, are dissolved.

The fusion in the ambiguous mode of the frequently covert philosophical concerns of explained Gothic and supernaturalist Gothic is a major achievement of fiction of the Romantic Age. Ambiguous Gothic is one of the finest expressions of the ontological crisis of Romanticism. Aesthetically, the writer's problem was to blend the sense of insoluble mystery with the impending revelation of an ultimate secret—the very revelation of which, however, threatens the sense of mystery. In lesser writers, the results are often very flat as works of narrative art. But sometimes the result is spectacular, as in the works of writers like Ludwig Tieck, E. T. A. Hoffmann,

Charles Brockden Brown, Nathaniel Hawthorne, Edgar Allan Poe, and, in a different way, Herman Melville—writers who came more and more to believe that whatever secrets of existence do exist can be found in the mind, especially at deep preconscious or unconscious levels, and also in philosophical perplexity, if they are to be found at all.

Romantic fascination with the lower layers of consciousness and philosophical problems of the nature of existence is inextricably linked with its obsession with the puzzle of external nature. Central to the Romantic mind-set is the sense that some further "natural" mystery will always open out from a newly comprehended mystery, the whole series having a total unity that is almost, but not quite, revealed. One is always *about* to comprehend some never-to-be-imparted ultimate secret. This sense of being on the very edge of vast physical, psychological, and metaphysical discoveries permeated the age. Much of the fiction of the time aimed at the dramatization of apparent mystery that would not be explained away at the end, but instead would open up new vistas that would include the mystery as part of its meaning rather than dissolving it.

Although not quite in the ambiguous mode, *Frankenstein* is an example of the literary exploration of what was called "the nightside of natural science" at the end of the eighteenth century and the beginning of the nineteenth. The novel is based not on scientific procedure but on esoteric pseudoscience. The pseudoscience of the time (such as mesmerism, animal magnetism, phrenology) provided an additional source of wonder lore to sacred and demonic myths from the Christian Middle Ages, to Gnosticism from early Christian Rome, and to the more ancient myths of Egypt. All, in essence, are in the esoteric tradition associated with the black arts—incantation, devil-worship, witchcraft, alchemy, and, later, Rosicrucianism. Their strong romantic appeal is easily seen in the fact that they have their origins in dim antiquity and yet point forward to stupendous future discoveries. From a literary point of view, of course, the pseudosciences are most useful, for they provide an effective blend of the sense of incomprehensible mystery and almost comprehensible natural law. In fact, they provide a new mythology to replace the waning Classical myths that formed such a great part of the allusive context of eighteenth-century literature.

In the 1790's writers were fascinated with the seemingly related discoveries in astronomy, gravitational attraction, acoustical vibration, galvanic and voltaic electricity, animal magnetism, hypnotism, states of suspension between waking and sleeping, and the possibility of the existence of an entire independent world of subconscious activity, the world of dreams and of madness. There seemed, moreover, to be an occult relationship between the physical world of Nature and some unifying force below or behind or within Nature. This speculation on the unity of existence was surrounded by mystery, by a sense of the infinite gulf of the unknown compounded by a Christian legacy of fearfulness that perhaps humankind was not meant to know God's secrets. Jean Paul Friedrich Richter, for example, developed the idea of myth into a conception of the Unconscious Archetype, into a depth psychology not unlike C. G. Jung's concept of the collective unconscious memory of humankind. But Jean Paul (as he was known) wrote of this unconscious realm as an abyss, wherein lay the common origin of dreams, of terror, of guilt, of demonology, as much as of myth itself. This realm has many names, he wrote, but its essential qualities are double—the

Terrifying and the Sublime. Sometimes the Unconscious shows itself as a Being, before whose presence we feel horror, guilt, and terror. "This feeling we call the fear of ghosts." At other times: "The spirit shows itself as The Infinite, and man prays."

But the duality goes further. Looking at his body, one of Jean Paul's fictional characters remarks that he has the sense that someone else is sitting in himself and that *he,* in turn, is in *him.* Insisting on this philosophical awareness of the doubleness of existence and of perception, Jean Paul made use of the *Doppelgänger* to suggest a split dissociated ego. His characters become terrified of their images in mirrors, meet their doubles on the street, or compulsively make their own wax likenesses. This motif suggests a mind in confrontation with itself, spinning inward in its attempt to define its dissociation by reference to a universe that is only incompletely perceived.

Blending the two modes of the supernatural and the explained supernatural, but effecting subtle shifts back and forth across the wavering border, the ambiguously explained Gothic tale presents the observable facts of the situation while simultaneously casting doubt upon them. While the reader is left to choose between alternatives, he is not given sufficient data to make such a choice with confidence. Thus the impact of the ambiguous tale is multiple. Its strength resides in forcing the reader to hold a delicate balance of possibilities in his mind, to apprehend intellectually the weird effects of a tale as products of a diseased imagination, but to feel them as supernatural phenomena. Or vice versa.

Whereas the supernatural is an "actuality" in Beckford's *Vathek,* Lewis's *The Monk,* Maturin's *Melmoth,* and is actually the preternatural in Mary Shelley's *Frankenstein,* in the ambiguous mode of the Gothic romance the relationship between the natural and the supernatural is uncertain—as is their relation to the mediating function of the human mind. What exactly *is* the white whale in Herman Melville's *Moby-Dick?* Mere brute animal? An actual demonic agent? A cipher into which a madman projects his frustrated hate? All three at once? Repeatedly in the works of writers like Tieck, Hoffmann, Brown, Washington Irving, Hawthorne, Théophile Gautier, Poe, and others, the treatment of the supernatural results in so intricate a pattern of ambiguity that a metaphysical and epistemological mystery not only comprehends the conscious and subconscious perceptions of the characters but also engulfs us as readers as well.

Especially in America and Germany did Gothic works tend to be in the ambiguously explained mode—such as Ludwig Tieck's "The Fair-Haired Eckbert" (1797) and E. T. A. Hoffmann's "The Sand-man" (1817), Charles Brockden Brown's *Wieland* (1798), the elder Richard Henry Dana's *Paul Felton* (1821), and the tales of Irving, Hawthorne, and Poe in the 1820's, 30's, and 40's. A good example of the ambiguous mode is Brown's *Wieland,* a famous novel admired by the Shelleys and said to have provided a point of departure for *Frankenstein.* The persistent question throughout is whether the younger Wieland acts under the influence of a demonic agent when he murders his family or whether his was the act of a madman influenced by environmental forces. We are never quite sure, despite the explanations involving religious mania, ventriloquism, and even spontaneous combustion, just as we are never quite sure how distorted a picture the narrator (ironically named Clara) provides for us, for she herself is a feverish neurotic. All we know is that the results are disastrous for all concerned.

The ambiguous mode seems not to have been so popular in Great Britain, though what some regard as a masterpiece of Gothic, *Private Memoirs and Confessions of a Justified Sinner* (1824), was written by the Scots author James Hogg. This work—also published in a revised form in 1837 as *The Confessions of a Fanatic*—tells the complicated stories, in several different forms, of three interrelated figures who become sequentially doubles of one another, one of whom may or may not be the half brother of the other and one of whom may or may not be Satan. Brought up in a household where he is taught to think of himself as one predestined to be saved, the principal of these becomes the friend of a young man who looks like himself. He also meets a third man, who, after the murder of the second, begins to take on the second's characteristics, and thus comes more and more to seem like the protagonist, who finds himself accused of crimes he cannot remember having committed. At the end, even though he is not sure if the third figure is not a projection of his own mind, he nonetheless enters into a suicide pact with him and thereby conclusively ensures his own damnation. Hogg also wrote a number of shorter works about *Doppelgängers* and dreamselves and thoses shape-shifting incubi that come in dreams, such as "The Hunt of Eildon" and "George Dobson's Expedition to Hell."

But Hawthorne, Poe, and Melville provide the most accessible points of reference for American readers attempting to understand the ambiguous Gothic tale. Hawthorne's metaphysical, epistemological, and psychological concerns—as well as his moralizing allegorical tendency—are well represented in an early brief sketch about the dream-states of the unconscious he called "The Haunted Mind" (1835). The narrator pictures himself, or the reader, as having suddenly awakened from a midnight slumber to see a procession of allegorical figures who exhibit various aspects of the demonic for the guilty heart that "holds its hell within itself." Even without such a burden of guilt, this midnight time is "the nightmare of the soul"—this "heavy, heavy sinking of the spirits; this wintry gloom about the heart; this indistinct horror of the mind, blending itself with the darkness of the chamber." It is important to observe Hawthorne's underscoring of the ambiguous relationship of the inner darkness of the mind "blending" with the outer darkness of the "real" world, revealed "on the borders of sleep and wakefulness." He vaguely modifies this gloom with a suggestion of a further dreamvision, contained in the image of a beautiful, pure woman, who involves the dreamer in *her* dream. But even in this better dream, the sleeper has "an involuntary start" and finds himself "running a doubtful parallel" between "human life and the hour which has now elapsed."

The didactic allegory that seems the initial impulse of the sketch is dissolved. In such a midnight hour, Hawthorne writes, "you emerge from mystery, pass through a vicissitude that you can but imperfectly control, and are borne onward to another mystery." Romantic desire for clear reciprocity between the subjective and the objective here becomes a guilt-laden "doubtful parallel" between the "subconscious" realm of the "other" and the conscious world. In story after story by Hawthorne—from "Roger Malvin's Burial" (1832) and "My Kinsman, Major Molineux" (1832), to "Young Goodman Brown" (1835) and "The Minister's Black Veil" (1836), to "Rappaccini's Daughter" (1844) and "Ethan Brand" (1850)—this doubtful parallel of subjective and objective, the central dread of the dark Romantic world view, is embedded in ambiguous Gothic narrative. (pp. 26-33)

G. Richard Thompson, in an introduction to Romantic Gothic Tales: 1790-1840, *edited by G. Richard Thompson, Harper & Row, Publishers, 1979, pp. 1-43.*

ROBERT D. HUME

[*An American scholar, Hume is a specialist in seventeenth- and eighteenth-century English drama. In the following excerpt, he defines the nature of the Gothic novel, contrasting it with works of Romanticism.*]

The Gothic novel has not fared well among literary critics, even in this age of sympathetic evaluations of largely forgotten minor works. Literary histories treat the subject with chilly indifference or condescension, granting it only cursory attention.

It is usually assumed that all Gothic novels are much the same, and that the form is defined by the presence of some stock devices. These "Gothic trappings" include haunted castles, supernatural occurrences (sometimes with natural explanations), secret panels and stairways, time-yellowed manuscripts, and poorly lighted midnight scenes. Such "Gothicism" is only too often ridiculous, even in the hands of its leading exponents. In consequence, the Gothic novel writers have been associated with [in the words of Samuel Chew] "the subliterary depths of romanticism . . . into [whose] noisome fastnesses we need not descend."

The object of this essay is to suggest that the Gothic novel is more than a collection of ghost-story devices, "the product of a dilettante interest in the potentialities of the Middle Ages for picturesque horror." Specifically, I wish to do three things: to analyze the characteristics and development of the Gothic novel; to define the essence of that "Gothic" which can be significant for Walpole, Melville, and Faulkner alike; and to set the original Gothic novels in better historical perspective by defining their relation to the romantic literature of the same period.

As a historical form the Gothic novel flourished between 1764 and 1820; Walpole's *The Castle of Otranto* and Maturin's *Melmoth the Wanderer* are its limits of demarcation. The appearance of the form has been variously accounted for. But in general it can be seen as one symptom of a widespread shift away from neoclassical ideals of order and reason, toward romantic belief in emotion and imagination. Horace Walpole saw his novel as part of a resurgence of romance against neoclassical restrictions: "the great resources of fancy have been dammed up, by a strict adherence to common life." Within the limits of the cliché, we can view the Gothic novel as a manifestation of Northrop Frye's age of growing "sensibility" to aesthetic impressions. Like the work of Ossian, Smart, and Sterne, the Gothic novel is part of the new "literature of process" which reflects its creator's mind.

The literature of the later eighteenth century attempts to rouse the reader's imaginative sympathies; the particular device employed toward this end by the Gothic novel writers is terror, which Burke had stressed as a factor in emotional involvement in his *A Philosophical Enquiry into the Origin of our Ideas of the Sublime and Beautiful* (1757). By Walpole's account in his "Preface to the First Edition," "terror" is "the author's principal engine" and serves to grip and affect the reader. To what end we will have to see. First, some discriminations must be attempted.

There were three varieties of novel widely current in the late eighteenth century, sentimental-domestic (the novel of manners), "Gothic," and didactic. *The Vicar of Wakefield* (1766), *The Castle of Otranto* (1764), and *Caleb Williams* (1794) are examples of each type respectively. The popularity of "Gothic" trappings quickly brought about their absorption into the other varieties of novel. (*Caleb Williams* exhibits some of them.) In consequence it is sometimes said that there are several kinds of Gothic novel. These are usually described as (1) Sentimental-Gothic, novels which utilize ghosts and gloomy-castle atmosphere to enliven sentimental-domestic tales (e.g., Clara Reeve's *The Old English Baron*). (2) Terror-Gothic, the most nearly "pure" Gothic novel (e.g., Mrs. Radcliffe's *The Mysteries of Udolpho*). (3) Historical-Gothic, in which the Gothic atmosphere is used in a historical setting (e.g., Sophia Lee's *The Recess*). These divisions are unsatisfactory. "Terror-Gothic" is too inclusive a category, lumping Radcliffe and Lewis together as it does. And the historical novel must at some point be distinguished from the Gothic.

J. M. S. Tompkins [see Further Reading] speaks of the "historical novel or Gothic Romance" which "in their origin . . . are not easily distinguishable." It is perhaps more accurate to say that the historical novel is an offshoot or development of the Gothic novel. The relationship is essentially accidental. Gothic novels are set in the past and are, as Tompkins says, at least "nominally historic," but they show no serious interest in veracity of fact or atmosphere. For Mrs. Radcliffe, the sixteenth century is as Gothic as the thirteenth. Walpole dabbled in the genuinely medieval, but his good characters, like those of the other Gothic novelists, are simply a projection of late eighteenth-century ideals, while his villain is a later development of the villain-hero of Jacobean drama. The historical element in the Gothic novel does little more than contribute to the freedom conferred by distance in time and space. A novel like *The Recess* (1785), which makes use of historical personages, is in reality a sentimental-domestic novel transposed into a supposedly historical situation with Gothic trimmings added for savor. If wearing a wool tie makes me a sheep, then *The Recess* is a Gothic novel. The novels of Jane Porter and Scott are the first novels whose *basis* is a specific historical setting.

I am suggesting, in short, that some Gothic novels are more than the sentimental fiction of the day fitted with outlandish trappings, in which case "sentimental-Gothic" and "historical-Gothic" are misnomers.

What are the distinctive characteristics of the "Gothic" novel? What features in common are to be found in the obviously dissimilar works of Walpole, Beckford, Lewis, Radcliffe, Mary Shelley, and Maturin? Answering these questions involves us in a dual task. First we must trace the evolution of the form, trying to see what produces its unity of impression. Second, we must attempt simultaneously to recognize the serious features of Gothic writing, distinguishing between the trappings which gave the eighteenth-century form its name and the essentials which the early examples share with novels in entirely different periods.

What techniques, objectives, and concerns do these novels have in common? One of their most prominent concerns, though seldom discussed, might grandiosely be called a psychological interest. As early as Walpole (1764) there is a considerable amount of concern for *interior* mental processes. Justifying his use of the supernatural, Walpole says, "Allow the possibility of the facts, and all the actors comport them-

selves as persons would do in their situation." The true Gothic novels pick up and advance the sort of psychologizing which Richardson began in *Clarissa* (1748). I say "advance" because, while they are neither so thorough nor so subtle as Richardson, they move into deeper and more emotionally complex situations. Robert Lovelace is a simpler character than Lewis' Ambrosio. But although Ambrosio is a more repulsive person, his responses to his own urges and actions are far more complicated and meaningful than Lovelace's irresistible impulse and consequent remorse.

Gothic novels display the reactions of their characters to trying or appalling situations. But their heroes and heroines are not subjected to trials merely for the sake of exhibiting fine feeling, as in the sentimental novels of the period—*The Old English Baron* (1777), for example, whose hero Edmund is truly a trial of the reader's patience. Mrs. Radcliffe enjoys something of the sentimental outlook, but she seldom indulges in Mackenziesque feeling for its own sake. It should not be forgotten that at one of the key points in *The Mysteries of Udolpho,* M. St. Aubert, on his deathbed, gives his daughter the following advice:

> "Above all, my dear Emily," said he, "do not indulge in the pride of fine feeling, the romantic error of amiable minds. Those, who really possess sensibility, ought early to be taught, that it is a dangerous quality, which is continually extracting the excess of misery, or delight, from every surrounding circumstance. And, since, in our passage through this world, painful circumstances occur more frequently than pleasing ones, and since our sense of evil is, I fear, more acute than our sense of good, we become the victims of our feelings, unless we can in some degree command them."

Another distinctive feature of the early Gothic novel is its attempt to *involve* the reader in a new way. In the sentimental literature of the age one is invited to admire fine feelings; in Gothic writing the reader is held in suspense with the characters, and increasingly there is an effort to shock, alarm, and otherwise rouse him. Inducing a powerful emotional response in the reader (rather than a moral or intellectual one) was the prime object of these novelists. In this endeavor they prepared the way for the romantic poets who followed them.

Gothic novels are often ridiculed for their use of the supernatural, though no one condemns Coleridge, say, for introducing it in "The Rime of the Ancient Mariner." The supernatural can be used crudely (witness Walpole's gigantic helmet), but this is no reason to condemn it outright. In his review of *The Monk* Coleridge gives an excellent defense of the use of the supernatural in fiction:

> The romance-writer possesses an unlimited power over situations; but he must scrupulously make his characters act in congruity with them. Let him work *physical* wonders only, and we will be content to *dream* with him for a while; but the first *moral* miracle which he attempts, he disgusts and awakens us. Thus our judgment remains unoffended, when, announced by thunders and earthquakes, the spirit appears to Ambrosio involved in blue fires that increase the cold of the cavern. . . . But when a mortal, fresh from the impression of that terrible appearance . . . is represented as being at the same moment agitated by so fleeting an appetite as that of lust, our own feelings convince us that this is not improbable, but impossible; not preternatural, but contrary to nature. The extent of the powers that

may exist, we can never ascertain; and therefore we feel no great difficulty in yielding a temporary belief to any, the strangest, situation of *things*. But that situation once conceived, how beings like ourselves would feel and act in it, our own feelings sufficiently instruct us; and we instantly reject the clumsy fiction that does not harmonize with them.

Direct use of the supernatural in fiction contravenes our ingrown idea of the essential realism of narrative fiction; symbolic use of the supernatural bothers us much less, particularly in poetry. But where realism is not the desired object—and it is not in the Gothic novel—supernaturalism seems a valid enough device for removing the narrative from the realm of the everyday. And this the Gothic novels clearly try to do. What Coleridge says about his part of the *Lyrical Ballads* is applicable:

> The incidents and agents were to be, in part at least, supernatural; and the excellence aimed at was to consist in the interesting of the affections by the dramatic truth of such emotions, as would naturally accompany such situations, supposing them real. And in *this* sense they have been to every human being who, from whatever source of delusion, has at any time believed himself under supernatural agency. . . . my endeavors should be directed to persons and characters supernatural . . . so as to transfer from our inward nature a human interest and a semblance of truth sufficient to procure for these shadows of imagination that willing suspension of disbelief for the moment, which constitutes poetic faith.

Among the significant Gothic novelists, only Ann Radcliffe bothers to produce natural explanations for all seemingly supernatural effects, and many readers find her explanations more distracting than the apparent events which occasion them. Too much attention has been paid to a convention which we should accept as readily as we accept the authorial presence in *Tom Jones* or the symbolic levels of *Ulysses*.

The distinguishing mark of the early Gothic novel is its atmosphere *and* the use to which that atmosphere is put. The involvement of the reader's imagination is central to the Gothic endeavor, even in an attempt as relatively crude as Walpole's. In retrospect the Gothic atmosphere seems mechanical, even in the greatest of these novels, but originally its purpose was to arouse and sensitize the reader's imagination, giving it further play than it ordinarily enjoyed, and the use of the supernatural was clearly meant to contribute to this imaginative stimulus.

Among the novels of the period 1764-1820 a distinction seems necessary between the novel of "terror" and the novel of "horror." This distinction has its origin in the aesthetics of the mid-eighteenth century. As Mrs. Radcliffe puts it, "Terror and horror are so far opposite, that the first expands the soul, and awakens the faculties to a high degree of life; the other contracts, freezes, and nearly annihilates them. . . . neither Shakespeare nor Milton by their fictions, nor Mr. Burke by his reasoning, anywhere looked to positive horror as a source of the sublime, though they all agree that terror is a very high one." In short, terror opens the mind to the apprehension of the sublime, while (according to Mrs. Radcliffe) the repugnance involved in horror closes it.

Terror dependent on suspense or dread is the *modus operandi* of the novels of Walpole and Radcliffe. *The Castle of Otranto* holds the reader's attention through dread of a series of terri-

ble possibilities—Theodore's execution, the (essentially) incestuous marriage of Manfred and Isabella, the casting-off of Hippolita, and so on. Mrs. Radcliffe's use of dramatic suspension is similar but more sophisticated. She raises vague but unsettling possibilities and leaves them dangling for hundreds of pages. Sometimes the effect is artificial, as in the case of the black-veiled "picture" at Udolpho, but in raising and sustaining the disquieting possibility of an affair between St. Aubert and the Marchioness de Villeroi, for instance, she succeeds splendidly. Mrs. Radcliffe's easy manipulation of drawn-out suspense holds the reader's attention through long books with slight plots.

The method of Lewis, Beckford, Mary Shelley, and Maturin is considerably different. Instead of holding the reader's attention through suspense or dread they attack him frontally with events that shock or disturb him. Rather than elaborating possibilities which never materialize, they heap a succession of horrors upon the reader. Lewis set out, quite deliberately, to overgo Mrs. Radcliffe. *The Monk* (1796), like *Vathek* (1786), *Frankenstein,* and *Melmoth the Wanderer,* gains much of its effect from murder, torture, and rape. The difference from terror-Gothic is considerable; Mrs. Radcliffe merely threatens these things, and Walpole uses violent death only at the beginning and end of his book. The reader is prepared for neither of these deaths, which serve only to catch the attention and to produce a climax, respectively.

Obviously a considerable shift has occurred. Is its purpose merely ever greater shock? Or has the Gothic novelists' aesthetic theory changed? Terror-Gothic works on the supposition that a reader who is repelled will close his mind (if not the book) to the sublime feelings which may be roused by the mixture of pleasure and pain induced by fear. Horror-Gothic assumes that if events have psychological consistency, even within repulsive situations, the reader will find himself involved beyond recall.

This change is probably related to a general shift in conceptions of good and evil. Regarded in the Renaissance as philosophically and practically distinct, they drew ever closer in the next two centuries. This movement culminated in the "confusions" of good and evil common among some romantics and epitomized in Blake's *The Marriage of Heaven and Hell* and Byron's *Cain.* No Augustan would have felt that Satan was the hero of *Paradise Lost.* Walpole and Mrs. Radcliffe maintain the proprieties of a strict distinction between good and evil, though in Manfred and Montoni they created villain-heroes whose force of character gives them a certain fearsome attractiveness, even within this moral context. But with the villain-heroes of horror-Gothic we enter the realm of the morally ambiguous. Ambrosio, Victor Frankenstein, and Melmoth are men of extraordinary capacity whom circumstance turns increasingly to evil purposes. They are not merely monsters, and only a bigoted reading makes them out as such.

To put the change from terror-Gothic to horror-Gothic in its simplest terms, the suspense of external circumstance is deemphasized in favor of increasing psychological concern with moral ambiguity. The horror-Gothic writers postulated the relevance of such psychology to every reader; they wrote for a reader who could say with Goethe that he had never heard of a crime which he could not imagine himself committing. The terror novel prepared the way for a fiction which though more overtly horrible is at the same time more serious and more profound. It is with *Frankenstein* and *Melmoth the Wanderer* that the Gothic novel comes fully into its own.

Because *Frankenstein* (1817) continues to be read as a horror story, serious critical discussion of it is rare. But it is both a skillfully constructed book and one of real psychological insight. The presence of an explorer (Robert Walton) as narrator is not merely a device for transmitting the story, but serves also as a parallel and reinforcement for the book's main themes. The idea which pervades the book is that of Promethean overreaching. Victor Frankenstein tries to become a god, and the endeavor destroys him. "Life and death appeared to me ideal bounds, which I should first break through, and pour a torrent of light into our dark world. A new species would bless me as its creator and source. . . . No father could claim the gratitude of his child so completely as I should deserve theirs." Victor Frankenstein is a figure similar to Thomas Mann's Adrian Leverkühn; he destroys his humanity for the sake of a "break through" not properly belonging to man.

The being which Victor Frankenstein creates (and meant to be beautiful) mirrors in its outward form his own inward deformity. The early history of the monster, which craves love, is an ironic reflection of Frankenstein's personality, for he can neither love nor respond properly to human feeling. The present-day confusion in comic-book terminology between Frankenstein and his monster is not surprising, for Frankenstein is a monster, and in a real sense he *is* the monster. Again and again Frankenstein calls himself the murderer of his family and friends; at first he is blaming himself for having let loose so dangerous a being, but as the novel advances we recognize that he has a half-mad understanding that the monster is enacting in objective form the implications of his own inhumanity. This is what makes the story seem truly uncanny. Senseless butchery by an inhuman monster would be frightening, but no more; here it is not senseless, but all too reasonable.

Victor Frankenstein is explicitly described as a man with originally benevolent impulses and great potentiality for good. His striving for a more than human greatness destroys the warmth of his humanity, and gradually he becomes totally involved with the monster which objectifies all his own inadequacies. Their final, mad chase to the north reflects literally their abandonment of society and their total absorption with their mutual self.

Melmoth the Wanderer is the last and clearly the greatest of the Gothic novels of this period. Melmoth himself is the epitome of the romantic villain-hero, a hybrid of the Wandering Jew and Milton's Satan with a bit of the Flying Dutchman thrown in. The book's structure is thematically simple but narratively elaborate; it consists of a series of tales inside each other, each told from a different standpoint. The theme is sadism, moral and physical, religious and social. Melmoth wanders, destructive and self-damned, fruitlessly seeking a salvation which his self-willed character prevents. The reader is repelled by his sadism, but cannot help feeling the tragic stature given Melmoth by the immensity of his suffering. This ambiguity in the reader's response Melmoth shares with such characters as Frankenstein and his monster, Macbeth, Captain Ahab, and Leverkühn. The reader sees clearly that Melmoth, like Marlowe's Faustus, is damned not by what he does, but by his own proud despair of forgiveness and salvation. In the love of Immalee Melmoth is offered redemption;

he is a Dutchman who cannot believe in the efficacy of his Senta.

What then in these Gothic novels is mere mummery and what, if anything, is more than that? The prime feature of the Gothic novel, I believe, is its attempt to involve the reader in special circumstances. Terror-Gothic plays on the reader's response to suspense, while horror-Gothic attempts to involve him with the villain-hero protagonist. Both types share an interest in the characters' psychology, and both kinds may be regarded as statements or correlatives of the author's state of mind.

This last point requires amplification. The key characteristic of the Gothic novel is not its devices, but its atmosphere. The atmosphere is one of evil and brooding terror; the imaginary world in which the action takes place is the author's objectification of his imaginative sense of the atmosphere. In other words, the setting exists to convey the atmosphere. Neither suspense nor horror is dependent upon a particular setting or atmosphere. *The Hound of the Baskervilles* and *Last Exit to Brooklyn* are not Gothic novels. The Gothic novel uses its atmosphere for ends which are fundamentally psychological, though its actual use ranges from the relative crudity of Walpole to the subtlety of Mary Shelley and Maturin.

Wild landscapes, ruined abbeys, and the like, were merely a convenient convention, a standardized method of achieving the desired atmosphere. The more significant components of the Gothic novel are as follows. (1) A setting in space or time or both sufficiently removed from the reader of 1800 that there would be no intrusion of everyday standards of factual probability and morality. Thus most of the stories are set in Southern France, Spain, Italy, or Germany, and usually in the sixteenth century or earlier. Time and place are irrelevant (real historicity is very slight) as long as they are vague or remote. Beckford's *Vathek* is sometimes discussed as an "oriental tale" in the tradition of *Rasselas,* but it is basically a Gothic novel whose oriental setting provides the necessary "distance." (2) There is a moral norm present in the story. The villain-hero is thus measured against a standard which the reader recognizes as close to his own everyday outlook. Walpole's Theodore and Isabella, Mrs. Radcliffe's Emily St. Aubert and Adeline (the latter in *The Romance of the Forest*), and Lewis' Raymond de las Cisternas and Lorenzo de Medina all serve this normative function. Mary Shelley presents Frankenstein's friend Clerval as an ordinary, decent man. Maturin's use of multiple narrators fulfills the same function. Although the reader is to be immersed in an extraordinary world, he must not feel that its psychological (as distinct from its factual) bounds are utterly foreign to him. If he does, then the story loses its immediacy for him; any application to his own mind is ruled out. (3) The action derives from a complex villain-hero. Even in stories as relatively black and white as *The Castle of Otranto* and *The Mysteries of Udolpho,* Manfred and Montoni are much more than stock villains, just as Ambrosio is much more than a stock hypocrite in *The Monk.* Frankenstein and Melmoth are impressively grandiose characters whose undoubted stature is compounded of dark aspirations and great force of character. The world and atmosphere of the Gothic novel are like its "terrific" protagonists—fearsome and profoundly ambiguous. (4) The confusion of evil and good which the Gothic novel reflects in its villain-heroes produces a non-Christian or anticlerical feeling. Coleridge seriously accused Lewis of blasphemy in *The Monk,* and the book long remained expurgated under the odium of blasphemy. Mrs. Radcliffe (particularly in *The Italian*) is sometimes anticlerical. To some extent the feeling is simply anti-Catholic. Maturin (a clergyman) is extremely critical of all churches, but particularly the Catholic Church. Mary Shelley, her mother's daughter, largely ignores religion. These writers simply cannot find in religion acceptable answers to the fundamentally psychological questions of good and evil which they were posing. This failure is reflected in their satire on both religious institutions and the simplicity of a religious morality.

Seen in these terms the Gothic novel becomes one kind of treatment of the psychological problem of evil. In its earliest form it is filled with "crude claptrap," but increasingly it takes on a "symbolic resonance" as external suspense is subordinated to involvement in moral ambiguity. This analysis pushes the case for these novels rather hard. I am offering it in an attempt to offset the common view that they have nothing but amusement value. Emphasis on the serious quality of these early Gothic novels makes their relationship to the later Gothic novels much clearer.

Wuthering Heights, Moby Dick, and Faulkner's *Sanctuary* are all Gothic novels. Each one creates a very distinct world of its own—as novels of manners or social conditions do not. All three novels possess a distinctive and pervasive atmosphere. Though all occur in contemporary time, each is isolated in space; Faulkner's decaying South, Melville's whaling ship, and Brontë's desolate country residences are far removed from the reader's sphere of experience. Similarly, each novel presents a clear standard of the ordinary. Melville's Ishmael and Brontë's Mr. Lockwood serve as both narrators and moral norms. Faulkner's scheme is more complex, but Horace Benbow and his sister Narcissa may be seen as the twin poles of ordinary morality. Ahab, Heathcliff, and Popeye are in their different ways the villain-heroes around whom each book is built. And each novel has an anti-Christian element: Joseph in *Wuthering Heights;* Melville's fighting Quakers; Faulkner's savage portrayal of a Baptist minister and typical Christian charity.

Moby Dick is perhaps the greatest of Gothic novels, and an almost perfect example of the form. In the microcosmic world of the whaling ship Ahab is the completely dominant villain-hero. He is a figure of immense stature, a good man, a kindly man of real humanity (witness his relations with Starbuck), but a man gripped by a deadly monomania which will destroy him and his companions with him. Symbolic-critical readings of the book always break down after a certain point, for like other Gothic novels *Moby Dick* ends in moral ambiguity; there is no message, no moral, no final statement of right and wrong. Moby Dick is for Ahab what the monster is for Frankenstein. In the literal sense he is only a whale, and Ahab's vengeance is ridiculous. In a symbolic sense, who can say? The white whale may be the symbol of evil in the world—or not. Ahab is a madman, and yet he remains a complex and tragic figure. Like Melmoth he wilfully persists in his own delusion. Yet he succeeds in carrying his crew with him, and the reader follows, irresistibly drawn into a mad and exalted quest. Ahab is a Promethean figure: if the sun insults him, he will strike at it, come what may. Very skillfully, Melville involves the reader with Ahab; we follow the narration of Ishmael into the situation, and then the narration vanishes, leaving us immersed in Ahab's world. In a similar manner we are drawn by Lockwood's narration into the self-contained world of *Wuthering Heights.* Both books

leave us with great ambiguities; good and evil, love and hate are intertwined until they are inseparable. Motives which we might praise or blame without a second thought in our everyday worlds appear to us in the Gothic context as beyond judgment. We are brought to see the hurts of Ahab and Heathcliff, to appreciate their complexities, and ultimately to decline judgment on the damage they do to themselves and to others. As is the case with Melmoth, tragic stature compensates for apparent inhumanity.

Sanctuary (1931) is quite differently constructed, and yet certainly remains a Gothic novel. It is a book about the pervasiveness of moral evil. Like some of the early Gothic novels it has been popular on account of its sensational elements: rape with a corncob, brothel scenes, and mob-burning of an innocent man—and this has hampered serious discussion of the book.

Faulkner dispenses with the convention of a heroic villain; Popeye is an impotent, vicious monster. But Faulkner went to some pains, in a chapter (xxxi) he added when revising the book, to make it clear that even Popeye cannot be held morally responsible for his actions. He is merely the victim of a syphilitic father and an insane grandmother. The novel's point is that all men are victims of the evil in human nature: there can be no good distinct from evil, and so there can be no definitive distinction between them. Systematically, Faulkner demolishes the illusions of the idealistic Horace Benbow, whose belief in justice and the distinction between good and evil collapses as he is forced to recognize his own suppressed potentiality for violent sexual response.

Sanctuary is an extreme and violent book, but a powerful one. The world Faulkner creates is diseased and disgusting; its effectiveness depends on the reader's willingness to be drawn into a world of evil in which nothing admirable is effective. There is no tragic grandeur here, no compensatory greatness. Faulkner's novel is a statement of despair over the inescapability of evil. The pervasive atmosphere of perversion and the macabre is the backdrop to Faulkner's demand that we recognize and agonize over the evil which is inextricably bound up with the good in every human being. If the book can be said to have a message, it is simply that there are no answers; even Popeye must be absolved of personal responsibility.

This much should be clear by now: the Gothic novel offers no conclusions. In its fully developed form it attempts to involve the reader in a special world in whose atmosphere of evil man is presented under trying circumstances. It emphasizes psychological reaction to evil and leads into a tangle of moral ambiguity for which no meaningful answers can be found.

With a clearer idea of the essentials of the Gothic novel we are ready to return to problems set aside earlier—the origin of the Gothic novel and its relation to romanticism. It is plain enough that the early Gothic novel is part of the movement away from neoclassicism and toward romanticism. Walpole subtitled his novel "A Gothic Story"; in the mid-eighteenth century "Gothic" meant basically antique and barbarous with reference to architecture. In this context it carried the connotation of the rude, wild, and irregular—by eighteenth-century standards, the Shakespearean. Walpole's imaginative excesses are part of a widespread reaction against the dominance of Locke's mechanistic concept of the mind. Even Mrs. Radcliffe, whose sense of decorum and propriety is notorious, was closer to Wordsworth than to Pope in her admiration of the sublime. The early Gothic novels, to borrow Walpole's terms again, were "romances," unrestrained exercises of that imagination against whose excesses Dr. Johnson warned so sternly.

Gothic and romantic writing are closely related chronologically and share some themes and characteristics, such as the hero who is a guilt-haunted wanderer. Both have a strong psychological concern with interior mental processes. The realistic novel, the novel of manners, and neoclassical poetry generally lead the reader to contemplate the exterior actions of the life around him. In sharp contradistinction, Gothic and romantic writing usually lead the reader to consider internal mental processes and reactions. The one sort of writing is basically social in its concern, the other essentially individual. It is from this absorption with the individual that Gothic and romantic writing gain their preoccupation with the mind.

Yet though the same set of conditions gave rise to both Gothic and romantic writing, and though they share many characteristics, they remain quite distinct. Their difference has always been easier to recognize than to define; here I wish to attempt the distinction with reference to some Coleridgean literary theory.

The key characteristics of Gothic and romantic writers are concern with ultimate questions and lack of faith in the adequacy of reason or religious faith to make comprehensible the paradoxes of human existence. English romanticism in its first form (early Wordsworth and Coleridge; Keats and Shelley) can be viewed as an attempt to find the emotional certainty of revealed religion directly from nature rather than from God. From nature alone the romantics attempt to derive feelings which earlier in European history were organized and sustained in a supernatural Christian framework. The romantics turn to "imagination," which, according to Coleridge, recasts the objects of the exterior world into a new and more profoundly "true" reality, giving the materials with which it chooses to work a unity and meaning which they do not possess in their original form. It is the imagination which serves the romantics as their vehicle of escape from the limitations of the human condition.

The Gothic writers, though possessed by the same discontent with the everyday world, have no faith in the ability of man to transcend or transform it imaginatively. Their explorations lie strictly within the realm of this world and they are confined to the limits of reason. Thus the writers of Gothic never offer intuitive solutions; they cannot present the sensed order found by the romantics in their highest flights. The Gothic literary endeavor is not that of the transcendent romantic imagination; rather, in Coleridge's terms, Gothic writers are working with fancy, which is bound to the "fixities and definites" of the rational world.

In saying this I do not mean to denigrate the Gothic novel. Within the *Biographia Literaria* fancy is sharply distinguished from imagination, but its present connotation of frivolous and whimsical is by no means necessary. Secondary imagination is that faculty of the mind which may surmount the limitations of this world to seek clarity and truth in a world of permanence beyond it. Fancy, on the other hand, however seriously it is used, can find only paradox, never high truth. Fancy will never appear to resolve the deepest conflicts and contradictions of this world; this is precisely what the romantics try to do, and what the Gothic novel never does.

The early Gothic novels can be considered the precursors of romanticism in their concern with sensibility, the sublime, and the involvement of the reader in a more than rational way. Gothic also prepares the way for and shares the romantic "confusion" of good and evil. But where Gothic remains darkened by the necessary ambiguities of its conclusions, romantic writing assumes the ultimate existence, if not the easy accessibility, of clear answers to the problems which torment man in this world.

From this perspective a writer like Byron seems closer to the Gothic camp than to the romantics. Biographically, he is practically the archetype of the Gothic-romantic hero, but as a romantic poet he fits only uneasily the type delimited by Wordsworth, Keats, and Shelley. Perhaps it is his Augustan affinities which so severely undermine his faith in the transcendent power of imagination, but Byron's cosmic despair is not offset even by his glorying in the mysterious grandeur of heroes modeled on himself. *Manfred, Cain,* and *Childe Harold* are all more Gothic than romantic in their moral confusions and ultimate paradoxes. Byron shows few signs of faith in the romantic metaphysic; his escape from his existential predicament, if it comes at all, comes in the comic perspective of *Don Juan.*

In the twentieth century most writers have accepted human limitations and uncertainty more easily than those writers of earlier centuries who believed that man is intrinsically a great and noble being. Yeats was perhaps the last great romantic writer. Gothic writing too has been on the decline, for evil is explained away sociologically today. Yet occasionally, as with *Sanctuary* and perhaps Thomas Mann's *Dr. Faustus* (1947), a novel is still written with the Gothic aims and characteristics.

Looking back, it may seem that we have come a long way from the Gothic novels of Horace Walpole and Mrs. Radcliffe. So indeed we have. But it is not always easy to see in a single work all of the implications which attach to it. *The Castle of Otranto* is a terror story, but it is also the beginning of a form. Walpole opened possibilities of which he was but dimly aware. Yet, in speaking of a new kind of "romance" in which the "fancy" is freed from restraint to treat the psychological reactions of men and women in "extraordinary positions," Walpole says that "if the new route he [Walpole] has struck out shall have paved a road for men of brighter talents, he shall own with pleasure and modesty, that he was sensible the plan was capable of receiving greater embellishments than his imagination or conduct of the passions could bestow on it." He was quite correct.

I have tried to treat the early Gothic novels less as terror stories than as experiments in a literary form which later came to full flower. Knowing the overall development of the form is a great aid to recognizing the promise of the early novels. We look now at Shakespeare's first plays and see signs of the coming greatness we know is there; looking at Marlowe's work we have no idea whether he would have developed further. With the great Gothic novels—*Frankenstein, Melmoth the Wanderer, Moby Dick*—to open our eyes, we can see the considerable aesthetic potential latent in the form crudely forged by Walpole and developed by Radcliffe and Lewis. The later, greater Gothic novels do not appear full-blown from nowhere. They inherited a form and tradition which had undergone half a century of exploratory development.

Gothic and romantic writing spring alike from a recognition

of the insufficiency of reason or religious faith to explain and make comprehensible the complexities of life. We may distinguish between Gothic and romantic in terms of what they do within this situation. The imagination, Coleridge tells us, reveals its presence "in the balance or reconciliation of opposite or discordant qualities." Romantic writing reconciles the discordant elements it faces, resolving their apparent contradictions imaginatively in the creation of a higher order. Gothic writing, the product of serious fancy, has no such answers and can only leave the "opposites" contradictory and paradoxical. In its highest forms romantic writing claims the existence of higher answers where Gothic can find only unresolvable moral and emotional ambiguity. (pp. 282-90)

Robert D. Hume, "Gothic versus Romantic: A Revaluation of the Gothic Novel," in PMLA, Vol. 84, No. 2, March, 1969, pp. 282-90.

S. L. VARNADO

[*In the following excerpt, Varnado defines Gothic fiction with reference to theologian Rudolf Otto's theories of the 'numinous.'*]

One of the engaging aspects of modern literary criticism has been the enthusiastic acceptance of aid from nonliterary disciplines. Psychoanalysis, anthropology, sociology, and semantics have undoubtedly enriched our understanding and influenced our critical response to literature. One suspects, however, that such methodologies are best applied to works which are more or less subjective in nature. The Gothic tradition in British and American literature, for instance, offers itself as a prime candidate. Critical appraisal of Gothic literature has sometimes been marked by an ambiguity, as though critics found difficulty in coming to terms with the material. In a well-known pronouncement on Edgar Allan Poe, T. S. Eliot has stated a common attitude toward Gothic fiction: "The forms which his lively curiosity takes are those in which a pre-adolescent mentality delights: wonders of nature and of mechanics and of the supernatural, cryptograms and cyphers, puzzles and labyrinths, mechanical chess-players, and wild flights of speculation. . . . There is just that lacking which gives dignity to the mature man: a consistent view of life. . . ." The Gothic elements in Poe's writings seem to be at the root of Eliot's rejection. On the other hand, a writer whom Eliot admires, Charles Baudelaire, takes a different view toward this same sort of material. For Baudelaire, "what will always make him [Poe] worthy of praise is his preoccupation with all the truly important subjects and those which are *alone* worthy of the attention of a spiritual man: probabilities, mental illnesses, scientific hypotheses, hopes and considerations about a future life, analysis of the eccentrics and pariahs of this world. . . . "

Such an antinomy raises, in fact, the central question about the Gothic spirit as it is reflected in the work of early novelists such as Horace Walpole, Ann Radcliffe, and Mary Shelley, as well as later writers like Charlotte Brontë, Edgar Allan Poe, Algernon Blackwood, and Franz Kafka. What, precisely, is the common denominator of a literary tradition that includes such a diverse company, and that has attracted, at least for a time, such dissimilar minds as those of Charles Dickens, Henry James, Joseph Conrad, and William Faulkner? The answer, as suggested, demands in part an analysis by way of nonliterary disciplines, since it is evident that the literary powers of such writers are not in question.

The particular nonliterary discipline that I propose for analyzing the Gothic tradition consists of the impressive body of work left by the late German theologian and philosopher Rudolf Otto (1869-1937). In his major work, *The Idea of the Holy* (1917), Otto attempted to analyze religious experience by means of what he termed the numinous. His central concern in the book is indicated by its subtitle: "The nonrational factor in the idea of the divine and its relation to the rational." The numinous, the word he coined to represent this nonrational factor, is man's underlying sense of supernatural fear, wonder, and delight when he is confronted by the divine. Although the several elements in numinous feeling may be analyzed, the numinous is essentially nonrational—that is, not able to be fully understood conceptually. It is a "feeling" but a feeling that has innate connections with the intellect. The numinous, which in its more primitive forms gives rise to the belief in ghosts and other supernatural fantasies, is still present in purified form in the higher manifestations of religion. This experience, with its associated forms and connections, its dichotomies between "sacred and profane," between "natural and supernatural," "rational and non-rational," and its often fragile but sometimes strong relations to the human sense of the "holy" is, I believe, the essential goal of the Gothic writer, and so far as it is achieved, his central distinction.

Otto's terminology and some of his ideas have appeared in works of literary criticism. There is, for instance, a very sound discussion of Otto's works in Maud Bodkin's *Archetypal Patterns in Poetry*. Both G. Wilson Knight and Walter Kaufman have used Otto's terminology in exploring certain aspects of Shakespeare. But even if the legitimacy of the numinous as a literary concept is granted, the question of relating it to the Gothic tale may appear doubtful. In what sense, it will be asked, does the preternatural element in Gothic fiction enter into the psychology of religious experience? Indeed, it will appear almost paradoxical to attempt to relate the two, since the more evident varieties of religious experience—prayer, contemplation, and mysticism—whether orthodox or otherwise, seem remote from the Gothic experience of Romantic literature.

It is in answer to this problem that the insights of Rudolf Otto are applicable. For Otto was certain that the area of religious experience which he termed the numinous is, in its early stages, closely associated with the preternatural; and that while some religions in their more advanced stages outgrow this association, they still retain vestiges of it. In fact, Otto was convinced that the preternatural as a condition of human consciousness is intimately connected with the whole phenomena of religion.

Otto begins *The Idea of the Holy* by distinguishing conceptual from nonconceptual statements about religion. Theistic religion, he believes, characterizes God by various conceptual statements about his nature, for example, his spirituality, power, and unity. Such conceptual statements Otto terms rational, and he makes it clear that they are of first importance in religious discussion. On the other hand, the nature of God is such that these rational attributes do not fully comprehend Him. "For so far are these 'rational' attributes from exhausting the idea of deity, that they in fact imply a non-rational or supra-rational Subject of which they are predicates." This nonrational element, however, must be apprehended in some way "else absolutely speaking nothing could be asserted of it."

To characterize this nonrational element or "unnamed Something" as he calls it, Otto coins the word *numinous,* from the Latin *numen* (a god or power). "I shall speak, then, of a unique 'numinous' category of value and of a definitely 'numinous' state of mind, which is always found wherever the category is applied. This mental state is perfectly *sui generis* and irreducible to any other; and therefore, like every absolutely primary and elementary datum, while it admits of being discussed, it cannot be strictly defined." But if the numinous cannot be defined it can, nevertheless, be suggested. "We must once again endeavour, by adducing feelings akin to them for the purpose of analogy or contrast and by the use of metaphor and symbolic expressions, to make the states of mind we are investigating ring out, as it were, of themselves."

In attempting to suggest these numinous states of mind, Otto uses as an ideogram the Latin phrase *mysterium tremendum.* "Conceptually *mysterium* is merely that which is hidden and esoteric, that which is beyond conception or understanding, extraordinary and unfamiliar. The term does not define the object more positively in its qualitative character. But though what is enunciated in the word is negative, what is meant is something absolutely and intensely positive. This pure positive we can experience in feelings, feelings which our discussion can help make clear to us, in so far as it arouses them actually in our hearts."

A number of distinct "notes" or feeling-states enter into Otto's analysis of the phrase *mysterium tremendum.* Tremor, for example, is the Latin word for the familiar experience of the natural emotion of fear. However, Otto uses it to suggest "a quite specific kind of emotional response, wholly distinct from that of being afraid. . . . There are in some languages special expressions which denote, either exclusively or in the first instance, this 'fear' that is more than fear proper. The Hebrew *Hiqdīsh* (hallow) is an example. To 'keep a thing holy in the heart' means to mark it off by a feeling of peculiar dread, not to be mistaken for any ordinary dread, that is, to appraise it by the category of the numinous."

The subtle, but distinct, qualitative difference between this feeling and ordinary human fear is suggested by an analysis of the physical reactions that accompany these states.

> We say: 'my blood ran icy cold,' and 'my flesh crept.' The 'cold blood' feeling may be a symptom of ordinary, natural fear, but there is something non-natural or supernatural about the symptom of 'creeping flesh.' And any one who is capable of more precise introspection must recognize that the distinction between such a 'dread' and natural fear is not simply one of degree and intensity. The awe or 'dread' *may* indeed be so overwhelmingly great that it seems to penetrate to the very marrow, making the man's hair bristle and his limbs quake. But it may also steal upon him almost unobserved as the gentlest of agitations, a mere fleeting shadow passing across his mood. It has therefore nothing to do with intensity, and no natural fear passes over into it merely by being intensified.

The accuracy of Otto's description is attested to by a number of passages from Gothic fiction. Cold blood and creeping flesh are, in fact, staples of Gothic literature, but it is the exceptional reader who has distinguished between "ordinary human fear" and the numinous emotions. A passage from Algernon Blackwood's short story "The Willows" suggests some remarkable parallels with what Otto has to say about numinous awe. In this tale, the narrator and a companion proceed by canoe into the upper reaches of the Danube where, amidst the loneliness of the primitive forest and a rising windstorm, they come upon a remote island entirely covered by small willow trees. They make camp, and as night falls the narrator attempts to analyze the alien emotions aroused in him by the island.

> Great revelations of nature, of course, never fail to impress in one way or another, and I was no stranger to moods of the kind. Mountains overawe and oceans terrify, while the mystery of great forests exercises a spell peculiarly its own. But all these, at one point or another, somewhere link on intimately with human life and human experience. They stir comprehensible, even if alarming, emotions. They tend on the whole to exalt.
>
> With this multitude of willows, however, it was something far different, I felt. Some essence emanated from them that besieged the heart. A sense of awe awakened, true, but of awe touched somewhere by a vague terror. Their serried ranks, growing everywhere darker about me as the shadows deepened, moving furiously yet softly in the wind, woke in me the curious and unwelcome suggestion that we had trespassed here upon the borders of an alien world, a world where we were intruders, a world where we were not wanted or invited to remain—where we ran grave risks perhaps!

This sense of the "uncanny" or "awesome" does not, however, exhaust the feeling states aroused by the ideogram *tremendum.* Otto perceives another element in it, namely the sense of "might," "power," "absolute overpoweringness," to which he gives the name of *majestas.*

> This second element of majesty may continue to be vividly preserved, where the first, that of unapproachability, recedes and dies away, as may be seen for example in mysticism. It is especially in relation to this element of majesty or absolute overpoweringness that the creature-consciousness, of which we have already spoken, comes upon the scene, as a sort of shadow or subjective reflection of it. Thus, in contrast to the 'overpowering' of which we are conscious, as an object over against the self, there is the feeling of one's own submergence, of being not 'dust and ashes' and nothingness. And this forms the numinous raw material for the feeling of religious humility.

Otto's representation of *majestas* must not be confused with the sense of "natural" majesty, although such awareness may be its starting point. This fugitive feeling-state is hard to depict in a single passage of literature. It generally finds its context in a cumulative series of narrations, as in the final chapters of *Moby-Dick.* The emotion does seem well focussed, however, in the description of the first sight of the numinous and nearly supernal whale.

> A gentle joyousness—a mighty mildness of repose in swiftness, invested the gliding whale. Not the white bull Jupiter swimming away with ravished Europa clinging to his graceful horns; his lovely, leering eyes sideways intent upon the maid; with smooth bewitching fleetness, rippling straight for the nuptial bower in Crete; not Jove, not that great majesty Supreme! did surpass the glorified White Whale as he so divinely swam.
>
> On each soft side—coincident with the parted swell, that but once leaving him, then flowed so wide away—on each bright side, the whale shed off

enticings. No wonder there had been some among the hunters who namelessly transported and allured by all this serenity, had ventured to assail it; but had fatally found that quietude but the vesture of tornadoes. Yet calm, enticing calm, oh, whale! thou glidest on, to all who for the first time eye thee, no matter how many in that same way thou may'st have bejuggled and destroyed before.

A final element suggested by the ideogram *tremendum* is termed by Otto the "urgency" or "energy" of the numinous object. This element is sometimes projected symbolically as the "wrath of God," and in qualities of vitality, passion, emotional temper, will-force, movement, excitement, activity, and impetus. Such a feeling, Otto tells us, makes its appearance in mysticism, especially "voluntaristic" mysticism and "the mysticism of love." It appears in Fichte's speculations on the Absolute as the gigantic, never-resting, active world-stress, and in Schopenhauer's daemonic "Will." In Goethe, too, the same note is sounded in his strange description of the "daemonic." The quality isolated here is prominent in Gothic fiction. Some of it enters into the characterization of Mr. Rochester in *Jane Eyre,* and of the monster in Mary Shelley's *Frankenstein.* It appears in rather melodramatic form in the final chapter of *The Monk* when the fiend carries Ambrosio out of the dungeon and across the mountain peaks. And it certainly contributes to the character of Captain Ahab, the "grand ungodly god-like man" of *Moby-Dick.*

Thus Otto distinguishes three distinct, but related, moments suggested by the ideogram *tremendum:* awfulness, majesty, and energy. He now proceeds to an analysis of the substantive *mysterium,* which stands as the form of the numinous experience. The mental reaction to this "moment" in the numinous consciousness is best described analogically by the word "stupor." "Stupor is plainly a different thing from *tremor;* it signifies blank wonder, an astonishment that strikes us dumb, amazement absolute." Its objective concomitant, the *mysterium,* suggests that which is "wholly other" (*anyad, alienum*) or in other words "that which is quite beyond the sphere of the usual, the intelligible, and the familiar, which therefore falls quite outside the limits of the 'canny' and is contrasted with it, filling the mind with blank wonder and astonishment."

To suggest this sense of the "wholly other" Otto undertakes an analysis of the fear of ghosts—a subject obviously quite germane to the Gothic.

> The ghost's real attraction . . . consists in this, that of itself and in an uncommon degree it entices the imagination, awakening strong interest and curiosity; it is the weird thing itself that allures the fancy. But it does this, not because it is 'something long and white' (as someone once defined a ghost) nor yet through any of the positive conceptual attributes which fancies about ghosts have invented, but because it is a thing that 'doesn't really exist at all,' the 'wholly other,' something which has no place in our scheme of reality but belongs to an absolutely different one and which at the same time arouses an irrepressible interest in the mind.

The accuracy of Rudolf Otto's analysis of such ghostly matters is attested to by a great deal of literature of the supernatural, but no better paradigm is available than Henry James' classic ghost story "The Jolly Corner." The description of Spencer Brydon's encounter with his horrific doppelgänger clearly depicts both the "wholly other" character of the spirit as well as the sense of blank wonder and stupor.

> The hands, as he looked, began to move, to open; then, as if deciding in a flash, dropped from the face and left it uncovered and presented. Horror, with the sight, had leaped into Brydon's throat, gasping there in a sound he couldn't utter; for the bared identity was too hideous as *his,* and his glare was the passion of his protest. The face, *that* face, Spencer Brydon's?—he searched it still, but looking away from it in dismay and denial, falling straight from his height of sublimity. It was unknown, inconceivable, awful, disconnected from any possibility—! He had been "sold," he inwardly moaned, stalking such game as this: the presence before him was a presence, the horror within him a horror, but the waste of his nights had been only grotesque and the success of his adventure an irony. Such an identity fitted his at *no* point, made its alternative monstrous. A thousand times yes, as it came upon him nearer now—the face was the face of a stranger. It came upon him nearer now, quite as one of those expanding fantastic images projected by the magic lantern of childhood; for the stranger, whoever he might be, evil, odious, blatant, vulgar, had advanced as for aggression, and he knew himself give ground . . . he felt the whole vision turn to darkness and his very feet give way. His head went round; he was going; he had gone.

In this passage, as in the entire story, the *mysterium* is transformed into and partakes of James' private universe, with all its exquisite values and peculiar defects. No writer could be further, in some ways, from the "average Gothic," and yet the numinous qualities provide a link. The apparition is "unknown, inconceivable, awful, disconnected from any possibility—!" which one takes to be a Jamesian rendition of the "wholly other." In fact, as James himself attests in several of his prefaces, the supernatural tale fascinated him.

It is the sense of fascination that forms the final strand in Otto's analysis of numinous feeling. Having analyzed what might be termed the daunting aspect of the numinous (*mysterium tremendum*), Otto discusses another element that stands at the opposite pole. This element Otto designates by the term *fascinans,* a kind of fascination, attraction, or allurement in the numinous. This *fascinans* is "a bliss which embraces all those blessings that are indicated or suggested in a positive fashion by any 'doctrine of salvation,' and it quickens all of them through and through; but these do not exhaust it. Rather by its all pervading, penetrating glow it makes of these very blessings more than the intellect can conceive in them or affirm of them."

Thus, Otto groups in what he calls a "harmony of contrasts" the various moments in the numinous experience; and these he indicates by the phrase (or ideogram as he terms it) *mysterium tremendum et fascinosum.*

> These two qualities, the daunting and the fascinating, now combine in a strange harmony of contrasts, and the resultant dual character of the numinous consciousness, to which the entire religious development bears witness, at any rate from the level of the 'daemonic dread' onwards, is at once the strangest and the most noteworthy phenomenon in the whole history of religion. The daemonic-divine object may appear to the mind an object of horror and dread, but at the same time it is no less something that allures with a potent charm, and

the creature who trembles before it, utterly cowed and cast down, has always at the same time the impulse to turn to it, nay even to make it somehow his own. The 'mystery' is for him not merely something to be wondered at but something that entrances him; and beside that in it which bewilders and confounds, he feels a something that captivates and transports him with a strange ravishment, rising often enough to the pitch of intoxication: it is the Dionysiac-element in the numen.

The peculiar "harmony of contrasts" is a prominent feature in the work of Edgar Allan Poe, who certainly had an intuitive grasp of the numinous consciousness as Otto expounds it, and explains, to some degree, Poe's puzzling ideas concerning "perversity" ("The Imp of the Perverse"), ideas which interested Baudelaire. But on a higher plane this daunting-attracting quality of the numinous infuses most of Poe's tales and poems. A striking example is his tale "A Descent Into the Maelström." As the protagonist finds himself drawn into the immense and terrifying depths of the maelström, his reflections vary from awe and terror before this nearly preternatural manifestation to a strange sense of fascination.

> It may look like boasting—but what I tell you is truth—I began to reflect how magnificent a thing it was to die in such a manner, and how foolish it was in me to think of so paltry a consideration as my own individual life, in view of so wonderful a manifestation of God's power. I do believe that I blushed with shame when this idea crossed my mind. After a little while I became possessed with the keenest curiosity about the whirl itself. I positively felt a *wish* to explore its depths, even at the sacrifice I was going to make; and my principal grief was that I should never be able to tell my old companions on shore about the mysteries I should see.

Throughout his book, Otto continually emphasizes that the numinous is not identical with the fully developed sense of the Holy. The concept of Holiness must of necessity include theological and moral elements. The numinous may thus be seen as bearing intrinsic relationship with and even providing a definition for a number of works, both literary and artistic, which might not generally be termed religious. For what else is one to say of the castles and mountain crags of Mrs. Radcliffe's novels, the glaciers, ice-floes, and desolate Scottish islands of *Frankenstein,* or the spectral sea-scapes of *The Narrative of Arthur Gordon Pym* but that they summon up many of the moods and tones that Otto has analyzed? Thus, by making use of Otto's insights, one is able to sense a new and more profound note in some very good literature of this kind that has sometimes been looked at with bewilderment if not downright condescension by certain critics.

Another fruitful link between the numinous and the Gothic tradition is to be found in Otto's remarks about preternatural events and magic. Preternaturalism has, of course, been a source of annoyance to some critics of the Gothic; and it does, indeed, require a strong palate to accept all the bleeding portraits, animated skeletons, lycanthropes, rattling chains, and vampires that infest Gothic literature, especially the older novels. But the artistic incorporation of the preternatural into literature should not, in itself, form a barrier to critical appreciation. It is on this point that Otto supplies a strong apologetic. "Now the magical," he says, "is nothing but a suppressed and dimmed form of the numinous, a crude form

of it which great art purifies and ennobles." He adds, "To us of the West the Gothic appears as the most numinous of all types of art. This is due in the first place to its sublimity; but Worringer in his *Problem der Gotik* has done a real service in showing that the peculiar impressiveness of Gothic does not consist in its sublimity alone, but draws upon a strain inherited from primitive magic, of which he tries to show the historical derivation."

The magical or preternatural event, then, if introduced artistically may serve to reinforce the numinous quality of the work. Nathaniel Hawthorne, who was sparing in his use of the preternatural, seems to achieve the proper effect in a passage from *The Marble Faun.* Donatello, Miriam, and Kenyon approach the open bier of a dead monk who lies in the Church of the Capuchins in Rome.

> And now occurred a circumstance that would seem too fantastic to be told, if it had not actually happened, precisely as we set it down. As the three friends stood by the bier, they saw that a little stream of blood had begun to ooze from the dead monk's nostrils; it crept slowly towards the thicket of his beard, where, in the course of a moment or two, it hid itself.
>
> "How strange!" ejaculated Kenyon. "The monk died of apoplexy, I suppose, or by some sudden accident, and the blood has not yet congealed."
>
> "Do you consider that a sufficient explanation?" asked Miriam, with a smile from which the sculptor involuntarily turned away his eyes. "Does it satisfy you?"
>
> "And why not?" he inquired.
>
> "Of course, you know the old superstition about this phenomenon of blood flowing from a dead body," she rejoined. "How can we tell but that the murderer of this monk (or, possibly, it may be only that privileged murderer, his physician) may have just entered the church?"

The Idea of the Holy contains chapters, of special interest to the literary critic, on the means of arousing the numinous consciousness by artistic works. "Of directer methods our Western art has only two," Otto says, "and they are in a noteworthy way negative, viz. *darkness* and *silence.*" His discussion of the artistic use of darkness conjures up many images of the "haunted castle" theme so dear to the tale of terror: "The semi-darkness that glimmers in vaulted halls, or beneath the branches of a lofty forest glade, strangely quickened and stirred by the mysterious play of half-lights, has always spoken eloquently to the soul, and the builders of temples, mosques and churches have made full use of it." Silence is "what corresponds to this in the language of musical sounds. . . . It is a spontaneous reaction to the feeling of the actual *numen praesens.*" Both of these "artistic means" are native to Western art; but Oriental art makes continual use of a third, namely, empty distance and emptiness. "Empty distance, remote vacancy, is, as it were, the sublime in the horizontal. The wide-stretching desert, the boundless uniformity of the steppe, have a real sublimity, and even in us Westerners they see vibrating chords of the numinous along with the note of the sublime, according to the principle of the association of feelings."

Perhaps Otto is right in concluding that most Western art has generally failed to make consistent use of emptiness, but the

Gothic literary tradition has, indeed, effectively utilized this method as a means to register a sense of the numinous. The vacant loneliness associated with sea, desert, mountain prospects, or the night sky is a constant theme. This characteristic is especially true of Coleridge's *Ancient Mariner* ("Alone, alone, all, all alone/ Alone on a wide wide sea!") and Poe's *Narrative of Arthur Gordon Pym,* as well as of several of Joseph Conrad's novels in which brooding descriptions of the sea stimulate the numinous sense of emptiness and silence. In *Victory,* for instance, a work which contains certain strong numinous elements, the lonely protagonist Heyst is a man who feels this numinous call of the sea.

> Like most dreamers, to whom it is given sometimes to hear the music of the spheres, Heyst, the wanderer of the Archipelago, had a taste for silence which he had been able to gratify for years. The islands are very quiet. One sees them lying about, clothed in their dark garments of leaves, in a great hush of silver and azure, where the sea without murmurs meets the sky in a ring of magic stillness. A sort of smiling somnolence broods over them; the very voices of their people are soft and subdued, as if afraid to break some protecting spell.

Thus, it seems clear that Otto's work provides many insights into the spirit of Gothic literature. The mountain gloom, lonely castles, phantom ships, violent storms, and the vastness of sea and polar regions correspond closely with Otto's description of the numinous. Likewise, the preternatural machinery of Gothicism, whether magical lore, apparitions, ghouls, vampires, or revenants, finds its explanation not in an over-ripe fantasy, but in an effort to instill a sense of the numinous.

We have seen several ways in which the numinous plays a part both in background and event in the Gothic tale. But the numinous is not confined to ontological reality; Otto contends that it also has an axiological character. This is to say, the numinous exists as a category of value within its own right; and as a consequence it can be used in analyzing character and moral value.

According to Otto, the numinous experience in itself is not an ethical manifestation and may exist without any relation to morality, as for instance in the case of certain primitive religions. When the numinous is commingled with moral and rational elements it becomes something different—namely *The Holy.* On the other hand, the numinous in its pure form, and without moral connotations, is still permeated by certain axiological elements. The numinous "object" produces in the percipient a sense of "creature feelings"; in fact, this result is one of the essential ways in which it impinges upon the individual consciousness. Out of such a feeling grows the sense of numinous value and of numinous disvalue. In opposition to this sense of "disvalue" or the profane stands the sacred. "This sanctus is not merely 'perfect' or 'beautiful' or 'sublime' or 'good,' though, being like these concepts also a value, objective and ultimate, it has a definite, perceptible analogy with them. It is the positive numinous value or worth, and to it corresponds on the side of the creature a numinous disvalue or 'unworth'."

The sense of numinous value, the sacred, is recognized as standing outside the sphere of morality as such. "In every highly-developed religion the appreciation of moral obligation and duty, ranking as a claim of the deity upon man, has been developed side by side with the religious feeling itself.

Nonetheless, a profoundly humble and heartfelt recognition of 'the holy' may occur in particular experiences without being always definitely charged or infused with the sense of moral demands. The 'holy' will then be recognized as that which commands our respect, as that whose real value is to be acknowledged inwardly." Likewise, the opposite pole, the numinous "disvalue" or sense of the profane, is not intrinsically a moral category. "Mere 'unlawfulness' only becomes 'sin,' 'impiety,' 'sacrilege,' when the character of *numinous unworthiness or disvalue* goes on to be transferred to and centered in moral delinquency. . . ."

Otto's explanation of numinous value and disvalue, if viewed as a phenomenological description, applies with equal force to many Gothic works which might otherwise appear to be morally neutral and therefore, at best, mere entertainment. There are, it is true, certain patent moral lessons attached to Mary Shelley's *Frankenstein,* but the categories of the sacred and profane, if applied to the hero's unholy experiments, add a new dimension to the story.

To explore this interpretation briefly, we must remember that the story projects a feeling of horror and evil that is disproportionate to the moral framework out of which Mary Shelley worked. The crimes of the monster and the ultimate ruin of his creator Frankenstein are the results of an experiment begun, perhaps, in good conscience. Mary Shelley suggests, in fact, that some of the evil nature of the monster is the result of economic and moral dislocations in society. Then, too, as a rationalist and liberal who followed the views of her father, she would have rejected a belief in the innate evil of man. What then is responsible for the brooding sense of profanity

Mary Shelley.

and unhallowed occupation that characterizes the inception of the monster?

> Who shall conceive the horrors of my secret toil, as I dabbled among the unhallowed damps of the grave, or tortured the living animal to animate the lifeless clay? My limbs now tremble and my eyes swim with the remembrance; but then a resistless, and almost frantic, impulse urged me forward; I seemed to have lost all soul or sensation but for this one pursuit. . . . I collected bones from charnel-houses, and disturbed, with profane fingers, the tremendous secrets of the human frame. In a solitary chamber, or rather cell, at the top of the house, and separated from all the other apartments by a gallery and staircase, I kept my workshop of filthy creation: my eye-balls were starting from their sockets in attending to the details of my employment.

There is really no "rational" explanation for such feelings, given the moral views of Frankenstein. He feels, rather, the sense of numinous "disvalue" attendant upon his profane experiments, a feeling that Mary Shelley shared despite her liberal and utopian sentiments to the contrary. The famous description of the animation of the monster heightens this sense of profanity.

> It was already one in the morning; the rain pattered dismally against the panes, and my candle was nearly burnt out, when, by the glimmer of the half-extinguished light, I saw the dull yellow eye of the creature open; it breathed hard, and a convulsive motion agitated its limbs.
>
> How can I describe my emotions at this catastrophe, or how delineate the wretch whom with such infinite pains and care I had endeavoured to form? His limbs were in proportion, and I had selected his features as beautiful. Beautiful!—Great God! His yellow skin scarcely covered the work of muscles and arteries beneath; his hair was of a lustrous black, and flowing; his teeth of a pearly whiteness; but these luxuriances only formed a more horrid contrast with his watery eyes, that seemed almost of the same colour as the dun white sockets in which they were set, his shrivelled complexion and straight black lips.

The question of Frankenstein's guilt in tampering with the well-springs of life is not treated directly. The consequent crimes and atrocities perpetrated by the monster are the results of "man's inhumanity to man," the evils of society and, to a certain extent, mere chance. Even at the last, Frankenstein absolves himself of direct guilt: "During these last days I have been occupied in examining my past conduct; nor do I find it blameable. In a fit of enthusiastic madness I created a rational creature, and was bound towards him, to assure, as far as was in my power, his happiness and well-being. This was my duty; but there was another still paramount to that. My duties towards the beings of my own species had greater claims to my attention, because they included a greater proportion of happiness or misery." Thus, on the merely rational level, *Frankenstein* expounds some rather patent moral truths which are perhaps most interesting from a historical standpoint. But in a deeper sense, the book portrays the mysterious sense of "profanity" and numinous disvalue which, according to Otto, is part of man's spiritual life.

It is upon such a system of thought, profound and original, that a new survey of Gothic literature may be conducted. Otto's description of the numinous, self-authenticating and convincing, suggests a new dimension to the literature of the preternatural. (pp. 11-21)

> S. L. Varnado, "The Idea of the Numinous in Gothic Literature," in The Gothic Imagination: Essays in Dark Romanticism, *edited by G. R. Thompson, Washington State University Press, 1974, pp. 11-21.*

THEMES AND TECHNIQUES

ELIZABETH MacANDREW

[*In the following excerpt, MacAndrew discusses the development of the Gothic conventions begun by Walpole in* The Castle of Otranto.]

The highly conventionalized nature of the settings and characters, structures and imagery of Gothic fiction has always been recognized. All too frequently, however, these features have been dubbed "Gothic machinery" or "claptrap" because, like other forms of popular literature, Gothic fiction has been seen as fare for a sensation-seeking audience and not, therefore, worth literary analysis. As a result, the course of the convention has not been traced. Instead, Gothic fiction has been called escape literature, intended to inspire terror for terror's sake. Such descriptions have concealed the important ideas these tales contain. The view of the early Gothic romances as "just" a form of escape does not adequately explain why they appeared when they did or why their appeal was so immediate and so strong. Descriptions of the genre as a literature of violence reflecting a violent age, or as a literature of sensation needed to perk up a jaded age are circular as well as contradictory. Recent attempts to treat Gothic literature as an aspect of Romanticism also fail to see its significance as a convention. When we see that Gothic tales have continued to appear for two hundred years, and that the convention has been put to use by major writers as different from each other as Emily Brontë and Henry James, it is evident that something more is involved than a continuing taste for a ghoulish kind of bedside reading, and that these works are not confined to a single period of literature.

From Walpole's maddened and murderous princeling in *The Castle of Otranto* to the self-tormented scientist in Robert Louis Stevenson's *Dr. Jekyll and Mr. Hyde,* the same conventional features keep reappearing because ideas of the same kind lie behind these works. That is, these and other writers chose the Gothic tale as a vehicle for ideas about psychological evil—evil not as a force exterior to man, but as a distortion, a warping of his mind. Walpole's slight romance yields such an interpretation, so does Stevenson's novel, so do the Gothic tales that appeared in the long stretch of time between them.

This is not to say that Stevenson and Walpole held the same view of evil, or of man's psychology in general. Indeed, their ideas on the subject form a sharp contrast. The great interest in tracing this literary convention lies in the changes that take place within it, which correspond to the changes in thought on the subject that have occurred since Locke first set forth his theory of the workings of the mind. What seems to have happened is this: following Locke (who was to the eighteenth century what Freud has been to the twentieth), eighteenth-century thinkers had devoted a great deal of their energies to the study of the mind, the nature of perception, the means to knowledge, expanding, adapting, and modifying Locke's ideas. It was the first era in which the mind was studied inductively, and the changes in world view, especially in ideas about the moral nature of Man, that such thinking reflected and also helped bring about were given literary expression in a number of different genres, but most directly in the Sentimental fiction of the time, of which Gothic literature is a part. Within this general literary development, Gothic fiction first made its appearance when Horace Walpole, his head full of a romanticized, eighteenth-century medievalism, awakened from a dream of which he could remember only a scrap and, under its influence, turned out *The Castle of Otranto,* at white heat. Though he himself felt the importance of this slight work, which, to the end of his life remained his favorite among his writings, he expected his fellow literati would scorn it as a "romance." Instead, his anonymous tale received high praise from literati and reading public alike. He had given fictional treatment to some of the major preoccupations of his time that were also his own concerns, and, after an interval, others began to copy his work—many a castle, many a tyrant, many a hero and heroine of perfect virtue and courage appeared. Naturally, however, Walpole's successors each took his devices and used them a little differently. Clara Reeve declared *Otranto* was too extravagant and confined herself wherever possible to the "Natural"; William Beckford, romping off into the Arabian Nights, introduced the grotesque into the genre; Matthew Lewis added the tormented monk who was immediately picked up by Ann Radcliffe, herself the chief among terror-mongers, whose villains had influenced Lewis in the first place.

In this rush of authors making use of and modifying one another's devices, there is more than a simple desire to share in the latest literary fad. Different though they were as personalities, these writers recognized the possibilities of the new genre for the expression of some of the prevailing views of their age, which they all shared, views not previously given fictional form. Each uncovered the implications of preceding works, recognizing the intuitions behind them. Thus, each delved deeper into the common subject, adding new devices to the convention as they were needed and producing works whose further implications could again be picked up by a successor to add a new round to the developing spiral of the genre. This process continued throughout the nineteenth century, as writers embodied the views of the later age in the same way. Thus, Mary Shelley, Edgar Allan Poe, and Nathaniel Hawthorne added twisted scientists to the mad monks of Lewis and Radcliffe. Among distorted human shapes inherited from the eighteenth century, monsters and demonic animals appeared in the nineteenth. The ghosts and devils of Walpole, Reeve, Lewis, and Radcliffe reappeared considerably modified in Maturin, Le Fanu, Brontë, and James, and to them and Beckford's Giaour were added vampires and witches. Settings were changed from medieval to contemporary, a man's house turned out to be still his Gothic castle and his soul, already reflected in paintings and statues, began to look back at him from mirrors and, worse still, from his double, a living, breathing copy of himself.

Gradually, if we follow the course of the convention as it winds through the nineteenth century, feeding its weird tales into the mainstream of realistic fiction, we can trace changes in ideas about the place of evil in the mind. The moral absolutes of eighteenth-century thought crumble before a shifting, relative morality. Soon Edgar Allan Poe is playing with ideas of evil and madness. By mid-nineteenth century, Emily Brontë has evoked a primitive *spiritus loci* to confound earlier notions of evil as unnatural; by the 1890s Henry James is placing evil in the eye of the moral arbiter. In tracing the convention, we can see the developing ideas that preoccupied the late eighteenth century and obsessed the nineteenth. In Gothic literature of those years, with its monsters and madmen, we find suggested imaginatively writers' intuitive understanding of human evil.

Thus, within this literary convention, as in any other, changes and developments have occurred while it has retained its basically stable and recognizable outlines. Individual works within the convention embody the particularities of the author's thought in the devices common to the whole convention and thereby reveal both the ideas of the particular moment and the overall purpose of the convention itself. That common purpose, which ties these works together, emerges from the peculiar form of symbolism found in Gothic tales. In this literature, the entire tale is symbolic. In analyzing it, one has to speak of storms that "stand for" the villain's anger or heroines that more closely represent a concept of virtue than flesh-and-blood women. Unlike the artfully buried symbols customary to a realistic work, the flagrant, all-pervading symbolism of a Gothic tale is almost, though not quite, allegorical. This literature is not allegory because its referents are deliberately hazy. The surface fiction is full of vague, unexplained horrors designed, not to render a precise meaning, but to evoke the emotion of "terror." Yet, these effects of "terror" in Gothic tales refer to something beyond the fictional devices that produce them. The quasi-allegorical effect derives from what lies behind the terror-inspiring fictional devices. These tales make use of the realization that monsters in fiction frighten because they are already the figments of our dreaming imaginations.

They are the shapes into which our fears are projected and so can be used in literature to explore the subterranean landscape of the mind. Terror is evoked when the ghost, the double, or the lurking assassin correspond to something that is actually feared, known or unknown. The fictional beings of Gothic fiction, whether they be human or animal, or manifestations from the "Beyond," whether they be universal archetypes or the pettiest of childhood bogies, symbolize real but vague fears that the reader recognizes as his own and all men's. Beneath the surface fiction there is a probing of humanity's basic psychological forces, an exploration of the misty realm of the subconscious, and the symbols correspond to psychological phenomena that yield to literary analysis. Yet it is probably this quasi-allegorical nature of Gothic symbolism, with its meaning lying almost entirely outside the fictional surface, that has caused this convention to be read only for its surface fiction, about which, it is true, little more can be said than that it evokes fear for fear's sake.

The authors of Gothic fiction, in writing their symbolic fantasies, necessarily chose a deliberately artificial form, for which they took their materials from earlier literature. *The Castle of Otranto* has several immediate antecedents—works that show an early use of historical setting, a ghost here and there, occasional sinister and supernatural happenings, and it has remote ancestors in Shakespeare and medieval romance. These and other predecessors have, of course, been traced. Thorough studies have been made of the relationship of

Gothic fiction to the graveyard poets, to Shakespeare and Spenser, and to the combination of antiquarianism and the movement of Sentimentalism that swept the late eighteenth century. But all this is mere learned lumber unless it shows how Gothic fiction does something new. Since Gothic fiction was, as has been generally recognized, a new genre, it follows that it was doing something different with the materials of its predecessors. To discover what that is, it is necessary to uncover the ideas and aesthetic principles that gave rise to these works by analyzing them as symbolic constructs and to trace the convention with all its accretions through time and space. When this is done, the heritage on which Gothic authors drew throws further light on the meaning and purposes of their works.

The source and fountainhead of the entire Gothic tradition, Walpole's *The Castle of Otranto,* appeared in 1764, twelve years before its first important successor, Clara Reeve's *The Old English Baron* (1771), twenty-two years before William Beckford's *Vathek* (1786), and nearly thirty before the first works of Ann Radcliffe. It is a rather frothy little romance, so crammed with events and relationships that it reads like a plot summary of itself. If Walpole had set out to stock a warehouse of Gothic materials for his successors, he could hardly have done better. *Otranto* is peopled with two-dimensional characters embodying virtue and vice; its setting constitutes a representation of the villain's character; it is an indirect narration, a story mediated through two voices before it reaches the reader; and its imagery and supernatural events lead to an interpretation of its meaning as an eighteenth-century psychological tale. All these features reappear in later works. Thus, an examination of *Otranto* tells a great deal about the convention to which it gave rise.

The medieval setting, the thunderous villain, the sensitive hero and heroine, the ghosts and other wonders that identify *The Castle of Otranto* as a Gothic tale were at least supposed to have been adopted from medieval romance. Here and elsewhere the relationship is tenuous at best, as the eighteenth century probably knew. A Gothic novel is to a medieval romance what an artificial ruin in an eighteenth-century garden was to a genuine one, and Walpole's romance is like his house, consciously fanciful in its medievalism. He himself said of Strawberry Hill, the house he transformed into a "Gothic" mansion: "Every true Goth must perceive" that the early rooms "are more the works of fancy than of imitation." The medieval setting of *Otranto,* too, is largely a creation of its author's imagination. Walpole uses his medieval tale to make a fictional reality of evil as a psychological state; not for historical accuracy, but to appeal to eighteenth-century sensibilities. He employs it in accordance with the late eighteenth century's aesthetic concept of the sublime as evoking pity and terror to draw the reader out of himself.

The first Gothic characteristic of *Otranto* is its presentation as an ancient manuscript rediscovered. This produces an indirect, mediated narration that imparts an air of strangeness to the exotic setting. Medieval Italy is already distant from the reader in time and space and, when he is asked to suppose himself imaginatively to be reading a manuscript of shadowy authorship unearthed and presented to him by an unidentified "editor," a sense is imparted that he is about to delve into a world that will be difficult to understand. In the preface to the first edition, Walpole's "editor" surmises that the story, the work of an unknown chronicler, is possibly by "an artful priest." He speculates about the date of composition, estab-

lishing a sense of obscurity by preventing the reader from pinpointing the origin of the manuscript and by remarking on the quality of the original Italian of which his "translation," he says, is a poor rendering. All this puts us on notice that a mysterious world is about to be revealed.

Sentimental and Gothic novelists frequently use fictitious editors of this sort. They are more than just a means for the author to conceal his identity. The statements these "editors" put into their "prefaces" must not be taken at face value. Rather, they are the first of many signals alerting us to the kind of reading required of us. For instance, by setting the "editor" between us and the "chronicler," who is himself relaying the story and, besides, is presented as suspect, Walpole guards against our rejecting the story because of its blatant artificiality, by putting us on notice that we must follow it according to its own rules.

Thus alerted, we can see that the "editor's" criticism of the writer's "moral" and his surmise that the suspect monk was attempting to "confirm the populace in their ancient errors and superstitions" is not a straightforward statement but a device of irony designed to attract our attention to that "moral." The "editor" remarks that the benighted medieval chronicler has erred in basing his work on so flimsy a precept as "that *the sins of fathers are visited on their children*" (Walpole's italics). Yet, in fact, the psychological aberration of incest—also a staple item in Gothic tales—is Walpole's central theme and he is using the editor's words to attract our attention to it. The plot is, in fact, an unravelling of the effect on children of their fathers' deeds, good and bad. From the crushing of Manfred's frail son Conrad under the giant helmet and Manfred's murder of his daughter to the hero Theodore's fulfillment of the prophecy, the children's lives are affected by their fathers' lives. And Manfred himself is driven by the demon of inherited evil. He is presented as not intrinsically wicked but as ruled by passions aroused by his obsession with the prophecy that his line will not retain its unlawful rule over the princedom. He was, we are told, naturally humane, "when his passion did not obscure his reason," but it does, in fact, obscure his reason throughout the novel. Like a medieval Oedipus, he tries to prevent the prophecy from coming true and his own evil deeds and his downfall are the result of his desperate effort to maintain the position he holds through his grandfather's crimes. Thus, the sins of the fathers are visited on the children in his case, too, but not in the sense that Manfred himself or his children have the divine wrath visited upon them. The awareness that his deeds are wrong and the sense that he is forced farther and farther down the path of evil maddens him and is actually the cause of his crimes. Thus, in this first of the Gothic novels, the problem of evil is already presented as a psychological problem created in the ambience of the family.

The characters who must carry the burden of this theme of inherited evil are also typically Gothic, being highly simplified figures useful for the embodiment of ideas. They are eighteenth-century, not medieval, figures, and, like the characters of Sentimental novels, their physical appearance corresponds to their spiritual state. The hero Theodore, his noble nature shining through his peasant's disguise, represents the Right and the Good. A handsome physical reincarnation of his grandfather Alfonso, the virtuous usurped prince whose giant ghost is haunting the castle, Theodore is nobility itself. The three women, all perfectly virtuous, are also perfectly beautiful. The son and heir is physically weak and puny, representing the weakness of Manfred's usurping claim in the face of just retribution. Manfred has more substance than they, because he is a figure torn by the conflict of good and evil within himself, but he is still a beetle-browed villain, also drawn without subtlety. These romance characters are like figures in a crowded tapestry. They talk in declamatory, set speeches that make the novel, crammed with action though it is, seem slow-moving, almost static. Hardly effective as a tale of adventure, it envelopes the reader, as in a dream, a sort of symbolic nightmare.

Otranto has a considerable stock of stage effects that became typical of Gothic fiction, not just in themselves, but in the way they are used. The portrait of Manfred's grandfather is not a Gothic device just because it supernaturally steps out of its frame and disgustedly slams a door in Manfred's face. It is typical of Gothic fiction because its gesture of scorn shows us Manfred's degeneration. It reveals that he has slipped lower morally than his grandfather. His ancestor's sins weigh so heavily upon him that they torment him into evil greater than his grandfather's original usurpation. The portrait serves as a reflection of Manfred, just as the statue of Alfonso reflects Alfonso's grandson Theodore. Typically, the device that gives us the reflection of the villain is a distorting mirror, giving the wicked man a monstrous shape, while the hero is mirrored faithfully. The way the statue shows signs of life, bleeds when Manfred stabs Matilda, is an example, like the action of the portrait, of the way the quasi-allegorical aspect of Gothic fiction works. These supernatural happenings are "translatable"; for example, the significance of the statue's bleeding can be restated as: "the spirit of Goodness (Alfonso) bleeds metaphorically in compassion at the piteous sight of Virtue (Matilda) destroyed." (It is unfortunate, but beside the point, that Walpole chose to make it a nosebleed.) The other supernatural phenomena in the novel work in the same way.

The central device in *Otranto* became the most famous of all Gothic devices: the identity of the castle or house with its owner. The castle in Walpole's novel *is* Manfred. The wife and daughter he dominates so completely are confined to it almost entirely, as if they lived and breathed and had their being within his personality. The comings and goings of other characters, demanding entrance, fleeing secretively, appearing suddenly, directly reflect their relations with him. And finally, as the novel ends in Manfred's moral collapse, the castle, disobeying the laws of nature, collapses too, disintegrating into rubble as other such buildings would do in later novels.

The identification of castle and man make the castle a manifestation of Manfred's mind. In turn, this causes the giant ghost, with which Walpole again risks making the reader laugh, to render its meaning. Appearing in pieces though it does—first the enormous, sable-plumed helmet, then an arm, then a leg—it is the ghost of Alfonso, a manifestation of "the real owner . . . grown too large to inhabit [the castle]" mentioned in the prophecy. Haunting the castle of Manfred's mind, it is his own awareness of the right and the noble that have been usurped by evil. The animated pieces of the giant suit of armor, unintentionally comic though they are, have a significance in relation to the overall meaning of the novel. Thus: the helmet crushes the weakling Conrad; that is, the first sign that Manfred's unlawful claim is to be wrested from him—the helmet—kills the son through whom that claim was to be maintained. The helmet is too big for ordinary

princelings, that is, Manfred's and Conrad's heads are figuratively too small to bear their responsibilities as princes. Conrad is too feeble physically to sustain even the first blow of retribution; that is, Manfred's claim to the castle is too weak to endure. The successive appearances of the giant mailed hand and the leg in armor and, finally, the full armored figure of Alfonso continue this theme.

Conrad's death renders Manfred more frantic than ever and so more villainous, showing how he continues to spin the web of evil out of himself. Because this event leaves him without an heir he sets in train the other dire events of the novel, all of which ultimately add pieces to the central portrait of Manfred himself. Other features of the tale also serve to characterize him. Theodore, the hero, for instance, embodies not merely nobility in the abstract but that noble sense of honor that Manfred has had to repress in himself to commit his evil deeds. It makes sense, consequently, that the villain should try to imprison the hero under the same giant helmet; that is, the threat of retribution makes Manfred aware of the unlawfulness of his position. This, in turn, awakens his sense of honor (Theodore speaks up from among the bystanders), which he immediately tries to repress. Theodore escapes temporarily through the hole the helmet has made in the paving of the courtyard, bringing him into the subterranean passages. That is, as Manfred's honor, he is confined in the dark recesses of the castle or Manfred's mind. And here he helps Isabella, the heroine, to escape from Manfred's lustful and incestuous pursuit, Manfred's sense of honor being, indeed, the only impulse that might lead him to spare her. The evil in Manfred, however, is more powerful than his honor, as we see when he angrily imprisons Theodore again, or in other words, again shuts up, represses, his sense of honor.

These correspondences between the characters and abstract qualities give this and other Gothic tales their quasi-allegorical air, but in the scenes that yield this kind of interpretation there is also a great deal of sexual symbolism that adds a rather different dimension, turning the interplay of abstract qualities into an exploration of Manfred's aberrant psychology. Much of the sexual symbolism revolves around Isabella. The daughter figure, who was to have married Conrad, becomes the object of Manfred's incestuous lust, and eventually marries the hero. When, fleeing Manfred, she comes upon Theodore in the subterranean passages, Isabella directs Theodore to open a secret lock in a trapdoor leading to a tunnel, although both are strangers to the place and the only light is a single moonbeam. Should we miss the sexual undertones to this scene, we later find her, in that incident frequently cited by critics, refusing out of maidenly modesty to follow Theodore into the depths of the caves, where they may take refuge from imminent danger. This moment in the novel is often pointed out as an example of the ridiculous lengths to which the authors of Gothic tales go to emphasize the "purity" of their heroines. But the whole scene has sexual significance. Isabella's refusal to go deep into the caves with Theodore can be seen as a refusal of sexual advances rendered symbolically in a tale in which actual sexual advances by these embodiments of Virtue would be impossible.

As a result of her refusal, her father finds the two of them at the mouth of the cave and there is an immediate clash between him and Theodore, who almost kills him—with a sword. Thus, the handsome, youthful hero has been brought into direct conflict with both the father figures in the novel, Manfred and Isabella's father, who are contending for both

Isabella and hegemony over the principality to which Theodore is, in fact, heir. The story reenacts the myth of power wrested from the old king by the young prince. In its association with the incest theme, the conflict over the daughter figure between the boyish hero and the two father figures suggests an Oedipal struggle between son and father for sexual possession of the woman. We should note here that the open conflict between the young and the old man is precipitated by the "over-niceness" of the young woman in her relations with the young man. This sort of subtlety pervades the entire Gothic tradition. There are many other features of the novel that have distinct sexual overtones, such as the stabbing of the second daughter figure, Matilda, the giant sword, and more.

The rest of the novel also lends itself to this sort of interpretation. In summary, the cardboard characters of *Otranto,* moving through improbable supernatural events, tell us that Manfred, a good character at heart, has been driven and twisted into evil in his attempt to maintain his inheritance, which is the character (castle) passed on to him from his grandfather whose enthroned wickedness usurped the place of the Good (Alfonso) within him. Driven wild by his sense of his own impotence (his barren wife Hippolyta and his feeble son who is destroyed), Manfred descends to incest. This sin, which mirrors the self, is presented first explicitly in his attempt to marry Isabella then symbolically when he stabs his daughter Matilda. This is again a self-destructive impulse to repress all goodness within himself, for Matilda, an entirely spiritual being who wished to devote her life to God by entering a convent, represents goodness itself, divorced from the entanglements of worldly life. She recognizes Alfonso in Theodore, instantly loves him (the Good), and so releases him from the prison in which Manfred has confined him. Thus, Manfred's good daughter, whom he spurns when his evil is upon him, releases his sense of honor again, but it only plagues him the more. As a consequence, after many a complication, Theodore (Manfred's honor) again rescues Isabella (the object of Manfred's incestuous lust). Honor, however, is once more negated when Manfred kills Matilda, mistaking her for Isabella as she talks with Theodore before the statue of Alfonso. This murder of his own spiritual being brings about both the collapse and the regeneration of Manfred. When the enormity of the deed bursts upon his consciousness, Manfred and the castle collapse simultaneously. The spirit of Alfonso (Manfred's spirit of Goodness) is translated into heaven as Manfred recognizes his own evil and the destruction he has brought on himself, and retires to a spiritual life in a monastery.

As the successive generations of Manfred's line have become increasingly degenerate under the distorting pressure of evil, so the descendants of Alfonso have grown increasingly noble through suffering. The spirit of nobility bursts asunder the walls of the castle, the closed world of Manfred's evil, and Theodore stands forth, not as the inheritor of a crumbled ruin, but as the personification of triumphant nobility above and greater than the worldly power represented by the principality of Otranto.

Thus, the apparently tragic ending of the novel is symbolically optimistic. The view of good and evil it conveys is consonant with the deistic outlook of Walpole and many of his contemporaries and the otherwise incongruous comic resolution in the final paragraph, in which Theodore and Isabella decide on marriage to be sustained by contemplation of the beloved spirit of Matilda, makes sense as a symbolic rendering of moral order restored.

It may be objected that this sort of interpretation reads more into Walpole's tale than is really there. Eighteenth-century novelists are not usually thought of as dredging up subconscious sexual images, or writing dream fantasies, or fictionalizing psychological ideas. Yet what we know of the late eighteenth century and of Walpole himself provides evidence to support these possibilities. All Walpole remembered of his dream was the giant hand on the stair rail, but his own feeling that he wrote the novel under the pressure of that dream indicates that he was able to release his imagination and allow the story to well up in his mind, rather than starting with an idea and a conscious plan. That he should have chosen a medieval setting for it was, he said, natural to a mind afloat in the Gothic atmosphere of Strawberry Hill, and, indeed, he was just the person to invent the device of the identification of the villain and his castle, regarding his own house, as he did, as an expression of his personality, an indulgence of his fancy. At the same time, the sort of personal expression this suggests was quite naturally welded in Walpole's work with the fictionalization of ideas. His interests lay with the antiquarianism that was part of the Sentimentalist movement of the day, a movement that, in its many aspects, was bent on exploring the emotions. In literature, Sentimentalism was embodying ideas about human nature, and Walpole was part of that movement.

Thus, personal reasons account for Walpole's having been the one to produce the tale that began the whole tradition, while the age he lived in accounts for the genre's having appeared when it did. No such work, after all, appeared from the pens of authors under similar personal pressures in earlier times. The late eighteenth century was an era of interested inquiry into the nature of the human mind and of an interest in the inner self that was also manifested in other new genres appearing at the time which probe and reveal the psyche.

Although Walpole and his contemporaries cannot have known his work would establish a literary convention, they were aware of the nature of the work itself. We can already see in the preface to the second edition of *Otranto* what Walpole saw himself as having achieved in the novel. He states explicitly that when he blended "the two kinds of romance, the ancient and the modern," the ancient, which was fantasy, freed his imagination, while the modern, reflecting the real world, lent reality to his characters. The characters are not very convincingly real, of course, but they are recognizably eighteenth-century figures embodying current ideas about the human mind. By placing them in the world of dreams and fairy tales, Walpole was able to present his age's concept of human evil—pride, hatred, violence, cruelty, incest—as part of man's psychology. The one kind of romance enabled him to delve into his own subconscious, the other helped him to relate what he found there to the human condition in general. (pp. 4-19)

Otranto is just the first of many a fictional plunge into the subconscious mind. Some later Gothic novels owe their origins, as it does, to actual dreams. Others result from their authors' conscious dredging up of dream symbols from their own minds. The later authors added new devices to fit their particular needs, but all these works are set up as revelations of horror. They present as psychological evil a sexual obsession, overwhelming guilt, or pride that defies the limits God has set for man, and they seek to arouse fear and sickening horror in the reader. These tales may see evil as an aberration in man or as an inherent part of his nature, they may question the value judgments placed on the phenomena they are symbolizing, but they all show the world its own dreams, drawing the reader into their closed worlds, playing on his emotions, and preventing him from denying that what he experiences in the novel may also be within himself.

It seems almost paradoxical that this depiction of man's nightmares should have grown out of the gentle tenets of Benevolism and the Sentimentalist movement. Yet the works of the first Gothic authors are based on the Benevolist view of man. The central belief of that view is that man, though fallen indeed, still has the potential for Good. An infinitely benevolent Creator has not abandoned his creature to inevitable depravity; man is born, not inherently evil, but with a nature that, if he is properly nurtured, enables him to live the virtuous life and so be happy. These ideas, held by the Sentimentalists, have been traced back to the Cambridge Platonists, a group of theologians at Cambridge University in the late seventeenth century. Their followers, the Latitudinarians, were active in both Church and State during and after the Restoration period, preaching religious tolerance and an active charity, and were highly influential. With help from Shaftesbury and the deists, they were primarily responsible for the widespread acceptance of Benevolism, as Louis Bredvold, among others, has shown. The Platonists, as Bredvold notes, were explicit about man's natural goodness. He quotes Henry More as saying, "Virtue . . . is the health of the soul, its natural state of well-being," and Benjamin Whichcote as writing: "Nothing is more certainly true than that all Vice is unnatural and contrary to the nature of Man. . . . A depraved and vicious Mind is as really the Sickness and Deformity thereof, as any foul and loathsome disease is to the body. . . . The good Man is an Instrument in Tune."

If he lives in conformity with the nature with which God has endowed him, man will be in harmony with Nature, the natural order, and so be happy. To accomplish this he must nurture and cultivate his innate good feelings. Social virtue springs from love of one's fellow man which must be fostered by developing the good feelings of the heart. The Sentimental movement that grew out of these ideas is thus a system of thought that makes "virtue" manifest in "good feelings," in pleasurable inward sensations. The protagonists of the Sentimental novels, the man and woman of feeling, are repositories of such virtuous feelings and the inner content that goes with them. Demonstrating, through the emotions they express and through their occasional actions, a natural benevolence uncorrupted by a faulty upbringing, they are oversimplified as characters. Objections were made, in the eighteenth century, as they are today, to the self-indulgent effusions and apparent smugness of these characters. Even those who admired Sentimental literature did so for the "fine feelings" to which it gave expression. Yet those heroes and heroines who exclaim about their own feelings and, in fact, do little else but emote, reflect the Benevolists' replacement of the traditional faith in Reason as the foundation stone of morality with the concept of feeling (Sentiment) as man's moral arbiter. All men are endowed by their Creator with a Moral Sense, the innate power that enables them to tell right from wrong instantaneously. Properly cultivated sensibilities keep people sensitive to this monitor and enable them to "sympathize," to feel with and for others. It was the didactic duty of literature to direct the "passions" toward the good ends for which God implanted them in man by drawing models of refined sensibility. The

Sentimental novel educates the reader's emotions by embodying in these characters correctly cultivated feeling, which the reader shares as he reads.

Evil, in this system of thought, is that which mars the harmony of the universe. It is the twisting and distortion of the potentially good feelings into destructive impulses that render the individual unhappy by setting him at war with God's harmony within and outside himself. Both good and evil are inner states of man's mind and, since beauty lies in God's order, the good and the beautiful are one, and evil is monstrous. These equations of goodness with beauty and wrongdoing with ugliness, which by mid-century were appearing in the writings of Adam Smith and others, were put to use by the authors of Sentimental and Gothic literature. They made their good characters physically lovely and gave the evil ones twisted bodies and ugly faces. The Gothic novel, in making monstrosity the outward show of the terrible inner distortion of man's innate good nature into evil, is thus an expression of the other side of the benevolist ideas reflected in the Sentimental novel. It forms a variant of the Sentimental genre, with related structures, forms, and devices. Sentimental novels reflect an ideal that, coming from God, is possibly realizable; the Gothic represents the distortion of that ideal.

Sentimental and Gothic literature is, as a result, highly paradigmatic. The characters are more nearly representations of the general human state than depictions of individual human beings. They are not personifications of good and evil nor yet either type characters or highly individualized portrayals. Occupying the hazy no-man's land between the abstraction of allegory and the "reality" of social and comic novels, they are manifestations of the semi-abstract, semi-real area occupied by concepts of the place of good and evil in the human mind. These characters are not realistically drawn because, to represent what all men are like, they must be drawn without strongly individual quirks; yet they are also not allegorical figures, because they do represent people, however simplified. They are strictly limited portrayals and their reference beyond themselves to the ideas they embody makes their outlines fuzzy. Plot, setting, structure in this literature are also determined by such outside reference to Sentimentalist concepts, lending an insubstantiality to the whole work that is desirable because it is conducive to evocation of the sublime, and so a prime means for catching the reader up in the work. These characteristics bring about the special kind of symbolism found in Gothic tales, which, directed to the reader's feelings, put him in touch with intuitively known aspects of his own nature. (pp. 22-5)

The Gothic authors, writing a new type of romance that would free the imagination of the author and engage the emotions of the reader, consciously wrote fantasy in the face of the rising taste for the social novel. The actual terms "romance" and "novel" were unstable at the time, as can be seen from Clara Reeve's effort to "fix" them in her *Progress of Romance*. They were at times used interchangeably, as they can be today, and at others to differentiate the two kinds. The kinds themselves, however, were consistently seen as separate, the one "fabulous" and the other a "picture of real life." As Walpole and Clara Reeve claimed, the Gothic was a new type combining techniques of the new novel writing with the fantasy of the "old" romance. It thus put the ordinary world in touch with the mysterious. This linking of the techniques of "new" and "old" romance (or "novel" and "romance") reflects the increasingly inductive study of the human mind.

The fictional form would educate the reader by manifesting the connection between abstract concepts and general human reality. Through the isolated world, ostensibly remote in space or time, the Gothic novels explore the dark aspects of the mind and, through their characters, they locate that world within everyday experience. The paradigmatic, eighteenth-century European types who people Gothic fiction are frightened almost witless by the impingement of supernatural horrors and diabolical cruelty on their neat, virtuous, and orderly lives. They are thus half figures of the imagination, half representations of ordinary people.

The Gothic authors used their devices to make manifest the effects and sometimes the cause of evil in the mind of a creature (man) with a potential to be free of it. The Fall of man was still the cause of his evil—this is why the problem is abysmal and the abyss itself used as a metaphor throughout the tradition—but since the Fall had not resulted in inevitable depravity and evil was unnatural, a fresh delineation of the psychology of good was needed, which, in turn, inevitably meant a new formulation of the psychology of evil. These authors wished to show their readers the "myself am Hell" of Milton's Satan and the "paradise within thee, happier far" of his new Man. The attempts to portray the "Good" inevitably opened up the problem of the nature of human evil. Indeed, among the early Gothic novels, there are two kinds: those that use the Gothic supernatural to "ravish" and "transport" their readers by opposing the virtuous of Sentimentalism to Gothic evil and then conclude with a Sentimental resolution; and those that, using the Sentimental characters as contrast, focus their attention on the villain and conclude with the disaster that overwhelms him. (pp. 37-8)

Setting out to explore the place of evil in the mind, the Gothic novelists found that their expedition into unknown territory uncovered the dream landscape of a closed world separated from that of everyday. The setting of the first Gothic novels in a remote historical time seems in itself an almost symbolic reenactment of the need to go back from the concealing refinements of civilization to the fundamentals of human nature. It is part of the late eighteenth century's general turning away from the two classical periods, gilded or silvered over (as the eighteenth century saw them) by rational light, to the "barbaric" and "Gothic" myths. To uncover the symbolic manifestations that *are* the country of the mind, the heirs of the enlightenment brought back out of the wilderness, the bogs and mountain fastnesses, the most emotion-laden images they knew, symbolic figures and landscapes from the dark, irrational past.

Their characters are not natural inhabitants of the settings in which they are placed because the very purpose of the setting—itself derived from literature and painting, not from nature—is to create an isolated environment in which to show eighteenth-century readers figures they can recognize as familiar and accept as showing what they and all mankind are like. Authentically medieval characters would not fulfill this purpose because they would delineate the local, differentiating features of the denizens of the middle ages.

The medieval setting was soon abandoned for a contemporaneous one, however, as if to bring home the depicted evil to the reader's own time. When the tale is no longer set in the distant past, a system of "nested," concentric narration maintains the illusion of a strange world, isolating a symbolic landscape within the ordinary "world." In these settings, the inner spiritual state of the characters retains its physical manifestation. Their souls shine or glare from their eyes, revealing peace or torment, which, in correspondence to the concept of the Moral Sense, is instantly recognizable as the consequence of virtue or vice. The heroes and heroines continue to be portrayed as beautiful. The villains, being mixed characters, vary in appearance, and the split-off doubles are ugly.

The omnipresent old house or castle is one of the most stable characteristics of the Gothic. A dire and threatening place, it remains more than a dwelling. It starts out as a stone representation of the dark, tortured windings in the mind of those eminently civilized, and therefore "unnatural" vices, ambition and cruelty; it bears the whole weight of the ages of man's drift away from an ideal state; and it becomes a lasting representation of the torments of the subconscious pressing upon the conscious mind and making a prison of the self. The landscape it stands in also remains part of the weeping and storming Nature of the pathetic fallacy. The heavens rent by terrible storms contrive to express human torment and rage; sunshine and singing birds convey spiritual peace. And at the most intense moment of moral danger, there still appears in this landscape the terrible abyss of damnation.

The characters in this literature find themselves teetering with terrifying vertigo on the edge of this abyss or they leave the craggy moral landscape to grope through dank subterranean corridors of evil into which only an occasional ray of the sunlight of virtue can filter. And these characters are, on the one hand, sensitive, tearful, one-sided depictions of man's virtuous potential transported whole from the Sentimental novel and, on the other, towering villains caught in the fearful psychomachia of evil. Weeping and shuddering in weird surroundings quite foreign to their well-ordered personalities, the Sentimental protagonists contend by the sheer force of their virtue with the storms set up by the violent struggle in the villain between his Moral Sense and natural goodness and the evil within which contorts him into madness.

The Gothic villains have an interesting potential for ambiguous, suggested meanings. When provided with the necessary sublime setting, these villains of the early Gothic are paradoxically more nearly recognizable as depictions of human beings than the good Sentimental characters who are their victims. Derided though they have been as bugbears too exaggerated to frighten adults, they have elicited greater critical admiration than the Sentimental characters. Neither type, however, should be measured as nearer or farther from human "reality." The depiction of the human potential for goodness in the heroes and heroines and of that goodness in a struggle to the death with its own evil in the villain are special and highly symbolic forms of characterization. The first produces heroines whose veins are filled not with blood but with water that continually overflows at their eyes, and who have no spirit; heroes who weep unmanly tears and are extravagantly noble, too ethereal to sweat. The second draws an exaggerated villain deliberately made larger than life, a towering storm of torment, whose evil is as great as his crippled potential for good was large.

The implications of such portrayals were quickly picked up by later authors, who made them explicit in rather different characters. Since the villain, representing the place of evil in the mind gone wrong, is caught in his interesting, soul-searing conflict and unable to obliterate consciousness of the lost possibility of virtue, he always has a certain pathos. Consequently, he is quickly transformed from a giant figure to a man-sized one, corresponding to the realization that his condition and the human condition are analogous: man born good and driven half mad by the torture of the evil into which he has been twisted. The depiction of an ordinary man suffering the torments of evil in place of the towering Gothic villain, however, produced a new and special aesthetic problem. How could the reader be made to feel the pathos of a character whose crimes were to be presented as horrible and bloody and were supposed to fill the reader with horror? The solution to this problem is just one example of the way the entire tradition has undergone a gradual modification while remaining, in its essence, unchanged. Since the reader was to sympathize with the tormented man who replaced the villain and who was a victim of his own evil, the device was formed of projecting the evil in him out onto a separate character. The figure of the double was thus born from the split and warring factions of the personality of the Gothic villain. The doubles figure showed that it was the nature of every man that the good in him must struggle in unending battle against the distortions of evil. It did so in a way that would make the reader accept the terrible certainty that this was true of himself, for it not only prevented him from rejecting the central character as evil; but, to the extent that he sympathized with that character, the double became a potential mirror image of himself as well.

The nineteenth-century works of this literature have not met with the same reluctance to interpret them as their eighteenth-century forebears, but they have not been treated as belonging to a single convention. They have not been clearly seen as descending in a direct line from the eighteenth-century works, because the origins of Gothic literature in eighteenth-century ideas have not been adequately shown and its tradition and meaning as a convention have found little recognition. Readers, for instance, who see Walpole's walking portrait as just "machinery," have little trouble ascribing symbolic significance to the strange behavior of the portrait of Dorian Gray, which behaves as no ordinary painting would. They find Edgar Allan Poe's Ligeia more acceptable than Matilda in Lewis' *The Monk,* although Ligeia does not more closely represent an ordinary flesh and blood woman; indeed, she is the more fantastic of the two. Robert Louis Stevenson's Mr. Hyde is nerve-racking, even though no reader believes an English doctor can transform himself into his own hairy, evil counterpart; and Hyde is less not more "real" than, say, Lewis' Ambrosio. If these later works seem to be more acceptable today than the early Gothic novels, it is probably because what they symbolize is nearer to the modern reader's own time and thought. The fact that they are symbolic is more easily seen because they are more closely representative of the underlying "myths" of today's culture and so more directly available to modern imaginations and feelings. The methods of the later authors, nonetheless, are demonstrably the same as those of the early writers of Gothic fiction. Evil is still ugliness in Wilde's tale, as it is in *Frankenstein; The Turn of the Screw* sets forth repressed sexuality through ghosts, as *The Monk* does through demons. Throughout the nineteenth century, however, the referent level of the symbolism becomes increasingly specific, until, finally, in the 1890s, a character within a work, Dr. Jekyll, himself provides an explicit "scientific" explanation for everything that, up to that point in the tale, has been manifested symbolically.

In a series of developments parallel to the invention of the double, other characteristics of the Gothic novel were modified as the tradition continued through its unending hall of

mirrors in which the reflections, however weird, continued to be images of man. The process is one of gradual discovery, an expanding awareness modifying what has previously been intuitively known. It is a fresh formulation of ancient nightmares in the light of developing ideas. The Gothic moon, like any other celestial body, shines on nothing new. Man is as he has been, committing acts of greater or lesser nastiness, which he himself then dubs evil or otherwise with varying degrees of absoluteness. That moon, nevertheless, makes the world look different; having appeared in the second half of the eighteenth century, it has been casting strange shadows ever since. (pp. 47-52)

Elizabeth MacAndrew, in her The Gothic Tradition in Fiction, *Columbia University Press, 1979, 289 p.*

EINO RAILO

[In the following excerpt, Railo examines the conventional Gothic castle, villain, hero, and heroine.]

The stage-setting with which before long the student of horror-romanticism is inevitably confronted is a species of old "Gothic" castle, the scene of innumerable horrors, capable of touching the imagination each time we see it, as when the curtain rises on ramparts and towers bathed in the spectral moonlight of *Hamlet.* The reader quickly observes that this "haunted castle" plays an exceedingly important part in these romances; so important, indeed, that were it eliminated the whole fabric of romance would be bereft of its foundation and would lose its predominant atmosphere. The entire stock-in-trade of horror-romanticism in its oldest and purest form consists, as will be shown in the following pages, chiefly of the properties and staff of this haunted castle, and, as we proceed farther in time, of motives based in the first instance upon these, so that to my mind acquaintance with the materials of horror-romanticism is best begun with this central stage and its appurtenances. Let us start, therefore, with a visit to the ancient vaults of Otranto Castle.

Of the castle's outward appearance no actual description is given, nor does the rapidity of the narrator's style permit him to linger over a calm and detailed picture of his setting. Nevertheless, the reader's imagination is soon aware of a concentration on the limited sphere of what seems to be a medieval castle. We are taken into the castle-yard and the chapel, where a marriage is taking place, and into various rooms, of which one contains the collection of ancestral portraits indispensable to such an edifice. The underground portion is full of bewildering vaulted passages, one of which leads through a secret door to a cave beyond the castle confines, another to the church of St. Nicholas. An awesome silence reigns in these subterranean vaults, a silence broken only by the creak of rusty hinges as a breath of air somewhere sets an old door moving. In their gloomy shade the maiden, flying from the lord of the castle, can at first hardly make out the faintly gleaming object in some hiding-place, and then only with difficulty does she perceive it to be the key to the complicated lock of a secret trap-door. The banqueting-hall is fitted with galleries whence the young heroine can, unseen, regard her lover and where she can fall into the inevitable swoon when the tyrant sentences him to death or lifelong confinement in the deepest dungeon of the darkest tower. Over the gate hangs a brazen horn which one cannot fail to notice, especially as the reason for its being there is hard to understand.

With some few such strokes Walpole conjures up his castle before the reader, avoiding overmuch detail, but continually stimulating the imagination. It must be admitted, too, that he has succeeded, for some hint of strangeness and austere majesty is undoubtedly left in the mind. A good example of what his fantasy of a Gothic castle betokened to him in importance and atmosphere is provided by the opening lines of *The Mysterious Mother,* into which he has effectively condensed the whole of Gothic horror:

> What awful silence! How these antique towers
> And vacant courts chill the suspended soul,
> Till expectation wears the cast of fear;
> And fear, half-ready to become devotion,
> Mumbles a kind of mental orison,
> It knows not wherefore.

Clara Reeve did little to develop this side of romanticism, nor does Walpole's manner of introducing the chief setting of his book seem to have appealed to her. One invention, however, she did make, which was to become an essential ingredient of all tales of horror in which the stage is an old castle, or for that matter, any other ruined building. In *The Old English Baron* we find, for the first time, deliberate use of an empty suite of rooms supposed to be haunted. The castle of the deceased Lord Lovel, now occupied by a usurper, Baron Fitz-Owen, is little more than an ordinary country house, reminiscent rather of her own time than of the Middle Ages, yet it has the peculiarity that certain rooms, for some secret reason cautiously hinted at, have long been closed. We are finally informed that it was in these rooms that the castle's rightful owner, Sir Walter Lovel, was murdered and his body hidden. We understand also that it was fear of his ghost which gave them the reputation of being haunted. An old suit of armour is still preserved there, the breastplate of which is stained with blood; the murdered man's bones are under the floor. The furniture is decayed and falling to pieces; the fabrics moth-eaten. The portraits of the rightful owners are turned towards the wall, and everywhere we find mournful reminders of past happiness, love and passion. Into the framework supplied by Walpole, Clara Reeve thus pours the first leavening of female sensitivity. Little else of import—no subterranean passages, secret doors or similar contrivances—is to be found in her work.

If, as we have seen, Walpole gave us the first features of the haunted castle with the all-important inventions of secret passages and trap-doors, and Clara Reeve added the ghost-ridden suite, it was Ann Radcliffe who developed this series of imaginary pictures to the full. With powerful imagination and inventiveness and a melancholy poetry she enriches the outlines derived from her predecessors to such an extent that in this field there was little else to add.

To begin with, she gives the castle's silhouette in clear, strong lines. It can be situated, for instance, on the coast, on the highest peak of a steep mountain, where wild romantic tempests freely rage. The slopes of the mountain are abrupt and dangerous. The castle is built with Gothic magnificence, its high towers seeming in their proud inaccessible majesty to frown defiance on the whole world; the entire edifice bears witness to the power of its past owners. These outward traits, which in themselves possess an effectivity not to be denied, continue to expand in the writer's imagination, forming a solemn background for her scenes and plot. Everything in the castle, its towers, vaulted portals, drawbridge, moat, bear the stern impress of ancient might and splendour. As we ap-

proach the castle of Udolpho at sunset, in the fading light its stout towers, ramparts and breastworks stand threatening and cruel on the brink of a giddy precipice; it looms there silent and lonely and sublime, monarch of the whole scene, defying all who dare to penetrate its mysteries.

But as we approach closer, sadness fills our minds. In the magnificent yards the marble is shattered and weatherworn, and around the tall, broken windows grass has grown which now "waves to the lonely gale." Ivy has sprouted from the collapsing ramparts, bearing witness to the decline of former power. Above the gigantic gate, guarded of old by two strong towers, weeds and tall grass have replaced the waving flags, seeming to sigh in the wind over the surrounding desolation. A crenellated wall once joined together the towers, and below them was a stout breastwork; the walls stretched formerly along the edge of the precipice. Mrs. Radcliffe loves castles which are falling into ruin; ruins are, to her mind, more romantic than a sound building.

She is not yet, however, satisfied, but brings into the circle of the haunted castle the old abbey and monastery. The broken arches and solitary towers of these rise gloomily impressive among the twilit trees, producing an eerie atmosphere tinged with devotion. A monastery of this description can be a big group of Gothic buildings, whose dismal towers and fear-awakening walls rise proudly, lonely and uncrushed amidst the surrounding dark shadows. The old building in a romantic forest can also be a former monastery, the past magnificence of which awakens in the spectator a respectful, timid feeling of devoutness.

In these descriptions of Mrs. Radcliffe's, all specially long and detailed, the dominant feeling is one of a deep and penetrative romanticism, deliberately adapted to suit every circumstance of the story, all of which serves to show how dear this particular atmosphere was to the author and how prominent a place it occupied in her emotional life. Thus, the site of the monastery is sometimes a kind of natural meadow shadowed by tall, dense trees, as old perhaps as the building itself, which cast over the scene "a romantic gloom." Thick ivy covers the walls, and owls lodge in the deserted towers. Stones and fragments of the walls lie around in the grass, which gently waves in the wind. To describe the melancholy sense of desolation which broods there, the writer has recourse to Ossian's phrase: "The thistle shakes its lonely head, the moss whistles to the wind."

The halls are paved with marble, the rooms are large and high. In some the gloom is enhanced by the panelling, which is almost as dark as darkness itself. In solemn mood we pace the rooms and corridors, whose long perspectives display a simple nobility of line and breathe "a holy calm." The windows are high and arched, furnished with stained glass and often shadowed by ivy; into the spacious and gloomy chambers they emit a solemn twilight, capable of affecting the heart to the extremity of terror. "A melancholy silence dwells in these deserted rooms, the tall arches of which are upborne on pillars of black marble."

The embellishments include portraits and hangings. The castle bell or clock has its own peculiar significance, either as a proclaimer of the time or as the bearer of a message. It is, in a fashion, a personal being that closely follows the fate of the castle and its inhabitants. It is the "great clock" of the castle, the "ancient monitor of the hall below." "Ay, there is the old clock . . . there he is still; the cannons have not silenced him! . . . There he was roaring out in the hottest fire I have seen this many a day." To the prisoner under sentence of death who in the silence of the night hears it strike One, it is like an echo of the death-chimes. It awakens the persecuted maiden from her dreams, to remind her that hope is vain and that all that is left for her is to sink under her anguish. She hears it strike every quarter, but when it finally strikes One, its note sounds ominous and fatal to her last hope. On her arrival at the castle she had heard the bell and listened to it with a tremulous foreboding in her heart as its voice was borne to her on the wind. Chime followed chime, fading away in "sullen murmur" far behind the mountains, and in her heart the feeling was born that it tolled in the beginning of a fateful period.

An exceedingly important part is played in Mrs. Radcliffe's books by the castle doors and passages, which are extremely numerous, winding and narrow, so that they form a veritable labyrinth. There is a constant moving along dark and winding passages to remote parts of the castle, reached usually through a small, iron-bound door. On our escape from the dungeons we have the luck to find in the thick dust a trapdoor—our foot having previously caught in its ring—and summoning all our strength we are enabled at the last moment, as the steps of our pursuers echo nearer, to slip through into the castle vaults. Here we are uncertain at first what direction to take, until again our luck discloses a heavy door in the opposite wall. This leads to a new system of vaulted passages which stretches beyond the castle walls and contains a tunnel leading to a hidden cave somewhere in a forest. A tapestry often hides the little secret door to an inner room; at the other end of this there may be large double doors embellished with heavy carvings. A merciful ray of moonlight, piercing in some marvellous way through a chink in the wall of this vaulted labyrinth, often helps us at critical moments to find such secret roads to salvation.

To this romantic building of the trio Walpole—Reeve—Radcliffe belong important properties, atmospheric and otherwise, well adapted to heighten the desired impression. Walpole uses moonlight. At the very moment when the tyrant is engaged in blackest night on some deed of darkness, the moon emerges from behind a cloud, revealing a ghastly scene that alarms him and prevents the crime from being committed. Through the coloured windows of great churches it shines dim and mysterious, illuminating to the tyrant's view the glassy eyes of his dead heir, a witness to the violent and tragic end of his line. The moon is intended to awaken a nocturnal atmosphere fraught with mystery and tinged with fantasy, fear and sadness. It lends an indistinct and weird shape to each feature; it is a theatrical searchlight cast from the wings at suitable moments to reveal to the terror-stricken audience visions and scenes of fear.

We have already mentioned the wind which causes doors to creak on their old rusted hinges. As the draught that wanders through subterranean passages, the wind has a special duty assigned to it by Walpole; it has to sweep through the vaults in sudden gusts and, meeting the persecuted heroine just when her flight is at its climax, to extinguish, to the reader's terror, the lantern or candle in her hand, leaving her in awful, pitch-black darkness. When it whines in the night outside the despairing and trembling maiden's window, the loquacious chamber-maid takes it for a sighing ghost. Lightning is the mighty ally of wind and storm: at a critical moment there comes a sudden burst of thunder that shakes the foundations

of the haunted castle, hinting at the existence of avenging, eternal powers.

With regard to the surrounding landscape Walpole, who writes economically, has little to say, but in its way this little is very descriptive. Near to the castle there is a forest and behind this mountains which contain caves running down to the sea. These have formerly been tenanted by hermits, but are now regarded as the haunts of evil spirits. Clara Reeve, too, is sparing of such details. In her book there is hardly any moonlight or thunder, but there, likewise, a busy gust of wind does its duty. When the young hero attempts to open the door of the haunted chamber the wind immediately extinguishes his lamp, leaving him in darkness. And when the rightful heir arrives at the castle of his forefathers, a considerate squall seems to roar out a welcome to him.

Much more frequently does Mrs. Radcliffe use such aids. Her castles and monasteries are set in beautiful, often majestic surroundings. She is fond of guiding her readers through districts devoid of signs of human habitation. Only the roar of distant torrents and the cries of birds of prey break the awesome and oppressive silence. The valleys are surrounded by steep mountain ridges, along the slopes of which waterfalls dash at furious speed, only to calm down at their feet to placid lakes. The dismal twilight of the woods, the soft calm of evening and the tranquil peace and solemnity of the land-

Frontispieces for the four volumes of the 1799 edition of Ann Radcliffe's The Mysteries of Udolpho.

scape lull the soul to a pleasant sense of oblivion. We fare, to take an example, along a valley, on each side of which are steep mountains. The sublime silence of the scene is disturbed only by the noise of distant waters and the cry of a bird high in the air. Emerging from this austere neighbourhood, an idyllic landscape, in effective contrast to the former, opens out before us. Its hills and valleys are bedecked with fields, vineyards and orchards. The shaded valleys are frequently adorned by a gently meandering stream, or tiny dwellings half-hidden among foliage. Between the trees gleams the tower of a monastery, and a little lake mirrors on its clear surface the surrounding beauty. The green woods and fields, the flowering meadows, the musical tinkle of the translucent brook, the contented humming of insects—all seem to refresh the soul and to make of life a blessing. The rising sun has his part well rehearsed; over the horizon appears first an inexpressibly glowing line, which swiftly broadens until the sun has emerged in all his majesty, revealing the whole face of nature, brightening every tint of the landscape and scattering glittering beams over the dewy surface of the land. A kind of "sweet romanticism," to use the author's own words, breathes from these landscape paintings executed with so much feeling.

The hum of the wind in empty vaults, in forests, in the grass growing over ruins; the storm that shrieks around the castle set on a high mountain, and the ghastly moonlight—of all these Mrs. Radcliffe makes exceedingly rich use. Cold autumnal winds howl dismally; in mighty gusts they play an accompaniment to the lonely hours of night; in sudden squalls they tear over the waste of sea, dashing the foaming waves with unspeakable force against the rocks. When a deathly silence reigns in the castle halls one can hear an eddy of wind creep, as it were mysteriously, through the corridors. As a low and mournful murmur it comes from the mountains, speeding "hollowly" over the earth, bringing in its train mists and coldness. It extinguishes the heroine's lamp as though trying to crush in her the last beam of hope, until finally every sound is swallowed up in the mighty rumbling of thunder. Bleak clouds, dank and tattered, fly swiftly across the face of the moon, which intermittently casts its pale light between them, revealing a mournful and depressing scene. Sometimes, however, its rays fall with a gentler, more poetic radiance on the waves softly dying on a delightful sandy beach; sometimes they seem to linger over a dewy landscape in the solemn hush of midnight, and then of the moonlight, the waves and the night a "scene of tranquil beauty" is born. (pp. 7-13)

The chief character in *The Castle of Otranto* is its master Manfred, of whom a dark and forbidding picture is given. He is not the rightful heir to Otranto, but a descendant of the usurping family, and in consequence his mind is ceaselessly oppressed by the prophecy of Saint Nicholas that "the Castle and Lordship of Otranto should pass from the present family whenever the real owner should be grown too large to inhabit it."

The story begins at a point when the fulfilment of this prophecy is nigh; at a time, therefore, when according to the wish of Saint Nicholas the mastership of Otranto is about to pass to the rightful heir of Alfonso, whom Manfred's grandfather Ricardo had murdered. By these means Manfred is made to appear from the beginning as a character struggling against an inevitable fate. When his only son dies in consequence of a supernatural incident, he wishes to leave his wife, who can no longer be expected to provide him with an heir, and to wed the betrothed of his son. But divine and mortal powers are arrayed against him, and soon the rightful heir comes on the scene in the guise of a young peasant called Theodore. Theodore falls in love with Manfred's daughter Matilda, but as Alfonso's blood cannot mix with that of the murderer's family, the marriage is impossible. The wedding is prevented by Manfred's murdering his own daughter; the prophecy being then fulfilled by the disclosure of Theodore's birth. Manfred abdicates and with his wife enters a monastery. Such, in brief, is the plot of the book.

The interest centres chiefly around Manfred, for one reason, because he seems familiar. He is possessed by a single idea, the realization of which is a matter of life and death with him, viz., the retention of the family power. The prophecy and his knowledge of his grandfather's crime combine, however, in making him uncertain and illogical, and in exposing him to fierce, spiritual conflicts. He is transformed into a being inhuman, savage and passionate, occasionally capable of some slight show of feeling, though taciturn and gloomily silent. When he sees Theodore for the first time he flies into a rage because of the youth's resemblance to the picture of Alfonso. It is expressly stated that Manfred was not the type of tyrant who practises cruelty for his pleasure, and that only fate had made his character, which was otherwise humane, so stern and unbending, and that his virtues were ever awake when passion had not befogged his brain. His heart was sensitive to outside influences, but his pride forbade him to show it. Those who were ignorant of the cause of his secret agony could not understand his temper; in their eyes he was scarcely sane, deliberately ill-treated his daughter and was a gloomy and lonely man, oppressed by the consciousness of a coming unhappy fate. He is the luckless hero of a tragedy of destiny, for whom we can feel sympathy.

Compared with him, Clara Reeve's tyrant, Lord Walter Lovel, is on a much lower plane, hardly more than a common criminal. The goal of all his strivings is to amass riches and honours, and it is for this that he has recourse to crime. Only in the obstinacy with which he denies his guilt to the last does he show any firmness of character.

On the whole, Mrs. Radcliffe's tyrants revert to the type of Manfred, though the motives behind their deeds are often more insignificant in nature. The predominant passion is love of power and riches. As men of fierce and morose nature they are entirely in the grip of their passions, slaves to anger, the lust for revenge and pride; men from whom no good can be expected. We are told that in their moments of fury and revenge, their imagination is unable to conceive methods of torture to equal their desires. No gentler feeling or mode of thinking alleviates their tyrannic sense of power or guides them to good deeds; their every act is one of boundless oppression and unscrupulousness. Only the desire for revenge can restrain their cupidity. The hidden cause for their harshness is often, as in Manfred's case, a dark crime perpetrated either by the tyrant himself or by his family. It hardens the heart, leads to new crimes and is not confessed until on deathbed, from which all honest men naturally draw back in horror. Others, again, die proud and unrepentant. With such tyrants love is nothing but passion; one sight of the heroine is sufficient to inflame them, and their unbridled nature refuses to admit of any obstacle. Outwardly they are often handsome and stalwart. Thus we are given to understand that Montoni, the darkly-glancing lord of Udolpho, is a man of "an uncommonly handsome person," whose features are expressive and manly. They indicate a commanding and quick-tempered nature, but the chief impression they awaken is one of gloomy taciturnity and a meditativeness bordering on melancholy.

Of all Mrs. Radcliffe's characters Montoni is the one best adapted to awaken interest and the one for whom the author herself, despite her attitude of horror, has the greatest affection. The model for Montoni is to be sought in Manfred, but while in the latter we have a fairly uncomplicated character, whose aims and deeds are easy of comprehension, the silent and gloomy Montoni has something enigmatical about his person. The crimes of Manfred and his family are known to us, but whether Montoni or his family have anything on their consciences remains uncertain to the end. A strange, suspicious atmosphere is created around Montoni which causes us to believe anything of him without proof or reason. As he wanders through the passages of his dilapidated castle, silent and darkly defiant, brooding over some secret thought, yet noble and beautiful in appearance, or sits cold and mocking amongst his accomplices, gambling or drinking, he achieves in some way an effect of romantically majestic proportions which attracts our interest owing to its novelty. Curiosity inclines us to ask who and what he really is and what his thoughts are; what the reason for his return to the deserted castle of Udolpho and what his plans there; but the questions remain unanswered. Montoni remains to the end an enigma. The reader is left with the suspicion that the author had indeed been capable of constructing a romantic, enigmatical type, but that her talent had proved insufficient to provide this type with a tragic fate based on a true mission in life. He is married to a French noblewoman, Madame Cheron, whom he takes with her niece to Italy, to the castle of Udolpho. There he attempts to gain possession of his wife's entire fortune and failing in this, ill-treats her until she dies. In the end he is imprisoned by the Venetian government for political reasons and dies a mysterious death in prison, unrepentant, secretive in death as in life.

Mrs. Radcliffe's other tyrants are depicted in a feebler, more summary style. Malcolm, master of Dunbayne, is "proud, oppressive, revengeful," "mighty in injustice and cruel in power." He has seized his brother's lands, murdered him and cast his son out into the world; having murdered the Lord of Athlin he tries to murder the latter's son Osbert, and even attempts to compel the daughter Mary to become his mistress. He fails, however, in these schemes and meets his death. On his death-bed he repents: "I have understood virtue, but I have loved vice. I do not now lament that I am punished, but that I have deserved punishment."

The actual death of a tyrant of this description is something out of the ordinary: he invariably expires "with a strong sigh." The Marquis of Mazzini holds his wife confined in life-long imprisonment in the dungeons of his castle and intends marrying off his daughter Julia against her will; but he falls by the hand of his second wife Maria de Vellorno. He too repents on his deathbed: "The retribution of heaven is upon me. My punishment is the immediate consequence of my guilt." Such is the main story of *The Sicilian Romance.*

In *The Romance of the Forest* the Marquis de Montalt has murdered his brother and believes he has murdered his niece Adeline. She has, however, escaped with her life to be cast on the mercy of her uncle, who tries to seduce her. This proves to be the last of his crimes; he is imprisoned, takes poison and dies, tortured by the remembrance of his crimes. A more interesting figure is a secondary tyrant, a nobleman called de la Motte, in whose castle hidden away in the forest Adeline comes to dwell. De la Motte is a weak character who does not scruple to improve his position by common highway robbery, and for this reason falls into dangerous dependence on the Marquis de Montalt. Because of his poverty he is bitter and envious, without moral backbone and even cowardly, scorn tempered by pity being awakened in us by his craven spirit. Yet in these surroundings he is a new type whom we shall meet again in the future. Finally, I mention the impressive Jesuit Schedoni, of the long romance *The Italian,* whose tall apparition and fanatic glance, coupled with the terrors of the Inquisition, provide the essence of the work in question.

Such are the tyrants of these romances. Of all the masters of haunted castles to whom so many hundreds of pages have been devoted, the type most likely to adhere to the memory is that represented by Manfred-Montoni, the lonely, stalwart, saturnine and black-browed man of beautiful countenance, whose spiritual life is in the grip of some secret influence and who, by reason of his intelligence and strength of will and the volcanic nature of his passions, stands out from his surroundings as an independent individual. In this respect Mrs. Radcliffe, in particular, has had a vision of something superhuman, of a superman with uncommon qualities, whose soul and actions are dominated by passions unknown to the ordinary mortal, passions verging on the demoniac. (pp. 28-32)

A contrast to the tyrant's uncontrollable temper and gloom is furnished by the sunny humanity and joyous outlook, coupled with outward beauty, embodied in the young hero of these romances. On his brow there sits no stigma of crime and bad conscience; it shines clear, and he regards the world with open and candid gaze. The hero of Walpole's story, the peasant Theodore, rises to increasing importance. He falls in love with Manfred's daughter and saves Isabella from insult; Manfred sentences him to death, but at the very moment of his execution a birth-mark, a bloody arrow, is seen on his shoulder, and at the sight the pious Father Jerome is moved to cry out: "Gracious heaven, what do I see! It is my child! my Theodore!" Jerome, formerly Count Falconara, was once married to Alfonso's daughter, and his lost child is thus the rightful heir to Otranto. The gentleness of his birth has already been revealed in his manners, which display an aristocratic charm and a pleasing humility; he is ready to sacrifice his life in the service of the oppressed and fears no one when the persecuted maiden seeks his protection. It is expressly stated that his sins are no more numerous than can be expected of one of his age. When in love, he delights to wander in shady places, as these harmonize best with the pleasant melancholy that fills his soul—quite in the manner of Valentine in *Two Gentlemen of Verona,* who sighs amidst his love-sorrows:

> Here can I sit alone, unseen of any,
> And to the nightingale's complaining notes
> Tune my distresses and record my woes,

or of the lovelorn Orlando in *As You Like It,* who in the romantic forest of Arden will

> . . . carve on every tree
> The fair, the chaste, and unexpressive she . . . ,

or of Romeo, whose love-sickness the poet depicts in the following lines:

> —underneath the grove of sycamore
> So early walking did I see your son:

With tears augmenting the fresh morning's dew,
Adding to clouds more clouds with his deep sighes.

On the death of his beloved Matilda he marries her friend Isabella, the betrothed of Manfred's dead son—not because he loves her as well, but because, as the bosom friend of the departed, she can assist with her memories in keeping alight the eternal melancholy which now pervades his soul. In appearance he resembles the portrait of his ancestor Alfonso, which depicts "a lovely prince, with large black eyes, a smooth white forehead and manly curling locks like jet." With this description the outward appearance of the romantic hero was established once and for all.

Clara Reeve's hero, Edmund, appears in similar circumstances to those of Theodore. He too is of unknown birth; his mother has disappeared and he grows up a poor farmer. But his great gifts, his manly and open nature and unfaltering love of truth distinguish him from the crowd and procure him a better education and honours. Finally, in a marvellous manner, he too regains the titles and property of his ancestors. In his case, the clue to his identity is a necklace left him by his mother.

On the whole Mrs. Radcliffe's young heroes resemble those described above, but are still more romantic, braver and more "refined." Osbert, the young lord of Athlin, is especially prominent in military exercises, for as the son of a noble he has inherited qualities. His lively and warm imagination make him a lover of poetry, inclined to day-dreaming; his favourite pastime is to wander in the stern, romantic mountains of Scotland, much as Beattie's Edwin. The fearsome and sublime attract him more than the gentle and harmonious. "Wrapt in the bright visions of fancy" he often loses himself "in awful solitudes." In outward appearance he is tall and majestic, his behaviour and manners are tinged with nobility, while in his countenance manliness and dignity are combined. This earlier type of Mrs. Radcliffe's undergoes development in that it is later completed, as in the case of Valancourt in *The Mysteries of Udolpho,* by the addition of a rococo elegance of deportment, while in his manners, even in his speech, one discerns a touch of pastoral sensitivity which often degenerates into tearful sentimentality. Many of these heroes have familiar tasks assigned to them—their duty is to rise on the strength of their legal rights from insignificance to an influential position and great happiness. The mysterious birthmark is not lacking: "It is my Philip. That strawberry on his arm confirms the decision."

As a general rule the type appears in these romances as the protector and future husband of the persecuted heroine. (pp. 38-40)

Let us now improve our acquaintance with Walpole's persecuted maiden, with the virtuous Isabella. When, with evil purpose, Manfred seizes her hand, terror renders her half-dead; she screams and flees from him. Whither? Where find a shelter from the tyrant's clutch? In the castle's mysterious vaults, of course. Thither she hastens, but there new terrors assail her. Every little noise and breath of air fills her heart with dread. She walks on tiptoe and as slowly as her impatience will allow, stopping frequently to listen for pursuers. Suddenly she seems to hear a mysterious sigh. Trembling with fear she retreats a pace or two. Then it seems to her that someone approaches; her blood curdles, for she believes herself about to fall again into Manfred's power. All the horrors the imagination can call up rise before her mind, and at that very moment a gust of wind extinguishes her lamp (with which, despite the suddenness of her flight, she is provided) and she is left helpless in pitch darkness. At this critical moment the author skilfully guides to her side the young hero, who leads her through secret caves and passages to shelter. Even at such a moment as this, however, the maiden does not forget her womanly dignity and good reputation: "Alas! what mean you, sir?" said she. "Though all your actions are noble, though your sentiments speak the purity of your soul, is it fitting that I should accompany you alone into these perplexed retreats? Should we be found together, what would a censorious world think of my conduct?"

In spite of her many vicissitudes, Isabella finds happiness in the end. Otherwise is it with Manfred's daughter Matilda. Although she is of surpassing beauty and only eighteen, her father fails to show any interest in her. At the death of her brother she tries to restrain her own sorrow, the better to be able to console her despairing parents. A quiet timidity is part of her nature; she feels that her vocation is to become a nun. Hearing the sentence pronounced by Manfred, that Theodore's head is to fall "this very instant," she sinks into a swoon. And when she opens the door of Theodore's prison to set him free, it is with the remark: "Young man, though filial duty and womanly modesty condemn the step I am taking, yet holy charity, surmounting all other ties, justifies this act." She will not blame her father for her death, but forgives everything, like the "emanation of divinity" she is said to be.

Clara Reeve's Emma has nothing particularly romantic about her. She is an ordinary gentle and beautiful girl without even any remarkable adventures. After a happy childhood she marries the hero, presenting him, in the quickest possible time, with five sons and a daughter, all of which is carefully recorded by the author. The "persecuted female" in this romance is Edmund's mother.

In Mrs. Radcliffe's mind there was an especially clear picture of what a romantic maiden ought to be, which she presents with the gesture of one showing off an ideal. The type in question is about twenty, of medium height, slenderly built, but extremely well-proportioned. Her face is half-hidden by the dark hair which falls in plaits over her bosom. Her beauty is enhanced by the "soft and pensive melancholy" which lends to her blue eyes such an interesting air. Where the question is of two sisters, one of them, Emily, for instance, is of harmonious and feminine build and has a beautiful face, fair hair and a "sweet expression" in her dark-blue eyes, while Julia is airier and livelier, with dark and flashing eyes and dark auburn hair which curls in beautiful profusion upon her neck. An attempt is sometimes made to describe the heroine by relating how she tried to hide her face in her robe, and how, notwithstanding, the long auburn tresses which flowed in "beautiful luxuriance" over her throat and bosom revealed an inkling of her "glowing beauty." In danger or anguish her face takes on an expression of "captivating sweetness." Almost every one of Mrs. Radcliffe's maidens are described in this manner. "In person Emily resembled her mother, having the same elegant symmetry of form, the same delicacy of features, and the same blue eyes, full of tender sweetness." A brunette beauty is described thus: "Dark brown hair played carelessly along the open forehead; the nose was rather inclined to aquiline; the lips spoke in smile, but it was a melancholy one; the eyes were blue, and were directed upwards, with an expression of peculiar meekness; while the soft cloud of the brow spoke the fine sensibility of the temper."

We are even given a little information regarding their education. Nearly all are skilful in drawing and cannot look upon a "sublime landscape" without attempting to immortalize it with their pencil. Embroidery is another of their accomplishments, and they are exceedingly skilled in music. "Laura was particularly fond of the lute, which she touched with exquisite sensibility." The lute is the favourite instrument of persecuted maidens, for its sad tinkle when fingered in the twilight or in the pale moonlight under the influence of melancholy or grief or unhappy love accords well with their emotions and the melting tunes they are wont to hum.

Such is approximately the maiden of these romances. In Walpole's story she is still at the Ophelia-Imogen stage, but in Mrs. Radcliffe's works she becomes the realization of her own ideal of maidenhood, reflecting the qualities demanded in those days of a really refined young maiden. To the type attaches something of the mincing virtue, coyness and capacity for blushing at the right moment found in the heroines of pastoral poems and in rococo womanhood, all with good manners as their ultimate aim. The romantic maiden of impetuous and passionate type whom we might have expected to find, the maiden who loves rashly, is still unknown; though in Mrs. Radcliffe's habit of dividing her heroines into fair and dark types there is some indication of future developments in this quarter. Some amount of influence seems ultimately to have been exerted by a model from the immediately preceding period—by Samuel Richardson's type of young woman. If we divest Isabella of her medieval costume, listen to her conversation and take note of her fortunes, we soon discover "the virtuous maiden in distress." Both types are young and unusually beautiful, noble in their thoughts and exceedingly jealous of their virtue, which tyrants and wicked lords do their best to threaten. Their chastity is constantly in the greatest danger, but each time Pamela seems on the point of ruin, she manages to escape unharmed, exactly as Marina in *Pericles*. Both preserve their mental balance in the most delicate situations, until, mostly after countless tears, blushes, and moral sermons, they end up with a happy marriage. Richardson defines Clarissa Harlowe in the following terms: "A young Lady of great Delicacy, Mistress of all the Accomplishments, natural and acquired, that adorn the Sex, having the strictest Notions of filial Duty."

This existence of endless persecution was now laid by the Walpole-Reeve-Radcliffe trio in romantic surroundings, and given greater effectivity by real adventures, the chief feature of which is a perpetual flight from persecutors in circumstances of great romanticism and terror. The maiden with adventures is familiar from Shakespeare, but in his case the type is, so to speak, commonly active, and not, like the maiden of early romanticism, a passive figure. What makes the persecution and hairbreadth escapes of the romantic maiden interesting to the student of literature is that, as a factor of excitement added to the plot, they point the way to the novel of excitement, and can for this reason be regarded as constituting a practically new invention of great vitality. (pp. 40-3)

> Eino Railo, "The Haunted Castle," in his The Haunted Castle: A Study of the Elements of English Romanticism, *George Routledge & Sons, Ltd., 1927, pp. 1-80.*

DEVENDRA P. VARMA

[*An Indian-born Canadian educator and critic, Varma special-

izes in the study of British Gothic literature. In the following excerpt from his* The Gothic Flame: Being a History of the Gothic Novel in England *(1957), Varma investigates the techniques of the Gothic novelists.*]

"Beneath the multifarious crotchets and pinnacles, with which the Gothic novelists adorned his fictional fantasies, lay certain general principles of structure," says Michael Sadleir. In texture and design these novels echo the intricate workmanship of Gothic cathedrals. These authors build their tales around suggestive hints and dim pictures; their pastoral scenes and complicated adventures are deftly related to the final catastrophe. Their masterly ordering of incidents, their contribution to the structure of the novel as an art form, is distinctive and impressive. The Gothic novel was not a cul-de-sac, but an important arterial development of the novel.

These novelists were the first to perceive and emphasize the dramatic method which has since become a platitude of narrative theory. Their methods and technique inspired Scott's feelings for individual scenes, led to the use of dramatic methods by Victorian novelists, the use of suspense in short stories by Poe and his successors, and eventually the mystifications and solutions of the modern detective novels and thrillers.

To bring the supernatural palpably into a scene, requires a bold experiment on the part of the novelist, and necessitates a long note of preparation and a whole train of circumstances that may gradually and insensibly lull the mind to an implicit credence. A series of incidents alone is, however, not enough to evoke terror; these have to make a strong impression on the mind. The Gothic novelist knew the potentialities of his art, and achieved his effects by one of two methods: the realistic or the poetic. The first attempted to produce a semblance of fact by means of detailed description or by pretence to a logical sequence of reasoning; the second aimed at arousing a poetic faith of the kind that Coleridge called "a willing suspension of disbelief." The Gothic novelists adopted either or both methods and reinforced effects by skilfully and powerfully agitating the reader's feelings.

One may justly assert that the true interest in story form came only with Gothic fiction. By bringing in new interest and excitement, it gave the novel an unprecedented popularity which has not waned even to this day. The very titles of novels published between 1740 and 1760 show how realistic fiction veered round the life of an individual personality, the chief source of interest, while all the authors laid a general emphasis on the truthful portrayal of contemporary life. Dr. Huffman considers the "four broad principles" governing English novelists of the eighteenth century. They are: the statement of a moral purpose, the truthful depiction of contemporary English life, the constant predominance of reason and common sense, and the observance of probability in plot, characters and machinery.

Smollett, in his dedication in *Ferdinand Count Fathom*, defines the scope of a novel and states that although a novel should achieve the realistic portrayal of life, it must provide for a leading character as a focal point of production: "A Novel is a large diffused picture, comprehending the characters of life . . . for the purposes of an uniform plan, and general occurrence, to which every human figure is subservient. But this plan cannot be executed with propriety, probability, or success, without a principal personage to attract the attention, unite the incidents, unwind the clue of the labyrinth." The picaresque novel had emphasized action in and for itself, but the Gothic novelists used 'action' to contrive and resolve complications of plot. As Scott pointed out: "the force, therefore, of the production lies in the delineation of external incident, while the characters of the agents . . . are entirely subordinate to the scenes in which they are placed."

Now, when the force of production hinges upon external incident, there is a new emphasis upon a careful placing of the incidents, which are striking and impressive, so as to sustain the interest of the long narrative. According to Mrs. Barbauld: "the unpardonable sin in a novel is dullness: however grave or wise it may be, if its author possesses no powers of amusing, he has no business to write novels."

When Walpole added dramatic effects to the old fairy-tales, he evolved a new technique in fiction, based on the principle of suspense. These books were the first to establish 'suspense' as the major ingredient in a novel, and their deliberate and artistic manipulation of this new tool of their craft is something quite different from the methods of Richardson and Fielding. Dr. A. C. Kettle emphasizes that "the works of great novelists of the eighteenth century never depended for effect on the unexpected, except in the sense of verbal wit and incongruous situation in comedy." But the critics with their usual tardiness were not ready to accept the quality of suspense as a necessary concomitant of the novel: "The story of a novel should be formed of a variety of interesting incidents; a knowledge of the world and of mankind are essential requisites of the writer. . . . Sentiments should be moral, chaste and delicate . . . language easy, correct, elegant," we read in the *Monthly Review* (1790). There is no mention here of suspense or excitement.

The artistic manipulation of suspense in the Gothic tales developed along various lines. First we meet with "the black veil" method of Mrs. Radcliffe: Emily in *The Mysteries of Udolpho* quivers in front of a dark velvet pall which uncannily sways in the nocturnal wind. She draws aside the veil to confront a hideous corpse, putrid and dropping to decay. Again in the chamber of the dead Marchioness she shivers before the inky curtains, and perceives the folds moving unaccountably, when suddenly a repulsive face peers out at her. Inexplicable music forms another common device for creating suspense. Mysterious disappearances likewise increase the tension. Lights that glimmer and fade away, doors which open and close without any mortal aid, and groans and wails of unexplained origin heighten the effect. Dread secrets half-revealed at the hour of death, and mysterious manuscripts half-deciphered in failing light, likewise stimulate intense curiosity.

The technique of spot-lighting individual scenes [is] another contribution of the Gothic novel. Certain pictures do stand out from the rest strongly enough, amidst all the eddies and whirlpool of incidents, for the reader's imagination to remain focused on them.

Indirectly, by tracing in fiction the progress and consequence of one strong, indulged passion, another trait adopted from the drama, they gave an impetus towards that science of psychology which was to turn into a craze and fashion a hundred years hence. They forecast the technique of the future novel by presenting certain subtle studies of character-physiognomy. Thus, by portraying mental states and emotions of characters, they enlarged the scope of the novel, and by sounding the whole gamut of fear, pointed towards the psychological novel of over a century later.

The Gothic villains are a prime example of their creator's instinctive feeling for psychologically interesting characters who yet merge with the pervading theme of the supernatural. We can distinguish three types of Gothic villain: the character of Manfred fashioned by Walpole in 1764, a type composed of ambitious tyranny and unbridled passion, who developed through Lord Lovel of Clara Reeve's *The Old English Baron;* the early villains of Mrs. Radcliffe, culminating in Count Montorio of Maturin and the character of Guzman in *Melmoth the Wanderer,* and also another descended from Karl Moor, the chieftain of Schiller's *Robbers* (1781). The latter type presents an "imposing figure." He is an outlaw, a Rousseauistic sentimentalist, a humanitarian who combats life's injustices, follies, and hypocrisies. Haunted by a sense of loneliness, helplessness, and despair, similar Victims of Destiny are La Motte in *The Romance of the Forest,* Falkland in *Caleb Williams,* and in *St. Leon,* the disfigured, misanthropic outlaw captain.

The third type of Gothic villain is the terrible 'superman' whose ways lie in darkness and whose strength originates far beyond mortal thought. He is a new mintage of the Satan portrayed by Milton in *Paradise Lost*—the immortal outcast, a masterful, vaunting villain, his spirit unbroken even in defeat. He is the Rosicrucian, the Alchemist staking his very life on some dark hope, and behind him is all the mystery of Cabbala, Freemasonry, Medieval Satanism. This Miltonic superman appears in these novels for the first time in Eblis, ruler of the realm of despair in Beckford's *Vathek* (1786). Nine years later Lewis introduced Lucifer in *The Monk*. Schemoli, the villainous monk of Maturin's *Family of Montorio* (1807) is obviously modelled upon his formidable predecessor Schedoni, Mrs. Radcliffe's physical superman endowed with a ruined aristocratic past and mysterious intellectual power.

These three main types have been presented in order of increasing complexity. Manfred, a kind of wicked baron born out of fairy-tale, becomes the Victim of Destiny, a supersensitive being drawn to evil against his better will, impelled by blind Fate; a character who sentimentalizes over bygone days. The superman combines the qualities of both— Manfred assumes a gigantic physique and overwhelming motive, and the Victim of Destiny is now presented as the victim of injustice. Like Satan or the Ghost-Seer he has tempted fate, or has a Faustian compact imposed on him like the Wandering Jew. Paying an outrageous price for enormous benefits, he usurps his powers, then wraps his suffering in proud and lonely gloom. These three main types are fluid concepts which continually interact, though not annihilating distinction, for the Gothic villain remains to the last not a bundle of characteristics, but a set of characters. For the most part he is all melodrama and extravagant emotion, designed to excite the last possible twinge of sensation. His gradual development illustrates increasing skill in the art of romance. In him we see also the emergence of the 'Romantic' character—an alien soul solacing itself in occult experiments with forbidden sciences or unscrupulous deeds. Lastly, the Gothic villain, like Frankenstein's monster, destroyed its creator, the Gothic novel. (pp. 213-16)

The Gothic novelists produced surrealistic effects by the extensive use of grotesque contrast. Walpole had introduced the tricks of light and shade, colour and line, in his novel. Mrs. Radcliffe juxtaposed sound and silence, a kind of surrealism of atmospheric suggestion: a dead calm precedes the horrors of her tempest, sounds of retreating steps are followed by a stillness as of the grave, the music sinks low and faint as the afar off castle gates close at night and all grows still as death, a profound stillness marks the pauses of the surge breaking loud and hollow on the shore, the windows of the great hall are dark and, the torch being gone, nothing glimmers in the pitchy night save a solitary star. Even the faint, intermittent susurrus of leaves deepens the solemnity of silence. In the works of the Schauer-Romantiks, scenes of entrancing sweetness are balanced against episodes of gruesome horror; the macabre accompanies the voluptuous, as in the famous Dance of Death.

An important surrealistic technique of 'telescoping' images is also employed by these authors. These novels are neither historical nor descriptive of ancient medieval manners, but essentially descriptive of the eighteenth century; and the fantastic telescoping of the two may be called a surrealistic technique. (pp. 221-22)

The Gothic romance is not concerned with a realistic approach to life. Character study and the social emotion of humour did not appeal to its authors. They aimed at awakening the twin emotions of Pity and Fear, but mainly Fear, as being more sublime. It must be acknowledged that Fear exerts a potent spell upon the human mind: horrid stories do impart a fearful joy. Human nature craves not only for amusement and entertainment but also demands the more strenuous catharsis of pity and terror. The tale of terror appeals to some deeply rooted human instinct; an irresistible, inexplicable impulse drives us towards the macabre. Man in the darkness of his ignorance is attracted mothlike by the fascination of weird and eerie themes pertaining to his own death. As is the glory of the flame for the moth, so "our instincts of love and terror are the foundations respectively of our sense of beauty and the sublime," says Edward Niles.

The tempestuous loveliness of terror exerted a powerful fascination for the Gothic novelists. Alonso, the Spaniard, in *Melmoth the Wanderer*, remarks, in his description of the death of the parricide torn to pieces by the mob: "the drama of terror has the irresistible power of converting its audience into its victims", and "Alas! in what moment of success do we not feel a sensation of terror!"

The attempt to achieve Beauty through the medium of Terror, was ultimately an experiment with Burke's theory that everything calculated to awaken mental images of agony, of danger, or of things giving the effect of fear, remains a profound source of the sublime. We feel that they practically demonstrated Burke's theory of Fear and Sublimity. In his *Inquiry into the Origin of our Ideas of the Sublime and Beautiful* (1757), Burke had already defined the range and scope of the "Novel of Terror." Mrs. Radcliffe adhered to his doctrine of the equivalence of the obscure, the terrible, and the sublime when she invoked feelings of dread under the obscurity of the triple mantle of night, desolation, and gloom, and by not carrying the idea of pain and danger as far as violence sustained her sublimity, producing a delightful horror, a kind of tranquillity tinged with terror. In her introductory essay to *Sir Bertrand*, a fragment (1773), Mrs. Barbauld attempts to explain how and why scenes of terror excite pleasurable emotions. She also discriminates between the scene of natural horror in Smollett's *Ferdinand Count Fathom* and the marvellous and terrible incidents in Walpole's *Otranto*.

The Gothic novelists led the readers to an ultimate state of terror through slow degrees of mounting suspense. The sublime terrors excited by great passions and catastrophes, approximate to the tragic emotions of pity and exaltation. Around these works hovers a spirit akin to that of tragedy, at least in the medieval and commonly accepted sense of a fall from high estate to misery and a wretched end. We cannot but feel our emotion go out towards Schedoni, Montoni, or Ambrosio in their hour of death. Villains they may have been, but we have been the constant spectators of their crimes and motives, and at the time of retribution we feel a deepening of understanding and sympathy.

Other properties of Burke's *Inquiry*, the stern beauty of mountainous landscapes, cataracts, and soaring eagles, the grandeur of storms with clashing thunder and lightning, the conflict of mighty nature's elements, are used by the Gothic novelists to arouse the emotions of terror and horror. Threatening physical exposure to the harshness of Nature is purely agonizing, but when felt only by the imagination, the pain is overpowered by sublime pleasure.

This type of literature chiefly concerned with the primitive excitement born of danger, battle, pursuit, the supernatural, fearful events, and visions, and love, appeals to the widest circle and gratifies the desire of its readers for something greater than reality, something they may admire and in their dreams would emulate.

If a work of art is the complement of life and a compensation for reality, if it does satisfy the need for spiritual activity, which ordinary reality does not satisfy, and if its purpose be to purify language, then the Gothic novel is a legitimate art form. It revived our apprehension of life itself by enlarging our sensibility, making readers more conscious of the kinship of terror and beauty and renewing awestruck wonder at possible forms of being. (pp. 225-26)

> *Devendra P. Varma, in his* The Gothic Flame, *A. Barker, 1957, 264 p.*

CORAL ANN HOWELLS

> [*In the following excerpt, Howells describes the techniques used by Gothic novelists to suggest emotional states.*]

I want to adopt Horace Walpole's emphasis on feeling as the distinctive attribute of Gothic—feeling as it is explored and enacted in the fictions themselves, and feeling as the primary response elicited from the reader. As its name suggests with its medieval associations, Gothic is allied with everything which is the opposite of Augustan: instead of notions of order and decorum and rational judgement, it represents the darker side of awareness, the side to which sensibility and imagination belong, together with those less categorisable areas of guilt, fear and madness which are such important and terrifying components of the earlier Augustan anti-vision and of Romanticism. Gothic fiction with its castles and abbeys, persecuted heroines, ghosts and nightmares, projects a peculiarly fraught fantasy world of neurosis and morbidity, and if we take a close look at the kinds of feeling in which these novelists were especially interested we begin to perceive how anti-Enlightenment anxieties were actually 'felt on the pulses' of a whole generation. There is nothing confident or optimistic about Gothic fiction: its main areas of feeling treat of melancholy, anxiety-ridden sentimental love and horror; it is a shadowy world of ruins and twilit scenery lit up from time to time by lurid flashes of passion and violence. All the time we have the uncomfortable sense of being in a fantasy world which is about to reveal secrets of the human personality—indeed straining towards these revelations—and yet constantly kept in check by the negative forces of guilt and repression. It is this sense of an imprisonment which is both psychological and linguistic that Robert Kiely [see Further Reading] defines as a quality of all Romantic fiction:

> The emotions on which they dwelt were too imperfectly understood or too threatening to be systematically rationalised, except by someone as daring as the Marquis de Sade. They explored feelings and compulsions which were not merely impolite to mention but often difficult to label and describe.

His statement has particularly interesting implications for the Gothic novelists, the very bizarreness of whose fiction shows how daring their attempts were to articulate some of the more disconcerting features of the life of the feelings. It is their vocabulary of emotional and imaginative experience and what it reveals about the Gothic state of mind that I intend to explore.

Gothic fiction is a literature full of curiosity, doubt and anxiety, and at this distance in time we can see working through it the same subversive forces that produced the French Revolution, the Marquis de Sade and the Romantic poets. The trouble was that the Gothic novelists didn't know what to do with their feelings of frustration and rebelliousness. Many of them were middle-class women, while Lewis was the son of the Deputy Secretary of War and Maturin was an Irish clergyman; all they knew was that they were dissatisfied and anxious. Their fiction is both exploratory and fearful. They are not always totally in control of their fantasies, for having opened up new areas of awareness which complicate life enormously, they then retreat from their insights back into conventionality with the rescue of a heroine into happy marriage and the horrible death of a villain. There is a profound unease and fear of anarchy which runs side by side with expressions of frustration at conventional restraints throughout Gothic fiction. These novelists feared the personal and social consequences of any release of passion or instinctual drives, as we can see in those narratives where the action is taken to its conclusion in the self-destruction of Lewis's Monk or the damnation of Maturin's Melmoth. As the result of their deep suspicions of the affective life, what they frequently did was to betray the forces they felt so strongly for they suffered from the worst kind of fear which trivialises important issues and ends by being totally reactionary—socially, politically and morally.

These tensions may explain why the Gothic novelists chose romance as their fictional form. By adopting a mode which is recognised as being separate from everyday life, they were free to create a fictional world which embodied their fears and fantasies and offered a retreat from insoluble problems, while at the same time it rendered their fears ultimately harmless by containing and distancing them in a fantasy. Gothic fiction is a most ambiguous form, for like romance it emphasises the intuitive, the arbitrary and the supernatural—what Henry James calls 'the disconnected and uncontrolled experience' (Preface to *The American*). However, the feelings out of which such fantasies spring are recognisably late eighteenth-century: they are all areas of anxiety relating to the same dilemmas that Richardson and Jane Austen acknowledged—problems of personal moral responsibility and judgement, questionings of restrictive convention, and a troubled awareness of irrational impulses which threatened to subvert

orthodox notions of social and moral propriety. These anxieties occur with obsessional frequency in Gothic fiction and though sublimated into forms which appear fabulous and unlikely, they are at the same time distorted images of real emotional tensions and moral dilemmas. (pp. 5-7)

Perhaps the real embarrassment to Gothic writers was their sense of their duty as moralists, for as writers of quasi-romance they were caught in the difficult position of trying to satisfy two entirely different demands: on the one hand the claims of orthodox Christian morality and its extension into social propriety, and on the other hand their own imaginative imperatives leading them in the opposite direction into the dynamics of impulse and irrationality, aided and abetted, of course, by their reading public's appetite for excitement. The effect of these two conflicting pressures is frequently quite disastrous, robbing their work both of moral conviction and of imaginative truth. They still adhered to the Johnsonian doctrine of the didactic purpose of fiction:

> In narratives where historical veracity has no place, I cannot discover why there should not be exhibited the most perfect idea of virtue . . . Vice, for vice is necessary to be shown, should always disgust; nor should the graces of gaiety, or the dignity of courage, be so united with it as to reconcile it to the mind.
>
> (*Rambler* Essay no. 4, 31 March 1750)

All the Gothic novelists are inheritors of this moralistic doctrine, claiming as Richardson had done that their novels were written for the sake of 'Example and Warning' (Richardson's letter to Lady Bradshaigh, 15 December 1748). The only trouble was that in fiction whose appeal was so obviously to the imagination rather than to the judgement and where the criteria of judgement were themselves called into question, the interpretation of events at the end in Christian moral terms frequently looks inappropriate as a comment on the moral and emotional issues raised within the novels. They do not enact a moral argument as Richardson or Fielding had done in their very different ways; instead of the sense of a problem being worked through, what we have is a series of partial insights into dilemmas, the implications of which are finally abandoned as the writers give up and give in to conventions endorsed by society and by the traditions of novel writing.

The ambivalent attitude of Gothic writers inevitably affected the way they presented emotion. Though they always insist on the powers of feeling and imagination they tend to concentrate on external details of emotional display while leaving readers to deduce for themselves complex inner psychological movements, from such evidence as a 'certain wildness of aspect' or a 'settled paleness of the countenance'. Their splendid displays of strong feeling often seize our attention but only add to the mystery of the feelings which could have provoked them. Take the two following passages, written twelve years apart:

> The desperate courage which the Marchese had assumed now vanished; he threw himself back upon the pillow, his breath shortened, the cold dews paced each other down his forehead, he veiled his face, which exhibited a cadaverous paleness, with the coverture; and stifled groans, and irregular respiration, were all the symptoms of remaining existence.
>
> (Eleanor Sleath, *The Orphan of the Rhine*, 1798.)

Terrified by the sudden violence of her manner, the soul-harrowing expression of her yet supremely-lovely features, our heroine remained motionless—one hand of her mother she yet retained within her own tremulous grasp; but it was the next moment withdrawn, and the convulsed form of Madame de Saussure staggered toward the sofa.

> (A. F. Holstein,
> *Love, Mystery, and Misery!* 1810, i)

Both these descriptions are typical of the way Gothic novelists record emotion: there is a precise recognition of its violent physical effects and at the same time perceptible on the author's part a shocked withholding of sympathy or a perplexed incomprehension like that of 'our heroine' in the second passage. As readers we are consistently placed in the position of literary voyeurs, always gazing at emotional excess without understanding the why of it: what we are given are the gestures of feeling rather than any insight into the complexity of the feelings themselves. The springs of these emotions elude us, so that we can only look on with appalled fascination as floods of feeling rush through the characters distorting their physical features with alarming rapidity:

> Pride, grief, horror, amazement, indignation, dismay, alternately agitated, alternately glowed in every feature.
>
> (Louisa Sidney Stanhope,
> *The Confessional of Valombre*, 1812, i)

As the result of this preoccupation with externals Gothic novels have frequently been criticised for being sensational, theatrical and melodramatic. It seems to me that these three words ought not to be taken only as adverse criticism, for they exactly describe the peculiar quality and the contemporary appeal of Gothic fiction. Gothic techniques are essentially visual in their emphasis on dramatic gesture and action and in their pictorial effects, giving the reader an experience comparable to that of a spectator at the theatre. Indeed, at no other period has the English novel been so close to the drama as it was between 1790 and 1820. We may think that the wholesale transplanting of dramatic techniques into prose fiction is uncomfortable or inappropriate, but as an experiment in widening the emotional rhetoric of the novel what the Gothic writers did is undeniably interesting. When we consider that these novelists from Walpole to Maturin without exception acknowledged Shakespeare as the major influence on their work, and that some of them, for example Lewis and Maturin, wrote more plays and melodramas than novels, not to mention the ease with which Gothic novels were adapted for the stage (e.g. Boaden's melodramas *Fontainville Forest* and *The Italian Monk* from Mrs Radcliffe's novels, and *Aurelio and Miranda* from Lewis's *Monk*), we begin to realise how accurately the word 'theatrical' can be used to describe the techniques and the effects of Gothic fiction.

It is easy to understand the appeal that Shakespeare would have had for these novelists when we relate Walpole's remarks in his *Otranto* prefaces to the way in which Dr Johnson interprets the qualities of Shakespearean drama in his *Preface to Shakespeare* (1765). Both of them saw his genius as essentially English and outside the classical orders of art, belonging to the English nation and its literature in its infancy when people were mainly interested in tales of 'adventures, giants, dragons, and enchantments'. All that 'Gothick mythology of fairies', as Johnson calls it, was outside the ordered social and moral ethos of the modern age, back in the 'barbarous times':

> He had no regard to distinction of time or place, but gives to one age or nation, without scruple, the customs, institutions and opinions of another, at the expense not only of likelihood but of possibility.

Johnson's scrupulous weighing of Shakespeare's looseness against his 'endless variety' and his concern with 'the general passions and principles by which all minds are agitated' was assimilated by novelists later in the century in so far as they saw Shakespeare as the image of freedom in literature. His plays pointed to the direction they wanted to follow, in subject matter and in methods of presentation. Speaking of Shakespeare's use of the marvellous, Johnson said:

> His plots, historical or fabulous, are always crowded with incidents, by which the attention of a rude people was more easily caught than by sentiment or argumentation and such is the power of the marvellous, even over those who despise it, that every man finds his mind more strongly seized by the tragedies of Shakespeare, than of any other writer; others please us by particular speeches, but he always makes us anxious for the event, and has perhaps excelled all but Homer in securing the first purpose of a writer, by exciting restless and unquenchable curiosity and compelling him that reads his work to read it through.

What Johnson did was to free Shakespeare from the charges of irregularity brought against him by neo-classical formalism, while Walpole showed how his plays could be used as models for fiction. In so doing, they made Shakespeare available to a new generation of writers who interpreted him and used him according to their own liking. Using his plays as models they borrowed his plots, his dramatic situations and his character types. The most cursory glance through Gothic novels will reveal the extent of Shakespearean borrowings: three of the 'Horrid Novels' mentioned in *Northanger Abbey* are prefaced by Shakespearean quotations, even though they may be as inapposite as Francis Lathom's description of his Gothic thriller *The Midnight Bell* (1798) as a 'round unvarnish'd tale'; and Lewis actually reveals the secret of *The Monk* in his quotation from *Measure for Measure* at the head of Chapter I. Shakespearean scenery with its wild Scottish heaths, storms and shipwrecks, funereal vaults and castle ramparts, influenced the landscape of terror fiction, combining as it did with other current enthusiasms for Ossian, the sublime and medieval architecture.

Macbeth and *Hamlet* appear to have been the most popular plays with novelists, providing as they do models for almost every kind of dramatic crisis by which men's passions are revealed, from supernatural fear to murder, revenge, madness, distracted love, melancholia, and agonised penitence. There are an abundance of Gothic murder scenes which bear a close resemblance to Hamlet's midnight visit to Claudius or to the murder of Duncan, while Lady Macbeth's tormented vision of the blood on her hands is the model for all those scenes where women who have committed crimes of passion are tortured by their guilt. Signora Laurentini in *Udolpho* and Lady St Clair in Mrs Kelly's *Ruins of Avondale Priory* (1796) are women of the Lady Macbeth type, while in *The Midnight Bell* the image is used quite literally: the hero is awakened by his mother, her hands covered in blood, her eyes wildly fixed and her hair dishevelled, who tells him to fly the castle instantly, 'as you value life, as you value heaven'. Then of course there are any number of agonised villains like Macbeth, distracted lovers in the dishevelled Hamlet style, and heroines of a distinct Ophelia cast in their sweetly pathetic expressions of wandering wit. Ghosts wander on battlements in the moonlight world of *Udolpho* and of Mrs Sleath's *Nocturnal Minstrel* (1810), while Scottish heaths peopled by mysterious figures veiled in mist are regular scenic features from Mrs Radcliffe's *Castles of Athlin and Dunbayne* (1789) right through the 1790s and into the nineteenth century with novels like Mrs Kelly's *Baron's Daughter* (1802) and Horsley-Curteis's *Scottish Legend* (1802), Francis Lathom's *Romance of the Hebrides* (1809) and Jane Porter's *Scottish Chiefs* (1810). Sir Walter Scott's poems and the Waverley Novels when they began to appear in 1814 were enthusiastically received by a reading public who had become accustomed by a long literary tradition to associate Scotland with mystery and adventure.

These random examples suggest how pervasive the Shakespearean influence was, for Shakespeare's plays provided a picturesque vocabulary of feeling which satisfied the current taste for highly-wrought emotions and inflated language. The Gothic novelists imitated Shakespeare's methods for showing passions in action, though they ignored his subtle investigations of those passions which made violence convincing. They were also hampered by the moral restriction of dealing with passions only in order to condemn them, so the result was often a reduction of Shakespeare to eighteenth-century moral cliché. Perhaps the most complete example of Shakespeare *moralisé* was Mrs Eliza Parsons' *The Mysterious Warning* (1796) based on *Hamlet*. She took the play and transformed it into a moral fable about the destructive effects of the passions on man's happiness and hopes of salvation. Despite the nature of her original, she was able to declare her honourable intention and her own negative merits in her Dedication to the Princess of Wales: 'I have never written a line tending to corrupt the heart, sully the imagination, or mislead the judgment of my young readers.' Taking as her motto 'Thus conscience can [sic] make cowards of us all', Mrs Parsons shapes her narrative into a triumphant conclusion of virtue over vice which she then celebrates in the lines

> Foul deeds will rise
> Though all the earth o'erwhelms them, to men's eyes.

The balance of *Hamlet* is drastically altered to fit in with Mrs Parsons' moral thesis about the infallible workings of Providential justice, so that though the themes of revenge, incest and fraternal treachery are preserved, moral and emotional qualities are re-allotted. The revenge motif is transferred from the hero to his wicked brother, and Hamlet's gloom and cynicism become the dominant traits of the penitent villains. Ferdinand, Mrs Parsons' Hamlet figure, emerges as the noble sentimental hero, the champion of virtue who performs the sacred trust of bringing unnatural behaviour to light and seeing that it is punished. Unlike Hamlet he is a man of decisive action who accomplishes his purpose and is rewarded by marriage to the girl he loves. The ghost figure gives the mysterious warnings about his brother's treachery which the hero receives, though finally the phenomenon is revealed to have been extraordinary rather than supernatural. (All the time it was the voice of a faithful old retainer who, like the ghost of Hamlet's father, knew the truth about secret evil deeds done by members of the family.) Mrs Parsons' belief in the unsearchable ways of Providence has something in common with Hamlet's fatalism, recommending as it does endurance, patience and acceptance, though only, I feel, because she believed that Providence was synonymous with poetic justice:

> In vain may the wicked hope to deceive the virtuous and unsuspecting mind, unobserved and undiscovered; there is a watchful and unerring eye, to whom all their black and artful schemes are laid open, and who, in its own good time, defeats the machinations of the wicked, and brings the offenders to the punishment they deserve.
> (*The Mysterious Warning,* Folio Press, 1968, iv)

In comparison with its prototype, *The Mysterious Warning* is inferior in every respect except its sensationalism. (pp. 14-20)

Inevitably in the novels as in the theatre certain patterns of facial expression and gesture came to be associated with certain feelings just as appearance indicated certain character types, and it is needless to detail the many 'fearful despairing groans' of the villains, the 'chilly agues of terror', the 'distracted looks' and 'deathy cheeks', or 'streaming tears of rapture' that proceeded from true lovers reunited. There is no doubt some validity for depicting extreme states of emotion according to a fixed pattern; the very choice of extremes limits the possibility of varied reactions. As Virginia Woolf points out, there are not many possible ways of registering shock and terror:

> It is unlikely that a lady confronted by a male body stark naked, wreathed in worms, where she had looked, maybe, for a pleasant landscape in oils, *should* do more than give a loud cry and drop senseless. And women who give loud cries and drop senseless do it in much the same way. That is one of the reasons why it is extremely difficult to write a tale of terror which continues to shock and does not first become insipid and later ridiculous.
> (*Granite and Rainbow,* ed. L. Woolf, 1958)

The Gothic novelists always tended to exaggerate emotional responses, so we find them more often depicting unusual heights and depths than showing the vast intermediate area of variable feeling which constitutes much of everyday life experience. Their repertoire was in fact limited by their preference for hysteria and emotional violence, a feature which became exaggerated in the minor fiction written between 1800 and 1810 into a wallowing in emotional display. (Incidentally, similar criticisms of overacting in the theatre were more frequently made at the same time, against the successors of Mrs Siddons and J. P. Kemble.) Hysterical insistence on emotional reaction finds its most superb rationale in the statement made in 1810 by A. F. Holstein in *Love, Mystery, and Misery:* 'If a frame is convulsed by deepest emotion, and the countenance with anguished suffering, the depiction is too strong to be misinterpreted.'

The absurdity to which physical display could lead is illustrated in the amusing account of how Thomas Babington Macaulay once kept a list of the number of fainting fits which occurred in a five-volume Minerva novel of 1806 (Kitty Cuthbertson's *Santo Sebastiano*). His list of faintings reads as follows:

Julia de Clifford	11
Lady Delamore	4
Lady Theodosia	4
Lord Glenbrook	2
Lord Delamore	2
Lady Enderfield	1
Lord Ashgrove	1
Lord St. Orville	1
Henry Mildmay	1

Macaulay's sister ends the account by selecting a typical passage from the novel 'to serve as a specimen of these catastrophes': 'One of the sweetest smiles that ever animated the face of mortal now diffused itself over the face of Lord St. Orville, as he fell at the feet of Julia in a death-like swoon.'

Language is also affected by extensive borrowing from the drama so that like physical appearance and gesture it is a kind of attitudinising and cannot function as an individuated statement of feeling. The flexibility which we recognise in the dialogues of Richardson, Fielding or Sterne has vanished, for now heroes and heroines speak in elegant formulae while villains rant and rave in extravagant hyperbole. Walpole, conscientiously imitating Shakespeare, had made an attempt to give the servants dialectal speech and we find instances of liveliness in the speech of 'low' characters throughout the period, but apart from Maturin's convincing Irish peasant dialogues in *Melmoth,* it is humorous caricature rather than genuine speech. When we compare the effect of Gothic novelists' use of dialect with that of Scott or Dickens, we see very little of that delight in verbal inventiveness which characterised the greater writers. Instead of conversation giving us an insight into a character's mind and feelings, in the Gothic novel the effect is just the opposite: particulars of individual feeling are blurred by orthodox rhetoric, and conversation is restricted by decorum to being a statement of the outward appearance of emotion.

Another method much favoured by these novelists for suggesting emotional states and atmosphere was the presentation of landscape. The novels are full of sublime and picturesque scenic descriptions, sometimes evoking a purely aesthetic response in the reader, but more frequently used as a kind of visual correspondence suggestive of an inner psychological state. Like Jane Austen, we cannot imagine a Gothic novel which doesn't have a castle or an abbey—or at least a monastic cell—for there is a distinctive Gothic environment which is both fairytale and menacing. It is an aesthetically created world, a farrago of popular eighteenth-century pictorial images deriving from the paintings of Claude Lorrain and Salvator Rosa, the architectural fantasies of Piranesi, and a general enthusiasm for the medieval revival. Not only is it a world lacking in substance, but when we compare Gothic descriptions of houses and scenery with those in the novels of Fielding, Richardson or Jane Austen, we find a disturbing shift in the authors' imaginative response to the world outside themselves. Instead of a sense of stability and harmony what we find in Gothic fiction is a dreadful insecurity in the face of a contingent world which is entirely unpredictable and menacing.

It is interesting to speculate why Fielding gave Squire Allworthy a Gothic house to live in in *Tom Jones.* He called it Paradise Hall:

> The Gothic style of building could produce nothing nobler than Mr. Allworthy's house. There was an air of grandeur in it that struck you with awe, and rivalled the beauties of the best Grecian architecture; and it was commodious within as venerable without.

The contrast between what Gothic represents in this Augustan novel and the disturbing connotations which such architecture assumed in later novels is very revealing of the different authorial attitudes to the world in which they lived. Fielding transformed his Palladian models in order to emphasise certain anti-Augustan qualities about Squire Allworthy

which he admired. Paradise Hall as its name suggests is like Eden, 'awe-inspiring, grand, noble, venerable', and by making it Gothic rather than Palladian Fielding is defining its difference from the Augustan world. Gothic here is as much associated with feeling as it would be for Horace Walpole thirty years later, but Fielding sees feeling as a good value belonging to the expansive era of pre-Augustan innocence. Everything in the description of Allworthy's house and his park points to harmony and stability; Gothic actually enhances this by carrying within it the religious connotations of cathedrals and notions of pre-Lapsarian innocence. With Richardson something of the hole-and-corner nature of Gothic creeps in as we see Pamela imprisoned by Squire B. in an old rambling house with owls hooting; and certainly Clarissa shares the sense of nightmarish imprisonment with later Gothic heroines. However, for Richardson a house still has a solid existence of its own with its whole domestic organisation going on uninterruptedly, whatever its imaginative transformations within the heroine's mind. Jane Austen's Palladian houses withstand any disintegration in the order of things, Donwell Abbey, Pemberley and Mansfield Park remaining as the very emblems of stability and harmony. By the time we get to Jane Austen we notice that a radical change has taken place in attitudes to Gothic architecture, so that after the 1790s it would be impossible for a writer to contemplate a Gothic edifice as anything other than radically unsound.

With Gothic novels the stability of the external world breaks down in the way it had threatened to do in Richardson; it has become interiorised, translated into the private world of imagination and neurotic sensibility. Nothing is constant any more: an ordinary room can suddenly be transformed into nightmare by the unlooked-for appearance of a ghost in a chair or a waxen figure covered in worms hiding quietly behind a velvet curtain; objects look different in the moonlight from what they do in the daytime, and things are not necessarily what they seem. Stone walls are not solid any more but are full of sliding panels and secret doorways opening onto winding staircases, while the foundations of Gothic castles are honey-combed by endless labyrinthine passageways which end in cells or funeral vaults or perhaps open into the light of day. Scenery shifts arbitrarily from one episode to the next; this is not merely related to the conventions of romance landscape but more fundamentally to the general instability and impermanence of things, when even castles like Udolpho or the prisons of the Inquisition can fall down or suddenly lose their solidity and power, melting back into the landscape of nightmare. When I suggested earlier that the Gothic world was the external image of the characters' (or the novelists') own obsessions, I was trying to make clear how the configurations of Gothic have a psychological rather than a physical existence. When reading Gothic fiction we have no sense of the real world even in the passages of static picturesque description, partly because they derive from the imaginary landscapes of painting and partly because they have only the most illusory stability. Even life in the countryside so nostalgically conjured up by writers like Mrs Radcliffe and Mrs Roche no longer has the peace and predictability which Fielding gave to it, for heroines can be snatched away from this security at a moment's notice by the arbitrary will of some powerful figure of authority. Everything in the Gothic world is exaggerated: the tranquil beauty of the country, the seemingly infinite corridors of castles, the dimness of moonlit landscapes, the ferocity of storms, the ruggedness of mountains—so that what began as an aesthetic response to environment becomes an imaginative recreation of the world.

When we talk about dream landscape in Gothic novels we are talking about a fictive world whose topography is shaped by and is the shape given to emotional responses to uncertainty and threat—the world of nervous breakdown from which Pamela and Clarissa were saved. (pp. 22-7)

> Coral Ann Howells, "Gothic Themes, Values, Techniques," in her Love, Mystery, and Misery: Feeling in Gothic Fiction, *The Athlone Press, 1978, pp. 5-27.*

ELIZABETH R. NAPIER

[In the following excerpt, Napier analyzes techniques used in early Gothic novels to create formal resolution.]

Many Gothic novels, following a pattern made popular in eighteenth-century poetry and prose, exhibit a strong tendency towards closure, towards stabilization and formal resolution. In no other respect does the Gothic novel betray its kinship with previous fiction more clearly. The urge to stabilize, especially marked in the early Gothic, indeed is often so extreme that other facets of the work, such as character and probable plot, are sacrificed to it; the occasionally disjunctive results are rarely acknowledged or explored. (Mary-Anne Radcliffe is a hesitant exception: she concludes *Manfroné,* her sensational tale of evil, with the directive that the reader should attempt to extract from it lessons of virtue and happiness.) That closure should be insisted upon with such vehemence, and often with such *naïveté,* may strike one as surprising in view of the fact that these novels have repeatedly been called 'pre-romantic'. Structurally speaking, few of the early works exhibit designs that are consciously or coherently 'romantic' (at least in McFarland's or Weiskel's sense of the term). This failure to depart in any radical way from the structures of prevailing modes of fiction suggests the essentially conservative attitude of many of the first Gothic writers. Intent, it seems, on adapting to the current taste for the marvellous, or on stretching the limits of fictional design to see, for example, how extreme or remote an experience may still afford a lesson in moral sentiment, the early Gothic remains undisruptive because the basic structure of its experience is still so familiar.

The need to solve and resolve (seen most clearly in Ann Radcliffe's desire to explain the supernatural occurrences in her tales) is a striking feature of early Gothic. In *The Castle of Otranto, The Old English Baron, Longsword,* and the novels of Ann Radcliffe, the ultimate aim is a state of moral and social equilibrium. The vicious are punished, the virtuous are rewarded, and social and ethical imbalances are tidily corrected. *The Castle of Otranto* opens with a complex and mysterious tangle of political and familial relationships. Manfred, falsely reigning in Otranto after his grandfather's murder of Alfonso the Good, seeks to ensure the continuation of his princedom by uniting his line with that of the family he has wronged. Unable, finally, to forestall a mysterious prophecy about the loss of the kingdom he has usurped, the villain's plans collapse, and the story ends with the true heir of Alfonso restored and Manfred retired to do penance in a convent. *The Old English Baron* (a story that revolves similarly around a murder and an unjust usurpation) concludes with political and ethical inequities again set to rights: Edmund, the son of the murdered Lord Lovel, assumes his rightful title and marries the virtuous Emma, and Sir Walter, his crimes revealed, is permanently banished from England. Even the haunted

apartment undergoes a transformation: it is repaired and refurbished for the use of the faithful Sir Philip Harclay. Leland's *Longsword,* one of the earliest historical novels to exhibit 'Gothic' traits, in an effort to achieve a similar final equilibrium, even goes so far as to defy the historical events on which it is based. The Earl of Salisbury, who in actual fact died from the poison given him by Hubert de Burgh, triumphs over his enemy and lives on in fiction to a ripe and rewarding old age. The management of priorities is particularly interesting here. The demands for historical accuracy (despite the assertions at the opening of the story) are clearly not as strong as those for structural balance and ethical justice. Throughout these works, aesthetic pleasure seems to derive from simple—indeed, simplistic, and often forcible—resolutions of situations of imbalance: identities are confirmed, families reunited, and rightful heirs restored.

In this almost obsessive desire to mete out rewards and punishments at the works' ends, it is not unusual to encounter frequent allusions to a coming resolution: Reeve and Walpole (as, later, Radcliffe and Lewis) utilize prophecies and dreams to prepare the reader for the revelations of character and event that are to come, and both novelists make use of family resemblances (Theodore-Alfonso; Edmund-Lord Lovel) to foreshadow the relationships that lie at the centre of the novels' mysteries. The prediction of such resolutions is a relatively simple affair; it depends mainly, as Sedgwick has argued, upon the reader's ability to recognize superficial similarities among characters and events. In works in which characters are delineated with more subtlety, the achievement of resolution brings more dramatic procedures into play. In such works, sudden tonal shifts or abrupt flattenings of character may occur as the authors make decisions about their players' final destinies. Thus, La Motte, in Ann Radcliffe's *The Romance of the Forest,* whose weaknesses have given rise to a complex combination of sympathy and detestation on the part of the reader, is not permitted to share in the concluding celebration of Adeline and Theodore, despite his apparent reform. The novel's absolute polarization of good and evil necessitates that virtuous and erring characters finally remain permanently apart. Radcliffe's dismissal of La Motte from the novel he has helped to energize suggests the tensions inherent in such a situation:

> For La Motte, who had been condemned for the robbery on full evidence, and who had been also charged with the crime which had formerly compelled him to quit Paris, a pardon could not be obtained; but at the earnest supplication of Adeline, and in consideration of the service he had finally rendered her, his sentence was softened from death to banishment. This indulgence, however, would have availed him little, had not the noble generosity of Adeline silenced other prosecutions that were preparing against him, and bestowed on him a sum more than sufficient to support his family in a foreign country. This kindness operated so powerfully upon his heart, which had been betrayed through weakness rather than natural depravity, and awakened so keen a remorse for the injuries he had once meditated against a benefactress so noble, that his former habits became odious to him, and his character gradually recovered the hue which it would probably always have worn, had he never been exposed to the tempting dissipations of Paris.

La Motte, under the pressures of the happy ending that banishes misfortune and vice, virtually ceases at the finale of the novel to function as a character: he becomes, rather (through the subjunctive tense), something he 'might have been', and at last is erased: his response to his fate contributes not to an understanding of his own character, but highlights the charity of Adeline.

Radcliffe's experiments with ethically mixed figures (like La Motte) are usually this cautious. Though in *The Mysteries of Udolpho* there are brief moments that betray an admiration of Montoni, and though in *The Italian* she shows an increased interest in characters of this kind, in the end she is unwilling to confront the complex moral judgments such 'tainted' heroes would demand. As a literary character, Schedoni meets a fate more punishing than La Motte: allowed a generous share of the reader's sympathy as the novel progresses, he is made to sacrifice it at the close as Radcliffe causes him to perform a revenge against Nicola that erases any trace of goodness in his character. . . . Radcliffe's hestitation at working with 'mixed' characters is seen most complexly in *The Mysteries of Udolpho,* the most openly self-questioning of her novels, in the figures of Valancourt and St Aubert. Both these men, essentially good, are made to appear to err. St Aubert reveals a connection with the Marchioness de Villeroi that is mysterious and possibly romantic, and Valancourt during Emily's absence appears to have involved himself in a life of dissipation in Paris. For modern readers, these aspects of Valancourt's and St Aubert's characters are interesting, for they deepen and considerably humanize the two men. To discover that their suppositional deeds are, in effect, devices to delay the catastrophe of the story and to extend a sense of mystery that is one of plot, not of psychology, brings Radcliffe's priorities startlingly into focus. The issue of Valancourt's offences is settled, summarily, when it is discovered that his lapses have been unjustly exaggerated; the more tantalizing question of St Aubert's guilt, a possibility that Radcliffe keeps open almost to the end of *Udolpho,* is similarly closed when the identity of the Marchioness de Villeroi is revealed. In both of these cases, Radcliffe toys with, but ultimately retreats from, the creation of potentially complicated characters into the realm of moral absolutes.

The finales of many Gothic novels, particularly, underline the authors' special desire to impose stability and meaning upon the events they have created: 'Here', Radcliffe writes at the end of *A Sicilian Romance,* 'the manuscript annals conclude. In reviewing this story, we perceive a singular and striking instance of moral retribution. We learn, also, that those who do only THAT WHICH IS RIGHT, endure nothing in misfortune but a trial of their virtue, and from trials well endured, derive the surest claim to the protection of heaven.' 'All these [papers], when together,' concludes Reeve in like fashion in *The Old English Baron,* 'furnish a striking lesson to posterity, of the over-ruling hand of Providence, and the certainty of RETRIBUTION.' *The Mysteries of Udolpho* ends on a similarly resonant note: 'O! useful may it be to have shewn, that, though the vicious can sometimes pour affliction upon the good, their power is transient and their punishment certain; and that innocence, though oppressed by injustice, shall, supported by patience, finally triumph over misfortune!' Matilda, in Eliza Parsons's *Castle of Wolfenbach,* restored to her rights as the daughter of the Countess Berniti, enunciates the moral in a letter she writes to Mother St Magdalene: ' "From you," said she, "I learned resignation, and a dependence on that Being who never forsakes the virtuous; from you I learned never to despair . . . I shall ever remember the unfortunate have claims upon the hearts of those whom God has blessed with

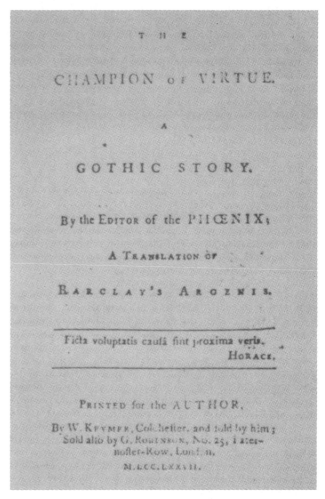

Title page of Clara Reeve's The Champion of Virtue: A Gothic Story, *later published as* The Old English Baron.

affluence; and that, through your means, reserved to experience every blessing of life, I shall feel it my duty, by active virtues, to extend, to the utmost of my abilities, those blessings to others less fortunate than myself." '

The strident tones and crude attempts at emphasis, often through typographical devices of capitalization, italics, and spacing, reveal a mingled determination to be explicit about the moral lessons to be gained from such tales of adventure and an uncertainty about the relevance of those 'lessons' to the narrative that has produced them. Mary-Anne Radcliffe thus concludes *Manfroné; or, The One-Handed Monk* by arguing that her unrelieved tale of the vices of mankind has been designed to show the beauty and superiority of goodness:

> Here the pen pauses: with its weak efforts it has endeavoured to delineate the vices of mankind, placing them in such a glaring view, with the hope of exciting in the bosom of the reader that horror and detestation which must make him studiously avoid giving way to those turbulent passions that vitiate the mind, and render it insensible to the charms of virtue; and may these pages, which shew him the misery attendant on evil actions, in all his researches after worldly enjoyment and felicity, deeply im-

> press on his mind, beyond the prevailing power of
> vice to erase, the never-failing maxim, that
>   *'To be good is to be happy!'*

In such Gothic novels as Sophia Lee's *The Recess* and Ann Radcliffe's *The Castles of Athlin and Dunbayne,* the tendency of the narrative voice to make confident generalizations about human behaviour has a similar stabilizing effect, because it suggests, as, for example, in Fielding's *Tom Jones,* that the reader is in the hands of a thoughtful and wise director, whose moral values resemble his own. Charlotte Dacre's *Zofloya* opens with a description of the main characters, doomed early in life because of their mother's transgression with an unprincipled count. Throughout the setting of this scene, Dacre intrudes to moralize on child-rearing, self-love, and depravity. (pp. 9-15)

In *Castle of Wolfenbach* there is a similar tendency to merge the dramatic with the authorial or editorial, so that what often begins as a conversation ends as a moral message delivered directly to the reader from the author. (p. 16)

The tendency of Gothic characters to speak in highly generalized, non-particularized terms is remarkable, for it emphasizes not only the relative flatness of their characters, but the inclination in Gothic works of the moral to intrude on—and often overshadow—the dramatic. In *Castle of Wolfenbach,* interestingly, most of the violent, Gothic elements of the novel are not presented by means of enacted situations at all, but through interpolated stories of injustice told by victims and perpetrators. The violence of the tale, with the exception of the bloody moment in which Matilda finds the servant of the Countess of Wolfenbach, is thus filtered for the reader because it is presented at a second remove from the actual event.

Radcliffe's novels also display this predilection: 'It is the peculiar attribute of great minds,' the author interrupts in *The Castles of Athlin and Dunbayne,* 'to bear up with increasing force against the shock of misfortune; with them the nerves of resistance strengthen with attack; and they may be said to subdue adversity with her own weapons.' In Radcliffe's later novels, authorial commentary becomes less frequent; the moralizing urge still exists, but its burden is increasingly shifted to her characters, who frequently utter generalizations about human nature in dialogues or sometimes wearying apostrophes. 'The world', muses St Aubert, in an example of such a passage, 'ridicules a passion which it seldom feels; its scenes, and its interests, distract the mind, deprave the taste, corrupt the heart, and love cannot exist in a heart that has lost the meek dignity of innocence. Virtue and taste are nearly the same, for virtue is little more than active taste, and the most delicate affections of each combine in real love. How then are we to look for love in great cities, where selfishness, dissipation, and insincerity supply the place of tenderness, simplicity and truth?' The slowing of pace and abstract quality of the diction here point to the difficulty of fitting the generalizing authorial voice to a character engaged in a dramatic situation. Such reflective interludes are frequent in Radcliffe's work and contribute to that quality of meditativeness that characterizes her novels; the intention, ultimately, seems to be to assure the reader that, even in the midst of events that defy his usual sense of what is possible, normal ethical codes are still in operation. The tacit assurance is that what appears on the surface to be a fantastic or unjust series of incidents will eventually be resolved, and in a fashion consistent with what is morally right.

What is sometimes perplexing about this moralizing tendency, however, is that in the lesser novels of the genre it often assumes a disjunctive relationship to the action that supposedly inspires it. Thus, in Mary-Anne Radcliffe's *Manfroné,* a rhapsodic speech on the transitory and delusive nature of human joys accords but ill with the adventures of dark forms and folded mantles that will shortly interrupt it. The disruptive combination of the two modes of narrating is seen in the description of Montalto's wounding: 'The soul of Montalto, calm and full of content, communicated its repose to its mortal habitation, and the happy lover, slumbering, became unconscious of what was passing around him—became unconscious of a dark savage form that hung over him, and who, putting his hand within the folds of his mantle, drew from thence a dagger!—Ah! where was then the guardian spirit which watches over the safety of the virtuous?' The hackneyed, metaphoric use of images of gulfs, brinks, and graves in such moralizing passages inadvertently calls to our attention how uncomfortably such idioms sit with narratives that resolve so insistently around the real thing:

> How transitory, how delusive are human joys!
> when we think we hold the phantom happiness in
> our grasp, it vanishes! Always in pursuit, yet we
> never attain it . . . Still, however, we fondly look
> forward, and in fancy see the air-formed gorgeous
> temple of human happiness rising stately before
> us—we see its wide-folding portals open to receive
> us—when, alas! we suddenly awake, and find it was
> but a mere delusion of the brain—a delusion which
> made us mindless of the wide-yawning gulf, on
> whose dreadful brink we totter, and often are lost.

The lack of self-consciousness in a passage such as this one is startling; the author shifts from one rhetorical mode to the next with no apparent awareness of disjunction or collision.

This tendency of a sermonizing tone to deepen the reader's sense of disruption is occasionally manifested on the level of the novel's plot. Sometimes, in fact, an author's moralizing serves as a mask beneath which he may adjust events to fit the forthcoming needs of the story. Thus, again in *Manfroné,* when Father Augustino dies, the narrator exclaims, 'What a pleasing, soul-elevating sight it is to behold the last sighs of the just!' The point of the scene, however, is not to moralize about death, but to remove Father Augustino from the story so that the Marchese de Montalto can appear at the attempted marriage of Rosalina and Manfroné.

In the novels of Lewis, Shelley, or Maturin, the difficulties of contending with such moral commentary increase. In Shelley's *Zastrozzi,* it is ominously absent; in *The Monk* and *Melmoth the Wanderer,* narrative interpolations have an effect of disturbing rather than orienting the reader:

> Scarcely had the Abbey-Bell tolled for five minutes
> [Lewis begins *The Monk*], and already was the
> Church of the Capuchins thronged with Auditors.
> Do not encourage the idea that the Crowd was assembled
> either from motives of piety or thirst of information.
> But very few were influenced by those
> reasons; and in a city where superstition reigns with
> such despotic sway as in Madrid, to seek for true
> devotion would be a fruitless attempt.

The opening of Melmoth's tale is similarly destructive to a full sense of participation on the part of the reader; it is interlarded with a puzzlingly irrelevant and unconnected profusion of literary allusions: 'No one knew so well as she', Maturin writes in a particularly garbled passage, 'to find where the four streams met, in which, on the same portentous season, the chemise was to be immersed, and then displayed before the fire, (in the name of one whom we dare not mention to "ears polite"), to be turned by the figure of the destined husband before morning.' Maturin's repeated intrusions of learned material into his supernatural narrative violate the tone in odd ways: John Melmoth is said to pore over the crumbling manuscript of Stanton's temptation like an antiquarian hoping to find 'some unutterable abomination of Petronius or Martial, happily elucidatory of the mysteries of the Spintriæ, or the orgies of the Phallic worshippers'. By the time Monçada's tale is introduced, Maturin's work has developed a sinister and unrelieved congruity of tone; the incongruities that precede it, however, are so extreme as to appear almost burlesque. (pp. 17-20)

Gothic novels may be generically stabilized by hearkening back to the procedures and language not only of history but of older, recognized fictional modes. Radcliffe's novels in particular, and the late 'sentimental Gothic' fiction of Roche and Parsons, exhibit a regard for providential meetings and rescues that recalls the works of Fielding or Goldsmith. Adeline, in *The Romance of the Forest,* persecuted by La Motte and the Marquis, is thus said at the end to survive by 'a destiny . . . to punish the murderer of her parent. When a retrospect is taken of the vicissitudes and dangers to which she had been exposed from her earliest infancy, it appears as if her preservation was the effect of something more than human policy, and affords a striking instance that Justice, however long delayed, will overtake the guilty.' Julia, in *A Sicilian Romance,* is similarly convinced that providence has 'conducted [her] through a labyrinth of misfortunes to this spot, for the purpose of delivering [her mother]'. The emphasis is even more overt in the earlier works of Leland and Reeve. 'I adored', proclaims Longsword, 'the preserving hand of heaven, whose influence had appeared so evidently in these events. The treachery of D'Aumont in seeking to destroy me, had opportunely conveyed me from the power of my enemies. The violence and oppression of Chauvigny, had proved the means of sending me deliverers, when fortune seemed most to frown upon me . . .' The passage sounds almost like Defoe: Longsword assumes the familiar retrospective stance that clarifies events that have been shrouded in mystery and speaks in syntactically balanced clauses that demonstrate the relationship between apparent evil and universal good.

Coincidences abound in Gothic fiction and are regularly attributed to the effects of providential supervision; heroes inevitably appear in the nick of time, at the most unlikely times, and in the most unlikely places. The reader is not meant to be surprised, but tantalized, when Manfroné discovers his own hand washed up on the shores of Lake Abruzzo. Even ghosts—the question of whose existence is often a source of embarrassment to Gothic writers—are tentatively put down to the infinite power of providence. As Madame de Menon muses to Emilia and Julia in an interesting passage in *A Sicilian Romance,*

> 'Who shall say that any thing is impossible to God? We know that he has made us, who are embodied spirits; he, therefore, can make unembodied spirits. If we cannot understand how such spirits exist, we should consider the limited powers of our minds, and that we cannot understand many things which are indisputably true. . . . Such spirits, if indeed

> they have ever been seen, can have appeared only by the express permission of God, and for some very singular purposes; be assured that there are no beings who act unseen by him; and that, therefore, there are none from whom innocence can ever suffer harm.'

These are curious observations, because Radcliffe finally in her novels regularly attributes all ghost-like effects to human agency; here, she seems to amuse herself with the thought that ghosts exist, but then evades the larger consequences of this view by attributing the possibility in the most conventional way to the hand of God. In *The Old English Baron,* Reeve's insistence on the effects of providential agency often creates—in a similar way to the works of Defoe and Smollett—interesting tensions between the stasis or stability achieved by the providential view and the forward impetus required by the narrative of adventure: 'Doubt not, said Oswald, but Heaven, who has evidently conducted you by the hand thus far, will compleat its own work; for my part, I can only wonder and adore!—Give me your advice then, said Edmund; for Heaven assists us by natural means'. The final sentence of *The Old English Baron* strikes an unmistakably Christian note: 'All these [papers], when together, furnish a striking lesson to posterity, of the overruling hand of Providence, and the certainty of RETRIBUTION. Thus one must be, perhaps, more cautious about generalizing, as do Nelson [see Further Reading] and Hume [see excerpt above], about the degree to which the Gothic is a form marked by the disappearance of God. Early Gothic works emphatically exhibit the same complex plots and the same attentiveness to providential coincidence as did their forebears and often adopt the same language to talk about it. Indeed, many of the first Gothic romances are simply moral tales in supernatural dress—the Gothic elements, that is, do not transform the structure of the narrative in any significant way; rather, they readorn and refurbish what to its readers would have been an old familiar form. This is certainly James R. Foster's view of the Gothic [see Further Reading]; to him, the mode is not revolutionary at all, but takes its place within a tradition of sentimental novel writing influenced primarily by Prévost:

> The true nature of the so-called Gothic novel has been misunderstood . . . The critics who have hit upon supernaturalism as the most distinctive and significant element, have done this in spite of the fact that a part of the body of the fiction they pretend to describe is plainly controlled by a rationalism that forbids anything more than a mere toying with the appearances of the marvellous . . .

The novel which reached a phase of its development with Ann Radcliffe played with ghosts, but its main purpose was obviously to tell a sentimental tale of adventure. . . .

(pp. 23-5)

[Many] Gothic novelists spoke openly about the sentimental nature of their endeavours. Many, like Clara Reeve, Regina Maria Roche, and Eliza Parsons, showed themselves adept at both genres, and many sentimental novelists (among them Charlotte Smith) in turn made free use of Gothic devices. The link, indeed, between Gothic and sentimental fiction is strong: both modes assume the primacy of feeling, and the pleasure of exercising it vicariously, and gain their effect by encouraging particularly strong emotional responses from their readers. The forms can overlap because it is the intensity of the response and not the type of experience eliciting the response (pleasurable, terrifying) that is in question. Gothic novels are, thus, replete with sentimental episodes: love affairs between young unfortunates generally occupy the centre of the plot and scenes of fainting and melancholy yearning are frequent. The plight of Parsons's Matilda in *Castle of Wolfenbach* is, in fact, more Richardsonian than Gothic. Pursued by the B-like Mr Weimar, Matilda has just overheard her uncle and his confidante, the Jewkes-like Agatha, plotting her ruin in the summer-house. Her response (like that of many of Parsons's and Roche's leading ladies) is directly in the sentimental tradition: 'Having heard thus far I tottered from the summer-house, and got into the shrubbery, where I threw myself on the ground, and preserved myself from fainting by a copious flood of tears!' Matilda escapes with her servant that night. Clara Reeve claimed in her dedication to *The Exiles* that 'it has always been my aim to support the cause of morality, to reprove vice, and to promote all the social and domestic virtues', and her *Old English Baron* originally bore a more adamant (if less romantic) title: *The Champion of Virtue*. Regina Maria Roche's highly popular *The Children of the Abbey,* a novel almost as beloved as Radcliffe's *Mysteries of Udolpho* in its time, and often described as Gothic in tone, is thoroughly sentimental in nature with only one incident—that of Amanda's discovery of Lady Dunreath in the castle—that could be called truly Gothic. (pp. 26-7)

[The] essentially decorative effect of the Gothic has repeatedly been condemned by critics and has made the form particularly vulnerable to satire. Most of the novels gain resonance and continuity by making use of the same devices: ruined castles, secret panels, concealed portraits, underground passageways. There is surprisingly little variation on this design. Even in more sophisticated examples of the genre, such as the novels of Maturin, where the devices, bolstered by other aspects of the narrative, become more psychologically suggestive, they occupy an undeniably prominent position. In extreme cases—those of Reeve or Lee, for example—the essential 'Gothicness' of the work attaches almost exclusively to these properties. An attempt to isolate the distinctive qualities of Gothic narrative brings the reader repeatedly back to this characteristic: Gothicism is finally much less about evil, 'the fascination of the abomination', than it is a standardized, absolutely formulaic system of creating a certain kind of atmosphere in which a reader's sensibility toward fear and horror is exercised in predictable ways. To include 'modern Gothic' novels such as *Wuthering Heights, Moby Dick,* and *Sanctuary* in the same category as Radcliffe's *The Italian* or Lewis's *The Monk* because they have in common 'a distinctive and pervasive atmosphere [of evil]' [Hume, see excerpt above] is to overlook the primacy of such a system. This is not a popular stand to take towards the Gothic because much of the more spirited recent criticism of the genre has been explicitly directed towards denying that it is 'a collection of ghost-story devices'. Underlying such reassessments is the assumption that psychological or moral ambiguity—of the kind present in *Wuthering Heights, Moby Dick,* and *Sanctuary,* but not in Ann Radcliffe's works—lends a dignity to the form that the emphasis on Gothic properties threatens to jeopardize. The devices, thus, in a critical sleight of hand that here seems particularly out of place, become necessarily signifiers of some deeper meaning. Any honest reading of Gothic fiction shows that the pleasure—and not the despair—of the text arises fairly forthrightly from the repetition of a certain series of extremely conventional scenes, events, and landscapes. The superficial and the formulaic thus, paradoxically, form the very heart of the Gothic, and because of this, the genre can acquire stability across itself (as television serials do) by making repeated use of the same interesting settings and events. Keats's letter to Reynolds of 1818 exhibits the kind of delight that an exaggerated attention to the formulaic can produce: ' . . . I am going among Scenery whence I intend to tip you the Damosel Radcliffe', he writes, '—I'll cavern you, and grotto you, and waterfall you, and wood you, and immense-rock you, and tremendous sound you, and solitude you. . . .' It was, of course, this predilection for the formula—and the ease with which it was copied—that allowed the proliferation and final degeneration of the form into the 'shilling shockers' or 'bluebooks' of the early nineteenth century.

The Gothic novelists' interest in the device may not at first appear to pose any particular problems—novels of this kind, the argument runs, exempt themselves from serious consideration because of their obvious superficiality. But the adherence to formulas (basically a technique of the surface) signals a concern with the superficial that, as Eve Sedgwick [see Further Reading] and Coral Ann Howells [see excerpt above] have pointed out, finds its way into other, more significant facets of the genre's form, and particularly into character. Sedgwick's exploration of this attribute of the Gothic illuminates the important repercussions of such a technique:

> . . . the fascination with the code in Gothic novels is so full and imperious that it weakens the verbal supports for the fiction of presence . . .
>
> It is in the insistence of this constitutive struggle, and the attenuated versions involving the veil and the habit rather than the countenance itself, that the Gothic novel makes its most radical contribution to the development of character in fiction. In a (novelistic) world of faces where the diacritical code is poor but where all nonlinguistic, or nonsignifying, discriminations are elided in its favor . . . two things will happen. First, there will be unbounded confusions of identity along the few diacritical axes: any furrowed man will be confusable with any other furrowed man (Schedoni with Zampari with Zeluca, for example), and so forth. Second, when the time comes to settle these confusions, the normal tools for doing so—nonce discriminations, the differentiations that happen not to be coded, 'This one has blue eyes and that one, I remember, had brown eyes . . .'—will be unavailable. The noncode level of discriminations having been vitiated by the fascination of the code, the only reliable basis for comparison will be one of those complete literal, ocular juxtapositions. And that will be reliable only to the degree that the two faces approach being line-for-line identical. (I.e., there is such a thing as a decided 'Yes! They are exactly the same' but no possible criterion for a decided 'No.') There seem to be no noncoded differences between persons that could not also occur in any one person over time.

The almost exclusive concern with two-dimensional characters in the Gothic becomes obvious when one attempts to discriminate between characters of different works: Radcliffe's heroines, Julia, Adeline, Emily, and Ellena, as was frequently observed by critics in Radcliffe's time, are a case in point. . . . Even conversation, muffled by the dictates of convention, provides no key to their inner minds [according to Coral Ann Howells]: ' . . . particulars of individual feeling are blurred by orthodox rhetoric, and conversation is restricted by decorum to being a statement of the outward appearance of emotion.' What we are finally given, in Howells's words, are 'gestures of feeling', 'external details of emotional display' rather than 'any insight into the complexity of the feelings themselves'. This emphasis on the superficial not only marks Gothic characters' personalities and actions; it is often used as a device to generate suspense about those characters. The supposed orphan Matilda in *Castle of Wolfenbach* (who at the end of the novel turns out to be the daughter of the Countess Berniti) is repeatedly referred to as gentle in countenance and bearing. '[H]er person, her figure, the extraordinary natural understanding she possesses', the Marquis exclaims, 'confirms my opinion that so many graces seldom belong to a mean birth or dishonest connexions'. The servant Bertha detects her goodness immediately, and the Countess of Wolfenbach, whose chambers are accidentally visited by Matilda, tells her that her countenance 'is a letter of recommendation to every heart'. The reader's recognition of Matilda's gentility, in a novel that places little emphasis on the exploration of internal states, must be accomplished through outward signs. Howells thus speaks convincingly of the 'theatricality' of the Gothic, of its emphasis on dramatic action and visual display. Walpole's characters, denied the language of the heart, act out the passions that move them in highly physical ways: Frederic, consumed with guilt at his passion for Matilda, falls to the ground 'in a conflict of penitence and passion'. A confusingly disproportionate relationship develops here that deserves examination: the more florid the emotional display, the more, as readers, we are discouraged from seeking the reasons for such a display. Our clues reduced to a series of conventional gestures (screams, shudders, faints, sighs), we are virtually prevented from developing anything more than a programmed response to stock Gothic situations. The satirical portrait, common in the criticism of the period, of two novel-reading ladies at the circulating library points to the (ironically) ineffective result of what appear to be situations calling for maximal emotional response:

> 'My dear Laura, have you read the new novel I recommended to you, The Animated Skeleton? I assure you it is the production of a very young lady, and is her first appearance in that character.'—*L.* 'Heaven grant it may be her last! What, a young lady in the character of an animated skeleton? I protest I shudder at the bare idea.'—'Pooh! You will know better soon! To be sure they used to frighten me a little at first, but it is nothing when you are used to it; there is nothing else now, and for my part I would not give a farthing for a novel that had not something about ghosts, and skeletons, and hobgoblins, and Emily walking alone with a great lamp in her hand through a parcel of damp cellars, in search of something to terrify her to her heart's content.'

In view of this kind of character (and reader) impoverishment, it becomes increasingly difficult to justify the application of such concepts as 'psychic archives' [see Hogle, Further Reading] or 'disintegration of identity' [Howells; see excerpt above] to Gothic fiction, for both these terms assume a depth of personality that characters in such works almost consistently lack. Indeed, in the early Gothic in particular, characters are systematically sacrificed to other, more highly valued, aspects of narrative such as moral or plot. This subordination of character in Gothic fiction recurs frequently enough to cast doubt on recent critical celebrations of the Gothic as psychologically exploratory. The extent to which

Gothic writers willingly analyse their characters obviously differs—Radcliffe's treatment of Schedoni in *The Italian* or Lewis's of Ambrosio in *The Monk* are obviously more complex—but it is one of the more perplexing and interesting characteristics of Gothic fiction that its practitioners become adept at retreating from a full exploration of the characters they create. Even in the case of Radcliffe's Schedoni or Lewis's Ambrosio, the villains lose much of their vitality by the end of the novel: Schedoni, in murdering Nicola, commits a revenge so horrible that it eliminates any trace of sympathy we might have had for him, and Ambrosio, like Victoria in Charlotte Dacre's *Zofloya,* is impoverished by his author's refusal to come to terms with his temptations as human ones. Like Dacre, Lewis at the close reveals the tempter to be Satan in disguise. Particularization of character is rare, which is why, in Sedgwick's view, there tends to be 'unbounded confusion along the diacritical axes'; most Gothic villains look alike and virtually all Gothic heroines do. Indeed, in an interesting, though understandable, slip of priorities, the real heroes of the Gothic may be, as Maurice Lévy has suggested, and as many titles of Gothic novels confirm, not people at all but buildings: the novelists' failure to explore internal psychological spaces is often more than compensated for by an intense interest in setting.

Characters in the Gothic are often, in fact, so highly generalized or idealized that no truly individual portraits emerge at all. Sir Philip, in Reeve's *Old English Baron,* is an example of such a figure. His reaction to the death of his friend, Lord Lovel ('The will of heaven be obeyed!'), is so impersonal and formulaic that we cease to be aware of him as a personality; he becomes, rather, a commentator on actions that are being performed by others.

Scott noted a similar subordination of character to scene in the work of Ann Radcliffe, commenting that the force of her production lay in 'the delineation of external incident' and not in character. Characters, indeed, are often lost sight of in moments of marked scenic intensity in Radcliffe's fiction. Her heroines respond to Alpine scenery with the same enthusiastic awe whatever their circumstances: even Ellena, as she is being abducted through the machinations of the Marchesa di Vivaldi, temporarily forgets her misfortunes in the face of a glorious mountain pass.

This same quick sacrifice of character may also occur as a response to the demands of plot. In such instances, characters will suddenly exhibit behaviour that has no relationship to their previous actions. Walpole's *Castle of Otranto* contains two such figures: Isabella's father, Frederic, who has not shown significant signs of weakness since his introduction in the novel, wavers in his mission in order to complicate the plot and increase the possibilities of Manfred's union with the heroine. Manfred himself repeatedly becomes sensitive when the plot requires it, when a period of respite is needed for Isabella, or when Walpole wants to strengthen the impact of a pathetic scene. In *The Mysteries of Udolpho,* Emily resists the evil reports of Montoni's character with a *naïveté* she exhibits nowhere else in the novel. Rosalina demonstrates the same unnatural stubbornness in *Manfroné,* refusing to leave a father who has imprisoned both her and her lover in a gloomy dungeon and is trying to force her into marriage with the hated and unprincipled Manfroné. (Rosalina's father later attempts her life with a dagger.) In Parsons's *Castle of Wolfenbach,* a previously gentle and benevolent character, Mrs Courtney, becomes increasingly and unusually jealous over the Count's affection for Matilda and tries to alienate the two, telling Matilda of the Count's attentions towards herself. In each of these cases, the desire for a more extended or complicated plot outweighs the sense that character should be consistent (or believable). The degree to which plot exercises pressure upon characters in the Gothic becomes most noticeable in instances like these, or at the conclusions of novels where heretofore complex characters, like La Motte or Schedoni, undergo the radical simplification that is necessary to conclude the novel neatly and justly. The more elaborate the plot, the more disposable the characters: the story of Regina Maria Roche's *Clermont* is so exceedingly complicated and based to such a degree on concealment and mystery that it is virtually impossible for her to develop more than a few characters in any detail, and the plot (one of treachery between brothers, fathers, sons, and between husbands and wives) is set in motion by a character—D'Alembert—whom we do not even actually meet until very near the novel's end. The psychological motivations for the tale, thus, as a partial consequence, remain an almost total mystery until the last volume, whereupon all is unravelled, almost exclusively through second-hand accounts of the action.

The dominance accorded scene, plot, and device in Gothic narrative imposes limitations on character and poses other, equally troubling, problems of interpretation. In the works of Walpole and Beckford, in particular, many properties or objects that appear to have symbolic qualities are found ultimately to be completely lacking in significant resonance. Thus, as Kiely argues [see Further Reading], the helmet and sword of *The Castle of Otranto,* because of a reduction of meaning in other parts of the narrative, do not function as true symbols; they are 'not phallic symbols because the characters have no lives to which they can refer'. The Gothic, indeed, repeatedly fails to operate on this more complex double level of significance. Symbolic equivalences or parallels are discouraged because they are supported on no other plane of the narrative. Thus, Julia's flight through the underground passages in *A Sicilian Romance* is not a descent into her subconscious because Radcliffe retreats throughout the novel from deepening character by posing specific analogues between personality and setting. The imagery in that section, indeed, leads us doggedly back to the surface, to the extent that the sequence unintentionally acquires the qualities of near slapstick:

> They *entered* the avenue, and locking the door after them, sought the flight of steps *down* which the count had before passed . . . They *now entered* upon a dark abyss; and the door which moved upon a spring, suddenly *closed* upon them. On *looking round* they beheld a large vault; and it is not easy to imagine their horror on discovering they were in a receptacle for the murdered bodies of the unfortunate people who had fallen into the hands of the banditti. . . .
>
> They had not been long in this situation, when they heard a noise which *approached gradually,* and which did not appear to come *from the avenue* they had passed.
>
> . . . Hippolitus believed the murderers were *returned;* that they had traced his retreat, and were coming *towards the vault* by some way unknown to him. He prepared for the worst—and drawing his sword, resolved to defend Julia to the last. Their apprehension, however, was soon dissipated by a trampling of horses, which sound had occasioned

his alarm, and which now seemed to come *from a courtyard above,* extremely *near the vault.* . . .

> The tumult had continued a considerable time, which the prisoners had passed in a state of *horrible suspence,* when they heard the uproar advancing *towards the vault* . . . Hippolitus again drew his sword, and placed himself *opposite the entrance,* where he had *not stood* long, when a violent push was made against the door; it flew open, and a party of men rushed *into the vault.*
>
> . . . the men *before him* were not banditti, but the officers of justice. . . .
>
> Hippolitus enquired for Ferdinand, and they all *quitted the vault* in search of him. . . .
>
> . . . On close examination [of the room in which Hippolitus had seen the dying cavalier], they perceived . . . a trap-door, which with some difficulty they lifted . . . They all *descended* . . .

This passage gains its effect from its precise delineation of physical space, not from its description of emotional response: Hippolitus and Julia register only the conventional emotions of 'horror' and 'horrible suspence'; Hippolitus, preparing 'for the worst', draws his sword and resolves 'to defend Julia to the last'. The unease in the situation appears to arise from the constantly shifting perimeters of space that surround them and which they traverse: they descend steps, enter an abyss, look around; noises approach from other avenues, from above; they leave the vault; then they all descend.

The amount of movement here is so obviously exaggerated that it impedes a reflective response on the part of the reader, a response of the kind that Maturin, in a similar section in *Melmoth the Wanderer,* clearly invites. The scene is Monçada's underground flight with the parricide. With its syntactic repetitions ('I listen . . . I speak to you . . . I hate . . . I dread you') and its emphasis on strong emotion, the passage gains a horrifying power that is missing from Radcliffe's drama:

> 'Though my blood [Monçada says to the parricide], *chilled* as it is by *famine and fatigue,* seems *frozen* in every drop while I *listen* to you, yet *listen* I must, and trust my *life and liberation* to you. *I speak to you* with the horrid confidence our situation has taught me,—*I hate,—I dread you. If we were to meet in life, I would shrink* from you with loathings of unspeakable abhorrence, *but here* mutual misery has mixed the most repugnant substances in unnatural coalition. The force of that alchemy must cease at the moment of my escape *from the convent and from you;* yet, for these miserable hours, *my life is as much dependent* on your exertions and presence, *as my power of supporting them is* on the continuance of your horrible tale . . .'

A tendency to tease the reader with effects is characteristic, especially, of the early Gothic and has misled many modern critics of the form: the genre's preoccupation with subterranean settings does not, in contrast to what some commentators have hopefully argued, necessarily point to a concern with human psychology, female physiology, or the unconscious. The genre, indeed, repeatedly fails to engage these deeper issues, and its failure involves a complex inability to confront both moral and aesthetic responsibilities: its often feverish search after sensation is puzzlingly joined with a deliberate retreat from meaning. This paradox is also the central one of the picturesque (and one about which Ruskin was particularly concerned). It is only by neatly (and naïvely) disjoining cause and effect that Gilpin, for example, can assert that Cromwell and Henry VIII were 'masters of ruins' or that trees with disease are often pictorially more desirable than healthy ones, 'capital sources of picturesque beauty'. Effect in such instances not only outweighs cause; it becomes a substitute for it, an excuse for not exploring more deeply the moral implications of a scene. Gilpin alludes periodically to this tension between aesthetic and moral categories, to the fact that, as he put it in *Cumberland,* 'moral and picturesque ideas do not always coincide', but he was reluctant to examine this interesting observation in any real detail.

Gothic novelists in a similar way often betray an attitude towards experience that emphasizes a disjunctive relationship between aesthetic and moral values. Radcliffe, whose theological distaste for Catholicism was acute, repeatedly uses Catholic settings in her novels, and on her journey through the Lake District in 1794, sought out and enjoyed scenes of lost Catholic splendour. '[T]hough reason rejoices that they no longer exist,' she remarked on the ruined monasteries on her tour, 'the eye may be allowed to regret'. Walpole's response (around the time of *Otranto*) to the news of a large wolf that had caused devastation in Languedoc suggests a similar inclination to evade the actual in favour of the ideal: if he had known about it earlier, he said, he might have included it in *The Castle of Otranto.* Beckford's reaction to the collapse of his tower at Fonthill shows a like self-absorbed disregard for practical consequences: he reported himself disappointed to have missed the spectacle. Distance, indeed, is a condition of aesthetic experience for Beckford: his travel diaries seldom contain direct observations about the towns he is visiting; instead, he coyly describes Flanders in Grecian terms, and Rome as if he were in Africa. He created another protective triangle in his relationship with Kitty Courtenay and Louisa Beckford, using Louisa, who loved him, as a shield for his correspondence with Kitty, with whom he was enamoured. This triangulating pattern marks all the major projects of Beckford's literary and personal life, allowing him the luxury of elaborate displays of wit without necessitating a close or spontaneous approach to his subject.

Such emphases on emotional displays and effects (often to the exclusion of causes) are complicated further by the distrust some Gothic writers display about emotion itself. In *The Mysteries of Udolpho,* the work in which Radcliffe seems most fully aware of the destructive side of the sensitivity with which her heroines are endowed, St Aubert utters his famous warning to Emily:

> 'Above all, my dear Emily . . . do not indulge in the pride of fine feeling, the romantic error of amiable minds. Those, who really possess sensibility, ought early to be taught, that it is a dangerous quality, which is continually extracting the excess of misery, or delight, from every surrounding circumstance. And, since, in our passage through this world, painful circumstances occur more frequently than pleasing ones, and since our sense of evil is, I fear, more acute than our sense of good, we become the victims of our feelings, unless we can in some degree command them. . . .
>
> . . . Always remember how much more valuable is the strength of fortitude, than the grace of sensibility. . . . Sentiment is a disgrace, instead of

an ornament, unless it leads us to good actions. . . .'

Radcliffe's insistence that her heroines display fortitude and withstand prolonged suffering has an interesting effect on our apprehension of the value she accorded emotion. As the example of the nun Agnes shows, and as the fate of many other high-tempered Gothic females such as Dacre's Victoria corroborates, the relinquishment of the self to passion is not intrinsically good:

> 'Sister! beware of the first indulgence of the passions; beware of the first! Their course, if not checked then, is rapid—their force is uncontroulable—they lead us we know not whither—they lead us perhaps to the commission of crimes, for which whole years of prayer and penitence cannot atone!—Such may be the force of even a single passion, that it overcomes every other, and sears up every other approach to the heart. Possessing us like a fiend, it leads us on to the acts of a fiend, making us insensible to pity and to conscience. And, when its purpose is accomplished, like a fiend, it leaves us to the torture of those feelings, which its power had suspended—not annihilated,—to the tortures of compassion, remorse, and conscience. . . . Remember, sister, that the passions are the seeds of vices as well as of virtues, from which either may spring, accordingly as they are nurtured. Unhappy they who have never been taught the art to govern them!'

Agnes's warning about the ungovernability of the passions is one that is reiterated throughout the Gothic: sensibility, it is stressed, is a particularly volatile quality that can easily become destructive. The Gothic heroine's job, then, seems to call into question the very novel that engendered her. Endowed with the sensitivity to be moved by the events around her, she must also, importantly, strive to resist their effects. It is thus not surprising to find that Radcliffe's heroines have a tendency to speak of their feelings in terms of restraint: 'Recollecting that she had parted with Valancourt, perhaps for ever, her heart sickened as memory revived. But she tried to dismiss the dismal forebodings that crowded on her mind, and to restrain the sorrow which she could not subdue; efforts which diffused over the settled melancholy of her countenance an expression of tempered resignation, as a thin veil, thrown over the features of beauty, renders them more interesting by a partial concealment.' The virtuous Matilda in *The Castles of Athlin and Dunbayne* is similarly admired for what she holds herself from doing: 'Overwhelmed by the news, and deprived of those numbers which would make revenge successful, Matilda forbore to sacrifice the lives of her few remaining people to a feeble attempt at retaliation, and she was constrained to endure in silence her sorrows and her injuries.' This linking of heroism with restraint poses some serious problems for Gothic narrative. As Radcliffe's heroines are allowed less access to their emotions, they become systematically less complex—more 'flat', more passive, and more reliant upon other characters (like Schedoni or Montoni) to provide a balanced dispersal of emotional energies within the narratives in which they act. This attempt to achieve balance, however, is rarely successful in Gothic fiction. The insistent internalizing of passion on the part of Radcliffe's heroines—and the author's ambivalent attitude towards the emotions—marks the movement of Radcliffean Gothic as one of repeated suppression and repression: events are withstood, secrets are internalized, fears remain unvoiced. A seeming attempt to stabilize here ranges strangely out of control: to try to govern, or suppress, the passions may lead to fixation (Emily looking at the corpse) or physical collapse (Emily at the veiled portrait).

The achievement of stabilization, or closure, in the Gothic thus becomes a curiously two-sided enterprise: desired because of its connections with resolution and the conquest of good over evil, it is nonetheless increasingly seen as an inadequate, or unrealistic, response to the pressures of passion and vice. Many illustrations of Gothic fiction seem (perhaps unconsciously) to stress this aspect of the mode: capturing the frozen gestures of astonishment on the part of the virtuous characters, they repeatedly display the helpless fixation or fainting away of women unable any longer to contain their physical or emotional responses to the evil that faces them. It is not until later, in the more psychologically complex works of William Godwin, James Hogg, and Mary Shelley, that this urge towards stabilization is relinquished in any comfortable way; no longer concerned with imposing a predetermined moral and structural order on the experiences they relate, their works gain a coherence, a sustained unity of tone that much earlier Gothic fiction lacks. (pp. 28-43)

> Elizabeth R. Napier, "Techniques of Closure and Restraint," in her The Failure of Gothic: Problems of Disjunction in an Eighteenth-Century Literary Form, Oxford at the Clarendon Press, 1987, pp. 9-43.

William Godwin.

THE GOTHIC NOVEL IN AMERICA

ORAL SUMNER COAD

[In the following excerpt, Coad surveys the Gothic novels of America, highlighting their similarities to and differences from English Gothic.]

The aim of this paper is to follow the Gothic convention during one of its most prolific periods as it manifested itself in America before reaching its apogee at the hands of Poe and Hawthorne. The limit of 1835 is chosen as marking approximately the beginning of the work of both these men in this field.

The writers and readers of America, in this as in all other literary matters, took their cue from England and made Gothic story-telling for many years one of the approved fashions in letters. As in England, this innovation was a natural reaction against the rationality, restraint and unimaginativeness of neo-classic literature. (p. 72)

The earliest trace of Gothic terror in our fiction appears in the first regular American novel, Mrs. Sarah Wentworth Morton's Richardsonian tale, *The Power of Sympathy, or the Triumph of Nature* (1789). One of the male characters has a Dantesque dream in which he visits the realm of departed sinners. The punishment meted out for seduction, the blackest crime on the blotter of Hell, impresses him with the extreme of fear. He is seized by a demon and thrust struggling into the midst of the group, but at this interesting moment he awakes.

The distinction of writing our first Gothic novel, however, belongs to Charles Brockden Brown. *Wieland, or the Transformation* (1798) is built around two decidedly terrifying phenomena: the inexplicable cremation of a man who at midnight is praying in an isolated pavilion; and mysterious voices that threaten and warn one character, and incite another to the murder of his wife and children. There is a more subtle sort of terror, too, in the foreboding, the spiritual devastation and the insane frenzy of one or other of these victims. For the emphasis on these psychological horrors Brown was probably indebted to Godwin's *Caleb Williams*.

Brown was convinced that the evocation of the reader's fear did not depend on medieval castles and superstitions. Accordingly he laid his scene in the America of his day. Moreover he gained his thrills by means befitting the time and place. His seeming supernaturalism is given not merely a natural, but even a scientific, explanation, and thus he took the next logical step beyond Mrs. Radcliffe. The cremation is found to be a result of spontaneous combustion—and the scrupulous author adds a foot-note citing exactly similar cases recorded in medical journals. The mysterious voices are produced by ventriloquism.

Wieland is far from a negligible representative of its class, even when compared with its English kindred. Its style, though stilted, serves by its preternatural seriousness to convey a mood of impending tragedy. The events, if melodramatic, are boldly imagined; and in all the strange sufferings of these tortured souls there is undeniable power. Even the modern reader glances uneasily from the palpitating page to the shadowy corners of the room.

Brown never again rose to the level of *Wieland*, but he continued its method in another early novel, *Edgar Huntly, or*

Memoirs of a Sleep-Walker (1799). Here the mysteries arise from the fact that both the young men in the story are afflicted with somnambulism, a much discussed subject of the time. One of the men, Clithero, is found at night digging under a tree where a murder had occurred. He later explains that this murder reminded him so forcibly of a crime of his own that in sleep he was drawn to the spot. Huntly awakes from one of his attacks of noctambulism to find himself in the blackness of a rocky cave. Before escaping he must kill a panther and several Indians. Exhausted in the fight he sinks to sleep, to awake with his head pillowed on a dead Indian. Thus the caverns of America's hills supplant the Gothic vaults of Europe, and the red-skin proves no less terrifying than the spectre of the castle.

Ormond, or the Secret Witness (1799), though not primarily a novel of terror, includes several incidents of that nature. There is a secret night burial of a ghastly-faced victim of yellow fever, that is described at length and with evident relish for all the gruesome and fear-inspiring details. Ormond, who has almost superhuman power over the heroine, by some unknown means learns everything she does. This, we discover, is accomplished through the agency of an unsuspected canvas door between their two houses. The book closes with a dreadful episode in which a desolate country house near Philadelphia does duty for the medieval hall, and the scene loses but little of its potency by the substitution.

Arthur Mervyn, or Memoirs of the Year 1793 (1799-1800) finds room for abundant frightfulness. The most telling passages are those which have to do with the yellow fever epidemic in Philadelphia. Here we find what might be called pathological Gothic. The physical and spiritual horror of the victims of the scourge is relentlessly described. Certain episodes are particularly dramatic. Mervyn enters a stricken house and, glancing into a mirror, sees, as though it were an apparition, a huge, misshapen, one-eyed man, who strikes him unconscious. On regaining his senses he finds himself on the point of being thrust into a coffin. He learns that the "apparition" was a thieving servant. On another occasion a figure glides into Mervyn's room with yellow and livid face, fleshless bones and ghastly, hollow eyes. At first he believes it to be the ghost of his friend, but it soon proves to be that friend himself, who has just escaped from the hospital.

Aside from his considerable skill as a narrator, Brown's importance for us consists in the fact that he always chose an American setting for his novels of the strange and marvelous, and that he offered, so far as was possible, a scientific explanation for his mysteries. By basing his effects on scientific phenomena of an uncanny nature he achieved a logically convincing terror that was a real contribution to Gothic literature.

Brown's partiality for native settings failed to affect Mrs. S. S. B. K. Wood, whose *Julia, or the Illuminated Baron* (1800) is a story of eighteenth century France. Its one scene of horror is in the Radcliffe manner. Julia, paying a nocturnal visit to a family tomb, touches the face of a corpse, long since interred, which instantly sinks to dust and ashes. Julia, not unnaturally, is petrified thereby. Nor is her perturbation lessened by a fleeting glimpse of a man's form in the shadows of the tomb. She believes it to be the phantom of her lover, who is thus apprising her of his demise. But a few nights later his living presence explains the apparition.

That Brown taught his countrymen something about horror

in fiction can be seen in *Glencarn, or the Disappointments of Youth* (1810), by George Watterston. Here again the thrills are extracted from such devices as are not inconsistent with the American setting. For our purpose the most significant episode is the hero's adventure with bandits on the banks of the Ohio. He is thrown into a cave and locked in, to discover that the floor is strewn with human skeletons and the walls besmeared with blood. Raising the lid of a coffin, that is to serve as his couch, he sees within the mangled body of a woman. After this manner the horror chamber of the medieval castle, favored of Mrs. Radcliffe, is transported to our own backyard.

The Asylum (1811), by Isaac Mitchell, is a title that implies no connection with a madhouse; it is merely the name that the maudlin lovers choose, not inappropriately, for their prospective home. The book illustrates a danger to which the American novelists' method of treating terror peculiarly exposed them. With astonishing incongruity the author by main force drags into the midst of his sentimental love story and tender scenery a bagful of the most shamelessly Radcliffian tricks. A ruinous mansion on the Connecticut coast—a complete copy of a medieval castle—which was built as a protection against Indians, becomes the temporary prison of the heroine. Here on successive nights she runs the gauntlet of Gothic terrors. After this grisly interlude, the story returns to its wonted course until the very last chapter, in which all these marvels are rationalized by the familiar robber explanation.

Of all our weavers of legends of fear prior to Poe, by far the most skillful, the most artistic, the most eery is Washington Irving. In his hands the story of terror for the first time becomes unmistakably literature. In his earliest work of fiction, *The Sketch Book* (1819-20), Irving proved himself a master of the sportive Gothic, a field in which he has scarcely been surpassed. Indeed "Rip Van Winkle," "The Spectre Bridegroom," and "The Legend of Sleepy Hollow" still remain the classic examples of this genre. As to "Rip Van Winkle" it is sufficient to say that a German superstition is transplanted to the Catskill Mountains and that in so doing Irving adhered to the Americanizing practice established by Brown, choosing for his setting a bit of wild native scenery admirably in keeping with the spirit of the tale. "The Spectre Bridegroom" is placed in medieval Germany, but the seeming supernaturalism is happily explained in the end. And the style, even in dealing with the apparently unearthly, is but mock-serious.

"The Legend of Sleepy Hollow" returns to the banks of the Hudson. The superstitions and ghost tales of the inhabitants create an appropriate atmosphere for the comic tragedy of Ichabod. "The Legend" might without injustice be called an American "Tam O'Shanter." In both much the same excellent balance of humor and terror is maintained. But, more to the point, they are similar in plan. The unlucky homeward ride in each case is preceded by an evening of merriment and story-spinning. Burns, like Irving, leads his hero to his undoing past various spots with superstitious associations. Both tales employ a haunted church, both include a demonic pursuit, and both terminate on or near a bridge over a stream, which, according to the belief of both Tam and Ichabod, fiends may not cross. Burns's fiends, however, are authentic inhabitants of the pit. Irving's, in keeping with the American practice of explaining such matters, is only a very human Dutchman armed with a pumpkin.

Bracebridge Hall (1822), aside from certain details in "The

Student of Salamanca," has but one story of the supernatural, "Dolph Heyliger." In this tale, which is located in Manhattan and again employs the sportive style, the most striking element is a phantom-ship with a silent and statue-like crew that once made its appearance in Manhattan Bay after a great storm. The spectre-bark, which seems to have owed its origin to colonial superstition and is perhaps also indebted to "The Ancient Mariner," is dealt with rather frequently in the literature of our period, but it was to have its finest presentment in Poe's "MS. Found in a Bottle."

Tales of a Traveller (1824) abounds in Gothic material. "The Adventure of My Uncle" and "The Adventure of My Aunt" are slight stories that rationalize the mystery. "The Bold Dragoon" and "Wolfert Webber" are tales of brisk fun, the former seeming to reveal some influence of "Tam O'Shanter," and the latter containing an episode possibly derived from Goethe's account of Mephistopheles's pranks in Auerbach's wine-cellar.

Much the best of the humorous stories in this volume is "The Devil and Tom Walker," a sort of comic New England *Faust,* which, in the happy blending of the terrifying and the ludicrous almost rivals "The Legend of Sleepy Hollow." The setting, a gloomy, snake-infested swamp, is excellently chosen. Here Tom encounters the Devil and seals his soul in exchange for pirate gold. After a career of iniquity, he is whisked back to the swamp on a black horse and never seen again.

If Irving's forte was the jesting Gothic, "The Adventure of the German Student" shows him to have a command of the sombre species as well. The student, finding a beautiful, homeless woman at the foot of the guillotine during the French Revolution, takes her to his room for the night. The next morning he finds her dead, and when he removes a black band from her throat her head falls to the floor. She had been beheaded the preceding day. Unlike some of Irving's stories already discussed, "The German Student" is direct, economical and grimly terrible.

The Alhambra (1832) contains a number of tales founded on local traditions that Irving picked up while visiting Granada. The spirit of these stories is inevitably that of *The Arabian Nights,* and their frank supernaturalism rests on magic treasure hidden in the bowels of the earth, demon steeds, flying carpets, palaces built by necromancy, enchanted beauties, and phantom armies that emerge from the heart of a mountain. The tone of the sketches is light and entertaining, but there is no unusual distinction about them. The chief importance of the volume lies in the fact that it is one of the few examples of Oriental Gothic in this country.

Irving's place in the field of our survey is large. In variety of tone and setting he is easily first, though his peculiar strain is humor and his predominant background is colonial America. Moreover he showed that an American writer could gain his ends without either crude melodrama or bogies fit only to frighten children.

The novels of John Neal suggest either that Gothic writing induces madness or that madness induces Gothic writing. His stories are the wildest, most incoherent pieces of imagination in American literature. It is as though they were the product of some of those crazed brains with which his books abound. No matter how soberly matter of fact his beginning may be, the tale soon trails off into confused raving and horror. His style is a perfect medium for his purpose: violent, hysterical, shrieking, it defies all laws of order and lucidity. Perhaps for

this reason, Neal's novels are not without melodramatic power. One can hardly fail to respond to their tremendous intensity and their devastating terror.

Though it is his first venture in the abnormal sphere, *Logan, the Mingo Chief* (1822) shows his peculiarities fully developed. There is evident some influence of Brown's rational explanations and American settings in the figure of an Indian who, surviving a supposedly fatal wound, like a genuine demon, for which he is mistaken, haunts the spot where he fell and shoots those who come near. But there are less rational elements, as in the scene in a European chamber where the hero goes through all the ghastly experiences common to the ghost-infested halls of the English romances. He later learns that a man had been killed in this room, and that the murderer, going insane, had sat all night watching the horrible swollen eyes of his victim.

Randolph (1823) is full of violence, murder and coffins. One portion is of particular significance. A murderer describes Annapolis, the scene of his crime, as a town of a strangely old-world air, of profound silence and solitude, of an almost baronial sullenness and gloom. The houses suggest manors and castles that were once the abode of the haughty and lonely nobility of Maryland. One night, so the murderer continues, while walking on a desolate street of the town, he perceived that he was followed by a silent form. He turned and struck his knife into the pursuer, but it merely walked on with long, noiseless strides. It seemed to him that the face was that of his victim. All this is especially interesting because the author is trying to impart to an American scene as much of the flavor of medieval Europe as possible in order to make it a fit setting for his Gothic terrors. Others, as we have seen, were doing the same thing, but Neal here elaborates his background more fully than had been done before.

Errata, or the Works of Will Adams (1823) is full of a vague horror. Two unusual figures are Adams's dwarfish brother and his dwarfish playmate, both of whom have an uncanny effect on him, the one being superhumanly malicious, the other superhumanly strong. In an illness Adams is seized with delirium and imagines himself first to be in a madhouse and then to have been buried alive. His mental agony is fearful in this state, and the style reaches a point of frenzy.

One of the few tales to use New England witchcraft as its theme is Neal's *Rachel Dyer* (1828). It tells of the cruel suffering and death of a woman accused of being a witch. There is considerable incidental witchery, which the author appears to accept as possible.

In general Neal followed the tendency of his predecessors by setting his novels in his native land, even though in certain episodes he wandered elsewhere. In the matter of supernaturalism he usually but not invariably explained his marvels. As to effect, Neal happily has no rivals in the school of frenzied fiction.

James Fenimore Cooper is never classed among the Gothic novelists, and yet several of his stories contain details, more or less prominent, unmistakably inspired by the prevailing fashion. *The Pilot* (1823) has a trace of it in the English abbey ruin where much of the action occurs. Here one of the girls is fear-struck on hearing the voice of the Pilot, whom she believes to be far away, until she learns that he has just been brought in a captive.

Lionel Lincoln (1825) is built about a mysterious old man

known as Ralph, who has unusual influence over Lionel and who is responsible for much apparent supernaturalism by his unexpected appearances and the marvelous power of his voice. Cooper frequently says that "his movements and aspect" have "the character of a being superior to the attributes of humanity." The explanation apparently lies in the discovery that Ralph is a madman who has escaped his keeper. His influence over Lionel arises from the fact that he is that hero's father. Another Gothic element is furnished by the strange idiot Job, Ralph's chief friend and companion.

Perhaps the most impressive examples of Cooper's natural supernaturalism are found in his finest novel, *The Prairie* (1827). In the first chapter, emigrants crossing the plain suddenly see the gigantic figure of a man standing in the center of the flood of sunset light. They regard it with superstitious awe, until they find that it is a mere human being named Leatherstocking. Near the end of the book is the powerfully described hanging of the murderer Abiram. After making all preparations for the hanging, his executioners depart, leaving him to choose the moment of his fatal leap. When they have withdrawn some distance and night has fallen, they hear a shriek which seems to come from the upper air, then a cry of horror as it were at their very ears, then a cry that exceeds horror, filling every cranny of the air, and they know that the criminal's day is done.

Among the least successful of Cooper's novels is *The Water-Witch* (1831), the only one in which he fails to explain his mysteries. Once again we encounter the ship of magical properties, which inexplicably eludes all pursuers, thanks to its presiding genius, a figure-head representing a malign water-witch.

The Heidenmauer (1832), a tale of sixteenth century Germany, has as setting a Gothic castle and abbey, and incorporates considerable medieval superstition. There is one effective and imaginative ghost scene, which explains itself away when it is discovered that the supposed ghost is a living man wrongly thought to have been killed.

Cooper contributed little that was new to Gothic methods. In the main he followed what was becoming the American practice of adhering to domestic settings and of explaining the supernatural. Commonly his effects are more satisfactory, dignified and poetic than those of his lesser contemporaries, but he too was capable of triviality.

A readable novel by a little known writer is *The Spectre of the Forest* (1823), by James McHenry. For us the interest centers in the "Spectre" a beneficent spirit who watches over the destinies of the hero. It being an American story, the "Spectre" is at last found to be a human being, the heroine's father and none other than Goffe, the regicide, who fled from England after the execution of Charles I. One architectural detail is significant: A man accused of witchcraft flees to a small cabin fitted with a secret door in the panel and with underground passages and rooms in the rock—a sort of transplanted medieval castle in little.

James K. Paulding was not only a friend but also an imitator of Irving. In *Koningsmarke, the Long Finne* (1823) the Gothic material is handled in the main humorously. The only figure with unearthly learnings is a sort of negro Meg Merrilies. After her death her ghost is believed to walk, and astonishing consequences follow, if we may believe a group of story tellers that assemble one night at the inn. But the recital of their grim adventures is rudely interrupted by a mighty shrieking

in the attic of the tavern. Something falls into the room, extinguishing the light and howling like a pack of demons. Of course it is only a cat fight. This is cruder than Irving, but it is in his vein.

A debt to Irving is again obvious in *The Dutchman's Fireside* (1831). A wild cry is heard at night on the shores of the Hudson. This reminds a Dutch captain of an Indian ghost said to invade these regions. As he starts the story, a scream is heard right over the ship, and the captain is slapped in the face. This is merely the doing of an owl, but the story never gets told.

Two semi-historical novels dealing with witchcraft are Lydia Maria Child's *Rebels, or Boston before the Revolution* (1825) and Catharine Maria Sedgwick's *Hope Leslie, or Early Times in the Massachusetts* (1827). In the former appears another imitation of Meg Merrilies, who can read the past and future. In the latter an old Indian woman is placed on trial as a witch because she has cured a rattlesnake victim with the aid of strange incantations. Shortly before her execution she is spirited away by the heroine, a deed for which Satan gets the credit.

Whittier's *Legends of New England* (1831), already referred to, contains several prose sketches of interest, in which, as in most preceding fiction, is seen the effort to create terror by natural causes. The two most striking tales are "The Haunted House," concerning an alleged witch who "haunts" her enemy's dwelling by entering it nightly and making various hair-raising noises—somewhat in the *Wieland* manner; and "A Night Among the Wolves," a story of rather potent psychological horror.

John Pendleton Kennedy like Paulding was a friend and follower of Irving. His *Swallow Barn, or a Sojourn in the Old Dominion* (1832) contains a legend resembling "The Devil and Tom Walker." The Goblin Swamp of Virginia is made the setting of a humorous story about a drunken blacksmith, upon whom the Devil plays numerous pranks. The episode has much of Irving's vigor, though lacking most of his intermixture of terror and his dramatic force.

Bryant is seen as the author of Gothic fiction in two stories in *Tales of the Glauber Spa* (1832), "By Several American Authors." In "The Skeleton's Cave" a party of three, while exploring a cavern containing a human skeleton, are immured by the fall of a large rock across the entrance. Before their release by a natural miracle, they suffer the most intense mental tortures, which even take the form of hallucinations and temporary insanity. "Medfield," our sole entry that would interest the Society for Psychical Research, tells of a man whose dead wife's spirit palpably but invisibly visits him to restrain his fierce temper. For these visitations and his early death, which results from them, the author suggests the explanation of monomania.

The only other story of terror in *Tales of the Glauber Spa* is "Boyuca," by R. C. Sands. It tells of a Spanish search for the fountain of youth in Florida through a trackless and funereal forest, which is described as a toweringly ominous and evil thing. A South American tiger that is encountered on the route produces the effect of a devil incarnate. Just as the explorers reach the fountain, a devastating tempest breaks upon them and kills their guide, an Indian hag reputed to be a witch. They bury her under the stars amid the dancing gleams of fireflies and the eldritch cries of the night creatures in the sinister old wood. The story is a skillful piece of exaggeration that does not fail to grip the imagination. Indeed, in its extravagant way, it is something of a masterpiece. The effect is obtained almost wholly by the weird nature descriptions, in which the influence of Coleridge may be suspected.

A narrative that does not lack haunting power in spite of its fantastic character is Richard Henry Dana's long short story, "Paul Felton" (in *Poems and Prose Writings,* 1833; reprinted from *The Idle Man,* a periodical of 1821-2). Paul, a moody young man tortured with jealousy of his wife, meets a demented boy of ghastly mien, who becomes his evil genius and by his malign influence leads Paul to murder his wife.

Robert Montgomery Bird, best known as the author of *Nick of the Woods* (1837), has a romance which falls within our period. *Calavar* (1834) goes to the unworked field of Spanish-America for its material. The hero, morbid and distracted because he has slain the woman he loves, construes natural appearances into supernatural; and in turn, because of his terrifying face, he is frequently taken for a spectre by the superstitious. An impressive bit of decoration is the description of the weird ceremonial rites of the natives against the background of a flaming volcano.

The foregoing discussion should have made it clear that our fiction writers were agreed in the main on two points. First, with considerable unanimity they explained away what at first appear to be supernatural phenomena. Secondly, they showed a common tendency toward locating their stories in America, choosing so far as possible gloomy surroundings, whether natural or architectural. The persistence with which they followed this practice, while the great majority of poets and playwrights went to Europe, is owing in no small measure to Brown. He, our first conspicuous novelist, was convinced of the possibilities that lay in American scenes, and his successors concurred in his declaration in the preface to *Edgar Huntly* that "for a native of America to overlook these would admit of no apology." This denatured Gothic is evidence of no little ingenuity. It is, in fact, more difficult to handle than the sort that depends on a medieval castle or abbey ruin, where, as the reader willingly admits, terror has its normal abode. The Americanized Gothic convinces, if at all, because of the author's skillful treatment; the medieval sort may take for granted our readiness, even our eagerness, to accept mystery and impossibility. But the American writers assigned themselves the harder task, and this fact should not be overlooked in estimating what they did. Perhaps they adopted this course because it seemed the likeliest way to gain new effects in an already well-worked form.

If Irving stands preeminent among these writers of Gothic tales, the reason is to be found partly in the form he chose. The short story is adapted to this kind of writing as the novel cannot be; the reader's credulity may be sustained for twenty pages, scarcely for four hundred. Furthermore the dramatic intensity necessary for success is best secured through the short story. Not without reason are the greatest marvel tales, from the *Arabian Nights* to Ambrose Bierce, short stories. Our novelists seem to have felt this too, for they approximated the short story in that they introduced the element of terror, as a rule, only in occasional and frequently complete episodes.

Between the poets on the one hand and the writers of plays and fiction on the other there is this distinction, that the latter usually explained their mysteries, whereas the former, in the majority of cases, treated them as beyond human ken. This point is emphasized by Whittier's *Legends of New England,* in which all the poems are frankly supernatural and all the prose tales find natural solutions for their strange happenings. The preponderance of these rationalized phenomena is proof that the dominant influence on the whole body of American Gothic literature was Mrs. Radcliffe. If her American disciples were often feeble followers, at least they showed discriminating taste in choosing as their model the most competent representative of the English school.

In the way of methods and devices the Americans did not contribute a great deal. Brown's scientific explanations are, to be sure, important. The sportive style was more frequently used here than in England, but the idea probably descended from "Tam O'Shanter." In the domesticating process our writers and especially our novelists discovered two new sources of terror: the Indian and New England witchcraft, both of which were often interestingly handled, but neither was developed to its full capacity. On the whole our most significant accomplishment was this very process of domestication. In a new land of but few traditions and legends, it was necessary to find or invent a new order of legend, an indigenous source of superstition and fear to serve the purpose of those that clustered about every castle and ruined abbey of Europe. To the imaginative Irving this condition offered a challenge that was eagerly accepted, and his success is attested by the fact that legends still cling to many places along the Hudson which he first imposed upon them. Lesser men found their readiest ally in our terrifying scenery and our no less terrifying aborigines. When nothing else offered, it was always possible to borrow details from the English romancers and transfer them bodily to America, sometimes with scant attention to congruity. For clumsy ineptitude in this particular *The Asylum* of Mitchell is unrivalled. For a wholly satisfying identification of terror them with native setting one must go outside our period to *The Scarlet Letter* and *The House of the Seven Gables.*

The extent to which terror caught the imagination of America is indicated though not defined by this study, for scarcely over half of the possible titles are mentioned here. With precedents so numerous it was almost inevitable that fiction writers like Poe and Hawthorne, beginning their work about the fourth decade of the nineteenth century, should be drawn in this direction. But, being geniuses, they were not content merely to repeat the formulas, crude as they usually were, of their fellow countrymen. Instead, they brought to the hackneyed idea a fresh creativeness, and to Gothic literature was added the grave moral beauty of Hawthorne and the exotic art of Poe. (pp. 80-93)

Oral Sumner Coad, "The Gothic Element in American Literature before 1835," in The Journal of English and Germanic Philology, *Vol. XXIV, 1925, pp. 72-93.*

GEORGE L. PHILLIPS

[*In the following excerpt, Phillips discusses why the Gothic novel was not more prevalent in the United States before 1830.*]

Oral Sumner Coad in an article, "The Gothic Element in American Literature before 1835," [see excerpt above] points out that the Gothic movement produced few results in American poetry and drama and that

only in fiction did Gothicism achieve anything approaching distinction in this country, probably for the simple reason that by 1835 we had produced almost no writers of real ability except writers of fiction.

Yet a study of Gothicism in early American fiction is necessarily limited when one considers that although Dr. Loshe [in *The Early American Novel*] lists 142 novels, written before 1830, only sixteen contain Gothic elements, and of these sixteen only Charles Brockden Brown can claim authorship of more than one.

The Gothic spirit was not unknown in the young republic: Jefferson, as early as 1771, had proposed some Gothic models of houses; and from 1812 on, Gothic churches sprang up in many cities. Washington Allston's macabre paintings, "Dead Man Revived by Touching Elisha's Bones," "Spalatro's Vision of the Bloody Hand," Rembrandt Peale's gruesome "Court of Death," and William Dunlap's weird "Death on the Pale Horse" show supernatural elements of Gothicism fixed by brush on canvas. Royall Tyler, in the introduction to *The Algerine Captive; or, The Life and Adventures of Doctor Updike Underhill, a Prisoner among the Algerines,* refers to the increasing popularity of the "gay stories and splendid impieties of the Traveller and Novelist" found in imported novels of terror:

> Dolly, the dairy maid, and Jonathan, the hired man, threw aside the ballad of the cruel stepmother, over which they had so often wept in concert, and now amused themselves into so agreeable a terrour, with the haunted houses and hobgobblins of Mrs. Ratcliffe [*sic*] that they were both afraid to sleep alone.

Since, by the turn of the century, Gothicism was finding increasing favor on the part of the American public in architecture, painting, and imported English novels, why did not the cult of the Gothic novel become fashionable among the American writers of fiction? The answer is, perhaps, not hard to find. In the first place, the comparatively recently colonized country could not offer to any would-be Walpoles, Lewises, or Mrs. Radcliffes such suitable medieval properties as ruined castles, hallowed by haunting armor-clanking ancestors; crumbling abbeys, undetermined by dark dangerous passages where ghosts of lovers long dead might cry aloud for vengeance; dark dungeons, inhabited by wicked monks, hellish spirits, and Lapland hags attended by their familiars. When an author like Daniel Jackson transplanted a Gothic castle to the bluffs overhanging the Hudson River, he was by no means convincing in describing the building which Melissa and her grim aunt approach as

> a large, old-fashioned, castle-like building, surrounded by a high, thick wall, and almost totally concealed on all sides from the sight, by irregular rows of large locusts and elm trees, dry prim hedges, and green shrubbery. . . . The house was of real Gothic architecture, built of rude stone, with battlements. . . . They ascended a flight of stairs, wound through several dark and empty rooms, till they came to one which was handsomely furnished. . . . "Here we are safe," said Melissa's aunt, "as I have taken pains to lock all the doors and gates after me; and here, Melissa, you are in the mansion of your ancestors. Your great grandfather, who came over from England, built this house in the earliest settlements of the country, and here he resided until his death. The reason why so high and thick a wall was built around it, and the

doors and gates so strongly fortified, was to secure it against the Indians. . . ."

What is more, democratic America could not vaunt aristocratic family legends of languishing maidens of noble birth or long-lost sons of kings, foully dispossessed of their rightful heritages. In the anonymously written *Margaretta: or, The Intricacies of the Heart* (1807) there is a satirical reference to the absurdities of transplanting the flamboyant English Gothic novel to America. A young English girl asks an American lady if she has no castles, spectres, or giants in her strange land. Her elder sister laughingly replies that their over-seas visitor was born in a North American castle, saw green spectres hopping about their pools, and giantesses nearly six feet in height.

In the second place, the writer of Gothic tales faced the discouraging Puritan belief that the novel, written only for amusement, was an idle waste of time for readers who might otherwise be profitably occupied. So powerful was the demand that a moral or utilitarian purpose be the determining factor of a story, based on facts, that Charles Brockden Brown thought it expedient to state in the preface to *Wieland* that his purpose was neither selfish nor temporary but illustrated some important branches of the moral constitution of man.

> The incidents related are extraordinary and rare. Some of them, perhaps, approach as nearly to the nature of miracles as can be done by that which is not truly miraculous. It is hoped that intelligent readers will not disapprove of the manner in which appearances are solved, but that the solution will be found to correspond with the known principles of human nature.

American novelists still paid homage to Richardson's moral principles, since he was probably the most popular novelist among the descendants of the Puritans.

In the third place, American patriotism demanded American scenes and incidents. The expanding frontiers invoked new phases of the dynamic present rather than attempts to rehabilitate the static medieval period. Brown saw the opportunities to use contemporary events and noted in the introduction to *Edgar Huntly* that he intended

> to exhibit a series of adventures, growing out of the condition of our country. One merit the writer may at least claim: that of calling forth the passions and engaging the sympathy of the reader by means hitherto unemployed by preceding authors. Puerile superstitions and exploded manners, Gothic castles and chimeras are the materials usually employed for this end. The incidents of Indian hostility, and the perils of the Western wilderness, are far more suitable, and for a native of America to overlook these would admit of no apology.

In *The Champions of Freedoms or, The Mysterious Chief* (1816), a novel based on episodes of the War of 1812, which were made to serve as an aegis for the spirit of Washington in the guise of an oracular corpse of an Indian chief, there is an elaborate homage to patriotism combined with the supernatural.

If, however, America could not offer her writers of fiction gory medieval legends and ivy-covered ruins, if she still bore a distrust, especially in New England, of improbable romances written to amuse and not to instruct, if she were over-eager to glory in her newly acquired liberty, still those of her writers who felt able to cope with this opposition found in English novels of Gothicism material upon which they might draw. They might choose to follow the unexplainable supernatural exuberances intricately embroidered in medieval material and displayed by such authors as Walpole, Lewis, or Maturin. They might prefer the more restrained effects secured oftentimes through the suggestive powers of Mrs. Radcliffe, who usually, but not always, tried to explain her horrors mechanically. They might be enticed, since they were living in a period rapidly becoming scientifically minded, by the psychological approach of securing the effects of terror and suspense revealed by Godwin in *Caleb Williams* with its contemporary background; nor would Mary Shelley's *Frankenstein* be less interesting because it suggested the lengths to which science might go. In its attempts, then, to arouse horror and suspense, the Gothic novel sought various channels. Ghosts and demons often gave way to scientific inventions; ruined castles were leveled for laboratories. Dr. Searborough sums up these factors:

> Daemonology manifests itself in the supernatural science in the Gothic novels as well as in the characterization of the devil and his confreres. We have diabolical chemistry, besides alchemy, astrology, hypnotism, ventriloquism, search for the philosopher's stone, infernal biology and other scientific twists of supernaturalism.

Nor were American writers hesitant in drawing upon these sources.

The first trace of Gothic horrors appears in Mrs. Morton's *The Power of Sympathy* (1789). In this tale of seduction the scheming Lovelace is so terrified by his dream of the harrowing fate for seducers in hell that he repents of his prurient schemes to undermine the virtue of the heroine. This interpolation of the supernatural permits Mrs. Morton to point her tale with a touch of "Monk" Lewis for the moral edification of her readers.

No doubt the best American exponent of Godwin's psychological and realistic type of Gothic novel is Charles Brockden Brown. Against an American background Brown weaves his weird and exciting plots. In *Wieland* he deals with ventriloquism, religious fanaticism, insanity, and spontaneous combustion; in *Arthur Mervyn,* with yellow fever and apparitions invoked by a diseased mind; in *Ormond,* again with yellow fever plagues; in *Edgar Huntly,* with Indian massacres, somnambulism, panthers, and insanity. Brown's dislike for the supernatural excesses of the Walpole-Lewis school and his predilection for making the mysterious appear natural through the use of ventriloquism, insanity, somnambulism, or the less frequent spontaneous combustion is manifested in *Wieland,* in which one of the characters declares:

> "Where is the proof," said I, "that demons may not be subjected to the control of men? This truth may be distorted and debased in the minds of the ignorant. The dogmas of the vulgar with regard to this subject are glaringly absurd; but, though these may be justly neglected by the wise, we are scarcely justified in totally rejecting the possibility that men may obtain supernatural aid. The dreams of superstition are worthy of contempt. Witchcraft, its instruments and miracles, the compact ratified by a bloody signature, the apparatus of sulphurous smells and thundering explosions, are monstrous. . . . That conscious beings, dissimilar from human, but moral and voluntary agents as we are, somewhere exist, can scarcely be denied."

In his attempt to associate his apparently supernatural incidents with everyday occurrences Brown does not hesitate to authenticate his details of spontaneous combustion by references to medical data; he explains the voice, "louder than human organs could produce, shriller than language can depict," as that of the ventriloquist who drives Wieland into a state of religious insanity; he describes an apparition as the result of weak nerves and flickering candle-light; he shows that Ormond's supernatural power to know what Constantia is doing exists solely because a secret canvas door connects their two houses; he discusses the horrors of the plague in Philadelphia in such a passage as:

> The door opened, and a figure glided in. The portmanteau dropped from my arms, and my heart's blood was chilled. If an apparition of the dead were possible, and that possibility I could not deny, this was such an apparition. A hue, yellowish and livid; bones, uncovered with flesh; eyes, ghastly, hollow, wobegone, and fixed in an agony of wonder on me. . . . My belief of something preternatural in his appearance, was confirmed by recollection of resemblance between these figures and those of one who was dead.

According to Loshe, Brown "achieved the really horrible which he and all the race of Gothic novelists had so long and industriously sought." Furthermore, Brown obtained his purpose of arousing his reader's terror and sympathy by the use of realistic American scenes, by drawing his main characters with psychological insight, by adhering to the scientific or rational form of Godwin's Gothic novels, and by taking the reader into his confidence through satirical tirades against the Walpole-Lewis type of Gothicism.

Mrs. Sally Sayward Barell Keating Wood's *Julia; or, The Illuminated Baron* (1800) contains only a suspicion of Gothic weirdness when the heroine touches the face of a corpse as she prowls about the ancestral tomb one night; moreover, she is again frightened by a ghost-like figure which turns out to be her absent lover. In 1804, Mrs. Wood's *Ferdinand and Elmira. A Russian Story* appeared with such definite touches of Mrs. Radcliffe apparent in the first few pages as a lonely maiden in a hall, without a light, with a locked door barring her escape, and with claps of thunder rendering the ghostly silence of the strange place. Gothic elements, even more fleshless than Mrs. Wood's, may be found in *Moreland Vale; or, The Fair Fugitive* (1801), written by a lady of New York State. In this novel a thief believes he sees the ghost of a man he has robbed. The supposed ghost assumes a sepulchral tone and makes the thief restore the stolen property.

George Watterston's *Glencarn; or, The Disappointments of Youth* (1810) has some bold Gothic strokes in a romance that is mainly sentimental. While the hero is discoursing on the beauty of the Ohio River along the banks of which roam wolves, bears, and tigers, his boat is captured by bandits who lead him through several dark passages into

> a narrow and filthy apartment which seemed to be in the extremity of the rock, the floor was covered with human skeletons, and the walls completely besmeared with human blood.

In a chest he finds the mangled body of a woman. Through his powers as a ventriloquist the hero makes his escape and learns the sad story of the bandit leader whom society forced to rob. Ventriloquism, contemporary American scenes, the cavern in the wilderness, the use of the first person, the bandit leader spurned by society, suggest Brown's influence on Watterston.

The anonymously written *The Sicilian Pirate; or, The Pillar of Mystery. A Terrific Romance* (1815) might be a travesty of the Walpole-Lewis type of Gothic romance. Adelmorn, already "black with perfidy . . . began to form dark plots, secretly planning how he might become red with murder." He murders his wife and sees before him his cast-off sweetheart, now an apparent phantom with crimson gore trickling from its breast. The phantom points and vanishes. Groans draw him to a thicket where he sees by the flashes of vivid lightning the airy form of his murdered wife which upbraids him for his miscreant deed. Overwhelmed, Adelmorn is about to commit suicide, but his mistress prevents him and receives the sword thrust. Adelmorn sails from Sicily to Norway, where he meets Oswang Furioso, whose magic mantle carries the men to Lapland, where Adelmorn vows to serve Lucifer and enjoys a banquet served by hags. He is stabbed by a jealous woman and disappears through spontaneous combustion.

Such novels as *Rosalvo Delmonmort. A Tale* (1818), John Neal's *Logan* (1822), James Fenimore Cooper's *Lionel Lincoln* (1825), James McHenry's *The Spectre of the Forest; or, Annals of the Housatonic* (1823), and James K. Paulding's *Koenigsmarke; or, Old Times in the New World* (1823) contain slight traces of Gothic influence in the use of ventriloquism, mysterious deaths, madmen, and superstitions.

One of the best Gothic episodes is found in the sentimental tale, *Alonzo and Melissa; or, The Unfeeling Father* (1824), by Daniel Jackson. Despite the solemn promise in the preface that the story holds no indecorous stimulants nor contains unmeaning and inexplicated incidents sounding upon the sense but imperceptible to the understanding, such Radcliffean elements as a "bodiless hand, cold as the icy fingers of death," candles which disappear, a peripatetic ball of fire that aimlessly meanders through the halls, and a human form with eyes burning like fire, and flames issuing from its head, are left unexplained. Melissa, the maiden immured in the castle, is subjected to these horrors by a band of robbers; but how these ingenious men contrived such unusual properties is not made clear by the author. Just as the spirit of Washington appeared in *The Champions of Freedom* to show the hero how he might best serve his country, so Dr. Franklin is introduced in *Alonzo and Melissa* to smooth the rough path of the hero and the heroine. The Gothic element in this patriotic tale is merely for adornment.

In conclusion, we find that Brown was the only early American novelist of importance before 1830 who was continually successful in domesticating the English Gothic novel. American writers recognized the lack of medieval settings, the Puritan antipathy for merely amusing tales, and the demand for patriotic motives; consequently, with ingenuity, a few tried to solve the problems confronting them either by writing novels which touched on contemporary events like wars and plagues and by explaining what appear to be superhuman agencies on psychological or scientific grounds; or, on the other hand, they might introduce Gothic episodes in tales of seduction, in sentimental romances, or in historical adventures. These episodes were imitations of the Walpole-Lewis, Mrs. Radcliffe, or Godwin-Shelley types of Gothic novel—

usually they belonged to the first two—but, in any case, they were parasitically attached to literature with an avowed didactic or moral purpose. (pp. 37-45)

George L. Phillips, "The Gothic Element in the American Novel before 1830," in West Virginia University Bulletin: Philological Studies, *Vol. 3, September, 1939, pp. 37-45.*

THE GOTHIC NOVEL IN SCOTLAND

FRANCIS RUSSELL HART

[In the following excerpt, Hart discusses the Scottish Gothic novel, paying particular attention to the works of Tobias George Smollett, Sir Walter Scott, and James Hogg.]

The early novels in Scotland are undeniably associated with what we may cautiously call the Gothic tendency in fiction of the late eighteenth century. Recent years have seen several attempts to define the Gothic novel, to distinguish what is essential from what is mere trapping, to separate serious from frivolous or popular Gothic, to insist on a hierarchy of generic elements, and to judge individual works according to their observance of such distinctions and priorities. My own view is that these efforts do not provide a fair critical approach to individual English novelists, let alone Scottish. We may learn something of the limits of generic definition, as well as something about the beginnings of a distinctive Scottish tradition in the novel, by viewing the novels of Smollett, Scott, and James Hogg—none of whom can be seen essentially as a Gothic novelist—in relation to a Gothic tendency. Smollett's variant of the tendency can be identified with the idea of the grotesque, Scott's with the idea of the historic, and Hogg's with the idea of the diabolic.

The Gothic tendency in the novel is normally seen to consist of five major elements, whichever predominates, however they are related: an antiquarian taste for what was taken to be the style or ornament of the late middle ages; an ambiguous taste for the preternatural, that is, a curious revival of the ghost story; a fascination with the mystery of human malevolence, perversity, sadism; a preference for the style or affective state called sublimity; and a shift of rhetorical aim away from the didactic and mimetic to the affective and expressive. A definition of genre or tendency cannot prematurely stipulate which emphasis is central, which element is mere trapping. What makes a novel in some sense Gothic is often closely related to what makes it interesting as a mixture of modes.

In his study of Smollett Robert Spector quotes two modern critical judgments of *The Adventures of Ferdinand Count Fathom* that, taken together, make a revealing paradox. Albrecht Strauss calls the book "a curious melange of incongruous fairy tale material and conventional claptrap," and this is accurate. Louis Martz sees Smollett turning away from the picaresque and "seeking new inspiration" in the horror tale, the fairy tale, Gothic, and fantastic narrative. This is true, too. The curious mixture and the new inspiration, however, should not conceal the degree to which Smollett is seeking new ways and matters for the expression of a vision he has had all along.

The conventional claptrap episodes have often been noted: the repeated visits of Renaldo to Monimia's supposed tomb; the awesome appearance of her "phantom"; and the flight of Fathom from the tempest in the dark wood to the old woman's bloody hut, which Scott praises as a "tale of natural wonder which rises into the sublime; and, though often imitated, has never been surpassed, or perhaps equalled." Spector adds to this last the episode of Celinda's seduction, finds here "the materials later exploited by Ann Radcliffe," and cites them both as examples of Smollett's satiric treatment of the Gothic:

> Smollett never simply yields to the devices of supernatural terror; indeed, he ridicules them even as he uses them . . . Smollett presents not Gothic terror, but the natural turmoil of the mind and actual physical dangers . . . If this is an early use of the Gothic in the English novel, it is one that takes little advantage of supernatural elements to harry the imagination . . . In a way these two satiric attacks on the Gothic illusion serve to undercut the terror in the one genuinely Gothic portion of the novel when Renaldo comes to what he believes to be the grave of Monimia . . . It is all a language . . . to set doubts on the authenticity of the horror; and, while Smollett gets the most out of the new taste for terror, he does it clearly with the touch of the satirist.

But this overlooks the way such episodes are related to other elements in the melange. Fathom's is the Hobbesian and mechanistic world of violent and gross physical needs, which Bruce rightly finds central to Smollett's vision. It is a world of warring animals, where the central symbol of depravity is the spectacle, at once horrible and ludicrous, of the close and violent interdependence of mind and body. It is a world where terror and horror are the strongest emotions, where man, preternaturally sensitized by extreme fear, supposes himself in hell, responds in part with religious awe, and thus affirms the preternatural workings of conscience. In such a world, Gothic suppositions are no mere claptrap excrescences. Nor does Smollett merely parody. The terror is nonetheless real for its ludicrous aspect; it is an antisublimity that is true grotesque. We have not gone far in interpreting Smollett's Gothic tendency if we reject as irrelevant the preclassical mode Smollett reintroduced into British fiction: that vision of a monstrously perverse, fallen, but animated world; that powerful conflation of the terrible, the horrible, and the ludicrous which we call the grotesque. In Scottish Gothic, the grotesque plays an essential role.

The grotesque in Smollett is inseparable from another modality which some (Kurt Wittig, for example) would see as distinctively Scottish, but which can also be identified with the later eighteenth century and its commitment to the theater of the mind, namely a radical and violent subjectivity of vision. One recalls the multiple distortions of subjectivity in the epistolary method of *Humphrey Clinker*. The grotesque and the radically distortive nature of subjectivity are theoretically linked by Smollett in a revealing passage in *Ferdinand Count Fathom:* "There is an affinity and short transition betwixt all the violent passions that agitate the human mind: They are all false perspectives, which though they magnify, yet perplex and render indistinct every object which they represent." The mixture is no mere satiric undercutting of terror, but an express fascination with the violent and grotesque subjectivity of extreme emotional states.

Roderick Random's outrage and despair at the gross caprice of the world cause him to see that world through the double lenses of infernal horror and sadistic glee. What Sedlmayr calls the "secularization of Hell" in Goya, often a central vision in Gothic fiction, is nowhere more striking than in the infernal grotesque of Random's descents—into the cockpit, into the London ordinary:

> [I] found myself in the middle of a cook's shop, almost suffocated with the steams of boiled beef . . . While I stood in amaze, undetermined whether to sit down or walk upwards again, Strap, in his descent, missing one of the steps, tumbled headlong into this infernal ordinary, and overturned the cook . . . In her fall, she dashed the whole mess against the legs of a drummer . . . scalded him so miserably, that he started up, and danced up and down, uttering a volley of execrations, that made my hair stand on end . . . This poultice [of salt] was scarce laid on, when the drummer . . . broke forth into such a hideous yell, as made the whole company tremble . . . grinding his teeth at the same time with a most horrible grin.

And the grotesque horror of the battle scene where Random lies stapled to the poop deck, blinded with blood and scattered brains, surely yields nothing in Gothic intensity to the gloomier scenes of charnel rape in *The Monk*. The effect is identical with what Kayser describes in Brueghel's secularizing of the infernal in Bosch: "the experience of the estranged world . . . the hellish torments, like the phantasmagoric, the ghostly, the sadistic, the obscene, the mechanical"—in short, "the terror inspired by the unfathomable, that is, the grotesque." The revival of the grotesque is part of the Gothic tendency.

But it goes further than that in Smollett. The grotesque may be grounded in a distinctive theology. The grotesque world reflects man's original and mysterious perverseness. Random's vision of subjective and sadistic violence may seem in part caused by the world's brutality, but this is clearly not the case in *Peregrine Pickle*. Pickle acts from what Poe will later call "a paradoxical something, which we may call *perverseness* . . . With certain minds, under certain conditions, it becomes absolutely irresistible. I am not more certain that I breathe, than that the assurance of the wrong or error of any action is often the one unconquerable *force* which impels us, and alone impels us to its prosecution . . . It is a radical, a primitive impulse—elementary." Perry's "preposterous and unaccountable passion" is to "afflict and perplex" his fellow creatures. Nor is this perversity separable from his creative exuberance, the humorous power that makes him a hero. He is a mysterious hero, to be sure, pawn of an infatuation of fancy and will, in a monstrous, potentially tragic world of "humors," of inexplicable hostilities, of "fantastic and maimed characters" such as Commodore Trunnion (V. S. Pritchett's phrase), whose fantastic maiming excites Perry to new heights of sadistic creativity. The moral mystery of cruel perverseness is, I think, far more central to *Peregrine Pickle* than is its philosophical morality, wherein the hero systematically discovers the destructive consequences of unbridled imagination. Perry is not a naif but a demonic scourge. He makes his world; it is his victim.

He torments his world not for its sordidness but for its solemnity, its conventional orders. His indefatigable intrigues have two essential effects: to expose the ludicrous in the solemn, and to invert or destroy the ordered reality of conventional society. The first gives the book its grotesqueness, the second its saturnalian humor. More often than judge or scourge, Perry is vice, demon, or lord of misrule. The example of Smollett's Perry suggests that we may have overlooked in the Gothic tendency a revival of saturnalian fantasy by overlooking its Scottish variations.

At any rate, here are two brief examples of the grotesque and the saturnalian in *Peregrine Pickle*. Nights at inns are filled with diabolical terror, ludicrous raptures. Gay and fantastic, ominous and sinister, the world loses all rational shape, and humans become helpless puppets. Pallet the painter, amorously invading his Dulcinea's chamber, stumbles instead on the hiding Capuchin

> so that the painter having stript himself to the shirt, in groping about for his Dulcinea's bed, chanced to lay his hand upon the shaven crown of the father's head, which by a circular motion, the priest began to turn round in his grasp, like a ball in a socket . . . one of his fingers happened to slip into his mouth, and was immediately secured between the Capuchin's teeth, with as firm a fixure, as if it had been screwed in a blacksmith's vice . . . the unfortunate painter was found lying naked on the floor, in all the agony of horror and dismay.

This same unfortunate painter stalks about in female costume at a masquerade and is gazed at by the multitude "as a preternatural phaenomenon." Peregrine delights in manipulating such spectacles. His grotesque taste is a function of his perversity. But his even stronger delight is in disorder—as in the marvelous dinner episode, where the whole table is involved "in havoc, ruin and confusion," and "before Pickle could accomplish his escape, he was sauced with the syrup of the dormouse pye, which went to pieces in the general wreck; and as for the Italian count, he was overwhelmed by the sow's stomach, which bursting in the fall, discharged its contents upon his leg and thigh, and scalded him so miserably, that he shrieked with anguish, and grinned with a most ghastly and horrible aspect." There is no sign here that the reader is to be morally concerned with imaginative excess. Rather, he is to share Perry's sadistic glee at monstrous disorder, and thus to recognize the "preposterous and unaccountable" fact of exuberant perverseness.

If the Gothic tendency in fiction of the late Enlightenment is to be restricted to ghost stories or to a modal unity of sublime awe, then Smollett's grotesque may be declared unrelated. But if it centers instead on the terror and horror aroused by the mysterious possibilities of alienation—perversity, monomania, diabolic possession—and on the power of such alienation to create and destroy, delude and fascinate, then *Peregrine Pickle* is pertinent indeed.

Although Sir Walter Scott does not use the word, Smollett's Gothic tendency was definitive for him. He stresses Smollett's sublimity, praises him as far above Fielding "in his power of exciting terror," refers to "the wild and ferocious Pickle" whose jokes resemble "those of a fiend in glee," and likens Smollett to Byron: "He was, like a pre-eminent poet of our own day, a searcher of dark bosoms, and loved to paint characters under the strong agitation of fierce and stormy passions. Hence misanthropes, gamblers, and duellists, are as common in his works, as robbers in those of Salvator Rosa, and are drawn, in most cases, with the same terrible truth and effect."

The same Gothic inclination is evident in Scott. But if Smol-

lett is excluded from the Gothic for his grotesque antisublimity, Scott is excluded for assimilating such Gothic elements into a historical realism. Is the distinction between the Gothic and the historic as real or significant as their kinship? Is historicity as essential to Scott as numerous commentators suggest? If we allow for the characteristically Scottish setting or atmosphere of local history, we may find Scott at his best more significantly related to the Gothic tendency than to the historic and thus understand Gothic less reductively.

Recent Scott criticism has argued otherwise. But I am increasingly impressed by earlier critics who saw Scott's historicism as dominantly aesthetic, his settings patterned on a macabre picturesque and conceived invariably, whatever the epochal surface, as timeless borderlands of romance where marvels jostle with human motives. It is the same in *Waverley*, where eighteenth-century enlightenment is stunned by the ambience of "romance," or in the late Renaissance of *Nigel*, which Scott saw spatially as foothills where the marvelous in incident still mixes with the subtly natural in character, or in the decaying Middle Ages of *Durward*, where romance ventures into a perilous, anarchic borderland between cynical pragmatism and ferocious quixotry. In all three, the same barbarousness and the same civility interplay in chiaroscuro, and the picturesque aesthetic renders historical confrontation as a haunted landscape. I may be overstating the case for emphasis, but my suggestion is that Scott inclined more to use history in the service of romance than to assimilate romance to the interpretation of history.

To view Scott otherwise is to be faced with the following critical situation, seen in three juxtaposed critical propositions: *The Bride of Lammermoor* is certainly one of Scott's best novels; *The Bride* is one of the most complete and effective syntheses of Gothic elements; *The Bride* is not really a Gothic novel. If the best of a genre or an author must be atypical, then definition has lost its usefulness. But some will object that this evidence is unfairly limited, so let me add two other novels also cited as "best" and also taken as illustrative of Gothic derivations in Scott: *Old Mortality* and *Redgauntlet*. I do not deny that Scott is a very interesting and hugely influential interpreter of the historic in experience. I mean merely to suggest, in a shift of emphasis, that the archetypal recurrences are more basic than discriminations of temporal or cultural setting. The recurrences are centrally Gothic: the macabre-picturesque ambience already mentioned, the definitive character relationship, the hereditary curse.

The central relationship in what is generally identified as the Gothic novel is a mutual fascination between fatalistic innocence and sublimely willful evil. The Gothic hero-villain alone is not definitive, and criticism that seeks moral interest in him alone mistakes the persistent Gothic characterology. Perilous innocence and demonic power are drawn to each other. Archetypally—some would say incestuously—akin, together they express or evoke the mysterious theodicy hinted at by even the most frivolously rationalized Gothic. As Anthony Winner puts it in a splendid essay on Hoffmann, "No one knows how the primal trespass comes about . . . We are paradoxically and unaccountably innocent and yet somehow guilty." We yearn in fantasy for both the pastoral idyll and the godlike power. As readers of Gothic novels we identify not with individual characters but with the painful division or the grotesque bond of infatuation between them: Emily and Montoni, Antonia and Ambrosio, Caleb and Falkland, Monster and Frankenstein, Immalee and Melmoth,

Cathy and Heathcliff—and some more mythic synthesists would add Christabel and Geraldine, Emanation and Spectre.

Such a bond is central in many Waverley novels. It is articulated, superficially at least, in terms of historical, cultural, or ideological division. The critical issue is whether the historic-cultural typology recently stressed in Scott's characterology has really displaced its antecedents in Gothic archetype or simply covered them up. The issue is not to be settled here in a few sentences. But having lengthily supported the earlier position elsewhere, I will briefly put the opposing case here.

The mutual fascinations in Scott are not really intercultural at all, and not between opposing epochs. They are the same in every age, and they are between moral and psychical poles: the meek but brave civility of moderation and the noble energy of monomania, the enlightened pragmatic and the barbaric idealistic, Sancho and Quixote. And in every age, says the ironic Stendhal, "the base Sancho Panza wins." At least on a conscious ideological level Scott evidently stood with Sancho and pragmatic civility. It is equally evident, as Scott sensed, that a semiconscious attraction to the charisma of the monomaniac, the demonic freedom of the antiempirical absolutist, reveals itself. Scott had a penchant for Gothic outlaws, humorous Jacobites, and fanatical Covenanters. That such figures are historicized into representative anachronisms sometimes seems little more than Scott's way of authenticating them—a familiarly Scottish way—and of saying that they are more ancient, more "given." What they really represent is a preenlightened persistence, a demonic element, in the human inheritance, to be sought out, exorcised, and not superficially denied or perilously overlooked. History itself is suspect. The absolutes of theological romance may be more basic.

Some such recognition is implicit in the quests and loyalties of Scott's protagonists, implicating them personally and irreversibly in the destinies of their demonic—that is, monomaniacal—counterparts. Henry Morton, barely known even as his legendary father's son, enters upon the destined path to his own identity, his birthright, by responding "helplessly" to the claim made in his father's name by the fanatical but compelling Burley. Morton suffers, but Burley is exorcised, dwindling at last into a mean devil at bay in a cave, a menace safely to be left behind. The tale of Wandering Willie sets a similar paradigm of exorcism for *Redgauntlet.* Steenie goes to hell and demands back his birthright from a satanic trickster-thief. Darsy Latimer likewise seeks his identity in a wild region dominated by his monomaniacal uncle; once more, the result is the exorcism, the comic diminution, of that demonic force. The exorcism in *The Bride of Lammermoor,* while tragically complex, is archetypally the same. The Master inherits a fanatical role he seeks to ignore, is fatefully attracted to a specious (because unstable, lifeless) innocence in Lucy Ashton. She is drawn for protection to his demonically divided inheritance. Trapped in his Gothic role, he simply disappears into the sands, as unreal at last as Caleb Balderstone's idolatrous illusion of a still noble house.

Idolatry and specious inheritance are closely linked in Scottish fiction. The role of the hereditary curse suggests as much. It is often the core of the protagonist's problem; it inheres in his disinheritance. Henry Morton lives in the ruins of his father's lost cause on the charity of his niggardly uncle. All that the Master has left are his name (hardly that), his ruined tower, and his quixotic fraud of a servant. Darsy Latimer has

a friend, a fatalistic curiosity, and not even his own name. Superficially the cause of disinheritance is "history," but "history" simply stands in for the evil—the idolatrous monomania, the inhumanity—in the past, the barbarism of man's moral youth. The curse of the past in Scott's Gothic is transmitted not in historic process, but in the warped and despotic personality of the past's monomaniacal devotee, the parental figure who sacrifices humanity to a cruelly quixotic idea. Yet the interdependence of innocence and monomania is powerful, fateful. Scott's relation to the Gothic is definitive for all his Scottish preoccupation with local history and legend. The mixture is a variant of the Gothic, expressive of a distinctive culture.

The same can be said for James Hogg, a third Gothic novelist in the early Scottish tradition. Least controversially yet most intriguingly Gothic, Hogg's *Private Memoirs and Confessions of a Justified Sinner* is a complex of diabolic possession, theological satire, and local legend. Hogg's landscape could hardly be more remote from the vague medieval sublimities or inquisitorial dungeons of Walpole, Radcliffe, Maturin. Yet it is, even more than Scott's, a haunted locale, and it is haunted chiefly by the terror of the diabolical. This, too, can have many meanings and shapes, and Hogg's diabolic principle is significantly different from the repressed, sadistic sublimity of the Miltonic or "sensibility" Gothic. In Hogg, the terror of the diabolic is at once more primitive and more explicitly theological—a mixture we will come to recognize as definitively Scottish. Hogg has conflated a terrible theological monomania with a grotesque folk diabolism; the result is a tale of diabolic possession whose current appeal seems wider, more various, than the appeal of almost any other Gothic novel of its period. It derives not just from the horror Gothic of Godwin and Lewis, but from the newly imported macabre of Hoffmann as well. It bears significant likeness, in its treatment of the diabolic compact, to *Melmoth the Wanderer* and, in form, to its other immediate predecessor, *Frankenstein.* And yet, as Dorothy Bussy told André Gide, "This book is Scotch to its very marrow; no Englishman could possibly have written it."

Gide's praise of the book centers on its conception of the diabolic. The devil, says Gide, is wholly believable in psychological terms without recourse to a simple supernaturalism; the end, which demands a more literal or naive credibility, is therefore weak. This is a major issue of interpretation in the book, and it is central to a conception of the Gothic as well: is the preternatural or the demonic to be consistently psychologized, naturalized, or is it to remain to some degree ontologically mysterious? The example of Hogg forces one to the latter position, for the very nature and experience of diabolic possession demand that the devil have some sort of metaphysically separate existence. And Hogg carefully verifies such separateness through the senses, however puzzled, of numerous observers.

The relation of possession in Hogg to the more familiar psychologized diabolism of other Gothic novels is not simple. Edwin Eigner, writing of Hogg as an antecedent to Stevenson, stresses the discovery of the power of darkness as another power or side of the self. For him, the discovery of one's shadowy double is essential to the moral shock that gives the Gothic its power: there was that *in me* that could love a murderer; part of *me* loved the spectacle of pain. Sometimes Hogg's sinner is sure that "I have two souls, which take possession of my bodily frame by turns," and the devil confirms the doctrine. But that is the point: the doctrine is diabolic and by no means the whole truth. In fact, it is crucial to diabolic possession in Hogg that possession is not mere "doubling"—that the self is possessed by an Other, that the story draws partly on the primitive fear of being bewitched, possessed, by the spirit or power of an Other, of being robbed of one's identity. The whole suspense of the struggle of Robert and Gil-Martin for Robert's soul hangs on the questions: Will Robert ultimately surrender his whole soul willingly to the Other and cease to be? When will human nature, as in *Melmoth,* relieve its torment by yielding to the ultimate horror? To identify this scourge of the proud and the damned too facilely with the German romantic doppelgänger is to ignore the more primordial fear of the metaphysical Other that robs one of oneself.

And yet Gil-Martin, whose reality is grounded throughout in folk diabolism, is highly sophisticated in his powers. What is most terrifying and bewildering about him (and terror and metaphysical bewilderment are inseparable in *The Sinner*) is his power of impersonation: "My countenance changes with my studies and sensations . . . It is a natural peculiarity in me, over which I have not full control. If I contemplate a man's features seriously, mine own gradually assume the very same appearance and character. And . . . by assuming his likeness I attain to the possession of his most secret thoughts." Via impersonation comes possession, and possession is power over the mind, capturing one's ideas and transforming them so as to damn one. The conception of evil here in Hogg, as in Smollett and Scott, is distinctively Scottish. In the English Gothic, with its concern for political and clerical tyranny, the power is more apt to be vaguely political, even when implicitly sexual; the devil is a tyrant over the will. In the Scottish Gothic the conception appears to be more intellectual; the power derives from the awful corruption of theological doctrine, from intellectual pride and sophistry. The tempter is a monomaniacal sophist whose power derives not from a sublimity of will, but from a sublimity of idea—and suitably, the word "sublime" or "sublimity" in Hogg's *Sinner* is reserved to describe diabolic ideas: "There is a sublimity in his ideas, with which there is to me a mixture of terror . . . I was greatly revived, and felt my spirit rise above the sphere of vulgar conceptions and the restrained views of unregenerate men . . . the ruinous tendency of the tenets so sublimely inculcated." The diabolic is the sublime power of theological doctrine impersonated by the devil.

But the diabolic in Hogg is a reality of folk legend and traditional Scottish culture as well. His novel is fixed in haunted locality. Localism is as essential to the book's credibility as its weird conflating of perspectives and its "swithering of modes" are to its rhetoric. Hogg speaks as an enlightened and distanced sceptic; he also speaks from within his traditional culture as the transmitter of legendary truth. His characteristic apologia is the passage at the end of a tale called "The Bridal of Polmood":

> Some may perhaps say, that this tale is ill-conceived, unnatural, and that the moral of it is not palpable; but let it be duly considered, that he who sits down to write a novel or romance—to produce something that is merely the creation of his own fancy, may be obliged to conform to certain rules and regulations; while he who transmits the traditions of his country to others, does wrong, if he do not transmit them as they are. He may be at liberty to tell them in his own way, but he ought by all

> means to conform to the incidents as handed down to him; because the greater part of these stories have their foundations in truth. That which is true cannot be unnatural, as the incidents may always be traced from their first principles—the passions and various prejudices of men; and from every important occurrence in human life a moral may with certainty be drawn.

In tales and novels alike, Hogg alternates among three narrative voices and methods. He speaks as the traditional collector divided in allegiance to modern enlightenment and to the truth of the archaic local storyteller, for whom traditional materials are matters of fact, who has inherited them primarily in dramatic anecdotes, and who traces his knowledge to kin and heir of participants. He speaks, on occasion, through dramatic narrators of the Galt sort—parochial memoirists who tell their adventures with faith in their general import and in their manifestation of providence. Or he speaks by wholly dramatic means through the expository dialogue of the ballad. Whichever he employs, he is experimenting with perspectives of local immediacy; and from such perspectives, time is less historic than legendary—the violent, often preternatural past of legend—while place is intensely, yet matter-of-factly, localized by name and topography. The result is closer to Galt than to Scott, yet different from both.

The Brownie of Bodsbeck (1817) provides an interesting counterpart to *Old Mortality* (1816) as well as to Galt's *Ringan Gilhaize* (1823). Its protagonist Walter Laidlaw is a curious analogue to Scott's Henry Morton; both are religious moderates who become involved with the Covenanters, during the "killing time," largely through the force and ruthlessness of Clavers. Hogg's Clavers is as distinct from Scott's romantic cavalier as Galt's is; yet he remains the brutal and capricious figure of local legends, legends recounting his raid through "the vales of Esk and Annan." "The narrator of this tale confesses that he has taken this account of his raid . . . solely from tradition . . . but these traditions are descended from such a source, and by such a line, as amounts with him to veracity." Hogg's is an attempt, as in Galt's *Ringan,* to do justice to the Covenanters by recounting their sufferings almost at first hand. His lack of narrative expertise results in an interesting confusion of point of view.

He wants evidently to speak in his own voice of the agonies and absurdities of the killing time, as one distanced and enlightened. Specifically, he treats with comic enlightenment the superstitions about a preternatural brownie who is actually a Covenanter in masquerade. He is offering historic truth to the curious but distanced modern reader. Yet he speaks as one in direct touch with the locale and its traditions; he has heard the descendants speak; he is closely acquainted with places that preserve local memories. Finally, he believes that Walter Laidlaw tells his own story best. In fact, he often reminds us that what is being narrated was preserved through Walter's repeated oral renditions: "as Walter was wont to relate the story himself, when any stranger came there on a winter evening, as long as he lived, it may haply be acceptable to the curious, and the lovers of rustic simplicity, to read it in his own words, although he drew it out to an inordinate length, and perhaps kept his own personal feelings and prowess too much in view for the fastidious or critical reader to approve." Upon reaching the climax of Walter's trial in Edinburgh, he insists, "the conclusion of this trial must be given in Walter's own phrase"—and it is, in pages of broad Scots, dialogue and all, including Walter's mimicry of the dialect of his humorous Highland friend Sergeant Macpherson. The whole book might well have been done in Walter's own voice. But had it been so, Walter could not have told the mysterious, sophisticated story of his daughter Katharine, supposed to have entered into diabolical communion with the brownie; and Hogg could not have intervened in the voice of the amused modern.

The narrator describes his homecoming, with a condescending view of the sentimental rustic: "With all these delightful and exhilarating thoughts glowing in his breast, how could that wild and darksome road, or indeed any road, be tedious to our honest goodman? . . . He crossed the Meggat about eleven o'clock in the night, just as the waning moon began to peep over the hills to the southeast of the lake." The topographical particularity is characteristic; the urbane narrator knows his country. Yet here he breaks off, for "such scenes and such adventures, are not worth a farthing, unless described and related in the language of the country to which they are peculiar." Walter takes over:

> I fand I was come again into the country o' the fairies an' the spirits . . . an' there was nae denying o't; for when I saw the bit crookit moon come stealing o'er the kipps o'Bowerhope-Law, an' thraw her dead yellow light on the hills o'Meggat, I fand the very nature an' the heart within me changed. A' the hills on the tae side o' the loch war as dark as pitch, an' the tither side had that ill-hued colour on 't, as if they had been a' rowed in their winding sheets; an' then the shadow o' the moon it gaed bobbing an' quivering up the loch fornent me, like a streek o' cauld fire.

He meets a white shape on the road, yet remains humorously half-sceptical—the moderate, somewhat enlightened protagonist, who is still the local farmer of his time. Hogg's comic preternaturalism is thus given dramatic reality—of a sort Burns, for example, never quite permits. "A' the stories that ever I heard about fairies in my life came linkin into my mind ane after anither, and I almaist thought I was already on my road to the Fairyland, an' to be paid away to hell, like a kane-cock, at the end o' seven years . . . Hout, thinks I, what need I be sae feared? They'll never take away ane o' my size to be a fairy—Od, I wad be the daftest-like fairy ever was seen."

The narrator is not so remote from Walter as his language suggests. In Hogg, the traditionary storyteller and the formal novelist are never reconciled, except perhaps in *The Justified Sinner.* In texture and proportion, the short dramatic tales are invariably well-shaped; but Hogg is unable to solve the problem of integrating them into the structural decorums of the novel. The apology for including all the incidents of Clavers' raids during the time Walter was his prisoner will often be repeated in kind in *The Three Perils of Man:* "It is necessary to mention all these, as they were afterwards canvassed at Walter's trial, the account of which formed one of his winter evening tales as long as he lived. Indeed, all such diffuse and miscellaneous matter as is contained in this chapter, is a great incumbrance in the right onward progress of a tale; but we have done with it, and shall now make haste to the end of our narrative in a direct uninterrupted line." Yet, in his uncertainty, this confused, would-be decorous narrator permits Hogg to have his traditions both ways. He gives the tradition, apologizes for it, recounts it in the character's own narrative, yet places himself where it happened and indicates his own sense of its reality. "These minute traditions are generally founded on truth; yet though two generations have

scarcely passed away since the date of this tale, tradition, in this instance, relates things impossible, else Clavers must indeed have been one of the infernals. Often has the present relator of this tale stood over the deep green marks of that courser's hoof, many of which remain on that hill, in awe and astonishment, to think that he was actually looking at the traces made by the devil's foot, or at least by a horse that once belonged to him."

The Brownie of Bodsbeck is a tale of specific locales, and Hogg delights in local distinctions of dialect. His tales are filled with them. Basil Lee recalls that when he went to America with a Highland lieutenant, "I could not speak English otherwise than in the broadest Border dialect, while he delivered himself in a broken Highland jargon." The "Love Adventures of Mr. George Cochrane" include a gypsy girl who speaks "in the true border twang," an "old wife of the same hamlet who spoke the border dialect in all its primitive broadness and vulgarity," and a Mary Park o' the Wolfcleuchhead, "who, having come from the head of Borthwick Water, did not speak with such a full border accent." *The Brownie* employs distinctive dialect narrators: Old Nanny mixes homely affection and covenant cant; Davie Tait produces a long prayer whose very language is to become local legend; John Hay, the shepherd, proves an impenetrable mystery to Clavers by virtue of the triumphant locality of his idioms and reflections. For Hogg local language is a force for the survival

While I fixed him without motion on the floor, Marguerite wresting the dagger from his hand plunged it repeatedly in his heart till he expired.

I now heard the heavy steps ascending the staircase : the door was thrown open and again the bleeding nun stood before me.

Two illustrations from the 1826 edition of Matthew Gregory Lewis's The Monk.

and integrity of local tradition; and thus, the integrity of his English narrator and of the structure that narrator seeks to impose becomes more problematical.

The same virtuosity of dialect fills *The Three Perils of Man* (1822). But the problem of formal integrity in this "comic, fantastic, and extravagant epic" is chiefly one of mode; and the authenticity of the book's storehouse of local legend is compromised by its derivation from literary convention, whose very sophistication makes us aware of the book's formal disunities and disproportions. Douglas Gifford feels that disunity of plot structure is irrelevant. But the narrator himself more than once likens his effort to that of a waggoner laden with rich merchandise and forced to carry it part by part up a steep ascent. And the dramatic storytellers of the book's several interpolated tales are severe critics of each other:

> "It is nae worth the name of a story that," said Tam Craik; "for, in the first place, it is a lang story; in the second place, it is a confused story; and, in the third place, it ends ower abruptly, and rather looks like half a dozen o' stories linkit to ane anither's tails."

> "Master Michael Scott," said Gibbie, "and my friends, I again appeal to you all if this man has not fallen through his tale."

Often it seems easy to turn such quips on Hogg himself; he invites them.

The framing romance is a courtly game of competing chivalric pledges, whose actual brutalities are often rendered in a grisly matter-of-fact style. The earl of Douglas vows to win Princess Margaret of Scotland by recapturing Roxburgh Castle from its English conqueror, Lord Musgrave, whose pledge to the Lady Jane Howard is to hold it until Christmas. These "two most beautiful ladies of England and Scotland" whimsically venture into the neighborhood in male disguise, and both are taken hostage; one appears to be executed, and Musgrave kills himself to save the other. An extravagant ethos of chivalric game combines with countless romance motifs of disguise, mistaken deaths, recognitions, metamorphoses, reunions, and restorations. Yet the plot is thinly historical and is allegedly taken from the manuscript of an old curate, recounted with the mock-romantic scepticism toward "the spirit of romance" characteristic of Scott. The siege plot takes up the first fifth and final quarter of this "most ambitious" of Hogg's novels. The long middle diverges from the siege plot to center on Sir Ringan Redhough, Warden of the Borders and supporter-rival of Douglas, and the prophecy that he will replace Douglas as lord of numerous Border baronies. Redhough sends an embassy to his kinsman, the grand warlock Michael Scott of Aikwood Castle, to learn his weird. The embassy, owing to Scott's magic contests with a mysterious friar and his struggle for power with his master the devil, is trapped on Scott's tower for several days, and engages in a competition of tales to determine who will be killed and eaten to save the rest. The competition is interwoven with the grotesque and farcical efforts of a rescue party. Ultimately, the ambassadors are made drunk by Scott and the devil and metamorphosed into cattle. The victory is celebrated by a visit from the king and queen, with chivalric games, knightings, and noble weddings. The book finishes with the awesome account of Michael Scott's climactic battles with the devil and his death.

Gifford praises "Hogg's courageous and epic attempt to work in the oral and popular tradition which had produced the ballads, folk-tales and legends." That he attempted to work in this tradition with frame and motif from chivalric romance makes for the work's intriguing peculiarity of mode, its "juxtaposition of romantic and realistic attitudes," its mingling—especially in the interpolated tales—of fabliau farce and demonic fantasy, its "unique blend of irony, racy humour, fantasy and romance." Not surprisingly, Gifford is reminded of both Dunbar and Smollett. And such associations as these, in the face of such combinations, mixtures, and formal problems, vividly imply the unique difficulties of the early Scottish novelist in search of a distinctive form. But the virtuoso diabolism, at once sublime and grotesque, Gothic and folkloristic, is what reminds us of the more assured author of *The Justified Sinner*: this, and the extravagant orchestration of contrasting styles and personae, and the effort to integrate traditionary tales and tellers into the form and mode of historical romance.

How much was sacrificed to make the more constrained and subtle achievement of the later book? It seems plausible to numerous commentators that a more sophisticated talent, that of Lockhart, took a hand in fashioning *The Justified Sinner.* Do the short stories, to which Hogg turned after this, "merely illustrate," as Gifford feels, "how grievous a loss the Scottish novel had suffered?" Or does Hogg's career in fiction, rather, illustrate the uncongeniality of the novel form to the fictional materials and impulses of Scottish tradition? (pp. 13-30)

> *Francis Russell Hart, "Scottish Variations of the Gothic Novel: Smollett, Scott, Hogg," in his* The Scottish Novel: From Smollett to Spark, *Cambridge, Mass.: Harvard University Press, 1978, pp. 13-30.*

INFLUENCE AND LEGACY

BRENDAN HENNESSY

[*In the following excerpt, Hennessy describes the absorption of Gothic elements into Romantic fiction and the Gothic novel's influence on modern supernatural stories and science fiction.*]

The term Romantic has been obscured and devalued by its loose application to literature of all ages that emphasises imagination and the subjective at the expense of the rational and ordered, which follows rules. But even in the stricter, late eighteenth-century and early nineteenth-century sense, and confining the term to those writers who were consciously following a definite, Romantic aim, the movement has a much less exact connotation of historical period than the Gothic. Romanticism is a current that can be traced right through to today, while Gothicism is a stream that goes underground, out of sight, for long periods, and then reappears in different forms. Part of the reason for the decline in Gothic as a genre was the absorption of many of its aspects by Romanticism.

Byron acknowledged that

> Otway, Radcliffe, Schiller, Shakespeare's art,
> Had stamped her image in me.

The Byronic, or Romantic, hero—the Fatal Man of the Romantics—in the form of the Giaour, the Corsair, Childe Harold, Lara, and Manfred—all pale, beautiful, haunted by guilt, with amazing eyes, melancholy, superior and proud, mostly also misanthropic, ruthless, mysterious, heroic and villainous—clearly derives from the writers he singles out. Most directly they come from Mrs Radcliffe's Montoni and Schedoni. The influence of Schiller's adventurous, suffering, robbers came both directly and from Lewis's *The Monk* via Schedoni, and Milton's Satan is a shadow over all. Setting Mrs Radcliffe's Schedoni—

> His cowl, too, as it threw a shade over the livid paleness of his face, increased its severe character, and gave an effect to his large melancholy eye, which approached to horror . . . his physiognomy . . . bore the traces of many passions, which seemed to have fixed the features they no longer animated . . . his eyes were so piercing that they seemed to penetrate, at a single glance, into the hearts of men, and to read their most secret thoughts; few persons could support their scrutiny, or even endure to meet them twice. . . .

beside Byron's Giaour—

> Dark and unearthly is the scowl
> That glares beneath his dusky cowl.
> The flash of that dilating eye
> Reveals too much of time gone by;
> Though varying, indistinct its hue,
> Oft will his glance the gazer rue,
> For in it lurks that nameless spell,
> Which speaks, itself unspeakable,
> A spirit yet unquell'd and high
> That claims and keeps ascendancy. . . .

—the correspondences are clear.

As well as drawing together all these sources, Byron added much of himself, a man who lived, loved and drank so hard that at his death at thirty-six his brain and heart showed the signs of very advanced age.

Byron's Manfred, talking of Astarte, provided the motto for the 'fatal men' of Romantic literature: 'I loved her, and destroy'd her'. Vampires are these fatal men in their most symbolic form. Byron mentions vampires in *The Giaour,* and, as mentioned, gave Polidori the sketch that became the first vampire novel in English. Vampires were invariably men in the first half of the eighteenth century; thereafter, they are mainly represented as women. Most vampire novels vulgarised Gothic themes.

The Wandering Jew, which became such a significant Gothic motif, has an unforgettable characterization in Coleridge's guilt-tortured *Ancient Mariner* (and later turns up in Keats's *Endymion* and Shelley's *Alastor*). Piranesi's etchings haunted Coleridge as well as Walpole and Beckford. In *Confessions of an Opium-Eater* Thomas De Quincey tells how Coleridge described to him Piranesi's etching entitled *Dreams:* staircases, one after the other, with Piranesi standing at the top of each one, before an abyss. (pp. 35-7)

Both interior and exterior settings in the Romantic poets often produce unmistakable echoes of the Gothic novels they consumed. Coleridge's ballad *Christabel* is a masterpiece of Gothic, with its haunted castle, and moonlight gleaming through torn clouds. Wordsworth in his verse play *The Borderers,* as well as borrowing a good deal of its content from

Schiller's *The Robbers* and from various Gothic fictions, has learned from Mrs Radcliffe how to put terror into the shapes and moods of natural scenery. Byron's drama, *Manfred,* has Gothic halls, a tower with a secret room, and demons, and his *Childe Harold* has picturesque passages that could have been written by Mrs Radcliffe, as could many of those in Keats and Shelley. Keats in *The Eve of St Agnes* plundered *Udolpho* for the castle, shadowy passages, moonlight and feudal jollifications. When he attempts gorgeous descriptions, as in *Lamia,* it is Beckford that comes to mind. Shelley, apart from his two Gothic novels *Zastrozzi* (1810) and *St Irvine* (1811), has bits of Gothic everywhere. The *Cenci,* in the words of Varma, has 'the ferocity of algolagnic sensibility'.

In early nineteenth-century prose fiction, the Gothic spirit, unmistakable as it is, manifests itself in different ways. Scott, the admirer of Mrs Radcliffe, took Gothic details to fill in his pictures and was rarely unfaithful to history. The Gothic manifestations of the Brontës are very interesting. Charlotte's Rochester in *Jane Eyre* and Emily's Heathcliff in *Wuthering Heights* have strong resemblances to Schedoni and Byron's Manfred: Rochester's locked-up mad wife is reminiscent of one in Mrs Radcliffe's *A Sicilian Romance,* and *Wuthering Heights* has nightmares and ghosts. Both novels have Gothic weather, and when Emily falters, she has Heathcliff 'crushing his nails into his palms, and grinding his teeth to subdue the maxillary convulsions'. But the stories, with all their passions, are rooted in the reality of the simple, domestic life of the English countryside: their emotive power is enhanced by their credibility.

It is appropriate to end this chapter with a Romantic-Gothic writer of great ability and seminal importance. With no author, perhaps, is the influences game easier to play than with the American Edgar Allan Poe (1809-49). His heroes have affinities with the lonely outsiders of the American literary tradition in Melville and Hawthorne, but more obviously and strikingly he learned a great deal from Coleridge, Byron, Keats, Shelley and De Quincey. The main impulse for his tales of horror was the German Gothic literature.

Poe's reputation is much higher in France than in Britain or the United States; he is regarded as the leading spirit of Symbolism, whom Baudelaire, Mallarmé, Verlaine and Rimbaud followed with reverence. Even more, if Jules Verne is the father of modern science fiction, Poe is the grandfather, and he also significantly developed the detective story, with lessons for Stevenson and Arthur Conan Doyle. 'The Murders in the Rue Morgue' (1841) was based on an actual American case, transposed to Paris. Poe's powers of deduction were such that he could work out the ending of a Dickens novel by reading the first chapter.

'The Rue Morgue' is as much a story of horror as of detection. It is the horror tale that is Poe's *forte*—his only attempt at a novel was unfinished. At the beginning, under the influence of German tales, he had all the familiar Gothic machinery, but very speedily developed his own, highly individual style. He then rejected the label of 'Germanic', with its associations of extravagant gloom and 'pseudo-horror', and wrote: 'I maintain that terror is not of Germany but of the soul— that I have deduced this terror only from its legitimate sources, and only to its legitimate results'.

Poe added psychology: his main interest, more so than Maturin's, was in what went on *inside* his protagonists' minds, and his descriptions of doom-laden settings and furniture are genuinely, and symbolically, relevant to the tale, not just spurious additions. The study is generally profound because most of the protagonists, like Usher in 'The Fall of the House of Usher' ('there were but peculiar sounds, and these from stringed instruments, which did not inspire him with horror') are endowed and cursed with an abnormally cultivated sensitivity. Estranged from reality, often inhabiting heavily curtained rooms, they lose their sanity and sometimes their lives. They are driven back into the prison of themselves. That is a horror symbolized in other tales by being drowned in whirlpools (as in 'A Descent into the Maelström'), being buried alive (as in 'The Cask of Amontillado'), being subjected to the most ingenious tortures the Spanish Inquisition could devise (as in 'The Pit and the Pendulum'). After Poe the Gothic spirit became diffused. The Romantic movement had particularly exploited its supernatural aspects, and many different kinds of novel and tale would do the same.

From the 1830s to today there has been a flood of literature descended from the Gothic. Most directly, there have been fiction about the supernatural, including stories of ghosts, vampires, werewolves and other weird transformations; detective and thriller fiction; fantasy and science fiction. Some of this is mediocre, escapist stuff, but there are more great names to put beside those already mentioned, and many other writers of exceptional interest.

The better writers on the supernatural achieve their effects with the minimum of props, and it is the interior, psychological effects that are significant. They learned from the great nineteenth-century novelists and some of the master storytellers how to do it. In *The Wild Ass's Skin (Le Peau de Chargrin,* 1831) [Balzac] uses a magic device. The hero, Raphael, shares many of the characteristics of Faust as well as of the author himself. The plot pivots round a magic piece of leather found in an antique shop, which grants its owner's wishes, but shrinks each time the spell is invoked, ironically shortening his life.

Another French writer, Alexandre Dumas, apart from his long list of historical novels, dealt with the supernatural. *The WolfLeader* (1857) uses that popular combination of Wandering Jew and werewolf themes, becoming a werewolf for periods being the Devil's condition for continuing life, and Dumas also wrote a number of vampire tales. The American Nathaniel Hawthorne, in both tales and novels, makes considerable use of the supernatural, or the weird, to symbolize evil. *The House of the Seven Gables* (1851) involves a family curse—the ghosts of ancestors haunting a house because one of the family condemned an innocent man—and this is a theme which Hawthorne handled in several works.

'The Queen of Spades' (1834), a short story by the greatest of Russian poets, Pushkin, uses the supernatural in a simple but masterly way, which combines irony and fantasy, and requires no aid from white sheets and clanking chains. It has reverberated in other literatures, was the basis of Tchaikovsky's opera and the ballet *The Three Card Trick.* Hermann, an army officer, is an austere, self-absorbed, obsessed 'hero' cast in a fatal, Romantic mould; he won Dostoyevsky's acclaim and may have suggested the latter's Raskolnikov in *Crime and Punishment.* Hermann threatens an old Countess with a pistol in order to get from her a card trick that will win him a fortune gambling, and she dies of shock. The pistol was unloaded. Her ghost reveals the card trick to him, but he is foiled by her at the last round of the card game, when instead of the Ace expected, the Queen of Spades appears. It

is her features which appear on the card: she winks, and he goes mad.

The Russian Gogol in his short stories develops a Hoffmann-like fantasy. Such stories as 'The Nose', in which that appendage, having been shaved off, takes on a life of its own and drives a carriage round St Petersburg, is whimsy rather than witty, but there are few doubts about 'The Portrait' (1835)—which continues living to express the evil of a wicked merchant—and 'The Overcoat' (1842), one of the most famous of all ghost stories.

Charles Dickens wrote many supernatural tales within the novels and for the magazines he edited between 1850 and 1870, encouraging contemporaries, notably Wilkie Collins and Bulwer Lytton to produce them. Henry James's *The Turn of the Screw* (1898) is about two children possessed by the evil spirits of dead servants. Franz Kafka, whose blend of allegory, fantasy and horror, defying easy categorization, has been a strong influence on so much modern fiction since, wrote three works that demand mention: *The Castle* (1930), *The Trial* (1937), and the long-short story *Metamorphosis* (1937), in which a young man becomes a cockroach. Like Poe and Kafka, Guy de Maupassant put many of his own phobias and nightmares into his tales of supernatural terror before he died in 1893, at 42, syphilitic and insane.

The Irishman Sheridan Le Fanu (1814-73) was, like Poe, a link between the Gothic and the psychological horror of modern times. In novels and numerous tales he dealt with all aspects of the supernatural, and his mastery of suspense and ability to sustain an atmosphere without slipping into bathos or unconscious humour (a tightrope for the best writers in the genre) have given him the status of a classic—though a neglected one. His tales show his strength, rather than his novels. Among his masterpieces are the short stories 'Carmilla', about a Countess vampire, which achieves psychological insight into lesbianism without detracting from or vulgarizing the horrific effect, and 'Green Tea', about a man haunted by a strange creature resembling a monkey.

Of the long list of British writers in this genre during the Victorian period, Lord Bulwer-Lytton, with the superb story 'The Haunted and the Haunters' (1859) among historical and occult works; Lord Dunsany (1878-1957) with his fantasies of other worlds, many containing a chilling evil presence at the heart of them; M. R. James (1862-1936), an ingenious but much less frightening version of Sheridan Le Fanu, his inspirer; and Walter de la Mare, the poet, who wrote various collections of ghost stories, and whose novels include *Memoirs of a Midget* (1921), about a woman two feet tall—all these are well worth reading.

Opinions vary on H. P. Lovecraft. His works, though readable, lack literary merit, and elements of racism and snobbery alienate many readers. But his fantasy worlds and weird tales are original, and enthusiasts for Gothic will admire his formidable knowledge of the literature of the supernatural. His critical work, *Supernatural Horror in Literature* was published in 1927 [see excerpt above]. More recent supernatural stories have shown an interest in magic, witchcraft and the occult in general.

A pattern for the development of the detective novel can be made out as follows: Godwin, Lewis, Poe (the key figure), Wilkie Collins, Sheridan Le Fanu. Le Fanu's *The House by the Churchyard* (1863) is a fine example. Collins wrote two compelling detective novels—*The Woman in White* (1860) and *The Moonstone* (1868), well written, well worked out, and sustaining the 'mysteries' (as much detective fiction used to be called) throughout. *The Woman in White* is one of the forerunners and best examples of what are called 'thrillers': added to the suspense/detection interest, there are adventures and more recognizable (though controlled) Gothic elements in this work, including a persecuted heroine and a devilish (though believable) criminal. *The Moonstone* is one of the best of detective novels.

These labels are only rough guides, particularly as detective fiction is so voluminous. Both detective novels and thrillers use such Gothic techniques as ingenious murder methods, the theft of wills and other documents, wrongful suspicion, suspense, mysteries explained at the end. City streets replace castle corridors. The persecuted heroine is still there, if dryer-eyed and more able to look after herself. The Gothic hero-villain may have become a mad scientist, a much nastier Frankenstein, as in Ian Fleming's thrillers, or he may be the detective, with an intellect far superior to that of anyone around him, and the evil refined down to mere eccentricity. Perhaps the most famous detective in fiction is Arthur Conan Doyle's egotistic Sherlock Holmes, a pale thin man, of astonishing deductive ability (like Poe's), who takes opium and plays the violin. He was the progenitor of a long line of detectives, including Dorothy L. Sayers's Lord Peter Wimsey, Agatha Christie's Hercule Poirot and the Belgian writer Simenon's Maigret.

The three English writers were generally concerned with plot rather than sensation, but they did write books that contained horror. One of Doyle's best novels, in fact, is *The Hound of the Baskervilles* (1901), a Sherlock Holmes story where the detective is confronted not by a werewolf but a vicious hound with a villainous master. Sayers put together large anthologies entitled *Great Short Stories of Detection, Mystery and Horror* (1929-34), and Agatha Christie also had a penchant for the weird, which surfaced in parts of many novels and in a fine volume of tales entitled *The Hound of Death* (1933).

Iris Murdoch, a philosopher as well as a novelist, uses Gothic elements in some of her novels, notably in *The Unicorn* and *The Time of the Angels,* the first set in a remote, coastal region, with a castle, a swamp and cliffs above the sea. She gives the landscape a romantic power over the characters, and the castle is a prison for the chief character, Hannah Crean-Smith, cursed by her husband to remain inside for seven years. The Gothic setting and situation enable the author to fabricate a mythical environment in which she can explore various ideas about good and evil, guilt and innocence, and freedom. *The Time of the Angels* is set in a rectory.

The earlier mention of 'mad scientists' suggests the link between the Gothic novel and science fiction. On the model of *Frankenstein* the best science fiction has some concern for science's role in the future and often has political and moral messages to deliver.

The works of Jules Verne, much of H. G. Wells, Aldous Huxley's *Brave New World* and George Orwell's *1984* are among the most original kinds, but in the past thirty or forty years, alongside an avalanche of SF pulp fiction, there has been a great variety of fascinating and vital literature in this sphere, on both sides of the Atlantic, the 'fantasy' and 'pure SF' labels becoming increasingly difficult to keep distinct. The work of the American Ray Bradbury (born 1920), mainly in short story form, is better described as fantasy. Kurt Vonne-

gut and Isaac Asimov, also American, are good as well as prolific.

Among the SF novels of Brian Aldiss is an ingenious commentary on Mary Shelley's novel called *Frankenstein Unbound* (1973), in which Joe Bodenland, owing to a space/time rupture, is transported back from the United States of the twenty-first century to the Switzerland of 1816. Here he meets Mary Shelley, the poet Shelley, whose wife she is about to become, Byron, and the characters of the novel *Frankenstein* that is being worked on. J. G. Ballard has concerned himself with what he calls 'inner space' (rather than outer). Many of his novels and stories deal with the effects on the mind of the environment and of natural disasters. Colin Wilson (born 1931) has written a combination of horror and SF in *Space Vampires* (1976). Michael Moorcock (born 1939) is an extremely prolific writer who exploits various techniques in fantasy, SF and traditional genres and is building a sizeable reputation. Angela Carter's writings have been called, in some desperation, 'Gothic science fiction'. Mostly her works are an unusual blend of the two. (pp. 38-45)

Finally, Frankenstein's monster, Radcliffe and Lewis's pale monks, Melmoth, the suffering outcasts of Poe and all the other Gothic hero-villains or anti-heroes that compel our attention and sympathy (even if also our condemnation), have strong links with the 'outsiders' in the novels of some of the greatest European writers of this century—Kafka, Camus, Sartre, Beckett and others.

The perpetual attraction of the tale of terror, H. P. Lovecraft said, was 'the scratching of unknown claws at the rind of the known world'. That is certainly what you hear in the best of the Gothic novels, and when you hear it in the passages of the great writers that have forced their way into this essay, the sound, however intermittent, is unmistakable and unforgettable. (p. 52)

Brendan Hennessy, in his The Gothic Novel, *Longman Group Ltd., 1978, 56 p.*

JAMES M. KEECH

[*In the following excerpt, Keech defines Gothic as a particular effect that has been used from the late eighteenth century to the present.*]

Traditionally, the Gothic novel has been regarded as a work defined by its common elements, a sort of formula novel employing standard atmospheric trappings and stereotyped characters. Conceptually, it has meant a set of stock devices used to evoke terror and horror: ruined castles and abbeys, dank dungeons, gloomy tyrants, mad monks, imperiled maidens, secret chambers, haunted galleries, creaking doors, mysterious portraits, ghosts, "skulls and coffins, epitaphs and worms." Scholars, such as Tompkins, Summers, and Varma, have divided it into types: the historical Gothic, the terror Gothic, and the horror Gothic, or "Schauer-Romantik"; but it has rarely been seen beyond these types as any more significant than those "horrid" novels that captivated Catherine Morland in Jane Austen's *Northanger Abbey*. Reeking of excessive romanticism, employing farfetched terrors, such as Walpole's statue with the nosebleed, and beset with imitation rather than creative originality, the Gothic novel has been viewed as little more than a literary curiosity.

It is not my purpose to revaluate the worth of the Gothic novels of the past, though this in many ways needs to be done, for they have received short shrift for too long in the literary marketplace. Rather, in this essay, I intend to focus on some of the limitations of the traditional perspective of the Gothic novel which blinds us to its consideration as an element of the literary vision after 1820. The Gothic novel needs redefinition in order for this to be done.

Recently there have been attempts to expand the range of the Gothic novel's definition and to broaden its application. Lowry Nelson, Jr. and Robert D. Hume, for example, have seen such novels as *Wuthering Heights, Moby-Dick,* and *Sanctuary,* as falling within the Gothic mold. Both critics have, essentially, chosen to see the Gothic novel not so much as a set of rigid trappings and devices as an effect produced by certain elements common to all Gothic novels. Though Nelson or Hume have not gone far enough in freeing the definition of the Gothic novel from its reliance upon traditional devices or in clarifying the distinction between the trappings and the effects these trappings produce, they have made significant steps toward a needed rethinking of what is called Gothic in fiction.

Basically, the Gothic novel should be seen as attempting to evoke a particularized response, and its stock devices as merely one means to that end. All literary artists attempt to involve the reader in a series of manipulated responses leading, hopefully, to an overall effect. The devices they use, call them setting, plot, character, imagery, shape the work to provoke that desired cumulative response. The response of the Gothic novel is fear, universally inherent in every man's nature, primitive and basic, and existing regardless of time, place, or culture. Imitation has rendered the traditional castle and Byronic villain, along with clanking ghosts, dungeons, and skeletons, as a hackneyed method of approaching that fear; and time, too, has changed the nature of what we regard as fearful. Certainly, at one time however, the stock devices worked. The early Gothic novels of the romantic period were not necessarily regarded as belonging to an inferior type of fiction. Until the flood of inferior Gothic imitations of the 1780-90s made the type recognizable and their inferior quality made them laughable enough to be ridiculed, as in *Northanger Abbey,* the first Gothic novels affected their readers with genuine power. Thomas Gray was made afraid of sleep at night by reading *The Castle of Otranto;* Byron called *Vathek* his Bible; Ann Radcliffe's novels established her to the age as a major novelist; Coleridge gave *The Monk* serious critical consideration in *The Critical Review* and thought it the "offspring of no common genius"; and genuine originality and serious literary skills were noted in Mary Shelley's *Frankenstein* and Maturin's *Melmoth the Wanderer.* That their power and emotional force can still be felt, in part, today gives added weight to the need for legitimate recognition of the Gothic as a meaningful literary experience.

The best of the Gothic novels were, and still are in part, successful works of art because they produced a universal and enduring response that is also inherent in later literature of Gothic nature: in "The Rime of the Ancient Mariner," *Wuthering Heights, Great Expectations, Moby-Dick, Heart of Darkness, Absalom, Absalom!,* and *Nineteen Eighty-Four.* The element common to all these is not a set of stock devices but the production of an effect of fear and foreboding that carries the reader to the realm of the nightmare by means of a variety of techniques of which the traditional Gothic trappings is but one. A definition of the Gothic novel should outline not the dated means but the simplest elements common to its effect.

One of these common elements is the particular quality of the Gothic response of fear, a fear characterized by a necessary presentiment of a somewhat vague but nevertheless real evil. It is a fear of shadows and unseen dangers in the night. Explicitness runs counter to its effectiveness, for Gothic fear is not so much what is seen but what is sensed beyond sight. The fearful inventions of J. R. R. Tolkien's imagination in *The Lord of the Rings,* the Night Riders and Gollum for example, are perfect illustrations of the power of the impressionistic over the concrete. Always seen as vague shapes or veiled in nebulous shadows, Tolkien's evil creations are genuinely fearful, and they impart a decidedly Gothic aura to his trilogy. In similar fashion, the fear in a traditional Gothic novel is created not only by that which frightens, the darkness of the underground passageways in Otranto's castle when the maiden's lamp is accidentally extinguished, but by the foreboding that magnifies its dangers: Isabella's apprehensions of her fate if captured by Manfred in this darkness. It is not only Victor Frankenstein's horror at the monster's brutal murder of his brother, but the premonition of those future atrocities which the monster's anguished hatred is both capable and desirous of inflicting. In *The Monk,* this fear is created not by Ambrosio's acts of murder and rape alone, but also by the presentiment that his process of moral corruption will intensify with further dreadful consequences. Thus, fear in a Gothic novel moves beyond the concrete in allowing the imagination to build upon and shape foreboding outlines into a sustained fear which is verified periodically by peaks of intense concrete terror or horror.

This association of fear and foreboding is not merely that suspense and dread to be found in those Gothic novels typed under the novel of terror, namely the works of Walpole and Radcliffe. It is present there in various plenty, of course, but it forms a vital part of the response in those novels classified by Varma as the "Schauer-Romantik," or romance of horror: the novels of Lewis, Shelley, Maturin. Horror does not negate fear, though Mrs. Radcliffe felt it did: "Terror and horror are so far opposite, that the first expands the soul, and awakens the faculties to a high degree of life; the other contracts, freezes, and nearly annihilates them. . . . " Rather, the repulsive horrors of Lewis, Shelley, and Maturin magnify the apprehensions that characterize Gothic fear. Agnes's awakening in the tomb and touching the maggots bred in the putrified flesh of adjacent corpses brings shudders of disgust and repulsion to *The Monk,* but it does not eliminate the dreaded fears of the future horrors that she might experience. Agnes can still suffer and the Prioress of St. Clare is still frighteningly capable of further atrocities. The mind is not closed by horror to the vicarious experience of the sublimity of fearful apprehensions (except to the reader who at this point closes the novel and reads no more), but rather enlarged by a greater intensity. The real distinction between novels of terror and of horror is not a difference in kind but in degree. D. P. Varma implies that the nature of the difference lies in their degree of intensity: "The difference between Terror and Horror is in the difference between awful apprehensions and sickening realization: between the smell of death and stumbling upon a corpse." Horror is not the finality of terror, but the magnification of it. Though we may be thoroughly shocked by man's, or a monster's, hitherto undreamt of acts, we also stand in greater fearful awe of the limits further acts may approach. The horrible sufferings of Moncada in *Melmoth the*

Wanderer do not end the reader's fears, but build them toward some awful crescendo that promises to reveal what man's final capacity for inflicting horror will be.

Indeed, the fearful response in the better Gothic novels is marked by the common element of intensity. They depict violations of moral and religious norms that are fearful by their excess. The acts that create fear and presage even more in the Gothic novel are supreme. They are grievous sins, not mere wrongs—the worst of what man or devil is capable. They stem not from accident or simple human frailty or corruption, but from an agency evaluated by the reader's moral perspective as approaching the ultimate in evil. The Gothic novel, therefore, deals not with gambling, thievery, or simple murder, but with matricide, rape, incest (*The Monk*); murders of innocent children and virginal brides (*Frankenstein*); blasphemy, infectious spiritual pollution, and damnation (*Vathek, Melmoth the Wanderer, Dracula*).

It is not surprising, therefore, that the best and most intense of Gothic novels employ hero-villains of Promethean proportions, giants among mortal men in their strength, in the intensity of their emotions, in their faculty for evil. They evoke terror not only by what they do but also by the presentiment of their dreadful capacities. Manfred, in *The Castle of Otranto,* fails materially to intensify the novel's effect, for he is merely a bad man, incapable of reaching beyond petty intrigue and impulsive murder. But Ann Radcliffe's Montoni in *The Mysteries of Udolpho* is truly fearful, for we sense that he is capable of extraordinary acts of human depravity. Shelley's monster, Maturin's Melmoth, and Stoker's Dracula are even more frightening, for, possessed of supernatural abilities, they possess a propensity for malevolence that exceeds human comprehension.

Though the better Gothic novels possess such Promethean hero-villains, they should not be seen as a basic defining characteristic of the Gothic, but merely a device for creating a high level of intensity of effect. Not all Gothic novels use them. They do not appear in *The Castle of Otranto, The Monk,* and *Vathek,* but the response of fear is still evoked, though at a somewhat lower level of intensity than, say, *Melmoth.* Any agency of absolute power would suffice to produce a similar intensity of fear, and the Inquisition was frequently so used in the Gothic novel, for example in *The Monk* and *Melmoth the Wanderer.*

Attendant to those novels that employ the hero-villain protagonist is the problem of what Robert Hume calls "moral ambiguity," a confusion in the reader's moral evaluation of the protagonist because of the coexistence of malevolent values and admirable heroic qualities. Though the reader may reject the evil the villain embodies, he is fascinated by his heroic greatness: by Montoni's strength of will and defiance of conventional moral and legal restraints, by Frankenstein's monster's alienation and superhuman physical powers, by Melmoth's tragic capacity for cynical suffering. This moral ambiguity imparts to the Gothic novel a greater complexity and dimension, and removes those novels which possess it from the morass of shallow sensationalism which is the major raison d'être of the inferior novel. It is not necessary for moral ambiguity to be present for a novel to be Gothic: there is no moral doubt of Dracula's status as monster, pure and simple. Ambrosio is also obviously corrupt and contemptible. But it seems vital for a great Gothic novel, accounting in great measure for the serious literary consideration given *Frankenstein* and *Melmoth the Wanderer.*

The term "Gothic," as I see it, consequently means a response, or effect, of fear characterized by foreboding and intensity rather than a set of traditional stock devices. The devices are merely a time-honored method of producing the effect with a minimum of artistic originality. Unfortunately, the word will never, perhaps, divorce itself from this association with ruined castles, graveyards, skeletons, ghosts, and imperiled maidens. It will always mean to some the stock elements. Perhaps, the modifier "traditional" should be used in conjunction with "Gothic" to imply, with some pejorative associations of imitative and hackneyed, the stock devices, and the term "Gothic" alone used to imply the response. Certainly, such a practice would emphasize that the traditional trappings are not necessary for a novel to be Gothic, but the response is, and it would distinguish between works which are Gothic by device, such as *The Old English Baron,* and works which are Gothic by effect, such as Conrad's *Heart of Darkness.*

Nevertheless, though the stock devices are neither primary nor exclusive to the Gothic novel, they cannot be dismissed, for their use does reflect another common element vital to the Gothic response. In order for the abbey, tower, tomb, skeleton, or ghost to activate the imagination and evoke the sense of fear, an appropriate atmosphere must be created. This atmosphere is primary to the necessary effect. With the proper atmosphere a child's playhouse can be chillingly terrifying and a castle safe, warm, beautiful, and romantic. Robert Hume has perceptively noted that "The key characteristic of the Gothic novel is not its devices, but its atmosphere. . . . The setting exists to convey the atmosphere."

The essential nature of the atmosphere which produces the Gothic response is ominousness. Redolent of isolation, evil, death, the images which convey this ominousness are those of darkness, danger, grotesqueness, and gloom. To the romantic sensibilities of the early Gothic novelists, medieval castles and wild scenery suggested this atmosphere, but it is by no means inherent solely in them. A scientist's laboratory, through emphasis of the proper atmosphere, can be just as Gothic as the Castle of Montoni:

> It was on a dreary night of November that I beheld the accomplishment of my toils. With an anxiety that almost amounted to agony, I collected the instruments of life around me, that I might infuse a spark of being into the lifeless thing that lay at my feet. It was already one in the morning; the rain pattered dismally against the panes, and my candle was nearly burnt out, when, by the glimmer of the half-extinguished light I saw the dull yellow eye of the creature open. . . .
>
> [Mary Shelley, *Frankenstein*]

In similar fashion, though the ostensible framework for *Vathek* is oriental, its basic character, as established by its atmosphere, is essentially Gothic:

> A death-like stillness reigned over the mountain and through the air; the moon dilated on a vast platform the shades of the lofty columns, which reached from the terrace almost to the clouds; the gloomy watch-towers, whose number could not be counted, were covered by no roof; and their capitals, of an architecture unknown in the records of the earth, served as an asylum for the birds of night, which, alarmed at the approach of such visitants, fled away croaking.

The more pervasive this ominous atmosphere and the greater its consistency of mood, the greater the sense of the Gothic response to the work. Manfred's dungeons in *The Castle of Otranto* are only mildly ominous: the passageways are intricate, silent, windy, dark, and ultimately "dismal," but so scant is the atmospheric detail that the novel's force is weakened. In comparison, the catacombs in Poe's "The Cask of Amontillado" are the essence of Gothic fear: dark, damp with dripping nitre, filled with skeletons and air so foul that torches glow instead of burn. The images that produce the atmosphere are so plentiful and so orchestrated in their connotative harmony that the story produces that supreme single effect that Poe demanded from a short story. Thus the extent of the development of atmosphere will, more than any other element, determine the placement of a work in the Gothic category, for it is the key distinguishing mark of the Gothic response.

Other key elements of the Gothic are certain basic characters or agents. These characters are not so much stereotypes as embodiments of traits whose conflict produces the feelings of apprehension and fear. First, there must be at least one character or agency, such as the hero-villain or the Inquisition, whose essence is unrestrained power or force or passion; and, secondly, at least one character who embodies meekness or helplessness and serves as the artistic surrogate for the reader's feelings of inadequacy. The agent of power is the focal point of the Gothic novel's production of apprehensive fear. His powers may stem from the human resources of strength, will, or intelligence, such as the powers of Manfred, Vathek, and Montoni, or they may be supernatural in origin, as are the powers of Ambrosio, Frankenstein's monster, Melmoth, and Dracula. In either case these powers are extraordinary and awesome. They are also powers either partially or totally perverted, even if innocent of conscious evil intent, as is Victor Frankenstein's pursuit of the secret of life. Only evil or misfortune comes from the exercise of these extraordinary powers, for some sort of moral corruption is at their core.

The character, or agent, or power appears magnified by his opposite, the character who represents helplessness, usually the persecuted maiden in the traditional Gothic novel but who can be any sort of victimized humanity. His helplessness stems either from the contrast of his ordinary mortality in conflict with superhuman powers or his meekness or vulnerability in conflict with greater human resources. This character reflects a moral norm which the reader finds acceptable, and consequently his persecution and his injuries seem terrifying or horrible when there is a shocking discrepancy between his moral position and undeserved calamities. This character's humanity and acceptable moral position enable the reader to identify with him and thus be drawn vicariously into the victim's world of fear and undeserved evil. There he finds himself in the frightening uncertainty of what appears to be a moral no-man's-land where ethical values and moral laws have no apparent weight, where the powerful ignore such standards with an ease and absence of conscience that bring the very validity or existence of the moral laws into question. If this process of victimization by the powerful is extended far enough, as it is in *The Monk, Frankenstein, Melmoth,* and in *Dracula,* the ultimate Gothic fear is momentarily reached, that surrealistically horrible recognition of a world of moral chaos where only power has meaning.

These, then, as I view them, are the basic defining characteristics of the Gothic novel: it evokes fear characterized by foreboding and intensity; this fear is created by an atmosphere of ominous detail and by the frightening supremacy of power and evil over weakness and good. If the concept of the Gothic can be divorced from the traditional reliance upon definition by stock devices, the word "Gothic" becomes liberated and timeless. It can be applied to identify minor effects or the essence of whole works, from the eighteenth century to the present. It also enables us to perceive something thematically meaningful in the writer's perception of terror and horror that goes beyond mere sensationalism, the traditionally regarded graveyard for the early Gothic novelists' attempts to approach sublimity through fear.

I suggest that the Gothic as a literary response neither ended with Maturin, nor did it degenerate further into the drugstore bookracks as cheap popular literature. Rather, I believe, serious novelists, after the traditional Gothic novel had ended its vogue, recognized something aesthetically meaningful in the Gothic novel: that it conveyed a universal and timeless response that could be used as a metaphor with thematic weight. Indeed, traditional Gothic novels such as *Frankenstein* and *Melmoth the Wanderer* employ the Gothic scene as metaphor. Mary Shelley used it to characterize the moral horror of Victor Frankenstein's experiments, and Maturin used the Gothic as a thematic reflection of the dark horror of spiritual despair. Later novelists, though not known as writers of Gothic novels, for example the Brontes, Dickens, Conrad, Wells, Faulkner, have utilized the Gothic response for thematic emphasis.

The Victorian novelists first saw the literary potential of the Gothic effect separated from its traditional heritage. Charlotte Bronte, perhaps more unconsciously than voluntarily, sensed within the Gothic novel certain symbolic elements that would convey thematic meanings of power, fear, and awe within a more realistic background. Mr. Rochester, ugly, powerful, willfully defying convention and law in his passionate love for Jane, is in direct descendency from Manfred, Montoni, and Melmoth. This Gothic hero-villain symbolized for Charlotte Bronte the power of the masculine essence and its sexual force: dominating, ugly yet fascinating, instilling a fearful helplessness in the female. In her novel Gothic fear metaphorically imparts a thematic moral perspective of complete free will divorced from social duty. Emily Bronte's Heathcliff is also a symbolic embodiment of power, will, sexual force, and passion—as perfect a Byronic hero-villain as any in a traditional Gothic novel. It is Heathcliff as Gothic villain, who stands as her central metaphor for fearful sexual passion, perhaps even a reflection of the subconscious sexual yearnings of Emily Bronte's own dark Id.

Charles Dickens also utilized the Gothic effect for its metaphorical meanings of fear and horror. Dickens was drawn not by the symbolic power or sexual energy inherent in the hero-villain, but by the metaphorical connotations of Gothic atmosphere. There is, however, a difficulty in determining Dickens's conscious use of the Gothic in his novels, for his symbolic atmosphere is complex, blending social misery with Gothic effect in such a way that it becomes impossible to separate his vision of bleak misery, imprisoned humanity, and spiritual poverty from that of horror and terror. The images of misery and Gothic fear are similar: decay, death, darkness, disease; they belong as much to slums such as Tom-all-Alone's as they do to castles and dungeons. There are occasions in Dickens's novels, however, when he seemed to be consciously thinking in terms of the traditional Gothic effect. This Gothic strain in Dickens's work runs from the inset stories of *Pickwick Papers* to the ominous cathedral crypt and tower of *Edwin Drood;* in the undertaker's shop and city slums of *Oliver Twist;* in the miserly decay of Scrooge's office of *A Christmas Carol;* in Krook and his shop, in the Ghost's Walk of *Bleak House;* in the grotesque specimens of Mr. Venus of *Our Mutual Friend;* in the gloomy prison of the Clennam house of *Little Dorrit;* and especially in Satis House of *Great Expectations.* In evoking the Gothic response to these settings, Dickens used thematic atmosphere to imply that fear and foreboding are integral elements of a society which esteems self or money more than people. The reader's expected shudder when encountering these settings of Dickens was to be one of moral horror, in the reflection that the Gothic was not necessarily an imaginary fancy in a cheap novel but a part of the very nature of normal society.

This influence of the Gothic novel upon the Brontes and Dickens has long been recognized; but, once this recognition has been noted and suitably filed in the correct pigeonhole of literary history, analysis of the author's purposeful uses of the Gothic fails to follow. The Gothic has, quite simply, too frequently been regarded as an end in itself. Thus the thematic intentions of the novelist's Gothic effects, that metaphorical equation through device and atmosphere of the fearful in the Gothic world and the fearful in his own world, becomes ignored. It is this thematic function of the Gothic that needs to be recognized in the fiction not generally associated with the Gothic tradition.

This metaphorical function of the Gothic becomes even more unnoticed in modern novels which produce the Gothic response without employing the traditional devices. It is with these works that a definition of the Gothic based on effect becomes critically meaningful. Joseph Conrad's *Heart of Darkness,* for example, is a novel colored throughout by a sense of the Gothic; and Kurtz's whispered cry, " 'The horror! The horror!' " at the thematic climax of the novel, precisely focuses the novel's essence. *Heart of Darkness* is a novel of Gothic horror.

Though it has no tormented victim and no Promethean villain of power (unless Kurtz can be seen as filling both roles simultaneously), the novel's atmosphere is profoundly Gothic. This atmosphere serves as an extended metaphor to characterize the dark submerged bestiality at the core of man's biological nature as fearful and horrible. Marlowe's search for Kurtz is like that of Browning's Childe Roland for the dark tower: a mythic quest through a frightening symbolic wasteland dominated by Gothic scenery which impressionistically imparts the work's theme. Atmosphere in *Heart of Darkness* is symbolically meaningful, and that atmosphere is decidedly and consistently Gothic.

The novel opens with the contrast of the morally neutral sea, luminous in the evening haze, with the land, long tainted by the darkness of man's potential for brutality: "The air was dark above Gravesend, and farther back still seemed condensed into a mournful gloom, brooding motionless over the biggest, and the greatest, town on earth." The symbolic landscape is further developed into a Gothic metaphor with Marlowe's summation of the historical heritage of England hidden behind its present civilized facade:

> "And this also . . . has been one of the dark places
> of the earth. . . . I was thinking of very old times,
> when the Romans first came here, nineteen hun-

dred years ago. . . . The very end of the world, a sea the color of lead, a sky the color of smoke. . . . Sandbanks, marshes, forests, savages—precious little to eat fit for a civilized man, nothing but Thames water to drink. No Falernian wine here, no going ashore. Here and there a military camp lost in the wilderness, like a needle in a bundle of hay—cold, fog, tempests, disease, exile, and death—death sulking in the air, in the water, in the bush."

This Gothic atmosphere metaphorically imparts its foreboding to all segments of Marlowe's quest: to the vision of the African river on the map as "an immense snake uncoiled . . . its tail lost in the depth of the land"; to the Belgian trading company on "a narrow and deserted street in deep shadow, high houses . . . a dead silence, grass sprouting between the stones," with its fatal women "guarding the door of darkness, knitting black wool as for a warm pall"; to the dark continent itself with its sense of decayed civilization imparted by ruined machinery, enslaved natives, solitude, and silence.

The forest itself is the principal Gothic metaphor in the novel, for its darkness, fearful and fascinating, conceals the mystery of Kurtz and of man that Marlowe seeks. The forest is the equivalent of the Gothic agent of power, suggesting the very strength of those primal urges to which Kurtz succumbs: "The great wall of vegetation, an exuberant and entangled mass of trunks, branches, leaves, boughs, festoons, motionless in the moonlight was like a rioting invasion of soundless life, a rolling wave of plants, piled up, crested ready to topple over the creek, to sweep every little man of us out of his little existence." Above all, the forest, symbol of concealment and strength, is fearful; for its black shadows hide mysteries far more ominous than those behind *The Mystery of Udolpho*'s black veiled recess: "the forest, the creek, the mud, the river—seemed to beckon with a dishonoring flourish before the sunlit face of the land a treacherous appeal to the lurking death, to the hidden evil, to the profound darkness of its heart."

Heart of Darkness is a Gothic novel. It is not traditional; it has no castles and dungeons, no skeletons and ghosts; but it fully embodies what is basically Gothic: apprehensive fear, ominous atmosphere, the sense of frightening power inherent in evil. Conrad saw this evil as an inherent part of man, not in a collection of literary trappings, and metaphorically used the Gothic effect in a meaningful way as the major symbolic force in his novel.

The fiction of William Faulkner has similar Gothic elements. Indeed, Faulkner was primarily regarded in the 1930s as a follower of Poe and Ambrose Bierce. Though this was a narrow perspective, the early critics of Faulkner perceived, even if they did not value, the Gothic strain that underlies much of Faulkner's chronicle of Yoknapatawpha County. An examination of the Gothic in his novels would show that Faulkner, rather than creating mere gory sensation, was artistically utilizing the Gothic to capitalize upon a stock response that metaphorically emphasizes the innate horror underlying certain aspects of Southern tradition.

Malcolm Cowley, in his famous introduction to *The Portable Faulkner,* first recognized this purposeful use of Gothic materials. In discussing *Absalom, Absalom!* he said: "It seems to belong in the realm of the Gothic romances, with Sutpen's Hundred taking the place of the haunted castle on the Rhine, with Colonel Sutpen as Faust and Charles Bon as Manfred. Then slowly it dawns on you that most of the characters and incidents have a double meaning; that besides their place in the story, they also serve as symbols or metaphors with a general application." These applications are varied, but they do form discernible thematic patterns in Faulkner's work.

One pattern can be noted in Faulkner's use, as metaphor, of an equivalent of the Gothic castle or haunted abbey: the ruined Southern antebellum mansion, such as the houses of Emily Grierson, Thomas Sutpen, Joanna Burden, the Compsons, the McCaslins, and the old Frenchman place. Each suggests a conventional Gothic device, yet the complex metaphorical implications go much further toward the suggestion of themes. The atmosphere of romantic decay accompanying the traditional device thematically conveys the sense of decline of the South's vanished glory, implying the need for the region to recognize the advent of a new age and to accept a new culture based on new values. Tragically, perhaps, neither the Compsons nor Emily Grierson can, and their Gothic houses symbolize the unyielding heritage of the past that plagues the South. But also, like the grandeur of a medieval castle, these mansions also convey other meanings: the worthy essence of a chivalric tradition, that gentleman's code of honor of the Compsons and Sartorises, which is crumbling under the less noble values of industrialization and the morally corrupt entrepreneurship symbolized by the rising Snopeses. There is also associated with these mansions a latent horror, a kind of Gothic curse, arising from their associations with slavery. The symbolic ghosts that haunt Sutpen's Hundred and the ledgers of the McCaslins are as fearful in their moral implications as the literal specters of Gothic galleries. The attitude toward the black man that evolved from slavery was the curse that doomed Thomas Sutpen, Joanna Burden, and Joe Christmas and which torments their descendents. The atmosphere surrounding the Gothic architectural setting was the perfect metaphor for Faulkner to use to convey the shadowy sense of doom and terror underlying Southern values.

The Gothic villain is another Gothic device that Faulkner employs for symbolic implications. As Robert Hume has argued, *Sanctuary*'s Popeye is the impotent, vicious monster symbolic of the inescapable evil in life. Thomas Sutpen, a more classic hero-villain of the Byronic stamp, represents the heroic will needed to create a civilization from raw wilderness, but he also serves as a metaphor symbolizing the fearful elements of Southern values: the self-destructive moral rigidity, the inhumanity of the South's caste system, the failure to acknowledge the brotherhood of all men because of race. Like Melmoth and Heathcliff, Thomas Sutpen belongs to the hazy regions of moral ambiguity. He is a gloriously dynamic mixture of admiration and Gothic horror who symbolized the ambiguity of the South, for Quentin Compson and also for William Faulkner.

The Gothic in nontraditional literature has, therefore, become a means of evoking a response, both emotional and moral, to those aspects of life which we fear, or ethically should fear, most. To the Brontes and Dickens Gothic fear was equated with sexual energy and inhuman materialism. To Conrad it was an integral element in the nature of man, and to Faulkner it was slavery and the distorted values of caste and honor. It may be interesting to now ask: what major fears of today find symbolic reflection as Gothic metaphors in our current fiction, and what does their use tell us about the way current novelists view contemporary society? Since the Gothic has become a metaphor for the ominous, destruc-

tive forces in life, the Gothic in today's art forms will point a finger of moral condemnation at those fearful elements of life that make man seem the impotent victim of the currently terrifying.

Novelists of today, I feel, find the Gothic responses of horror in an increasingly complex and amoral technology, in giant industry, giant government, and giant bureaucracy. When millions can die with the push of a single button on a machine, or fall victim to the perversity of a computer, or sense the very air they breathe is toxic, the Gothic becomes an apt evaluation for the nature of existence. The ordinary man is seen as a powerless victim of life's incomprehensible forces. The Byronic hero-villain recedes as an object of fear to be replaced by abstract agencies, evoking a correspondent Gothic horror, which, though more vague, are just as powerful, frightening, and inhuman. Instead of Manfreds, Montonis, and Melmoths, the new evil forces in life given Gothic substance by modern novelists are Big Brother government, scientifically controlled humanity, the suppression of individual freedom in a world grown too complex for ordinary comprehension.

Science, with its nuclear bombs and nerve gases, is one of today's monsters. The relationship between science and the Gothic response is an old one, existing as early as Mary Shelley's *Frankenstein* and continuing through nineteenth-century fiction with Wilkie Collins's depiction of the horrors of vivisection in *Heart and Science* and H. G. Wells's *Island of Doctor Moreau.* A Gothic atmosphere was thus seen very early as a means of symbolically expressing the cold objectivity of science and the sense of fearful power resident in the control of natural forces. In the twentieth century, this attitude toward science has been coupled with an awareness of the basic inhumanity of man's institutions; and novelists' projections of the future, in such novels as *Nineteen Eighty-Four, Fahrenheit 451,* and occasionally in *Brave New World,* significantly impart a sense of Gothic gloom and apprehension to their political-technological antiutopias. Each novel opens with the creation of a Gothic atmosphere which shapes initial attitudes to the narrative that follows: *Fahrenheit 451* with a glimpse of lurid, fiery destruction; *Brave New World* with the Central London Hatchery, a cold, grey skyscraper equivalent of the Gothic castle; and *Nineteen Eighty-Four* with scenes of ruin and decay. In addition, each novel contains scenes of a clearly Gothic horror: the mechanical hound in *Fahrenheit 451;* the Pavlovian conditioning room in *Brave New World;* Winston Smith's tortures in the Ministry of Love in *Nineteen Eighty-Four.* Thus each novel utilizes the metaphorical implications of the Gothic response thematically to project the sense of fear surrounding a future built upon our present tendencies and values.

Of the three novels, only *Nineteen Eighty-Four* can be called primarily Gothic, for only it contains all the elements necessary to place it within the Gothic type. The other novels use the Gothic as an occasional metaphor to suggest possible reactions to future life; *Nineteen Eighty-Four* sees a future under Big Brother government as synonymous with Gothic horror. Its passive victim is Winston Smith. Big Brother is the symbolic representative of ominous power. The prevailing atmosphere is one of gloom, decay, and fear. Its horrors are equal to any in *The Monk.* For example, the apprehensive terror of Room 101 in the Ministry of Love builds to a crescendo of genuine Gothic horror:

"The rat," said O'Brien, still addressing his invisible audience, "although a rodent is carnivorous. You are aware of that. You have heard of the things that happen in the poor quarters of this town: In some streets a woman dare not leave her baby alone in the house, even for five minutes. The rats are certain to attack it. Within quite a small time they will strip it to the bones. They also attack sick or dying people. They show astonishing intelligence in knowing when a human being is helpless." There was an outburst of squeals from the cage. . . .

· · · · ·

"I have pressed the first lever," said O'Brien. "You understand the construction of this cage. The mask will fit over your head, leaving no exit. When I press this other lever, the door of the cage will slide up. These starving brutes will shoot out of it like bullets. Have you ever seen a rat leap through the air? They will leap onto your face and bore straight into it. Sometimes they attack the eyes first. Sometimes they burrow through the cheeks and devour the tongue."

With this response of absolute horror evoked, the Gothic is seen as the prevailing metaphor characterizing the nature of existence under the political system of *Nineteen Eighty-Four.*

Undoubtedly, the Gothic will be used in other works as a metaphor for the scientific-bureaucratic future or for the present. Perhaps, like the absurd, it will become a dominant motif used to characterize perspectives of modern life by novelists who find our present existence not only meaningless but fearful or horrible. Kurt Vonnegut, in *Slaughterhouse Five* for example, demonstrates how the two metaphors can operate concurrently. In a description of an Iron Maiden, Vonnegut imparts a brief but powerful moment of traditional horror, thematically establishing an historical precedent for man's brutal nature, which is further augmented by a flippant repeated phrase which emphasizes the absurdity of his concomitant callousness:

> Weary's father once gave Weary's mother a Spanish thumbscrew in working condition—for a kitchen paperweight. Another time he gave her a table lamp whose base was a model one foot high of the famous "Iron Maiden of Nuremburg." The real Iron Maiden was a medieval torture instrument, a sort of boiler which was shaped like a woman on the outside—and lined with spikes. The front of the woman was composed of two hinged doors. The idea was to put a criminal inside and then close the door slowly. There were two special spikes where the eyes would be. There was a drain in the bottom to let out all the blood.
>
> So it goes.

Certainly the Gothic response offers significant potential to the modern writer, not only in conjunction with the absurd, but on its own as a metaphor of fear and horror. We have seen it advance from a perspective of the romantically fearful medieval past to a metaphor for contemporary evils and fears: sexual passion, materialism, the hereditary savagery of man. Today it reflects the individual's sense of impotence in a fearfully incomprehensible world. As a metaphor, the Gothic response is still alive and functioning with properly disturbing effectiveness. (pp. 130-44)

James M. Keech, "The Survival of the Gothic Response," in Studies in the Novel, *Vol. VI, No. 2, Summer, 1974, pp. 130-44.*

FURTHER READING

Baker, Ernest A. "The Gothic Novel." In his *The History of the English Novel: The Novel of Sentiment and the Gothic Romance,* pp. 175-227. London: H. F. and G. Witherby, 1934.
  Discusses the evolution of the Gothic novel from the novel of sensiblity and describes the major Gothic works and figures.

Bayer-Berenbaum, Linda. *The Gothic Imagination: Expansion in Gothic Literature and Art.* Rutherford, N. J.: Fairleigh Dickinson University Press, 1982, 155 p.
  Interdisciplinary study of Gothicism, in which Bayer-Berenbaum contends that "expansion and intensification are the essence of the Gothic experience, effected by a combination of the natural and supernatural into a continuous, immanent realm in which absolute separations between physical and spiritual or holy and profane are violated in order to create a single, greater domain."

Beers, Henry A. "The Gothic Revival." In his *A History of English Romanticism in the Eighteenth Century,* pp. 221-64. New York: Henry Holt and Co., 1916.
  Investigates the forerunners of Gothic fiction and architecture and provides a general overview of eighteenth-century Gothicism.

Birkhead, Edith. *The Tale of Terror: A Study of the Gothic Romance.* New York: E. P. Dutton and Co., 1921, 241 p.
  Survey of Gothic fiction which was one of the first serious critical studies to urge the importance of the Gothic genre to the development of literature.

Blondel, Jacques. "On 'Metaphysical Prisons'." *Durham University Journal* LXIII (n. s. XXXII), No. 2 (March 1971): 133-38.
  Investigates the motif of enclosure or imprisonment in Gothic novels, concluding that "Gothic art and its aftermath unweariedly [dug] beneath the level of conscience and consciousness, questioning the order of the age of Enlightenment."

Cooke, Arthur L. "Some Side Lights on the Theory of the Gothic Romance." *Modern Language Quarterly* 12, No. 4 (December 1951): 429-36.
  Examines a variety of aesthetic theories about Gothic fiction that Cooke feels have been given scant attention, such as the theory that the terror and pity evoked by Gothic works bring about an Aristotelian catharsis.

Doody, Margaret Anne. "Deserts, Ruins and Troubled Waters: Female Dreams in Fiction and the Development of the Gothic Novel." *Genre* X, No. 4 (Winter 1977): 529-72.
  Includes an analysis of dreams in the Gothic novels of Sophia Lee, Charlotte Smith, Ann Radcliffe, and others, concluding that they expressed women's feelings of guilt, rage, and inferiority and extended these feelings to the traditionally stalwart and rational male characters.

Duffy, Maureen. "Gothick Horror." In her *The Erotic World of Faery,* pp. 207-21. London: Hodder and Stoughton, 1972.
  Refers to the tradition of fairies in literature and Freudian theories about incest in analyzing the supernatural conventions in Gothic novels.

Fiedler, Leslie A. "Charles Brockden Brown and the Invention of the American Gothic" and "The Blackness of Darkness: Edgar Allan Poe and the Development of the Gothic." In his *Love and Death in the American Novel,* rev. ed., pp. 126-161, pp. 391-429. New York: Dell Publishing Co., 1966.
  Discusses the Gothic novel, as exemplified by the works of Brown and Poe, as an intrinsic part of the development of American literature.

Fiske, Christabel Forsythe. "The Tales of Terror." *The Conservative Review* III, No. 1 (March 1900): 37-74.
> Surveys types of Gothic fiction, criticizing the "stilted moral tone" and the "stock characters" of the novels of Walpole, Reeve, and Radcliffe, but praising Radcliffe's skill at description and Maturin's literary power and versatility.

Foster, James R. "D'Arnaud, Clara Reeve, and the Lees" and "Ann Radcliffe: End of a Phase." In his *History of the Pre-Romantic Novel in England,* pp. 186-224, pp. 261-76. New York: Modern Language Association of America, 1949.
> Discusses the Gothic novel as an offshoot of the sentimental novel, focussing on the careers of Clara Reeve and Ann Radcliffe.

Frank, Frederick S. *The First Gothics: A Critical Guide to the English Gothic Novel.* New York: Garland Publishing, 1987, 496 p.
> Comprehensive bibliography of Gothic fiction. Includes a glossary, a chronology, and an essay in which Frank examines the literary roots of Gothicism and the evolution of the Gothic novel into various forms.

Gose, Elliott B. "The Gothic Novel." In his *Imagination Indulged: The Irrational in the Nineteenth-Century Novel,* pp. 19-26. Montreal: McGill-Queen's University Press, 1972.
> Looks at the techniques used by Gothic authors to produce a combination of romance and reality.

Graham, John. "Character Description and Meaning in the Romantic Novel." *Studies in Romanticism* V, No. 4 (Summer 1966): 208-18.
> Studies the use in the Gothic novel of physiognomy, or "the art of judging character and disposition from the features of the face or the form and lineaments of the body generally."

Graham, Kenneth W., ed. *Gothic Fictions: Prohibition/ Transgression.* New York: AMS Press, 1989.
> Collection of studies on Gothic fiction, with essays both about the genre in general and about specific works.

Hart, Francis Russell. "The Experience of Character in the English Gothic Novel." In *Experience in the Novel,* edited by Roy Harvey Pearce, pp. 83-106. New York: Columbia University Press, 1968.
> Contends that the demonic in Gothic fiction is "virtually a function of [social] relationship" and that the reader must accept the characters as realistic as well as allegorical in order to fully understand this message.

———. "Limits of the Gothic: The Scottish Example." In *Racism in the Eighteenth Century,* edited by Harold E. Pagliaro, pp. 137-53. Cleveland: Press of Case Western Reserve University, 1973.
> Associates the Scottish novelists Smollett, Scott, and Hogg with the following characteristics respectively: grotesque, historic, and diabolic. Hart states that his "purpose is to understand the Gothic beginnings of the Scottish novel, but in furthering this purpose I may also use my Scottish example as a way of exploring the limits of the Gothic tendency."

Hogle, Jerrold E. "The Restless Labyrinth: Cryptonymy in the Gothic Novel." *Arizona Quarterly* 36, No. 4 (Winter 1980): 330-58.
> Analyzes the symbolism of the underground settings in Gothic novels.

Kaufman, Pamela. "Burke, Freud, and the Gothic." *Studies in Burke and His Time* XIII, No. 3 (Spring 1972): 2179-92.
> Uses the psychological theories of Edmund Burke and Sigmund Freud to explain the appeal of Gothic fiction.

Kiely, Robert. *The Romantic Novel in England.* Cambridge, Mass.: Harvard University Press, 1972, 275 p.
> In depth studies of twelve Gothic novels which emphasize the genre's importance in the development of the novel.

Le Tellier, Robert Ignatius. *Kindred Spirits: Interrelations and Affinities between the Romantic Novels of England and Germany, 1790-*

1820. Salzburg: Institut für Anglistik und Amerikanistik, 1982, 423 p.
> Seeks to clarify similarities in English and German Gothic fiction with relation to themes, structures, and devices.

Lewis, Paul. "Fearful Lessons: The Didacticism of the Early Gothic Novel." *CLA Journal* XXIII, No. 4 (June 1980): 470-84.
> Contends that the early Gothic works of Radcliffe, Lewis, and others cannot be considered as failed Romantic novels. Lewis concludes that even "as we are concentrating on the ambiguity and amorality of later Gothic works, we should remember that the founders of the movement in Britain and America insisted on the compatibility of intensity, mystery, and didacticism."

———. "Mysterious Laughter: Humor and Fear in Gothic Fiction." *Genre* XIV, No. 3 (Fall 1981): 309-27.
> Postulates that "if the Gothic is rooted in intense incongruity/mystery, then incongruity theory suggests that it is perched on the thin line between humor and fear and that there are a variety of ways in which the relationship between these emotions can be manipulated by writers."

Longueil, Alfred E. "The Word 'Gothic' in Eighteenth-Century Criticism." *Modern Language Notes* XXXVIII, No. 8 (December 1923): 453-60.
> Traces the evolution of the term Gothic from its reference to the "barbarous" northern tribes to "a sneering-word, from a sneering-word to a cool adjective, from a cool adjective to a cliché in criticism."

Lydenberg, Robin. "Gothic Architecture and Fiction: A Survey of Critical Responses." *Centennial Review* XXII, No. 1 (Winter 1978): 95-109.
> Investigates similarities in critical responses to Gothic architecture and literature.

Mayo, Robert D. "How Long Was Gothic Fiction in Vogue?" *Modern Language Notes* LVIII, 1 (January 1943): 58-64.
> Calculates the percentage of Gothic stories in *Lady's Magazine* during the late eighteenth and early nineteenth centuries, determining that the span of Gothic popularity encompassed the years 1791 to 1814. Mayo recommends that novels in the Gothic mode be categorized as "revivals" if they were published after 1814.

McIntyre, Clara F. "Were the 'Gothic Novels' Gothic?" *PMLA* XXXVI, No. 4 (December 1921): 644-67.
> Contends that "Gothic" is a misleading term for the eighteenth-century novels best represented by Ann Radcliffe. McIntyre suggests that while the trappings of these stories are derived from medieval times, the spirit of the genre was more influenced by the dramas of the Elizabethan Renaissance.

Nelson, Lowry, Jr. "Night Thoughts on the Gothic Novel." *Yale Review* LII, No. 2 (Winter 1963): 236-57.
> Analysis of the major Gothic novels which concludes, "we may well be convinced that the gothicists for all their outlandish oddities were in effect among the most fruitful literary explorers of the psyche."

Novak, Maximillian E. "Gothic Fiction and the Grotesque." *Novel: A Forum on Fiction* 13, No. 1 (Fall 1979): 50-67.
> Uses critic Wolfgang Kasper's theories of the grotesque to identify Gothicism as part of that category and to analyze various phases of Gothicism. Novak finds that "Gothic fiction is a grotesque distortion of anything resembling ordinary life."

Paulson, Ronald. "Gothic Fiction and the French Revolution." *ELH* 48, No. 3 (Fall 1981): 532-54.
> Argues that "Gothic did in fact serve as a metaphor with which some contemporaries in England tried to come to terms with what was happening across the Channel in the 1790s."

Platzner, Robert L., and Hume, Robert D. "Gothic Versus Romantic: A Rejoinder." *PMLA* 86, No. 2 (March 1971): 266-74.

Debate over the definition of Gothic and its relationship to Romanticism. Hume defends his article "Gothic Versus Romantic: A Revaluation of the Gothic Novel" (see excerpt above) against Platzner's objections.

Punter, David. *The Literature of Terror: A History of Gothic Fictions from 1765 to the Present Day.* London: Longman, 1980, 449 p.
Surveys Gothic novels in chronological groups, developing a theory of Gothic fiction based on psychology and Marxism.

Quennell, Peter. "The Moon Stood Still on Strawberry Hill." *Horizon* XI, No. 3 (Summer 1967): 113-19.
Describes the unique and shocking nature of Walpole's *Castle of Otranto,* Beckford's *Vathek,* Radcliffe's *Mysteries of Udolpho,* and Lewis's *The Monk,* as they appeared to contemporary readers, and provides biographical sketches of these authors at the time they wrote these works.

Ringe, Donald A. *American Gothic: Imagination and Reason in Nineteenth-Century Fiction.* Lexington: University Press of Kentucky, 1982, 215 p.
Analyzes the development of the Gothic novel in America, concluding that Americans "created a version of the Gothic mode which, without denying its European roots, became in time recognizably American."

Rustowski, Adam M. "Convention and Generic Instability of the English Gothic Novel." *Studia Anglica Posnaniensia* 8 (1976): 175-87.
Describes the conventions in Gothic novels that result in confusion of good and evil.

Sage, Victor. *Horror Fiction in the Protestant Tradition.* London: Macmillan Press, 1988, 262 p.
Hypothesizes that "the rise and currency of literary Gothic is strongly related to the growth of the campaign for Catholic Emancipation from the 1770s onward until the first stage ends temporarily with the Emancipation Act of 1829; but further, that continuance of the horror novel is equally, if not more strongly, related to the subsequent struggles, doctrinal and political, which flared up between Catholic and Protestant throughout the course of the nineteenth century and well into the twentieth."

Skilton, David. "Gothic, Romantic and Heroic." In his *Defoe to the Victorians: Two Centuries of the English Novel,* pp. 59-79. Harmondsworth, England: Penguin Books, 1977.
General overview of the Gothic novel, which emphasizes its contribution to Romantic novels and poetry and modern horror fiction.

Stevens, L. Robert. "The Exorcism of England's Gothic Demon." *Midwest Quarterly* XIV, No. 2 (Winter 1973): 151-64.
Contrasts the Anglo-American sense of the Gothic, in which Stevens perceives a fundamental sense of optimism, with the Continental variety, which he describes as "the underlying fear that the world 'out there' beyond the confines of the sanctuary is possessed of demons, that anyone might misstep at any time, that the rules for spiritual living are thin strands across the abyss."

Stevenson, Lionel. "Terror and Edification (1775-1800)." In his *The English Novel: A Panorama,* pp. 148-76. Boston: Houghton Mifflin Co., 1960.
Contends that the Gothic novel extended the values and situations of Richardson's sentimental novels.

Summers, Montague. *The Gothic Quest: A History of the Gothic Novel.* London: Fortune Press, 1938, 443 p.
Landmark study of Gothic literature which provides detailed descriptions of major and minor Gothic works, describes influences on the genre, and devotes a significant section to the study of Matthew Lewis's life and career.

Tarr, Sister Mary Muriel. *Catholicism in Gothic Fiction: A Study of the Nature and Function of Catholic Materials in Gothic Fiction in England, 1762-1820.* Washington: Catholic University of America Press, 1946, 141 p.
Concludes that references to Catholic clergy, services, and beliefs, although highly inaccurate, served the dual purpose of feeding anti-Catholic prejudices and providing a sentimental and romantic atmosphere.

Thompson, G. R., ed. *The Gothic Imagination: Essays in Dark Romanticism.* Pullman: Washington State University Press, 1974, 176 p.
Various studies of Gothic themes, conventions, and issues, including essays by Robert D. Hume and Maurice Levy.

Tompkins, J. M. S. "The Gothic Romance." In his *The Popular Novel in England: 1770-1800,* pp. 243-95. Westport, Conn: Greenwood Press, 1976.
Study of the Gothic novel's themes, techniques, and conventions, focusing on Ann Radcliffe's novels.

Tracy, Ann B. "Gothic, Had-I-But-Known, Damsel-in-Distress: Stalking the Elusive Distinction." In *Murderess Ink: The Better Half of the Mystery,* edited by Dilys Winn, pp. 14-17. New York: Workman Publishing, 1979.
Compares the Gothic heroine to the heroine of modern romance novels.

Tymn, Marshall B. *Horror Literature: A Core Collection and Reference Guide.* New York: R. R. Bowker Co., 1981, 559 p.
Includes annotated bibliographies of primary sources and essays on the Gothic romance and later works influenced by the Gothic genre.

Varnado, S. L. *Haunted Presence: The Numinous in Gothic Fiction.* Tuscaloosa: University of Alabama Press, 1987, 160 p.
Discusses Gothic fiction in the light of theologian Rudolph Otto's concept of the "numinous."

Wagenknecht, Edward. "The Renascence of Wonder." In his *Cavalcade of the English Novel,* pp. 110-33. New York: Henry Holt and Co., 1943.
Discussion of both well-known and less studied Gothic novels.

Watt, William W. *Shilling Shockers of the Gothic School: A Study of Chapbook Gothic Romances.* Cambridge, Mass.: Harvard University Press, 1932, 54 p.
Description of the short, cheaply published, and often plagiarized Gothic stories that were extremely popular in the late eighteenth and early nineteenth centuries.

Wright, Walter Francis. *Sensibility in English Prose Fiction, 1760-1814: A Reinterpretation.* Urbana: University of Illinois, 1937, 158 p.
Analyzes the Gothic novel as novel of sensibility, asserting that it "is the feelings which animated the novelists rather than the materials which the writers employed that reveal the nature of the development of fiction from the age of Walpole and Mrs. Brooke to that of Mrs. Radcliffe and Lewis."

Russian Nihilism

INTRODUCTION

For related criticism, see the entry on the Russian Civic Critics in *NCLC,* Volume 20.

Russian Nihilism is a term designating a broad social, political, and literary movement that flourished during the 1860s. The common aims of the Nihilists included the emancipation of the individual from political, social, and cultural restrictions and the material improvement of the backward Russian state; at the same time, the movement lacked a unified ideology, and the precise definition of nihilism in its Russian context is subject to dispute. Richard Stites, a scholar of the movement, voices the prevailing opinion that Nihilism "was not so much a corpus of formal beliefs and programs (like populism, liberalism, Marxism) as it was a cluster of attitudes and social values and a set of behavioral effects. In short, it was an ethos."

The Nihilist movement was inspired in part by the writings of Mikhail Bakunin, the leading European anarchist of the 1850s and 1860s, and Aleksandr Herzen, an emigré socialist whose periodical *Kolokol* (*The Bell*) popularized liberal ideas in the 1850s. Herzen's publication found a welcome reception among Russia's liberal aristocracy, who wanted to install a westernized parliamentary government in place of the unpopular czarist autocracy. While the repressive regime of Nicholas I (1825-55) prevented the ready dissemination of radical ideas, the accession of the liberal Alexander II in 1855 and a series of well-intended but insufficient reforms opened the door to widespread attack by intellectuals on existing conditions. As the result of educational reforms instituted by Alexander II, the intelligentsia now included members of the lower classes, the "rasnochintsy," who demanded drastic reform of the Russian state. This initiated what has become known as the Nihilist movement. Ivan Turgenev is credited with popularizing the archetypal "Nihilist" in his characterization of Bazarov in the novel *Ottsy i deti* (*Fathers and Sons*), published in 1862. Although Turgenev's intentions in creating this character were essentially satirical, Bazarov's intense individualism, total contempt for traditional values, and faith in scientific progress largely defined the Nihilist polemic of the 1860s.

Scholars generally agree that the Nihilist "doctrine" was most clearly expressed by the writers collectively referred to as Civic Critics: Nikolay Chernyshevsky, Nikolay Dobrolyubov, and Dmitry Pisarev, influential critics who combined literary exegesis with exposition of progressive philosophical and social theory. Chernyshevsky also wrote fiction, and his 1862 novel *Chto delat'* (*What Is to Be Done?*) is frequently cited as a key Nihilist work for its vivid portrait of radical youth and advocacy of feminism. With the increasing influence of the Civic Critics' ideas, Nihilism soon became established as a popular social movement, and young people, especially university students and the privileged sons and daughters of the aristocracy, sought to shock, outrage, and bemuse conventional society with their strangely austere life-style,

dishevelled appearance, and radical views on politics, ethics, and religion. As the decade progressed, the Nihilist movement lost its reformist and literary character and became increasingly identified with terrorism as the left wing of the intelligentsia embarked on a policy of sabotage and violence, including an attempt on the Czar's life by a Nihilist student in 1866.

The shift by Russia's intellectual elite toward an overtly revolutionary program in the 1870s has led to a common perception of Nihilism as a purely negative and destructive doctrine, rather than one of practical action and social reconstruction, as advocated by the Civic Critics. While some commentators suggest that Nihilism ought to be considered in the abstract—as a general philosophy of pessimism, or, alternatively, as an inherent spiritual condition caused by a harsh physical and political environment—the majority of scholars define Russian Nihilism as a progressive social movement with definite historical parameters.

REPRESENTATIVE WORKS

Chernyshevsky, Nikolay Gavrilovich
  Esteticheskie otnosheniia iskusstva k deistvitel'nosti
    (essay) 1855
  Chto delat' (novel) 1863
      [*What Is to Be Done?: Tales about New People,*
      1883]
  Polnoe sobranie sochinenii N. G. Chernyschevskogo. 10
    vols. (essays, novels, and criticism) 1905-06
  Selected Philosophical Essays (essays) 1953
Dobrolyubov, Nikolay Alexandrovich
  *"Chto takoye Oblomvschina?" (essay) 1859
      †["What is Oblomovism?" 1956]
  *"Tiomnoye Tzarstvo?" (essay) 1859
      †["The Kingdom of Darkness," 1956]
  *"Kogda zhe prediot nastroyashchi den?" (essay)
      1860
      †["When Will the Day Come?" 1956]
  *"Unizhonnye i oskorblyonne" (essay) 1861
  Izbrannye filosofskie sochineniia. 2 vols. (essays) 1948
  Selected Philosophical Essays (essays) 1956
Pisarev, Dmitry Ivanovich
  ‡"Bazarov" (essay) 1862
  ‡"Realisty" (essay) 1864
      ["The Realists," 1965]
  ‡"Pushkin i Belinsky" (essay) 1865
  ‡"Razrusenie èstetiki" (essay) 1865
  Sochineniya. 10 vols. (criticism and essays) 1866-69
  "Bor'ba za suscestvovanie" (essay) 1867-68
  Sochineniya. 6 vols. (criticism and essays) 1894
  Literaturno-kriticheskie stati (criticism) 1940
  Izbrannye filosofskie i obshchestvenno-politicheskie stati
    (essays) 1944
  Sochineniya. 4 vols. (criticism and essays) 1955-56

Selected Philosophical, Social, and Political Essays
(essays) 1958
Literaturnaya kritika (criticism) 1981
D. I. Pisarev ob ateizme, religii i tsetkvi (essays) 1984
Turgenev, Ivan
Ottsy i deti (novel) 1862
[*Fathers and Sons, 1867;* also published as *Fathers and Children* in *The Novels of Ivan Turgenev,* 1899]

*These essays were originally published in the journal *Sovremenik.*

†These essays were translated and published in *Selected Philosophical Essays* in 1956.

‡These essays were originally published in the journal *Russkoe Slovo.*

DEFINITIONS AND OVERVIEWS

MIKHAIL BAKUNIN

[*A leading revolutionary activist in Russia during the mid nineteenth century, Bakunin was the principal theorist of philosophical and political anarchism and a major influence on the development of the Nihilist movement during the 1860s. While Bakunin's anarchist vision of the overthrow of the reigning powers of Europe was largely superseded by the ideological program of Marxism, his stated goals—the destruction of established society and the institution of a federation of cooperative communities—have continued to influence radical thought. In the following speech, originally presented in 1868 in Geneva, Bakunin affirms the necessity of destroying traditional European religious and political structures in order to create a new society.*]

Brethren, I come to announce unto you a new gospel, which must penetrate to the very ends of the world. This gospel admits of no half-measures and hesitations. The old world must be destroyed, and replaced by a new one. The *Lie* must be stamped out and give way to Truth.

It is our mission to destroy the *Lie;* and, to effect this, we must begin at the very commencement. Now the beginning of all those lies which have ground down this poor world in slavery, is God. For many hundred years monarchs and priests have inoculated the hearts and minds of mankind with this notion of a God ruling over the world. They have also invented for the people the notion of another world, in which their God is to punish with eternal torture those who have refused to obey their degrading laws here on earth. This God is nothing but the personification of absolute tyranny, and has been invented with a view of either frightening or alluring nine-tenths of the human race into submission to the remaining tenth. If there were really a God, surely he would use that lightning which he holds in his hand, to destroy those thrones, to the steps of which mankind is chained. He would assuredly use it to overthrow those altars, where the truth is hidden by clouds of lying incense. Tear out of your hearts the belief in the existence of God; for, as long as an atom of that silly superstition remains in your minds, you will never know what freedom is.

When you have got rid of the belief in this priest-begotten God, and when, moreover, you are convinced that your existence, and that of the surrounding world, is due to the conglomeration of atoms, in accordance with the laws of gravity and attraction, then, and then only, you will have accomplished the first step towards liberty, and you will experience less difficulty in ridding your minds of that second lie which tyranny has invented.

The first lie is *God.* The second lie is *Right. Might* invented the fiction of Right in order to insure and strengthen her reign; that Right which she herself does not heed, and which only serves as a barrier against any attacks which may be made by the trembling and stupid masses of mankind.

Might, my friends, forms the sole groundwork of society. Might makes and unmakes laws, and that might should be in the hands of the majority. It should be in the possession of those nine-tenths of the human race whose immense power has been rendered subservient to the remaining tenth by means of that lying fiction of *Right* before which you are accustomed to bow your heads and to drop your arms. Once penetrated with a clear conviction of your own *might,* you will be able to destroy this mere notion of *Right.*

And when you have freed your minds from the fear of a God, and from that childish respect for the fiction of *Right,* then all the remaining chains which bind you, and which are called science, civilisation, property, marriage, morality, and justice, will snap asunder like threads.

Let your own happiness be your only law. But in order to get this law recognised, and to bring about the proper relations which should exist between the majority and minority of mankind, you must destroy everything which exists in the shape of State or social organisation. So educate yourselves and your children that, when the great moment for constituting the new world arrives, your eyes may not be blinded and deceived by the falsehoods of the tyrants of throne and altar.

Our first work must be destruction and annihilation of everything as it now exists. You must accustom yourselves to destroy everything, the good with the bad; for if but an atom of this old world remains, the new will never be created.

According to the priests' fables, in days of old a deluge destroyed all mankind, but their God specially saved Noah in order that the seeds of tyranny and falsehood might be perpetuated in the new world. When you once begin your work of destruction, and when the floods of enslaved masses of the people rise and engulf temples and palaces, then take heed that no ark be allowed to rescue any atom of this old world which we consecrate to destruction. (pp. 2-3)

> *Mikhail Bakunin, quoted in "Russian Nihilism" by Fritz Cunliffe-Owen, The Nineteenth Century, Vol. VII, No. XXXV, January, 1880, pp. 1-26.*

PETER KROPOTKIN

[*Kropotkin was a Russian sociologist, philosopher, geographer, essayist, and critic. Born of an aristocratic family, Kropotkin became an anarchist in the 1870s and later fled to Europe, where he composed several of his best-known works. Chief among these is his* Memoirs of a Revolutionist, *which is con-*

sidered a monumental autobiographical treatment of the revolutionary movement in Russia. In the following excerpt from that work, Kropotkin provides a contemporary account of the Nihilist movement in Russia during the first half of the 1860s.]

A formidable movement was developing in the [1860s] amongst the educated youth of Russia. Serfdom was abolished. But quite a network of habits and customs of domestic slavery, of utter disregard of human individuality, of despotism on the part of the fathers, and of hypocritical submission on that of the wives, the sons, and the daughters, had developed during the two hundred and fifty years that serfdom had existed. Everywhere in Europe, at the beginning of this century, there was a great deal of domestic despotism,—the writings of Thackeray and Dickens bear ample testimony to it; but nowhere else had that tyranny attained such a luxurious development as in Russia. All Russian life, in the family, in the relations between commander and subordinate, military chief and soldier, employer and employee, bore the stamp of it. Quite a world of customs and manners of thinking, of prejudices and moral cowardice, of habits bred by a lazy existence, had grown up. Even the best men of the time paid a large tribute to these products of the serfdom period.

Law could have no grip upon these things. Only a vigorous social movement, which would attack the very roots of the evil, could reform the habits and customs of everyday life; and in Russia this movement—this revolt of the individual— took a far more powerful character, and became far more sweeping in its criticisms, than anywhere in Western Europe or America. "Nihilism" was the name that Turguéneff gave it in his epoch-making novel, *Fathers and Sons.*

The movement is misunderstood in Western Europe. In the press, for example, nihilism is continually confused with terrorism. The revolutionary disturbance which broke out in Russia toward the close of the reign of Alexander II., and ended in the tragical death of the Tsar, is constantly described as nihilism. This is, however, a mistake. To confuse nihilism with terrorism is as wrong as to confuse a philosophical movement like stoicism or positivism with a political movement such as, for example, republicanism. Terrorism was called into existence by certain special conditions of the political struggle at a given historical moment. It has lived, and has died. It may revive and die out again. But nihilism has impressed its stamp upon the whole of the life of the educated classes of Russia, and that stamp will be retained for many years to come. It is nihilism, divested of some of its rougher aspects,—which were unavoidable in a young movement of that sort,—which gives now to the life of a great portion of the educated classes of Russia a certain peculiar character which we Russians regret not to find in the life of Western Europe. It is nihilism, again, in its various manifestations, which gives to many of our writers that remarkable sincerity, that habit of "thinking aloud," which astounds Western European readers.

First of all, the nihilist declared war upon what may be described as "the conventional lies of civilized mankind." Absolute sincerity was his distinctive feature, and in the name of that sincerity he gave up, and asked others to give up, those superstitions, prejudices, habits, and customs which their own reason could not justify. He refused to bend before any authority except that of reason, and in the analysis of every social institution or habit he revolted against any sort of more or less masked sophism.

He broke, of course, with the superstitions of his fathers, and in his philosophical conceptions he was a positivist, an agnostic, a Spencerian evolutionist, or a scientific materialist; and while he never attacked the simple, sincere religious belief which is a psychological necessity of feeling, he bitterly fought against the hypocrisy that lends people to assume the outward mask of a religion which they repeatedly throw aside as useless ballast.

The life of civilized people is full of little conventional lies. Persons who hate each other, meeting in the street, make their faces radiant with a happy smile; the nihilist remained unmoved, and smiled only for those whom he was really glad to meet. All those forms of outward politeness which are mere hypocrisy were equally repugnant to him, and he assumed a certain external roughness as a protest against the smooth amiability of his fathers. He saw them wildly talking as idealist sentimentalists, and at the same time acting as real barbarians toward their wives, their children, and their serfs; and he rose in revolt against that sort of sentimentalism which, after all, so nicely accommodated itself to the anything but ideal conditions of Russian life. Art was involved in the same sweeping negation. Continual talk about beauty, the ideal, art for art's sake, æsthetics, and the like, so willingly indulged in,—while every object of art was bought with money exacted from starving peasants or from underpaid workers, and the so-called "worship of the beautiful" was but a mask to cover the most commonplace dissoluteness,— inspired him with disgust, and the criticisms of art which Tolstóy, one of the greatest artists of the century, has now so powerfully formulated, the nihilist expressed in the sweeping assertion, "A pair of boots is more important than all your Madonnas and all your refined talk about Shakespeare."

Marriage without love, and familiarity without friendship, were equally repudiated. The nihilist girl, compelled by her parents to be a doll in a Doll's House, and to marry for property's sake, preferred to abandon her house and her silk dresses. She put on a black woolen dress of the plainest description, cut off her hair, and went to a high school, in order to win there her personal independence. The woman who saw that her marriage was no longer a marriage, that neither love nor friendship connected those who were legally considered husband and wife, preferred to break a bond which retained none of its essential features. Accordingly she often went with her children to face poverty, preferring loneliness and misery to a life which, under conventional conditions, would have given a perpetual lie to her best self.

The nihilist carried his love of sincerity even into the minutest details of every-day life. He discarded the conventional forms of society talk, and expressed his opinions in a blunt and terse way, even with a certain affection of outward roughness.

In Irkútsk we used to meet once a week in a club and have some dancing. I was for a time a regular visitor at these soirées, but afterwards, having to work, I abandoned them. One night, when I had not made my appearance for several weeks, a young friend of mine was asked by one of the ladies why I did not appear any more at their gatherings. "He takes a ride now when he wants exercise," was the rather rough reply of my friend. "But he might come and spend a couple of hours with us, without dancing," one of the ladies ventured to say. "What would he do here?" retorted my nihilist friend; "talk with you about fashions and furbelows? He has had enough of that nonsense." "But he sees Miss So-and-So occasionally," timidly remarked one of the young ladies present.

"Yes, but she is a studious girl," bluntly replied my friend; "he helps her with her German." I must add that this undoubtedly rough rebuke had its effect, for most of the Irkútsk girls soon began to besiege my brother, my friend, and myself with questions as to what we should advise them to read or to study.

With the same frankness the nihilist spoke to his acquaintances, telling them that all their talk about "this poor people" was sheer hypocrisy so long as they lived upon the underpaid work of these people whom they commiserated at their ease as they chatted together in richly decorated rooms; and with the same frankness a nihilist would declare to a high functionary that the latter cared not a straw for the welfare of those whom he ruled, but was simply a thief, and so on.

With a certain austerity the nihilist would rebuke the woman who indulged in small talk and prided herself on her "womanly" manners and elaborate toilette. He would bluntly say to a pretty young person: "How is it that you are not ashamed to talk this nonsense and to wear that chignon of false hair?" In a woman he wanted to find a comrade, a human personality,—not a doll or a "muslin girl,"—and he absolutely refused to join in those petty tokens of politeness with which men surround those whom they like so much to consider as "the weaker sex." When a lady entered a room a nihilist did not jump from his seat to offer it to her, unless he saw that she looked tired and there was no other seat in the room. He behaved towards her as he would have behaved towards a comrade of his own sex; but if a lady—who might have been a total stranger to him—manifested the desire to learn something which he knew and she did not, he would walk every night to the far end of a large city to help her.

Two great Russian novelists, Turguéneff and Goncharóff, have tried to represent this new type in their novels. Goncharóff, in "Precipice," taking a real but unrepresentative individual of this class, made a caricature of nihilism. Turguéneff was too good an artist, and had himself conceived too much admiration for the new type, to let himself be drawn into caricature painting; but even his nihilist, Bazároff, did not satisfy us. We found him too harsh, especially in his relations with his old parents, and, above all, we reproached him with his seeming neglect of his duties as a citizen. Russian youth could not be satisfied with the merely negative attitude of Turguéneff's hero. Nihilism, with its affirmation of the rights of the individual and its negation of all hypocrisy, was but a first step toward a higher type of men and women, who are equally free, but live for a great cause. In the nihilists of Chernyshévsky, as they are depicted in his far less artistic novel, "What is to be Done?" they saw better portraits of themselves.

"It is bitter, the bread that has been made by slaves," our poet Nekrásoff wrote. The young generation actually refused to eat that bread, and to enjoy the riches that had been accumulated in their fathers' houses by means of servile labor, whether the laborers were actual serfs or slaves of the present industrial system.

All Russia read with astonishment, in the indictment which was produced at the court against Karakózoff and his friends, that these young men, owners of considerable fortunes, used to live three or four in the same room, never spending more than five dollars apiece a month for all their needs, and giving at the same time their fortunes for starting coöperative associations, coöperative workshops (where they themselves

worked), and the like. Five years later, thousands and thousands of the Russian youth—the best part of it—were doing the same. Their watchword was, "V naród!" (To the people; be the people.) During the years 1860-65, in nearly every wealthy family a bitter struggle was going on between the fathers, who wanted to maintain the old traditions, and the sons and daughters, who defended their right to dispose of their lives according to their own ideals. Young men left the military service, the counter, the shop, and flocked to the university towns. Girls, bred in the most aristocratic families, rushed penniless to St. Petersburg, Moscow, and Kíeff, eager to learn a profession which would free them from the domestic yoke, and some day, perhaps, also from the possible yoke of a husband. After hard and bitter struggles, many of them won that personal freedom. Now they wanted to utilize it, not for their own personal enjoyment, but for carrying to the people the knowledge that had emancipated them.

In every town of Russia, in every quarter of St. Petersburg, small groups were formed for self-improvement and self-education; the works of the philosophers, the writings of the economists, the historical researches of the young Russian historical school, were carefully read in these circles, and the reading was followed by endless discussions. The aim of all that reading and discussion was to solve the great question which rose before them. In what way could they be useful to the masses? Gradually, they came to the idea that the only way was to settle amongst the people, and to live the people's life. Young men went into the villages as doctors, doctors' helpers, teachers, village scribes, even as agricultural laborers, blacksmiths, woodcutters, and so on, and tried to live there in close contact with the peasants. Girls passed teachers' examinations, learned mid-wifery or nursing, and went by the hundred into the villages, devoting themselves entirely to the poorest part of the population.

These people went without any ideal of social reconstruction in their mind, or any thought of revolution. They simply wanted to teach the mass of the peasants to read, to instruct them in other things, to give them medical help, and in any way to aid in raising them from their darkness and misery, and to learn at the same time what were *their* popular ideals of a better social life. (pp. 296-302)

Peter Kropotkin, "St. Petersburg: First Journey to Western Europe," in his Memoirs of a Revolutionist, *Dover Publications, Inc., 1988, pp. 224-342.*

CHARLES A. MOSER

[*Moser is the author of* Antinihilism in the Russian Novel of the 1860's *(1964). In the following excerpt from that work, he discusses the cultural background and popular definitions of Russian Nihilism in the 1860s, identifying the principal themes of the movement in the writings of the Civic Critics and other prominent literary figures of the period.*]

The term "nihilist" . . . has a long history. In the Middle Ages the word was used to designate a person who doubted the divinity of Christ and other articles of the Christian faith. It appeared in Russian as early as 1829 although in this instance the writer, assigning another sense to the meaning of the Latin root *nihil* "nothing," spoke of a "nihilist" as a worthless person or someone who knew nothing. In Belinskij's mind the word was allied to "emptiness", but before long the journalist Katkov and also Dobroljubov were using it with the connotations attached to it in the 1860's. Whatever the word's history, it is generally agreed that Ivan Turgenev fastened the label firmly on the younger generation through his novel *Fathers and Sons* (1862), with its famous passage in Chapter 5 where Pavel Petrovič and his nephew Arkadij discuss the younger, "nihilist" generation. *Fathers and Sons* was the first literary work to concentrate public attention on the rising progressives and the tag used by Turgenev to designate them remained fixed in the public mind.

If we strip the term "nihilism" of its contemporary existentialist encrustations, it should signify a doctrine advocating intellectual negation and the sheer destruction of whatever may in fact exist, be it material or spiritual. Such a theory would hold that it is of no interest whether or not anything replaces that which is to be annihilated. A thoroughly consistent nihilist would even consider it his duty to keep on ruining anything that had been constructed or that would be constructed in the future regardless of its utility. He should adhere to no positive philosophical or religious beliefs at all. In its pure form a doctrine of this type has been held by very few people; no society could tolerate a man who attempted seriously to put such theories into practice. Almost any historical personage who could be called a nihilist in the political sense limited himself in the extreme case to advocating the destruction of the existing order because it was evil, after which, he assumed, it would be replaced by something better, although this was not his concern. If the new proved to be too much less than ideal, it likewise could be annihilated until some satisfactory situation ultimately emerged from the alternation of destruction and creation. Though he might refuse to admit it, such a person would have to possess some sort of blueprint for the future society in order merely to recognize a "satisfactory situation".

Of course the Russian radicals of the 1860's were far from being total nihilists in the sense described above. In the first place, they had unbounded faith in themselves and their convictions. Politically, they looked in vague fashion toward a socialist system or, in infrequent cases perhaps, toward an anarchist society. As they thought the road to their ideal world would be long and arduous, however, the only path which seemed to lie immediately open to them was that of negating the existing order and clearing space so that something better might be established in its place. Their consequent negligence in elaborating any positive plans for the future gave their ideological opponents the opportunity to claim that they were nihilists of the purest type, interested only in negation for the sake of negation. Though this was an unjust accusation, the nihilists themselves were partially responsible for it.

The radicals, their allies and even some of their opponents protested against the application of the emotionally loaded term "nihilism" to their doctrines. Herzen, in a famous article on Bazarov, gave the following definition of nihilism:

> Nihilism . . . is logic without structure, it is science without dogmas, it is the unconditional submission to experience and the resigned acceptance of all consequences, whatever they may be, if they follow from observation, or are required by reason. Nihilism does not transform something into nothing, but shows that nothing which has been taken for something is an optical illusion, and that every truth, however it contradicts our fantastic ideas, is more wholesome than they are, and is in any case what we are in duty bound to accept.

Thus Herzen claimed that though nihilism would seem on the surface to be a negative doctrine, it is in fact a positive one. In his tendentious poem "Gazetnaja" ("The Reading Room", 1865), Nekrasov describes an elderly reactionary talking about his son. When he accused his son of being a nihilist, the latter replied that "nihilist is a stupid word" but that he was willing to accept the label if by it were understood a "straightforward person", one who "works, seeks truth", one who is ready to "hiss down rascals and on occasion is happy to thrash them a bit". Even the prolific journalist and author P. D. Boborykin, no friend of the radicals', in an article written for the foreign press, objected to the idea that "nihilism" in the Russia of the 1860's was a negative doctrine. Nihilism's "principles and tendencies", he asserted,

> are much more positive . . . than negative. If the Nihilists began with a destructive criticism, it was only to enable them to introduce with greater enthusiasm and a more ardent belief their own rules and doctrines into every part of their teaching. . . . Even the most negative principle of Nihilism—viz., that which relates to art—is in a certain sense a positive doctrine, because it *affirms* the inferiority of art to nature.

The radicals were understandably reluctant to apply the term "nihilist" to themselves and thus give it greater currency than it already possessed. The name placed in circulation by them as a counter-measure was the "new man" or the "new men", the implication being that these men, the radicals, had broken with the old ways and were searching for new concepts. Černyševskij's *What Is To Be Done?* is largely a eulogy of the "new men", and the term did acquire considerable popularity as a more satisfactory tag for the younger generation. Pisarev attempted to introduce the term "realism" to denote the approach of the younger generation: a "realist" was one who looked dispassionately on everything about him and evaluated it in objective fashion. However, the name "realist" did not gain wide acceptance. Pisarev wrote one very interesting article on the subject of the "new man" entitled "The Thinking Proletariat" (originally "A New Type", published in 1865). Some of the new men's altogether admirable characteristics, according to Pisarev, were the following:

> The new men have become passionately attached to generally useful work.

> The personal advantage of the new men coincides with the general advantage, and their egotism incorporates within itself the broadest possible love of humanity.

> The new men's intelligence is in the most complete harmony with their emotions, because with them neither the intelligence nor the emotions have been distorted by chronic enmity toward other people.

The radicals expended much effort in producing articles such as this one by Pisarev and fiction delineating the intellectual outlines of the "new men" of the future who would embody completely the ideals of the radical generation of the 1860's. The quarrel over the terminology to be applied to the young radicals of the decade was a fairly important one, although the doctrines espoused by them were the same whether they were pejoratively called "nihilists" or approvingly named the "new men".

The progressives of the 1860's, having received the radical tradition from the 1840's and placed their own stamp upon it, in turn yielded to the following stage, the generation which "went to the people" and eventually raised the theory of individual terrorism to the status of a basic tactic. On April 4, 1866, a shot fired at the Tsar by the radical student Karakozov initiated the era of terrorism which was to continue by fits and starts into the next century, during which no high official could feel certain of being protected against all the fanatics bent on taking his life. The high-water-mark of this current in the revolutionary movement was the successful assassination, after several failures, of the Tsar Alexander II in the middle of Petersburg in 1881. It was this more spectacular and romantic aspect of the Russian revolutionary movement, particularly in the 1870's and 1880's, which attracted the notice and in large measure the sympathy of the western public to the "nihilist" cause. In western minds the word "nihilist" conjured up visions of a wild-eyed bomb-thrower, which was not at all what the genuine "nihilist" of the 1860's was, although he certainly contained within himself the potentiality of development into a political assassin.

A less glamorous but far more widespread aspect of the revolutionary movement of the 1870's was the attempted "going to the people". Young intellectuals from the large city universities decided to don peasant dress, learn a trade if possible, gain the confidence of the peasantry and carry on revolutionary agitation among them. The entire movement reached its climax in the "mad summer" of 1874, when hordes of students swarmed into the countryside in pursuit of revolutionary aims. The peasants for the most part did not in the least understand what the students were about and turned many of them in to the police while ridiculing others, so that the whole idea fizzled. Turgenev portrayed the failure of some of the initiators of this *narodnik* (a *narodnik* was one who placed his confidence in the peasantry) movement in his novel *Virgin Soil.* (pp. 18-22)

Although, as with any intellectual movement, there were various and often contending currents in the nihilist milieu in the Russia of the 1860's, certain elements may be isolated as common to the bulk of the radicals of that time in one form or another. Since the Russia of that day lay open to an astonishingly large degree to all sorts of influences emanating from Western Europe, the initial formulation of certain doctrines or the first impulse for their development often came from western writers, publicists and thinkers. In most cases imported ideas found native interpreters in the persons of Russian journalists, especially Pisarev and Černyševskij, who acted as enthusiastic propagandists of new ideas emanating from the West and frequently added something of their own. Finally, theory was in some instances embodied in practice in Russian life, attempts were made to experiment on the basis of the new concepts in the hope that such experimentation would help prepare the way for a transformation of Russian life. These foreign and domestic theories and practice bestowed upon the nihilist milieu of the 1860's its peculiar shape and coloration.

Non-radical observers of intellectual life in the 1860's were struck very sharply by the nihilists' theories of negation and exposure. This approach was forced on the nihilists by the thought, mentioned above, that the road to the reconstruction of society would be long and arduous and that the first and most pressing task before the radical generation was that of clearing space for the new, sweeping away all that was corrupt in the old. This idea found one of its most explicit and extreme formulations in a well-known passage by Pisarev where he says that the younger generation should flail merci-

Dmitry Pisarev

lessly about itself, for what was healthy and strong in its surroundings would remain undamaged and what was unhealthy and rotten would be swept away, which was all to the good. The nihilists tended automatically to react negatively to whatever they saw about them in Russian life. They condemned out of hand anything that was an integral part of the contemporary order or that seemed to support it. As ideas of this sort could easily be applied to any and all cases, the negative approach soon came to be employed unthinkingly and almost universally. Even Pisarev, the leader of the negating party, on one occasion protested against too facile negation.

> When a person negates utterly everything, this means he negates precisely nothing and even that he knows and understands nothing. If the one who occupies himself with the facile business of complete negation is not a child but an adult, then one can even assert boldly that this flamboyant gentleman is endowed with such an immobile and lazy mind that he will never imbibe nor understand a single sensible thought.

Though Pisarev, a man with a certain amount of intellectual flexibility, could appreciate the value of selective negation, many of his followers were incapable of this. The totally negative attitude of the early nihilists provoked the following comment from A. V. Nikitenko, a moderate liberal who worked for reform within government circles:

> And what do you want, Mister Reds, if only you possess any definite aims? You would like to destroy the existing government. But whom will you put in its place? Of course you will experience no

difficulty in putting yourselves there. But others
may not want this. What then: struggle, war?

Nikitenko had considerable justification for his worry, for at
this early date negation pure and simple was one of the younger generation's most notable intellectual attributes.

The "exposure" of current abuses, a trend akin to that of negation, found its most prominent place in the fiction produced by the so-called "nihilist" authors. Two currents within the "nihilist" novel may be distinguished; the radical utopian trend, and the "critical realist" novel which cast a jaun-
diced eye on phenomena of Russian life. The tradition of
"critical realism" in Russian literature was well established
by the 1860's, as it is usually considered to derive from
Gogol's *Dead Souls* and "The Greatcoat", written about
1840. In the 1860's the tradition of the gloomy and negative
approach to Russian reality was continued by a group of
minor writers, most of whom lived wretchedly and died
young.

Nikolaj Pomjalovskij, for example, who was born in 1835,
died in 1863 from natural causes complicated by acute alcoholism, a disease shared by many of the nihilist authors of
the 1860's. He established his reputation with the savagely
gloomy *Seminary Sketches* (*Očerki bursy,* 1862-1863), in
which he pictured the degradation of young souls in seminary
schools, the merciless stifling of all that was good in them.
Two novelettes of his, *Bourgeois Happiness* (*Meščanskoe
sčast'e*) and *Molotov* (1861), describe the struggle of the hero
against the unreasonable restrictions laid upon him by society.

V. A. Slepcov (1836-1878) wrote a novel likewise in the critical tradition entitled *Hard Times* (*Trudnoe vremja,* 1865),
which is of literary interest if only for its brilliantly written
dialogue. The atmosphere is bleak, as usual; the hero, Rjazanov, is shown as a man of the highest ideals who is unable
to accomplish anything very solid. It is interesting that in this
work Slepcov slipped past the censor a number of enigmatic
and fragmentary references to governmental abuses which it
requires some analysis to discover.

A third writer who devoted most of his attention to unpleasant aspects of Russian life was Nikolaj Uspenskij (1837-
1889), whose peasant stories written at the end of the 1850's
were hailed by the radical critics as the harbinger of the new,
cruelly negative attitude toward the Russian countryside
which the radicals felt was required. Later in life Uspenskij
sank into pauperism and alcoholism, writing for extremely
conservative publications.

A quotation from the work of A. I. Levitov (1835-1877) may
demonstrate the debunking role played by the nihilist authors
at this time. In one of his sketches Levitov attacks the way
in which stories are usually written about student life in the
capital. As described by the non-radical school, the hero is
usually named Bogoblagodatov (a name which hints at the
ecclesiastical origin of many of the radical students) or
Somov. He is shown living in a dark hole, without bread or
tea, bundled up cozily reading Heine or the German materialist Büchner while the rain or snow beats against the win-
dowpanes. Then a friend bursts in with ten rubles he has acquired from somewhere, they sing "Gaudeamus igitur" and
entertain a dark-eyed Maša. In fact, says Levitov, student life
was nothing like that:

> In two years of such a life I heard nothing the least

like a feminine voice except for the voices of my numerous landladies. . . .

> You forget, not only how to study various sciences
> and to sing Gaudeamus, but even how to talk, when
> one's young soul is constantly and heavily bur-
> dened for two whole years by various bitter
> thoughts, and one's body—by hunger and cold,
> don't forget—a twenty-year-old body, one which
> would wish to see the sun's rays brighter than they
> are on the infrequent occasions when they pene-
> trate into the *furnished rooms* with their windows
> facing on filthy and stinking courtyards.

This was plain, unvarnished reality as it actually existed, oppressive and unbearable, which the "negaters" considered it
their duty to bring to public notice.

Allied to the negative attitude prevailing in the 1860's were
two other more superficial but still characteristic aspects of
the radical milieu: the juvenile approach of the radicals and
the intellectual intolerance prevailing among the "progressive" intelligentsia. It is striking that two of the outstanding
radical leaders of the 1860's, Dobroljubov and Pisarev, ended
their careers in their middle or late 20's after having exerted
great intellectual influence for several years. Many of the
other prominent radicals, such as Černyševskij, though
chronologically older, aimed their writings predominantly at
young people. V. V. Rozanov, a noted thinker of a later time,
commented on the fact that the radical critics of the 1860's
wrote for *youth* and it never occurred to them that adult standards might be applied to their production by men like Katkov and Dostoevskij. The radicals, Rozanov said, were "unconscious pedagogues". "An adult needs to know the *truth,*
while an adolescent needs to *deify* the instructor, without
which faith in him is lost and the teaching itself dissipated."
Rozanov also remarked that there was never a Herzen cult
although there was one of a sort for Pisarev:

> He [Herzen] was not only too complex, too devel-
> oped intellectually, but also insufficiently pure in-
> side for this. He would not have struck out a well-
> written witticism, even though he felt its inaccura-
> cy after having written it. Pisarev would never have
> acted the same way.

The simplicistic and therefore juvenile approach of the radicals was described many years later in memoirs by a woman
who was herself a member of this generation, E. Vodovozova.
She spoke of the "unshakeable faith" which her contemporaries had had in the power of reason to banish all the injustice and corruption which had accumulated in Russia
through the ages. All that was necessary was that intelligent
people should undertake the task of reform. The nihilists, she
wrote,

> believed passionately in the all-powerful signifi-
> cance of the natural sciences, in the great power of
> education . . . and with many of them this faith ex-
> tended to childish naiveté.

It is probably supportable to say that the 1860's phase of the
Russian revolutionary movement was the most thoroughly
youth-oriented period in its history.

The juvenile attitude toward the world was manifested especially in the virulent tone of the press, particularly in the early
1860's. The left-wing journals were chiefly to blame for this
even though the entire press was infected by it. During the
apogee of nihilism's influence, vitriolic journalistic polemics

were the order of the day. "People don't *quarrel over opinions* anymore", complained one observer in 1861, " . . . but straight out, *ex abrupto,* call an author 'narrow-minded', a 'blockhead', and his article 'rubbish', 'trash', . . ." Nor did journalists hesitate to make use of any information they possessed concerning the personal failings of an opposing writer. The critic N. N. Straxov, who devoted many contemporary articles to nihilism, remarked that he had nothing against polemics over ideas but that disputes based on personalities were useless. Furthermore, he thought, one journal prevailed over another, not because of the ideas expressed in it, but as the result of the prestige engendered by its previously established reputation. Straxov analyzed the situation rather well when he remarked that the leading radical journal *Sovremennik* "often reminds me of some fabulous, fantastic world in which great wonders are accomplished . . . [A writer for the journal] whistles—and dozens of scholars are annihilated." Straxov later made a very penetrating statement on the intellectual foundations of the radical attitude which he applied to Pisarev but which I think may be generalized to cover all the radical publicists of the time. Straxov decided that the guiding thread in Pisarev's thought could be expressed in the words: "I don't understand it, so it's nonsense." Such an approach led to extreme intellectual intolerance, for the views of any given radical were of course based on facts he could understand and were ordinarily combined into a fairly simple system. Anything which the radical was incapable of comprehending or which did not fit into his system was automatically considered as of no worth and as an object for derision. A clear-cut example of this intellectual intolerance, the exclusion in no uncertain terms of anything which does not jibe with one's preconceived notions, is to be found in Černyševskij. Černyševskij formulated his monistic and "scientistic" world-outlook on the basis of science as it existed around 1860 or so, after which time he was apparently unwilling to accept further scientific discoveries except insofar as they supported his already established system. Thus Černyševskij worked himself into a fury upon reading a popular essay by the physicist Helmholtz on the subject of non-Euclidean geometries. In 1878 Černyševskij wrote from exile a long letter to his sons attacking Helmholtz, his essay, and the very idea of non-Euclidian geometry in extremely intemperate language. He called Helmholtz an "ignoramus" and "country bumpkin of the male sex" and the theories he was setting forth "nonsense", "piffle". Since Černyševskij wrote all this in a personal letter not designed for publication, the only possible explanation for the venting of such spleen on Helmholtz—even if we allow for the harsh conditions of Černyševskij's Siberian exile—was Černyševskij's native intellectual rigidity. His attitude toward Helmholtz was a logical extrapolation of the attitudes to which he had adhered in the early 1860's and which were then the prevailing ones.

The tensions which arose between the younger generation of revolutionaries and the older ones, in this case represented by Herzen, are discussed in a chapter from the latter's autobiographical *Past and Thoughts.* A group of nihilists who had left Russia and come to England, where they sat around quarreling over revolutionary tactics, discovered that Herzen was in possession of a certain amount of money for use in emergencies. They demanded that funds be given them for revolutionary work within Russia, and when Herzen refused to accede to this request—for various reasons he did not feel free to dispose of the money entirely as he might have liked anyway—the young émigrés became highly indignant with him. The episode confirmed Herzen's forebodings about the re-

sults of a "mésalliance" between the younger and older revolutionaries.

Intellectual intolerance led to splits within the nihilist generation itself as well as to quarrels between the younger radicals and their intellectual forebears like Herzen. The most widely publicized disagreement between two wings of the radical camp, dubbed by Dostoevskij the "schism among the nihilists" (*raskol v nigilistax*), was that between the *Russkoe slovo* group, whose spokesman was Pisarev, and the *Sovremennik* group, led principally by the critic M. A. Antonovič and by M. E. Saltykov-Ščedrin. Differences between these two factions first became evident in 1862 after the publication of *Fathers and Sons,* which Pisarev accepted, with a few reservations, but which Antonovič fiercely decried as a slander against the nihilists. In 1864-1865 the quarrel, after having lain quiescent for a time during the first part of Pisarev's imprisonment, flared up again and became even more violent. One of the principal questions at issue in the latter part of the debate was Pisarev's contention that Saltykov-Ščedrin was betraying the radical cause by refusing to approve of Černyševskij's novel *What Is To Be Done?* unreservedly. Pisarev, a gifted polemist, emerged the victor from the fray, but not before the sight of bloody internecine strife had given the conservative camp great enjoyment. The acrimonious disputes did nothing to strengthen the radical cause and probably diminished its authority in the eyes of the general public. The quarrel, however, was a natural consequence of the "for or against" stance adopted by almost all the radical thinkers of the time: solidarity down to small details was felt to be required on all issues.

The central tenet of the nihilist outlook in the 1860's was a positivist, monistic philosophical materialism, in most cases fading into "scientism" (a belief that all philosophical problems not already resolved through the researches of natural science would eventually be solved and that, necessarily, in a materialistic sense). Western theoreticians of positivism, materialism and scientism were known inside Russia. Auguste Comte, the founder of positivism although he moved far away from his original views in his later years when he attempted to set himself up as the pope of a positivist religious body, was valued by the rising radical generation of the 1860's. *Sovremennik,* for example, published a long article on "Auguste Comte and the Positivist Philosophy" in 1865. The Englishman Henry Buckle, who attempted to place the writing of history on a scientifically sociological basis, was likewise highly esteemed.

The rise of a "scientistic" philosophical outlook was encouraged by the rapid development of the natural sciences in Europe. Many Russian students, encouraged to leave Russia by the closing of Petersburg University for two years, from 1861 to 1863, studied at Heidelberg and other German universities where such outstanding scientists as the chemist Bunsen, the physicists Kirchhoff and Helmholtz, and the mathematician Cantor were employed. Russia herself was producing at this time a number of famous natural scientists, including the chemist D. I. Mendeleev (1843-1907), the biologist I. I. Mečnikov (1845-1916), the woman mathematician Sof'ja Korvin-Krukovskaja (1850-1891), and the great investigator of behaviorism, I. P. Pavlov, who, though he died in 1936, was born in 1849. The publication of Charles Darwin's *Origin of Species* (1859) created as great a sensation in Russia as in other countries. Many young students absorbed his theories with avidity, especially after the book's appearance in Russian translation in 1864. Since biology, of all the branches of natural science, attracted the greatest attention from the radicals of the 1860's, Darwin's work was a very important factor in the intellectual milieu of the time.

The names of Comte, Darwin and other leading intellectuals of the 19th century carried great weight in Russia, but a group of now-forgotten German materialists—principally Jacob Moleschott (1822-1892), Karl Vogt (1817-1895), and Ludwig Büchner (1834-1899)—also enjoyed authority among Russian youth. These men, gathered around the great German scientific centers, expended most of their effort on writing philosophical works applying the latest results of natural science to human affairs. Vogt was a genuine physiologist as well as a philosopher, but he was better known in Russia for the philosophical inferences he drew from his own and others' researches than for his researches themselves. The emphasis placed by these men on the importance of physiology led them to espouse and propagate doctrines of "physiological determinism", the idea that the characteristics or capabilities of an individual or of a race are so determined by physiology that nothing can be done to alter these characteristics or capabilities. Such doctrines as these lead Soviet philosophers to look upon Vogt, Moleschott and Büchner with suspicion—the Soviets would like to think that man can be transformed through the manipulation of his social environment—and to tag them "vulgar materialists" as distinguished from "dialectical materialists". (pp. 23-31)

The "vulgar materialists" found ardent advocates within Russia in Černyševskij, Dobroljubov and especially Pisarev. Černševskij's most important philosophical essay, "The Anthropological Principle in Philosophy" (1860), develops at great length ideas of philosophical materialism and the view that natural science will eventually resolve all the unsettled problems of knowledge. In Černyševskij's opinion, all that exists, be it organic or inorganic, forms one great unity. In his own words,

> . . . the difference between the inorganic kingdom of nature and the vegetable kingdom is like the difference between a tiny blade of grass and a huge tree; it is a difference in quantity, in intensity, in complexity, but not in the fundamental character of the phenomena.

Thus, for instance, the oxidation of a piece of wood (rotting) takes place slowly and simply, whereas in living plants oxidation occurs in several forms and in much more complex fashion; but the basic process is still oxidation. In like manner the lowest animals are connected with the highest, viz. man, by a great chain of existence which is essentially uniform, only more complex at the upper extremity. To illustrate this concept Černyševskij drew a famous parallel between the thought processes of a Newton in discovering the law of gravity and "the process that takes place in the nervous system of the fowl that finds an oat grain in a dung heap"; however, he added the warning that though the central core of these processes is the same, it should be understood that there is a vast difference in dimensions between them. He ridicules the idea that animals do not possess consciousness or that they cannot reason, in order to support his theories.

Dobroljubov not only propagandized the achievements of the natural sciences but on one occasion skated dangerously close to accepting physiological determinism, rescuing himself by a parenthesis. It is significant, he wrote, that women's brains are generally smaller than men's.

> This is in complete conformity with their mental development: it is well known that (probably as a result of the conditions of our civilization) women's reasoning faculties are less developed than those of men.

The parenthetical remark comes closer to contradicting than to modifying the main thought.

Pisarev acted as the most enthusiastic propagandist of natural scientific ideas in Russia through his articles printed in *Russkoe slovo*. In 1861-1862 he published a series of articles which were little more than a rehash of works by the German scientistic philosophers: "Moleschott's Physiological Sketches" went over Moleschott's *Physiologisches Skizzenbuch;* "The Process of Life" discussed Vogt's *Physiologische Briefe;* and the article "Physiological Pictures" reviewed Büchner's *Physiologische Bilder.* Pisarev's articles added nothing to the sum of human knowledge but simply transmitted to the Russian public works popularizing the results of scientific investigations which had already appeared in western Europe. Pisarev not only expended a great deal of energy himself on the popularization of science, but he later even demanded that writers of fiction should do the same thing. (pp. 32-4)

The scientism, materialism and utilitarianism of the average nihilist were invariably accompanied by atheism, a component part of radical doctrines. Since the Russian Empire was officially founded on Russian Orthodoxy and philosophical articles at that time had to pass through a special ecclesiastical censorship, it was impossible to advocate atheism in so many words, but the doctrine was overwhelmingly implied in much that was then written. . . . [The] whole orientation of Büchner's *Kraft und Stoff* was: since science discovers no evidence for any "vital force" or any design in the universe, such things do not exist. Ludwig Feuerbach's attempt in *The Essence of Christianity* to prove that religions were simply the result of the projection of human needs was known and greeted with approbation in Russian radical circles. Černyševskij's "Anthropological Principle in Philosophy" is imbued with an atheism which emerges clearly in spite of the fact that the author was forced to use veiled language in order to get his article through the censorship. He employs the term "fantastic hypotheses" to refer to idealism and to religion and makes the following unmistakable though indirect attack on religion:

> It is said that the discoveries made by Copernicus in astronomy changed man's conception of things that are apparently very remote from astronomy. Exactly the same change, in exactly the same direction, but on a far more extensive scale, is now being brought about by discoveries in chemistry and physiology. They are changing man's conception of things that are apparently very remote from chemistry.

In the novel *Step by Step*, a work depicting the "new men" by Innokentij Fedorov-Omulevskij published in 1870, one deeply religious character, a friend of the hero's, is shown as a pitiable person. The hero, Svetlov, gives him Feuerbach to read in hopes of bringing him to the light. It is well known that Dobroljubov as a very young man was extremely religious and agonized greatly over his sins. In his memoirs the radical publicist A. M. Skabičevskij describes his own loss of religious faith. Although in his early university career he was an ardent Christian, he rose up from a close reading of the Bible convinced that the Old Testament presented a history of the Jews which was no different from the early stages of other religions. The doubts springing from this re-evaluation of the Bible later led Skabičevskij to reject the religious approach altogether. Sometimes the real-life nihilists flaunted their atheism openly and thereby caused scandals. An early example of this is to be found in the biography of the radical author Vasilij Slepcov. Once in 1853, while he was attending mass at the church attached to his school, he went up front during the singing of the Creed: "I believe in God the Father Almighty . . ." and announced: "But I don't believe in Him." For this insolence he was expelled from school.

The denial on the part of the radicals that anything at all could be attributed to a Divine Being led to a search for a new ethical basis for life, one not founded on revelation or on authority. If the promptings of a moral "conscience" were a figment of the imagination, a new ethic based on the rational intellect had to be constructed. The most common way in which this was done was to decide on some end for society as desirable, assume the desirable end as axiomatic, and then announce that all measures for the furthering of this end were moral and all actions hindering it, immoral. The Populist critic N. K. Mixajlovskij, deriving his central idea from Nožin, employed this concept of the new ethic in his famous definition of "progress":

> Progress is the gradual approximation to the unity of indivisibles, to the fullest and most all-embracing division of labor between organs possible and the least possible division of labor among people. Anything which delays this movement is immoral, unjust, harmful, irrational. Only that which diminishes the heterogeneity of society, at the same time strengthening the heterogeneity of its individual members, is moral, just, rational and useful.

Mixajlovskij's desirable aim for society is close to that envisaged by Marx when he looked for the all-around man to emerge in the future communist society, the man whose interests would be broad and talents varied. These talents would be exercised in freedom when the division of labor then existing in society was eliminated.

The extremist Russian radical thinker Petr Tkačev posited as his aim an absolute equalitarian ideal. The attainment of thorough-going equality between men would abolish many problems, in his view. For example, the problem of remuneration for labor will be solved

> . . . when everyone is unconditionally equal, when there is no difference between anyone either from the *intellectual, moral or physical* point of view. Then they will all have an exactly equal share in the returns of production, and any special valuation of their work will become entirely superfluous. [Italics mine.]

If this end were accepted, necessarily without proof, as desirable, then anything which furthered it was "progressive", or, we might say, "moral". Such a view of ethics was also apparent in the theories of the conspiratorial revolutionaries when it was preached that anything which brought the desired end, the revolution, closer was moral, no matter how repulsive it might seem by conventional standards.

One of the most interesting attempts at the construction of a new ethic made by a first-line "nihilist" is to be found in Pisarev's article "The Thinking Proletariat" (1865). Pisarev solves the ethical problem very neatly by equating "intellect" and "honesty". Guilt is abolished because sin is negated; the more intelligent a man is the more honorable he is. The new men, wrote Pisarev,

> do not sin and do not repent; they always cogitate and therefore merely make errors in calculation, but then they correct these errors and avoid them in their subsequent computations. With the new men the good and the truth, honesty and knowledge, character and intelligence turn out to be equivalent concepts; the more intelligent the new man the more honest he is because fewer mistakes creep into his calculations. With the new man there are no reasons for a rift between intelligence and emotion because the intelligence, oriented toward liked and useful labor, always advises only that which is consonant with personal advantage, which coincides with the genuine interests of humanity and, consequently, with the demands of the strictest justice and the most delicate moral feeling.

Pisarev was trying to establish the same sort of monolithic monism in man's spiritual world that Černyševskij preached with respect to the physical world. The unity of reason, wish and deed is complete when all is guided by the intellect alone.

The nihilists' primary interest, at least around 1860, was in the negation of the old order in preparation for some sort of new social structure, but the problem of the form of the future society was not entirely neglected. European utopian socialism possessed a powerful attraction for Russian minds both in the 1840's and the 1860's, although the utopian socialist schemes, concentrating as they did on the urban proletariat, were not immediately applicable to the Russian situation of that day, when the number of industrial workers was relatively small. The French socialist school was represented by Saint-Simon, Proudhon and Louis Blanc. In 1863-1864 Pisarev was very much under Saint-Simonian influence, although he never became his disciple. He accepted Saint-Simon's emphasis on industrialism but rejected his concept of state capitalism. Proudhon was widely appreciated in Russia as a socialist theoretician: in 1865 *Sovremennik* printed an article on "Proudhon and His System of Economic Contradictions". The German school was represented by Lassalle, with his proposals for widespread voluntary workers' organizations. Robert Owen, who combined practical good sense with socialist theories in his experiments at New Lanark showing how enlightened self-interest on the entrepreneurs' part could lead to better conditions for the workers, enjoyed great prestige. Dobroljubov devoted an article to him in 1859 and Gončarov drew some of the inspiration for his businesslike positive heroes Stolz (*Oblomov*) and Tušin (*The Precipice*) from Owen's example.

Even though there were not sufficient workers in Russia to motivate the intelligentsia to formulate definite schemes based on them, the radicals could still point the way to the social organization of the future, when the proletariat should have developed, through the formation of communes. Here the influence of Fourier may be discerned at work. Russian Fourierism attained its peak during the heyday of the Petraševskij circle in the 1840's, but in the 1860's enthusiasm for the communal mode of living took on concrete forms. In his novel *What Is To Be Done?* Černyševskij presented a detailed description of communal living quarters and sewing co-operatives. His progressive heroine, Vera Lopuxova, conceives the idea of founding a sewing establishment, the seed from which the future commune will grow. She is wise enough to exercise great care in selecting those girls who will form the nucleus of the project. "It seems to me", Vera tells her husband,

> that the main thing, when you are choosing just a few people, is to act cautiously from the very beginning, so that these will actually be honorable, good people, not scatter-brained, not unstable, but steady and at the same time gentle, so that there won't be any idle quarrels from them and so that they will be able to select others.

Vera with difficulty succeeds in locating three such girls. For the first month she maintains silence about her schemes and manages to gain the confidence of her seamstresses as a just employer. Then, when the soil has been well prepared, she persuades them to accept her idea of sharing the enterprise's profits among the workers and thereafter making all decisions only with the consent of the entire shop. When some time has elapsed and the establishment has expanded markedly, the girls come to the conclusion that the profits should be divided equally among all the workers because the more skilled seamstresses receive their proportionately greater rewards in higher wages. Vera is included as a wage-worker on the same footing as the others. Some of the profits are set aside as a fund from which individuals may borrow without payment of interest.

The establishment of this reserve fund gradually gives rise to the thought that it would be much cheaper to purchase provisions together and finally to dwell together. Many of the girls have relatives who are permitted to live in the commune then established, after the fixing of rate scales for room and board. The girls are able to reduce expenses in various ways: they rent a large bloc of living space at a lesser price and economize on food and clothing. One graphic example of a saving is furnished by the case of the communal umbrellas. It is discovered that out of 25 girls living in the commune, no more than five ever go out on a given rainy night. Therefore, instead of buying 25 cheap umbrellas at two rubles each, five expensive umbrellas at five rubles each are purchased; in this way every girl who uses an umbrella has a good one instead of a poor one at half the total cost for the commune. The rooms in which the commune members live are all excellently and individually furnished, with mirrors, mahogany or walnut furniture, and so forth.

One important point about this commune is that Vera, the instigator, is extremely careful to keep herself in the background and not claim any personal authority. When one of the girls is married Vera refuses, if asked, to be her wedding sponsor but instead accompanies her simply as a friend. "And in general", comments Černyševskij,

> she avoided in all possible ways any appearance of influence, tried to bring others forward and was so successful at this that many of the ladies who came to place orders at the shop could not tell her apart from the other two cutters.

In such fashion, like the unfolding of a blossom, the establishment of a model commune followed from the kernel idea of eliminating the entrepreneur's profits. At least it did if the initiator of the commune were as self-effacing as Vera Lopuxova and if the sociology of labor could be accurately analyzed along the following lines: the seamstresses

> work for themselves, they themselves are the bosses; therefore they receive that portion which the owner of the shop would have kept as profit. But

this isn't all: when working for their own benefit and at their own expense they are much more economical both of raw materials and of time: the work goes faster and involves fewer expenses.

In real life things did not develop so neatly as envisaged by Černyševskij. *What Is To Be Done?* served as the direct stimulus for the establishment of several communes in Petersburg and other cities during the 1860's. Most of the communes started around this time were set up with the limited, practical aim of reducing living expenses for their members. In 1863 one group of 13 artists did begin an "atelier" for work purposes which was not very successful. The best-known and most publicized of the communes formed around 1863 was the Znamenskaja commune, on the street of that name, founded by V. A. Slepcov. This commune, which lasted from the end of 1863 to the first part of 1864, has been described in sufficient detail to allow us to pass an informed judgement on the reasons for its failure. Černyševskij had looked upon the commune described in *What Is To Be Done?* as a stepping-stone to a world-wide upheaval introducing the future utopia, when re-educated mankind would perceive the advantages of communal living and embrace this form of existence enthusiastically. Slepcov, sharing these ideas with Fourier and Černyševskij, also wanted something of more widespread significance to emerge from his experiment, and in this his commune differed from others founded at that time simply to reduce living expenses. In spite of the fact that Slepcov himself possessed higher expectations for the future of his effort, he proceeded to admit to the commune persons who did not share his broader enthusiasm, who were in fact looking only for a cheaper place to live independently. Foremost among the weak reeds was Ekaterina Žukovskaja, but included in her faction were the more aristocratic (by conviction if not by descent) nihilists: Maša Kopteva, who had little sympathy for the common people; a lawyer named Jazykov, who joined only because he was a relative of Slepcov's; and possibly A. F. Golovačev, who believed in the cause but was entirely too weak-willed to do battle for it. This group was opposed by two genuine *nigilistki* (nihilist girls), Aleksandra Markelova and Princess (a fake title) Ekaterina Makulova. With two such antagonistic parties in the commune, Čukovskij asserts, its failure was guaranteed from the beginning. Nevertheless, there were other reasons for the commune's lack of success. One was that Slepcov apparently tried to arrogate excessive authority to himself as the leader of the commune, thus offending the more independent members. Slepcov chose an unnecessarily luxurious apartment for the group and incurred disproportionate expenses through the holding of frequent "open houses" designed to acquaint the public with the commune. Slepcov's known weakness for women, who outnumbered the men in the commune, gave rise to rumors that debauchery reigned there. Although this is probably not true, the actual situation lent some credence to the rumors. Finally, the police kept the house on Znamenskaja Street under close surveillance. As a consequence of all these disrupting elements the commune passed out of existence in the spring of 1864. Čukovskij makes a very apt comment on the gap between theory and practice in the case of the Znamenskaja commune:

> But this task [of constructing widespread phalansteries through the example of his commune] was carried out awkwardly. Slepcov's practice turned out to be out of step with his magnificent theory: he built this commune on such a shaky foundation

that it could not help falling apart in a very short time.

Such was the sad history of one of the most serious attempts in Russia to put utopian social theories into practice.

A "cause" which occupied an important place in the radical milieu of the 1860's was that of feminine emancipation. Here George Sand, whose name recurs constantly in the Russian writings of the period, was the great foreign exemplar. Through her novels and in her personal life she preached the doctrine that women should be sexually emancipated and socially independent. John Stuart Mill was also acclaimed as a supporter of feminine emancipation for such writings as his article "Enfranchisement of Women", published in 1851. In 1864 *Sovremennik* popularized his ideas in a piece entitled "John Stuart Mill on the Emancipation of Women". Most of the Russian radicals were indignant, however, at any pseudo-progressive girl who adopted such notions only as a justification for sexual license and did not take the additional step of subjecting her newly-won freedom to the service of the revolutionary cause.

The problem of feminine emancipation had been taken up at least as early as the 1840's in fiction with the appearance of Herzen's *Who Is To Blame?* (*Kto vinovat?*) and A. V. Družinin's *Polin'ka Saks.* In the 1860's it was well nigh impossible to find either a nihilist or an antinihilist novel which did not treat the subject in some degree. Černyševskij's *What Is To Be Done?,* Marko Vovčok's *A Live Soul* (*Živaja duša,* 1868), Fedor Rešetnikov's *One's Own Bread* (*Svoj xleb,* 1870) were all dedicated largely to pointing the way to freedom for enslaved Russian women. Černyševskij and others suggested that the easiest path for a girl trapped under despotic family discipline was a "front" marriage which would enable her to leave the parental roof. In like manner, if a woman were married to a husband so old-fashioned as to believe in the traditional view of woman, she should feel no compunction about abandoning him. A wife who did no useful work but merely saw to household affairs for her husband was no better than a kept woman; she should strive to achieve economic independence for herself.

Feminist propaganda in fiction and in magazine articles did not fail to lead to real-life dramas, for it was at this time that numbers of "emancipated women" left home to seek a new life. In her memoirs Avdot'ja Panaeva, perhaps exaggerating a bit, recounts the tale of one tragic family schism. The eldest daughter in a family wanted to continue her studies but her mother, fearing that she would become a nihilist, opposed this. After a stormy domestic scene, one day the mother finally drove the daughter from the house.

> The young girl, embittered by such an act, did not seek a reconciliation; she got along somehow or other for about a half a year, ran around in the cold after lessons that paid almost nothing in poor footgear and a thin coat, and came down with tuberculosis. When the mother was informed that her daughter was hopelessly ill, she rushed to her, brought her to the house, called in expensive doctors, but it was already too late, the daughter died and the mother soon went out of her mind with grief.

"Fictitious marriages" were also employed in actual fact by the nihilist girls. One of the first such operations was engineered by the sister of the radical critic Varfolomej Zajcev, whose father was demanding that she should return to the pa-

rental roof. In order to avoid this, Zajceva located a certain "young, wealthy, but not especially bright prince, inspired with good intentions of being useful to humanity", who was willing to marry her, though he had not known her before, and then let her go with a foreign passport immediately after the ceremony. In this way Zajceva became legally a free agent without suffering from the whims of a tyrannical husband.

Many of the "new women" who did leave home in one way or another gravitated to Petersburg, the source of radical doctrines, and tried to support themselves through translations or whatever other "honest" work they could find. It would seem that the capital at this time was greatly oversupplied with translators. In any event the emancipated young woman, the *nigilistka,* usually dressed and acted in bohemian fashion, whether living in Petersburg or in the provinces, and thus could be promptly recognized. The reactionary newspaper *Vest'* printed a description that, for all its disapproving tone, summarizes very succinctly the essential points concerning the emancipated woman. Most *nigilistki, Vest'* wrote, are

> usually very plain, exceedingly ungracious, so that they have no need to cultivate curt, awkward manners; they dress with no taste and in impossibly filthy fashion, rarely wash their hands, never clean their nails, often wear glasses, always cut their hair, and sometimes even shave it off. . . . They read Feuerbach and Büchner almost exclusively, despise art, use "ty" [the familiar form of address] with several young men, light their cigarettes, not from a candle, but from men who smoke, are uninhibited in their choice of expressions, live either alone or in phalansteries, and talk most of all about the exploitation of labor, the silliness of marriage and the family and about anatomy.

Close-cropped hair and glasses, usually dark glasses, were the most prominent trademarks of the nihilist girls. By way of contrast, incidentally, the nihilist men were usually easily identifiable because they wore their hair long. The nihilist girls' enthusiasm for anatomy—some wanted to and did go abroad to study for a medical degree—was especially shocking to the older generation, since young ladies were not supposed to be informed of the coarse physical facts of existence. All the characteristics listed in the quoted paragraph were elements of a demonstrative reaction on the part of the nihilists to the accepted moral and social norms of Russia.

E. P. Majkova (1836-1920), for several years a close friend of Gončarov's, was one member of the younger generation in the 1860's who put radical feminist doctrines into practice. Married to Vladimir Nikolaevič Majkov, she was the mother of three children by him. As early as 1862 she began to take an interest in radical literature and to travel abroad, while her husband and her family remained as conservative as ever. In 1864 the Majkovs took in as a boarder a young man named Ljubimov, about 9 years Majkova's junior, who at that time was unsuccessful in gaining admission to Petersburg University. An affair between Ljubimov and Majkova was begun. Majkova abandoned her husband and children in 1866, prepared for publication a primer entitled *The Alphabet and First Reading Lessons,* and helped Ljubimov gain admission to the university in September of 1867. In 1868 she bore her lover a child which they were unable to keep. In 1869 Ljubimov gave up his studies and the couple went off to the Caucasus, where he disappeared and she spent the next thirty years of her life operating a free public library in Soči. Majkova's actions illustrate many cherished radical notions of the 1860's: free love, the insignificance of family ties if they acted as a drag on one's convictions, a belief in education and the desire to do something "useful", for example the writing of a primer and the establishment of a public library for the enlightenment of the masses.

Another article in the nihilist creed which deserves more detailed attention is the intense faith in the beneficence of education and in its power to effect monumental changes in Russian life. If everyone were sufficiently educated society would come to understand what actions were in its own interest and would be prepared to take the necessary measures to improve its situation. Černyševskij was one of the chief propagandists of this view. Education, according to him, would bring people to the realization that their own personal interest coincided with the general interest, something which up to then had not been perceived. Once this insight had been attained, there would be no more "evil" people, people who were evil primarily because they were ignorant and did not comprehend that in exploiting others they were harming themselves as well as society at large. With the triumph of education the union of intellect and virtue and the coalescing of personal interest with the common good would be achieved. Pisarev, ringing a variation on this theme, was certain that the exploiting classes, if shown the light, would realize the iniquity of their self-seeking activities and would begin to reform Russia's social and economic system. They could accomplish this more rapidly than anyone else because their hands were already on the levers of power. The education of the masses was likewise of tremendous importance, for an educated proletariat could conceive and carry out many projects which would not so much as have occurred to it in a more ignorant state. All that was required for the transformation of society, cried Pisarev, was education in huge quantities:

> There exists only one evil among mankind—ignorance; for this evil there is only one remedy—science; however, this remedy must be taken, not in homeopathic doses, but by the bucketful, by the cask. This remedy taken timidly increases the sufferings of the sick organism. The remedy taken boldly leads to a radical recovery. But human cowardice is so great that a saving remedy is considered poisonous.

The nihilists made a serious attempt to raise the intellectual level of the masses through the establishment of the famous "Sunday schools" (*voskresnye školy*). The movement, which began in Kiev in 1859 and spread rapidly to other cities of the Empire, was sparked by Professor P. V. Pavlov (1823-1895), a man who obviously looked for great results from it since his slogan was reported to have been "La révolution par l'école". The schools, which met on Sundays so that workers unable to attend on any other day might come, were run by university students who were happy to insert anti-regime propaganda into their teaching wherever possible. At first there were elements in the government which looked with favor upon the Sunday schools, and permission for the founding of new ones was granted liberally. Even when warnings were sounded to the effect that propaganda unfavorable to the state was being carried on in them, they still found defenders in official circles. A. V. Nikitenko, at that time a man of influence in the government, was disinclined to believe the adverse reports on the schools, hoped that they would prove viable and considered that in the extreme case they should be taken over and run by the government itself. An attempt was made

to institute a measure of control over the schools by installing priests in them to supervise the ideological content of the instruction, but this proved to be an insufficient measure. In the summer of 1862 two Sunday schools in the capital were charged with spreading subversive propaganda and the whole system was shut down. Later manifestations of the Sunday-school philosophy were comparatively feeble, although some schools were established in after years. In spite of the enthusiasm evoked by the movement for Sunday schools, both among the young intellectuals who taught in them and the common people who studied in them, they failed in their purpose of bringing about any great improvement in Russian society. Although this can be attributed to governmental interference in some measure, the schools certainly would not have fulfilled the high hopes placed in them by the radicals even had they been left strictly alone.

Radical opinions differed markedly from the ideas of the general non-radical public in the area of esthetics. The radical critics and their followers had very definite theories about the place of the arts, particularly literature, in the society they were trying to create. The classical statement of nihilist esthetic doctrines was the work written by Černyševskij as a thesis for his master's degree entitled "The Esthetic Relations of Art to Reality" (published in 1855). Most of the comments on literature made by Dobroljubov and Pisarev afterwards were mere glosses, albeit sometimes interesting ones, on Černyševskij's essay. Černyševskij takes as his guiding principle the pre-eminence of real life over art and constructs his whole esthetic system on this foundation, attacking Hegelian esthetics as he goes through "bathetic" comparisons which bring apparently exalted intellectual concepts thudding down to earth. Černyševskij demonstrates to his own satisfaction that all objections which can be made against beauty in reality, for example that beauty in reality is transient, are groundless and that furthermore the same objections can be turned against beauty in art. The power of art is the power of generalization and also its ability to produce surrogates for reality. If a man cannot visit the sea he may satisfy himself with a painted seascape, although this is only because he cannot have the real thing. "The essential purpose of art is to reproduce everything in life that is of interest to man." Finally, art should not be ashamed to admit that it stands lower than reality, just as science is not reluctant to confess to this.

The radical critics waged a constant battle against that critical camp in Russian letters (Družinin, Annenkov, Botkin and others) which contended that art should have no ulterior purpose and that it should not be intentionally didactic. Černyševskij, Dobroljubov and their followers also faced the problem that most of the outstanding writers of the time were out of sympathy with radical aims and refused to produce the type of literature demanded. The radical attack was therefore two-pronged, designed to descredit those writers, both past and present, who did not write socially useful works, and to stimulate the appearance of that sort of literature which was considered desirable. Thus Černyševskij, who in the latter part of the 1850's, together with Dobroljubov, mounted a consistent campaign to undermine Turgenev's authority, made an ill-natured onslaught against the latter's story "Asja":

> The devil with these love questions—of what interest are they for the contemporary reader, who is absorbed in problems bound up with administrative and judiciary improvements, the financial reforms, the liberation of the peasants?

Dobroljubov had a strong tendency to evaluate a writer on the basis of the social utility of his work's content and not on esthetic grounds, which led him to praise the writings of second-rate radical authors and ignore or negate the works of top-flight literary men which did not fit his classifications or comply with his demands. Pisarev in the article "Puškin and Belinskij" (1865) set out to destroy Puškin as a writer worthy of any respect since the latter had been acclaimed by the supporters of the "pure art" school as their patron. Pisarev, operating with his wonderful polemical gifts, attempted to prove that Puškin was nothing more than an able versifier and that his ideas, when lifted out and examined, proved to be amazingly trivial, unimportant and even silly. Even today an admirer of Puškin's work can never feel quite the same about him after having read Pisarev's attack, so vigorously is it pressed. The unflagging enmity of the nihilist critics toward art without a social purpose, the social purpose prompted by the radicals themselves, led a number of the poets of that day who could not comply with such demands to retire from literature altogether for a time or else to limit their output sharply.

The radical critics had very definite opinions as to what literature should do as well as what it should not do. The idea in a work of art was of primary importance, and if this idea were harmful or incorrect the work of art was worthless no matter how esthetically pleasing it might be. Dobroljubov worked for the transformation of literature into a propaganda arm of a political cause, an arm which would be obliged to work for certain given political aims. Another task of literature, according to him, was to publicize the latest findings of science and make them understandable to the masses. Literature in the tradition of "critical realism" should flay social shortcomings and expose abuses of power. On the positive side, literature should exert its imagination in painting the world to come when radical ideals would have been implemented in all their fulness. These two strains are united in a passage from Pisarev's "Puškin and Belinskij" which sounds strangely contemporary:

> If he [Puškin] sang about the rights and duties of man, of the striving toward the bright future (*svetloe buduščee*), of the shortcomings of contemporary reality, of the struggle of the human intellect against ancient delusions, of conscious love for the Fatherland and for humanity, of the meaning of various critical historical events—then, of course, his singing would disturb and torture people's hearts, and at the same time the most stupid, the most indifferent, haughty and foolish public could not accuse this singing of not giving any instruction, not leading to any aim and not being of any use. If the poet's singing caused his hearers to meditate seriously, if it awakened or strengthened within them the love of truth, hatred of deceit and exploitation, contempt for duplicity and obtuseness, then all that would be left for the public to do would be to listen to him and to thank him. . . .

Through their critical writings Dobroljubov, Černyševskij and Pisarev were successful in encouraging the emergence of such authors as Nikolaj Uspenskij and A. I. Levitov, who wrote "sketches", in which artistic form played almost no role, depicting the dark sides of Russian life. The positive type of radical novel, however, was so slow in making its appearance that Černyševskij himself took up the task of writing the first one even though his talents as a novelist were of the most meagre. This work, *What Is To Be Done?*, opened

a new era in radical letters; its publication was a literary event of great magnitude and the novel was a general subject of conversation on all levels of Russian society. One contemporary who had been abroad for two years, out of contact with "progressive" Russian literature and, in particular, lacking knowledge of *What Is To Be Done?*, told of the embarrassment which his ignorance caused him:

> In the first place I was unable in conversation, whether fitting or not, to cite passages from these above-mentioned works [primarily *What Is To Be Done?*], which deprived my talk of both force and persuasiveness in the eyes of a certain type of listener. In the second place, I was unable to nod approvingly and smile when my interlocutor would speak in the tone and spirit of the works named. . . .

Černyševskij's main interest in his novel was the sketching of the "new man" who would be the inheritor of the future socialist earth. Such a man is the proto-positive hero Raxmetov, an absolutely upright and honorable person of undeviating devotion to the "cause", a cause which is understood to be the revolutionary transformation of Russian society. He disciplines himself through gymnastics, eats only food which the common people would eat, educates himself by reading the few classics which contain the kernels of truth merely elaborated upon by those who write the books filling libraries, vows sexual abstinence and denies himself all pleasures except for cigars, the one weakness he is unable or considers it unnecessary to overcome. His most peculiar exploit is a night spent on a bed of nails for the sake of self-discipline, to prove to himself that his body was completely subjected to his will. "Great is the mass of honest, good people", writes Černyševskij,

> but such people [the "new men"] are few; but in this mass they are the theine in the tea, the bouquet in a noble wine; from them come its power and aroma; they are the flower of the best people, they are the movers of movers, they are the salt of the salt of the earth.

A more fantastic peroration than this one concocted by a supposedly "sober realist" can hardly be imagined.

What Is To Be Done? inspired innumerable readers among the radical generation of the 1860's and among later radical generations; it also gave rise to a certain number of imitations in the literature of the 1860's. One of the most interesting works of this "radical utopian" kind was Innokentij Fedorov-Omulevskij's *Step by Step* (1870), which was very popular in its day and is not devoid of a certain interest even now. The central hero of the novel, Svetlov (his name is derived from *svetlyj*, "luminous"), although no fanatic ascetic like Raxmetov, comports himself ideally at all times and displays an admirable independence of mind. At one point he remarks in conversation with a kindly old general that he does not believe in letters of recommendation because nobody can guarantee another person's character. He himself might write recommendations for a limited number of his friends, but it is against his principles to place an acquaintance in a potentially embarrassing position by requesting a recommendation from him. When Svetlov returns from the university in Petersburg his parents expect him to be haughty because of his education, but instead he behaves very modestly. After having been arrested for what was in fact a peace-making role during a rebellion of local workers against a hated factory manager,

Svetlov announces to his worried mother, when she visits him in prison:

> . . . these dirty [prison] walls can't disgrace any-one, mother. . . . A man disgraces himself when he ceases to be a man! But I shall always remain a man: wherever I may be I shall always have my heart, my convictions, my attachments; and I shall always have my human dignity as well. . . .

At the end of the novel Svetlov goes abroad and there, the reader understands by implication, engages in tasks of a revolutionary nature.

Svetlov and Raxmetov, then, are two outstanding examples of the image of the radical, or "nihilist", as the radicals themselves demanded he should be portrayed. These characters served as examples, inspirations and spurs to the younger generation to develop in the way considered suitable by the radical critics and therefore the works in which they appeared were proclaimed by the radicals to be good art in the best sense of the word.

The radical critics and thinkers of the 1860's did not confine themselves merely to veiled propaganda in support of the revolutionary cause. They could on occasion write clearly revolutionary appeals and even participate in activities which could only be construed by the government as subversive.

In one of Pisarev's unpublished articles, for example, there is to be found the following unambiguous statement of revolutionary hostility to the existing regime:

> The Romanov dynasty and the Petersburg bureaucracy must perish. . . . That which is dead and rotten should fall into the grave of itself; all that is left for us to do is give them [i.e., the Romanovs and the bureaucracy] one last push and cast mud on their stinking corpses.

Černyševskij was arrested by the authorities in 1862 for having allegedly participated in revolutionary activities and there is at the very least a good chance that the government's suspicions were correct. In discussing this episode Soviet scholars are torn between the desire to show that Černyševskij was cruelly and unjustifiably persecuted and the wish to prove that he was such a consistent radical that he took the final step to revolutionary deeds and thus was a full participant in the revolutionary movement. If we define "revolutionary" to mean, not only those who at that time engaged in conspiratorial activities against the government, but also those who would have fought actively for the overthrow of the regime had the barricades gone up—and not remained passive or defended the government—then it would seem certain that Pisarev and Černyševskij, along with many of their followers, were "revolutionaries". For them the forcible overthrow of Tsarist power was a desirable objective. (pp. 36-52)

Charles A. Moser, "The Nihilist World of the 1860's: Nihilism in Its Historical Connections" and "The Nihilist Milieu of the 1860's," in his Antinihilism in the Russian Novel of the 1860's, *Mouton & Co., 1964, pp. 13-22, 23-60.*

WOMEN AND NIHILISM

RICHARD STITES

[*Stites is the author of* The Women's Liberation Movement in Russia: Feminism, Nihilism, and Bolshevism, 1860-1930 *(1978). In the following excerpt from that work, he elaborates on the ideological ties linking Chernyshevsky's socially progressive novel* What Is To Be Done? *to the proto-feminist program that emerged from the Nihilist movement.*]

In the broadest sense, Chernyshevsky's novel, *What Is To Be Done?* (1863) was a Bible for all advanced Russian women with aspirations toward independence, whether they thought and acted as organized feminists, as revolutionaries, or as "nihilist" women. To the feminists it reinforced their ideas on education and economic independence and on the moral imperative of helping other women struggle for these things. To the radical women whose life interests transcended the narrower aspiration of women's emancipation in order to embrace the cause of liberating the "people," the influence of the book was more subtle. Though necessarily muted by the problem of censorship, the theme of the radical remaking of Russian society was vividly implicit as was its summons to women to free themselves from social incarceration in order to join the ranks of the "new people" who would one day effect the social revolution. But the most direct impact of the novel was upon what came to be seen as the nihilist outlook on women and sex—a doctrine of personal emancipation and sexual freedom that was not only psychologically alien to the moderate feminism of Stasova and Trubnikova but also distinguishable (if not always distinguished) from female political radicalism.

By all accounts, the work exerted a colossal influence on the radical intelligentsia. On women's consciousness and on men's awareness of "the problem," it had both a short and a long range effect. To contemporary men and women of the so-called nihilist persuasion, it offered attractive and apparently rational solutions to such immediate problems as parental despotism, incompatible marriages, conflicting loves, and the true road to a life of fulfillment and meaning. These solutions are clearly mapped out in the rapidly developing consciousness of the central character, Vera Pavlovna. But beyond this, it also advanced a broader program of relations between the sexes and a view of erotic love that would command the unspoken allegiance of generations of revolutionaries.

Chernyshevsky, son of a priest, and hero of the radical "hotheads" of the day, was best known for his essays on philosophy, politics, and economics, and, during the halcyon days of *The Contemporary,* was the leading radical spokesman in Russia. His open contempt for liberalism and "small deeds" precluded any sympathy for the feminist approach to women's subjection. His major views on women had been fashioned years before, chiefly under the suggestive influence of George Sand and Fourier, whose teachings he first encountered from friends in the Petrashevsky Circle. Shortly before his marriage to Olga Sokratovna Vasileva—a most suitable subject for his theories—Chernyshevsky drafted a personal "program" of future relations with women. The program called for submission to his wife, full freedom of action for her, and unflagging fidelity for himself. He voiced the hope that the marriage would be a partnership of two intellectuals, but he also argued that women "occupied an insignificant place in the family," and that now "the reed should be bent back the other way." In line with this, he was prepared to offer his wife the freedom that he would deny to himself—inconstancy and adultery. As it happened, Olga Sokratovna was perfectly willing to avail herself of Chernyshevsky's broad-minded generosity.

This was a calculated moral act and not merely an indulgent gesture. It was meant to be an act of "rational egoism" resting on the supposition that his cuckolded feeling created less pain than that caused by his wife's lack of freedom. But Chernyshevsky felt pain none the less, and this perhaps induced him to avoid writing about the subject until his arrest. While endorsing Mikhailov's conclusions, he disagreed with his undue emphasis on the woman question, and told Shelgunov that such an emphasis was well enough when there were no other problems. But faced with the prospect of unlimited leisure in the Peter-Paul Fortress, Chernyshevsky turned once again to those enduring personal issues and sought to find answers for them. What prompted him? Retrospection? The novels of George Sand? Mikhailov's recent articles and their warm reception? We do not know. Perhaps all of them, combined with his personal acquaintance with advanced "nihilist" women striving for that consciousness he was about to describe in the person of Vera Pavlovna.

The unfolding of Vera Pavlovna's consciousness as a full human being is the dominant theme of *What Is To Be Done?* Its direct artistic inspiration may have been Pomyalovsky's *Molotov* (1861), which Chernyshevsky had with him in the cell. That story's main female character, her conversations with Molotov, and the author's soliloquies to the reader, all have their counterparts in Chernyshevsky's novel. Vera, like Pomyalovsky's Nadya, is a sensitive and well-educated girl, trapped in an obscurantist household, and seeking "her own way." Her mother is a model of crude ambition and ignorance ("Young girls shouldn't know about such things; it's their mother's business"), and is endeavoring to marry Vera to a well-heeled libertine. Vera's consciousness begins with one of those dreams that play such a crucial role in her development. In an allegory of her deliverance, she is released from a dark and stifling cellar by a figure who calls herself "Love of Mankind," then hastens to the myriads of dream prisons to liberate her sisters from their bondage. But at her level of development—and given the Russian legal code—she cannot extricate herself without the aid of an outside force. A medical student, Dmitry Lopukhov, offers her what came to be called a "fictitious marriage," a legal convenience to enable her to leave the house of her parents but with no connubial obligations.

The device of the "fictitious marriage" was already in use among Russian youth by the time Chernyshevsky wrote the novel. One of his real life models for Vera Pavlovna was Mariya Obrucheva, sister of a well-known radical. At Chernyshevsky's suggestion, the medical student Peter Bokov agreed to tutor her; later he offered her a fictitious marriage (1851), so that she could break with her family and study medicine in St. Petersburg. Vera Pavlovna, like her prototype, fell in love with her obliging liberator, though this was by no means part of the agreement. But, in spite of an ideal arrangement of marital equality, including separate rooms, Vera later fell in love with her husband's best friend, Kirsanov, an instructor at the medical academy. In real life, this was the noted physiologist, Ivan Sechenov, who won the heart of his student, and settled down with the Bokovs in a *ménage à trois* in the early 1860's. This, the Mikhailov-Shelgunova-Shelgunov triangle, and his own broodings provided ample material for Chernyshevsky's literary triangle.

Vera had advanced to the point where she could recognize that Lopukhov did not love her (a combination of friendship and sex was not enough for her), and that she was attracted to the more sociable Kirsanov. But she could not solve the problem; this was still left to the initiative of the male principles. After a brief struggle with the arcane complexities of "rational egoism," Lupukhov cut the knot neatly, if melodramatically, by feigning suicide and disappearing. His motivation was the same utilitarian theory that had undergirded Chernyshevsky's own marital "program." The latter had once hinted to Olga Sokratovna that if he were too much in the way, he might emulate the hero of George Sand's *Jacques* and do away with himself.

In the course of her struggle for freedom to love, Vera discovers that love, marriage, and even total erotic fulfillment are not enough to make her a free woman. Like many women in Russian life at that moment, she sensed that economic independence was even more fundamental than sexual freedom and equality. "Everything is based on money," her first husband tells her. "He who has money has power and rights"; and "as long as woman lives off a man, she is dependent on him." Julie Letellier, the lady of easy virtue, put it another way: "I am depraved not because they call me an immoral woman; not for what I have done or what I have lost or what I have suffered; not because my body has been desecrated. No, I am depraved because I have become accustomed to idleness and luxury without being able to live independent of others." Vera already knows this. "I want to be independent and live in my own way," she says. "I do not want to submit to anyone. I want to be free, to be obligated to no one, so that no one dare say to me: you must do this or that for me."

Vera's second dream shows her that work, the social equivalent of motion in nature, is the central force in life. Drawing partly on socialist theory and partly on the practice of Russian *artels*, Chernyshevsky constructs for her a fictional sewing cooperative, which begins as a limited profit-sharing enterprise and develops into a full-scale residential producers' and consumers' commune in the heart of St. Petersburg. Vera Pavlovna, recalling her dream-given injunction to liberate other women, uses the sewing *artel* to raise the consciousness of her female employees. She makes partners of them, shares the profits, draws them into the administration, and gradually educates them to self-reliance through carefully programmed readings of "progressive" literature. She is the fictional predecessor of the Zhenotdel organizers who, sixty years later, were using similar techniques in "consciousness raising" throughout the length and breadth of the Soviet Republic. It is here among the needles and the brochures of her sewing establishment that Vera Pavlovna reaches that level of awareness and activism that makes her one of the earliest agents of women's liberation in European fiction.

Yet even this activity, together with her household duties (performed with the aid of a servant!) and her lessons, is not sufficient to absorb her self-generating energies and sublimate her confessed surplus of passion. She needs "a personal occupation, something important, on which [her] whole existence would hang." But she realizes the obstacles to a higher role for women: "The rule of force has deprived her both of the means for development and the motivation for it." Her level of consciousness will not allow her to be content with a governess job, an overcrowded occupation in any case. She decides to study medicine, with the aid of her husband, just as the real Bokova studied with Sechenov before the academy excluded her. "It would be very important," says Vera Pavlovna, "if we finally had women doctors. They would be very useful for all women. Women can talk with other women much better than they can with men. How much suffering, pain, and sorrow could be avoided. It must be tried." Will power, social consciousness, action—the salient features of the New Woman—are all on display. In pursuing medicine, Vera Pavlovna was following, not setting, a trend; but her imitators in the next two decades would be legion.

Chernyshevsky's approach to women's liberation has a different style from that of the organized feminists. In education, his stress was on individual effort: books, tutoring by friends, and circles. No scenes in university halls, no struggling female students, no petitions. As for charity, the author's view is given subtle expression in the following passage about Polozova, a minor character: "Her father gave her a good deal of pocket money and she, as any good woman would do, gave to the poor. But she also read and thought, and she began to notice that what she did give had a much smaller effect than it ought to have had; that too many of her 'poor' were fakers and good-for-nothings, and that the really deserving . . . almost never received enough to have any long-range effect on their condition." The *artel* was meant to be the nucleus of a fundamental reordering of society that would give decent work to all, and thus obviate the need for such demeaning activity as philanthropy. But even to some contemporary readers, the contrast was not entirely convincing in the novel, for a good deal of patronizing took place even in the egalitarian atmosphere of the *artel.* This was especially apparent in the parable of the redeemed prostitute, Nastya Kryukova. Chernyshevsky's teaching, reduced to its essentials, is this: men must cease being the clients of prostitutes and thus eliminate the market; women must help the victims by giving them work. Any feminist from 1860 right up to the Revolution could have said (and did say) the same thing.

Commenting both on the bleakness of the Russian social landscape and on the significance of his heroine, Chernyshevsky says of Vera Pavlovna that she is "one of the first women whose life is well arranged. First examples possess historical interest; and 'a first swallow' is of special interest to us denizens of northern climes." She is to be the harbinger of a warm springtime in human relations that will succeed the harsh winters of class and sexual subjugation. Her well ordered life is rooted in her ability to make social activity a pendant to her erotic life, to counterpoise will against passion. In a scene, cunningly interrupted by intervals of sexual intimacy, Chernyshevsky has her utter the following words to her husband: "If a person thinks to himself 'I can't,' then he can't. It has been suggested to women that they are weak; so they feel weak, and then actually become weak." Vera's strength lies in her profound consciousness of the power of her will and her ability to act. Throughout the story, she endeavors to impart this same consciousness to other members of her sex. The novel thus becomes, among other things, a celebration of the latent power of woman, and a flattering summons to take her life into her own hands. Vera Pavlovna's positive outlook and her towering self-confidence constituted a legacy to the nihilists of the 1860's who would see in her the proper model of action, will, and sexual identification.

This was Chernyshevsky's parting gift to the women of his generation.

In view of the great debates on sex and marriage that occupied his revolutionary grandchildren some sixty years after he wrote *What Is To Be Done?*, Chernyshevsky's views on these matters, strewn through the novel, need to be brought into sharper focus. Some of these required little comment on his part; for example the ideas of freely contracted unions and of equality in marriage that included privacy and "a room of one's own." Others, like his unqualified rejection of possessiveness and jealousy, evoked a storm of verbal emotion. "O filth, filth! 'to possess.' Who dares possess a human being? A robe or a pair of slippers, yes. But this is nonsense! Almost all of us men possess some of you, our sisters. But this is nonsense too. How can we call you our sisters? You are our lackeys! Some of you, even many of you, dominate us. But that means nothing; don't lackeys dominate their masters?" As to jealousy: "A developed man shouldn't have it. It is a distorted emotion, a false emotion, a vile emotion; a phenomenon of that social order under which I let no one wear my linen or smoke my pipe; it is a vestige of that view of man which sees him as property, as a thing."

Thus divorce or its non-juridical equivalents is not only permissable but also necessary in Chernyshevsky's sexual world. When two halves of a union do not "fit," there should be neither blame nor guilt nor any effort to cripple the personality of one by remodeling it to fit the other. Indeed, Chernyshevsky unabashedly tells his reader that the "secret" of enduring and loving partnerships is the awareness of both members that the other is free "at any moment" to bid farewell, without regret or rancor, once the free bond of love has eroded. Only in the case of children, he says, should the parents make every effort to avoid separation if such an act would have harmful consequences for them. These remarks and the lives of his characters leave no doubt that Chernyshevsky looked upon divorce as an exception, a necessary escape hatch for those who had come together through error. Divorce, or its nihilist equivalent, was not to be construed as an everyday convenience to be invoked repeatedly in order to satisfy promiscuous inclinations.

What of sex itself? Does Chernyshevsky ignore it, as some commentaries and abridged translations would lead us to believe? Was the puritanical Rakhmetov, who eschewed wine and women, the *alter ego* of Chernyshevsky? Hardly so. For the author does not merely rail against "abnormal thirst" and loveless carnal possession; against them he poises an acutely sensitive appreciation of amorous eroticism. It is given first utterance when he describes how Kryukova, the ex-prostitute, achieves sensual arousal for the first time in the arms of the loving Kirsanov. And it reaches its apogee in Vera Pavlovna's triumphant depiction of sexual ecstacy as an act of love:

> The power of sensation is commensurate with the depth of the organism out of which it rises. If aroused only by an external cause, an external object, it is fleeting and it embraces only a limited portion of life. He who drinks wine only because someone offers him the glass will not have much appreciation of its taste and will derive little satisfaction from it. Pleasure is much more intense when it is rooted in the imagination, when the imagination seeks out the object and agent of its pleasure. Then the blood rises more noticeably and you can feel its warmth, a feeling which heightens the impression

of ecstasy. But even this is very weak in comparison with what happens when the root of the relationship is planted deep in the soil of a moral life. Then passion penetrates the entire nervous system with extraordinary force over a long period of time.

Chernyshevsky moors the idea of erotic love to other aspects of a healthy social life in essentially Fourierist terms. "Unless work precedes them," says Lopukhov, "diversion, relaxation, fun, and festivity have no reality." And elsewhere: "A person who manages his life correctly divides his time into three parts: work, pleasure, and rest or recreation." This notion is given full play in the great commune of Vera's fourth dream, with its futuristic visions of golden fields, fertile valleys, workers singing in the sun and returning home to their glass and crystal communal dwellings to receive bounteous meals prepared by the children and the old people. Hard work has prepared them for an augmented enjoyment of pleasure. And here Vera's guide, now "the beautiful tsaritsa" now the "Goddess of Sexual Equality" speaks with the voice of Eros: "I rule here. Here all is dedicated to me: Work—to prepare fresh feelings and energy for me; Play—to get in readiness for me; Rest—to enjoy after me. Here I am the goal of life. Here I am life itself."

Thus we have in Chernyshevsky not only the moral mechanics of sexual freedom, equality, and mobility but also the centrality of sex itself. Even Lenin, who admired him deeply, might have admitted that the author of *What Is To Be Done?* had spent more than a little time in ventilating questions which Lenin felt to be too much in the forefront. As a matter of fact, Chernyshevsky's basic views are not greatly different from those of Alexandra Kollontai whose writings were to bring down upon her the moral wrath of Leninists in the 1920's, and neither Chernyshevsky nor Kollontai were on the extreme sexual left of their respective revolutionary cultures. Chernyshevsky would not have dreamed of allowing the communitarian couples of Vera's fourth dream to emerge from their connubial alcoves in order to change partners.

But the line between promiscuity and ease of divorce is a difficult one to draw. Like Herzen, Mikhailov, and the others who wrote before him, Chernyshevsky, by insisting on freedom in love and at the same time celebrating the joys of a lasting union, left the door open for conflicting interpretations. Otherwise it could not be. Chernyshevsky knew this. He was writing for New People who were endowed with realism, rational egoism, and the "correct" moral vision. For the still corrupted generality no program, no credo, no novel could chart the way to a new sexual basis for society. Nor, as it happened, could either the fortified monogamy of tsarist society or the permissive atmosphere of post-revolutionary Russia bring and keep together what the laws of ordinary psychology would rend asunder.

Reactions to the novel were immediate and strong. Fëdor Tolstoy, a conservative writer for *The Northern Bee,* accused Chernyshevsky of recommending "every comfort and seduction for shopgirls and streetwalkers, removing all obstacles for them, and giving them the right to take lovers into their rooms." Askochensky, in *Household Conversation,* suggested that Chernyshevsky's characters belonged in a workhouse where the meager diet and hard labor would help them unlearn their stupid emancipatory notions. A conservative priest, N. Soloviev, used his review of *What Is To Be Done?* as an occasion to strike at the entire phenomenon of women's emancipation in Russia, including higher education. His

major concern was the moral laxness of "modern" women who, he claimed, had adopted the harmful idea of George Sand that since men have sexual freedom, women should have it too. Soloviev insisted that Chernyshevsky's *What Is To Be Done?* preached a brand of "free love" that was hardly distinguishable from prostitution and "the debasement of woman's noble nature by means of cunning theoretical positions." He concluded from the drift of the novel that Vera Pavlovna would fall in love with Rakhmetov and then cohabit with all three of her admirers, or so the philosophy of the author would allow.

One of the most violent critical reactions was a polemical tract entitled *What They Did in "What Is To Be Done?"* written in the 1870's by Professor Tsitovich of Odessa University. In a deliberate effort to distort and discredit the meaning of the book, by means of a dubious exegesis of the Russian law codes, Tsitovich accused the characters of committing abduction, bigamy, pimping, and fornication, among other things. His bitterest comments, including some vile remarks about the heroine, were directed at the alleged Darwinian spirit of the novel. Vera Pavlovna's choice of Kirsanoy over Lopukhov, he said, was no more than a mechanical act of sexual selection, a human version of the beastly behavior described in *The Origin of Species.* Tsitovich was particularly distressed by the fact that, as he said, every schoolgirl and student knew the book intimately and was "considered a dunce if she was not acquainted with the exploits of Vera Pavlovna." From this no doubt accurate observation, he concluded that the female defendants in the recent political trials were the latest embodiments of the characters in Chernyshevsky's book.

Conservatives were unanimous in imputing to the novel an open endorsement of sexual license. The term "free love," used all over the Western world as a weapon against emancipation, was defined as complete promiscuity. But of course neither George Sand's "freedom of the heart" nor Chernyshevsky's version of it was any such thing. It simply meant that a young woman should be allowed to follow her romantic (not merely physical) inclinations, including, if necessary, the desertion of one man for another. But the love knot of each relationship would be as binding on the members as that made by any matrimonial contract, indeed more so. Freedom of love could only be sequential, never simultaneous. Even Enfantin stopped short of polygamous behavior for his Don Juan types. But most conservatives could not or would not see this truth. The cynical obscurantists, as Plekhanov pointed out years later, understood full well the real morality of the novel which menaced their Philistine life style of secret affairs and "boudoir visits." Thus the identification of the moral formulas of *What Is To Be Done?* with the worst kind of debauchery and carnal license was to be the hall-mark of anti-nihilist criticism for decades.

Reviews of the novel in the "progressive" camp were generally favorable. Pisarev's "Thinking Proletariat," the most influential, welcomed the heroes to the world of Russian letters and praised Vera Pavlovna as "the new woman." He defended them against the critics' charge of immorality by contrasting their honest behavior to that of the conventional cad, Storeshnikov, who lewdly dreams of seducing Vera. But Shelgunov was not so enthusiastic. He saw Vera Pavlovna as an undeveloped woman, still moving in the rarefied atmosphere of love that suffuses the works of Turgenev and George Sand, a transitional figure, trained for love and not for work rather than a New Woman. Being one of the real life models for the novel, Shelgunov also found fault with the "chivalrous relations" among the principals. "Even our best people have not yet been able to free themselves from their false relations with women. . . . " Among simple people, he said, were simple desires, based on physiology and not on the exalted and excessively "feminine atmosphere" of this book.

But it was Pisarev's view which prevailed overwhelmingly among the young radicals and nihilists. Skabichevsky recalled the impact that Chernyshevsky's novel made upon his circle:

> We read the novel almost like worshippers, with the kind of piety with which we read religious books, and without the slightest trace of a smile on our lips. The influence of the novel on our society was colossal. It played a great role in Russian life, especially among the leading members of the intelligentsia who were embarking on the road to socialism, bringing it down a bit from the world of drama to the problem of our social evils, sharpening its image as the goal which each of us had to fight for.

Vodovozova recalled how the gentry, returning from their summer homes in the fall of 1863, were greeted everywhere with discussions of *What Is To Be Done?*. Young girls would pay up to twenty-five rubles for a copy composed of serial issues of *The Contemporary* bound together. Although most of its ideas were already current, she said, its literary form provided a synthesis that opened people's eyes and "gave a vigorous push to the mental and moral development of Russian society." As the literary historian, Ovsyaniko-Kulikovsky observed many years later, "Vera Pavlovna symbolized the women's movement of the 1860's; in her aspirations and her enterprises were reflected the stage which the woman question had reached at that time."

When Chernyshevsky was led out of the fortress to his place of civil execution in 1864, two young women, one the sister of Lyudmila Shelgunova, threw bouquets of flowers at him. This act of gratitude and admiration symbolized the belief of a large number of women in the Russia of the 1860's that he had shown them "the right path" to the future emancipation. Although it is true that Chernyshevsky had worked up themes and techniques already in use among the younger generation, it was clear that he had offered the most comprehensive set of answers to date to the "burning questions." Even Shelgunov admitted that in *What Is To Be Done?*, Chernyshevsky was describing life and not creating it. What Sergei Aksakov, Goncharov, and Turgenev had done to describe the ethos of the pre-emancipation gentry, Chernyshevsky had done for the would-be destroyers of that ethos. Herzen, no great friend of Chernyshevsky at the time (1866), named him and Mikhailov as those who had done the most to help liberate women from the humiliating yoke of the family.

Although cultural anthropologists might not agree, the concept of ethnicity need not be confined to national, regional, or linguistic groups but ought to be applied to any category of human beings that constitutes a more or less clearly defined cultural community visibly distinguishable from the surrounding society. Indeed, when applied to communities with a homogeneous culture—whether political, social, or religious—it can have far more meaning than when used to conceptualize such internally diverse categories as "Jews," "Southern Blacks," or "Irish Catholics." The term "nihil-

ists" has long been employed by both sympathizers and critics to describe a large, diffuse group of Russians who made their appearance in the late 1850's and early 1860's and who formed the pool out of which radical movements emerged. There have been many attempts to define Russian nihilism, but I think Nikolai Strakhov came close to the truth when he said that "nihilism itself hardly exists, although there is no denying the fact that nihilists do." Nihilism was not so much a corpus of formal beliefs and programs (like populism, liberalism, Marxism) as it was a cluster of attitudes and social values and a set of behavioral affects—manners, dress, friendship patterns. In short, it was an ethos.

The origin of the term *nigilistka* (female nihilist) is just as difficult to trace as that of the word *nigilist*. One thing is certain: it was a derivative of the masculine word and followed it into the language of popular usage. But just as nihilists existed before the word was popularized in Turgenev's *Fathers and Children* (1861), so the women nihilist was on the scene before the birth of Kukshina, the caricature of her from the same novel. Although the word has been used previously in Russian thought, it was in the 1860's that it assumed its familiar meaning. "In those days of national renewal," wrote Elizaveta Vodovozova, a representative woman of the 1860's, "the young intelligentsia was moved by ardent faith, not by sweeping negation." For many young women of the 1860's, embarrassed by the restrictions, real or imaginary, which Russian society imposed upon them, and impatient with the pace of feminism, the philosophic posture and the social attitudes of the people who were called nihilists had an enormous attraction. Only they, it seemed, were trying to put into practice the grandiose notions of equality and social justice which the publicists of recent years had preached.

Lev Deutsch, the well-known revolutionary and pioneer of Russian Marxism, made the following observation:

> By rejecting obsolete custom, by rising up against unreasonable opinions, concepts, and prejudices, and by rejecting authority and anything resembling it, nihilism set on its way the idea of the equality of all people without distinction. To nihilism, incidentally, Russia owes the well-known and remarkable fact that in our culturally deprived country, women began, earlier than in most civilized states, their surge toward higher education and equal rights—a fact which already [as of 1926] has had enormous significance and which in the future will obviously play a great role in the fate of our country and even perhaps throughout the civilized world.

"The idea of the equality of all people without distinction" was the magnet which drew so many young idealistic women into the "nihilist" camp. When it became clear that nihilism was the only intellectual movement which emphatically included women in its idea of emancipation, the way was opened for a coalition of the sexes.

Nihilist women, whatever their age or costume, approached the problem of their rights as women with an outlook basically different from that of the feminists. If the feminists wanted to change pieces of the world, the nihilists wanted to change the world itself, though not necessarily through political action. Their display of will and energy was more visible; and their attitude toward mere charity was similar to that of Thoreau—that it was better to *be* good than to *do* good. The feminists wanted a moderate amelioration of the condition of women, especially in education and employment opportunities, assuming that their role in the family would improve as these expanded. The nihilists insisted on total liberation from the yoke of the traditional family (both as daughters and as wives), freedom of mating, sexual equality—in short, personal emancipation. Better education and jobs were simply the corollaries of this. Though they thirsted after learning, nihilist women often preferred to seek it abroad than to join the slow struggle for higher education in Russia itself. Where the feminists may have seen complete liberation as a vague apparition, the nihilist saw it as an urgent and realizable task. This is one reason why the social and personal behavior of the *nigilistka* was more angular and more dramatic than that of the feminist.

The outlook of the woman-as-nihilist has been differentiated here from that of the woman-as-radical. . . . This differentiation is only slightly artificial for, while it is true that many women nihilists of the 1860's were drawn to radical causes, political radicalism as such was not a necessary condition for choosing "nihilist" solutions to the woman question. The techniques employed by the nihilists did not in themselves imply a politico-revolutionary view of life. Indeed there were some nihilists of both sexes whose extreme individualism, though drawing them to socially and sexually radical attitudes, actually prevented them from embracing causes, ideologies, or political action. Like the individualist sexual rebels of early nineteenth-century Europe, many women nihilists avoided organized movements, whether feminist or radical. Their "feel-yourself orientation" was at odds with the imperatives of underground activity. "Inner rebellion" and personal identification were sufficient, and they avoided revolutionary circles out of fear, lack of awareness, or plain distaste. Sexually emancipated behavior in a woman—to say nothing of a man—has never been a necessary indication of her political "modernity."

Precisely when the people of St. Petersburg began using the word *nigilistka* to describe the progressive, advanced, or educated woman is difficult to say. We can only be sure that after the publication of *Fathers and Children,* the image of the "female nihilist" (Turgenev did not use the word) was firmly fixed in the public eye. Much has been written about Turgenev's attitude to his hero, Bazarov, and the nihilists he seemed to represent; but there was no doubt that Evdoksiya Kukshina was an unflattering caricature. She surpassed the ludicrous in her attitudes and behavior. Her cigarette smoking, her slipshod attire, and her brusque manner were affected gestures of modernity, accompanying her shallow passion for chemistry. When asked why she wanted to go to Heidelberg, her answer was the hilarious. "How can you ask! Bunsen lives there!" She is beyond George Sand ("a backward woman, knows nothing about education or embryology") and correctly denounces Proudhon, but in the same breath praises Michelet's *L'amour!*

Dostoevsky called Kukshina "that progressive louse which Turgenev combed out of Russian reality." Pisarev pointed out that her counterparts in real life were not nihilists, but "false nihilists" and "false *emancipées.*" The radical critic, Antonovich, however, blasted the novel in *The Contemporary,* and berated the author for his unfair portrayal of contemporary women. Seeing that the cartoon figure of Kukshina would be used as a weapon of ridicule against all advanced women, he suggested that, however ridiculous the unripe, progressive female might appear, the traditional upperclass woman was even more ridiculous. "Better to flaunt a book than a petticoat," he said. "Better to coquette with science than with a dandy. Better to show off in a lecture hall than at a ball."

The nihilist view of women was further crystallized in the following year by the discussion of a satirical anti-nihilist play, *Word and Deed,* by Ustryalov. Its hero is stern, unbending, thoroughly unromantic; his credo is "to believe what I know, acknowledge what I see, and respect what is useful." Like Bazarov, he scorns love, only to be swept off his feet by a conventional young damsel. This buffoonery prompted Andrei Gieroglifov, a member of Pisarev's circle, to face the issue squarely in an essay bearing the title "Love and Nihilism," written just as Chernyshevsky was completing his novel, and drawn largely from Schopenhauer's "Metaphysics of Love." Gieroglifov proposed a thoroughgoing anti-idealistic explanation of love as no more than the awakening of the reproductive instinct, however innocent it might appear. Going well beyond Chernyshevsky, he insisted that love was not to be seen as a purely personal and individual pleasure. In it "the will of each person becomes the agent of the race," and "there is no participation by the individual will of man." All mating and the feelings that accompany it were based on nature's need to continue the species. Can a nihilist love? Yes, answered Gieroglifov, "for reason does not negate feeling;" but the nihilist must recognize love's relationship to nature. What kind of woman can he love? Not a doll or a plaything, says Gieroglifov, but a woman of knowledge who rejects the archaic, the passive, and the impotent and embraces the new, the creative, and the forceful. "Then there will be a greater correspondence and harmony between the men and women of the new generation. Without this it is impossible to reach that mutual happiness which nature itself demands."

One of the most interesting and widely remarked features of the *nigilistka* was her personal appearance. Discarding the "muslin, ribbons, feathers, parasols, and flowers" of the Russian lady, the archetypical girl of the nihilist persuasion in the 1860's wore a plain dark woolen dress, which fell straight and loose from the waist with white cuffs and collar as the only embellishments. The hair was cut short and worn straight, and the wearer frequently assumed dark glasses. This "revolt in the dress" was part of the *nigilistka's* repudiation of the image of the "bread-and-butter miss," that pampered, helpless creature who was prepared exclusively for attracting a desirable husband and who was trained at school to wear *décolletée* even before she had anything to reveal. These "ethereal young ladies" in tarlatan gowns and outlandish crinolines—the phrase is Kovalevskaya's—bedecked themselves with jewelry and swept their hair into "attractive" and "feminine" coiffures. Such a sartorial ethos, requiring long hours of grooming and primping, gracefully underlined the leisure values of the society, the lady's inability to work, and a sweet, sheltered femininity. The *nigilistka's* rejection of all this fit in with her desire to be functional and useful, and with her repugnance for the day-to-day existence of "the superfluous woman."

But it was also a rejection of her exclusive role as a passive sexual object. Long luxuriant tresses and capacious crinolines, so obviously suggestive of fertility, were clearly parts of the feminine apparatus of erotic attraction. The traditional results were romance, courtship, and marriage, followed by years of disappointing boredom or domestic tyranny. The machinery of sexual attraction through outward appearance that led into slavery was discarded by the new woman whose

Engraving of three leading contributors to The Contemporary: *Chernyshevsky, Dobrolyubov, and Mikhaylov.*

nihilist creed taught her that she must make her way with knowledge and action rather than feminine wiles. Linked to the defeminization of appearance was the unconscious longing to resemble the man, for the distinctive garb of the nihilist girl—short hair, cigarettes, plain garments—were boyish affectations. These, together with intensity of interest in academic and "serious" matters, tended to reduce the visible contrasts between the sexes and represented the outward form of her inner desire—to diminish the sharp social and cultural difference between men and women.

Beneath her new costume, the nihilist of the 1860's also assumed a new personality and self-image. The sickly romanticism and sentimentality are gone. She realized that true personal autonomy required psychological independence, though not separation, from men. To establish her identity, she needed a cause or a "path," rather than just a man. So, in rejecting chivalric or tender attention from men, she often seemed blunt, for she deeply longed to be received as a human being, not simply as a woman. This also explains why she cut or hid her pretty hair beneath a cap and covered her eyes with smoked lenses. "Value us as comrades and fellow workers in life," she seemed to be saying to men; "as your equals with whom you can speak simply and plainly."

The new attitude was vividly reflected in her social behavior.

The typical *nigilistka,* like her male comrade, rejected the conventional hypocrisy of interpersonal relations and tended to be direct to the point of rudeness, unconcerned with the ordinary amenities, and often enough unconcerned with cleanliness as well. The insistence upon complete equality of the sexes also induced men of the new generation to cast overboard the ballast of chivalry and stylized gallantry. As one of Kropotkin's acquaintances observed, they would not stand up when a woman entered the room, but they would often travel halfway across the city to help a girl in her studies. The new woman was anxious to be respected for her knowledge and not for the size of her bust or the plenitude of her skirts.

The costumes and customs of the new culture were assumed, sometimes temporarily, by so many faddists that it was often difficult to tell the nihilist from the *poseur.* The term nihilist was flung about as indiscriminately then as it was in the 1870's and 1880's when it became a synonym for assassin. Leskov, for instance, reported in 1863 that "short haired young ladies who married at the first chance" were considered nihilists. Like many such terms, it was loosely applied and was fluid enough to serve many purposes—most of them pejorative: A *nigilistka* could be an auditor at the university, a girl with bobbed hair, a grown woman with "advanced" ideas (whether or not she understood them), or a volunteer in one of the feminist or philanthropic bodies, depending upon the point of view of the describer.

What Is To Be Done? bequeathed to the woman of the 1860's not only a self-image but also some specific devices for liberation as well, particularly the fictitious marriage as a means of escape, and the *artel*-commune as a mode of social action. Though both pre-dated the novel, their incidence increased with its publication and with the growth of family discord that formed its social background. The great schism between fathers and sons, which has received much scholarly attention, also affected the daughters and drew them into a "struggle between the Domostroi and the nineteenth century," as Pisarev neatly if oversimply put it. That there was a genuine family upheaval among the gentry, there can be no doubt. "Girls, bred in the most aristocratic families," wrote Kropotkin [see essay above], "rushed penniless to St. Petersburg, Moscow, and Kiev, eager to learn a profession which would free them from the domestic yoke, and some day, perhaps, from the possible yoke of a husband." Sofya Kovalevskaya recalled the same phenomenon from the days before her own deliverance: "Children especially girls, were seized by a virtual epidemic of running away from home . . . we would hear how the daughter of this or that landowner had fled, perhaps abroad to study, or to Petersburg—to the 'nihilists'."

The adventures of Kovalevskaya's circle offer an array of influences and motivations that were fermenting among the privileged young ladies of the time. Her sister, Anna Korvin-Krukovskaya, grew up in the sheltered idyll of a country estate, far from "the stream of new currents." Spoiled and petted, she roamed like a "free cossack" through her childhood, untouched by any ideas other than an adolescent spell of religious mysticism. But in the summer of 1862, when she was nineteen, the son of the village priest, on vacation from his scientific studies in Petersburg, regaled her with the "materialist" theories of Darwin and Sechenov, and introduced her to the thick journals. Anyuta was transformed. She donned a black dress and stuffed her hair into a severe net; she started teaching village children, refused to attend balls, and filled her room with the acoutrements of scientific learning. When her father, the stern commanding general of the St. Petersburg Arsenal, denied her plea to study medicine in the capital, she turned her hand to fiction and, after titanic battles with her family, eventually freed herself.

Sofya Kovalevskaya's childhood was as unhappy as her sister's was carefree. The feeling of being unloved haunted her early years and was the key to her subsequent emotional difficulties. Envy of her sister filled her with malaise and was given expression in possessive puppyloves and sexual longing in the form of a three-legged man who pursued her in dreams. But by the time she was eighteen, she was under Anyuta's nihilist spell and had developed her own consuming passion for mathematics. The sisters with a friend hatched a plan to secure a "fictitious" husband for Anyuta who would take them to Europe. Their first candidate, Sechenov himself, refused at the insistence of his "wife" Bokova, who opposed the project despite her reputation as the inventor of fictitious marriages. They found a "brother"—code word for fictitious husband—in Vladimir Kovalevsky, who agreed to marry, not Anyuta, but Sonya. She expressed her regret "that brother is not a Muslim," so that he could marry all three of them. Kovalevsky agreed, in accordance with the code, that he would not exercise his conjugal rights. The marriage took place, over strenuous objections from the family, in 1868. All the

parties hastened abroad to carve out for themselves separate careers in literature and science. Sonya and her husband remained friends, but only after the death of her adored father did she allow him "full" relations with her.

Anna Evreinova (1844-1919), offered another variant. Though the daughter of the high-ranking commandant of Pavlovsk, she acquired an early aversion for balls and gowns and refused to become "a drawing-room lady." Closely guarded by her imperious father who abhorred "superfluous" learning, she would study classical languages by candlelight after returning from the hated galas. She tried to acquire a fictitious husband, writing to her cousin that "we are seeking people like ourselves, warmly devoted to a cause and whose principles are identical to ours, who would not so much marry us as liberate us, and who would understand our needs and be useful to us in our present circumstances." Failing to find one, she crossed the frontier illegally and, after a few years study at the University of Leipzig, became the first woman doctor of laws in Russia. Like Kovalevskaya, she avoided radical activity and in later years became an active proponent of women's rights and publisher of *The Northern Messenger.*

Vodovozova described some of the difficulties of fictitious marriages in the 1860's. A young man, hearing of a woman who wished to leave home in order to study and develop herself, would offer himself as a fictitious husband. After the wedding there was immediate separation, without consummation of the marriage, and often without any contact at all. The girl would typically go abroad; the man would fall in love with someone else and wish to marry. A long correspondence and a drawn-out divorce would ensue. In the meantime, both couples might have illegitimate children. For those who continued to reject conventional morality, of course, such conditions offered little hardship, especially if they dwelt in the half-world of underground or émigré circles. But for "May nihilists" who later returned to the world of more conventional norms—and there were many—the situation was more painful. Sometimes a "fictitious" husband, hiding his real designs, would attempt to extract his conjugal rights from the deceived girl after the ceremony had taken place. But the fictitious marriage remained for a long time a favorite method among women who wished to escape from uncomfortable nests.

There were also wives who left husbands for failing to offer them the kind of life promised by the teachings of the New People. Sleptsov's novel, *A Difficult Time,* accurately portrays an advanced woman, disillusioned with her husband from whom she had expected "significant things" and a partnership in a life of excitement. About to leave him to go to St. Petersburg, she says:

> When you wanted to marry me, what did you tell me? Just remember! You said, "We will work together and do great things which might even bring us and our dear ones to ruin, but I'm not afraid of that. If you feel you have the strength, then let's go on together"—and I went. Of course then I was just a foolish girl and didn't fully understand what you were talking about; I simply felt and guessed. And I would have gone anywhere . . . because I thought and believed that we would do real things. And what has it all amounted to? You curse at your peasants for every copeck; and I stand here salting pickles.

A real life example was Ekaterina Maikova (1836-1920), wife of the well-known literary figure Vladimir Maikov. The marriage was a happy and stable one, but there was clearly something missing in Maikova's life. In the early 1860's, she began re-examining her married life in the light of ideas, particularly those of *What Is To Be Done?*. Her life no longer fulfilled her needs. In the end she went off with a student, bore him a child, and began to study at the Alarchin Courses in Petersburg. Her case was a common one in those days.

There was a rumor abroad among the provincial gentry in the middle of the 1860's about a communist community in St. Petersburg to which all young girls of good family were invited after escaping from home. There both sexes and all classes lived together in "complete communism" with well-born ladies taking their turns washing the floors. At the root of this rumor was the fact that both the nihilists and the radicals had adopted the *artel* and the commune as a means of assisting women along their new path. This development preceded *What Is To Be Done?* by about two years. Since 1861, Petersburg was rapidly filling up with women and most of them did not find suitable outlets for their energies through the feminist organizations. Most were too poor to act as leaders in these enterprises and too proud to play the passive role in feminism by accepting charity from the grand ladies of the capital. What they wanted desperately was intellectual work, freedom, and a decent place to live. None of the ordinary channels of female employment could offer this combination to all the recent immigrants to the city. Rents were high, wages low, jobs, especially white collar ones, very hard to get—for men as well as women. The cooperative and its variants emerged as a partial solution to this problem.

The best-known commune, which appeared before Chernyshevsky's novel, was the Grech Commune. According to Nikolai Leskov, who fictionalized it in "The Enigmatic Man," a number of journalists who favored women's emancipation decided to put their theories into practice and extend a hand to the numerous unemployed, educated women in the capital by hiring them as typesetters, translators, and writers. Most of these men, said Leskov, a tendentious witness, were mainly interested in seducing their female clients. An exception was Arthur Benni, a Polish-born British citizen, who moved in and out of radical circles in the 1860's until his death on a Risorgimento battlefield in 1867. In 1862 he conceived of the idea of hiring women as translators, and established a "commune" for them in his quarters in the Grech lodging house—thus the "Grech Commune" or "Grech Phalanstery," a share-the-expense living arrangement with take-home work. Again according to Leskov, the communalists spent most of their time debating the woman question and very little time translating. Benni was forced to do most of the work himself and pay the women out of his own pocket until he could do so no longer. Then the commune dissolved.

Far more famous was the commune organized by Benni's friend, Vasily Sleptsov (1836-1878), the author of *A Difficult Time*. His yearning to help the "working masses" fused with his growing interest in the woman question, and he played a leading role in giving education, work, and independence to young women of the capital. Some critics have stressed that it was only the *young* women of the capital who attracted his attention, but other accounts do not seem to bear this out. He organized popular lectures for women on scientific subjects. They drew large crowds, until rumors of a police raid and the hostility of some of the female auditors to the presence of *aris-*

tokratki (i.e., well-dressed ladies) hurt the attendance. He also founded bookbinding workshops for women and set up mutual aid funds to supply them with cheap credit. In short, Sleptsov, though not the first to take up the problem of women's independence as his mother claimed, was the most energetic example of the advanced man of the 1860's who endeavored to help women without patronizing them.

In 1863, he established a residential commune, inspired directly by *What Is To Be Done?* and partly also no doubt by Fourier whose works on women he had studied. The commune consisted of seven men and women in a large apartment on Znamenskaya Street where the members had separate bedrooms but shared expenses, meals, and housework. Two of the women were described by Kornei Chukovsky, who wrote a history of the commune, as genuine, militant nihilists: One, Alexandra Markelova, had been left unmarried with a baby; the second, Ekaterina Makulova, ironically called "the princess," was coarse and unattractive and wholly incapable of earning a living on her own. The other two women were of a different sort. Mariya Kopteva came of good parents, had had an institute education but, because of her "turbulent imagination," had fled her parental home and come to Petersburg to support herself. Ekaterina Tsenina, later Zhukovskaya, had travelled a route typical for advanced women in the sixties: escape from her family through marriage, desertion of her husband, odd jobs in the provinces, and some translation work in Petersburg for Vernadsky's *Economic Index*. While seeking additional work, she met Sleptsov through Markelova and was invited into the commune. Though happy to cut her rental expenses, she was reluctant and suspicious from the very outset. When Sleptsov, welcoming her into the commune, tried to kiss her hand, she withdrew it angrily and said: "I must warn you that I do not subscribe to Fourier's theory of sexual relations, even in the abstract, and I also forewarn you that if any member of the commune intends to put this theory into practice, I refuse to join."

The Znamenskaya Commune lasted about a year and became a well-known haunt for the Petersburg intellectuals, Lavrov, Sechenov, and Panaeva. Benni courted Kopteva; and the economist Yuly Zhukovsky won the hand of Tsenina. But friction grew up, partly because none of the women cared to help in the housework, but mostly because of the deeper hostility between the two factions: Kopteva and Tsenina on one side, all the rest on the other. The former two viewed with scorn Sleptsov's obviously sincere attempt at social experimentation. They also retained the fashionable dress habits of their upbringing, while the other two women assumed the more typical unsightly appearance of nihilists: Thus Tsenina called herself and Kopteva "aristocratic nihilists" and Markelova and the princess "sloppy nihilists." One need not go so far as Chukovsky's characterization of these women as "the Mensheviks and Bolsheviks of nihilism" in order to recognize that there were fundamental differences in outlook between them. The commune also invited gossip. Nikolai Uspensky called it the Muslim harem of Sultan Sleptsov; Saltykov-Shchedrin made the appropriate analogies with Ménilmontant and Enfantin. Leskov claimed that Sleptsov had entered Kopteva's room in a state of partial undress. But scholars as well as other contemporaries insist, no doubt correctly, that the commune was monastic. The real cause of its dissolution were the personal animosity, the marriage plans, and the familiar rumors of a police raid.

Another experiment inspired by *What Is To Be Done?* was a laundry *artel* for women, organized in the spring of 1864 by a Mme. Garshina. The overenthusiastic patroness, in an obvious effort to emulate Vera Pavlovna, overpaid her women (even when they did not work) and introduced prostitutes into the establishment in order to rehabilitate them through useful labor. The results were both disastrous and comic. Her employees, suspicious of the high wages and good treatment, refused to listen to Garshina's sermons on cooperation, demanded an end to equality of wages, and began, in emulation of the prostitutes, drinking and carousing with soldiers on the premises of the *artel*. In relating her sad story, Mme. Garshina also took a swipe at the hypocritical liberals who sympathized with women's rights but who never paid their laundry bills. Similar episodes were reported in other parts of Russia.

Vodovozova recalled how young people would sit around a table with a copy of *What Is To Be Done?* in front of them and laboriously plan an *artel*. One of these *artels* collapsed because of conflicting interpretations of the novel. Its organizer insisted that it be lavishly furnished and designed to make large profits; the New People, he said, were egoists, not ascetics. But when he introduced a contingent of prostitutes, citing Vera Pavlovna's love for Kryukova and Julie Letellier, the refined widow who acted as his manager resigned and the *artel* ran aground. Vera Zasulich, who recalled that such enterprises grew up like mushrooms after the appearance of *What Is To Be Done?*, mentioned one where the seamstresses broke away and demanded the sewing machines on the principle—which they had just learned—that "machinery belongs to labor."

Communes and *artels* became a kind of fad in the 1860's. Ilya Repin lived for a while in a commune of painters; Modest Musorgsky lived in another. But their god, as Chukovsky reminds us with gentle irony, was Flaubert and not Feuerbach. The idea received another boost in 1866 when Eduard Pfeiffer's *Zur Genossenschafttum* (1865) appeared in a Russian translation. But after 1866, with the onset of reaction, the fad died and *artels* and communes became almost the exclusive preserve of radical circles.

If the important publicists of the 1860's were in favor of the New Woman, most of the literary figures were against her. Tolstoy, who nourished a warm loathing for the ideas of George Sand, wrote an anti-nihilist play, *The Infected Family*. Pisemsky, Leskov, Goncharov, and Dostoevsky all wrote novels attacking nihilism and its doctrines on women. These, and a dozen other minor representatives of the genre, are discussed together in Charles Moser's *Antinihilism in the Russian Novel of the 1860s* [excerpted above]. The book demonstrates how deeply these Russian writers, who clearly voiced the sentiments of a large sector of "society," were distressed by what they took to be the immoral antics of the nihilists. But it also demonstrates, if taken together with the historical reality, how distorted and muddled was their view of nihilist behavior.

Pisemsky's *Troubled Sea* (1863), and Nikolai Akhsharumov's story "A Delicate Affair" (1864) merely documented the harmful effect of the idea of "free love" on a circle of nihilists. Klyushnikov's *Mirage* (1864) was more devastating. In it, a *nigilistka*, in whose room hang portraits of George Sand and Jenny d'Héricourt, is seduced politically by an evil Polish intriguer, and physically by a Russian radical working with the Poles. These corrupted people are contrasted with the upright, slavophiloid hero, Rusanov, who rescues the girl after her fall. Pisarev, Zaitsev, and Saltykov-Shchedrin roasted the novel in their reviews, while the conservative critic, Edelsohn of *The Readers' Library*, saw it as a healthy antidote to the toxic effects of *What Is To Be Done?* Leskov's *No Exit* of the same year, was a fictionalized treatment of the Znamenskaya Commune where Sleptsov is cast as a lecher, and "Princess" Makulova—Bertholdi in the novel—is made to voice the view that "the family is the most disgusting form of what fools call civilization."

The complete parody of the nihilist idea of love was Avenarius' *Disease* (1867) in whose sensational seduction scene a "progressive student" explains to his victim, a sincere but misled young girl, why she should make love with him. "Without this sympathy [between the sexes] the world would die out," he explains; "but it is instilled by nature, as an instinctive striving, into every living thing, and every four-footed animal, every stupid bird, every insect even upon maturity searches for a sympathetic heart. Do you mean to say that man, the highest feature in the organic world, should flout the laws of nature?" The passage was a paraphrase of Gieroglifov's "Love and Nihilism," and the message was that the New People, afflicted with these contagious ideas, were "infecting" innocent girls. It was hardly a novelty in Russian intellectual or political history to compare a new idea to some raging disease, for the analogy had the advantage of invoking some kind of quarantine.

But the physiological cynicism depicted by Avenarius was not a feature of the nihilist love ethos. It was, however, an accurate foreshadowing of the outlook of the "Saninists" of 1908-1914—the Soviet "drink of water" enthusiasts of the 1920's whose brutish attitude toward sex would evoke indignant attacks from the spiritual descendants of the nihilists of the 1860's. For the nihilists, sexual morality signified a liaison with one person, based on love and lasting only as long as love lasted; it did not permit casual conquests, unfair seductions, the patronizing of prostitutes, or even adultery (in their sense of the word)—in short any of the conventional immoralities recognized as such in the bourgeois moral code.

The anti-nihilist writers were as tendentious as the nihilists themselves. Their characters were caricatures, not portraits. The anti-nihilists were not, however, necessarily hostile to women's emancipation, but rather to the nihilist men who showed them the wrong way. Leskov's *The Bypassed*, for instance, described a workshop that combined feminism, charity, and religion, and was designed to look after the welfare of young girls. It was in sharp contrast to Vera Pavlovna's wondrous arcadia of reason and self-interest. Goncharov, whose anti-nihilist novel, *The Precipice* was among the most scorching, explained his position on the matter: "Isn't it a fact," he asked, "that women disregarded their loved ones, were seduced away from respectable life, society, and family by the crude heroes of the 'new force,' the 'new course' and by the idea of some sort of 'great future'? Isn't it a fact that fine young girls followed them into their cellars and garrets, abandoning parents, husbands, and worse, children?" These women had been corrupted, he said. But there were others, genuinely serious women who were working to prepare themselves for an independent life by discipline and education. "In the hands of these women," said Goncharov, "lies the correct solution of the so-called woman question."

Nihilist teaching on the woman question, for all its egalitarian and liberationist sweep, did not provide a very solid theoretical or social base for the further emancipation of women. The Chernyshevsky synthesis—brothers liberating sisters (the fictitious marriage), women liberating women, freedom of choice in love and marriage, cooperative work and communal life for both sexes, full development of the mind and the personality of women—was officially adopted by the revolutionary intelligentsia of the 1870's and after, though parts of it were obscured or downplayed by the imperatives of a desperate struggle for power. Indeed, much of it was absorbed into the ethos of the non-radical progressive intelligentsia. But opposition to the nihilist view of sexual equality among the conservative elements of the empire remained very potent; and revolt against the established order in this domain of human relations had to be personal, sporadic, and often traumatic. The fictitious marriage, though regularly used by later radicals to recruit women, was an individual and not always successful device outside the radical fold. Free unions and freedom of love had little relevance to economic or professional development of upper-class women; none at all to the masses of female peasants. And cooperative and communal experiments—an attempt to adapt popular forms (*artel* and *obshchina*) to the life of the repenting privileged—did not enjoy great success in the 1860's, even when employed by outright radical groups. . . . They were swept away in the "white terror" of 1866 and replaced in the 1870's by underground conspirative cells.

Nihilism, as a way of life distinct from radicalism, began to dissolve at the end of the 1860's. Various historical punctuation marks have been offered: the so-called "white terror" of 1866, the shutting down of *The Russian Word* and *The Contemporary,* Pisarev's death in 1868, Lavrov's *Historical Letters* with its new ethic of populism, and so on. Those who had brandished nihilist ideas and habits in the early 1860's tended either to join the revolution—with which society identified them anyway—or pass back into the mainstream of Russian life, retaining only superficial vestiges of their non-conformist youth. But nihilism, in its isolated form, had to end in a *cul de sac* as far as the general emancipation of women was concerned. Refusing to accept or to destroy the culture, the nihilists had only the alternative of disobeying it. Their active responses to the woman question, taken by themselves, could not lead to its solution. The radicals came to recognize that the superficial "nihilist" devices of *What Is To Be Done?* could have no long range effect unless its central, socialist ideas were realized in Russian life. The nihilists, however, did pass on their sexual ideas and practices to generations of revolutionaries who, after some fifty years of struggle, would attempt to translate them into public policy. (pp. 89-114)

Richard Stites, "The Nihilist Response," in his The Women's Liberation Movement in Russia: Feminism, Nihilism, and Bolshevism, 1860-1930, *Princeton University Press, 1978, pp. 89-114.*

LITERATURE AS REFORM: THE CIVIC CRITICS

MARC SLONIM

[*Slonim was a Russian-born American critic who wrote extensively on Russian literature. In the following excerpt from his survey of Russian literature of the nineteenth and twentieth*
centuries, The Epic of Russian Literature: From Its Origins through Tolstoy *(1950), Slonim outlines the careers of the Civic Critics Chernyshevsky, Dobrolyubov, and Pisarev and discusses the role of their thought and writings in the development of the Nihilist movement.*]

The most typical and influential representative of the new spirit [of the 1860s] was certainly Nicholas Chernyshevsky, economist, historian, novelist, philosopher, and critic. The son of a well-to-do priest, he was born in 1828 in Saratov, on the Volga River. He attended a theological seminary and, at the age of eighteen, was a student at the University of St. Petersburg. In 1848 he came in contact with the group that later was to be called the 'circle of Petrashevsky.' Most of its members were Utopian Socialists and ardent admirers of Robert Owen, George Sand, Saint-Simon, and Fourier. Chernyshevsky shared their tendencies; but while the young men who gathered in the evenings at the house of Petrashevsky were such idealists and enthusiasts as Dostoevsky or Pleshcheyev (who subsequently became well known as a poet), he defined himself as Realist and Rationalist. Petrashevsky and his friends were arrested, tried, and subjected to the torture of a mock capital execution in 1849; but Chernyshevsky fortunately escaped arrest. Four years later he made his literary debut and soon became one of the editors of *The Contemporary,* the influential organ of liberal Westernizers and radicals, published by Nekrassov. Almost immediately he was recognized as the leader of the young generation, and his authority remained unchallenged for more than two decades.

Widely read in Feuerbach, the German materialists, and the French socialists, Chernyshevsky had laid a firm foundation for his philosophical and historical materialism. Metaphysics were for him the 'pre-history' of science, and he refused to admit any source of knowledge outside of experience. A firm believer in the unity of mind and body, Chernyshevsky defined pleasure and interest as the main determinants of human behavior. Man has all sorts of needs, ranging from such primary ones as breathing, eating and drinking, to secondary ones of an emotional and intellectual nature. Happiness implies the satisfaction of most human needs and ought to be the goal of any well-organized society. As long as human beings are the agents of progress it is of the utmost importance to have a clear idea of historical events and of contemporary social, economic, and political issues. Any individual who wants to help progress along must have a definite program of potential improvements. Social rationalism is a prerequisite of any public action.

This analysis of contemporary life led Chernyshevsky to the conclusion that the causes of poverty, injustice, oppression, calamities, and deviations from that which is right were mainly economic. Class struggle, social inequality, the competition of groups and governments, the unequal distribution of capital and land, were all deeply rooted in economics and could be eradicated only if the whole structure of society was transformed. According to Chernyshevsky, this could be brought about only under Socialism, which he defined as a government of co-operation, solidarity, and popular ownership of capital, land, and factories.

In his famous *Comments on the Political Economy of John Stuart Mill* he made a penetrating analysis of contemporary economic theories and formulated his conviction of the inevitability of Socialism as a result of social development. In this, as well as in his recognition of the progressive role of capitalism in its early stages, he came very close to Marxism—both

Marx and Engels valued him highly. His position, however, was between Marxism and Populism (or Russian Socialism). Chernyshevsky criticized Herzen's 'utopias' and scouted all talk of Russia's 'mission' and the collapse of Europe. This staunch Westernizer and positivist admitted, however, that the *mir,* or rural commune, that 'relic of the past doomed in the long run to disappear,' could render invaluable service in the transition to Socialism. He was, on the whole, of the opinion that Russian agriculture would not follow the European pattern of concentration of capital, and he studied carefully 'the particularities' of Russia's social structure. Without raising the problem of moral or political superiority, he recognized that Europe and America had their own courses of development, while Russia, owing to her traditions and her own ways of life, would reach the same objectives in a different manner. This attitude made Chernyshevsky equally opposed to the Slavophiles and to the revolutionary messianism of Herzen and Bakunin.

A foe of historic fatalism, Chernyshevsky shared the faith of Herzen and the Populists that the 'human will, guided by reason,' could intervene in current history; despite his positivism he asserted that progress could be ultimately explained by the superiority of human intelligence. 'Everything in human life can be reduced to moral issues,' he wrote to his son in 1877. This moral approach formed a link between Chernyshevsky and his forerunners, such as Belinsky and Herzen, although his socialism was distinctly more realistic and economic. His political diagnoses were based upon hard facts, and his surveys show a sober, clear intelligence coupled with an acute perception of political realities. In 1862, when even Herzen doubted the victory of the North in the American Civil War, Chernyshevsky was calmly confident and predicted correctly the general course of events.

For many years Chernyshevsky led a campaign against serfdom. He believed in a peasant revolution following the emancipation, and wanted the Russian youth to be prepared for a great upheaval. Of course, the censorship prevented him from fully expressing his belief, but his readers understood all his allusions and were never mistaken in regard to his radical opinions.

Chernyshevsky's influence as a literary critic was no less important than his role as an ideological leader; moreover, his articles on contemporary writers advanced many points of his political and social doctrines. Two of his books, *Essays on the Gogol Period in Russian Literature* (1855), and the dissertation for his doctorate in philosophy, *The Esthetic Relationship between Art and Reality* (1853-5) became classics of sociological criticism and later provided the philosophical foundations for Marxist literary criticism in the Soviet era. Rejecting idealistic esthetics, Chernyshevsky proclaimed the supremacy of life over art. His point of departure was reality, and this materialistic concept determined all his conclusions. Real life in nature and society finds representation in art. Not infrequently such representation—which is the fundamental goal of art—assumes the character of interpretation or indictment of various phenomena; in that case we have critical Realism, as in Russian literature during and after the time of Gogol. The theory of art for art's sake is nonsense; the concept of abstract beauty is as preposterous as the illusion of objectivity in history. Each historian, from Tacitus to Macaulay, not only reports facts but also evaluates them according to his political and social opinions. Writers in general are also not dispassionate: Hobbes was an Absolutist, Milton a Republican, and Rousseau a Revolutionary Democrat. Whenever an artist represents Beauty with a capital 'B' he really reflects the feeling of a social group or class.

Each century, according to Chernyshevsky, had its historic mission. 'The life and glory of our times are two drives: humanism, and the endeavor to improve the conditions of human life.' This forms the content of contemporary art, from which everything useless should be banned: art must be socially significant. 'Literature and criticism have for us Russians an enormous importance such as they surely have nowhere else.'

In 1862 Chernyshevsky was arrested, in connection with the unrest among university students, and thrown into the Fortress of SS. Peter and Paul. There he wrote his novel *What Is To Be Done?,* which was to become a gospel to the young generation. This didactic work, poor in characterization, structure, and language, happened to have a tremendous public appeal. Its main theme is feminine emancipation, which is discussed at some length by the heroine, Vera Pavlovna, with her first husband, the medical student Lopukhov, whom she marries to escape the sordid environment of her family. Subsequently she debates the same question with her second husband, Kirsanov, who is also a physician. Vera Pavlovna symbolized the New Woman, whose primary concern is not with her good looks but with equality and economic independence. An active, practical person, she organizes a cooperative dressmaking shop. When Lopukhov realizes that she no longer loves him he stages a pretended suicide and goes to America to leave the field clear for his friend and rival Kirsanov.

These three characters represented the young generation with all its typical traits—and it was the pleasure of recognition that made the novel so popular. Another reason for its success were the allusions to the radical and revolutionary ideas of the time. In one of her dreams, Vera Pavlovna not only sees the stages of the progress of feminism but also has a vision of an ideal society, based on reason, science, freedom, and social service. The most appealing pages of the novel, however, are those devoted to Rakhmetov—a young nobleman who turns Spartan, renouncing woman, wine, and pleasure of any kind (except smoking!) in order to dedicate himself completely to The Cause. Although his mysterious activities are never explained in the novel, its readers then understood very well that the strong, unemotional, highly rationalistic Rakhmetov was a revolutionary. Chernyshevsky wrote with admiration that Rakhmetov 'did not spend a quarter of an hour a month on relaxation or rest.'

This perfectly self-controlled and never-erring hero subordinated all his acts to the supreme goal he had set for himself—the triumph of revolution and Socialism. As a contrast to all the superfluous men of Russian literature he was truly a new hero—and as such fired the imagination of young people throughout Russia. It is extremely revealing that this schematic image of action, logic, and virtue could mean so much to Chernyshevsky's contemporaries. The first revolutionary socialist in Russian fiction appeared as an intransigent extremist, ready for renunciation and sacrifice and resembling in his monastic austerity religious fanatics. The radicals aspired to serve as soldiers of the revolution and brothers of a socialistic order: for many years to come Rakhmetov remained their ideal, and the students sang of 'the man who wrote *What Is To Be Done?*' Officially the name of Chernyshevsky had been banned from the press. In 1863, a year after his arrest, he was branded a political criminal and deprived of all civil rights. Although no specific charge was brought against him and despite the absence of any evidence, Chernyshevsky was accused of 'pernicious influence on the young' and sentenced to penal servitude. He spent twenty-one years in mines and prisons as an exile in Siberia.

These ordeals did not, however, impair his moral integrity, his absolute devotion to science and Socialist ideals, and his puritanical attitude toward duty and work. But they did ruin him as a writer and as a scholar; after 1864 his scattered articles and essays never equaled the writings he had published at the peak of his career. He was not allowed to return to Russia until 1883, and died six years later, in 1889, in his native town of Saratov.

Chernyshevsky's ideas were popularized in literary criticism by his most talented disciple, Nicholas Alexandrovich Dobroliubov (1836-61). This young man, who died of tuberculosis at the age of twenty-five, and whose literary activity lasted only five years, was the most influential Russian critic after Belinsky.

Born into the family of a humble priest at Nizhni Novgorod (now Gorky), Dobroliubov, like Chernyshevsky, studied in a theological seminary, and later attended the Teachers' College in St. Petersburg. In 1856 he published his first article in *The Contemporary,* and the next year was appointed editor of its critical and bibliographical sections.

This stern-looking, bespectacled, prematurely aged young man, with a long face framed in side whiskers, had a powerful mind, a phenomenal memory, and a capacity for working at all hours of the day and night. The Patrician Writers felt uncomfortable in his presence: they were slightly awed by this 'democratic peasant,' who was unbending in his revolutionary faith and puritanical in his moral judgments. Here was the true representative of the young socialist and radical, so uncompromising, rigid, and vehement that he made even Herzen thoughtful and uneasy.

Dobroliubov's articles on Turgenev, Goncharov, Ostrovsky, Saltykov and others assured his reputation. They were generally lengthy essays, the springboard for which was provided by some novel, play, or tale. Dobroliubov was interested in art as a form of social communication and argued fiercely against the art-for-art's-sake theory, so prevalent among the liberal gentry. When discussing a writer or a book he always considered to what extent they expressed the natural yearnings of a period and of a people. Art had the duty, declared Dobroliubov, of dealing with social phenomena and, if it did not reflect them truthfully, completely, and profoundly it was undesirable and should be discarded. The critic's task was to help the reader to comprehend the social and artistic meaning of a book: 'Real criticism deals with works of art in the same manner as with the facts of life.' His articles did not analyze merely *Oblomov,* or *On the Eve,* or *The Thunderstorm,* but also the segment of Russian life each work portrayed and the social ideas it touched upon. Dobroliubov was a sociological critic, for whom literature represented a part of the broader unity of life and at the same time was an implement for transforming life. Like Chernyshevsky, he associated literature and revolution, and demanded from writers a conscientious service to society.

He was an excellent writer, and his articles were brilliant with civic indignation, sarcasm, wit, and pathos. No less successful were his satirical poems against the moderates, Slavo-philes, or pseudo-liberals, which he regularly published in the *Whistle* (a supplement to *The Contemporary*) and in the *Spark* (a satirical magazine directed by Vassily Kurochkin, the poet, whose masterly translations of Béranger made the latter extremely popular with the Russian readers). The tradition of satirical periodicals, dating back to Catherine's reign, was resumed and revived in the 'sixties, and Dobroliubov, Nekrassov, Kurochkin, and a number of others were successful in this genre. For fourteen years *The Spark* (banned by the censors in 1873) served as a mouthpiece for the democratic revolutionary movement and was highly influential in educated society.

Chernyshevsky and Dobroliubov determined the tendency and the tone of literary criticism for generations to come. Their ideas were accepted as a sort of obligatory credo by the radical intelligentsia. Thus, sixty years before the Revolution the two writers had established the foundations of what today determines the literary policy of the Communist party and of the Soviet critics.

Chernyshevsky and Dobroliubov represented the 'revolutionary democracy' of the 'sixties. It was another critic, Dimitry Ivanovich Pisarev (1840-68), who gained acclaim and an enthusiastic following as the exponent of Nihilism.

By an odd coincidence Pisarev's life was almost as short as Dobroliubov's: he drowned at twenty-eight, while swimming in the Baltic Sea. Unlike his two great contemporaries, he belonged to a rich and noble family, received excellent education in the gymnasia and the University of St. Petersburg, spoke several foreign languages fluently, and was destined by his family to have a diplomatic career. He turned to writing instead, and proved to be an indefatigable worker during the nine years of his literary activity. After Dobroliubov's death and Chernyshevsky's exile he occupied the first place in Russian journalism, although he was badly handicapped by political persecutions. In 1862 he was arrested and put in solitary confinement, and most of his sensational articles were written in a prison cell. They were published in *The Russian Word,* a monthly review founded in 1860 and second in influence only to *The Contemporary.*

Pisarev, a consistent materialist, shared the revolutionary bent of *The Contemporary* group but, while Dobroliubov and Chernyshevsky were mainly concerned in social issues on a large scale, Pisarev devoted his attention to the problems of the individual. Pisarev believed that natural sciences offered the only 'safe ground for a truly rational and wide outlook on nature, man, and society.' For the sake of complete independence and freedom of thought, Pisarev, who had a strong critical sense, denied all authority in morality, society, or literature. His ideal man was a 'thinking realist' who would accept only what was within the bounds of reason, logic, and utility. Pisarev's attitude toward life and art was strictly utilitarian. In his challenging articles 'The Realists' and 'The Destruction of Esthetics' he discarded sentimentalism, platonic love, romanticism, idealism, mysticism, and poetry as 'sheerest drivel.' Novels, poems, and paintings were, in his opinion, far too often mere conglomerations of words or colors. 'Thinking realists' had no time to play with such rubbish. 'We are poverty-stricken and stupid,' declared Pisarev, 'and whatever distracts us from our main tasks—education, scientific development, material and social progress—is useless and therefore obnoxious.' Money spent for ballets, theaters, or books of poetry should be used for building railroads and factories. A pair of boots was of more importance than a tragedy of Shakespeare's, and a shoemaker was superior to Raphael, since the work of the former had a practical purpose. Pisarev attacked Pushkin's poetry as something that merely helped the drones to kill time.

He undoubtedly enjoyed making such controversial statements and, feeling himself an *enfant terrible,* deliberately made them in a coarse and crude manner. But his witty, vigorous, and caustic articles were not merely challenging or exaggerated; they expressed the feelings of the generation that admired the Rakhmetovs and did not want to waste their time reading love poems or waxing rapturous over the purple hues of a sunset. As Bazarov in Turgenev's *Fathers and Sons* said: 'Nature is not a temple but a workshop, where man should stick to his job.' Pisarev declared that Bazarov was a 'thinking realist,' and that the younger generation, instead of reviling him, ought to adopt Turgenev's term and call themselves 'Nihilists.'

The Nihilism of Pisarev and of the thousands upon thousands of his followers was not the outright revolutionary doctrine that in Europe and America it is generally assumed to be. The vast movement of the 'sixties, of which Nihilism was but one facet, was in the main a revolt of the individual against any restrictions—moral, political, or personal—and against any authority—of the State, the Church, or the family. It was a kind of intellectual terrorism, which was to be replaced ten years later by a political one. The Nihilist was fundamentally a materialist and an atheist. For him experimental science took the place of God. 'Everyone of us,' wrote Bartholomew Zaitzev (1842-82), journalist and one of the leaders of the movement, 'was ready to be hanged for Moleschott or Darwin.'

A Nihilist who respected himself had to repudiate any connection with the idealism and estheticism of the preceding generation. A university student who discussed the problem of the immortality of the soul committed a grave sin in the eyes of his comrades. The Nihilists were intransigent and dogmatic, as so many iconoclasts are. Together with Pisarev they were overthrowing all the idols in such a frenzy that their supposed freedom of thought, for them, became a more powerful idol.

In the beginning the Nihilists were aware of social conditions, without being expressly socialistic. Pisarev himself, for instance, did not believe in the masses: he called the toilers the passive material, the nebula of history, incapable of struggle for a better life. He considered only the members of the intelligentsia, composed of thinking realists, as a driving force in human progress. The Nihilists' claims of equal rights for both sexes, their high talk of free love and the economic independence of women, and their criticism of marriage as merely another form of sale and purchase provoked more stir in society than the most daring political utterances of the radicals. The Nihilists loved to stress their contempt of good manners and all the 'useless frippery' of the leisure classes. The men affected Russian blouses and spoke loudly, using coarse expressions. The girls smoked, cut their hair short, and, to the horror of their parents, stayed till dawn in the quarters of their male companions. It was difficult to convince the shocked fathers and mothers that this highly suspicious behavior only involved orgies of talk: the Nihilists, despite all their posing, were rather puritanical and ascetic in matters of sex. Whatever their blunders and exaggerations, however, they greatly contributed to the movement of feminine emancipation, which was one of the most significant trends of the period.

As a result of a vigorous campaign in the press and in society women gained admission to the institutions of higher learning, and universities for women were founded in Russia.

Nihilism was just a growing pain, according to Mikhailovsky, the great sociologist: under the disguise of youthful fanaticism, rudeness, and exaggeration there was a real and very reasonable desire for work and practical action. After the emancipation of the serfs, the younger generation believed that an unlimited field of activity had opened to them. As Katherine Breshko-Breshkovskaya described it in her *Memoirs,* her contemporaries went into all sorts of professions and positions; they established schools and model farms, taught technical sciences in towns and the *a-b-c's* in villages, invaded governmental offices and the *zemstvos;* the women as well as the men became physicians, engineers, teachers, lawyers. Some of the Nihilists regarded their activities from a purely practical side, emphasizing that they were free from 'altruism, sentimentalism, and other rubbish of the past,' but the majority dreamed of serving the people.

At the beginning the Nihilists attempted to act in a perfectly legal and normal way. These attempts seemed, however, highly suspicious to the authorities, and all sorts of regulations and restrictions thwarted the efforts of thousands of well-intentioned young men and women. The government feared their enthusiasm and energy and had no desire to 'crown the reforms' by a transformation of the monarchy. Reactionary measures followed the abolition of serfdom; as far back as 1862 students were beaten up by the police for demonstrations for academic freedom. The arrests of leaders such as Chernyshevsky and Pisarev added to the discontent of the younger generation, pushing it towards radicalism—and toward Socialism, since in Russia the Socialists were the vanguard of public opinion. This agitation, which manifested itself in proclamations, student strikes, and demonstrations, and in the activities of numerous secret circles, reached its peak by 1866, when Karakozov, a student, fired at the Czar as he was riding through the capital. Karakozov was hanged, and, although his attempt was an individual action without accomplices, innumerable arrests were made throughout the country. To be found in possession of a photograph of Chernyshevsky was enough to send a man to prison. The government reverted to an openly reactionary policy. The Socialist-Populists in their turn adopted revolutionary and terroristic tactics, which made the 'seventies a period of desperate underground activity.

'Russia is being thrust toward a catastrophe,' wrote Alexander Herzen: 'my heart bleeds at this sad spectacle.' (pp. 210-18)

Marc Slonim, *"The Critics and the Nihilists,"* in his The Epic of Russian Literature: From Its Origins through Tolstoy, *Oxford University Press, 1950, pp. 203-18.*

E. LAMPERT

[In the following excerpt from Sons against Fathers: Studies in Russian Radicalism and Revolution *(1965), a critical history of the Civic Critics, Lampert delineates the Nihilist components of Pisarev's critical essays, arguing that his ideological stance lies somewhere between that of Turgenev and Chernyshevsky.]*

Among the men of the sixties, Pisarev belonged to the ex-

treme champions of the human person against the encroachments of the environment, of that very objective world of phenomena, conditioned, caused, determined. . . . It is this
world that stood in danger from Pisarev's plea for the human
world of 'free subjectivity'. Indeed, it stood in danger from
his own acute rationalistic mind, assailed by the sinister
charms of untrammelled human existence, even while producing the mechanistic conviction that it was nothing but an
elaborate calculating machine.

In a later essay on the conflict between Church and State in
medieval Europe Pisarev wrote: 'Despite my respect for general causes, I must state categorically that the major conflict
between the emperors and the popes which had such far-
reaching consequences was brought about by the personality
of the monk Hildebrand. And it seems to me that his personality was not only the occasion but the actual cause of the
conflict.' Without its impact 'the conflict might not have aris-
en at all, and the whole history of European civilization
would have taken another, unknown course'. The shape of
Cleopatra's nose, after all, influenced not only wars but civilizations. And Pisarev proceeds to insert a question mark
against the cast-iron determinism of the scientific evolution
of mankind that he held in such high esteem: 'How far', he
asks, 'does the impact of man's individual spirit and character impinge on the general course of historical events? The
question is of the utmost importance and difficulty: It has not
been solved and cannot be solved with monolithic simplicity.'

It is true that such questions arose in Pisarev's mind chiefly
when dealing with matters of history. 'The natural sciences',
he wrote, 'must not be on any account identified with history,
although Buckle attempts to reduce both to a common denominator. In history everything is in the idea, everything is
in the person. . . . In natural science everything is in the
fact. . . .' And this led him to an insistence on the priority
of ideas and intellectual attitudes in a historian's account of
human affairs. Yet even here Pisarev failed to be consistent.
His frequent protests against the cultivation of science divorced from human ends made him push historical causes,
like everything else, into the sphere of material facts. 'Cold
and hunger!', he exclaims. 'It is these two simple causes
which explain all the real sufferings of mankind, all the vicissitudes of history, all the crimes of individuals and all the immorality of social relations.' It was the business of science to
deal with these material facts and to deduce valid action from
their analysis. But, by the same token, science and the work
of scientists were not, for Pisarev, something apart from their
conduct as human beings. He realized that the clash and
combination of human agencies were not so dispassionate a
matter as the combination of chemical substances. In the end,
it proved blasphemous to bottle the infinite variety of life even
in scientific jars, prepared by professionals claiming 'a monopoly of learning and oracular authority'. True, the value
of science remained unimpaired, but primarily as a means of
fostering 'the cold criticism of the sceptical mind', as an abro-
gation of pre-scientific wisdom and humility, of intellectual
passivity and wonder. Apart from this, science, too, turned
into a 'beautiful anachronism'. Even Comte, whom Pisarev
admired, is urged to watch the spectacle of science with less
of the reverence appropriate to a Church and with more of
the freedom of the spirit appropriate to those who promote
'the cause of denial', from which Comte and Buckle alike
were as far removed as possible, and whose object could not
in any case be scientific in the sense of 'undeniable'. 'Denial',
'nihilism' was perhaps the only cause in which Pisarev found

complete self-expression and where his mind did not wander
into a kind of universal schizophrenia.

The term 'nihilism', though applied to some rationalists in
the Middle Ages, and later to various 'negative' trends among
the French Encyclopædists, has become a term of abuse. A
French dictionary published in the latter half of the last century defined a nihilist as 'une personne non civilisée' ['an uncivilized person']; an English dictionary about the same time
preferred the description 'a worldly, dissipated, riotous person'; while Bismarck announced in the German *Reichstag* in
1884 that 'der russische Nihilismus ist eine . . . Abart des
Fortschritts' ['Russian nihilism is a . . . degenerate variety
of progress']. In Russia, Pushkin had already been nick-
named 'nihilist' by his adversaries. To judge from the caricatures of the official Russian press of the sixties, a nihilist represented something akin to a contemporary version of a 'beat-
nik'. A report of the Third Section gave the following description of the species, or rather of its female representative: 'She
has cropped hair, wears blue glasses, is slovenly in her dress,
rejects the use of comb and soap, and lives in civil matrimony
with an equally repellent individual of the male sex or with
several such.' The Russian promoters of the terror of established moral and political principle saw this appearance as
leading in some obscure way to the established principle of
terror itself, and 'nihilism' became the shibboleth attached to
Russian revolutionaries, especially, though quite improperly,
to those of the terrorist wing.

In literature . . . the term was first introduced by Turgenev
in *Fathers and Sons,* to describe a new type among the intelligentsia—men who, in the words of one of the novel's characters (Arkady), 'bow before no authority of any kind, and accept no faith, no principle, whatever veneration surrounds it'.
But few among Pisarev's contemporaries understood the significance of nihilism better than Herzen, although some nihilists, particularly the nihilistic *émigrés* in Geneva who spent
their time in badgering him, roused his resentment. 'What a
pity', Herzen wrote to Ogarev at the beginning of 1868, 'that
I have come to know properly this Maccabaeus of Petersburg
nihilism [Pisarev] so late. This is where true awareness and
vindication of oneself lies—spoken out not by a fool or a
wretch, but by a keen-sighted young man.' Earlier on, he
wrote that 'nihilism is a remarkable phenomenon in the intellectual history of Russia':

> 'Nihilism' is force of logic without restraint; it is
> science without dogma; it is unconditional alle-
> giance to experience and a ready acceptance of all
> consequences, wherever they may lead. . . . Nihil-
> ism does not turn 'something' into 'nothing', but
> shows that 'nothing' that has been taken for 'some-
> thing' is an optical illusion, and that every truth,
> however it contradicts our comfortable notions, is
> more wholesome than they are. Whether the name
> be appropriate or not does not matter. We are ac-
> customed to it. It is accepted by friend and foe, it
> has become a police label, it has become a denunci-
> ation, an insult with some, a word of praise with
> others. . . . When Belinsky, on hearing a friend's
> lengthy explanation to the effect that 'Mind' attains
> self-consciousness in man, indignantly replied: 'So,
> I am not supposed to be conscious on my own be-
> half but on behalf of 'Mind'! . . . But why should
> I be taken advantage of ? I'd better not be conscious
> at all. What do I care for the 'Mind's' conscious-
> ness?'—when he said this, he spoke as a *nihilist.*
> When Bakunin convicted the Berlin professors of
> being frightened by negation, and the Parisian rev-

olutionaries of conservatism, he was a *nihilist* in the fullest sense. . . . When the Petrashevskists went to forced labour for seeking, in the words of their sentence, 'to overthrow all divine and human laws and destroy the foundations of society' . . . they were *nihilists*.

This may also be taken as a summary of Pisarev's position. But his nihilism had an accent of its own, and its moral and intellectual setting was a personal one. It contained, broadly speaking, three elements. In his early writings, particularly in 'The Scholasticism of the Nineteenth Century', but also in the later 'Our Academic Learning', nihilism was predominantly intellectual and critical. It was a form of scepticism carried to the point of iconoclasm, in his attitude to axioms, dogmas, and to everything that had been taken for granted. The troubles of man were analysed by him in this connexion mainly as under-education, starved imagination, privation of light, and so on. This was linked with an open-mindedness that verged on naïve credulity towards new concepts, especially scientific concepts, which seemed to hold out a promise to Pisarev's search for new forms of life. The credulity served to enhance the force of denial: it involved a regression to a more primitive level, quite unknown to Herzen, a new innocence of perception liberated from the cataract of all traditional ideas, a kind of 'drawing back to take a better leap'. At this point, Pisarev showed none of that sense of the hopeless suffering of the people which filled Chernyshevsky and Dobrolyubov with an urge for destruction; and it had little in common with the moral convictions in which their rebellion was set. But it was also devoid of any note of disillusionment of the kind which makes a creed out of necessity and accuses life of nothingness, from ceaseless brooding on man's terrible fate. Pisarev intellectualized: hence the contempt for fluff and flurry, the acid manner, the urge to expose authoritative ideas and utterances to intellectual ignominy. Frequently, an imp of youthful mischief broke out from the spirit of denial, although his personal biography shows that underneath there ran a dark stream of unrest and self-searching to the point of self-destruction. As mental revolt against all kinds of intellectual values his nihilism threatened not so much the prevailing social and political order as this order's balance of mind. But in this Pisarev went further than any of his contemporaries.

> If authority proves mendacious [he wrote in a celebrated passage], doubt will destroy it, and this will do immense good. If it should prove indispensable or useful, doubt will subject it to radical criticism and re-instate it. In a word, here is our ultimatum: what can be smashed, must be smashed. What stands the blow is good; what flies into smithereens is rubbish. In any case, hit out right and left: no harm will or can come of it.

It is a mystery how the 'ultimatum' could have passed the censor. It caused jubilation among the young radicals whose mood it reflected, and extreme confusion in the Censorship Department. The liberal censor Nikitenko was beside himself. His *démarche* against the 'Russian Word', and Pisarev in particular, provoked the latter's biting remark that his opponents sought 'to make literature a department of the police'. He also wrote about reactions in the Moscow press: 'It pleases me that my ideas displease the Muscovite pundits, and I am sure that many writers wish, as I do, to provide the 'Russian Messenger' [Katkov's paper] with as many opportunities as possible to display its peevishness.' However, he added a plea for the negators, and for the reasons that drove

them to negate: they were, he said, up against 'the tragic enthralment of Russian thought'.

The other elements of nihilism appear in Pisarev's examination of two literary characters—Turgenev's Bazarov and Chernyshevsky's Rakhmetov—and in his 'destruction of aesthetics'. . . . [It] will be convenient to isolate here from his treatment of the two literary characters the specifically nihilistic features.

In his essay on 'Bazarov', written in 1862, Pisarev deliberately presented nihilism without regard to any sensibilities. The Bazarovs 'lend themselves to no compromise and no hopes of any kind'. They are 'strangers', not because they are victims of circumstances, but because they are men who have consciously expelled themselves from their surroundings and circumstances and whose isolation is evidence of freedom. They are 'lonely individuals', deprived of the support of the multitude, deprived even of much pride in the existence of the self, but sticking stubbornly, none the less, to their independence. Their nihilism excludes every attitude that is likely to serve as a prop to confidence. Even denial is denied if it is sustained by love of the image which it destroys, or if it becomes a satisfying edifice to dwell in. Their pursuit of scientific knowledge is a form of 'hygiene', directed towards the elimination of any odd entity which can be found cumbering man's free thought and his ability to see reality as it is. 'Nature', Pisarev says, 'must be explored. Instead, we enter into pathetic relations with her, we lose time in wonder, we obfuscate our minds with all sorts of illusory images, in which some claim to discover beauty, others consolation, still others even meaning and logic.'

Bazarov's free-thinking, as Pisarev presents it, is remote from the secure and balanced rationalism of the eighteenth century. He lacks the optimistic belief of the men of the Enlightenment in their own age and civilization, their historical self-satisfaction, their sense of prestige and status. And, though Pisarev commended Voltaire and Diderot for not having felt 'the slightest pity or sympathy for the things they negated and destroyed', he ascribed to them a nihilism that would have filled them with despondency. True, Pisarev's nihilism did not at this stage amount to a doctrine of social and political revolt. But instead of being, as before, merely or mainly an extreme form of scepticism, it became a kind of denuded amoral morality, in which human acts appear as arbitrary gestures: Bazarov 'thinks what he wills to think' and 'does what he chooses to do'. He is completely independent even of the few things he believes in. He deliberately suppresses his moral imagination; he is tough and matter-of-fact; and the daring defiance of any real or imaginary gods is replaced by the habit of doing without either the gods or the stimulus of defying them.

Pisarev was anxious not to turn nihilism into a romantic posture, which is often only a form of dramatized opportunism. He examined it with simple exactitude and a remarkable absence of emotion. 'Denial', he said, 'is a hard, tedious and deadly task.' The earnestness as well as the vigour with which he denied saved Pisarev from being just an iconoclast swinging a sword at respectable opinions. As it was, his nihilism even became a heroic creed, an exhortation to live with one's ailments, to master one's plight in an imperfect world by being aware of it. It could not heal wounds, nor, as the fate of Turgenev's Bazarov showed, remove the bitterness of death. It was, in Pisarev's words, nothing more than 'stark realism'. Its only apparent moral or social reference consisted in that it marked a turning inside out of falsehoods which had lasted for centuries and on which it took revenge through Bazarovian extremes of discourtesy: 'a malady, perhaps', Pisarev said, 'but a malady of our time which we must live through', 'a pathological phenomenon, as pathological as the world which [the nihilist] denies'. But even the exposure of falsehood entailed no sense of tragedy, which, to be absorbed, calls for pity, terror, and forgiveness. 'Much may change with time', Pisarev concluded, 'but . . . we have, meanwhile, to console ourselves with the supremely fruitless realization that we do to a certain extent comprehend the incongruity of life.' " 'And that is nihilism?' ", he ends by asking in the words of Bazarov's outraged interlocutor. " 'That is nihilism", Bazarov [and Pisarev] repeated, this time with pointed insolence.'

The conclusion suggests a moral and social wasteland—the nemesis perhaps of an inveterate rationalist at the end of his tether, grasping nothing at all and ignorant of what he is to do. In point of fact, Pisarev was more or less confident and more or less successful in grasping reality, and he claimed that nihilism leads in the end to a discovery of true humanity and even of true social relations. The connexion was never properly worked out by him: paradox continued to have its arresting effect on him. Broadly speaking, the connexion was indicated by a shift of emphasis from nihilism to revolution, from a feeling that the old world was doomed to a realization that it must be changed. Revolutionary elements can be found in Pisarev's early writings, notably in the document which was responsible for his imprisonment. Admittedly, such elements referred in the main to his concern for the liberation of the human mind. They owed little to any positive examination of contemporary social problems. But even those who pursue, as Pisarev pursued, destruction by 'hitting right and left' cannot fail to create: it suffices to create new words and new valuations in order in the long run to create new things. In any case, the new things were already emerging; the settled habits of thought and behaviour against which Pisarev maintained an incessant protest had begun already to be shaken by the rapid differentiation and disintegration of post-Reform Russian society. The function of the rebel was becoming significantly different by being more self-controlled and less arbitrary. Furthermore, Pisarev could not eliminate in himself the moral fervour which he condemned in others but which impelled him to seek a reconciliation between 'egotism and altruism'. Even his ambivalent attitude to the impersonal forces at work in life, in which, none the less, man remained conscious of his own free will and rationality and ability to change it, had obvious moral and social implications. Even science to him was not so much research as application of research to purposes which were moral, a way of behaviour taking place in human society, rather than a mere method of understanding the mechanics of the world.

All this prepared the transition from nihilism to social revolution, and it found its symbolic expression in that Pisarev turned his attention from Bazarov to Rakhmetov. There is some evidence that Chernyshevsky himself conceived his novel *What Is to Be Done?* as a kind of counterblast to Turgenev's *Fathers and Sons*. It will be remembered that the latter caused surprise and indignation to some radicals, particularly those around the 'Contemporary', for Bazarov was taken to be a deliberate caricature of the 'sons' precisely on account of those extreme nihilistic and egotistic features with which Turgenev endowed him and which Pisarev extolled. Chernyshevsky's Rakhmetov, who does not stand artistic compar-

ison with Turgenev's hero, shares some of the latter's characteristics. But, unlike Bazarov, he is first and foremost a revolutionary, dedicated to the subversion of the existing order: he is a man without a private past, present, or future, without emotional needs and satisfactions; he is completely and selflessly identified with the fate of his fellow men. Pisarev tried to draw a kind of composite portrait, combining the nihilism and individualistic non-conformity of Bazarov with the revolutionary socialism and sense of solidarity of Rakhmetov. He did this in an essay entitled 'The New Type' (*Novyi tip*) or 'The Thinking Proletariat' (*Myslyashchii proletariat*) and written in prison in 1865. Its ostensible aim was to examine and commend Chernyshevsky's novel, but it can be regarded as a definitive statement of his own beliefs. (pp. 308-16)

E. Lampert, "Dimitry Pisarev (1840-1868)," in his Sons against Fathers: Studies in Russian Radicalism and Revolution, *Oxford at the Clarendon Press, 1965, pp. 295-316.*

NIHILISM AND THE RUSSIAN NOVEL: TURGENEV AND DOSTOEVSKY

CHARLES I. GLICKSBERG

[*In the following excerpt from his critical survey* The Literature of Nihilism *(1975), Glicksberg discusses the principles of Russian Nihilism and notes Nihilist themes in novels by Turgenev.*]

The nihilist is a man in perpetual conflict with himself. One day, he knows not quite how it happened, he finds himself convinced of the fact that his life is utterly without meaning or purpose. For him this fact, however shattering its impact, constitutes an incontrovertible truth. This nadaistic epiphany did not come upon him suddenly; it was a slow, cumulative growth, like the insidious spread of cancer in the human body. Once the metaphysical infection set in, there was no arresting its malignant advance.

The curious thing about this process of inner conversion to a nihilist position is that the postulant who joins this order does not immediately question the truth of his belief. It is for him a universal, not a narrowly personal or neurotic truth. All men, he feels certain, are secretly of this persuasion, though they try to hide it from themselves. They are guilty of bad faith. They embrace consolatory faiths, they hail the promise of supernatural reward for all the suffering they have had to endure on earth, or they invent some myth that celebrates the glory and fullness of life and somehow manages to deny the reality of death.

But no man is a nihilist for long before a violent reaction sets in. He begins to fight against his recurrent moods of fatalistic despair. He has lost all incentives for living. The sky, as far as his eye can reach, is dark and overcast. Spiritually paralyzed like one of the living dead, he attempts to overcome this unbearable condition of life-in-death by resorting to a logical ploy. It is a contradiction in terms to argue that everything in the last resort is meaningless. If that is so, then his belief that everything is absurd is a questionable if not erroneous assumption. The grounds on which he based his nihilistic faith prove treacherous. But this is not enough to change his mind for good. He resists the mandate of logic by the simple Pascalian expedient of asserting that logic is not the ruler of life. He remains stricken, disconsolate, not to be comforted. Let others partake of whatever nostrums are offered them; he will refuse to blind himself to the truth of being: the truth of ultimate nothingness. To assume that existence is a fortuitous, purposeless explosion of biological energy is to commit intellectual suicide; it is to reduce man, the one creature who strives persistently toward the goal of transcendence, to the same order of importance as the amoeba, the worm, and the ant. It is to strip him completely of a sense of destiny.

The literary nihilists constitute an aberrant and self-defeating minority. Their situation is indeed a hopeless one. Despairing (though they profess to have gone beyond despair) and desperate, yet not knowing what to do if they are to save themselves, they have no alternative but to reject everything that makes up the body of values mankind cherishes in life. In doing so, they leave themselves exposed to the charge of sheer irrationality. This does not disturb them in the least, for the irrational reaches to the very heart of their complaint: the death of God, the total absence of purpose, the absurdity of a universe that manifests no concern for the fate of man. Despite the teleological pattern some philosophers are able to piece together, there is no good reason for the experiment of life on earth—none that the mind of the nihilist can grasp.

Nihilism goes beyond the most extreme form of pessimism, for the pessimist still adheres to some standard. He simply finds that life fails to measure up to the human ideal. Death is an outrage to which he cannot reconcile himself. Even if he recommends universal suicide, he does so for the sake of relieving men of senseless suffering. But the nihilist repudiates all standards—reason, ideals, purpose, meaning, truth. Hence he cannot take anything seriously. Love is a biological illusion, the quest for fame is an expression of vanity, the ambitious projects men undertake are designed to hide the emptiness of existence. Trapped in this state of utter disenchantment, he lacks the incentive to act. If he goes on living, it is because he cannot summon up the energy to take his own life. Besides, he realizes that individual suicide is an absurd and futile gesture: it solves no problem.

He is like Stavrogin, Dostoevski's nihilistic hero, devoid of will. He has no aim in life. He is tormented by his vision of the void, the *néant,* nada, the Nothing. The secret of his being is that he is bored by the spectacle life has to offer. He is alienated from his fellow men by his contempt for human nature's daily food. He suffers from the spleen, from acedia, the deadly sin of sloth. He abides by no moral law. He blows neither hot nor cold. Maurice Friedman, in *Problematic Rebel,* declares:

> The secret of Stavrogin's boredom and his passionless indifference lies, more than anything, in the fact that he is not only cut off and detached but irreparably divided. He cannot do anything with his whole being and his whole heart. One part of him always looks on as the bored and listless observer, knowing that there is no extreme that can ever catch him up in such a way that he may really give himself to anyone or lose himself in anything.

But Dostoevski's nihilists—the obsessed atheist Kirillov, "this maniac of a theophobe whose suicide is a protest against God's world" and Ivan Karamazov, the rebel who believes that "everything is permissible"—do not conform to a single

Ivan Turgenev

fixed pattern. Ivan, in many of his rebellious utterances, gives expression to "the essence of Russian nihilistic atheism." The Russian nihilist in the second half of the nineteenth century was infected with a skepticism that poisoned his system and blighted his whole life. "The nihilistic superman recognizes no ethical truths, rejects all moral codes: nothing at all can be denied him." He is the Man-God, satanic in his revolt, but his hubristic presumption in seeking to gain mastery over life and death results in a despair so extreme that it leads him to commit suicide. Dostoevski here confesses the split in his own being. He interprets nihilism not as a subversive philosophy imported from abroad but as a diabolical temptation that dwells in the breast of Russian intellectuals.

The nihilist is thus caught in the trap set and sprung by his own contradictions. In condemning life for its lack of purpose, he is betraying a religious hunger for ultimate meaning, but it is a metaphysical hunger which, on his terms, he can never hope to satisfy. He can deal with this problem in one of four ways. He can remain indifferent to it, deliberately ignoring, like the logical positivists, what cannot be solved. The scientist keeps silent about that which cannot be known. Or he can adopt a despairing hedonism, seeking to live feverishly in the present moment. Or, like Unamuno, he can affirm a transcendental faith in the face of all rational objections, creating the God he needs in order to triumph over death. Or, like Kafka, he can reject the Absolute and the world in an ironic gesture of impotence. Or he can revolt against the myth of the absurd by means of a humanistic affirmation of solidarity with mankind. In the last case, the nihilist realizes that if life is to have any positive meaning it must be one that man himself imposes on it. In this way he is able to fulfill his destiny, instead of being the architect of his own misfortunes. He does so without necessarily compromising his nihilist principles. Whatever may be the fate meted out to the race of man in the fullness of time, he will bear his existential burden in the problematical present and summon up the courage, like his forbears, to create art as well as shape the course of his own life. Perpetually confronted by the precariousness of existence, the nihilist who, in literature or life, seeks authenticity of being, never shuts the door completely on hope.

Throughout the course of history, from the dawn of civilization, man has recurrently harbored the suspicion that life is a cruel and hideous joke, a meaningless episode in a meaningless dream. Resigned to this knowledge, the Oriental mind transforms nothingness into an absolute, making a veritable religion out of Nirvana, the blessed symbol of ultimate nonbeing. The texture of reality was woven of the stuff of illusion. The West countered the threat of nothingness by adopting the Christian mythos that promised the gift of immortality to mortal man. When the myth collapsed, when belief in God as a causal agent in the arena of history largely vanished, the Christian ideal was secularized, supplanted by the Promethean goal of striving for mastery of the world of Nature. The cult of progress was best exemplified in the Marxianized version of the Kingdom Come finally established in Soviet Russia.

Yet it was Russia that, paradoxically, was the generative ground of both nihilism and revolutionary messianism. It gave birth to the superfluous man and the positive hero, to Oblomov and Bazarov. Though Turgenev held that he coined the term *nihilism,* it was used as far back as 1790 in Germany. Though the term *nihilism* existed long before Turgenev made it popular, it was not used in the sense ascribed to it in *Fathers and Sons* until the eighteen sixties. The new generation was radical in its demands, impatient of intellectuals who theorized but failed to act. The young critics Chernyshevski, Dobrolyubov, and Pisarev used literature as a springboard for trenchant sociological preachment. Art was meant to serve the cause of political emancipation and social betterment. The Russian nihilists were political extremists who fought to establish a better life for the masses. Not that they went to extreme lengths in carrying out their program. They believed, most of them, in a future socialist or anarchist society. Thus their negativism was, in fact, balanced by a positive, if vaguely formulated, hope. According to Moser, the basic tenet of the nihilistic outlook in the sixties was "a positivist, monistic philosophical materialism, in most cases fading into 'scientism' (a belief that all philosophical problems not already resolved through the researches of natural science would eventually be solved and that, necessarily, in a materialist sense)" [see excerpt by Moser above]. The nihilist movement in Russia was influenced by the work of Auguste Comte, Charles Darwin, and Ludwig Büchner. Büchner labored to demolish the pretensions of idealism and religion. Thus, to the regnant faith in materialism and utilitarianism, the nihilists added the evangelical motif of atheism. Chernyshevski boldly proclaimed his adherence to atheism. The Russian nihilists drew the logical conclusion that if God did not exist, a new basis for ethics, not grounded in supernatural revelation, had to be found. Fourier's influence, which had been strong in the forties, still persisted. Chernyshevski's commune, described in his didactic novel *What Is to Be Done?,* was intended to start a movement of communal living that could spread throughout the world. The novel he composed drew the portrait of "the new man," the positive hero who would inherit the socialist world of the future. The nihilist as secular saint is embodied in the character of Rakhmetov, who lives abstemiously like the poor, though not abandoning his sole luxury—a cigar.

Russian nihilism promulgated a methodological skepticism. It hailed scientific naturalism as the sovereign method of arriving at the truth—that is the chief identifying characteristic of the nihilistic concept among the Russian intelligentsia, which distinguished it from the philosophical nihilism of a Schopenhauer or Nietzsche. Though the doctrine embraced positivism and the ideal of scientific exactitude, in practice the writers who accepted the doctrine became accusers of the established order. Believing as they did that science offered the best available means of attaining salvation, the Bazarovs of Russia warred against the abstract, the metaphysical, the mystical; the truth they believed in was always concrete, factual, and practical. Inspired by the work of Comte, John Stuart Mill, Taine, Littré, Büchner, Moleschott, and Vogt, especially the last three, they exalted the figure of the natural scientist, the Prometheus of the modern age. They also derived ideological support for their outlook from Darwin's theory of evolution and from the writings of Feuerbach and Stirner.

The philosophy of materialism, which led to atheism, strengthened the critical spirit in the nihilists to such a degree that they questioned all things. As Masaryk remarks [in his *Spirit of Russia,* excerpted below]: "Atheism and materialism are at once preconditions and logical consequences of nihilist criticism and negation." On the whole, however, nihilism in Russia was social and political in character; it aimed to overthrow the absolutism of the Czar and the power of the theocracy. Not until the appearance of Andreyev was nihilism couched in metaphysical terms. The Russian nihilists, whose portrait Turgenev drew faithfully with a mixture of sympathy and distaste, never gave way to despair; they submitted to a kind of revolutionary discipline; in conformity with their ruling mystique of "the people," they sought to identify themselves with the peasants. "Since the sixties, nihilism had become the question of questions for thoughtful Russians—and for thoughtful Europeans."

Fathers and Sons introduces a tragic protagonist. It was Turgenev's fundamental belief, which shaped his aesthetic of fiction, that there existed a tragic element in every human being. As he declared: "we are all condemned to die. Can there be anything more tragic than that?" The pessimism that informs his major novels grows out of his constant awareness that the most precious achievement of the history of culture, the development of the unique human personality, is negated by the doom of death. Turgenev asked himself repeatedly what lay beyond the grave. Perhaps nothing but the void. Like Bazarov, he realized that Nature was unaffected by the aspirations and ideals of humanity. Bazarov, a man of strong will, is unsparing in his search for knowledge, yet it avails him naught: he must perish at the end. Turgenev, though himself not a rebel, admired the heroic individual. Unlike Dostoevski, he wanted the truth, not the assurance of salvation. When the novel was published, a storm of detraction broke out, the reactionaries seizing on the invidious term *nihilism* as their target for a heavy barrage of abuse.

In focusing attention on the difficult problem the Russian intellectual then faced, his role in life and his relation to society. Turgenev anticipated the modern dilemma. He had arrived at the conclusion that life was not made for happiness. Freedom of will was but an illusion. His Schopenhauerian *Weltanschauung* is evident in his interpretation of Nature as indifferent to human hopes and needs. The individual counts for naught; he vanishes, leaving no trace behind him, as if to confirm the lesson of his utter insignificance in the cosmic scheme of things. No matter how beautiful Nature appears at times, it oppresses man with the sense of his own mortality. Whatever fate befalls man, Nature remains imperturbable, unmoved by his quest for ultimate meaning. Turgenev offers no hope of redemption through Christ. Death is incontestably the victor in every encounter with the human adventurer; whatever fulfillment man is able to attain lasts but a moment and then is rudely taken away. Death, the conqueror, wins every battle. Bazarov, like the Communist protagonists in *Man's Fate,* attaches no importance to his own personality; he tries hard to be self-sufficient. Since he believes in nothing, he must believe in himself as God. Freeborn points out: "Bazarov, the nihilist, has no belief beyond himself, no will greater than his own, and in this self-sufficiency he exhibits that 'bottomless abyss' of arrogance and self-will which is characteristic of the man-God." He recognizes no higher law. Once death overtakes him, then he ceases to be; there is no resurrection.

This is a recurrent motif in Turgenev's work. In *On the Eve* (1859), Turgenev introduced the character of a patriot, Insarov, who is unlike Bazarov or Rudin, the dreamer and enthusiast. Turgenev foreshadows the death of this Bulgarian hero. This is how Yelena, the Russian woman whom Insarov has married, broods while he is ill:

> why is there such a thing as death, why is there parting, sickness, and tears? Or otherwise why is there this beauty, this sweet feeling of hope, why the reassuring consciousness of a firm refuge, of constant defence, immortal protection? What is the meaning of this smiling, benedictory heaven, this happy, quietly resting earth? Or is it all really only within us, while outside us is eternal cold and silence? Are we really alone—alone—and out there, everywhere, in all those inaccessible abysses and depths—everything, everything is alien to us?

Here, as in other novels he wrote, Turgenev ends on the note that death comes to all. In *Smoke* (1886), the hero, Litvinov, realizes the evanescence of life; everything human and particularly everything Russian seemed as fugitive as smoke. It was while depicting the suffering of his characters that Turgenev voiced his perception of the perishability of all things beautiful, the impassivity of Nature, the defeat of man by powers he cannot cope with. Nevertheless, affirming his faith in man, Turgenev underlined the importance of the individual self. He insisted that he was not prejudiced against his hero, Bazarov. In striving to capture the truth of the imagination, he had to include bad as well as good traits. (pp. 74-82)

> Charles I. Glicksberg, "Nihilism in the Russian Soul," in his The Literature of Nihilism, *Bucknell University Press, 1975, pp. 73-94.*

WILLIAM C. BRUMFIELD

[*In a comparative analysis of Turgenev's* Fathers and Sons *and Vasily Slepcov's novel* Hard Times, *Brumfield argues that Turgenev's characterization of the Nihilist Bazarov ultimately derives from the Romantic individualism of the 1830s and 1840s.*]

In his essay "Bazarov Again" ("Ešče raz Bazarov," 1862), Alexander Herzen writes: "This mutual interaction of people and books is a strange thing. A book takes its whole shape from the society that spawns it, then generalizes the material, renders it clearer and sharper, and as a consequence reality

is transformed." It is generally accepted that in Russia the mutual interaction of people and books has been intense, particularly in the realm of social and political commentary, and there is, no doubt, considerable truth in Herzen's observation that under such conditions "real people take on the character of their literary shadows." Whether or not young Russians after 1862 were "almost all out of *What Is to Be Done?* with the addition of a few of Bazarov's traits," such was frequently assumed to be the case, as the statements of critics and political activists attest. Dmitrij Pisarev, for example, in an article entitled "We Shall See" ("Posmotrim," 1865), raises the specter of hundreds of Bazarovs: "the Bazarov type is growing constantly, not by days, but by the hour, in life as well as in literature." But as Herzen recognized, Pisarev's Bazarov owes more to the critic's own vision of the Russian intelligentsia than to the text of *Fathers and Sons:* "Whether Pisarev understood Turgenev's Bazarov correctly does not concern me. What is important is that he recognized *himself* and *others like him* in Bazarov and supplied what was lacking in the book."

Many of the novel's exegetes have continued to supply "what was lacking" in order to portray Bazarov as a representative of radical tendencies in the sixties. And yet Bazarov is defined to a much greater degree by a literary archetype deriving from European Romanticism and clearly delineated in certain of Turgenev's earliest writings. The case for this derivation can be made within Turgenev's works, but the extent to which it forms his portrayal of the nihilist is all the more clearly revealed when one compares *Fathers and Sons* (*Otcy i deti,* 1862) with another novel written during the same period and centered around a similar (that is, radical) protagonist. Its author, Vasilij Slepcov, was well known for his participation in radical causes during the sixties (as the fame of his Petersburg commune attests), and he presumably had a more intimate knowledge of the radical milieu than did Turgenev. Furthermore Slepcov, who began his career as a writer in the early sixties, lacked the Romantic apprenticeship which was to have such a pervasive influence on Turgenev's later work. Consequently, in his novel *Hard Times* (*Trudnoe vremja,* published in *Sovremennik,* 1864), Slepcov presents the Russian radical from a different literary perspective.

The similarity between *Fathers and Sons* and *Hard Times* was first noted, appropriately enough, by Pisarev, in an article entitled "Flourishing Humanity" ("Podrastajuščaja gumannost," 1865). Pisarev characterizes Slepcov's protagonist, Rjazanov, as "one of the brilliant representatives of my beloved Bazarov type." Although one might question the accuracy of this statement, the resemblance between the two protagonists certainly provides a basis for comparison. Both Bazarov and Rjazanov are *raznočincy* (the latter a priest's son), disaffected intellectuals who intend to destroy so that others may build, although neither is certain as to how the destruction will occur or who will do the building. Both represent the rise of a new class and a new military in Russia's educational system. Both are products of the urban intellectual milieu—although their origins link them to the provinces of central Russia ("Rjazanov"). Both are intruders in a rural backwater, which is itself beset with problems of social reform.

On this last point even the details correspond: the principle landowners in both novels—Nikolaj Kirsanov and Ščetinin—attempt to introduce agricultural improvements and reforms in their dealings with the peasants, but their efforts are viewed with suspicion by neighboring landowners and with indifference by the peasants (a reaction familiar to Tolstoj's repentant landowners). Kirsanov and Ščetinin are swindled by their laborers and are baffled by their ignorance, superstition, and resistance to the reforms. Descriptions of rural poverty are frequent, particularly in *Hard Times,* while attempts to implement a rational system of agricultural productivity are continually frustrated. (In both works a new threshing machine, purchased at great expense, proves too heavy for local conditions.) The similarity extends to the physical setting as well: the same dilapidated church, the same peasant huts clustered in a village near a manor house with the same arbors and acacias.

Once placed in this setting, both protagonists are led into a situation which pits their urban radicalism against a form of gentry liberalism. As would be expected, each novelist relies heavily on dialogue to develop a conflict which arises from ideological antagonism, but there is a difference in the function of these verbal confrontations. In *Hard Times* they so dominate the core of the work that plot is relatively unimportant and the narrator's comments are little more than extended stage directions. In *Fathers and Sons,* which has a plot of greater complexity, the narrator's intrusions direct the reader's perception of events, while ideological arguments serve primarily to motivate a course of action which eventually has little to do with ideology. Nevertheless, both works begin with a similar conflict, and they present it in much the same terms.

From the moment Pavel Kirsanov first hears the word "nihilist," until Bazarov's interview with Odincova in chapter sixteen, Turgenev's radical periodically expresses views which cannot be reconciled with the idea of social progress through gradual reform. Bazarov's political rhetoric is too well known to require lengthy quotation, but two passages—both in chapter ten—are particularly close to the views Rjazanov will express in *Hard Times.* In the first Bazarov dismisses the vocabulary of liberalism (as expressed by Pavel Kirsanov): "Aristocracy, liberalism, progress, principles . . . if you think about it, how many foreign . . . and useless words!" In the second, he makes one of the most common accusations directed against Russian liberalism—its inability to act:

> Then we figured out that talking, always talking about our sores wasn't worth the effort, that it only led to banality and doctrinairism. We saw that even our smart ones, so-called progressive people and exposers of abuses, were fit for nothing; that we were occupied with nonsense, were harping about some sort of art, unconscious creativity, parliamentarianism, the legal profession, and the devil knows what else, while it's a question of daily bread. . . .

In one passage from *Hard Times* Rjazanov develops a similar argument as he explains to Ščetinin's wife the uselessness of progressive articles she has been reading:

> You see, it's all the same. You have these signs, and on them its written 'Russian Truth' or 'White Swan.' So you go looking for a white swan—but it's a tavern. In order to read these books and understand them, you have to be practiced. . . . If you have a fresh mind and you pick up one of these books, then you really will see white swans: schools, and courts, and constitutions, and prostitutions, and Magna Chartas, and the devil knows what else. . . . But if you look into the matter, you'll see that it's nothing but a carry-out joint.

In the same vein Bazarov states that "at the present time, negation is the most useful action," that before construction "the ground has to be cleared", while Rjazanov gives Ščetinina a paraphrase of one of his radical pamphlets: "If you want to build a temple, first take measures so that the enemy cavalry doesn't use it as a stable." When Ščetinina asks, what is to be done, Rjazanov answers: " 'All that's left is to think up, to create a new life; but until then . . .' he waved his hand." Rjazanov's manner of expression may be earthier than Bazarov's, yet the ideas are the same. Bazarov's rage against useless talk notwithstanding, neither radical goes beyond the rhetoric of frustration.

But however similar that rhetoric, the ensuing development reveals a fundamental difference between the novels. Turgenev, it would seem, is less interested in Bazarov the nihilist (understood as a product of ideology) than in Bazarov the Romantic rebel. For by the middle of *Fathers and Sons* the ideological element begins to recede and it becomes clear that Bazarov's radical views, rather than determining his actions, have served to establish a position of isolation from which he can offer his challenge to the order of the universe. Turgenev has endowed his hero with a matrix of current political opinions, only to lead him toward a confrontation between his "fathomless" ego and his "intimation of mortality"—a confrontation inherent in Bazarov's aggressive determination to understand the essence of nature through a type of scientific materialism. If in his challenge Bazarov has lost a sense of oneness with nature (the talisman scene), Turgenev effects a final reconciliation which in itself implies a Romantic view of the unity between man and nature—or a longing for that unity:

> However passionate, sinning, and rebellious the heart concealed in the tomb, the flowers growing over it look at us serenely (*bezmjatežno*) with their innocent eyes: they tell us not of eternal peace alone, of that great peace of 'indifferent' nature; they tell us also of eternal reconciliation and of life without end. . . .

Such lines have a distinctly Wordsworthian ring—if not in diction, then certainly in thought.

The evidence for viewing Bazarov's nihilism as one component of a Romantic image is grounded in Turgenev's own statements on the subject, particularly in his preparatory remarks for *Virgin Soil* (*Nov,* 1877). He writes that there are "Romantics of Realism," who "long for the real and strive toward it as former Romantics did toward the 'ideal,' " who seek in this reality "something grand and significant (*nečto velikoe i značitel noe*)." After characterizing the type as a prophet, tormented and anguished, Turgenev adds: "I introduced an element of *that* Romanticism into Bazarov as well—a fact that only Pisarev noticed."

This reference to the hero as a Romantic of Realism is the most explicit statement of the relation between Bazarov's faith in materialism and the Romantic spirit which informs his behavior. But that spirit is clearly defined within the novel itself—defined, in part, by Bazarov's use of terms such as "romantic" and "romanticism." In chapter four he says of the elder Kirsanovs: "These elderly romantics! They develop their nervous systems to the point of irritation . . . and so their equilibrium is destroyed." Commenting on the nature of love he tells Arkadij: "Study the anatomy of the eye a bit; where does the enigmatic glance you talk about come in? That's all romanticism, nonsense, rot, art (*xudožestvo*)." During the dispute in chapter ten the narrator remarks: "This last phrase [spoken by Arkadij] apparently displeased Bazarov; there was a flavor of philosophy, that is to say, romanticism about it, for Bazarov called philosophy, too, romanticism. . . ." In his presentation of Bazarov's thoughts on Odincova, the narrator comments: "In his conversations with Anna Sergeevna he expressed more strongly than ever his clam contempt for everything romantic; but when he was alone, with indignation he recognized the romantic in himself." And in chapter nineteen Bazarov tells Arkadij: " 'In my opinion it's better to break stones on the road than to let a woman gain control over even the end of your little finger. That's all . . .' Bazarov was on the point of uttering his favorite word, 'romanticism,' but he checked himself and said 'nonsense'." Pisarev is very much to the point when he says, in an 1862 article entitled "Bazarov": "Pursuing romanticism, Bazarov with incredible suspicion looks for it where it has never even existed. Arming himself against idealism and smashing its castles in the air, he at times becomes an idealist himself. . . ." Indeed, Bazarov's path to self-knowledge (and spiritual crisis) is associated with the developing awareness of "the romantic within himself," however contemptuously he may react to that element.

Bazarov, of course, does not use words such as "romanticism" in a specifically literary sense. And P. G. Pustovojt has noted that Turgenev's application of the terms "romantic" and "romanticism" in his critical writings often refers to a "romantic" disposition rather than to Romanticism as a literary method. But from a structural point of view the two are inextricably connected: the literature and rhetoric of Romanticism provide the model for this romantic disposition. In fact the model is delineated in Turgenev's work well before *Fathers and Sons.* In a review of Vrončenko's translation of *Faust* (*Otečestvennye zapiski,* 1845, No. 2), Turgenev describes the Romantic hero in the following terms:

> He becomes the center of the surrounding world; he . . . does not submit to anything, he forces everything to submit to himself; he lives by the heart, but by his own, solitary heart—not another's—even in love, about which he dreams so much; he is a romantic, and romanticism is nothing more than the apotheosis of personality (*apofeoz ličnosti*). He is willing to talk about society, about social questions, about science; but society, like science, exists for him—not he for them.

Much in this description could well be applied to Bazarov: the last sentence is reminiscent of his outburst against concern for the peasants' well-being in the face of his own inevitable death, while the phrase "apotheosis of personality" identifies one of the dominant motifs in Bazarov's character. In chapter ten Pavel Petrovič remarks Bazarov's "almost Satanic pride," while Arkadij, in chapter nineteen, notices "the fathomless depths of Bazarov's conceit," and asks him whether he considers himself a god. Whatever the difficulties in establishing a typology for *homo romanticus,* the passage quoted above suggests that in his commentary on Faust, Turgenev presented an interpretation of the Romantic hero which reached its culmination in the creation of Bazarov.

But one can find the type still earlier—in Turgenev's verse drama *Steno* (1837). Despite differences in plot and circumstance both Steno and Bazarov suffer much the same spiritual malaise—an awareness of great strength, coupled with a sense of isolation and impotence before the totality of nature. In act one Steno muses: "Rome passed . . . and we too shall disappear, leaving nothing behind us. . . . What does life signify? What death? I inquire of you, the sky, but you are silent in your cold magnificence!" Similar rhetorical passages occur throughout the play: Steno speaks of the loss of faith, of the insignificance of man, and yet there is a hint of reconciliation in death. In act two Turgenev characterizes his hero through the voice of the monk Antonio: "How much strength he has! How much suffering. In him the Creator has shown us an example of the torments of those with a mighty soul, when they, relying on their strength, go alone to meet the world and embrace it." (See also Turgenev's description of Bazarov in a letter to Konstantin Slučevskij, "I conceived of a figure gloomy, wild, enormous, half-grown from the soil, strong, caustic, honest—and all the same condemned to destruction . . .".) And since *Steno* is little more than a paraphrase of *Manfred* (as Turgenev readily admitted), it would seem that the portrait of Bazarov owes much to the Byronic variant of European romanticism—particularly in its concept of the alienated but defiant hero.

Turgenev would later ridicule his youthful enthusiasm for Manfred, as he would the play which arose from this infatuation. But the evidence of his fiction shows a reworking, an adaptation of certain fundamental concerns—and modes of expression—contained within the juvenilia. It might be argued that Turgenev had sufficiently detached himself from his early derivative Romanticism to judge it in *Fathers and Sons.* Yet the narrative rhetoric of that novel, especially in the concluding paragraph, leads one to assume that the Romantic element was still very much a part of his vision. As M. O. Geršenzon has noted, much in Turgenev's later work is organically related to *Steno,* and Bazarov must be considered evidence of that continuity.

In view of these antecedents it would seem that the conflict between Bazarov and Pavel Kirsanov is an antagonism not so much between the idealistic liberal of the forties and the materialistic radical of the sixties, as between two "generations" of Romantics—both derived from variations of Romanticism prevalent in the thirties and forties. This common element in Turgenev's conception of Bazarov and Kirsanov has not been sufficiently acknowledged, despite the fact that it is developed through an extensive system of parallels in their characterization as well as their fate. Each is passionate in his defense of certain principles, abstractions, ideals (and Bazarov's "materialism" is just as idealistic as Kirsanov's liberalism). But for all of their apparent dedication to an ideological position, each is led to believe that his life is without purpose. To be sure, there is a difference in their expression of this belief: Kirsanov's resignation as opposed to the anger and defiance of Bazarov's metaphysical nihilism.

In each case Turgenev motivates the crisis with a passionate, desperate affair which represents his conception of the incomprehensible power of love—love unattainable, which can end only in death. Pavel Kirsanov, shattered by his attraction to the "mysterious" Princess R. (chapter seven), enters a period of decline in which his former hopes and ambitions are abandoned. Kirsanov is consigned to an existence which has all the appearance of a romantic cliché: "Ladies considered him an enchanting *melanxolik* ['melancholic'], but he did not associate with ladies . . ." And Bazarov claims to see through the cliché. After the account of Kirsanov's life (ostensibly told by Arkadij) Bazarov responds: "And what about these mysterious relations between a man and a woman? We physiologists know what such relations are. Study the anatomy of the eye. . . . " But Kirsanov's affair is merely a prelude to Bazarov's confrontation with Odincova, during which Turgenev will invest the cliché with a pathos appropriate to his hero's strength. Both Bazarov and Kirsanov die in the course of the novel; but Kirsanov, trapped within his image of fatal passion, is granted only a lingering death in life (see the final lines of chapter twenty-four). Bazarov, however, transcends the motif of destructive love by the strength of a rebellion which reflects the egocentric Romantic anguish so imperfectly realized in *Steno*.

Turgenev, then, has isolated Bazarov and Pavel Kirsanov within an intensely subjective, individual crisis that has little direct relation to an ideological dispute between opposing generations. Indeed, the entire notion of generational conflict in *Fathers and Sons* is open to question. It is often assumed that the title implies sons against fathers, yet the Kirsanovs are quite reconciled at the end of the novel and the affection between Bazarov and his parents is beyond doubt. Furthermore, Pavel Kirsanov and Bazarov reach a tenuous reconciliation of their own, following the duel which again reveals the Romantic principle in both—Bazarov's rationalizations notwithstanding. Whatever the initial opposition (based on role stereotypes—youth rebelling against its elders), it is affinity between the generations that defines the basic pattern of relations between fathers and sons (Bazarov's father shouting at the end of chapter twenty-seven, "I rebel, I rebel").

Rather, the book's irreconcilable conflict is surely between the two sons, and it is all the deeper—and more subversive—for not being expressed in ideological terms. Arkadij, whose political views are dismissed early in the novel, is representative of the "honest consciousness," one who accepts his role within the family and its process of biological continuity. Bazarov, well aware of his companion's apostasy ("You're not made for our bitter, rough, lonely existence"), consigns him to his domestic, jackdaw happiness, thus intensifying the isolation so necessary for his own image. Indeed, Arkadij has replaced his "radical" opinions with a desire to turn a profit on the family estate—and in so doing illustrates Turgenev's statement in the letter to Slučevskij: "My entire story is directed against the gentry as a progressive class." As Arkadij and Katja enter Arcadia in fulfillment of roles appropriate to pastoral comedy, Bazarov, the Romantic radical, is left to his tragic destiny. Like Rudin, he is remembered by the happy at their feast (discreetly, to be sure). But also like Rudin, he can have no place with the settled and unrebellious.

In comparison with Turgenev's romanticized view of revolt, Slepcov's approach to radicalism is rather prosaic. One could point to an element of the Romantic in Rjazanov—like Bazarov, a rebel and prey to the *ressentiment* which accompanies his rebellion—that wave of the hand. But Slepcov undercuts the element by his laconic narrative tone as well as by the structure of a plot which can be reduced to the simplest of outlines: Rjazanov, a radical *intelligent* escaping Petersburg in the wake of a new period of repression (1863), arrives at the estate of his university acquaintance, Sčetinin, now married and settled into what he hopes will be the morally and financially satisfying role of enlightened landowner. Rjazanov and Sčetinin engage in a series of arguments during which the radical attempts to demolish the liberal's belief in gradual social progress through reform. But the focus of the novel eventually shifts to Sčetinin's wife.

Under the sway of Rjazanov's nihilistic opinions, Sčetinina can no longer accept what she now sees as her husband's im-

potent liberalism. She decides to abandon her role as benevolent estate mistress and devote herself to another cause. Yet, when she turns to Rjazanov for the emotional and moral support to sustain her in this decision, she is rebuffed. In an intertwining of sexual and ideological elements characteristic of the relations within this *menage á trois,* Rjazanov rejects her sexual advances as well as her desire to aid him in his vaguely defined radical activity. Sčetinina, however, perseveres in her resolve to leave the estate for Petersburg, where she will attempt to join the ranks of the "new people," despite Rjazanov's dim view of this fashionable radicalism (an echo, perhaps, of Bazarov's attitude toward Sitnikov and Kukšina).

The novel ends in a standoff. Sčetinin takes refuge in his reform projects, and a liberated Marja Sčetinina goes to Petersburg in search of her cause. Rjazanov, committed to a distant and uncertain revolution, leaves the estate with his one trophy, a deacon's son who intends to enroll in a provincial school against his father's wishes (another *raznočinec* activist in the making). Slepcov has clarified relations between the characters only to leave them on the threshold of other ambiguities. In a literary variant of his own nihilism he offers no positive solution to the questions the work raises, nor does he imply that his characters are capable of finding such solutions.

It should be clear then that Slepcov, in contrast to Turgenev, adheres to the ideological conflict posed at the beginning of the work, while avoiding a romanticized image of the radical which would focus attention on character rather than ideology. Such an approach has implications not only for the significance of the protagonist, but also for the development of the novel. For while Turgenev directs his work to a consideration of Bazarov and his fate, Slepcov, focusing on the problem of radical response during a period of "hard times," begins where Turgenev leaves off: in the liberal gentry's arcadia. In Sčetinin, Rjazanov faces not a Pavel Kirsanov but his own contemporary, a new type of liberal—practical (or so he thinks), optimistic, willing to accept emancipation reforms with the understanding that they should be made to work in his own interests. The question is will they? and at what cost to the peasants who supply the labor?

Turgenev, in a final, brief gesture of concern with social issues indicates that there will be problems in adjusting to the reforms, but couples his remark with references to the Kirsanov's growing prosperity. Beyond this such problems do not interest him, because they provide no scope for the greater struggle which is his true concern. Bazarov merely dismisses Arkadij's new role as benevolent landowner, he does not challenge it. The Romantic rebel is not concerned with the details or pretensions of land reform, and he does not return to accuse Arkadij of hypocrisy in his dealings with the peasants—indeed, he cannot return. His isolation must be maintained in the interests of a conclusion beyond specific considerations of politics and ideology.

This analysis has attempted to interpret *Fathers and Sons,* in particular the relation between radicalism and literary archetype, by offering a contrast with another work which deals with many of the same issues. It would be pointless to claim that Slepcov, a talented minor writer, has given a more truthful representation of the *nigilist* as a social phenomenon. But he has written a novel which reflects and comments his views as a radical intellectual. In presenting a form of radical ideology peculiar to the sixties, Slepcov shows little tendency to idealize its proponents, with the result that he is able to offer a radical critique without transforming his characters into advocates of a simplistic, utopian solution in the manner of Černyševskij.

Turgenev's achievement, however, is of a different order—one in which the role of ideology is more tenuous. His political and philosophical views and his ambivalence toward Bazarov have received much attention; but efforts to interpret *Fathers and Sons* solely in terms of the "liberal predicament" or a specific philosophical system are, finally, inadequate. It has been noted that Turgenev's correspondence during the latter part of 1860 contains frequent references to a sense of depression, and although this is not an uncommon mood in his writings one such letter (to Fet) does suggest a link between this despondency and his irritation with the young critics then in control of *Sovremennik* who wished to consign their elders to oblivion. It may well be that Bazarov represents Turgenev's attempt to come to terms with the radical spirit which both fascinated and repelled him.

But in doing so Turgenev returned to a problem which had occupied him at the earliest stages of his literary career: the challenge and the *ressentiment* of the Romantic hero, the apotheosis of self. When Antonovič labels Bazarov a "caricature" trying to imitate a demonic or Byronic nature, and Turgenev, in a letter to Ludwig Pietsch, writes, "ich den ganzen Kerl viel zu heldenhaft—idealistisch (read "romantisch") aufgefasst habe" ["I conceived of the fellow far too heroically—idealistically (read 'romantically')], both are admitting the same thing from different points of view. Bazarov is not a caricature, but it is equally true that Turgenev attached ideological positions to a Romantic archetype, only to submerge them in other, literary and metaphysical concerns inherent in the type. Yet, in an irony entirely appropriate to the complexity of relations between literature and society, it is Turgenev (not Slepcov) who defined the image of radicalism with his Romantic nihilist. (pp. 495-504)

> *William C. Brumfield, "Bazarov and Rjazanov: The Romantic Archetype in Russian Nihilism," in* Slavic and East-European Journal, *n.s. Vol. 21, No. 4, Winter, 1977, pp. 495-505.*

THOMAS GARRIGUE MASARYK

[*Masaryk was a Czech man of letters and president of the Czechoslovak republic from 1918 to 1935. In the following excerpt from his three-volume study of Russian history and culture,* The Spirit of Russia: Studies in History, Literature and Philosophy, *originally published in Germany in 1913, Masaryk analyzes the interrelationship between atheism and radical nihilism in novels by Dostoevsky.*]

No sooner had Dostoevsky finished *The Idiot* in 1868 than he was confiding in his friend Maykov a plan for a "tremendous" new novel to be concerned with the very foundations of the author's own being. The work was originally to be called "Atheism."

"I have the central character," Dostoevsky wrote:

> A Russian of our own social background, middle-aged, not overly erudite but not entirely without education or standing. All of a sudden, in middle age, he loses his faith in God. Throughout his life he has done nothing but work; he has never thought of departing from the well-trodden path, till the age of 45 he does absolutely nothing that would call attention to himself. . . . Loss of faith produces a pow-

erful effect on him. . . . He consorts with the new generation, with atheists, Slavs and Europeans, with superstitious Russians, ascetics, priests; in particular, he succumbs to the propaganda of a Polish Jesuit and then falls into the depths of flagellantism. At the very end, he discovers both Christ and the Russian earth, the Russian Christ and the Russian God.

Dostoevsky adds: "I beg you to tell no one about this, but I must write this novel; even if I should die I will have expressed the very essence of my own being."

Two years later, when he was actually at work on *The Possessed,* Dostoevsky again reveals his plan to his friend Maykov. The work is to be entitled *The Life of a Great Sinner* and is eventually to comprise five large novels. "The key issue, to be taken up in each one of the parts, is the very one which has, consciously or unconsciously, tortured me all my life: the question of God's existence. The hero, in the course of his life, becomes successively an atheist, a believer, a fanatic, a sectarian and, once again an atheist."

In these two letters to his friend we have the whole of Dostoevsky as a man as well as his novels in a nutshell: especially so *The Brothers Karamazov* which proved to be the final outcome of these plans.

The book presents four brothers and the old man Karamazov; we are shown a collective phenomenon as well as a generation which displays a whole spectrum of romantic shades and gradations. We are shown the father who, in his appearance and way of life, reminds us of the perverse and demented Roman emperors; we have Dmitri, a blindly instinctive person, but also the philosophical Ivan who, in the face of the atheist's dilemma (either the Jesuitism of the Grand Inquisitor or suicide), wants to live to be at least thirty because he loves life more than he loves the purpose of life and who thus continues to live in defiance of logic. Alyosha, the clean, monastic novice, is conscious of being just as much of a Karamazov while Smerdyakov, as his name suggests, is supposed to be the basest of the species. After all, he is the illegitimate offspring born of intercourse with a feeble-minded woman, the product, therefore, of a perverted passion. Theism and atheism were always the central question for Dostoevsky—a question bearing upon the very being or non-being of man, the individual, the Russian people and humanity in general.

The letter which sketches the plan for his major life work also discloses that Dostoevsky intended to prepare himself for the task by reading the entire Russian and European literature on atheism. As a result, Dostoevsky arrived at his conclusions not alone from the premises postulated by Feuerbach, Schopenhauer, Buechner, Belinsky, Herzen, Bakunin and their Russian disciples. He was quite as aware of the Fausts, Manfreds and Rollas in European literature. The reader of Dostoevsky will, in fact, discover echoes of and references to the most diverse sources in world literature.

Now, to me the cardinal issue is to understand both the genesis of atheism and the process by which it is transformed into the politics of revolution. The crucial point is, of course, that this is no academic matter. It has a direct bearing on living reality. In metaphysical terms, it seems to me that Dostoevsky is unable to tell us very much more than Kant and every other important theist, namely, that the world is, or at least appears to be, a teleological whole. Atheism, on the other hand, devolves from a realisation and conviction that the world is, at bottom, devoid of harmony. It is as simple as that. In a more formal sense, Dostoevsky may be said to espouse the teleological argument. In his theodicy he attempts to understand the existence of evil very much as Leibnitz and other optimists did. I say, "in his theodicy," because the works of Dostoevsky, especially *The Brothers Karamazov* and *The Idiot,* are a marvellous modern theodicy, which attempts a psychological and sociological analysis of atheism.

The Russian atheist is not the kind of man who simply manages to talk himself out of a belief in God and then goes on to enjoy a good meal and a bottle of wine, even though such types do exist in Russia and are portrayed in Dostoevsky. The Russian atheist becomes not a hedonist but a pessimist and his pessimism can be of two types: either he works himself into a titanic all-consuming anger, or he falls into literal and total despair. In either case, he does not confine his sentiments merely to the written word. The palliatives of conventional optimism have no effect on him whatever.

On this point, certainly, Belinsky had laid the groundwork for the analysis later offered by Dostoevsky. He had begun with a Hegelian belief in gradual evolution which had reconciled him with life and the world. Yet, once he had acquired a more intimate knowledge of that life, and Russian life in particular, Belinsky had done with theoretical optimism for good and all. Consider this passage for instance:

> I am told: Develop all the treasures of thy spirit that thou mayest achieve free self-satisfaction for that spirit; weep to console thyself; mourn to bring thyself joy; strive towards perfection; mount towards the highest steps upon the staircase of development; and shouldst thou stumble—well, thou wilt fall! The devil take thee then, for thou wert fit for nothing better. . . . Most humble thanks, Egor Feodorovic Gegel [Hegel], I bow before your philosophic philistinism. I must dutifully assure you that if I should succeed in creeping up the developmental stairs to attain the topmost step I would endeavour, even there, to take into the reckoning all the victims of vital conditions and of history, all the victims of misfortune, of superstition, of the inquisition of Philip II, and so on—and in default would hurl myself headlong from the summit. I do not desire happiness in any other terms, and I must be tranquillised concerning the fate of every one of my blood brothers.

Here, indeed, you have the main theme of Ivan Karamazov. And who can wonder that Dostoevsky was so much impressed by Belinsky just before his own personal catastrophe, the arrest in 1849. Let the reader turn to Book V of Part II in *The Brothers Karamazov.* He will find there nothing less than the holy scripture of Russian atheism. Chapter IV in particular reveals its inner core and is entitled "Rebellion" by anything but chance. The Russian atheist quite literally does rebel against his God and carries that rebellion on *usque ad finem* ["into infinity"].

The brothers Ivan and Alyosha—one the philosophical atheist, the other a religious theist—are discussing God in a tavern. (How very Russian!) Ivan is elaborating on Belinsky's thought. He is commenting on the harmony of the spheres and of the world by offering his believing brother the example of the General who orders a small boy torn to pieces by dogs before his mother's eyes because the child in throwing a stone had struck the General's favourite dog on its paw. In the account, Ivan himself is killing two birds with one stone. First,

he is characterising the social "order" under serfdom (the incident he is relating pre-dates 1861) and then he confronts the optimist who always defends absolutely love of one's neighbour with a stark question. Can and will Alyosha also love this General? What about a cosmic harmony in which innocent, unknowing children undergo such inhuman suffering? What becomes of the teaching about forgiveness of sin? What, indeed, is one to do with the General? Shall one not shoot him to assuage one's sense of moral justice? "Speak, Alyosha!" he cries.

"Yes, shoot him," Alyosha whispered, while looking at his brother with a pale and crooked smile.

"Bravo!" shouts Ivan, almost triumphantly. "If even you say so, well then. . . . And behold the strict monk! Behold that little demon in your heart, Alyosha Karamazov."

Alyosha concedes the particular disharmony and a host of others but seeks consolation in the thought that the totality is, after all, still harmonious. He derives peace of soul particularly from Christian teaching on the forgiveness of sin and the dead Christ as redeemer. What matters to Alyosha is that Christ does belong to the whole, that He indeed exists and has the right to bestow forgiveness.

But it is precisely this Christian teaching that Ivan turns on with his "Euclidian," positivist and utilitarian reasoning! He sees nothing but discord and the recognition of it somehow fills him with malicious joy. What use, he asks, is punishment in the afterlife and what meaning can forgiveness have if so many have already endured the most frightful of tortures?

Fyodor Dostoevsky

Clearly, it is impossible to cause all that suffering to be undone.

> "I don't want harmony, I don't want it out of love of mankind. I prefer to stay with unavenged suffering. I would rather have my own unavenged suffering continue, with my unassuaged bitterness, even if I should, perhaps, prove wrong. They have set too high a price on harmony; the price being asked just for admission is just too high for us. So I hurry to return my admission ticket. If I am an honourable man, I must return my ticket as soon as possible. Alyosha, I am not refusing to accept God, I am just most respectfully returning to him the ticket."

> "That," Alyosha says in a low voice and with bowed head, "is rebellion!"

Here indeed is the essence of Russian nihilistic atheism. It is not merely an academic doctrine: it is one's very own fate in life. It has nothing whatever to do with an attitude of mere indifference. It is not positivist agnosticism but rather a kind of embittered scepticism which revels in the laceration of the soul. The Russian atheist carries out his Promethean revolt in full consciousness. He literally bristles with hatred, is saturated in revenge and falls into despair with real passion. The Russian atheist is hardly the product of a general and vague awareness of cosmic disharmony: his points of departure are the actual Russian world and the past history of Russia. Thus, the Russian atheist is essentially an ethical and social being rather than a metaphysical one. He is, quite forthrightly, preoccupied with the ethical aspect of religion.

The immediate consequence of his own position for any Russian atheist must be the apotheosis of his own ego. Indeed, that is precisely what Stirner and other German radical subjectivists had taught. Still, the Russian atheist is neither a subjectivist nor an idealist who supposes that the external world exists only in his own imagination and as an expression of his own will. On the contrary, the world exists all too evidently; it does exist in all its social worthlessness. That is why a merely conceptual negation of God will not lead very far: God must be literally dethroned. Above all, it is essential to eradicate the Christian deity, the God-man and to put in his place the Man-god who will be able to bring order out of chaos.

Thus, the Russian Man-god craves neatness and a new world order. The old ethical and social precepts are useless to him. The nihilistic superman recognises no ethical truths, rejects all moral codes: nothing at all can be denied him. This Pauline assertion is repeated constantly in *The Brothers Karamazov:* if there is no God and no immortality (identical concepts for Dostoevsky) then, too, there is nothing immoral, there are no ethical commands and prohibitions. Everything is permitted.

Freedom, equality, brotherhood: these signify liberty and power for Dostoevsky's superman. Raskolnikov and the hero of *The Raw Youth* dream of becoming Napoleons and Rothschilds. Both were entirely unto themselves and quite unique. By analogy, the nihilist who has read his Stirner also craves the same sense of uniqueness and even if he never does achieve the position of a Napoleon or Rothschild, the "idea" becomes sufficient unto itself. His intense and passionate desire is enough to place him outside and above society:

> I was seized by the idea of conceiving an average person of no special gifts, standing before the world

and saying with a smile: 'You, Galileos, Copernicuses, Charlemagnes, Napoleons; you, Pushkins and Shakespeares, Field-Marshals, and Chamberlains of the royal courts: look at me, untalented and illegitimate, yet I stand above you because you have subordinated yourselves to me!'

Ivan's philosophy is thus easily understood: in a disordered world he feels that to love one's neighbour becomes quite meaningless. The all-powerful and almighty superman can act without the least restraint even if this should entail the most extreme measures. He is lord of life and death. He may kill as well as perish by his own hand.

In the final analysis, therefore, atheism can only lead either to murder or to suicide. This is the theme of *Crime and Punishment* and it reappears in each of Dostoevsky's subsequent books.

The right to commit either murder or suicide is, of course, a total negation of Russia: it is a denial of its history and culture, of the nation and the fatherland and above all of its religion. The meaning of Russian life and civilisation, the individual Russian as well as the immense whole, the Czar himself, intoxicated by the thought that his realm is the sixth continent of the world, all of these and a millennium of history are reduced to nonsense.

Thus, the radical nihilist is led inexorably by his antipathy toward Russian civilisation to a hatred of his fatherland, its history and people to hatred of himself. Russian history and civilisation, millions upon millions of Russians—and he himself among them—signify nothing and have no meaning.

For Dostoevsky himself, it is precisely religion which imparts meaning to life, whether it is that of an individual, a whole people, or of all mankind. The meaning and substance of Russian civilisation devolves from faith: a deep and pervasive faith, the real and solely Russian Orthodox faith. Hence, to him, the negation or denial of Russia can only mean the rejection of the Russian faith.

"He who has no nation, has no God." That is the concise and pragmatic way in which he sees the close connection between patriotism and theism and conversely, between atheism and revolution. In *The Possessed,* atheism, nihilism, and revolution are treated as synonyms by Dostoevsky.

Moreover, the negation of Russia by the nihilist clearly means the acceptance of Europe. Russia is nothing, Europe is everything, and if not literally everything then certainly a good deal or at least something. And acceptance of Europe means pre-eminently acceptance of the Catholic religion since Protestantism, in Dostoevsky's view, always remained a negligible force. Yet, by this logic, it follows that since the Europeanised Russian is a nonbeliever, European Catholicism is therefore proven to be no true religion, in fact, not a religion at all but instead a form of atheism and naturalism. Hence, in political terms, a nihilistic Europeanisation of Russia can result only in socialism which turns out to be nothing so much as a social form of atheism.

The nihilist's disbelief is also synonymous with acceptance of European pseudo-science, or rather of its half-science and half-education and for that reason the nihilistic atheist, is, strictly speaking, no more than a half-atheist in the sense that he always remains only half-educated. There are, after all, atheists who *believe* in the Devil! Hence, Dostoevsky tells us often that a Russian simply cannot become a real atheist at all. He draws his own principal atheistic character accordingly: Ivan Karamazov remains simply a sceptic and a rebel against God. He does recognise God even though he turns in the admission ticket to his world. The quasi-educated atheists thus usually turn out to be nothing more than feeble little devils, badly possessed of genuine demonic qualities. In *The Possessed* they are portrayed as semi-literate, unbelieving and yet superstitious.

Dostoevsky refers often to this pseudo-sophistication of the nihilist and sees in this kind of semi-literacy the bane of the nineteenth century. What he particularly deplores is the resulting inner schizophrenia, that half-way house of the contemporary Russian: part Russian, part European, part believer, part secular philosopher, part saint, part demon. . . .

In the letter to Maykov announcing his plan for *The Great Sinner,* as the work was then called, we read about a 13-year-old boy who has already been involved in crime. The parents send him to a monastery where the juvenile nihilist encounters the great man of God, Tikhon. Dostoevsky places much stress on the fact that the boy comes from "our educated classes" by which he means to show that pseudo-literacy can result only in moral turpitude. In fact, Dostoevsky always and with unflagging zeal points to the connection between atheism and moral anarchy. The relationship, however, is not such that atheism merely creates anarchy; on the contrary, it is moral degeneracy which leads to atheism and atheism thus becomes a disguise for infamy. This atheism of semi-education springs not so much from philosophy as from immorality. The revolt of the semi-educated nihilists, as Dostoevsky once put it, is the atheism of "an idea sunk into the gutter."

Dostoevsky singles out sexual promiscuity as the great moral failing of his time. Ivan Karamazov is Faust and Don Juan in one and the same person and the Don remains the stronger of the two. The brothers Karamazov and their father are made the very symbols of the disease: Karamazovites.

By "semi-education" Dostoevsky means liberalism, the Petersburg Russo-European learning which has turned against the indigenous religion—that Westernising liberalism for which he castigates Turgenev so mercilessly in *The Possessed*. Indeed, when his friend Maykov recognised some of Turgenev's heroes in the characters of the novel, Dostoevsky was delighted by the discovery. (pp. 6-14)

Thomas Garrigue Masaryk, "The Life of the Great Sinner: Atheism, Nihilism, and 'The Brothers Karamazov'," in his The Spirit of Russia, Vol. 3, *edited by George Gibian, translated by Robert Bass, George Allen & Unwin Ltd., 1967, pp. 6-98.*

CHARLES A. MOSER

[*In the following analysis of Dostoevsky's novel* The Idiot, *Moser examines Dostoevsky's treatment of moral and aesthetic issues that served as sources of conflict between the radical Nihilists and their conservative opponents.*]

It is hazardous to approach any novel of Dostoevskij's from one point of view only, and this is certainly true of a work as complex—not to say confusing—as *The Idiot*. And yet critics and literary historians may sometimes utilize such an approach to good and quite legitimate effect, provided that they remember that they are elucidating only a facet of the work, and not the work in its entirety. I shall try to bear that

in mind in this discussion of Dostoevskij's great novel *The Idiot*.

As I approached it within the context of Russia of the 1860's, the decade in which it was written and first read, *The Idiot* intrigued me because superficially it seemed to have so little in common with the radical intellectual currents swirling through the country in that day. It is, after all, the second of a series of three novels, of which the first and third clearly have much to do with 'nihilism' as an intellectual and cultural phenomenon. Indeed, so obsessive was Dostoevskij's concern with the intellectual trends of the 1860's that even his fourth great novel, *The Brothers Karamazov,* which articulates his religious views in a manner unsurpassed in world literature, is still set in the Russia of the 1860's.

Dostoevskij began planning *The Idiot* in 1867, one of the decade's central years, began writing specifically on it in September of that year, and worked most intensively on the text as we now know it from the following December until about January of 1869. A major impetus for the novel flowed from his attendance at a Peace Congress in Geneva from September 9 to 12, 1867, in which he had the chance to observe at first hand that gathering of radicals chaired by Garibaldi. He found the European radicals distinctly repulsive and muddleheaded, good embodiments of traits which he found so ridiculous and yet dangerous in the Russian radicals of his day. Despite all this, it seems, he then wrote a novel with rather few overt connections to the assault upon political and philosophical radicalism which he had undertaken in *Crime and Punishment* and would intensify in *The Possessed*. This is a circumstance which calls for some investigation and explanation.

To begin with, there are clearly *some* openly antinihilist elements in *The Idiot;* indeed they are quite obvious. For example, the description of Antip Burdovskij, Pavliščev's putative son, who arrives with a small group of radicals to confront Prince Myškin with an article exposing and upbraiding him for living off his father's wealth without providing for Pavliščev's natural son, is a *locus classicus* of the description of the young radical in the antinihilist literature of the 1860's. Burdovskij's personal cleanliness leaves much to be desired (his hands are dirty, as were supposedly those of all nihilists); his clothing is both filthy and untidy. Although Dostoevskij emphasizes the young man's 'innocence', he also detects in him an element common to his entire generation, a "strange and consistent need both to be and to feel himself to be eternally offended". Somehow reality has done the younger generation wrong, and can never be forgiven. Also, Burdovskij shares with most of his nihilist contemporaries a severe inability to express himself verbally: he spoke 'hurriedly', Dostoevskij writes, and could scarcely get his words out, "just as if he were tongue-tied, or even a foreigner, although as a matter of fact he was of purely Russian extraction". Dostoevskij was fully capable of delving more deeply than this into the social psychology of the nihilist, but he did not think this necessary in describing the meeting between the Prince and the nihilist group. He simply pointed to Burdovskij's traits of personal uncleanliness, verbal inadequacy, and psychological sensitivity, and passed on.

Dostoevskij also underlined the crude straightforwardness of the radical generation in other portions of the novel. During their meeting with the Prince, the young radicals "do not request, but rather demand": they advance a claim to what is theirs by right, and which they do not intend to be denied.

They have long ago condemned the formalities of civilized discourse, and spare no one's feelings in their dedication to the truth. A young man very much one of them, Ippolit Terent'ev, considers this a positive trait. When he wishes to discover precisely how much time is left to him, he summons the student Kislorodov (his very surname is a satirical thrust at the radicals):

> A week or so ago the student Kislorodov was brought to see me; his convictions have made him a materialist, atheist and nihilist, which was why I asked him to come; I needed a man who finally would tell me the unadorned truth, without formalities and ceremony. That is precisely what he did, and not only readily and without ceremony, but even with evident satisfaction (which I thought was a little excessive). He blurted out to me that I had about a month to live . . .

Thus even Ippolit complains a bit about the relish with which the radicals bear evil tidings to others.

The 'woman question', intellectually quite fashionable in the 1860's, also emerges in *The Idiot,* as one might expect from a novel in which beautiful and modern women play such important roles, but it is never examined in great depth. Thus it occurs in the amusing passage early on in which the cynical Ganja Ivolgin declares to Myškin his willingness to marry Nastas'ja Filippovna for her money (he can be as rudely straightforward as any radical):

> She thinks me a scoundrel because I'm so openly ready to take her for her money even though she was another man's mistress, without realizing that a lot of other men would deceive her even worse; they would attach themselves to her and start spouting all the liberal and progressive phrases, including all this stuff about feminism. . . . They'd swear to the self-centered fool . . . that they were taking her because of her "noble heart and her misfortunes", when in fact they'd be marrying her for her money too.

Dostoevskij probably believed, then, that the enthusiastic adherents of 'women's rights'—among men, at any rate—simply utilized currently popular ideas for the purpose of deceiving gullible women.

Dostoevskij's treatment of the 'woman question', though it is mentioned here and there in the novel, reaches its apogee in the description of Myškin just before his intended wedding, when the inveterate gossipers and misinterpreters of reality who inhabit Dostoevskij's fictional world decide that he is attempting to prove a radical point by marrying Nastas'ja Filippovna instead of Aglaja:

> And to this was added, by way of characterizing contemporary morals, that the muddle-headed young man [Myškin] had in fact been in love with his fiancée, the general's daughter, but that he had rejected her purely out of nihilism and for the sake of the scandal he would create when he allowed himself the satisfaction of marrying a fallen woman in front of everyone and thereby to show that as far as he was concerned there exist neither fallen nor virtuous women, but only free women, nothing more . . .

Shortly before this passage Dostoevskij links Myškin—at least as interpreted by the crowd—to the "nihilism detected by Mr. Turgenev", and so to the antinihilist current in literature generally. Furthermore, recognizing that the phrase "out of nihilism" (*iz nigilizma*) may sound a trifle strange to the untutored ear, Dostoevskij offers a gloss on it: "out of nihilism, that is, for insult and humiliation's sake". Through this gloss Dostoevskij identifies the nihilists as individuals who systematically and deliberately employed scandal as a means of subverting accepted social customs, and thereby society itself: if the general rules of a society come to be seriously questioned, then the society itself is in danger of toppling. The reader of *The Idiot* realizes that Prince Myškin's motivations in marrying Nastas'ja Filippovna are not the same as those attributed to him by the crowd—and yet there *is* some justification for its interpretation of the facts.

Here we touch upon a deeper problem of Dostoevskij's fictional approach to reality, one which is for him a constant but which, in the confrontation between Myškin and the young nihilists, he connects to the nihilist intellectual movement: the question of truth. Precisely this feature of Dostoevskij's art—his profound sense of the contingency of truth, the relativity of reality—makes him the most modern of nineteenth century writers despite his overtly conservative beliefs and his conscious desire to preach the eternal verities. It also makes him one of the most intellectually unsettling writers in literature, for in reading him we can rarely be certain that we have achieved a 'true' comprehension of reality. To be sure, we may come to know the 'facts', bare and unadorned, but the human mind cannot content itself with a jumble of facts: it must also have an interpretive framework in which to arrange them. The problem is that different people erect different frameworks, and the interpretations of events which emerge from those frameworks may diverge sharply from one another and from actual 'reality'. For example, all the 'facts' the rumormongers cite in describing Prince Myškin's courtship are 'true': he had had a relationship of sorts with Aglaja, he had declared his intention of marrying Nastas'ja Filippovna, he had broken a valuable Chinese vase, and he had appointed a date for the wedding. In fact he had asked his nihilist friend Burdovskij to act as the wedding attendant (*šafer*) for Nastas'ja Filippovna. Thus the facts given in the popular account of Myškin's marriage are all correct so far as they go, but they seem to yield false conclusions when arranged in an interpretive framework which assumes that Myškin is motivated by 'nihilism'.

Myškin deals with precisely this same issue when he encounters the young nihilists and their article in chapter 8 of part two. A number of the 'facts' contained in the article, if viewed simply as facts, are arguably correct; and yet the author of the article interprets them in a framework which makes the whole piece emerge as, in Myškin's word, 'untruth' (*nepravda*). To be sure, the Prince shows that certain key 'facts' given in the article are pure distortions. Backed into a corner, Keller admits he wrote most of the article, but still defends its overall effect:

> As for certain inaccuracies—hyperboles, so to say—why you will surely agree that the most important thing is initiative, the most important thing is aim and purpose; the important thing is to provide a beneficent example, and then later on we can worry about particular details, and then finally it's a matter of style (*slog*) . . .

Thus, Keller argues, the chief thing in a piece of writing is its central theme: does it promote the 'good of society'? The reader should consider 'initiative', motivation, the author's good intentions, even 'style', or the generally accepted manner of writing on a particular topic. Under such conditions the question of factual accuracy recedes to a position of secondary importance.

In this case, however, the 'aim and motivation' of the entire piece depend on one 'fact': is Burdovskij indeed Pavliščev's illegitimate son? Here Myškin produces his trump card when Ivolgin demonstrates by the scientific laws of mathematics and human gestation that Burdovskij could not be Pavliščev's son. Burdovskij has no choice but to accept this proof, and to withdraw any demands made in the article on his behalf. But the problem of factual accuracy reappears at the end of the confrontation, when Burdovskij returns to the Prince a sum of money which the latter had sent him as 'charity'. Doktorenko declares the sum to be 250 rubles, one participant indignantly recalls that the article had reported the sum as only 50 rubles, and actual examination of the money determines that it consists of 100 rubles. One radical, Lebedev's nephew, protests that in essence all such figures are equivalent: "Of course 100 rubles is not the same thing as 250 rubles", he says:

> and the whole matter is not one of indifference, but the principle is important; the important thing here is the initiative, and it's merely a detail that the sum is 150 rubles short. The important thing is that Burdovskij refuses to accept your charity, Your Highness, that he throws it back in your face, and in this sense it's all the same whether it's 100 or 250 rubles.

Here Lebedev's nephew asserts the superiority of moral criteria over bare facts in determining truth, and he defends factual inaccuracy much as Keller has done before him: 'initiative', 'intention' are the vital factors, more important perhaps than the laws of mathematics or of reality which are subject to empirical verification. What is important is that Burdovskij returns money to Myškin out of a sense of self-respect; the amount of the money in question is a mere detail.

The difficulty of interpreting reality—exemplified by the popular rumors about Myškin's marriage at the end of the novel and the discussion of Keller's article in the middle—is a central one in Dostoevskij's fictional world: the reader can rarely be certain of what has happened there, for Dostoevskij untiringly undercuts what the reader thinks he knows. However, this problem deserves far more extended treatment than can be provided in a paper of this length.

Still another element in Dostoevskij's thought plays a very important role in *The Idiot,* and defines a major area of conflict between the radical intellectuals of the 1860's and their opponents: aesthetics, or the science of the beautiful.

The aesthetic conflict had begun to emerge openly in the 1850's, with the formation of what came to be called the Gogolian and Pushkinian schools in Russian criticism. The Gogolian camp, represented by Černyševskij and his followers, believed that art should be socially useful, and decried purely aesthetic values in art and literature. By the mid-1860's the radicals had reached the point where they rejected aesthetics altogether: in 1865 Dmitrij Pisarev could write in a retrospective article on Černyševskij's master's essay that "aesthetics, to our immense satisfaction, has been absorbed into physiology and hygiene". The Pushkinian school, on the other hand, preached the primacy of art over reality and praised Puškin for what they interpreted as his dedication to the ideal of pure art. These two camps among Russian intellectuals diverged

sharply in the 1860's: as a consequence of this disagreement the radicals belittled Puškin as a poet, and Nekrasov was constrained to repress his natural affinity for Puškin for some 15 years, while the controversy was at its height.

The radicals' campaign against aesthetics in the 1860's engendered some extreme reactions from their opponents. The poet Afanasij Fet devised a literary theory which asserted the absolute primacy of aesthetic considerations in art, finding strong support for his position from such critics as Aleksandr Družinin and Vasilij Botkin. And the little-known critic Nikolaj Solov'ev, in an article of 1864 published in Dostoevskij's journal *Èpocha,* went so far as to argue that aesthetics should serve as the basis for human ethics and morality. Since this was the first article Solov'ev had published in *Èpocha,* Dostoevskij appended a note to it in which he welcomed it, but added that he could not agree with all its conclusions.

In all probability one of the things Dostoevskij rejected in Solov'ev's piece was his central idea of founding ethics upon aesthetic feeling. Both the radicals and the extreme aesthetic camp tended to reject supernatural revelation as an ethical foundation. The radicals were atheists almost as a matter of course: they sought to base a new ethic on scientific rationalism or on utilitarianism. In like manner, the extreme aesthetic camp felt no need for the hypothesis of God: Fet, for instance, was a well-known and quite open atheist. Dostoevskij, on the other hand, defended the traditional view of ethics and morality as based upon Divine revelation and sanction, and therefore found himself at odds with both the radical and aesthetic camps. In *Crime and Punishment* and *The Possessed* Dostoevskij sought to demonstrate that a moral code based upon the rational and scientific presuppositions of the radicals could only lead to destruction; in *The Idiot,* in my view, whatever may have been his initial intentions, he ends by demonstrating that a code of morality based upon aesthetics alone (as Solov'ev would have it) also results in destruction. Therefore, by a process of elimination, the only sound basis remaining for a code of morality is a belief in immortality and in God as revealed to mankind through Christ.

If we realize that the destructive power of beauty is a major theme within *The Idiot,* then certain important aspects of the novel become much more comprehensible than they may be otherwise. For instance Puškin, the patron of the aesthetic camp, is a central presence in the novel: near its mid-point Aglaja recites his poem "The Poor Knight" in its entirety, and Myškin is closely associated with both the poem and its hero. Aglaja summarizes her view of the poem's meaning in the following very significant words:

> In this poem we have the direct depiction of a man who first of all is capable of having an ideal, and who in the second place, once he has found an ideal, can put his faith in it, and having done that, can blindly dedicate his entire life to it. . . . It is not said there, in the poem, what exactly the "poor knight's" ideal consisted of, but it's obvious that it was some bright image, "an image of pure beauty" . . .

No matter what we may think of Aglaja's interpretation of the poem, her words may be applied rather directly to Myškin, who indeed is enamored of all things beautiful. Very early in the novel we learn of the Prince's attraction to the beauties of calligraphy: he writes a beautiful hand himself, and is happy to expatiate at great length on the achievements of great calligraphic masters of the past. He ends his discourse on this topic with the revealing peroration:

> A flourish (*rosčerk*) is a highly perilous thing! A flourish demands extraordinary taste; but if it should be successful, if the right proportions should be found, why such a script is beyond compare, so much so that *one could fall in love with it* (italics added).

In view of this, it is scarcely astonishing that when Myškin first sees Nastas'ja Filippovna's portrait, he is struck by her extraordinary beauty: the author's description of the impression the portrait makes upon the Prince includes the adjectives 'strange', 'blinding', and—most important—'unbearable' (*nevynosimyj*) attached to the noun 'beauty'. Shortly thereafter, in speaking of Nastas'ja Filippovna, Adelaida remarks that "such beauty is power . . . with beauty like that one could transform (*perevernut'*) the world!" And Myškin does in fact succumb to the power of Nastas'ja Filippovna's beauty: like Puškin's poor knight, he dedicates himself to the ideal of pure beauty as embodied in Nastas'ja Filippovna. However, there is one crucial difference between the poor knight and Myškin: the former acts within a religious context, while the latter remains on a secular plane, no matter how exalted it may be.

Myškin's tragedy lies in the fact that his dedication to an ideal of "unbearable beauty" is simply the prelude to illness—his personal affliction—and ultimately to destruction. The famous passage in which the narrator describes the onset of Myškin's epileptic attacks contains elements very like those used in describing his reaction to Nastas'ja Filippovna's portrait:

> His mind and heart were illuminated with an extraordinary light; all his unease, all his doubts, all his worries were somehow eliminated at one stroke, were resolved into some sort of higher peace, full of clear and harmonious joy. . . . But these moments, these flashes were only harbingers of that ultimate second . . . which led to the attack itself. This second was, of course, *unbearable.* . . . "What difference does it make if this is an illness?" he finally decided. "Why should it matter that this tension is abnormal if its result, if the moment of sensation, recalled and examined later when I am restored to health, turns out to be *harmony* and *beauty* in the highest degree . . .?"

No matter how the Prince may extol the ecstasy of the instant before the onset of an epileptic seizure, the fact remains that the attack entails the temporary obliteration of his normal faculties; and, if the attacks continue without hindrance, they will cause their permanent destruction.

This context makes even more understandable the significance of Nastas'ja Filippovna's efforts to attain the apex of her beauty on the eve of her projected marriage. To be sure, any woman seeks to be at her most beautiful on her wedding day, and Myškin is told that Nastas'ja Filippovna is "as busy as only a great beauty can be in dressing for her wedding". When she emerges from the house on her way to church, the narrator describes her beauty, not so much directly as indirectly, through its powerful effect on the clownish bystanders; and a familiar word appears in the single brief passage which speaks directly of her beauty: "her large dark eyes flashed out at the crowd like red-hot coals; and that glance was *unbearable* for the crowd. The symbolism of the scene,

however, lies in this, that it is precisely at the instant of her supreme beauty that Nastas'ja Filippovna flings herself into Rogožin's arms and sets off to her doom. Nastas'ja Filippovna's beauty leads to her physical destruction, and Prince Myškin's dedication to that beauty causes his intellectual and moral destruction in the novel's unforgettable concluding scene. It is fatal, Dostoevskij thus demonstrates, to base one's moral life on a sense of beauty: an ethical and moral system cannot be built upon an aesthetic foundation, for the immoral, the abnormal, even the ugly may sometimes appear beautiful to certain individuals.

If this interpretation is correct, then one must reassess Myškin's otherwise puzzling reactions to Hans Holbein's famous painting of Christ taken from the cross, a copy of which he sees in Rogožin's house. Holbein depicts the body of the dead Christ with such excruciating realism that Myškin exclaims: "Some people could lose their faith by looking at that picture!" Moreover, Myškin offers this comment after he—nearly alone among Dostoevskij's major characters—has refused to reply by changing the subject when Rogožin puts the central question of Dostoevskij's universe to him: does he believe in God? What faith in God Myškin has must be founded upon beauty and harmony; in all probability it cannot survive a sustained challenge from unlovely reality, as exemplified by Holbein's crucified Christ. We have the contemporary witness of Dostoevskij's wife that when she and her husband first viewed the original painting, despite the fact that she reacted to it much as Myškin did, it overwhelmed Dostoevskij, filling him with 'ecstasy', so that he ended by declaring Holbein a "remarkable artist and poet". In his book *Dostoevskij's Quest for Form,* Robert L. Jackson deals with the place of Holbein's painting in *The Idiot* in a manner which leaves an unresolved contradiction. "Holbein's 'Christ in the Tomb' was", he writes,

> —from the point of view of Dostoevsky's Christian aesthetic—. . . a caricature of the supreme symbol and embodiment of transfiguration, Jesus Christ; its message was death and disfiguration. Dostoevsky's commitment to the notion of ideal beauty is a commitment . . . to the ideal of ethical beauty. To give de jure recognition to Holbein's disfigured Christ, to call it beauty, would not merely destroy the notion of an aesthetic ideal—it would deny the notion of an ethical ideal . . .

If the analysis proffered here is correct, then Jackson is wrong in equating the aesthetic and ethical ideals in Dostoevskij's thought. Dostoevskij's own ethical ideal was based upon a commitment to Christ, who lived in this world as a man, who suffered and died as a man; and Dostoevskij knew very well that suffering and death are rarely lovely. That is why Dostoevskij was so taken with Holbein's painting, and why Myškin's response to it does not coincide with his own. For in *The Idiot,* among many other things, Dostoevskij occupied the aesthetic no-man's-land located between the radicals and their opponents: while affirming the importance of art for the elaboration of human ideals, he denied with equal vigor that man could build a moral code for himself on an aesthetic foundation. Ethics could only be founded on true religion: "Morality and faith are one" he wrote in the notebooks to *The Possessed.*

In *The Idiot,* then, Dostoevskij grappled with two of the central intellectual cleavages of the 1860's: the problem of morality and the question of aesthetics. Thus *The Idiot* is just as firmly rooted in the intellectual soil of that remarkable decade as are *Crime and Punishment* and *The Possessed*. (pp. 377-87)

Charles A. Moser, "Nihilism, Aesthetics, and 'The Idiot'," in Russian Literature, *Vol. XI, No. IV, May 15, 1982, pp. 377-88.*

FURTHER READING

Barghoorn, Frederick C. "D. I. Pisarev: A Representative of Russian Nihilism." *The Review of Politics* 10, No. 2 (April 1948): 190-211.

    A survey of the radical milieu of the 1860s, focusing on the Nihilist aspects of Pisarev's writings.

Brower, Daniel R. *Training the Nihilists: Education and Radicalism in Tsarist Russia.* Ithaca, N.Y.: Cornell University Press, 1975, 248 p.

    Examines the role of the Russian educational system in the formation of Russia's radical intelligentsia from the 1840s to the 1870s.

Dryzhakova, Elena. "Dostoevsky, Chernyshevsky, and the Rejection of Nihilism." In *Oxford Slavonic Papers* n.s. XIII, edited by J. L. I. Fennell, A. E. Pennington, and I. P. Foote, pp. 58-79. Oxford: Clarendon Press, 1980.

    Traces the development of Dostoevsky's critical perspective on the work of Chernyshevsky, arguing that "in his attitude to Chernyshevsky he showed respect, consideration, and a desire to understand him fully—while at the same time totally rejecting his aesthetic, ideological, and moral views."

Frank, Joseph. "Nihilism and *Notes from Underground*." *The Sewanee Review* LXIX, No. 1 (Winter 1961): 1-33.
    Argues that *Notes from Underground* "was conceived and executed as one magnificent satirical parody" of Russian Nihilism.

Freeborn, Richard. "Egoistic Nihilism and Revolutionary Nihilism." In his *The Russian Revolutionary Novel: Turgenev to Pasternak*, pp. 4-38. Cambridge: Cambridge University Press, 1982.

    Studies the evolution of the literary tradition of Russian Nihilism, accentuating the central role played by Turgenev's *Fathers and Sons* and Chernyshevsky's *What Is to Be Done?*

Hingley, Ronald. *Nihilists: Russian Radicals and Revolutionaries in the Reign of Alexander II (1855-81)*. London: Weidenfeld and Nicolson, 1967, 128 p.

    A general history of the Russian Nihilist movement addressing its literary, social, and political aspects.

Ponomareff, Constantin V. *On the Dark Side of Russian Literature. 1709-1910.* New York: Peter Lang, 1987, 261 p.

    Thematic study of Russian literature from the classical age to the demise of Symbolism that highlights "the predominantly nihilist inspiration and vision in the best of Russian writing."

Rogers, James Allen. "Darwinism, Scientism, and Nihilism." *The Russian Review* 19, No. 1 (January 1960): 10-23.

    Assesses the influence of German scientism and Darwin's theory of natural selection on the Russian radical intelligentsia of the 1860s.

Stacy, R. H. "The Civic Critics." In his *Russian Literary Criticism: A Short History,* pp. 55-65. Syracuse: Syracuse University Press, 1974.

    Outlines the literary careers of Chernyshevsky, Dobrolyubov, and Pisarev.

Venturi, Franco. *Roots of Revolution: A History of the Populist and Socialist Movements in Nineteenth Century Russia.* Translated by Francis Haskell. New York: Alfred A. Knopf, 1964, 850 p.

    A highly regarded study of Russian revolutionary history that includes a chapter on Chernyshevsky and numerous references to the other Civic Critics.

Nineteenth-Century Literature Criticism

Topics Volume

Cumulative Indexes

Volumes 1-28

This Index Includes References to Entries in These Gale Series

Contemporary Literary Criticism

Presents excerpts of criticism on the works of novelists, poets, dramatists, short story writers, scriptwriters, and other creative writers who are now living or who have died since 1960.

Twentieth-Century Literary Criticism

Contains critical excerpts by the most significant commentators on poets, novelists, short story writers, dramatists, and philosophers who died between 1900 and 1960.

Nineteenth-Century Literature Criticism

Offers significant passages from criticism on authors who died between 1800 and 1899.

Literature Criticism from 1400 to 1800

Compiles significant passages from the most noteworthy criticism on authors of the fifteenth through eighteenth centuries.

Classical and Medieval Literature Criticism

Offers excerpts of criticism on the works of world authors from classical antiquity through the fourteenth century.

Short Story Criticism

Compiles excerpts of criticism on short fiction by writers of all eras and nationalities.

Children's Literature Review

Includes excerpts from reviews, criticism, and commentary on works of authors and illustrators who create books for children.

Contemporary Authors Series

Encompasses five related series. *Contemporary Authors* provides biographical and bibliographical information on more than 95,000 writers of fiction, nonfiction, poetry, journalism, drama, motion pictures, and other fields. Each new volume contains sketches on authors not previously covered in the series. *Contemporary Authors New Revision Series* provides completely updated information on active authors covered in previously published volumes of *CA*. Only entries requiring significant change are revised for *CA New Revision Series*. *Contemporary Authors Permanent Series* consists of updated listings for deceased and inactive authors removed from the original volumes 9-36 when these volumes were revised. *Contemporary Authors Autobiography Series* presents specially commissioned autobiographies by leading contemporary writers. *Contemporary Authors Bibliographical Series* contains primary and secondary bibliographies as well as analytical bibliographical essays by authorities on major modern authors.

Dictionary of Literary Biography

Encompasses four related series. *Dictionary of Literary Biography* furnishes illustrated overviews of authors' lives and works and places them in the larger perspective of literary history. *Dictionary of Literary Biography Documentary Series* illuminates the careers of major figures through a selection of literary documents, including letters, notebook and diary entries, interviews, book reviews, and photographs. *Dictionary of Literary Biography Yearbook* summarizes the past year's literary activity with articles on genres, major prizes, conferences, and other timely subjects and includes updated and new entries on individual authors. *Concise Dictionary of American Literary Biography* comprises six volumes of revised and updated sketches on major American authors that were originally presented in *Dictionary of Literary Biography*.

Something about the Author Series

Encompasses three related series. *Something about the Author* contains heavily illustrated biographical sketches on juvenile and young adult authors and illustrators from all eras. *Something about the Author Autobiography Series* presents specially commissioned autobiographies by prominent authors and illustrators of books for children and young adults. *Authors & Artists for Young Adults* provides high school and junior high school students with profiles of their favorite creative artists in the mediums of print, film, television, drama, song lyrics, and cartoons.

Yesterday's Authors of Books for Children

Contains heavily illustrated entries on children's writers who died before 1961. Complete in two volumes.

Literary Criticism Series
Cumulative Author Index

This index lists all author entries in the Gale Literary Criticism Series and includes cross-references to other Gale sources. References in the index are identified as follows:

AAYA: *Authors & Artists for Young Adults,* Volumes 1-3
CAAS: *Contemporary Authors Autobiography Series,* Volumes 1-11
CA: *Contemporary Authors* (original series), Volumes 1-130
CABS: *Contemporary Authors Bibliographical Series,* Volumes 1-3
CANR: *Contemporary Authors New Revision Series,* Volumes 1-29
CAP: *Contemporary Authors Permanent Series,* Volumes 1-2
CA-R: *Contemporary Authors* (revised editions), Volumes 1-44
CDALB: *Concise Dictionary of American Literary Biography,* Volumes 1-6
CLC: *Contemporary Literary Criticism,* Volumes 1-60
CLR: *Children's Literature Review,* Volumes 1-21
CMLC: *Classical and Medieval Literature Criticism,* Volumes 1-5
DLB: *Dictionary of Literary Biography,* Volumes 1-92
DLB-DS: *Dictionary of Literary Biography Documentary Series,* Volumes 1-7
DLB-Y: *Dictionary of Literary Biography Yearbook,* Volumes 1980-1988
LC: *Literature Criticism from 1400 to 1800,* Volumes 1-13
NCLC: *Nineteenth-Century Literature Criticism,* Volumes 1-28
SAAS: *Something about the Author Autobiography Series,* Volumes 1-9
SATA: *Something about the Author,* Volumes 1-59
SSC: *Short Story Criticism,* Volumes 1-6
TCLC: *Twentieth-Century Literary Criticism,* Volumes 1-37
YABC: *Yesterday's Authors of Books for Children,* Volumes 1-2

A. E. 1867-1935 . . . . TCLC 3, 10
See also Russell, George William
See also DLB 19

Abbey, Edward 1927-1989 . . . . . . CLC 36, 59
See also CANR 2; CA 45-48;
obituary CA 128

Abbott, Lee K., Jr. 19??- . . . . CLC 48

Abe, Kobo 1924- . . . . CLC 8, 22, 53
See also CANR 24; CA 65-68

Abell, Kjeld 1901-1961 . . . . CLC 15
See also obituary CA 111

Abish, Walter 1931- . . . . CLC 22
See also CA 101

Abrahams, Peter (Henry) 1919- . . . . . CLC 4
See also CA 57-60

Abrams, M(eyer) H(oward) 1912- . . . CLC 24
See also CANR 13; CA 57-60; DLB 67

Abse, Dannie 1923- . . . . CLC 7, 29
See also CAAS 1; CANR 4; CA 53-56;
DLB 27

Achebe, (Albert) Chinua(lumogu)
1930- . . . . CLC 1, 3, 5, 7, 11, 26, 51
See also CLR 20; CANR 6, 26; CA 1-4R;
SATA 38, 40

Acker, Kathy 1948- . . . . CLC 45
See also CA 117, 122

Ackroyd, Peter 1949- . . . . CLC 34, 52
See also CA 123, 127

Acorn, Milton 1923- . . . . CLC 15
See also CA 103; DLB 53

Adamov, Arthur 1908-1970 . . . . . . CLC 4, 25
See also CAP 2; CA 17-18;
obituary CA 25-28R

Adams, Alice (Boyd) 1926- . . . CLC 6, 13, 46
See also CANR 26; CA 81-84; DLB-Y 86

Adams, Douglas (Noel) 1952- . . . CLC 27, 60
See also CA 106; DLB-Y 83

Adams, Henry (Brooks)
1838-1918 . . . . TCLC 4
See also CA 104; DLB 12, 47

Adams, Richard (George)
1920- . . . . CLC 4, 5, 18
See also CLR 20; CANR 3; CA 49-52;
SATA 7

Adamson, Joy(-Friederike Victoria)
1910-1980 . . . . CLC 17
See also CANR 22; CA 69-72;
obituary CA 93-96; SATA 11;
obituary SATA 22

Adcock, (Kareen) Fleur 1934- . . . . . . CLC 41
See also CANR 11; CA 25-28R; DLB 40

Addams, Charles (Samuel)
1912-1988 . . . . CLC 30
See also CANR 12; CA 61-64;
obituary CA 126

Adler, C(arole) S(chwerdtfeger)
1932- . . . . CLC 35
See also CANR 19; CA 89-92; SATA 26

Adler, Renata 1938- . . . . CLC 8, 31
See also CANR 5, 22; CA 49-52

Ady, Endre 1877-1919 . . . . TCLC 11
See also CA 107

Agee, James 1909-1955 . . . . TCLC 1, 19
See also CA 108; DLB 2, 26;
CDALB 1941-1968

Agnon, S(hmuel) Y(osef Halevi)
1888-1970 . . . . CLC 4, 8, 14
See also CAP 2; CA 17-18;
obituary CA 25-28R

Ai 1947- . . . . CLC 4, 14
See also CA 85-88

Aickman, Robert (Fordyce)
1914-1981 . . . . CLC 57
See also CANR 3; CA 7-8R

Aiken, Conrad (Potter)
1889-1973 . . . . CLC 1, 3, 5, 10, 52
See also CANR 4; CA 5-8R;
obituary CA 45-48; SATA 3, 30; DLB 9,
45

Aiken, Joan (Delano) 1924- . . . . CLC 35
See also CLR 1; CANR 4; CA 9-12R;
SAAS 1; SATA 2, 30

Author Index

Author Index

Enright, D(ennis) J(oseph)
1920- .... CLC **4, 8, 31**
See also CANR 1; CA 1-4R; SATA 25;
DLB 27

Enzensberger, Hans Magnus
1929- .... CLC **43**
See also CA 116, 119

Ephron, Nora 1941- .... CLC **17, 31**
See also CANR 12; CA 65-68

Epstein, Daniel Mark 1948- .... CLC **7**
See also CANR 2; CA 49-52

Epstein, Jacob 1956- .... CLC **19**
See also CA 114

Epstein, Joseph 1937-............. CLC **39**
See also CA 112, 119

Epstein, Leslie 1938- .... CLC **27**
See also CANR 23; CA 73-76

Erdman, Paul E(mil) 1932- .... CLC **25**
See also CANR 13; CA 61-64

Erdrich, Louise 1954-.......... CLC **39, 54**
See also CA 114

Erenburg, Ilya (Grigoryevich) 1891-1967
See Ehrenburg, Ilya (Grigoryevich)

Eseki, Bruno 1919-
See Mphahlele, Ezekiel

Esenin, Sergei (Aleksandrovich)
1895-1925 .... TCLC **4**
See also CA 104

Eshleman, Clayton 1935-.......... CLC **7**
See also CAAS 6; CA 33-36R; DLB 5

Espriu, Salvador 1913-1985........ CLC **9**
See also obituary CA 115

Estleman, Loren D. 1952-........ CLC **48**
See also CA 85-88

Evans, Marian 1819-1880
See Eliot, George

Evans, Mary Ann 1819-1880
See Eliot, George

Evarts, Esther 1900-1972
See Benson, Sally

Everett, Percival L. 1957?- .... CLC **57**
See also CA 129

Everson, Ronald G(ilmour) 1903- ... CLC **27**
See also CA 17-20R

Everson, William (Oliver)
1912- .... CLC **1, 5, 14**
See also CANR 20; CA 9-12R; DLB 5, 16

Evtushenko, Evgenii (Aleksandrovich) 1933-
See Yevtushenko, Yevgeny

Ewart, Gavin (Buchanan)
1916- .... CLC **13, 46**
See also CANR 17; CA 89-92; DLB 40

Ewers, Hanns Heinz 1871-1943 ... TCLC **12**
See also CA 109

Ewing, Frederick R. 1918-
See Sturgeon, Theodore (Hamilton)

Exley, Frederick (Earl) 1929-.... CLC **6, 11**
See also CA 81-84; DLB-Y 81

Ezekiel, Tish O'Dowd 1943-....... CLC **34**

Fagen, Donald 1948-............. CLC **26**

Fair, Ronald L. 1932-............ CLC **18**
See also CANR 25; CA 69-72; DLB 33

Fairbairns, Zoe (Ann) 1948- .... CLC **32**
See also CANR 21; CA 103

Fairfield, Cicily Isabel 1892-1983
See West, Rebecca

Fallaci, Oriana 1930-............. CLC **11**
See also CANR 15; CA 77-80

Faludy, George 1913-............. CLC **42**
See also CA 21-24R

Fante, John 1909-1983............ CLC **60**
See also CANR 23; CA 69-72;
obituary CA 109; DLB-Y 83

Farah, Nuruddin 1945-............ CLC **53**
See also CA 106

Fargue, Leon-Paul 1876-1947 ..... TCLC **11**
See also CA 109

Farigoule, Louis 1885-1972
See Romains, Jules

Farina, Richard 1937?-1966......... CLC **9**
See also CA 81-84; obituary CA 25-28R

Farley, Walter 1920- .... CLC **17**
See also CANR 8; CA 17-20R; SATA 2, 43;
DLB 22

Farmer, Philip Jose 1918-....... CLC **1, 19**
See also CANR 4; CA 1-4R; DLB 8

Farrell, J(ames) G(ordon)
1935-1979 .... CLC **6**
See also CA 73-76; obituary CA 89-92;
DLB 14

Farrell, James T(homas)
1904-1979 .... CLC **1, 4, 8, 11**
See also CANR 9; CA 5-8R;
obituary CA 89-92; DLB 4, 9; DLB-DS 2

Farrell, M. J. 1904-
See Keane, Molly

Fassbinder, Rainer Werner
1946-1982 .... CLC **20**
See also CA 93-96; obituary CA 106

Fast, Howard (Melvin) 1914- ...... CLC **23**
See also CANR 1; CA 1-4R; SATA 7;
DLB 9

Faulkner, William (Cuthbert)
1897-1962 .... CLC **1, 3, 6, 8, 9, 11, 14,
18, 28, 52; SSC 1**
See also CA 81-84; DLB 9, 11, 44;
DLB-Y 86; DLB-DS 2

Fauset, Jessie Redmon
1884?-1961................ CLC **19, 54**
See also CA 109; DLB 51

Faust, Irvin 1924-................ CLC **8**
See also CA 33-36R; DLB 2, 28; DLB-Y 80

Fearing, Kenneth (Flexner)
1902-1961 .... CLC **51**
See also CA 93-96; DLB 9

Federman, Raymond 1928- ...... CLC **6, 47**
See also CANR 10; CA 17-20R; DLB-Y 80

Federspiel, J(urg) F. 1931-........ CLC **42**

Feiffer, Jules 1929-............. CLC **2, 8**
See also CA 17-20R; SATA 8; DLB 7, 44

Feinberg, David B. 1956-......... CLC **59**

Feinstein, Elaine 1930-............ CLC **36**
See also CAAS 1; CA 69-72; DLB 14, 40

Feldman, Irving (Mordecai) 1928-.... CLC **7**
See also CANR 1; CA 1-4R

Fellini, Federico 1920-............ CLC **16**
See also CA 65-68

Felsen, Gregor 1916-
See Felsen, Henry Gregor

Felsen, Henry Gregor 1916- .... CLC **17**
See also CANR 1; CA 1-4R; SAAS 2;
SATA 1

Fenton, James (Martin) 1949-...... CLC **32**
See also CA 102; DLB 40

Ferber, Edna 1887-1968........... CLC **18**
See also CA 5-8R; obituary CA 25-28R;
SATA 7; DLB 9, 28

Ferlinghetti, Lawrence (Monsanto)
1919?- .... CLC **2, 6, 10, 27**
See also CANR 3; CA 5-8R; DLB 5, 16;
CDALB 1941-1968

Ferrier, Susan (Edmonstone)
1782-1854 .... NCLC **8**

Feuchtwanger, Lion 1884-1958 ..... TCLC **3**
See also CA 104; DLB 66

Feydeau, Georges 1862-1921 ...... TCLC **22**
See also CA 113

Ficino, Marsilio 1433-1499 .... LC **12**

Fiedler, Leslie A(aron)
1917- .... CLC **4, 13, 24**
See also CANR 7; CA 9-12R; DLB 28, 67

Field, Andrew 1938-............. CLC **44**
See also CANR 25; CA 97-100

Field, Eugene 1850-1895 .... NCLC **3**
See also SATA 16; DLB 21, 23, 42

Fielding, Henry 1707-1754 .... LC **1**
See also DLB 39

Fielding, Sarah 1710-1768........... LC **1**
See also DLB 39

Fierstein, Harvey 1954-........... CLC **33**
See also CA 123

Figes, Eva 1932-................. CLC **31**
See also CANR 4; CA 53-56; DLB 14

Finch, Robert (Duer Claydon)
1900- .... CLC **18**
See also CANR 9, 24; CA 57-60

Findley, Timothy 1930- .... CLC **27**
See also CANR 12; CA 25-28R; DLB 53

Fink, Janis 1951-
See Ian, Janis

Firbank, Louis 1944-
See Reed, Lou
See also CA 117

Firbank, (Arthur Annesley) Ronald
1886-1926 .... TCLC **1**
See also CA 104; DLB 36

Fisher, Roy 1930-................ CLC **25**
See also CANR 16; CA 81-84; DLB 40

Fisher, Rudolph 1897-1934 .... TCLC **11**
See also CA 107; DLB 51

Fisher, Vardis (Alvero) 1895-1968.... CLC **7**
See also CA 5-8R; obituary CA 25-28R;
DLB 9

FitzGerald, Edward 1809-1883 .... NCLC **9**
See also DLB 32

Fitzgerald, F(rancis) Scott (Key)
1896-1940 .... **TCLC 1, 6, 14, 28; SSC 6**
See also CA 110, 123; DLB 4, 9, 86;
DLB-Y 81; DLB-DS 1;
CDALB 1917-1929

Fitzgerald, Penelope 1916- ...... **CLC 19, 51**
See also CA 85-88; DLB 14

FitzGerald, Robert D(avid) 1902- ... **CLC 19**
See also CA 17-20R

Fitzgerald, Robert (Stuart)
1910-1985 .... **CLC 39**
See also CANR 1; CA 2R;
obituary CA 114; DLB-Y 80

Flanagan, Thomas (James Bonner)
1923- .... **CLC 25, 52**
See also CA 108; DLB-Y 80

Flaubert, Gustave
1821-1880 .... **NCLC 2, 10, 19**

Fleming, Ian (Lancaster)
1908-1964 .... **CLC 3, 30**
See also CA 5-8R; SATA 9

Fleming, Thomas J(ames) 1927- .... **CLC 37**
See also CANR 10; CA 5-8R; SATA 8

Fletcher, John Gould 1886-1950... **TCLC 35**
See also CA 107; DLB 4, 45

Flieg, Hellmuth
See Heym, Stefan

Flying Officer X 1905-1974
See Bates, H(erbert) E(rnest)

Fo, Dario 1929- .... **CLC 32**
See also CA 116

Follett, Ken(neth Martin) 1949- .... **CLC 18**
See also CANR 13; CA 81-84; DLB-Y 81

Fontane, Theodor 1819-1898 ..... **NCLC 26**

Foote, Horton 1916- .... **CLC 51**
See also CA 73-76; DLB 26

Forbes, Esther 1891-1967.......... **CLC 12**
See also CAP 1; CA 13-14;
obituary CA 25-28R; SATA 2; DLB 22

Forche, Carolyn 1950- .... **CLC 25**
See also CA 109, 117; DLB 5

Ford, Ford Madox 1873-1939 ... **TCLC 1, 15**
See also CA 104; DLB 34

Ford, John 1895-1973............. **CLC 16**
See also obituary CA 45-48

Ford, Richard 1944- .... **CLC 46**
See also CANR 11; CA 69-72

Foreman, Richard 1937-.......... **CLC 50**
See also CA 65-68

Forester, C(ecil) S(cott)
1899-1966 .... **CLC 35**
See also CA 73-76; obituary CA 25-28R;
SATA 13

Forman, James D(ouglas) 1932- .... **CLC 21**
See also CANR 4, 19; CA 9-12R; SATA 8,
21

Fornes, Maria Irene 1930-........ **CLC 39**
See also CA 25-28R; DLB 7

Forrest, Leon 1937- .... **CLC 4**
See also CAAS 7; CA 89-92; DLB 33

Forster, E(dward) M(organ)
1879-1970 .... **CLC 1, 2, 3, 4, 9, 10, 13,
15, 22, 45**
See also CAP 1; CA 13-14;
obituary CA 25-28R; DLB 34

Forster, John 1812-1876 .... **NCLC 11**

Forsyth, Frederick 1938- ...... **CLC 2, 5, 36**
See also CA 85-88

Forten (Grimke), Charlotte L(ottie)
1837-1914 .... **TCLC 16**
See also Grimke, Charlotte L(ottie) Forten
See also DLB 50

Foscolo, Ugo 1778-1827.......... **NCLC 8**

Fosse, Bob 1925-1987............ **CLC 20**
See also Fosse, Robert Louis

Fosse, Robert Louis 1925-1987
See Bob Fosse
See also CA 110, 123

Foster, Stephen Collins
1826-1864 .... **NCLC 26**

Foucault, Michel 1926-1984 .... **CLC 31, 34**
See also CANR 23; CA 105;
obituary CA 113

Fouque, Friedrich (Heinrich Karl) de La
Motte 1777-1843 .... **NCLC 2**

Fournier, Henri Alban 1886-1914
See Alain-Fournier
See also CA 104

Fournier, Pierre 1916- .... **CLC 11**
See also Gascar, Pierre
See also CANR 16; CA 89-92

Fowles, John (Robert)
1926- .... **CLC 1, 2, 3, 4, 6, 9, 10, 15, 33**
See also CANR 25; CA 5-8R; SATA 22;
DLB 14

Fox, Paula 1923-................. **CLC 2, 8**
See also CLR 1; CANR 20; CA 73-76;
SATA 17; DLB 52

Fox, William Price (Jr.) 1926- ..... **CLC 22**
See also CANR 11; CA 17-20R; DLB 2;
DLB-Y 81

Frame (Clutha), Janet (Paterson)
1924- .... **CLC 2, 3, 6, 22**
See also Clutha, Janet Paterson Frame

France, Anatole 1844-1924 .... **TCLC 9**
See also Thibault, Jacques Anatole Francois

Francis, Claude 19??-............. **CLC 50**

Francis, Dick 1920- .... **CLC 2, 22, 42**
See also CANR 9; CA 5-8R

Francis, Robert (Churchill)
1901-1987 .... **CLC 15**
See also CANR 1; CA 1-4R;
obituary CA 123

Frank, Anne 1929-1945 .... **TCLC 17**
See also CA 113; SATA 42

Frank, Elizabeth 1945-........... **CLC 39**
See also CA 121, 126

Franklin, (Stella Maria Sarah) Miles
1879-1954 .... **TCLC 7**
See also CA 104

Fraser, Antonia (Pakenham)
1932- .... **CLC 32**
See also CA 85-88; SATA 32

Fraser, George MacDonald 1925-.... **CLC 7**
See also CANR 2; CA 45-48

Frayn, Michael 1933-...... **CLC 3, 7, 31, 47**
See also CA 5-8R; DLB 13, 14

Fraze, Candida 19??- .... **CLC 50**
See also CA 125

Frazer, Sir James George
1854-1941 .... **TCLC 32**
See also CA 118

Frazier, Ian 1951-................ **CLC 46**

Frederic, Harold 1856-1898...... **NCLC 10**
See also DLB 12, 23

Fredman, Russell (Bruce) 1929-
See also CLR 20

Fredro, Aleksander 1793-1876..... **NCLC 8**

Freeling, Nicolas 1927- .... **CLC 38**
See also CANR 1, 17; CA 49-52

Freeman, Douglas Southall
1886-1953 .... **TCLC 11**
See also CA 109; DLB 17

Freeman, Judith 1946-........... **CLC 55**

Freeman, Mary (Eleanor) Wilkins
1852-1930 .... **TCLC 9; SSC 1**
See also CA 106; DLB 12

Freeman, R(ichard) Austin
1862-1943 .... **TCLC 21**
See also CA 113; DLB 70

French, Marilyn 1929-...... **CLC 10, 18, 60**
See also CANR 3; CA 69-72

Freneau, Philip Morin 1752-1832.. **NCLC 1**
See also DLB 37, 43

Friedman, B(ernard) H(arper)
1926- .... **CLC 7**
See also CANR 3; CA 1-4R

Friedman, Bruce Jay 1930-.... **CLC 3, 5, 56**
See also CANR 25; CA 9-12R; DLB 2, 28

Friel, Brian 1929-........... **CLC 5, 42, 59**
See also CA 21-24R; DLB 13

Friis-Baastad, Babbis (Ellinor)
1921-1970 .... **CLC 12**
See also CA 17-20R; SATA 7

Frisch, Max (Rudolf)
1911- .... **CLC 3, 9, 14, 18, 32, 44**
See also CA 85-88; DLB 69

Fromentin, Eugene (Samuel Auguste)
1820-1876 .... **NCLC 10**

Frost, Robert (Lee)
1874-1963 ... **CLC 1, 3, 4, 9, 10, 13, 15,
26, 34, 44**
See also CA 89-92; SATA 14; DLB 54

Fry, Christopher 1907-....... **CLC 2, 10, 14**
See also CANR 9; CA 17-20R; DLB 13

Frye, (Herman) Northrop 1912- .... **CLC 24**
See also CANR 8; CA 5-8R

Fuchs, Daniel 1909-............ **CLC 8, 22**
See also CAAS 5; CA 81-84; DLB 9, 26, 28

Fuchs, Daniel 1934-.............. **CLC 34**
See also CANR 14; CA 37-40R

Fuentes, Carlos
1928- ...... **CLC 3, 8, 10, 13, 22, 41, 60**
See also CANR 10; CA 69-72

Fugard, Athol 1932-... **CLC 5, 9, 14, 25, 40**
See also CA 85-88

Hamner, Earl (Henry), Jr. 1923- . . . **CLC 12**
See also CA 73-76; DLB 6

Hampton, Christopher (James)
1946- . . . . **CLC 4**
See also CA 25-28R; DLB 13

Hamsun, Knut 1859-1952 . . . . . . **TCLC 2, 14**
See also Pedersen, Knut

Handke, Peter 1942- . . **CLC 5, 8, 10, 15, 38**
See also CA 77-80

Hanley, James 1901-1985 . . . **CLC 3, 5, 8, 13**
See also CA 73-76; obituary CA 117

Hannah, Barry 1942- . . . . **CLC 23, 38**
See also CA 108, 110; DLB 6

Hansberry, Lorraine (Vivian)
1930-1965 . . . . **CLC 17**
See also CA 109; obituary CA 25-28R;
DLB 7, 38; CDALB 1941-1968

Hansen, Joseph 1923- . . . . **CLC 38**
See also CANR 16; CA 29-32R

Hansen, Martin 1909-1955 . . . . **TCLC 32**

Hanson, Kenneth O(stlin) 1922- . . . . **CLC 13**
See also CANR 7; CA 53-56

Hardenberg, Friedrich (Leopold Freiherr) von
1772-1801
See Novalis

Hardwick, Elizabeth 1916- . . . . **CLC 13**
See also CANR 3; CA 5-8R; DLB 6

Hardy, Thomas
1840-1928 . . . **TCLC 4, 10, 18, 32; SSC 2**
See also CA 104, 123; SATA 25; DLB 18,
19

Hare, David 1947- . . . . **CLC 29, 58**
See also CA 97-100; DLB 13

Harlan, Louis R(udolph) 1922- . . . . . **CLC 34**
See also CANR 25; CA 21-24R

Harling, Robert 1951?- . . . . **CLC 53**

Harmon, William (Ruth) 1938- . . . . . **CLC 38**
See also CANR 14; CA 33-36R

Harper, Frances Ellen Watkins
1825-1911 . . . . **TCLC 14**
See also CA 111, 125; DLB 50

Harper, Michael S(teven) 1938- . . **CLC 7, 22**
See also CANR 24; CA 33-36R; DLB 41

Harris, Christie (Lucy Irwin)
1907- . . . . **CLC 12**
See also CANR 6; CA 5-8R; SATA 6

Harris, Frank 1856-1931 . . . . **TCLC 24**
See also CAAS 1; CA 109

Harris, George Washington
1814-1869 . . . . **NCLC 23**
See also DLB 3, 11

Harris, Joel Chandler 1848-1908 . . . **TCLC 2**
See also YABC 1; CA 104; DLB 11, 23, 42

Harris, John (Wyndham Parkes Lucas)
Beynon 1903-1969
See Wyndham, John
See also CA 102; obituary CA 89-92

Harris, MacDonald 1921- . . . . **CLC 9**
See also Heiney, Donald (William)

Harris, Mark 1922- . . . . **CLC 19**
See also CAAS 3; CANR 2; CA 5-8R;
DLB 2; DLB-Y 80

Harris, (Theodore) Wilson 1921- . . . . **CLC 25**
See also CANR 11; CA 65-68

Harrison, Harry (Max) 1925- . . . . . . **CLC 42**
See also CANR 5, 21; CA 1-4R; SATA 4;
DLB 8

Harrison, James (Thomas) 1937-
See Harrison, Jim
See also CANR 8; CA 13-16R

Harrison, Jim 1937- . . . . **CLC 6, 14, 33**
See also Harrison, James (Thomas)
See also DLB-Y 82

Harrison, Tony 1937- . . . . **CLC 43**
See also CA 65-68; DLB 40

Harriss, Will(ard Irvin) 1922- . . . . . . **CLC 34**
See also CA 111

Harte, (Francis) Bret(t)
1836?-1902 . . . . **TCLC 1, 25**
See also CA 104; SATA 26; DLB 12, 64,
74; CDALB 1865-1917

Hartley, L(eslie) P(oles)
1895-1972 . . . . **CLC 2, 22**
See also CA 45-48; obituary CA 37-40R;
DLB 15

Hartman, Geoffrey H. 1929- . . . . **CLC 27**
See also CA 117, 125; DLB 67

Haruf, Kent 19??- . . . . **CLC 34**

Harwood, Ronald 1934- . . . . **CLC 32**
See also CANR 4; CA 1-4R; DLB 13

Hasek, Jaroslav (Matej Frantisek)
1883-1923 . . . . **TCLC 4**
See also CA 104

Hass, Robert 1941- . . . . **CLC 18, 39**
See also CA 111

Hastings, Selina 19??- . . . . **CLC 44**

Hauptmann, Gerhart (Johann Robert)
1862-1946 . . . . **TCLC 4**
See also CA 104; DLB 66

Havel, Vaclav 1936- . . . . **CLC 25, 58**
See also CA 104

Haviaras, Stratis 1935- . . . . **CLC 33**
See also CA 105

Hawkes, John (Clendennin Burne, Jr.)
1925- . . . . . . **CLC 1, 2, 3, 4, 7, 9, 14, 15,
27, 49**
See also CANR 2; CA 1-4R; DLB 2, 7;
DLB-Y 80

Hawthorne, Julian 1846-1934 . . . . . **TCLC 25**

Hawthorne, Nathaniel
1804-1864 . . . **NCLC 2, 10, 17, 23; SSC 3**
See also YABC 2; DLB 1, 74;
CDALB 1640-1865

Hayashi Fumiko 1904-1951 . . . . . . **TCLC 27**

Haycraft, Anna 19??-
See Ellis, Alice Thomas

Hayden, Robert (Earl)
1913-1980 . . . . **CLC 5, 9, 14, 37**
See also CANR 24; CA 69-72;
obituary CA 97-100; CABS 2; SATA 19;
obituary SATA 26; DLB 5, 76;
CDALB 1941-1968

Hayman, Ronald 1932- . . . . **CLC 44**
See also CANR 18; CA 25-28R

Haywood, Eliza (Fowler) 1693?-1756 . . **LC 1**
See also DLB 39

Hazzard, Shirley 1931- . . . . **CLC 18**
See also CANR 4; CA 9-12R; DLB-Y 82

H(ilda) D(oolittle)
1886-1961 . . . . **CLC 3, 8, 14, 31, 34**
See also Doolittle, Hilda

Head, Bessie 1937-1986 . . . . **CLC 25**
See also CANR 25; CA 29-32R;
obituary CA 109

Headon, (Nicky) Topper 1956?-
See The Clash

Heaney, Seamus (Justin)
1939- . . . . **CLC 5, 7, 14, 25, 37**
See also CANR 25; CA 85-88; DLB 40

Hearn, (Patricio) Lafcadio (Tessima Carlos)
1850-1904 . . . . **TCLC 9**
See also CA 105; DLB 12

Hearne, Vicki 1946- . . . . **CLC 56**

Heat Moon, William Least 1939- . . . **CLC 29**

Hebert, Anne 1916- . . . . **CLC 4, 13, 29**
See also CA 85-88; DLB 68

Hecht, Anthony (Evan)
1923- . . . . **CLC 8, 13, 19**
See also CANR 6; CA 9-12R; DLB 5

Hecht, Ben 1894-1964 . . . . **CLC 8**
See also CA 85-88; DLB 7, 9, 25, 26, 28

Hedayat, Sadeq 1903-1951 . . . . **TCLC 21**
See also CA 120

Heidegger, Martin 1889-1976 . . . . . . **CLC 24**
See also CA 81-84; obituary CA 65-68

Heidenstam, (Karl Gustaf) Verner von
1859-1940 . . . . **TCLC 5**
See also CA 104

Heifner, Jack 1946- . . . . **CLC 11**
See also CA 105

Heijermans, Herman 1864-1924 . . . **TCLC 24**
See also CA 123

Heilbrun, Carolyn G(old) 1926- . . . . . **CLC 25**
See also CANR 1; CA 45-48

Heine, Harry 1797-1856
See Heine, Heinrich

Heine, Heinrich 1797-1856 . . . . **NCLC 4**

Heinemann, Larry C(urtiss) 1944- . . **CLC 50**
See also CA 110

Heiney, Donald (William) 1921-
See Harris, MacDonald
See also CANR 3; CA 1-4R

Heinlein, Robert A(nson)
1907-1988 . . . . . . **CLC 1, 3, 8, 14, 26, 55**
See also CANR 1, 20; CA 1-4R;
obituary CA 125; SATA 9; DLB 8

Heller, Joseph
1923- . . . . **CLC 1, 3, 5, 8, 11, 36**
See also CANR 8; CA 5-8R; CABS 1;
DLB 2, 28; DLB-Y 80

Hellman, Lillian (Florence)
1905?-1984 . . . . . **CLC 2, 4, 8, 14, 18, 34,
44, 52**
See also CA 13-16R; obituary CA 112;
DLB 7; DLB-Y 84

Helprin, Mark 1947- . . . . . **CLC 7, 10, 22, 32**
See also CA 81-84; DLB-Y 85

Hemingway, Ernest (Miller)
1899-1961 . . . **CLC 1, 3, 6, 8, 10, 13, 19,
30, 34, 39, 41, 44, 50; SSC 1**
See also CA 77-80; DLB 4, 9; DLB-Y 81;
DLB-DS 1

Author Index

Immermann, Karl (Lebrecht)
  1796-1840 .... NCLC 4

Ingalls, Rachel 19??- .... CLC 42
  See also CA 123

Ingamells, Rex 1913-1955 .... TCLC 35

Inge, William (Motter)
  1913-1973 .... CLC 1, 8, 19
  See also CA 9-12R; DLB 7;
  CDALB 1941-1968

Innaurato, Albert 1948- .... CLC 21, 60
  See also CA 115, 122

Innes, Michael 1906-
  See Stewart, J(ohn) I(nnes) M(ackintosh)

Ionesco, Eugene
  1912- .... CLC 1, 4, 6, 9, 11, 15, 41
  See also CA 9-12R; SATA 7

Iqbal, Muhammad 1877-1938 ..... TCLC 28

Irving, John (Winslow)
  1942- .... CLC 13, 23, 38
  See also CA 25-28R; DLB 6; DLB-Y 82

Irving, Washington
  1783-1859 .... NCLC 2, 19; SSC 2
  See also YABC 2; DLB 3, 11, 30, 59, 73,
  74; CDALB 1640-1865

Isaacs, Susan 1943- .... CLC 32
  See also CANR 20; CA 89-92

Isherwood, Christopher (William Bradshaw)
  1904-1986 .... CLC 1, 9, 11, 14, 44
  See also CA 13-16R; obituary CA 117;
  DLB 15; DLB-Y 86

Ishiguro, Kazuo 1954- ...... CLC 27, 56, 59
  See also CA 120

Ishikawa Takuboku 1885-1912 .... TCLC 15
  See also CA 113

Iskander, Fazil (Abdulovich)
  1929- .... CLC 47
  See also CA 102

Ivanov, Vyacheslav (Ivanovich)
  1866-1949 .... TCLC 33
  See also CA 122

Ivask, Ivar (Vidrik) 1927- .... CLC 14
  See also CANR 24; CA 37-40R

Jackson, Jesse 1908-1983 .... CLC 12
  See also CA 25-28R; obituary CA 109;
  SATA 2, 29, 48

Jackson, Laura (Riding) 1901-
  See Riding, Laura
  See also CA 65-68; DLB 48

Jackson, Shirley 1919-1965 ..... CLC 11, 60
  See also CANR 4; CA 1-4R;
  obituary CA 25-28R; SATA 2; DLB 6;
  CDALB 1941-1968

Jacob, (Cyprien) Max 1876-1944 ... TCLC 6
  See also CA 104

Jacob, Piers A(nthony) D(illingham) 1934-
  See Anthony (Jacob), Piers
  See also CA 21-24R

Jacobs, Jim 1942- and Casey, Warren
  1942- .... CLC 12

Jacobs, Jim 1942-
  See Jacobs, Jim and Casey, Warren
  See also CA 97-100

Jacobs, W(illiam) W(ymark)
  1863-1943 .... TCLC 22
  See also CA 121

Jacobsen, Josephine 1908- .... CLC 48
  See also CANR 23; CA 33-36R

Jacobson, Dan 1929- .... CLC 4, 14
  See also CANR 2, 25; CA 1-4R; DLB 14

Jagger, Mick 1944- .... CLC 17

Jakes, John (William) 1932- .... CLC 29
  See also CANR 10; CA 57-60; DLB-Y 83

James, C(yril) L(ionel) R(obert)
  1901-1989 .... CLC 33
  See also CA 117, 125

James, Daniel 1911-1988
  See Santiago, Danny
  See also obituary CA 125

James, Henry (Jr.)
  1843-1916 .... TCLC 2, 11, 24
  See also CA 104; DLB 12, 71, 74;
  CDALB 1865-1917

James, M(ontague) R(hodes)
  1862-1936 .... TCLC 6
  See also CA 104

James, P(hyllis) D(orothy)
  1920- .... CLC 18, 46
  See also CANR 17; CA 21-24R

James, William 1842-1910 ..... TCLC 15, 32
  See also CA 109

Jami, Nur al-Din 'Abd al-Rahman
  1414-1492 .... LC 9

Jandl, Ernst 1925- .... CLC 34

Janowitz, Tama 1957- .... CLC 43
  See also CA 106

Jarrell, Randall
  1914-1965 .... CLC 1, 2, 6, 9, 13, 49
  See also CLR 6; CANR 6; CA 5-8R;
  obituary CA 25-28R; CABS 2; SATA 7;
  DLB 48, 52; CDALB 1941-1968

Jarry, Alfred 1873-1907 .... TCLC 2, 14
  See also CA 104

Jeake, Samuel, Jr. 1889-1973
  See Aiken, Conrad

Jean Paul 1763-1825 .... NCLC 7

Jeffers, (John) Robinson
  1887-1962 .... CLC 2, 3, 11, 15, 54
  See also CA 85-88; DLB 45

Jefferson, Thomas 1743-1826 .... NCLC 11
  See also DLB 31; CDALB 1640-1865

Jellicoe, (Patricia) Ann 1927- ...... CLC 27
  See also CA 85-88; DLB 13

Jenkins, (John) Robin 1912- .... CLC 52
  See also CANR 1; CA 4Rk; DLB 14

Jennings, Elizabeth (Joan)
  1926- .... CLC 5, 14
  See also CAAS 5; CANR 8; CA 61-64;
  DLB 27

Jennings, Waylon 1937- .... CLC 21

Jensen, Laura (Linnea) 1948- ...... CLC 37
  See also CA 103

Jerome, Jerome K. 1859-1927 ..... TCLC 23
  See also CA 119; DLB 10, 34

Jerrold, Douglas William
  1803-1857 .... NCLC 2

Jewett, (Theodora) Sarah Orne
  1849-1909 .... TCLC 1, 22; SSC 6
  See also CA 108, 127; SATA 15; DLB 12,
  74

Jewsbury, Geraldine (Endsor)
  1812-1880 .... NCLC 22
  See also DLB 21

Jhabvala, Ruth Prawer
  1927- .... CLC 4, 8, 29
  See also CANR 2; CA 1-4R

Jiles, Paulette 1943- .... CLC 13, 58
  See also CA 101

Jimenez (Mantecon), Juan Ramon
  1881-1958 .... TCLC 4
  See also CA 104

Joel, Billy 1949- .... CLC 26
  See also Joel, William Martin

Joel, William Martin 1949-
  See Joel, Billy
  See also CA 108

Johnson, B(ryan) S(tanley William)
  1933-1973 .... CLC 6, 9
  See also CANR 9; CA 9-12R;
  obituary CA 53-56; DLB 14, 40

Johnson, Charles (Richard)
  1948- .... CLC 7, 51
  See also CA 116; DLB 33

Johnson, Denis 1949- .... CLC 52
  See also CA 117, 121

Johnson, Diane 1934- .... CLC 5, 13, 48
  See also CANR 17; CA 41-44R; DLB-Y 80

Johnson, Eyvind (Olof Verner)
  1900-1976 .... CLC 14
  See also CA 73-76; obituary CA 69-72

Johnson, James Weldon
  1871-1938 .... TCLC 3, 19
  See also Johnson, James William
  See also CA 104, 125; DLB 51

Johnson, James William 1871-1938
  See Johnson, James Weldon
  See also SATA 31

Johnson, Joyce 1935- .... CLC 58
  See also CA 125

Johnson, Lionel (Pigot)
  1867-1902 .... TCLC 19
  See also CA 117; DLB 19

Johnson, Marguerita 1928-
  See Angelou, Maya

Johnson, Pamela Hansford
  1912-1981 .... CLC 1, 7, 27
  See also CANR 2; CA 1-4R;
  obituary CA 104; DLB 15

Johnson, Uwe
  1934-1984 .... CLC 5, 10, 15, 40
  See also CANR 1; CA 1-4R;
  obituary CA 112; DLB 75

Johnston, George (Benson) 1913- ... CLC 51
  See also CANR 5, 20; CA 1-4R

Johnston, Jennifer 1930- .... CLC 7
  See also CA 85-88; DLB 14

Jolley, Elizabeth 1923- .... CLC 46

Jones, D(ouglas) G(ordon) 1929- .... CLC 10
  See also CANR 13; CA 113; DLB 53

Jones, David
1895-1974 . . . . **CLC 2, 4, 7, 13, 42**
See also CA 9-12R; obituary CA 53-56;
DLB 20

Jones, David Robert   1947-
See Bowie, David
See also CA 103

Jones, Diana Wynne   1934- . . . . **CLC 26**
See also CANR 4; CA 49-52; SATA 9

Jones, Gayl   1949- . . . . **CLC 6, 9**
See also CA 77-80; DLB 33

Jones, James   1921-1977. . . . **CLC 1, 3, 10, 39**
See also CANR 6; CA 1-4R;
obituary CA 69-72; DLB 2

Jones, (Everett) LeRoi
1934- . . . . **CLC 1, 2, 3, 5, 10, 14, 33**
See also Baraka, Amiri; Baraka, Imamu
Amiri
See also CA 21-24R

Jones, Madison (Percy, Jr.)   1925- . . . **CLC 4**
See also CANR 7; CA 13-16R

Jones, Mervyn   1922- . . . . **CLC 10, 52**
See also CAAS 5; CANR 1; CA 45-48

Jones, Mick   1956?-
See The Clash

Jones, Nettie   19??- . . . . **CLC 34**

Jones, Preston   1936-1979 . . . . **CLC 10**
See also CA 73-76; obituary CA 89-92;
DLB 7

Jones, Robert F(rancis)   1934- . . . . **CLC 7**
See also CANR 2; CA 49-52

Jones, Rod   1953- . . . . **CLC 50**

Jones, Terry   1942?-
See Monty Python
See also CA 112, 116; SATA 51

Jong, Erica   1942- . . . . **CLC 4, 6, 8, 18**
See also CANR 26; CA 73-76; DLB 2, 5, 28

Jonson, Ben(jamin)   1572-1637. . . . . . . **LC 6**
See also DLB 62

Jordan, June   1936- . . . . **CLC 5, 11, 23**
See also CLR 10; CANR 25; CA 33-36R;
SATA 4; DLB 38

Jordan, Pat(rick M.)   1941- . . . . **CLC 37**
See also CANR 25; CA 33-36R

Josipovici, Gabriel (David)
1940- . . . . **CLC 6, 43**
See also CA 37-40R; DLB 14

Joubert, Joseph   1754-1824 . . . . **NCLC 9**

Jouve, Pierre Jean   1887-1976 . . . . . . **CLC 47**
See also obituary CA 65-68

Joyce, James (Augustine Aloysius)
1882-1941 . . . . . . **TCLC 3, 8, 16, 26, 35;
SSC 3**
See also CA 104, 126; DLB 10, 19, 36

Jozsef, Attila   1905-1937. . . . . **TCLC 22**
See also CA 116

Juana Ines de la Cruz   1651?-1695 . . . . **LC 5**

Julian of Norwich   1342?-1416? . . . . **LC 6**

Just, Ward S(wift)   1935- . . . . **CLC 4, 27**
See also CA 25-28R

Justice, Donald (Rodney)   1925- . . **CLC 6, 19**
See also CANR 26; CA 5-8R; DLB-Y 83

Kacew, Romain   1914-1980
See Gary, Romain
See also CA 108; obituary CA 102

Kacewgary, Romain   1914-1980
See Gary, Romain

Kadare, Ismail   1936- . . . . **CLC 52**

Kadohata, Cynthia   19??- . . . . **CLC 59**

Kafka, Franz
1883-1924 . . . . **TCLC 2, 6, 13, 29; SSC 5**
See also CA 105, 126; DLB 81

Kahn, Roger   1927- . . . . **CLC 30**
See also CA 25-28R; SATA 37

Kaiser, (Friedrich Karl) Georg
1878-1945 . . . . **TCLC 9**
See also CA 106

Kaletski, Alexander   1946- . . . . **CLC 39**
See also CA 118

Kallman, Chester (Simon)
1921-1975 . . . . **CLC 2**
See also CANR 3; CA 45-48;
obituary CA 53-56

Kaminsky, Melvin   1926-
See Brooks, Mel
See also CANR 16; CA 65-68

Kaminsky, Stuart   1934- . . . . **CLC 59**
See also CA 73-76

Kane, Paul   1941-
See Simon, Paul

Kanin, Garson   1912- . . . . **CLC 22**
See also CANR 7; CA 5-8R; DLB 7

Kaniuk, Yoram   1930- . . . . **CLC 19**

Kant, Immanuel   1724-1804 . . . . . . **NCLC 27**

Kantor, MacKinlay   1904-1977 . . . . . . **CLC 7**
See also CA 61-64; obituary CA 73-76;
DLB 9

Kaplan, David Michael   1946- . . . . . . **CLC 50**

Kaplan, James   19??- . . . . **CLC 59**

Karamzin, Nikolai Mikhailovich
1766-1826 . . . . **NCLC 3**

Karapanou, Margarita   1946- . . . . **CLC 13**
See also CA 101

Karl, Frederick R(obert)   1927- . . . . . **CLC 34**
See also CANR 3; CA 5-8R

Kassef, Romain   1914-1980
See Gary, Romain

Katz, Steve   1935- . . . . **CLC 47**
See also CANR 12; CA 25-28R; DLB-Y 83

Kauffman, Janet   1945- . . . . **CLC 42**
See also CA 117; DLB-Y 86

Kaufman, Bob (Garnell)
1925-1986 . . . . **CLC 49**
See also CANR 22; CA 41-44R;
obituary CA 118; DLB 16, 41

Kaufman, George S(imon)
1889-1961 . . . . **CLC 38**
See also CA 108; obituary CA 93-96; DLB 7

Kaufman, Sue   1926-1977 . . . . **CLC 3, 8**
See also Barondess, Sue K(aufman)

Kavan, Anna   1904-1968 . . . . **CLC 5, 13**
See also Edmonds, Helen (Woods)
See also CANR 6; CA 5-8R

Kavanagh, Patrick (Joseph Gregory)
1905-1967 . . . . **CLC 22**
See also CA 123; obituary CA 25-28R;
DLB 15, 20

Kawabata, Yasunari
1899-1972 . . . . **CLC 2, 5, 9, 18**
See also CA 93-96; obituary CA 33-36R

Kaye, M(ary) M(argaret)   1909?- . . . . **CLC 28**
See also CANR 24; CA 89-92

Kaye, Mollie   1909?-
See Kaye, M(ary) M(argaret)

Kaye-Smith, Sheila   1887-1956. . . . . **TCLC 20**
See also CA 118; DLB 36

Kazan, Elia   1909- . . . . **CLC 6, 16**
See also CA 21-24R

Kazantzakis, Nikos
1885?-1957. . . . . **TCLC 2, 5, 33**
See also CA 105

Kazin, Alfred   1915- . . . . **CLC 34, 38**
See also CAAS 7; CANR 1; CA 1-4R

Keane, Mary Nesta (Skrine)   1904-
See Keane, Molly
See also CA 108, 114

Keane, Molly   1904- . . . . **CLC 31**
See also Keane, Mary Nesta (Skrine)

Keates, Jonathan   19??- . . . . **CLC 34**

Keaton, Buster   1895-1966 . . . . **CLC 20**

Keaton, Joseph Francis   1895-1966
See Keaton, Buster

Keats, John   1795-1821. . . . . **NCLC 8**

Keene, Donald   1922- . . . . **CLC 34**
See also CANR 5; CA 1-4R

Keillor, Garrison   1942- . . . . **CLC 40**
See also Keillor, Gary (Edward)
See also CA 111; DLB 87

Keillor, Gary (Edward)
See Keillor, Garrison
See also CA 111, 117

Kell, Joseph   1917-
See Burgess (Wilson, John) Anthony

Keller, Gottfried   1819-1890 . . . . **NCLC 2**

Kellerman, Jonathan (S.)   1949- . . . . . **CLC 44**
See also CA 106

Kelley, William Melvin   1937- . . . . . . **CLC 22**
See also CA 77-80; DLB 33

Kellogg, Marjorie   1922- . . . . **CLC 2**
See also CA 81-84

Kelly, M. T.   1947- . . . . **CLC 55**
See also CANR 19; CA 97-100

Kelman, James   1946- . . . . **CLC 58**

Kemal, Yashar   1922- . . . . **CLC 14, 29**
See also CA 89-92

Kemble, Fanny   1809-1893 . . . . **NCLC 18**
See also DLB 32

Kemelman, Harry   1908- . . . . **CLC 2**
See also CANR 6; CA 9-12R; DLB 28

Kempe, Margery   1373?-1440? . . . . **LC 6**

Kempis, Thomas á   1380-1471 . . . . **LC 11**

Kendall, Henry   1839-1882 . . . . **NCLC 12**

Keneally, Thomas (Michael)
1935- . . . . . . **CLC 5, 8, 10, 14, 19, 27, 43**
See also CANR 10; CA 85-88

Author Index

Lindsay, (Nicholas) Vachel
    1879-1931 .... TCLC 17
    See also CA 114; SATA 40; DLB 54;
    CDALB 1865-1917

Linney, Romulus 1930- .... CLC 51
    See also CA 1-4R

Li Po 701-763 .... CMLC 2

Lipsyte, Robert (Michael) 1938-.... CLC 21
    See also CANR 8; CA 17-20R; SATA 5

Lish, Gordon (Jay) 1934-......... CLC 45
    See also CA 113, 117

Lispector, Clarice 1925-1977...... CLC 43
    See also obituary CA 116

Littell, Robert 1935?-............ CLC 42
    See also CA 109, 112

Liu E 1857-1909 .... TCLC 15
    See also CA 115

Lively, Penelope 1933-......... CLC 32, 50
    See also CLR 7; CA 41-44R; SATA 7;
    DLB 14

Livesay, Dorothy 1909- .... CLC 4, 15
    See also CA 25-28R

Llewellyn, Richard 1906-1983....... CLC 7
    See also Llewellyn Lloyd, Richard (Dafydd
    Vyvyan)
    See also DLB 15

Llewellyn Lloyd, Richard (Dafydd Vyvyan)
    1906-1983
    See Llewellyn, Richard
    See also CANR 7; CA 53-56;
    obituary CA 111; SATA 11, 37

Llosa, Mario Vargas 1936-
    See Vargas Llosa, Mario

Lloyd, Richard Llewellyn 1906-
    See Llewellyn, Richard

Locke, John 1632-1704 .... LC 7
    See also DLB 31

Lockhart, John Gibson
    1794-1854 .... NCLC 6

Lodge, David (John) 1935-........ CLC 36
    See also CANR 19; CA 17-20R; DLB 14

Loewinsohn, Ron(ald William)
    1937- .... CLC 52
    See also CA 25-28R

Logan, John 1923- .... CLC 5
    See also CA 77-80, 124; DLB 5

Lo Kuan-chung 1330?-1400? .... LC 12

Lombino, S. A. 1926-
    See Hunter, Evan

London, Jack
    1876-1916 .... TCLC 9, 15; SSC 4
    See also London, John Griffith
    See also SATA 18; DLB 8, 12;
    CDALB 1865-1917

London, John Griffith 1876-1916
    See London, Jack
    See also CA 110, 119

Long, Emmett 1925-
    See Leonard, Elmore

Longbaugh, Harry 1931-
    See Goldman, William (W.)

Longfellow, Henry Wadsworth
    1807-1882 .... NCLC 2
    See also SATA 19; DLB 1, 59;
    CDALB 1640-1865

Longley, Michael 1939-........... CLC 29
    See also CA 102; DLB 40

Lopate, Phillip 1943- .... CLC 29
    See also CA 97-100; DLB-Y 80

Lopez Portillo (y Pacheco), Jose
    1920- .... CLC 46

Lopez y Fuentes, Gregorio
    1897-1966 .... CLC 32

Lord, Bette Bao 1938- .... CLC 23
    See also CA 107

Lorde, Audre (Geraldine) 1934-..... CLC 18
    See also CANR 16, 26; CA 25-28R;
    DLB 41

Loti, Pierre 1850-1923 .... TCLC 11
    See also Viaud, (Louis Marie) Julien

Lovecraft, H(oward) P(hillips)
    1890-1937 .... TCLC 4, 22; SSC 3
    See also CA 104

Lovelace, Earl 1935-.............. CLC 51
    See also CA 77-80

Lowell, Amy 1874-1925 .... TCLC 1, 8
    See also CA 104; DLB 54

Lowell, James Russell 1819-1891 .. NCLC 2
    See also DLB 1, 11, 64; CDALB 1640-1865

Lowell, Robert (Traill Spence, Jr.)
    1917-1977 ... CLC 1, 2, 3, 4, 5, 8, 9, 11,
                                    15, 37
    See also CANR 26; CA 9-12R;
    obituary CA 73-76; CABS 2; DLB 5

Lowndes, Marie (Adelaide) Belloc
    1868-1947 .... TCLC 12
    See also CA 107; DLB 70

Lowry, (Clarence) Malcolm
    1909-1957 .... TCLC 6
    See also CA 105; DLB 15

Loy, Mina 1882-1966............. CLC 28
    See also CA 113; DLB 4, 54

Lucas, George 1944-.............. CLC 16
    See also CA 77-80

Lucas, Victoria 1932-1963
    See Plath, Sylvia

Ludlam, Charles 1943-1987..... CLC 46, 50
    See also CA 85-88; obituary CA 122

Ludlum, Robert 1927- .... CLC 22, 43
    See also CANR 25; CA 33-36R; DLB-Y 82

Ludwig, Ken 19??- .... CLC 60

Ludwig, Otto 1813-1865......... NCLC 4

Lugones, Leopoldo 1874-1938 ..... TCLC 15
    See also CA 116

Lu Hsun 1881-1936 .... TCLC 3

Lukacs, Georg 1885-1971.......... CLC 24
    See also Lukacs, Gyorgy

Lukacs, Gyorgy 1885-1971
    See Lukacs, Georg
    See also CA 101; obituary CA 29-32R

Luke, Peter (Ambrose Cyprian)
    1919- .... CLC 38
    See also CA 81-84; DLB 13

Lurie (Bishop), Alison
    1926- .... CLC 4, 5, 18, 39
    See also CANR 2, 17; CA 1-4R; SATA 46;
    DLB 2

Lustig, Arnost 1926-............. CLC 56
    See also CA 69-72; SATA 56

Luther, Martin 1483-1546.......... LC 9

Luzi, Mario 1914-............... CLC 13
    See also CANR 9; CA 61-64

Lynn, Kenneth S(chuyler) 1923-.... CLC 50
    See also CANR 3; CA 1-4R

Lytle, Andrew (Nelson) 1902-...... CLC 22
    See also CA 9-12R; DLB 6

Lyttelton, George 1709-1773........ LC 10

Lytton, Edward Bulwer 1803-1873
    See Bulwer-Lytton, (Lord) Edward (George
    Earle Lytton)
    See also SATA 23

Maas, Peter 1929- .... CLC 29
    See also CA 93-96

Macaulay, (Dame Emile) Rose
    1881-1958 .... TCLC 7
    See also CA 104; DLB 36

MacBeth, George (Mann)
    1932- .... CLC 2, 5, 9
    See also CA 25-28R; SATA 4; DLB 40

MacCaig, Norman (Alexander)
    1910- .... CLC 36
    See also CANR 3; CA 9-12R; DLB 27

MacCarthy, Desmond 1877-1952 .. TCLC 36

MacDermot, Thomas H. 1870-1933
    See Redcam, Tom

MacDiarmid, Hugh
    1892-1978 .... CLC 2, 4, 11, 19
    See also Grieve, C(hristopher) M(urray)
    See also DLB 20

Macdonald, Cynthia 1928-...... CLC 13, 19
    See also CANR 4; CA 49-52

MacDonald, George 1824-1905..... TCLC 9
    See also CA 106; SATA 33; DLB 18

MacDonald, John D(ann)
    1916-1986 .... CLC 3, 27, 44
    See also CANR 1, 19; CA 1-4R;
    obituary CA 121; DLB 8; DLB-Y 86

Macdonald, (John) Ross
    1915-1983 ...... CLC 1, 2, 3, 14, 34, 41
    See also Millar, Kenneth

MacEwen, Gwendolyn (Margaret)
    1941-1987 .... CLC 13, 55
    See also CANR 7, 22; CA 9-12R;
    obituary CA 124; SATA 50; DLB 53

Machado (y Ruiz), Antonio
    1875-1939 .... TCLC 3
    See also CA 104

Machado de Assis, (Joaquim Maria)
    1839-1908 .... TCLC 10
    See also CA 107

Machen, Arthur (Llewellyn Jones)
    1863-1947 .... TCLC 4
    See also CA 104; DLB 36

Machiavelli, Niccolo 1469-1527 ...... LC 8

MacInnes, Colin 1914-1976...... CLC 4, 23
    See also CA 69-72; obituary CA 65-68;
    DLB 14

MacInnes, Helen (Clark)
1907-1985 . . . . **CLC 27, 39**
See also CANR 1; CA 1-4R;
obituary CA 65-68, 117; SATA 22, 44

Macintosh, Elizabeth 1897-1952
See Tey, Josephine
See also CA 110

Mackenzie, (Edward Montague) Compton
1883-1972 . . . . **CLC 18**
See also CAP 2; CA 21-22;
obituary CA 37-40R; DLB 34

Mac Laverty, Bernard 1942- . . . . **CLC 31**
See also CA 116, 118

MacLean, Alistair (Stuart)
1922-1987 . . . . **CLC 3, 13, 50**
See also CA 57-60; obituary CA 121;
SATA 23

MacLeish, Archibald
1892-1982 . . . . **CLC 3, 8, 14**
See also CA 9-12R; obituary CA 106;
DLB 4, 7, 45; DLB-Y 82

MacLennan, (John) Hugh
1907- . . . . **CLC 2, 14**
See also CA 5-8R

MacLeod, Alistair 1936- . . . . **CLC 56**
See also CA 123; DLB 60

MacNeice, (Frederick) Louis
1907-1963 . . . . **CLC 1, 4, 10, 53**
See also CA 85-88; DLB 10, 20

Macpherson, (Jean) Jay 1931- . . . . . . **CLC 14**
See also CA 5-8R; DLB 53

MacShane, Frank 1927- . . . . **CLC 39**
See also CANR 3; CA 11-12R

Macumber, Mari 1896-1966
See Sandoz, Mari (Susette)

Madach, Imre 1823-1864 . . . . **NCLC 19**

Madden, (Jerry) David 1933- . . . . **CLC 5, 15**
See also CAAS 3; CANR 4; CA 1-4R;
DLB 6

Madhubuti, Haki R. 1942- . . . . **CLC 6**
See also Lee, Don L.
See also CANR 24; CA 73-76; DLB 5, 41

Maeterlinck, Maurice 1862-1949 . . . **TCLC 3**
See also CA 104

Mafouz, Naguib 1912-
See Mahfuz, Najib

Maginn, William 1794-1842 . . . . **NCLC 8**

Mahabharata
c. 400 B.C.-c. 400 A.D. . . . . **CMLC 5**

Mahapatra, Jayanta 1928- . . . . **CLC 33**
See also CANR 15; CA 73-76

Mahfuz Najib 1912- . . . . **CLC 52, 55**
See also DLB-Y 88

Mahon, Derek 1941- . . . . **CLC 27**
See also CA 113; DLB 40

Mailer, Norman
1923- . . . . . . **CLC 1, 2, 3, 4, 5, 8, 11, 14,
28, 39**
See also CA 9-12R; CABS 1; DLB 2, 16,
28; DLB-Y 80, 83; DLB-DS 3

Maillet, Antonine 1929- . . . . **CLC 54**
See also CA 115, 120; DLB 60

Mais, Roger 1905-1955 . . . . **TCLC 8**
See also CA 105

Maitland, Sara (Louise) 1950- . . . . . . **CLC 49**
See also CANR 13; CA 69-72

Major, Clarence 1936- . . . . **CLC 3, 19, 48**
See also CAAS 6; CANR 13; CA 21-24R;
DLB 33

Major, Kevin 1949- . . . . **CLC 26**
See also CLR 11; CANR 21; CA 97-100;
SATA 32; DLB 60

Malamud, Bernard
1914-1986 . . . . . **CLC 1, 2, 3, 5, 8, 9, 11,
18, 27, 44**
See also CA 5-8R; obituary CA 118;
CABS 1; DLB 2, 28; DLB-Y 80, 86;
CDALB 1941-1968

Malherbe, Francois de 1555-1628 . . . . . **LC 5**

Mallarme, Stephane 1842-1898 . . . . **NCLC 4**

Mallet-Joris, Francoise 1930- . . . . . . **CLC 11**
See also CANR 17; CA 65-68

Maloff, Saul 1922- . . . . **CLC 5**
See also CA 33-36R

Malone, Louis 1907-1963
See MacNeice, (Frederick) Louis

Malone, Michael (Christopher)
1942- . . . . **CLC 43**
See also CANR 14; CA 77-80

Malory, (Sir) Thomas ?-1471 . . . . **LC 11**
See also SATA 33

Malouf, David 1934- . . . . **CLC 28**

Malraux, (Georges-) Andre
1901-1976 . . . . . . **CLC 1, 4, 9, 13, 15, 57**
See also CAP 2; CA 21-24;
obituary CA 69-72; DLB 72

Malzberg, Barry N. 1939- . . . . **CLC 7**
See also CAAS 4; CANR 16; CA 61-64;
DLB 8

Mamet, David (Alan)
1947-1987 . . . . **CLC 9, 15, 34, 46**
See also CANR 15; CA 81-84, 124; DLB 7

Mamoulian, Rouben 1898- . . . . **CLC 16**
See also CA 25-28R

Mandelstam, Osip (Emilievich)
1891?-1938? . . . . **TCLC 2, 6**
See also CA 104

Mander, Jane 1877-1949 . . . . **TCLC 31**

Mandiargues, Andre Pieyre de
1909- . . . . **CLC 41**
See also CA 103

Mangan, James Clarence
1803-1849 . . . . **NCLC 27**

Manley, (Mary) Delariviere
1672?-1724 . . . . **LC 1**
See also DLB 39

Mann, (Luiz) Heinrich 1871-1950 . . . **TCLC 9**
See also CA 106; DLB 66

Mann, Thomas
1875-1955 . . . . . . **TCLC 2, 8, 14, 21, 35;
SSC 5**
See also CA 104, 128; DLB 66

Manning, Frederic 1882-1935 . . . . . **TCLC 25**

Manning, Olivia 1915-1980 . . . . . . **CLC 5, 19**
See also CA 5-8R; obituary CA 101

Mano, D. Keith 1942- . . . . **CLC 2, 10**
See also CAAS 6; CANR 26; CA 25-28R;
DLB 6

Mansfield, Katherine
1888-1923 . . . . **TCLC 2, 8**
See also CA 104

Manso, Peter 1940- . . . . **CLC 39**
See also CA 29-32R

Mapu, Abraham (ben Jekutiel)
1808-1867 . . . . **NCLC 18**

Marat, Jean Paul 1743-1793 . . . . **LC 10**

Marcel, Gabriel (Honore)
1889-1973 . . . . **CLC 15**
See also CA 102; obituary CA 45-48

Marchbanks, Samuel 1913-
See Davies, (William) Robertson

Marie de l'Incarnation 1599-1672 . . . . **LC 10**

Marinetti, F(ilippo) T(ommaso)
1876-1944 . . . . **TCLC 10**
See also CA 107

Marivaux, Pierre Carlet de Chamblain de
(1688-1763) . . . . **LC 4**

Markandaya, Kamala 1924- . . . . . . **CLC 8, 38**
See also Taylor, Kamala (Purnaiya)

Markfield, Wallace (Arthur) 1926- . . . **CLC 8**
See also CAAS 3; CA 69-72; DLB 2, 28

Markham, Robert 1922-
See Amis, Kingsley (William)

Marks, J. 1942-
See Highwater, Jamake

Marley, Bob 1945-1981 . . . . **CLC 17**
See also Marley, Robert Nesta

Marley, Robert Nesta 1945-1981
See Marley, Bob
See also CA 107; obituary CA 103

Marmontel, Jean-Francois
1723-1799 . . . . **LC 2**

Marquand, John P(hillips)
1893-1960 . . . . **CLC 2, 10**
See also CA 85-88; DLB 9

Marquez, Gabriel Garcia 1928-
See Garcia Marquez, Gabriel

Marquis, Don(ald Robert Perry)
1878-1937 . . . . **TCLC 7**
See also CA 104; DLB 11, 25

Marryat, Frederick 1792-1848 . . . . **NCLC 3**
See also DLB 21

Marsh, (Dame Edith) Ngaio
1899-1982 . . . . **CLC 7, 53**
See also CANR 6; CA 9-12R; DLB 77

Marshall, Garry 1935?- . . . . **CLC 17**
See also CA 111

Marshall, Paule 1929- . . . . . **CLC 27; SSC 3**
See also CANR 25; CA 77-80; DLB 33

Marsten, Richard 1926-
See Hunter, Evan

Martin, Steve 1945?- . . . . **CLC 30**
See also CA 97-100

Martin du Gard, Roger
1881-1958 . . . . **TCLC 24**
See also CA 118

Martineau, Harriet 1802-1876 . . . . **NCLC 26**
See also YABC 2; DLB 21, 55

Martinez Ruiz, Jose 1874-1967
See Azorin
See also CA 93-96

Martinez Sierra, Gregorio
1881-1947 .... TCLC 6
See also CA 104, 115

Martinez Sierra, Maria (de la O'LeJarraga)
1880?-1974.................. TCLC 6
See also obituary CA 115

Martinson, Harry (Edmund)
1904-1978 .... CLC 14
See also CA 77-80

Marvell, Andrew 1621-1678......... LC 4

Marx, Karl (Heinrich)
1818-1883 .... NCLC 17

Masaoka Shiki 1867-1902 .... TCLC 18

Masefield, John (Edward)
1878-1967 .... CLC 11, 47
See also CAP 2; CA 19-20;
obituary CA 25-28R; SATA 19; DLB 10,
19

Maso, Carole 19??-.............. CLC 44

Mason, Bobbie Ann
1940- .... CLC 28, 43; SSC 4
See also CANR 11; CA 53-56; SAAS 1;
DLB-Y 87

Mason, Nick 1945-............... CLC 35
See also Pink Floyd

Mason, Tally 1909-1971
See Derleth, August (William)

Masters, Edgar Lee
1868?-1950.......... TCLC 2, 25
See also CA 104; DLB 54;
CDALB 1865-1917

Masters, Hilary 1928- .... CLC 48
See also CANR 13; CA 25-28R

Mastrosimone, William 19??- ...... CLC 36

Matheson, Richard (Burton)
1926- .... CLC 37
See also CA 97-100; DLB 8, 44

Mathews, Harry 1930-.......... CLC 6, 52
See also CAAS 6; CANR 18; CA 21-24R

Mathias, Roland (Glyn) 1915-...... CLC 45
See also CANR 19; CA 97-100; DLB 27

Matthews, Greg 1949- .... CLC 45

Matthews, William 1942-......... CLC 40
See also CANR 12; CA 29-32R; DLB 5

Matthias, John (Edward) 1941-...... CLC 9
See also CA 33-36R

Matthiessen, Peter 1927-... CLC 5, 7, 11, 32
See also CANR 21; CA 9-12R; SATA 27;
DLB 6

Maturin, Charles Robert
1780?-1824.................. NCLC 6

Matute, Ana Maria 1925- .... CLC 11
See also CA 89-92

Maugham, W(illiam) Somerset
1874-1965 .... CLC 1, 11, 15
See also CA 5-8R; obituary CA 25-28R;
DLB 10, 36

Maupassant, (Henri Rene Albert) Guy de
1850-1893 .... NCLC 1; SSC 1

Mauriac, Claude 1914-............. CLC 9
See also CA 89-92

Mauriac, Francois (Charles)
1885-1970 .... CLC 4, 9, 56
See also CAP 2; CA 25-28; DLB 65

Mavor, Osborne Henry 1888-1951
See Bridie, James
See also CA 104

Maxwell, William (Keepers, Jr.)
1908-....................... CLC 19
See also CA 93-96; DLB-Y 80

May, Elaine 1932- .... CLC 16
See also CA 124; DLB 44

Mayakovsky, Vladimir (Vladimirovich)
1893-1930 .... TCLC 4, 18
See also CA 104

Maynard, Joyce 1953-............CLC 23
See also CA 111

Mayne, William (James Carter)
1928-....................... CLC 12
See also CA 9-12R; SATA 6

Mayo, Jim 1908?-
See L'Amour, Louis (Dearborn)

Maysles, Albert 1926- and **Maysles, David**
1926- .... CLC 16

Maysles, Albert 1926-
See Maysles, Albert and Maysles, David
See also CA 29-32R

Maysles, David 1932-
See Maysles, Albert and Maysles, David

Mazer, Norma Fox 1931- .... CLC 26
See also CANR 12; CA 69-72; SAAS 1;
SATA 24

McAuley, James (Phillip)
1917-1976 .... CLC 45
See also CA 97-100

McBain, Ed 1926-
See Hunter, Evan

McBrien, William 1930- .... CLC 44
See also CA 107

McCaffrey, Anne 1926-........... CLC 17
See also CANR 15; CA 25-28R; SATA 8;
DLB 8

McCarthy, Cormac 1933-........ CLC 4, 57
See also CANR 10; CA 13-16R; DLB 6

McCarthy, Mary (Therese)
1912-1989-... CLC 1, 3, 5, 14, 24, 39, 59
See also CANR 16; CA 5-8R; DLB 2;
DLB-Y 81

McCartney, (James) Paul
1942- .... CLC 12, 35

McCauley, Stephen 19??-.......... CLC 50

McClure, Michael 1932- .... CLC 6, 10
See also CANR 17; CA 21-24R; DLB 16

McCorkle, Jill (Collins) 1958-...... CLC 51
See also CA 121; DLB-Y 87

McCourt, James 1941-............. CLC 5
See also CA 57-60

McCoy, Horace 1897-1955 .... TCLC 28
See also CA 108; DLB 9

McCrae, John 1872-1918........ TCLC 12
See also CA 109

McCullers, (Lula) Carson (Smith)
1917-1967 .... CLC 1, 4, 10, 12, 48
See also CANR 18; CA 5-8R;
obituary CA 25-28R; CABS 1; SATA 27;
DLB 2, 7; CDALB 1941-1968

McCullough, Colleen 1938?- .... CLC 27
See also CANR 17; CA 81-84

McElroy, Joseph (Prince)
1930-....................... CLC 5, 47
See also CA 17-20R

McEwan, Ian (Russell) 1948- ...... CLC 13
See also CANR 14; CA 61-64; DLB 14

McFadden, David 1940-............ CLC 48
See also CA 104; DLB 60

McGahern, John 1934-........ CLC 5, 9, 48
See also CA 17-20R; DLB 14

McGinley, Patrick 1937-.......... CLC 41
See also CA 120

McGinley, Phyllis 1905-1978 ...... CLC 14
See also CANR 19; CA 9-12R;
obituary CA 77-80; SATA 2, 44;
obituary SATA 24; DLB 11, 48

McGinniss, Joe 1942-............. CLC 32
See also CA 25-28R

McGivern, Maureen Daly 1921-
See Daly, Maureen
See also CA 9-12R

McGrath, Patrick 1950-.......... CLC 55

McGrath, Thomas 1916- .... CLC 28, 59
See also CANR 6; CA 9-12R, 130;
SATA 41

McGuane, Thomas (Francis III)
1939- .... CLC 3, 7, 18
See also CANR 5; CA 49-52; DLB 2;
DLB-Y 80

McGuckian, Medbh 1950-......... CLC 48
See also DLB 40

McHale, Tom 1941-1982........ CLC 3, 5
See also CA 77-80; obituary CA 106

McIlvanney, William 1936-........ CLC 42
See also CA 25-28R; DLB 14

McIlwraith, Maureen Mollie Hunter 1922-
See Hunter, Mollie
See also CA 29-32R; SATA 2

McInerney, Jay 1955-............ CLC 34
See also CA 116, 123

McIntyre, Vonda N(eel) 1948- ..... CLC 18
See also CANR 17; CA 81-84

McKay, Claude 1890-1948........ TCLC 7
See also CA 104; DLB 4, 45

McKuen, Rod 1933-............. CLC 1, 3
See also CA 41-44R

McLuhan, (Herbert) Marshall
1911-1980 .... CLC 37
See also CANR 12; CA 9-12R;
obituary CA 102

McManus, Declan Patrick 1955-
See Costello, Elvis

McMillan, Terry 19??-............ CLC 50

McMurtry, Larry (Jeff)
1936- .... CLC 2, 3, 7, 11, 27, 44
See also CANR 19; CA 5-8R; DLB 2;
DLB-Y 80, 87

McNally, Terrence 1939-...... CLC 4, 7, 41
See also CANR 2; CA 45-48; DLB 7

McPhee, John 1931-.............. CLC 36
See also CANR 20; CA 65-68

McPherson, James Alan 1943-..... CLC 19
See also CANR 24; CA 25-28R; DLB 38

McPherson, William 1939- .... CLC 34
See also CA 57-60

McSweeney, Kerry 19??- .... CLC 34

Mead, Margaret 1901-1978 .... CLC 37
See also CANR 4; CA 1-4R;
obituary CA 81-84; SATA 20

Meaker, M. J. 1927-
See Kerr, M. E.; Meaker, Marijane

Meaker, Marijane 1927-
See Kerr, M. E.
See also CA 107; SATA 20

Medoff, Mark (Howard) 1940- ... CLC 6, 23
See also CANR 5; CA 53-56; DLB 7

Megged, Aharon 1920- .... CLC 9
See also CANR 1; CA 49-52

Mehta, Ved (Parkash) 1934- .... CLC 37
See also CANR 2, 23; CA 1-4R

Mellor, John 1953?-
See The Clash

Meltzer, Milton 1915- .... CLC 26 13
See also CA 13-16R; SAAS 1; SATA 1, 50;
DLB 61

Melville, Herman
1819-1891 .... NCLC 3, 12; SSC 1
See also DLB 3; CDALB 1640-1865

Membreno, Alejandro 1972- .... CLC 59

Mencken, H(enry) L(ouis)
1880-1956 .... TCLC 13
See also CA 105; DLB 11, 29, 63

Mercer, David 1928-1980 .... CLC 5
See also CA 9-12R; obituary CA 102;
DLB 13

Meredith, George 1828-1909 ...... TCLC 17
See also CA 117; DLB 18, 35, 57

Meredith, William (Morris)
1919- .... CLC 4, 13, 22, 55
See also CANR 6; CA 9-12R; DLB 5

Merezhkovsky, Dmitri
1865-1941 .... TCLC 29

Merimee, Prosper 1803-1870 ...... NCLC 6

Merkin, Daphne 1954- .... CLC 44
See also CANR 123

Merrill, James (Ingram)
1926- .... CLC 2, 3, 6, 8, 13, 18, 34
See also CANR 10; CA 13-16R; DLB 5;
DLB-Y 85

Merton, Thomas (James)
1915-1968 .... CLC 1, 3, 11, 34
See also CANR 22; CA 5-8R;
obituary CA 25-28R; DLB 48; DLB-Y 81

Merwin, W(illiam) S(tanley)
1927- ...... CLC 1, 2, 3, 5, 8, 13, 18, 45
See also CANR 15; CA 13-16R; DLB 5

Metcalf, John 1938- .... CLC 37
See also CA 113; DLB 60

Mew, Charlotte (Mary)
1870-1928 .... TCLC 8
See also CA 105; DLB 19

Mewshaw, Michael 1943- .... CLC 9
See also CANR 7; CA 53-56; DLB-Y 80

Meyer-Meyrink, Gustav 1868-1932
See Meyrink, Gustav
See also CA 117

Meyers, Jeffrey 1939- .... CLC 39
See also CA 73-76

Meynell, Alice (Christiana Gertrude
Thompson) 1847-1922 .... TCLC 6
See also CA 104; DLB 19

Meyrink, Gustav 1868-1932 ...... TCLC 21
See also Meyer-Meyrink, Gustav

Michaels, Leonard 1933- .... CLC 6, 25
See also CANR 21; CA 61-64

Michaux, Henri 1899-1984 ...... CLC 8, 19
See also CA 85-88; obituary CA 114

Michelangelo 1475-1564 .... LC 12

Michener, James A(lbert)
1907- .... CLC 1, 5, 11, 29, 60
See also CANR 21; CA 5-8R; DLB 6

Mickiewicz, Adam 1798-1855 ..... NCLC 3

Middleton, Christopher 1926- ...... CLC 13
See also CA 13-16R; DLB 40

Middleton, Stanley 1919- .... CLC 7, 38
See also CANR 21; CA 25-28R; DLB 14

Migueis, Jose Rodrigues 1901- ..... CLC 10

Mikszath, Kalman 1847-1910 ..... TCLC 31

Miles, Josephine (Louise)
1911-1985 .... CLC 1, 2, 14, 34, 39
See also CANR 2; CA 1-4R;
obituary CA 116; DLB 48

Mill, John Stuart 1806-1873 ..... NCLC 11

Millar, Kenneth 1915-1983 .... CLC 14
See also Macdonald, Ross
See also CANR 16; CA 9-12R;
obituary CA 110; DLB 2; DLB-Y 83

Millay, Edna St. Vincent
1892-1950 .... TCLC 4
See also CA 104; DLB 45

Miller, Arthur
1915- .... CLC 1, 2, 6, 10, 15, 26, 47
See also CANR 2; CA 1-4R; DLB 7;
CDALB 1941-1968

Miller, Henry (Valentine)
1891-1980 .... CLC 1, 2, 4, 9, 14, 43
See also CA 9-12R; obituary CA 97-100;
DLB 4, 9; DLB-Y 80

Miller, Jason 1939?- .... CLC 2
See also CA 73-76; DLB 7

Miller, Sue 19??- .... CLC 44

Miller, Walter M(ichael), Jr.
1923- .... CLC 4, 30
See also CA 85-88; DLB 8

Millhauser, Steven 1943- .... CLC 21, 54
See also CA 108, 110, 111; DLB 2

Millin, Sarah Gertrude 1889-1968 .. CLC 49
See also CA 102; obituary CA 93-96

Milne, A(lan) A(lexander)
1882-1956 .... TCLC 6
See also CLR 1; YABC 1; CA 104; DLB 10

Milner, Ron(ald) 1938- .... CLC 56
See also CANR 24; CA 73-76; DLB 38

Milosz Czeslaw
1911- .... CLC 5, 11, 22, 31, 56
See also CANR 23; CA 81-84

Milton, John 1608-1674 .... LC 9

Miner, Valerie (Jane) 1947- .... CLC 40
See also CA 97-100

Minot, Susan 1956- .... CLC 44

Minus, Ed 1938- .... CLC 39

Miro (Ferrer), Gabriel (Francisco Victor)
1879-1930 .... TCLC 5
See also CA 104

Mishima, Yukio
1925-1970 .... CLC 2, 4, 6, 9, 27; SSC 4
See also Hiraoka, Kimitake

Mistral, Gabriela 1889-1957 .... TCLC 2
See also CA 104

Mitchell, James Leslie 1901-1935
See Gibbon, Lewis Grassic
See also CA 104; DLB 15

Mitchell, Joni 1943- .... CLC 12
See also CA 112

Mitchell (Marsh), Margaret (Munnerlyn)
1900-1949 .... TCLC 11
See also CA 109; DLB 9

Mitchell, S. Weir 1829-1914 ...... TCLC 36

Mitchell, W(illiam) O(rmond)
1914- .... CLC 25
See also CANR 15; CA 77-80

Mitford, Mary Russell 1787-1855 .. NCLC 4

Mitford, Nancy 1904-1973 .... CLC 44
See also CA 9-12R

Miyamoto Yuriko 1899-1951 ...... TCLC 37

Mo, Timothy 1950- .... CLC 46
See also CA 117

Modarressi, Taghi 1931- .... CLC 44
See also CA 121

Modiano, Patrick (Jean) 1945- ..... CLC 18
See also CANR 17; CA 85-88

Mofolo, Thomas (Mokopu)
1876-1948 .... TCLC 22
See also CA 121

Mohr, Nicholasa 1935- .... CLC 12
See also CANR 1; CA 49-52; SATA 8

Mojtabai, A(nn) G(race)
1938- .... CLC 5, 9, 15, 29
See also CA 85-88

Moliere 1622-1673 .... LC 10

Molnar, Ferenc 1878-1952 .... TCLC 20
See also CA 109

Momaday, N(avarre) Scott
1934- .... CLC 2, 19
See also CANR 14; CA 25-28R; SATA 30,
48

Monroe, Harriet 1860-1936 .... TCLC 12
See also CA 109; DLB 54

Montagu, Elizabeth 1720-1800 .... NCLC 7

Montagu, Lady Mary (Pierrepont) Wortley
1689-1762 .... LC 9

Montague, John (Patrick)
1929- .... CLC 13, 46
See also CANR 9; CA 9-12R; DLB 40

Montaigne, Michel (Eyquem) de
1533-1592 .... LC 8

Montale, Eugenio 1896-1981 ... CLC 7, 9, 18
See also CA 17-20R; obituary CA 104

Montgomery, Marion (H., Jr.)
1925- .... CLC 7
See also CANR 3; CA 1-4R; DLB 6

Montgomery, Robert Bruce 1921-1978
See Crispin, Edmund
See also CA 104

O'Dell, Scott 1903-.............. CLC 30
See also CLR 1, 16; CANR 12; CA 61-64;
SATA 12; DLB 52

Odets, Clifford 1906-1963 ...... CLC 2, 28
See also CA 85-88; DLB 7, 26

O'Donovan, Michael (John) 1903-1966
See O'Connor, Frank
See also CA 93-96

Oe, Kenzaburo 1935-.......... CLC 10, 36
See also CA 97-100

O'Faolain, Julia 1932-....... CLC 6, 19, 47
See also CAAS 2; CANR 12; CA 81-84;
DLB 14

O'Faolain, Sean 1900- ..... CLC 1, 7, 14, 32
See also CANR 12; CA 61-64; DLB 15

O'Flaherty, Liam
1896-1984 .... CLC 5, 34; SSC 6
See also CA 101; obituary CA 113; DLB 36;
DLB-Y 84

O'Grady, Standish (James)
1846-1928 .... TCLC 5
See also CA 104

O'Grady, Timothy 1951-......... CLC 59

O'Hara, Frank 1926-1966 ..... CLC 2, 5, 13
See also CA 9-12R; obituary CA 25-28R;
DLB 5, 16

O'Hara, John (Henry)
1905-1970 ...... CLC 1, 2, 3, 6, 11, 42
See also CA 5-8R; obituary CA 25-28R;
DLB 9; DLB-DS 2

O'Hara Family
See Banim, John and Banim, Michael

O'Hehir, Diana 1922-............ CLC 41
See also CA 93-96

Okigbo, Christopher (Ifenayichukwu)
1932-1967 .... CLC 25
See also CA 77-80

Olds, Sharon 1942-........... CLC 32, 39
See also CANR 18; CA 101

Olesha, Yuri (Karlovich)
1899-1960 .... CLC 8
See also CA 85-88

Oliphant, Margaret (Oliphant Wilson)
1828-1897 .... NCLC 11
See also DLB 18

Oliver, Mary 1935-............ CLC 19, 34
See also CANR 9; CA 21-24R; DLB 5

Olivier, (Baron) Laurence (Kerr)
1907-...................... CLC 20
See also CA 111

Olsen, Tillie 1913-............ CLC 4, 13
See also CANR 1; CA 1-4R; DLB 28;
DLB-Y 80

Olson, Charles (John)
1910-1970 ..... CLC 1, 2, 5, 6, 9, 11, 29
See also CAP 1; CA 15-16;
obituary CA 25-28R; CABS 2; DLB 5, 16

Olson, Theodore 1937-
See Olson, Toby

Olson, Toby 1937- .... CLC 28
See also CANR 9; CA 65-68

Ondaatje, (Philip) Michael
1943- .... CLC 14, 29, 51
See also CA 77-80; DLB 60

Oneal, Elizabeth 1934-
See Oneal, Zibby
See also CA 106; SATA 30

Oneal, Zibby 1934-.............. CLC 30
See also Oneal, Elizabeth

O'Neill, Eugene (Gladstone)
1888-1953 .... TCLC 1, 6, 27
See also CA 110; DLB 7

Onetti, Juan Carlos 1909-....... CLC 7, 10
See also CA 85-88

O'Nolan, Brian 1911-1966
See O'Brien, Flann

O Nuallain, Brian 1911-1966
See O'Brien, Flann
See also CAP 2; CA 21-22;
obituary CA 25-28R

Oppen, George 1908-1984 .... CLC 7, 13, 34
See also CANR 8; CA 13-16R;
obituary CA 113; DLB 5

Orlovitz, Gil 1918-1973 .... CLC 22
See also CA 77-80; obituary CA 45-48;
DLB 2, 5

Ortega y Gasset, Jose 1883-1955 ... TCLC 9
See also CA 106

Ortiz, Simon J. 1941-............. CLC 45

Orton, Joe 1933?-1967....... CLC 4, 13, 43
See also Orton, John Kingsley
See also DLB 13

Orton, John Kingsley 1933?-1967
See Orton, Joe
See also CA 85-88

Orwell, George
1903-1950 .... TCLC 2, 6, 15, 31
See also Blair, Eric Arthur
See also DLB 15

Osborne, John (James)
1929- .... CLC 1, 2, 5, 11, 45
See also CANR 21; CA 13-16R; DLB 13

Osborne, Lawrence 1958- .... CLC 50

Osceola 1885-1962
See Dinesen, Isak; Blixen, Karen
(Christentze Dinesen)

Oshima, Nagisa 1932- .... CLC 20
See also CA 116

Oskison, John M. 1874-1947...... TCLC 35

Ossoli, Sarah Margaret (Fuller marchesa d')
1810-1850
See Fuller, (Sarah) Margaret
See also SATA 25

Otero, Blas de 1916- .... CLC 11
See also CA 89-92

Owen, Wilfred (Edward Salter)
1893-1918 .... TCLC 5, 27
See also CA 104; DLB 20

Owens, Rochelle 1936-............ CLC 8
See also CAAS 2; CA 17-20R

Owl, Sebastian 1939-
See Thompson, Hunter S(tockton)

Oz, Amos 1939-... CLC 5, 8, 11, 27, 33, 54
See also CA 53-56

Ozick, Cynthia 1928-......... CLC 3, 7, 28
See also CANR 23; CA 17-20R; DLB 28;
DLB-Y 82

Ozu, Yasujiro 1903-1963 .... CLC 16
See also CA 112

Pa Chin 1904-.................. CLC 18
See also Li Fei-kan

Pack, Robert 1929-.............. CLC 13
See also CANR 3; CA 1-4R; DLB 5

Padgett, Lewis 1915-1958
See Kuttner, Henry

Padilla, Heberto 1932-............ CLC 38
See also CA 123

Page, Jimmy 1944-............... CLC 12

Page, Louise 1955-............... CLC 40

Page, P(atricia) K(athleen)
1916-...................... CLC 7, 18
See also CANR 4, 22; CA 53-56; DLB 68

Paget, Violet 1856-1935
See Lee, Vernon
See also CA 104

Palamas, Kostes 1859-1943 .... TCLC 5
See also CA 105

Palazzeschi, Aldo 1885-1974....... CLC 11
See also CA 89-92; obituary CA 53-56

Paley, Grace 1922-........... CLC 4, 6, 37
See also CANR 13; CA 25-28R; DLB 28

Palin, Michael 1943- .... CLC 21
See also Monty Python
See also CA 107

Palma, Ricardo 1833-1919........ TCLC 29
See also CANR 123

Pancake, Breece Dexter 1952-1979
See Pancake, Breece D'J

Pancake, Breece D'J 1952-1979 .... CLC 29
See also obituary CA 109

Papadiamantis, Alexandros
1851-1911 .... TCLC 29

Papini, Giovanni 1881-1956....... TCLC 22
See also CA 121

Parini, Jay (Lee) 1948- .... CLC 54
See also CA 97-100

Parker, Dorothy (Rothschild)
1893-1967 .... CLC 15; SSC 2
See also CAP 2; CA 19-20;
obituary CA 25-28R; DLB 11, 45

Parker, Robert B(rown) 1932-...... CLC 27
See also CANR 1, 26; CA 49-52

Parkin, Frank 1940-.............. CLC 43

Parkman, Francis 1823-1893..... NCLC 12
See also DLB 1, 30

Parks, Gordon (Alexander Buchanan)
1912-...................... CLC 1, 16
See also CANR 26; CA 41-44R; SATA 8;
DLB 33

Parnell, Thomas 1679-1718......... LC 3

Parra, Nicanor 1914-.............. CLC 2
See also CA 85-88

Pasolini, Pier Paolo
1922-1975 .... CLC 20, 37
See also CA 93-96; obituary CA 61-64

Pastan, Linda (Olenik) 1932- ...... CLC 27
See also CANR 18; CA 61-64; DLB 5

Pasternak, Boris 1890-1960... CLC 7, 10, 18
See also obituary CA 116

Squires, (James) Radcliffe 1917-.... **CLC 51**
See also CANR 6, 21; CA 1-4R

Stael-Holstein, Anne Louise Germaine Necker, Baronne de 1766-1817....... **NCLC 3**

Stafford, Jean 1915-1979..... **CLC 4, 7, 19**
See also CANR 3; CA 1-4R;
obituary CA 85-88; obituary SATA 22;
DLB 2

Stafford, William (Edgar)
1914-.................... **CLC 4, 7, 29**
See also CAAS 3; CANR 5, 22; CA 5-8R;
DLB 5

Stannard, Martin 1947-.......... **CLC 44**

Stanton, Maura 1946-............. **CLC 9**
See also CANR 15; CA 89-92

Stapledon, (William) Olaf
1886-1950.................. **TCLC 22**
See also CA 111; DLB 15

Starbuck, George (Edwin) 1931-.... **CLC 53**
See also CANR 23; CA 21-22R

Stark, Richard 1933-
See Westlake, Donald E(dwin)

Stead, Christina (Ellen)
1902-1983............. **CLC 2, 5, 8, 32**
See also CA 13-16R; obituary CA 109

Steele, Timothy (Reid) 1948-....... **CLC 45**
See also CANR 16; CA 93-96

Steffens, (Joseph) Lincoln
1866-1936.................. **TCLC 20**
See also CA 117; SAAS 1

Stegner, Wallace (Earle) 1909-... **CLC 9, 49**
See also CANR 1, 21; CA 1-4R; DLB 9

Stein, Gertrude 1874-1946... **TCLC 1, 6, 28**
See also CA 104; DLB 4, 54

Steinbeck, John (Ernst)
1902-1968..... **CLC 1, 5, 9, 13, 21, 34,
                    45, 59**
See also CANR 1; CA 1-4R;
obituary CA 25-28R; SATA 9; DLB 7, 9;
DLB-DS 2

Steiner, George 1929-............. **CLC 24**
See also CA 73-76

Steiner, Rudolf(us Josephus Laurentius)
1861-1925.................. **TCLC 13**
See also CA 107

Stendhal 1783-1842............. **NCLC 23**

Stephen, Leslie 1832-1904........ **TCLC 23**
See also CANR 9; CA 21-24R, 123;
DLB 57

Stephens, James 1882?-1950....... **TCLC 4**
See also CA 104; DLB 19

Stephens, Reed
See Donaldson, Stephen R.

Steptoe, Lydia 1892-1982
See Barnes, Djuna

Sterling, George 1869-1926....... **TCLC 20**
See also CA 117; DLB 54

Stern, Gerald 1925-............. **CLC 40**
See also CA 81-84

Stern, Richard G(ustave) 1928-... **CLC 4, 39**
See also CANR 1, 25; CA 1-4R

Sternberg, Jonas 1894-1969
See Sternberg, Josef von

Sternberg, Josef von 1894-1969..... **CLC 20**
See also CA 81-84

Sterne, Laurence 1713-1768......... **LC 2**
See also DLB 39

Sternheim, (William Adolf) Carl
1878-1942 .... **TCLC 8**
See also CA 105

Stevens, Mark 19??-.............. **CLC 34**

Stevens, Wallace 1879-1955..... **TCLC 3, 12**
See also CA 104, 124; DLB 54

Stevenson, Anne (Katharine)
1933-.................... **CLC 7, 33**
See also Elvin, Anne Katharine Stevenson
See also CANR 9; CA 17-18R; DLB 40

Stevenson, Robert Louis
1850-1894 .... **NCLC 5, 14**
See also CLR 10, 11; YABC 2; DLB 18, 57

Stewart, J(ohn) I(nnes) M(ackintosh)
1906-.................... **CLC 7, 14, 32**
See also CAAS 3; CA 85-88

Stewart, Mary (Florence Elinor)
1916-.................... **CLC 7, 35**
See also CANR 1; CA 1-4R; SATA 12

Stewart, Will 1908-
See Williamson, Jack
See also CANR 23; CA 17-18R

Still, James 1906-................ **CLC 49**
See also CANR 10; CA 65-68; SATA 29;
DLB 9

Sting 1951-
See The Police

Stitt, Milan 1941-................ **CLC 29**
See also CA 69-72

Stoker, Abraham
See Stoker, Bram
See also CA 105

Stoker, Bram 1847-1912 .... **TCLC 8**
See also Stoker, Abraham
See also SATA 29; DLB 36, 70

Stolz, Mary (Slattery) 1920-...... **CLC 12**
See also CANR 13; CA 5-8R; SAAS 3;
SATA 10

Stone, Irving 1903-1989........... **CLC 7**
See also CAAS 3; CANR 1; CA 1-4R;
SATA 3

Stone, Robert (Anthony)
1937?-................ **CLC 5, 23, 42**
See also CANR 23; CA 85-88

Stoppard, Tom
1937-...... **CLC 1, 3, 4, 5, 8, 15, 29, 34**
See also CA 81-84; DLB 13; DLB-Y 85

Storey, David (Malcolm)
1933-................ **CLC 2, 4, 5, 8**
See also CA 81-84; DLB 13, 14

Storm, Hyemeyohsts 1935-......... **CLC 3**
See also CA 81-84

Storm, (Hans) Theodor (Woldsen)
1817-1888 .... **NCLC 1**

Storni, Alfonsina 1892-1938 .... **TCLC 5**
See also CA 104

Stout, Rex (Todhunter) 1886-1975 ... **CLC 3**
See also CA 61-64

Stow, (Julian) Randolph 1935- .. **CLC 23, 48**
See also CA 13-16R

Stowe, Harriet (Elizabeth) Beecher
1811-1896 .... **NCLC 3**
See also YABC 1; DLB 1, 12, 42;
CDALB 1865-1917

Strachey, (Giles) Lytton
1880-1932 .... **TCLC 12**
See also CA 110

Strand, Mark 1934-......... **CLC 6, 18, 41**
See also CA 21-24R; SATA 41; DLB 5

Straub, Peter (Francis) 1943-...... **CLC 28**
See also CA 85-88; DLB-Y 84

Strauss, Botho 1944-............. **CLC 22**

Straussler, Tomas 1937-
See Stoppard, Tom

Streatfeild, (Mary) Noel 1897- ..... **CLC 21**
See also CA 81-84; obituary CA 120;
SATA 20, 48

Stribling, T(homas) S(igismund)
1881-1965 .... **CLC 23**
See also obituary CA 107; DLB 9

Strindberg, (Johan) August
1849-1912 .... **TCLC 1, 8, 21**
See also CA 104

Stringer, Arthur 1874-1950 .... **TCLC 37**
See also DLB 92

Strugatskii, Arkadii (Natanovich)
1925-..................... **CLC 27**
See also CA 106

Strugatskii, Boris (Natanovich)
1933-..................... **CLC 27**
See also CA 106

Strummer, Joe 1953?-
See The Clash

Stuart, (Hilton) Jesse
1906-1984 .... **CLC 1, 8, 11, 14, 34**
See also CA 5-8R; obituary CA 112;
SATA 2; obituary SATA 36; DLB 9, 48;
DLB-Y 84

Sturgeon, Theodore (Hamilton)
1918-1985 .... **CLC 22, 39**
See also CA 81-84; obituary CA 116;
DLB 8; DLB-Y 85

Styron, William
1925-.......... **CLC 1, 3, 5, 11, 15, 60**
See also CANR 6; CA 5-8R; DLB 2;
DLB-Y 80; CDALB 1968-1987

Sudermann, Hermann 1857-1928 .. **TCLC 15**
See also CA 107

Sue, Eugene 1804-1857 .... **NCLC 1**

Sukenick, Ronald 1932-..... **CLC 3, 4, 6, 48**
See also CA 25-28R; DLB-Y 81

Suknaski, Andrew 1942- .... **CLC 19**
See also CA 101; DLB 53

Sully-Prudhomme, Rene
1839-1907 .... **TCLC 31**

Su Man-shu 1884-1918.......... **TCLC 24**
See also CA 123

Summers, Andrew James 1942-
See The Police

Summers, Andy 1942-
See The Police

Summers, Hollis (Spurgeon, Jr.)
1916-...................... **CLC 10**
See also CANR 3; CA 5-8R; DLB 6

Thompson, Ernest 1860-1946
See Seton, Ernest (Evan) Thompson

Thompson, Francis (Joseph)
1859-1907 .... **TCLC 4**
See also CA 104; DLB 19

Thompson, Hunter S(tockton)
1939- .... **CLC 9, 17, 40**
See also CANR 23; CA 17-20R

Thompson, Judith 1954- .... **CLC 39**

Thomson, James 1834-1882 ...... **NCLC 18**
See also DLB 35

Thoreau, Henry David
1817-1862 .... **NCLC 7, 21**
See also DLB 1; CDALB 1640-1865

Thurber, James (Grover)
1894-1961 .... **CLC 5, 11, 25; SSC 1**
See also CANR 17; CA 73-76; SATA 13;
DLB 4, 11, 22

Thurman, Wallace 1902-1934 ..... **TCLC 6**
See also CA 104, 124; DLB 51

Tieck, (Johann) Ludwig
1773-1853 .... **NCLC 5**

Tillinghast, Richard 1940- .... **CLC 29**
See also CANR 26; CA 29-32R

Timrod, Henry 1828-1867 ...... **NCLC 25**

Tindall, Gillian 1938- .... **CLC 7**
See also CANR 11; CA 21-24R

Tiptree, James, Jr. 1915-1987 ... **CLC 48, 50**
See also Sheldon, Alice (Hastings) B(radley)
See also DLB 8

**Tocqueville, Alexis (Charles Henri Maurice
Clerel, Comte) de** 1805-1859 .. **NCLC 7**

Tolkien, J(ohn) R(onald) R(euel)
1892-1973 .... **CLC 1, 2, 3, 8, 12, 38**
See also CAP 2; CA 17-18;
obituary CA 45-48; SATA 2, 32;
obituary SATA 24; DLB 15

Toller, Ernst 1893-1939 .... **TCLC 10**
See also CA 107

Tolson, Melvin B(eaunorus)
1900?-1966 .... **CLC 36**
See also CA 124; obituary CA 89-92;
DLB 48, 124

Tolstoy, (Count) Alexey Nikolayevich
1883-1945 .... **TCLC 18**
See also CA 107

Tolstoy, (Count) Leo (Lev Nikolaevich)
1828-1910 .... **TCLC 4, 11, 17, 28**
See also CA 104, 123; SATA 26

Tomlin, Lily 1939- .... **CLC 17**

Tomlin, Mary Jean 1939-
See Tomlin, Lily
See also CA 117

Tomlinson, (Alfred) Charles
1927- .... **CLC 2, 4, 6, 13, 45**
See also CA 5-8R; DLB 40

Toole, John Kennedy 1937-1969 .... **CLC 19**
See also CA 104; DLB-Y 81

Toomer, Jean
1894-1967 ..... **CLC 1, 4, 13, 22; SSC 1**
See also CA 85-88; DLB 45, 51

Torrey, E. Fuller 19??- .... **CLC 34**
See also CA 119

Tournier, Michel 1924- ...... **CLC 6, 23, 36**
See also CANR 3; CA 49-52; SATA 23

Townshend, Peter (Dennis Blandford)
1945- .... **CLC 17, 42**
See also CA 107

Tozzi, Federigo 1883-1920 .... **TCLC 31**

Trakl, Georg 1887-1914 .... **TCLC 5**
See also CA 104

Transtromer, Tomas (Gosta)
1931- .... **CLC 52**
See also CA 117

Traven, B. 1890-1969 .... **CLC 8, 11**
See also CAP 2; CA 19-20;
obituary CA 25-28R; DLB 9, 56

Tremain, Rose 1943- .... **CLC 42**
See also CA 97-100; DLB 14

Tremblay, Michel 1942- .... **CLC 29**
See also CA 116; DLB 60

Trevanian 1925- .... **CLC 29**
See also CA 108

Trevor, William 1928- ..... **CLC 7, 9, 14, 25**
See also Cox, William Trevor
See also DLB 14

Trifonov, Yuri (Valentinovich)
1925-1981 .... **CLC 45**
See also obituary CA 103, 126

Trilling, Lionel 1905-1975 .... **CLC 9, 11, 24**
See also CANR 10; CA 9-12R;
obituary CA 61-64; DLB 28, 63

Trogdon, William 1939-
See Heat Moon, William Least
See also CA 115, 119

Trollope, Anthony 1815-1882 ..... **NCLC 6**
See also SATA 22; DLB 21, 57

Trotsky, Leon (Davidovich)
1879-1940 .... **TCLC 22**
See also CA 118

Trotter (Cockburn), Catharine
1679-1749 .... **LC 8**

Trow, George W. S. 1943- .... **CLC 52**
See also CA 126

Troyat, Henri 1911- .... **CLC 23**
See also CANR 2; CA 45-48

Trudeau, G(arretson) B(eekman) 1948-
See Trudeau, Garry
See also CA 81-84; SATA 35

Trudeau, Garry 1948- .... **CLC 12**
See also Trudeau, G(arretson) B(eekman)

Truffaut, Francois 1932-1984 ...... **CLC 20**
See also CA 81-84; obituary CA 113

Trumbo, Dalton 1905-1976 .... **CLC 19**
See also CANR 10; CA 21-24R;
obituary CA 69-72; DLB 26

Tryon, Thomas 1926- .... **CLC 3, 11**
See also CA 29-32R

Ts'ao Hsueh-ch'in 1715?-1763 .... **LC 1**

Tsushima Shuji 1909-1948
See Dazai Osamu
See also CA 107

Tsvetaeva (Efron), Marina (Ivanovna)
1892-1941 .... **TCLC 7, 35**
See also CA 104, 128

Tunis, John R(oberts) 1889-1975 ... **CLC 12**
See also CA 61-64; SATA 30, 37; DLB 22

Tuohy, Frank 1925- .... **CLC 37**
See also DLB 14

Tuohy, John Francis 1925-
See Tuohy, Frank
See also CANR 3; CA 5-8R

Turco, Lewis (Putnam) 1934- ...... **CLC 11**
See also CANR 24; CA 13-16R; DLB-Y 84

Turgenev, Ivan 1818-1883 .... **NCLC 21**

Turner, Frederick 1943- .... **CLC 48**
See also CANR 12; CA 73-76; DLB 40

Tutuola, Amos 1920- .... **CLC 5, 14, 29**
See also CA 9-12R

Twain, Mark
1835-1910 ... **TCLC 6, 12, 19, 36; SSC 6**
See also Clemens, Samuel Langhorne
See also YABC 2; DLB 11, 12, 23, 64, 74

Tyler, Anne
1941- .... **CLC 7, 11, 18, 28, 44, 59**
See also CANR 11; CA 9-12R; SATA 7;
DLB 6; DLB-Y 82

Tyler, Royall 1757-1826 .... **NCLC 3**
See also DLB 37

Tynan (Hinkson), Katharine
1861-1931 .... **TCLC 3**
See also CA 104

Tytell, John 1939- .... **CLC 50**
See also CA 29-32R

Tzara, Tristan 1896-1963 .... **CLC 47**
See also Rosenfeld, Samuel

Uhry, Alfred 1947?- .... **CLC 55**
See also CA 127

Unamuno (y Jugo), Miguel de
1864-1936 .... **TCLC 2, 9**
See also CA 104

Underwood, Miles 1909-1981
See Glassco, John

Undset, Sigrid 1882-1949 .... **TCLC 3**
See also CA 104

Ungaretti, Giuseppe
1888-1970 .... **CLC 7, 11, 15**
See also CAP 2; CA 19-20;
obituary CA 25-28R

Unger, Douglas 1952- .... **CLC 34**

Unger, Eva 1932-
See Figes, Eva

Updike, John (Hoyer)
1932- ...... **CLC 1, 2, 3, 5, 7, 9, 13, 15,
23, 34, 43**
See also CANR 4; CA 1-4R; CABS 2;
DLB 2, 5; DLB-Y 80, 82; DLB-DS 3

Urdang, Constance (Henriette)
1922- .... **CLC 47**
See also CANR 9, 24; CA 21-24R

Uris, Leon (Marcus) 1924- .... **CLC 7, 32**
See also CANR 1; CA 1-4R; SATA 49

Ustinov, Peter (Alexander) 1921- .... **CLC 1**
See also CANR 25; CA 13-16R; DLB 13

Vaculik, Ludvik 1926- .... **CLC 7**
See also CA 53-56

Valenzuela, Luisa 1938- .... **CLC 31**
See also CA 101

Valera (y Acala-Galiano), Juan
1824-1905 .... **TCLC 10**
See also CA 106

Wallace, David Foster   1962- . . . . **CLC 50**

Wallace, Irving   1916- . . . . **CLC 7, 13**
See also CAAS 1; CANR 1; CA 1-4R

Wallant, Edward Lewis
1926-1962 . . . . **CLC 5, 10**
See also CANR 22; CA 1-4R; DLB 2, 28

Walpole, Horace   1717-1797 . . . . **LC 2**
See also DLB 39

Walpole, (Sir) Hugh (Seymour)
1884-1941 . . . . **TCLC 5**
See also CA 104; DLB 34

Walser, Martin   1927- . . . . **CLC 27**
See also CANR 8; CA 57-60; DLB 75

Walser, Robert   1878-1956 . . . . **TCLC 18**
See also CA 118; DLB 66

Walsh, Gillian Paton   1939-
See Walsh, Jill Paton
See also CA 37-40R; SATA 4

Walsh, Jill Paton   1939- . . . . **CLC 35**
See also CLR 2; SAAS 3

Wambaugh, Joseph (Aloysius, Jr.)
1937- . . . . **CLC 3, 18**
See also CA 33-36R; DLB 6; DLB-Y 83

Ward, Arthur Henry Sarsfield   1883-1959
See Rohmer, Sax
See also CA 108

Ward, Douglas Turner   1930- . . . . **CLC 19**
See also CA 81-84; DLB 7, 38

Warhol, Andy   1928-1987 . . . . **CLC 20**
See also CA 89-92; obituary CA 121

Warner, Francis (Robert le Plastrier)
1937- . . . . **CLC 14**
See also CANR 11; CA 53-56

Warner, Marina   1946- . . . . **CLC 59**
See also CANR 21; CA 65-68

Warner, Rex (Ernest)   1905-1986 . . . . **CLC 45**
See also CA 89-92; obituary CA 119;
DLB 15

Warner, Sylvia Townsend
1893-1978 . . . . **CLC 7, 19**
See also CANR 16; CA 61-64;
obituary CA 77-80; DLB 34

Warren, Mercy Otis   1728-1814 . . . **NCLC 13**
See also DLB 31

Warren, Robert Penn
1905-1989 . . . **CLC 1, 4, 6, 8, 10, 13, 18,**
39, 53, 59; SSC 4
See also CANR 10; CA 13-16R. 129. 130;
SATA 46; DLB 2, 48; DLB-Y 80;
CDALB 1968-1987

Washington, Booker T(aliaferro)
1856-1915 . . . . **TCLC 10**
See also CA 114, 125; SATA 28

Wassermann, Jakob   1873-1934 . . . . . **TCLC 6**
See also CA 104; DLB 66

Wasserstein, Wendy   1950- . . . . . . **CLC 32, 59**
See also CA 121; CABS 3

Waterhouse, Keith (Spencer)
1929- . . . . **CLC 47**
See also CA 5-8R; DLB 13, 15

Waters, Roger   1944-
See Pink Floyd

Wa Thiong'o, Ngugi
1938- . . . . **CLC 3, 7, 13, 36**
See also Ngugi, James (Thiong'o); Ngugi wa
Thiong'o

Watkins, Paul   1964- . . . . **CLC 55**

Watkins, Vernon (Phillips)
1906-1967 . . . . **CLC 43**
See also CAP 1; CA 9-10;
obituary CA 25-28R; DLB 20

Waugh, Auberon (Alexander)   1939- . . **CLC 7**
See also CANR 6, 22; CA 45-48; DLB 14

Waugh, Evelyn (Arthur St. John)
1903-1966 . . . **CLC 1, 3, 8, 13, 19, 27, 44**
See also CANR 22; CA 85-88;
obituary CA 25-28R; DLB 15

Waugh, Harriet   1944- . . . . **CLC 6**
See also CANR 22; CA 85-88

Webb, Beatrice (Potter)
1858-1943 . . . . **TCLC 22**
See also CA 117

Webb, Charles (Richard)   1939- . . . . . . **CLC 7**
See also CA 25-28R

Webb, James H(enry), Jr.   1946- . . . . **CLC 22**
See also CA 81-84

Webb, Mary (Gladys Meredith)
1881-1927 . . . . **TCLC 24**
See also CA 123; DLB 34

Webb, Phyllis   1927- . . . . **CLC 18**
See also CANR 23; CA 104; DLB 53

Webb, Sidney (James)
1859-1947 . . . . **TCLC 22**
See also CA 117

Webber, Andrew Lloyd   1948- . . . . . . **CLC 21**

Weber, Lenora Mattingly
1895-1971 . . . . **CLC 12**
See also CAP 1; CA 19-20;
obituary CA 29-32R; SATA 2;
obituary SATA 26

Wedekind, (Benjamin) Frank(lin)
1864-1918 . . . . **TCLC 7**
See also CA 104

Weidman, Jerome   1913- . . . . **CLC 7**
See also CANR 1; CA 1-4R; DLB 28

Weil, Simone   1909-1943 . . . . **TCLC 23**
See also CA 117

Weinstein, Nathan Wallenstein   1903?-1940
See West, Nathanael
See also CA 104

Weir, Peter   1944- . . . . **CLC 20**
See also CA 113, 123

Weiss, Peter (Ulrich)
1916-1982 . . . . **CLC 3, 15, 51**
See also CANR 3; CA 45-48;
obituary CA 106; DLB 69

Weiss, Theodore (Russell)
1916- . . . . **CLC 3, 8, 14**
See also CAAS 2; CA 9-12R; DLB 5

Welch, (Maurice) Denton
1915-1948 . . . . **TCLC 22**
See also CA 121

Welch, James   1940- . . . . **CLC 6, 14, 52**
See also CA 85-88

Weldon, Fay
1933- . . . . **CLC 6, 9, 11, 19, 36, 59**
See also CANR 16; CA 21-24R; DLB 14

Wellek, Rene   1903- . . . . **CLC 28**
See also CAAS 7; CANR 8; CA 5-8R;
DLB 63

Weller, Michael   1942- . . . . **CLC 10, 53**
See also CA 85-88

Weller, Paul   1958- . . . . **CLC 26**

Wellershoff, Dieter   1925- . . . . **CLC 46**
See also CANR 16; CA 89-92

Welles, (George) Orson
1915-1985 . . . . **CLC 20**
See also CA 93-96; obituary CA 117

Wellman, Manly Wade   1903-1986 . . **CLC 49**
See also CANR 6, 16; CA 1-4R;
obituary CA 118; SATA 6, 47

Wells, Carolyn   1862-1942 . . . . **TCLC 35**
See also CA 113; DLB 11

Wells, H(erbert) G(eorge)
1866-1946 . . . . . . **TCLC 6, 12, 19; SSC 6**
See also CA 110, 121; SATA 20; DLB 34,
70

Wells, Rosemary   1943- . . . . **CLC 12**
See also CLR 16; CA 85-88; SAAS 1;
SATA 18

Welty, Eudora (Alice)
1909- . . . . **CLC 1, 2, 5, 14, 22, 33; SSC 1**
See also CA 9-12R; CABS 1; DLB 2;
DLB-Y 87; CDALB 1941-1968

Wen I-to   1899-1946 . . . . **TCLC 28**

Werfel, Franz (V.)   1890-1945 . . . . . . **TCLC 8**
See also CA 104

Wergeland, Henrik Arnold
1808-1845 . . . . **NCLC 5**

Wersba, Barbara   1932- . . . . **CLC 30**
See also CLR 3; CANR 16; CA 29-32R;
SAAS 2; SATA 1; DLB 52

Wertmuller, Lina   1928- . . . . **CLC 16**
See also CA 97-100

Wescott, Glenway   1901-1987 . . . . **CLC 13**
See also CANR 23; CA 13-16R;
obituary CA 121; DLB 4, 9

Wesker, Arnold   1932- . . . . **CLC 3, 5, 42**
See also CAAS 7; CANR 1; CA 1-4R;
DLB 13

Wesley, Richard (Errol)   1945- . . . . **CLC 7**
See also CA 57-60; DLB 38

Wessel, Johan Herman   1742-1785 . . . . **LC 7**

West, Anthony (Panther)
1914-1987 . . . . **CLC 50**
See also CANR 3, 19; CA 45-48; DLB 15

West, Jessamyn   1907-1984 . . . . . . **CLC 7, 17**
See also CA 9-12R; obituary CA 112;
obituary SATA 37; DLB 6; DLB-Y 84

West, Morris L(anglo)   1916- . . . . . **CLC 6, 33**
See also CA 5-8R; obituary CA 124

West, Nathanael   1903?-1940 . . . . **TCLC 1, 14**
See also Weinstein, Nathan Wallenstein
See also CA 125; DLB 4, 9, 28

West, Paul   1930- . . . . **CLC 7, 14**
See also CAAS 7; CANR 22; CA 13-16R;
DLB 14

West, Rebecca   1892-1983 . . **CLC 7, 9, 31, 50**
See also CANR 19; CA 5-8R;
obituary CA 109; DLB 36; DLB-Y 83

Wilson, Sloan 1920-.............. CLC 32
See also CANR 1; CA 1-4R

Wilson, Snoo 1948-.............. CLC 33
See also CA 69-72

Wilson, William S(mith) 1932-..... CLC 49
See also CA 81-84

Winchilsea, Anne (Kingsmill) Finch, Countess
of 1661-1720.................. LC 3

Winters, Janet Lewis 1899-
See Lewis (Winters), Janet
See also CAP 1; CA 9-10

Winters, (Arthur) Yvor
1900-1968 .... CLC 4, 8, 32
See also CAP 1; CA 11-12;
obituary CA 25-28R; DLB 48

Wiseman, Frederick 1930-........ CLC 20

Wister, Owen 1860-1938 .... TCLC 21
See also CA 108; DLB 9

Witkiewicz, Stanislaw Ignacy
1885-1939 .... TCLC 8
See also CA 105

Wittig, Monique 1935?-........... CLC 22
See also CA 116

Wittlin, Joseph 1896-1976........ CLC 25
See also Wittlin, Jozef

Wittlin, Jozef 1896-1976
See Wittlin, Joseph
See also CANR 3; CA 49-52;
obituary CA 65-68

Wodehouse, (Sir) P(elham) G(renville)
1881-1975 ... CLC 1, 2, 5, 10, 22; SSC 2
See also CANR 3; CA 45-48;
obituary CA 57-60; SATA 22; DLB 34

Woiwode, Larry (Alfred) 1941-... CLC 6, 10
See also CANR 16; CA 73-76; DLB 6

Wojciechowska, Maia (Teresa)
1927-....................... CLC 26
See also CLR 1; CANR 4; CA 9-12R;
SAAS 1; SATA 1, 28

Wolf, Christa 1929- .... CLC 14, 29, 58
See also CA 85-88

Wolfe, Gene (Rodman) 1931-....... CLC 25
See also CANR 6; CA 57-60; DLB 8

Wolfe, George C. 1954-........... CLC 49

Wolfe, Thomas (Clayton)
1900-1938 .... TCLC 4, 13, 29
See also CA 104; DLB 9; DLB-Y 85;
DLB-DS 2

Wolfe, Thomas Kennerly, Jr. 1931-
See Wolfe, Tom
See also CANR 9; CA 13-16R

Wolfe, Tom 1931-... CLC 1, 2, 9, 15, 35, 51
See also Wolfe, Thomas Kennerly, Jr.

Wolff, Geoffrey (Ansell) 1937- ..... CLC 41
See also CA 29-32R

Wolff, Tobias (Jonathan Ansell)
1945-....................... CLC 39
See also CA 114, 117

Wolfram von Eschenbach
c. 1170-c. 1220 .... CMLC 5

Wolitzer, Hilma 1930-............ CLC 17
See also CANR 18; CA 65-68; SATA 31

Wollstonecraft (Godwin), Mary
1759-1797 .... LC 5
See also DLB 39

Wonder, Stevie 1950-............ CLC 12
See also Morris, Steveland Judkins

Wong, Jade Snow 1922-.......... CLC 17
See also CA 109

Woodcott, Keith 1934-
See Brunner, John (Kilian Houston)

Woolf, (Adeline) Virginia
1882-1941 .... TCLC 1, 5, 20
See also CA 104; DLB 36

Woollcott, Alexander (Humphreys)
1887-1943 .... TCLC 5
See also CA 105; DLB 29

Wordsworth, Dorothy
1771-1855 .... NCLC 25

Wordsworth, William 1770-1850.. NCLC 12

Wouk, Herman 1915-........ CLC 1, 9, 38
See also CANR 6; CA 5-8R; DLB-Y 82

Wright, Charles 1935- .... CLC 6, 13, 28
See also CAAS 7; CA 29-32R; DLB-Y 82

Wright, Charles (Stevenson) 1932-.. CLC 49
See also CA 9-12R; DLB 33

Wright, James (Arlington)
1927-1980 .... CLC 3, 5, 10, 28
See also CANR 4; CA 49-52;
obituary CA 97-100; DLB 5

Wright, Judith 1915- .... CLC 11, 53
See also CA 13-16R; SATA 14

Wright, L(aurali) R. 1939-........ CLC 44

Wright, Richard B(ruce) 1937- ...... CLC 6
See also CA 85-88; DLB 53

Wright, Richard (Nathaniel)
1908-1960 ... CLC 1, 3, 4, 9, 14, 21, 48;
SSC 2
See also CA 108; DLB-DS 2

Wright, Rick 1945-
See Pink Floyd

Wright, Stephen 1946-........... CLC 33

Wright, Willard Huntington 1888-1939
See Van Dine, S. S.
See also CA 115

Wright, William 1930-............ CLC 44
See also CANR 7, 23; CA 53-56

Wu Ch'eng-en 1500?-1582? .... LC 7

Wu Ching-tzu 1701-1754 .... LC 2

Wurlitzer, Rudolph 1938?-..... CLC 2, 4, 15
See also CA 85-88

Wycherley, William 1640?-1716 ...... LC 8

Wylie (Benet), Elinor (Morton Hoyt)
1885-1928 .... TCLC 8
See also CA 105; DLB 9, 45

Wylie, Philip (Gordon) 1902-1971... CLC 43
See also CAP 2; CA 21-22;
obituary CA 33-36R; DLB 9

Wyndham, John 1903-1969 .... CLC 19
See also Harris, John (Wyndham Parkes
Lucas) Beynon

Wyss, Johann David 1743-1818 .. NCLC 10
See also SATA 27, 29

Yanovsky, Vassily S(emenovich)
1906-1989 .... CLC 2, 18
See also CA 97-100

Yates, Richard 1926-......... CLC 7, 8, 23
See also CANR 10; CA 5-8R; DLB 2;
DLB-Y 81

Yeats, William Butler
1865-1939 .... TCLC 1, 11, 18, 31
See also CANR 10; CA 104; DLB 10, 19

Yehoshua, A(braham) B.
1936-.................... CLC 13, 31
See also CA 33-36R

Yep, Laurence (Michael) 1948-..... CLC 35
See also CLR 3; CANR 1; CA 49-52;
SATA 7; DLB 52

Yerby, Frank G(arvin) 1916-... CLC 1, 7, 22
See also CANR 16; CA 9-12R; DLB 76

Yevtushenko, Yevgeny (Alexandrovich)
1933-........... CLC 1, 3, 13, 26, 51
See also CA 81-84

Yezierska, Anzia 1885?-1970....... CLC 46
See also CA 126; obituary CA 89-92;
DLB 28

Yglesias, Helen 1915-........... CLC 7, 22
See also CANR 15; CA 37-40R

Yorke, Henry Vincent 1905-1974
See Green, Henry
See also CA 85-88; obituary CA 49-52

Young, Al 1939-................. CLC 19
See also CANR 26; CA 29-32R; DLB 33

Young, Andrew 1885-1971......... CLC 5
See also CANR 7; CA 5-8R

Young, Edward 1683-1765........... LC 3

Young, Neil 1945-............... CLC 17
See also CA 110

Yourcenar, Marguerite
1903-1987 .... CLC 19, 38, 50
See also CANR 23; CA 69-72; DLB 72

Yurick, Sol 1925-................ CLC 6
See also CANR 25; CA 13-16R

Zamyatin, Yevgeny Ivanovich
1884-1937 .... TCLC 8, 37
See also CA 105

Zangwill, Israel 1864-1926....... TCLC 16
See also CA 109; DLB 10

Zappa, Francis Vincent, Jr. 1940-
See Zappa, Frank
See also CA 108

Zappa, Frank 1940- .... CLC 17
See also Zappa, Francis Vincent, Jr.

Zaturenska, Marya 1902-1982.... CLC 6, 11
See also CANR 22; CA 13-16R;
obituary CA 105

Zelazny, Roger 1937-............. CLC 21
See also CANR 26; CA 21-24R; SATA 39;
DLB 8

Zhdanov, Andrei A(lexandrovich)
1896-1948 .... TCLC 18
See also CA 117

Ziegenhagen, Eric 1970-.......... CLC 55

Zimmerman, Robert 1941-
See Dylan, Bob

Author Index

Literary Criticism Series
Cumulative Topic Index

This index lists all topic entries in the Gale Literary Criticism Series *Contemporary Literary Criticism, Literature Criticism from 1400 to 1800, Nineteenth-Century Literature Criticism,* and *Twentieth-Century Literary Criticism.*

NCLC Cumulative Nationality Index

Nationality Index